Life-Span Human Development Sixth Edition

Carol K. Sigelman
The George Washington University

Elizabeth A. Rider
Elizabethtown College

WADSWORTH
CENGAGE Learning

Australia · Brazil · Japan · Korea · Mexico · Singapore ·
Spain · United Kingdom · United States

WADSWORTH
CENGAGE Learning

**Life-Span Human Development,
Sixth Edition
Carol K. Sigelman and Elizabeth A. Rider**

Publisher: Michele Sordi

Development Editor: Kristin Makarewycz

Assistant Editor: Magnolia Molcan

Managing Technology Project Manager:
Amy Cohen

Marketing Manager: Sara Swangard

Marketing Assistant: Melanie Cregger

Marketing Communications Manager: Linda
Yip

Project Manager, Editorial Production: Mary
Noel

Creative Director: Rob Hugel

Art Director: Vernon T. Boes

Print Buyer: Karen Hunt

Permissions Editors: Deanna Ettinger,
Mardell Glinski Schultz

Production Service: Dan Fitzgerald, Graphic
World Inc.

Text Designer: Jeanne Calabrese

Photo Researcher: Kim Adams

Copy Editor: Graphic World Publishing
Services

Cover Designer: Paula Goldstein

Cover Images (clockwise from top left):
Jeremy Woodhouse/Getty; Darwin
Wiggett/Firstlight; Alexander
Makarewycz; Chris Whitehead/Getty;
JupiterImages/i2i/Alamy; Nancy Nev/
Getty; Lisa Petkau/First Light; PhotoDisc

Compositor: Graphic World Inc.

For product information and technology assistance, contact us at
Cengage Learning Customer & Sales Support, 1-800-354-9706
For permission to use material from this text or product,
submit all requests online at **cengage.com/permissions.**
Further permissions questions can be e-mailed to
permissionrequest@cengage.com.

Library of Congress Control Number: 2007938973

Student Edition:
ISBN-13: 978-0-495-55340-3
ISBN-10: 0-495-55340-9

Loose-leaf Edition:
ISBN-13: 978-0-495-50615-7
ISBN-10: 0-495-50615-X

Wadsworth Cengage Learning
10 Davis Drive
Belmont, CA 94002-3098
USA

Cengage Learning is a leading provider of customized learning solutions
with office locations around the globe, including Singapore, the United
Kingdom, Australia, Mexico, Brazil, and Japan. Locate your local office at
international.cengage.com/region.

Cengage Learning products are represented in Canada by Nelson Education,
Ltd.

For your course and learning solutions, visit **academic.cengage.com.**

Purchase any of our products at your local college store or at our preferred
online store **www.ichapters.com.**

Printed in Canada
2 3 4 5 6 7 12 11 10 09 08

To our partners in development, Lee Sigelman and Corbett Rider

Brief Contents

Contents

9 Intelligence and Creativity 244

Preface

This book is about the development of human beings—from their days as fertilized eggs to their last days. It highlights regularities in development as well as differences among individuals in different social contexts, and it asks fundamental questions about why we humans develop as we do. The field of life-span human development is a dynamic one, and we attempt to keep up with the change in this, the sixth edition of *Life-Span Human Development.*

This new edition incorporates many exciting changes, yet it retains the core features valued by students and instructors over the years. In this edition, we remain firmly committed to three key features: (1) our unique integrated topical–chronological approach, (2) a presentation that is both research-based and relevant to the "real world," and (3) emphasis on the all-important nature–nurture issue throughout the book. In addition, we update coverage of key topics and controversies in life-span human development, introduce a new appendix on careers in life-span human development, and add new pedagogical features and supplements to enhance the teaching–learning process.

A Topical and Chronological Approach

The most distinctive feature of this book is its unique *integrated topical–chronological approach.* Almost all other life-span development textbooks adopt a chronological or "age–stage" approach, carving the life span into age ranges and describing the prominent characteristics of individuals within each age range. In contrast, we adopt a topical approach for the overall organization of the book blended with a chronological approach within chapters. Each chapter focuses on a domain of development, such as physical growth, cognition, or personality, and traces developmental trends and influences in that domain from infancy to old age. Each chapter calls attention to age groups through major sections on infancy, childhood, adolescence, and adulthood.

Why Topical?

Why have we fought the tide? Like many other instructors, we have typically favored topically organized textbooks when teaching child-, adolescent-, or adult-development courses. As

a result, it seemed natural to use that topical approach in introducing students to the whole life span. Besides, chronologically organized texts often have to repeat themselves as they remind readers of where development left off in an earlier age period (that was covered in a previous chapter).

More important, a topic-by-topic organization conveys the flow of development in each area—the systematic, and often dramatic, transformations that take place as well as the developmental continuities. The topical approach also helps us emphasize developmental *processes*—how nature and nurture interact over the life span to bring change.

Finally, a predominantly topical approach is more compatible with a *life-span perspective*, which views any period of life in relation to what comes before and what is yet to come. In chronologically organized textbooks, many topics are described only in connection with the age group to which they seem most relevant—for example, attachment in relation to infancy, or sexuality in relation to adolescence and adulthood. A topical organization makes readers ask intriguing questions that they might otherwise not ask, such as these about attachment relationships:

- What do infants' attachments to their parents have in common with, and how do they differ from, attachments between childhood friends or between adult romantic partners?
- Do securely attached infants later have a greater capacity to form and sustain friendships or romantic partnerships than infants whose early social experiences are less favorable?
- What are the consequences at different points in the life span of lacking someone to be closely attached to?

Attachments are important throughout the life span, and a topical organization helps make that clear.

Why Chronological?

We adopted a topical approach because we consider it the best way to introduce the how and why of human development. We also appreciate the strengths of the chronological approach, particularly its ability to portray the whole person in each period of the life span. For this reason, we integrated the age–stage approach with the topical organization, aiming to have the best of both worlds.

Each topical chapter contains major sections on infancy, childhood, adolescence, and adulthood. The existence of these sections is proof that the chapters consider development in each of the domains covered across the *whole* life span. These age–stage sections call attention to the distinctive qualities of each phase of life and make it easier for students to find material on an age period of particular interest to them. We allow our degree of emphasis on each period of the life span to vary depending on the significance of the developments in each period.

We believe that our integrated topical–chronological approach allows us to convey the flow of life-span development in particular areas and the factors influencing it while highlighting the major physical, cognitive, and psychosocial developments within any particular developmental period.

Adaptability of the Integrated Topical–Chronological Approach

Even though links among chapters are noted throughout the book, instructors who are teaching short courses or who are otherwise pressed for time can omit a chapter without fear of rendering other chapters incomprehensible. For example:

- A cognitively oriented course might omit one or more of the socially oriented chapters (Chapters 11, 12, and 14–17).
- A socially oriented course might omit one or more of the cognitively oriented chapters (Chapters 6–10).

Moreover, this approach allows instructors enough flexibility to cover infancy, childhood, and adolescence in the first portion of the course, if they prefer, and to save the material on adulthood for the end.

RESEARCH-ORIENTED AND REAL COVERAGE

We have worked hard to create a text that is rigorous yet readable—research-oriented yet "real" to students. The sixth edition of *Life-Span Human Development* tackles complex theoretical controversies and presents the best of both classic and contemporary research from multiple disciplines in a way that is accessible and relevant to students' life experiences and career development.

We believe that it is critical for students to understand how we know what we know about development—to appreciate the research process. With that in mind, we describe illustrative studies and present their data in graphs and tables, and we cite the authors and dates of publication for a large number of books and articles, all fully referenced in the bibliography at the end of the book. Some students may wonder why they are there. It is because we are committed to the value of systematic research, because we are bound to give credit where credit is

due, and because we want students and their professors to have the resources they need to pursue their interests in human development during and after the course.

We also appreciate that solid scholarship is of little good to students unless they want to read it, can understand it, and see its relevance. We maintain that even the most complex issues in human development can be made understandable through clear and organized writing. To make the material more "real," we clarify developmental concepts through examples and analogies, connect topics in the text to topics in the news, and highlight the practical implications of research findings. We also incorporate material relevant to students' current and future roles as parents, teachers, psychologists, health professionals, and other human service professionals. And we help students see that major theories of human development do not just guide researchers but can help anyone analyze issues that we all face—including such practical matters as raising children, working with troubled adolescents, or coping with Alzheimer's disease in the family.

NATURE–NURTURE THEME

If students gain nothing else from their study of human development, we hope they gain a deeper understanding of the nature–nurture issue and of the many interacting forces affecting the developing person. We want students to understand that human development is an incredibly complex process that grows out of transactions between a changing person and a changing world and out of dynamic relationships among biological, psychological, and social influences. No contributor to development—a gene, a temperament, a parent, a culture—acts alone and is unaffected by other influences on development.

We introduce the nature–nurture issue in Chapter 1. Each subsequent chapter includes one or more illustration of the intertwined contributions of nature and nurture to development. Along the way, we describe some exciting studies involving molecular genetics that compare individuals with and without particular genes and with and without particular life experiences to bring home what it means to say that genes and environment interact to influence development. It becomes clear in Chapter 3, for example, that the odds of depression become high only when a person is at genetic risk for depression *and* experiences multiple stressful events. We grapple with nature–nurture as it pertains to everything from physical growth and the effects of prenatal alcohol exposure, to temperament and parenting behavior, to autism and aging. In this edition, we have expanded coverage of evolution, genes, hormones, and other biological forces in development; enriched descriptions of how ethnic group, social class, community, and the larger cultural context modify development; and, most importantly, illuminated the complex interrelationships between biological and environmental influences that are at the heart of the developmental process.

The following theme index shows the scope of coverage of the nature–nurture issue in this text:

ORGANIZATION OF THE TEXT
Core Concepts: Chapters 1 to 4

The book begins by orienting students to the life-span perspective on human development and to approaches to the scientific study of development (Chapter 1), as well as to the central issues and theoretical perspectives that have dominated the field (Chapter 2). It then explores developmental processes in some depth, examining genetic influences (Chapter 3) and early environmental influences (Chapter 4) on development. These chapters establish how both genes and environments contribute to typical changes and individual differences throughout the life span.

Development of Basic Human Capacities: Chapters 5 to 10

Chapters on the growth and aging of the body and nervous system (Chapter 5) and on the development of sensory and perceptual capacities (Chapter 6) launch our examination of the development of basic human capacities. Chapter 7 covers Jean Piaget's perspective on cognitive development and the quite different perspective offered by Lev Vygotsky; Chapter 8 views memory and problem solving from an information-processing perspective; Chapter 9 highlights the psychometric approach to cognition, exploring individual differences in intelligence and creativity; and Chapter 10 explores language development and the roles of language and cognition in educational achievement.

Development of Self in Society: Chapters 11 to 17

The next three chapters concern the development of the self: changes in self-conceptions and personality, including vocational identity (Chapter 11); in gender roles and sexuality (Chapter 12); and in social cognition and morality (Chapter 13). The self is set more squarely in a social context as we trace life-span changes in attachment relationships (Chapter 14) and in roles and relationships within the family (Chapter 15). Finally, we offer a life-span perspective on developmental problems and disorders (Chapter 16) and examine why people die and how they cope with death (Chapter 17).

Getting the Big Picture

To help students pull together the "big picture" of life-span human development at the end of the course, we remind students of some of the major themes of the book at the end of Chapter 17 and offer a chart inside the back cover that summarizes major developments in each of seven periods of the life span.

NEW TO THIS EDITION

In this edition, we have organized chapters into numbered chapter sections with their own Summing Up and Critical Thinking sections, include an appendix on Careers in Human Development, and introduce new material reflecting the latest in life-span development research.

Numbered Major Chapter Headings

To help students navigate and learn from the book, and also to help instructors more easily assign sections within chapters, we have numbered the major headings of each chapter and have carried this numbering into the Chapter Summary.

Section-Ending Critical Thinking Questions

At the end of each major section, bulleted Summing Up summaries help students pull together the main points, and new section-ending Critical Thinking questions invite students to reflect on the material or apply it to a problem.

Appendix on Careers in Human Development

New to this edition is an appendix laying out possibilities for translating an interest in life-span human development into a career in research, teaching, or professional practice. We clarify what types of careers are available with a bachelor's, master's, or doctoral degree; suggest steps students can take now to position themselves for success; and provide a list of resources to assist students in their career exploration and development.

Updates

As always, the book has been thoroughly updated from start to finish; it conveys the most recent discoveries and insights developmentalists have to offer. We take pride in having written a well-researched and well-referenced book that professors and students can use as a resource. We have added some exciting new topics and greatly revised, expanded, and updated coverage of other topics. A sampling:

Chapter 1. Understanding Life-Span Human Development

- Elaboration of the introductory presentation of the nature–nurture issue using Bronfenbrenner's bioecological model and a new example of the model's application
- Coverage of a newly identified period of the life span, "emerging adulthood"
- Updates on research ethics and the need for cultural sensitivity in research

Chapter 2. Theories of Human Development

- Use of the examples of school phobia in a 6-year-old and teenage pregnancy to help students think like theorists and appreciate differences in the ways different theorists explain the same developmental phenomena
- Revision of the Systems Theories section to focus more squarely on Gilbert Gottlieb's epigenetic psychobiological systems theory

Chapter 3. Genes, Environment, and Development

- The latest from the Human Genome Project and molecular genetics research
- Highlighting of the importance of gene expression—the turning on and off of genes over the course of development, partly in response to environmental influences
- New table clarifying the difference between mitosis and meiosis

Chapter 4. Prenatal Development and Birth

- The latest research on prenatal development and teratogens, including the effect of 9/11 on children born to women who were pregnant at the time
- Expanded coverage of the birthing experience and the father's experience of birth
- New section on breastfeeding

Chapter 5. Health and Physical Development

- A whole new emphasis on health and wellness to supplement the chapter's focus on physical and neural development, including a new section on health and wellness in each developmental period and greater attention to the importance of activity throughout the life span
- More on the dynamic systems perspective on the emergence of motor skills

Chapter 6. Perception

- New slant on the roles of nature and nurture in perception emphasizing the debate between constructivists and nativists
- More on the everyday implications of perceptual abilities and changes in them with age

Chapter 7. Cognition

- More discussion of criticisms of Piaget's theory
- Elaboration of Vygotsky's views on tool use among humans
- Expanded discussion of cognitive development in relation to children's beliefs in Santa Claus and changing tastes in humor

Chapter 8. Memory and Information Processing

- More on the neural basis of memory
- More on adolescents as information processors

- More on autobiographical memory in adulthood
- Use of the selection, optimization, compensation model to discuss coping with diminishing cognitive resources in old age

Chapter 9. Intelligence and Creativity

- New sections on creativity in each developmental period
- A new box on "Fostering Creativity"

Chapter 10. Language and Education

- Reorganized coverage of language development
- Discussion of what makes for an effective school in the context of the No Child Left Behind Act

Chapter 11. Self and Personality

- Introduction of five principles of personality set forth by McAdams and Pals to highlight the multifaceted nature of personality
- Inclusion of the increasingly influential approach to the study of temperament developed by Mary Rothbart and her colleagues and its relationship to the "Big Five" personality dimensions
- Research on life stories and the narrative identity approach to personality

Chapter 12. Gender Roles and Sexuality

- The latest findings on the nature and extent of gender differences
- Sharpened discussion of patterns of gender role behavior over the life span and the reasons why gender roles are sometimes strictly adhered to, sometimes viewed more flexibly
- Major revision and updating of the sections on sexual development and behavior, including new research on the social and cultural contexts of sexuality and new findings on downward trends in sexual activity and pregnancy among teens, accompanied by increased oral sex
- New figure and two new tables to enrich coverage

Chapter 13. Social Cognition and Moral Development

- Evolutionary perspective on social cognition and morality and lessons from research with chimpanzees
- Exploration of whether the brain has a special module that allows us to understand human behavior, including recent work on mirror neurons
- New table summarizing theories of moral development
- More on the role of emotion in moral development

Chapter 14. Attachment and Social Relationships

- New chapter opener about social relationships and the Virginia Tech massacre
- The latest from the National Institute of Child Health and Human Development study of the effects of day care on infants and young children
- New findings on the implications of infant attachment for adult romantic relationships
- New box on the dark side of peer relations in childhood and adolescence

Chapter 15. The Family

- Addition of the concept of coparenting to the discussion of the family system
- The latest thinking on social class differences in parenting
- New material on cultural differences in parenting and the effectiveness of different parenting styles in different cultural contexts

Chapter 16. Developmental Psychopathology

- Box on reasons behind the apparent epidemic of autism
- The emerging mirror neuron hypothesis about why autistic individuals have difficulty relating to other people
- The dangers of ruminating and co-ruminating about problems for adolescent girls
- New research on preventing eating disorders
- New data on the prevalence of psychological disorders in adulthood

Chapter 17. The Final Challenge: Death and Dying

- The latest on why we age and die and on the prospects for extending life
- New challenges to traditional assumptions about how people grieve
- A new box on what to say to the bereaved
- A closing reminder of the book's major themes

Appendix: Careers in Human Development

- A brand new appendix outlining different careers in human development, with a focus on research, teaching, and professional practice and the levels of education required for different jobs
- A robust list of additional student resources, including websites and supplemental books

CHAPTER ORGANIZATION

The chapters of this book use a consistent format and contain the following:

A *chapter outline* orients students to what lies ahead.

Introductory material stimulates interest, lays out the plan for the chapter, and introduces key concepts, theories, and issues relevant to the area of development to be explored.

Developmental sections (Chapters 5–17) describe key changes and continuities, as well as the mechanisms underlying them, during four developmental periods: infancy, childhood, adolescence, and adulthood.

"Explorations" boxed features allow more in-depth investigation of research on a topic (for example, reproductive technologies, sleep deprivation in adolescence, aging drivers, language acquisition among deaf children, cultural differences in moral thinking, the harmful side of peer relationships, culture and parenting, and euthanasia).

"Applications" boxed features examine how knowledge has been used to optimize development in a domain of development (for instance, to treat genetic defects, promote lifelong health, improve cognitive functioning across the life span, combat the effects of stereotypes of aging on the self-perceptions of older adults, treat aggressive youth, help social isolates, prevent family violence, treat children with psychological disorders, and lengthen life).

The bulleted *"Summing Up"* sections within each chapter and the *"Chapter Summary"* section at the end of each chapter give an overview of the chapter's main themes to facilitate student learning and review of the material.

"Critical Thinking" questions after each major chapter section challenge students to think about or apply the chapter material in new ways.

The *"Key Terms"* section lists the new terms introduced in the chapter in the order in which they were introduced and with the page number on which they were introduced. The terms are printed in boldface, defined when they are first presented in a chapter, and included in the glossary at the end of the book.

The *"Media Resources"* section describes selected websites that offer further information about chapter topics and are accessible from the book's website at academic.cengage.com/psychology/sigelman. Students are also directed to the other resources available at that site, including *Understanding the Data: Exercises on the Web* and the online diagnostic study tool *CengageNOW*.

SUPPLEMENTS

The sixth edition of *Life-Span Human Development* is accompanied by a better array of supplements prepared for both the instructor and the student to create the best learning environment inside and outside the classroom. All the supplements have been thoroughly revised and updated. Especially noteworthy are the media and Internet-based supplements. We invite instructors and students to examine and take advantage of the teaching and learning tools available.

For the Instructor

Instructor's Manual with Test Bank. Revised by Bradley Caskey, University of Wisconsin, River Falls. This manual contains chapter-specific outlines; a list of print, video, and online resources; and student learning objectives. The manual has a special emphasis on active learning with suggested student activities and projects for each chapter. The test bank, in both print and computerized form, consists of 135 multiple-choice, 20 true or false, 20 fill-in-the-blank, and 10 essay questions for each chapter. Questions are marked with the correct answer, main text page reference, and difficulty and are keyed to the Learning Objectives. This edition also contains suggested answers to the main text's Critical Thinking questions.
ISBN-10: 0-495-50893-4; ISBN-13: 978-0495-50893-9

PowerLecture with JoinIn™ and ExamView®. PowerLecture includes preassembled Microsoft® PowerPoint® lecture slides with graphics from the text by Suzanne Krinsky of Colorado State University. These lecture slides contain figures from the text and videos, allowing you to bring together text-specific lecture outlines and art from the text, along with video and animations from the web or your own materials—culminating in a powerful, personalized, media-enhanced presentation. In addition to a full Instructor's Manual and Test Bank, PowerLecture also includes:

- JoinIn™ Student Response System, a book-specific system that allows you to transform your classroom and assess your students' progress with instant in-class quizzes and polls. This program lets you pose book-specific questions and display students' answers seamlessly within the Microsoft® PowerPoint® slides of your own lecture, in conjunction with the "clicker" hardware of your choice.
- ExamView® testing software with all the test items from the printed Test Bank in electronic format enables you to create customized tests of up to 250 items in print or online.

ISBN-10: 0-495-50894-2; ISBN-13: 978-0-495-50894-6

ABC® Videos for Lifespan Development. The ABC videos feature short, high-interest clips about current studies and research in psychology. These videos are perfect for discussion starters or to enrich lectures. Some topics include:

- Infant Mental Health
- Fathers and Autism
- Foster Care
- Child and Adult Daycare
- Midlife Memory
- Alzheimer's Test

Contact your sales representative to order.

DVD ISBN-10: 0-495-50315-0; ISBN-13: 978-0-495-50315-6
VHS ISBN-10: 0-495-00328-X; ISBN-13: 978-0-495-00328-1

Wadsworth Developmental Psychology Video Library. Bring developmental psychology concepts to life with videos from Wadsworth's Developmental Psychology Video Library, which includes thought-provoking offerings from Films for Humanities and other excellent educational video sources. This extensive collection illustrates important developmental psychology concepts covered in many life-span courses. Certain adoption conditions apply.

For the Student

Study Guide. Written by coauthor Elizabeth A. Rider of Elizabethtown College, the *Study Guide* is designed to promote active learning through a guided review of the important principles and concepts in the text. The study materials for each chapter include a comprehensive multiple-choice self-test and exercises that challenge students to think about and to apply what they have learned.
ISBN-10: 0-495-50846-2; ISBN-13: 978-0495-50846-5

Internet-Based Supplements

Book Companion Website at academic.cengage.com/psychology/sigelman. This website provides instructors and students with a wealth of free information and resources, including tutorial quizzes, web links, essay questions, critical thinking exercises, and *Understanding the Data* exercises.

CengageNOW. Not only is CengageNOW a valuable course management and time-saving tool for instructors, it also offers many features that provide students with efficient ways to study for success in the course. CengageNOW includes diagnostic pre-tests and post-tests, with resulting *Personalized Study Plans*. For every chapter, students' unique *Personalized Study Plans* enable them to focus on what they need to learn and select the activities that best match their learning styles. CengageNOW includes an integrated e-book, videos, simulations, and animations—all designed to help students gain a deeper understanding of important concepts. Prompts at the end of each chapter guide students online to CengageNOW.

CengageNOW includes pre-tests and post-tests written by Jori Reijonen. If the textbook does not include an access code card, students can go to www.ichapters.com to order an access code.
Printed Access Card: ISBN-10: 0-495-59691-4; ISBN-13: 978-0-495-59691-2
Instant Access Code: ISBN-10: 0-495-59692-2; ISBN-13: 978-0-495-59692-9

Audio Study Tools. Audio Study Tools provides audio reinforcement of key concepts that students can listen to from their personal computer or MP3 player. Created specifically for

Sigelman and Rider's *Life-Span Human Development, Sixth Edition*, Audio Study Tools provides approximately 10 minutes of audio content for each chapter, giving students a quick and convenient way to master key concepts. Audio content allows students to test their knowledge with quiz questions, listen to a brief overview reflecting the major themes of each chapter, and review key terminology. Order Audio Study Tools directly at www.ichapters.com.
ISBN-10: 0-495-50897-7; ISBN-13: 978-0-495-50897-7

iChapters. At www.ichapters.com, students can select from more than 10,000 print and digital study tools, including the option to buy individual e-chapters and e-books. The first e-chapter is free.

WebTutor™ Toolbox on WebCT and Blackboard. This online supplement helps students succeed by taking them into an environment rich with study and mastery tools, communication aids, and additional course content. For students, WebTutor Toolbox offers real-time access to a full array of study tools, including flashcards (with audio), practice quizzes, Internet exercises, asynchronous discussion, a whiteboard, and an integrated e-mail system. Instructors can use WebTutor Toolbox to offer virtual office hours, to post syllabi, to set up threaded discussions, to track student progress on quizzes, and more. You can customize the content of WebTutor Toolbox in any way you choose, including uploading images and other resources, adding web links, and creating course-specific practice materials.
ISBN-10: 0-495-63882-X; ISBN-13: 978-0-495-63882-7
WebCT™ ISBN-10: 0-495-63880-3; ISBN-13: 978-0-495-63880-3

ACKNOWLEDGMENTS

We would like to express our continuing debt to David Shaffer of the University of Georgia for allowing his textbook to inform the first and second editions of this book.

Credit for excellent supplementary materials goes to Bradley Caskey, who revised the *Instructor's Manual with Test Bank*, and coauthor Elizabeth Rider, who wrote the *Study Guide* that accompanies this book.

Producing this book required the joint efforts of Wadsworth and Graphic World Publishing Services. We thank our editor, Michele Sordi, for her capable leadership of the project, and Kristin Makarewycz, our development editor, for her thorough and thoughtful readings of each chapter and special efforts to make this edition the most visually appealing and pedagogically effective edition yet. We thank Dan Fitzgerald at Graphic World for outstanding management of the book's production; Cheryl Whitley, Michele Margenau, and Jackie Favazza at Graphic World for composition of the book; Jeanne Calabrese for her creative work on the graphic design; and Kim Adams for photo research. All of these pros were a joy to work with, and the book is much better because of them. We are

grateful, as well, for the able assistance of Mary Noel, production project manager; Vernon Boes, art director; Amy Cohen, managing technology project manager; and Magnolia Molcan, assistant editor. We also appreciate the strong support of Linda Yip, advertising project manager; Sara Swangard, marketing manager; and Melanie Cregger, marketing assistant.

We remain deeply indebted to sponsoring editors past—to C. Deborah Laughton, who insisted that this project be undertaken, and to Vicki Knight, who skillfully shepherded the first edition through its final stages and oversaw the second edition. Finally, Lee Sigelman is always there, Gooseberry and Doughy Sigelman deserve thanks yet again for putting up with their distracted and unamusing companion, and Corby Rider and Tucker deserve deepest appreciation for their patience, understanding, and ability to entertain themselves (quietly) while mom works.

Reviewers

We are very grateful to six "cohorts" of reviewers for the constructive criticism and great suggestions that have helped us make each edition of this book better than the one before:

Barinder Bahvra, *Macomb Community College*
David Beach, *University of Wisconsin–Parkside*
Howard Bierenbaum, *College of William & Mary*
Fredda Blanchard-Fields, *Louisiana State University*
Cheryl Bluestone, *Queensborough Community College*
Tracie Blumentritt, *University of Wisconsin La Crosse*
Denise Ann Bodman, *Arizona State University*
Bob Bornstein, *Miami University–Oxford*
Kim G. Brenneman, *Eastern Mennonite University*
Donna Brent, *Hartwick College*
Mary Ann Bush, *Western Michigan University*
Elaine H. Cassel, *Lord Fairfax Community College*
Yiwei Chen, *Bowling Green State University*
Shelley Drazen, *Binghamton University (SUNY)*
Michelle R. Dunlap, *Connecticut College*
Marion Eppler, *East Carolina University*
Dan Florell, *Eastern Kentucky University*
James N. Forbes, *Angelo State University*
Claire Ford, *Bridgewater State College*
Carie Forden, *Clarion University*
Jody S. Fournier, *Capital University*
Janet Fritz, *Colorado State University*
Rebecca J. Glover, *University of North Texas*
Cheryl Hale, *Jefferson College*
Charles Harris, *James Madison University*
Karen Hartlep, *California State University at Bakersfield*
Debra L. Hollister, *Valencia Community College*
Stephen Hoyer, *Pittsburg State University*
Malia Huchendorf, *Normandale Community College*
David P. Hurford, *Pittsburg State University*
Vivian Jenkins, *University of Southern Indiana*
Linda Jones, *Blinn College*
Wayne G. Joosse, *Calvin College*

John Klein, *Castleton State College*
Jim Korcuska, *University of San Diego*
Suzanne Krinsky, *University of Southern Colorado*
Brett Laursen, *Florida Atlantic University*
Sherry Loch, *Paradise Valley Community College*
Becky White Loewy, *San Francisco State University*
Rosanne Lorden, *Eastern Kentucky University*
Nancy Macdonald, *University of South Carolina–Sumter*
Susan Magun-Jackson, *University of Memphis*
Robert F. Marcus, *University of Maryland*
Gabriela A. Martorell, *Portland State University*
Rebecca Kang McGill, *Temple University*
Russell Miars, *Portland State University*
Ann K. Mullis, *Florida State University*
Ronald L. Mullis, *Florida State University*
Bridget C. Murphy-Kelsey, *University of Oklahoma*
Susan L. O'Donnell, *George Fox University*
Shirley M. Ogletree, *Southwest Texas State University*

Jim O'Neill, *Wayne State University*
Rob Palkovitz, *University of Delaware*
Suzanne Pasch, *University of Wisconsin at Milwaukee*
Louise Perry, *Florida Atlantic University*
Mark Rafter, *College of the Canyons*
Marjorie Reed, *Oregon State University*
Eileen Rogers, *University of Texas at San Antonio*
Mark Runco, *California State University at Fullerton*
Pamela Schuetze, *Buffalo State College*
Matt Scullin, *West Virginia University*
Timothy Shearon, *Albertson College of Idaho*
Luis Terrazas, *California State University at San Marcos*
Polly Trnavsky, *Appalachian State University*
Katherine Van Giffen, *California State University at Long Beach*
Catherine Weir, *Colorado College*
Ruth Wilson, *Idaho State University*
Robin Yaure, *Penn State Mont Alto*

About the Authors

Carol K. Sigelman is associate vice president for graduate studies and academic affairs and professor of psychology at The George Washington University. She earned her bachelor's degree from Carleton College and a double-major doctorate in English and psychology from George Peabody College for Teachers. She has also been on the faculty at Texas Tech University, Eastern Kentucky University (where she won her college's Outstanding Teacher Award), and the University of Arizona. She has taught courses in child, adolescent, adult, and life-span development and has published research on such topics as the communication skills of individuals with developmental disabilities, the development of stigmatizing reactions to children and adolescents who are different, and children's emerging understandings of diseases and psychological disorders. Through a grant from the National Institute of Child Health and Human Development, she studied children's intuitive theories of AIDS and developed and evaluated a curriculum to correct their misconceptions and convey the facts of HIV infection. Through a grant from the National Institute on Drug Abuse, she and her colleagues explored children's and adolescents' understandings of the effects of alcohol and drugs on body, brain, and behavior. For fun, she enjoys hiking, biking, and just being with her husband.

Elizabeth A. Rider is professor of psychology and Registrar at Elizabethtown College in Pennsylvania. She has also been on the faculty at the University of North Carolina at Asheville. She earned her undergraduate degree from Gettysburg College and her doctorate from Vanderbilt University. She has taught courses on child and life-span development, women and gender issues, applied developmental psychology, and genetic and environmental influences on development. She has published research on children's and adults' spatial perception, orientation, and ability to find their way. Through a grant from the Pennsylvania State System for Higher Education, she studied factors associated with academic success. The second edition of her text on the psychology of women, *Our Voices*, was published by John Wiley & Sons in 2005. When she is not working, her life revolves around her son and a fun-loving springer spaniel.

1
CHAPTER

Understanding Life-Span Human Development

BORN IN TENNESSEE IN 1880—15 years after the Civil War, 2 years before Franklin Delano Roosevelt was born, and years before the automobile, much less the Internet—Mrs. Ella Miller was the eldest daughter of former slaves. She had only two dresses as a child, and she recalls seeing her first airplane and thinking it was going to fall on her (Tousignant, 1995). She married but had no children. After her husband, Isaac, died at age 70, she worked as a domestic helper for two elderly women until she retired (at age 107!).

One of the growing number of **centenarians** (people age 100 or older) in the United States, Mrs. Miller spent her last years with her niece, remained active in church, spoke to elementary school children about life in the late 1800s, and stocked up on candy and cookies whenever she went grocery shopping (Frost, 2000).

Mrs. Miller attributed her long life to never worrying: "I try to make life more jolly than sad" (Tousignant, 1996). She was pleased to share her rules of living: "Be on time, save your money, care about one another, love life, love people and have a desire to be somebody. All living is about love. Joy is in helping others" (Frost, 2000). Just entering the third century she had seen a part of, she died in 2000 of heart failure at age 119, as old as humans get ("Ella Galbraith Miller," 2000).

■ ■ ■

This book is about the development of humans like Ella Miller—and you—from conception to death. Among the fascinating and important questions it addresses are these: How do infants perceive the world around them and how do their minds develop? Does the divorce of a child's parents have lasting effects on the child's personality or later romantic relationships? Why do some college students have more trouble than others deciding on a major or committing themselves to a serious relationship? Do most adults experience a midlife crisis in which they question what they have done with their lives? How do people typically change physically and mentally as they age, and how does retirement affect them? It also takes on more fundamental questions: How in the world does a single fertilized egg cell evolve into an adult human being? How do genetic and environmental influences shape human development? How can we use the findings of research to optimize development?

Do any of these questions intrigue you? Probably so, because we are all developing persons interested in ourselves and the other developing people around us. Most college students want to understand how they and those they know have been affected by their experiences, how they have changed over the years, and where they may be headed. Many students also have practical motivations for learning about human development—for example, a desire to be a better parent or to pursue a career as a psychologist, nurse, teacher, or other human services professional.

This introductory chapter lays the groundwork for the remainder of the book by addressing some basic questions: How should we think about development and influences on it? What is the science of life-span development? How is development studied? And what are some of the challenges in studying human development?

Centenarian Ella Miller, daughter of former slaves, at age 115.

© James A. Parcell/*The Washington Post*

1.1 | HOW SHOULD WE THINK ABOUT DEVELOPMENT?

We begin by asking what it means to say that humans "develop" over the life span, how we can conceptualize the life span, and how we can approach the single biggest issue in the study of development, the nature–nurture issue, and understand developing humans in their environments.

Defining Development

Development can be defined as systematic changes and continuities in the individual that occur between conception and death, or from "womb to tomb." Development entails many changes; by describing these changes as systematic, we imply that they are orderly, patterned, and relatively enduring—not fleeting and unpredictable like mood swings. Development also involves continuities, ways in which we remain the same or continue to reflect our past selves.

The systematic changes and continuities of interest to students of human development fall into three broad domains:

1. *Physical development.* The growth of the body and its organs, the functioning of physiological systems, physical signs of aging, changes in motor abilities, and so on.
2. *Cognitive development.* Changes and continuities in perception, language, learning, memory, problem solving, and other mental processes.
3. *Psychosocial development.* Changes and carryover in personal and interpersonal aspects of development, such as motives, emotions, personality traits, interpersonal skills and relationships, and roles played in the family and in the larger society.

Even though developmentalists often specialize in one of these three aspects of development, they appreciate that humans are whole beings and that changes in one area affect the others. The baby who develops the ability to crawl, for example, has new opportunities to develop her mind by exploring kitchen cabinets and to hone her social skills by trailing her parents from room to room.

How do you picture typical changes from birth to old age? Many people picture tremendous positive gains in capacity from infancy to young adulthood, little change during early adulthood and middle age, and loss of capacities in the later years. This stereotyped view of the life span is largely false, but it also has some truth in it, especially with respect to biological development. Traditionally, biologists have defined **growth** as the physical changes that occur from conception to maturity. We indeed become biologically mature and physically competent during the early part of the life span. **Biological aging** is the deterioration of organisms (including humans) that leads inevitably to their death. Biologically, development does involve growth in early life, stability in early and middle adulthood, and declines associated with aging in later life.

Many aspects of development do not follow this "gain–then stability–then loss" model, however. Modern developmental scientists recognize that developmental change at any age involves both gains and losses. For example, child development is not all about gain; children gain many cognitive abilities as they get older, but they also lose self-esteem and become more prone to depression (Gotlib & Hammen, 2002; Robins et al., 2002). Nor should we associate aging only with loss: expertise and wisdom often increase from early adulthood to middle and later adulthood (Baltes, Lindenberger, & Staudinger, 1998), and adults age 60 and older score higher on vocabulary tests than adults ages 18 to 30 (Verhaeghen, 2003).

In addition, people do not always improve or worsen but instead just become different than they were (as when a child who once feared loud noises comes to fear hairy monsters under the bed instead). Development clearly means more than positive growth during infancy, childhood, and adolescence. And **aging** involves more than biological aging; it refers to a range of changes, *positive and negative,* in the mature organism. In short, development involves gains, losses, neutral changes, and continuities in each phase of the life span.

Conceptualizing the Life Span

If you were to divide the human life span into periods, how would you do it? ● **Table 1.1** lists the periods that many of today's developmentalists regard as distinct. You will want to keep them in mind as you read this book, because we will constantly be speaking of infants, preschoolers, school-age children, adolescents, and young, middle-aged, and older adults. Note, however, that the given ages are approximate. Age is only a rough indicator of developmental status; there are huge differences in functioning and personality among individuals of the same age. Interestingly, the most diverse of all age groups appears to be elderly adults (Andrews, Clark, & Luszcz, 2002). Yet many people stereotype all old people as forgetful, frail, or cranky.

Table 1.1 represents only one view of the periods of the life span. Age—like gender, race, and other significant human characteristics—means different things in different societies. Each society has its own ways of dividing the life span and of treating the people in different age groups. Each socially defined age group in a society—called an **age grade** or age stratum—is assigned different statuses, roles, privileges, and responsibilities. Segregating children into grades in school based on age is one form of age grading. Just as high schools have "elite" seniors and "lowly" freshmen, whole societies are

What periods of the life span do you distinguish?

● TABLE 1.1   AN OVERVIEW OF PERIODS OF THE LIFE SPAN

PERIOD OF LIFE	AGE RANGE
Prenatal period	Conception to birth
Infancy	First 2 years of life
Preschool period	2 to 5 or 6 years (some prefer to describe as *toddlers* children who have begun to walk and are age 1 to 3)
Middle childhood	6 to about 12 (or until the onset of puberty)
Adolescence	Approximately 12 to 20 (or when the individual becomes relatively independent of parents and begins to assume adult roles)
Early adulthood	20 to 40 years
Middle adulthood	40 to 65 years
Late adulthood	65 years and older

© AP/Wide World Photos

Each January 15 in Japan, 20-year-olds are officially pronounced adults in a national celebration and enter a new age grade. Young women receive kimonos, young men receive suits, and all are reminded of their responsibilities to society. Young adults also gain the right to drink, smoke, and vote. The modern ceremony grew out of an ancient one in which young samurai became recognized as warriors (Reid, 1993). The age-grading system in Japanese culture clearly marks the beginning of adulthood

layered into age grades. We, for example, grant "adults" (18-year-olds by law in the United States) a voting privilege not granted to children. Legal definitions of the boundary between adolescence and adulthood vary, though. In most states in the United States, the legal age for marrying is lower than the legal ages for voting or serving in the military, and the right to drink alcohol is granted last, commonly at age 21 (Settersten, 2005). Similarly, although many of us define age 65 as the boundary between middle age and old age, in fact the ages at which people become eligible for Medicare, Social Security benefits, and "senior discounts" at restaurants and stores vary.

In certain other cultures, the recognized periods of the life span include a period before birth and an afterlife, or the life span may be pictured as a circle that includes reincarnation or some other way of being "recycled" and born again (Fry, 1985, 1999; Kojima, 2003). The St. Lawrence Eskimo simply distinguish between boys and men (or between girls and women), whereas the Arusha people of East Africa have six socially meaningful age grades for males: youths, junior warriors, senior warriors, junior elders, senior elders, and retired elders (Keith, 1985).

Once a society has established age grades, it defines what people should and should not do at different points in the life span (Elder & Shanahan, 2006). According to pioneering gerontologist Bernice Neugarten and her colleagues (Neugarten, Moore, & Lowe, 1965), these expectations, or **age norms,** are society's way of telling people how to act their age. In our culture, for example, most people agree that 6-year-olds are too young to date or drink beer but are old enough to attend school. We also tend to agree that adults should think about marrying

around age 25 and should retire around age 65 (Neugarten, Moore, & Lowe, 1965; Settersten, 1998). In less industrialized countries, where couples typically have children in their teens and often become ill, disabled, and unable to work in middle age, age norms typically call for earlier achievement of these milestones (Shanahan, 2000).

Why are age norms important? First, they influence people's decisions about how to lead their lives. They are the basis for what Neugarten (1968) called the **social clock**—a person's sense of when things should be done and when he or she is ahead of or behind the schedule dictated by age norms. Prompted by the social clock, for example, an unmarried 25-year-old may feel that he should propose to his girlfriend before she gives up on him, or a childless 35-year-old might fear that she will miss her chance at parenthood unless she has a baby soon. Second, age norms affect how easily people adjust to life transitions. Normal life events such as having children typically tend to affect us more negatively when they occur "off time" than when they occur "on time," at socially appropriate ages (McLanahan & Sorensen, 1985). It can be challenging indeed to experience puberty at either age 8 or age 18 or to become a new parent at 13 or 48.

Age grades, age norms, social clocks, and the meanings of age differ not only from culture to culture but also from subculture to subculture. Our own society is diverse socioeconomically, racially, and ethnically, and African American, Hispanic American, Native American, Asian American, and European American individuals sometimes hold different age norms and have different developmental experiences. Within each of these broad racial and ethnic groups there are immense variations associated with such factors as specific national origin, length of time in North America, degree of integration into mainstream society, language usage, and socioeconomic status.

Generally, individuals from lower-income families in our society tend to reach milestones of adulthood such as starting work, marrying, and having children earlier than those from middle-income and upper-income families do (Elder & Shanahan, 2006). Linda Burton (1996a) studied age norms in a low-income African American community and found it was considered appropriate there for a young woman to become a mother at 16 and a grandmother at 34—earlier than in most middle-class communities, white or black. Teenage mothers in this community looked to their own mothers and, especially, their grandmothers to help them care for their children. Similar norms prevail among low-income European Americans in rural Appalachia. It may seem unusual from a middle-class perspective for children to be born to mothers so young and then to be raised largely by people other than their mothers and fathers. Yet it is not unusual in many cultures around the world for child care responsibilities to be shared like this with grandmothers and other relatives (Rogoff, 2003). Nor is there evidence that such care is damaging to development.

As the Explorations box on "Historical Changes in Periods of the Life Span" (page 8) illustrates, the meanings of childhood, adolescence, and adulthood also differ from historical period to historical period. Not until the 17th and 18th centuries in Western cultures were children viewed as innocents to be protected rather than as potential workers who should grow up quickly; not until the late 19th century was adolescence recognized as a distinct phase of the life span; and not until the 20th century has our society begun to define a period of emerging adulthood, a period of middle age in which the nest is emptied of children, and a period of old age characterized by retirement.

The broader message is clear: *We must view development in its historical, cultural, and subcultural context.* We must bear in mind that each social group settles on its own definitions of the life span, the age grades within it, and the norms appropriate to each age range, and that each social group experiences development differently. We must also appreciate that the major periods of the life span recognized today—adolescence, middle age, and so on—have not always been considered distinct. One of the most fascinating challenges in the study of human development is to understand which aspects of development are universal and which aspects differ in different social contexts (Norenzayan & Heine, 2005; Shweder et al., 2006).

Framing the Nature–Nurture Issue

Developmental scientists seek to understand the processes that shape human development, which means grappling with *the* major issue in the study of human development—the **nature–nurture issue,** or the question of how biological forces and environmental forces act and interact to make us what we are. We highlight this central issue in development throughout this book, because understanding the causes of development is "one of the foremost intellectual challenges of modern science" (Gottlieb, Wahlsten, & Lickliter, 2006).

On the *nature* side of the debate are those who emphasize the influence of heredity, universal maturational processes guided by the genes, biologically based predispositions produced by evolution, and biological influences such as hormones and brain growth spurts. To those who emphasize *nature,* development is largely a process of **maturation,** the biological unfolding of the individual according to a plan contained in the **genes** (the hereditary material passed from parents to child at conception). Just as seeds turn into mature plants through a predictable process, humans "unfold" within the womb (assuming that they receive the necessary nourishment from their environment). Their genetic program then makes it likely that they will walk and utter their first words at about 1 year of age, achieve sexual maturity between 12 and 14, and gray in their 40s and 50s. Maturational changes in the brain contribute to cognitive changes such as increased memory and problem-solving skills and to psychosocial changes such as increased understanding of other people's feelings. Genetically influenced maturational processes guide all of us through many of the same developmental changes at about the same points in our lives, while individual hereditary endowment is making each person's development unique.

On the *nurture* side of the nature–nurture debate are those who emphasize change in response to **environment**—all the external physical and social conditions, stimuli, and events that can affect us, from crowded living quarters and polluted air, to social interactions with family members, peers, and teachers, to the neighborhood and broader cultural context in which we develop. We know that the physical environment matters—for example, that exposure to lead in the paint in old buildings can stunt children's intellectual development or that living near a noisy airport can interfere with their progress in learning to read (Evans, 2006). And we will see countless examples in this book of how the social environment—the behavior of other people—shapes development. Rather than seeing maturation as the process driving development, those on the nurture side of the nature–nurture debate emphasize **learning**—the process through which experience (that is, environmental stimuli) brings about relatively permanent changes in thoughts, feelings, or behavior. A certain degree of physical maturation is clearly necessary before a child can dribble a basketball, but careful instruction and long, hard hours of practice are just as clearly required if the child is to excel in basketball (see ● **Table 1.2** for a summary of the nature-nurture debate).

If nature is important in development, we would expect all children to achieve similar developmental milestones at similar times because of maturation, and we would expect differences among individuals to be largely caused by differences in their genetic makeup. If nurture is important in development, we would expect humans to be alike if their environments are alike but would also expect human development to take different forms depending on the individual's life experiences. Let's settle the nature–nurture debate right now: Developmental changes are generally the products of a complex interplay between nature (genetic endowment, biological influences, and maturation) and nurture (environmental influences, experi-

● TABLE 1.2 THE LANGUAGE OF NATURE AND NURTURE

NATURE	NURTURE
Heredity	Environment
Maturation	Learning
Genes	Experience
Biologically based predispositions	Cultural influences

■ **FIGURE 1.1** Aggression among children in four cultures.
SOURCE: Based on means reported in Munroe et al. (2000)

ences, and learning). It is not nature *or* nurture; it is nature *and* nurture. To make matters more complex, it is nature affecting nurture and nurture affecting nature! For example, biology (nature) provides us with a brain that allows us to learn from our experiences (nurture), experiences which in turn change our brains. Much of the joy of studying human development comes from trying to understand more precisely how these two forces combine to make us what we are.

Ponder this sample nature–nurture question. In the United States, there is consistent evidence that, on average, boys are more likely than girls to engage in physically aggressive behavior and men commit more violent crimes than women (Hyde, 1984; Quinsey et al., 2004). Does this sex difference reflect nature (biological differences between the sexes, such as different hormone balances) or nurture (for example, a tendency of parents to tolerate or even encourage aggression in boys but to suppress it in girls)? How might you try to answer this nature–nurture question?

One approach is to find out whether sex differences in physical aggression are evident in societies quite different from our own. This question is what prompted Robert Munroe and his colleagues (2000) to study aggression among 3- to 9-year-old children in four nonindustrialized societies from diverse parts of the globe: Belize, Kenya, Nepal, and American Samoa. In each society, 24 girls and 24 boys were studied. Residents of the communities studied were trained to observe children's social behavior, including their aggressive behavior. Aggressive behavior was defined as assaulting (hitting, kicking, or otherwise attacking someone), horseplay (roughhousing), and symbolic aggression (making insulting or threatening gestures or statements).

As ■ **Figure 1.1** shows, boys exhibited more aggression than girls in all four societies. Overall, about 10% of boys' social behaviors, compared with 6% of girls' behaviors, were aggressive. Boys, and girls too, were especially likely to behave aggressively when they were in a group with a relatively large number of boys. Munroe and his colleagues noted that male play groups in which young males compete for dominance are observed in primate species other than human beings. Establishing dominance in the peer group gives males an edge in competing for mates and reproducing. Possibly, then, genes that predispose males to be aggressive have been built into the human genetic code over the course of evolution (Barash,

2002). The evidence in support of nature in Munroe's study is not strong, but it hints that genes could contribute to gender differences in aggression.

However, cultural differences in aggression—as well as in the size of the gender difference in aggression—were also evident in this study. The two most patrilineal cultures (cultures in which families are organized around male kin groups) were Kenya and Nepal. These proved to be the cultures in which aggressive behavior was most frequent (10–11% of social acts, as opposed to 4–6% in Belize and American Samoa). Moreover, sex differences in aggression were sharpest in these patrilineal cultures. As is often the case when we ask whether nature or nurture is more important in development, these findings, like those of other studies, suggest that both nature and nurture contribute to gender differences in aggression. The findings also make us want to conduct more research, including studies examining both biological and environmental differences between the sexes, to understand more fully why males, especially in some cultural contexts, are more physically aggressive than females.

Grasping the Ecology of Development

If we take seriously the concept that human development is shaped by interacting biological and environmental factors, we need a way to conceptualize a changing person in a changing and multifaceted environment. To help you think about this, we will consider an influential conceptual model of development formulated by Russian-born American psychologist Urie Bronfenbrenner (1917–2005). Decades ago, Bronfenbrenner became disturbed that many developmentalists were studying human development out of context, expecting it to be universal and failing to appreciate how much it could vary from culture to culture, from neighborhood to neighborhood, and from home to home. Bronfenbrenner formulated an ecological model to describe how the environment is organized and how it affects development. He later renamed it a **bioecological model** of development to stress how biology and environment interact to produce development (Bronfenbrenner, 1979, 1989; Bronfenbrenner & Morris, 2006).

In Bronfenbrenner's view, the developing person, with his or her genetic makeup and biological and psychological characteristics, is embedded in a series of environmental systems. These systems interact with one another and with the individual over time to influence development. Bronfenbrenner described four environmental systems that influence, and are influenced by, the developing person, as shown in ■ **Figure 1.2.**

1. A **microsystem** is an immediate physical and social environment in which the person interacts face-to-face with other people and influences and is affected by them. The primary microsystem for a firstborn infant is likely to be the family—perhaps infant, mother, and father, all reciprocally influencing one another. The developing child may also experience other microsystems such as a day care center or grandmother's house. We have much evidence that the family environment is an important influence on child development and have come to appreciate the importance of peer groups, schools, and neighborhood environments.

2. The **mesosystem** consists of the interrelationships or linkages between two or more microsystems. For example, a marital conflict in the family (one microsystem) could make a child withdraw from staff members and other children at the day care center (a second microsystem) so that her experience there becomes less intellectually stimulating. A loving home environment, by contrast, is likely to allow a child to benefit more from experiences in the day care center—or later, in school, at college, or on the job.

3. The **exosystem** consists of linkages involving social settings that individuals do not experience directly but that can still influence their development. For example, children can be affected by how their parents' day at work went or by a decision by the local school board to focus instruction almost entirely on getting more children to pass the state reading examination.

4. The **macrosystem** is the larger cultural context in which the microsystem, mesosystem, and exosystem are embedded. **Culture** is often defined as the shared understandings and way of life of a people, including beliefs and practices concerning the nature of humans in different phases of the life span, what children need to be taught to function in society, and how people should lead their lives as adults. Although the United States has a high standard of living, it is not a very family-friendly cultural environment in many ways, as

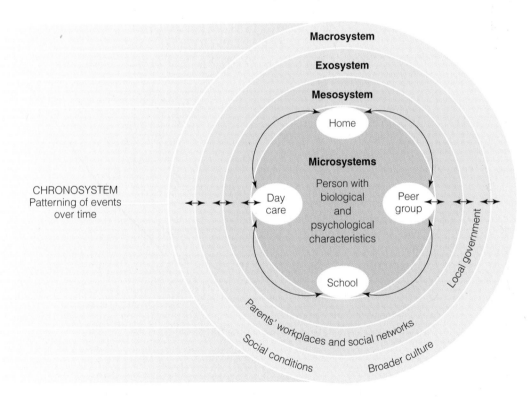

■ **FIGURE 1.2** Urie Bronfenbrenner's bioecological model of development pictures environment as a series of nested structures. The microsystem refers to relations between the developing person and her immediate environment, the mesosystem to connections among microsystems, the exosystem to settings that affect but do not contain the individual, the macrosystem to the broader cultural context of development, and the chronosystem to the patterning over time of historical and life events. Researchers face many challenges in studying the developing person in context.
SOURCE: Adapted from Kopp & Krakow (1982)

HISTORICAL CHANGES IN PERIODS OF THE LIFE SPAN

The quick historical tour that you are about to take should convince you that the historical context in which humans develop matters and that the phases of the life span recognized today were not always perceived as distinct—and may not always be perceived as they are today.

Childhood

Phillippe Ariès (1962) conducted an ambitious historical analysis and concluded that, before 1600, European societies had little concept of childhood as we know it. Until then, he believed, children were viewed as miniature adults. In medieval Europe (A.D. 500–1500), for example, 6-year-olds were dressed in miniature versions of adult clothing and expected to work alongside adults at home, at a shop, or in the fields (Ariès, 1962). Moreover, a 10-year-old convicted of stealing could be hanged (Kean, 1937).

It is now clear that it is an exaggeration to say that pre–17th-century adults held a miniature-adult view of childhood (Cunningham, 1996; Hanawalt, 2003). Parents throughout history seem to have recognized that children are different from adults. Nevertheless, before the 17th and 18th centuries, people in Western societies pressured children to grow up, adopt adult roles, and contribute economically to the family's survival as soon as possible. During the 17th and 18th centuries, the modern concept of childhood gradually came into being. Children came to be seen as more distinctly childlike—as innocent beings who should be protected, given a proper moral and religious education, and taught skills such as reading and writing so that they would eventually become good workers (Cunningham, 1996).

The historical context of child development continues to change. Some observers argue

that modern society has been reverting to a medieval view of childhood—asking children to grow up quickly and to cope with terrorists, drugs dealers, gun violence, and other social ills (Elkind, 1992; Koops, 2003). Might we be exposing children to too many "adult" issues and situations too early in life? Maybe, but consider that the age of consent for sexual relations was 12 or younger as late as the end of the 19th century (Coontz, 2000b).

Adolescence

If the modern concept of childhood arose only during the 17th century, perhaps it is not surprising that **adolescence**—the transitional period between childhood and adulthood that begins with puberty and ends when the individual has acquired adult competencies and responsibilities—came to be viewed as a distinct period of the life span in Western societies only at the end of the 19th century and beginning of the 20th century (Hine, 1999; Kett, 1977). Before the industrial revolution, work took place within the family household; families farmed, built furniture, or engaged in other trades at home. Children contributed as they became able; age mattered little (Gillis, 2003). Early in the industrial revolution, factories needed cheap labor. At first they could make do with children; later they used immigrants. But as industry advanced, an educated labor force was needed, so laws were passed restricting child labor and making schooling compulsory. By the middle of the 20th century, adolescence had become a distinct life stage in which youths spent their days in school—separated from the adult world and living in their own peer culture (Furstenberg, 2000).

After World War II, adolescents began to attend college in large numbers and to postpone marriage and parenthood, delaying their entry into the adult world still further (Furstenberg et al., 2004; Keniston, 1970). Today, Jeffrey Arnett

How might your childhood have been different if you had worked in the coal mines like these boys?

and others are talking about the appearance in developed countries of a new period of development called **emerging adulthood,** extending from about age 18 to age 25, when young people are neither adolescents nor adults. According to Arnett (2006), this is a distinctive phase of life in which youth:

- explore their identities;
- lead unstable lives filled with job changes, new relationships, and moves;
- are self-focused, relatively free of obligations to others, and therefore free to focus on their own psychological needs;
- feel in between—adultlike in some ways but not others; and
- believe they have limitless possibilities ahead (Arnett, 2000; Arnett & Tanner, 2006).

What do you regard as key markers of adulthood, and how many of them do you believe you have achieved? When Frank Furstenberg and his colleagues (2004) conducted a survey on the matter, they found that only 31% of 30-year-old men and 46% of 30-year-old women in the United States in the year 2000 had achieved all of what the researchers considered to be the traditional markers of adulthood:

Bronfenbrenner himself often lamented (Bronfenbrenner & Morris, 2006). For example, the United States is one of only 4 countries out of 168 studied that does not provide paid maternity leave to female employees; the Family and Medical Leave Act provides for 12 weeks of leave, but it is *unpaid* leave and it is not available to workers in small companies (Heymann, Penrose, & Earle, 2006). Nor does the United States do as much as many other nations to ensure that workers

can take leave to care for sick children or ailing elders or that children of all income levels have appropriate preschool and after-school programs.

In addition to the microsystem, mesosystem, ecosystem, and macrosystem, Bronfenbrenner introduced the concept of the **chronosystem** to capture the idea that changes in people and their environments occur in a time frame ("chrono" means completing an education, being financially independent, leaving home, marrying, and having children. Back in 1960, by contrast, 65% of men and 77% of women age 30 had passed these milestones. Granted, many people today no longer consider marriage and parenthood to be markers of adulthood. However, even focusing on the other markers, young people in 2000 were making slower progress toward adulthood than young people in 1960. Not everyone agrees that emerging adulthood is a truly distinct period of development, but there is much agreement that adolescents are taking longer these days to become adults, largely because they are spending more time getting an education and taking longer to accumulate enough money to live independently and support a family.

Adulthood

Adulthood is also different today than it was in past eras. In ancient Rome, the average age of death was 20 to 30 years old; in the late 17th century, it was 35 to 40 years (Dublin & Lotka, 1936). These figures, which are *averages*, are low mainly because so many more infants died in the past. However, even those lucky enough to make it through early childhood had relatively low odds, by modern standards, of living to be 65 or older.

The average life expectancy continued to increase dramatically during the 20th century in many countries—at first because more babies survived infancy and early childhood, more recently because more people lived into old age (National Research Council, 2001). In 1900, the average life expectancy for a newborn born in the United States was about 47 years; in the early 21st century, it is 77.5 years overall—over 80 for a white female, 76 for a black female, 75 for a white male, and 69 for a black male (National Center for Health Statistics, 2005). The difference in life expectancy between the longest living Americans (Asian women, over 87 years on average) and the shortest living Americans (urban black males, 67 on average) is over 20 years (Murray et al., 2006).

The makeup of the U.S. population changed accordingly in the 20th century. In 1900, about 4% of the population was 65 and older. By 2000, the percentage was close to 13% and still climbing (Satariano, 2006). Census takers are closely watching the **baby boom generation**—the huge number of people born between 1946 and 1964—move through middle age. The first wave of baby boomers turned 60 in 2006: George W. Bush, Laura Bush, and Bill Clinton, along with Dolly Parton, Donald Trump, and Cher, not to mention the senior (in more ways than one) author of this book (Adler, 2005). They were a year old when Howdy Dowdy first appeared on TV and 17 when John F. Kennedy was assassinated; they grew up fearing nuclear bombs and Russians; and many of them protested the Vietnam War or fought in it (Adler, 2005). As Gail Sheehy (2005, p. 4) notes, "By taking longer to grow up and delaying marriage, parenting and retirement, [the Baby Boomers] have shifted all the stages of adulthood ahead by 10 to 15 years." And now policy makers will be watching closely as the boomers age. By 2030, when most baby boomers will have retired from work, adults 65 or older will represent more than 20% of the U.S. population (Satariano, 2006).

As 20th-century parents began to bear fewer children and live long enough to see their children empty the nest, Western societies began to recognize middle age as a distinct period between early adulthood and old age (Moen & Wethington, 1999). Middle age has been stereotyped as either a time of midlife crisis and turmoil or a time of stability and little developmental change. It is now understood to be a time of good health, stable relationships, many responsibilities, and high satisfaction for most people. It is also a time when people cope successfully with changes such as menopause and other signs of aging and achieve peak levels of cognitive functioning (Whitbourne & Willis, 2006; Willis & Schaie, 1999).

The experience of old age also changed during the 20th century, with the introduction of Social Security, Medicare, and other such programs for the elderly (Cole, 1992). In earlier centuries, people who survived to old age literally worked until they dropped; now they retire in their 60s if they have the means to do so. As a result, we have come to view old age as the retirement phase of life. Today's elderly adults also have fewer chronic diseases and disabilities, and are less affected by the ones they have, than elderly adults even a century ago (Satariano, 2006).

Yet as more people reach older ages, more will have diseases and disabilities. Aging in the 21st century will mean being part of an increasingly large group of people with chronic diseases and disabilities who depend on an increasingly small group of younger, working adults to support them by paying Social Security taxes and funding pensions, Medicare, social services, and other support programs (Wilmoth & Longino, 2006). This "graying of America," along with societal changes we cannot yet anticipate, will make the aging experience by the end of the 21st century quite different than it is today. The United States and other developed economies are now struggling with the challenges of meeting the needs of their graying populations, but the issue is a global one. Soon developing nations such as China (where a policy limiting families to one child will mean fewer adult children to support their aging parents) and India (where poverty is widespread) may struggle even more with these challenges (Eberstadt, 2006).

In sum, age—whether it is 7, 17, or 70—has meant something different in each historical era. And most likely, the experience of being 7, 17, or 70 will be different in the 21st century than it was in the 20th.

time) and unfold in particular patterns or sequences over a person's lifetime. We cannot study development by taking still photos; we must use a video camera and understand how one event leads to another. Thus conflict between husband and wife leads to divorce and to changes in family members and their relationships, or societal events such as economic depressions, wars, and technological breakthroughs alter individual development while individuals, in turn, affect the course of history (Modell & Elder, 2002). Each of us functions in particular microsystems linked through the mesosystem and embedded in the larger contexts of the exosystem and the macrosystem, all in continual flux.

Consider this example of how to analyze a problem using Bronfenbrenner's ecological model: If you wanted to optimize development by preventing or reducing drinking among teenagers, how might you intervene in each of Bronfenbrenner's environmental systems? Thinking of the family and peer group microsystems in which adolescents develop, you could provide an alcohol and drug prevention program to parents of teenagers, or you could recruit high school students who are peer leaders to influence other high school students to stay alcohol free. Thinking of the mesosystem, you could focus on strengthening the connections between the microsystem of the high school and the microsystem of the peer group. You might decide to offer more alcohol-free social events at school in hopes of reducing the number of peer-organized parties that involve drinking outside of school.

Focusing on the exosystem, if the police in your community have been lax in enforcing rules forbidding the sale of alcohol to minors, an intervention aimed at getting police officers to clamp down might be effective. Even adolescents who do not interact directly with either the police or managers of bars and liquor stores could be affected by such a clampdown if it makes alcohol less available to them. Finally, you may conclude that the real source of the problem is a whole culture (macrosystem) that tolerates drinking to excess among both adults and youth. A broad community campaign against irresponsible drinking may be needed.

The bioecological model suggests that the study of human development will not be easy. According to Bronfenbrenner and Morris (2006), researchers need to consider the relationships among and effects of key characteristics of the *person*, the *context*, the *time* dimension, and the *processes* through which an active person and his or her environment interact (for example, parent–infant interaction or play with peers). The bioecological model suggests that the contributions of nature and nurture cannot be separated easily because they are part of a dynamic system, continually influencing one another (Lerner, 2006). Complex research designs and complex statistical techniques will be needed to assess the many interacting influences on development portrayed in Bronfenbrenner's model (Lerner, Dowling, & Chaudhuri, 2005). It is appropriate, then, that we look next at the science of life-span human development and whether it is up to the challenge.

Summing Up

▍ Development is systematic changes and continuities over the life span, involving gains, losses, and neutral changes in physical, cognitive, and psychosocial functioning.

▍ Development occurs in an historical and cultural context and is influenced by age grades, age norms, and social clocks.

▍ Concepts of the life span and its distinctive periods differ in different periods of history and cultures. In the 17th and 18th centuries, children came to be seen as innocents; in the late 19th century, adolescence emerged as a distinct phase; and in the 20th century, emerging adulthood, the "empty nest" period, and an old-age retirement period have appeared.

▍ Understanding the nature–nurture issue means understanding the interaction of biology and maturation with environment and

learning. In Bronfenbrenner's bioecological model, individuals, with their biological and psychological characteristics, interact with the microsystem, mesosystem, exosystem, and macrosystem over time (chronosystem).

Critical Thinking

1. Given the age grades and age norms that prevail in our society, how would you compare the advantages and disadvantages of being (a) an adolescent as opposed to an adult, (b) an elderly adult as opposed to a young adult?

2. Ask a few people of different ages how they would define "middle age." Compile your results and analyze how much agreement there is among the answers.

3. Using Bronfenbrenner's bioecological model, characterize the environmental systems in which you are currently developing, giving an example of how each of Bronfenbrenner's systems may have affected you within the past year.

<table>
<tr><td>1.2</td><td>

What Is the Science of Life-Span Development?

</td></tr>
</table>

If development consists of systematic changes and continuities from conception to death brought about by multiple factors, the science of development consists of the study of those changes and continuities. In this section we consider the goals of the science of life-span development, its origins, and the modern life-span perspective on development.

Goals of Study

The goals driving the study of life-span development are describing, explaining, and optimizing development (Baltes, Reese, & Lipsitt, 1980). To achieve the goal of *description*, developmentalists characterize the behavior of humans of different ages and trace how that behavior changes with age. They describe both normal development and individual differences, or variations, in development. Although average trends in human development across the life span can be described, it is clear that no two people (even identical twins) develop along precisely the same pathways. Some babies are considerably more alert and active than others. Some 80-year-olds are out on the dance floor; others are home in bed.

Description is the starting point in any science, but scientists ultimately strive to achieve their second goal, *explanation*. Developmentalists seek to understand why humans develop as they typically do and why some individuals develop differently than others. To do so, developmentalists study the contributions of nature and nurture to development.

The third goal is *optimization* of human development. How can humans be helped to develop in positive directions? How can their capacities be enhanced, how can developmental difficulties be prevented, and how can any developmental problems that emerge be overcome? Pursuing the goal of optimizing development might involve evaluating ways to stimulate intellectual growth in preschool programs, to prevent alcohol abuse among college students, or to support elderly adults after the death of a spouse. To those who are or aspire to be teachers, psychologists or counselors, nurses or occupational therapists, or other helping professionals, applied research on optimizing development is especially relevant. (Note that the appendix of this book discusses careers related to life-span human development.)

Early Beginnings

Just as human development has changed through the ages, attempts to understand it have evolved over time (Cairns & Cairns, 2006). Although philosophers have long expressed their views on the nature of humans and the proper methods of raising children, it was not until the late 19th century that the first scientific investigations of development were undertaken. Several scholars began to carefully observe the growth and development of their own children and to publish their findings in the form of **baby biographies.** Perhaps the most influential baby biographer was Charles Darwin (1809–1882), who made daily records of his son's development (Darwin, 1877; see also Charlesworth, 1992). Darwin's curiosity about child development stemmed from his interest in evolution. He believed that infants share many characteristics with their nonhuman ancestors and that understanding the development of the individual embryo and child can offer insights into the evolution of the species. Darwin's evolutionary perspective and studies of the development of embryos strongly influenced early theories of human development, which emphasized universal, biologically based maturational changes (Cairns & Cairns, 2006; Parke et al., 1994).

Baby biographies left much to be desired as works of science, however. Because different baby biographers emphasized different aspects of their children's behavior, baby biographies were difficult to compare. Moreover, parents are not entirely objective observers of their own children, and early baby biographers may have let their assumptions about evolution and development bias their observations. Finally, because each baby biography was based on a single child—often the child of a distinguished family—it was not clear whether the findings would generalize to other children.

The **case study method**—an in-depth examination of an individual that often involves compiling and analyzing information from a variety of sources, such as observation, testing, and interviewing the person or people who know her—is still used today. The case study method can provide rich information about the complexities of an individual's development and the influences on it. It is particularly useful in studying people with rare conditions and disorders, when it is simply not possible to assemble a large sample of people to study, and it can be a good source of hypotheses that can be examined further in larger-scale studies. The main limitation of case studies is that conclusions based on a single case may not generalize to other individuals.

Although Darwin and other baby biographers deserve credit for making human development a legitimate topic of study and influencing early views of it, the man most often cited as the founder of developmental psychology is G. Stanley Hall (1846–1924), the first president of the American Psychological Association. Well aware of the shortcomings of baby biographies, Hall attempted to collect more objective data on large samples of individuals. He developed a now all-too-familiar research tool, the questionnaire, to explore "the contents of children's minds" (Hall, 1891). By asking children questions about every conceivable topic, he discovered that children's understanding of the world grows rapidly during childhood and that the "logic" of young children is often not logical.

Hall went on to write an influential book, *Adolescence* (1904). Strongly influenced by Darwin's evolutionary theory, Hall drew parallels between adolescence and the turbulent period in the evolution of human society during which barbarism gave way to modern civilization. Adolescence, then, was a tempestuous period of the life span, a time of emotional ups and downs and rapid changes—a time of what Hall called **storm and stress.** Thus it is Hall we have to thank for the notion that most teenagers are emotionally unstable—a largely inaccurate notion, as it turns out (Arnett, 1999). Yet as this book will reveal, Hall was right to mark adolescence as a time of dramatic change; substantial changes in the brain and in cognitive and social functioning do take place during this period.

Hall capped his remarkable career by turning his attention to the end of the life span in *Senescence* (1922), an analysis of how society treats (or, really, mistreats) its older members. His methods were limited by modern standards; he was mainly concerned with describing development, whereas today's developmentalists are more concerned with explaining it (Shanahan, Erickson, & Bauer, 2005). Hall's ideas about evolution and its relation to periods of human development were also flawed. Yet he deserves much credit for stimulating scientific research on the entire human life span and for raising many important questions about it (Shanahan, Erickson, & Bauer, 2005).

The Modern Life-Span Perspective

Although a few early pioneers of the study of human development like G. Stanley Hall viewed all phases of the life span as worthy of study, the science of human development began to break into age-group specialty areas during the 20th century. Some researchers focused on infant or child development, others specialized in adolescence, and still others formed the specialization of **gerontology,** the study of aging and old age. In the 1960s and 1970s, however, a true **life-span perspective** on human development began to emerge. In an influential paper, Paul Baltes (1987) laid out seven key assumptions of the life-span perspective (see Baltes, Lindenberger, & Staudinger, 1998, 2006, for elaborations). These are important themes that

G. Stanley Hall is widely recognized as the founder of the scientific study of human development.

you will see echoed throughout this book. They will also give you a good sense of the challenges facing researchers who study human development.

1. *Development is a lifelong process.* Today's developmentalists appreciate that human development is not just "kid stuff," that we change throughout the life span. They also believe that development in any period of life is best seen in the context of the whole life span. For instance, our understanding of adolescent career choices is bound to be richer if we concern ourselves with formative influences in childhood and the implications of such choices for adult career development.

2. *Development is multidirectional.* To many pioneers of its study, development was a universal process leading toward more "mature" functioning. Today's developmentalists recognize that different capacities show different patterns of change over time; for example, some intellectual skills decline faster than others in late adulthood; some don't change much; and some even continue to improve, as we'll see in Chapter 9. Different aspects of human functioning have different trajectories of change.

3. *Development involves both gain and loss.* As we have noted already, development is not just gain in childhood and loss in later life. Rather, gain and loss are intertwined during every phase of the life span. Baltes claims that gain inevitably brings with it loss of some kind, and loss brings gain—that gain and loss occur jointly. Examples? As infants gain command of the sounds of the language they hear spoken, they lose their early ability to "babble" sounds heard in other languages of the world (see Chapter 10); gaining a capacity for logical thought as a school-age child means losing some of the capacity for fanciful, imaginative think-

ing one had as a preschooler (Chapter 7); and choosing to specialize in one area in one's career often means losing command of other specialized skills (Chapter 11).

4. *Development is characterized by lifelong plasticity.* **Plasticity** refers to the capacity to change in response to positive or negative environmental influences. Developmental scholars have long known that child development can be damaged by a deprived environment and optimized by an enriched one. It is now understood that this plasticity continues into later life—that the aging process is not fixed but rather can be altered considerably depending on the individual's experiences. For example, elderly adults who have been losing intellectual abilities can, with special training and practice, regain some of those abilities or at least lose them more slowly (Baltes, Lindenberger, & Staudinger, 2006; Willis et al., 2006). Older adults who regularly engage in mentally stimulating activities such as playing chess, playing a musical instrument, and dancing (the dancer has to think about the steps) even appear to be less likely than their mentally inactive peers to develop Alzheimer's disease and other forms of dementia (Verghese et al., 2003). Studies of animals tell us this may be because mental stimulation results in the formation of new connections among neurons in the brain—even an aging brain (see Chapter 5).

5. *Development is shaped by its historical–cultural context.* This theme, a big message of Bronfenbrenner's bioecological model, is illustrated by a study conducted in China, where capitalism has increasingly been taking root and children are increasingly being trained to be competitive and self-reliant. (Chen, Cen, Li, & He, 2005). For school-aged children assessed in 1990, shyness and sensitivity—traits traditionally valued in Chinese children—were assets; shy and sensitive children were found to be well-adjusted academic achievers. However, for children assessed in 2002, shyness and sensitivity did not fit as well to the demands of a more capitalistic society; now this trait was associated with rejection by peers, problems in school, and depression. Thus the implications of certain

The plasticity of the brain is evident even in old age if people remain intellectually active.

personality traits for adjustment can change as a society changes.

The importance of historical–cultural context is also illustrated beautifully by the pioneering work of Glen Elder and his colleagues on how the Great Depression of the 1930s affected the later life courses and development of the era's children and adolescents (Elder, 1998; Elder, Liker, & Cross, 1984). A few years after the stock market crashed in 1929, one of three workers was unemployed and many families were tossed into poverty (Rogler, 2002). Although many families survived the hardships of the Great Depression nicely, this economic crisis proved to be especially difficult for children if their out-of-work and demoralized fathers became less affectionate and less consistent in disciplining them. When this was the case, children displayed behavior problems and had low aspirations and poor records in school, and they turned into men who had erratic careers and unstable marriages and women who were seen by their own children as ill tempered. Clearly the trajectories our lives take can be affected for years by the social context in which we grow up. How do you think your generation will be affected by such events as 9/11, Hurricane Katrina, and the Iraq War?

6. *Development is multiply influenced.* Today's developmental scientists share Urie Bronfenbrenner's belief that human development is the product of many interacting causes—both inside and outside the person, both biological and environmental. It is the often-unpredictable outcome of ongoing interactions between a changing person and her changing world. Some influences are experienced by all humans at similar ages, others are common to people of a particular generation, and still other are unique to the individual (Baltes, 1987).

7. *Understanding development requires multiple disciplines.* Because human development is influenced by everything from biochemical reactions to historical events, it is impossible for one discipline to have all the answers. A full understanding of human development will come only when many disciplines, each with its own perspectives and tools of study, join forces. Where we once talked of developmental psychology as a field of study, we now talk of *developmental science* (Lerner, 2006). Not only psychologists but also biologists, neuroscientists, historians, economists, sociologists, anthropologists, and many others have something to contribute to our understanding. Some universities have established interdisciplinary human development programs that bring members of different disciplines together to forge more integrated perspectives on development. The study of human

How might the historical event Hurricane Katrina alter the development of the members of this family?

AP Images/Ben Sklar

development is more interdisciplinary now than ever before (Cairns & Cairns, 2006).

SUMMING UP

❙ The study of life-span development pursues the goals of description, explanation, and optimization, and began with the baby biographies written by Charles Darwin and others.

❙ Through his use of questionnaires and study of all phases of the life span, including the storm and stress of adolescence, G. Stanley Hall came to be regarded as the founder of developmental psychology.

❙ The life-span perspective on human development set forth by Baltes assumes that development (1) is lifelong, (2) takes many directions, (3) involves gains and interlinked losses at every age, (4) is characterized by plasticity, (5) is affected by its historical and cultural context, (6) is influenced by multiple interacting causal factors, and (7) requires study by multiple disciplines.

CRITICAL THINKING

1. Create specific examples that would show how each of the seven principles of the life-span perspective might apply to Mrs. Ella Miller, the woman introduced at the beginning of the chapter.

1.3 | HOW IS DEVELOPMENT STUDIED?

How do developmental scholars gain understanding of the complexities of life-span development? They use the scientific method used in any physical or social science. Let us review for you, briefly, some basic concepts of scientific research and then turn to research strategies devised specifically for describing, explaining, and optimizing development (see Creasey, 2006; Teti, 2005).

The Scientific Method

There is nothing mysterious about the **scientific method.** It is both a method and an attitude—a belief that investigators should allow their systematic observations (or data) to determine the merits of their thinking. For example, for every "expert" who believes that psychological differences between males and females are largely biological in origin, there is likely to be another expert who just as firmly insists that boys and girls differ because they are raised differently. Whom should we believe? It is in the spirit of the scientific method to believe the data—that is, the findings of research. The scientist is willing to abandon a pet theory if the data contradict it. Ultimately, then, the scientific method can help the scientific community and society at large weed out flawed ideas.

The scientific method involves a process of generating ideas and testing them by making observations. Often, preliminary observations provide ideas for a **theory**—a set of concepts and propositions intended to describe and explain certain phenomena. Jean Piaget, for instance, observed his own children's development and used these observations as the basis for his influential theory of cognitive development (see Chapter 7).

Theories generate specific predictions, or **hypotheses,** regarding a particular set of observations. Consider, for example, a theory claiming that psychological differences between the sexes are largely caused by differences in their social environments. Based on this theory, a researcher might hypothesize that if parents grant boys and girls the same freedoms, the two sexes will be similarly independent, whereas if parents let boys do more things than they let girls do, boys will be more independent than girls. Suppose that the study designed to test this hypothesis indicates that boys are more independent than girls no matter how their parents treat them. Then the hypothesis would be disconfirmed by the findings, and the researcher would want to rethink this theory of sex-linked differences. If other hypotheses based on this theory were inconsistent with the facts, the theory would have to be significantly revised or abandoned in favor of a better theory.

This, then, is the heart of the scientific method: theories generate hypotheses, which are tested through observation of behavior, and new observations indicate which theories are worth keeping and which are not (see ■ **Figure 1.3**).

Sample Selection

Any study of development focuses on a particular research **sample** (the group of individuals studied) with the intention of generalizing to a larger **population,** a well-defined group (such as premature infants, American high school students, or Chinese elders) from which the sample is drawn and about

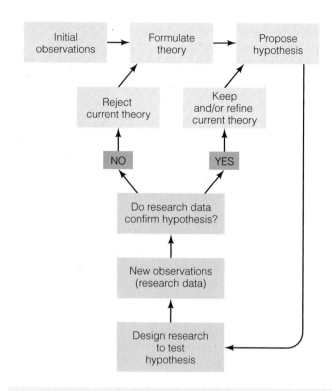

■ **FIGURE 1.3** The scientific method in action.

which we want to draw conclusions. Although it is probably advocated more than it is used, the best approach is to study a **random sample** of the population of interest—a sample formed by identifying all members of the larger population and then, by a random means (such as drawing names blindly), selecting a portion of that population to study. Random sampling increases confidence that the sample studied is representative of the larger population of interest and therefore that conclusions based on studying the sample will be true of the whole population.

In practice, developmentalists often draw their samples—sometimes random, sometimes not—from their local communities. Thus, researchers might survey students at local high schools about their drug use but then be unable to make statements about American teenagers in general if, for example, the school is in a suburb where drug-use patterns are different than they might be in an inner-city area. They would certainly be unable to generalize about Kenyan or Brazilian high school students. All researchers must be careful to describe the characteristics of the sample they studied and to avoid overgeneralizing their findings to populations that might be socioeconomically or culturally different from the research sample (Rogoff, 2003).

Data Collection

No matter what aspect of human development we are interested in—the formation of bonds between infants and their parents, adolescent sexual behavior, memory skills in elderly adults—we must find appropriate ways to measure what interests us. The methods used to study human development are varied, depending on the age group and aspect of development of interest (Creasey, 2006). Here we will look at some pros and cons of three major methods of data collection used by developmental researchers: self-report measures, behavioral observations, and physiological measurements. We illustrate these methods with a study by Julie Hubbard and her colleagues (2002) that used all three approaches. Hubbard was interested in the relationship between anger and two styles of aggression in 8-year-olds, as determined by teachers' responses to questions about children's behavior in the classroom: a "hot" kind of aggression in which children hit, pinch, and otherwise abuse other children when provoked, and a cooler, more calculating style of aggression in which children use aggression to get what they want. The researchers expected aggressive children of the first type to be more likely than aggressive children of the second type to become angry in a laboratory situation in which another child (a confederate of the researchers) cheated shamelessly in a board game about astronauts and won.

Obviously the researchers needed a way to measure anger in the anger-provoking situation. Before reading further, think about how you would measure it.

Verbal Reports

Interviews, written questionnaires or surveys, ability and achievement tests, and personality scales all involve asking people questions either about themselves (self-report measures) or about someone else (for example, child behavior as reported by parents or teachers). These verbal report measures are often standardized, meaning that they ask the same questions in precisely the same order of everyone so that the responses of different individuals can be directly compared.

Hubbard's research team used a verbal report measurement to assess anger. The researchers had the children in the study watch a videotape of all the turns in the game they played with the cheating confederate, stopped the tape at each turn, and asked each child, "How angry did you feel now?" The child responded on a four-point scale ranging from 1 (not at all) to 4 (a lot). The researchers were able to use these ratings to calculate for each child an average degree of self-reported anger over the entire game and to look at changes in degree of anger as the game progressed.

Although self-report and other verbal report methods are widely used to study human development, they have shortcomings. First, self-report measures typically cannot be used with infants, young children, cognitively impaired elders, or other individuals who cannot read or understand speech well. Informant surveys, questionnaires, or interviews are often used in these situations instead. Second, because individuals of different ages may not understand questions in the same way, age differences in responses may reflect age differences in comprehension or interpretation rather than age differences in the quality of interest to the researcher. Finally, respondents may try to present themselves (or those they are providing information about) in a positive or socially desirable light.

Behavioral Observations

Naturalistic observation involves observing people in their common, everyday (that is, natural) surroundings (Pellegrini, 1996). Ongoing behavior is observed in homes, schools, playgrounds, workplaces, nursing homes, or wherever people are going about their lives. Naturalistic observation has been used to study child development more often than adult development, largely because infants and young children often cannot be studied through self-report techniques that demand verbal skills. The greatest advantage of naturalistic observation is that it is the only technique that can reveal what children or adults do in everyday life.

Yet naturalistic observation has its limitations. First, some behaviors (for example, heroic efforts to help other people) occur too infrequently and unexpectedly to be observed in this manner. Second, it is difficult to pinpoint the causes of the behavior, or of any developmental trends in the behavior, because in a natural setting many events are usually happening at the same time, any of which may affect behavior. Finally, the presence of an observer can sometimes make people behave differently than they otherwise would. Children may "ham it up" when they have an audience; parents may be on their best behavior. Therefore, researchers sometimes videotape the proceedings from a hidden location or spend time in the setting before they collect their "real" data so that the individuals they are observing become used to their presence and behave more naturally.

To achieve greater control over the conditions under which they gather behavioral data, researchers often use **structured observation**; that is, they create special conditions designed to elicit the behavior of interest. Hubbard used structured observation by setting up the astronaut game situation and having the confederate cheat to provoke children's anger. The confederate was carefully trained to behave exactly the

Naturalistic observation of young children is done in day care centers, preschools, homes, and other everyday settings.

same with each of the 272 participants in the study. Sessions were videotaped; Hubbard then trained graduate and undergraduate students to code second by second whether the participants' facial expressions were angry, sad, happy, or neutral and whether they showed nonverbal signs of anger (for example, slamming game pieces on the table). Pairs of observers coded some of the same videotapes to ensure that they would come to similar conclusions about what facial emotion or nonverbal behavior was being expressed. Structured observation permits the study of behaviors rarely observable in natural settings. By exposing all research participants to the same stimuli, this approach also increases the investigator's ability to compare the effect of a stimulus on different individuals. Concerns about this method center on whether conclusions based on behavior in specially designed settings will generalize to behavior in natural settings.

Physiological Measurements

Finally, developmental scientists sometimes take physiological measurements to assess variables of interest to them; for example, they use brain-scanning techniques to measure the activity in particular parts of the brain while children or adults engage in learning tasks, chart changes in hormone levels in menopausal women, or collect measurements of heart rate and other signs of arousal to assess emotions.

Hubbard's team collected data on two physiological measures of anger by attaching electrodes to children's hands and chests (after convincing the children that astronauts normally wear sensors when they go into space!). Emotionally aroused people, including angry ones, often have sweaty palms and low

Physiological measurement techniques include measuring brain activity through electrodes attached to the scalp as infants respond to different stimuli.

© Bob Daemmrich/PhotoEdit

skin conductance, or electrical resistance of the skin, as measured by electrodes attached to their hands. Emotional arousal is also given away by a high heart rate, measured through electrodes on the chest.

Physiological measurements have the advantage of being hard to fake; the person who tells you she is not angry may be physiologically aroused, and the adolescent who claims not to take drugs may be given away by a blood test. Physiological measurements are also particularly useful in the study of infants because infants cannot tell us verbally what they are thinking or feeling. The main limitation of physiological measurements is that it is not always clear what they are assessing. In Hubbard's study, for example, skin conductance was related to the other measures of anger as expected but heart rate was not. The researchers noted that individuals' heart rates slow when they are interested in something and that a slow heart rate in their study may therefore have signaled either high interest or low anger, making its meaning ambiguous.

These, then, are the most commonly used techniques of collecting data about human development: verbal report measures (interviews, questionnaires, and tests), behavioral observation (both naturalistic and structured), and physiological measures. Because each method has its limitations, knowledge is advanced the most when *multiple* methods are used to study the same aspect of human development and these different methods lead to similar conclusions. In the Hubbard study, the use of multiple methods of assessing anger did indeed help the researchers distinguish between children showing "hot" and "cool" types of aggression. As expected, children who engaged in "hot" aggression in the classroom showed more anger during the game, especially as revealed by their skin conductance and nonverbal behavior.

Whatever the basic techniques used, unique challenges may arise in collecting data from humans of different ages (Creasey, 2006). Studying young infants, whose attention is sometimes hard to capture and who cannot answer questions, calls for plenty of ingenuity, as illustrated by some of the work on infant perception in Chapter 6. Assessing the abilities of young children can be tricky as well. For example, presenting information to toddlers through videos may seem like a good approach until you consider the findings of a recent study of 2-year-olds (Troseth, Saylor, and Archer, 2006). Children told face-to-face where to find a hidden toy could find it, but children given precisely the same information by a woman on a video screen could not. Why? Unless toddlers were given an opportunity to interact with the woman on the video through closed circuit television before the hidden toy task and hear her call them by name and respond to what they said and did, they apparently tuned her out, figuring that whatever she was talking about on the TV screen was irrelevant to them!

At the other end of the life span, researchers face many challenges gathering data from elderly adults. For instance, they must ensure that elderly adults who have sensory impairments can see and hear stimuli; that elderly adults are as comfortable as younger adults performing tasks on the computers used so commonly today in cognitive psychology laboratories;

and that elderly adults do not feel they are being treated like children, as when they are asked ridiculously easy questions on tests that are often used by researchers to screen for Alzheimer's disease and other cognitive impairments (Creasey, 2006).

The Experimental and Correlational Methods

Once developmental scientists have formulated hypotheses, chosen a sample, and figured out what to measure and how to measure it, they can test their hypotheses. The most powerful research method for explaining behavior and identifying the causes of developmental changes in behavior is the experiment. When experiments cannot be conducted, correlational research techniques may suggest answers to important *why* questions.

The Experimental Method

In an **experiment,** an investigator manipulates or alters some aspect of the environment to see how this affects the behavior of the sample of individuals studied. Consider an experiment conducted by Lynette Friedrich and Aletha Stein (1973) some years ago to study how different kinds of television programs affect the social behavior of preschool children. These researchers divided children in a nursery school into three groups: one group was exposed to violent cartoons such as *Superman* and *Batman* (aggressive treatment condition), another group watched episodes of *Mister Rogers' Neighborhood* portraying many helpful and cooperative acts (prosocial treatment condition), and a third group saw programs featuring circuses and farm scenes with neither aggressive nor altruistic themes (neutral control condition).

The goal of an experiment is to see whether the different treatments that form the **independent variable**—the variable manipulated so that its causal effects can be assessed—have

Many studies demonstrate that observational learning of aggression occurs when children watch a lot of violence on television.

differing effects on the behavior expected to be affected, the **dependent variable** in the experiment. The independent variable in Friedrich and Stein's experiment was the type of television children watched—a variable with three possible values in their study: aggressive, prosocial, or neutral. One dependent variable that Friedrich and Stein chose to study was aggressive behavior. Any variable represents one specific way of measuring a concept of interest. Friedrich and Stein chose to use a complicated naturalistic observation system to count several types of aggressive actions toward classmates in the nursery school. Behavior was observed before each child spent a month watching daily episodes of one of the three kinds of television programs and was recorded again after that period to see if it had changed. The independent variable is the hypothesized cause, and the dependent variable is the effect, when cause–effect relationships are studied. Similarly, if researchers were testing drugs to improve memory function in elderly adults with Alzheimer's disease, the type of drug administered (for example, a new drug versus a placebo with no active ingredients) would be the independent variable and performance on a memory test would be the dependent variable.

So, did the number of aggressive behaviors observed "depend on" the independent variable, the type of television watched? Children who watched violent programs became more aggressive than children who watched prosocial or neutral programs—but this was only true of the children in the study who were already relatively aggressive. Thus, this experiment demonstrated a clear cause–effect relationship, although only for some children, between the kind of behavior children watched on television and their own subsequent behavior.

This study has the three critical features shared by any true experiment:

1. *Manipulation of the independent variable.* Investigators must arrange for different groups to have different experiences so that the effects of those experiences can be assessed. If investigators merely compare children who already watch a lot of violent television and children who watch little, they cannot establish that violent television watching *causes* increased aggression.

2. *Random assignment of individuals to treatment conditions.* **Random assignment** of participants to different experimental conditions (for example, by drawing names from a jar) is a way of making the treatment groups similar in all respects at the outset (in previous tendencies to be aggressive or helpful, in socioeconomic status, and in all other individual characteristics that could affect social behavior). Only if experimental groups are similar in all respects initially can researchers be confident that differences among groups at the end of the experiment were caused by differences in the experimental treatments they received.

3. *Experimental control.* In a true experiment with proper **experimental control**, all factors other than the independent variable are controlled or held constant so that they cannot contribute to differences among the treatment groups. Friedrich and Stein ensured that children in the three treat-

ment conditions were treated similarly except for the type of television they watched. It would have ruined the experiment, for example, if the children exposed to violent programs had to watch them in a small, crowded room where tempers might flare but the children in the other two groups watched in larger, less crowded rooms. The variable of interest, the type of TV watched, would then be confounded, or entangled, with the degree of crowding in the room, and the researchers would have been unable to separate the effects of one from those of the other.

The greatest strength of the experimental method is its ability to establish unambiguously that one thing causes another—that manipulating the independent variable causes a change in the dependent variable. When experiments are properly conducted, they contribute to our ability to *explain* human development and sometimes help us to *optimize* it.

Does the experimental method have limitations? Absolutely! First, the findings of laboratory experiments do not always hold true in the real world, especially if the situations created in laboratory experiments are artificial and unlike the situations that people encounter in everyday life. Urie Bronfenbrenner (1979), who was critical of the fact that so many developmental studies are contrived experiments, once charged that developmental psychology had become "the science of the strange behavior of children in strange situations with strange adults" (p. 19). Experiments often show what can cause development but not necessarily what *does* most strongly shape development in natural settings (McCall, 1977).

A second limitation of the experimental method is that it cannot be used to address many significant questions about human development for ethical reasons. How would you conduct a true experiment to determine how older women are affected by their husbands' deaths, for example? You would need to identify a sample of elderly women, randomly assign them to either the experimental group or the control group, then manipulate the independent variable by leaving the control group participants alone but killing the husband of each woman in the experimental group! Ethical principles obviously demand that developmentalists use methods other than true experimental ones to study questions about the effect of widowhood—and a host of other important questions about development.

Researchers sometimes study how a program or intervention affects development through a **quasi experiment**—an experiment-like study that evaluates the effects of different treatments but does not randomly assign individuals to treatment groups (see Pitts, Prost, & Winters, 2005). A gerontologist, for example, might conduct a quasi experiment to compare the adjustment of widows who choose to participate in a new support group for widows and those who do not. When individuals are not randomly assigned to treatment groups, however, uncontrolled differences among the groups studied could influence the results (for example, the widows who seek help might be more sociable than those who do not). As a result, the researcher is not able to make strong statements about what caused what, as in a true experiment.

The Correlational Method

Largely because of ethical issues, most developmental research today is correlational rather than experimental. The **correlational method** generally involves determining whether two or more variables are related in a systematic way. Researchers do not randomly assign participants to treatment conditions, manipulate the independent variable, or control other factors, as in an experiment. Instead, researchers take people as they are and attempt to determine whether there are relationships among their experiences, characteristics, and developmental outcomes.

How might a correlational study of the effects of television on children's aggressive behavior differ from Friedrich and Stein's experiment on this topic? In a well-designed correlational study, L. Rowell Huesmann and his colleagues (2003) correlated children's TV viewing between the ages of 6 and 9 with their aggressive behavior as adults 15 years later. Children picked their favorites from lists of TV programs and indicated how often they watched each program so that a self-report measure of the amount of violent TV watched could be created. The researchers then correlated the TV-watching measure with a measure of adult aggressive behavior that combined in one index criminal behavior, traffic violations, spouse abuse, and physical aggression, as well as more indirect forms of aggression such as trying to get other people to dislike someone.

Huesmann and his colleagues were then able to determine the strength of the relationship between these two variables by calculating a **correlation coefficient**—a measurement of the extent to which individuals' scores on one variable are systematically associated with their scores on another variable. A correlation coefficient (symbolized as r) can range in value from $+1.00$ to -1.00. A positive correlation between TV viewing and aggression would indicate that as the number of hours of TV children watch increases, so does the number of aggressive acts they commit (see ■ **Figure 1.4**, Panel A). A positive correlation of $r = +0.90$ indicates a stronger, more predictable positive relationship than a smaller positive correlation such as $r = +0.30$. A negative correlation would result if the heaviest TV viewers were consistently the least aggressive children and the lightest viewers were the most aggressive children (see Panel B). A correlation near 0.00 would be obtained if there was no relationship between the two variables—if one cannot predict how aggressive children are based on their TV-viewing habits (see Panel C).

Huesmann's team found the positive relationship they hypothesized between watching violent TV as a child and engaging in aggressive and antisocial behavior as an adult. The correlation was $+.21$ for men and $+.19$ for women—not very large but still indicative of a meaningful relationship. People who watched a great deal of violent TV as children, whether male or female, had higher composite aggression scores as adults than did people who had watched less violence as children. But does this correlational study firmly establish that watching action-packed programs causes children to become more aggressive? Or can you think of alternative explanations for the correlation between watching TV and aggression?

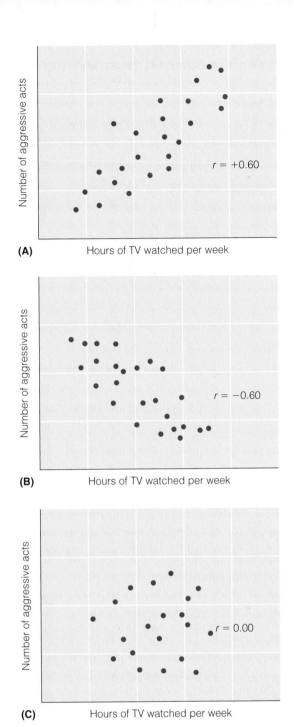

(A) Hours of TV watched per week

$r = +0.60$

(B) Hours of TV watched per week

$r = -0.60$

(C) Hours of TV watched per week

$r = 0.00$

Number of aggressive acts

■ **FIGURE 1.4** Plots of hypothetical correlations between the amount of TV children watch and the number of aggressive acts they display. Each dot represents a specific child who watches a high, medium, or low amount of TV and commits a high, medium, or low number of aggressive acts. Panel A shows a positive correlation between television watching and aggression: the more TV children watch, the more aggressive they are. Panel B shows a negative correlation: the more TV children watch, the less aggressive they are. Finally, Panel C shows zero correlation: the amount of TV watched is unrelated to the amount of aggression displayed.

One possibility in correlational studies is that *the direction of the cause–effect relationship is reversed.* That is, exposure to violent TV may not cause children to become aggressive; rather, being aggressive may cause children to seek out blood and gore on TV. However, this problem of determining the directionality of causation was not as bothersome in Huesmann's study as it is in correlational studies that measure both variables of interest at the same time. It is difficult to argue that aggression in adulthood caused violent TV watching in childhood. Moreover, Huesmann collected data on how aggressive children in his sample were during childhood. He was then able to demonstrate that, although highly aggressive children watch more violent TV than other children do, watching violent TV predicts becoming an aggressive adult, even when controlling statistically for how aggressive these adults were as children.

A second possibility in correlational studies is that *the association between the two variables is caused by some third variable.* An example of such a third variable might be parental rejection. Some children might have parents who are harsh and rejecting, and they might watch more TV than most children in order to avoid unpleasant interactions with their parents. They may be aggressive because they are angry and upset about being rejected. If so, watching TV did not cause these children to become more aggressive than their peers. Rather, a third variable—parental rejection—may have caused both their aggressive ways and their TV-viewing habits.

Thus, the correlational method has one major limitation: it cannot unambiguously establish a causal relationship between one variable and another the way an experiment can. Correlational studies can *suggest* that a causal relationship exists, however. Indeed, Huesmann's team used complex statistical techniques in which a correlation is corrected for the influence of other variables to show that watching violent television in childhood probably contributed to aggression in adulthood. Several potential third variables, including parental rejection, low socioeconomic status, and low intelligence quotient (IQ)—all correlated with both watching violent TV and aggression—were ruled out as explanations of the relationship between TV viewing and aggression. Still, despite all their efforts to establish that the direction of the cause–effect relationship is from watching violent TV to aggression rather than vice versa, and to rule out possible third variables that could explain the TV–aggression relationship, Huesmann's team could not establish a definite cause–effect link because of the correlational nature of the study.

Despite this key limitation, the correlational method is extremely valuable. First, as already noted, many problems can be addressed only through the correlational method (or through quasi experiments) because it would be unethical to conduct certain experiments. Second, complex correlational studies and statistical analyses allow researchers to learn about how multiple factors operating in the "real world" combine to influence development. Because life-span development is influenced by multiple factors rather than one or two factors at a time, experiments are not enough. See ● **Table 1.3** for a comparison of experimental and correlational methods.

● TABLE 1.3   A COMPARISON OF THE EXPERIMENTAL METHOD AND THE CORRELATIONAL METHOD

Experimental Method	Correlational Method
Manipulation of an independent variable (investigator exposes participants to different experiences)	Study of people who have already had different experiences
Random assignment to treatment groups to ensure similarity of groups	Assignment by "nature" to groups (groups may not be similar in all respects)
Experimental control of extraneous variables	Lack of control over extraneous variables
Can establish a cause–effect relationship between independent variable and dependent variable	Can suggest but not firmly establish that one variable causes another
May not be possible for ethical reasons	Can be used to study issues that cannot be studied experimentally for ethical reasons
May be artificial (findings from contrived experimental settings may not generalize well to the "real world")	Can study multiple influences operating in natural settings (findings may generalize better to the "real world")

Overall, understanding of why humans develop as they do is best advanced when the results of different kinds of studies *converge*—when experiments demonstrate a clear cause–effect relationship under controlled conditions and correlational studies reveal that the same relationship seems to be operating in everyday life, even in the context of other possible causes. The results of multiple studies addressing the same question can be synthesized to produce overall conclusions through the research method of **meta-analysis** (Glass, McGaw, & Smith, 1981; Lipsey & Wilson, 2001). A meta-analysis of multiple studies of the link between watching violence on television and aggression showed a reliable relationship between the two (Anderson & Bushman, 2002; Bushman & Anderson, 2001). The magnitude of the correlation was usually between +0.10 and +0.30. That may seem small, but it is larger than the average correlation between calcium intake and bone mass or between time spent doing homework and academic achievement (Huesmann & Taylor, 2006). Moreover, the relationship shows up in studies using the correlational method, in studies using the experimental method, and in both laboratory and naturalistic settings (see Huesmann & Taylor, 2006; Kirsh, 2006).

Developmental Research Designs

Along with the experimental and correlational methods used by all kinds of researchers to study relationships between variables, developmental researchers need specialized research designs to study how people change and remain the same as they get older (Creasey, 2006; Schaie, 2000). To describe development, researchers have relied extensively on two types of research designs: the cross-sectional design and the longitudinal design. A third type of design, the sequential study, has come into use in an attempt to overcome the limitations of the other two tech-

niques. First we will look at three influences on the outcomes of developmental studies, then we explore the strengths and weaknesses of the cross-sectional and longitudinal designs.

Age, Cohort, and Time of Measurement Effects

Developmental studies can be influenced by three factors: age effects, cohort effects, and time of measurement effects. **Age effects** are the effects of getting older. What interests developmental researchers is the relationship between age (or really the biological and environmental changes that come about with age) and a particular aspect of development. **Cohort effects** are the effects of being born as a member of a particular generation in a particular historical context. Any **cohort** is a group of people born at the same time, either in the same year or within a specified span of years (that is, as part of a particular generation like the baby boomers born after World War II, the Generation Xers born in the late 1960s and 1970s, or the members of the millennial generation, the "baby boomlet" generation born in the 1980s and 1990s). People who are in their 80s today not only are older than people in their 50s and 20s but belong to a different cohort or generation and have had different formative experiences.

Finally, **time of measurement effects** in developmental research are the effects of historical events and trends occurring when the data are collected (for example, effects of a traumatic event like 9/11, advances in health care, or technological advances such as the introduction of the World Wide Web). Time of measurement effects are not unique to a particular cohort but can affect anyone alive at the time. Once you are aware that age, cohort, and time of measurement can all influence developmental research findings, you can appreciate that both the cross-sectional and the longitudinal designs have their limitations.

Cross-Sectional and Longitudinal Designs

In a **cross-sectional design,** the performances of people of different age groups, or cohorts, are compared. A researcher interested in the development of vocabulary might gather samples of speech from several 2-, 3-, and 4-year-olds; calculate the mean (or average) number of distinct words used per child for each age group; and compare these means to describe how the vocabulary sizes of children age 2, 3, and 4 differ. Another researcher may calculate the average reaction times of adults who are in their 60s, 70s, and 80s. The cross-sectional study provides information about *age differences.* By seeing how different age groups differ, researchers can attempt to draw conclusions about how performance changes with age.

In a **longitudinal design,** the performance of one cohort of individuals is assessed repeatedly over time. The language development study just described would be longitudinal rather than cross-sectional if a researcher identified a group of 2-year-olds, measured their vocabulary sizes, waited a year until they were age 3 and measured their vocabularies again, did the same thing a year later when they were age 4, then compared the mean scores of these same children at the three ages. In any longitudinal study, whether it covers only a few months in infancy or 50 years, the same individuals are studied as they develop. Thus, the longitudinal design provides information about *age changes* rather than age differences.

Now, does it matter whether researchers choose the cross-sectional or the longitudinal design to describe development? Suppose a team of researchers was interested in whether attitudes about the roles of men and women in society typically become more traditional or more liberated over the adult years. Suppose they conducted a longitudinal study by administering a gender-role questionnaire three times to a group of men and women: in 1970 (when the men and women were 30), in 1990 (when they were 50), and in 2010 (when they were 70). Suppose that in 2010 another research team conducted a cross-

sectional study of this same question, comparing the gender-role attitudes of adults 30, 50, and 70 years old at that time. ■ **Figure 1.5** illustrates these two designs, and ■ **Figure 1.6** portrays the hypothetical age trends they might generate.

What is going on in Figure 1.6? The cross-sectional study seems to say that as people get older, their attitudes about gender roles become more traditional. The longitudinal study suggests precisely the opposite: as people get older, their attitudes about gender roles seem to become more liberated. How could a cross-sectional study and a longitudinal study on the same topic lead to such different conclusions?

Strengths and Weaknesses of the Cross-Sectional Design

In the cross-sectional study of gender attitudes, the three age groups being compared represent three cohorts of people. The 70-year-olds were born in 1940, the 50-year-olds in 1960, and the 30-year-olds in 1980. The cross-sectional study tells how people of different ages (cohorts) differ, and this can be useful information. But the cross-sectional technique does not necessarily tell how people develop as they get older. Do 70-year-olds hold more conservative gender-role attitudes than 30-year-olds because people become more conservative as they get older or because 70-year-olds are members of a cohort raised in a traditional period when women mainly stayed home and raised children? We cannot tell. *Age effects and cohort effects are confounded, or entangled.*

Possibly, then, older adults' unliberated responses to the questionnaire in 2010 reflect views they learned early in life and maintained for the rest of their lives. Perhaps their views did not become more traditional as they got older. And per-

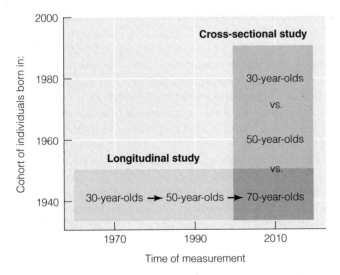

■ **FIGURE 1.5** Cross-sectional and longitudinal studies of development from age 30 to age 70.

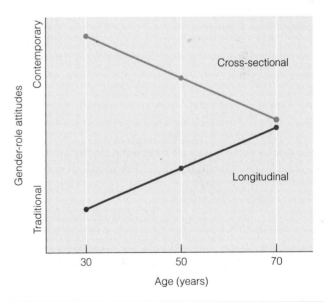

■ **FIGURE 1.6** Conflicting findings of hypothetical cross-sectional and longitudinal studies of gender-role attitudes. How could the two studies produce different age trends?

For baby boomers growing up in the 1950s, gender roles were more traditional than they are now.

haps the 30-year-old cohort, which grew up when the women's movement had had major impacts on society, formed liberated gender-role attitudes early in life and retained those liberated attitudes as they grew older. Perhaps, then, what initially looked like a developmental trend toward greater traditionalism (an age effect) is actually a cohort effect resulting from differences in the formative experiences of the different generations studied.

The problem of cohort effects is the central problem in cross-sectional research. As you will see in Chapter 9, it was once believed, based on cross-sectional studies of performance on intelligence tests, that people experience significant declines in intellectual functioning starting in middle age; later longitudinal studies told a much more positive story about intellectual aging (Schaie, 2000). The problem was that the older adults in cross-sectional studies grew up in a time when many people did not graduate from high school. Subsequent longitudinal studies have shown that these older people probably did not experience steep losses of intellectual abilities during adulthood (a true developmental or age effect); they merely performed less well than younger cohorts because they received less education in their youth (a cohort effect).

Despite this central problem, developmentalists still commonly use the cross-sectional design. Why? Because it has the great advantage of being quick and easy: researchers can go out this year, sample individuals of different ages, and be done with it. Moreover, this design should yield valid conclusions if the cohorts studied are likely to have had similar growing-up experiences—as when 3- and 4-year-olds rather than 30- and 40-year-olds are compared. It is when researchers attempt to make inferences about development over the span of many years that cohort effects in cross-sectional studies, interesting as they may be, can yield a misleading picture of development.

The second major limitation of the cross-sectional design is that, because each person is observed at only one point, researchers learn nothing about how different individuals change with age. They cannot see, for example, whether different people show divergent patterns of change in their gender-role attitudes over time or whether individuals who are especially liberated in their attitudes as 30-year-olds are also especially liberated at 70. To address issues like these, researchers need longitudinal research.

Strengths and Weaknesses of the Longitudinal Design

Because the longitudinal design traces changes in individuals as they age, it can tell whether most people change in the same direction or whether different individuals travel different developmental paths, especially when modern techniques for analyzing individual growth curves are applied to the data (Schaie, 2000). It can indicate whether the characteristics and behaviors measured remain consistent over time—for example, whether bright, aggressive, or dependent young people retain those same traits in later life. And it can tell whether experiences early in life predict traits and behaviors later in life. The cross-sectional design can do none of these.

What, then, are the limitations of the longitudinal design? In our hypothetical longitudinal study of gender-role attitudes, adults were first assessed at age 30 then reassessed at age 50 and age 70. The study centered on *one cohort* of individuals: members of the 1940 birth cohort. These people were raised in an historical context in which gender-role attitudes were traditional and then saw the women's movement change many of those attitudes considerably. Their responses in 2010 may have been more liberal than their responses in 1970 not because gender-role attitudes *typically* become more liberal as people get older but because major societal changes occurred from one time of measurement to the next during the time frame of the study. In the longitudinal study, then, *age effects and time of measurement effects are confounded*. The researchers would not be able to tell for sure whether the age-related changes observed are true developmental trends that might be evident in any historical context; instead, they may reflect historical events occurring during a particular study.

The problem, then, is that researchers may not be able to generalize what they find in a longitudinal study to people developing in other historical periods. Gender-role attitudes became considerably more liberal in the United States from the 1970s to the 1990s. For example, in 1977, more than half of respondents to a survey said it was more important for a wife to help her husband's career than to have her own; by 1996, only about one in five agreed (Brewster & Padavic, 2000). But perhaps we would obtain different "developmental" trends if we were to conduct a longitudinal study in an era in which traditional gender roles suddenly became popular again.

The longitudinal design has other disadvantages. One is fairly obvious: this approach is costly and time-consuming, particularly if it is used to trace development over a long span and at many points in time. Second, because knowledge is constantly changing, measurement methods that seemed good at the start of the study may seem dated or incomplete by the end. Third, participants drop out of long-term studies; they may move, lose interest, or, especially in studies of aging, die during the course of the study. The result is a smaller and often less representative sample on which to base conclusions. Finally, there may be effects of repeated testing; sometimes simply taking a test improves performance on that test the next time around.

Are both the cross-sectional and the longitudinal designs hopelessly flawed, then? That would be overstating their weaknesses. Cross-sectional studies are very efficient and informative, especially when the cohorts studied are not widely different in age or formative experiences. Longitudinal studies are extremely valuable for what they can reveal about how people change as they get older—even though it must be recognized that the cohort studied may not develop in precisely the same way that an earlier or later cohort does. Still, in an attempt to overcome the limitations of both cross-sectional and longitudinal designs, developmentalists have devised a more powerful method of describing developmental change: the sequential design.

Sequential Designs: The Best of Both Worlds

A **sequential design** combines the cross-sectional approach and the longitudinal approach in a single study (Schaie, 1994; Schaie & Caskie, 2005). A sequential study of gender-role attitudes might begin in 1970 as a longitudinal study of a cohort of 30-year-olds. In 1980, the researchers would reassess these adults at age 40 and start studying a second group of 30-year-olds longitudinally. ■ **Figure 1.7** shows how this study might unfold. Notice that it involves multiple longitudinal studies, that it also involves multiple cross-sectional studies in which we can compare different age groups at a particular point in time, and that it even allows comparison of 30-years-olds who were born and lived at different times. In Chapter 9, you will read about an ambitious sequential study of changes in IQ test performance during adulthood conducted by K. Warner Schaie (1996). Adults ranging in age from 22 to 70 were tested and then retested every 7 years, and at each testing a new sample of adults in their 20s to 70s was added to the study, making for an elaborate study providing many insights into the relationships between IQ scores and age, cohort of birth, and time of measurement.

Sequential designs, by combining the cross-sectional and longitudinal approaches, improve on both. They can tell researchers (1) which age-related trends are truly developmental in nature and reflect how most people, *regardless of cohort*, can be expected to change over time (age effects); (2) which age trends differ from cohort to cohort and suggest that each generation is affected by its distinct growing-up experiences (cohort effects); and (3) which trends suggest that events during a specific period of time similarly affect all cohorts alive at the time (time of measurement effects). In short, sequential designs can begin to untangle the effects of age, cohort, and time of mea-

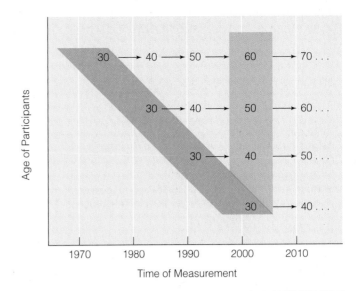

■ **FIGURE 1.7** A sequential study. This study begins in 1970 with a group of 30-year-olds studied longitudinally every 10 years thereafter. In 1980, a second longitudinal study is launched, in 1990 a third, and so on. Notice that at a point in time such as 2000 (orange shading), age groups can be compared in a cross-sectional study. Notice too that 30-year-olds from different cohorts can be compared (blue shading).

surement. Yet they are extremely complex and expensive. See ● **Table 1.4** for a summary of the three basic developmental designs. Generally, the study of life-span human development has progressed from early (and sometimes misleading) cross-sectional studies to more and more long-term longitudinal studies and, increasingly, to more complex sequential studies (Baltes, Lindenberger, & Staudinger, 2006).

SUMMING UP

■ The scientific method involves testing hypotheses based on theories by conducting research with a sample from a larger population.

■ Common data collection methods include verbal reports, behavioral observations, and physiological measures.

■ Experiments involving random assignments to conditions, manipulation of the independent variable, and experimental control help identify cause–effect relationships, whereas in correlational studies, it is difficult both to determine the direction of influence and to rule out third variables.

■ Cross-sectional developmental designs compare age groups but confound age effects and cohort effects; longitudinal studies describe age change but confound age effects and time of measurement effects; and sequential studies combine the cross-sectional and longitudinal approaches to improve on both.

	CROSS-SECTIONAL DESIGN	LONGITUDINAL DESIGN	SEQUENTIAL DESIGN
Procedure	Observe people of different cohorts at one point in time	Observe people of one age group repeatedly over time	Combine cross-sectional and longitudinal approaches; observe different cohorts on multiple occasions
Information Gained	Describes age differences	Describes age changes	Describes age differences and age changes
Advantages	Demonstrates age differences in behavior and hints at developmental trends Takes little time to conduct and is inexpensive	Indicates how individuals are alike and different in the way they change over time Can reveal links between early behavior or experiences and later behavior	Helps separate the effects of age, cohort, and time of measurement Indicates whether developmental changes experienced by one generation or cohort are similar to those experienced by other cohorts
Disadvantages	Age trends may reflect cohort effects rather than true developmental change Provides no information about change in individuals over time	Age trends may reflect time of measurement effects during the study rather than true developmental change Relatively time-consuming and expensive Measures may later prove inadequate Participants drop out Participants can be affected by repeated testing	Complex and time-consuming Despite being the strongest method, may leave questions about whether a developmental change can be generalized

CRITICAL THINKING

1. Select one of the research studies described in this chapter and discuss how it could be used to optimize development.

2. You are interested in developmental changes in moodiness from age 12 to age 20. Design both a cross-sectional and a longitudinal study of this question, and weigh the advantages and disadvantages of the two designs. Also, using the material on verbal report, behavioral observation, and physiological measurements, develop two distinct approaches to measuring moodiness for use in your research.

3. Does the adequacy of the nutrition a child receives during the prenatal period affect the child's IQ test performance at age 5? Suggest both an experimental design and a correlational design to study this question. What features make the two designs different, and what are their pros and cons? Hint: Do not forget to consider ethical issues.

1.4 | WHAT SPECIAL CHALLENGES DO DEVELOPMENTAL SCIENTISTS FACE?

We conclude this chapter by discussing two complex challenges in the study of human development: being sensitive to cultural and subcultural differences and protecting the rights of research participants.

Conducting Culturally Sensitive Research

Both Bronfenbrenner's bioecological model and Baltes's life-span perspective emphasize that development is shaped by its cultural context. They imply that we need to study development in a variety of contexts using culturally sensitive research methods and measurements to understand both what is universal and what is culturally specific about human development (Lonner, 2005). Easier said than done!

Developmentalists now appreciate the need to study samples of developing persons from a variety of ecological settings, not just white middle-class America. A particularly important aspect of the ecology of human development is **socioeconomic status (SES)**, the status in society of an individual or family based on such indicators as occupational prestige, education, and income. We know that low-income families are often exposed to more stress but have fewer coping resources than higher-income families (Heymann, Penrose, & Earle, 2006). We know too that the developmental experiences and trajectories of children are significantly affected by whether they grow up in poverty or affluence. On average, although there are many exceptions, parents of middle or high socioeconomic status tend to provide more stimulating and supportive home environments for their children than low-socioeconomic status (low-SES) parents do. The result is higher academic achievement and better adjustment among higher-SES children than among lower-SES children, as well as better health, cognitive

Findings of research conducted in one culture may not hold true in another culture.

functioning, and adjustment in adulthood (Bornstein & Bradley, 2003; Conger & Donnellan, 2007; Luo & Waite, 2005).

Studying different subcultural and cultural groups is also critical. However, ensuring that questionnaire and interview questions and testing and observation procedures are meaningful in a culture, and that they mean the same thing for individuals from different subcultural and cultural groups if comparisons are to be made, can be extremely challenging (Rogoff, 2003). Here is an illustration of this challenge. When one organization translated a survey into 63 languages and then had the questions translated back into English, strange things happened: "married or living with a partner" was translated as "married but have a girlfriend," and "American ideas and customs" became "the ideology of America and border guards" (Morin, 2003). When another team sought to conduct a cross-cultural study of caregiver–infant interactions, they faced a dilemma about whether to observe such interactions when the caregiver and infant were alone (typical in American homes) or when the caregiver and infant were in a group (typical in Micronesia). They settled on observing in both social contexts to avoid findings that might be biased toward one cultural group or the other (Sostek et al., 1981).

In addition, researchers who study cultural influences on development or racial, ethnic, and socioeconomic differences in development must work hard to keep their own cultural values from biasing their perceptions of other groups. Too often, Western researchers have let **ethnocentrism**—the belief that one's own group and its culture are superior—creep into their research designs, procedures, and measures. And too often, researchers in the United States have judged minority group children and adults according to white middle-class standards, have labeled them "deficient" when they would better be described as "different," and have looked more at their vulnerabilities than at their strengths (Ogbu, 1981; Spencer, 2006). Also

too often, researchers have assumed that all African Americans or Asian Americans or Hispanic Americans are alike psychologically when in fact there is great diversity within each racial or ethnic group (Helms, Jernigan, & Mascher, 2005). Today's developmentalists appreciate the importance of understanding human development in its ecological context, but actually doing so is a tremendous challenge.

Protecting the Rights of Research Participants

Developmental researchers must also be sensitive to issues involving **research ethics**—the standards of conduct that investigators are ethically bound to honor to protect their research participants from physical or psychological harm (Kodish, 2005; Sales & Folkman, 2000). Recall the study by Hubbard and colleagues (2002) described earlier in this chapter, in which 8-year-olds were deliberately provoked to become angry after witnessing another child cheat them and win a board game unfairly. The researchers recognized that their study raised ethical issues. As a result, they arranged for the following: (1) children's parents observed the session through a one-way mirror so that they could call a halt to it if they thought their child was becoming too upset; (2) so that children would not leave with bad feelings about losing, they played another game with the confederate that was rigged so that they would win; (3) children were debriefed about the real purposes of the study; and (4) children enjoyed snack and play time with the confederate (who, by the way, was very concerned not to be branded a cheater).

Many ethical issues arise in research. For example, is it ethical to tell children that they performed poorly on a test to create a temporary sense of failure? Is it an invasion of a family's privacy to ask adolescents questions about conversations they have had with their parents about sex? Should a study of how a hormone replacement pill affects menopausal women be halted if it appears that the drug is having harmful effects? If a drug to treat memory loss in elderly adults with Alzheimer's disease appears to be working, should it be withheld from the control group in the study?

Such issues have led the federal government (through the Office for Human Research Protections), the American Psychological Association, the Society for Research in Child Development, the American Geriatrics Society, and other organizations and agencies to establish guidelines for ethical research with humans. Federal regulations require universities and other organizations that conduct research with humans to have institutional review boards (IRBs) that determine whether proposed research projects conform to ethical standards and to approve the projects only if they comply. The federal government has tightened its oversight of research in recent years as a result of past abuses.

Deciding whether a proposed study is on safe ethical ground involves weighing the possible benefits of the research (gains in knowledge and potential benefits to humanity or to the participants) against the potential risks to participants. If the potential benefits greatly outweigh the potential risks, and if there are no other, less risky procedures that could produce these same benefits, the investigation is likely to be viewed as ethical. The investigator's ethical responsibilities boil down to respecting the rights of research participants by (1) allowing them to make informed and uncoerced decisions about taking part in research, (2) debriefing them afterward (especially if they are not told everything in advance or are deceived), (3) protecting them from harm, and (4) treating any information they provide as confidential. We will examine each of these responsibilities in detail.

1. *Informed consent.* Researchers generally should inform potential participants of all aspects of the research that might affect their decision to participate so that they can make a voluntary decision based on full knowledge of what the research involves. But are young children or mentally impaired children or adults capable of understanding what they are being asked to do and of giving their *informed* consent? Probably not. Therefore, researchers who study such "vulnerable" populations should obtain informed consent both from the individual (if possible) and from someone who can decide on the individual's behalf—for example, the parent or guardian of a child or the legal representative of a nursing home resident. Investigators also must take care not to pressure anyone to participate and must respect participants' right to refuse to participate, to drop out during the study, and to refuse to have their data used by the investigator.

Researchers face many challenges in deciding when children are old enough to understand what is involved in a study, in communicating the basics of the study as simply and clearly as possible, and in ensuring that children really understand what they have been told (e.g., see Burke, Abramovitch, & Zlotkin, 2005; Kodish, 2005). They must take similar care in studying elderly adults to ensure that the individual is capable of giving informed consent or to obtain consent from someone who can speak for an individual with cognitive impairments (Kim et al., 2004). Cultural differences must also be considered; for example, people in non-Western societies may have difficulty understanding the difference between research and medical or psychological treatment and may have different ideas than we do about who should give consent for participation or how best to protect research participants (Molyneux et al., 2005). For this reason, more and more researchers are now trying to involve community members in the planning and design of their studies (Martin & Lantos, 2005).

2. *Debriefing.* Researchers generally tell participants about the purposes of the study in advance, but in some cases doing so would ruin the study. If you told college students in advance that you were studying moral development and then gave them an opportunity to cheat on a test, do you think anyone would cheat? Instead, you might set up a situation in which students believe they can cheat without being detected and then debrief them afterward, explaining the true purpose of the study. You would also have an obligation to make sure that participants do not leave feeling upset about cheating.

3. *Protection from harm.* Researchers are bound not to harm research participants either physically or psychologically. Infants may cry if they are left in a room with a stranger, adolescents may be embarrassed if they are asked about their sex lives, adults who are depressed may experience negative side effects when given experimental antidepressants. Investigators must try to anticipate such consequences and weigh the risks of the research against its benefits to society.

If physical or psychological harm to the participants seems likely, the researcher should consider another way of answering the research question. Federal regulations provide special protection to children; if a research project does not benefit child participants directly, they should be exposed to only minimal levels of risk—not much more than the risks of daily life or of undergoing routine physical and psychological tests and examinations (Kodish, 2005). Moreover, if participants of any age become upset or are harmed, the researcher must take steps to undo the damage.

4. *Confidentiality.* Researchers also have an ethical responsibility to keep confidential the information they collect. It would be unacceptable, for example, to tell a child's teacher that the child performed poorly on an intelligence test or to tell an adult's employer that a drinking problem was revealed in an interview. The confidentiality of medical records concerning a person's physical and mental health is now particularly well protected by the Health Insurance Portability and Accountability Act of 1996, or HIPAA (Gostin, 2001). Only if participants give explicit permission to have information about them shared with someone else, or in rare cases if the law requires disclosure of information (such as when a researcher learns that a child is being abused), can that information be passed on.

Clearly, developmental researchers have some serious issues to weigh if they want their research to be not only well designed but also culturally sensitive and ethically responsible. Understanding life-span human development and the complexities of interactions between nature and nurture is an incredibly complex undertaking. It would be impossible if researchers merely conducted study after study without guiding ideas. Theories of human development provide those guiding ideas and are the subject of Chapter 2.

SUMMING UP

▌ Developmental researchers strive to study humans in a variety of ecological contexts, develop culturally sensitive methods and measures, and keep their own cultural values and ethnocentrism from biasing their conclusions.

▌ Researchers must adhere to standards of ethical research practice, with attention to informed consent, debriefing participants, protecting participants from harm, and maintaining confidentiality.

1. Now that you have your PhD in life-span developmental psychology, you want to interview elderly widows in Japan and in the United States about their emotional reactions to widowhood shortly after the deaths of their husbands. Based on the material on ethical issues in developmental research, what steps would you take to make your study as ethical as possible? And what might you do to make the research as culturally sensitive as possible?

CHAPTER SUMMARY

1.1 How Should We Think about Development?

- Development is systematic changes and continuities over the life span, involving gains, losses, and neutral changes in physical, cognitive, and psychosocial functioning; it is more than growth in childhood and biological aging in adulthood.
- Development takes place in an historical and cultural context and is influenced by age grades, age norms, and social clocks.
- Concepts of the life span and its distinctive periods have changed over history and differ from culture to culture. In the 17th and 18th centuries, children came to be seen as innocents; in the late 19th century, adolescence emerged as a distinct phase; and only in the 20th century have we recognized emerging adulthood, a middle-aged "empty nest" period, and an old age characterized by retirement.
- Understanding the nature–nurture issue means understanding the interaction of biology and maturation with environment and learning. The complexities of transactions between people and their environment are captured in Bronfenbrenner's bioecological model, in which the individual, with his or her biological and psychological characteristics, interacts with environmental systems called the microsystem, mesosystem, exosystem, and macrosystem over time (chronosystem).

1.2 What Is the Science of Life-Span Development?

- The study of life-span development, guided by the goals of description, explanation, and optimization, began with the baby biographies written by Charles Darwin and others.
- Through his use of questionnaires and attention to all phases of the life span, including the storm and stress of adolescence, American psychologist G. Stanley Hall came to be regarded as the founder of developmental psychology.
- By adopting the modern life-span perspective on human development set forth by Baltes, we assume that development (1) occurs throughout the life span, (2) can take many different directions, (3) involves gains and interlinked losses at every age, (4) is characterized by plasticity, (5) is affected by its historical and cultural context, (6) is influenced by multiple interacting causal factors, and (7) can best be understood if scholars from multiple disciplines join forces to understand it.

1.3 How Is Development Studied?

- The scientific method involves formulating theories and testing hypotheses by conducting research with a sample (ideally a random sample) from a larger population.

- Common data collection methods include verbal reports, behavioral observations, and physiological measures.
- The goal of explaining development is best achieved through experiments involving random assignments to conditions, manipulation of the independent variable, and experimental control. In correlational studies, it is difficult to determine the direction of influence and to rule out third variables.
- Developmental research designs seek to describe age effects on development. Cross-sectional studies compare different age groups but confound age effects and cohort effects. Longitudinal studies study age change but confound age effects and time of measurement effects. Sequential studies combine the cross-sectional and longitudinal approaches.

1.4 What Special Challenges Do Developmental Scientists Face?

- To understand human development in its ecological context, researchers must study humans in a variety of ecological contexts, develop culturally sensitive methods and measures, and keep their own cultural values and ethnocentrism from biasing their conclusions.
- Researchers must adhere to standards of ethical research practice, with attention to ensuring informed consent, debriefing individuals from whom information has been withheld, protecting research participants from harm, and maintaining confidentiality of data.

KEY TERMS

centenarian 2
development 2
growth 3
biological aging 3
aging 3
age grade 3
age norms 4
social clock 4
nature–nurture issue 5
maturation 5
genes 5
environment 5
learning 5
bioecological model 7
microsystem 7
mesosystem 7
exosystem 7
macrosystem 7
culture 7
adolescence 8
emerging adulthood 8
chronosystem 8
baby boom generation 9
baby biographies 11
case study method 11
storm and stress 11
gerontology 11
life-span perspective 11
plasticity 12
scientific method 14

theory 14
hypothesis 14
sample 14
population 14
random sample 14
naturalistic observation 15
structured observation 15
experiment 17
independent variable 17
dependent variable 17
random assignment 17
experimental control 17
quasi experiment 18
correlational method 18
correlation coefficient 18
meta-analysis 20
age effects 20
cohort effects 20
cohort 20
time of measurement effects 20
cross-sectional design 21
longitudinal design 21
sequential design 23
socioeconomic status (SES) 24
ethnocentrism 25
research ethics 25

MEDIA RESOURCES

BOOK COMPANION WEBSITE

academic.cengage.com/psychology/sigelman
Find online quizzes, flash cards, animations, video clips, experiments, interactive assessments, and other helpful study aids for this text at **academic.cengage.com/psychology/sigelman**. You can also connect directly to the following sites:

ABOUT DEVELOPMENTAL PSYCHOLOGY

The about.com: Psychology site contains links to articles on most classic theories of human development (e.g., Piaget, Kohlberg). It also has links to articles on key developmental topics like stages of prenatal development and research methods.

APA ETHICAL STANDARDS

The American Psychological Association maintains an excellent website describing the ethical principles and code of conduct for psychologists. This code addresses both research and professional standards of behavior.

CENSUS DATA

The website of the U.S. Census Bureau provides a wealth of statistical information about the population of the United States, including information about different age groups.

SOCIAL PSYCHOLOGY NETWORK-DEVELOPMENTAL PSYCHOLOGY

For a large menu of resources on life-span human development on the Social Psychology network (maintained by Scott Plous of Wesleyan University), simply type in "Developmental Psychology" in the "Search Social Psychology Network" Q (question box) on the homepage and hit the quick search button.

UNDERSTANDING THE DATA: EXERCISES ON THE WEB

academic.cengage.com/psychology/sigelman
For additional insight on the data presented in this chapter, try out the exercises for these figures at **academic.cengage.com/psychology/sigelman**:

Figure 1.1 Aggression among children in four cultures

Figure 1.6 Conflicting findings of hypothetical cross-sectional and longitudinal studies of gender-role attitudes

CENGAGENOW

academic.cengage.com/login
Go to **academic.cengage.com/login** to link to CengageNOW, your online study tool. First take the Pre-Test for this chapter to get your Personalized Study Plan, which will identify topics you need to review and direct you to online resources. Then take the Post-Test to determine what concepts you have mastered and what you still need work on.

© Ronnie Kaufman/Corbis

2 CHAPTER

Theories of Human Development

TERRELL, AGE 6, just started first grade last week, all decked out in his new shirt and pants. Now he is begging his mother each morning to let him stay home. He cries and says that he has a terrible stomachache, and a headache and a sore foot besides, and is going to throw up any second so please, please, can he stay home. Because his symptoms clear up quickly if he is allowed to stay home, it is clear that Terrell's problem is not a physical illness. But what *is* wrong?

SHERRY IS ONLY 15 YEARS OLD and is pregnant. Her relationship with Robert had become the center of her life. The sex "just happened" one night after a party and continued. Neither Sherry nor Robert wanted a baby, but neither used a contraceptive, so here they are.

Teenage pregnancy is also common, although rates in the United States have decreased since the mid-1990s, when 1 in 10 females aged 15 to 19 became pregnant each year and more than half gave birth (Connolly, 2005; Farber, 2003). Valued in many societies, pregnancy during the teen years is generally discouraged in ours and many teenage pregnancies are unplanned and unwanted. Having a child as a teenager can have positive or negative effects on a young woman's life course depending on the circumstances. Sometimes it mobilizes her support network and helps her focus on school and work; other times it interrupts her education, limits her job prospects, and leaves her living in poverty and raising a child by herself (Furstenberg, 2005).

■ ■ ■

School refusal (sometimes called school phobia), a reluctance or refusal to go to school, affects from 1% to as many as 5% of school-age children, and is most common among 5- to 7-year-olds like Terrell who are venturing off to school for the first time (Fremont, 2003; Heyne, King, & Tonge, 2004). It can have a number of different causes, and it can involve considerable anxiety and emotional distress for the child.

How might we explain a 6-year-old's school refusal or a 15-year-old's unwanted pregnancy from a developmental perspective? What are your theories? What explanations might the leading theories of human development offer? We attempt to answer these questions in this chapter to illustrate that different theories of human development offer different lenses through which to view the same developmental phenomena.

2.1 DEVELOPMENTAL THEORIES AND THE ISSUES THEY RAISE

As noted in Chapter 1, a theory is a set of ideas proposed to describe and explain certain phenomena—in this book, the phenomena of human development. In science, it is not enough simply to catalog facts without organizing this information around some set of concepts and propositions. Researchers would soon be overwhelmed by trivia and would lack "the big picture." A theory of human development provides needed organization, offering a lens through which researchers can interpret any number of specific facts or observations. A theory also guides the collection of new facts or observations, making clear (1) what is most important to study, (2) what can be hypothesized or predicted about it, and (3) how it should be studied. Because different theorists often have different views on these critical matters, what is learned in any science greatly depends on which theoretical perspectives become dominant, which largely depends on how well they account for the facts.

All of us hold some basic beliefs about human development—for example, about the importance of genes versus good parenting in healthy development. Reading this chapter should make you more aware of your own assumptions about human development and how they compare with those of the major theorists. Scientific theories are expected to be more rigorous than our everyday theories, however; theories are not just speculations, hunches, or unsupported opinions. A good developmental theory should be:

- *Internally consistent.* Its different parts and propositions should hang together and should not generate contradictory hypotheses or predictions.

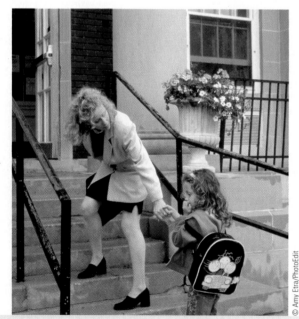

School refusal (or school phobia) is quite common among children starting school. Why might this child be reluctant to go to school?

© Amy Etra/PhotoEdit

WHERE DO YOU STAND ON MAJOR DEVELOPMENTAL ISSUES?

Choose one option for each statement, and write down the corresponding letter or fill it in at the end of the box. See Table 2.4 to compare your results with how the theorists described in this chapter view development.

1. Biological influences (heredity and maturational forces) and environmental influences (culture, parenting styles, and learning experiences) are thought to contribute to development. Overall,
    a. biological factors contribute far more than environmental factors.
    b. biological factors contribute somewhat more than environmental factors.
    c. biological and environmental factors are equally important.
    d. environmental factors contribute somewhat more than biological factors.
    e. environmental factors contribute far more than biological factors.

2. Children are innately
    a. mostly bad; they are born with basically negative, selfish impulses.
    b. neither good nor bad; they are tabula rasae (blank slates).
    c. both good and bad; they are born with predispositions that are both positive and negative.
    d. mostly good; they are born with many positive tendencies.

3. People are basically
    a. active beings who are the prime determiners of their own abilities and traits.
    b. passive beings whose characteristics are molded either by social influences (parents, other significant people, and outside events) or by biological changes beyond their control.

4. Development proceeds
    a. through stages so that the individual changes rather abruptly into a different kind of person than she was in an earlier stage.
    b. in a variety of ways—some stagelike and some gradual or continuous.
    c. continuously—in small increments without abrupt changes or distinct stages.

5. When you compare the development of different individuals, you see
    a. many similarities; children and adults develop along universal paths and experience similar changes at similar ages.
    b. many differences; different people often undergo different sequences of change and have widely different timetables of development.

Statement

| 1 | 2 | 3 | 4 | 5 |

Your pattern of choices:

___ ___ ___ ___ ___

-   *Falsifiable.* It can be proved wrong; that is, it can generate specific, testable hypotheses that can be studied and either supported or not supported by data. If a theory is vague or generates contradictory or ambiguous hypotheses, it cannot guide research, cannot be tested, and therefore will not be useful in advancing knowledge.
-   *Supported by data.* A good theory should help us better describe, predict, and explain human development; that means its predictions should be confirmed by research results.

Theories that fail to meet these evaluation criteria—theories that are not internally consistent, falsifiable, and supported by data—need to be revised or discarded.

In this chapter, we examine four major theoretical viewpoints, each with different messages about the nature of human development:

1. The *psychoanalytic* viewpoint developed by Sigmund Freud and revised by Erik Erikson and other followers
2. The *learning* perspective developed by B. F. Skinner, Albert Bandura, and others
3. The *cognitive developmental* viewpoint associated with Jean Piaget
4. The *systems theory* approach, exemplified by Urie Bronfenbrenner (see Chapter 1) and Gilbert Gottlieb

To aid comparison of these theories, we outline five key developmental issues on which theorists—and people in general—often disagree (P. H. Miller, 2002; Parke et al., 1994): the goodness and badness of human nature, nature and nurture, activity and passivity, continuity and discontinuity, and universality and context specificity. We invite you to clarify your stands on these issues by completing the brief questionnaire in the Explorations box. Table 2.4 indicates how the major developmental theorists might answer the questions, so you can compare your assumptions with theirs. In Explorations boxes throughout this chapter, we imagine some major points each theorist might make about the causes of school refusal or teenage pregnancy. We suggest that you predict what each theorist would say before you read each of these boxes to see whether you can successfully apply the theories to a specific problem. It is our hope that when you master the major theories, you will be able to draw on their concepts and propositions to make sense of your own and other people's development.

Nature and Nurture

Is development primarily the product of nature (biological forces) or nurture (environmental forces)? As you saw in Chapter 1, the nature–nurture issue is the most important and most complex issue in the study of human development. A strong believer in nature—in individual genetic makeup, universal maturational processes guided by genes, biologically based predispositions built into genes over the course of evolution, and other biological influences—would claim that all normal children achieve the same developmental milestones at similar times because of maturational forces, that major changes in functioning in late adulthood are biologically based, and that differences among children or adults are largely because of differences in genetic makeup and physiology.

By contrast, a strong believer in nurture would emphasize environment—the range of influences outside the person. Nurture includes influences not only of the physical environment such as crowding and pollution, but also of the social environment consisting of learning experiences, child-rearing methods, societal changes, and the cultural context in which the person develops. Like the English philosopher John Locke (1632–1704), a strong believer in nurture would argue that human development can take many forms depending on the individual's experiences over a lifetime.

The Goodness and Badness of Human Nature

Are people inherently good, inherently bad, or neither? Well before modern theories of human development were proposed, philosophers of the 17th and 18th centuries were taking stands on the nature of humans. Thomas Hobbes (1588–1679), for one, portrayed children as inherently selfish and bad and believed that it was society's responsibility to teach them to behave in civilized ways. By contrast, Jean Jacques Rousseau (1712–1778) argued that children were innately good, that they were born with an intuitive understanding of right and wrong, and that they would develop in positive directions as long as society did not interfere with their natural tendencies. In the middle was John Locke, who maintained that infants are **tabula rasae,** or "blank slates," waiting to be written on by their experiences. That is, children were neither innately good nor innately bad but could develop in any direction depending on their experiences.

These different visions of human nature are all represented in one or more theories of development. These views have radically different implications for how people should raise children. In teaching children to share, for example, should adults assume that their innate selfish tendencies must be battled at every step, that they are predisposed by nature to be helpful and caring, or that they have the potential to become either selfish beasts or selfless wonders depending on how they are brought up? Recent evidence of biologically based tendencies, good and bad, has challenged the popular belief that humans are blank slates who have no biologically based predispositions and can become anything they are raised to become (Pinker, 2002).

Activity and Passivity

The **activity–passivity issue** focuses on whether people are active in their own development or passively shaped by forces outside themselves. Some theorists believe that humans are curious, active creatures who orchestrate their own development by exploring the world around them and shaping their environ-

ments. The girl who asks for dolls at the toy store and the boy who clamors instead for toy machine guns are actively contributing to their own gender-role development. Both the budding scientist who experiments with chemicals in the basement and the sociable adolescent who spends hours on the phone are seeking out and creating a "niche" that suits their emerging traits and abilities—and that further develops those traits in the process (Harris, 2006).

Other theorists view humans as passive beings shaped largely by forces beyond their control—usually environmental influences but possibly strong biological forces. From this vantage point, children's academic failings might be blamed on the failure of their parents and teachers to provide them with the right learning experiences, and the problems of socially isolated older adults might be attributed to societal neglect of the elderly rather than to deficiencies within the individual. Theorists disagree about how active individuals are in creating and influencing their own environments and, in the process, in producing their own development.

Continuity and Discontinuity

Do you believe that humans change gradually, in ways that leave them not so different from the way they were before, or do you believe humans change abruptly and dramatically? One aspect of the **continuity–discontinuity issue** focuses on whether the changes people undergo over the life span are gradual or abrupt. Continuity theorists view human development as a process that occurs in small steps, without sudden changes, as when grade school children gradually gain weight from year to year. In contrast, discontinuity theorists picture the course of development as more like a series of stair steps, each of which elevates the individual to a new (and often more advanced) level of functioning. When an adolescent boy rapidly shoots up 6 inches in height, gains a bass voice, and grows a beard, the change seems discontinuous (see ■ Figure 2.1).

A second aspect of the continuity–discontinuity issue focuses on whether changes are quantitative or qualitative in nature. Quantitative changes are changes in *degree* and indicate

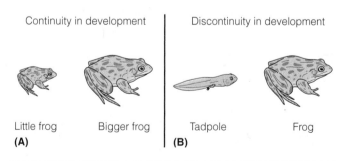

Continuity in development   Discontinuity in development

Little frog   Bigger frog   Tadpole   Frog
(A)   (B)

■ **FIGURE 2.1** Is development continuous (A) or discontinuous (B)? That is, do people change quantitatively, becoming different in degree (as shown in Panel A with size), or do they change qualitatively, becoming different in kind (as shown in Panel B when a tadpole becomes a frog)?

continuity: a person gains more wrinkles, grows taller, knows more vocabulary words, or interacts with friends less frequently. By contrast, qualitative changes are changes in *kind* and suggest discontinuity. They are changes that make the individual fundamentally different in some way. The transformations of a caterpillar into a butterfly rather than just a bigger caterpillar, of a nonverbal infant into a speaking toddler, and of a prepubertal child into a sexually mature adolescent are examples of qualitative changes.

So, continuity theorists typically hold that developmental changes are gradual and quantitative, whereas discontinuity theorists hold that they are more abrupt and qualitative. Discontinuity theorists often propose that people progress through **developmental stages.** A stage is a distinct phase of the life cycle characterized by a particular set of abilities, motives, emotions, or behaviors that form a coherent pattern. Each stage is viewed as qualitatively different from the stage before or the stage after. Thus, the preschool child may be said to have a fundamentally different approach to solving problems than the infant, adolescent, or adult.

Universality and Context Specificity

Finally, developmental theorists often disagree on the **universality–context-specificity issue**—on the extent to which developmental changes are common to all humans (universal) or different from person to person (context specific). Stage theorists typically believe that the stages they propose are universal. For example, a stage theorist might claim that virtually all children enter a new stage in their intellectual development as they enter adolescence or that most adults, sometime around age 40, experience a midlife crisis in which they raise major questions about their lives. From this perspective, development proceeds in certain universal directions.

But other theorists believe that human development is far more varied. Paths of development followed in one culture may be quite different from paths followed in another culture.

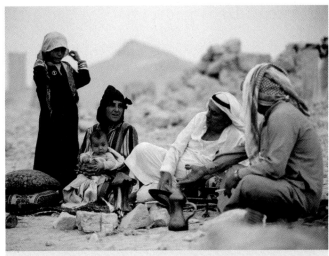

To what extent is human development universal and to what extent is it culture specific? Only cross-cultural research can tell us.

For example, preschool children in the United States sometimes believe that dreams are real but give up this belief as they age. By contrast, children raised in the Atayal culture of Taiwan have been observed to become more and more convinced as they get older that dreams are real, most likely because that is what adults in their culture believe (Kohlberg, 1966b). Within a single culture, developmental change may differ from subcultural group to subcultural group, from family to family, or from individual to individual. There seems to be both universality and context specificity in human development. As American poet Mark Van Doren once said, "There are two statements about human beings that are true: that all human beings are alike, and that all are different" (cited in Norenzayan & Heine, 2005, p. 763).

Now that you are familiar with some major issues of human development that different theories resolve in different ways (see ● Table 2.1), we will begin our survey of the theories, starting with Freud's well-known psychoanalytic perspective.

● TABLE 2.1 ISSUES IN HUMAN DEVELOPMENT

ISSUE	DESCRIPTION
1. Nature–Nurture	Is development primarily the product of genes, biology, and maturation—or of experience, learning, and social influences?
2. Goodness–Badness of Human Nature	Are humans innately good, innately bad, neither (tabula rasae), or both?
3. Activity–Passivity	Do humans actively shape their own environments and contribute to their own development—or are they passively shaped by forces beyond their control?
4. Continuity–Discontinuity	Do humans change gradually and in quantitative ways—or do they progress through qualitatively different stages and change dramatically into different beings?
5. Universality–Context Specificity	Is development similar from person to person and from culture to culture—or do pathways of development vary considerably depending on the social contexts?

- Theories organize and explain the facts of human development and are adequate if they are internally consistent, falsifiable, and supported by data.

- The major issues confronted by developmental theorists are nature and nurture, the goodness and badness of human nature, activity and passivity, continuity and discontinuity, and universality and context specificity.

CRITICAL THINKING

1. Professor Whitehead has developed a theory of aging emphasizing (1) nature *and* nurture, (2) the goodness of human nature, (3) activity, (4) continuity, and (5) context specificity in development. Develop five sentences, one for each of the five issues in human development, that would illustrate the Professor's views on aging.

2.2 | FREUD: PSYCHOANALYTIC THEORY

It is difficult to think of a theorist who has had a greater effect on Western thought than Sigmund Freud, the Viennese physician who lived from 1856 to 1939. This revolutionary thinker's **psychoanalytic theory** challenged prevailing notions of human nature and human development by proposing that people are driven by motives and emotional conflicts of which they are largely unaware and that they are shaped by their earliest experiences in life (Hall, 1954). Freud's ideas continue to influence thinking about human development, even though they are far less influential

© Mary Evans Picture Library/Alamy

Sigmund Freud's psychoanalytic theory was one of the first, and one of the most influential, theories of how the personality develops from childhood to adulthood.

today than they once were. Because you have undoubtedly been introduced to this theory before, we cover it only briefly.

Instincts and Unconscious Motives

Central to Freudian psychoanalytic theory is the notion that humans have basic biological urges or drives that must be satisfied. Freud viewed the newborn as a "seething cauldron," an inherently selfish creature "driven" by **instincts,** or inborn biological forces that motivate behavior. These biological instincts are the source of the psychic (or mental) energy that fuels human behavior and that is channeled in new directions over the course of human development.

Freud strongly believed in **unconscious motivation**—the power of instincts and other inner forces to influence behavior without awareness. A preadolescent girl, for example, may not realize that she is acting in babyish ways in order to regain the security of her mother's love, and a teenage boy may not realize that his devotion to body building is a way of channeling his sexual and aggressive urges. So, you immediately see that Freud's theory emphasizes the nature side of the nature–nurture issue: biological instincts—forces that often provide an unconscious motivation for actions—are said to guide human development.

Id, Ego, and Superego

According to Freud (1933), each individual has a fixed amount of psychic energy that can be used to satisfy basic urges or instincts and to grow psychologically. As a child develops, this psychic energy is divided among three components of the personality: the id, the ego, and the superego. At birth, all psychic energy resides in the **id**—the impulsive, irrational part of the personality whose mission is to satisfy the instincts. It seeks immediate gratification, even when biological needs cannot be realistically or appropriately met. If you think about it, young infants do seem to be all id in some ways. When they are hungry or wet, they fuss and cry until their needs are met. They are not known for their patience.

The second component of the personality is the **ego,** the rational side of the individual that tries to find realistic ways of gratifying the instincts. According to Freud (1933), the ego begins to emerge during infancy when psychic energy is diverted from the id to energize cognitive processes such as perception, learning, and problem solving. The hungry toddler may be able to do more than merely cry when she is hungry; she may be able to draw on the resources of the ego to hunt down Dad, lead him to the kitchen, and say "cookie." However, toddlers' egos are still relatively immature; they want what they want *now*. As the ego matures further, children become more capable of postponing their pleasures until a more appropriate time and of devising logical and realistic strategies for meeting their needs.

The third part of the Freudian personality is the **superego,** the individual's internalized moral standards. The superego develops from the ego as 3- to 6-year-old children internalize

The three parts of the personality proposed by Freud are inevitably in conflict.

(take on as their own) the moral standards and values of their parents. Once the superego emerges, children have a parental voice in their heads that keeps them from violating society's rules and makes them feel guilty or ashamed if they do. The superego insists that people find socially acceptable or ethical outlets for the id's undesirable impulses.

Conflict among the id, ego, and superego is inevitable, Freud said. In the mature, healthy personality, a dynamic balance operates: the id communicates its basic needs, the ego restrains the impulsive id long enough to find realistic ways to satisfy these needs, and the superego decides whether the ego's problem-solving strategies are morally acceptable. The ego must strike a balance between the opposing demands of the id and the superego while accommodating the realities of environment.

According to Freud (1940/1964), psychological problems often arise when the individual's supply of psychic energy is unevenly distributed among the id, the ego, and the superego. For example, a person diagnosed as an antisocial personality, or sociopath, who routinely lies and cheats to get his way, may have a weak superego, whereas a married woman who cannot undress in front of her husband may have an overly strong superego, perhaps because she was made to feel ashamed about any interest she took in her body as a young girl. Through analysis of the dynamics operating among the three parts of the personality, Freud and his followers attempted to describe and understand individual differences in personality and the origins of psychological disorders.

Psychosexual Development

Freud (1940/1964) maintained that as the child matures biologically, the psychic energy of the sex instinct, which he called **libido,** shifts from one part of the body to another, seeking to gratify different biological needs. In the process, as outlined in ● **Table 2.2,** the child moves through five **psychosexual stages:** oral, anal, phallic, latent, and genital.

Freud emphasized the role of nature over that of nurture in development, maintaining that inborn biological instincts drive behavior and that biological maturation guides all children through the five psychosexual stages. Yet he also viewed nurture—especially early experiences within the family—as an important contributor to individual differences in adult personality. At each psychosexual stage, the id's impulses and social demands come into conflict. Harsh child-rearing methods can heighten this conflict and the child's anxiety.

To defend itself against anxiety, the ego adopts unconscious coping devices called **defense mechanisms** (Freud, 1940/1964). Consider the defense mechanism of **fixation**—arrested development in which part of the libido remains tied to an early stage. A baby boy who was rarely allowed to linger at the breast, was screamed at for mouthing and chewing paychecks and other fascinating objects left lying around the house, or was otherwise deprived of oral gratification might become fixated at the oral stage. He would then seek to satisfy unmet oral needs and to avoid the potentially more agonizing conflicts of the anal stage. He might display this oral fixation by becoming a chronic thumb sucker and, later in life, by chain-smoking, talking incessantly (as college professors are prone to do), or depending too much on other people.

Similarly, the 3-year-old who is harshly punished for toileting accidents may become fixated at the anal stage and turn into an inhibited or stingy adult. Or she may deal with her anxiety through another defense mechanism, **regression,** which involves retreating to an earlier, less traumatic stage of development. She may revert to infantile behavior—cooing like a baby and demanding juice from a baby bottle. Similarly, the man who has had a terrible day at work may want his wife to act like his mother and "baby" him. In this way, Freud argued, early experiences may have long-term effects on personality development.

The phallic stage from age 3 to age 6 is an especially treacherous time, according to Freud. Youngsters develop an incestuous desire for the parent of the other sex. (A boy's Oedipus complex and a girl's Electra complex are discussed in Chapter 12.) If all goes well, they resolve the emotional conflict they experience by identifying with the same-sex parent and in the process incorporating that parent's values into the superego. After the lull of the latent period, during which sexual urges are tame and 6- to 12-year-olds invest psychic energy in schoolwork and play, adolescents experience new psychic conflicts as they reach puberty and enter the final stage of psychosexual development, the genital stage. They may have difficulty accepting their new sexuality, may reexperience some conflicting feelings toward their parents that they felt during the phallic stage, and may distance themselves from their parents to defend themselves against these anxiety-producing feelings. During adulthood, people may develop a greater capacity to love and typically satisfy the mature sex instinct by having children. However, Freud believed that psychosexual development stops with adolescence and that the individual remains in the genital stage throughout adulthood.

In the Explorations box on page 37 we imagine the notes that Freud might have scribbled down to explain Terrell's

FREUD'S PSYCHOSEXUAL THEORY		ERIKSON'S PSYCHOSOCIAL THEORY	
STAGE (AGE RANGE)	DESCRIPTION	STAGE (AGE RANGE)	DESCRIPTION
Oral stage (birth to 1 year)	Libido is focused on the mouth as a source of pleasure. Obtaining oral gratification from a mother figure is critical to later development.	Trust vs. mistrust (birth to 1 year)	Infants must learn to trust their caregivers to meet their needs. Responsive parenting is critical.
Anal stage (1 to 3 years)	Libido is focused on the anus, and toilet training creates conflicts between the child's biological urges and the society's demands.	Autonomy vs. shame and doubt (1 to 3 years)	Children must learn to be autonomous—to assert their wills and do things for themselves—or they will doubt their abilities.
Phallic stage (3 to 6 years)	Libido centers on the genitals. Resolution of the Oedipus or the Electra complex results in identification with the same-sex parent and development of the superego.	Initiative vs. guilt (3 to 6 years)	Preschoolers develop initiative by devising and carrying out bold plans, but they must learn not to impinge on the rights of others.
Latent period (6 to 12 years)	Libido is quiet; psychic energy is invested in schoolwork and play with same-sex friends.	Industry vs. inferiority (6 to 12 years)	Children must master important social and academic skills and keep up with their peers; otherwise, they will feel inferior.
Genital stage (12 years and older)	Puberty reawakens the sexual instincts as youths seek to establish mature sexual relationships and pursue the biological goal of reproduction	Identity vs. role confusion (12 to 20 years)	Adolescents ask who they are and must establish social and vocational identities; otherwise, they will remain confused about the roles they should play as adults.
		Intimacy vs. isolation (20 to 40 years)	Young adults seek to form a shared identity with another person, but may fear intimacy and experience loneliness and isolation.
		Generativity vs. stagnation (40 to 65 years)	Middle-aged adults must feel that they are producing something that will outlive them, either as parents or as workers; otherwise, they will become stagnant and self-centered.
		Integrity vs. despair (65 years and older)	Older adults must come to view their lives as meaningful to face death without worries and regrets.

school refusal and Sherry's pregnancy, as described at the start of the chapter. What might you say if you were Freud?

Strengths and Weaknesses

Many developmentalists fault Freud for proposing a theory that is ambiguous, internally inconsistent, difficult to pin down and test, and therefore not easily falsifiable (Fonagy & Target, 2000).

Testing hypotheses that require studying unconscious motivations and the workings of the unseen id, ego, and superego has been challenging. Freud himself offered little hard evidence to support his theory. Moreover, when the theory has been tested, many of its specific ideas have not been supported (Crews, 1996; Fisher & Greenberg, 1977). As a result, one critic called it "a theory in search of some facts" (Macmillan, 1991, p. 548).

To illustrate, Freud initially concluded that many of his patients had been sexually or physically abused during child-

EXPLORATIONS

FREUD: NOTES ON SCHOOL REFUSAL AND TEENAGE PREGNANCY

Notes on School Refusal

Terrell's problem may not be fear of school as much as separation anxiety—fear of leaving his mother originating from an unresolved Oedipal conflict, an incestuous desire for his mother in the phallic stage of psychosexual development. School refusal can indeed be caused by separation anxiety rooted in problems in the parent–child relationship and emotional difficulties such as anxiety and depression in the child (Elliott, 1999).

We should analyze the mother–son relationship from birth to find the source of this boy's problems. Lack of gratification, or too much gratification, during the oral or anal stages may have contributed to his current difficulty resolving his Oedipal conflict.

Notes on Teenage Pregnancy

Teenagers experience intense emotional conflicts during the genital stage of psychosexual development. Their new sexual urges are anxiety-provoking and may reawaken the sexual conflicts of earlier psychosexual stages. For example, Robert might have been seeking to gratify his unconscious desire for his mother by possessing Sherry (or Sherry may have been seeking to possess her father).

Teenagers who engage in risky sex may not have strong enough egos (to analyze the consequences) and superegos (to arouse guilt) to keep their selfish ids in check.

---

hood but had repressed their traumatic experiences. Because this was difficult to accept, he later said that children in the phallic stage wished for and fantasized about, but did not actually experience, seduction by their parents (Masson, 1984). There is still controversy about whether Freud meant to deny the reality of incest and other forms of child sexual abuse or to call attention to the importance of fantasy in his later writings (Ahbe-Rappe, 2006). Moreover, it is still debated whether Freud's patients were really sexually abused or whether his therapeutic techniques planted thoughts in their minds and created false memories of abuse. Overall, Freud's claims about the role of sexual fantasy in child development have not received much support (Crews, 1996), although psychologists do recognize that sexual abuse in childhood can contribute to later psychological problems (see Chapter 12).

Although many of Freud's specific ideas have been difficult to test or have not been supported by research when they have been tested, many of his general insights have stood up well and have profoundly influenced theories of human development and psychotherapy (Fonagy & Target, 2000). First, Freud called attention to *unconscious processes* underlying human behavior, to inner conflicts of which we are not aware; some of his insights in this area are supported by modern neuropsychological research (Guterl, 2002), and they have profoundly influenced psychotherapy by making the goal to bring unconscious motivations to the surface where they can be confronted and changed. Second, he was one of the first to highlight the importance for later development of *early experiences* in the family. Finally, he pointed out the important role of *emotions* in development. Developmentalists have often slighted emotional development, focusing instead on observable behavior or on rational thought processes.

SUMMING UP

▌ Freud's psychoanalytic theory characterizes humans as driven by inborn biological instincts of which they are largely unconscious and divides the personality into the id, ego, and superego.

▌ The five psychosexual stages involve emotional conflicts that create the need for defense mechanisms and have lasting effects on personality.

▌ Biological needs drive development, but parents can contribute to emotional problems, especially if they are overly restrictive.

▌ Although Freud called attention to the unconscious, early experience, and emotions, many specifics of his theory lack support.

CRITICAL THINKING

1. In 2006, Congressman Mark Foley from Florida resigned from office in disgrace after it was revealed that he wrote sexually suggestive e-mails to adolescent males serving as congressional pages. Foley also chaired the House Caucus on Missing and Exploited children, speaking often on the need to protect children from sexual predators. What might Freud hypothesize about Foley's personality?

2.3 ERIKSON: NEO-FREUDIAN PSYCHOANALYTIC THEORY

Another sign of Freud's immense influence is that he inspired so many disciples and descendants to make their own contributions to the understanding of human development. Among these well-known neo-Freudians were Alfred Adler, who suggested that siblings (and rivalries among siblings) are significant in development; Carl Jung, a pioneer in the study of adult development who claimed that adults experience a kind of midlife crisis (see Chapter 11) and then become freer to express both the "masculine" and the "feminine" sides of their personalities; Karen Horney, who challenged Freud's ideas about sex differences; Harry Stack Sullivan, who argued that close friendships in childhood set the stage for intimate relationships later in life (see Chapter 14); and Freud's daughter Anna, who developed techniques of psychoanalysis appropriate for children.

ERIKSON: NOTES ON SCHOOL REFUSAL AND TEENAGE PREGNANCY

Notes on School Refusal

Like a good Freudian, check for unresolved conflicts from earlier stages of development. For example, might Terrell have developed a sense of shame and doubt owing to negative reactions from his parents when he tried to assert himself as a toddler?

Focus on his current psychosocial stage, industry versus inferiority. Might Terrell have performed poorly on school tasks during the first week of school and concluded that he is inferior to the other children?

Like a good Freudian, focus on the parent–child relationship, but recognize that other relationships count too. Something going on in Terrell's relationships with his peers or teacher, or even something happening in the wider culture, may be affecting him.

Notes on Teenage Pregnancy

Like a good Freudian, check for unresolved conflicts from earlier stages. Adolescents who never developed a strong sense of trust in other people during infancy, for example, may fear abandonment and may try to use sex to keep from being abandoned.

Or focus on the adolescent psychosocial conflict of identity versus role confusion: Adolescents seek a sense of identity by experimenting with different roles and behaviors to see what suits them. They try drugs, dye their hair orange, join radical groups, change majors every semester, and yes, have sex.

Maybe Sherry and Robert tried to find an easy resolution to their role confusion by latching prematurely onto an identity as the other's boyfriend or girlfriend rather than going through the hard work of experimenting to find out who they are (Erikson, 1968).

But the neo-Freudian who most influenced thinking about life-span development was Erik Erikson (1902–1994; see Chapter 11). Erikson studied with Anna Freud and emigrated from Germany to the United States when Hitler rose to power (Friedman, 1999). Like Sigmund Freud, Erikson (1963, 1968, 1982) concerned himself with the inner dynamics of personality and proposed that the personality evolves through systematic stages. However, compared to Freud, Erikson:

- Placed less emphasis on sexual urges as the drivers of development and more emphasis on social influences such as peers, teachers, schools, and the broader culture.
- Placed less emphasis on the unconscious, irrational, and selfish id and more on the rational ego and its adaptive powers.
- Held a more positive view of human nature, seeing people as active in their development, largely rational, and able to overcome the effects of harmful early experiences.
- Put more emphasis on development after adolescence.

As one scholar put it, Erikson shifted Freudian thought "upward in consciousness, outward to the social world, and forward throughout the complete life span" (Hoare, 2005, p. 19).

Psychosocial Stages

Erikson believed that humans everywhere experience eight major **psychosocial stages,** or conflicts, during their lives. (Erikson's psychosocial stages are next to Freud's in Table 2.2.) Whether the conflict of a particular stage is successfully resolved or not, the individual is pushed by both biological maturation and social demands into the next stage. However, the unsuccessful resolution of a conflict will influence how subsequent stages play out.

For example, the first conflict, *trust versus mistrust*, revolves around whether or not infants become able to rely on other people to be responsive to their needs. To develop a sense of

Erik Erikson built on Freudian theory and proposed that people experience eight psychosexual crises over their life span.

© UPI-Bettmann/Corbis

trust, infants must be able to count on their primary caregivers to feed them, relieve their discomfort, come when beckoned, and return their smiles and babbles. Whereas Freud focused on the significance of the caregiver's feeding practices, Erikson believed that the caregiver's general responsiveness was critical to later development. If caregivers neglect, reject, or respond inconsistently to infants, infants will mistrust others. A healthy balance between the terms of the conflict must be struck for development to proceed optimally. Trust should outweigh mistrust, but an element of skepticism is also needed: an overindulged infant may become too trusting (a gullible "sucker").

So it goes for the remaining stages of childhood. If all goes well as children confront and resolve each conflict, they will gain a sense of self and develop *autonomy* (rather than shame and doubt about their ability to act independently), develop the *initiative* (as opposed to guilt) that allows them to plan and tackle big projects, and acquire the sense of *industry* (rather than inferiority) that will result in mastering important academic and social skills in school. This will position adolescents to successfully resolve the conflict for which Erikson (1968) is best known, *identity versus role confusion*. Erikson characterized adolescence as a time of "identity crisis" in which humans attempt to define who they are (in terms of career, religion, sexual identity, and so on), where they are heading, and how they fit into society. As part of their search, they often change their minds and experiment with new looks, new majors, new relationships, and new group memberships. Erikson should know: He was the tall, blond stepson of a Jewish doctor who wandered all over Europe after high school, trying out a career as an artist and several other possibilities before he ended up studying child psychoanalysis under Anna Freud and finally found his calling in his mid-20s (Friedman, 1999).

Whereas Freud's stages stopped with adolescence, Erikson believed that psychosocial growth continues during the adult years. Successfully resolving the adolescent conflict of identity versus role confusion paves the way for resolving the early adulthood conflict of *intimacy versus isolation* and for becoming ready to participate in a committed, long-term relationship. Successful resolution of the middle-age conflict of *generativity versus stagnation* involves individuals gaining a sense that they have produced something that will outlive them, whether by successfully raising children or by doing something meaningful through work or volunteer activities. Finally, elderly adults who resolve the psychosocial conflict of *integrity versus despair* find a sense of meaning in their lives that will help them face death.

Erikson clearly did not agree with Freud that the personality is essentially "set in stone" during the first 5 years of life. Yet he, like Freud and other psychoanalytic theorists, believed that people progress through systematic stages of development, undergoing similar personality changes at similar ages. Individual differences in personality presumably reflect the different experiences individuals have as they struggle to cope with the challenges of each life stage. Both biological maturation and demands of the social environment influence the individual's progress through Erikson's sequence of psychosocial stages. As an illustration, the Explorations box on page 38 shows what Erikson might have said about Terrell's school refusal and Sherry's pregnancy.

Strengths and Weaknesses

Many people find Erikson's emphasis on our rational, adaptive nature and on an interaction of biological and social influences easier to accept than Freud's emphasis on unconscious, irrational motivations based in biological needs. Erikson also seems to have captured some central developmental issues in his eight stages. He has had an especially great impact on ideas about and research on adolescent identity formation and issues faced during adulthood (see Chapter 11). Still, Erikson's theory has many of the same shortcomings as Freud's. It is sometimes vague and

difficult to test. And although it provides a useful *description* of human personality development, it does not provide an adequate *explanation* of how this development comes about. Important psychoanalytic theorists such as Erikson continue to shape understanding of human development (Austrian, 2002), but many developmentalists have rejected the psychoanalytic perspective in favor of theories that are more precise and testable.

SUMMING UP

▌ Compared to Freud, neo-Freudian Erik Erikson placed more emphasis on social influences, the rational ego, the potential for overcoming early problems, and the whole life span.

▌ Erikson's eight psychosocial stages involve issues of trust, autonomy, initiative, industry, identity, intimacy, generativity, and integrity. Parents, peers, and the larger culture influence how conflicts are resolved.

▌ The theories of both Freud and Erikson, though influential, are difficult to test and describe development better than they explain it.

CRITICAL THINKING

1. How might Erikson's view of Congressman Foley's development differ from Freud's (return to the Critical Thinking question from the previous section)?

2.4 LEARNING THEORIES

Give me a dozen healthy infants, well formed, and my own specified world to bring them up in, and I'll guarantee to take any one at random and train him to become any type of specialist I might select—doctor, lawyer, artist, merchant, chief, and yes, even beggar-man and thief, regardless of his talents, penchants, tendencies, abilities, vocations, and race of his ancestors. (Watson, 1925, p. 82)

This bold statement—that nurture is everything and that nature, or genetic endowment, counts for nothing—was made by John B. Watson, a strong believer in the importance of learning in human development and a pioneer of learning theory perspectives on human development. Early learning theorists such as Watson emphasized that human behavior changes in direct response to environmental stimuli; later learning theorists such as Albert Bandura grant humans a more active and cognitive role in their own development but still believe that their development can take different directions depending on their experiences.

Watson: Classical Conditioning

Watson's (1913) **behaviorism** rested on his belief that conclusions about human development and functioning should be based on observations of overt behavior rather than on speculations about unobservable cognitive and emotional processes. Watson rejected psychoanalytic theory and devoted a good deal of his time to trying to explain Freud's fascinating discoveries about humans in terms of basic learning principles (Rilling, 2000). He maintained that learned associations between external stimuli and observable responses are the building blocks of both normal and abnormal human development. Like John Locke, Watson believed that children have no inborn tendencies and that how they turn out depends entirely on the environment in which they grow up and the ways in which their parents and other significant people in their lives treat them.

To make his point, Watson and colleague Rosalie Raynor (1920) set out to demonstrate that fears can be learned—that they are not necessarily inborn as was commonly thought. They used the principles of **classical conditioning,** a simple form of learning in which a stimulus that initially had no effect on the individual comes to elicit a response through its association with a stimulus that already elicits the response. The Russian physiologist Ivan Pavlov first called attention to classical conditioning. In a famous experiment, Pavlov demonstrated how dogs, who have an innate (unlearned) tendency to salivate at the sight of food, could learn to salivate at the sound of a bell if, during a training period, the bell was regularly sounded just before they were given food.

Watson and Raynor presented a gentle white rat to a now-famous infant named Albert, who showed no fear of it. However, every time the rat was presented, Watson would slip behind Albert and bang a steel rod with a hammer. The loud noise served as an **unconditioned stimulus (UCS)**—that is, an unlearned stimulus-for fear; fear in turn is an automatic, unlearned, or **unconditioned response (UR)** to loud noises (babies are naturally upset by them). During conditioning, the stimuli of the white rat and the loud noise were presented together several times. Afterward, Watson presented the white rat to Albert without banging the steel rod. Albert now whimpered and cried in response to the white rat alone. His behavior had changed as a result of his experience. Specifically, an initially neutral stimulus, the white rat, had become a **conditioned stimulus (CS)** for a **conditioned response (CR),** fear, as shown in ■ **Figure 2.2.** This learned response generalized to other furry items such as a rabbit and a Santa Claus mask. By today's standards, Watson's experiment would be viewed as unethical, but he had made his point: *emotional responses can be learned.* Fortunately, fears learned through classical conditioning can be unlearned if the feared stimulus is paired with an unconditioned stimulus for happy emotions (Jones, 1924).

Classical conditioning is undoubtedly involved when infants learn to love their parents, who at first may be neutral stimuli but who become associated with the positive sensations of receiving milk, being rocked, and being comforted. And classical conditioning helps explain why adults find certain songs on the radio, scents, or articles of clothing "turn them on." A range of emotional associations and attitudes are acquired through classical conditioning.

According to the learning theory perspective, then, it is a mistake to assume that children advance through a series

■ **FIGURE 2.2** The three phases of classical conditioning.

of distinct stages guided by biological maturation, as Freud, Erikson, and other stage theorists have argued. Instead, learning theorists view development as nothing more than learning. It is a continuous process of behavior change that is context specific and can differ enormously from person to person. Watson's basic view was advanced by B. F. Skinner.

Skinner: Operant Conditioning

B. F. Skinner (1905–1990), probably the most famous American psychologist, had a long, distinguished career at Harvard University. Through his research with animals, Skinner (1953) gained understanding of another important form of learning, **operant conditioning,** in which a learner's behavior becomes either more or less probable depending on the consequences it produces. A learner first behaves in some way and then comes to associate this action with the positive or negative consequences that follow it. The basic principle behind operant conditioning makes sense: people tend to repeat behaviors that have pleasant consequences and cut down on behaviors that have unpleasant consequences. Through operant conditioning, individuals learn new skills and a range of habits, both good and bad.

In the language of operant conditioning, *reinforcement* occurs when a consequence strengthens a response, or makes it more likely to occur. If a preschool child cleans his room, receives a hug, then cleans his room more frequently thereafter, the hug provided **positive reinforcement** for room cleaning. *Positive* here means that something has been added to the situation, and *reinforcement* means that the behavior is strengthened. Thus a positive reinforcer is an event that, when introduced following a behavior, makes that behavior more probable. (Note that the effect on the child's behavior, not the parent's belief that the child might find a hug reinforcing, defines the consequence as reinforcing.)

Behaviorists have found that it is best to provide continuous positive reinforcement when a new skill or habit is first being learned, reinforcing every occurrence. Then, to maintain the behavior, it is best to shift to a "partial reinforcement schedule" in which only some occurrences of the behavior are reinforced and the pattern of reinforcement is unpredictable. Then the learner is likely to continue performing even if reinforcement stops.

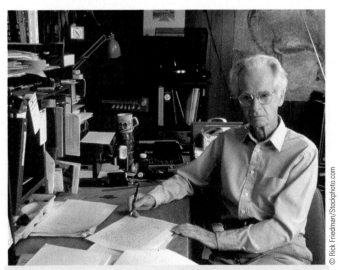

B. F. Skinner's operant conditioning theory emphasized the role of environment in controlling behavior.

Negative reinforcement (which is *not* a fancy term for punishment) occurs when a behavioral tendency is strengthened because something negative or unpleasant is removed from the situation, or is escaped or avoided, after the behavior occurs. Have you been in a car in which an obnoxious buzzer sounds until you fasten your seat belt? The idea is that your "buckling up" behavior will become a habit through negative reinforcement: buckling your seat belt allows you to escape the unpleasant buzzer. No candy or hugs follow the action, so negative rather than positive reinforcement makes you likely to buckle your seat belt. Many bad habits develop because they allow people to avoid or escape unpleasant events; they were learned through negative reinforcement. Teenagers may learn to lie to avoid long lectures from their parents or to drink because it allows them to escape feelings of anxiety at parties. In each case, a behavior is strengthened through negative reinforcement—through the removal or elimination of something unpleasant like a lecture or anxiety.

Contrast reinforcement, whether it is positive or negative, with punishment: Whereas reinforcement increases the strength of the behavior that preceded it, *punishment* decreases the strength of the behavior or weakens it. Two forms of punishment parallel the two forms of reinforcement. **Positive punishment** occurs when an unpleasant event is added to the situation following a behavior (for example, a child is spanked for misbehaving, a cashier is criticized for coming up short of cash at the end of the day). **Negative punishment** occurs when something pleasant is removed from the situation following the behavior (a child loses the privilege of staying up late on Saturday night, the amount the cashier was short is deducted from her pay). Both positive and negative punishment decrease the likelihood that the punished behavior will be repeated.

The four possible consequences of a behavior are summarized in ■ **Figure 2.3.** In addition, some behavior has no consequence. Behavior that is ignored, or no longer reinforced, tends to become less frequent through a process called **extinction.** Indeed, a good alternative to punishing a child's misbehavior is ignoring it and instead reinforcing desirable behavior that is incompatible with it. Too often, the well-behaved child is ignored and the misbehaving child gets the attention—attention that can serve as positive reinforcement for the misbehavior.

Skinner and other behavioral theorists have emphasized the power of positive reinforcement and have generally discouraged the use of physical punishment in child rearing. By contrast, many parents believe that physical punishment of bad behavior is necessary in raising children; indeed, in a 2004 national survey 77% of men and 69% of women agreed that a child sometimes needs a "good, hard spanking" (Child Trends Databank, undated). What does research say about who is right?

Although it is generally best to use more positive approaches before resorting to punishment, punishment makes children comply with parents' demands in the short run (Benjet & Kazdin, 2003). Spanking or another form of physical punishment can be effective in changing behavior in the longer run if it (1) is administered immediately after the act (not hours

	PLEASANT STIMULUS	UNPLEASANT STIMULUS
ADMINISTERED	**Positive reinforcement, adding a pleasant stimulus** (strengthens the behavior) Dad gives in to the whining and lets Moosie play Nintendo, making whining more likely in the future.	**Positive punishment, adding an unpleasant stimulus** (weakens the behavior) Dad calls Moosie a "baby." Moosie does not like this at all and is less likely to whine in the future.
WITHDRAWN	**Negative punishment, withdrawing a pleasant stimulus** (weakens the behavior) Dad confiscates Moosie's favorite Nintendo game to discourage whining in the future.	**Negative reinforcement, withdrawing an unpleasant stimulus** (strengthens the behavior) Dad stops joking with Lulu. Moosie gets very jealous when Dad pays attention to Lulu, so his whining enables him to bring this unpleasant state of affairs to an end.

■ **FIGURE 2.3** Possible consequences of whining behavior. Moosie comes into the TV room and sees his father talking and joking with his sister, Lulu, as the two watch a football game. Soon Moosie begins to whine, louder and louder, that he wants them to turn off the television so he can play Nintendo games. If you were Moosie's father, how would you react? Here are four possible consequences of Moosie's behavior. Consider both the type of consequence—whether it is a pleasant or aversive stimulus—and whether it is administered ("added to" the situation) or withdrawn. Notice that reinforcers strengthen whining behavior, or make it more likely in the future, whereas punishers weaken it.

later when the child is being an angel), (2) is administered consistently after each offense, (3) is not overly harsh, (4) is accompanied by explanations, (5) is administered by an otherwise affectionate person, and (6) is combined with efforts to reinforce more acceptable behavior (Domjan, 1993; Gershoff, 2002; Perry & Parke, 1975).

Frequent physical punishment can have undesirable effects, however. Although researchers cannot always be sure whether punishment causes problem behavior, problem behavior causes punishment, or both, research suggests that physical punishment may make children resentful and anxious and may breed aggression by teaching them that hitting is an appropriate way to solve problems. The negative effects of physical punishment are especially clear when the child punished is older than 6 years (Benjet & Kazdin, 2003).

In sum, Skinner, like Watson, believed that the course of human development depends on the individual's learning experiences. One boy's aggressive behavior may be reinforced over time because he gets his way with other children and because his parents encourage his "macho" behavior. Another boy may quickly learn that aggression is prohibited and punished. The two may develop in different directions based on their different histories of reinforcement and punishment.

Skinner's operant conditioning principles can help explain many aspects of human development and are still studied by psychologists (Staddon & Cerutti, 2003). Yet some developmentalists believe that Skinner placed too much emphasis on a single type of learning and too little emphasis on the role of cognitive processes such as attention, memory, and reflection in learning. Therefore, today's developmental scholars are more attracted to Albert Bandura's cognitive brand of learning theory than to Skinner's operant conditioning emphasis.

Bandura: Social Cognitive Theory

In his **social cognitive theory** (formerly called social learning theory), Stanford psychologist Albert Bandura (1977, 1986, 1989, 2000, 2006) claims that humans are cognitive beings whose active processing of information plays a critical role in their learning, behavior, and development. Bandura argues that human learning is very different from rat learning because humans have far more sophisticated cognitive capabilities. He agrees with Skinner that operant conditioning is an important type of learning, but he notes that people think about the connections between their behavior and its consequences, anticipate the consequences likely to follow from their behavior, and often are more affected by what they believe will happen than by the consequences they actually encounter. Individuals also reinforce or punish themselves with mental pats on the back and self-criticism, and these cognitions also affect behavior. More generally, Bandura wanted his position to be called *social cognitive theory* rather than *social learning theory* for a reason: to distance himself from some early, behavioral learning theories and to emphasize that his theory was about the motivating and self-regulating role of cognition in human behavior (Bandura, 1986).

By highlighting observational learning as the most important mechanism through which human behavior changes, Bandura made his cognitive emphasis clear. **Observational learning** is simply learning by observing the behavior of other people (called *models*). By imitating other people, a child may learn how to speak a language and tackle math problems, as well as how to swear, snack between meals, and smoke. Observational learning is regarded as a more cognitive form of learning than conditioning because learners must pay attention, construct and

Albert Bandura highlighted the role of cognition in human learning. He is on the faculty at Stanford University.

responses. Whether they will perform what they learn depends partly on the process of **vicarious reinforcement,** in which learners become more or less likely to perform a behavior based on the consequences experienced by the model they observe.

In recent years, Bandura (2000, 2006) has emphasized the concept of **human agency,** ways in which people deliberately exercise cognitive control over themselves, their environments, and their lives. From the time they are infants recognizing that they can make things happen in their worlds, people form intentions, foresee what will happen, evaluate and regulate their actions as they pursue plans, and reflect on their functioning. These cognitions play a real causal role in influencing their behavior and that of other people. Most importantly, individuals develop a high or low sense of **self-efficacy,** the belief that one can effectively produce desired outcomes in a particular area of life. Whether you undertake an action such as going on a diet or studying for a test and whether you succeed depend greatly on whether you have a sense of self-efficacy with respect to that behavior.

Watson and Skinner may have believed that people are passively shaped by environment to become whatever those around them groom them to be, but Bandura does not. Because he views humans as active, cognitive beings, he holds that human development occurs through a continuous reciprocal interaction among the person (the individual's biological and psychological characteristics and cognitions), his or her behavior, and his or her environment—a perspective he calls **reciprocal determinism** (see ■ Figure 2.4). As Bandura sees it, environment does not rule, as it did in Skinner's thinking: people choose, build, and change their environments; they are not just shaped by them. Nor does biology rule; genetic influences on human behavior are evident, but cultural forces also change human environments (as when humans devised airplanes, indoor heating, and vaccines). The environments shaped by humans then influence biological evolution by influencing which traits increase the odds of survival (Bandura, 2000). And peo-

remember mental representations (images and verbal summaries) of what they saw, retrieve these representations from memory later, and use them to guide behavior. It is an especially important form of learning in less industrialized societies, where children learn not in schools where they are segregated from adults and given formal instruction but through participation in everyday activities in which they actively observe and listen to their elders and learn skills such as weaving and hunting without adults intentionally teaching them (Rogoff et al., 2003).

In a classic experiment, Bandura (1965) set out to demonstrate that children could learn a response neither elicited by a conditioned stimulus (as in classical conditioning) nor performed and then strengthened by a reinforcer (as in operant conditioning). He had nursery school children watch a short film in which an adult model attacked an inflatable "Bobo" doll: hitting the doll with a mallet while shouting "Sockeroo," throwing rubber balls at the doll while shouting "Bang, bang, bang," and so on. Some children saw the model praised, others saw him punished, and still others saw no consequences follow his violent attack. After the film ended, children were observed in a playroom with the Bobo doll and many of the props the model had used to work Bobo over.

What did the children learn? The children who saw the model rewarded and the children in the no-consequences condition imitated more of the model's aggressive acts than did the children who had seen the model punished. But interestingly, when the children who had seen the model punished were asked to reproduce all of the model's behavior they could remember, they showed that they had learned just as much as the other children. Apparently, then, children can learn from observation without necessarily imitating (performing) the learned

A person is never too old to learn by observing others.

LEARNING THEORISTS: NOTES ON SCHOOL REFUSAL AND TEENAGE PREGNANCY

Notes on School Refusal

Anxiety disorders and phobias can be learned in a variety of ways; modern learning theorists also appreciate that genetics, personality, and other personal characteristics can affect such learning (Mineka & Zinbarg, 2006).

Watson might hypothesize that Terrell had a traumatic experience at school—maybe a fire drill alarm scared him or he had an accident in the bathroom. Through classical conditioning, the school building might become a conditioned stimulus for anxious responses.

As Skinner would note, if Terrell's act of entering the classroom results in punishing consequences (a punch from a bully, harsh words from the teacher), the frequency of going to school will decline. And if acting sick is negatively reinforcing because it helps Terrell avoid the anxiety associated with going to school, "sick" behavior will become more frequent.

Perhaps Terrell's mother is positively reinforcing stay-at-home behavior by allowing Terrell to spend quality time with her doing fun things when he is "sick."

Through observational learning, Bandura would add, a child who witnesses another child's anxious behavior at school may learn to behave anxiously.

Notes on Teenage Pregnancy

Through Watson's classical conditioning, Sherry and Robert may have learned to associate the very presence of the other with the pleasurable sensations associated with sexual activity.

As Skinner might observe, teenagers have unprotected sex because having sex is reinforcing, whereas using contraceptives is not.

According to Bandura, expectations about the consequences of our actions can be more important than the reinforcers and punishers actually operating in the situation. Thus, if Robert *believes* that using a condom will decrease his sexual enjoyment, his belief may decrease the chances that he and his partner will use protection.

Bandura would also emphasize observational learning—teens who are exposed to a lot of sexually explicit material on television, in the movies, in music, and in magazines are more sexually active than other teens (Brown et al., 2006). Observing the sexual attitudes and behaviors of parents, siblings, and friends also influences teenagers.

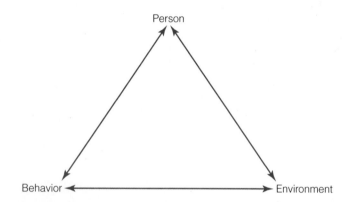

■ **FIGURE 2.4** Bandura's reciprocal determinism involves mutual influence of the person, the person's behavior, and the environment.

ple's personal characteristics and behaviors affect the people around them, just as these people are influencing their personal characteristics and future behaviors.

Like Watson and Skinner, Bandura doubts that there are universal stages of human development. He maintains that development is context specific and can proceed along many paths. It is also continuous, occurring gradually through a lifetime of learning. Bandura acknowledges that children's cognitive capacities mature, so they can remember more about what they have seen and can imitate a greater variety of novel behaviors. Yet he also believes that children of the same age will be dissimilar if their learning experiences have differed considerably.

Obviously there is a fundamental disagreement between stage theorists such as Freud and Erikson and learning theorists such as Bandura. Learning theorists do not give a general description of the normal course of human development because they insist that there is no such description to give. Instead, they offer a rich account of the mechanisms through which behavior can change, using principles of learning that are universal in their applicability to understand how each individual changes with age in unique ways (Goldhaber, 2000). We imagine what Watson, Skinner, and Bandura would say about school refusal and teenage pregnancy in the Explorations box.

Strengths and Weaknesses

Watson's and Skinner's behavioral learning theories and Bandura's modern social cognitive theory have contributed immensely to the understanding of development and continue to be influential. Learning theories are precise and testable. Carefully controlled experiments have shown how people might learn everything from altruism to alcoholism. Moreover, learning principles operate across the life span and can be used to understand behavior at any age. Finally, learning theories have practical applications; they have been the basis for many highly effective behavioral and cognitive-behavioral techniques for optimizing development and treating developmental problems.

Still, learning theories, even Bandura's more recent social cognitive theory, leave something to be desired as explanations of human development. Consider the following demonstration. Paul Weisberg (1963) reinforced 3-month-old infants with smiles and gentle rubs on the chin whenever they happened to make babbling sounds such as "bababa." He found that these infants babbled more often than did infants who received the same social stimulation randomly rather than only after each babbling sound they made. But does this mean that infants normally begin to babble *because* babbling is reinforced by their caregivers? Not necessarily. All normal infants, even deaf ones, babble around 4 months of age. Moreover, no matter what experiences are provided to newborns, they will not be maturationally ready to babble. We must suspect, then, that the maturation of the neural and muscular control required for babbling has more than a little to do with the onset of babbling during infancy.

This example highlights two criticisms of learning theories as theories of human development. First, learning theorists rarely demonstrate that learning is responsible for commonly observed developmental changes; they show through their experiments only that learning *might* have resulted in developmental change, as in the case of reinforcement increasing the frequency of babbling. Some critics wish that learning theorists would provide a fuller account of normal changes across the life span. Second, early learning theorists, and even Bandura, probably put too little emphasis on biological influences on development such as genetic endowment and maturational processes that affect how people respond to learning experiences. We may learn to fear snakes, for example. However, probably because snakes were a threat to our ancestors, we have evolved so that we learn to fear snakes more easily than we learn to fear bunnies or flowers (Ohman & Mineka, 2003). Today's learning theorists view learning as more complex than pioneers like Watson and Skinner did; they appreciate that factors such as genetic endowment, previous learning history, personality, and social context affect how humans react to their learning experiences (Mineka & Zinbarg, 2006).

SUMMING UP

▌ Learning theorists maintain that humans change gradually and can develop in many directions depending on environmental influences.

▌ Watson focused on the role of classical conditioning in the learning of emotional responses; Skinner highlighted operant conditioning involving reinforcement and punishment; and Bandura's social cognitive theory emphasizes observational learning, human agency and self-efficacy, and reciprocal determinism.

▌ Learning theories are well supported but do not necessarily explain normal developmental changes and underemphasize biological influences.

CRITICAL THINKING

1. Gert, age 78, fell and broke her hip recently and has become overly dependent on her daughter for help ever since, even though she can get around quite well. How might (1) Freud or Erikson, and (2) Watson, Skinner, or Bandura explain her old-age dependency?

2.5 PIAGET: COGNITIVE DEVELOPMENTAL THEORY

After behavioral learning theories dominated the study of development in the 1950s and 1960s, many developmentalists began to look for a theory that was both more cognitive and more clearly developmental. They found what they wanted in the groundbreaking work of Jean Piaget. No theorist has contributed more to the understanding of children's minds than Piaget (1896–1980), a Swiss scholar who began to study children's intellectual development during the 1920s. This remarkable man developed quickly himself, publishing his first scientific work (a letter to the editor about an albino sparrow) at age 11. Eventually, Piaget blended his interest in zoology and the adaptation of animals to their environments with his interest in philosophy. He then devoted his career to the study of how humans acquire knowledge and use it to adapt to their world.

Piaget's lifelong interest in cognitive development emerged while he worked at the Alfred Binet laboratories in Paris on the first standardized IQ test. IQ tests estimate individuals' intelligence based on the number and types of questions they answer correctly. Piaget soon became interested in children's wrong answers and noticed that children of about the same age gave the same kinds of wrong answers. By questioning them to find out how they were thinking about the problems presented to them, he began to realize that young children do not simply know less than older children do; instead, they think in a qualitatively different way. Eventually Piaget developed a theory to account for changes in thinking from infancy to adolescence.

Constructivism

Influenced by his background in biology, Piaget (1950) viewed intelligence as a process that helps an organism adapt to its environment. The infant who grasps a cookie and brings it to her mouth is behaving adaptively, as is the adolescent who solves algebra problems or the mechanic who fixes cars. As hu-

Swiss psychologist Jean Piaget revolutionized the field of human development with his theory of cognitive growth.

mans mature, they acquire ever more complex cognitive structures, or organized patterns of thought or action, that aid them in adapting to their environments.

Piaget insisted that children are not born with innate ideas about reality, as some philosophers claim. Nor did he think children are simply filled with information by adults, as learning theorists believe. Piaget's position, called **constructivism,** was that children actively construct new understandings of the world based on their experiences. Some preschool children, for example, invent on their own ideas such as that the sun is alive because it moves across the sky, that children may get diseases if they tell lies or otherwise misbehave, and that babies come from the baby store.

How do children construct more accurate understandings of the world? By being curious and active explorers: watching what is going on around them, seeing what happens when they experiment on the objects they encounter, and recognizing instances in which their current understandings are inadequate to explain events. Children use their current understandings of the world to help them solve problems, but they also revise their understandings to make them fit reality better (Piaget, 1952). The *interaction* between biological maturation (most importantly, a developing brain) and experience (especially discrepancies between the child's understanding and reality) is responsible for the child's progress from one stage of cognitive development to a new, qualitatively different, stage.

Stages of Cognitive Development

Piaget proposed four major periods of cognitive development: the sensorimotor stage (birth to age 2), the preoperational stage (ages 2 to 7), the concrete operations stage (ages 7 to 11), and the formal operations stage (ages 11 to 12 or older). These stages form what Piaget called an *invariant sequence;* that is, all children progress through the stages in the order they are listed with-

Jean Piaget believed that children are naturally curious explorers who try to make sense of their surroundings.

out skipping stages or regressing to earlier stages. The ages given are only guidelines; different children progress at different rates.

The key features of each stage are summarized in ● **Table 2.3;** we will describe them in more depth in Chapter 7. The core message is that humans of different ages think in qualitatively different ways (Inhelder & Piaget, 1958).

Infants in the **sensorimotor stage** deal with the world directly through their perceptions (senses) and actions (motor abilities). They are unable to use symbols (gestures, images, or words representing real objects and events) to help them solve problems mentally. However, they learn a great deal about the

● **TABLE 2.3 JEAN PIAGET'S FOUR STAGES OF COGNITIVE DEVELOPMENT**

STAGE (AGE RANGE)	DESCRIPTION
Sensorimotor (birth to 2 years)	Infants use their senses and motor actions to explore and understand the world. At the start they have only innate reflexes, but they develop increasingly "intelligent" actions. By the end, they are capable of symbolic thought using images or words and can therefore plan solutions to problems mentally.
Preoperational (2 to 7 years)	Preschoolers use their capacity for symbolic thought to develop language, engage in pretend play, and solve problems. But their thinking is not yet logical; they are egocentric (unable to take others' perspectives) and are easily fooled by perceptions because they cannot rely on logical operations.
Concrete operations (7 to 11 years)	School-age children acquire concrete logical operations that allow them to mentally classify, add, and otherwise act on concrete objects in their heads. They can solve practical, real-world problems through a trial-and-error approach but have difficulty with hypothetical and abstract problems.
Formal operations (11 to 12 years and older)	Adolescents can think about abstract concepts and purely hypothetical possibilities and can trace the long-range consequences of possible actions. With age and experience, they can form hypotheses and systematically test them using the scientific method.

PIAGET: NOTES ON SCHOOL REFUSAL AND TEENAGE PREGNANCY

Notes on School Refusal

Cognition is an important influence on behavior; we need to understand how Terrell is thinking about both his home life and school.

We should assess his stage of cognitive development. Especially if he has not yet made the transition from the preoperational stage to the concrete-operational stage, his anxiety may be rooted in a faulty cause–effect analysis or a misunderstanding (e.g., the belief that the serial murderer or terrorist he saw on TV will kill his mother next or that the school shooting that happened in another state will happen at his school).

Notes on Teenage Pregnancy

Cognitive limitations, failure to anticipate consequences, and lack of knowledge may all influence sexual decision making. Sherry and Robert may not yet be solidly into the stage of formal operations and therefore may not be able to think through all of the long-range consequences of their sexual behavior.

Misconceptions (pun intended!) about sex and contraception are common among adolescents (Aarons & Jenkins, 2002). In one study of 13- to 15-year-olds, more than 60% did not know that urinating after sex will not prevent pregnancy (Carrera et al., 2000).

world by exploring it, and they acquire tools for solving problems through their sensory and motor experiences.

The preschooler who has entered the **preoperational stage** of cognitive development has developed the capacity for symbolic thought but is not yet capable of logical problem solving. The 4- or 5-year-old can use words as symbols to talk about a problem and can mentally imagine doing something before actually doing it. However, lacking the tools of logical thought, preoperational children must rely on their perceptions and as a result are easily fooled by appearances. For example, they tend to think that large objects will sink in water, even if they are lightweight, and that water poured from a short, wide glass to a taller, thinner glass has magically become more water. According to Piaget, preschool children are also egocentric thinkers who have difficulty adopting perspectives other than their own. As a result, they may cling to incorrect ideas simply because they want them to be true.

School-age children who have advanced to the **concrete operations stage** are more logical than preschoolers. They use a trial-and-error approach to problem solving and do well on problems that involve thinking about concrete objects. These children can perform many important logical actions, or operations, in their heads on concrete objects (hence, the term *concrete operations*, and Piaget's description of the preschool child as *pre*operational). For example, they can mentally categorize or add and subtract objects. They can also draw sound, general conclusions based on their concrete or specific observations. However, they have difficulty dealing with abstract and hypothetical problems.

Adolescents who reach the **formal operations stage** are able to think more abstractly and hypothetically than school-age children. They can define *justice* abstractly, in terms of fairness, rather than concretely, in terms of the cop on the corner or the judge in the courtroom. They can formulate hypotheses or predictions in their heads, plan how to systematically test their ideas experimentally, and imagine the consequences of their tests. It often takes some years before adolescents can adopt a thoroughly systematic and scientific method of solving problems and can think logically about the implications of purely hypothetical ideas. Then they may be able to devise grand theories about what is wrong with parents, the school system, or the federal government.

Obviously, children's cognitive capacities change dramatically between infancy and adolescence as they progress through Piaget's four stages of cognitive development. Infants, young children, school-age children, and adolescents and adults simply do not think the same way. What, then, do you suppose Piaget would have said about school refusal and teenage pregnancy? The Explorations box sketches his possible thoughts. Where Freud and Erikson might have looked to personality disorders or emotional conflicts for explanations, and Skinner and Bandura would have looked to specific learning experiences, Piaget probably would have hypothesized that cognitive immaturity, lack of knowledge, and faulty beliefs underlie many developmental problems.

Strengths and Weaknesses

Like Freud, Piaget was a true pioneer whose work has left a deep and lasting imprint on thinking about human development. You will see his influence throughout this text, for the mind that "constructs" understanding of the physical world also comes, with age, to understand sex differences, moral values, emotions, death, and a range of other important aspects of the human experience. Piaget's cognitive developmental perspective dominated the study of child development for about 3 decades, until the 1980s. Most developmentalists today continue to accept Piaget's basic beliefs that thinking changes in qualitative ways during childhood, that children are active in their own development, and that development occurs through an interaction of nature and nurture. Piaget's description of intellectual development has been tested and has been largely, although not wholly, supported. Finally, Piaget's ideas have influenced education and child rearing by encouraging teachers and parents to pitch their educational programs to children's levels of understanding and to stimulate children to discover new concepts through their own direct grappling with problems.

Still, Piaget has had his share of criticism (Lourenco & Machado, 1996; also see Chapter 7). For example, critics fault him for saying too little about the influences of motivation and emotion on thought processes. Based on research evidence, they also question whether Piaget's stages really hang together as coherent and general modes of thinking that can be applied to a variety of types of problems; instead, the thinking skills needed to solve different types of problems seem to be acquired at different rates. Critics also conclude that Piaget underestimated the cognitive abilities of young children and put too little emphasis on the role of parents and other more knowledgeable people in nurturing cognitive development. And they challenge the idea that all humans in every culture develop through the same stages toward the same endpoints. As a result, developmentalists began to seek theoretical perspectives that allowed more diversity in the pathways that human development could take while retaining Piaget's theme that nature and nurture interact to produce developmental change.

Other Perspectives on Cognitive Development

Two important approaches to cognitive development that challenged some of Piaget's thinking will be discussed in more detail later in this book: Vygotsky's *sociocultural perspective* (see Chapter 7) and the *information-processing approach* (see Chapter 8). However, we briefly touch on each here.

The **sociocultural perspective** on cognitive development offered by a contemporary of Piaget, Russian psychologist Lev Vygotsky, has become quite influential in recent years. Disagreeing with Piaget's notion of universal stages of cognitive development, Vygotsky maintained that cognitive development is shaped by the sociocultural context in which it occurs and grows out of children's interactions with members of their culture. Each culture provides its members with certain tools of thought—most notably a language but also tools such as pencils, art media, mathematical systems, and computers. The ways in which people in a particular culture approach and solve problems are passed from generation to generation through oral and written communication. Hence culture, especially as it is embodied in language, shapes thought. As a result, cognitive development is not the same universally; it varies across social and historical contexts. And whereas Piaget tended to see children as independent explorers, Vygotsky saw them as social beings who develop their minds through their interactions with parents, teachers, and other knowledgeable members of their culture.

Other challenges to Piaget came from scholars who saw a need to look more closely at the processes involved in thinking and factors affecting those processes. The **information-processing approach** to cognition, which became the dominant perspective starting in the 1980s, likens the human mind to a computer with hardware and software and emphasizes fundamental mental processes such as attention, memory, decision making, and the like. Development involves changes in the capacity and speed of the information-processing machine we call the brain and in the strategies we use to process information. This approach is the focus of Chapter 8 and has guided research not only on attention, memory, and problem solving but also on gender, social cognition, and many other topics addressed in this book.

SUMMING UP

▌ Piaget's cognitive developmental perspective views intelligence as an adaptive process of creating new understandings (constructivism).

▌ Biological maturation and experience interact to push children through four universal, invariant, and qualitatively different stages of thinking: sensorimotor, preoperational, concrete operational, and formal operational.

▌ Despite Piaget's immense influence, developmentalists question whether development is as stagelike and universal as he claimed.

CRITICAL THINKING

1. How do you think Piaget would explain why adolescents are more able than preschool children to participate in coherent conversations with a social partner?

2.6 | SYSTEMS THEORIES

Systems theories of development (some are called contextual theories, some systems theories or dynamic systems theories) generally claim that changes over the life span arise from the ongoing transactions between a changing organism and a changing world (see, for example, Gottlieb, Wahlsten, & Lickliter, 2006; Howe & Lewis, 2005; Lerner, 2006; Li, 2003). Changes in the person produce changes in his environment; changes in the environment produce changes in the person. The individual and the physical and social contexts with which he or she interacts are inseparable parts of a larger system. Moreover, development does not always leads in one direction toward some mature endpoint like formal-operational thought, as stage theorists tend to believe. It can proceed in a variety of directions and take a variety of forms depending on the complex interplay between biological and environmental influences.

Urie Bronfenbrenner's bioecological model, introduced in Chapter 1, illustrates a systems perspective on development. The individual, with her biologically based characteristics, is embedded in and interacts with four environmental systems. Here, we highlight another theorist who emphasized the idea that development grows out of systems of interacting influences, Gilbert Gottlieb (1929–2006), a developmental psychobiologist. He emphasized that human development takes place in the context of our evolutionary history as a species and arises from ongoing interactions between biological and environmental influences. Although Bronfenbrenner started out interested in the environment and increasingly realized that biological influences on development were equally important, Gottlieb started out as a biologist and increasingly became convinced of the importance of environmental influences.

Similarities between animals and humans make us suspect that many aspects of human development are the product of evolution.

Evolutionary Theory and Ethology

Gilbert Gottlieb's perspective grew out of earlier work looking at human development in the context of evolutionary theory (Bjorklund & Pellegrini, 2002; Burgess & MacDonald, 2005; Gottlieb, Wahlsten, & Lickliter, 2006). In his tremendously influential theory of evolution, Charles Darwin (1859) maintained that genes that aid their bearers in adapting to their environment will be passed on to future generations more frequently than genes that do not (see Chapter 3). Evolutionary theory therefore prompts us to ask how the characteristics and behaviors we commonly observe in humans today may have helped our ancestors adapt to their environment and consequently may have become part of the shared genetic endowment of our species.

Researchers inspired by Darwin's theory founded the field of **ethology,** the study of the evolved behavior of various species in their natural environments (J. Archer, 1992; Hinde, 1983). Noted ethologists Konrad Lorenz and Niko Tinbergen asked how many apparently innate, species-typical animal behaviors might be adaptive in the sense that they contribute to survival. Ethologists maintain that behavior is adaptive only in relation to a particular environment (for example, nomadic wandering makes sense in an environment in which food is scarce but not in an environment in which it is abundant); as a result, they believed that it was essential to study behavior and development in its natural contexts using naturalistic observation. So, for example, they have recorded birdsongs in the wild, analyzed their features carefully, explored how male birds learn

the songs characteristic of their species, and attempted to understand how songs aid birds in reproduction and survival. And they have studied the role of environmental stimuli in triggering instinctive behaviors such as the tendency of young birds to follow their mothers, dominance hierarchies in groups of chimpanzees, and parenting behavior in a variety of species. Sometimes ethologists just observe, and sometimes they conduct experiments to determine how different environmental stimuli affect the development of species-typical patterns of behavior.

Ethologists suggest that humans, like other species, display species-specific behaviors that are the products of evolution and assist them in adapting to their environment. In Chapter 3, we will look at the basics of Darwinian evolutionary theory, and in Chapter 14, we will discuss attachment theory, an influential perspective rooted in both psychoanalytic theory and ethological theory. Attachment theorists view the formation of close relationships between human infants and their caregivers as evolved behavior that increases the odds that the young will survive. We will also discuss throughout this book the work of modern evolutionary psychologists, which raises fundamental questions about why humans think and behave as they do (Bjorklund & Pellegrini, 2002; Ellis & Bjorklund, 2005).

Gottlieb's Epigenetic Psychobiological Systems Perspective

While ethologists were examining the evolutionary roots of human behavior, developmental psychobiologist Gilbert Gottlieb studied how products of evolution such as genes and hormones interact with environmental factors to guide the individual's development (1992, 2000, 2002, 2003; Gottlieb, Wahlsten, & Lickliter, 1998, 2006). According to Gottlieb's **epigenetic psychobiological systems perspective,** development is the product of interacting biological and environmental forces that

Gilbert Gottlieb sought to understand how biology and environment interact to produce development.

form a larger system. It is possible to focus on the interplay of nature and nurture both at the level of the species interacting with its environment over the course of evolution and at the level of the individual, with his unique genetic makeup, interacting with his unique environment over the course of a lifetime (Li, 2003).

The starting point in the epigenetic psychobiological systems perspective is recognition that evolution has endowed us with a human genetic makeup. We do not start out as *tabula rasae*. Rather, we are predisposed to develop in certain directions rather than in others—for example, to develop so that we master language, use tools, display guilt, act aggressively, mate and bear children, and do the other things that humans do (Pinker, 2002). However, genes do not dictate anything; they only make certain developmental outcomes more probable than others. What happens in development depends on **epigenesis,** the process through which nature and nurture, genes and environment, *jointly* bring forth particular developmental outcomes—sometimes surprising outcomes that are not easily predicted. In describing the epigenetic process, Gottlieb emphasized mutual influences over time involving (1) the activity of genes, which turn on and off at different points during development; (2) the activity of neurons; (3) the organism's behavior; and (4) environmental influences of all kinds, as shown in ■ **Figure 2.5.**

Gottlieb accused biologists of the past of wrongly claiming that genes dictate what happens in development in a one-directional and deterministic way and that genetic and physiological influences are therefore more causally important than environmental ones. We need to appreciate, he said, that each of his four levels is important and must be understood in its own

right. Behavior cannot be explained, he argued, by reducing it to simpler components such as genes or neurons. In addition, we need to appreciate that behavior and environment influence the activity of genes and the functioning of the brain, just as genes and the brain influence behavior and the environment.

Some examples will help illustrate these points. The biochemical environment of a cell in a human embryo, as influenced by factors such as the nutrition it receives, can influence whether and how the genes in that cell express themselves and, in turn, how they influence an individual's emerging traits. Stimulation from the *environment*, gained partly through the infant's exploratory *behavior*, not only produces *neural activity* and changes the brain but also affects the *activity of genes*, which in turn influence the production of proteins that contribute to the building of the neural networks necessary for normal sensory systems (Johnston & Edwards, 2002). If an individual grows up in a species-typical environment that supplies normal sensory experiences, all is likely to go well in development; but if an individual is deprived of sensory stimulation, the outcome may be different.

Gottlieb made his case by demonstrating that behavior that most people assume is innate or instinctive—etched in the genetic code of all members of a species in the course of evolution—may or may not occur depending on the organism's early environment. He showed, for example, that the tendency of young ducks to prefer their mothers' vocal calls to those of other birds such as chickens is not as automatic as you might guess (Gottlieb, 1991). Duckling embryos that were exposed to chicken calls before they hatched and then were prevented from vocalizing at birth actually came to prefer the call of a chicken to that of a mallard duck. Similarly, baby rats do not instinctively seek water when they are dehydrated; they will not seek water unless they have had at least one experience of being dehydrated and then are able to drink water (Hall, Arnold, & Myers, 2000). A behavior as basic as drinking water when thirsty, then, requires not only a biologically based sensitivity to dehydration but also specific early learning experiences that allow the organism to associate drinking with overcoming dehydration.

The message is clear: genes do not determine anything. They are partners with environment in directing organisms, including humans, along certain universal developmental pathways as well as in unique directions (Gottlieb, Wahlsten, & Lickliter, 2006). Even seemingly instinctive, inborn patterns of behavior will not emerge unless the individual has both normal genes and normal early experiences. And there is no point trying to figure out how much of an individual's traits and behavior is caused by nature and how much is caused by nurture because genes and environment "coact." They are inseparable parts of the larger developmental system.

Now let's leave ducks and rats behind and think about humans. We actively and deliberately change our environments by farming, urbanizing, polluting, fighting infectious diseases, and so on. As we change our environments, through cultural evolution, we may actually change the course of biological evolution. How? Because our new environments may make

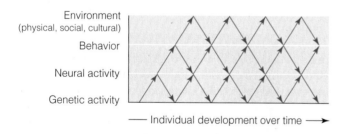

BIDIRECTIONAL INFLUENCES

Environment (physical, social, cultural)
Behavior
Neural activity
Genetic activity

—— Individual development over time ⟶

■ **FIGURE 2-5** Gottlieb's model of bidirectional influences. Genes do not determine development; rather, genetic influences interact with environmental influences, the individual's behavior, and activity at the neural level to make certain developmental outcomes more or less probable in the epigenetic process. Psychologists often focus on behavior–environment interactions, and biologists on genetic–neural interactions, but ALL parts of the system influence every other part (Gottlieb, 2003). Can you think of an example of each type of influence?
SOURCE: *Individual development and evolution: The genesis of novel behavior* by Gilbert Gottlieb copyright © 1991 by Oxford University Press, Inc. Used by permission of Oxford University Press, Inc.

GOTTLIEB: NOTES ON SCHOOL REFUSAL AND TEENAGE PREGNANCY

Notes on School Refusal

First place behavior in its evolutionary context: There are good reasons why we might have evolved to be anxious in unfamiliar situations.

Consider all possible influences of each of the following factors on the others: (1) genes (a genetic predisposition to be anxious?), (2) neural activity (overarousal in response to a noisy, chaotic classroom?), (3) behavior (immature coping skills?), and (4) the environment (mean teacher? bullies? overprotective parents?).

Cultural influences may be important: School refusal is increasing in Japan as mothers increase the pressure on their children to succeed in school (Kameguchi & Murphy-Shigematsu, 2001).

Analyze the whole person–environment system over time, expecting reciprocal influences among multiple influences—not one simple cause.

Notes on Teenage Pregnancy

Place behavior in its evolutionary context: Sexual behavior is adaptive, afterall; it has allowed humans to reproduce themselves for centuries!

Look for multiple, interacting causes, analyzing the ongoing interactions between these developing adolescents (the activity of their genes, their hormones, their brains and neural activity, and their behavior are all rapidly changing) and the changing world in which they are developing (their physical, social, and cultural environment). Keep in mind, for example, that just as poor parent and peer relations can increase the likelihood of risky sexual behavior, risky sexual behavior negatively affects parent and peer relations (Henrich et al., 2006).

Ask whether these teenagers' cultural environment is one that considers teenage pregnancy a normal step in development or a social problem; in some cultures, including some lower-income subcultures in the United States, early motherhood is viewed as adaptive (Davies et al., 2003; Farber, 2003).

Recognize that there is not *one* cause of teenage pregnancy; there is a whole system of interacting causes.

---

different genes critical to survival than our previous environments did. Here's an intriguing example: genes associated with a high tolerance to lactose in milk have become far more prevalent in human populations that have a tradition of dairy farming than in other human populations (Aoki, 1986; Voight et al., 2006). Over time, in the context of plenty of milk to drink, people with these gene variants were apparently more likely to survive than people without them.

Because genes only make particular developmental outcomes more or less probable in epigenesis, we cannot tell how the developmental story will end until we see what emerges from epigenesis, the long history of interactions among the multiple factors influencing development. The epigenetic psychobiological systems perspective helps us appreciate that each person's development takes place in the context of our evolutionary history as a species. That is, we share many genes with other humans because those genes enabled our ancestors to adapt to their environments. This perspective also helps us appreciate that the development of the individual arises from complex interactions over time among genetic, neural, behavioral, and environmental influences—interactions in which genes affect environment and, importantly, environment affects whether particular genes are activated and how they affect development.

No matter how systems theorists define the forces that interact to shape development, they believe that people and their environment are in continual flux, and that changes in one inevitably produce changes in the other because they are all part of a larger system. Modern theorists cannot ignore that people develop in a changing cultural and historical context—something that Piaget and other stage theorists tended to do. Nor can they focus all of their attention on environmental influ-

ences and ignore that humans are biological organisms whose genes contribute to their development and influence the experiences they have—something that early learning theorists tended to do. Interestingly, Urie Bronfenbrenner, who initially emphasized cultural influences on development, and Gottlieb, who initially emphasized biological influences, ended up in close agreement that it is the system of interactions among biological and environmental forces that counts. In the Explorations box, we imagine what Gottlieb might have thought about contributors to school refusal and teenage pregnancy.

Strengths and Weaknesses

Systems theories of development are complex, but that is because life-span human development is complex. We can applaud Gottlieb, Bronfenbrenner, and like-minded theorists for conceptualizing development as the often unpredictable product of biological and environmental forces interacting within a complex system and challenging us to look closely at ongoing transactions between the individual and his or her environment.

Yet systems theories can be faulted for failing to provide a clear picture of the course of human development and for being only partially formulated and tested at this point. But a more serious criticism can be made: systems perspectives may never provide any coherent developmental theory. Why? If we take seriously the idea that development can take a range of paths depending on a range of interacting influences both within and outside the person, how can we ever state generalizations about development that will hold up for most people? If change over a lifetime depends on the ongoing transactions between a unique person and a unique environment, is each life span unique? The problem is this: "For the contextual or systems theorist, often the only generalization that holds is, 'It depends.'" (Goldhaber, 2000, p. 33).

In light of these concerns, some theorists have proposed combining systems perspectives with the best features of stage theories that propose universal paths of development (Lerner & Kauffman, 1985). They argue that development may be more predictable than Gottlieb's theory implies when children with normal human biological endowments develop in normal human environments (MacDonald & Hershberger, 2005). Perhaps it is still possible to see humans as moving in orderly directions in many aspects of their development while also appreciating diversity in development. Perhaps it is possible to view developmental attainments such as formal-operational thinking not as inevitable, universal achievements but as attainments that are more or less *probable* depending on the individual's genetic endowment and life experiences.

SUMMING UP

▌ Systems theories such as those of Bronfenbrenner and Gottlieb view development as the product of ongoing transactions between person and environment.

▌ Ethology asks how species-specific behaviors may have evolved, and Gottlieb's epigenetic psychobiological systems perspective highlights interactions among genes, neural activity, behavior, and environment.

▌ Systems theories are incomplete, however, and do not provide a coherent picture of human development.

CRITICAL THINKING

1. Revisit Figure 2.5 showing Gottlieb's model of bidirectional influence. Choosing either the neural activity and environment levels, or the genetic activity and behavior levels, develop an example showing how the two levels could reciprocally influence each other and what this means for understanding development.

2. Looking at all the possible paths of influence in Figure 2.5, identify and illustrate with examples two paths of influence that seem well-established and obvious and two that seem surprising and not so obvious.

2.7 | THEORIES IN PERSPECTIVE

That completes this survey of some grand and emerging theories of human development. These theories can be grouped into even grander categories based on the broad assumptions they make about human development (Goldhaber, 2000; Pepper, 1942; Reese & Overton, 1970).

Stage theorists such as Freud, Erikson, and Piaget form one broad group and have much in common. They believe that development is guided in certain universal directions by biological–maturational forces within the individual. Humans unfold—much as a rose unfolds from its beginnings as a seed—according to a master plan carried in their genes, assuming that they grow up in a reasonably normal environment. They evolve through distinct or discontinuous stages that are universal and lead to the same final state of maturity. Parents who subscribe to the stage theory perspective on development are likely to see themselves as *supporters* of development. They would tend to trust their children's biologically based tendencies to seek the learning opportunities they most need at each stage in their growth. They would respond to their children's changing needs and interests but they would not feel compelled to structure all their children's learning experiences. This position is like the philosophy of education incorporated in Montessori schools (Lillard, 2005).

By contrast, learning theorists such as Watson, Skinner, and Bandura emphasize the role of environment more than the role of biology in development. Parents who subscribe to a learning theory model of human development are not likely to trust genetically guided maturational forces to ensure that their children develop in healthy directions. Such parents are likely to act as *trainers*, assuming that their children will not develop properly (or at least will never be Harvard material) unless they are systematically exposed to particular learning experiences at particular times. These parents are likely to take deliberate steps to shape desirable behaviors and eliminate undesirable ones in their offspring.

Finally, systems theorists emphasize both biology and environment as inseparable components of a larger system. Humans contribute actively to the developmental process (as stage theorists such as Piaget maintain), but environment is also an active participant in the developmental drama (as learning theorists maintain). The potential exists for both qualitative (stagelike) change and quantitative change. Development can proceed along many paths depending on the intricate interplay of nature and nurture. Parents who adopt a systems theory of development, such as Gottlieb's epigenetic psychobiological systems view, are likely to appreciate that their children are influencing them just as much as they are influencing their children. They are likely to view themselves as *partners* with their children in the developmental process.

It is because different theories rest on different basic assumptions that they offer such different pictures of human development and its causes. Theorists who view the world through different lenses not only study different things but are likely to disagree even when the same "facts" are set before them because they will interpret those facts differently. This is the nature of science. Our understanding of human development has changed, and will continue to change, as one prevailing view gives way to another. From the beginning of the study of human development at the turn of the 20th century through the heyday of Freud's psychoanalytic theory, a stage theory perspective prevailed, emphasizing biological forces in development (Parke et al., 1994). In the 1950s and 1960s, learning theories came to the fore, and attention shifted from biology

USING DEVELOPMENTAL THEORIES TO PREVENT TEENAGE PREGNANCY

Although views vary across societies, teenagers in our society are generally encouraged to postpone parenthood so that they can complete their educations and begin their work lives before taking on the responsibilities of parenthood. If different developmental theorists were asked to recommend to policy makers strategies for lowering the rate of teenage pregnancy in the United States, what do you think they would recommend?

Psychoanalytic theorists tend to locate the causes of problems within the person. Sigmund Freud might want to identify and target for intervention teenagers who have especially strong ids and weak egos and superegos or who are experiencing extremes of anxiety and strained relationships with their parents during their teen years. Erik Erikson might want to identify teenagers who are troubled by a crisis of identity versus role confusion. High-risk teenagers might then be treated through psychoanalysis; the aim would be to help them resolve the inner conflicts that might influence their sexual behavior. The psychoanalytic approach might work with teenagers who are psychologically disturbed. However, teenagers who become pregnant do not really have higher rates of psychopathology overall than teenagers who do not become pregnant (Farber, 2003).

Adopting Jean Piaget's cognitive developmental perspective might make us pessimistic that young teenagers can learn to engage in long-term planning and rational decision making about sexual issues until they are solidly into the formal operations stage of cognitive development. However, if we could identify the kinds of faulty cognitive structures or misunderstandings that young adolescents have about their risks of pregnancy and about contraceptive methods, we could attempt to correct their mistaken ideas using concrete examples and simple explanations. The solution to teenage pregnancy, then, would be improved sex education programs—programs that provide teenagers with accurate information and help them think clearly about the long-term consequences of their sexual decisions. Sex education programs that are carefully designed and teach decision-making and communication skills can indeed increase the use of contraceptives and reduce pregnancy rates (Franklin & Corcoran, 2000). However, education alone is often not enough, so perhaps we need to consider solutions that locate the causes of teenage pregnancy in the environment rather than in the individual's psychological weaknesses or cognitive deficiencies.

Learning theorists strongly believe that changing the environment will change the person. In support of this belief, it appears that the most effective approach to teenage pregnancy prevention is to make contraceptives readily available to teens through health clinics and to teach them how to use them (Franklin & Corcoran, 2000; Kirby, 2002). This approach reflects a Skinnerian philosophy of encouraging the desired behavior by making it more reinforcing and less punishing. Albert Bandura's social cognitive theory suggests that it might also help to provide teenagers with more role models of responsible sexual behavior. Through the right observational learning experiences, teenagers might develop more sexually responsible behavior and learn that the consequences of safer sex are likely to be more desirable than the consequences of early parenthood (Unger, Molina, & Teran, 2000).

Systems theorists such as Gilbert Gottlieb would aim to change *both* the person and the environment—to change the whole system of interacting biological and environmental forces. Quick fixes are unlikely to work. The solution may require focusing on the adolescent as a whole person and aiming not to change sexual behavior alone but to address teenagers' broader socioemotional needs and enhance their overall adjustment (Allen, Seitz, & Apfel, 2007). The solution may also require changing the social context in which adolescents develop, with attention to how adolescents and their parents, peers, and partners influence one another. Looking at the cultural environment in the United States might lead one to conclude that teenage pregnancy in poverty areas may not be reduced significantly until poor parents face fewer stresses, schools are safe and stimulating, jobs are available, and more disadvantaged young people gain confidence that they can climb out of poverty if they pursue an education and postpone parenthood (Farber, 2003).

You can see, then, that the theoretical position one takes has a profound effect on how one attempts to optimize development. Yet, as you have also seen, each theory may offer only a partial solution to the problem being addressed. In all likelihood, multiple approaches will be needed to address complex problems such as unwanted teenage pregnancy—and to achieve the larger goal of understanding human development.

© Bubbles Photolibrary/Alamy

What approaches might you consider if you were a school nurse charged with reducing the pregnancy rate in the local high school?

● TABLE 2.4 COMPARE YOURSELF WITH THE THEORISTS

In the Explorations box at the beginning of this chapter, you were asked to indicate your position on basic issues in human development by answering five questions. If you transcribe your answers (a, b, c, d, or e) in the appropriate boxes in the first column below, you can compare your stands with those of the theorists described in this chapter—and review the theories. With whom do you seem to agree the most?

THEORY: THEORIST

	Your Answers (from the Explorations box on Page 31)	Psychoanalytic Theory: Freud's Psychosexual Theory	Psychoanalytic Theory: Erikson's Psychosocial Theory	Learning Theory: Skinner's Behavioral Theory	Learning Theory: Bandura's Social Cognitive Theory	Cognitive Developmental Theory: Piaget's Constructivism	Systems Theories: Gottlieb's Epigenetic Psychobiological Systems Perspective
MESSAGE		Biologically based sexual instincts motivate behavior and steer development through five psychosexual stages, oral to genital	Humans progress through eight psychosocial conflicts, from trust vs. mistrust to integrity vs. despair	Development is the product of learning from the consequences of one's behavior through operant conditioning	Development is the product of cognition, as illustrated by observational learning and human agency	Development proceeds through four stages of cognitive development, from sensorimotor to formal operations	Development takes many directions depending on transactions between a changing person and a changing environment
NATURE–NURTURE	Question 1	b. More nature (biology drives development; early experience in the family influences it, too)	c. Nature and nurture equally	e. Mostly nurture	d. More nurture	b. More nature (maturation interacting with experience guides all through the same stages)	c. Nature and nurture equally
GOODNESS–BADNESS OF HUMAN NATURE	Question 2	a. Bad (selfish, aggressive urges)	d. Good (capable of growth)	b. Neither good nor bad	b. Neither good nor bad	d. Good (curious)	c. Both good and bad (people have biologically based predispositions toward both)
ACTIVITY–PASSIVITY	Question 3	b. Passive (humans are influenced by forces beyond their control)	a. Active	b. Passive (humans are shaped by environment)	a. Active (humans influence their environments)	a. Active	a. Active
CONTINUITY–DISCONTINUITY	Question 4	a. Discontinuous (stagelike)	a. Discontinuous (stagelike)	c. Continuous (habits gradually increase or decrease in strength)	c. Continuous	a. Discontinuous (stagelike)	b. Both continuous and discontinuous
UNIVERSALITY–CONTEXT SPECIFICITY	Question 5	a. Universal	a. Universal (although stages may be expressed differently in different cultures)	b. Context specific (direction of development depends on experiences)	b. Context specific	a. Universal	b. Context specific

toward environment and toward the view that children are blank tablets to be written on. Then, with the rising influence of cognitive psychology and Piaget's theory of cognitive development in the late 1960s and 1970s, a stage theory model emphasizing the interaction of nature and nurture gained prominence. Finally, in the 1980s and 1990s, we gained a fuller appreciation of both biological–genetic and cultural–historical influences on development.

Where are we today? The broad perspective on key developmental issues taken by systems theorists such as Bronfenbrenner and Gottlieb is the perspective that most 21st-century developmentalists have adopted. The field has moved beyond the extreme, black-or-white positions taken by many of its pioneers. We now appreciate that humans, although not tabula rasae, have evolved so that they have the potential to develop in good and bad directions; that human development is always the product of nature and nurture; that both humans and their environments are active in the developmental process; that development is both continuous and discontinuous in form; and that development has both universal aspects and aspects particular to certain cultures, times, and individuals. In short, the assumptions and theories that guide the study of human development have become increasingly complex as the incredible complexity of human development has become more apparent.

As we have emphasized, a main function of theories in any science is to guide research. Thus Freud stimulated researchers to study inner personality conflicts, Skinner inspired them to analyze how behavior changes when its environmental consequences change, and Piaget inspired them to explore children's thinking about every imaginable topic. Different theories stimulate different kinds of research and yield different kinds of facts, as you will see throughout this book.

Theories also guide practice. As you have seen, each theory of human development represents a particular way of defining developmental issues and problems. Often, how you define a problem determines how you attempt to solve it. To illustrate, take one last look at teenage pregnancy. As you have seen, different theorists hold radically different opinions about the causes of teenage pregnancy. How do you think each would go about trying to reduce the rate of teenage pregnancy in our society? The Applications box on page 53 offers some ideas.

Just as developmental scientists need theories to guide their work, every parent, teacher, human services professional, and observer of humans is guided by some set of basic assumptions about how humans develop and why they develop as they do. We hope that reading this chapter will stimulate you to think about your own theory of human development. One way to start is by comparing the answers you gave to the questions in this chapter's first Explorations box with the summary information in ● **Table 2.4** and seeing which theorists' views are most compatible with your own.

You need not choose one theory and reject others. Because different theories often highlight different aspects of development, one may be more relevant to a particular issue or to a particular age group than another. Many developmentalists today are theoretical **eclectics** who rely on many theories, recog-

nizing that no major theories of human development can explain everything but that each has something to contribute to our understanding. In many ways, emerging systems perspectives on development provide the broadest point of view yet proposed. There is no reason many of the insights offered by Erikson, Piaget, Bandura, and others cannot be incorporated within this perspective to help us understand changing people in their changing worlds.

Summing Up

▎ During the 20th century, stage theories emphasizing biological forces gave way to learning theories emphasizing environmental influences, then to Piaget's cognitive developmental theory emphasizing the interaction of nature and nurture, and finally to complex systems theories in which developmental outcomes are more or less probable depending on multiple factors.

▎ Many developmentalists today are theoretical eclectics.

Critical Thinking

1. You have decided to become an eclectic and to take from each of the four major perspectives in this chapter (psychoanalytic, learning, cognitive developmental, and systems theory) only one truly great insight into human development. What four ideas would you choose, and why?

2. How might two of the theoretical perspectives discussed in this chapter explain the causes of and treat Terrell's case of school refusal (see chapter opening)?

CHAPTER SUMMARY

2.1 Developmental Theories and the Issues They Raise

- Theories organize and explain the facts of human development and are adequate to the extent that they are internally consistent, falsifiable, and supported by data.
- The five major issues in the study of human development are nature and nurture, the goodness and badness of human nature, activity and passivity, continuity and discontinuity, and universality and context specificity.

2.2 Freud: Psychoanalytic Theory

- In Freud's psychoanalytic theory, humans are irrational beings largely driven by inborn biological instincts of which they are largely unconscious. The personality is partitioned into the id, ego, and superego (which emerge in that order).
- Libido is rechanneled across five psychosexual stages—oral, anal, phallic, latent, and genital—each of which involves psychic conflicts that create the need for defense mechanisms and have lasting effects on personality.
- Biological needs drive development, but parents affect a child's success in dealing with conflicts and can contribute to emotional problems if they are overly restrictive.

- Although Freud called attention to the unconscious, early experiences in the family, and emotional development, his theory is not easily falsifiable and many of its specifics lack support.

2.3 ERIKSON: NEO-FREUDIAN PSYCHOANALYTIC THEORY

- Compared to Freud, neo-Freudian Erik Erikson emphasized biological urges less and social influences more; emphasized id less and ego more; held a more optimistic view of human nature and people's ability to overcome early problems; and theorized about the whole life span.
- According to Erikson, development proceeds through eight psychosocial stages involving issues of trust, autonomy, initiative, industry, identity, intimacy, generativity, and integrity. Parents, peers, and the larger culture influence how conflicts are resolved.
- The theories of both Freud and Erikson have been influential but are difficult to test and tend to describe development better than they explain it.

2.4 LEARNING THEORIES

- Learning theorists maintain that humans change gradually and can develop in many directions depending on environmental influences.
- Behaviorist Watson focused on the role of classical conditioning in the learning of emotional responses, and Skinner highlighted operant conditioning and the roles of reinforcement in strengthening behavior and punishment in weakening behavior.
- Bandura's social cognitive theory emphasizes the importance of cognitive processes in observational learning, as well as human agency, including self-efficacy, and reciprocal determinism among person, behavior, and environment.
- Learning theories are well supported and applicable across the life span, but they do not necessarily explain normal developmental changes and early theories especially underemphasized biological influences on development.

2.5 PIAGET: COGNITIVE DEVELOPMENTAL THEORY

- Piaget's cognitive developmental perspective holds that intelligence is an adaptive process in which humans create new understandings of the world through their active interactions with it (constructivism).
- The interaction of biological maturation and experience causes children to progress through four universal, invariant, and qualitatively different stages of thinking: sensorimotor, preoperational, concrete operational, and formal operational.
- Despite Piaget's immense influence, developmentalists question whether development is as stagelike and universal as he claimed.

2.6 SYSTEMS THEORIES

- Systems theories view development as the product of ongoing transactions and mutual influence between the individual and his environment.
- Ethology asks how species-specific behaviors may have evolved, and Gottlieb's epigenetic psychobiological systems perspective highlights mutual influences among genes, neural activity, behavior, and environment—both over the course of evolution and during the epigenetic process.
- Systems theories are incomplete, however, and do not provide a coherent picture of human development.

2.7 THEORIES IN PERSPECTIVE

- During the 20th century, stage theories such as Freud's emphasizing biological forces gave way to learning theories emphasizing environmental influences and then to Piaget's cognitive developmental theory, which emphasizes the interaction of nature and nurture.
- Piaget's concept of universal stages has given way to more complex systems theories such as those of Bronfenbrenner and Gottlieb, who expect developmental outcomes to be more or less probable depending on multiple factors.
- Theories influence both research and practice, and many developmentalists are theoretical eclectics.

KEY TERMS

tabula rasae 32
activity–passivity issue 32
continuity–discontinuity issue 32
developmental stage 33
universality–context-specificity
    issue 33
psychoanalytic theory 34
instinct 34
unconscious motivation 34
id 34
ego 34
superego 34
libido 35
psychosexual stages 35
defense mechanisms 35
fixation 35
regression 35
psychosocial stages 38
behaviorism 39
classical conditioning 40
unconditioned stimulus
    (UCS) 40
unconditioned response
    (UR) 40
conditioned stimulus (CS) 40
conditioned response (CR) 40

operant conditioning 41
positive reinforcement 41
negative reinforcement 41
positive punishment 41
negative punishment 41
extinction 41
social cognitive theory 42
observational learning 42
vicarious reinforcement 43
human agency 43
self-efficacy 43
reciprocal determinism 43
constructivism 46
sensorimotor stage 46
preoperational stage 47
concrete operations stage 47
formal operations stage 47
sociocultural perspective 48
information-processing
    approach 48
systems theories 48
ethology 49
epigenetic psychobiological
    systems perspective 49
epigenesis 50
eclectic 55

MEDIA RESOURCES

BOOK COMPANION WEBSITE

academic.cengage.com/psychology/sigelman
Find online quizzes, flash cards, animations, video clips, experiments, interactive assessments, and other helpful study aids for this text at **academic.cengage.com/psychology/sigelman.** You can also connect directly to the following sites:

ERIKSON

The mythosandlogos.com website contains almost 40 links to information on the life and theory of Erik Erikson. The site also contains a list of books on Erikson and the psychoanalytic approach to development.

FREUD

This site of the Abraham A. Brill Library of the New York Psychoanalytic Institute and Society (see especially "Sigmund Freud on the Internet") offers biographical information and excerpts from a few of the writings of the founder of psychoanalytic theory.

PIAGET

The Jean Piaget Society provides biographical information, links to other Piaget resources on the web, and lists of suggested readings for those who would like to learn more about Piaget's research and writings.

SKINNER

The B. F. Skinner Foundation works with Harvard University to archive Skinner's literary estate and publishes significant works in the study of behavior. Its website contains a brief biography of the late behaviorist by his daughter, Julie S. Vargas, and a non-technical summary of operant conditioning.

TEENAGE PREGNANCY

For those interested in the topic of teenage pregnancy, the website for the National Campaign to Prevent Teenage Pregnancy offers a wealth of statistics and information about approaches to preventing teenage pregnancy.

CENGAGENOW

academic.cengage.com/login
Go to **academic.cengage.com/login** to link to CengageNOW, your online study tool. First take the Pre-Test for this chapter to get your Personalized Study Plan, which will identify topics you need to review and direct you to online resources. Then take the Post-Test to determine what concepts you have mastered and what you still need work on.

3

CHAPTER

Genes, Environment, and Development

A **NEWSPAPER STORY** about Jim Lewis and Jim Springer inspired Thomas Bouchard Jr. and his associates (Bouchard, 1984; Bouchard et al., 1990) to undertake a study in which they reunited identical twins who had been separated soon after birth and asked them to complete a 50-hour battery of tests. Together after spending all but the first 4 weeks of their 39 years apart, Jim and Jim discovered that they had both married women named Linda—and then women named Betty. They named their first sons James Alan and James Allan, had dogs named Toy, and liked Miller Lite beer and Salem cigarettes.

Barbara Herbert and Daphne Goodship, also reunited after 39 years apart, both wore a beige dress and a brown velvet jacket when they met for the first time in London. They shared a habit of "squidging" (pushing up their noses), had fallen down the stairs at age 15, laughed more than anyone they knew, and never voted.

Yet identical twins Jessica and Rachel Wessell, despite growing up together and being close, are far from identical. One excels in math, the other in English. One has cerebral palsy and is in a wheelchair, possibly because of lack of oxygen to her brain at birth; the other twin was in the marching band in high school (Helderman, 2003).

■ ■ ■

The influence of genes on development must be taken seriously—but so must the influence of environment. How do nature and nurture, heredity and environment, contribute to the shaping of physical and psychological characteristics? That is the complex puzzle we grapple with in this chapter. Many people are environmentalists at heart, believing that there is no such thing as a "bad seed," that proper parenting and a stimulating environment can make any child develop well, and that most of the psychological differences among people reflect their experiences over a lifetime. Reading this chapter should increase your appreciation of genetic contributions to development and give you new insights into the importance of environmental influences.

We begin with a brief look at ways in which genes make humans similar. Then the chapter turns to what each person inherits at conception and how this genetic endowment influences traits. Then it explores research findings on how genes and environment make individuals different from one another in intelligence, personality, and other important characteristics. Finally, we draw some general conclusions about heredity and environment from a life-span perspective.

3.1 | EVOLUTION AND SPECIES HEREDITY

Most descriptions of heredity focus on its role in creating differences among people. Some individuals inherit blue eyes, others brown eyes; some inherit blood type O, others blood type A or B. But isn't it remarkable that almost every one of us has two eyes and that we all have blood coursing through our veins? Virtually all of us also develop in similar ways at similar ages—walking and talking around 1 year, maturing sexually from 12 to 14, watching our skin wrinkle in our 40s and 50s. Such similarities in development and aging are a product of **species heredity**—the genetic endowment that members of a species have in common, including genes that influence maturation and aging processes. Humans can feel guilty but cannot fly; birds can fly but cannot feel guilty. Each species has a distinct heredity. Species heredity is one reason certain patterns of development and aging are universal.

To understand where we got our species heredity, we must turn to evolutionary theory. We introduced Gilbert Gottlieb's modern epigenetic psychobiological systems theory in Chapter 2. Here we go back to basics—to the pathblazing work of Charles Darwin (1809–1882). Darwin's theory of evolution sought to explain how the characteristics of a species change over time and how new species can evolve from earlier ones (Darwin, 1859). The theory has been and continues to be controversial, but it is tremendously important to our understanding of why humans de-

Identical twins share some remarkable similarities, even when separated early in life, but differ as well.

© JUPITERIMAGES/Brand X/Alamy

velop as they do. And it is not "just a theory," not just speculation; rather, it is a well-supported theoretical account, described by one evolutionary psychologist as "as close to truth as any science is ever likely to get" (Barash, 2006, p. B10). Darwin's theory makes these main arguments:

1. *There is genetic variation in a species.* Some members of the species have different genes (and therefore different genetically influenced traits) than other members of the species do. If all members of the species were genetically identical, there would be no way for the genetic makeup of the species to change over time. Because novel genes arise through errors in cell division all the time (see later section on mutations), genetic variation is assured.

2. *Some genes aid adaptation more than others do.* Suppose that some members of a species have genes that make them strong and intelligent, whereas others have genes that make them weak and dull. Those with the genes for strength and intelligence would likely be better able to adapt to their environment—for example, to win fights for survival or to figure out how to obtain food.

3. *Genes that aid their bearers in adapting to their environment will be passed to future generations more frequently than genes that do not.* This is the principle of **natural selection**—the idea that nature "selects," or allows to survive and reproduce, those members of a species whose genes permit them to adapt to their environment. By contrast, genes that reduce the chances that an individual will survive and reproduce will become rarer over time because they will not be passed to many offspring. Through natural selection, then, the genetic makeup of a species slowly changes—and will continue to change as long as individuals with certain genetic makeups reproduce more frequently than individuals with other genetic makeups. Change can eventually be sufficient to produce a new species. The result is what Darwin marveled at when he conducted observations in the Galapagos Islands: the incredible diversity of species on earth, each well adapted to its environment.

Consider a classic example of evolution. H. B. D. Kettlewell (1959) carefully studied moths in England. There is genetic variation among moths that makes some dark and others light. By placing light and dark moths in several sites, Kettlewell found that in rural areas light-colored moths were most likely to survive but that in industrial areas dark moths were most likely to survive. The explanation? In rural areas, light-colored moths blend in well with light-colored trees and are therefore better protected from predators. Natural selection favors them. However, in sooty industrial areas, lightcolored moths are easy pickings against the darkened trees, whereas dark moths are well disguised. When industry came to England, the proportion of dark moths increased; as pollution was brought under control in some highly industrialized areas, the proportion of light-colored moths increased (Bishop & Cooke, 1975).

Notice, then, that evolution is not just about genes. It is about the *interaction between genes and environment.* A particular genetic makeup may enhance survival in one kind of envi-

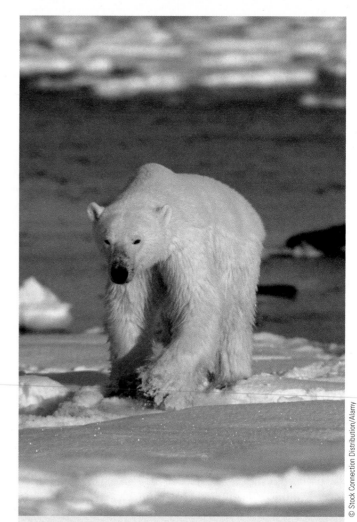

Each species has evolved through natural selection to be adapted to its environment.

© Stock Connection Distribution/Alamy

ronment but prove maladaptive in another. Which genes are advantageous, and therefore which become more common in future generations, depends on what environment a group experiences and what traits that environment demands. Genes that helped our ancestors hunt prey may not be as important in today's environment as genes that help people master cell phones and computers. Humans, like other species, are continuing to evolve as their environments change (Voight et al., 2006).

According to evolutionary theory, then, humans, like any other species, are as they are and develop as they do partly because they have a shared species heredity that evolved through natural selection. Solutions to problems faced by our ancestors thousands of years ago in such important areas as mate selection, childbearing, and parenting may have become built into the human genetic code. Not all human similarity is because of genes, however. Through the process of cultural evolution, we "inherit" from previous generations a characteristically human environment and tried and true ways of adapting to it (Bjorklund & Pellegrini, 2002). Indeed, the most significant legacy of biological evolution may be a powerful and very flexible brain that allows humans to learn from their experiences, to find better ways of adapting to their environment and even changing it to suit them better, and, with the help of language, to share what they have learned with future generations (Bjorklund & Pellegrini, 2002; Ellis & Bjorklund, 2005).

SUMMING UP

■ Humans develop similarly partly because of a shared species heredity produced by biological evolution.

■ According to Darwin's evolutionary theory, genes that aid members of the species in adapting to their environment and reproducing will become more common through natural selection.

■ Humans are also similar because they inherit a characteristically human environment through cultural evolution.

CRITICAL THINKING

1. Think of two or three human behaviors that you believe are so universal that they are probably built into our species heredity. Why might genes underlying these behaviors have been selected for in the course of evolution?

3.2 INDIVIDUAL HEREDITY

To understand how genes contribute to *differences* among humans, we must start at **conception**—the moment when an egg is fertilized by a sperm—look at the workings of genes, and then consider the mechanisms through which genes can influence traits.

The Genetic Code

A few hours after sperm penetrates ovum, the sperm cell begins to disintegrate, releasing its genetic material. The nucleus of the ovum releases its own genetic material, and a new cell nucleus is created from the genetic material provided by mother and father. This new cell, called a **zygote** and only the size of a pinhead, is the beginning of a human. Conception has occurred.

A sperm cell and an ovum each contribute 23 chromosomes to the zygote to give it 46 chromosomes total, organized into 23 pairs. **Chromosomes** are the threadlike bodies in the nucleus of each cell that are made up of genes, the basic units of heredity. Thus, of each chromosome pair—and of each pair of genes located on corresponding sites on a chromosome pair—one member came from the father and one member came from the mother. Sperm and ova, unlike other cells, have only 23 chromosomes because they are produced through the specialized process of cell division called **meiosis**. At the start of this process, a reproductive cell in the ovaries of a female or the testes of a male that contains 46 chromosomes splits to form two 46-chromosome cells, and then these two cells each split again to form a total of four cells. In this last step, though, a special cell division process occurs in which each resulting cell receives only 23 chromosomes. The end product is one egg (and three nonfunctional cells that play no role in reproduction) in a female or four sperm in a male. Each resulting sperm cell or ovum thus has only one member of each of the parent's 23 pairs of chromosomes.

The single-celled zygote formed at conception becomes a multiple-celled organism through the more usual process of cell division, **mitosis**. During mitosis, a cell (and each of its 46 chromosomes) divides to produce two identical cells, each containing the same 46 chromosomes. As the zygote moves through the fallopian tube toward its prenatal home in the uterus, it first divides into two cells; the two then become four, the four become eight, and so on, all through mitosis. Except for sperm and ova, all normal human cells contain copies of the 46 chromosomes provided at conception (see ● **Table 3.1**). Mitosis continues throughout life, creating new cells that enable us to grow and replacing old cells that are damaged.

Both members of a chromosome pair influence the same characteristics. Each chromosome consists of strands of deoxyribonucleic acid (DNA), the double helix molecule whose chemical code is our genetic endowment. DNA is made up of

● **TABLE 3.1 MITOSIS AND MEIOSIS COMPARED**

	MITOSIS	MEIOSIS IN MALES	MEIOSIS IN FEMALES
BEGINS	Conception	Puberty	Early in prenatal period when unripened ova form
CONTINUES	Throughout life span	Throughout adolescence and adulthood	Through the reproductive years; an ovum ripens each month of the menstrual cycle
PRODUCES	Two identical daughter cells, each with 46 chromosomes like its parent	Four sperm, each with 23 chromosomes	One ovum and 3 nonfunctional polar bodies, each with 23 chromosomes
ACCOMPLISHES	Growth of human from fertilized egg, renewal of the body's cells	Formation of male reproductive cells	Formation of female reproductive cells

SOURCE: From Yvonna S. Lincoln & Egon G. Guba, *Naturalistic inquiry* Copyright © 1985 Sage Publications. Reprinted with permission of Sage Publications.

sequences of the chemicals A (adenine), C (cytosine), G (guanine), and T (thymine). Some of these sequences are functional units called genes (see ■ Figure 3.1). Genetic scientists used to think humans had about 100,000 genes but research now suggests that the number of genes is probably no more than 20,000–25,000 (International Human Genome Sequencing Consortium, 2004).

Each gene, of which there can be several variants, provides instructions that lead to the production of particular amino acids, which in turn form proteins, the building blocks of all bodily tissues and of essential substances such as hormones, neurotransmitters, and enzymes (Rutter, Moffitt, & Caspi, 2006). Other stretches of DNA are involved in regulating genes; they, along with environmental influences, affect the processes involved in the production of amino acids.

The Human Genome Project

Through the **Human Genome Project,** researchers have mapped the sequence of the chemical units or "letters" that make up the strands of DNA in human chromosomes. They still needed to do some "spell checking" when they made their initial announcement, but they had a pretty good draft of the human genome (Weiss & Gillis, 2000). The drudgery of this monstrous task was done by supercomputers and robots the size of small cars working alongside human technicians. The raw material analyzed was DNA samples from a few humans of diverse racial backgrounds.

It is estimated that the human genome has 3.1 billion of the chemical constituents A, C, G, and T. Interestingly, only about 3 to 4% of the human genome—1 inch out of an estimated 6 feet of DNA—is believed to consist of genes, each of which is a specific sequence of from 1000 to 100,000 of these chemical "letters" (Weiss, 2000). Other stretches of DNA were at first called "junk DNA," but then it became clear that they have important functions in regulating the activity of the genes, in turning them on and off (Rutter et al., 2006).

The Human Genome Project and the massive genome analysis projects that have followed it are yielding astounding new discoveries every year. The International HapMap Project, for example, described the genetic similarities and differences among 270 people from a variety of racial and ethnic groups around the world (Turnpenny & Ellard, 2005). It turns out that about 999 of 1000 base chemicals are identical in all humans; it is the remaining 1 of 1000 that makes us different (see ■ Figure 3.2 on DNA fingerprinting). At the same time, geneticists are discovering that genetic diversity among individuals is greater than anyone appreciated. For example, as the result of copying errors in mitosis, people differ considerably with respect to whether they have fewer than or more than the "normal" two copies of various genes (Redon et al., 2006). The number of copies a person has may influence the diseases and disorders the person experiences.

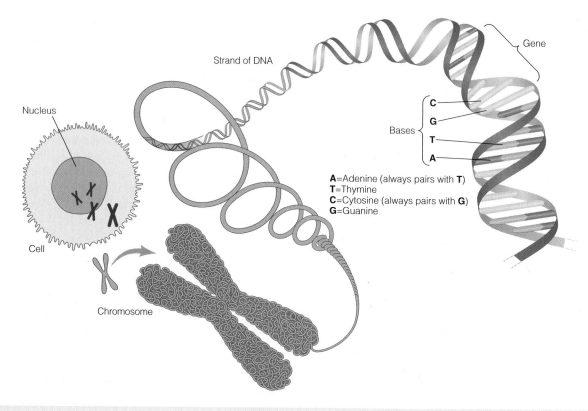

A=Adenine (always pairs with **T**)
T=Thymine
C=Cytosine (always pairs with **G**)
G=Guanine

■ **FIGURE 3.1** The chromosomes in each cell consist of strands of DNA made up of sequences of the bases A, T, C, and G, some of which are functional units called genes.
SOURCE: Adapted from Weiss, R. (2000, May 23). For DNA, a defining moment: With code revealed, challenge will be to find its meaning and uses. *Washington Post*, p. A16.

FIGURE 3.2 DNA fingerprinting allows determination of a child's father, matching of DNA from a crime scene to a suspect, and analysis of disease risk. Here, each column is a graphic representation, something like a bar code, of particular sequences of DNA known to vary a good deal from person to person. [Shown in order are samples from: (A) an unrelated person, (B) the father of a family, (C) his first son, (D) his second son, and (E) his wife. Looking at the sons, one can recognize bands that appear in either their father's or their mother's fingerprint.]
(Courtesy of Professor A. Markham, St. James Hospital, Leeds.)

Genetic research involving analysis of DNA also has shown that we share most of our genes not only with other humans but also with other primates and even mice. For example, humans and chimpanzees share about 96% of their genetic material in common (Chimpanzee Sequencing and Analysis Consortium, 2005). Moreover, analysis of DNA from the bone of a Neanderthal who lived almost 40,000 years ago is being conducted and is shedding light on human evolution and the capabilities of Neanderthals in comparison to humans (Green et al., 2006).

Researchers have also been conducting analyses of DNA samples from groups around the world to identify gene variants that have evolved in recent centuries, most likely in response to changes in the environments of modern humans. For example,

gene variants that make people tolerate lactose in milk spread among Europeans as dairy farming became common and being able to tolerate milk presumably became adaptive (Voight et al., 2006). Similar changes in the prevalence of specific genes detected in other populations appear to be adaptations to changes in food sources, disease threats, and other life conditions. By comparing the genes of humans, human ancestors, chimpanzees, and other species, and by analyzing human DNA for signs of genetic change, researchers are able to test in new ways some of the predictions of Darwin's theory of evolution and are gaining new insights into how the human species evolved and how humans are unique.

Finally, researchers are applying the findings of the Human Genome Project to better identify and screen for genes associated with diseases and with good or poor reactions to drugs used in treating diseases (Goldstein & Cavalleri, 2005). When a gene associated with a disease or disorder is located on a particular chromosome, much remains to be done before this information can be usefully applied. Researchers may devise a test for the gene, study the functions of the gene's products so that they can begin to understand how the disease or disorder comes about, and only then attempt to develop new drugs and other means of preventing or curing the dysfunction associated with the gene (Weiss, 2003b). As James Watson, codiscoverer of the double helix structure of DNA, put it, "We have the book, and now we've got to learn how to read it" (Weiss & Gillis, 2000, p. A12).

Genetic Uniqueness and Relatedness

To understand how people are both different from and like others genetically, consider that when a pair of parental chromosomes separates during meiosis, which of the two chromosomes will end up in a particular sperm or ovum is a matter of chance. And, because each chromosome pair separates independently of all other pairs, and because each reproductive cell contains 23 pairs of chromosomes, a single parent can produce 2^{23}—more than 8 million—different sperm or ova. Any couple could theoretically have at least 64 trillion babies without producing 2 children with identical genes.

The genetic uniqueness of children of the same parents is even greater than this because of a quirk of meiosis known as **crossing over.** When pairs of chromosomes line up before they separate, they cross each other and parts of them are exchanged, much as if you were to exchange a couple of fingers with a friend at the end of a handshake. Crossing over increases even more the number of distinct sperm or ova that an individual can produce. In short, it is incredibly unlikely that there ever was or ever will be another human exactly like you genetically. The one exception is **identical twins** (or identical triplets, and so on), also called monozygotic twins because they result when one fertilized ovum divides to form two or more genetically identical individuals. This happens in about 1 of every 250 births (Segal, 2005).

How genetically alike are parent and child or brother and sister? You and either your mother or your father have 50% of your genes in common because you received half of your chromosomes (and genes) from each parent. But if you have followed our mathematics, you will see that siblings may have many genes in common or few depending on what happens during meiosis. Because siblings receive half of their genes from the same mother and half from the same father, their genetic resemblance to each other is 50%, the same genetic resemblance as that of parent and child. The critical difference is that they share half of their genes *on the average*; some siblings share more and others fewer. Indeed, we have all known some siblings who are almost like twins and others who could not be more different if they tried.

Fraternal twins (also called dizygotic twins because two eggs are involved) result when two ova are released at approximately the same time and each is fertilized by a different sperm, as happens in about 1 of every 125 births (Plomin, 1990). Fraternal twins are no more alike genetically than brothers and sisters born at different times and need not even be of the same sex. Fraternal twins tend to run in families and have become more common in recent years because more couples are undergoing in vitro fertilization (Segal, 2005; and see Explorations box on "Prenatal Detection of Abnormalities" later in this chapter). Grandparent and grandchild, aunt or uncle and niece or nephew, and half brothers and half sisters have 25% of their genes in common on average. Thus, everyone except an identical twin is genetically unique, but each person also shares genes with kin that contribute to family resemblances.

Determination of Sex

Of the 23 pairs of chromosomes that each individual inherits, 22 (called *autosomes*) are similar in males and females. The chromosomes of the 23rd pair are the sex chromosomes. A male child has one long chromosome called an **X chromosome** because of its shape, and a short, stubby companion with far fewer genes called a **Y chromosome.** Females have two X chromosomes. The photos of the male and female karyotypes show chromosomes that have been photographed through a powerful microscope, then arranged in pairs and rephotographed in a pattern called a **karyotype** that allows their number and form to be studied.

Thanks to the Human Genome Project, we now know a good deal about the composition of the X chromosome. Each X chromosome has almost 1100 genes, compared to only about 80 on a Y chromosome, many of which are involved in the production of sperm (Brown, 2005). It seems that X and Y chromosomes have evolved along their own paths and share very few genes with similar functions. Moreover, we now know that one of a female's two X chromosomes is normally inactivated early in the prenatal period (and then that X chromosome remains inactive in cells subsequently produced through mitosis), but that about 15% of the genes on the inactivated X chromosome remain active and may contribute to sex differences (Ross et al., 2005).

Because a mother has only X chromosomes and a father's sperm cell has either an X chromosome or a Y chromosome

(A)

(B)

© CNRI/Science Photo Library/Photo Researchers, Inc.

The male karyotype (A) shows the 22 pairs of autosomal chromosomes and the 2 sex chromosomes—an elongated X and a shorter Y chromosome. The photographic arrangement of a female's chromosomes (B) shows 2 X chromosomes.

(depending on which sex chromosome a sperm receives during meiosis), it is the father who determines a child's gender. If an ovum with its one X chromosome is fertilized by a sperm bearing a Y chromosome, the product is an XY zygote—a genetic male. A gene on the Y chromosome then sets in motion the biological events that result in male sexual organs (Hawley & Mori, 1999; and see Chapter 12). If a sperm carrying an X chromosome reaches the ovum first, the result is an XX zygote—a genetic female. Perhaps if these facts had been known in earlier eras, women would not have been criticized, tortured, divorced, and even beheaded for failing to bear male heirs.

So, a genetically unique boy or girl has roughly 20,000–25,000 genes on 46 chromosomes arranged in 23 pairs. How do these genes influence the individual's characteristics and development? It is still a mystery, but understanding is increasing rapidly.

Translation and Expression of the Genetic Code

One does not have to understand cell biology to appreciate that environmental factors help determine which genetic potentials are translated into physical and psychological realities and which are not. Consider the genes that influence height. Some people inherit genes calling for exceptional height, and others inherit genes calling for a short stature. But **genotype,** the genetic makeup a person inherits, is different from **phenotype,** the characteristic or trait the person eventually has (for example, a height of 5 feet 8 inches). An individual whose genotype calls for exceptional height may or may not be tall. Indeed, a child who is severely malnourished from the prenatal period onward may have the genetic potential to be a basketball center but may end up too short to make the team. Environmental influences combine with genetic influences to determine how a particular genotype is translated into a particular phenotype—the way a person looks, thinks, feels, or behaves.

As you have seen, genes provide instructions for development by calling for the production of chemical substances. For example, genes set in motion a process that lays a pigment called *melanin* in the iris of the eye. Some people's genes call for much of this pigment, and the result is brown eyes; other people's genes call for less of it, and the result is blue eyes. Genetically coded proteins also guide the formation of cells that become neurons in the brain, influencing potential intelligence and personality.

But genes both influence, and are influenced by, the biochemical environment surrounding them during development and the behavior of the developing organism (Gottlieb, 2002). As a result, a particular cell can become part of an eyeball or part of a kneecap depending on what cells are next to it during embryonic development and what they are doing. You should therefore think of the genetic "code" as written in erasable pencil rather than in indelible ink, and of both genes and environment as active forces in development throughout the life span.

A multitude of environmental factors not only in the womb but throughout life influence which genes are activated when (Gottesman & Hanson, 2005). Because all cells have the same genes on the same chromosomes, what makes brain, blood, and other cells different from each other is not what genes they contain, but which genes are *expressed.*

Gene expression is the activation of particular genes in particular cells of the body at particular times in the life span; only if a gene is "turned on" is it influential. Gene expression, then, is what ultimately determines our traits, and it is affected by both genetic factors (mainly the action of regulatory DNA) and environmental factors such as diet and stress (Rutter et al., 2006). If different life experiences cause the genes of identical twins to express themselves differently, this could help explain some of the many differences we see in their characteristics and behavior, as the Explorations box on page 66 reveals.

In the end, no one completely understands the remarkable epigenetic process that transforms a single cell with its genetic endowment into millions of diverse cells—blood cells, nerve cells, skin cells, and so on—all organized into a living, behaving human. Nor do we fully understand how genes help bring about certain developments at certain points in the life span. Yet it is becoming clearer that genes are active players along with environment in the developmental process and that having this gene or that gene may be less important than how the individual's genotype is expressed.

Mechanisms of Inheritance

Another way to approach the riddle of how genes influence human development is to consider the major mechanisms of inheritance—how parents' genes influence their children's traits. There are three main mechanisms of inheritance: single gene-pair inheritance, sex-linked inheritance, and polygenic (or multiple gene) inheritance.

Single Gene-Pair Inheritance

Through **single gene-pair inheritance,** each of thousands of human characteristics are influenced by only one pair of genes—one from the mother, one from the father (Turnpenny & Ellard, 2005). Although he knew nothing of genes, a 19th-century monk named Gregor Mendel contributed greatly to our knowledge of single gene-pair inheritance and earned his place as the father of genetics by cross-breeding different strains of peas and carefully observing the outcomes (Henig, 2000). He noticed a predictable pattern to the way in which two alternative characteristics would appear in the offspring of cross-breedings—for example, smooth seeds or wrinkled seeds, green pods or yellow pods. He called some characteristics (for example, smooth seeds) *dominant* because they appeared more often in later generations than their opposite traits, which he called *recessive.*

As an illustration of the principles of Mendelian heredity, consider the remarkable fact that about three-fourths of us can

THE NEXT CHALLENGE: UNDERSTANDING GENE EXPRESSION

Researchers have long been curious about why identical twins differ from each other in so many ways. How *do* we explain how, despite having identical genes, one identical twin can have schizophrenia, autism, or another significant disorder while the other does not? Environment has to be the answer, but the story is a little more complicated.

Mario Fraga and his colleagues (2005) suspected that the answer might lie partly in gene expression—in which genes are turned on or off in each twin. They conducted analyses of the DNA and RNA of 40 pairs of identical twins ranging in age from 3 to 74 in order to shed light on the epigenetic process through which genetic and environmental influences translate genotype into phenotype. They found that older twin pairs were more different from each other than younger twin pairs in the patterns of activation of their genes. For example, a close analysis of the RNA of 3-year-old twins and 50-year-old twins showed that the genes of the young children had almost identical patterns of expression. If a gene was turned on in one twin, it was turned on in the other; if it was turned off in one twin, it was turned off in the other. By contrast, the genes of the 50-year-old twins were expressed very differently; many

genes that were activated in one twin were deactivated in the other.

What's more, those twins who had spent less of their lives together and had lived different lifestyles (for example, as indicated by their eating habits, levels of physical activity, and use of tobacco, alcohol, drugs) showed greater differences in their patterns of gene activation than did twins who had led similar lives. This finding suggests that environment influences gene expression, which in turn influences a person's traits and behavior. There is now plenty more such evidence, some of it coming from experiments with animals (Rutter et al., 2006).

Imagine, then, that as identical twins go through life their genes become more and more different—not in their chemical makeup but in which of them are expressed when and in what cells of the body. Think of chromosomes as something like strings of Christmas tree lights whose bulbs turn on and off in intricate patterns over a lifetime. Although identical twins share the same genotype, epigenesis increasingly results in an activated genome in one twin that is quite different from that in the other twin. Differences in gene expression may then contribute, along with environmental

influences, to some of the differences in appearance, health, and behavior we see between identical twins. It could be that some diseases and disorders arise not because a normal gene is missing but because it is not expressed normally, possibly because of disruptions in epigenesis associated with a poor diet, toxins, or stressful experiences (Whitelaw & Garrick, 2006). We know, for example, that stress can affect patterns of gene activation, patterns which are then transmitted from cell to cell during mitosis and even appear to be transmitted across generations from mother to child through the mother's egg (Harper, 2005; Rutter et al., 2006).

If we want to understand human development, it is clearly not going to be sufficient to know what genetic makeup a person has. We must also understand which of his or her genes are turned on or off, and when, during development, and what genetic and environmental factors are at work to shape these patterns of gene expression. What's clear is that genes are not fixed entities that never change from conception on. Instead, they are highly changeable, and their changeability enhances our ability to adapt to changing environments over our lives (Gottesman & Hanson, 2005).

---

curl our tongues upward into a tubelike shape, whereas one-fourth of us cannot. It happens that there is a gene associated with tongue curling; it is a **dominant gene,** meaning that it will be expressed when paired with a **recessive gene,** a weaker gene that can be dominated (like one associated with the absence of tongue-curling ability).

The person who inherits one "tongue-curl" gene (label it U) and one "no-curl" gene (call it -) would be able to curl his tongue (that is, would have a tongue-curling phenotype) because the dominant, tongue-curl gene overpowers the recessive, no-curl gene. Using ■ **Figure 3.3** as a guide, you can calculate the odds that parents with various genotypes for tongue curling will have children who can or cannot curl their tongues. Each cell of the figure shows what will happen when a father contributes one of his two genes to a sperm and a mother contributes one of her two genes to an ovum and each of four children they have inherits one of the mother's genes and one of the father's.

Dominant genes triumph over recessive genes. If a father with the genotype UU (a tongue curler) and a mother with the genotype - - (a non–tongue curler) have children, each child

they produce will have one gene for tongue curling and one for a lack of tongue curling (genotype U-) and each will be a tongue curler. Because the tongue-curl gene dominates, you can say that this couple has a 100% chance of having a tongue-curling child. Notice that two different genotypes, UU and U-, both produce the same phenotype: an acrobatic tongue.

A tongue-curling man and a tongue-curling woman can surprise everyone and have a child who lacks this amazing talent. These two parents both must have the U- genotype. If the father's recessive gene and the mother's recessive gene happen to unite in the zygote, they will have a non–tongue-curling child (with the genotype - -). The chances are 25%—one out of four—that this couple will have such a child. Of course, the laws of conception are much like the laws of cards. This couple could beat the odds and have a whole family of non–tongue-curling children or they could have none. Because people who cannot curl their tongues must have the - - genotype, two non–tongue-curling parents will have only non–tongue-curling (- -) children.

● **Table 3.2** lists several other examples of dominant and recessive traits associated with single gene-pair inheritance.

■ **FIGURE 3.3** Can you curl your tongue as shown? Tongue-curling ability is determined by a dominant gene; if you can curl your tongue, then either your mother or your father can, because one of them must have the dominant gene. All possibilities are shown in the figure; each of the nine boxes shows the gene combinations of the four possible children a particular mother and a particular father can have.

Some physical characteristics in this table (such as eye color and hair color and curliness) are in fact influenced by more than a single pair of genes. Also, in some cases, a dominant gene incompletely dominates a recessive partner gene and the result is a new trait that blends the parents' traits—as when crossing red and white flowers produces pink ones or when dark-skinned and light-skinned parents have a child with light brown skin. This phenomenon is called **incomplete dominance**. In other cases of single gene-pair heredity, two genes influence a trait but each is expressed in the product, as when crossing red and white flowers produces flowers with red and white streaks—a phenomenon called **codominance**. For example, an AB blood type is a mix of A and B blood types (both A and B proteins appear on blood cells). In short, single gene-pair inheritance is a bit more complex than Mendel realized.

Sex-Linked Inheritance

Sex-linked characteristics are influenced by single genes located on the sex chromosomes rather than on the other 22 pairs of chromosomes. Indeed, you could say *X-linked* rather than *sex-linked* because most of these attributes are associated with genes located only on X chromosomes.

Why do far more males than females display red–green color blindness? The inability to distinguish red from green is caused by a recessive gene that appears only on X chromosomes. Recall that Y chromosomes are shorter than X chromosomes and have fewer genes. If a boy inherits the recessive color-blindness gene on his X chromosome, there is no color-vision gene on the Y chromosome that could dominate the color-blindness gene. He will be color blind. By contrast, a girl who inherits the gene usually has a normal color-vision gene on her other X chromosome that can dominate the color-blindness gene (see ■ **Figure 3.4**). She would have to inherit two of the recessive color-blindness genes (one from each parent) to be color blind. Which parent gives a boy who is color blind his color-blindness gene? Definitely his mother, for she is the source of his X chromosome. **Hemophilia,** a deficiency in the blood's ability to clot, is also far more common among males than females because it is a sex-linked disorder associated with a recessive gene on X chromosomes.

Polygenic Inheritance

So far we have considered only the influence of single genes or gene pairs on human traits. Every week, it seems, we read in the newspaper that researchers have identified "the gene" for

● TABLE 3.2   EXAMPLES OF TRAITS INFLUENCED BY DOMINANT AND RECESSIVE GENES

DOMINANT TRAIT	RECESSIVE TRAIT
Brown eyes	Gray, green, hazel, or blue eyes
Dark hair	Blond hair
Nonred hair	Red hair
Curly hair	Straight hair
Normal vision	Nearsightedness
Farsightedness	Normal vision
Roman nose	Straight nose
Broad lips	Thin lips
Extra digits	Five digits
Double jointed	Normal joints
Pigmented skin	Albinism
Type A blood	Type O blood
Type B blood	Type O blood
Normal hearing	Congenital deafness
Normal blood cells	Sickle-cell disease*
Huntington's disease*	Normal physiology
Normal physiology	Cystic fibrosis*
Normal physiology	Phenylketonuria (PKU)*
Normal physiology	Tay-Sachs disease*

*Condition described in this chapter.
SOURCES: Burns & Bottino, 1989; McKusick, 1990.

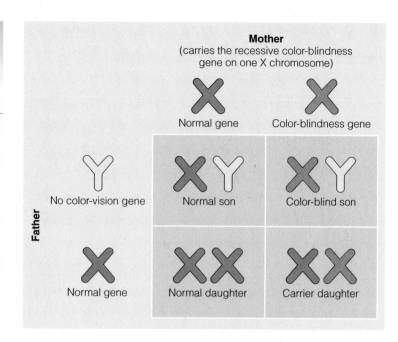

■ **FIGURE 3.4** The workings of sex-linked inheritance in red–green color blindness.

This is the way intelligence and most other measurable human traits are distributed. At this point, we do not know how many gene pairs influence intelligence or other polygenic traits. What we can say is that unknown numbers of genes, interacting with environmental forces, create a range of individual differences in most important human traits.

Mutations

We have described the three major mechanisms by which the genes inherited at conception influence traits: single gene-pair, sex-linked, and polygenic inheritance. Occasionally, however, a new gene appears as if out of nowhere; it is not passed on by a parent. A **mutation** is a change in the structure or arrangement of one or more genes that produces a new phenotype. For example, experts believe that the recessive gene for the sex-linked disorder hemophilia was first introduced into the royal families of Europe by Queen Victoria. Because no cases of hemophilia could be found in the queen's ancestry, the gene may have been a mutation that she passed to her offspring (Massie & Massie, 1975). New cases of hemophilia, then, can be caused by either spontaneous mutations or sex-linked inheritance. The odds that mutations will occur are increased by environmental hazards such as radiation and toxic industrial waste; yet most mutations are just spontaneous errors (Turnpenny & Ellard, 2005).

Some mutations have beneficial effects and become more common in a population over time through natural selection. A good example is the gene associated with **sickle-cell disease,** a blood disease common among African Americans in which red blood cells take on a sickle shape (described in more detail

cancer, bed-wetting, happiness, or some other phenomenon. However, most important human characteristics are **polygenic traits;** they are influenced by multiple pairs of genes, interacting with environmental factors, rather than by a single pair of genes (Turnpenny & Ellard, 2005). Examples of polygenic traits include height, weight, intelligence, personality, and susceptibility to cancer and depression.

When a trait is influenced by multiple genes, many degrees of the trait are possible, depending on which combinations of genes individuals inherit. The trait (for example, intelligence) tends to be distributed in the population according to the familiar bell-shaped or normal curve. Many people are near the mean of the distribution; fewer are at the extremes.

later in the chapter). It probably arose as a mutation but became more prevalent in Africa, Central America, and other tropical areas over many generations through natural selection because having one of the recessive sickle-cell genes protected people from malaria and allowed them to live longer and produce more children than people without the protective gene. Unfortunately, the sickle-cell gene does more harm than good where malaria is no longer a problem. Thus, mutations can be either beneficial or harmful, depending on their nature and on the environment in which their bearers live.

Chromosome Abnormalities

Genetic endowment can also influence human development through **chromosome abnormalities,** in which a child receives too many or too few chromosomes (or abnormal chromosomes) at conception. Most such abnormalities are caused by errors in chromosome division during meiosis. Through an accident of nature, an ovum or sperm cell may be produced with more or

Children with Down syndrome have distinctive eyelid folds, short limbs, and thick tongues.

© Peter Casolino/Alamy

fewer than the usual 23 chromosomes. In most cases, a zygote with the wrong number of chromosomes is spontaneously aborted; chromosome abnormalities are the main cause of pregnancy loss. However, around 1 child in 160 is born with more or, rarely, fewer chromosomes than the normal 46 (Simpson & Elias, 2003).

One familiar chromosome abnormality is **Down syndrome,** also known as *trisomy 21* because it is associated with three rather than two 21st chromosomes. Children with Down syndrome have distinctive eyelid folds, short stubby limbs, and thick tongues. Their levels of intellectual functioning vary widely, but they are typically mentally retarded to some degree and therefore develop and learn at a slower pace than most children. In some parts of the world, over half die in infancy, most often because of heart defects (Christianson, Howson, & Modell, 2006), but in the United States and other wealthy nations many people with Down syndrome are now living into middle age, when they commonly develop Alzheimer's disease, the degenerative brain disease which is sometimes traceable to a gene on Chromosome 21 (see Chapter 16). Improved medical care has lengthened their lives, and special education and other training programs have improved their functioning (Roizen & Patterson, 2003).

What determines who has a child with Down syndrome and who does not? Chance, partly. The errors in meiosis responsible for Down syndrome can occur in any mother—or father. However, the chances of chromosome abnormalities of various kinds and other birth defects increase as a parent's age increases (Cleary-Goldman et al., 2005). The chances of having a baby with Down syndrome are higher than previously thought—about 13 births in 10,000, or 1 birth in 733, in the United States (Centers for Disease Control and Prevention, 2006a). The odds increase with the mother's age, especially from about age 35 on (see ■ Figure 3.5). A father's age also has a bearing on the odds of a Down syndrome birth, especially if his partner is at least 35 years old. Indeed, couples older than 40 have about 6 times the risk of Down syndrome as couples younger than 35 (Fisch et al., 2003).

Why? As they age, ova and sperm are increasingly likely to be abnormal; mothers' eggs, which begin forming in the prenatal period, have more years to degenerate than sperm, which do not begin to be produced until puberty and are produced continuously thereafter. Older mothers and fathers are also more likely than younger ones to have been exposed to environmental hazards that can damage ova or sperm, such as radiation, drugs, chemicals, and viruses (Strigini et al., 1990). Finally, older mothers' bodies may be less likely than young mothers' bodies to spontaneously abort abnormal fetuses (Fisch et al., 2003). For a host of reasons, then, the fact that many adults today are delaying parenthood until their 30s or 40s is likely to translate into increased numbers of chromosome abnormalities.

Most chromosome abnormalities other than Down syndrome involve a child's receiving either too many or too few sex chromosomes (Wodrich, 2006). Like Down syndrome, these sex chromosome abnormalities can be attributed mainly to er-

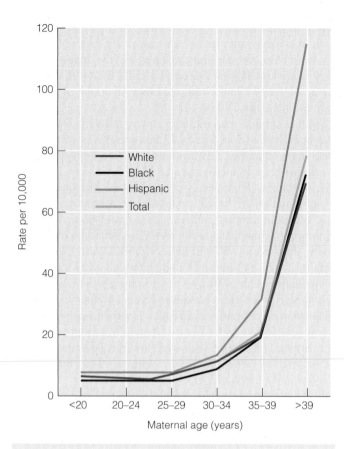

FIGURE 3.5 The rate of Down syndrome births increases steeply as the mother's age increases.
SOURCE: "Down Syndrome Prevalence at Birth" (1994).

rors in meiosis that become increasingly likely in older parents and in parents whose chromosomes have been damaged by environmental hazards. One well-known example is **Turner syndrome,** in which a female (about 1 in 3000) is born with a single X chromosome (XO). These girls remain small and often have stubby fingers and toes, a "webbed" neck, a broad chest, and underdeveloped breasts. They are unable to reproduce, typically favor traditionally feminine activities, and often have lower-than-average spatial and mathematical reasoning abilities (Downey et al., 1991).

Another example is **Klinefelter syndrome,** in which a male (1 in 200) is born with one or more extra X chromosomes (XXY). Klinefelter males tend to be tall and generally masculine in appearance, but they are sterile and at puberty develop feminine sex characteristics such as enlarged breasts. Most have normal general intelligence test scores, but many are below average in language skills and school achievement (Mandoki et al., 1991).

Finally, **fragile X syndrome** is worth noting because it is the most common hereditary cause of mental retardation (McConkie-Rosell et al., 2005). In this condition, one arm of the X chromosome is only barely connected to the rest of the chromosome and looks as if it is about to break off (hence the term *fragile*). Some affected individuals have large jaws and ears; most are mentally retarded. The abnormal X chromo-

some is caused by sex-linked inheritance and therefore is more common among males than females. The root of the condition is too many repeats or duplications of a sequence of three letters in the genetic code. The result is lack of a protein important to the formation of connections between neurons of the brain (O'Donnell & Warren, 2002). The number of repeats of the DNA segment responsible for fragile X syndrome increases from generation to generation if people with the sex-linked gene behind fragile X syndrome bear children, causing more serious mental retardation in later generations of an affected family.

Genetic Diagnosis and Counseling

Although 97% or more of babies will *not* be born with major birth defects, diseases and disorders associated with a single gene or pair of genes, polygene disorders, and chromosome abnormalities can profoundly affect human development (Brown, 2003; Simpson & Elias, 2003). **Genetic counseling** is a service that "helps people understand and adapt to the medical, psychological, and familial implications of genetic contributions to disease" (Resta et al., 2006, p. 77). Genetic counselors provide information on the nature, likelihood, and effects of genetic diseases and disorders to people who suspect or learn that they or their unborn children are at risk for some genetically based problem. They provide the information their clients need to make decisions but are careful not to make the decisions for them (Turnpenny & Ellard, 2005).

Thanks to the Human Genome Project and related research, today's genetic counselors have access to more information than ever about the nature, detection, and treatment of genetic defects and can quickly and inexpensively analyze a person's DNA from a cheek swab. Although we advise caution if you choose this option, you can even order a test kit and mail in a sample of your DNA to be analyzed—for a price, of course—to determine whether you have any of a number of genes associated with diseases and disorders (Boodman, 2006). To illustrate issues in genetic diagnosis and counseling, we focus on sickle-cell disease and Huntington's disease. Several other genetic diseases, including cystic fibrosis, hemophilia, phenylketonuria (PKU), and Tay-Sachs disease, are described in ● **Table 3.3.**

Suppose an African American couple visits a genetic counselor, takes a genetic test, and learns that they both are carriers of the recessive gene for sickle-cell disease. Individuals with this disease have sickle-shaped blood cells that tend to cluster together and distribute less oxygen through the circulatory system than normal cells do (Davidson, 2002). They have great difficulty breathing and exerting themselves, experience painful swelling of their joints, and often die early from heart or kidney failure. The genetic counselor might tell the couple that about 9% of African Americans in the United States have the genotype we will call *Ss*; they carry one dominant gene (S) that calls for round blood cells and one recessive gene (*s*) that calls for sickle-shaped blood cells (Thompson, 1975). Such people are called **carriers** because, although they do not have

DISEASE	DESCRIPTION	GENETIC MECHANISM	DIAGNOSIS AND TREATMENT
CYSTIC FIBROSIS	Glandular problem results in mucus buildup in lungs that makes breathing difficult and shortens life; common among Caucasians	Recessive gene pair; carriers were protected from epidemics of diarrhea in Europe	DNA test can identify most carriers, but so many mutations are possible that the tests for all are not feasible. Hours of physical therapy and antibiotics delivered by aerosol spray to keep lungs clear can prolong life, and experimental gene therapy has had some success
PHENYLKETONURIA (PKU)	Lack of enzyme needed to metabolize phenylalanine in milk and many other foods results in conversion of phenylalanine into an acid that attacks the nervous system and causes mental retardation	Recessive gene pair	Routinely screened for with a blood test at birth; special diet low in phenylalanine prevents brain damage
HEMOPHILIA	Deficiency in blood's ability to clot; more common in males than in females	Sex-linked inheritance (gene on X chromosome)	DNA analysis of cells obtained through CVS or amniocentesis can detect it; blood transfusions can improve clotting and reduce the negative effects of internal bleeding
HUNTINGTON'S DISEASE	Deterioration of the nervous system in middle age, associated with dementia, jerky movements, personality changes	Dominant gene	Test enables relatives to find out whether they have the gene; preimplantation genetic diagnosis of embryonic cells may be used to ensure a healthy child
SICKLE-CELL DISEASE	Blood cells are sickle-shaped rather than round, stick together, make breathing difficult, and cause painful swelling of joints; common in African Americans	Recessive gene pair; carriers were protected from malaria in Africa	Blood test can determine whether parents are carriers (newborns in the United States are screened with a blood test); antibiotics and blood transfusions relieve symptoms
TAY-SACHS DISEASE	Metabolic defect results in accumulation of fat in a child's brain, degeneration of the nervous system, and early death; common in Jewish people from Eastern Europe	Recessive gene pair	Blood test can determine whether parents are carriers, and fetal DNA analysis can determine whether a child is affected; medication may help, but most victims die in childhood

SOURCES: Davidson, 2002; Kingston, 2002; Simpson & Elias, 2003; Turnpenny & Ellard, 2005.

the disease, they can transmit the gene for it to their children. The child who inherits two recessive sickle-cell genes *(ss)* will have sickle-cell disease. The genetic counselor would therefore explain that an *Ss* father and an *Ss* mother (two carriers) have a one-in-four, or 25%, chance of having a child with sickle-cell disease *(ss)*.

This couple also has a two-in-four, or 50%, chance of having a child who will be a carrier like themselves. This is significant, the counselor would say, because the dominant gene associated with round blood cells shows incomplete dominance. As a result, carriers of the sickle-cell gene have many round blood cells and some sickle-shaped cells (see the photo on this page). When they are at high altitudes, are given anesthesia, or are otherwise deprived of oxygen, carriers may experience symptoms of sickle-cell disease—painful swelling of the joints and severe fatigue.

Sickle-shaped (elongated) and normal (round) blood cells from a carrier of the sickle-cell gene.

PRENATAL DETECTION OF ABNORMALITIES

Pregnant women today, especially those over 35 or 40, turn to a variety of medical techniques to tell them in advance whether their babies are likely to be normal (Simpson & Elias, 2003; Turnpenny & Ellard, 2005). The easiest and most commonly used method is **ultrasound** (also called sonography), the use of sound waves to scan the womb and create a visual image of the fetus on a monitor screen. Ultrasound can indicate how many fetuses are in the womb and whether they are alive, and it can detect genetic defects that produce visible physical abnormalities. Prospective parents often enjoy "meeting" their child and can find out (when the pregnancy is far enough along) whether their child is going to be a girl or a boy. Ultrasound is now widely used even when abnormalities are not suspected because it is considered very safe (Simpson & Elias, 2003).

To detect chromosome abnormalities such as Down syndrome and to determine, through DNA analysis, whether the genes for particular single gene-pair disorders are present, **amniocentesis** is commonly used. A needle is inserted into the abdomen, a sample of amniotic fluid is withdrawn, and fetal cells that have been shed are analyzed. The risk of miscarriage associated with amniocentesis turns out to be not the commonly cited 1 of 200 cases but as few as 1 in 1600 cases, no more than the risk for women who do not undergo amniocentesis (Eddleman et al., 2006). Thus the procedure can be considered safe and is often recommended for older mothers. Its main disadvantage is that it is not considered safe until the 15th week of pregnancy (Simpson & Elias, 2003).

Chorionic villus sampling (CVS) involves inserting a catheter through the mother's vagina and cervix (or, less commonly, through her abdomen) into the membrane called the *chorion* that surrounds the fetus, and then extracting tiny hair cells from the chorion that contain genetic material from the fetus. Sample cells are then analyzed for the same genetic defects that can be detected using amniocentesis. The difference is that chorionic villus sampling can be performed as early as the 10th week of pregnancy, allowing parents more time to consider the pros and cons of continuing the pregnancy if an abnormality is detected (Simpson & Elias, 2003). The risks of CVS are only slightly greater than those of amniocentesis; CVS is recommended more and more frequently today because it is quite safe and can be done earlier than amniocentesis.

Parents who have reason to believe they are at high risk to have a baby with a serious condition can minimize their risk by using new assisted reproductive technologies (see Chapter 4). **Preimplantation genetic diagnosis** involves fertilizing a mother's eggs with a father's sperm in the laboratory using in vitro fertilization (IVF) techniques, conducting DNA tests on the first cells that result from mitosis of each fertilized egg, and implanting in the mother's uterus only eggs that do not have chromosome abnormalities or genes associated with disorders (Bick & Lau, 2006; Simpson & Elias, 2003). Although costly, this option may appeal to couples who would not consider abortion but do not want to have a child with a serious defect. Preimplantation genetic diagnosis can now screen for more than 90% of the most common genetic disorders (Adams, 2003). It is controversial because it could be used not only to prevent disorders and diseases but also to try to create "designer" children with the characteristics parents want (Braude, 2006).

Finally, **maternal blood sampling** can yield fetal cells that slipped through the placenta into the mother's blood—cells that can then be analyzed with no risk at all to the fetus (Chiu & Lo, 2006; Yang, Kim, & Jung, 2002). This method is not yet accurate enough for regular use in clinical practice, however. Fetal cells only rarely make it to the mother's bloodstream and may be hard to distinguish from fetal cells left behind from previous pregnancies. Still, this noninvasive method of prenatal diagnosis will probably improve and become more common.

Prenatal diagnostic techniques such as ultrasound, amniocentesis, CVS, preimplantation genetic diagnosis, and maternal blood sampling can provide tremendously important information when there is reason to suspect a problem. Yet most couples can look forward to immense relief when they are told that their babies are just fine.

Ultrasound monitoring.

© PHOTOTAKE Inc./Alamy

After providing the couple with this information, the genetic counselor might discuss prenatal screening procedures that can detect many genetic abnormalities prenatally. Three widely used techniques—amniocentesis, chorionic villus sampling, and ultrasound—as well as the newer methods of preimplantation genetic diagnosis and maternal blood sampling, are described in the Explorations box on prenatal detection of abnormalities. For the parents whose tests reveal a normal embryo or fetus, the anxiety of undergoing the tests and waiting for the results gives way to relief. For parents who learn that their fetus has a serious defect, the experience can be agonizing. The alternatives may be abortion or the challenges of raising a child with a serious disorder. In the case of sickle-cell disease, a blood test is used to screen newborns for the disease, and affected children begin a life of treatment with blood transfusions and antibiotics to prevent infections (Davidson, 2002).

Now consider **Huntington's disease,** a famous (and terrifying) example of a genetic defect associated with a single dominant gene. It typically strikes in middle age and steadily deteriorates the nervous system. Among the effects are motor disturbances such as slurred speech, an erratic and seemingly drunken walk, grimaces, and jerky movements; personality changes such as increased moodiness and irritability; and dementia or loss of cognitive abilities (Bishop & Waldholz, 1990; Sutton-Brown & Suchowersky, 2003). Any child of a parent with Huntington's disease is almost certain to develop the disease if she receives the dominant (but fortunately rare) Huntington's gene rather than its normal counterpart gene at conception; the risk for an individual who has a parent with Huntington's disease is therefore one out of two, or 50%. (You may wish to work the odds for yourself using the approach shown in Figure 3.3.)

In 1983, James Gusella and his colleagues applied then emerging techniques for locating specific genes on specific chromosomes to study a large family with many cases of Huntington's disease and traced the gene for it to Chromosome 4 (Bishop & Waldholz, 1990). This discovery led to the development of a test to enable the relatives of Huntington's victims to find out whether or not they inherited the gene; some want to know, others do not (Sutton-Brown & Suchowersky, 2003; Wiggins et al., 1992). If it turns out that a prospective parent has the gene and the couple wishes to have children, preimplantation genetic diagnosis (see the Explorations box) can be used to test fertilized eggs for the presence of the Huntington's gene, and the doctor can then implant only eggs without the gene in the mother's uterus.

Genetic counselors must keep up with breakthroughs in prevention, diagnosis, and treatment of genetically related diseases and disorders. For the many conditions that are polygenic in origin, it is usually not possible to do a definitive test or even give solid odds, but genetic counselors nonetheless can educate families and attempt to correct their misunderstandings.

SUMMING UP

▌ Each person inherits a genotype contained in 20,000–25,000 genes on 23 pairs of chromosomes (including the sex chromosomes, XX or XY), half of which come from each parent.

▌ The Human Genome Project has revealed much about the human genome and research points to the importance of environment in influencing gene expression over a lifetime.

▌ Genotype influences phenotype (actual traits) through single gene-pair, sex-linked, and polygenic inheritance; mutations; and chromosome abnormalities such as Down syndrome.

▌ Genetic counseling provides information about genetic contributions to diseases and disorders; techniques of prenatal diagnosis include amniocentesis, chorionic villus sampling, ultrasound, preimplantation genetic diagnosis, and maternal blood sampling.

CRITICAL THINKING

1. Hairy forehead syndrome (we made it up) is caused by a single dominant gene, *H*. Using diagrams such as those in Figure 3.3 and Figure 3.4, figure out the odds that Herb (who has the genotype *Hh*) and Harriet (who also has the genotype *Hh*) will have a child with hairy forehead syndrome. Now repeat the exercise, but assume that hairy forehead syndrome is caused by a recessive gene, *h*, and that both parents again have an *Hh* genotype.

2. Alan is color blind, and we know that red–green color blindness is a sex-linked trait associated with a recessive gene. Knowing that he is color blind, what can you infer about Alan's parents and about his brothers and sisters?

3.3 | STUDYING GENETIC AND ENVIRONMENTAL INFLUENCES

How do researchers study the contributions of genes and environment to the normal range of variation among us in physical and psychological traits? **Behavioral genetics** is the scientific study of the extent to which genetic and environmental differences among people or animals are responsible for differences in their traits (Plomin et al., 2001, 2003). It is impossible to say that a given person's intelligence test score is the result of, say, 80%, 50%, or 20% heredity and the rest environment. The individual would have no intelligence without both genetic makeup and experiences. It is, however, possible for behavioral geneticists to estimate the **heritability** of measured IQ and of other traits or behaviors. Heritability has a specific meaning: the proportion of all the variability in the trait within a large sample of people that can be linked to genetic differences among those individuals. To say that measured intelligence is *heritable*, then, is to say that differences in tested IQ within a particular group of people are to some degree attributable to the different genetic endowments of these individuals. It is critical to understand that estimates of heritability differ from study to study depending on what sample is studied and how (Maccoby, 2000).

It may seem from their title that *behavioral geneticists* tell us only about genetic contributions to development, but in fact their work tells us about the contributions of both genetic and environmental factors to differences among people. The variability in a trait that is not associated with genetic differences is associated with differences in experiences and other environmental influences. Behavioral geneticists gather evidence through experimental breeding, family, and adoption studies. Their work is now being supplemented by use of techniques to study specific genes.

Experimental Breeding

To study the relative influence of genes and environment on animal behavior, behavioral geneticists sometimes design breeding experiments, much like those Gregor Mendel conducted to discover the workings of heredity in plants. For example, **selective breeding** involves attempting to breed animals for a particular trait to determine whether the trait is heritable. In a classic study, R. C. Tryon (1940) tested numerous rats for the ability to run a complex maze. Rats that made few errors were labeled *maze bright*; those that made many errors were termed *maze dull*. Then, across several generations, Tryon mated bright rats with bright rats and dull rats with dull rats. If differences in experience rather than differences in genetic makeup had accounted for maze performance differences in the first generation of rats studied, selective breeding would have had no effect. Instead, across generations, the differences in learning performance between the maze-bright and maze-dull groups of rats became increasingly larger. Tryon demonstrated that maze-learning ability in rats is influenced by genetic makeup.

Selective breeding studies have also shown that genes contribute to such attributes as activity level, emotionality, aggressiveness, and sex drive in rats, mice, and chickens (Plomin et al., 2001). Because people do not take kindly to the idea of being selectively bred, such research cannot be done with humans. Instead, research on genetic influence in humans has relied primarily on determining whether the degree of genetic similarity between pairs of people is associated with the degree of physical or psychological similarity between them.

Twin, Adoption, and Family Studies

Twins have long been recognized as important sources of evidence about the effects of heredity. A simple type of *twin study* involves determining whether identical twins reared together are more similar to each other in certain traits than fraternal twins reared together. If genes matter, identical twins should be more similar because they have 100% of their genes in common, whereas fraternal twins share only 50% on average.

Today, most sophisticated twin studies include not only identical and fraternal twin pairs raised together but also identical and fraternal twins reared apart—four groups in all, differing in both the extent to which they share the same genes and the extent to which they share the same home environment (Bouchard & Pedersen, 1999). Identical twins separated near birth and brought up in different environments—like the twins introduced at the beginning of the chapter—are particularly fascinating and informative because any similarities between them cannot be attributed to common family experiences.

Yet the twin method has been criticized. Some have charged that identical twins are treated more similarly than fraternal twins and that their more similar environment contributes to their greater similarity. Identical twins *are* treated more similarly. However, there appears to be little relationship between how similarly twins are treated and how similar they turn out to be psychologically (Loehlin, 1992). The more similar treatment identical twins receive is most likely caused by their genetic and psychological similarity (Reiss, 2005). Critics also charge that behavioral geneticists underestimate the role of prenatal influences and the possibility that identical twins are more psychologically similar than fraternal twins, even if they are separated after birth, because they share a more similar prenatal environment than fraternal twins or other siblings do (Devlin, Daniels, & Roeder, 1997). Finally, it has been charged that the twin method is more suited to identifying genetic influences than to identifying environmental ones. It asks whether twins who share 100% of their genes are more similar to one another than twins who share 50% of their genes, but it does not allow us to determine whether pairs of individuals who share exactly the same environment are more similar than pairs who share 50% of their experiences (Turkheimer, 2000).

A second commonly used method is the *adoption study*. Are children adopted early in life psychologically similar to their biological parents, whose genes they share, or are they similar to their adoptive parents, whose environment they share? If adopted children resemble their biological parents in intelligence or personality, even though those parents did not raise them, genes must be influential. If they resemble their adoptive parents, even though they are genetically unrelated to them, a good case can be made for environmental influence. Like the twin method, the adoption method has proved useful in estimating the relative contributions of heredity and environment to individual differences, but it also has been criticized. Researchers must appreciate that not only the genes of a biological mother but also the prenatal environment she provides could influence how an adopted child turns out (Gottlieb, Wahlsten, & Lickliter, 2006). They must also be careful to correct for the tendency of adoption agencies to place children in homes similar to those they were adopted from. In addition, researchers must recognize that because adoptive homes are generally above-average environments, adoption studies may underestimate the effect on human differences of the full range of variation in the environments families provide for children (Stoolmiller, 1999).

Finally, researchers are conducting complex *family studies* that include pairs of siblings who have different degrees of genetic similarity—for example, identical twins, fraternal twins, full biological siblings, half siblings, and unrelated stepsiblings who live together in stepfamilies (Reiss, 2000; Segal, 2000). They are also measuring qualities of these family members' experiences to determine how similar or different the environments of siblings are. Researchers are even looking at all of this longitudinally so that they can assess the extent to which both genes and environment contribute to continuity and change in traits as individuals develop (Reiss, 2000).

Estimating Influences

Having conducted a twin, adoption, or family study, behavioral geneticists use statistical calculations to estimate the degree to which heredity and environment account for individual differences in a trait of interest. When they study traits that a person either has or does not have (for example, a smoking habit or diabetes), researchers calculate and compare **concordance rates**—the percentage of pairs of people studied (for example, pairs of identical twins or adoptive parents and children) in which, if one member of a pair displays the trait, the other does, too. If concordance rates are higher for more genetically related than for less genetically related pairs of people, the trait is heritable.

Suppose researchers are interested in whether homosexuality is genetically influenced. They might locate men who are gay and who have twins, either identical or fraternal, locate their twin siblings, and find out whether they, too, are gay. In one study of this type (Bailey & Pillard, 1991), the concordance rate for identical twins was 52% (29 of the 56 twins of gay men

Twins are concordant if they both display a trait of interest such as smoking.

were also gay), whereas the concordance rate for fraternal twins was 22% (12 of 54 twins of gay men were also gay). This finding and others suggest that genetic makeup contributes to both men's and women's sexual orientation (Bailey, Dunne, & Martin, 2000). But notice that identical twins are *not* perfectly concordant. Environmental factors must also affect sexual orientation. After all, Bailey and Pillard found that, in 48% of the identical twin pairs, one twin was gay but the other was not, despite their identical genes.

When a trait can be present in varying degrees, as is true of height or intelligence, correlation coefficients rather than concordance rates are calculated (see Chapter 1). In a behavioral genetics study of IQ scores, a correlation would indicate whether the IQ score of one twin is systematically related to the IQ score of the other, such that if one twin is bright, the other is bright, and if one is not so bright, the other is not so bright. The larger the correlation for a group of twins, the closer the resemblance between members of twin pairs.

To better appreciate the logic of behavioral genetics studies, consider what Robert Plomin and his colleagues (Plomin et al., 1988) found when they assessed aspects of personality among twins in Sweden whose ages averaged 59. One of their measures assessed an aspect of emotionality—the tendency to be angry or quick tempered. The scale was given to many pairs of identical twins and fraternal twins—some pairs raised together, others separated near birth and raised apart. Correlations reflecting the degree of similarity between twins are presented in ● **Table 3.4.** From such data, behavioral geneticists can estimate the contributions of three factors to individual differences in emotionality: genes, shared environmental influences, and nonshared environmental influences.

1. *Genes.* In the example in Table 3.4, genetic influences are clearly evident, for identical twins are consistently more

● **TABLE 3.4   CORRELATIONS FROM A TWIN STUDY OF THE HERITABILITY OF ANGRY EMOTIONALITY**

	RAISED TOGETHER	RAISED APART
Identical twin pairs	0.37	0.33
Fraternal twin pairs	0.17	0.09

By dissecting this table, you can assess the contributions of genes, shared environment, and nonshared environment to individual differences in angry emotionality.
Genes. Are identical twins more similar than fraternal twins? Yes: 0.37 is greater than 0.17, and 0.33 is greater than 0.09; therefore greater genetic similarity is associated with greater emotional similarity.
Shared environment. Are twins who grow up together more similar than twins raised apart? Only a small effect of shared environment is evident: 0.37 is slightly greater than 0.33, and 0.17 is slightly greater than 0.09.
Nonshared environment. Are identical twins raised in the same home dissimilar, despite sharing 100% of their genes and the same environment? Yes: a correlation of .37 is far less than a perfect correlation of 1.00, suggesting a good deal of nonshared environmental influence.
SOURCE: From EAS temperaments during the last half of the life span: Twins reared apart and twins reared together by R. Plomin, et al. from *Psychology and Aging, 3,* 1988. Copyright 1988 by The American Psychological Association. Reprinted by permission.

similar in emotionality than fraternal twins are. The correlation of 0.33 for identical twins reared apart also testifies to the importance of genetic makeup. If identical twins grow up in different families, any similarity in their psychological traits must be caused by their genetic similarity. These data suggest that emotionality is heritable; about a third of the variation in emotionality in this sample can be linked to variations in genetic endowment.

2. *Shared environmental influences.* Individuals living in the same home environment experience **shared environmental influences,** common experiences that work to make them similar—for example, a common parenting style or exposure to the same toys, peers, schools, and neighborhood. Do you see evidence of shared environmental influences in the correlations in Table 3.4? Notice that both identical and fraternal twins are slightly more similar in emotionality if they are raised together than if they are raised apart (0.37 exceeds 0.33, 0.17 exceeds 0.09). However, these correlations tell us that shared environmental influences are weak: twins are almost as similar when they grew up in different homes as when they grew up in the same home.

3. *Nonshared environmental influences.* Experiences unique to the individual—those that are not shared by other members of the family and that work to make individuals different from each other—are referred to as **nonshared environmental influences.** Whether they involve being treated differently by parents, having different friends or teachers, undergoing different life crises, or even being affected differently by the same events, nonshared environmental influences make members of the same family different (Rowe, 1994). In Table 3.4, notice that identical twins raised together are not the same, even though they share 100% of their genes *and* the same family environment; a correlation of 0.37 is much lower than a perfect correlation of 1.00. Any differences between

If you have brothers and sisters, do you think your parents treated you better or worse than they treated your siblings? If so, what might have been the effects of these nonshared environmental influences on your development?

identical twins raised together must be either because of differences in their unique, or nonshared, experiences or because of errors in measuring the trait.

Anyone who has a brother or sister can attest that different children in the same family are not always treated identically by their parents. Moreover, studies of identical twins have revealed systematic relationships between differences in their birth weight and early family experiences and differences in such characteristics as their levels of anxiety, conduct problems, and academic achievement (Asbury, Dunn, & Plomin, 2006). Thus, failing to find strong shared environmental influences on a trait does not mean that family influences are unimportant. There could be nonshared environmental influences, both within and outside the home, working to make children in the same family different rather than similar.

Despite their weaknesses, twin, adoption, and family studies have taught us a great deal about the contributions of genes, shared environment, and nonshared environment to similarities and differences among humans. Some developmentalists, because they believe that genetic and environmental influences are intertwined, fault the methods used by behavioral geneticists and their approach of trying to separate the contributions of nature and nurture (Gottlieb, 2002; Lewontin, Rose, & Kamin, 1984). We will return to these criticisms later.

Molecular Genetics

The Human Genome Project, by providing a map of the human genome, has opened the door to exciting new approaches to studying genetic and environmental influence. **Molecular genetics** is the analysis of particular genes and their effects, including identification of specific genes that influence particular traits and comparison of animals or humans who have these specific genes with those who do not. Once a specific gene's location and role are known, it is possible to test people's DNA samples for the presence of the gene and study how people who have a particular variant of a gene differ from those who have different variants of it.

Methods based on molecular genetics are being used to identify the multiple genes that contribute to polygenic traits (Plomin et al., 2003; Rende & Waldman, 2006). The goal is to say things such as "this gene accounts for 20% of the variation, and these two other genes account for 10% of the variation each," in a phenotype or trait of interest (for example, reading ability or depression). So far, analyses based on molecular genetics suggest that many genes contribute to each polygenic trait or disorder and that each gene's contribution is very small—less than 1% of the variation each in the case of genes potentially influencing intelligence (Plomin, Kennedy, & Craig, 2006).

Consider Alzheimer's disease, the most common cause of dementia in later life (Williams, 2003; also see Chapter 16). Twin studies indicate that it is herita-

© Bubbles Photolibrary/Alamy

ble (Gatz et al., 2006), but what genes are behind it? Molecular genetics can help answer that question. Researchers have been looking closely at a gene called *apolipoprotein E*, or *apoE*. One of several variants of apoE, apoE4, has been linked to a higher-than-normal risk of Alzheimer's. Although apoE4 is only one contributor to Alzheimer's disease and many Alzheimer's patients do not have the gene, researchers can now test research participants for the presence of apoE4, then study differences between individuals with the gene and individuals without it. In one such study (Hofer et al., 2002), elderly adults with the apoE4 gene showed greater memory deterioration over a 7-year period than did individuals without it, even though none of the participants had diagnosable Alzheimer's disease yet. Other researchers are finding that certain environmental factors such as head injury and a high cholesterol level increase the odds that a person with the apoE4 gene will develop Alzheimer's disease (Williams, 2003). Genetic research may soon make it possible to identify early, based on their genetic makeup and their cognitive functioning, people who will develop Alzheimer's disease and who can benefit from treatment for it (see Chapter 16).

Because it is now possible to compare large samples of people who do or do not have particular gene variants using molecular genetics, researchers may not need to rely as much in the future on studies of twins and adopted individuals. They will also become better able to answer important questions about how specific genes and combinations of genes interact with specific environmental factors to shape development (Hutchinson et al., 2004; Posthuma & de Geus, 2006).

SUMMING UP

▪ Behavioral genetics studies the heritability of a trait (the percentage of variability in a population that can be linked to genetic differences among individuals), as well as the contributions of shared environmental influences that make individuals in the same family similar and of the nonshared environmental influences that make family members different.

▪ Methods of study include selective breeding studies of animals, and twin, adoption, and family studies of humans in which concordance rates and correlation coefficients are calculated.

▪ Molecular genetics is used to identify specific gene variants that contribute to traits and to compare people who do or do not have these variants.

CRITICAL THINKING

1. Design a twin study and an adoption study to study the contributions of genes and environment to whether or not a person smokes. Explain what patterns of results would provide evidence of a genetic influence on smoking.

2. Focusing on families you know, illustrate how genes, shared environmental influences, and nonshared environmental influences could each help explain why some teenagers are more talkative than others are.

3.4 | ACCOUNTING FOR INDIVIDUAL DIFFERENCES

Findings from behavioral genetics studies have challenged and changed understandings of human development, as you will see throughout this book. We give a few examples here, drawn from studies of intellectual abilities, temperament and personality, and psychological disorders (see Plomin et al., 2001, 2003; Rowe, 1994, for reviews). Expect some surprises.

Intellectual Abilities

How do genes and environment contribute to differences in intellectual functioning, and how do their relative contributions change over the life span? Consider the average correlations between the IQ scores of different pairs of relatives presented in ● Table 3.5. These averages are primarily from a review by Thomas Bouchard Jr. and Matthew McGue (1981) of studies involving 526 correlations based on 113,942 pairs of children, adolescents, and adults. Clearly, correlations are higher when people are closely related genetically than when they are not and are highest when they are identical twins. Overall, the heritability of IQ scores is about 0.50, meaning that genetic differences account for about 50% of the variation in IQ scores and environmental differences account for the other half of the variation in the samples studied (Plomin, 1990).

Can you detect the workings of environment in the table? Notice that (1) pairs of family members reared together are somewhat more similar in IQ than pairs reared apart; (2) frater-

● TABLE 3.5 AVERAGE CORRELATIONS BETWEEN THE IQ SCORES OF PAIRS OF INDIVIDUALS

FAMILY PAIRS	RAISED TOGETHER	RAISED APART
Identical twins	0.86	0.72
Fraternal twins	0.60	0.52
Biological siblings	0.47	0.24
Biological parent and child	0.42	0.22
Half siblings	0.31	—
Adopted siblings	0.34	—
Adoptive parent and adopted child	0.19	—
Unrelated siblings (same age, same home)	0.26	—

SOURCE: All but two of these averages were calculated by Bouchard and McGue (1981) from studies of both children and adults. The correlation for fraternal twins reared apart is based on data reported by Pedersen et al. (1985); that for unrelated children in the same home is based on data reported by Segal (2000).

nal twins, who should have especially similar family experiences because they grow up at the same time, tend to be more alike than siblings born at different times; and (3) the IQs of adopted children are related to those of their adoptive parents. All of these findings suggest that *shared* environmental influences tend to make individuals who live together more alike than if they lived separately. Notice, however, that genetically identical twins reared together are not perfectly similar. This is evidence that their unique or *nonshared* experiences have made them different.

Do the contributions of genes and environment to differences in intellectual ability change over the life span? You might guess that genetic influences would decrease as children accumulate learning experiences, but you would be wrong. Genetic endowment appears to gain rather than lose importance from infancy to adulthood as a source of individual differences in intellectual performance (McCartney, Harris, & Bernieri, 1990; Plomin & Spinath, 2004).

In a longitudinal study of identical and fraternal twins conducted by Ronald Wilson (1978, 1983), identical twins scored no more similarly than fraternal twins on a measure of infant mental development during the first year of life; thus, evidence of heritability was lacking in infancy. This may be because powerful maturational forces keep redirecting infants back to the same species-wide developmental pathway, regardless of specific genetic makeup or experiences (McCall, 1981). The influence of individual heredity began to show by around 18 months of age. Identical twins even experienced more similar spurts in intellectual development than fraternal twins.

The identical twins in Wilson's study stayed highly similar throughout childhood and into adolescence, the correlation between their IQ scores averaging about 0.85. Meanwhile, fraternal twins became *less* similar over the years; the correlation between their IQ scores had dropped to 0.54 by adolescence. As a result, the heritability of IQ scores increased from infancy to adolescence. The contribution of genes to individual differences in IQ remains high during adulthood, and even in old age, although some studies suggest that genetic influence may diminish somewhat as chronic diseases become more common and make even identical twins more dissimilar (Vogler, 2006). Studies using the techniques of molecular genetics are beginning to identify specific genes on several chromosomes that make at least a small contribution to intelligence and that can now be studied in interaction with specific environmental factors (Posthuma & de Geus, 2006).

Whereas the heritability of intelligence test performance increases with age, shared environmental influences become less significant with age, explaining about 30% of the variation in IQ in childhood but close to 0% in adulthood (McGue et al., 1993; Plomin & Spinath, 2004). Why might this be? Siblings are probably exposed to similar (shared) learning experiences when they are young. As they age, partly because of their different genetic makeups, they may seek and have different (nonshared) life experiences. They may elicit different reactions from their parents, join different peer groups, encounter different teachers, and so on.

Does evidence of the heritability of IQ scores mean that we cannot improve children's intellectual development by enriching their environment? Not at all. True, the IQs of adopted children are, by adolescence, correlated more strongly with the IQs of their biological parents than with the IQs of their adoptive parents. However, the *level* of intellectual performance that adopted children reach can increase dramatically (by 20 points on an IQ test) if they are adopted into more intellectually stimulating homes than those provided by their biological parents (Scarr & Weinberg, 1978, 1983; Van IJzendoorn & Juffer, 2005). Most likely, then, stimulating environments help children realize more fully their genetically based potentials. It is critical for parents, teachers, and others concerned with optimizing development to understand that genetically influenced qualities can very often be altered.

Temperament and Personality

As parents know well, different babies have different personalities. In trying to describe infant personality, researchers have focused on aspects of **temperament**—tendencies to respond in predictable ways, such as sociability and emotional reactivity, that serve as the building blocks of later personality (see Chapter 11 for a fuller description of temperament). Behavioral genetics research indicates that genes contribute to individual differences in temperament in infancy and to not only continuity but also change in later personality (Ebstein, Benjamin, & Belmaker, 2003; Krueger, Johnson, & Kling, 2006).

Arnold Buss and Robert Plomin (1984) reported average correlations from around 0.50 to 0.60 between the temperament scores of identical twins. The corresponding correlations for fraternal twins were not much greater than zero. Think about that: a zero correlation is what you would expect if they were strangers living in different homes rather than fraternal twins who, on average, share half their genes, the same home, and often the same bedroom! It does not seem to matter

The temperament of infants is genetically influenced. (These twins look a bit wary.)

whether researchers look at fraternal twin pairs, ordinary siblings, or unrelated children adopted into the same family, *living in the same home does not seem to make children more similar in personality* (Dunn & Plomin, 1990).

Similar conclusions have been reached about the contributions of genes and environment to adult personality (Krueger, Johnson, & Kling, 2006; Loehlin et al., 1998; see also Chapter 11). The same major dimensions of personality are evident in people from a variety of cultures and appear to have a genetic basis (Yamagata et al., 2006). Of all the differences among adults on major dimensions of personality, about 40% of the variation is attributable to genetic differences (Loehlin, 1985). Only 5% of the variation reflects the effects of shared family environment. Indeed, identical twins are about as similar in personality when they are raised apart as when they grow up in the same home (Bouchard et al., 1990). The remaining 55% of the variability in adult personalities is associated with nonshared environmental influences, ways in which experiences within or outside the family make siblings different from each other.

Family environment is important in personality development but usually not because it has a standard effect on all family members that makes them alike. Parents do appear to influence their children to adopt attitudes and interests similar to their own, at least while they are living at home (Eaves et al., 1997; Plomin et al., 2001). Shared environment also helps make adolescent siblings similar in the extent to which they engage in delinquent behavior (Rowe, 1994) and smoke, drink, and use other substances, mostly because siblings influence one another (Hopfer, Crowley, & Hewitt, 2003). Yet behavioral geneticists have discovered repeatedly that environment often plays a more important role in creating differences among family members than in creating similarities among them (Reiss, 2000; Rowe, 1994). When it comes to many personality traits, unique, nonshared environmental influences rather than shared ones, along with genes, seem to be most significant.

Researchers who once assumed that parents molded all their children's personalities in similar directions are now trying to link differences in the personalities of brothers and sisters to differences in their experiences (Dunn & Plomin, 1990; Reiss, 2000). In one study of identical twins, for example, negative parental feelings toward and harsh discipline of one identical twin were correlated with more acting out by that twin than by the twin who was treated more kindly (Asbury et al., 2003). Because identical twins have identical genes, this finding cannot be interpreted as an example of genes influencing parents' reactions to a child.

Much more needs to be understood about nonshared environmental influences. Developmentalists have assumed for too long that parents treat all their children much the same and steer them along similar developmental paths (Harris, 1998). Increasingly, it seems more useful to ask how genetic differences and nonshared experiences, both inside and outside the home, steer brothers and sisters along *different* developmental paths.

Psychological Disorders

As you will see in this book, both genes and environment contribute to psychological disorders across the life span—to alcohol and drug abuse, autism, depression, attention deficit hyperactivity disorder, eating disorders, aggressive and criminal behavior, Alzheimer's disease, and every other psychological disorder that has been studied (Plomin & McGuffin, 2003; Rende & Waldman, 2006; Rutter et al., 2006; and see Chapter 16 for information about the heritability of several of these disorders). Usually it's a matter of multiple genes, each fairly common, making a small contribution, along with multiple environmental factors, to the development of a disorder (Rutter et al., 2006).

Here consider just one example. **Schizophrenia** is a serious mental illness that involves disturbances in logical thinking, emotional expression, and social behavior and that typically emerges in late adolescence or early adulthood. In the 1950s and 1960s, experts were convinced it was caused by mothers who were cold and inconsistent in their parenting style but that has been proven wrong (Rowe & Jacobson, 1999). Now we know that genes contribute substantially to this disorder, although there are probably many genes and it is not yet clear which are most influential (Gottesman & Hanson, 2005). The average concordance rate for schizophrenia in identical twin pairs is 48%; if one twin has the disorder, in 48% of the pairs studied, the other has it, too (Gottesman, 1991; Owen & O'Donovan, 2003). By comparison, the concordance rate for fraternal twins is only 17%. In addition, children who have at least one biological parent who is schizophrenic have an increased risk of schizophrenia *even if they are adopted away early in life* (Heston, 1970). Thus, the increased risk these children face has more to do with their genes than with being brought up by a schizophrenic adult.

It is easy to conclude, mistakenly, that any child of a person with schizophrenia is doomed to become schizophrenic. But here are the facts: Whereas about 1% of people in the general population develop schizophrenia, about 13% of children who have a schizophrenic parent become schizophrenic (Cardno & Murray, 2003; Gottesman, 1991). So, although children of people with schizophrenia are at greater risk for schizophrenia than other children, 87% or so of the children of one schizophrenic parent do *not* develop the disorder. Even for the child of two parents with schizophrenia or for an identical twin whose twin develops the disorder, the odds of developing schizophrenia are only about one in two.

Clearly, then, environmental factors also contribute significantly to this mental illness. People do not inherit psychological disorders; they inherit *predispositions* to develop disorders. Genes and environment then interact so that a person who has inherited a genetic susceptibility to schizophrenia will likely not develop the disorder unless he also has stressful experiences that trigger the illness. For example, genetically at-risk children who are exposed to an infectious disease prenatally or who experience oxygen deprivation during delivery are more likely to develop schizophrenia (Cannon et al., 2003). And adopted children who have a biological parent with schizophrenia are at greater risk of developing schizophrenia if they grow up in a dysfunctional adoptive home than if they grow up in a healthy family environment (Tienari et al., 2004). Adopted children without a genetic risk for schizophrenia are unlikely to develop the disorder even if they grow up in a dysfunctional family.

In short, children may inherit predispositions to develop several problems and disorders and their experiences will interact with their genetic makeup to determine how well adjusted they turn out to be. Such research also shows that it is overly simple and often wrong to assume that any behavioral problem a child displays must be the result of bad parenting.

The Heritability of Different Traits

Although genes contribute to variation in virtually all human traits that have been studied, some traits are more heritable than others (Bouchard, 2004). ■ **Figure 3.6** presents some correlations obtained in the Minnesota Twin Study between the traits of identical twins raised apart and reunited later in life.

Observable physical characteristics, from eye color to height, are strongly associated with individual genetic endowment. Even weight is heritable; adopted children resemble their biological parents but not their adoptive parents in weight (Grilo & Pogue-Geile, 1991). Certain aspects of physiology,

such as measured brain activity and reactions to alcohol, are highly heritable, too (Lykken, Tellegen, & Iacono, 1982; Neale & Martin, 1989), as is level of physical activity (Eriksson, Rasmussen, & Tynelius, 2006). In addition, genetic differences among older adults contribute to differences in their functioning and rates of aging (Arking, 2006; Vogler, 2006). For example, genes influence both levels of performance and changes in performance over time in markers of aging such as lung capacity and arterial blood pressure (Finkel et al., 2003a). Genes also contribute to susceptibilities to many diseases associated with aging, and genetic differences account for about one-third of the variation in longevity (Arking, 2006; see also Chapter 17).

If physical and physiological characteristics are strongly heritable, general intelligence is moderately heritable: 50% or more of the variation among people (almost 70% in the study summarized in Figure 3.6) is attributable to genes. Somewhat less influenced by genes are aspects of temperament and personality, for which about 40 to 50% of the variation can be traced to genes, and susceptibility to many psychological disorders, for which heritability varies widely from condition to condition. Genetic endowment contributes, but only modestly, to differences in attitudes and interests, which are influenced primarily by nonshared experiences (Olson et al., 2001; Rowe, 1994). Even politically liberal or conservative attitudes are partly influenced by genes, possibly through genetic influence on personality (Alford, Funk, & Hibbing, 2005).

What *isn't* influenced by genes? Political party is one example; it is more influenced by shared environment than by genes (Alford, Funk, & Hibbing, 2005). The security of a child's attachment to parents is another. In one study of identical and fraternal twins (Fearon et al., 2006), a mother's degree of sensitivity affected the security of attachment of both her twin infants to her, but this shared environmental influence was evident whether the twins were identical or fraternal. Identical twins were not more similar than fraternal twins in attachment security the way they should be if genes were the determining factor. Nonshared experiences were even more important in shaping security of attachment.

Individual differences in creativity also do not appear to be closely tied to genes. Identical twins are not much more alike than fraternal twins, so heritability is low. However, twins of both sorts are similar to one another, suggesting that the shared environment is somehow important in nurturing creativity, possibly because certain parents give their children a good deal of freedom to be inventive and others make their children color within the lines (Plomin et al., 2001; Reznikoff et al., 1973). The case is not closed, however; recent research using molecular genetics has revealed possible associations between specific genes and performance on tests of creativity (Reuter et al., 2006).

In sum, heredity influences physical traits more than intelligence; intelligence more than personality, certain attitudes, and interests; and some traits such as political party, security of attachment, and creativity

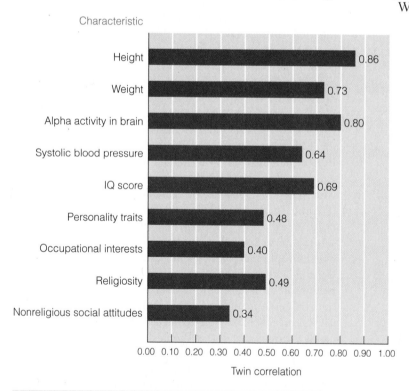

Characteristic

	Twin correlation
Height	0.86
Weight	0.73
Alpha activity in brain	0.80
Systolic blood pressure	0.64
IQ score	0.69
Personality traits	0.48
Occupational interests	0.40
Religiosity	0.49
Nonreligious social attitudes	0.34

0.00 0.10 0.20 0.30 0.40 0.50 0.60 0.70 0.80 0.90 1.00

Twin correlation

■ **FIGURE 3.6** Correlations between the traits of identical twins raised apart in the Minnesota Twin Study.

SOURCE: From T.J. Bouchard Jr., D.T. Lykken, M. McGue, N.L. Segal, & A. Tellegen, Sources of psychological differences: The Minnesota Study of Twins Reared Apart, *Science, 250,* pp. 223–228. Copyright © 1990, The American Association for the Advancement of Science. Reprinted with permission.

even less. However, the vast majority of psychological traits are heritable to some extent, with genes accounting for up to half of the variation in a group and environmental factors (shared environmental ones in childhood but more often nonshared environmental ones) accounting for the other half or more of the variation (Plomin et al., 2001; Wachs, 2000).

Influences on Heritability

Heritability is not a fixed quality; rather it varies depending on the sample studied. First, it varies in relation to the age of the sample, as you have already seen. In a particularly striking example of this, an eating disorders survey was administered to female twins who were age 11 and prepubertal, age 11 and pubertal, and age 17 and pubertal (Klump, McGue, & Iacono, 2003). Genes explained 54% of the variation in survey responses indicative of high risk for eating disorders among girls who had reached puberty but 0% among the 11-year-old girls who had not yet reached puberty. For prepubertal girls, shared environmental factors were the most important influence on responses. This study hints that genes that help trigger eating disorders in adolescence may be activated by the biochemical changes associated with puberty and may not be expressed before adolescence.

Second, heritability estimates differ depending on the environment of the individuals studied. Many classic twin and adoption studies have involved children and adults from middle-class environments, and they have shown that genetic differences among children have a lot to do with IQ differences. However, Eric Turkheimer and his colleagues (2003) studied the heritability of IQ in a sample that included many children from very low-income families as well as children from affluent homes. As shown in ■ **Figure 3.7**, among children from wealthy

families, genes accounted for 72% of the variation in IQ, whereas shared environment was not important—as in most previous studies. By contrast, genes explained only about 10% of the variation in IQ among children from poor families; instead, shared environmental influences accounted for almost 60% of the variation.

This finding could mean that a deprived and unstimulating environment drags most children down, regardless of whether their genetic potential is high or low, but that some families living in poverty are able to offer a home environment that helps their children thrive despite their economic disadvantage. In more affluent environments, children may have more freedom to build niches that suit their genetically based predispositions and that then make them more or less intellectually inclined depending on their unique genetic makeup (Kendler, 2003). It is too early to tell; not all studies of socioeconomic differences in heritability agree (Rutter et al., 2006). It is clear, though, that the heritability of a trait is not one fixed number. It is a range of numbers affected by the age, socioeconomic status, and other qualities of the individuals studied (Rutter et al., 2006).

Low SES   **High SES**

■ Genes   □ Shared environment   ■ Nonshared environment

■ **FIGURE 3.7** The proportions of variance in child IQ scores explained by genes, shared environment, and nonshared environment differ for children from low or high socioeconomic status (SES) environments.
SOURCE: From E. Turkheimer, M. Haley, B. D'Onofrio, & I.I. Gottesman, Socioeconomic status modifies heritability of IQ in young children, *Psychological Science*, 9, 623–628. Copyright © 2003 Blackwell Publishing. Reprinted with permission.

SUMMING UP

▌ Behavioral genetics research shows that intellectual abilities are heritable and that the contribution of genes increases with age, whereas the contribution of shared environment decreases with age.

▌ Differences in infant temperament and adult personality are largely attributable to genes and nonshared, but not shared, environment.

▌ Many psychological disorders such as schizophrenia are rooted in an interaction of genes and environmental stressors.

▌ Physical and physiological characteristics are more strongly influenced by genes than are intellectual abilities and, in turn, personality and attitudes; certain traits such as security of attachment and creativity do not seem to be heritable.

▌ Heritability differs depending on the age and socioeconomic status of the sample studied.

CRITICAL THINKING

1. There's surely no gene that makes people politically liberal or politically conservative; yet political liberalism–conservatism is heritable. Develop an explanation of how genes could influence it. While you're at it, how might shared environment and nonshared environment influence it?

2. Alan's biological parents both had schizophrenia, so he was placed in an adoptive home when he was only 1 year old. He grew up with his adoptive parents (neither of whom had psychological disorders) from then on. What would you tell Alan about his chances of becoming schizophrenic if you were a genetic counselor?

What should we conclude overall about the influences of genes and environment and about the ways in which these two great forces in development conspire to make us what we are? Genes clearly do not orchestrate our growth before birth and then leave us alone. Instead, they are "turning on" and "turning off" in patterned ways throughout the life span, helping shape the attributes and behavioral patterns that we carry with us through our lives and changing their activity in response to environmental stimuli (Gottlieb, 2002). An evolved and shared species heredity makes us similar in the ways we develop and age. Unique individual genetic makeups cause us to develop and age in our own ways. No less important are environmental influences, from conception to death.

From infancy through childhood and adolescence, children's unique genetic potentials increasingly show themselves in their behavior. Identical twins start out similar and remain similar, but fraternal twins, like brothers and sisters generally, go their own ways and become increasingly dissimilar. Shared environmental influences—the forces that make children in the same family alike—are stronger early in life than they are later in life. Nonshared environmental influences—those unique experiences that make members of the family different—remain important throughout the life span. In short, as we move out of the home and into the larger world, we seem to become, increasingly, products of our unique genes and our unique experiences. But the two do not operate independently. Genes and environment are interrelated in interesting and important ways.

As you have seen throughout this chapter, behavioral geneticists try to establish how much of the variation observed in human traits such as intelligence can be attributed to individual differences in genetic makeup and how much can be attributed to individual differences in experience. Useful as that research is, it does not take us far in understanding the complex interplay between genes and environment over the life span (Turkheimer, 2000). As Ann Anastasi (1958) asserted many years ago, instead of asking *how much* is because of genes and how much is because of environment, researchers should be asking *how* heredity and environment work together to make us what we are. With that in mind, consider the workings of two tremendously important developmental mechanisms: gene–environment interactions and gene–environment correlations (Rowe, 2003; Rutter et al., 2006).

Gene–Environment Interactions

Genes do not determine anything; instead, they provide us with potentials that are realized or not depending on the quality of our experiences. Consider an interesting study using modern molecular genetics techniques that allow one to look at the effects of a specific gene in combination with a specific environmental risk factor (also see Rutter et al., 2006). Avshalom Caspi and his colleagues (2003) sought to understand why stressful experiences cause some people but not others to become depressed. Using a large sample of New Zealanders who had been studied longitudinally, Caspi's team performed DNA analysis to determine which variants of a gene known to affect levels of the neurotransmitter serotonin in the brain each person in the sample had (serotonin level has been linked to depression). They also administered surveys to measure the stressful events each person had experienced between ages 21 and 26, and whether, at age 26, each person had experienced a diagnosable case of depression in the past year.

In ■ **Figure 3.8,** you can see that genes matter (having genes that predispose a person to depression results in a slightly higher probability of depression overall than having genes that protect against depression). You also see that environment matters (overall, depression becomes more likely as the number of stressful events a person experiences increases). The real message in the figure, however, is embodied in the concept of **gene–environment interaction**: how our genotypes are expressed depends on what kind of environment we experience, and how we respond to the environment depends on what kind of genes we have. In Figure 3.8, you see that individuals with two of the high-risk variants of the gene studied are more vulnerable to depression than people with two of the protective variants of the gene, but *only* if they experience multiple stressful events. By comparison, even multiple stressful events will not easily cause people with the protective genes to become depressed. Thus the genes people have make a difference only when their environment is stressful, and a stressful environment

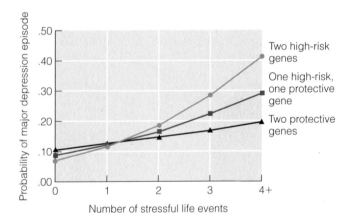

FIGURE 3.8 The odds of a depressive episode at age 26 are highest for individuals who: (1) inherit two genes known to increase the risk of depression rather than two genes known to protect against depression, and (2) experience four or more stressful life events between ages 21 and 26. This is an example of gene–environment interaction: the effects of genetic makeup on depression depend on how stressful a person's environment is, and the effects of stressful life events depend on the person's genotype.

SOURCE: Reprinted with permission from Caspi et al. (2003). Influences of life stress on depression. *Science*, July 18, Vol 301, p 388, Figure 1B. Copyright © 2003 AAAS. http://www.sciencemag.org.

has an effect only on individuals with a genotype that predisposes them to depression. Genes and environment interact.

It may turn out to be this way for many disorders: it often takes a combination of high-risk genes and a high-risk environment to trigger problems (Caspi et al., 2003). For example, the odds of depression also increase if children with a predisposing gene (a gene different from the gene discussed above) are neglected or abused (Caspi, Sugden, et al., 2003), and conduct disorders in children are especially likely when children who are at genetic risk for conduct problems are physically abused (Jaffee et al., 2005). For some time, researchers believed that gene–environment interactions were rare, but more and more evidence of them is now emerging as researchers look, as in Figure 3.8, at interactions between specific genes and specific environmental factors (Rutter et al., 2006).

Gene–Environment Correlations

Each person's genetic makeup also influences the kinds of experiences she seeks and has. Sandra Scarr and Kathleen McCartney (1983), drawing on the theorizing of Robert Plomin, John DeFries, and John Loehlin (1977), have proposed three kinds of **gene–environment correlations,** or ways in which a person's genes and his environment or experiences are systematically interrelated: passive, evocative, and active. The concept of gene–environment *interactions* tells us that people with different genes react differently to the environments they encounter. By contrast, the concept of gene–environment *correlations* says that people with different genes encounter different environments (Loehlin, 1992). As an illustration, imagine children with a genetic potential to be highly sociable and other children whose genes are likely to make them shy.

Passive Gene–Environment Correlations

The kind of home environment that parents provide for their children is influenced partly by the parents' genotypes. Because parents provide children not only with a home environment but also with their genes, the rearing environments to which children are exposed are correlated with (and are likely to suit) their genotypes.

For instance, sociable parents not only transmit their "sociable" genes to their children but also, because they have "sociable" genes, create a social home environment—inviting their friends over frequently, taking their children to social events, and so on. These children inherit genes for sociability, but they also experience an environment that matches their genes and that may make them more sociable than they would otherwise be. By contrast, the child with shy parents is likely to receive genes for shyness *and* a correlated environment—one without as much social stimulation.

Evocative Gene–Environment Correlations

A child's genotype also *evokes* certain kinds of reactions from other people. The smiley, sociable baby is likely to get more smiles, hugs, and social stimulation than the wary, shy baby.

Similarly, the sociable child may be sought more often as a playmate by other children, the sociable adolescent may be invited to more parties, and the sociable adult may be given more job assignments involving public relations. In short, genetic makeup may affect the reactions of other people to a child and, hence, the kind of social environment that the child will experience.

Active Gene–Environment Correlations

Finally, children's genotypes influence the kinds of environments they *seek*. The individual with a genetic predisposition to be extraverted is likely to go to every party in sight, invite friends to the house, join organizations, and otherwise build a "niche" that is highly socially stimulating. The child with genes for shyness may actively avoid large group activities and instead develop solitary interests.

Passive, evocative, and active genotype–environment correlations can all operate to influence a trait as parents and children choose and influence their environments (Rutter et al., 2006). However, Scarr and McCartney suggest that the balance of the three types of genotype–environment correlations shifts during development. Because infants are at home a good deal, their environment is largely influenced by their parents through passive influences. Evocative influences operate throughout life; our characteristic, genetically influenced traits consistently prompt characteristic reactions in other people. Finally, as humans develop, they become increasingly able to build their own niches, so active gene–environment correlations become increasingly important.

Rhoda Sidney/PhotoEdit

If the son of a basketball player turns out to be a good basketball player, is it because of genetic endowment or experience? We cannot say because genes and environment are correlated. Through passive gene–environment correlation, the children of athletes not only inherit their parent's genes but also grow up in sports-oriented family environments.

Genetic Influences on Environment

Is there much evidence supporting Scarr and McCartney's claim that people's genes are correlated with, and possibly influence, their experiences in life? Indeed there is. Behavioral geneticists are discovering that measures of environment are themselves heritable. What this means is that identical twins are more similar than fraternal twins, and biological siblings are more similar than adoptive siblings, in the environments they experience and in their perceptions of these environments, for example in:

- Both objective and perceived aspects of parenting style, such as warmth and the quality of the parent–child relationship (Plomin & Bergeman, 1991; Reiss, 2005)
- Time spent watching television (Plomin et al., 1990)
- Number of stressful life events experienced (Kendler et al., 1993)

If our genetically influenced personality traits affect how others treat us and what experiences we seek and have, these findings make sense. For example, identical twins who are irritable and difficult could help create a conflict-ridden family environment, whereas calm and controlled children could help create a cohesive family environment, even if they are raised apart (Krueger, Markon, & Bouchard, 2003).

Such findings challenge some of our most fundamental assumptions about human development. After all, they say that what we regard as purely environmental influences on development partly reflect the workings of heredity (Reiss, 2000; Rowe, 1994). Robert Plomin (1990) suggests that we must question our assumptions. Suppose, he says, we find that parents who read to their children have brighter children than parents who do not read to their children. In the not-so-distant past, most developmentalists would have interpreted this finding rather uncritically as evidence that parents make important contributions to their children's intellectual development by reading to them. Without denying the importance of parents, suppose we offer this alternative interpretation: Parents and children whose genes predispose them to be highly intelligent are more likely to seek opportunities to read than parents and children who are less intellectually inclined. If this is the case, can we be so sure that reading to children *causes* them to be brighter? Would we be able to show that reading to children is beneficial even when the parents and children involved are genetically unrelated? One more example: If we observe that aggressive children tend to have parents who are negative and hostile toward them, can we be sure that the children's aggression is because of the experiences they have had growing up with negative parents? Is it not also possible that they inherited genes from their irritable and aggressive parents that predisposed them to be irritable and aggressive themselves or even made their parents hostile toward them (O'Connor et al., 1998)?

Perhaps the most convincing evidence of the importance of gene–environment correlations comes from an ambitious study by David Reiss, Jenae Neiderhiser, E. Mavis Hethering-ton, and Robert Plomin, summarized in their book *The Relationship Code* (2000). The sample for this study consisted of 720 pairs of same-sex adolescents who differed in their degree of biological relationship from identical twins to biological siblings to unrelated stepsiblings. The researchers measured environmental factors such as parent–child and sibling–sibling interaction and adolescent adjustment variables such as self-esteem, sociability, depression, and antisocial behavior.

This major study suggested that family processes are important, but not for the reasons developmentalists have traditionally assumed. Family processes, Reiss and his colleagues argue, appear to be a mechanism through which the genetic code is expressed. Repeatedly, the study revealed that genes shared by parents and children partly or even largely accounted for relationships between children's experiences and their developmental outcomes—for example, between negative parenting tactics and antisocial behavior on the part of adolescents. In 44 of 52 instances in which significant relationships between measures of the family environment and adolescent adjustment were detected, genes influenced both family environment and adolescent adjustment and accounted for most of the relationship between the two (Reiss & Neiderhiser, 2000).

So genes and environment conspire to shape development. Genes influence how parents, peers, and others treat children. These environmental influences—usually nonshared ones that differ from sibling to sibling—then influence the individual's development, often reinforcing genetically based predispositions. This means that behavioral geneticists, who often emphasize the importance of genes, and socialization researchers, who stress the role of experiences in development, are both right. And it means that caregivers sensitive to a child's genetically based predispositions will be in a good position to strengthen a child's adaptive tendencies and suppress or work around the maladaptive ones.

Controversies Surrounding Genetic Research

As illustrated by public policy debates over reproductive technologies, cloning, and stem cell research, society is grappling with the complex and troubling ethical issues that have arisen as geneticists have gained the capacity to identify the carriers and potential victims of diseases and disorders, to give parents information that might prompt them to abort a pregnancy, and to experiment with techniques for altering the genetic code through gene therapy. As the Applications box illustrates, applications of gene therapy to humans have not yet been very successful but are likely to be pursued more vigorously as knowledge expands. Some observers worry about Nazi-like attempts to create a super race of clones. For these and other reasons, genetic research is controversial and will remain so.

Likewise, behavioral genetics research is controversial among developmental scientists. On the one hand, it has provided some important insights into human development: that genes are important, that the unique experiences of siblings are

PREVENTION AND TREATMENT OF GENETIC CONDITIONS

Ultimately, genetic researchers want to know how the damaging effects of genes associated with diseases and disorders can be prevented, cured, or at least minimized. One of the greatest success stories in genetic research involves **phenylketonuria (PKU),** a disorder caused by mutations in a single pair of recessive genes (Turnpenny & Ellard, 2005). Affected children lack a critical enzyme needed to metabolize phenylalanine, a component of many foods (including milk). As phenylalanine accumulates in the body, it is converted to a harmful acid that attacks the nervous system and causes children to be mentally retarded and hyperactive.

In the mid-1950s, scientists developed a special diet low in phenylalanine, and in 1961, they developed a simple blood test that could detect PKU soon after birth, before any damage had been done. Today, newborn infants are routinely screened for PKU, and affected children are immediately placed on the special (and, unfortunately, distasteful) diet (Miller, 1995). They must stay on it for their entire lives or risk deterioration in cognitive functioning, although other therapies are also being developed (National Institutes of Health, 2000; Santos et al., 2006). Here, then, genetic research led to the prevention of one of the many causes of mental retardation. And here is a clear-cut example of the interaction between genes and environment: a child will develop the condition and become mentally retarded only if he inherits the PKU genes *and* eats a normal (rather than a special) diet.

Guided by the Human Genome Project, medical researchers today are actively experimenting with **gene therapy**—interventions that involve substituting normal genes for the genes associated with a disease or disorder or otherwise altering a person's genetic makeup.

In some experiments, viruses are used to carry normal replacement genes into an individual's cells (Turnpenny & Ellard, 2005). Gene therapy experiments to treat such genetic disorders as hemophilia (through infusions of normal genes into the blood) and the lung disease cystic fibrosis (using aerosol sprays to deliver normal genes to the lungs) are under way and are having some success (Griesenbach, Geddes, & Alton, 2006; Park & Gow, 2006; Walsh, 2003).

Yet progress in gene therapy has been slow because of a host of problems (Park & Gow, 2006; Weiss, 2003a). The death of Jesse Gelsinger, the first person to die in a gene therapy trial, was a sobering reminder of the risks. His immune system attacked the viruses that were to carry normal genes into his malfunctioning liver and destroyed not only the viruses but his own organs (Fischer, 2000). This 1999 tragedy resulted in stricter controls on gene therapy research and increased concern about ethical issues.

Although effective gene therapies undoubtedly will be developed, it is simpleminded to think that gene therapies will prevent or cure most diseases and disorders. Why? Because as you now understand, most conditions are the product of genes and environment interacting. Researchers not only must deliver the right genes to the body in sufficient number to have the desired effect but also must get them to turn on and off when they should to produce normal functioning (Weiss, 2003a). Preventing or curing polygenic disorders such as schizophrenia will be especially hard because this will require a better understanding of how multiple genes *and* multiple environmental risk factors contribute to disorders. No "quick fix" such as the PKU diet will be possible. Still, the pace of breakthroughs in gene therapy research will increase, and societies will continue to grapple with the ethical issues these advances raise.

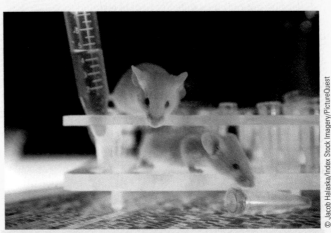

Gene therapy experiments with mice promise to yield treatments that could benefit humans.

more influential than those they share, that children influence parents just as parents influence children. Behavioral genetics research sometimes provides more compelling evidence of the effects of the environment on development than studies that do not take genes into account do. For example, one study that included twins showed that even controlling for genetic influences on a parent's tendency to use harsh punishment and a child's tendency to be aggressive, harsh punishment is associated with negative outcomes such as aggression and drug and alcohol use (Lynch et al., 2006). Similarly, by studying the children of twin pairs in which one twin experienced divorce and the other did not, Brian D'Onofrio and his colleagues (2006) were able to show a link between experiencing divorce and both engaging in early sexual behavior and experiencing emotional difficulties, but not to certain other outcomes associated with divorce in previous studies.

Nonetheless, a number of respected researchers continue to question the validity of some behavioral genetics research surveyed in this chapter. They believe that techniques for calculating heritability attribute too much importance to genes and too little to environment because they credit to genes some variance caused by a combination of genetic and environmental influence (McCartney, 2003; van Os & Sham, 2003). They doubt that the influences of genes and environment on individual differences can ever be cleanly separated and maintain that parents have far more important effects on their children's development than some behavioral geneticists acknowledge (Collins et al., 2000; Lerner, 2003). They also insist that behavioral genetics research tells us little about what we should really want to understand: *epigenesis*, the long and complex process through which genotypes are translated into phenotypes (Gottlieb, Wahlsten, & Lickliter, 2006).

Still, parents may be in a better position to be good parents if they understand their children's genetically based predispositions and how to respond appropriately to them. Providing children with optimal experiences, of course, depends on knowing which environments stimulate healthy development and which do not. It is fitting, then, that the next chapter takes a closer look at early environmental influences on development.

SUMMING UP

▌ From infancy to adolescence, genetic influences gain importance and shared environmental influences become less significant.

▌ Genes help determine not only how different people respond to experiences (through gene–environment interactions) but also what experiences they have (through passive, evocative, and active gene–environment correlations).

▌ It is not nature *or* nurture but an incredibly complex interplay of genetic and environmental influences from conception to death that is important.

CRITICAL THINKING

1. Evidence suggests that children who are physically punished by their parents tend to behave more aggressively around their peers than children who are not. What explanation for this finding might a social cognitive learning theorist such as Albert Bandura (see Chapter 2) propose? What alternative explanations does research on behavioral genetics, including work on gene–environment correlations, suggest?

2. Assume that genes predispose some people to be highly religious and some people to be unreligious and that some environments nurture religiosity and others do not. Explain how a gene–environment interaction and a gene–environment correlation could each make Peter more religious than Paul.

CHAPTER SUMMARY

3.1 EVOLUTION AND SPECIES HEREDITY

• As humans, we develop similarly in part because we share a species heredity, the product of evolution.

• According to Darwin's theory of evolution, if there is genetic variation in a species—and if some genes aid members of the species in adapting to their environment and reproducing—those genes will become more common in the population over time through natural selection.

• Humans are also similar because they inherit a characteristically human environment through cultural evolution.

3.2 INDIVIDUAL HEREDITY

• Each human has an individual heredity provided at conception, when sperm and ovum, each with 23 chromosomes because of meiosis, unite to form a single-cell zygote with 46 chromosomes. Parent and child share 50% of their genes in common; siblings share 50% on average.

• The chromosomes contain some 20,000–25,000 genes mapped by the Human Genome Project, which has revealed similarities and differences between the genes of different human groups and different species.

• Environmental factors influence how a genotype (genetic makeup) is translated into a phenotype (actual traits); genes provide a "code" that influences, with environmental factors, how cells are formed and function; regulator DNA influences the important process of gene expression throughout the life span.

• The three main mechanisms of inheritance are single gene-pair inheritance, sex-linked inheritance, and polygenic (multiple gene) inheritance. Some children are also affected by noninherited changes in gene structure (mutations); others, because of errors in meiosis, have chromosome abnormalities such as Down, Turner, Klinefelter, and fragile X syndromes.

• Genetic counseling offers information and guidance to people at risk for genetic conditions; abnormalities can be detected prenatally through amniocentesis, chorionic villus sampling, ultrasound, preimplantation genetic diagnosis, and maternal blood sampling.

3.3 STUDYING GENETIC AND ENVIRONMENTAL INFLUENCES

• Behavioral geneticists conduct selective breeding and twin, adoption, and other family studies that describe resemblances between pairs of people using concordance rates and correlation coefficients. They then estimate the heritability of traits and the contributions of shared (with siblings) and nonshared (unique) environmental influences.

• Techniques of molecular genetics are used to identify and study particular gene variants and to compare people who do and do not have them.

3.4 ACCOUNTING FOR INDIVIDUAL DIFFERENCES

• Performance on measures of intelligence is a heritable trait. Infant mental development is strongly influenced by a species-wide maturational plan, but over the course of childhood and adolescence, individual differences in mental ability more strongly reflect both individual genetic makeup and nonshared environmental influences, whereas shared environmental influences wane.

• Aspects of temperament and personality are also genetically influenced, and nonshared environmental influences are significant but shared environmental influences are not.

• Similarly, psychological disorders such as schizophrenia have a genetic basis but it often takes an interaction of genes and environmental stressors to produce disorder.

- Overall, physical and physiological characteristics are more strongly influenced by genetic endowment than are intellectual abilities and, in turn, personality traits or social attitudes. Certain traits such as creativity and security of parent–child attachment do not seem to be genetically influenced, but heritability differs depending on characteristics of the sample studied.

3.5 HEREDITY AND ENVIRONMENT CONSPIRING

- Both genes and nonshared environment are influential over the life span, but shared environmental influences become less important after childhood.
- Gene–environment interactions mean that environment influences how genes are expressed and that genes influence how people react to the environment. Passive, evocative, and active gene–environment correlations suggest that people experience and seek environments that match and reinforce their genetic predispositions. Thus, people are shaped by a complex interplay of genetic and environmental influences over the life span.

KEY TERMS

MEDIA RESOURCES

BOOK COMPANION WEBSITE

academic.cengage.com/psychology/sigelman
Find online quizzes, flash cards, animations, video clips, experiments, interactive assessments, and other helpful study aids for this text at academic.cengage.com/psychology/sigelman. You can also connect directly to the following sites:

CRACKING THE CODE OF LIFE-NOVA

This Public Broadcasting Service (PBS) program, originally aired on *NOVA* in April 2001, chronicles the race to complete the human genome map. You can watch the entire 2-hour program on its companion website, which contains links for learning more about DNA sequencing, exploring the issues surrounding genetic manipulation, and revisiting the nature versus nurture debate.

GENETIC EDUCATION AND COUNSELING

The Genetics Education Center at the University of Kansas Medical Center also has a website with a wealth of good materials on the Human Genome Project and on genetic disorders and conditions. It is aimed at educators and genetic counselors. Among its features are a glossary of genetic terms; a page on the ethical, legal, and social implications of genetic research; and up-to-date information about the Human Genome Project.

GENETESTS

To learn about a particular disease and its diagnosis and symptoms and to find whether a test for it exists, consult GeneTests, which, although aimed at doctors, is readable. Click on "Gene Reviews" and search for a disease.

HUMAN GENOME PROJECT

The Human Genome Project is an international research effort aimed at characterizing the makeup of all 46 human chromosomes by mapping sequences of their DNA. For a look at how this is done, as well as the latest in efforts to understand and prevent genetic defects and diseases, check out the website for the National Human Genome Research Institute.

MINNESOTA TWIN FAMILY STUDY

The Minnesota twin family study website contains information on twin research begun in the 1980s and which continues today. Key information includes a list of current researchers and some of their most recent publications and a great brochure "What's Special about Twins to Science?"

UNIVERSE OF GENETIC TESTS

Lab tests online is a great public resource for those interesting in current genetic testing procedures. The Universe of Genetic Tests area of the site includes both basic information and advanced articles on numerous types of tests (e.g., clinical genetic testing, percentage testing, cytogenetics). You can also read about the pros and cons of genetics testing.

UNDERSTANDING THE DATA: EXERCISES ON THE WEB

academic.cengage.com/psychology/sigelman
For additional insight on the data presented in this chapter, try out the exercises for these figures at academic.cengage.com/psychology/sigelman:

Table 3.5 Average Correlations between the IQ Scores of Pairs of Individuals

Figure 3.7 The proportions of variance in child IQ scores explained by genes, shared environment, and nonshared environment differ for children from low or high socioeconomic status (SES) environments

Figure 3.8 The odds of a depressive episode at age 26 are highest for individuals who: (1) inherit two genes known to increase the risk of depression rather than two genes known to protect against depression, and (2) experience four or more stressful life events between ages 21 and 26. This is an example of gene–environment interaction: the effects of genetic makeup on depression depend on how stressful a person's environment is, and the effects of stressful life events depend on the person's genotype.

CENGAGENOW

© Plush Studios/Getty Images

CHAPTER

4

Prenatal Development and Birth

■ ■ ■

What are the possible effects of prenatal exposure to maternal stress? How might Florence's daughter Emily be affected by her mother's exposure to the dust, debris, and asbestos released that day? These are the sorts of questions we address in this chapter as we explore prenatal development and the environment of the womb.

4.1 PRENATAL DEVELOPMENT

Perhaps at no time in the life span does development occur faster, or is environment more important, than between conception and birth. What maturational milestones normally occur during this period?

Conception

Midway through the menstrual cycle, every 28 days or so, females ovulate: An ovum (egg cell) ripens, leaves the ovary, and begins its journey through the fallopian tube to the uterus. Usually the egg disintegrates and leaves the body as part of the menstrual flow. However, if the woman has intercourse with a fertile man around the time of ovulation, the 300 million or so sperm cells in his seminal fluid swim, tadpole style, in all directions. Of the 300 to 500 sperm that survive the long, 6-hour journey into the fallopian tubes, one may meet and penetrate the ovum on its descent from the ovary (Sadler, 2006; see also ■ **Figure 4.1**). Once this one sperm penetrates the egg cell, a biochemical reaction occurs that repels other sperm and keeps them from

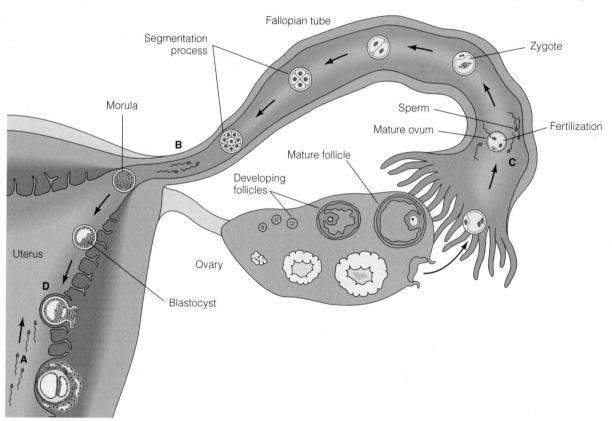

■ **FIGURE 4.1** Fertilization and implantation. (A) Millions of sperm cells have entered the vagina and are finding their way into the uterus. (B) Some spermatozoa are moving up the fallopian tube (there is a similar tube on the other side) toward the ovum. (C) Fertilization occurs. The fertilized ovum drifts down the tube, dividing and forming new cells as it goes, until it implants itself in the wall of the uterus (D) by the seventh or eighth day after fertilization.

REPRODUCTIVE TECHNOLOGIES: NEW CONCEPTIONS OF CONCEPTION

Many couples have no trouble conceiving children, but as many as one in four couples experience difficulties conceiving a child despite desperately wanting one (Schmidt, 2006). Infertility is equally likely to be traced to the man as the woman and stems from a variety of causes. For example, adolescents and adults who have contracted sexually transmitted diseases may become infertile (Steinberg et al., 1998). Some couples are helped to conceive in relatively simple ways. A man may be advised to wear looser pants and underwear because an unusually high temperature in the testes interferes with sperm production. A woman may be asked to take her temperature to determine when she ovulates and is therefore most likely to become pregnant.

When simpler methods fail, some couples move on to more elaborate (and expensive) **assisted reproductive technologies (ARTs),** medical techniques used to increase fertility. ART techniques typically start with or include prescription drugs for the woman to stimulate her ovaries to ripen and release several eggs. Although this is the least invasive and least expensive ART, it has come under fire because of its connection to multiple births. Pregnancies involving multiples almost always result in premature deliveries that are costly financially, emotionally, and physically. Several highly visible cases of multiple births—the McCaughey's septuplets in 1997, Nkem Chukwu's octuplets in December 1998, and the Qahtani septuplets in 2001—resulted after the mothers had taken "fertility drugs." Chukwu's eight babies all weighed less than 2 pounds at birth (the smallest one—just over 10 ounces—died soon after birth) and racked up medical bills of about $400,000 *each* before going home (Nichols, 1999). Health problems are likely with such births. Two of the McCaughey children, for example, had feeding problems and two others suffer from cerebral palsy.

Emotionally, research shows that even having twins can be stressful and challenging for parents compared to having a singleton birth (Oliveness et al., 2005). Ruth Feldman and Arthur Eidelman (2005) compared triplets to twins and singletons on various measures.

They found cognitive delays among the triplets throughout infancy, which seemed to be associated with less responsive parenting. The authors concluded that parents of triplets struggle to provide sensitive, personalized attention to three infants simultaneously, a situation that negatively affects developmental outcomes.

To reduce the chances of such risky higher-order multiple births, physicians may suggest "selective reduction" in which some embryos are aborted to improve the outcome for the remaining embryos. Some families, though, refuse this option for personal or religious reasons.

Another ART is **artificial insemination,** which involves injecting sperm, either from a woman's partner or from a donor, into her uterus. In **in vitro fertilization (IVF),** several eggs are removed from a woman's ovary, fertilized by sperm in a petri dish in the laboratory, then transferred to the woman's uterus in hopes that one will implant on the wall of the uterus. Often, though, more than one fertilized egg would implant and multiple births would result. Mindful of the complications associated with multiples, many physicians are now limiting the number of fertilized eggs that are implanted during IVF procedures. Italy, for example, passed a law in 2004 restricting the number of eggs that can be implanted at one time to three (La Sala et al., 2006).

We should note that there are many variations of IVF, depending on who provides the eggs and the sperm. A couple wanting to have a child (the would-be biological mother and father) could donate both eggs and sperm and the biological mother carries the baby to term. At the other end of the spectrum, an infant conceived through IVF could wind up with five "parents": a sperm donor, an egg donor, a surrogate mother in whom the fertilized egg is implanted, and a caregiving mother and father. Pursuing IVF is not cheap; it costs about $12,400 a try in the United States! The success rate for women who use their own fresh (rather than frozen) eggs is about 1 in 4 overall, but decreases as mothers get older (Centers for Disease Control, 2005; Van Voorhis, 2006). For women over the age of 42, the odds of a live birth following ART are about 1 in 10.

What are the implications for the new family of using IVF and other reproductive technologies? Infertile couples may experience many heartbreaks in their quest for parenthood if try after try fails. Couples report that infertility is stressful, and unsuccessful treatment has long-term psychosocial effects (Verhaak et al., 2005). Still, even couples who have not successfully conceived following infertility treatment are found to be well adjusted and stable and, looking back on the experience, they report positive growth in their lives as a result of this experience (Daniluk, 2001). Although their attempts to conceive were unsuccessful, they may feel satisfied that they actively pursued available options.

What about couples who succeed in having children through IVF? Are their children and their relationship with them any different than for children conceived the "old-fashioned" way? To find out, Susan Golombok and her colleagues (2005, 2006) have conducted numerous studies comparing family relationships and child outcomes in families where the children were conceived through IVF (with either egg donation or sperm donation) or where children were conceived the usual way. Parents in both groups were remarkably similar in their parenting behaviors. In one study that used teacher ratings, teachers thought that the IVF mothers were more openly affectionate with their children (Hahn & DiPietro, 2001). And IVF mothers reported greater warmth and protectiveness toward their children, possibly because they had tried so hard and paid so much to become parents and undoubtedly wanted their children very much. In other research, parents reported caring just as much for children conceived with the help of someone else's sperm or egg (and therefore genetically unrelated to them) as for children conceived through IVF using their own sperm and egg (Golombok et al., 2005, 2006).

Thus, children conceived through today's reproductive technologies do not appear to be disadvantaged in any way by their unique start in life. Ultimately, how a child is conceived may be inconsequential relative to how a child is raised.

entering the already fertilized egg. As explained in Chapter 3, conception, the beginning of life, occurs when the genetic material of the sperm and egg unite to form a single-celled zygote. The process may sound simple, but, as you can see in the Explorations box on page 91, some couples cannot conceive a child, much as they want to, and seek medical help.

Prenatal Stages

The zygote contains the 46 chromosomes that are the genetic blueprint for the individual's development. It takes about 266 days (about 9 months) for the zygote to become a fetus of billions of cells that is ready to be born. This prenatal development is divided into three stages or periods: the germinal period, the embryonic period, and the fetal period.

The Germinal Period

The **germinal period** lasts approximately 2 weeks; the important events of this period are outlined in ● **Table 4.1**. For the first week or two, the zygote divides many times through mitosis, forming the **blastocyst,** a hollow ball of about 150 cells that is the size of the head of a pin. When the blastocyst reaches the uterus around day 6, it implants tendrils from its outer layer into the blood vessels of the uterine wall. This is quite an accomplishment; only about half of all fertilized ova are successfully implanted in the uterus. In addition, not all implanted embryos survive the early phases of prenatal development. Approximately 15% of recognized pregnancies end in miscarriage, and many unrecognized pregnancies—perhaps as many as 50%—are believed to terminate with miscarriage (Sadler, 2006). Many of these early losses are because of genetic defects.

● **TABLE 4.1 EVENTS OF THE GERMINAL PERIOD**

DAY	EVENT
1	Fertilization usually occurs within 24 hours of ovulation.
2	The single-celled zygote begins to divide 24–36 hours after fertilization.
3–4	The mass has 16 cells and is called a morula; it is traveling down the fallopian tube to the uterus.
5	An inner cell mass forms; the entire mass is called a blastocyst and is the size of a pinhead.
6–7	The blastocyst attaches to the wall of the uterus.
8–14	The blastocyst becomes fully embedded in the wall of the uterus. It now has about 250 cells.

The Embryonic Period

The **embryonic period** occurs from the third to the eighth week after conception. During this short time, every major organ takes shape, in at least a primitive form, in a process called **organogenesis.** The layers of the blastocyst differentiate, forming structures that sustain development. The outer layer becomes both the **amnion,** a watertight membrane that fills with fluid that cushions and protects the embryo, and the **chorion,** a membrane that surrounds the amnion and attaches rootlike extensions called *villi* to the uterine lining to gather nourishment for the embryo. The chorion eventually becomes the lining of the **placenta,** a tissue fed by blood vessels from the mother and connected to the embryo by the **umbilical cord.** Through the placenta and umbilical cord, the embryo receives oxygen and nutrients from the mother and eliminates carbon dioxide and metabolic wastes into the mother's bloodstream. A membrane called the *placental barrier* allows these small molecules to pass through, but it prevents the large blood cells of embryo and mother from mingling. It also protects the developing child from many harmful substances, but as you will see shortly, it is not infallible; some dangerous substances slip through.

Meanwhile, the cells in the interior of the blastocyst give rise to the ectoderm, mesoderm, and endoderm. These will eventually evolve into specific tissues and organ systems, including the central nervous system (brain and spinal cord) from the ectoderm; muscle tissue, cartilage, bone, heart, arteries, kidneys, and gonads from the mesoderm; and gastrointestinal tract, lungs, and bladder from the endoderm (Sadler, 2006).

Development proceeds at a breathtaking pace (see ● **Table 4.2**). The beginnings of a brain are apparent after only 3 to 4 weeks, when the neural plate folds up to form the neural tube (see ■ **Figure 4.2**). The bottom of the tube becomes the spinal cord. "Lumps" emerge at the top of the tube and form the forebrain, midbrain, and hindbrain (see ■ **Figure 4.3**). The so-called primitive or lower portions of the brain develop earliest. They regulate such biological functions as digestion, respiration, and elimination; they also control sleep–wake states and permit simple motor reactions. These are the parts of the brain that make life possible.

In as many as 5 out of 1000 pregnancies, the neural tube fails to fully close (Birnbacher, Messerschmidt, & Pollak, 2002). When this happens at the bottom of the tube, it can lead to **spina bifida,** in which part of the spinal cord is not fully encased in the protective covering of the spinal column. Failure to close at the top of the neural tube can lead to **anencephaly,** in which the main portion of the brain above the brain stem fails to develop. Neural tube defects occur 25 to 29 days after conception and are more common when the mother is deficient in folic acid, a substance critical for normal gene function (Percy, 2007). This illustrates the importance of good maternal nutrition for development, which we will have more to say about in a later section.

Other critical organs are also taking shape. Just 4 weeks after conception, a tiny heart not only has formed but also has

● TABLE 4.2 EVENTS OF THE EMBRYONIC PERIOD

WEEK	EVENT
3	Now an embryo, the person-to-be is just 1/10 of an inch (2 mm) long. It has become elongated, and three layers emerge—the ectoderm, mesoderm, and endoderm.
4	The embryo is so curved that the two ends almost touch. The outer layer (ectoderm) folds into the neural tube. From the mesoderm, a tiny heart forms and begins to beat. The endoderm differentiates into a gastrointestinal tract and lungs. Between days 21 and 28, eyes develop.
5	Ears, mouth, and throat take shape. Arm and leg buds appear. The handplate from which fingers will emerge appears. The heart divides into two regions, and the brain differentiates into forebrain, midbrain, and hindbrain.
6–7	The embryo is almost 1 inch long. The heart divides into four chambers. Fingers emerge from the handplate, and primitive facial features are evident. The important process of sexual differentiation begins.
8	Most structures and organs are present. Ovaries and testes are evident. The embryo begins to straighten and assumes a more human appearance.

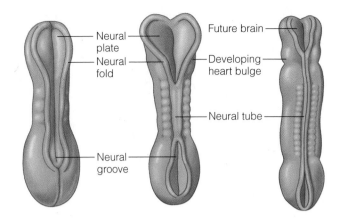

■ **FIGURE 4.2** The nervous system emerges from the neural plate, which thicken and folds to form the neural groove. When the edges of the groove meet, the neural tube is formed. All of this takes place between 18 and 26 days after conception.

begun to beat. The eyes, ears, nose, and mouth rapidly take shape in the second month, and buds appear that will become arms and legs. During the second month, a primitive nervous system also makes newly formed muscles contract. Only 60 days after conception, at the close of the embryonic period, the organism is a little over an inch long and has a distinctly human appearance.

The important process of sexual differentiation begins during the seventh and eighth prenatal weeks. First, undifferentiated tissue becomes either male testes or female ovaries: If the embryo inherited a Y chromosome at conception, a gene on it calls for the construction of testes; in a genetic female with two X chromosomes, ovaries form instead. The testes of a male embryo secrete **testosterone,** the primary male sex hormone that stimulates the development of a male internal reproductive system, and another hormone that inhibits the development of a female internal reproductive system. In the absence of these hormones, the embryo develops the internal reproductive system of a female.

Clearly, the embryonic period is dramatic and highly important because it is when the structures that make us human evolve. Yet many pregnant women, either because they do not yet know they are pregnant or do not appreciate the value of

By 5 to 6 weeks after conception, head, torso, and limbs have formed, a tiny heart has begun to beat, and the umbilical cord (lower center) has taken shape to transport nutrients. By the end of the embryonic period (8 weeks), all major organs have formed.

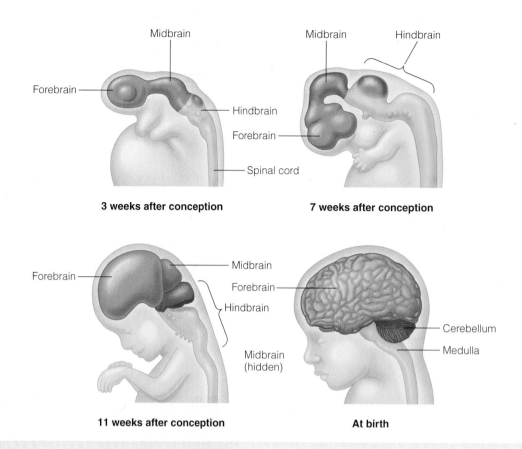

■ FIGURE 4.3 The brain at four stages of development, showing hindbrain, midbrain, and forebrain.

early prenatal care, do not go to a doctor until *after* the eighth week of prenatal development, often too late to prevent the damage that can be caused by an unhealthy lifestyle.

The Fetal Period

The **fetal period** lasts from the ninth week of pregnancy until birth (see ● **Table 4.3**). Neurons continue to proliferate (i.e., multiply) at a staggering rate during this period; by one estimate, the number of neurons increases by hundreds of thousands every minute throughout all of pregnancy, with a concentrated period of proliferation occurring between 10 and 20 weeks after conception (Nelson, Thomas, & deHaan, 2006). As a result of this rapid proliferation, the young infant has around 100 billion neurons. Another period of proliferation takes place after birth, but this produces an increase in glial cells, not nerve cells. Glial cells function primarily as support cells for neurons. Once formed, neurons migrate from their place of origin to particular locations within the brain where they will become part of specialized functioning units. The impetus for migration is influenced by genetic instructions and by the biochemical environment in which brain cells find themselves. Neurons travel along the surface of glial cells and detach at programmed destinations in the developing brain. Neurons migrate to the closest or innermost parts of the brain first and to the farthest or outermost parts last, and much of this occurs between 8 and 15 weeks after conception.

In addition to multiplication and migration of cells, **differentiation** is occurring. Early in development, every neuron starts with the potential to become any specific type of neuron; what it becomes—how it differentiates—depends on where it migrates. Thus, if a neuron that would normally migrate to the visual cortex of an animal's brain is transplanted into the area of the cortex that controls hearing, it will differentiate as an auditory neuron instead of a visual neuron (Johnson, 2005). These early cells that have not yet specialized are known as **stem cells.** In 1998, researchers discovered how to separate stem cells from human embryos and grow these cells in the laboratory. This procedure has been controversial because of its use of aborted human embryos, but it shows great promise for someday treating serious diseases such as Parkinson's disease, diabetes, and Alzheimer's disease by engineering specialized cells from stem cells.

Organ systems that formed during the embryonic period continue to grow and begin to function. Harmful agents will no longer cause major malformations because organs have already formed, but they can stunt the growth of the fetus and interfere with the wiring of its rapidly developing nervous system.

In the third month of pregnancy, distinguishable external sex organs appear, the bones and muscles develop, and the fe-

● TABLE 4.3   EVENTS OF THE FETAL PERIOD

WEEK	EVENT
9	Bone tissue emerges and the embryo becomes a fetus. The head of the fetus looks huge relative to the rest of the body—it takes up about half of the total length of the fetus. The fetus can open and close its mouth and turn its head.
10–12	Fingers and toes are clearly formed. External genitalia have developed. Movements have increased substantially—arms and legs kick vigorously, but the fetus is still too small for the mother to feel all these movements. The fetus also shows "breathing" movements with its chest and some reflexes.
13–16	The heartbeat should be audible with a stethoscope. Fetal movements may become apparent to the mother. The fetus is about 4½ inches long and the skeleton is becoming harder.
17–22	Fingernails and toenails, hair, teeth buds, and eyelashes grow. Brain development is phenomenal, and brain waves are detectable.
23–25	These weeks mark the age of viability, when the fetus has a *chance* of survival outside the womb. It is about 12 inches long and weighs about 1 pound.
26–32	The fetus gains weight, and its brain grows. The nervous system becomes better organized.
33–38	The last 6 weeks of a full-term pregnancy bring further weight gain and brain activity. The lungs mature and begin to expand and contract.

tus becomes frisky: By the end of the third month (that is, by the end of the first third of pregnancy, or *trimester*), it moves its arms, kicks its legs, makes fists, and even turns somersaults. The mother probably does not yet feel all this activity because the fetus is still only about 3 inches long. Nonetheless, this tiny being can swallow, digest food, and urinate. All this "behaving" contributes to the proper development of the nervous system, digestive system, and other systems of the body (Smotherman & Robinson, 1996).

During the *second trimester* (the fourth, fifth, and sixth months), more refined activities appear (including thumb sucking), and by the end of this period the sensory organs are functioning: Premature infants as young as 25 weeks respond to loud noises and bright lights (Allen & Capute, 1986; Sadler, 2006). At about 23 weeks after conception, midway through the fifth month, the fetus reaches the **age of viability,** when survival outside the uterus is possible *if* the brain and respiratory system are well enough developed. The age of viability is earlier today than at any time in the past because medical techniques for keeping fragile babies alive have improved considerably over the past few decades. In 2007, a baby girl believed to be the most premature baby to survive went home after 4 months of neonatal intensive care. She was born at 21 weeks and 6 days, weighing just 10 ounces. Despite this miracle, many infants born at 22–25 weeks do not survive, and of those who do, many experience chronic health or neurological problems (Hack & Fanaroff, 1999; Paul et al., 2006). Thus, the age of viability is an indicator of when survival *may be possible,* but it is by no means a guarantee of life or health.

During the *third trimester* (the seventh, eighth, and ninth months), the fetus gains weight rapidly. This time is also criti-

By 16 weeks, the fetus has a distinctly human appearance.

During the fetal period, growth is substantial and there is little room for the fetus to move in the womb. This 20-week-old fetus is curled into the classic "fetal position" in its tight quarters.

At 24 weeks of gestation, this fetus has reached the age of viability, when it might have a chance to survive outside the womb if born early.

cal in the development of the brain, as is the entire prenatal period (see Chapter 5). Early in pregnancy, the basic architecture of the nervous system is laid down. During the second half of pregnancy, neurons not only multiply at an astonishing rate (proliferation) but they also increase in size and develop an insulating cover, **myelin,** that improves their ability to transmit signals rapidly. Most importantly, guided by both a genetic blueprint and early sensory experiences, neurons connect with one another and organize into working groups that control vision, memory, motor behavior, and other functions. For good reason, parents should be concerned about damage to the developing human during the first trimester, when the brain and other organs are forming. However, they should not overlook the significance of the second and third trimesters, which are critical to normal brain functioning and therefore to normal development.

As the brain develops, the behavior of the fetus becomes more like the organized and adaptive behavior seen in the newborn. For example, Janet DiPietro and her colleagues (2002, 2006) assessed heart rates and activity levels in fetuses at various prenatal intervals (between 20 and 38 weeks after conception) and at 2 weeks following birth. Only at 36 weeks of gestation did heart rate activity and movement become increasingly organized into coherent patterns of waking and sleeping known as **infant states.** Fetuses whose heart rates and movements were concordant (that is, matched) at 36 weeks showed better regu-

lation of their behavioral states 2 weeks following birth. They were more alert, less irritable, better able to sustain their attention, and more likely to maintain control even during stressful parts of the postnatal examination.

DiPietro and her colleagues (1996b) also found that, with age, fetal heart rates become increasingly responsive to such stimuli as a vibrator placed on the mother's abdomen. Fetuses moved, on average, about once a minute and were active 20 to 30% of the time. As ■ **Figure 4.4** shows, at 20 weeks, fetuses spent only about 17% of their time in an organized infant state such as quiet sleep, active sleep, or active waking. By the end of the prenatal period, they were in one distinct state or another at least 85% of the time. They spent most of their time snoozing, especially in active sleep. Whereas in the 20th week of pregnancy they were almost never active and awake, by the 32nd week they spent 11 to 16% of their time in an active, waking state. The patterns detected in this and other studies suggest that important changes in the nervous system occur 28 to 32 weeks after conception, when premature infants are typically well equipped to survive. As the nervous system becomes more organized, so does behavior.

Interestingly, different fetuses displayed consistent differences in their patterns of heart rate and movement, and the researchers detected correlations between measures of fetal physiology and behavior and measures of infant temperament (DiPietro et al., 1996a). For example, active fetuses turned out

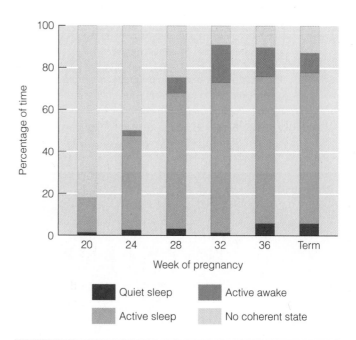

■ **FIGURE 4.4** The percentage of time the fetus spends in different states from the 20th week until the end of pregnancy. Time in one coherent state or another increases with age, and most time is spent in a state of sleep.
SOURCE: From Fetal neurobehavioral development by J. A. DiPietro, et al. from *Child Development*, 67. © 1996 Society for Research in Child Development, Inc. Reprinted by permission.

As it nears the end of the gestational period (38–40 weeks for a full-term infant), the fetus engages in many behaviors observed in newborns (here, it sucks its thumb).

to be active, difficult, and unpredictable babies, and fetuses whose states were better organized were also better regulated at 3 months following birth, as indicated by their waking fewer times during the night. The message is clear: Newborn behavior does not spring from nowhere; it emerges long before birth. There is a good deal of continuity between prenatal behavior and postnatal behavior.

By the middle of the ninth month, the fetus is so large that its most comfortable position in cramped quarters is head down with limbs curled in (the "fetal position"). The mother's uterus contracts at irregular intervals during the last month of pregnancy. When these contractions are strong, frequent, and regular, the mother is in the first stage of labor and the prenatal period is drawing to a close. Under normal circumstances, birth will occur within hours.

SUMMING UP

▌ Conception occurs when an egg is fertilized by a sperm. The resulting zygote rapidly undergoes cell division and forms a blastocyst, which makes its way to the uterus where it implants itself.

This first phase of development is the germinal period and lasts about 2 weeks.

▌ The embryonic stage occurs from the third to the eighth week after conception. During this time, every major organ begins to take shape through the process of organogenesis. Toward the end of this period, the important process of sexual differentiation begins.

▌ During the last prenatal stage—the fetal stage—the fetus increases in size and undergoes tremendous brain development. Cells proliferate (i.e., multiply), migrate to their final location in the brain, and differentiate into specialized functions. At around 23 weeks, the fetus reaches the age of viability, when survival outside the womb may be possible.

CRITICAL THINKING

1. If you had to select one of the three periods of prenatal development as the most important, which would it be? What are your reasons for your choice?

2. What ethical concerns should be considered with the use of artificial reproductive technologies? As technologies become more advanced in the future, what additional concerns may arise?

4.2   THE PRENATAL ENVIRONMENT

The mother's womb is the **prenatal environment** for the unborn child. Just as children are influenced by their physical and social environments, so too is the fetus affected by its surroundings. The physical environment includes everything from the molecules that reach the fetus's bloodstream before birth to the architecture of a home to the climate outside it. The social environment includes all the people who can influence and be influenced by the developing person and the broader culture. Although early theorists tended to view environment as a set of forces that shaped the individual, as though a person were just a lump of clay to be molded, we now know this is not the case. Recall the explanation from Chapter 1 of *reciprocal influences*: people shape their physical and social environments and are, in turn, affected by the environments they have helped create. For example, if a woman uses cocaine during pregnancy, her newborn may be extraordinarily fussy: environment has affected development. But a fussy baby is likely to affect his environment by irritating his mother, who then expresses her tenseness in her interactions with him; this makes him fussier, which aggravates his mother even more, and her aggravation, in turn, makes him even crankier. Such transactions between person and environment begin at the moment of conception.

The developing embryo-then-fetus is a vulnerable little creature. How can its development be optimized? What hazards does it face? "Experts" throughout history have offered several odd ideas about the effects of the prenatal physical environment on growth. For example, it was once believed that pregnant women could enhance their chances of bearing sons if they ate red meat and salty snacks, whereas eating vegetables and sweet snacks would supposedly increase the likelihood of having daughters (Springen, 2004). And until the early 1940s, it was widely—and wrongly—believed that the placenta was a marvelous screen that protected the embryo and fetus from nicotine, viruses, and all kinds of other hazards. In her book *Message in a Bottle: The Making of Fetal Alcohol Syndrome,* Janet Golden (2005) describes how experts and "regular folk" alike were reluctant to accept the findings that alcohol consumption during pregnancy could be harmful to the developing fetus because of the strongly held belief throughout much of history that the womb was a protective barrier. It wasn't until the early 1970s that we had the first official acknowledgment that this was not the case when researchers identified a collection of symptoms in children whose mothers had consumed alcohol during pregnancy. (We will come back to this topic later in this section.)

Today, we understand that transactions between the organism and its environment begin at conception. When all is right, the prenatal environment provides just the stimulation and support needed for the fetus to mature physically and to develop a repertoire of behaviors that allow it to seek more stimulation, which in turn contributes to the development of more sophisticated behavior. When the prenatal environment is abnormal, development can be steered far off track, as you will now see as we examine the influence of various substances. But just as exposure to some substances can place children at risk, other factors can enhance their developmental outcome, as you will see in later sections of this chapter.

Your main mission here is to discover the extent to which early environmental influences, interacting with genetic influences, make or break later development. The nature–nurture issue, then, is the central issue to consider when thinking about prenatal development and its influence on the developing person. Early environmental influences on development—bad and good—demand serious attention. Such influences interact with genetic makeup throughout the life span to make us who we are. If a common genetic heritage can make different human beings alike in some respects, so can similar environments. If unique genes make one person different from another, so do unique experiences.

Teratogens

A **teratogen** is any disease, drug, or other environmental agent that can harm a developing fetus (for example, by causing deformities, blindness, brain damage, or even death). The list of teratogens has grown frighteningly long, and the environment contains many potential teratogens whose effects on development have not yet been assessed. Before considering the effects of some major teratogens, however, let us emphasize that only 15% of newborns have *minor* problems and even fewer—perhaps 5%—have more significant anomalies (Sadler, 2006). We will start with a few generalizations about the effects of teratogens, which we will then illustrate with examples:

- *Critical period.* The effects of a teratogenic agent are worst during the critical period when an organ system grows most rapidly.

- *Dosage and duration.* The greater the level of exposure and the longer the exposure to a teratogen, the more likely it is that serious damage will occur.
- *Genetic makeup.* Susceptibility to harm is influenced by the unborn child's and by the mother's genetic makeup. Some fetuses are more (or less) resistant to teratogens and some mothers are more (or less) able to detoxify teratogens (Percy, Lewkis, & Brown, 2007). Therefore, not all embryos and fetuses are affected, nor are they affected equally, by a teratogen.
- *Environment.* The effects of a teratogen depend on the quality of both the prenatal and the postnatal environments.

Look more closely at the first generalization, which is particularly important. A period of rapid growth is a **critical period** for an organ system—a time during which the developing organism is especially sensitive to environmental influences, positive or negative. As you will recall, organogenesis takes place during the embryonic period (weeks 3–8 of prenatal development). As ■ **Figure 4.5** shows, it is during this time—before many women even realize they are pregnant—that most organ systems are most vulnerable to damage. Moreover, each organ has a critical period that corresponds to its own time of most rapid development (for example, weeks 3–6 for the heart and 4–7 for the arms and fingers). Once an organ or body part is fully formed, it is usually less susceptible to damage. However, because some organ systems—above all, the nervous system—can be damaged throughout pregnancy, *sensitive periods* might be a better term than *critical periods.*

Drugs

The principles of teratology can be illustrated by surveying just a few of the many drugs—prescription, over-the-counter, and social—that can disrupt prenatal development. More than half of pregnant women take at least one prescription or over-the-counter drug during pregnancy (Kacew, 1999). Under a doctor's close supervision, medications used to treat ailments and medical conditions are usually safe for mother and fetus. However, certain individuals exposed to certain drugs in certain doses at certain times during the prenatal period are damaged for life.

Thalidomide. In the late 1950s, a West German drug company sold large quantities of **thalidomide,** a popular tranquilizer said to relieve morning sickness (the periodic nausea many women experience during the first trimester of pregnancy). Presumably, the drug was safe; it had no ill effects in tests on pregnant rats. Tragically, however, the drug had adverse effects on humans. Indeed, more than any other drug, thalidomide alerted the world to the dangers of taking drugs during pregnancy.

Thousands of women who used thalidomide during the first 2 months of pregnancy gave birth to babies with all or parts of their limbs missing, with the feet or hands attached directly

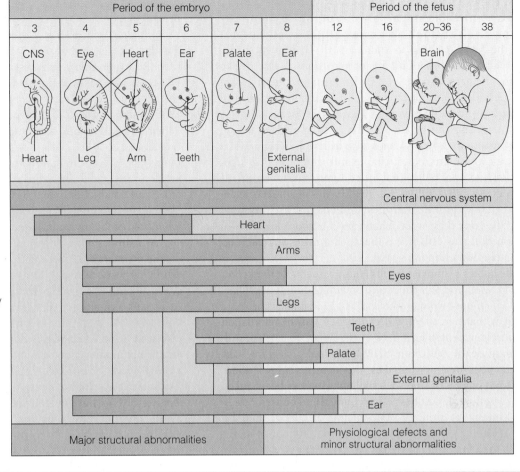

	Period of the embryo						Period of the fetus			
Prenatal week	3	4	5	6	7	8	12	16	20–36	38

Site of birth defect (the part of the embryo or fetus where damage is most likely to occur)

CNS — Heart; Eye — Leg; Heart — Arm; Ear — Teeth; Palate; Ear — External genitalia; Brain

Severity of defects (dark orange shading indicates the most highly sensitive period for teratogenic effects)

Central nervous system
Heart
Arms
Eyes
Legs
Teeth
Palate
External genitalia
Ear

Major structural abnormalities | Physiological defects and minor structural abnormalities

■ **FIGURE 4.5** The critical periods of prenatal development. Teratogens are more likely to produce major structural abnormalities during the third through the eighth prenatal week. Note, however, that many organs and body parts remain sensitive to teratogenic agents throughout the 9-month prenatal period.
SOURCE: Adapted from Moore, K. L. (1988). *The developing human*. Philadelphia: W. B. Saunders.

to the torso like flippers, or with deformed eyes, ears, noses, and hearts (Knightley et al., 1979). It soon became clear that there are critical periods for different deformities. If the mother had taken thalidomide 20 to 22 days after conception (34 to 36 days after the first day of a woman's last menstrual period), her baby was likely to be born without ears. If she had taken it 22 to 27 days after conception, the baby often had missing or small thumbs; if thalidomide was taken between 27 and 33 days after conception, the child was likely to have stunted legs or no legs. And if the mother waited until 35 or 36 days after conception before using thalidomide, her baby was usually not affected. Thus, thalidomide had specific effects on development, depending on which structures were developing when the drug was taken.

Thalidomide, banned for years, is again being prescribed by physicians, this time for treatment of conditions associated with leprosy, acquired immunodeficiency syndrome (AIDS), tuberculosis, and some forms of cancer (Wright, 2000). Given its tragic past association with birth defects, the manufacturers of thalidomide have stamped each pill with a drawing of a pregnant woman inside a circle with a diagonal line through it (the universal "no" symbol) and have included a picture of a baby with the characteristic stunted limbs on the packaging accompanying the pills. Critics, however, worry that these measures will not be enough to prevent future birth defects.

Tobacco. Warning labels on cigarette packages that smoking may damage fetuses have resulted in a decline, but not an absence, of smoking during pregnancy (Centers for Disease Control, 2007b). In the United States, about 1 out of every 10 women report smoking during pregnancy. Among teens (15–19 years), the rate is higher—about 17% smoke during pregnancy (Centers for Disease Control, 2007b). In England, as many as 25% of women smoke during pregnancy, with teen rates even higher than this (Owen, McNeill, & Callum, 1998). Women who smoke experience higher rates of miscarriage than nonsmokers, and babies born to mothers who smoke grow more slowly in the womb and are at risk for prematurity, low birth weight, cleft lips (an opening in the top lip), and cleft palates (an opening in the roof of the mouth; Habek et al., 2002; Little, Cardy, & Munger, 2004). Smoking restricts blood flow to the fetus, which in turn reduces the levels of growth factors, oxygen, and nutrients that reach the fetus, leading to smaller size (Huijbregts et al., 2006). More than half of infants born to women who smoke 20 or more cigarettes a day end up in neonatal intensive care and experience some degree of central nervous system impairment. Women do not even have to be heavy smokers during pregnancy for behavioral effects to be evident among their offspring. Newborns exposed to as few as 5 cigarettes a day in the womb are more irritable and score lower on standard assessments of behavioral functioning than other infants (Mansi et al., 2007). Often the small babies of smokers experience catch-up growth after they are born and reach normal size by the time they enter school, but the more their mothers smoked, the less likely it is that their growth will catch up completely (Kanellopoulos et al., 2007).

The babies of smokers are also more susceptible than other babies to respiratory infections and breathing difficulties (Diaz, 1997). The more a woman smokes during pregnancy, the more likely it is that her infant will experience growth retardation and neurological problems (Law et al., 2003). The risk of **sudden infant death syndrome (SIDS),** in which a sleeping baby suddenly stops breathing and dies, also increases as the amount of smoking increases. And maternal smoking has been linked to mild cognitive difficulties and to conduct and behavior problems (Kotimaa et al., 2003; Wakshlag et al., 2006a, 2006b). These effects appear to last at least into childhood. Finally, findings from longitudinal studies have led some researchers to conclude that chronic prenatal exposure to nicotine—a legal substance—may have more negative effects on central nervous system development than sporadic exposure to the illegal drug cocaine (Bada et al., 2005; Slotkin, 1998).

In sum, maternal smoking during pregnancy is unwise because it slows fetal growth and contributes to respiratory, cognitive, and conduct problems. These effects may be caused not only by nicotine and other chemicals in cigarettes but also by toxic by-products of smoking, such as carbon monoxide, that reduce the flow of blood and oxygen to the fetus. Further, we must consider that women who smoke during pregnancy are likely to be white, young, low-income, and less educated than women who do not smoke during pregnancy (Whalen et al., 2006). It may be that some of these other factors act independently or in conjunction with cigarette smoking to create the less than ideal outcomes seen among these exposed infants (Huijbregts et al., 2006).

Alcohol. Alcohol consumed by the mother readily crosses the placenta, where it can directly affect fetal development and disrupt hormone functions of the placenta (Gabriel et al., 1998). Prenatal alcohol exposure disrupts the normal process of neuronal migration, leading to several outcomes depending on the severity of the effects. The most severe is a cluster of symptoms dubbed **fetal alcohol syndrome (FAS),** with noticeable physical symptoms such as a small head and distinctive facial abnormalities (see ■ Figure 4.6). Children with FAS are smaller and lighter than normal, and their physical growth lags behind that of their age-mates.

Children with FAS also show signs of central nervous system damage. As newborns, they are likely to display excessive irritability, hyperactivity, seizures, or tremors. Most children with FAS score well below average on IQ tests throughout childhood and adolescence, and many are mentally retarded (Howell et al., 2006; Nulman et al., 2007). Hyperactive behavior and attention deficits are also common among these children (Bhatara, Loudenberg, & Ellis, 2006). Longitudinal research indicates that more than 90% of children born with FAS have mental health problems later in life, including attention deficit hyperactivity disorder and conduct disorders (Fryer et al., 2007). They are also likely to get into trouble at school, break the law, and experience job-related problems (Autti-Rämö, 2000; Merrick et al., 2006).

As many as 30% of pregnant women drink some alcohol during pregnancy; 12% admit to "risk drinking" (seven or more drinks per week or five drinks on one occasion); and up to 4% abuse alcohol (Aros et al., 2006; O'Connor & Whaley, 2003). As a result, as many as 3 in 1000 babies in the United States are born with FAS and suffer its symptoms all their lives. Children who were exposed prenatally to alcohol but do not have FAS experience milder alcohol-related effects labeled either *fetal alcohol effects* or *alcohol-related neurodevelopmental disorder* (Nulman et al., 2007). These individuals do not have all the features of FAS but have physical, behavioral, cognitive, or a combination of these problems. In Italy, where many people indulge in daily alcohol consumption with meals, the incidence of FAS and its milder forms is roughly 35 out of 1000 children (May et al., 2005).

How much drinking does it take to harm an unborn baby? In keeping with the dosage principle of teratology, mothers who consume larger quantities of alcohol are at greater risk for having children with alcohol-related complications (Roccella & Testa, 2003; Streissguth et al., 1999). The pattern of drinking is also important. Binge drinking (consuming five or more drinks during a single session) has more negative effects on fetal development than consuming the same number of drinks across multiple sessions (Jacobson & Jacobson, 1999). Consuming five drinks in one evening results in higher blood alcohol levels for both mother and fetus than consuming one drink on each of five evenings. Finally, in keeping with the critical-period principle of teratogens, the effects of alcohol depend on which systems are developing at the time of exposure. The facial abnormalities associated with FAS result from consumption during the first trimester, when the face and skull bones are forming. During the second and third trimesters, there is much fetal growth as well as rapid brain development; thus, alcohol consumption during this latter part of pregnancy is likely to stunt growth and brain development.

No amount of drinking seems to be entirely safe. Even a mother who drinks less than an ounce a day is at risk to have a sluggish or placid newborn whose mental development is slightly below average (Jacobson et al., 1993). Other research shows that exposure to less than one drink per week during pregnancy is associated with mental health problems during

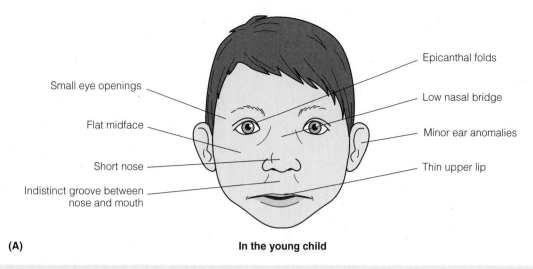

Small eye openings

Flat midface

Short nose

Indistinct groove between
nose and mouth

Epicanthal folds

Low nasal bridge

Minor ear anomalies

Thin upper lip

(A)

In the young child

■ **FIGURE 4.6** (A) Characteristic features of a child with fetal alcohol syndrome (FAS).
SOURCE: From T.W. Sadler, Characteristic features of a child with fetal alcohol syndrome, *Langman's medical embryology* (9th ed.). Copyright © 2004, Lippincott, Williams, & Wilkins.
Reprinted with permission.

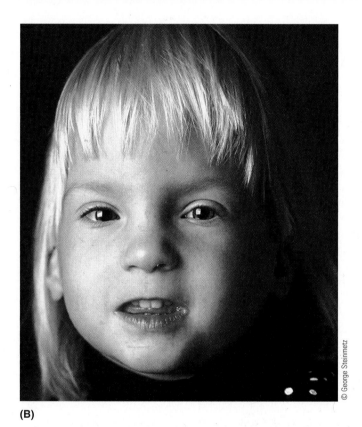

© George Steinmetz

(B)

(B) Child with FAS, illustrating many features in the drawing.
Such children may also have cardiovascular and limb defects.

childhood, at least among girls (Sayal et al., 2007). What is more, there is no well-defined critical period before or after which fetal alcohol effects cannot occur; drinking late in pregnancy can be as risky as drinking soon after conception.

Why do some babies of drinking mothers suffer ill effects but others do not? To answer this, you need to consider the nature–nurture issue again. First, the chances of damage depend partly on the mother's physiology—for example, on how efficiently she metabolizes alcohol and, therefore, how much is passed to the fetus (Shepard & Lemire, 2004). Complicating the situation, problem drinkers often have other problems that can aggravate the effects of alcohol on the fetus or cause damage—among them, malnutrition, use of drugs other than alcohol, cigarette smoking, and lack of prenatal care (Armstrong, 2003). In addition, consistent with the third principle of teratogenic effects, the embryo's genetic makeup and physical condition influence its ability to resist and recover from damage. So, for example, one fraternal twin may show all the physical abnormalities associated with FAS but the other twin, although exposed to the same prenatal environment, may show almost none; by contrast, identical twins respond similarly when exposed to alcohol prenatally (Streissguth & Dehaene, 1993). As the third principle of teratology states, both the child's and the mother's characteristics influence the extent to which a given teratogen proves damaging. Thus, the genetic makeup of both the mother and the child interact with environmental forces to determine the effects of alcohol on development.

Finally, note that it is not just the mother's use of alcohol that can adversely affect development. Some research suggests that a father's use of alcohol can influence fetal development. Other research, however, shows that paternal drinking does not affect fetal development so much as it adversely affects later development through poor parenting (Leonard & Das Eiden, 2002). Also, fathers who abuse alcohol or drugs are often with partners who abuse alcohol or drugs, making it difficult to separate the effects of the mother's use of these substances from the father's use (Frank, Brown et al., 2002). So researchers still do not know whether a father's consumption of alcohol causes the problems or whether the problems arise from things often associated with a father's abuse of alcohol.

Cocaine. Although there is no "cocaine syndrome" with characteristic physical abnormalities such as those associated with FAS, cocaine use can damage the fetus. It can cause spontaneous abortion in the first trimester of pregnancy and premature detachment of the placenta or fetal strokes later in pregnancy (Diaz, 1997). Cocaine also contributes to fetal malnourishment, retarded growth, and low birth weight (Bada et al., 2005). At birth, a small proportion of babies born to cocaine users experience withdrawal-like symptoms such as tremors and extreme irritability and have respiratory difficulties (Diaz, 1997).

Cocaine-exposed infants show deficits on several measures of information processing (Singer et al., 1999) and sensory motor skills during their first year (Arendt et al., 1998). Fortunately, most problems caused by prenatal cocaine exposure do not persist into childhood (Frank, Jacobs et al., 2002; Miller-Loncar et al., 2005). For problems that persist, it is unclear whether they are caused by the prenatal exposure to cocaine or by other prenatal or postnatal risk factors that affected infants may experience as the children of substance-abusing parents. For instance, many pregnant women who use cocaine also tend to smoke or drink alcohol during pregnancy (Nordstrom et al., 2005). In addition, cocaine-using mothers are less attentive to their babies and engage in fewer interactions with them during the first year than non–drug-using mothers or mothers who use drugs other than cocaine (Minnes et al., 2005).

● **Table 4.4** catalogs several substances and their known or suspected effects on the child. What should you make of these findings? You now understand that drugs do not damage all fetuses exposed to them in a simple, direct way. Instead, complex transactions between an individual with a certain genetic makeup and the prenatal, perinatal, and postnatal environ-

---

● **TABLE 4.4   SOME DRUGS TAKEN BY THE MOTHER THAT AFFECT THE FETUS OR NEWBORN**

DRUG	EFFECTS
Alcohol	Results include a small head, facial abnormalities, heart defects, low birth weight, and intellectual retardation (see main text).
Antiepileptic drugs	Drugs such as Dilantin, Luminal, and Tegretol, used to treat seizures, increase the incidence of cleft lip and palate, neural tube defects, kidney disease and restricted growth (Kothare & Kaleyias, 2007).
Aspirin and nonsteroidal and anti-inflammatory drugs	An occasional low dose is OK, but used in large quantities, such drugs may cause neonatal bleeding and gastrointestinal discomfort. Large amounts of these over-the-counter pain killers (e.g., Advil) have been associated with low birth weight and increased risk of miscarriage (Li, Liu, & Odouli, 2003).
Chemotherapy drugs	Such drugs cross the placenta and attack rapidly dividing cells. They can increase malformations and lead to miscarriage.
Marijuana	Heavy use of marijuana has been linked to premature birth, low birth weight, and mild behavioral abnormalities such as irritability at birth.
Narcotics	Addiction to heroin, codeine, methadone, or morphine increases the risk of premature delivery and low birth weight. The newborn is often addicted and experiences potentially fatal withdrawal symptoms (e.g., vomiting and convulsions). Longer-term cognitive deficits are sometimes evident.
Sex hormones	Birth control pills containing female hormones have been known to produce heart defects and cardiovascular problems, but today's pill formulas are safer. Progesterone in drugs used to prevent miscarriage may masculinize the fetus. Diethylstilbestrol, once prescribed to prevent miscarriage, increased the risk of cervical cancer and created infertility and pregnancy problems in exposed daughters (DESAction, 2007; Kaufman et al., 2000).
Stimulants	Heavy caffeine use has been linked to miscarriages, higher heart rates, and abnormal reflexes and irritability at birth, but it does not seem to have long-lasting effects on development (Barr & Streissguth, 1991). Cocaine use can cause premature delivery, spontaneous abortion, and low birth weight, and it may result in later learning and behavioral problems (see main text). Amphetamine use has been linked to aggressive behavior and low school achievement (Billing et al., 1994).
Tobacco	Babies of smokers tend to be small and premature, have respiratory problems, and sometimes show intellectual deficits or behavioral problems later in development (see main text). Sons whose mothers smoked during their pregnancy may later have fertility problems (Storgaard et al., 2003). Secondhand smoke in the pregnant woman's environment can increase her risk of miscarriage (George et al., 2006).

SOURCES: Based partly on information from Batshaw, 2002; Diaz, 1997; Friedman & Polifka, 1996; Winn & Hobbins, 2000.

ments influence whether or not prenatal drug exposure does lasting damage (Van Beveren, Little, & Spence, 2000). Still, women who are planning to become pregnant or who are pregnant should avoid all drugs unless they are prescribed by a physician and essential to health.

Diseases

Just as drugs can jeopardize the prenatal environment, so can diseases. Here, we take a look at three diseases—rubella, syphilis, and AIDS—that illustrate principles of teratogens. ● Table 4.5 summarizes these and other maternal conditions that may affect prenatal development.

Rubella. In the early 1940s, a doctor discovered that many infants born to women affected by **rubella** (German measles) during pregnancy had one or more of a variety of defects, including blindness, deafness, heart defects, and mental retardation. Because rubella was fairly common, there were enough cases for doctors to see that the environment of the womb leaves the fetus vulnerable to outside influences. Rubella is most dangerous during the first trimester, a critical period in which the eyes, ears, heart, and brain are rapidly forming. Nearly 15% of pregnant women with rubella miscarry or experience a fetal death (Andrade et al., 2006). Yet not all babies whose mothers had rubella, even during the most critical period of prenatal development, will have problems. Birth de-

● TABLE 4.5 MATERNAL DISEASES AND CONDITIONS THAT MAY AFFECT AN EMBRYO, FETUS, OR NEWBORN

DISEASE OR CONDITION	EFFECTS
SEXUALLY TRANSMITTED DISEASES (STDs)	
Acquired immunodeficiency syndrome (AIDS)	If transmitted from mother to child, AIDS destroys defenses against disease and may lead to death. Mothers can acquire it through sexual contact or contact with contaminated blood (see main text).
Chlamydia	Chlamydia can lead to premature birth, low birth weight, eye inflammation, or pneumonia in newborns. This most common STD is easily treatable.
Gonorrhea	This STD attacks the eyes of the child during birth; blindness is prevented by administering silver nitrate eyedrops to newborns.
Herpes simplex (genital herpes)	This disease may cause eye and brain damage or death in the first trimester. Mothers with active herpes are advised to undergo cesarean deliveries to avoid infecting their babies during delivery, because 85% of infants born with herpes acquire the virus during birth through the birth canal.
Syphilis	Untreated, it can cause miscarriage or serious birth defects such as blindness and mental retardation (see main text).
OTHER MATERNAL CONDITIONS OR DISEASES	
Chicken pox	Chicken pox can cause spontaneous abortion, premature delivery, and slow growth, although fewer than 2% of exposed fetuses develop limb, facial, or skeletal malformations.
Cytomegalovirus	This common infection shows mild flulike symptoms in adults. About 25% of infected newborns develop hearing or vision loss, mental retardation, or other impairments, and 10% develop severe neurological problems or even die.
Influenza (flu)	The more powerful strains can cause spontaneous abortions or neural abnormalities early in pregnancy.
Rubella	Rubella may cause vision and hearing loss, mental retardation, heart defects, cerebral palsy, and microcephaly (see main text).
Toxemia	Affecting about 5% of mothers in the third trimester, its mildest form, preeclampsia, causes high blood pressure and rapid weight gain in the mother. Untreated, preeclampsia may become eclampsia and cause maternal convulsions, coma, and death of the mother, the unborn child, or both. Surviving infants may be brain damaged.
Toxoplasmosis	This illness, caused by a parasite in raw meat and cat feces, leads to blindness, deafness, and mental retardation in approximately 40% of infants born to infected mothers.

SOURCES: Based partly on information from Batshaw, 2002; Ratcliffe, Byrd, & Sakornbut, 1996; Simpson & Creehan, 1996; and Winn & Hobbins, 2000.

fects occur in 60 to 85% of babies whose mothers had the disease in the first 2 months of pregnancy, in about 50% of those infected in the third month, and in only 16% of those infected in the fourth or fifth months (Kelley-Buchanan, 1988). Consistent with the critical-period principle, damage to the nervous system, eyes, and heart is most likely during that part of the first 8 weeks of pregnancy when each of these organs is forming, whereas deafness is more likely when the mother contracts rubella in weeks 6 to 13 of the pregnancy. Today, doctors stress that a woman should not try to become pregnant unless she has been immunized against rubella or has already had it. As a result of successful immunization programs, many women are now immune to this previously common infection. Nevertheless, recent outbreaks of rubella have been reported in several countries, including the Netherlands, Brazil, and Spain (de Mol et al., 2006; Torner et al., 2006).

Syphilis. Now consider another teratogen, the sexually transmitted disease **syphilis**. Syphilis during pregnancy can cause miscarriage or stillbirth (Genc & Ledger, 2000). Babies born alive to mothers who have syphilis, like those born to mothers who have rubella, often suffer blindness, deafness, heart problems, or brain damage. This shows that different teratogens—here, syphilis and rubella—can be responsible for the same problem. However, whereas rubella is most damaging in the early stage of pregnancy, syphilis is most damaging in the middle and later stages of pregnancy. This is because syphilitic organisms cannot cross the placental barrier until the 18th prenatal week, providing a window of opportunity for treating the mother-to-be who finds out she has the disease. Even with appropriate treatment—penicillin—some infants are infected or die (Genc & Ledger, 2000).

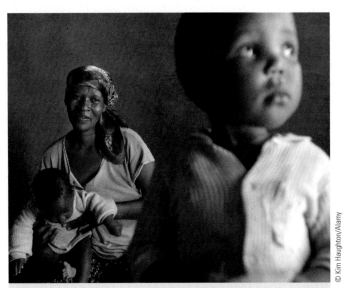

Women with HIV, the virus that causes AIDS, can transmit this to their babies prenatally through the placenta, during birth, or post-natally during breastfeeding.

AIDS. The sexually transmitted disease of greatest concern in recent decades is **acquired immunodeficiency syndrome (AIDS),** the life-threatening disease caused by the human immunodeficiency virus (HIV). AIDS destroys the immune system and makes victims susceptible to "opportunistic" infections that eventually kill them unless they are treated with multiple drugs. HIV-infected mothers can transmit the virus to their babies (1) prenatally, if the virus passes through the placenta; (2) perinatally, when blood may be exchanged between mother and child as the umbilical cord separates from the placenta; or (3) postnatally, if the virus is transmitted during breast-feeding. Without treatment, somewhere between 15 and 35% of babies born to HIV-infected mothers will become infected (Newell, 2003). The rate is much lower if these mothers take azidothymidine, also called AZT or zidovudine, to treat the HIV or if they and their newborns are given a drug called nevirapine, which helps block transmission of HIV at birth (Newell, 2003; Stringer et al., 2004). Bottle-feeding further reduces the rate of HIV transmission from affected mothers to their infants (Magoni et al., 2005). Infected infants now live longer than they did at the outset of the AIDS epidemic because of the development of appropriate treatments—75% are alive at age 5, and many survive into adolescence (King et al., 2002).

Although mother-to-child transmission of HIV in the United States has decreased significantly since peaking in 1992, it continues to be a tremendous problem in Africa and other parts of the world with AIDS epidemics. In 2005, for example, about 700,000 infants worldwide became infected with HIV from their mothers, most in sub-Saharan Africa (Avert, 2006).

Environmental Hazards

A mother can control what she ingests, but sometimes she cannot avoid a hazardous external environment. Here, we discuss two environmental conditions—radiation and pollutants—that may endanger the unborn child.

Radiation. After atomic bombs were dropped on Hiroshima and Nagasaki in 1945, not one pregnant woman who was within one-half mile of the blasts gave birth to a live child, and 75% of those who were within a mile and a quarter of the blasts had stillborn infants or seriously handicapped children who died soon after birth (Apgar & Beck, 1974). Surviving children of these mothers had a higher-than-normal rate of mental retardation and greater incidence of leukemia and cancers later in life (Centers for Disease Control, 2007a; Kodama, Mabuchi, & Shigematsu, 1996). Even clinical doses of radiation, such as those used in X-rays and cancer treatment, are capable of causing mutations, spontaneous abortions, and a variety of birth defects, especially if the mother is exposed between weeks 8 and 15 (Hill & Haffner, 2002). Therefore, expectant mothers are routinely advised to avoid X-rays unless they are essential to their own survival, as might be the case with women undergoing certain cancer treatments.

GETTING LIFE OFF TO A GOOD START

The more we learn about important environmental influences on human development, the better able we are to optimize environment and therefore to optimize development. Although the nature and quality of an individual's environment matters throughout the life span, it seems sensible to do as much as possible to get a baby's life off to a good start.

For starters, it would be good for babies if more of them were planned and wanted. Moreover, a woman should begin making positive changes in her lifestyle, such as giving up smoking, before she even thinks about becoming pregnant. Once a woman is pregnant, she should seek good prenatal care as quickly as possible so that she will learn how to optimize the well-being of both herself and her unborn child and so that any problems during the

pregnancy can be managed appropriately. The guidelines for pregnant women are not that complicated, although they are often violated. They boil down to such practices as eating an adequate diet, taking prenatal vitamins, protecting oneself against diseases, and avoiding drugs. Research suggests that social support and clear communication between health-care providers and pregnant women can go far to improve prenatal care (Bennett et al., 2006; Harley & Eskenazi, 2006).

Today, many couples also enroll in classes that prepare them for childbirth. These classes started in the 1940s to help reduce the fear and pain experienced by many women during labor and delivery. The **Lamaze method** of prepared childbirth teaches women to associate childbirth with pleasant feelings and to ready themselves for the process by learning exercises,

breathing and pushing methods, and relaxation techniques that make childbirth easier (Lamaze, 1958). Parents typically attend Lamaze classes for 6 to 8 weeks before the delivery. The father or another supportive person becomes a coach who helps the mother train her muscles and perfect her breathing for the event that lies ahead. Couples who participate in childbirth preparation classes report a greater sense of control during labor and delivery, and this sense of control is associated with higher levels of satisfaction with the childbirth experience (Hart & Foster, 1997). Unfortunately, following their delivery, many women say that their prenatal classes did not go as far as they could have in providing practice with the coping strategies useful for a smooth delivery (Spiby et al., 1999).

Pollutants. Recall our chapter opener about Florence Engoran, who was pregnant at the time of the 9/11 attacks. The collapse of the World Trade Center (WTC) exposed those living in the vicinity to large amounts of potentially toxic pollutants. In the months following 9/11, researchers enrolled pregnant women in a longitudinal study to track potential effects of prenatal exposure to pollution on a variety of infant outcomes. So far, this research has revealed that infants born to women living near the World Trade Centers in the months after the destruction were born lighter, shorter, and slightly earlier than a control group of babies whose mothers were not living near the WTC (Lederman et al., 2004). Further research will examine whether prenatal exposure to the WTC pollution affected children's neurocognitive development.

Exposure to "heavy metals," such as lead in the air we breathe and the water we drink, is an ongoing concern. Children exposed prenatally to lead are smaller at birth and may be born preterm (Jelliffe-Pawlowski et al., 2006; Schell et al., 2006). They also show impaired intellectual functioning as infants in proportion to the amount of lead in their umbilical cords (Bellinger et al., 1987; Canfield et al., 2003). This finding holds true even after controlling for other differences among children, such as socioeconomic status. Lead exposure postnatally is also dangerous. It is estimated that one in four children under age 6 in the United States lives in a home with lead dust from old paint (Rogan & Ware, 2003). Exposure to even low levels of lead—lower than previously thought to be safe—is associated with IQ decreases of 4 to 7 points (Rogan & Ware, 2003). Prenatal exposure to mercury, dioxins, and polychlorinated biphenyls (PCBs) has also been associated with

perinatal and postnatal problems (e.g., Jedrychowski et al., 2006; Nakajima et al., 2006).

Clearly, there is a critical need for more research aimed at identifying a huge number of chemicals, wastes, and other environmental hazards that may affect unborn children. One expert estimates that there are 70,000 synthetic chemicals "out there" to which children may be exposed, but that fewer than 20% of these have been evaluated for toxicity (Morris, 1999).

The message is unmistakable: The chemistry of the prenatal environment often determines whether an embryo or fetus survives and how it looks and functions after birth. A variety of teratogens can affect development, although as you have learned, the influence of teratogens varies. Effects are worst in critical periods when organ systems are growing most rapidly, and effects are more serious with greater exposure to teratogens. Not all embryos or fetuses are equally affected by the same teratogen; the genetic makeup of both the mother and her unborn child and the quality of the prenatal and postnatal environments all play a role in determining the effects. By becoming familiar with the information here, and by keeping up with new knowledge, parents-to-be can do much to increase the already high odds that their unborn child will be normal as it approaches its next challenge: the birth process.

The Mother's State

What can parents, especially the mother-to-be, do to sustain a healthy pregnancy? The Applications box on "Getting Life Off to a Good Start" explores how parents can set the stage for a healthy pregnancy. Here, we describe three characteristics of the mother—age, emotional state, and nutritional status—that can affect the quality of the prenatal environment.

Age

At one end of the age spectrum, 11- and 12-year-old girls have given birth; at the other end of the spectrum, a 67-year-old Spanish woman and a 60-year-old American woman made the record books in their respective countries by giving birth to twins after in vitro fertilization. These are, however, unusual cases. The safest, and more typical, time to bear a child appears to be from about age 16 to age 35. One analysis of more than 73,000 birth records suggests an even narrower age band for "optimal" pregnancy during a woman's 20s: Women between the ages of 20 and 30 had the lowest rates of low–birth-weight babies and premature deliveries compared to younger and older women (Machado, 2006).

Very young mothers have higher-than-normal rates of birth complications, including premature deliveries and stillbirths (Salihu et al., 2006). The reproductive system of the teenager (19 years or younger) may not be physically mature enough to sustain a fetus to full term, making this group more vulnerable to having a low–birth-weight baby. However, the greater problem appears to be that teenagers often do not seek prenatal care, and they are more likely to live in poverty than mothers in their 20s and older. Unfortunately, these conditions are likely to persist after the birth, leading to increased death rates before their first birthday among infants born to mothers 15 years or younger (Phipps, Blume, & DeMonner, 2002).

As for older women, they are more likely to experience trouble getting pregnant. For those who do conceive, there is an increased risk of stillbirth, miscarriage, and low–birth-weight babies, as shown in ■ **Figure 4.7** (Borders et al., 2007; Reddy, Ko, & Willinger, 2006). In the past, many fetal deaths in older women were caused by congenital abnormalities. With today's extensive prenatal testing of women older than 35, however, fewer babies are dying from congenital problems, partly because many such fetuses are identified early and aborted. Still, fetal death rates remain higher for older women, particularly for those beyond age 50 (Salihu et al., 2003). Compared with younger women, women over the age of 35 are more likely to release more than a single egg during ovulation, which increases their chances of conceiving fraternal twins (Beemsterboer et al., 2006). Though some women may be thrilled to learn that they are carrying twins, any multiple pregnancy and delivery carries additional health risks for the mother and the babies. Finally, keep in mind that despite the increased risks of childbearing among older women, most have normal pregnancies and healthy babies.

Does the mother's age have any effect on her parenting skills once the baby arrives? Marc Bornstein and colleagues (2006) found that parenting skills improved from adolescence through a woman's mid-20s, but beyond the age of about 30, increasing age did not offer any additional benefits in terms of parenting skills. Possibly this is because, by age 30, women

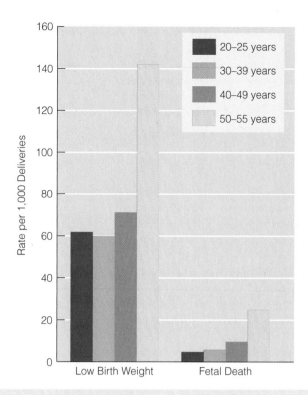

■ **FIGURE 4.7** Low birth weight and fetal death increase after maternal age 40, with marked increases after age 50. SOURCE: Adapted from Salihu, H. M., Shumpert, M. N., Slay, M., Kirby, R. S., & Alexander, G. R. (2003). Childbearing beyond maternal age 50 and fetal outcomes in the United States. *Obstetrics and Gynecology*, 102, 1006–1014.

have developed more awareness of their own strengths and weaknesses and have acquired greater knowledge about child development.

Emotional Condition

Is the prenatal environment affected by how the mother feels about being pregnant or how her life is going while she is pregnant? Life is filled with many stressors—both chronic (poverty, for example, or ongoing job stress) and acute (experiencing a serious car accident, for example, or witnessing the mass murders at Virginia Tech on April 16, 2007). Being pregnant does not make stress disappear; for some women with unintended or mistimed pregnancies, pregnancy may increase stress levels. How might the fetus be affected by the mother's experience of stress?

When a woman such as Florence Engoran, introduced at the beginning of the chapter, becomes emotionally aroused, her glands secrete powerful hormones such as adrenaline (also called epinephrine) that may cross the placental barrier and enter the fetus's bloodstream. At the least, these hormones temporarily increase the fetus's motor activity. A temporarily stressful experience such as falling or receiving a scare will generally not damage mother or fetus. It is only when a mother experiences *prolonged and severe* emotional stress and anxiety during her pregnancy (as a result, for example, of the death of her husband, chronic illness of another child, or unemployment) that damage may be done (Borders et al., 2007; Hansen, Lou, & Olsen, 2001). The most likely effects are a faster and more irregular heart rate and stunted prenatal growth, which can lower birth weight; premature birth; and birth complications (Berkowitz et al., 2003). Following birth, babies whose mothers had been highly stressed during pregnancy tend to be smaller, more active, more irritable, and more prone to crying than other babies (de Weerth, van Hees, & Buitelaar, 2003; Wurmser et al., 2006). Stress during pregnancy can also cause delays in cognitive development (Buitelaar et al., 2003).

How might maternal stress stunt fetal growth and contribute to the offspring's irritability and anxiety? The mechanisms are not yet clear. The link between the mother's stressful experiences and small, premature babies may involve stress hormones, changes in the immune system, reduced blood flow through the arteries in the uterus, or even a poor diet (see, for example, DiPietro, Costigan, & Gurewitsch, 2003). Whatever the mechanism, it is clear that not all stressed mothers have babies who are small and arrive early. Indeed, Janet DiPietro and her colleagues (2006) found that mild to moderate stress experienced by otherwise healthy mothers during pregnancy may actually enhance fetal development. How can we reconcile these seemingly contradictory findings? What can we tell potential parents about the effects of stress—is it beneficial or harmful? It may depend on the effect that the stressful event has on the woman's daily life. If the event significantly disrupts daily life, child outcomes may be worse than if the mother's daily life is affected very little by the event (Laplante et al., 2004).

Stress and anxiety are not the only maternal emotional states to consider. Maternal depression during pregnancy may lead to motor delays in newborns (Lundy et al., 1999). Depression affects levels of neurotransmitters (brain chemicals) in both mothers and their newborns. Researchers have found a connection between these changes in neurotransmitter levels and certain immature motor responses of newborns. They do not yet know, however, whether these effects persist.

Nutritional Condition

At the turn of the last century, doctors advised mothers to gain a mere 10 to 15 pounds while pregnant. With better understanding of nutrition and pregnancy, doctors now recommend a healthy, high-protein, high-calorie diet with a total weight gain of 25 to 35 pounds for normal-weight women—and many women gain more than this recommended weight during their pregnancy (Olson, 2002). Doctors know that inadequate prenatal nutrition and lack of weight gain can be harmful. Severe maternal malnutrition, which occurs during famine, stunts prenatal growth and produces small, underweight babies (Stein et al., 1975; Susser & Stein, 1994). The effects of malnutrition depend on when it occurs. During the first trimester, malnutrition can disrupt the formation of the spinal cord, result in fewer brain cells, and even cause stillbirth (Susser & Stein, 1994). Restrictive dieting, use of diuretics, and disor-

dered eating behaviors during the first trimester can also cause serious problems, such as neural tube defects (Carmichael et al., 2003). During the third trimester, malnutrition is most likely to result in smaller neurons, a smaller brain, and a smaller child overall.

The offspring of malnourished mothers sometimes show cognitive deficits as infants and children. Poor prenatal nutrition may also put some children at risk for certain diseases in adulthood, especially hypertension, coronary heart disease, and diabetes (Barker, 1998; Goldberg & Prentice, 1994). Some research challenges these conclusions, however. In many cases prenatal malnutrition does not have serious long-term effects on development, and among women who are adequately nourished, it is difficult to establish a connection between specific nutrients and birth outcome or later behaviors (Langley-Evans & Langley-Evans, 2003; Mathews, Youngman & Neil, 2004). One exception to this is a deficiency of folic acid, which, as mentioned earlier, has been linked to neural tube defects. In 1998, the United States and Canada initiated mandatory folate enrichment of cereal products (look for fortified breakfast cereals and breads) in an effort to increase folate levels of women of childbearing age. As ■ Figure 4.8 shows, these fortification programs have been associated with a decrease in the incidence of neural tube defects such as spina bifida, particularly among Hispanics and Whites, who had higher rates of spina bifida prior to the start of the program than Blacks (Williams et al., 2005). Although such fortification programs help, it may still be difficult to consume the "perfect" combination of foods to provide the full measure of recommended vitamins and minerals. Consequently, most health-care professionals prescribe prenatal vitamins for their pregnant patients.

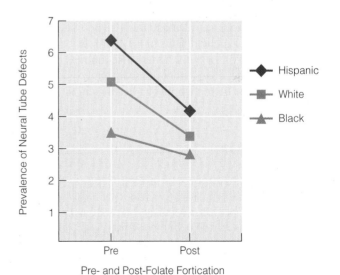

■ **FIGURE 4.8** The prevalence of neural tube defects such as spina bifida has decreased in the United States and Canada since these countries began fortifying cereals with folate.
SOURCE: Adapted from Williams, I. J., Rasmussen, S. A., Flores, A., Kirby, R. S., Edmonds, L. D. (2005). Decline in the prevalence and anencephaly by race/ethnicity: 1995–2002. *Pediatrics, 116*, 580–586.

Although prenatal nutrition is clearly important, much depends on whether a child receives an adequate diet and good care after birth. Dietary supplements, especially when combined with stimulating day care, can go a long way toward heading off the potentially damaging effects of prenatal malnutrition. Best, of course, is good nourishment before *and* after birth.

The Father's State

What about characteristics of the fathers? Does the father's state have any influence on the quality of the prenatal environment or birth outcome? Unfortunately, there is not a lot of research on the father's contributions to prenatal development beyond his genetic contribution. But researchers know that the father's age, just like the mother's age, can influence development. We noted earlier that women older than 35 are at greater risk of miscarriage than younger mothers. Similarly, the odds of miscarriage increase with paternal age (Kleinhaus et al., 2006). The risk of congenital heart defects is also greater for children of older fathers (Olshan, Schnitzer, & Baird, 1994). In addition, there is an elevated risk of neural tube defects, kidney problems, and Down syndrome among children born to older fathers (McIntosh, Olshan, & Baird, 1995). Like the risk of miscarriage, the likelihood of Down syndrome is greater when both mother and father are older (Fisch et al., 2003). Finally, researchers have consistently identified advanced paternal age (i.e., 50 and older) as a risk factor for schizophrenia (see Chapter 3; Rasmussen, 2006; Tsuchiya et al., 2005).

A father's exposure to environmental toxins can also affect a couple's children. A father's prolonged exposure to radiation, anesthetic gases used in operating rooms, pesticides, or other environmental toxins can damage the genetic material in his sperm and cause genetic defects in his children (Stone, 1992; Strigini et al., 1990). In short, fathers, like mothers, should assess and, if need be, change their lifestyles and exposure to risk factors to optimize their chances of a healthy child.

SUMMING UP

▌ The womb is an environment that can influence the unborn child in favorable or unfavorable ways. As an environment, the womb can influence the developing child and can be influenced by the child-to-be as well as by the mother.

▌ Teratogens are environmental factors that can harm a developing fetus. There are numerous teratogens, such as alcohol, tobacco, diseases, and environmental toxins, that can adversely affect prenatal development.

▌ Four principles help researchers understand the effects of teratogens: effects are worst when organ systems are growing most rapidly, effects are more serious with greater exposure to teratogens, harmful effects depend on the genetic makeup of both the mother and her unborn child, and the effects of terato-

gens often depend on the quality of the prenatal and postnatal environments.

▌ The mother's emotional and nutritional state can influence the unborn child, as can the age of both the mother and the father.

CRITICAL THINKING

1. There seem to be so many things that have the potential to adversely affect prenatal development. Put these in perspective and summarize three or four things that prospective parents should be most concerned about when considering their unborn baby's environment.

2. Imagine you are asked to speak with a group of mothers-to-be about the possible hazards influencing prenatal development. Describe for them the four principles of teratogens and illustrate each principle with an example.

4.3 THE PERINATAL ENVIRONMENT

The **perinatal environment** is the environment surrounding birth; it includes influences such as drugs given to the mother during labor, delivery practices, and the social environment shortly after birth. Like the prenatal environment, the perinatal environment can greatly affect human development.

In most Western cultures, a dramatic shift in birthing practices occurred during the 20th century. In 1930, 80% of births took place at home; by 1990, this figure had plummeted to 1% (Zander & Chamberlain, 1999). This change in birth setting was accompanied by a shift from thinking about birth as a natural family event that occurred at home to thinking that birth is a medical event to be solved with high technology (Cassidy, 2006). In most cases, doctors assumed full authority for decisions regarding delivery.

Despite the continued medical setting of most births today, many couples want to give birth in a situation that combines the security of modern technology with a comfortable homelike feeling. Many hospitals have responded by restructuring their labor and delivery rooms and practices to give parents greater flexibility and control when it comes time to deliver. Today's parents are also pushing for greater voice in their delivery experiences (Carmichael, 2004). Mothers-to-be have several choices when it comes to who will assist with their delivery, including family physicians, obstetricians, specialists in maternal–fetal medicine, and midwives. For high-risk pregnancies associated with delivery complications, a maternal–fetal specialist, or perinatologist, is recommended. However, for the majority of women, personal preference can determine the best caregiver for pregnancy and delivery. In many countries, such as England and France, midwives have been the traditional pregnancy caregivers. For the past century, most (around 90%) women in the United States have relied on physicians or obstetricians for pregnancy care, but the use of midwives is slowly increasing, from 4% in 1990 to 8% more recently (Centers for Disease Control, 2006b). In general, midwives view

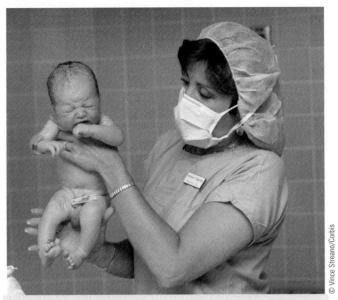

Most newborns have not yet acquired the "cuteness" of somewhat older babies. Instead, they are often red, wrinkled, and swollen in places, and they may be covered with amniotic fluid, blood, fine downy hair (lanugo), and a white greasy substance (vernix). Their heads may even be misshapen from coming through the birth canal or from the use of forceps or suction during delivery.

pregnancy and delivery as natural life events rather than as medical events requiring medical intervention. They partner with the laboring mother-to-be to assist her with delivery but do not dictate the conditions of labor and delivery.

Another change in the delivery room is the presence of a spouse, partner, mother, sister, and/or friend to provide support and share in the miracle of birth. Most women find the support provided by this familiar person helpful and reassuring. Some women have the support of a *doula*—an individual trained to provide continuous physical and emotional support throughout the childbirth process. Such support tends to shorten labor by as much as half and to reduce the need for pain medication and assisted delivery such as use of forceps or vacuum (Hodnett et al., 2003; Scott, Klaus, & Klaus, 1999). The rate of cesarean sections is lower among women continuously supported by a doula or midwife (Dickinson et al., 2002). Mothers with continuous labor support also report more positive feelings about the birth experience, fewer symptoms of postnatal depression, and greater likelihood of breast-feeding than nonsupported mothers (Scott, Klaus, & Klaus, 1999). Clearly, then, the context surrounding labor and delivery is important: Women who receive more support during childbirth have more positive experiences.

Childbirth is a three-stage process (see ■ Figure 4.9). The first stage of labor begins as the mother experiences regular contractions of the uterus and ends when her cervix has fully dilated (widened) so that the fetus's head can pass through. This stage of labor lasts an average of 9 hours for firstborn children and 4 to 6 hours for later-born children, but it may last much longer (or shorter) depending on the individual and her circumstances

(Albers, 1999; Jones & Larson, 2003). It ends when the cervix has dilated to 10 centimeters. The second stage of labor is delivery, which begins as the fetus's head passes through the cervix into the vagina and ends when the baby emerges from the mother's body. This is when the mother is often told to "bear down" (push) with each contraction to assist her baby through the birth canal. For first deliveries, this stage takes about 1 hour; for later deliveries, it can be 15 to 20 minutes (Albers, 1999; Jones & Larson, 2003). Finally, the third stage of the birth process is the delivery of the placenta, which lasts only a few minutes.

When the birth process is completed, the mother (and often the father, if he is present) is typically physically exhausted, relieved to be through the ordeal of giving birth, and exhilarated all at once. Meanwhile, the fetus has been thrust from its carefree but cramped existence into a strange new world.

Possible Hazards

In most births, the entire process goes smoothly, and parents and newborn quickly begin their relationship. Occasionally, however, problems arise.

Anoxia

One clear hazard during the birth process is **anoxia,** or oxygen shortage (also called *asphyxia*). Anoxia can occur for any number of reasons—for example, because the umbilical cord becomes pinched or tangled during birth, because sedatives given to the mother reach the fetus and interfere with the baby's breathing, because mucus lodged in the baby's throat prevents normal breathing, or because the baby is in a **breech presentation** (feet or buttocks first) during a vaginal delivery. If identified in advance, fetuses in breech position can be safely delivered by cesarean section to avoid possible anoxia that may occur with a vaginal delivery. Anoxia is dangerous primarily because brain cells die if they are starved of oxygen for more than a few minutes. Severe anoxia can initially cause poor reflexes, seizures, heart rate irregularities, and breathing difficulties. In the long run, severe anoxia can lead to memory impairment or **cerebral palsy,** a neurological disability associated with, primarily, difficulty controlling muscle movements; it also increases the risk of learning or intellectual disabilities and speech difficulties (Fehlings, Hunt, & Rosenbaum, 2007). Milder anoxia makes some infants irritable at birth or delays their motor and cognitive development, but usually does not lead to permanent problems.

Fetal monitoring procedures during labor and delivery can alert caregivers to the possibility of anoxia and allow them to take preventative measures. For example, a vaginal delivery is nearly impossible for the 1 fetus in 100 that is found lying sideways in the uterus. The fetus must be turned to assume a head-down position or be delivered by **cesarean section,** a surgical procedure in which an incision is made in the mother's abdomen and uterus so that the baby can be removed. Now, consider the potential hazards associated with delivery procedures and technologies.

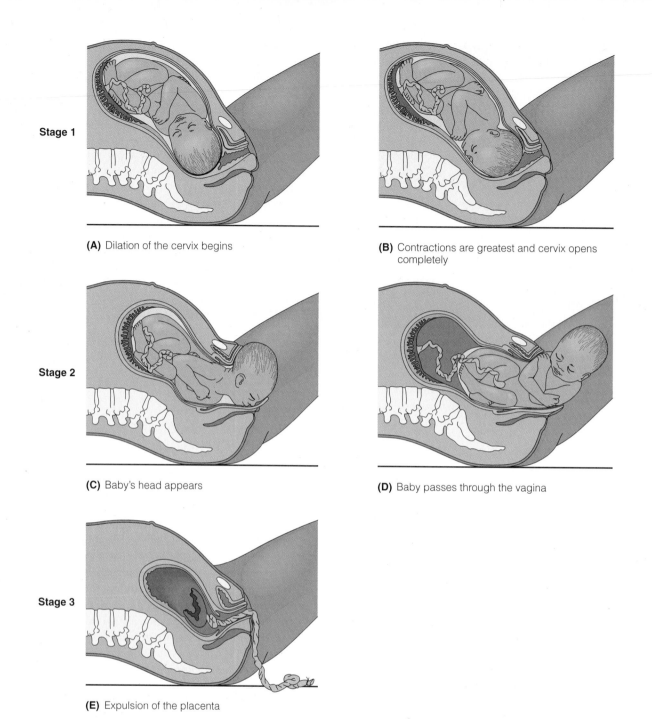

(A) Dilation of the cervix begins

(B) Contractions are greatest and cervix opens completely

(C) Baby's head appears

(D) Baby passes through the vagina

(E) Expulsion of the placenta

■ **FIGURE 4.9** The three stages of labor. Stage 1: (A) Contractions of the uterus cause dilation and effacement of the cervix. (B) Transition is reached when the frequency and strength of the contractions are at their peak and the cervix opens completely. Stage 2: (C) The mother pushes with each contraction, forcing the baby down the birth canal, and the head appears. (D) Near the end of stage 2, the shoulders emerge and are followed quickly by the rest of the baby's body. Stage 3: (E) With a few final pushes, the placenta is delivered.

Complicated Delivery

In some cases, mothers may need assistance with delivery, possibly because labor has proceeded too long with too little to show for it or because of concern about the well-being of the baby or mother. There is much debate in the medical literature about whether delivery is better assisted with forceps or with vacuum extraction (Johanson & Menon, 2000; O'Grady, Pope, & Patel, 2000). For years, doctors frequently used forceps (an instrument resembling an oversized pair of salad tongs). However, forceps on the soft skull of the newborn occasionally caused serious problems, including cranial bleeding and brain damage. Alternatively, doctors may use vacuum extraction ("suction") to assist difficult deliveries. This procedure has fewer risks associated with it, although it is not risk free. In a vacuum extraction, a cup is inserted through the opening of the birth canal and attached to the baby's head. Suction is applied to make the cup adhere to the baby's scalp; during each contraction and with the mother bearing down, the doctor uses the traction created by the suction to help deliver the baby. From the mother's point of view, vacuum extraction is less traumatic than forceps because the vacuum extractor takes up less space in the birth canal (and therefore is felt less) than forceps (Shihadeh & Al-Najdawi, 2001). For the baby, however, there is likely to be swelling of the scalp and some marking where the vacuum cup was attached. More serious injuries are possible if the vacuum is not properly used. Unfortunately, women who deliver with vacuum assistance report less satisfaction with the overall birth experience than mothers who deliver by other methods (Schindl et al., 2003).

Cesarean sections, too, have been controversial. Use of this alternative to normal vaginal delivery has prevented the death of many babies—for example, when the baby is too large or the mother is too small to permit normal delivery, when a fetus out of position cannot be repositioned, or when fetal monitoring reveals that a birth complication is likely. Medical advances have made cesarean sections about as safe as vaginal deliveries, and few ill effects on mothers and infants have been observed. But mothers who have "C-sections" do take longer to recover from the birth process and are sometimes less positive toward and involved with their babies, at least during the first month of life (DiMatteo et al., 1996). Nonetheless, the development of babies born by cesarean appears to be perfectly normal (Durik, Hyde, & Clark, 2000).

Many observers have questioned why cesarean deliveries have become so much more common—to the point that they accounted for 30% of births in the United States in 2005 (Hamilton et al., 2007). By one estimate, 11% of first-time cesarean sections are unnecessary and 65% of second-time cesareans are unnecessary (Kabir et al., 2005). Some obstetricians readily opt for C-section deliveries because it protects them from the costly malpractice suits that might arise from complications in vaginal deliveries (Childbirth Connection, 2007). C-sections also generate more revenue than vaginal deliveries. On average, a cesarean without complications costs about $12,600 in the United States, compared with $6,700 for a vaginal delivery (Childbirth Connection, 2007). Contributing to the high rate of C-sections is the tendency for women who have had one C-section to deliver subsequent babies by C-section rather than attempting a vaginal delivery. Although there is a very small risk of complications with a vaginal delivery following a C-section, it is safe for the large majority of women (Landon et al., 2004). Finally, the high rate of C-section deliveries also reflects the fact that some mothers—and their doctors—prefer having a scheduled birth rather than contending with the unscheduled vaginal delivery. Around 28% of C-sections are elective, not medically necessary (Meikle et al., 2005). Mothers who undergo planned (as opposed to emergency) C-sections rate the birth experience more positively than any other group, including those who deliver vaginally (Schindl et al., 2003).

In a few instances, tension between the hospital's concerns and the mother's wishes related to delivery practices can put them at odds. In one case, a hospital sought and received permission from a judge for guardianship of a fetus so that it could force the mother to deliver her baby by cesarean section (Associated Press, 2004). The hospital argued that a vaginal delivery would endanger the life of the child because an ultrasound showed that it was large. The mother, on the other hand, feared having a C-section and had successfully delivered six previous children vaginally. By the time the hospital obtained the court order for guardianship, the parents had gone to another hospital, where the mother vaginally delivered a healthy 11-pound baby girl. In another case, a mother carrying twins was advised to have a cesarean section. She refused and several weeks later gave birth to a healthy girl and a stillborn boy (Miller, 2005). When an autopsy revealed that the boy had been alive at the time doctors advised her to have a C-section and had died only 2 days prior to the natural delivery, the mother was charged with first-degree criminal homicide, charges that were later dropped when she pled guilty to child endangerment. Cases such as these raise questions about whether institutions can force women to undergo a surgical procedure against their wishes, and more generally, questions about who charts the course of pregnancy and delivery—mother or other?

Medications

Some of us were delivered in an era when mothers were routinely drugged into unconsciousness during delivery so that they would not experience any pain, or if they did, they wouldn't remember it. Not surprisingly, concerns have been raised about medications given to mothers during the birth process—analgesics and anesthetics to reduce their pain, sedatives to relax them, and stimulants to induce or intensify uterine contractions. Sedative drugs that act on the entire body cross the placenta and can affect the baby. Babies whose mothers receive large doses of sedative medications during delivery are generally sluggish and irritable, are difficult to feed or cuddle during the first few days of life, and smile infrequently (Elbourne & Wiseman, 2000). In short, they act as though they are drugged. Think about it: Doses of medication large enough to affect mothers can have much greater effects on newborns who weigh only 7 pounds and have immature circulatory and excretory systems that cannot get rid of drugs for days.

Regional analgesics, such as epidurals and spinal blocks, reduce sensation in specific parts of the body. Because they do not cross the placenta, they have fewer ill effects on babies and are preferred by many physicians over sedative drugs that *do* cross the placenta. Epidurals are also rated by mothers as more effective for pain control than other forms of analgesics (Macario et al., 2000; Sheiner et al., 2000). But with these advantages mothers and physicians must weigh disadvantages, including longer labor times and increased need for forceps or vacuum assistance with epidurals (Cassidy, 2006; Halpern et al., 1998).

One of the most commonly used drugs is oxytocin (brand name "Pitocin"), which can initiate and speed up contractions—moving labor along more quickly. Oxytocin may be administered if a woman's labor seems to have stalled or if she is beyond her due date or the amniotic sac has broken without contractions. The body naturally produces low levels of oxytocin throughout pregnancy and administering synthetic oxytocin to assist delivery is considered very safe.

In sum, taking obstetric medications is not as risky a business today as it once was, but it is still a decision that requires the pros and cons to be weighed carefully. The effects depend on which drug is used, how much is taken, when it is taken, and by which mother.

Possible hazards during birth, then, include anoxia; breech presentation; the need for assisted delivery through forceps, vacuum extraction, or cesarean section; and the use of medications for pain relief or to speed up labor. Fortunately, most deliveries, although unique from the parents' perspective, are routine from a clinical perspective. In the next section, we consider the birth experience from a family perspective.

The Mother's Experience

What is it really like to give birth to a child? For every woman who has given birth, you are likely to hear a unique birth story (Savage, 2001). Most mothers admit that they experienced severe pain and a good deal of anxiety, including feelings of outright panic (Waldenström et al., 1996). Yet most also emerged from the delivery room feeling good about their achievement and their ability to cope ("I did it!"). Overall, 77% felt the experience was positive and only 10% said it was negative. And, despite longer labors and more medication, first-time mothers did not perceive labor and delivery much differently than experienced mothers did.

What factors influence a mother's experience of birth? Psychological factors such as the mother's attitude toward her pregnancy, her knowledge and expectations about the birth process, her sense of control over childbirth, and the social support she receives from her partner or someone else are important determinants of her experience of delivery and of her new baby (Waldenström et al., 1996; Wilcock, Kobayashi, & Murray, 1997). Social support can be especially important. When the father, or another supportive person whose main role is to comfort the mother, is continuously present during labor and delivery, women experience less pain, use less medication, are less likely to have cesarean sections, and are more likely to feel good about the birth process (Hodnett & Osborn, 1989; Kennell et al., 1991).

Cultural Factors

The experience of childbearing is shaped by the cultural context in which it occurs. For example, different cultures have different views of the desirability of having children. In some, a large family is a status symbol, whereas in the People's Republic of China, a "one-child policy" discourages multiple childbearing in hopes of slowing population growth and rais-

ing the standard of living. As a result of this policy, the average number of children a Chinese woman bears dropped from nearly five children in 1970 to fewer than two in recent years. The ratio of boys to girls has also changed; many parents want their one child to be a boy who can support them in old age and therefore abort female fetuses identified through ultrasound tests or abandon their female babies after they are born.

Practices surrounding birth also differ widely. Consider three different birth scenarios that reflect different cultural beliefs about pregnancy and delivery. Among the Pokot people of Kenya, there is strong social support of the mother-to-be (O'Dempsey, 1988). The community celebrates the coming birth, and the father-to-be stops hunting lest he be killed by animals. As a result, he is available to support his wife. A midwife, aided by female relatives, delivers the baby. The placenta is buried in the goat enclosure, and the baby is washed in cold water and given a mixture of hot ash and boiled herbs so that it will vomit the amniotic fluid it has swallowed. Mothers are given plenty of time to recover. They go into seclusion for 1 month and devote themselves entirely to their babies for 3 months.

By contrast, in Uttar Pradesh in northern India, the blood associated with childbirth is viewed as polluting, and the whole event as shameful (Jeffery & Jeffery, 1993). A *dai*, a poorly paid attendant hired by the woman's mother-in-law, delivers the baby. The *dai* typically hates her menial, disgusting job, provides no pain relievers, discourages the mother from crying out in pain, and offers little emotional support. The mother is kept in the house for several days and in the family compound for weeks so that she will not pollute others. Because the baby is also believed to be polluted, its hair is shaved off.

Finally, among the !Kung San of Namibia, women typically labor by themselves (Cassidy, 2006). Giving birth alone is considered to be a strength. When labor begins, the !Kung woman goes off on her own and is expected to labor quietly. To do otherwise is considered a sign of weakness and possibly shows indifference toward the baby.

In contrast to these examples, childbirth in highly industrialized Western societies is highly "medicalized," with women hospitalized, hooked up to monitors, and separated from most friends and family members. Should we return to more traditional ways of birthing that view delivery less like a major medical event and more like a typical life event? As the Indian example illustrates, not all "traditional" practices are in the best interests of parents and babies. Also, Western societies do a far better job than developing countries of preventing mother and infant mortality. In some areas of sub-Saharan Africa, for example, about 15% of babies die during childbirth or in the first year of life (Caldwell, 1996). In Western, industrial societies, infant mortality rates have dropped from almost 30 infants out of 1000 (3%) in 1950 to 7 infants out of 1000 (0.7%) in 2004 (Division of Vital Statistics, 2004). Unfortunately, infant mortality is twice as high for black infants as for white infants (Guyer et al., 2000). The secret to a more optimal birth experience may be to blend beneficial traditional practices such as offering emotional support to new mothers with modern medical know-how.

Postpartum Depression

Some new mothers suffer from depression following the birth of their baby. As many as 60% of all new mothers report feeling tearful, irritable, moody, anxious, and depressed within the first few days after birth (Najman et al., 2000). This condition—the baby blues—is relatively mild, passes quickly, and is probably linked to the steep drops in levels of female hormones that normally occur after delivery and to the stresses associated with delivering a child and taking on the responsibilities of parenthood (not to mention coping with the lack of sleep experienced by many new mothers).

A second, and far more serious, condition is **postpartum depression**—an episode of clinical depression that lasts months rather than days in a woman who has just given birth. It affects approximately 1 in 10 new mothers (Cooper & Murray, 1998). Only rarely does a woman who has never had significant emotional problems become clinically depressed for the first time after giving birth. Most affected women have histories of depression, and many were depressed during pregnancy. Also, women vulnerable to depression are more likely to become depressed if they are experiencing other life stresses on top of the stresses of becoming a mother (Honey, Bennett, & Morgan, 2003). Lack of social support—especially a poor relationship with a partner—also increases the odds (Boyce, 2003; Heh, 2003).

Postpartum depression has significant implications for the parent–infant relationship. One study compared the children of 58 mothers who experienced postpartum depression with the children of 42 nondepressed mothers over a 5-year period (Murray et al., 1999). The children of the depressed mothers were less securely attached to their mothers during infancy and were less responsive during interactions with their mothers at age 5. They also tended to respond negatively when another child approached them in a friendly manner.

Mothers who had been postnatally depressed report greater behavioral problems by their children. At age 11, children of postnatally depressed mothers show more violent behavior even when researchers control for family characteristics and later episodes of maternal depression (Hay et al., 2003). The violence exhibited by these children is associated with anger management problems, attention problems, and hyperactive behavior. In another study, adolescents whose mothers had been postnatally depressed showed elevated levels of cortisol, which is associated with major depression (Halligan et al., 2004). The implication of these results is that early experiences with a depressed mother might predispose these children to later depression.

How exactly might maternal depression in the weeks and months following delivery affect children's behavior and increase their odds of developing depression? Mothers who are depressed tend to be relatively unresponsive to their babies and may even feel hostility toward them. They are tired, distracted, and often lack the energy needed to be fully engaged with their infants. Even though mothers typically recover from postnatal depression, research suggests that their early attitudes about their babies and the resulting pattern of early mother–child interactions set the stage for ongoing interaction problems that affect the child's behavior (Murray et al., 1999; Weinberg et al., 2006). The contribution of genes inherited from their depression-prone mothers and of stressful experiences before birth, after birth, or both can combine to precipitate depression in the child (Goodman, 2002). Thus, for their own sakes and for the sakes of their infants, mothers experiencing more than a mild case of the baby blues should seek professional help in overcoming their depression.

The Father's Experience

When birthing moved into hospitals, the medical establishment aggressively prohibited fathers from participating in their children's birth on the grounds that they would contaminate the sterile environment needed for a safe birth (Cassidy, 2006). It would take many decades, many lawsuits, and more progressive views about birth support before men were routinely accepted—and expected—in the delivery room. Today, many men prepare for fatherhood before delivery, attend prenatal classes with their partner, and are present for their child's birth. Fathers report that they want to be involved with their partner's pregnancy, although they don't always know how to make this happen (Draper, 2002).

Like mothers, fathers experience the process of becoming a parent as a significant event in their lives that involves a mix of positive and negative emotions. Also like mothers, fathers tend to be anxious during pregnancy and birth and some even experience some of the same physiological symptoms as their pregnant partner. These symptoms, called **couvade** (from the French word meaning "to hatch"), include bloating, weight gain, fatigue, insomnia, and nausea (Cassidy, 2006). And before you conclude that these symptoms must be "all in their heads," consider that some research shows hormonal shifts among expectant fathers that are similar to the hormonal shifts experienced by pregnant women (Cassidy, 2006).

As for the labor period, new fathers report feeling scared, unprepared, helpless, and frustrated (Chandler & Field, 1997; Chapman, 2000; Hallgren et al., 1999). They find labor to be more work than they had expected and sometimes feel excluded as the nurses take over. For most men, attending prenatal classes with their partner improves their experience of childbirth, although for a few men, the added knowledge that comes with these classes increases their anxiety (Greenhalgh, Slade, & Spiby, 2000). Stress levels among men tend to be highest during their partner's pregnancy and then decrease after the birth of the baby (Condon, Boyce, & Corkindale, 2004). Despite the stresses, negative emotions usually give way to relief, pride, and joy when the baby finally arrives (Chandler & Field, 1997). Indeed, most fathers find early contact with their babies special. As one father put it, "when my wife handed Anna to me, I was completely unprepared for the intense experience of fatherhood. I was overwhelmed by my feeling of belonging to and with this new child" (Reed, 1996, p. 52).

The thrill of having a new baby often intermingles with other emotions in the weeks and months after delivery as fathers struggle to become comfortable and confident in their new role as parent (Barclay & Lupton, 1999; St. John, Cameron, & McVeigh, 2005). Recent research reveals that nearly as many new fathers as new mothers experience symptoms of depression following the birth of their children (Paulson, Dauber, & Leiferman, 2006; Pinheiro et al., 2006; Wang & Chen, 2006). Fathers who are depressed interact less with their children. And like depressed mothers, depressed fathers report a lack of social support, suggesting that the postnatal period could be enhanced for both mothers and fathers with stronger support systems in place.

One particular area that seems to trouble first-time fathers is their sexual relationship with their partners. Men expect their sex life to return to its prepregnancy state after the birth of their baby and are disappointed when it does not (Condon, Boyce, Corkindale, 2004). They must forge a relationship with a new child as well as renegotiate their relationship with their partner.

SUMMING UP

▌ The perinatal environment, or the environment surrounding birth, influences both newborns and their parents. Parents increasingly want the flexibility to choose a birthing option that fits their lifestyle and expectations.

▌ Childbirth is a three-step process consisting of labor, delivery of the baby, and expulsion of the placenta. Despite recent concerns about overuse, cesarean sections are common.

▌ Perinatal risks to the baby include anoxia, assisted delivery (for example, forceps, vacuum extraction, and cesarean section), and the effects of medications given to the mother.

▌ Both new mothers and fathers report a variety of emotions in response to their child's birth. Their interpretation of the experience is influenced by the views of their surrounding culture.

CRITICAL THINKING

1. Considering the research on birth and the perinatal environment, arrange the perfect birth experience for you and your baby and justify its features. Where would you be, who would be with you, and what would be done?

2. Some experts worry that cesarean sections are overused. What do you think? Should a woman be able to choose whether she delivers vaginally or by cesarean section? Should hospitals be permitted to force a woman to deliver by cesarean if they believe the fetus is in danger?

4.4 | THE NEONATAL ENVIRONMENT

So now that parents have a baby, what do they do? Here we will look at the **neonatal** environment—the events of the first month and how parents might optimize the development of young infants.

There are marked differences in how parents interact with their newborns. As Meredith Small (1999) characterizes it, "our ideas about parenting and infant care are as culturally constructed as what we wear, what we eat, or how we dance" (p. 41). For example, in societies where infant mortality is high, babies may not even be named or viewed as people until they seem likely to survive (Nsamenang, 1992). The Beng, who are concentrated in small farming towns along the Ivory Coast, believe that newborns are not entirely in this world but exist in the world the babies will eventually inhabit after death (L. Gottlieb, 2000). Once their umbilical cord stump falls off on the 4th or 5th day of life, they begin to inhabit this world but still vacillate between the two worlds for another 4 to 5 years. During this time, the Beng regard their children as vulnerable. Spiritual beliefs influence their child care practices, leading for example, to twice daily enemas for infants using a chili pepper solution.

Among the !Kung, a hunting and gathering society of the Kalahari Desert in southern Africa, babies are carried upright in slings during the day and they sleep in the same bed with their mothers at night. They are touched more than 70% of daytime hours and are breast-fed whenever they want (usually 20 to 40 times per day), and may not be weaned until the age of 4 (Hewlett, 1995). In general, infants in hunter–gatherer so-

In many cultures, mothers keep their babies close to them all day and night to ensure their survival.

© P. Amranand/SuperStock

cieties are indulged considerably, at least until their survival is assured.

Infant care practices are considerably different in modern, industrialized societies where infant mortality is lower. In the United States, babies may sleep in the same bed or room as their parents for just a few weeks before being settled into a crib in their own room, a practice that mothers in many other cultures, who sleep in the same bed with their babies until they are toddlers, find quite bizarre. Infants in industrialized nations like the United States are touched only 12 to 20% of daytime hours and they are often trained to breast-feed or bottle-feed on a schedule, usually 5 to 7 times a day (Hewlett, 1995).

Regardless of where they live, new parents are often uncertain about how to relate to their babies and may find the period after birth stressful. T. Berry Brazelton (1979) has devised a way to help parents appreciate their baby's competencies and feel competent themselves as parents. He developed a newborn assessment technique, the Brazelton Neonatal Behavioral Assessment Scale, that assesses the strength of infant reflexes and the infant's responses to 26 situations (for example, reactions to cuddling, general irritability, and orienting to the examiner's face and voice). Brazelton uses this test to teach parents to understand their babies as individuals and to appreciate many of the pleasing competencies that they possess. During "Brazelton training," parents observe the test being administered and learn how to administer it themselves to elicit smiles and other heartwarming responses from their babies.

Breast or Bottle?

Over time and across cultures, feeding practices vary considerably. Without question, breastfeeding is the most natural form of nutrition for newborns. And until modern times, it was the

Breastmilk provides the perfect balance of nutrients for the developing infant.

© Photoinfusion Picture Library/Alamy

sole source of nourishment until solid foods were introduced. For a variety of reasons, breastfeeding in the United States reached an all-time low in the early 1970s, when only 1 in 4 mothers attempted to nurse their newborn infants. Bottle-feeding with formula had become the norm (Eiger and Olds, 1999). Since then, research has shown numerous advantages of breast milk over formula and all major health organizations (e.g., the American Academy of Family Physicians, Canadian Paediatric Society, National Health Service of Great Britain, World Health Organization, and more) have advocated for exclusive breastfeeding for the first 6 months of life. As a result of public awareness campaigns regarding the advantages of breastfeeding, nearly 7 in 10 mothers now attempt to nurse their newborns (Ahluwalia, Morrow, & Hsia, 2006). But only 50% are still breastfeeding after a month and less than one-third are still at it by 6 months (Wellbery, 2006).

The health benefits of breastfeeding are numerous and include fewer ear infections and respiratory tract problems for children and lower risk of ovarian cancer and early breast cancer for mothers (MMWR, 2006a). Breast milk contains several substances that protect nursing infants from infections and it has the perfect blend of nutrients for a quickly developing little person. Another bonus for mothers is faster weight loss when they breastfeed following childbirth. For premature babies, breast milk has been referred to as "more of a medicine than a food" because of its positive effects on their immune systems and weight gain (Gross-Loh, 2006, p. 38).

Given the health benefits of breastfeeding, why don't more women breast-feed? Women cite a number of reasons for not continuing with breastfeeding, including issues related to self (e.g., sore nipples) and issues related to the baby (e.g., concerns that baby is not getting adequate nutrition) (Ahluwalia, Morrow, & Hsia, 2006; Baxter, 2006). Young women, those from low socioeconomic backgrounds, and those with less education are less likely to breast-feed than other women (Ryan & Zhou, 2006). Being employed outside the home is also associated with lower breastfeeding rates, presumably because of the logistical problems of breastfeeding while at work (Ryan & Zhou, 2006). Finally, fewer black mothers breastfeed than white mothers (MMWR, 2006a). Interestingly, Hispanic mothers have a fairly high rate of breastfeeding until they immigrate to the United States and then the rate decreases with the amount of time in the United States (Gibson-Davis & Brooks-Gunn, 2006). This likely reflects U.S. cultural values toward breastfeeding, which are more ambivalent than those in many other countries. To improve breastfeeding rates, ambivalent (and in some cases, downright negative) views of breastfeeding need to be addressed so that women view breastfeeding as *the* option not just *an* option.

Identifying At-Risk Newborns

A few infants will be considered **at risk** for either short-term or long-term problems because of genetic defects, prenatal hazards, or perinatal damage. It is essential to these infants' survival and well-being that they be identified as early as possible. Newborns are routinely screened using the **Apgar test,** which provides a quick assessment of the newborn's heart rate, respiration, color, muscle tone, and reflexes (see ● Table 4.6). The test has been used for more than 50 years and, despite its "low-tech" nature, is still considered a valuable diagnostic tool (Casey, McIntire, & Leveno, 2001). The simple test is given immediately and 5 minutes after birth. It yields scores of 0, 1, or 2 for each of the five factors, which are then added to yield a total score that can range from 0 to 10. Infants who score 7 or higher are in good shape. Infants scoring 4 or lower are at risk—their heartbeats are sluggish or nonexistent, their muscles are limp, and their breathing is shallow and irregular, if they are breathing at all. These babies will immediately experience a different postnatal environment than the normal baby experiences because they require medical intervention in intensive care units to survive, as you will see at the end of the chapter.

One particular group of at-risk babies that should be examined more closely are those with **low birth weight (LBW).** As ● Table 4.7 illustrates, the younger (and smaller) babies are at birth, the lower their chances of survival. Approximately 8% of babies born in the United States have a low birth weight (less than 2500 grams, or 5½ pounds). Some of these babies are born at term and are called "small for date," but many are born preterm (less than 37 weeks of gestation) and are more at risk as a result (see ■ Figure 4.10). The survival and health of these small infants is a concern, particularly for infants who are very small (less than 1500 grams or just over 3 pounds at most). Prematurity is the leading cause of infant mortality (Callaghan et al., 2006). Although LBW infants account for about 8% of all births, they account for 65% of all infant deaths and nearly 60% of the money spent on pregnancies and deliveries (Callaghan et al., 2006; Schmitt, Sneed, & Phibbs, 2006). Very LBW infants are even more costly: they account for less than 1% of all births but 36% of the total hospital costs (Schmitt, Sneed, & Phibbs, 2006). The high emotional and economic costs of LBW have made this an important medical and societal issue.

We don't always know what causes LBW, but research has identified a number of factors regularly associated with it. For starters, LBW is strongly linked to low socioeconomic status, probably because poor women are more likely to have poor nutrition and inadequate prenatal care (Goldenberg & Culhane, 2007; Hughes & Simpson, 1995). In addition, many other risk factors that we have already described, such as smok-

● TABLE 4.6   THE APGAR TEST

FACTORS	SCORE		
	0	1	2
HEART RATE	Absent	Slow (under 100 beats per minute)	Moderate (over 100 beats per minute)
RESPIRATORY EFFORT	Absent	Slow or irregular	Good; baby is crying
MUSCLE TONE	Flaccid; limp	Weak; some flexion	Strong; active motion
COLOR	Blue or pale	Body pink, extremities blue	Completely pink
REFLEX IRRITABILITY	No response	Frown, grimace, or weak cry	Vigorous cry

● TABLE 4.7   SURVIVAL AND HEALTH OF PREMATURE BABIES BY GESTATIONAL AGE

FACTOR	RESULTS (IN WEEKS AND %)			
Number of completed weeks since last menstruation	<23 weeks	23 weeks	24 weeks	25 weeks
Percentage of babies who survive	0–15%	2–35%	17–58%	35–85%
Percentage of survivors with chronic lung disease	89%	57–70%	33–89%	16–71%
Percentage of survivors with a severe neurodevelopmental disability*	69%	30%	17–45%	12–35%

*Includes cerebral palsy, mental retardation, blindness or severe myopia, and deafness.
SOURCE: Based on data from Hack & Fanaroff, 1999.

1999). Higher-order multiples spend 8 times as long in the hospital as singleton infants and cost more than 6 times as much in hospital costs (Henderson et al., 2004).

The good news is that most LBW babies born since the advent of neonatal intensive care in the 1960s function within the normal range of development and experience significant catch-up growth (Wilson-Costello et al., 2007; Xiong et al., 2007). However, compared with normal–birth-weight children, LBW children, especially those with extremely LBW (less than 1000 grams, or 2 pounds 3 ounces) are at greater risk for blindness, deafness, cerebral palsy, poor academic achievement, autism, and health problems (e.g., Platt et al., 2007; Tommiska et al., 2007). Respiratory difficulties are likely because premature babies have not yet produced enough **surfactant,** a substance that prevents the air sacs of the lungs from sticking together and therefore aids breathing. Surfactant therapy for LBW infants became common practice around 1990 and seems to improve the survival rate among the sickest infants. However, it has not entirely improved health or long-term achievement scores of LBW babies in general, perhaps because smaller and earlier-born babies, who have the most complications, are now surviving to be among the school-age population of LBW survivors (Hagen et al., 2006; Paul et al., 2006).

ing and stress, are linked to LBW. And not surprisingly, the more risk factors experienced during pregnancy, the greater the likelihood of delivering a small baby (Rosenberg, 2001).

Low birth weight is also associated with multiple births, which have increased substantially over the past several decades largely because of increased use of ovulation-stimulating drugs to treat infertility. In 1980, there were 37 higher-order multiple births (three or more) in every 100,000 births; by 1998, this figure had jumped to 194 higher-order multiples in every 100,000 births (Martin et al., 2005). Among single-birth infants, approximately 5% are LBW, but among twins, nearly half are LBW. Among higher-order multiples, 86% are low birth weight (Cohen et al.,

Modern technology permits the survival of younger and smaller babies, but many experts believe we have reached the lowest limits of viability between 23 and 24 weeks of gestation.

In addition to the advances made thanks to the high-tech interventions now available in most neonatal intensive care units (NICU), research has shown that several low-tech interventions can go far in improving the developmental outcomes of LBW, premature infants. For starters, these vulnerable infants benefit from their mother's breast milk even if they can't effectively nurse when they are hooked up to tubes and machines in the NICU. Mothers can pump their breast milk to provide nutrient-rich nourishment that helps boost their infant's fledgling immune system. Babies with extremely LBW who receive breast milk later score about 5 points higher on the Bayley Scale of Mental Development than similar babies who receive no breast milk (Vohr et al., 2006). And among babies receiving breast milk, there are measurable differences between those who consumed the largest quantities and those who consumed the least.

There is also evidence that skin-to-skin contact is therapeutic for these infants. Sometimes called kangaroo care, resting on a parent's chest helps maintain body temperature, heart rate, and oxygen levels in the blood (Feldman & Eidelman, 2003), and the rhythmic sound of the parent's heartbeat calms the infant and may help simulate the environment of the womb. Premature infants who experience kangaroo care settle into more mature patterns of quiet sleep and alert wakefulness than premature infants who do not receive this treatment. One of the nice things about kangaroo care is that both mothers and fathers can participate. Doing so improves parents' sensitivity to their infant and makes the dynamics among the trio more positive (Feldman et al., 2003).

In addition to skin-to-skin contact, Tiffany Field and her colleagues (Diego, Field, & Hernandez-Reif, 2005; Field et al., 2006) have shown that premature infants benefit from massage therapy. For example, in one study, premature babies received either light or moderate massage 3 times per day for 5 days

(Field et al., 2006). Those who received moderate-pressure massage gained significantly more weight on each of the days of the therapy than the premature babies in the light-massage group. Babies receiving moderate massage seemed to be more relaxed and less aroused, which may have facilitated greater weight gain (Field et al., 2006). In addition, the massage increased the efficiency of the digestive system, which is also associated with greater weight gain (Diego, Field, & Hernandez-Reif, 2005).

Although the long-term health prognosis for LBW babies is now good, many children born with an extremely LBW continue to experience neurosensory impairments and academic problems throughout their childhood and teen years (Doyle & Anderson, 2005; Saigal et al., 2007). These cognitive deficits in childhood can be traced to deficits in attention, speed, and memory evident in preterm infants during their first year (Rose et al., 2005). The fate of premature and LBW babies depends considerably on two factors. The first is their biological condition—their health and neurological status in particular. The second is the quality of the postnatal environment they experience. For instance, in a study of more than 8000 infants, Dennis Hogan and Jennifer Park (2000) found that the disadvantages of LBW were amplified for children of minority status growing up in poverty with a single parent. In contrast, LBW babies who live with two parents and whose mother is well educated, although they start out with delays, improve and may even catch up to the average child by age 8 (Ment et al., 2003). And children born with very LBW whose mothers are consistently responsive to them throughout infancy and toddlerhood attain higher levels of cognitive achievement than similar children with less responsive mothers (Smith, Landry, & Swank, 2006). In contrast, premature infants whose mothers are "out of synch" with them exhibit less mature outcomes at age 2 (Feldman & Eidelman, 2006).

Other research shows that at-risk infants can benefit from programs that teach their parents how to provide responsive care and appropriate intellectual stimulation to them once they are home. Home visits to advise parents, combined with a stimulating day care program for LBW toddlers, can teach mothers how to be better teachers of their young children and stimulate these children's cognitive development. In an ambitious project called the Infant Health and Development Program, premature and LBW infants at eight sites have benefited from such early intervention (McCormick et al., 2006). The program involves weekly home visits during the first year of life and then biweekly home visits and attendance by the infant at a special day care center for half a day every day from age 1 to age 3. Mothers are given child care education and support.

The program appears to help parents provide a more growth-enhancing home environment—for example, to give their babies appropriate toys and learning materials and to interact with them in

Research shows that skin-to-skin contact can help babies regulate body temperature and maintain a regular heart rate and oxygen levels in the blood.

© UKraft/Alamy

stimulating ways. The intervention also helped these at-risk babies, especially the heavier ones, achieve more cognitive growth by age 3 than they would otherwise have achieved. An impressive 14-point boost in IQ scores at age 3 for heavier LBW children who received the intervention had dropped to a 4-point advantage at age 8 but this small advantage was still evident at age 18 (McCarton et al., 1997; McCormick et al., 2006). Children who weighed 2000 grams (4 pounds 6 ounces) or less at birth did not get much benefit from the program. Other research similarly shows that early intervention effects on premature infants fade over time (Johnson et al., 2005). Researchers have more to learn, then, about what it takes to keep the development of at-risk children on a positive track after the perinatal period comes to a close. However, everything we know about life-span environmental forces suggests that supportive parents and programs can do a great deal to optimize every child's development. It seems that premature, LBW babies can achieve normal levels of intellectual functioning during childhood when they live in middle-class homes, when their mothers are relatively educated, and most importantly, when their mothers, rich or poor, are consistently attentive and responsive when interacting with them (Smith, Landry, & Swank, 2006).

Studies such as these raise a larger issue about the importance of early experience. Some developmentalists take seriously the concept of critical (or sensitive) periods in early development. Others stress the resilience of human beings, their ability to rebound from early disadvantages and to respond to environmental influences throughout their lives rather than only during so-called critical periods. Which is it?

Risk and Resilience

To what extent does harm done in the prenatal or perinatal period last, and to what extent can postnatal experiences make up for it? You have encountered many examples in this chapter of what can go wrong before or during birth. Some damaging effects are clearly irreversible: The thalidomide baby will never grow normal arms or legs, and the child with FAS will always be mentally retarded. Yet throughout history, many children turned out fine even though their mothers—unaware of many risk factors—smoked and drank during their pregnancies, received heavy doses of medication during delivery, or experienced serious illness. So, although many factors place a fetus at risk and increase the likelihood of problems after birth, not all at-risk infants end up with problems (Fraser, 2004). Is it also possible that some babies exposed to and clearly affected by risks recover from their deficiencies later in life?

Indeed it is, and researchers now have the results of major longitudinal studies that say so. Emmy Werner, with her colleague Ruth Smith, studied a group of babies born in 1955 on the island of Kauai in Hawaii for 40 years (Werner, 1989a, 1989b; Werner & Smith, 1982, 1992, 2001). This was a monumental undertaking. All women of Kauai who were to give birth in 1955 were interviewed in each trimester of preg-

nancy, and physicians noted any prenatal, perinatal, or postnatal complications. On the basis of this information, each baby was categorized as having been exposed to severe, moderate, mild, or no prenatal or perinatal stress. At ages 1, 2, 10, 18, 32, and 40 years, researchers diligently tracked down their participants and conducted interviews (initially with the mothers and later with the children), administered psychological and cognitive tests, rated the quality of the family environment, and conducted medical examinations. Remarkably, at the 40-year follow-up, the researchers still had 70% (489 of 698) of their original group of babies born in 1955 in the study.

One-third of the children classified as at risk showed considerable resilience, getting themselves back on a normal course of development. Through this self-righting capacity, they were able to mature into competent, successful adults with no evident learning, social, or vocational problems despite being at risk for poor outcomes. Two major findings emerge from this research:

- The effects of prenatal and perinatal complications decrease over time.
- The outcomes of early risk depend on the quality of the postnatal environment.

The postnatal environments of these successful at-risk children included two types of **protective factors**, influences that prevent the damaging effects of risk factors or help children overcome disadvantages. These are:

- *Personal resources.* Possibly because of their genetic makeup, some children have qualities such as intelligence, sociability, and communication skills that help them choose or create more nurturing and stimulating environments and cope with challenges. For example, parents and other observers noted that these children were agreeable, cheerful, and self-confident as infants, which elicited positive caregiving responses. They also believed that they were in control of their own fates—that through their actions, they could bring about positive outcomes.
- *Supportive postnatal environment.* Some at-risk children receive the social support they need within or outside the family. Most importantly, they are able to find at least one person who loves them unconditionally and with whom they feel secure.

Clearly, hazards during the important prenatal and perinatal periods can leave lasting scars, and yet many children show remarkable resilience. There seem to be some points in the life span, especially early on, in which both positive and negative environmental forces have especially strong effects. Yet *environment matters throughout life.* It would be a mistake to assume that all children who have problems at birth are doomed. In short, early experience by itself can, but rarely does, make or break development; later experience counts, too, sometimes enough to turn around a negative course of development.

CHAPTER SUMMARY

4.1 PRENATAL DEVELOPMENT

- Prenatal development begins with conception and proceeds through the germinal, embryonic, and fetal periods.

- The germinal period lasts about 2 weeks. During this time, the single-celled zygote created when a sperm penetrates an egg repeatedly multiples and travels to the uterus where it implants itself.

- The embryonic period lasts through the eighth week after conception. Every major organ takes shape during this time in a process called organogenesis. The placenta forms and connects the embryo to its mother through the umbilical cord. Major developments occur during this time, including formation and beating of the heart and the start of sexual differentiation.

- The fetal period lasts from the ninth week after conception until the end of pregnancy. The body and brain undergo much growth during this time. Neurons multiply, migrate, and differentiate into what they will finally become. The age of viability is reached at around 23–24 weeks of gestation.

- Growth during the prenatal period is faster than during any other period of the life span.

4.2 THE PRENATAL ENVIRONMENT

- The womb is an environment and can affect the embryo/fetus in positive as well as negative ways.

- Teratogens include diseases, drugs, or other environmental agent that can harm the developing fetus. Teratogens are most damaging to an organ during the time when the organ is developing most rapidly. In addition, the longer and stronger the exposure to a teratogen, the more likely that damage will occur to the developing child. The genetic makeup of both mother and unborn baby influence the effect of a teratogen, as does the quality of the prenatal and postnatal environments.

- Numerous drugs—prescription, over-the-counter, and recreational—have been found to have teratogenic effects. One of the most widely used drugs—alcohol—results in a cluster of symptoms that have life-long effects on the children who are exposed prenatally.

- Diseases such as rubella (German measles), syphilis, and AIDS can adversely affect the developing baby, as can environmental hazards such as radiation and pollution.

- Some aspects of the mother can influence the quality of the prenatal environment, including her age, emotional state, and nutritional status. Women in their 20s have the lowest rates of pregnancy and birth complications. Women who experience prolonged and severe emotional stress during pregnancy may give birth to smaller babies. Good nutrition is important throughout pregnancy and is often supplemented with vitamins and fortified foods.

- Characteristics of the father, such as his age, may also affect the baby.

4.3 THE PERINATAL ENVIRONMENT

- The perinatal environment includes delivery practices and drugs used to assist with delivery. Many births today take place in the medical setting of a hospital or birthing center.

- Childbirth is a three-stage process that begins with regular contractions of the uterus and dilation of the cervix. The second stage of labor is the actual delivery of the baby out of the woman's body. The third stage is the delivery of the placenta.

- Among the possible birth complications is anoxia, or an oxygen shortage, which may occur for a variety of reasons. Anoxia can lead to brain damage or cerebral palsy if the brain is deprived of oxygen for more than a few minutes.

- Some babies must be assisted through the birth canal with vacuum extraction or forceps. Some women undergo a cesarean section, or surgical removal of the baby. Many women in Western cultures are given medications to assist with delivery. Most common are epidural or spinal blocks to reduce pain and oxytocin to promote contractions.

- The experience of pregnancy and childbirth vary widely, across cultures as well as across women within a culture. Some women experience mild to moderate depression following childbirth. Fathers, too, often need time to adjust to the life changes that accompany becoming a parent.

4.4 THE NEONATAL ENVIRONMENT

- The neonatal environment refers to the events of the first month or so after delivery. Caring for a newborn varies across cultures. Nearly all cultures promote breastfeeding as the ideal way to nourish the young infant. For a variety of reasons, some mothers bottle-feed their newborns or switch to bottle-feeding after a trial run with breastfeeding.

- Some infants are considered to be at risk for short-term or long-term problems and must receive extra care during the neonatal period. Babies born prematurely and who have low birth weight are at risk for a number of complications.

- Many at-risk babies show remarkable resilience and outgrow their problems, especially if they have personal resources, such as sociability and intelligence, and grow up in stimulating and supportive postnatal environments where someone loves them.

KEY TERMS

assisted reproductive
    technologies (ARTs) 91
artificial insemination 91
in vitro fertilization (IVF) 91
germinal period 92
blastocyst 92
embryonic period 92
organogenesis 92
amnion 92
chorion 92
placenta 92
umbilical cord 92
spina bifida 92
anencephaly 92
testosterone 93
fetal period 94
differentiation 94
stem cells 94
age of viability 95
myelin 96
infant states 96
prenatal environment 97
teratogen 98
critical period 98

thalidomide 98
sudden infant death syndrome
    (SIDS) 100
fetal alcohol syndrome
    (FAS) 100
rubella 103
syphilis 104
acquired immunodeficiency
    syndrome (AIDS) 104
Lamaze method 105
perinatal environment 108
anoxia 109
breech presentation 109
cerebral palsy 109
cesarean section 109
postpartum depression 113
couvade 113
neonatal 114
at risk 115
Apgar test 116
low birth weight (LBW) 116
surfactant 117
protective factors 119

MEDIA RESOURCES

BOOK COMPANION WEBSITE

academic.cengage.com/psychology/sigelman
Find online quizzes, flash cards, animations, video clips, experiments, interactive assessments, and other helpful study aids for this text at academic.cengage.com/psychology/sigelman. You can also connect directly to the following sites:

BIRTH DEFECTS

The website for the National Center on Birth Defects and Developmental Disabilities includes links to information on birth defects and disabilities, press releases, and current health news.

18 WAYS TO MAKE A BABY-NOVA

Originally broadcast by PBS in October 2001, this NOVA program investigates the world of assisted reproduction. A companion website contains interactive and multimedia opportunities to explore topics related to fertility and reproduction, such as human cloning and cell division.

LIFE'S GREATEST MIRACLE-NOVA

Using the microimagery of Swedish photographer Lennart Nilsson, the PBS NOVA program Life's Greatest Miracles tracks the growth of a baby from embryo to newborn. Winner of an Emmy award, it is available to watch in its entirety on the companion website. The site also provides background on the stem-cell debate and contains related multimedia resources for further exploration.

PREGNANCY/CHILDBIRTH

The childbirth.org site provides practical advice on a variety of pregnancy- and birth-related topics, including childbirth classes, choices in birth, complications of labor, and pain relief in labor. It also provides advice on early feeding issues like breastfeeding and when to introduce solid food.

VISIBLE EMBRYO

The visible embryo is a multiple award winning site that offers an amazing amount of text and graphic information on the human organism as it develops from ovulation through the fetal stage. One nice element is the visible "spiral" depicting 23 distinct stages of prenatal change. The site also features links to information on key pregnancy issues.

UNDERSTANDING THE DATA: EXERCISES ON THE WEB

academic.cengage.com/psychology/sigelman
For additional insight on the data presented in this chapter, try out the exercises for these figures at academic.cengage.com/psychology/sigelman:

> **Figure 4.4** The percentage of time the fetus spends in different states from the 20th week until the end of pregnancy. Time in one coherent state or another increases with age, and most time is spent in a state of sleep.

> **Table 4.7** Survival and Health of Premature Babies by Gestational Age

CENGAGENOW

academic.cengage.com/login
Go to **academic.cengage.com/login** to link to CengageNOW, your online study tool. First take the Pre-Test for this chapter to get your Personalized Study Plan, which will identify topics you need to review and direct you to online resources. Then take the Post-Test to determine what concepts you have mastered and what you still need work on.

© Simon Marcus/Corbis

5 CHAPTER

Health and Physical Development

"**JOSH IS A 12-YEAR-OLD BOY** with constitutional growth delay. Although he has grown at a normal rate throughout childhood, his height is below the 5th percentile line on the growth chart. His bone age is delayed by 2 to 3 years, so he is unlikely to reach a normal adult height. He has always been the smallest child in his class, and the size difference is getting more noticeable as some of his classmates begin their growth spurts: Josh looks more like a 4th grader than a 7th grader. He is having school problems this year, after moving into a new school. His teachers report that 'he's either a clown or a bully in class, and he just does not pay attention.' He likes sports and is good at soccer, but the coach does not want to let him try out for the team—he is afraid Josh will get hurt. The older boys at school sometimes pick him up and carry him around, calling him 'Pee-wee' and 'Squirt.' He has started spending a lot of time alone in his room and does not seem interested in anything. After his last visit to the doctor, he said, 'I'm sick of hearing how tall I'll be in 10 years. I'm a shrimp now, and that is all that matters.'" (Rieser & Underwood, 2004)

Josh's case illustrates the complexity as well as the significance of growth and development. Although he is growing at the normal *rate* of development, he is still markedly shorter than other boys his age. What are the processes underlying Josh's growth? And what are the psychological implications for Josh and other children, adolescents, and adults of the physical and health changes that occur throughout the life span?

These are the sorts of questions that we address in this chapter on health and physical development. We start with an overview of the major physical systems that underlie human functioning. We also look at the reproductive system as it matures during adolescence and then changes during adulthood. And we watch the physical self in action, as motor skills develop during childhood and as physical fitness and motor behaviors change during adulthood. We identify influences on health, physical development, and aging so that you can better understand why some children develop—and some older adults age—more rapidly than others.

5.1 BUILDING BLOCKS OF GROWTH AND DEVELOPMENT

Physical capabilities are fundamental to what people are able to do in life. A 5-year-old child is physically able to experience the world in ways markedly different from those available to a 5-month-old infant. Mariah, for example, can throw a ball with her mom, run with her dog, play hopscotch with her friends, feed and dress herself, and enjoy many of the rides at the amusement park. Changes in her brain have increased her memory abilities and capacity to think, and her language skills are astounding compared with those of the 5-month-old. Yet Mariah and other 5-year-olds are limited by their physical selves. It will be years before their brains are fully developed, allowing greater concentration and more sophisticated thought processes. Their strength and coordination on motor tasks will continue to improve, and their bodies will grow taller and heavier and will mature sexually.

Human growth and development is an incredibly complex process, influenced by both genetic and environmental factors.

At certain times and for certain developments, genetic influences dominate, whereas at other times, environmental influences are more powerful. But as we have explained in previous chapters, genetic and environmental forces are always working together. Consider height. The average female in the United States is about 5 feet 4 inches (162 cm) and the average male is 5 feet 9 inches (175 cm), but there is considerable variability. Sandy Allen from the state of Indiana, for instance, is considered the tallest living woman in the world at just over 7 feet 7 inches; most women with Turner syndrome (see Chapter 3) are nearly 3 feet shorter than this—4 feet 8 inches on average (Kochi et al., 2007). Even among those considered within the average range of height, there is variability. Genes account for some of this: Tall people tend to have tall parents, whereas short people often have "short genes" hanging on their family tree. Research with twins confirms a fairly strong genetic influence in height (Estourgie-van Burk et al., 2006).

But as noted in Chapter 3, even if you inherit the genetic propensity to be tall (or short), environment can influence the expression of those genes. If you lack adequate nutrition, for example, you may not realize your full growth potential. And consider the case of children with celiac disease. An abnormality with their stomach lining leaves them unable to absorb nutrients from food despite adequate consumption. Their disease leads to malnutrition, which stunts growth. As ■ **Figure 5.1** shows, however, treatment that restores absorption of nutrients leads to dramatic **catch-up growth.** This catch-up growth after a period of malnutrition or illness reflects the body's struggle to get back on the growth course it is genetically programmed to follow.

To understand how growth can be influenced by genes and environments, we need to consider the workings of the endocrine and nervous systems.

The Endocrine System

The endocrine, or hormonal, system consists of a group of **endocrine glands** that secrete chemicals called *hormones* directly into the bloodstream. Perhaps the most critical of the endocrine glands is the **pituitary gland,** the so-called master gland located at the base of the brain. Directly controlled by the hypothala-

■ FIGURE 5.1 This shows the catch-up growth that has occurred in a girl following treatment at around age 11 for her celiac disease.

SOURCE: From *Human growth and development,* N. Cameron, Ed. NY: Academic Press. Copyright © 2002. Reprinted with permission of Elsevier.

mus of the brain, it triggers the release of hormones from all other endocrine glands by sending hormonal messages to those glands. Moreover, the pituitary produces **growth hormone,** which triggers the production of specialized hormones that directly regulate growth. Children who lack adequate growth hormone are unlikely to exceed 4 feet (or 130 cm) in height as adults if left untreated. Treatment with synthetic growth hormones can lead to near-expected adult height if administered early—well before the start of puberty (Bajpai et al., 2006; Reiter et al., 2006). By contrast, administering growth hormones to children who are simply short and do not have an endocrine problem is likely to do no good and can even backfire. Hormone treatment tends to induce an early and short puberty, and treated children either attain the height they would have reached anyway early or end up smaller than they would otherwise have been (Rosenfeld, 1997). Adults who use human growth hormone in an attempt to enhance their athletic performance are at risk for a variety of health conditions, including cardiac problems and insulin resistance. Despite widespread beliefs about its potential performance-enhancing benefits, there are no clinically documented benefits to athletes who inject human growth hormone (O'Mathúna, 2006).

The thyroid gland also plays a key role in physical growth and development and in the development of the nervous system. Children whose mothers had a thyroid deficiency during pregnancy can experience intellectual problems (LaFranchi, Haddow, & Hollowell, 2005). Thyroid deficiency during infancy can also lead to mental retardation and slow growth if unnoticed and untreated (Robertson, 1993). Children who develop a thyroid deficiency later in life will not suffer brain damage, because most of their brain growth has already occurred, but their physical growth will slow drastically.

In Chapter 4, you learned about another critical role of the endocrine system. A male fetus will not develop male reproductive organs unless (1) a gene on his Y chromosome triggers the development of the testes (which are endocrine glands), and (2) the testes secrete the most important of the male hormones, testosterone. Male sex hormones become highly important again during adolescence. When people speak of adolescence as a time of "raging hormones," they are quite right. The testes of a male secrete large quantities of testosterone and other male hormones (called **androgens**). These hormones stimulate the production of growth hormone, which in turn triggers the adolescent growth spurt. Androgens are also responsible for the development of the male sex organs and contribute to sexual motivation during adulthood.

Meanwhile, in adolescent girls, the ovaries (also endocrine glands) produce larger quantities of the primary female hormone, **estrogen,** and of progesterone. Estrogen increases dramatically at puberty, stimulating the production of growth hormone and the adolescent growth spurt, much as testosterone does in males. It is also responsible for the development of the breasts, pubic hair, and female sex organs and for the control of menstrual cycles throughout a woman's reproductive years. Finally, the adrenal glands secrete androgen-like hormones that contribute to the maturation of the bones and muscles in both sexes. There is also evidence that the maturation of the adrenal glands during middle childhood results in sexual attraction well before puberty in both boys and girls (McClintock & Herdt, 1996) and relates to sexual orientation in adulthood (Arlt et al., 1999). The roles of different endocrine glands in physical growth and development are summarized in ● Table 5.1.

In adulthood, endocrine glands continue to secrete hormones, under the direction of the hypothalamus and the pituitary gland, to regulate bodily processes. For example, thyroid hormones help the body's cells metabolize (break down) foods into usable nutrients, and the adrenal glands help the body cope with stress. Throughout the life span, then, the endocrine system works with the nervous system to keep the body on an even keel. Yet changes occur; for example, declines in levels of sex hormones are associated with menopause. And, as you will see in Chapter 17, some theorists believe that changes in the functioning of the endocrine glands late in life help bring about aging and death.

In short, the endocrine system, in collaboration with the nervous system, is centrally involved in growth during childhood, physical and sexual maturation during adolescence, functioning over the life span, and aging later in life.

● TABLE 5.1 HORMONAL INFLUENCES ON GROWTH AND DEVELOPMENT

ENDOCRINE GLAND	HORMONES PRODUCED	EFFECTS ON GROWTH AND DEVELOPMENT
Pituitary	Growth hormone	Regulates growth from birth through adolescence; triggers adolescent growth spurt
	Activating hormones	Signal other endocrine glands (such as ovaries and testes) to secrete their hormones
Thyroid	Thyroxine	Affects growth and development of the brain and helps regulate growth of the body during childhood
Testes	Testosterone	Are responsible for development of the male reproductive system during the prenatal period; directs male sexual development during adolescence
Ovaries	Estrogen and progesterone	Are responsible for regulating the menstrual cycle; estrogen directs female sexual development during adolescence
Adrenal glands	Adrenal androgens	Play a supportive role in the development of muscle and bones; contribute to sexual motivation

The Nervous System

None of the physical or mental achievements that we regard as human would be possible without a functioning nervous system. Briefly, the nervous system consists of the brain and spinal cord (central nervous system) and the neural tissue that extends into all parts of the body (peripheral nervous system). Its basic unit is a **neuron** (see ■ **Figure 5.2**). Although neurons come in many shapes and sizes, they have some common features. Branching, bushy dendrites receive signals from other neurons, and the long axon of a neuron transmits electrical signals to other neurons or, in some cases, directly to a muscle cell. The axon of one neuron makes a connection with another neuron at a tiny gap called a **synapse.** By releasing neurotransmitters stored at the ends of its axons, one neuron can either stimulate or inhibit the action of another neuron. The axons of many neurons become covered by a fatty sheath called *myelin*, which acts like insulation to speed the transmission of neural impulses. The process of **myelination**—neurons becoming encased in this protective substance that speeds transmission—begins prenatally but continues for many years after birth, proceeding from the spinal cord to the hindbrain, midbrain, and forebrain.

Now imagine a brain with as many as 100 billion neurons and each neuron communicating through synapses to thousands of others. How does this brain develop to make adults more physically and mentally capable than infants? Is it that adults have more neurons than infants do? Do they have more synapses connecting neurons or a more organized pattern of connections? And what happens to the brain in later life?

Brain Development

In Chapter 4, we traced the amazing evolution of the brain during the prenatal period. Here, we pick up the story by looking at what goes on in the brain from birth onward. Although the brain is proportionately the largest and most developed part of the body at birth, much of its development takes place after birth. At birth, the brain weighs about 25% of its adult weight; by age 2, it reaches 75% of its adult weight; and by age 5, the brain has achieved 90% of its adult weight. The myelination of neurons continues throughout childhood and into adolescence, and the different areas of the brain become more specialized.

The development of the brain early in life is heavily influenced by the unfolding of a genetic program that has evolved over many generations (Nelson, Thomas, & De Haan, 2006). But genes are not the only influence—an individual's experiences are also crucial to brain development. As Charles Nelson and colleagues (2006) describe it, "the brain's circuitry must rely on experience to customize connections to serve the needs of the individual" (p. 3). Assuming that the infant has normal opportunities to explore and experience the world, the result will be a normal brain and normal development.

Thus, the brain, especially early in its formation, has great **plasticity;** that is, it is responsive to the individual's experiences and can develop in a variety of ways (Kolb & Whishaw, 2006). On the negative side, the developing brain is highly vulnerable to damage if it is exposed to drugs or diseases (recall the description of teratogens in Chapter 4) or if it is deprived of sensory and motor experiences. On the positive side, this highly adaptable brain can often recover successfully from injuries. Neurons that are not yet fully committed to their specialized functions can often take over the functions of damaged neurons. Moreover, the immature brain is especially able to benefit from stimulating experiences. Rats that grow up in enriched environments with plenty of sensory stimulation develop larger, better-functioning brains with more synapses than rats that grow up in barren cages (Greenough, Black, & Wallace, 1987; Nilsson et al., 1999). Brain plasticity is greatest early in development. However, the organization of synapses within the nervous system continues to change in response to experience

■ **FIGURE 5.2** Parts of a neuron. (A) Although neurons differ in size and function, they all contain three main parts: the dendrites, which receive messages from adjacent neurons; the cell body; and the axon, which sends messages across the synapse to other neurons. (B) The formation of dendrites leading to new connections among existing neurons, as well as the myelination of neural pathways, accounts for much of the increase in brain weight during a baby's first two years.

throughout the life span. Animals put through their paces in mazes grow bushier dendrites, whereas their brains lose some of their complexity if the animals are then moved to less stimulating quarters (Thompson, 2000).

In short, the critical or sensitive period for brain development—the time when it proceeds most rapidly—is during the late prenatal period and early infancy. The developing brain is characterized by a good deal of plasticity: normal genes may provide rough guidelines about how the brain should be configured, but early experience determines the architecture of the brain.

One important feature of the developing organization of the brain is the **lateralization,** or asymmetry and specialization of functions, of the two hemispheres of the cerebral cortex. Instead of developing identically, the functions controlled by the two hemispheres diverge. In most people, the left cerebral hemisphere controls the right side of the body and

is adept at the *sequential* (i.e., step-by-step) processing needed for analytic reasoning and language processing. The right hemisphere generally controls the left side of the body and is skilled at the *simultaneous* processing of information needed for understanding spatial information and processing visual–motor information. Although it is an oversimplification, the left hemisphere is often called the *thinking* side of the brain, whereas the right hemisphere is called the *emotional* brain.

Having two hemispheres of the brain is not the same as having two brains. The hemispheres "communicate" and work together through the corpus callosum, "the super-highway of neurons connecting the halves of the brain" (Gazzaniga, 1998, p. 50). Even though one hemisphere might be more active than the other during certain tasks, they both play a role in all activities. For example, the left hemisphere is considered the seat of language because it controls word content, grammar, and syntax, but the right hemisphere processes melody, pitch, sound intensity, and the affective content of language.

If one hemisphere is damaged, it may be possible for the other hemisphere to "take over" the functions lost. For example, in a small sample of children who had their left hemispheres removed to try to reduce or eliminate severe seizures, all regained normal use of language (Vining et al., 1997; de Bode & Curtiss, 2000). The sample included two children who were 12 and 13 years old at the time of surgery—fairly old in terms of brain development. Thus, although the left hemisphere processes language in most people (perhaps 92%), the right hemisphere may also be able to fill this function, although it is not yet known how this possibility might be limited—or enhanced—by age or other characteristics of the individual (Gazzaniga, 1998; Knecht et al., 2000).

When does the brain become lateralized? Signs of brain lateralization are clearly evident at birth. Newborns are more likely to turn their heads to the right than to the left (Thompson & Smart, 1993), and one-quarter clearly prefer the right hand in their grasp reflex (Tan & Tan, 1999). Left hemispheric specialization is evident among 5- to 12-month-old babies who engage in babbling, thought by many to be a precursor of language (Holowka & Petitto, 2002). This evidence suggests that young brains are already organized in a lateralized fashion. Still, preference for one side of the body over the other (being right-handed or left-handed) becomes more stable and systematic throughout childhood.

Signs of lateralization so early in life suggest that it has a genetic basis. Further support for the role of genes comes from family studies of handedness. Overall, about 9 in 10 people rely on their right hands (or left hemispheres) to write and perform other motor activities. In families where both parents are right-handed, the odds of having a left-handed child are only 2 in 100. These odds increase to 17 in 100 when one parent is left-handed and to 46 in 100 when both parents are left-handed (Springer & Deutsch, 1997). This suggests a genetic basis to handedness, although it could also indicate that children become left-handed because of experiences provided by left-handed parents. However, experience would not account for head-turning preferences in young infants or for the differential activation of the left and right hemispheres observed in newborns when listening to speech sounds. Thus, nature seems to account better than nurture for much of the lateralization of the brain.

Overall, then, the brain appears to be structured very early so that the two hemispheres of the cortex will be capable of specialized functioning. As we develop, most of us come to rely more on the left hemisphere to carry out language processing and more on the right hemisphere to do such things as perceive spatial relationships and emotions. We also come to rely more consistently on one hemisphere, usually the left, to control many of our physical activities.

When does the brain complete its development? In the past, we might have answered that the brain was fully developed by the end of infancy, or even by the end of pregnancy. Today, however, the answer is that brain development is never truly complete; the brain changes across the life span. Nonetheless, there are periods when the brain experiences growth spurts. These growth spurts seem to occur at the times in infancy, childhood, and adolescence when Jean Piaget and others believe major cognitive breakthroughs occur (see, for example, Epstein, 2001; Kwon & Lawson, 2000). For example, toddlers experience a vocabulary spurt following a period of rapid myelination of those parts of the brain involved in language development (Pujol et al., 2006). And teenagers are more likely than children to ask hypothetical "what if" questions and to reason about weighty abstractions such as truth and justice, which corresponds to maturation of the prefrontal lobes during adolescence. Such changes may also allow adolescents to focus better on task-relevant material and block task-irrelevant information (Durston et al., 2006; Paus, 2005).

Other changes in the brain also take place between ages 12 and 20. Myelination of certain pathways, including those that allow people to concentrate for lengthy periods, continues during adolescence, which may help explain why infants, toddlers, school-age children, and even young adolescents have shorter attention spans than do older adolescents and adults (Tanner, 1990). Further, myelination continues well into adulthood, which may explain why adults are better able than teenagers to integrate thoughts and emotions (Benes, 1998; Nelson, Thomas, & de Haan, 2006). The speed at which the nervous system processes information also continues to increase during adolescence.

Finally, although 12-year-olds, even those who are intellectually gifted, are often "clever" or smart, they are rarely what people would call "wise." They can solve many problems correctly, but they are not as skilled as older adolescents or adults at demonstrating insight, foresight, or a broad perspective on a problem (see Brugman, 2006). Although changes in the brain during adolescence are less dramatic than those earlier in life, it is likely that some of the cognitive growth researchers observe during the teenage years becomes possible only because of further brain development. For instance, when coupled with appropriate physical, cognitive, and social experiences, maturation of the brain contributes to the development of scientific reasoning ability. Changes in the brain during adolescence may also account for some of the risky behaviors associated with this period (see the Explorations box on page 128).

The Aging Brain

Many people fear that aging means losing brain cells and ultimately becoming "senile." As you will see in Chapter 16, Alzheimer's disease and other conditions that cause serious brain damage and dementia are not part of normal aging; they do not affect most older people. Normal aging is associated with gradual and relatively mild degeneration within the nervous system—some loss of neurons, diminished functioning of many remaining neurons, and potentially harmful changes in the tissues surrounding and supporting the neurons, such as the protective myelin covering (Hof & Mobbs, 2001; Peters, 2002). Just as brain weight and volume increase over the childhood years,

CAN BRAIN DEVELOPMENT EXPLAIN WHY ADOLESCENTS TAKE MORE RISKS THAN ADULTS?

Adolescents are notorious for taking chances that most adults would not take. They often display poor judgment and decision making when it comes to alcohol, drug, and cigarette use, sexual activities, and driving. According to the Department of Health and Human Services (Centers for Disease Control, 2007d), risky behaviors during adolescence include the following:

- Smoking frequently (reported by 19% of adolescents) or occasionally (23%)
- Drinking alcohol (43%)
- Drinking and driving (10%)
- Riding with a driver who has been drinking (29%)
- Using marijuana (20%)
- Carrying weapons (19% overall but 30% among males)
- Having sex without a condom (37%)
- Using alcohol or drugs before sexual intercourse (23%)
- Getting into a physical fight (36%)

Various explanations have been offered for adolescents' risk taking, including the need to separate from parents and the influence of the peer group (for example, Arnett, 2002). However, several researchers are also beginning to find connections between brain development and risky behavior during adolescence. Linda Spear (2000b) found that the prefrontal cortex—that part of the brain involved in control of emotions and decision making—decreases in size and undergoes a reorganization of neural connections during adolescence. The prefrontal cortex appears to be particularly important in planning and thinking through the consequences of decisions.

Adriana Galvan and her colleagues (2007) found a connection among anticipation of outcomes as positive or negative, brain activity, and engaging in risky behavior. The researchers measured activity in a part of the brain called the accumbens (thought to be associated with reward, pleasure, and addiction) and found that adolescents, relative to children and adults, exhibited higher levels of activity. Activity in the accumbens increased when adolescents anticipated both negative and positive consequences of risk taking. Importantly, though, the researchers found individual differences across all ages, showing that although adolescents as a group may be more prone to risk-taking behaviors, this is not true of all adolescents.

In other research, teenagers displayed less activity than adults in a part of the brain that has been associated with a desire for reward (Bjork et al., 2004). This underactivity may mean that teens need more stimulation to achieve the same level of reward that others achieve with less stimulation, leading them to engage in more risky behaviors. And research conducted by the National Institutes of Health shows that the area of the brain involved in inhibiting risky behavior is not fully developed until around age 25 (Giedd, 2004).

Thus, a growing body of research suggests some connection between brain activity and risk-taking behavior during the teen years. Neurotransmitters (brain chemicals) may help explain this link. Animal research reveals that one chemical, dopamine, reaches peak levels during adolescence in the prefrontal cortex and limbic system before dropping and then leveling off (Lewis et al., 1998). This chemical is involved in novelty seeking and in determin-

© Sebastien Baussais/Alamy

ing the motivational value of activities (Spear, 2000a). If this holds true for human adolescents, then their risky behaviors may reflect a combination of seeking new experiences and a changing incentive value of stimuli—both influenced by changes in brain chemistry and incomplete development of the prefrontal cortex during adolescence. So far, the research with humans seems to support this brain–behavior connection. The adolescent brain, then, is still a work in progress, and some risk taking by teenagers may be par for the course until further brain developments, such as maturation of the prefrontal cortex, refine their good judgment and decision making (Steinberg, 2007).

---

they decrease over the adult years, especially after age 50 (Courchesne et al., 2000; Resnick, 2000). As people age, more of their neurons atrophy or shrivel, transmit signals less effectively, and ultimately die (Hof & Mobbs, 2001). Elderly adults may end up with 5 to 30% fewer neurons, depending on the brain site studied, than they had in young adulthood. Neuron loss is greater in the areas of the brain that control sensory and motor activities than in either the association areas of the cortex (involved in thought) or the brain stem and lower brain (involved in basic life functions such as breathing) (Whitbourne, 2005).

Other signs of brain degeneration besides neuron loss include declines in the levels of important neurotransmitters; the formation of "senile plaques," hard areas in the tissue surrounding neurons that may interfere with neuronal functioning and are seen in abundance in people with Alzheimer's disease; and reduced blood flow to the brain, which may starve neurons of the oxygen and nutrients they need to function (Hof & Mobbs, 2001). One of the main implications of such degeneration, as you will see later, is that older brains typically process information more slowly than younger brains do.

Mental "exercise" later in life is likely to contribute to neural growth in the aging brain and compensate for neural degeneration.

On the positive side, research shows that the brain can change in response to experience and develop new capabilities *throughout the life span* (see Nelson & Luciana, 2001). Middle age brings greater integration of the left and right hemispheres, which may help increase creativity and cognitive functioning (Cohen, 2005). Older adults who engage in high levels of aerobic activity show enhanced mental performance and corresponding increases in activity in certain regions of the brain (Colcombe et al., 2004). In addition, neurons can form new synapses and extend their dendrites (Kolb & Whishaw, 2006), thus filling in gaps left by dying neurons. This self-repair demonstrates at least some degree of plasticity in the aging brain, just as in the young brain.

What does it mean for older adults that both degeneration and plasticity—both losses and gains—characterize the aging brain? In some people, degeneration may win and declines in intellectual performance will occur. In other people, plasticity may prevail; their brains may form new and adaptive neural connections faster than they are lost so that performance on some tasks may actually improve with age (at least until very old age). For example, in his book *The Mature Mind: The Positive Power of the Aging Brain*, Gene Cohen (2005) argues that several forms of more sophisticated thinking only emerge during middle and older adulthood. These include dualistic thinking, systematic thinking, and relativistic thinking, which we will discuss in Chapter 7. Also, as you will see in Chapters 7, 8, and 9, older adults vary widely in how effectively they learn, remember, and think, and in how well their intellectual abilities hold up as they age. On average, however, plasticity and growth may make up for degeneration until people are in their 70s and 80s. One key to maintaining or even improving performance in old age is to avoid the many diseases that can interfere with nervous system functioning. Another key is to remain intellectually active—to create an "enriched environment" for the brain. You can reject the view that aging involves nothing but a slow death of neural tissue. Old brains *can* learn new tricks.

Principles of Growth

Now that you know something about the endocrine and nervous systems, and how they contribute to growth early in life, is it possible to make general predictions about growth patterns? To do so, researchers often apply three general principles that underlie growth. It is easiest to see these principles in action during infancy when growth is fast. For instance, you have probably noticed that young infants seem to be all head compared with older children and adults. That is because growth follows the **cephalocaudal principle,** according to which growth occurs in a head-to-tail direction. This pattern is clear in ■ **Figure 5.3**: The head is far ahead of the rest of the body during the prenatal period and accounts for about 25% of the newborn's length and 13% of total body weight. But the head accounts for only 12% of an adult's height and 2% of an adult's weight (Zemel, 2002). During the first year after birth, the trunk grows the fastest; in the second year, the legs are the fastest growing part of the body.

While infants are growing from the head downward, they are also growing and developing muscles from the center outward to the extremities. This **proximodistal principle** of growth can be seen during the prenatal period, when the chest and internal organs form before the arms, hands, and fingers. During the first year after birth, the trunk is rapidly filling out but the arms remain short and stubby until they undergo their own period of rapid development.

A third important principle of growth and development is the **orthogenetic principle.** This means that development starts globally and undifferentiated and moves toward increasing differentiation and hierarchical integration (Werner, 1957). Consider a human who starts as a single, undifferentiated cell at conception. As growth proceeds, that single cell becomes billions of highly specialized cells (neurons, blood cells, liver cells, and so on). These differentiated cells become organized, or integrated, into functioning systems such as the brain or the digestive system.

Having looked at the building blocks of growth and development, you are ready to examine the development, aging, and health of the physical self. We concentrate on the body (its size, composition, and functioning) and the use of body and brain in physical activities such as locomotion and finely controlled movements. We also consider factors that are important to health at different ages. In doing so, we turn once again to a life-span model.

A Life-Span Developmental Model of Health

The life-span developmental perspective introduced in Chapter 1 can be applied to a consideration of health and physical change as we age. We can summarize a life-span model of health as follows:

- Health is a lifelong process. It is influenced by personal choices over the life span and is constantly changing in response to these choices.

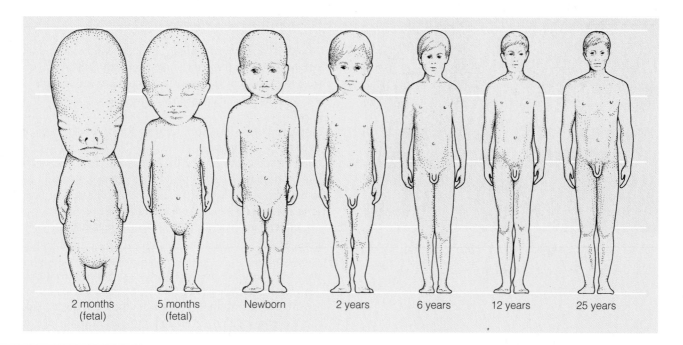

■ **FIGURE 5.3** Changes in the proportions of the human body from the fetal period through adulthood. The head represents 50% of body length at 2 months after conception but only 12–13% of adult height. By contrast, the legs constitute only about 12–13% of the length of a 2-month-old fetus but 50% of an adult's height.

- Health is determined by both genetic and environmental influences. "It has genetic origins; it develops during infancy, childhood, and adulthood as a result of gene-environment interactions" (Aldwin, Spiro, & Park, 2006; p. 85).
- Health—and its study—is multidimensional. Health is a constellation of "physical, mental, and social well-being and not merely the absence of disease or infirmity" (Aldwin, Spiro, & Park, 2006; p. 86).
- Changes in health involve both gains and losses; it both improves and declines over the life span in response to many factors.
- Health occurs in a sociohistorical context and can be enhanced or constrained by the social and historical factors that contribute to it. Especially important is socioeconomic status. Lower socioeconomic status is associated with poorer health and well-being and shorter life expectancy (Aldwin, Spiro, & Park, 2006).

Thus, an individual's health is determined by genetic factors, personal choice, and environmental influences working in concert across the life span. The importance of a life-span model of health will be clear as we view health in each of the following sections.

SUMMING UP

■ Each of the many systems of the human body develops and ages at its own rate, guided by a genetic program set into action by the brain and the hormones released by the endocrine system.

■ The nervous system consists of the brain, the spinal cord, and peripheral neurons. The workings of the endocrine and nervous systems can be hindered or enhanced by environmental forces.

■ During childhood, neural transmission speeds up and lateralization of various brain functions, although present at birth, becomes more evident in behavior.

■ During adolescence, the brain (especially the prefrontal cortex) continues to develop, permitting sustained attention and strategic planning.

■ The aging brain exhibits both degeneration and plasticity. Neurons atrophy and die, and blood flow to the brain decreases; but the aging brain forms new synapses to compensate for neural loss and reorganizes itself in response to learning experiences.

■ Physical growth proceeds according to the cephalocaudal (head-to-tail), proximodistal (center outward), and orthogenetic (global and undifferentiated to differentiated and integrated) principles.

■ Health is best viewed from a life-span developmental perspective emphasizing genes, personal choice, and environmental factors in interaction.

CRITICAL THINKING

1. In what ways is brain plasticity an advantage and in what ways might it be a disadvantage to the developing human?

2. Why is it important to view health from a life-span developmental perspective? Can you illustrate three aspects or components of this perspective as they apply to you or members of your family?

5.2 THE INFANT

Infancy is characterized by rapid growth, continued brain development, emergence of locomotor skills, and impressive sensory and reflexive capabilities. Understanding the newborn's capacities and limitations brings a fuller appreciation of the dramatic changes that take place between birth and adulthood.

Rapid Growth

Newborns are typically about 20 inches long and weigh 7 to 7½ pounds. However, weight and length at birth can mislead about eventual weight and height because the growth of some fetuses is stunted by a poor prenatal environment (Lejarraga, 2002). Size during the first few months after birth is related more to prenatal experiences (environment) than to size of parent (genes). This is easy to see in twins and other multiple births, because their prenatal growth is significantly restricted by siblings competing for the limited space in the mother's womb.

In the first few months after birth, infants grow rapidly, gaining nearly an ounce of weight a day and an inch in length each month. By age 2, they have already attained about half of their eventual adult height and weigh 27 to 30 pounds on average. Although we usually think of growth as a slow and steady process, daily measurements of infant length show that babies grow in fits and starts (Lampl, 2002). They may go weeks with no growth and then shoot up half an inch in 24 hours! Not surprisingly, these growth spurts are often accompanied by irritability that many parents, unaware of the phenomenal growth taking place, find puzzling. In the end, 90 to 95% of an infant's days are growth free, but their occasional bursts of physical growth add up to substantial increases in size.

Bones and muscles are also developing quickly during infancy. At birth, most bones are soft, pliable, and difficult to break. They are too small and flexible to allow newborns to sit up or balance themselves when pulled to a standing position. The soft cartilage-like tissues of the young infant gradually ossify (harden) into bony material as calcium and other minerals are deposited into them. In addition, more bones develop, and they become more closely interconnected. As for muscles, young infants are relative weaklings. Although they have all the muscle cells they will ever have, their strength will increase only as their muscles grow.

Newborn Capabilities

Newborns used to be viewed as helpless little organisms ill prepared to cope with the world outside the womb. We now know that they are quite well equipped to begin life. Just what can a newborn do? Among the most important capabilities are reflexes, functioning senses, a capacity to learn, and organized, individualized patterns of waking and sleeping.

Reflexes

One of the newborn's greatest strengths is a set of useful reflexes. A **reflex** is an unlearned and involuntary response to a stimulus, such as when the eye automatically blinks in response to a puff of air. ● **Table 5.2** lists some reflexes that can be readily observed in all normal newborns. These seemingly simple reactions are quite varied and complex patterns of behavior and they provide infants with a way to begin interacting with their world (von Hofsten, 2007).

Some reflexes are called *survival reflexes* because they have clear adaptive value. Examples include the breathing reflex (useful for obvious reasons), the eye-blink reflex (which protects against bright lights or foreign particles), and the sucking reflex (needed to obtain food). Those called *primitive reflexes* are not clearly useful; many are believed to be remnants of evolutionary history that have outlived their purpose (but see Schott & Rossor, 2003, for another perspective). The Babinski reflex is a good example. Why would it be adaptive for infants to fan their toes when the bottoms of their feet are stroked? Frankly, we don't know. Other primitive reflexes may have some adaptive value, at least in some cultures. For example, the grasping reflex may help infants carried in slings or on their mothers' hips to hang on. Finally, some primitive reflexes—for example, the stepping reflex—are forerunners of useful voluntary behaviors that develop later in infancy. The expression of primitive reflexes at age 6 weeks, however, is not related to the expression of later motor behaviors (Bartlett, 1997). Thus, infants who demonstrate a strong primitive grasping reflex at 6 weeks are not necessarily the infants who demonstrate a strong voluntary grasp later in infancy.

Primitive reflexes typically disappear during the early months of infancy. For instance, the grasping reflex becomes weak by 4 months and is replaced by voluntary grasping. These primitive reflexes are controlled by the lower, subcortical areas of the brain and are lost as the higher centers of the cerebral cortex develop and make voluntary motor behaviors possible. Even though many primitive reflexes are not very useful to infants, they have proven to be useful in diagnosing infants' neurological problems. If such reflexes are not present at birth—or if they last too long in infancy—physicians know that something is wrong with a baby's nervous system. The existence of reflexes at birth tells them that infants are ready to respond to stimulation in adaptive ways. The disappearance of certain reflexes tells them that the nervous system is developing normally and that experience is affecting both brain and behavior. Thus, we see that the presence and then the absence of reflexes can serve as a general indicator of neurological health.

Behavioral States

Another sign that newborns are healthy and equipped for life is their ability to establish organized and individualized patterns of daily activity. Settling into an organized sleep–wake pattern is an indication that the baby is integrating biological, physiological, and psychosocial information (Sadeh, Raviv, & Gruber,

REFLEXES	DEVELOPMENTAL COURSE	SIGNIFICANCE
SURVIVAL REFLEXES		
Breathing reflex	Permanent	Provides oxygen; expels carbon dioxide
Eye-blink reflex	Permanent	Protects eyes from bright light or foreign objects
Pupillary reflex: Constriction of pupils to bright light; dilation to dark or dimly lit surroundings	Permanent	Protects against bright light; adapts visual system to low illumination
Rooting reflex: Turning a cheek toward a tactile (touch) stimulus	Weakens by 2 months; disappears by 5 months	Orients child to breast or bottle
Sucking reflex: Sucking on objects placed (or taken) into mouth	Is gradually modified by experience over the first few months after birth; disappears by 7 months	Allows child to take in nutrients
Swallowing reflex	Is permanent but modified by experience	Allows child to take in nutrients; protects against choking
PRIMITIVE REFLEXES		
Babinski reflex: Fanning then curling toes when bottom of foot is stroked	Disappears 12–18 months after birth	Presence at birth and disappearance in first year indicate normal neurological development
Grasping reflex: Curling fingers around objects (such as a finger) that touch the baby's palm	Disappears in first 3–4 months; is replaced by a voluntary grasp	Presence at birth and later disappearance indicate normal neurological development
Moro reflex: Loud noise or sudden change in position of baby's head will cause baby to throw arms outward, arch back, then bring arms toward each other	Disappears by 4 months; however, child continues to react to unexpected noises or a loss of bodily support by showing startle reflex (which does not disappear)	Presence at birth and later disappearance (or evolution into startle reflex) indicate normal neurological development
Swimming reflex: Infant immersed in water will display active movements of arms and legs and will involuntarily hold breath (thus staying afloat for some time)	Disappears in first 4–6 months	Presence at birth and later disappearance indicate normal neurological development
Stepping reflex: Infants held upright so that their feet touch a flat surface will step as if to walk	Disappears in first 8 weeks unless infant has regular opportunities to practice it	Presence at birth and later disappearance indicate normal neurological development

Preterm infants may show little to no evidence of primitive reflexes at birth, and their survival reflexes are likely to be irregular or immature. However, the missing reflexes will typically appear soon after birth and will disappear a little later than they do among full-term infants.

Rooting reflex.

Grasping reflex.

Stepping reflex.

2000). Infants must move from short sleep–wake cycles distributed throughout the day and night to a pattern that includes longer sleep periods at night with longer wake periods during the day. Much to their tired parents' dismay, newborns have no clear sense of night or day and may wake every 1 to 4 hours. By 3 months, infants begin to establish a predictable sleep–wake cycle; by 6 months three-quarters have settled into a fairly consistent pattern (Minard, Freudigman, & Thoman, 1999). They spend more time asleep at night and awake during the day, and many sleep through the night. Newborns spend half of their sleeping hours in active sleep, also called **REM sleep** (for the rapid eye movements that occur during it). Infants older than 6 months spend only 25 to 30% of their total sleep in REM sleep, which more closely resembles the 20% that adults spend in REM sleep.

Why do young infants sleep so much and spend so much more time in REM sleep than adults? Some research suggests that sleep patterns in infancy are associated with brain maturation and plasticity (e.g., Dang-Vu et al., 2006). REM sleep in particular may be important for learning and memory processes, which may help explain why infants, who have so much to learn, spend more time in this sleep. Daphne and Charles Maurer (1988) suggest that infants use sleep to regulate sensory stimulation. Being bombarded by too much stimulation can "overload" the immature nervous system. To reduce the stimulation, infants tend to become less active, grow quieter, and shift into sleep. This may explain why infants are notoriously fussy at the end of a busy day—often at dinnertime when parents are tired and hoping for some peace. The infant's nervous system can be overstimulated by the flood of stimulation received during the day. Somehow, the arousal needs to be reduced—perhaps by crying and then sleeping. Adults sometimes marvel at how infants can sleep through the loudest noises and the brightest lights, but being able to do so may serve a valuable function. As the Applications box on page 134 shows, sleep is important across the life span and inadequate sleep can take its toll in a variety of ways.

Observations of newborns also make it clear that they have a great deal of individuality. Research confirms this. For instance, in one study one newborn was observed to be in an alert waking state for almost 9 hours out of a 24-hour period, whereas another was in an alert waking state for only about an hour during a 24-hour period (Brown, 1964). Similarly, one newborn cried only 17% of the time, but another spent 39% of the time crying! Premature babies spend more time in transitions from one state to another, and the time they spend in any particular state is shorter than it is for full-term infants (Wyly, 1997). Such variations among infants have obvious implications for parents. It is likely to be far more pleasant to be with a baby who is often alert and rarely cries than it is to interact with a baby who is rarely attentive and frequently fussy. As you saw in Chapter 3, both genetic endowment and environment contribute to these kinds of differences in infant temperament.

Life becomes easier for parents (in some ways) as infants age. As ● **Table 5.3** shows, infants gradually spend more time awake and less time eating, fussing, and crying. Although their sleep times do not change much, their sleep patterns do: they sleep for longer periods at night and take fairly predictable naps during the day.

Sensing and Learning

As you saw in Chapter 4, the sensory systems are developing before birth, and all of the senses are functioning reasonably well at birth. Newborns see and hear, and they respond to tastes, smells, and touches in predictable ways. For instance, newborns can visually track slow-moving objects, they can turn in the direction of sounds, they can turn from unpleasant odors, they are responsive to touch, and they show preferences for sweet tastes (Wyly, 1997). We will explore these sensory capabilities further in Chapter 6.

Another strength of newborns is their ability to learn from their experiences. They can, for example, learn to suck faster if sucking produces pleasant-tasting sugary liquid rather than plain water (Lipsitt, 1990). In other words, they can change their behavior according to its consequences. This is an example of the process of operant conditioning introduced in Chapter 2.

Newborn infants are competent and ready for life. They have a range of reflexes, functioning senses, a capacity to learn, and an organized and unique pattern of waking and sleeping. But when you think about newborns in comparison with adults, it is also clear that newborns are limited beings. Their brains are not nearly as developed as they will be by the end of infancy. Their capacity to move voluntarily and intentionally is limited, and although their senses are working, they cannot interpret stimuli as well as an older individual can. They can learn, but they are slow learners compared with older children, often requiring many learning trials before they form an association between stimulus and response. And they clearly lack important social and communication skills. In short, newborns have strengths and limitations—strengths that can serve as building blocks for later development and limitations that show much remains to be accomplished.

● **TABLE 5.3 PERCENTAGE OF DAY (24-HOUR PERIOD) SPENT IN VARIOUS BEHAVIORAL STATES AT 2, 6, 12, AND 40 WEEKS**

BEHAVIOR	2 WEEKS	6 WEEKS	12 WEEKS	40 WEEKS
Sleeping	59%	56%	57%	55%
Awake	14	19	25	34
Feeding	17	15	11	8
Fussing	5	6	5	3
Crying	4	3	2	<1

Note especially the increase in time awake. Because of rounding, the columns do not total 100%.
SOURCE: Adapted from St. James-Roberts & Plewis, 1996, Table 2.

ARE TODAY'S CHILDREN (AND ADULTS) SLEEP DEPRIVED?

"Impaired by sleep loss, individuals start a task feeling fine. Minutes later, however, heads begin to nod, and the rate of deterioration accelerates. Instead of being able to sustain attention for a 45-minute lecture in a classroom, for example, a student might be able to manage only 3 to 5 minutes" (National Academy of Sciences, 2000, p. 15).

How much sleep do people need, and what happens when they do not get enough? As the graph in this Applications box illustrates, sleep needs change with age, with infants needing the most and adults the least number of hours per night. Experts recommend that 2- to 5-year-olds should get about 12 hours of sleep every night, school-age children should get about 10 hours, teens should get about 9 hours of sleep, and adults should get roughly 8 hours (National Sleep Foundation, 2007). Reports from children and their parents suggest that sleeping problems are common (Gregory, Fijsdijk, & Eley, 2006).

Among preschoolers, lack of a good night's sleep is associated with behavioral problems such as acting out and not complying with requests (Lavigne et al., 1999). Teachers report that at least 10% of their elementary school–age students have trouble staying awake in the classroom (Owens et al., 2000). School-age children who do not get adequate sleep at night perform poorly on a variety of memory tasks and experience problems at school (Smaldone, Honig, & Byrne, 2007; Steenari et al., 2003).

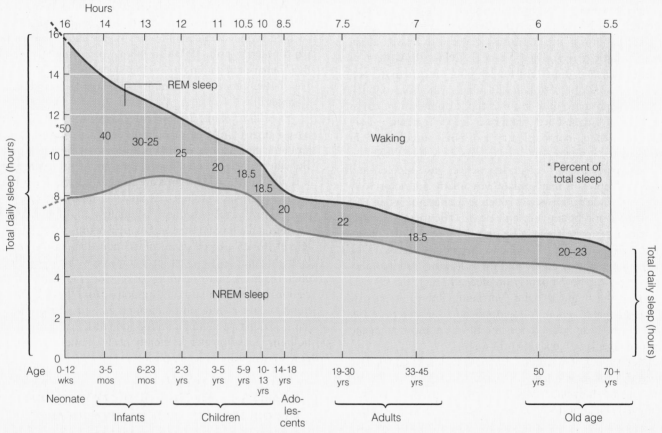

Graph showing changes with age in the total amount of daily sleep and the percentage of REM sleep. There is a sharp drop in the amount of REM sleep after the early years, falling from 8 hours at birth to less than 1 hour in old age. The change in the amount of non-REM (NREM) sleep is much less marked, falling from 8 hours to about 5 hours over the life span.

SOURCE: http://www.sleephomepages.org.

Physical Behavior

The motor behaviors of newborns are far more organized and sophisticated than they appear at first glance, but newborns are not ready to dance or thread needles. By age 2, however, immobile infants have become toddlers, walking up and down stairs by themselves and using their hands to accomplish simple self-care tasks and to operate toys. How do the motor skills involved in walking and manipulating objects develop?

Locomotor Development

● **Table 5.4** shows the age at which half of U.S. infants master particular motor milestones. This average age of mastery is

Getting a good night's sleep only seems to get more difficult as children move into middle school. Katia Fredriksen and her colleagues (2004) found that sixth-graders who got too little sleep had lower self-esteem, poorer grades, and more depression symptoms than their well-rested peers. Furthermore, hours of sleep obtained declined during middle school; girls were more likely than boys to cut their sleep short by getting up earlier in the morning. By extending their sleep just 40 to 60 minutes, 9- to 12-year-olds can increase their performance significantly (Sadeh, Gruber, & Raviv, 2003).

Teenagers are especially likely to be at risk for daytime sleepiness and the consequences associated with fatigue. Changes in the sleep–wake cycle, melatonin production, and circadian rhythms during adolescence mean that the "natural" time for falling asleep shifts later. Research shows that the level of melatonin (a sleep-promoting hormone) rises later at night for teens than for children or adults (National Sleep Foundation, 2007). Teens report later bedtimes from age 12 to age 18 and only 20% of them get the optimal amount of sleep on school nights (National Sleep Foundation, 2007). Although psychosocial factors may also contribute to later bedtimes than in childhood (for example, doing homework or text messaging with friends late into the night), biological factors—puberty in particular—seem primarily responsible. Teens who go to bed at 11 p.m. should not wake up until around 8 a.m. if they are to get the recommended amount of sleep. However, most teens find themselves getting out of bed around 6:30 a.m. to get to school on time (see the graph in this box). High schools typically start earlier than middle or elementary schools, often by 7:30 a.m. to accommodate bus schedules. Thus, just when their biological clocks are pushing back sleep times at night, schools are getting teens up earlier in the morning.

What are the consequences for teens who do not get enough sleep? Teens report greater sleepiness during the day and are quicker to fall asleep than younger children who get the same amount of sleep. Sleepiness is associated with decreased motivation or trouble initiating and maintaining activity, especially on "boring" tasks (Dahl, 1999). Tired teens may be able to successfully navigate a favorite class or read a particularly good book, but these same teens may have trouble completing an assignment in their least favorite subject or studying for an exam. Teens who have had their sleep restricted display increased sleepiness in proportion to the number of nights that their sleep is reduced. But surprisingly—at least to many adults—these same teens "perk up" in the evenings and show high levels of energy that discourage them from going to bed early (National Academy of Sciences, 2000).

Teens who sleep less at night or who stay up later on the weekends than their peers report higher levels of depression, irritability, and lack of tolerance for frustration (Dahl, 1999; Wolfson & Carskadon, 1998). They may also have difficulty controlling their emotional responses, which leads to greater expression of aggression or anger (Dahl, 1999). As happens with younger children, teens who do not get enough sleep have trouble concentrating in school, experience short-term memory problems, and may doze off in class (National Sleep Foundation, 2007).

In addition to causing lapses of attention, sleep deprivation also slows reaction times. Together, these changes increase the likelihood of accidents, which may help explain why adolescents have higher rates of car accidents than any other age group. Becoming drowsy or falling asleep behind the wheel of a car contributes to more than 100,000 accidents every year, and more than half of these accidents involve young drivers (National Sleep Foundation, 2007). Another 1 million car crashes

every year are caused by driver inattention, a correlate of sleepiness.

Finally, what happens when adults are sleep deprived? Young adults sleep 7 to 8 hours per night; this decreases to 6½ to 7½ hours during middle age and drops even further during old age. When they are raising children, which corresponds to the time career demands are likely to be high, many adults (about two-thirds) report that they do not get enough sleep (National Sleep Foundation, 2007). And one out of every five parents reports that daily functioning is impaired at least several days a week because that person feels so tired. The implications of this for worker productivity and safety are tremendous.

Older adults, although they sleep less at night, often compensate by taking a nap during the day. They are also more likely to report sleep problems such as difficulty staying asleep and repeated awakenings during the night. Changes in physiology, such as decreased production of melatonin and growth hormone, both of which help regulate sleep, contribute to the sleep problems experienced by older adults. In addition, older adults are more likely to experience health problems such as arthritis and congestive heart failure that disrupt sleep and to take medications that decrease sleep (National Sleep Foundation, 2007).

For all ages, learning more about sleep needs and the effects of sleep deprivation can lead to healthy lifestyle changes. Adhering to a regular bedtime and wake time on the weekends and on school and work days can help maintain healthy sleep habits. Unfortunately, "sleeping in" on the weekends alters the sleep–wake cycle and makes it more difficult to get up early for work or school Monday morning. So, next time you find yourself dozing off in class or at work, do not jump to the conclusion that the work you are doing is boring. It may be that your sleep–wake cycle is out of sync with the schedule imposed on you by school or work.

called the **developmental norm** for a skill. Developmental norms such as these must be interpreted carefully. They depend on the group studied (children walk earlier today than they used to and walk earlier in some cultures than in others), and they hide a good deal of variation among children, even in the sequence in which skills are mastered (von Hofsten, 1993). Finally, most children who master a skill earlier or later than

the developmental norm are still within the normal range of development. Parents should not be alarmed if their child is 1 or 2 months "behind" the norm; only significantly delayed achievement of key skills such as sitting up or walking is cause for concern.

Can you recognize the workings of the cephalocaudal and proximodistal principles of development in the milestones in

AGE (IN MONTHS)	MILESTONE
2	Lifts head up when lying on stomach
3	Rolls over from stomach to back; holds head steady when being carried
4	Grasps a cube or other small object
5	Sits without support toward end of month
6	Stands holding on to something
7	Rolls over from back to stomach and may begin to crawl or creep; shows thumb opposition
8	Pulls self up to standing position
9	Walks holding on to furniture; bangs two objects together
10	Plays clapping games (e.g., pat-a-cake)
11	Stands alone
12	Walks well alone; drinks from a cup

Based on European American, Hispanic, and African American children in the United States. Indicates the age at which 50% of infants have demonstrated the skill. Keep in mind that there are large individual differences in when infants display various developmental milestones.
SOURCES: Bayley, 1993; Frankenburg et al., 1992; WHO Multicentre Growth Reference Study Group, 2006.

Table 5.4? Early motor development follows the cephalocaudal principle because the neurons between the brain and the muscles acquire myelin sheaths in a head-to-tail manner. Thus, infants can lift their heads before they can control their trunks enough to sit, and they can sit before they can control their legs to walk. The proximodistal principle of development is also evident in early motor development. Activities involving the trunk are mastered before activities involving the arms and legs, and activities involving the arms and legs are mastered before activities involving the hands and fingers or feet and toes. Therefore, infants can roll over before they can walk or bring their arms together to grasp a bottle, and children generally master **gross motor skills** (skills such as kicking the legs or drawing large circles that involve large muscles and whole body or limb movements) before mastering **fine motor skills** (skills such as picking Cheerios off the breakfast table or writing letters of the alphabet that involve precise movements of the hands and fingers or feet and toes). As the nerves and muscles mature downward and outward, infants gradually gain control over the lower and the peripheral parts of their bodies.

The orthogenetic principle is also evident in early motor development. A young infant is likely to hurl his body as a unit at a bottle of milk held out to him (a global response). An older infant gains the ability to move specific parts of her body separately (a differentiated response); she may be able to extend one arm toward the bottle without extending the other arm, move the hand but not the arm to grasp it, and so on, making distinct, differentiated movements. Finally, the still older infant is able to coordinate separate movements in a functional sequence—reaching for, grasping, and pulling in the bottle while opening his mouth to receive it and closing his mouth when the prize is captured (an integrated response).

Crawling. Life changes dramatically for infants and their parents when the infants first begin to crawl or creep, normally around 7 months. Crawling is highly variable: one infant may slither on her belly in a kind of combat crawl, another may use only his forearms to pull ahead, and another may chug backward (Adolph & Berger, 2006). However, most infants around 10 months old end up crawling on their hands and knees, and they all seem to figure out that the best way to keep their balance is to move the diagonal arm and leg at the same time (Adolph & Berger, 2006).

With their new mobility, infants are better able to explore the objects around them and to interact with other people. Experience moving through the spatial world contributes to cognitive, social, and emotional development (Adolph & Berger, 2006). For example, crawling contributes to more frequent social interactions with parents and to the emergence of a healthy fear of heights.

It is interesting to note that fewer infants crawl today as a result of spending less time on their stomachs since the "Back to Sleep" campaign, aimed at reducing sudden infant death syndrome (SIDS), was introduced in the United States and Britain in the early 1990s. Although some parents are concerned when their infants do not crawl at the age suggested by many baby manuals, it turns out that there is no great developmental significance to crawling. Babies can go directly from sitting to walking.

Walking. Although parents must be on their toes when their infants first begin walking, they take great delight in witnessing this new milestone in motor development, which occurs around infants' first birthday. According to Esther Thelen (1984, 1995), the basic motor patterns required for walking are present at birth. They are evident in the newborn's stepping reflex and in the spontaneous kicking of infants lying down. Indeed, Thelen noticed that the stepping reflex and early kicking motions were identical. She began to question the traditional understanding that early reflexes, controlled by subcortical areas of the brain, are inhibited once the cortex takes control of movements. Thelen showed that it simply requires more strength to make the walking motion standing up (as in the stepping reflex) than to make it lying down (as in kicking). She demonstrated that babies who no longer showed the stepping motion when placed standing up on a table did show it when suspended in water because less muscle power was needed to move their chunky legs. The upshot? Infants need more than a more mature nervous system to walk; they must also develop more muscle and become less top-heavy. Even when they begin to walk, they lack good balance partly because of their big heads and short legs. Steps are short; legs are wide apart; and hips, knees, and ankles are flexed. There is much teetering and falling, and a smooth gait and good balance will not be achieved for some time. Thelen's point is that adults would walk funny, too, if they, like infants, were "fat, weak, and unstable" (Thelen, 1984, p. 246; see also Spencer et al., 2006).

It's very possible that some of you reading this book spent time in an infant "walker" before the American Academy of Pediatrics denounced them as unsafe in 2001 (AAP, 2001). What effect did these walkers have on the emergence of walking? Did they enhance walking, perhaps by allowing infants to exercise their legs without having to support the full weight of their bodies? To answer these questions, Andrea Siegel and Roger Burton (1999) studied three groups of infants: One group used no walkers; a second group used older-model walkers that had large leg openings and allowed the infants to see their legs and feet; and a third group used newer-model walkers designed to be safer than the older model with small leg openings and large opaque trays. These newer walkers helped prevent infants from slipping out of the seat, but they blocked the infants' view of their legs and feet. Infants who did not use either type of walker sat up, crawled, and walked earlier than infants with the old-style walkers, and they in turn walked earlier than infants with newer walkers. Why? Infants in the newer walkers with the opaque trays did not receive sensory feedback about their movements; they could not see how their movements altered the positions of their legs relative to other body parts and to the stationary environment, the way infants in the older walkers could. Meanwhile, infants who did not use walkers at all enjoyed unrestricted movement and sensory feedback about the effects of their movement. So, not only are baby walkers unsafe because infants can tumble out of them or propel them down steps, but regular use of them can actually delay motor development. As you will see later in this section, infants need feedback to learn how to coordinate their body movements with the demands of their environment.

In many cases, the infant who has recently impressed her parents by staggering across the room in an upright position seems to regress by reverting to crawling. From the infant's perspective, this apparent regression is quite logical. They have mastered crawling and are quite fast at it, whereas walking on two legs is hard work and can slow them down (Adolph & Berger, 2006). So if they have important things to do, they might find it more efficient to use their reliable crawling skills than to labor at walking. With a little bit of practice, walking will soon become routine and then infants will move on to mastering other skills as well.

Grasping and Reaching

If you look at what infants can do with their hands, you will find another progression from reflexive activity to more voluntary, coordinated behavior. As you have seen, newborns come equipped with a grasping reflex. It weakens from age 2 to 4 months, and for a time infants cannot aim their grasps well. They take swipes at objects and even make contact more than you would expect by chance, but they often miss. And rather than opening their hands to grasp what they are reaching for, they make a fist (Wallace & Whishaw, 2003).

By the middle of the first year, infants grasp objects well, although they use a rather clumsy, clamp-like grasp in which they press the palm and outer fingers together—the ulnar grasp. Initially, they reach for objects using jerky movements and a locked elbow (Berthier & Keen, 2006). By 6 months of age, they are able to bend their elbow, and their reaching movements become increasingly smooth over the next 18 months. They anticipate how they need to adjust their hand so that it can effectively grasp an approaching object (von Hofsten, 2007). We can again see the workings of the proximodistal principle of development as we watch infants progress from controlling their arms, then their hands, and finally their individual fingers enough to use a **pincer grasp,** involving only the thumb and the forefinger (or another finger). The pincer grasp appears as early as 5 months and is reliable by the infant's first birthday (Wallace & Whishaw, 2003).

By 16 months, infants can scribble with a crayon, and by the end of the second year they can copy a simple horizontal or vertical line and even build towers of five or more blocks. They are rapidly gaining control of specific, *differentiated* movements, then *integrating* those movements into whole, coordinated actions. They use their new locomotor and manipulation skills to learn about and adapt to the world around them. By cornering bugs and stacking Cheerios, they develop their minds.

Once infants have mastered the pincer grasp, they can pick up all sorts of objects.

Motor Skills as Dynamic Action Systems

How do motor skills emerge? Thelen (1995, 1996) observed infants throughout their first year and discovered that they spent a great deal of time engaged in **rhythmic stereotypies.** That is, the infants moved their bodies in repetitive ways—rocking, swaying, bouncing, mouthing objects, and banging their arms up and down. Thelen found that infants performed these rhythmic stereotypies shortly before a new skill emerged but not after the skill had become established. Thus, infants might rock back and forth while on their hands and knees, but once they were crawling, they no longer rocked.

Esther Thelen's work has culminated in the development of the **dynamic systems theory** to explain such motor developments (Thelen & Smith, 1994; see also Spencer et al., 2006). According to dynamic systems theory, developments take place over time through a "self-organizing" process in which children use the sensory feedback they receive when they try different movements to modify their motor behavior in adaptive ways (Smith & Thelen, 1993; von Hofsten, 2007). Behaviors that seem to emerge in a moment of time are actually the cumulative effects of motor decisions that the infant makes over a longer time (Spencer et al., 2006). In this view, motor milestones such as crawling and walking are the learned outcomes of a process of interaction with the environment in which infants do the best they can with what they have in order to achieve their goals (Thelen, 1995). Thus, development is highly individualistic: "infants must explore a wide range of behaviors to discover and select their own unique solutions in the context of their intrinsic dynamics and movement history" (Spencer et al., 2006; p. 1528). Neural maturation, physical growth, muscle strength, balance, and other characteristics of the child interact with gravity, floor surfaces, and characteristics of the specific task to influence what children can and cannot learn to do with their bodies. Recall the infants who could not see their legs or feet in the newer walkers: it took them longer to achieve certain motor milestones than infants who could see their legs and learn how their movements affected their relationship to their environment.

Consistent with the dynamic systems approach, Karen Adolph and Anthony Avolio (2000) found that young toddlers could adjust their walking to changes in both body dimensions and the slope of a walkway. The researchers had young toddlers walk on slopes of different degrees while wearing a vest with removable "saddlebags" that could be weighted to simulate changes in their body dimensions (see ■ **Figure 5.4**). The weights added mass and shifted the toddlers' center of gravity, akin to what happens when toddlers grow. Would toddlers be able to compensate for the changes in their body and their environment? Yes—they adjusted their motor skills to adapt to rapid "growth" of their bodies and to changes in their environment (Adolph & Berger, 2006). Like adults carrying a heavy load on their shoulders, toddlers bent their knees and kept their upper bodies stiffly upright to maintain their balance with heavier loads. Toddlers with greater walking experience did better than those with less experience (Garciaguirre, Adolph,

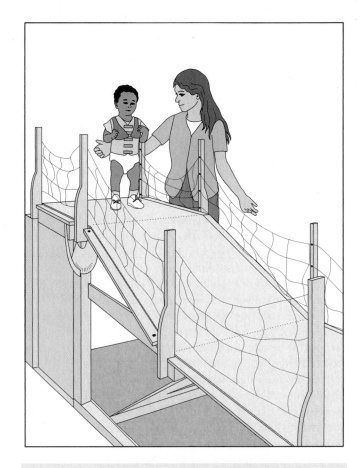

■ **FIGURE 5.4** Adolph and Avolio's walkway with adjustable slope. Infants are outfitted with weighted saddlebags to alter their body mass and center of gravity. While an experimenter stays beside infants to ensure safety, parents stand at the end of the walkway and encourage their child to walk toward them.
SOURCE: From K.E. Adolph & A.M. Avolio, Walking infants adapt locomotion to changing body dimensions, *Journal of Experimental Psychology: Human Perception and Performance*, 26, p. 1148–1166. Copyright © 2000 by The American Psychological Association. Reprinted with permission of the American Psychological Association.

& Shrout, 2007). Toddlers also seemed to recognize when the walkway was too steep to travel safely—they either avoided it or scooted down on their bottoms or on their hands and knees. Young walkers (16 months) are also clever enough to figure out that they can use handrails to help maintain their balance while walking across bridges (Berger & Adolph, 2003). Further, they quickly discover that a sturdy handrail offers more support than a "wobbly" handrail and they are more adventuresome when they can use a sturdy handrail for support (Berger, Adolph, & Lobo, 2005).

As every parent knows, toddlers do not become proficient walkers without experiencing a few falls. As it turns out, these tumbles may help walkers learn which surfaces are safe and which ones may be problematic (Joh & Adolph, 2006). With age, toddlers become increasingly adept at figuring out how to avoid falls. Finally, changes in one area of the dynamic system influence other areas. When toddlers start to walk, it temporarily disrupts their previously established balance during sitting (Chen et al., 2007). It's as if toddlers experience a "recalibration of an internal model for the sensorimotor control" of their bodies (Chen et al., p. 16).

What does this dynamic systems perspective say about the contribution of nature and nurture to development? According to Thelen (1995), toddlers walk not because their genetic code programs them to do so but because they learn that walking works well given their biomechanical properties and the characteristics of the environments they must navigate. In the dynamic systems approach, nature (e.g., maturation of the central nervous system) and nurture (sensory and motor experience) are both essential and largely inseparable. Feedback from the senses and from motor actions is integrated with the ever-changing abilities of the infant. Having learned how to adjust one motor skill (such as crawling) to successfully navigate environmental conditions, however, does not mean that infants will generalize this knowledge to other motor skills (such as walking; see Adolph & Berger, 2006). Different motor skills present different challenges. Crawling infants, for instance, must learn to avoid such dangers as bumping their head on table legs. Walking infants face other challenges, such as not toppling over when turning around. To master these challenges, infants need opportunities to gather feedback from each motor activity.

Finally, an important contribution of the dynamic systems approach to motor development is its integration of action with thought (von Hofsten, 2007). The motor behaviors we have been describing are not separate and distinct from the child's knowledge. Children have to think about how to organize their movements to optimize what they are able to get from their ever-changing environment. Thus, there is far more to motor development than implied by norms indicating when we might expect infants to sit up, stand alone, or walk independently. The emergence of motor skills is complex and is closely connected to perceptual–cognitive developments.

Health and Wellness

What typical health issues must infants—and their parents—navigate? As noted in the previous chapter, modern medicine has made it possible for smaller and smaller babies to survive premature delivery, but sadly, most babies born weighing less than 750 grams (1 pound 10½ ounces) die within the first year (MacDorman et al., 2005). The health problems associated with premature delivery and low birth weight often continue to challenge infants throughout their first year and beyond, illustrating one of the principles of the life-span model of health: Events can have lifelong effects on health. Only about 12% of babies in the United States are premature but as many as one-third of infant deaths are caused by complications of premature birth, making this the second leading cause of infant death (Callaghan et al., 2006). **Congenital malformations**—defects that are present at birth, either from genetic factors or prenatal events—are the leading cause of death during the first year

(National Center for Injury Prevention and Control, 2007). Such malformations include heart defects, spina bifida, Down syndrome, cleft palates, and more.

Infant health has been dramatically improved in recent decades by administering vaccinations aimed at protecting infants from a variety of diseases (e.g., diphtheria, pertussis, polio, and measles). The approximately 20% of infants who do *not* receive the recommended immunizations are more likely to contract illnesses that can compromise their health (National Center for Health Statistics, 2005). Unfortunately, socioeconomic status in the United States often determines who has access to health-care services that cover immunizations. As the life-span model predicts, one's sociohistorical context influences health.

Thus, health during infancy starts well before birth with prenatal care that helps prevent and/or treat potential congenital anomalies and preterm birth. Health after birth is enhanced by well-baby visits to the doctor to ensure that development is proceeding normally and by following recommendations for prevention of illness.

Summing Up

▌ The physical changes that occur during the short period of infancy are awe-inspiring. Infants gain significant height and weight, their bones harden, and their muscles become stronger.

▌ Reflexes, sensory capabilities, and organized waking and sleeping states allow infants to gather information from their surroundings and interact in increasingly meaningful ways with their environments.

▌ According to dynamic systems theory, children "self-organize" their motor development by using sensory feedback they receive from their movements to modify their motor behavior in adaptive ways.

▌ Congenital malformations and complications of preterm birth are the leading causes of infant mortality. Preventative medicine such as well-baby visits to the doctor and vaccinations can improve infant health.

Critical Thinking

1. How do infants' sensory abilities and reflexes equip them to function and learn about their world?

2. Recall a time when you learned a new motor skill—for example, how to inline skate or hit a golf ball. Can you apply the dynamic systems approach to understand how your skill developed over time and what influenced its development?

5.3 THE CHILD

Development of the body and of motor behavior during childhood is slower than it was during infancy, but it is steady. You need only compare the bodies and the physical feats of the

2-year-old and the 10-year-old to be impressed by how much change occurs over childhood.

Steady Growth

From age 2 until puberty, children gain about 2 to 3 inches in height and 5 to 6 pounds in weight every year (National Center for Health Statistics, 2007a). During middle childhood (ages 6–11), children may seem to grow little, probably because the gains are small in proportion to the child's size (4–4½ feet and 60–80 pounds on average) and therefore harder to detect. The cephalocaudal and proximodistal principles of growth continue to operate. As the lower parts of the body and the extremities fill out, the child takes on more adultlike body proportions. The bones continue to grow and harden, and the muscles strengthen.

Physical Behavior

Infants and toddlers are capable of controlling their movements in relation to a *stationary* world, but children master the ability to move capably in a *changing* environment (Sayre & Gallagher, 2001). They must learn to modify their movements to adapt to changes in environment. This allows them to bring their hands together at just the right time to catch a ball and to

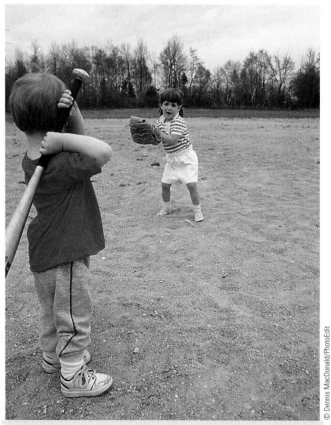

Children are not as coordinated in preschool as they will be a few years later.

© Dennis MacDonald/PhotoEdit

avoid bumping into moving people when walking through a crowded mall. They also refine many motor skills. For example, young children throw a ball only with the arm, but older children learn to step forward as they throw. Their accuracy throwing a ball increases around age 7, as does their speed of throwing (Favilla, 2006). Thus, older children can throw a ball farther than younger ones can, not just because they are bigger and stronger but also because they can integrate multiple body movements—raising their arm, turning their body, stepping forward with one foot, and pushing their body forward with the other foot (Sayre & Gallagher, 2001).

The toddler in motion appears awkward compared with the older child, who takes steps in more fluid and rhythmic strides and is better able to avoid obstacles. And children quickly become able to do more than just walk. By age 3, they can walk or run in a straight line, although they cannot easily turn or stop while running. By age 4, children are getting so talented with their motor skills that they can trace a figure with one hand while tapping a pen with their other hand (Otte & van Mier, 2006). Kindergarten children can integrate two motor skills—hopping on one foot with walking or running—into mature skipping (Loovis & Butterfield, 2000). With each passing year, school-age children can run a little faster, jump a little higher, and throw a ball a little farther. Their motor skills are also responsive to practice. In one study, children improved their arm movements 25 to 30% with practice—an impressive accomplishment compared with the 10% improvement shown by adults who practiced (Thomas, Yan, & Stelmach, 2000). There are some gender differences in motor skills, with boys slightly ahead in throwing and kicking and girls somewhat ahead in hopping and tasks that require manual dexterity (Junaid & Fellowes, 2006; van Beurden et al., 2002). These differences seem to arise primarily from practice and different expectations for males and females rather than from inherent differences between the two groups.

From age 3 to age 5, eye–hand coordination and control of the small muscles are improving rapidly, giving children more sophisticated use of their hands. At age 3, children find it difficult to button their shirts, tie their shoes, or copy simple designs. Their drawings often look more like scribbles than pictures. By age 5, children can accomplish all of these feats and can cut a straight line with scissors or copy letters and numbers with a crayon. Their drawings become recognizable and are increasingly realistic and detailed (see ■ **Figure 5.5**). The typical 5- to 6-year-old can also tie her shoes and even use a knife to cut soft foods. By age 8 or age 9, children can use household tools such as screwdrivers and have become skilled performers at games that require eye–hand coordination. Handwriting quality and speed also improve steadily from age 6 to age 15 (van Galen, 1993).

Finally, older children have quicker reactions than young children do. When dogs suddenly run in front of their bikes, they can do something about it. In studies of **reaction time**, a stimulus, such as a light, suddenly appears and the subject's task is to respond to it as quickly as possible—for example, by pushing a button. These studies reveal that reaction time im-

■ **FIGURE 5.5** Children's fine motor control and cognitive skills develop throughout childhood, allowing them to progress from making circles, lines, and scribbles at age 2 (drawing on the left) to meaningful pictures at age 6 (drawing on the right).

proves steadily throughout childhood (Eaton & Ritchot, 1995; Yan et al., 2000). As children age, they can carry out any number of cognitive processes more quickly. This speeding up of neural responses with age contributes in important ways to steady improvements in memory and other cognitive skills from infancy to adolescence (see Chapter 8).

Health and Wellness

Children's health is influenced by a multitude of factors, some of which are beyond their control. For instance, parents' education and socioeconomic status affect their children's health (Chen, Martin, & Matthews, 2006). Children whose parents are less educated are more likely to experience poor or fair health than children with more educated parents. This is particularly true for black children and white children, but less true for Hispanic children and Asian children, whose health outcomes may be buffered by strong social networks that cut across educational and socioeconomic levels (see ■ **Figure 5.6**). Clearly, then, the sociohistorical context of development plays a role in children's health and well-being.

Nutrition continues to be an important contributor to health throughout childhood, as it was during infancy. Much to parents' dismay, though, the toddler who sampled all sorts of new foods may turn into a picky eater during childhood. One reason for this is that the rate of growth has slowed down, diminishing children's appetites. Still, they need to have a well balanced diet that addresses their nutritional needs. Unfortunately, societal influences often inadvertently encourage poor eating habits rather than good ones. Many children eat fast foods, which are often fried, and snack on foods high in carbohydrates and low on nutritional value. Parents can help by regularly offering a variety of healthy foods and modeling healthy eating

habits. There are lifelong benefits: Boys who maintain a low-fat diet from infancy through childhood lower their risk of heart disease and stroke later in life (Stephenson, 2006). The same benefits are not found among girls, perhaps because of their different hormonal profile.

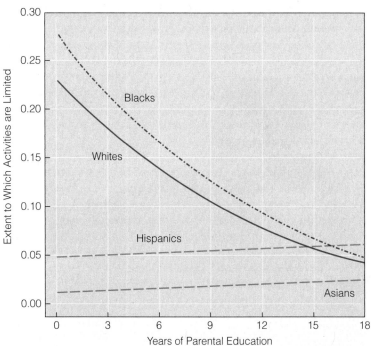

■ **FIGURE 5.6** Among white families and black families, parent's education level influences the extent to which children's activities are limited by poor or fair health: Children have more limitations when their parents are less educated. This is not true among Hispanic families and Asian families.

Chen, E., Martin, A. D., & Matthews, K. A. (2006). Understanding health disparities: The role of race and socioeconomic status in children's health. *American Journal of Public Health, 96,* 702–705.

Accidents constitute a major category of negative influences on children's health and well-being. Childhood is unfortunately marked by numerous unintentional injuries, making this the leading cause of death throughout the childhood years (Centers for Disease Control, 2007c). Crashes involving motor vehicles cause the largest number of fatal injuries during childhood. Parents can reduce the possibility of motor vehicle injuries by properly strapping their infants and young children into car seats, or as they get older, insisting that they sit in the backseat with a shoulder strap seat belt.

Health during childhood can also be fostered by regular physical activity. For instance, children who participate in a systematic exercise program are more physically fit than children who lead a more sedentary lifestyle (see Tuckman, 1999, for a review). The benefits of exercise go beyond physical fitness; physical activity may enhance cognitive and psychological functioning. In a review of studies on children's participation in physical activity and their academic performance, Roy Shepard (1997) concluded that increased physical activity was associated with improved academic skills. But these data are largely correlational, and many factors may explain the connection between physical activity and academic performance. For instance, Mark Tremblay and colleagues (Tremblay, Inman, & Willms, 2000) found that although regular participation in physical activity did not strongly influence 12-year-olds' academic performance, it did positively affect their self-esteem. Students who are healthier and feel better about themselves may perform better in the classroom.

Unfortunately, our contemporary lifestyles may inadvertently promote physical inactivity. The average child spends 5 to 6 hours every day watching television or videos, playing video games, and working or playing on the computer (Roberts & Foehr, 2004). At the same time, some schools have reduced recess time and physical education requirements (Kaiser Family Foundation, 2004). Most kids get chauffeured everywhere they need to go in the family car, further decreasing their opportunities for walking and physical activity. As a result, as many as 30 to 40% of American children are estimated to be overweight or at risk for being overweight, and being an overweight child or adolescent usually means becoming an overweight adult (Freedman et al., 2006; Vieweg et al., 2007).

Children who watch more than 5 hours of television a day are about 5 times more likely to be overweight than children who watch 0 to 2 hours a day, perhaps because they get little exercise and eat the junk foods they see advertised on TV. According to recent research by the Kaiser Foundation, elementary school children see an average of 21 food advertisements on television every day (Kaiser Family Foundation, 2007). As ● **Table 5.5** shows, most food advertisements are for candy and snacks or cereals. The researchers found that none of the 8854 advertisements included in the study were for fruits and vegetables.

Does watching television, with all its junk food ads, lead to obesity or do obese children simply like to watch more television, perhaps because the sedentary nature of television suits them? Most of the research on this has been correlational, which does not allow us to establish a cause–effect connection (e.g., Gortmaker et al., 1996; Proctor et al., 2003). But several experimental interventions that have reduced TV time (rather than eliminating it entirely, which is nearly impossible to do in this day and age) suggest that the amount of time spent watching television can affect weight. For example, in one study, a group of third-graders and fourth-graders had their television time eliminated for 10 days and then limited to 7 hours per week for 6 months. Compared to a matched group of children

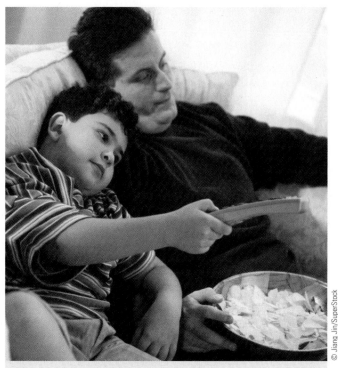

Many children today put on excess weight because of a combination of poor diet choices and lack of exercise.

● **TABLE 5.5 DISTRIBUTION OF TELEVISION ADVERTISEMENTS FOR FOOD APPEARING DURING CHILDREN'S PROGRAMS**

TYPE OF FOOD	PERCENTAGE OF ADVERTISEMENTS
Candy and Snacks	34%
Cereals	28
Fast Food	10
Dairy Products	4
Fruit Juices	1
Fruit or Vegetables	0

SOURCE: From Kaiser Family Foundation Television Food Advertising to Children in The United States, Publication # 7618. Copyright © 2007 Kaiser Family Foundation. Reprinted with permission.

whose time was not changed, the intervention children had decreased their body weight by the end of the 6-month period (Robinson, 1999). So, changing the amount of children's television viewing can impact their weight, although we still don't know for sure whether this is caused by the decreased time in front of the television set, the decreased viewing of ads for junk foods, or some combination of these and other factors.

SUMMING UP

- There is steady and marked improvement in all aspects of physical growth and motor behavior over the childhood years.
- Accidental injuries are the leading cause of death during childhood, with motor vehicle accidents topping the list of injury causes.
- Health is enhanced with proper nutrition and regular physical activity. Current lifestyles have decreased physical activity and increased sedentary media time, which is associated with increased weight among today's children.

CRITICAL THINKING

1. Develop a model for reducing childhood injuries. Based on children's burgeoning physical and motor skills, what would be your focus for helping parents, schools, and neighborhoods keep their children as safe as possible?

2. Design an intervention to reduce childhood obesity and indicate how you will assess the effectiveness of your intervention.

5.4   THE ADOLESCENT

Adolescents are intensely focused on their physical self, and rightly so—dramatic physical changes are taking place during this period. Consider your own transformation from child to adult. You rapidly grew taller and took on the body size and proportions of an adult during your growth spurt. Moreover, you experienced **puberty**—the processes of biological change that result in an individual's attaining sexual maturity and becoming capable of producing a child. We look at both of these processes.

The Growth Spurt

As noted earlier in the chapter, the **adolescent growth spurt** is triggered by an increase in the level of growth hormones circulating through the body during adolescence. Boys and girls grow at different rates, as do different body parts. Girls' peak rate of growth for height is just under 12 years; for boys it is 13.4 years (Geithner et al., 1999). The peak rate of growth for weight is 12.5 years for girls and 13.9 years for boys. Thus, boys lag behind girls by 1 to 2 years. Both sexes return to a slower rate of growth after the peak of their growth spurts. Like infants, ado-

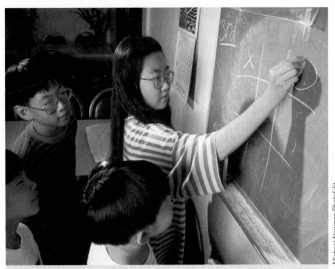

Although there are large individual differences, girls typically mature earlier than boys, which sometimes leads to girls' towering over the boys in their classes.

Michael Newman/PhotoEdit

lescents may grow in spurts rather than continuously (Lampl, 2002). Girls achieve their adult height by around 16 years; boys are still growing at 18, 19, or even 20 years (National Center for Health Statistics, 2007a).

Muscles also develop rapidly in both sexes, with boys normally gaining a greater proportion of muscle mass than girls do. Total body weight increases in both sexes, but it is distributed differently: girls gain extra fat, primarily in the breasts, hips, and buttocks; boys develop broader shoulders.

Sexual Maturation

Long before the physical signs of puberty are evident, the body is changing to prepare for sexual maturity. The adrenal glands increase production of adrenal androgens as early as age 6 to age 8, which contributes partly to such secondary sex characteristics as pubic and axillary (underarm) hair (Spear, 2000a). But the more obvious signs of sexual maturity emerge with increased production of gonadal hormones (those produced by the testes or ovaries): androgens in males and estrogen and progesterone in females. The gonadal hormones are primarily responsible for the development of secondary sexual characteristics and sexual maturity.

For girls, the most dramatic event in the sexual maturation process is **menarche**—the first menstruation—normally between ages 11 and 14 with an average of 12½ years for non-Hispanic white girls, 12 years for non-Hispanic black girls, and somewhere between these ages for Hispanic and Asian American girls (Anderson, Dallal, & Must, 2003; Chumlea et al., 2003). Menstruation is the process of shedding the lining of a uterus prepared to support a fertilized egg. However, young girls often begin to menstruate before they have begun to ovulate, so they may not be capable of reproducing until several years after menarche (Spear, 2000a).

After decreasing during the first half of the 20th century, the average age of menarche has not changed much in recent decades, at least in industrialized nations (Chumlea et al., 2003; Viner, 2002). However, there is a great deal of variability in when secondary sex characteristics (such as breast buds and pubic hair) appear. Sexual maturation also proceeds at different rates in different ethnic groups. Several studies have found that African American and Mexican American girls begin to experience pubertal changes earlier than European American girls (Chumlea et al., 2003; Wu, Mendola, & Buck, 2002). At age 9, for example, 49% of African American girls have begun to develop breasts compared with only 16% of European American girls and 25% of Mexican American girls (Wu, Mendola, & Buck, 2002). A few girls (1% of European Americans and 3% of African Americans) show signs of breast or pubic hair development at age 3, and a few have not begun to mature even at age 12 (Herman-Giddens et al., 1997). In addition, a girl's weight at birth as well as the amount of weight she gains during childhood both influence the timing of menarche: the lighter she is at birth and the more weight she gains during childhood, the earlier she tends to begin menstruating (Sloboda et al., 2007; Tam et al., 2006).

For the average boy, the sexual maturation process begins around age 11 to age 11½ with an initial enlargement of the testes and scrotum (the saclike structure that encloses the testes). Unpigmented, straight pubic hair appears soon thereafter, and about 6 months later, the penis grows rapidly about the same time that the adolescent growth spurt begins (see ■ Figure 5.7). The marker of sexual maturation most like menarche in girls is **semenarche,** or a boy's first ejaculation—the emission of seminal fluid in a "wet dream" or while masturbating. It typically occurs around age 13. Just as girls often do not ovulate until some time after menarche, boys often do not produce viable sperm until some time after their first ejaculation.

Somewhat later, boys begin to sprout facial hair, first at the corners of the upper lip and finally on the chin and jawline. As the voice lowers, many boys have the embarrassing experience of hearing their voices "crack" uncontrollably up and down between a squeaky soprano and a deep baritone, sometimes within a single sentence. Boys may not see the first signs of a hairy chest until their late teens or early 20s, if at all.

What determines an adolescent's rate of development? Genes are part of the answer: identical twins typically experience changes at similar times, and early or late maturation tends to run in families (Tanner, 1990). In both sexes, the changes involved in physical and sexual maturation are triggered when the hypothalamus of the brain stimulates activity in the endocrine system (see the description at the beginning of this chapter). Boys and girls have similar levels of both male and female sex hormones during childhood. By the time sexual maturation is complete, however, males have larger quantities of male hormones (androgens, including testosterone) circulating in their blood than females do, whereas females have larger quantities of female hormones (estrogen, progesterone, and others).

(A) Females

(B) Males

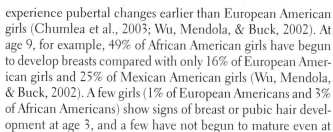

■ **FIGURE 5.7** Sexual maturation of females (A) and males (B): The numbers represent the age range at which each aspect of maturation begins or ends. For example, growth of the penis may begin as early as age 10½ or as late as age 14½.

Physical and sexual maturation, then, are processes set in motion by the genes and executed by hormones. But environment also plays its part in the timing of maturation. This is dramatically illustrated by the **secular trend**—the historical trend in industrialized societies toward earlier maturation and greater body size. In 1840, for example, the average age of menarche was 16½ years, a full 4 years later than it is today (Rees, 1993). Today, researchers can still find cultures in which sexual maturity is reached much later than it is in Western nations. For example, in one region of Saudi Arabia the average age of menarche is 15, and in one part of Papua New Guinea the average girl does not reach menarche until age 18 (Dosoky & Amoudi, 1997; Tanner, 1990).

What explains the secular trend? Better nutrition and advances in medical care seem to be the major factors (Gluckman & Hanson, 2006). Worldwide, the age of menarche is earlier in countries with good nutrition, long life expectancies, and high literacy rates, reflecting the effect of both biological and environmental factors (Thomas et al., 2001). In industrialized nations, today's children are more likely than their parents or grandparents to reach their genetic potential for maturation and growth because they are better fed and less likely to experience growth-retarding illnesses. Even within the relatively affluent U.S. society, poorly nourished adolescents—both boys and girls—mature later than well-nourished ones do. Girls who are taller and heavier as children tend to mature earlier than other girls (Lee et al., 2007). By contrast, girls who engage regularly in strenuous physical activity and girls who suffer from anorexia nervosa (the life-threatening eating disorder that involves dieting to the point of starvation) may begin menstruating late or stop menstruating after they have begun. These variations seem to be tied not to overall weight but to skeletal development, particularly maturation of the pelvic bones necessary for delivering a baby (Ellison, 2002).

Research by Bruce Ellis and Judy Garber (2000) shows that family stress can also affect the timing of puberty in girls. Girls whose mothers were depressed were likely to experience early puberty, as were girls who had a stepfather or mother's boyfriend present in the home. In particular, girls who were relatively young when an unrelated male moved into the house and whose mothers and stepfathers or boyfriends had a more conflicted, stressful relationship were likely to experience early sexual maturity. However, girls from lower socioeconomic backgrounds lag several months behind their higher socioeconomic counterparts, possibly because of less adequate nutrition and health care (Dosoky & Amoudi, 1997). Truly, then, physical and sexual maturation are the products of an interaction between heredity and environment, with some environments delaying maturation and others hastening it.

Psychological Implications

As noted previously, there are large individual differences in the timing of physical and sexual maturation. An early-maturing girl may develop breast buds at age 8 and reach menarche at age 10, whereas a late-developing boy may not begin

to experience a growth of his penis until age 14½ or a height spurt until age 16. Within a middle school, then, there is a wide assortment of bodies, ranging from entirely childlike to fully adultlike. No wonder adolescents are self-conscious about their appearance.

What psychological effects do the many changes associated with puberty have on adolescents? In many cultures, girls approaching or experiencing puberty tend to become concerned about their appearance and worry about how others will respond to them. One adolescent girl may think she is too tall, another that she is too short. One may try to pad her breasts; another may hunch her shoulders to hide hers. Not surprisingly, research confirms that individual reactions to menarche vary widely, with many girls reporting a mixture of positive and negative feelings and some confusion about the process (Koff & Rierdan, 1995; Moore, 1995). Unfortunately, cultural views about menstruation are often negative, and girls internalize these negative myths about what to expect. Many also develop poor body images because they are bothered by the weight gains that typically accompany menarche (Seiffge-Krenke, 1998).

What about boys? Their body images are more positive than those of girls, and they are more likely to welcome their weight gain and voice changes (Benjet & Hernández-Guzmán, 2002; Martin, 1996). But they hope to be tall, hairy, and handsome, and they may become preoccupied with their physical and athletic prowess. Whereas menarche is a memorable event for girls, boys are often unaware of some of the physical changes they are experiencing. They notice their first ejaculation, but they rarely tell anyone about it and often were not prepared for it (Stein & Reiser, 1994). Although males express a mix of positive and negative reactions to becoming sexually mature, they generally react more positively to semenarche than girls do to menarche; 62% of boys regard semenarche positively, whereas only 23% of girls view menarche positively (Seiffge-Krenke, 1998).

Pubertal changes may prompt changes in family relations. Adolescents physically distance themselves from their parents by engaging in less body contact, especially with fathers, and they go to great lengths to avoid being seen naked by their parents (Schulz, 1991, in Seiffge-Krenke, 1998). Likewise, parents seem to restructure the parent–child relationship, placing greater distance between themselves and their children. Perhaps as a result of the barriers erected between adolescents and their parents, teens become more independent and less close to their parents (Steinberg, 1989). They are also more likely to experience conflicts with their parents, especially with their mothers—more often about minor issues such as unmade beds, late hours, and loud music than about core values. Hormone changes in early adolescence may contribute to this increased conflict with parents and to moodiness, bouts of depression, lower or more variable energy levels, and restlessness (Buchanan, Eccles, & Becker, 1992). However, cultural beliefs about family relations and about the significance of becoming an adult also influence parent–child interactions during adolescence. For example, many Mexican American boys and their parents appear to become closer rather than more distant during the peak of pubertal changes (Molina & Chassin, 1996).

Even when parent–child relationships are disrupted during early adolescence, they become warmer once the pubertal transition is completed. Parents—mothers and fathers alike—can help adolescents adjust successfully to puberty by maintaining close relationships and helping adolescents accept themselves (Swarr & Richards, 1996). Overall, you should not imagine that the physical and hormonal changes of puberty cause direct and straightforward psychological changes in the individual. Instead, biological changes interact with psychological characteristics of the person and with changes in the social environment to influence how adolescence is experienced (Magnusson, 1995; Paikoff & Brooks-Gunn, 1991).

Early versus Late Development

If "timely" maturation has psychological implications, what is it like to be "off time"—to be an especially early or late developer? The answer depends on whether we are talking about males or females and also on whether we examine their adjustment during adolescence or later on.

Consider the short-term effect of being an early-developing or late-developing boy. Early-developing boys are judged to be socially competent, attractive, and self-assured, and they enjoy greater social acceptance by their peers (Bulcroft, 1991). The only negative aspect of being an early-maturing boy is increased risk of earlier involvement in substance use and other problem behaviors such as bullying (Kaltiala-Heino et al., 2003). By comparison, late maturation in boys has more negative effects. Late-maturing boys tend to be more anxious and less sure of themselves, and they experience more behavior and adjustment problems (Dorn, Susman, & Ponirakis, 2003). As a group, they even score lower than other students do, at least in early adolescence, on school achievement tests (Dubas, Graber, & Petersen, 1991). However, on the positive side, late-maturing boys are less likely to drink alcohol during adolescence (Bratberg et al., 2005).

Now consider early-maturing and late-maturing girls. Traditionally, physical prowess has not been as important in girls' peer groups as in boys', so an early-developing girl may not gain much status from being larger and more muscled. In addition, because girls develop about 2 years earlier than boys do, a girl may be subjected to ridicule for a time—the only one in her grade who is developed and thus the target of some teasing. Perhaps for some of these reasons, early maturation appears to be more of a disadvantage than an advantage for girls. Many studies report an association between early maturation and lower self-esteem among girls (see, for example, Forys & Rider, 2000; Williams & Currie, 2000). The early-maturing girl tends to be less popular than her prepubertal classmates, and she is more likely to report symptoms of depression and anxiety, especially if she had psychological problems as a child (Graber et al., 1997; Hayward et al., 1997). In addition, early-maturing girls often end up socializing with an older peer group; consequently, they are likely to become involved in dating, smoking, drinking, having sex, and engaging in minor troublemaking at an early age (Bratberg et al., 2005; Burt et al., 2006; Deardorff et al., 2005).

Late-maturing girls (like late-maturing boys) may experience some anxiety as they wait to mature, but they do not seem to be as disadvantaged as late-maturing boys. Indeed, whereas later-developing boys tend to perform poorly on school achievement tests, later-developing girls outperform other students (Dubas, Graber, & Petersen, 1991). Perhaps late-developing girls focus on academic skills when other girls have shifted some of their focus to extracurricular activities.

Do differences between early and late developers persist into later adolescence and adulthood? Typically, they fade with time. By late high school, for example, differences in academic performance between early and late maturers have already disappeared (Dubas, Graber, & Petersen, 1991), and early-maturing girls are no longer less popular than other girls (Hayward et al., 1997). However, there may be lasting effects of some of the risky behaviors engaged in by early-maturing girls (such as sex and drinking). And some research shows that early-maturing girls have a greater likelihood than all other groups of experiencing lifetime adjustment problems, including both anxiety and depression (Graber et al., 1997). Some of the advantages of being an early-maturing boy may carry over into adulthood, but early-maturing boys also seem to be more rigid and conforming than late-maturing ones, who may learn some lessons about coping in creative ways from their struggles as adolescents.

Overall, then, late-maturing boys and early-maturing girls are especially likely to find the adolescent period disruptive. However, psychological differences between early-maturing and late-maturing adolescents become smaller and more mixed in quality by adulthood. It is also important to note that differences between early and late maturers are relatively small and that many factors besides the timing of maturation influence whether this period goes smoothly or not. For example, girls who make the transition from elementary to middle school at the same time they experience puberty exhibit greater adjustment problems than girls who do not experience a school transition and pubertal changes simultaneously (Simmons & Blyth, 1987).

Finally, and perhaps most important, the effects of the timing of puberty depend on the adolescent's perception of whether pubertal events are experienced early, on time, or late (Seiffge-Krenke, 1998). Thus, one girl may believe she is a "late bloomer" when she does not menstruate until age 14. But another girl who exercises strenuously may believe that menarche at age 14 is normal because delayed menarche is typical of serious athletes. Peer and family-member reactions to an adolescent's pubertal changes are also instrumental in determining the adolescent's adjustment. This may help explain the difference in adjustment between early-maturing boys and early-maturing girls. Parents may be more concerned and negative about their daughter's emerging sexuality than they are about their son's. These attitudes may be inadvertently conveyed to teens, affecting their experience of puberty and their self-concept.

Physical Behavior

The dramatic physical growth that occurs during adolescence makes teenagers more physically competent than children. Rapid muscle development over the adolescent years makes both boys and girls noticeably stronger than they were as children (Seger & Thorstensson, 2000). Their performance of large-muscle activities continues to improve: An adolescent can throw a ball farther, cover more ground in the standing long jump, and run much faster than a child can (Keough & Sugden, 1985). However, as the adolescent years progress, the physical performance of boys continues to improve, whereas that of girls often levels off or even declines (Seger & Thorstensson, 2000).

Clearly, larger muscles enable boys to outperform girls in activities that require strength. But biological differences cannot entirely explain sex differences in physical performance (Smoll & Schutz, 1990). Gender-role socialization may be partly responsible. As girls mature sexually and physically, they are often encouraged to be less "tomboyish" and to become more interested in traditionally "feminine" (often more sedentary) activities. Studies of world records in track, swimming, and cycling suggest that as gender roles have changed in the past few decades, women have been improving their performances, and the male–female gap in physical performance has narrowed dramatically (Sparling, O'Donnell, & Snow, 1998; Whipp & Ward, 1992). A small gender gap remains in some areas of physical activity, largely related to biological differences—greater muscle mass in males, greater body fat in females, and differences in oxygen transport capacity (Sparling, O'Donnell, & Snow, 1998). But as today's girls participate more often in sports and other strenuous physical activities, their performance on tests of large-muscle activity is likely to remain stable or improve during adolescence, rather than declining as it did in previous generations. Then both young women and young men will be likely to enter adulthood in peak physical condition.

Health and Wellness

Adolescents should be reaching their peak of physical fitness and health and, indeed, many adolescents are strong, fit, and energetic. Unfortunately, the sedentary lifestyle of modern society may be undermining the health and fitness of an increasing number of teens. Fitness tests of American teenagers show that an alarming one-third of them have poor physical fitness (Carnethon, Gulati, & Greenland, 2005). Teens may be doing well in school, but they are flunking treadmill tests that measure heart and lung function. Today's teens are showing up with high blood pressure, high cholesterol, and high blood sugar, putting them at risk for heart disease at earlier ages than previous generations of teens.

The number of teens who meet the criteria for obesity has also increased in recent decades. **Obesity**—being 20% or more above the "ideal" weight for your height, age, and sex—is clearly a threat to health. Obese people do not live as long as their normal-weight peers, and they are at greater risk for such problems as heart and kidney disease, high blood pressure, diabetes, liver problems, and even arthritis. Obesity is usually the product of both nature and nurture: heredity is perhaps the most important factor, but poor eating habits, inactivity, and even parenting beliefs contribute (Gable & Lutz, 2000). Individuals who are overweight as adolescents—even those who slim down as adults—run a greater-than-average risk of coronary heart disease and a host of other health problems some 55 years later (Must et al., 1992).

The leading causes of death among teens are unintentional injuries (mostly from motor vehicles) and violence, including homicides and suicides (Centers for Disease Control, 2007c). Other health risks that may originate during adolescence include alcohol and drug use and cigarette smoking. Lifestyle choices made by adolescents have important implications for their health, both in the short term and in the long term. Consider the one out of four high school students who report occasional heavy or binge drinking (Centers for Disease Control, 2006e). Teens under the influence of alcohol are more likely to make additional risky choices: (1) They are more likely to smoke cigarettes and the more they smoke, the more likely they are to become addicted to nicotine. (2) They are more likely to engage in risky sexual behaviors including sex with multiple partners and unprotected sex. In turn, these behaviors are associated with unintended pregnancies and sexually transmitted diseases. (3) They are more likely get into a car where the driver has been drinking, which greatly increases the risk of an accident. (4) They are more likely to get into physical fights, experience academic problems, and engage in illegal behaviors. These behaviors, or the predisposition to these behaviors, may have been present before the alcohol use, but alcohol use can still exacerbate the problems. By some analyses, making the decision not to drink during adolescence may be one of the teen's most important health decisions.

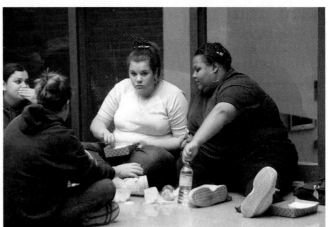

Sedentary lifestyles have led to an increasing number of teens who are overweight or obese.

SUMMING UP

▌ The adolescent period is marked by physical growth—the adolescent growth spurt—and attainment of puberty or sexual maturity. Girls experience their growth spurt at a younger age than do boys. The major milestone of sexual maturity for girls is menarche—their first menstruation. For boys, it is the less noted experience of semenarche, or first ejaculation. A combination of genes, hormones, and environmental factors determine the timing and rate of growth and puberty.

▌ The physical changes of adolescence are significant and have psychological implications. Girls' experience is often on the negative side, whereas boys tend to report a more positive reaction to growth and puberty. Boys who mature early experience largely positive benefits whereas late-maturing boys have a more negative experience. In contrast, girls who mature early are sometimes disadvantaged by teasing from their peers and the influence of the older peers with whom they often socialize. Late-maturing girls seem to benefit academically, possibly because they continue to spend more time on schoolwork than their early-maturing peers.

▌ Adolescents are a relatively healthy bunch, but the fitness level of some teens is poor because of a lack of physical activity. Accidental injuries and violence are the leading causes of death during adolescence and include motor vehicle accidents, suicides, and homicides.

CRITICAL THINKING

1. What are the most significant health concerns during adolescence? If you could get adolescents to change one or two behaviors to improve their health, what would they be and why?

2. How would you counsel the parents of an early-maturing girl so that they understand the risks she may face and what they can do to help her adjust successfully?

5.5 | THE ADULT

The body of the mature adolescent or young adult is at its prime in many ways. It is strong and fit; its organs are functioning efficiently; it is considered to be in peak health. But it is aging, as it has been all along. Physical aging occurs slowly and steadily over the life span. Physical and health changes begin to have noticeable effects on appearance and functioning in middle age and have an even more significant effect by the time old age is reached, although more so in some people than in others.

In the next sections, we discuss typical changes that occur as we progress through middle adulthood and old age. We also look at health issues that can challenge us and consider what it takes to age successfully.

Typical Changes

What changes can we expect across adulthood and old age? There are usually some changes in appearance, physical functioning, and the reproductive system, as well as a slowing of motor responses. Let's look at each of these areas in more detail.

Appearance and Physical Functioning

Only minor changes in physical appearance occur in the 20s and 30s, but many people notice signs that they are aging as they reach their 40s. Skin becomes wrinkled, dry, and loose, especially among people who have spent more time in the sun. Hair thins and often turns gray from loss of pigment-producing cells. And to most people's dismay, they put on extra weight throughout much of adulthood as their metabolism rate slows but their eating and exercise habits do not adjust accordingly. This "middle-aged spread" could be controlled by regular exercise but it occurs when many adults feel they have little time to exercise because family and work responsibilities demand a great deal of their time. Among middle-aged adults, the majority are overweight or obese and only 20% are considered to be in a healthy weight range (Centers for Disease Control, 2007).

The body shows additional effects of aging in old age. After gaining weight throughout early and middle adulthood, people typically begin to lose weight starting in their 60s (Whitbourne, 2005). Unfortunately, this loss of weight in old age is not from losing the fat gained in middle age but from losing valuable muscle and bone. Importantly, it is not age per se that reduces muscle mass but rather the sedentary lifestyle adopted by many older adults. When Abby King and colleagues (2000) surveyed nearly 3000 women in middle and later adulthood, they found that only 9% met the criteria for being regularly active. And as age increased, level of activity decreased. Age is not the only culprit, however, in making adults less active; low level of education, poor neighborhood characteristics, and personal factors (such as caregiving responsibilities and lack of energy) also influence whether or not adults exercise (King et al., 2000).

Aging also involves a gradual decline in the efficiency of most bodily systems from the 20s on. Most systems increase to a peak sometime between childhood and early adulthood and decline slowly thereafter. No matter what physical function you look at—the capacity of the heart or lungs to meet the demands of exercise, the ability of the body to control its temperature, the ability of the immune system to fight disease, or strength—the gradual effects of aging are evident. For example, Monique Samson and her colleagues (2000) assessed handgrip strength in healthy men and women between ages 20 and 80. Women showed only small decreases in muscle strength before age 55 but much larger decreases after age 55. Men showed steady loss of muscle strength across all ages studied.

It should be noted, however, that individual differences in physiological functioning increase with age (Harris et al., 1992). That is, aerobic capacity and other physiological measurements vary more widely among 70-year-olds than among 20-year-olds. Even though the average old person is less physiologically fit than the average young person, not all older people have poor physiological functioning. Older adults who remain physically active retain greater strength (Amara et al., 2003).

Some older adults have a good deal of reserve capacity and can perform strenuous activities even in their 80s and 90s.

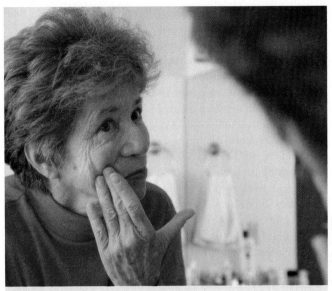
Older adults, like adolescents, often struggle to come to terms with the physical changes they experience as they get older.

Another fact of physical aging is a decline in the **reserve capacity** of many organ systems—that is, their ability to respond to demands for extraordinary output, such as in emergencies (Goldberg & Hagberg, 1990). For example, old and young people do not differ much in resting heart rates, but older adults, even if they are disease-free, will have lower maximal heart rates (Lakatta, 1990). This means that older adults who do not feel very old as they go about their normal routines may feel very old indeed if they try to run up mountains.

Older adults are often less fit than younger ones because they decrease their involvement in vigorous physical activity as they get older—females earlier than males (Ruchlin & Lachs, 1999). By late adulthood, they may find that they get tired just climbing stairs or carrying groceries; running a marathon is out of the question. The average older person tires more quickly and needs more time to recover after vigorous activity than the average younger person.

Psychological Implications

Some people, influenced by societal stereotypes to equate "old" with "unattractive," find the physical changes in their appearance and functioning that occur with age difficult to accept. American society values youth and devalues old age and the physical changes that often accompany it. What are the psychological implications of growing older under these conditions? Negative stereotypes about older adults abound—they are sickly, frail, forgetful, unattractive, dependent, or otherwise incompetent. Such stereotypes can lead to **ageism,** or prejudice against elderly people. Most elderly adults have internalized these negative views but believe they apply to other older adults and not to themselves.

Laura Hurd (1999) interviewed women between ages 50 and 90 who attended programs at a "senior center." She found that the women actively worked to distance themselves from the "old" category and to remain in the "not old" category. These categories were defined not by age but by what individuals can and cannot do. Generally, the women believed that

they were not old because they had the physical and mental abilities to avoid nursing home care. In particular, they believed that remaining active—both physically and socially—was the key to avoiding becoming old. Women who considered themselves "not old" believed that men and women who were old had given in to the stereotypes of aging by being inactive and solitary.

As you have seen, many older adults, even those who consider themselves "not old," have chronic diseases and impairments. Still, the majority of people 65 and older say they are in excellent, very good, or good health (Federal Interagency Forum, 2007). Whites are more likely to report they are in good health than Blacks or Hispanics (76% compared to 60% and 62%). Relatively few older adults say they need assistance with daily activities, although the figure climbs with age—from 9% of those age 65 to age 69 to 50% of those age 85 and older (Hobbs, 1996). Although having a chronic disease or disability tends to lower an older person's sense of well-being, many people with arthritis, diabetes, and other difficulties are no less content with their lives than anyone else (Kempen et al., 1997). Clearly, most older people are able to retain their sense of well-being and their ability to function independently despite an increased likelihood of impairments.

The Reproductive System

During most of adulthood, the sex hormones that start to be secreted during adolescence help ensure interest in sexual behavior and the ability to have children, but they also have psychological implications and affect the experience of aging. In men, testosterone levels fluctuate annually, with the highest levels detected in June and July (Andersson et al., 2003), and daily (Harman & Talbert, 1985). Men with high levels of testostcrone tend to be more sexually active and aggressive than other men (Archer, 1991; Schiavi et al., 1991). Otherwise, it is not clear that changes in men's hormone levels are tied to changes in their moods and behavior.

By contrast, hormone levels in women shift drastically each month as they progress through their menstrual cycles. These shifts have psychological implications for some women. Estrogen and progesterone levels rise to a peak at midcycle, when a woman is ovulating, and decline as she approaches her menstrual period. The cyclic changes in hormones may lead to such symptoms as bloating, moodiness, breast tenderness, and headaches during the days just before the menstrual flow, symptoms collectively referred to as **premenstrual syndrome (PMS).** Among women age 21 to age 64, 41% report that they experience PMS and another 17% report at least some symptoms before menstruation (Singh et al., 1998). Many adolescent women (88%) report moderate or severe symptoms (Cleckner-Smith, Doughty, & Grossman, 1998).

However, there is some debate about the validity of PMS. In research where women are simply asked to complete mood surveys every day and do not know that their menstrual cycles are being studied, most report little premenstrual mood change (Englander-Golden et al., 1986). This suggests that expectations and not hormones play a role in many cases of PMS. Only a few women—probably fewer than 5%—experience significant PMS. Changes in estrogen and progesterone levels may be responsible for the severe PMS these women experience (Schmidt et al., 1998). Women with severe PMS may find relief when treated with antidepressant drugs such as Prozac (Dimmock et al., 2000). For women with milder forms of PMS, treatment with calcium and vitamin D may alleviate symptoms because low estrogen levels experienced prior to menstruation can interfere with the absorption of these substances by the body (Thys-Jacobs, 2000). Clearly, individuals vary in how they experience menstrual cycles.

Genetic endowment influences the extent to which a woman experiences both premenstrual and menstrual distress (Condon, 1993; Kendler et al., 1992). Social factors also play a role. Learned societal stereotypes of what women "should" experience at different phases of the menstrual cycle appear to influence what women experience and report (Ainscough, 1990; Englander-Golden et al., 1986). Most likely, then, biological, psychological, social, and cultural factors all contribute to a woman's experience of the menstrual cycle during her adult life (McFarlane & Williams, 1990).

Female Menopause

Like other systems of the body, the reproductive system ages. The ending of a woman's menstrual periods in midlife is called **menopause.** The average woman experiences menopause at age 51, and the usual age range is from 45 to 54. The process takes place gradually over 5 to 10 years as periods become either more or less frequent and less regular. Levels of estrogen and other female hormones decline so that the woman who has been through menopause has a hormone mix that is less

"feminine" and more "masculine" than that of the premenopausal woman. When menopause is completed, a woman is no longer ovulating, no longer menstruating, and no longer capable of conceiving a child.

The age at which a woman reaches menopause is somewhat related to both the age at which she reached menarche and the age at which her mother reached menopause (Varea et al., 2000). Although life expectancy has increased and the age of menarche has decreased over history as part of the secular trend, the age of menopause does not appear to have changed much and is similar from culture to culture (Brody et al., 2000). What has changed is that women are now living long enough to experience a considerable period of postmenopausal life.

Society holds rather stereotypic views of menopausal women. They are regarded as irritable, emotional, depressed, and unstable. How much truth is there to this stereotype? Not much. About two-thirds of women in U.S. society experience **hot flashes**—sudden experiences of warmth and sweating, usually centered around the face and upper body, that occur at unpredictable times, last for a few seconds or minutes, and are often followed by a cold shiver (Whitbourne, 2005). Many also experience vaginal dryness and irritation or pain during intercourse. Still other women experience no symptoms.

What about the psychological symptoms—irritability and depression? Again, researchers have discovered wide variation among menopausal women—and not much truth to the negative stereotypes. In a particularly well-designed study, Karen Matthews and her associates (Matthews, 1992; Matthews et al., 1990) studied 541 initially premenopausal women over a 3-year period, comparing those who subsequently experienced menopause with women of similar ages who did not become menopausal. The typical woman entering menopause initially experienced some physical symptoms such as hot flashes. Some women also reported mild depression and temporary emotional distress, probably in reaction to their physical symptoms, but only about 10% could be said to have become seriously depressed in response to menopause. Typically, menopause had no effect on the women's levels of anxiety, anger, perceived stress, or job dissatisfaction. When women do experience severe psychological problems during the menopausal transition, they often had those problems well before the age of menopause (Greene, 1984).

Women who have been through menopause generally say it had little effect on them or that it even improved their lives; they are usually more positive about it than women who have not been through it yet (Gannon & Ekstrom, 1993; Wilbur, Miller, & Montgomery, 1995). For most women, menopause brings no changes in sexual interest and activity, although sexual activity gradually declines in both women and men over the adult years (Laumann, Paik, & Rosen, 1999). In short, despite all the negative stereotypes, menopause seems to be "no big deal" for most women. Indeed, many women find the end of monthly periods to be quite liberating.

Why do some women experience more severe menopausal symptoms than others do? Again, part of the answer may lie with biology. Women who have a history of menstrual prob-

CULTURAL DIFFERENCES IN THE EXPERIENCE OF MENOPAUSE

The physical changes involved in menopause are universal, but the psychological experience of it is not. Consider hot flashes, the most frequent complaint of menopausal women. Nearly three-quarters of American and Canadian women report experiencing at least one hot flash during the menopausal period, but only one in five Japanese women recall having had any (Lock, 1993; Shaw, 1997). Even within the United States, Japanese and Chinese women report fewer menopausal symptoms than African American, European American, and Hispanic women (Gold et al., 2000). In Zimbabwe, women experience the same symptoms as reported by women in Western cultures, but they view these as part of a normal and healthy stage of life and not as an unhealthy sign of loss

(McMaster, Pitts, & Poyah, 1997). Thus, they tend not to seek treatment or complain about their "symptoms."

Marcha Flint (1982) surveyed women of a high and socially advantaged caste in India and found that women who had not reached menopause looked forward to it and that women who had reached it were pleased that they had. Why? According to Flint, menopause brought social rewards to these Indian women. They were freed from the taboos associated with menstruation that had kept them veiled and segregated from male society as younger women. They could now mingle with men other than their husbands and fathers and even drink the local brew with the fellows. Moreover, they still had meaningful work roles and were seen as wise by virtue of their years. In North

American society, by comparison, aging often means a loss of status for older women, and menopause is regarded as a medical condition of aging to be treated with hormones.

Not all women share this negative and medical view of menopause, even when the broader culture around them embraces this view. Some American women, for instance, report that menopause is insignificant relative to other things going on in their lives (Winterich & Umberson, 1999). Others regard menopause as a normal life transition, even an opportunity to embark on new life options (Adler et al., 2000). So again, biological, psychological, and social factors all play parts in how a seemingly common event is interpreted differently by different individuals.

---

lems (such as PMS) report more menopausal symptoms, both physical and psychological (Morse et al., 1998). Thus, some women may experience greater biological changes. But psychological and social factors of the sort that influence women's reactions to sexual maturation and to their menstrual cycles also influence the severity of menopausal symptoms. For example, women who expect menopause to be a negative experience are likely to get what they expect (Matthews, 1992). There is also a good deal of variation across cultures in how menopause is experienced (see the Explorations box). It appears that the effect of menopause is colored by the meaning it has for the woman, as influenced by her society's prevailing views of menopause and by her own personal characteristics.

For years, **hormone replacement therapy,** or **HRT** (taking estrogen and progestin to compensate for hormone loss at menopause), was considered an effective cure for the symptoms that many women experience with menopause. HRT relieves physical symptoms of menopause, such as hot flashes and vaginal dryness, and prevents or slows osteoporosis. Unfortunately, this trust in HRT was shattered in 2002 by a large government study that found that HRT increases women's chances of developing breast cancer and experiencing heart attacks and strokes (Women's Health Initiative, 2004). For most women, these risks outweigh the benefits of HRT, particularly if the hormones estrogen and progestin are taken over a long period. For women with severe menopausal symptoms associated with decreasing production of hormones, short-term HRT (for example, up to 2 years) may be warranted. In the year following publication of the research, sales of hormones dropped by 40% (Grady, 2006) and women and their physicians have been scrambling for alternative treatments. To date, however, the benefits and pitfalls of these alternatives, such as soy, have not been documented. Lifestyle changes such as exercising and getting adequate sleep may

be the best options for menopausal women because they alleviate some complaints and are safe.

Male Andropause

Obviously, men cannot experience menopause because they do not menstruate. They also do not experience the sharp drop in hormones that accompanies menopause in women. But over the past decade, some research has pointed to the possibility that men experience andropause as they age. **Andropause,** slower and not as dramatic as menopause in women, is characterized by decreasing levels of testosterone and a variety of symptoms including low libido, fatigue and lack of energy, erection problems, memory problems, and loss of pubic hair (Tan & Pu, 2004; Vermeulen, 2000; Wu, Yu, & Chen, 2000). By age 80, men have between 20 and 50% of the testosterone that they had at age 20. The sperm produced by older men may not be as active as those produced by younger men. Still, men can father children long after women become incapable of bearing children.

Some research reports that testosterone levels are markedly lower among men over age 50 with symptoms of andropause than among men without symptoms (Wu, Yu, & Chen, 2000). But other research does not show a clear connection between andropause symptoms and testosterone levels (see, for example, Vermeulen, 2000). In one study, for example, half of 50- to 70-year-old men complained of erectile dysfunction despite having sufficient levels of testosterone; most of these cases of erectile dysfunction are caused by medical conditions such as diabetes and not by lower hormone production (Gould, Petty, & Jacobs, 2000).

In sum, the changes associated with andropause in men are more gradual, more variable, and less complete than those associated with menopause in women. As a result, men experience fewer psychological effects. Frequency of sexual activity does decline as men age. However, this trend cannot be blamed entirely on decreased hormone levels, because sexual activity often declines even when testosterone levels remain high (Gould, Petty, & Jacobs, 2000; see also Chapter 12 on sexuality).

Slowing Down

You may have noticed, as you breeze by them on the sidewalk, that older adults often walk more slowly than young people do. Indeed, research suggests that the amount of time stoplights provide for pedestrians to cross the street is not enough for the 99% of people age 72 or older who walk at a pace slower than 4 feet per second (Langlois et al., 1997). Some older adults also walk as if they were treading on a slippery surface—with short, shuffling steps and not much arm movement.

It's not just walking that slows with age. On average, older adults perform many motor actions more slowly and with less coordination than younger adults do (Whitbourne, 2005). In a study comparing younger adults (18–24 years) with older adults (62–72 years) on five motor tasks, the older adults performed more slowly on all five (Francis & Spirduso, 2000). The older adults were especially slow on fine motor tasks requiring object manipulation, such as inserting pegs in holes. They also have more trouble when tasks are novel and when they are complex—for example, when any one of several stimuli might appear on a screen and each requires a different response (Sliwinski et al., 1994; Spirduso & MacRae, 1990). On average, older adults take 1½ to 2 times longer than young adults to respond on a range of cognitive tasks that require speedy answers (Lima, Hale, & Myerson, 1991).

What accounts for the slowing of motor performance in old age? One hypothesis is that the ability to produce complex behavior declines with age (Newell, Vaillancourt, & Sosnoff, 2006). Putting together the multiple components that comprise complex tasks becomes increasingly difficult as we age (Kolev, Falkenstein, & Yordanova, 2006; Shea, Park, & Braden, 2006). Motor responses also likely slow because the brain itself slows. Gerontologist James Birren has argued that *the* central change that comes about as people age is a slowing of the nervous system (Birren & Fisher, 1995). It affects not only motor behavior but also mental functioning, and it affects most elderly people to at least some degree.

You should not expect all old people to be slow in all situations, however. The reaction times of older adults vary greatly (Yan, Thomas, & Stelmach, 1998; Yan et al., 2000). Physically fit older people and those free from cardiovascular diseases have quicker reactions than peers who lead sedentary lives or have diseases, although they are still likely to be slower than they were when they were younger (Earles & Salthouse, 1995; Spirduso & MacRae, 1990). Aerobic exercise or experience playing video games can also speed the reactions of older adults (Dustman et al., 1989, 1992). In addition, experience can help elderly people compensate for a slower nervous system so that they can continue to perform well on familiar motor tasks.

Disease, Disuse, or Abuse?

Many aspects of physical functioning seem to decline over the adult years in many individuals. But an important question arises: when researchers look at the performance of older people, are they seeing the effects of aging alone or the effects of something else? The "something else" could be disease, disuse of the body, abuse of the body—or all three.

Most older people have at least some chronic *disease* or impairment, such as arthritis or heart disease. How would an elderly person function if she could manage to stay disease-free? Birren and his colleagues (1963) addressed this question in a classic study of men age 65 to 91. Extensive medical examinations were conducted to identify two groups of elderly men: (1) those who were almost perfectly healthy and had no signs of disease and (2) those who had slight traces of some disease in the making but no clinically diagnosable diseases. Several aspects of physical and intellectual functioning were assessed in these men, and the participants were compared with young men.

The most remarkable finding was that the healthier group of older men hardly differed from the younger men. They were equal in their capacity for physical exercise, and they beat the younger men on measures of intelligence requiring general information or knowledge of vocabulary words. Their main limitations were the slower brain activity and reaction times that seem to be so basic to the aging process. Overall, aging in the absence of disease had little effect on physical and psychological functioning. However, the men with slight traces of impending disease were deficient on several measures. Diseases that have progressed to the point of symptoms have even more serious consequences for performance.

So it is possible that disease, rather than aging, accounts for many declines in functioning in later life. We must note, however, that Birren and his colleagues had a tough time finding the perfectly healthy older people they studied. Most older people experience both aging and disease, and it is difficult to separate the effects of the two. Although aging and disease are distinct, increased vulnerability to disease is one part—and an important part—of normal aging.

Disuse of the body also contributes to steeper declines in physical functioning in some adults than in others. John Masters and Virginia Johnson (1966) proposed a "use it or lose it" maxim to describe how sexual functioning deteriorates if a person engages in little or no sexual activity. The same maxim can be applied to other systems of the body. Muscles atrophy if they are not used, and the heart functions less well if a person leads a sedentary life (Rosenbloom & Bahns, 2006). Changes such as these in some aging adults are much like the changes observed in people of any age confined to bed for a long time (Goldberg & Hagberg, 1990). The brain also needs "mental exercise" to display plasticity and to continue to function effectively in old age (Black, Isaacs, & Greenough, 1991). In short, most systems of the body seem to thrive on use, but too many people become inactive as they age (Rosenbloom & Bahns, 2006).

Finally, *abuse* of the body contributes to declines in functioning in some people. Excessive alcohol consumption, a high-fat diet, and smoking are all clear examples (Haber, 1994). In addition, although elderly adults are rarely recreational drug abusers, many take several prescribed medications. Drugs typically affect older adults more powerfully than they do younger adults; they can also interact with one another and with the aging body's chemistry to impair functioning (Cherry & Morton, 1989; Lamy, 1986).

Overall, then, poor functioning in old age may represent any combination of the effects of aging, disease, disuse, and abuse. We may not be able to do much to change basic aging processes but as you will see in the next section, we can change our lifestyles to optimize the odds of a long and healthy old age.

Health and Wellness

By the time people are 65 or older, it is hard to find many who do not have something wrong with their bodies. Acute illnesses such as colds and infections become less frequent from childhood on, but chronic diseases and disorders become more common. National health surveys indicate that many of the 70-and-older age group have at least one chronic impairment—whether a sensory loss, arthritis, hypertension, or a degenerative disease (Federal Interagency Forum, 2006). Arthritis alone affects 43% of elderly men and 55% of elderly women; in addition, about half have hypertension (high blood pressure), and about one-third have heart disease (Federal Interagency Forum, 2006). Among older adults who live in poverty, many of whom are members of a minority group, health problems and difficulties in day-to-day functioning are even more common and more severe (Clark & Maddox, 1992; Hobbs, 1996). Still, as ● **Table 5.6** shows, most adults maintain the physical capabilities that allow them to function successfully.

Again, though, it is important to note that there is tremendous variability in the health, wellness, and functioning of older adults. Some are limited by health problems, but others enjoy active, healthy lives. Indeed, some older adults are far more active than younger ones! For instance, Michael Stones and Albert Kozma (1985) cite the example of a 98-year-old man who could run a marathon (26.2 miles) in 7½ hours! And former president George Bush marked the occasion of his 80th birthday by skydiving and has plans to skydive again for his 85th birthday.

What factors might account for such differences and what do we know about staying healthy in older adulthood? For one, older adults who exercise reap many benefits. Exercise can improve cardiovascular and respiratory functioning, slow bone loss, and strengthen muscles. In one study, older athletes (average age 69 years) were compared with older nonathletes on several physiological measures following exercise. The athletes showed better oxygen uptake capacity and greater cardiovascular stamina than the nonathletes (Jungblut et al., 2000). In another study, elderly adults who did low-intensity exercise and weight lifting for 1 year became stronger and more flexible and

● **TABLE 5.6** **PERCENTAGE OF OLDER ADULTS (65 PLUS) WHO CAN SUCCESSFULLY ACHIEVE EACH TASK**

SKILL	MEN	WOMEN
Walk one-quarter mile	86%	76%
Climb 10 stairs without resting	93%	85%
Stoop, crouch, or kneel	91%	82%
Reach over head	97%	96%

SOURCE: Federal Interagency Forum on Aging-Related Statistics, 2006, p. 29.

experienced less pain as a result (Sharpe et al., 1997). Exercise can make aging adults feel less stressed and happier, and it can enhance their cognitive functioning (Barnes et al., 2003; Rowe & Kahn, 1998; Yaffe et al., 2001). Physical activity is also associated with a lower incidence of depression among older adults (Lampinen, Heikkinen, & Ruoppila, 2000). Overall, it is estimated that regular exercise by older adults can delay the onset of physical disabilities by up to 7 years (Vita et al., 1998).

Exercise is clearly beneficial to physical and mental health over the life span. What exercise cannot do is halt the inevitable aging process. Even frequent joggers gain weight and add inches to their waists as they enter middle age (Williams, 1997). True, people who exercise generally weigh less and have slimmer waists than those who do not, but a 30-year-old man who runs 20 to 30 miles a week until he is 50 would add almost 2 inches to his waist anyway; he would have to run farther each year to avoid it. To try to beat aging, then, it is not enough to remain active; a person must become *more* active over the years (Williams, 1997).

Another factor that contributes to health and wellness is the presence or absence of disease. There are a number of diseases that become more prominent with age. Among the most common diseases of old age are osteoporosis and osteoarthritis.

Extreme bone loss in later life results from **osteoporosis** (meaning "porous bone"), a disease in which a serious loss of minerals leaves the bones fragile and easily fractured. It involves pain and can result in death if the victim falls and fractures a hip. Nearly one-third of elderly adults who fracture a hip die within 1 year; hip fractures are also a leading cause of nursing home admissions (Whitbourne, 2005). One fall can change an older person's entire lifestyle, requiring a shift from independent living to assisted living. Not surprisingly, adults who have experienced a fall often begin to restrict their activities out of fear of falling again. Unfortunately, less activity can make them more vulnerable because it can lead to further decreases of muscle and bone mass (Whitbourne, 2005). Osteoporosis is a special problem for older women, who never had as much bone mass as men and whose bones tend to thin rapidly after menopause. European and Asian women with light frames, those who smoke, and those with a family history of osteoporosis are especially at risk.

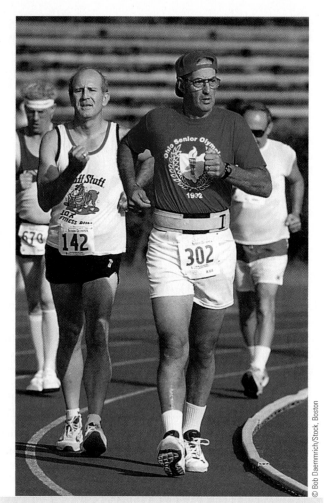

Physical activity throughout adulthood is strongly associated with better health and longer life.

What can be done to prevent osteoporosis? For starters, dietary habits can influence a person's risk for osteoporosis. Many individuals do not get enough calcium to develop strong bones when they are young or to maintain bone health as they age (Kart, Metress, & Metress, 1992). Weight-bearing exercises such as walking or jogging can help prevent osteoporosis, as can the hormone replacement therapy (HRT) that some women take following menopause (but see this chapter's earlier section, "Female Menopause," for a discussion of concerns about HRT). It is increasingly evident that good bone health starts in childhood and adolescence (Krucoff, 2000). Girls and young women who are physically active and eat a healthy diet develop higher bone density that protects them from bone loss in later life.

The joints also age over the adult years. The cushioning between bones wears out, and the joints stiffen. Many older adults experience pain or discomfort from arthritis, or joint inflammation. The most common joint problem among older adults is **osteoarthritis,** which results from gradual deterioration of the cartilage that cushions the bones from rubbing against one another. For some older adults, joint disease is deforming and painful and limits their activities. The older person who can no longer fasten buttons, stoop to pick up dropped items, or even get into and out of the bathtub may easily feel incompetent and dependent (Whitbourne, 2005).

Successful Aging

Everyone wants to age "successfully"; that is, maintain good health and be free of diseases that might limit physical and mental skills and the ability to actively participate in desired daily activities (Rowe & Kahn, 1998). Older adults want to be as independent as possible and pursue a lifestyle that makes them feel satisfied. Researchers are beginning to learn some of the secrets to successful aging.

In 1986, David Snowdon (2002) began the Nun Study with 678 nuns ranging in age from 75 to 106 years. Snowdon, an epidemiologist, chose to study the nuns because they were very similar with respect to socioeconomic status, housing, health care, and diet. In this remarkable longitudinal study, participants underwent annual mental and physical testing, provided complete access to a lifetime of health records, and agreed to donate their brains for examination following their deaths.

The first finding to emerge from the Nun Study was that level of education affected longevity and health. Those with a college degree lived longer and were more likely to remain independent. The risk of death among the college-educated nuns was lower at every age. Another major finding was that the nuns who were active, both physically and mentally, lived longer and healthier than nuns who were not as active.

A unique aspect of the Nun Study was that each nun had written an autobiography prior to taking her vows (average age of 22 years) and, decades later, these autobiographies became part of the data analyzed for the study. This analysis revealed that older nuns who were healthy had used more complex vocabulary in their autobiographies decades earlier (on average, 60 years earlier). They used words such as "particularly, privileged, and quarantined" as opposed to simple words such as "girls, boys, and sick" that were used by nuns who later developed symptoms of Alzheimer's disease (Snowdon, 2002, p. 107). In particular, idea density, a measure of language-processing ability, measured in early adulthood predicts mental functioning in later adulthood. In addition, nuns whose autobiographies expressed more positive emotions lived longer than nuns whose autobiographies expressed fewer positive emotions.

The message to take away from such research is that both physical and mental activity, along with a positive attitude, can help slow the effects of aging on both the body and brain. As noted earlier, we can't avoid the biological reality of aging, but we can make choices across the life span that will increase the odds of aging successfully. Clearly, then, our health and well-being are influenced by an interaction of environmental and genetic factors.

© Bob Daemmrich/Stock, Boston

SUMMING UP

▌ Declines in physical systems and capabilities begin in early adulthood, with steeper declines evident among older adults.

▌ As people age, their nervous systems, reaction times, and motor behavior slow; their capacity for vigorous activity is also reduced.

▌ For both sexes, changes in the reproductive system are a normal part of aging. Neither women nor men seem to suffer much as their ability to have children wanes or disappears. Sexual activity becomes less frequent, but it remains an important part of life for most older adults.

▌ Aging, disease, disuse, and abuse of the body all affect performance in later life. Healthy older people function much like younger people except for their slower reactions, but the development of chronic diseases is a fact of aging for most people.

▌ Health and well-being during adulthood are influenced by genetic predispositions acting in concert with the environment and lifestyle choices. Exercise can enhance both physical and mental functioning. Common diseases among older adults include osteoporosis, which leads to fragile bones, and osteoarthritis, or joint inflammation.

▌ Physical and mental activity, as well as a positive attitude, improve the odds of successful aging.

CRITICAL THINKING

1. Many (indeed, most) stereotypes of the physical aging process are negative and depressing. What in this chapter gives you reason to be more optimistic about aging, and why? Cite specific concepts and research findings.

2. Suppose you set as your goal reaching age 100 in superb physical condition. Describe and justify a plan for achieving your goal, then indicate why you might not make it despite your best efforts.

CHAPTER SUMMARY

5.1 BUILDING BLOCKS OF GROWTH AND DEVELOPMENT

• Growth is influenced by genes and environments, through the working of the endocrine and nervous systems. Endocrine glands such as the pituitary, thyroid, testes, and ovaries regulate behavior by secreting hormones directly into the bloodstream.

• Brain development is most evident during the late prenatal period and infancy when there is a good deal of plasticity of brain functions but continues through the life span.

• Physical growth proceeds according to the cephalocaudal (head-to-tail), proximodistal (center outward), and orthogenetic (global and undifferentiated to integrated and differentiated) principles.

• Health is multidimensional, influenced by an individual's genetic makeup, life-style choices, and sociohistorical context.

5.2 THE INFANT

• Growth during infancy is impressive, with noticeable increases in height and weight between birth and 2 years of age. Infants come into the world equipped with reflexes, sensory capabilities, organized states, and an ability to learn from their experiences.

• Major motor milestones are achieved during infancy, including crawling, walking, reaching, and grasping. These accomplishments are best understood within a dynamic systems model.

• Health during infancy may be challenged by congenital malformations and the lingering effects of preterm delivery and low birth weight.

5.3 THE CHILD

• The physical changes during childhood are not as dramatic as those witnessed during infancy or those that will occur during the adolescent years, but they bring the child closer to becoming a full-fledged adult.

• Children's health is influenced by their parents' socioeconomic status and lifestyle choices.

• Unintentional injuries involving motor vehicles are the leading cause of death during childhood.

• Physical activity is an important component of health during childhood.

5.4 THE ADOLESCENT

• Adolescents undergo major physical changes as they experience a growth spurt and sexual maturation.

• Most adolescents, but especially girls, react to the maturation process with mixed feelings and worry about their physical appearance and capabilities. Early maturation tends to give boys an advantage over their peers but appears to be disadvantageous for girls. For girls, the best course would be to mature "on time," that is, when peers are experiencing the same changes.

• Overall, adolescents are healthy and fit, although sedentary lifestyles can lead to overweight and health problems for some.

• Lifestyle choices made by adolescents can have both short-term and long-term effects on health.

5.5 THE ADULT

• Changes in appearance and functioning start to become evident during middle adulthood, and declines are noticeable in most older adults. There are large individual differences in physical functioning of older adults. Negative stereotypes about aging may lead many older adults to negatively interpret the natural changes that accompany aging.

• Women experience menopause, a cessation of menstruation and an end of child-bearing years. Men experience andropause, a more gradual change in their reproductive system. The experience of menopause is variable and a variety of treatments are available to treat the symptoms.

• In general, older adults respond more slowly than they did when they were younger, particularly with respect to motor actions.

• Adults who engage in regular physical activity are more likely to be healthier and live longer than adults who are sedentary. Although disease may account for some of the changes seen among some elderly individuals, disuse and abuse of the physical systems of the body also contribute to symptoms of aging.

• Overall, older adults have more physical ailments than younger adults, but there is tremendous variability in health and physical abilities during older adulthood. Common diseases in older adulthood include osteoporosis and osteoarthritis.

KEY TERMS

MEDIA RESOURCES

BOOK COMPANION WEBSITE

academic.cengage.com/psychology/sigelman
Find online quizzes, flash cards, animations, video clips, experiments, interactive assessments, and other helpful study aids for this text at **academic.cengage.com/psychology/sigelman**. You can also connect directly to the following sites:

AGING BODY AND MIND

The National Institute on Aging website offers publications on health and aging issues in adulthood including a number of articles on applied topics like caregiving and making sense of healthcare information.

DELAYED SEXUAL MATURATION

Information on the cause of delayed sexual maturation can be found at the Merck online Medical Library site. The site also discusses possible intervention strategies.

HEALTH AND WELLNESS

Medline Plus provides extensive information on "health topics" across the life-span and includes recent scholarly research on each covered topic.

NEWBORN AND INFANT DEVELOPMENT

The newborn and infant section of the MedlinePlus website summarized key milestones in sensory, physical, and language development during the months following birth. There are also several excellent illustrations of key elements of early development.

SECRET LIFE OF THE BRAIN-NOVA

In 2002, PBS premiered *The Secret Life of the Brain* that tracked the development of the human brain from baby through adulthood. Its companion website summarizes each of the five episodes and offers web-exclusive features such as a three-dimensional exploration of the brain.

UNDERSTANDING THE DATA: EXERCISES ON THE WEB

academic.cengage.com/psychology/sigelman
For additional insight on the data presented in this chapter, try out the exercises for these figures at **academic.cengage.com/psychology/sigelman**:

Figure 5.1 Catch-up growth in a girl following treatment for celiac syndrome at around age 11

Table 5.3 Percentage of Day (24-Hour Period) Spent in Various Behavioral States at 2, 6, 12, and 40 Weeks

Figure 5.7 Sequence of events in the sexual maturation of females and males

CENGAGENOW   CENGAGENOW™

academic.cengage.com/login
Go to **academic.cengage.com/login** to link to CengageNOW, your online study tool. First take the Pre-Test for this chapter to get your Personalized Study Plan, which will identify topics you need to review and direct you to online resources. Then take the Post-Test to determine what concepts you have mastered and what you still need work on.

© Jim Sugar/Stockphoto.com

6 CHAPTER

Perception

157

EQUIPPED WITH AN IMMATURE nervous system, a baby arrives into a clamorous world of stimuli that come both from within and without her growing body. In the early months of life, a normally developing child begins the task of making order out

of the sensations that stream unbidden and unchanneled through her maturing senses. First she must attain control over her body's motions and internal sensations and over her own attention. . . . these abilities to process sights, sounds, and other

sensations and to organize responses in a calm, focused manner support mastery of further basic skills of development (Greenspan, 1997, p. 45).

Psychologists have long distinguished between sensation and perception. **Sensation** is the process by which sensory receptor neurons detect information and transmit it to the brain. From birth, infants sense their environment. They detect light, sound, odor-bearing molecules in the air, and other stimuli. But do they make "sense" of it? **Perception** is the interpretation of sensory input: recognizing what you see, understanding what is said to you, knowing that the odor you have detected is a sizzling steak, and so on. It is affected by the individual's history of learning experiences. Does a newborn perceive the world, then, or merely sense it? And what happens to sensory and perceptual capacities as the person ages? Perhaps we should start with a more basic question: Why should you care about the development of sensation and perception?

Sensation and perception are at the heart of human functioning. Everything you do depends on your ability to perceive the world around you. You would have a tough time as a student if you could neither read printed words nor understand speech. Indeed, you would not be able to walk to class without the aid of the body senses that control movement. Possibly one

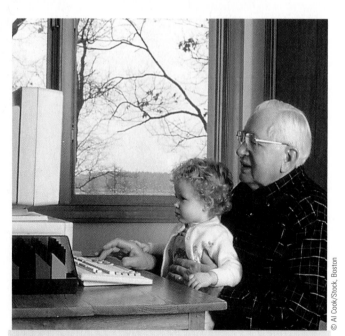

In what ways are the perceptual experiences of infants and adults similar, and in what ways are they different because of the adult's greater experience with the world?

reason that sensation and perception may not seem important is that they occur so effortlessly for most people. And as long as the sensory–perceptual systems are in good working order, we tend to take them for granted. But as soon as there is a "glitch" in the system, we become painfully aware of the limitations imposed when, for example, we lose our vision or sense of smell.

There is another reason to be interested in sensation and perception. They have long been at the center of a debate among philosophers and, more recently, developmental scientists about how we gain knowledge of reality.

6.1 ISSUES OF NATURE AND NURTURE

Does the ability to perceive the world around us depend solely on innate biological factors, or is this ability acquired through experience and learning? **Constructivists** come down on the side of nurture (Kellman & Arterberry, 2006). They argue that our perception of the world is constructed over time through learning. Yes, we come equipped at birth with functioning sensory systems, but understanding the input coming in through our senses requires interacting with the environment and "learning to infer the meanings of our sensations" (Kellman & Arterberry, 2006, p. 112). For instance, the retinal image of an object located 50 feet from an observer is different from the retinal image of the same object located just 10 feet from the observer. According to the constructivists, we need experience with viewing objects at various distances to learn how to interpret the different retinal images that they project.

On the nature side of the issue are the **nativists** who argue that perception is *not* created by interpreting external input—that instead innate capabilities and maturational programs are the driving forces in perceptual development (Kellman & Arterberry, 2006). Infants come equipped with basic sensory capabilities, which are further refined according to an innate plan. Nativists would argue that the infant does not need experience to learn how to interpret different retinal images cast by the same object at different distances. Information available in the constantly changing retinal images created as we move about our world provides this understanding. Thus, from the nativist perspective, perception is direct—it does not require interpretation based on previous experience (Kellman & Arterberry, 2006).

Although the constructivist view of perception has long been popular, more sophisticated methods of assessing infants' capabilities are yielding new findings about their perceptual abilities. As a result, some researchers have shifted toward a more nativist perspective to understand the origins of some aspects of perception.

Nature–nurture issues also arise in the study of declines in sensory and perceptual abilities in later life. Are these declines universal, suggesting that they are the product of fundamental aging processes? Or do they differ greatly from person to person and result from factors other than aging, such as disease, exposure to ultraviolet rays, loud noise, or other environmental influences known to damage the senses? Just as researchers must pin down the contributions of nature and nurture to early perceptual development, they must clarify their roles in perceptual aging.

In the next section, we look closely at sensation and perception in infancy because this is when most fundamental perceptual capacities emerge. Later, you will see how much more "intelligent" the senses become during childhood and adolescence and will question the image of old age as a time of little more than sensory decline.

SUMMING UP

▪ Constructivists argue that the newborn is a "blank slate" and must acquire an understanding of the world through experience with sensory inputs. Thus, according to the constructivist perspective, nurture drives the development of perception.

▪ Nativists believe that each person is born with some innate understanding of how to interpret sensory information. Thus, according to the nativists, the origin of perception is largely nature.

CRITICAL THINKING

1. What sort of evidence would you need to gather to demonstrate that the origin of perception is innate rather than constructed through experience?

6.2 | THE INFANT

The pioneering American psychologist William James (1890) claimed that sights, sounds, and other sensory inputs formed a "blooming, buzzing confusion" to the young infant. James was actually noting that impressions from the several senses are fused rather than separable, but his statement has since been quoted to represent the view that the world of the young infant is hopelessly confusing.

Today, the accepted view is that young infants have far greater perceptual abilities than anyone suspected. Their senses are functioning even before birth, and in the first few months of life they show many signs that they are perceiving a coherent rather than a chaotic world. Why the change in views? It is not that babies have become smarter. It is that researchers have

become smarter. They have developed more sophisticated methods of studying what infants can and cannot do. Infants, after all, cannot tell researchers directly what they perceive, so the trick has been to develop ways to let their behavior speak for them.

Assessing Perceptual Abilities

As researchers have devised more ingenious ways of testing the perceptual capacities of young infants, they have uncovered more sophisticated capacities at younger ages. The main methods used to study infant perception are the habituation, preferential looking, evoked potentials, and operant conditioning techniques (Cohen & Cashon, 2006; Gibson & Pick, 2000).

Habituation

Humans of all ages lose interest in a stimulus if it is presented repeatedly. This process of learning to be bored is called **habituation.** Researchers can use this process to uncover what is going on inside the infant's mind. Suppose researchers repeatedly present the same visual stimulus (such as a blue circle) to an infant; eventually the infant becomes bored and looks away—the infant habituates. If the researchers then present a different stimulus (such as a red circle) and the infant regains interest, researchers know that the infant has discriminated between the two stimuli (Cohen & Cashon, 2006). This procedure can be used to test for discrimination of stimuli by all the senses—vision, hearing, touch, and even taste and smell.

Preferential Looking

Alternatively, researchers can present an infant with two stimuli at the same time and measure the length of time the infant spends looking at each. A preference for one over the other, like responding to a novel stimulus in the habituation paradigm, indicates that the infant discriminates between the two stimuli. What if the infant looks equally long at the two stimuli? Then it is unclear what researchers can conclude; the infant may discriminate between the stimuli but may simply not like one better than the other. It is also possible that infants have a preference but do not display it with preferential looking (Rovee-Collier, 2001). They may reveal this preference when tested with an alternative method, such as an opportunity to interact with the preferred object.

Evoked Potentials

Researchers can get an idea of how the brain responds to stimulation by measuring its electrical activity with small metal disks (electrodes) attached to the skin's surface. The infant simply sits in a comfortable seat and watches or listens to various stimuli. The electrodes and computer record the brain's response to these stimuli so that researchers can "see" what is going on inside the brain.

Operant Conditioning

As you learned in Chapter 2, humans will repeat a response that has a pleasant consequence; that is, they are capable of learning through operant conditioning. Young infants are not easily conditioned, but they can learn to suck faster or slower or to turn their head to the side when a certain stimulus is presented if they are reinforced for that response. Suppose that you want to determine whether infants can distinguish between two speech sounds. First, an infant might be conditioned over several trials to turn his head every time he hears a sound—perhaps by being shown an interesting toy or being given a taste of milk. Then, a second sound would be presented; if the infant turns his head, it suggests that the two sounds are perceived as equivalent; if the infant does *not* turn his head, you can conclude that the two sounds have been discriminated.

Methods for studying infant perception have their limitations. For example, infants may not respond to a difference between stimuli for reasons unrelated to an inability to discriminate between them. Still, these techniques, with others, have revealed a good deal about what infants perceive and what they do not, as you will now see.

Vision

Most of us tend to think of vision as our most indispensable sense. Because vision is indeed important, we examine its early development in some detail before turning to the other major senses.

Basic Capacities

The eye functions by taking in stimulation in the form of light and converting it to electrochemical signals to the brain. How well does the newborn's visual system work? From the first minutes of life, the infant can detect changes in brightness and can visually track a slow-moving picture or object (Slater, 2004). Still, the newborn's visual capabilities are lacking when compared to those of an adult—their **visual acuity,** or the ability to perceive detail, is 40 times worse than an adult's (Lewis & Maurer, 2005). Objects are blurry to young infants unless they are about 8 inches from the face or are bold patterns with sharp light–dark contrasts—the face of a parent, for example. The young infant's world is also blurred because of limitations in **visual accommodation**—the ability of the lens of the eye to change shape to bring objects at different distances into focus. It is likely to take 6 months to 1 year before the infant can see as well as an adult (Slater, 2004).

Very young infants also see the world in color, not in black and white as some early observers thought (Zemach, Chang, & Teller, 2006). How do researchers know this? Suppose they accustom an infant to a blue disk using the habituation technique. What will happen if they then present either a blue disk of a different shade or a green disk? Infants 4 months old will show little interest in a disk of a different blue but will be attentive to a green disk—even when the light reflected from these two stimuli differs in wavelength from the original blue stimulus by the same amount (Schiffman, 2000). Thus, 4-month-olds appear to discriminate colors and categorize portions of the continuum of wavelengths of light into the same basic color categories (red, blue, green, and yellow) that adults do. Color vision is present at birth, but newborns cannot discriminate some color differences well because their receptors are not yet mature. By 2 to 3 months, however, color vision is mature (Goldstein, 2007). Like adults, 4-month-old infants can detect a colored stimulus on a background that is a different shade of the same color (Franklin, Pilling, & Davies, 2005). However, like adults, they are *faster* at detecting the stimulus on a background of a different color.

In short, the eyes of the young infant are not working at peak levels, but they are working. As one researcher summarizes it: Infants are able to see what they need to see (Hainline, 1998). Even newborns can perceive light and dark, focus on nearby objects, distinguish colors, and see simple patterns. But does all this visual stimulation make any sense?

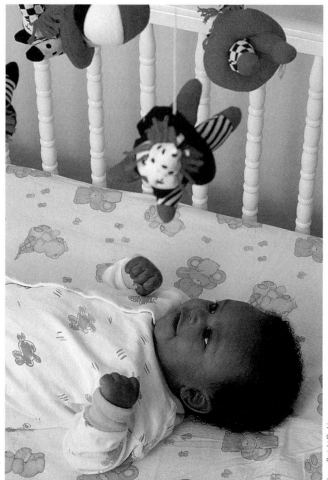

At 2 months, Jordan is attracted to the mobile's well-defined contours (or light–dark contrasts) and bold patterns (which are neither too simple nor too complex).

Pattern Perception

Over years of testing, researchers have found that even young infants prefer to look at certain patterns more than others. What are the properties of patterns that "turn infants on"? For one thing, young infants are attracted to patterns that have a large amount of light–dark transition, or **contour;** they are responsive to sharp boundaries between light and dark areas (Banks & Shannon, 1993; Farroni et al., 2005). This is perhaps why it was once mistakenly thought that infants could only see in black and white. They can detect color, but often the pastel colors presented to young infants do not have enough contrast to be interesting. Black and white objects, however, offer this contrast.

Second, young infants are attracted to displays that are dynamic (as opposed to static) or contain *movement* (Courage, Reynolds, & Richards, 2006; Kavsek & Yonas, 2006). Newborns can and do track a moving target with their eyes, although their tracking at first is imprecise and likely to falter unless the target is moving slowly (Easterbrook et al., 1999; Slater, 2004). Infants also look longer at moving objects and perceive their forms better than those of stationary ones (Johnson & Aslin, 1995; Slater 2004).

Finally, young infants seem to be attracted to *moderately complex* patterns. They prefer a clear pattern (for example, a bold checkerboard pattern) to either a blank stimulus or an elaborate one such as a page from the *New York Times* (Fantz & Fagan, 1975). As infants mature, they prefer more complex stimuli.

One special pattern that has garnered much attention from researchers is the human face. Early research showed that young infants preferred to look at schematic drawings of faces rather than other patterned stimuli and that faces elicited more visual tracking by young infants than other targets (Gamé, Carchon, & Vital-Durand, 2003). Other research shows that within hours of birth, infants prefer their mother's face to a strange woman's face (see Sai, 2005). These findings seem to suggest an inborn tendency to orient to faces and to even recognize a particular face. But as you have just learned, infants prefer contour, movement, and moderate complexity. Human faces have all of these physical properties. In addition, research shows that newborns have a preference for patterns that have more information in their upper visual field, that is, patterns that are "top-heavy" (Cassia et al., 2006; Cassia, Turati, & Simion, 2004; Turati, 2004). Again, faces are top-heavy. As for being able to visually pick out their mother's face from a lineup, it turns out that newborns can only do this when they have been exposed to their mother's face *along with her voice*. Without this auditory–visual coupling, neonates fail to recognize their mother's face (Sai, 2005).

To recap what has been covered up to this point, researchers know that infants younger than 2 months have visual preferences, and they also know something about the physical properties of stimuli that attract infants' attention. Martin Banks and his colleagues have offered a simple explanation for these early visual preferences: Young infants prefer to look at what-

ever they can see well (Banks & Ginsburg, 1985). Based on a complex mathematical model, Banks has been able to predict how different patterns might look to a young infant. ■ **Figure 6.1** gives an example. Because the young infant's eye is small and its neural receptors are immature, it has poor visual acuity and sees a highly complex checkerboard as a big, dark blob. The pattern in a moderately complex checkerboard can be seen. Less-than-perfect vision would therefore explain why young infants prefer moderate complexity to high complexity. Indeed, limited vision can account for several of the infant's visual preferences. Young infants seem to actively seek the visual input they can see well—input that will stimulate the development of the visual centers of their brains (Banks & Shannon, 1993; Hainline, 1998).

Finding that young infants discriminate patterns and prefer some over others raises another question. Can infants really perceive forms or patterns? For example, do they just see an angle or two when they view a triangle, or do they see a whole triangular form that stands out from its background as a distinct shape? Some research suggests that even newborns are sensitive to information about whole shapes or forms (Valenza et al., 2006). But most studies point to an important breakthrough in the perception of forms starting around 2 or 3 months (see Colombo, 2001; Courage, Reynolds, & Richards, 2006). Part of the story is told in ■ **Figure 6.2**. One-month-olds focus on the outer contours of forms such as faces (Johnson, 1997).

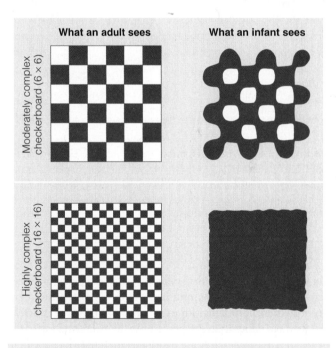

■ **FIGURE 6.1** What the young eye sees. By the time these two checkerboards are processed by eyes with undeveloped vision, only the checkerboard at top left may have a pattern remaining. Blurry vision in early infancy helps explain a preference for moderately complex rather than highly complex stimuli.
SOURCE: Adapted from Banks & Salapatek (1983).

1-month-old   2-month-old

Visual scanning of a geometric figure by 1- and 2-month-old infants

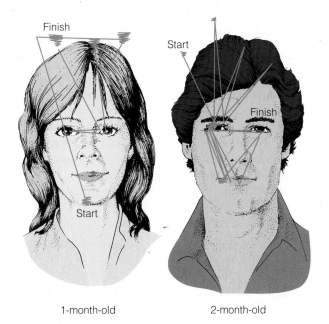

1-month-old   2-month-old

Visual scanning of the human face by 1- and 2-month-old infants

■ **FIGURE 6.2** Visual scanning in early infancy. The 1-month-old seems to be trying to locate where an object begins and ends, whereas the 2-month-old seems to be on the way to figuring out what an object is by exploring it inside and out.
SOURCE: Adapted from Salapatek (1975).

Starting around 2 months, infants no longer focus on some external boundary or contour; instead, they explore the interiors of figures thoroughly (for example, looking at a person's facial features rather than just at the chin, hairline, and top of the head). It is as though they are no longer content to locate where an object starts and where it ends, as 1-month-olds tend to do; they seem to want to know what it is. During this time, infants also become better at shifting their attention or disengaging from a stimulus (Colombo, 2001; Courage, Reynolds, & Richards, 2006). Initially, their gaze seems to become "stuck" on the fixated object, and they have difficulty shifting it to another object. As you might imagine, this difficulty with shifting gaze limits what young infants can take in from their environment.

Much remains to be learned about early perception of faces. An intense nature–nurture debate still rages about whether infants have an innate ability to perceive faces or can do so only after they have had some experience looking at faces (Cassia et al., 2006; Johnson & de Haan, 2001; Slater, 2004). Still, we can conclude that infants truly perceive a meaningful face, not merely an appealing pattern, by 2 to 3 months of age. Infants smile when they see faces as though they recognize them as familiar and appreciate their significance. So it goes with pattern perception more generally: As infants gain experience with different objects, their attention is drawn to certain objects not only because they have certain physical properties, but also because their forms are recognized as familiar.

Depth Perception

Another important aspect of visual perception involves perceiving depth and knowing when objects are near or far. Although it can take years to learn to judge the size of objects in the distance, very young infants have some intriguing abilities to interpret spatial cues involving nearby objects. For example, they react defensively when objects move toward their faces; blinking in response to looming objects first appears around 1 month and becomes more consistent over the next few months (Kayed & van der Meer, 2007; Nanez & Yonas, 1994).

Moreover, even newborns seem to operate by the principle of **size constancy:** They recognize that an object is the same size despite changes in its distance from the eyes. In one study, 4-month-olds were habituated to either a 6-cm disk or a 10-cm disk presented at different distances (see ■ **Figure 6.3;** Granrud, 2006). They were then tested to see whether they would prefer to look at a disk that was the same size but cast a different retinal image or one that was a different size but cast the same retinal image. The infants responded on the basis of actual object size, not size of the retinal image cast by the object. They preferred to look at the disk that was a novel size rather than the one that cast the same retinal image as during the habituation phase. This indicates that infants recognize the size of an object even when the object is presented at different distances and thus produces different images on the retina.

Does this evidence of early spatial perception mean that infants who have begun to crawl know enough about space to avoid crawling off the edges of beds or staircases? The first attempt to examine depth perception in infants was carried out in classic research by Eleanor Gibson and Richard Walk (1960) using an apparatus called the **visual cliff.** This cliff consists of an elevated glass platform divided into two sections by a center board. On the "shallow" side a checkerboard pattern is placed directly under the glass. On the "deep" side the pattern is several feet below the glass, creating the illusion of a drop-off or "cliff." Infants are placed on the center board and coaxed by their mothers to cross both the shallow and the deep sides. Testing infants 6½ months of age and older, Gibson and Walk found that 27 of 36 infants would cross the shallow side to reach Mom, but only 3 of 36 would cross the deep side. Most

Habituation Phase:

A   18-cm distance   6-cm disk

OR

B   50-cm distance   10-cm distance

Retinal Image of Habituated Disk

Test Phase:

A   30-cm distance
Same-size object; different retinal image
Different-size object; same retinal image

OR

B   30-cm distance
Different-size object; same retinal image
Same-size object; different retinal image

■ **FIGURE 6.3** Which disk will infants prefer? The one that is the same size as what they were habituated to in the previous phase, or the one that projects the same retinal image as in the habituation phase? Whether they were in condition A or B, they preferred the different sized object in the test phase.

SOURCE: From C.E. Granurd, Size constancy in infants: 4-month-olds' responses to physical versus retinal image size, *Journal of Experimental Psychology: Human Perception and Performance, 32,* pp. 1398–1404. Copyright © 2006 American Psychological Association

infants of crawling age (typically 7 months or older) clearly perceive depth and are afraid of drop-offs.

But the testing procedure used by Gibson and Walk depended on the ability of infants to crawl. Would younger infants who cannot yet crawl be able to perceive a drop-off? Joseph Campos and his colleagues (Campos, Langer, & Krowitz, 1970) found that when they slowly lowered babies over the shallow and deep sides of the visual cliff, babies as young as 2 months had a slower heart rate on the deep side than on the shallow side. Why slower? When we are afraid, our hearts beat faster, not slower. A slow heart rate is a sign of interest. So, 2-month-old infants *perceive a difference* between the deep and the shallow sides of the visual cliff, but they have not yet learned to *fear* drop-offs.

Fear of drop-offs appears to be learned through crawling— and perhaps falling now and then, or at least coming close to it (Campos, Bertenthal, & Kermoian, 1992). Some beginning crawlers will shuffle right off the ends of beds or the tops of stairwells if they are not watched carefully. However, fear of drop-offs is stronger in infants who have logged a few weeks

of crawling than in infants of the same age who do not yet crawl. Both maturation and normal experiences moving about contribute to the perception and interpretation of depth, it seems.

Organizing a World of Objects

Another challenge in perceptual development is to separate the visual field into distinct objects, even when parts of objects are hidden behind other objects. From an early age, infants show remarkable abilities to organize and impose order on visual scenes in much the same way that adults do. For example, Katherine Van Giffen and Marshall Haith (1984) reported that 3-month-olds, but not 1-month-olds, will focus their attention on a small irregularity in an otherwise well-formed circle or square pattern, as if they appreciated that it is a deviation from an otherwise well-formed and symmetrical pattern.

Infants must also determine where one object ends and another begins. Elizabeth Spelke and her colleagues (Kellman & Spelke, 1983; Spelke, 1990) have concluded that young infants are sensitive to several cues about the wholeness of ob-

An infant on the edge of a visual cliff, being lured to cross the "deep" side.

jects, especially cues available when an object moves. For example, 4-month-olds seem to expect all parts of an object to move in the same direction at the same time, and they therefore use common motion as an important cue in determining what is or is not part of the same object (Kellman & Spelke, 1983). It takes infants longer, until about 6 months of age, to determine the boundaries or edges of stationary objects (Gibson & Pick, 2000). Amy Needham (1999) has found that 4-month-old babies, like adults, use object shape to figure out that two objects side by side are separate. They also use *good form* (for example, logical continuation of a line) to perceive an object's unity or wholeness (Johnson et al., 2000). Thus, babies appear to have an innate ability to organize a visual scene into distinct objects, and they are better able to make sense of a world in motion—a world like the one they live in—than to make sense of a stationary world.

The Infant as an Intuitive Theorist

That is not all. Researchers have been exploring infants' understandings of the physical laws that govern objects. For example, Elizabeth Spelke and her colleagues have been testing infants to determine what they know of Newtonian physics and the basic laws of object motion (Spelke & Hermer, 1996). Do babies know that a falling object will move downward along a continuous path until it encounters an obstruction? Spelke's studies suggest that infants only 4 months of age seem surprised when a ball dropped behind a screen is later revealed below a shelf rather than resting on it. They look longer at this "impossible" event than at the comparison event in which the ball's motion stops when it reaches a barrier. By 6 months, infants seem surprised when a ball drops behind a screen and then, when the screen is lifted, appears to be suspended in midair rather than lying at the bottom of the display unit (Kim & Spelke, 1992; Spelke et al., 1992). This hints that they know something about the laws of gravity. Do infants understand any other simple principles of physics? Yes; 4-month-olds watching a moving object disappear behind the left side of a screen seem to expect to see the object reappear from the right side of the screen (Bremner et al., 2005). And 4-month-olds are also surprised when a wide object disappears into a narrow container (Wang, Baillargeon, & Brueckner, 2004).

Findings from such violation-of-expectation tasks have led some developmentalists to conclude that young infants do more than just sense the world—that they come equipped with organized systems of knowledge, called **intuitive theories,** that allow them to make sense of the world (Wellman & Gelman, 1992; Gelman, 1996). From an early age, children distinguish between the domains of knowledge adults know as physics, biology, and psychology. They organize their knowledge in each domain around causal principles and seem to understand that different causal forces operate in different domains (for example, that desires influence the behavior of humans but not of rocks). According to this intuitive theories perspective, young infants have innate knowledge of the world, and they perceive and even reason about it much as adults do. Coming to know the physical world is then a matter of fleshing out understandings they have had all along rather than constructing entirely new ones as they age (Spelke, 1994).

As you will see in the Explorations box, some researchers also believe that babies understand number concepts long before they ever step into a math class. All in all, it is becoming clearer that young infants know a good deal more about the world around them than anyone imagined, although they learn more as they get older.

From birth, infants will look in the direction of an interesting sound. This ability to localize sound improves and becomes more voluntary by 4 months.

CAN BABIES COUNT?

Although you may think it ridiculous to ask whether babies can count, some developmentalists have discovered that very young infants have some impressive understandings of the abstract quality we call *number*. Karen Wynn (1992, 1995) sought to determine whether 5-month-old infants could add and subtract numbers by seeing how long infants looked at different addition and subtraction "problems." Her test procedure, summarized in the illustration in this Explorations box, involved showing the infant a display area with a single Mickey Mouse doll in it, raising a screen to hide the doll, and having the infant watch as a hand placed a second doll in the display area and came out empty. The infant was then observed to see how long she looked at each of two outcomes when the screen was dropped again: a correct outcome in which two dolls were in the display area when the screen was removed (1 + 1 = 2) or an incorrect outcome in which only one doll was present (1 + 1 = 1).

Which of these two events attracted more attention? Infants looked longer at the incorrect outcome, as though surprised by the mathematical error it represented. They also looked longer at a 1 + 1 = 3 scenario than at the correct 1 + 1 = 2 outcome. These 5-month-olds also seemed able to subtract: They were surprised when one doll removed from a pair of dolls resulted in two dolls rather than one.

Further research with displays of larger numbers sheds additional light on infants' number sense. Infants can distinguish 8 from 16 objects and 16 from 32 objects, but cannot discriminate 8 from 12 or 16 from 24 (Xu & Spelke, 2000; Xu, Spelke, & Goddard, 2005). Similarly, research using auditory sequences shows that 6-month-old infants can distinguish between 16 and 8 sounds and 9-month-old infants can tell the difference between 12 and 8 sounds, although they cannot distinguish 10 from 8 sounds (Lipton & Spelke, 2003). This research suggests a general understanding of numbers that becomes increasingly precise over the first year.

But do such findings really show that babies can count and understand numerical functions? In Wynn's research, the finding that infants look more at incorrect mathematical outcomes than at correct ones is difficult to interpret (Canfield & Smith, 1996): What competencies are babies actually showing? Some research has replicated Wynn's findings (see, for example, Moore & Cocas, 2006; Simon, Hespos, & Rochat, 1995), lending support to the idea that infants have an innate sensitivity to numerical knowledge. The picture becomes muddled, however, when we look at other research. Tony Simon (1997, 1999) suggests that these findings show babies come equipped with—or quickly develop—an ability to distinguish "same" from "different" but do not yet understand numbers or precise addition and subtraction (see also Lécuyer et al., 2004). According to this view, at steps 3 and 4 in Wynn's experiment (see the illustration), babies develop some sort of mental representation of two objects. When the screen drops and two objects are revealed (the correct outcome), the image in front of the infant matches the mental representation he formed. But in the incorrect outcome, the screen drops to reveal one object, which does not match the infant's mental representation. Thus, longer looking times in the incorrect conditions may reveal only a general understanding of same versus different, not of mathematical processes.

Although the jury may still be out on whether babies can count, this research reveals an impressive ability, at least, to mentally represent and distinguish complex displays during the first year.

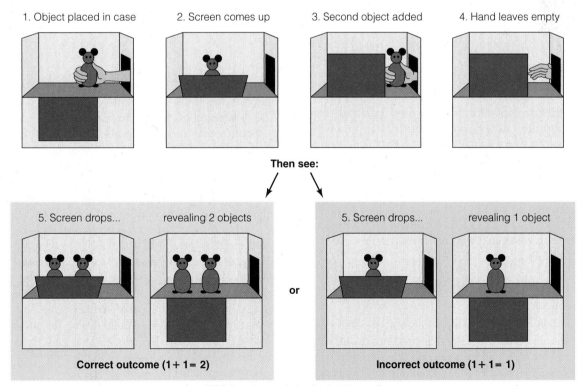

Sequence of events:

1. Object placed in case
2. Screen comes up
3. Second object added
4. Hand leaves empty

Then see:

5. Screen drops... revealing 2 objects

Correct outcome (1 + 1 = 2)

or

5. Screen drops... revealing 1 object

Incorrect outcome (1 + 1 = 1)

Which outcome is looked at longer?

AIDING INFANTS AND CHILDREN WITH HEARING IMPAIRMENTS

Although sensory impairments can change the course of normal life-span development, much can be done to help even those individuals born totally deaf or blind develop in positive directions and function effectively in everyday life. Let's briefly examine interventions for infants and children who have hearing impairments. Why tackle hearing impairments and not another sensory system? Because several estimates suggest that hearing impairments take a heavy toll on the individual and on society. Researchers at Johns Hopkins University, for example, estimate that more than $1 million will be spent over the lifetime of each infant or child who becomes deaf before acquiring language (Mohr et al., 2000).

For the 2 to 3 in 1000 infants born deaf or hearing impaired, early identification and treatment are essential if they are to master spoken language. Until recently, the average hearing-impaired child was not identified until age 2½ or older, usually when it became clear that his language skills had not developed normally (National Institutes of Health, 2006; Saffran, Werker, & Werner, 2006). Because children who receive no special intervention before age 3 usually have lasting difficulties with speech and language, most states have now mandated that all newborns be screened for hearing loss before they leave the hospital. How do you test the hearing of newborns? By using the auditory evoked potentials described at the beginning of the chapter and determining whether sounds trigger normal activity in the brain. Infants' behaviors also give physicians clues about their hearing. Does she turn her head when spoken to? Does he react to loud noises? Is she soothed by your voice? If the answers to these questions are no, a more thorough examination is warranted.

Once hearing-impaired infants are identified, interventions can be planned. Many programs attempt to capitalize on whatever residual

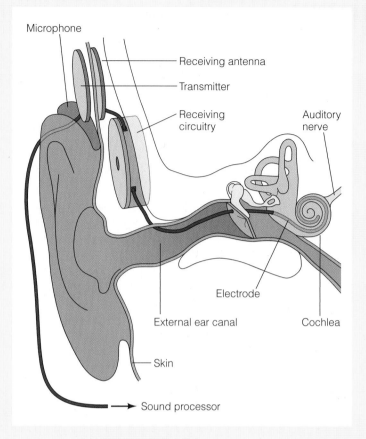

Hearing

Hearing is at least as important to us as vision, especially because we depend on it to communicate with others through spoken language. As Anne Fernald (2004) notes, "while vision may be primary in enabling infants to learn about the physical world, audition plays a powerful role in initiating infants into a social world" (p. 37).

The process of hearing begins when moving air molecules enter the ear and vibrate the eardrum. These vibrations are transmitted to the cochlea in the inner ear and are converted to signals that the brain interprets as sounds.

Basic Capacities

Newborns can hear well—better than they can see. They can also localize sounds: They are startled by loud noises and will turn from them, but they will turn toward softer sounds (Field et al., 1980; Morrongiello et al., 1994). Even unborn infants can

hear some of what is going on in the world outside the womb as much as 3 months before birth (Saffran, Werker, & Werner, 2006). Researchers have detected changes in fetal heart rates that correspond to changes in sounds they are exposed to while in their mother's womb (Fifer, Monk, & Grose-Fifer, 2004; Saffran, Werker, & Werner, 2006). Infants seem to prefer listening to auditory stimuli that are relatively complex, a finding that is consistent with the preference for moderate complexity that we saw with visual stimuli (Richard et al., 2004).

Although the auditory sense is working before birth, infants appear to be a little less sensitive to very soft sounds than adults are (Saffran, Werker, & Werner, 2006). As a result, a soft whisper may not be heard. Still, newborns can discriminate among sounds within their range of hearing that differ in loudness, duration, direction, and frequency or pitch, and these basic capacities improve rapidly during the first months after birth (Fernald, 2004). In general, the sounds that penetrate the womb before birth are the ones that are the easiest for the infant to hear after birth (Eliot, 1999).

hearing these children have by equipping them with hearing aids. Today, even profoundly deaf children can be helped to hear through an advanced amplification device called the **cochlear implant** (see the illustration in this Applications box). The device is implanted in the inner ear through surgery and connected to a microphone worn outside the ear. It works by bypassing damaged hair cells (sensory receptors located in the inner ear) and directly stimulating the auditory nerve with electrical impulses.

Deaf children provided with cochlear implants by age 4 recognize more spoken words and speak more intelligibly than do children who receive them later in childhood, though even children given implants later in life can benefit (Harrison, Gordon, & Mount, 2005). Indeed, research shows that the rate of language development among children with cochlear implants is similar to that of children with normal hearing (Miyamoto, Houston, & Bergeson, 2005; Schery & Peters, 2003). In addition, speech production and speech perception are improved in deaf children who have cochlear implants compared with deaf children who have traditional hearing aids but are still less than the speech production and perception of normal hearing children (Houston et al., 2005; Schery & Peters, 2003). Performance is especially enhanced if there is earlier implantation and more auditory training following the implant. For some, cochlear implants have truly opened up new horizons that they thought were not possible before the implant (e.g., Denworth, 2006; Mishori, 2006).

Why, then, are not all hearing-impaired children provided with cochlear implants? First, they require surgery and are expensive—although the expense of cochlear implants may be offset by educational savings down the road (Cheng et al., 2000). Also, despite their benefits, cochlear implants do not have the full support of the deaf community (Bollag, 2006; Tucker, 1998). Deaf children who use them, some say, will be given the message that they should be ashamed of being deaf. They

will be deprived of participation in the unique culture that has developed in communities of deaf people who share a common language and identity. Because their hearing will still be far from normal, they may feel they do not belong to either the deaf or the hearing world (Arana-Ward, 1997; Fryauf-Bertschy et al., 1997).

Another important element in early intervention programs for hearing-impaired children is parent involvement (Maxon & Brackett, 1992). In one program for hearing-impaired children, infants are fitted with hearing aids and teachers then go into the home to show parents how to make their children more aware of the world of sound (Bess & McConnell, 1981). For instance, on hearing the screech of a car's brakes outside, parents might put their hands to their ears, rush their child to the window, and talk about the noise. Similarly, parents are urged to slam doors, deliberately rattle pots and pans, and create other such opportunities for the child to become alert to sounds. All the while, parents are using words to describe everyday objects, people, and events.

This combination of the right amplification device and auditory training in the home has proven effective in improving the ability of hearing-impaired infants and preschoolers to hear speech and learn to speak. Yet for other deaf and severely hearing-impaired children, the most important thing may be early exposure to sign language. Early intervention programs for parents of deaf infants can teach them strategies for getting their infants' attention and involving them in conversations using sign (Chen, 1996). The earlier in life deaf children acquire some language system, whether spoken or signed, the better their command of language is likely to be later in life (Mayberry & Eichen, 1991). Deaf children whose parents are deaf and use sign language with them, as well as deaf children of hearing parents who participate in early intervention programs, generally show normal patterns of development, whereas children who are not exposed to any language system early in life suffer for it (Marschark, 1993).

Speech Perception

Young infants seem to be well equipped to respond to human speech and, indeed, show a preference for speech over non-speech sounds (Vouloumanos & Werker, 2007). They can discriminate basic speech sounds—called **phonemes**—very early in life. Peter Eimas (1975b, 1985) pioneered research in this area by demonstrating that infants 2 to 3 months old could distinguish similar consonant sounds (for example, *ba* and *pa*). In fact, infants seem to detect the difference between the vowels *a* and *i* from the second day after birth (Clarkson & Berg, 1983). They can even distinguish between standard sounds (those that occur regularly in a language) and deviant sounds (those that occur rarely) in the first few days after birth (Ruusuvirta et al., 2003). By 3 months, they have developed a sound category system that allows them to recognize a phoneme even when it is spoken by different people (Marean, Werner, & Kuhl, 1992; Winkler et al., 2003). These are impressive accomplishments.

Infants can actually make some speech sound discriminations better than adults (Werker & Desjardins, 1995). They be-

gin life biologically prepared to learn any language humans anywhere speak. As they mature, they become especially sensitive to the sound differences significant in their own language and less sensitive to sound differences irrelevant to that language. For example, young infants can easily discriminate the consonants *r* and *l* (Eimas, 1975a). So can adults who speak English, French, Spanish, or German. However, the Chinese and Japanese languages make no distinction between *r* and *l*, and adult native speakers of those languages cannot make this particular auditory discrimination as well as young infants can (Miyawaki et al., 1975). Similarly, infants raised in English-speaking homes can make discriminations important in Hindi but nonexistent in English, but English-speaking adults have trouble doing so (Werker et al., 1981).

By 1 year of age, when infants are just beginning to utter their first words, they have already become insensitive to contrasts of sounds that are not made in their native language (Rivera-Gaxiola, Silva-Pereyra, & Kuhl, 2005; Werker & Desjardins, 1995). Further, they show *increased* sensitivity to native language sounds (Kuhl et al., 2006). Their early auditory experiences have shaped the formation of neural connections, or synapses, in the auditory areas of their brains so that they are optimally sensitive to the sound contrasts that they have been listening to and that are important in the language they are acquiring (see Chapter 10).

Newborns are especially attentive to female voices (Ecklund-Flores & Turkewitz, 1996), but can they recognize their mother's voice? Indeed they can. Even unborn fetuses can distinguish their mother's voice from a stranger's voice. How do we know this? Canadian researchers measured fetal heart rate in response to a tape recording (played over the mother's stomach) of either their mother's voice or a stranger's voice (Kisilevsky et al., 2003). Heart rates increased in response to their mother's voice and decreased in response to the stranger's voice, indicating that fetuses detected a difference between the two. Following birth, newborns will learn to suck faster on a special pacifier when it activates a recording of the mother's voice (DeCasper & Fifer, 1980).

Does this early recognition extend to fathers' voices? Sorry, men, apparently not. Even by 4 months, infants show no preference for their father's voice over the voice of a strange man (Ward & Cooper, 1999). They can detect differences between various male voices, however, indicating that the lack of preference for the father's voice is not because of a failure to distinguish it.

Why would infants prefer their mother's but not their father's voice? We need to look at what is happening before birth to answer this. Anthony DeCasper and Melanie Spence (1986) had mothers recite a passage (for example, portions of Dr. Seuss's *The Cat in the Hat*) many times during the last 6 weeks of their pregnancies. At birth, the infants were tested to see if they would suck more to hear the story they had heard before birth or to hear a different story. Remarkably, they preferred the familiar story. Somehow these infants were able to recognize the distinctive sound pattern of the story they had heard in the womb. Auditory learning before birth could also explain why newborns prefer to hear their mother's voice to those of unfamiliar women but do not show a preference for their father's voice. They are literally bombarded with their mother's voice for months before birth, giving them ample opportunity to learn its auditory qualities.

So hearing is more developed than vision at birth. Infants can distinguish among speech sounds and recognize familiar sound patterns such as their mother's voice soon after birth. Within the first year, they lose sensitivity to sound contrasts insignificant in the language they are starting to learn, and they further refine their auditory perception skills. Unfortunately, some infants experience hearing problems, placing them at risk for language and communication problems. The Applications box on page 166 examines the importance of early identification and treatment of hearing problems.

Taste and Smell

Can newborns detect different tastes and smells? Both of these senses rely on the detection of chemical molecules. The sensory receptors for taste—taste buds—are located mainly on the

From birth, infants respond to tastes. In response to a sugar solution, newborns part their lips, lick their upper lips, make sucking movements, and sometimes smile. In response to bitter tastes, they purse their lips or open their mouths with the corners down and drool.

tongue. In ways not fully understood, taste buds respond to chemical molecules and produce perceptions of sweet, salty, bitter, or sour tastes. At birth, babies can clearly distinguish sweet, bitter, and sour tastes and show a preference for sweets. Indeed, sugar water—but not plain water—seems to have a marvelous ability to calm even premature babies and can help them cope with painful events such as needle pricks (Barr et al., 1999; Smith & Blass, 1996).

Different taste sensations also produce distinct facial expressions in the newborn. Jacob Steiner and his colleagues (Ganchrow, Steiner, & Daher, 1983; Steiner, 1979) have found that newborns lick their lips and sometimes smile when they are tasting a sugar solution but purse their lips and even drool to get rid of the foul taste when they are given a bitter solution. Their facial expressions become increasingly pronounced as a solution becomes sweeter or more bitter, suggesting that newborns can discriminate different concentrations of a substance. Even before birth, babies show a preference for sweets when they swallow more amniotic fluid that contains higher concentrations of sugars than amniotic fluid with lower concentrations of sugar (Fifer, Monk, & Grose-Fifer, 2004).

Although we may have a general—and innate—preference for sweets and avoidance of bitters, flavor preferences are highly responsive to learning (Myers & Sclafani, 2006). Research by Julie Mennella and her colleagues (2004, 2006) suggests that food preferences may be influenced by early tastes that we are exposed to during infancy. Starting at 2 weeks of age, Mennella fed infants one of two formulas for 7 months. One formula was bland, and the other was bitter and tasted sour, at least to most adults. After this period, the babies who had been fed the sour formula continued to consume it, but the other infants refused when it was offered to them. By 4 to 5 years, children fed the unpleasant-tasting formula were more likely to consume other sour-tasting foods (for example, a sourflavored apple juice) than children exposed to only bland-tasting formula (Mennella & Beauchamp, 2002).

Such research may be key to helping researchers understand why some people are picky eaters, whereas others are open to a wide variety of tastes. Greater exposure to a variety of flavors during infancy—what a breast-fed baby with a mother who eats many different foods might experience—may lead to a more adventuresome eater later on. These early experiences with different flavors may also extend to the prenatal period and exposure to different chemicals in the amniotic fluid (Fifer, Monk, & Grose-Fifer, 2004). Although learning plays a role in taste preferences, we cannot discount genetic predispositions. Discovery of a "taste gene" has shown that genetic variation can account for a lot of the variation in children and adults' perception of bitterness and some of the variation in children's perception of sweetness (Mennella, Pepino, & Reed, 2005).

The sensory receptors for smell, or **olfaction,** are located in the nasal passage. Like taste, the sense of smell is working well at birth. Newborns react vigorously to unpleasant smells such as vinegar or ammonia and turn their heads away (Rieser, Yonas, & Wilkner, 1976). Even premature babies (born at 28 weeks of gestation) are capable of detecting various odors. Newborns also reliably prefer the scent of their own amniotic fluid over that of other amniotic fluid, suggesting that olfactory cues are detectable prenatally (Schaal, Barlier, & Soussignan, 1998). Exposure to a familiar odor—their own amniotic fluid or their mother's breast milk—can also calm newborns, resulting in less crying when their mothers are absent or when they undergo a painful procedure (Rattaz, Goubet, & Bullinger, 2005; Varendi et al., 1998). All babies also show a preference for the smell of human milk over formula, even if they have only consumed formula (Delaunay-El Allam, Marlier, & Schaal, 2006; Marlier & Schaal, 2005). Furthermore, babies who are breast-fed can recognize their mothers solely by the smell of their breasts or underarms within 1 or 2 weeks of birth (Cernoch & Porter, 1985; Porter et al., 1992). Babies who are bottle-fed cannot, probably because they have less contact with their mothers' skin. On the flip side, mothers can identify their newborns by smell and they are less repulsed by the odor of their own infant's dirty diaper than one from an unfamiliar infant (Case, Repacholi & Stevenson, 2006; Porter, 1999). Thus, the sense of smell we often take for granted may help babies and their parents get to know each other.

Touch, Temperature, and Pain

Receptors in the skin detect touch or pressure, heat or cold, and painful stimuli. The sense of touch seems to be operating nicely before birth and, with the body senses that detect motion, may be among the first senses to develop (Eliot, 1999; Field, 1990). You saw in Chapter 5 that newborns respond with reflexes if they are touched in appropriate areas. For example, when touched on the cheek, a newborn will turn its head and open its mouth. Even in their sleep, newborns will habituate to strokes of the same spot on the skin but respond again if the tactile stimulation is shifted to a new spot—from the ear to the lips, for example (Kisilevsky &

Muir, 1984). And like the motor responses described in Chapter 5, sensitivity to tactile stimulation develops in a cephalocaudal (head to toe) direction, so the face and mouth are more sensitive than lower parts of the body. No wonder babies like to put everything in their mouths—the tactile sensors in and around the mouth allow babies to collect a great deal of information about the world. Most parents quickly recognize the power of touch for soothing a fussy baby. Touch has even greater benefits. Premature babies who are systematically stroked over their entire body gain more weight and exhibit more relaxed behavior and more regular sleep patterns than premature babies who are not massaged (Field et al., 2006; Scafidi, Field, & Schanberg, 1993).

Newborns are also sensitive to warmth and cold; they can tell the difference between something cold and something warm placed on their cheeks (Eliot, 1999). Finally, young babies clearly respond to painful stimuli such as needle pricks. For obvious ethical reasons, researchers have not exposed infants to severely painful stimuli. However, analyses of babies' cries and facial movements as they receive injections and have blood drawn leave no doubt that these procedures are painful. Even premature babies show cortical responses to pain (Slater et al., 2006). And pain is responsive to learning. For example, researchers have compared infants born to diabetic mothers, who have their heels pricked every few hours after birth to test their blood sugar levels, with infants born to nondiabetic mothers (Taddio, 2002). Both groups of infants have blood drawn from the back of their hands before they leave the hospital so several routine tests can be conducted. The infants who have already had their heels pricked show a larger response to having blood drawn than the infants who have never experienced the presumably painful needle pricks in their feet. Indeed, some infants who had already experienced the heel pricks began to grimace when the nurse was preparing their skin for the needle prick, indicating that they had learned from their prior experiences that a painful moment was coming.

Such research challenges the medical wisdom of giving babies who must undergo major surgery little or no anesthesia. It turns out that infants are more likely to survive heart surgery if they receive deep anesthesia that keeps them unconscious during the operation and for a day afterward than if they receive light anesthesia that does not entirely protect them from the stressful experience of pain (Anand & Hickey, 1992). And the American Academy of Pediatrics (2000) recommends that local anesthesia be given to newborn males undergoing circumcision.

You have now seen that each of the major senses is operating in some form at birth and that perceptual abilities improve dramatically during infancy. Let us ask one final question about infant perception: Can infants meaningfully integrate information from the different senses?

Integrating Sensory Information

It would obviously be useful for an infant attempting to understand the world to be able to put together information gained from viewing, fingering, sniffing, and otherwise exploring objects. It now seems clear that the senses function in an integrated way at birth. For instance, newborns will look in the direction of a sound they hear, suggesting that vision and hearing are linked. Moreover, infants 8 to 31 days old expect to feel objects that they can see and are frustrated by a visual illusion that looks like a graspable object but proves to be nothing but air when they reach for it (Bower, Broughton, & Moore, 1970). Thus, vision and touch, as well as vision and hearing, seem to be interrelated early in life. This integration of the senses helps babies perceive and respond appropriately to the objects and people they encounter (Hainline & Abramov, 1992; Walker-Andrews, 1997).

A more difficult task is to recognize through one sense an object familiar through another; this is called **cross-modal perception.** This capacity is required in children's games that involve feeling objects hidden in a bag and identifying what they are by touch alone. Some researchers (for example, Streri, 2003; Streri & Gentez, 2004) report that newborns can recognize an object by sight that they had previously touched with their hand. But other researchers have had trouble demonstrating cross-modal perception in such young infants (for example, Maurer, Stager, & Mondloch, 1999). Apparently, early cross-modal perception is a fragile ability dependent on various task variables such as which hand is used to manipulate the object (Streri & Gentez, 2004). Consistent oral-to-visual cross-modal transfer is shown by 3 months of age (illustrated by infants' ability to visually discriminate an object previously experienced by mouthing or sucking it), and other forms of cross-modal per-

ception are reliably displayed at 4 to 7 months (Streri & Pecheux, 1986; Walker-Andrews, 1997). By that age, for example, infants integrate vision and hearing to judge distance; they prefer to look at an approaching train that gets louder and a departing one that gets quieter rather than at videos in which sound and sight are mismatched (Pickens, 1994). Nevertheless, performance on more complex cross-modal perception tasks that require matching patterns of sounds with patterns of visual stimuli continues to improve throughout childhood and even adolescence (Bushnell & Baxt, 1999).

Researchers now conclude that impressions from the different senses are "fused" early in life, much as William James believed, but they do not create the "blooming, buzzing confusion" he described. Rather, this early sensory integration may make it easier for babies to perceive and use information that comes to them through multiple channels simultaneously (Walker-Andrews, 1997). Then, as the separate senses continue to develop and each becomes a more effective means of exploring objects, babies become more skilled at cross-modal perception and are able to coordinate information gained through one sense with information gained through another.

Influences on Early Perceptual Development

The perceptual competencies of even very young infants are remarkable, as is the progress made within the first few months of life. All major senses begin working before birth and are clearly functioning at birth; parents would be making a huge mistake to assume that their newborn is not taking in the sensory world. Many perceptual abilities—for example, the ability to perceive depth or to distinguish melodies—emerge within just a few months of birth. Gradually, basic perceptual capacities are fine-tuned, and infants become more able to interpret their sensory experiences—to recognize a pattern of light as a face, for example. By the end of the second year, the most important aspects of perceptual development are complete. The senses and the mind are working to create a meaningful world of recognized objects, sounds, tastes, smells, and bodily sensations.

The fact that perceptual development takes place so quickly can be viewed as support for the "nature" side of the nature–nurture debate. Many basic perceptual capacities appear to be innate or to develop rapidly in all normal infants. What, then, is the role of early sensory experience in perceptual development?

Early Experience and the Brain

Classic studies conducted by David Hubel and Torsten Wiesel showed that depriving newborn kittens of normal visual experience by suturing one eye closed for 8 weeks resulted in a lack of normal connections between that eye and the visual cortex—and blindness even after the eye had been reopened (Hubel & Wiesel, 1970). Even as little as 1 week of deprivation during

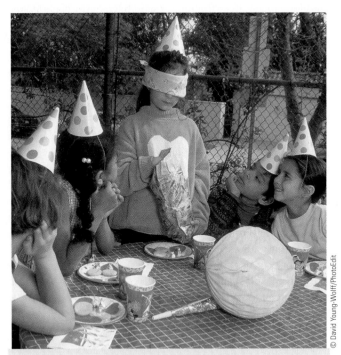

Intersensory perception. The ability to recognize through one sense (here, touch) what has been learned through another (vision) increases with age during infancy and childhood. Here, the birthday girl must identify prizes in the bag by touch alone.

© David Young-Wolff/PhotoEdit

the critical period of the first 8 weeks of life can lead to permanent vision loss in the kitten (Kandel & Jessell, 1991). By contrast, depriving an adult cat's eye of light does not lead to permanent damage.

In humans, it is probably more accurate to characterize the effects of early experience on vision in terms of **sensitive periods** rather than critical periods (Armstrong et al., 2006). Accordingly, a sensitive period is "a window of time during which an individual is *more* affected by experience, and thus has a higher level of plasticity than at other times throughout life" (p. 326). Terri Lewis and Daphne Maurer (2005) provide evidence for multiple sensitive periods during which vision can be influenced by experience. First, there is the period they call visually driven normal development. This is when expected developmental changes in vision will occur with exposure to "normal" visual input; these changes will not occur if visual input is absent. Second, there is a sensitive period for damage; that is, there is a period when abnormal or absent visual input is likely to lead to permanent deficits in some aspect of vision. Third, there is a sensitive period for recovery when the visual system has the potential to recover from damage (Lewis & Maurer, 2005, p. 164).

Sensory experience is vital in determining the organization of the developing brain. Imagine what visual perception would be like in an infant who was blind at birth but later had surgery to permit vision. This is the scenario for perhaps 3 of every 5000 infants with congenital **cataracts,** a clouding of the lens that leaves these infants nearly blind from birth if it is not corrected. In the past, surgery to remove cataracts was often delayed until infants were older. But such delays meant that infants had weeks, months, or even years with little or no visual input. Consequently, some never developed normal vision even after the lens defect was removed.

It turns out that the visual system requires stimulation early in life, including patterned stimulation, to develop normally. Although the visual system has some plasticity throughout childhood, the first 3 months of life are considered critical (Lambert & Drack, 1996). During this time, the brain must receive clear visual information from both eyes. Unfortunately, not all infants with cataracts are identified early enough to benefit from surgery. One recent study found that even with visual screening programs for newborns before they leave the hospital, the vast majority of congenital cataracts are still not identified during the neonatal (first month) period (Sotomi et al., 2007). Early identification is essential. Identification and removal by 10 weeks of age is associated with better long-term outcomes than identification and removal after this age (Lambert et al., 2006). Even after surgery restores their sight, these infants have difficulty, at least initially, perceiving their visual world clearly (Maurer, Mondloch, & Lewis, 2007). Acuity after surgery is what you might find in a newborn without cataracts—in other words, rather poor (Maurer et al., 1999). But it improves significantly during the month following surgery.

Years after corrective surgery, individuals who missed out on early visual experience because of congenital cataracts show normal visual abilities in some areas, such as sensitivity to low spatial frequencies (e.g., wide stripes) and recognition of faces based on the *shape* of facial features. However, they struggle with certain other visual tasks including the ability to distinguish between mid and high spatial frequencies (e.g., medium and narrow strips) as well as holistic face processing and recognizing faces based on *spacing* of facial features. What might account for this pattern?

Daphne Maurer and her colleagues (2007) argue that the deficits reflect sleeper effects of early visual deficits. Thus, patterned visual input early in life is critical to developing later sensitivity to detail and holistic face processing. Even though these abilities do not normally develop until after early infancy—and after corrective surgery has occurred—early visual deprivation likely affects the brain in a way that prevents infants from developing these abilities even when normal visual input is restored (Maurer, Mondloch, & Lewis, 2007). Clearly, then, early visual experiences influence later visual perception.

The same message about the importance of early experience applies to the sense of hearing: Exposure to auditory stimulation early in life affects the architecture of the developing brain, which in turn influences auditory perception skills (Finitzo, Gunnarson, & Clark, 1990). Children with hearing impairments who undergo cochlear implant, which bypasses damaged nerve cells in their inner ear, may struggle for months to understand the meaning of signals reaching their brain through the implant before they derive benefits (Allum et al., 2000; see also the Applications box). Although the brain is being fed information, it must learn how to interpret these signals. Otherwise, the signals are a crashing jumble of nonsense that can be worse than not hearing (Colburn, 2000). The conclusion is clear: Maturation alone is not enough; normal perceptual development also requires normal perceptual experience. The practical implication is also clear: Visual and hearing problems in children should be detected and corrected as early in life as possible (Joint Committee on Infant Hearing, 2000).

The Infant's Active Role

Parents need not worry about arranging the right sensory environment for their children because young humans actively seek the stimulation they need to develop properly. Infants are active explorers and stimulus seekers; they orchestrate their own perceptual, motor, and cognitive development by exploring their environment and learning what it will allow them to do (Gibson, 1988; Gibson & Pick, 2000).

According to Eleanor Gibson (1988), infants proceed through three phases of exploratory behavior:

1. From birth to 4 months infants explore their immediate surroundings, especially their caregivers, by looking and listening, and they learn a bit about objects by mouthing them and watching them move.

2. From 5 to 7 months, once the ability to voluntarily grasp objects has developed, babies pay far closer attention to objects, exploring objects with their eyes as well as with their hands.

3. By 8 or 9 months, after most have begun to crawl, infants extend their explorations into the larger environment and carefully examine the objects they encounter on their journeys, learning all about their properties. Whereas a 4-month-old infant may merely mouth a new toy and look at it now and then, a 12-month-old will give it a thorough examination—turning it, fingering it, poking it, and watching it intently (Ruff et al., 1992).

By combining perception and action in their exploratory behavior, infants actively create sensory environments that meet their needs and contribute to their own development (Eppler, 1995). As children become more able to attend selectively to the world around them, they become even more able to choose the forms and levels of stimulation that suit them best.

Cultural Variation

Do infants who grow up in different cultural environments encounter different sensory stimulation and perceive the world in different ways? Perceptual preferences obviously differ from culture to culture. In some cultures, people think heavier women are more beautiful than slim ones or relish eating sheep's eyeballs or chicken heads. Are more basic perceptual competencies also affected by socialization?

People from different cultures differ little in basic sensory capacities, such as the ability to discriminate degrees of brightness or loudness (Berry et al., 1992). However, their perceptions and interpretations of sensory input can vary considerably. For example, you have already seen that children become insensitive, starting at the end of the first year after birth, to speech sound contrasts that they do not hear regularly because they are not important in their primary language. Michael Lynch and his associates (1990) have shown that the same is true for perceptions of music. Infants from the United States, they found, noticed equally notes that violated either Western musical scales or the Javanese pelog scale. This suggests that humans are born with the potential to perceive music from a variety of cultures. However, American adults were less sensitive to bad notes in the unfamiliar Javanese musical system than to mistuned notes in their native Western scale, suggesting that their years of experience with Western music had shaped their perceptual skills.

Another example of cultural influence concerns the ability to translate perceptions of the human form into a drawing. In Papua New Guinea, where there is no cultural tradition of drawing and painting, children ages 10 to 15 who have had no schooling do not have much luck drawing the human body; they draw scribbles or tadpolelike forms far more often than children in the same society who have attended school and have been exposed many times to drawings of people (Martlew & Connolly, 1996; see ■ **Figure 6.4**). We all have the capacity to create two-dimensional representations, but we apparently develop that capacity more rapidly if our culture provides us with relevant experiences. Many other examples of the effects of cultural learning experiences on visual and auditory perception can be cited (Berry et al., 1992).

■ **FIGURE 6.4** Children ages 10 to 15 in Papua New Guinea, unless they have attended school, lack experience with drawings of the human form and produce drawings much like those done by far younger children (such as 4-year-olds) in U.S. society. Cultural experience influences the ability to translate visual perceptions into representations on the page.
SOURCE: From Human figure drawings by schooled and unschooled children in Papua New Guinea by M. Matthew and K. J. Connolly from *Child Development, 67.* © 1996 Society for Research in Child Development, Inc. Reprinted by permission.

SUMMING UP

▌ The visual system is fairly well developed at birth. Infants under 2 months of age discriminate brightness and colors and are attracted to contour, moderate complexity, and movement. Starting at 2 or 3 months, infants more clearly perceive whole patterns such as faces and seem to understand a good deal about objects and their properties, guided by intuitive theories of the physical world.

▌ Spatial perception develops rapidly, and by about 7 months infants not only perceive drop-offs but also fear them.

▌ Young infants can recognize their mother's voice and distinguish speech sounds that adults cannot discriminate.

▌ The senses of taste and smell are also well developed at birth. In addition, newborns are sensitive to touch, temperature, and pain.

▌ The senses are interrelated at birth, but as infants develop, performance on cross-modal perception tasks improves.

CRITICAL THINKING

1. Drawing on your knowledge of the sensory and perceptual capacities of newborns, put yourself in the place of a newborn just emerging from the womb and describe your perceptual experiences.

There are some refinements of the sensory systems during childhood. For example, visual acuity improves to adult-levels sometime between 4 and 6 years, and sensitivity to contrasts develops completely by about 7 years of age (Maurer, Mondloch, & Lewis, 2007). Recognition of odors improves between ages 6 and 11, at which point it is comparable to adult levels (Stevenson, Mahmut, & Sundqvist, 2007). For the most part, though, sensory and perceptual development is largely complete by the end of infancy. Is there anything left to accomplish during childhood? Mostly, sensory and perceptual development during this time is a matter of children learning to use their senses more intelligently. For example, children rapidly build knowledge of the world so that they can recognize and label what they sense, giving it greater meaning. As a result, it becomes even harder to separate perceptual development from cognitive development.

The Development of Attention

Much of perceptual development in childhood is really the development of **attention**—the focusing of perception and cognition on something in particular. Youngsters become better able to use their senses deliberately and strategically to gather the information most relevant to a task at hand.

Infants actively use their senses to explore their environment, and they prefer some sensory stimuli to others. Still, there is some truth to the idea that the attention of the infant or very young child is "captured by" something and that of the older child is "directed toward" something. Selective as they are, 1-month-old infants do not deliberately choose to attend to faces and other engaging stimuli. Instead, a novel stimulus attracts their attention and, once their attention is "caught," they sometimes seem unable to turn away (Butcher, Kalverboer, & Geuze, 2000; Ruff & Rothbart, 1996). As children get older, three things change: their attention spans become longer, they become more selective in what they attend to, and they are better able to plan and carry out systematic strategies for using their senses to achieve goals.

Longer Attention Span

Young children have short attention spans. Researchers know that they should limit their experimental sessions with young children to a few minutes, and nursery-school teachers often switch classroom activities every 15 to 20 minutes. Even when they are doing things they like, such as watching a television program or playing with a toy, 2- and 3-year-olds spend far less time concentrating on the program or the toy than older children do (Ruff & Capozzoli, 2003; Ruff & Lawson, 1990). In one study of sustained attention, children were asked to put strips of colored paper in appropriately colored boxes (Yendovitskaya, 1971). Children ages 2 to 3 worked for an average of 18 minutes and were easily distracted; children ages 5 to

6 often persisted for 1 hour or more. Further improvements in attention span occur later in childhood as those parts of the brain involved with attention become further myelinated (see Chapter 5).

More Selective Attention

Although infants clearly deploy their senses in a selective manner, they are not good at controlling their attention—deliberately concentrating on one thing while ignoring something else, what is known as **selective attention.** With age, attention becomes more selective and less susceptible to distraction. As infants approach 2 years, they become able to form plans of action, which then guide what they focus on and what they ignore (Ruff & Rothbart, 1996).

Between approximately 3½ and 4 years, there is a significant increase in focused attention. Kathleen Kannass and John Colombo (2007) tested 3½- and 4-years-olds while they worked on a task under one of three conditions: no distraction, constant distraction (a TV program in an unfamiliar language played continuously in the background), or intermittent distraction (the same TV program played in the background but was frequently turned on and off as the children worked). Among the 3½-year-olds, the two groups working with any distraction had more trouble completing their task than the group working without distraction. Among the 4-year-olds, only the group working with constant distraction had trouble finishing the task. Those working with intermittent distraction were able to stay as focused on the task as children working without distraction. Finally, the researchers found that when a distracter was present, looking away from their task led to worse performance, whereas looking away when there was no distraction did not impair performance. These findings should suggest to parents and teachers of young children that performance will be better if distractions in task materials and in the room are kept to a minimum. In particular, the presence of a continuous distracter will lead to trouble completing tasks (Kannass & Colombo, 2007).

More Systematic Attention

Finally, as they age, children become more able to plan and carry out systematic perceptual searches. You have already seen that older infants are more likely than younger ones to thoroughly explore a pattern. Research with children in the former Soviet Union reveals that visual scanning becomes considerably more detailed and exhaustive over the first 6 years of life (Zaporozhets, 1965). But the most revealing findings come from studies of how children go about a visual search. In general, children search more slowly than adults (Donnelly et al., 2007) but they are also less efficient. Elaine Vurpillot (1968) recorded the eye movements of 4- to 10-year-olds trying to decide whether two houses, each with several windows containing various objects, were identical or different. As ■ **Figure 6.5** illustrates, children ages 4 and 5 were not systematic. They often looked at only a few windows and, as a result, came to wrong

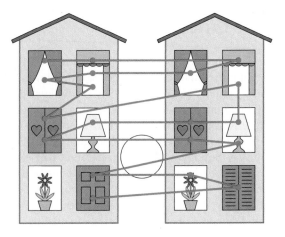

5-year-old: "The same"   8-year-old: "Not the same"

■ **FIGURE 6.5** Are the houses in each pair identical or different? As indicated by the lines, 8-year-olds are more likely than 5-year-olds to answer correctly because they systematically scan the visual features of the two pictures.
SOURCE: Adapted from Vurpillot (1968).

conclusions. In contrast, most children older than 6 were very systematic; they typically checked each window in one house with the corresponding window in the other house, pair by pair. Improvements in visual search continue to be made throughout childhood and into early adulthood (Burack et al., 2000).

SUMMING UP

▪ Learning to control attention is an important part of perceptual development during childhood. Infants and young children are selectively attentive to the world around them, but they have not fully taken charge of their attentional processes.

▪ With age, children become more able to concentrate on a task for a long period, to focus on relevant information and ignore distractions, and to use their senses in purposeful and systematic ways to achieve goals.

▪ Infants and children who can control and sustain their attention are more successful at problem solving.

CRITICAL THINKING

1. You have an unlimited budget for redesigning a local child care center that serves children 6 weeks to 6 years old. Given what you know about sensory and perceptual capabilities of infants and young children, what equipment and toys will you purchase, and how will you remodel and redecorate the rooms?

6.4 | THE ADOLESCENT

There is little news to report about perception during adolescence, except that some developments of childhood are not completed until then. There are two changes during this time, though, that warrant discussion. First are refinements in attention and second are potential insults to hearing from exposure to loud noise.

Attention

It is fairly clear that adolescents have longer attention spans than children. They can, for example, sit through longer classes, work on papers or study for lengthier periods of time, and take tests that last as long as 3 to 4 hours (e.g., the SAT). The ability to sustain attention improves considerably between childhood and adulthood (McKay et al., 1994). This seems to be tied to increased myelination of those portions of the brain that help regulate attention (Tanner, 1990). As we noted in Chapter 5, a myelin coating on neurons helps insulate them to speed up transmission of neural impulses.

In addition, adolescents become still more efficient at ignoring irrelevant information so that they can concentrate on the task at hand. Not only do they learn more than children do about material they are supposed to master, but they also learn *less* about distracting information that could potentially interfere with their performance (Miller & Weiss, 1981). Children have the rudimentary skills to adapt to distractions, but compared to adolescents and adults, they are slowed down and more likely to be thrown off track by distracters. Similarly, adolescents can divide their attention more systematically between two tasks. For instance, Andrew Schiff and Irwin Knopf (1985) watched the eye movements of 9-year-olds and 13-year-olds during a two-part visual search task. Children were to push a response key when particular symbols appeared at the center of a screen and to remember letters flashed at the corners of the screen. The adolescents developed efficient strategies for switching their eyes from the center to the corners and back at the right times. The 9-year-olds had an unfortunate tendency

Adolescents are skilled at dividing their attention among several tasks.

to look at blank areas of the screen or to focus too much attention on the letters in the corners of the screen, thereby failing to detect the symbols in the center.

Hearing

Adolescence should be a period of optimal acuity of all the senses, but in today's world of rock concerts, MP3 players, power equipment, and so on, auditory acuity can become compromised in some adolescents. As ● **Table 6.1** shows, loud sounds—those above 75 decibels—may leave the listener with a loss of hearing. Fans of loud music, beware: The noise at rock concerts and night clubs is often in the 120-decibel to 130-decibel range, well above the level where damage may occur. And if you can

● TABLE 6.1 NOISE LEVELS	
NOISE	NUMBER OF DECIBELS
Whisper	30
Quiet room	40
Normal speech	60
City traffic	80
Lawnmower	90
Rock concerts	110–140
Jet plane takeoff	120
Jackhammer	130
Firearm discharge	140

The healthy ear can detect sounds starting at 0 decibels. Damage to hearing can start between 75 and 80 decibels and is more likely with long-term exposure to loud sounds.

hear the music coming from the headset of your friend's MP3 player, your friend may be damaging her hearing.

The most common outcome of noise exposure is **tinnitus,** or ringing sounds in one or both ears that can last for days, weeks, or indefinitely. A majority—as many as 85%—of concert attendees report experiencing tinnitus (Bogoch, House, & Kudla, 2005; Chung et al., 2005). Hearing problems associated with short periods of exposure to loud sounds may be temporary, but damage from regular exposure to these same sounds can accumulate over time, leading to moderate or even severe hearing loss by adulthood.

Many teens report that they are aware of the potential for hearing loss from exposure to loud sounds, but they do not believe that hearing loss is a serious health concern for them (Chung et al., 2005). Thus, despite their own awareness that noise exposure can lead to hearing loss and warnings from parents and health officials that noise can be hazardous, teens do little to protect their hearing because hearing loss is not perceived as an important issue. Few wear ear plugs at concerts or ear protectors when operating power equipment (Bogoch, House, & Kudla, 2005; Chung et al., 2005). Part of the problem is the perception that ear protection is not "cool." Teens who are more open to behavioral change and those who are less concerned about appearance are more willing to use ear protection (Bogoch, House, & Kudla, 2005). In addition, teens from higher socioeconomic backgrounds tend to rate noise exposure as more negative, and therefore are more open to ear protection, than teens from lower socioeconomic backgrounds (Widén & Erlandsson, 2004).

Educational programs to improve hearing protection among teens need to focus on several issues to be effective. They need to help teens recognize that there may be long-term consequences of noise exposure; damage to the auditory system can accumulate over time. Second, they need to address teens' perception that hearing loss is not an important health issue. Until hearing is perceived as a priority, teens and others will have little motivation to protect this sensory system. And finally, education programs need to reduce the stigma associated with wearing hearing protection so teens feel comfortable making the decision to protect their hearing when they are in settings with loud noise.

SUMMING UP

▌ Basic perceptual and attentional skills are perfected during adolescence. Adolescents are better than children at sustaining their attention and using it selectively and strategically to solve the problem at hand.

▌ Exposure to loud noise can cause tinnitus or ringing sounds in the ear that can be temporary or permanent. Damage to the auditory system from exposure to loud noise can accumulate over time, leading eventually to hearing impairment. Teens are aware that loud noise can cause hearing loss, but most do not rate this as a serious health concern and do not take measures to protect their hearing.

1. You are a tutor and want a 5-year-old and a 13-year-old to systematically compare pairs of maps to determine whether they are similar or different. What can you expect of each child and what can you do to optimize the performance of the younger child?

2. Design an educational unit for a high school health class that is aimed at reducing the incidence of noise-induced hearing loss.

6.5 THE ADULT

What becomes of sensory and perceptual capacities during adulthood? There is good news and bad news, and we might as well dispense with the bad news first: Sensory and perceptual capacities decline gradually with age in the normal person. Whispers become harder to hear, seeing in the dark becomes difficult, food may not taste as good, and so on. Often these declines begin in early adulthood and become noticeable in the 40s, sometimes giving middle-aged people a feeling that they are getting old. Further declines take place in later life, to the point that you would have a hard time finding a person age 65 or older who does not have at least a mild sensory or perceptual impairment. The good news is that these changes are gradual and usually minor. As a result, we can usually compensate for them, making small adjustments such as turning up the volume on the TV set or adding a little extra seasoning to food. Because the losses are usually not severe, and because of the process of compensation, only a minority of old people develop serious problems such as blindness and deafness.

The losses we are describing take two general forms. First, sensation is affected, as indicated by raised **sensory thresholds**. The threshold for a sense is the point at which low levels of stimulation can be detected—a dim light can be seen, a faint tone can be heard, a slight odor can be detected, and so on. Stimulation below the threshold cannot be detected, so the rise of the threshold with age means that sensitivity to very low levels of stimulation is lost. (You saw that the very young infant is also insensitive to some very low levels of stimulation.)

Second, perceptual abilities decline in some aging adults. Even when stimulation is intense enough to be well above the detection threshold, older people sometimes have difficulty processing or interpreting sensory information. As you will see, they may have trouble searching a visual scene, understanding rapid speech in a noisy room, or recognizing the foods they are tasting.

So, sensory and perceptual declines are typical during adulthood, although they are far steeper in some individuals than in others and can often be compensated for. These declines involve both a rise of thresholds for detecting stimulation and a loss of some perceptual abilities.

Vision

We begin with a question that concerns many people as they get older: Will I lose my eyesight? For most people, the answer is no. Fewer than 2% of adults older than 70 are blind in both eyes, and only 4.4% are blind in one eye, but these numbers increase as we go through our 80s and 90s (Campbell et al., 1999). Although most adults will not be blind, many experience some vision problems. As ● Table 6.2 shows, 9 in 10 people will wear corrective lenses; 1 in 4 will have cataracts, or cloudiness of the normally clear lens; and some will need to use a magnifying glass to help them see. Why do these changes in the visual system occur, and is there anything you can do to prevent losses? Before we answer these questions, we need to briefly review the basic workings of the visual system.

As ■ Figure 6.6 shows, light enters the eye through the cornea and passes through the pupil and lens before being projected (upside down) on the retina. From here, images are relayed to the brain by the optic nerve at the back of each eye. The pupil of the eye automatically becomes larger or smaller depending on the lighting conditions, and the lens changes shape, or accommodates, to keep images focused on the retina. In adolescents and young adults, the visual system is normally at peak performance. Aging brings changes to all components of the visual system.

Changes in the Pupil

As we age, our pupils become somewhat smaller and do not change as much when lighting conditions change. As a result, older adults experience greater difficulty when lighting is dim, when it is bright, and when it suddenly changes. Approximately one-third of adults older than 85 exhibit a tenfold loss of the ability to read low-contrast words in dim lighting (Brabyn, 2000). ■ Figure 6.7 shows how visual acuity decreases only

● **TABLE 6.2 PERCENTAGE OF ADULTS 70 YEARS AND OLDER WHO EXPERIENCE VISION PROBLEMS**

VISION CONDITION	PERCENTAGE OF ADULTS 70 AND OLDER
Cataract(s)	57%
Visual Impairment	20%
Glaucoma	9%
Macular Degeneration	6%
Retinopathy from Diabetes	4%
Workplace Eye Injury	4%

SOURCE: Adapted from MMWR Weekly, 2006b.

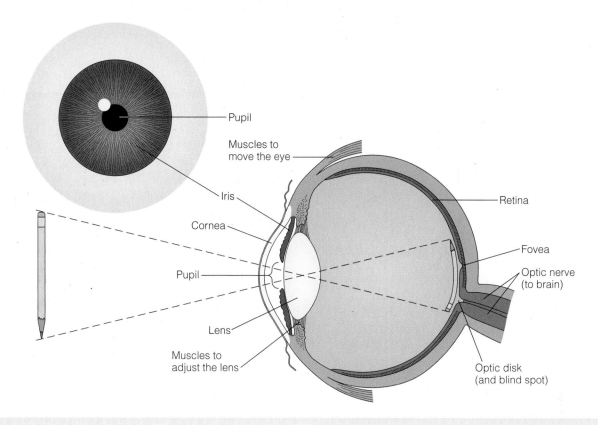

■ FIGURE 6.6 The human eye and retina. Light passes through the cornea, pupil, and lens and falls on the light-sensitive surface of the retina, where images of objects are projected upside down. The information is relayed to the brain by the optic nerve.

slightly with age under ideal conditions—strong contrast and bright light. But when contrast is poor, and especially when poor contrast is combined with low light levels, the drop in visual acuity is sharper (Haegerstrom-Portnoy, Schneck, & Brabyn, 2000). Findings such as these explain why older adults often have difficulty reading menus in restaurants with "mood" lighting. To compensate, they might use a small flashlight. And restaurants could help by providing menus printed with sharp contrast (black print on a pure white background).

When walking into the sunlight after watching a movie in a darkened theater, older adults' pupils are slower than younger adults' to change from large to small, a process that helps reduce the glare of bright lights. In one study, adults older than 85 years took more than 2 minutes to recover from glare, whereas adults younger than 65 needed less than 15 seconds (Brabyn, 2000).

Similarly, **dark adaptation**—the process in which the eyes adapt to darkness and become more sensitive to the low level of light available—occurs more slowly in older individuals than in younger ones (Fozard & Gordon-Salant, 2001). As a result, the older person driving at night may have special problems when turning onto a dark road from a lighted highway.

Changes in the Lens

The lens of the eye also undergoes change with age. It has been gaining new cells since childhood, making it denser and less flexible later in life. It cannot change shape, or accommodate, as well to bring objects at different distances into focus. The lens is also yellowing, and both it and the gelatinous liquid behind it are becoming less transparent. The thickening of the lens with age leads to **presbyopia,** or the decreased ability of the lens to accommodate objects close to the eye (Scheiber, 2006). Over the years, an adult may, without even being aware of it, gradually move newspapers and books farther from the eye to make them clearer—a form of compensation for decline. Eventually, however, the arms may simply be too short to do the trick any longer. Middle-aged adults cope with problems of near vision by getting reading glasses (or, if they also have problems with distance vision, bifocals); reading fine print may still be a problem, however.

As for distance vision, visual acuity as measured by standard eye charts increases in childhood, peaks in the 20s, remains steady through middle age, and steadily declines in old age (Evans et al., 2002; Klein et al., 2001). The implications for the average adult are fairly minor. For example, in one major study, three out of four older adults (75 years and older) had good corrected vision (Evans et al., 2002). At worst, most of them could see at 20 feet what a person with standard acuity can see at 25 feet—not a big problem. Among the oldest adults—those in their 90s—37% are visually impaired, but only 7% have lost all functional vision. Several studies show that women experience greater declines in visual acuity than men (see, for example, Bailey et al., 2006). Older women with

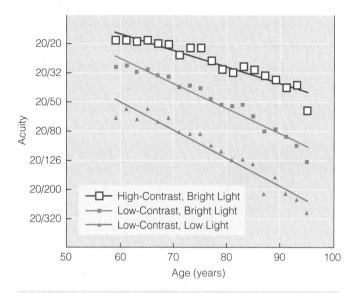

■ FIGURE 6.7 Visual acuity of older adults under optimal (high contrast and bright light), average (low contrast and bright light), and poor (low contrast and low light) stimulus conditions.

Adapted from Haegerstrom-Portnoy, G., Schneck, M. E., and Brabyn, J. A. (1999). Seeing into old age: Vision function beyond acuity. *Optometry and Vision Science, 76,* 141–158.

As adults age, they typically find they are more bothered by glare and need corrective lenses.

declining vision are more susceptible to falling and fracturing a bone, which is a serious threat to their independence (Pedula et al., 2006). Fracturing a hip often triggers a shift from independent to assisted living and can even be fatal. And poor vision that is not correctable can seriously decrease older adults' quality of life. According to one estimate, older adults with poor visual acuity (20/40 or worse) were as impaired as those with a major medical problem such as stroke (Chia et al., 2004).

Thus, even though most of us will not be blind, we will need to wear corrective lenses and regularly monitor our vision. The minority of elderly people who experience serious declines in visual acuity typically suffer from pathological conditions of the eye. These conditions become more prevalent in old age but are not part of aging itself. For example, cataracts are the leading cause of visual impairment in old age. Most older adults have some degree of lens clouding, and significant clouding is present in roughly half of adults older than 75 years, often from lifelong heavy exposure to sunlight and its damaging ultraviolet rays (Fozard & Gordon-Salant, 2001). Fortunately, cataracts can be removed through surgery, which can improve vision and prevent blindness.

Retinal Changes

Researchers also know that the sensory receptor cells in the retina may die or not function in later life as efficiently as they once did. The serious retinal problem **age-related macular degeneration** results from damage to cells in the retina responsi-

ble for central vision. Thus, vision becomes blurry; it also begins to fade first from the center of the visual field, making reading and many other activities impossible. Because cataracts are now often successfully corrected with surgery, age-related macular degeneration has become a leading cause of blindness in older adults (Congdon et al., 2004). The causes of macular degeneration are largely unknown, but some research points to a genetic contribution; other research shows a connection with cigarette smoking (Evans, 2001). Currently, there is no treatment for macular degeneration, but several researchers are working to develop retinal implants that would stimulate the remaining cells of the retina and restore some useful vision (Boston Retinal Implant Project, 2004).

Changes in the retina also lead to decreased visual field, or a loss of peripheral (side) vision (Fozard & Gordon-Salant, 2001). Looking straight ahead, an older adult may see only half of what a young adult sees to the left and the right of center. Can you think of activities that might be hindered by a decreased visual field? Driving a car comes to mind. For example, when approaching an intersection, you need to be able to see what is coming toward you as well as what is coming from the side roads. The Explorations box describes some other sensory changes that might make driving more hazardous for older people.

Significant loss of peripheral vision can lead to tunnel vision, a condition often caused by retinitis pigmentosa or by glaucoma. **Retinitis pigmentosa (RP)** is a group of hereditary disorders that all involve gradual deterioration of the light-sensitive cells of the retina. Symptoms of RP can appear as

AGING DRIVERS

Older drivers are perceived by many as more accident prone and slower than other drivers. Perhaps you have had the experience of zipping down the interstate when a slow-moving car driven by an elderly adult pulls into your path, forcing you to brake quickly. Is this experience representative, and is the stereotype of older drivers accurate? This is an important question, because 20% of all drivers will be older than 65 years by 2030 (Braver & Trempel, 2004; Lyman et al., 2002).

It is true that older adults (70 years and older) are involved in more automobile fatalities than middle-aged adults (see the graph in this Explorations box). But the most accident-prone group is young drivers between ages 16 and 24 (Insurance Institute for Highway Safety, 2007). When you take into account that young people drive more than elderly people do, it turns out that both elderly drivers and young drivers have more accidents *per mile driven* than middle-aged drivers have (Insurance Institute for Highway Safety, 2007).

Why is driving hazardous for elderly adults? Clearly, vision is essential to driving; vision accounts for approximately 90% of the information necessary to operate and navigate a car (Messinger-Rapport, 2003). Visual acuity or clarity is one component of problematic driving, but as noted in the main text, poor acuity is fairly easy to correct. Therefore, although older adults cite concerns about eyesight as one reason to limit or avoid driving, it cannot account for all the problems older drivers

have (Ragland, Satariano, & MacLeod, 2004).

Diminished peripheral vision also makes driving hazardous (Owsley et al., 1998). Good drivers must be able to see vehicles and pedestrians approaching from the side. Half of the fatal automobile accidents involving older drivers occur at intersections, and older drivers are more than twice as likely as young drivers to have problems making left turns (Uchida, Fujita, & Katayama, 1999). Not only must drivers see obstacles moving toward them, they must evaluate the speed and trajectory of these objects and integrate this information with their own speed and trajectory to determine a course of action. For example, is the car approaching from the left going to hit my car, or will I be through the intersection before it reaches me? Unfortunately, perceiving moving objects is a problem for older adults, even those who have good visual acuity (Erber, 2005). And simultaneously processing multiple pieces of information is also difficult for older adults. Thus, older drivers have trouble reading street signs while driving (Dewar, Kline, & Swanson, 1995), and they are less able than younger adults to quickly change their focus from the dashboard to the rearview mirror to the road ahead.

After understanding the dynamics of a potentially dangerous situation, the driver must be able to react quickly to threats (for example, a child chasing a ball into the street). As you learned in Chapter 5, older adults typically have

slower response times than younger adults; thus, they need more time to react to the same stimulus. Finally, older adults are slower to recover from glare and to adapt to the dark, which makes night driving problematic. But the driving records of older adults are not as bad as might be expected, because many of them compensate for visual and other perceptual difficulties and slower reactions by driving less frequently, especially in conditions believed to be more hazardous—at night, during rush hour, and when the weather is poor (Messinger-Rapport, 2003). Older adults with visual problems such as cataracts and those with cognitive problems are more likely to limit their driving than older adults without these problems (Messinger-Rapport, 2003). Some states have responded to concerns about elderly drivers with mandatory road retesting for license renewal (Cobb & Coughlin, 1998). But most states have no distinct policies about license renewal for older adults. It is not that states do not care; rather, they face strong opposition from groups such as the American Association of Retired Persons and individual older adults (Cobb & Coughlin, 1998). To give up driving is to give up a big chunk of independence, something anyone would be loath to do. Most people want to find ways to drive safely as long as possible. By understanding the strengths and limitations of their sensory–perceptual abilities, older adults will be in a good position to keep driving safely. Remember that the next time you are stuck behind a slow driver.

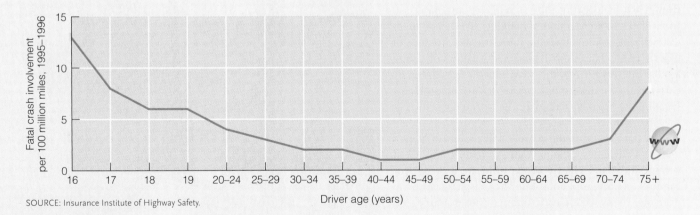

SOURCE: Insurance Institute of Highway Safety.

early as childhood, but it is more likely to be diagnosed in adulthood, when the symptoms have become more apparent. Individuals with RP often have a history of visual problems at night and a gradual loss of peripheral vision. There is no cure for retinal deterioration, but some promising research suggests that treatment with vitamin A can slow (not eliminate) the progress of the disease (Berson, 2000; Sibulesky et al., 1999).

In **glaucoma,** increased fluid pressure in the eye can damage the optic nerve and can cause a progressive loss of peripheral vision and, ultimately, blindness. It becomes more common over age 50. The key is to prevent the damage before it occurs, using eyedrops or surgery to lower eye fluid pressure. In many cases, however, the damage is done before people experience visual problems; only regular eye tests can reveal the buildup of eye pressure that spells trouble (Fozard & Gordon-Salant, 2001).

To recap, you can expect some changes in vision as you age. Sensory thresholds increase with age so that you need higher levels of stimulation than when you were young. Acuity, or sharpness of vision, decreases, and it takes longer for eyes to adapt to changes. Fortunately, it is possible to correct or compensate for most of these "normal" changes. Some older adults will experience more serious visual problems, such as those caused by changes in the retina, but early detection and treatment can preserve vision in most adults.

Attention and Visual Search

As you learned earlier in this chapter, perception is more than just seeing. It is using the senses intelligently and allocating attention efficiently. Young children have more difficulty performing complex visual search tasks and ignoring irrelevant information than older children do. Do older adults also have more difficulty than younger adults?

Older adults do worse than younger ones on several tests that require dividing attention between two tasks (divided attention) or selectively attending to certain stimuli while ignoring others (selective attention; see Juola et al., 2000; Madden & Langley, 2003). The more distracters a task involves, the more the performance of elderly adults falls short of the performance of young adults. In everyday life, this may translate into difficulty carrying on a conversation while driving or problems locating the asparagus amid all the frozen vegetables at the supermarket.

In one test of visual search skills, Charles Scialfa and his colleagues (Scialfa, Esau, & Joffe, 1998) asked young adults and elderly adults to locate a target (for example, a blue horizontal line) in a display where the distracter items were clearly different (for example, red vertical lines) or in a more difficult task where the distracters shared a common feature with the target (for example, blue vertical and red horizontal lines). Older adults were slower and less accurate on the more challenging search task. They were also more distracted by irrelevant information; they were especially slow com-

pared with young adults when the number of distracter items in the display was high. In some situations, elderly people appear to have difficulty inhibiting responses to irrelevant stimuli so that they can focus their attention more squarely on relevant stimuli (Erber, 2005). Older adults can improve their visual search performance with practice, and they are more successful when they strategically use a feature of the display (for example, color) to help guide their search (Madden, Gottlob, & Allen, 1999).

In short, older adults have their greatest difficulties in processing visual information when the situation is *novel* (when they are not sure exactly what to look for or where to look) and when it is *complex* (when there is a great deal of distracting information to search through or when two tasks must be performed at once). By contrast, they have fewer problems when they have clear expectations about what they are to do and when the task is not overly complicated (Madden, 2007). Thus, an older factory worker who has inspected radios for years may be just as speedy and accurate as a younger worker at this well-practiced, familiar task, but he might perform relatively poorly if suddenly asked to inspect pocket calculators and look for a much larger number of possible defects—a novel and complex task.

Hearing

There is some truth to the stereotype of the hard-of-hearing older person. The older the age group, the greater the percentage of people who have at least mild hearing loss: as many as 90% of individuals older than 65 have impaired hearing (Fozard & Gordon-Salant, 2001). Most older people experience mild to moderate hearing impairments, some experience severe hearing loss, and only a few are deaf (Dalton et al., 2004).

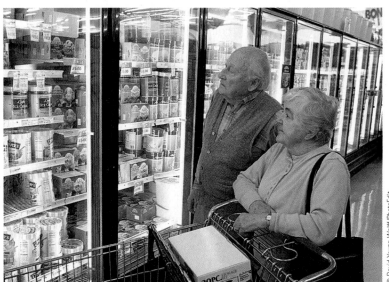

An older adult is likely to find the ice cream as efficiently as a younger adult in a familiar supermarket but may have difficulty with this visual search task if the supermarket is unfamiliar.

Basic Capacities

Sources of hearing problems range from excess wax buildup in the ears to infections to a sluggish nervous system. Most age-related hearing problems seem to originate in the inner ear, however (Fozard & Gordon-Salant, 2001). The cochlear hair cells that serve as auditory receptors, their surrounding structures, and the neurons leading from them to the brain degenerate gradually over the adult years. The most noticeable result is a loss of sensitivity to high-frequency or high-pitched sounds, the most common form of **presbycusis,** or problems of the aging ear. Thus an older person may have difficulty hearing a child's high voice, the flutes in an orchestra, and high-frequency consonant sounds such as *s*, *z*, and *ch* (Whitbourne, 2005) but may have less trouble with deep voices, tubas, and sounds such as *b*. After age 50, lower-frequency sounds also become increasingly difficult to hear (Kline & Scialfa, 1996). Thus, to be heard by the average older adult, a sound—especially a high-pitched sound but ultimately any sound—must be louder than it needs to be to exceed the auditory threshold of a younger adult.

Is this loss of hearing with age the inevitable result of basic aging processes, or is it caused by other factors? Researchers know that the loss is more noticeable among men than among women, that men are more likely to work in noisy industrial jobs, and that those who hold such jobs experience more hearing loss than other men (Martin & Clark, 2002; Reuben et al., 1998). But even when adults who have held relatively quiet jobs are studied, men show detectable hearing losses earlier in life (in their 30s) and lose hearing sensitivity at a faster rate than women do (Pearson et al., 1995). It seems, then, that most people, men more than women, will experience some loss of sensitivity to high-frequency sounds as part of the basic aging process, but that certain people will experience more severe losses because of their experiences.

Speech Perception

Perhaps the most important thing we do with our ears in everyday life is listening to other people during conversations. The ability to hear is one requisite for understanding speech, but this complex auditory perception task also depends on cognitive processes such as attention and memory. How well do aging adults do?

Older adults typically have more difficulty understanding conversation than younger adults do, even under ideal listening conditions. This age difference becomes smaller when differences in hearing are controlled but it does not entirely disappear (Schneider, Daneman, et al., 2000). Under poor listening conditions—for example, loud background noise—group differences between older and young adults are larger even when individual differences in hearing are accounted for (Schneider, Daneman, et al., 2000). Thus, older adults may recall fewer details of a conversation that takes place in a crowded, noisy restaurant. Age-related declines in hearing are partly responsible, but difficulty with segmenting the different sources of

speech in a conversation also seems to contribute to the observed declines in speech perception among older adults (Murphy, Daneman, & Schneider, 2006).

In addition, auditory perception tasks, like visual perception tasks, are more difficult for older people when they are novel and complex. In familiar, everyday situations, older adults are able to use contextual cues to interpret what they hear (Fozard & Gordon-Salant, 2001). In one study, for example, elderly adults were about as able as young adults to recall meaningful sentences they had just heard (Wingfield et al., 1985). However, they had serious difficulty repeating back grammatical sentences that made no sense or random strings of words, especially when these meaningless stimuli were spoken rapidly. So, an older person may be able to follow an ordinary conversation but not a technical presentation on an unfamiliar topic—especially if the speaker makes the task harder by talking too fast.

Overall, then, most older adults have only mild hearing losses, especially for high-frequency sounds, and only minor problems understanding everyday speech; in addition, they can compensate for their difficulties successfully—for example, by reading lips and relying on contextual cues. Novel and complex speech heard under poor listening conditions is likely to cause more trouble. Fortunately, there are ways older people can improve their hearing or compensate for its loss, as the Applications box on page 182 describes.

Taste and Smell

Does the aging of sensory systems also mean that older people become less able to appreciate tastes and aromas? Studies designed to measure taste thresholds suggest that with increasing age, some of us have more difficulty detecting weak taste stimulation—for example, a small amount of salt on food or a few drops of lemon juice in a glass of water (Mattes, 2002; Schiffman, 1997). Thus, older adults may report that food tastes bland and use larger amounts of salt and seasonings than they used when they were younger. In addition, both middle-aged and older adults sometimes have difficulty discriminating among tastes that differ in intensity (Nordin et al., 2003). In one study, for example, adults over 70 were less able than young adults to reliably judge one solution to be saltier, more bitter, or more acidic than another (Weiffenbach, Cowart, & Baum, 1986). Interestingly, older adults did not have difficulty distinguishing degrees of sweetness; people do not seem to lose the sweet tooth they are born with.

The ability to perceive odors also typically declines with age. Sensitivity to odors increases from childhood to early adulthood then declines during adulthood, more so with increasing age (Finkelstein & Schiffman, 1999; Ship et al., 1996). However, differences among age groups are usually small, and many older people retain their sensitivity to odors. The age decline depends on the type of odor: older adults can identify unpleasant odors just as well as younger adults, although they show some decline in their ability to identify pleasant odors

AIDING ADULTS WITH HEARING IMPAIRMENTS

In the earlier Applications box, we examined ways to help infants and children who have hearing impairments, often from birth. Here, we consider the other end of the life span. What can be done to assist hearing-impaired adults, most of whom were born with normal hearing? Unfortunately, many older adults are reluctant to admit that they have a hearing problem and do not seek assistance. And among those who admit to having a hearing problem, many refuse to wear a hearing aid because they feel it stigmatizes them as old, or they report that hearing aids do not work or do not help them to hear better (Lupsakko, Kautiainen, & Sulkava, 2005).

Those who do not have their hearing corrected may suffer depression, decreased independence, and strained relationships (Appollonio et al., 1996). Imagine how hard social interaction can become if you cannot understand what is being said, misinterpret what is said, or have to keep asking people to repeat what they said. One 89-year-old woman became extremely depressed and isolated: "There is an *awfulness* about silence. . . . I am days without speaking a word. It is affecting my voice. I fear for my mind. I cannot hear the alarm clock, telephone ring, door bell, radio, television—or the human voice" (Meadows-Orlans & Orlans, 1990, pp. 424–425). In contrast, among those older adults who do use hearing aids, quality of life improves (Vuorialho, Karinen, & Sorri, 2006). We tend to think of vision as our most important sense, but hearing impairments may be more disruptive than visual impairments to cognitive and social functioning. Still, many individuals cope well with their hearing impairments and maintain active, satisfying lifestyles.

Hearing aids, although beneficial, cannot restore normal hearing; they tend to distort sounds and to magnify background noise as well

as what the wearer is trying to hear. In addition, many older people are ill served by hearing aids that are of poor quality or that are poorly matched to their specific hearing problems. Because cochlear implants work best for individuals exposed to spoken language before they lost their hearing, elderly people are ideal candidates for them. They tolerate the surgical procedure required for implantation well, and their hearing-test scores increase significantly (Kelsall, Shallop, & Burnelli, 1995). In addition, adults who receive cochlear implants report that their quality of life improves significantly (Faber & Grontved, 2000). Cochlear implants, however, cannot work overnight miracles; it can take months, even years, to learn how to interpret the messages relayed by the implant to the brain (Colburn, 2000).

Finally, the physical and social environment can be modified to help people of all ages with hearing losses. For example, furniture can be arranged to permit face-to-face contact; lights can be turned on to permit use of visual cues such as gestures and lip movements. Then there are the simple guidelines we can follow to make ourselves understood by hearing-impaired people. One of the most important is to avoid shouting. Shouting not only distorts speech but also raises the pitch of the voice (therefore making it more difficult for elderly people to hear); it also makes it harder for the individual to read lips. It is best to speak at a normal rate, clearly but without overarticulating, with your face fully visible at a distance of about 3 to 6 feet.

With modern technology, appropriate education, effective coping strategies, and help from those who hear, hearing-impaired and deaf individuals of all ages can thrive.

(Konstantinidis, Hummel, & Larsson, 2006). Women are more likely than men to maintain their ability to label odors in scratch-and-sniff tests (Ship & Weiffenbach, 1993), partly because they are less likely than men to have worked in factories and been exposed to chemicals that could damage the chemical receptors involved in odor perception (Corwin, Loury, & Gilbert, 1995). Also, healthy adults of both sexes retain their sense of smell better than do those who have diseases, smoke, or take medications (Wilson et al., 2006). Again, then, perceptual losses in later life are part of the basic aging process but vary from person to person depending on environmental factors.

How do declines in the senses of taste and smell affect the older person's enjoyment of food? Susan Schiffman (1977) blindfolded young adults and elderly adults and asked them to identify blended foods by taste and smell alone. As ● Table 6.3 reveals, the older people were correct less often than the college students were. But was this because of a loss of taste sensitivity or smell sensitivity? Or was it a cognitive problem—difficulty coming up with the name of a food that was sensed?

Claire Murphy (1985) attempted to shed light on these questions by presenting young and elderly adults with 12 of the blended foods used by Schiffman. She observed that older

people often came up with the wrong specific label but the right idea (identifying sugar as fruit or salt as peanuts, for example). Thus, at least some of their difficulty may have been cognitive. Murphy also tested women whose nostrils were blocked and found that both young and elderly women did miserably when they could not smell and had to rely on taste alone. These findings suggest that a reduced ability to identify foods in old age is less because of losses in the sense of taste than because of the small losses in the sense of smell as well as declines in the cognitive skills required to remember and name what has been tasted (Murphy, Nordin, & Acosta, 1997).

If foods do not have much taste, an older person may lose interest in eating and may not get proper nourishment (Rolls, 1999). Alternatively, an older person may overuse seasonings such as salt or may eat spoiled food, which can threaten health in other ways. Yet these problems can be remedied. For example, when flavor enhancers were added to the food in one nursing home, elders ate more, gained muscle strength, and had healthier immune system functioning than they did when they ate the usual institutional fare (Schiffman & Warwick, 1993).

Conclusions about changes in taste and smell must be considered in perspective. These sensory and perceptual abilities are highly variable across the life span, not just in older

● TABLE 6.3   AGE DIFFERENCES IN RECOGNITION OF FOODS

PERCENTAGE RECOGNIZING FOOD

PUREED FOOD SUBSTANCE	COLLEGE STUDENTS (AGES 18–22)	ELDERLY PEOPLE (AGES 67–93)
FRUITS		
Apple	93%	79%
Banana	93%	59%
Pear	93%	86%
Pineapple	93%	86%
Strawberry	100%	79%
Tomato	93%	93%
VEGETABLES		
Broccoli	81%	62%
Cabbage	74%	69%
Carrot	79%	55%
Celery	89%	55%
Corn	96%	76%
Cucumber	44%	28%
Green bean	85%	62%
Green pepper	78%	59%
Potato	52%	59%
MEAT/FISH		
Beef	100%	79%
Fish	89%	90%
Pork	93%	72%
OTHER		
Rice	81%	55%
Walnut	33%	28%

Elderly adults have more difficulty than young college students in identifying most blended foods by taste and smell alone. Percentages of those recognizing food include reasonable guesses such as "orange" in response to "apple." Notice that some foods (for example, cucumber) are difficult for people of any age to identify by taste and smell alone. Appearance and texture are important to the recognition of such foods.

SOURCE: Schiffman, S. (1977). Food recognition by the elderly. *Journal of Gerontology, 32.* Reprinted by permission.

adulthood. Many older adults will not experience deficits: They can continue to smell the roses and enjoy their food.

Touch, Temperature, and Pain

By now, you have seen numerous indications that older adults are often less able than younger adults to detect weak sensory stimulation. This holds true for the sense of touch. The detection threshold for touch increases and sensitivity is gradually lost from middle childhood on (Erber, 2005). It is not clear that minor losses in touch sensitivity have many implications for daily life, however.

Similarly, older people may be less sensitive to changes in temperature than younger adults are (Frank et al., 2000). Some keep their homes too cool because they are unaware of being cold; others may fail to notice that it is too hot. Because older bodies are less able than younger ones to maintain an even temperature, elderly people face an increased risk of death in heat waves or cold snaps (Worfolk, 2000).

It seems only fair that older people should also be less sensitive to painful stimulation, but are they? They are indeed less likely than younger adults to report *weak* levels of stimulation as painful, although the age differences in pain thresholds are not large or consistent (Verrillo & Verrillo, 1985). Yet older people seem to be no less sensitive to stronger pain stimuli. Unfortunately, older adults are more likely to experience chronic pain than younger adults but are less likely to obtain adequate pain relief (Gloth, 2000). Adults with arthritis, osteoporosis, cancer, and other diseases who also experience depression and anxiety are especially likely to perceive pain. Treating these secondary conditions and administering effective pain relief can improve the daily functioning and psychological well-being of older adults.

The Adult in Perspective

Of all the changes in sensation and perception during adulthood that we have considered, those involving vision and hearing appear to be the most important and the most universal. Not only do these senses become less keen, but older people also use them less effectively in such complex perceptual tasks as searching a cluttered room for a missing book or following rapid conversation in a noisy room. Declines in the other senses are less serious and do not affect as many people.

Although people compensate for many sensory declines, their effects cannot be entirely eliminated. At some point, aging adults find that changes in sensory abilities affect their activities. As ● Table 6.4 shows, older adults with one or two sensory impairments are more likely to experience difficulty with basic tasks of living—walking, getting outside, getting in or out of bed or a chair, taking medicines, or preparing meals. Notice, however, that even older adults without sensory impairments report some difficulty with these tasks. People who are limited by sensory impairments usually have physical or intellectual impairments as well, most likely because of general declines in neural

ACTIVITY	WITH VISUAL IMPAIRMENTS	WITH HEARING IMPAIRMENTS	WITH BOTH VISUAL AND HEARING IMPAIRMENTS	WITHOUT VISUAL OR HEARING IMPAIRMENTS
Difficulty walking	43.3%	30.7%	48.3%	22.2%
Difficulty getting outside	28.6%	17.3%	32.8%	11.9%
Difficulty getting in or out of a bed or chair	22.1%	15.1%	25.0%	10.4%
Difficulty taking medicines	11.8%	7.7%	13.4%	5.0%
Difficulty preparing meals	18.7%	11.6%	20.7%	7.8%

SOURCE: Adapted from Campbell et al., 1999.

functioning that affect both perception and cognition (Baltes & Lindenberger, 1997; Salthouse et al., 1996). Most older adults, even those with sensory impairments, are engaged in a range of activities and are living full lives. Thus, although most adults will experience some declines in sensory abilities with age, these changes do not need to detract from their quality of life.

SUMMING UP

▌ During adulthood, sensory and perceptual capacities gradually decline in most individuals, although many changes are minor and can be compensated for. Changes in the lens, pupil, cornea, and retina of the eye contribute to decreased vision as we age.

▌ Hearing difficulty associated with aging most commonly involves loss of sensitivity to high-frequency (high-pitched) sounds. Hearing aids can significantly improve older adults' abilities to detect sounds. Even elderly people without significant hearing losses may experience difficulty understanding novel and complex speech spoken rapidly under poor listening conditions.

▌ Many older people have difficulty recognizing or enjoying foods, largely because of declines in the sense of smell and memory; touch, temperature, and pain sensitivity also decrease slightly, but intense pain stimuli still hurt.

CRITICAL THINKING

1. You have been hired to teach a cooking course to elderly adults. First, analyze the perceptual strengths and weaknesses of your students: What perceptual tasks might be easy for them, and what tasks might be difficult? Second, considering at least three senses, think of five strategies you can use to help your students compensate for the declines in perceptual capacities that some of them may be experiencing.

2. You are the coordinator for social and educational activities at your community center, which means you work with people of all ages, ranging from the youngest infants to the oldest adults. In planning activities, what is important to know about capturing and holding the attention of different age groups?

CHAPTER SUMMARY

6.1 ISSUES OF NATURE AND NURTURE

• Sensation is the detection of sensory stimulation and perception is the interpretation of what is sensed.

• Developmentalists and philosophers differ about whether basic knowledge of the world is innate (the nativist position) or must be acquired through the senses (the constructivist position).

6.2 THE INFANT

• Methods of studying infant perception include habituation, evoked potentials, preferential looking, and operant conditioning techniques.

• From birth, the visual system is working reasonably well, although improvements in visual acuity, visual accommodation, and color vision will occur over the first 6 to 12 months of life. Infants display certain visual preferences, including patterns that have contour, movement, and moderate complexity. Infants can perceive depth during their first year, but must learn how to use this information in order to steer clear of drop-offs once they begin to crawl.

• The auditory sense is well developed at birth. Very young infants can recognize their mother's voice and can make distinctions among speech sounds that adults may no longer be able to make. The other senses are also well developed at birth and become refined by the end of infancy.

• Infants develop cross-modal perception around 3 to 6 months of age, although this ability to recognize through one sense what was learned by a different sense continues to develop through later infancy and childhood.

• The early presence of sensory and perceptual abilities suggests that they are innate, but they are also clearly influenced by early experiences. Certain experiences may be necessary for normal visual perception to develop, suggesting a sensitive period for the visual system.

• Infants actively seek out stimulation by exploring their environments, which typically provides them with the stimulation they need to develop normal sensory and perceptual skills.

6.3 THE CHILD

- Sensory skills undergo little change during childhood, although children learn better how to use the information coming in through their senses.
- During childhood we learn to sustain attention for longer periods, to direct it more selectively (filtering out distracting information), and to plan and carry out more systematic perceptual searches.

6.4 THE ADOLESCENT

- During adolescence, the ability to sustain and control attention improves further, and sensation and perception are at peak levels.
- Exposure to loud noise, especially over an extended period of time, can lead to noise-induced hearing loss. Adolescents understand that this loss can occur, but do not rate it as an important health concern. Few teens take steps to protect their hearing.

6.5 THE ADULT

- Throughout adulthood, sensory abilities gradually decline. Sensory thresholds—the amount of stimulation required for detection—rise and perceptual processing of sensory information often declines.
- Visual changes include cataracts (clouding of the lens), reduced ability of the pupil to change in response to changes in light, thickening of the lens leading to decreased acuity (presbyopia), and retinal changes such as age-related macular degeneration and retinitis pigmentosa. Glaucoma, increased fluid pressure in the eye, becomes more common with age and can lead to blindness if untreated.
- Presbycusis—changes in hearing associated with aging—affects many older adults and most commonly leads to trouble detecting high-pitched sounds. Older adults have more difficulty with speech perception, especially under noisy conditions, than younger adults.
- Taste and smell decline slightly with old age, and sensitivity to touch, temperature, and pain also decrease.
- Changes in the sensory–perceptual systems can often be compensated for with, for example, corrective lenses for the eyes, amplification devices for the ears, and more spices for the taste buds. Moderate to severe declines that are not corrected can lead to declines in activities and quality of life among older adults.

KEY TERMS

MEDIA RESOURCES

BOOK COMPANION WEBSITE

academic.cengage.com/psychology/sigelman
Find online quizzes, flash cards, animations, video clips, experiments, interactive assessments, and other helpful study aids for this text at **academic.cengage.com/psychology/sigelman.** You can also connect directly to the following sites:

AGING BODY FUNDAMENTALS

This Merck Manual website contains a nice summary of the major physiological changes that occur with advancing age. Be sure to check out the chart describing common changes in specific body systems and the consequences of these changes.

AUDITORY DEVELOPMENTAL SCALE

This site contains a great summary of developmental milestones concerning listening, receptive language, and auditory memory skills from birth through age 6 years.

THE EYE DIGEST

This University of Illinois Eye & Ear Infirmary physicians-sponsored site contains information on all of the major age-related visual problems (e.g., cataracts, senile macular degeneration).

THE HUMAN BODY'S SENSES: HEARING THEME PAGE

A one-stop shop for web links on hearing including sites on the physiology of the ear and the basic auditory process.

UNDERSTANDING THE DATA: EXERCISES ON THE WEB

academic.cengage.com/psychology/sigelman
For additional insight on the data presented in this chapter, try out the exercise for this figure at **academic.cengage.com/psychology/sigelman:**

> **Unnumbered figure** in Explorations box titled "Aging Drivers"

CENGAGENOW

academic.cengage.com/login
Go to **academic.cengage.com/login** to link to CengageNOW, your online study tool. First take the Pre-Test for this chapter to get your Personalized Study Plan, which will identify topics you need to review and direct you to online resources. Then take the Post-Test to determine what concepts you have mastered and what you still need work on.

© Paul Conklin/PhotoEdit

LAURA (3 YEARS OLD), removing an opened can of soda from the refrigerator, to her mother: "Whose is this? It's not yours 'cause it doesn't have lipstick."

Matt (11 years old) wanted to go to a hobby store on Memorial Day. His mother, doubting it was open, told him to call. Matt went to the phone, returned, and said, "Let's go." They arrived to find the store

closed. The frustrated mother: "I thought you called." Matt: "I did, but they didn't answer, so I figured they were too busy to come to the phone" (DeLoache, Miller, & Pierroutsakos, 1998, p. 801).

▪ ▪ ▪

From an early age, humans think and reason about the world around them—sometimes coming to logical conclusions. At age 3, Laura shows remarkable logic when she concludes that a soda cannot be her mother's because it does not have lipstick on it. By contrast, Matt, age 11, does not use the rational powers we assume 11-year-olds possess, perhaps because his wishes get in the way.

In this chapter, we begin to examine the development of **cognition**—the activity of knowing and the processes through which knowledge is acquired and problems are solved. Humans are cognitive beings throughout the life span, but as the preceding examples suggest, their minds change in important ways. We concentrate on the influential theory of cognitive development proposed by Jean Piaget, who traced growth in cognitive capacities during infancy, childhood, and adolescence, and then ask what becomes of these capacities during adulthood. We also consider an alternative view: Lev Vygotsky's sociocultural perspective on cognitive development. Both theorists have changed how we think about cognitive functioning and education. We explore Piaget and Vygotsky's ideas for improving cognitive skills at the end of this chapter; we will revisit these ideas in Chapter 10 when we cover language and education.

7.1 PIAGET'S CONSTRUCTIVIST APPROACH

Piaget was an exceptional person. As you learned in Chapter 2, Piaget became intrigued by children's mistakes because he noticed that children of the same age often made similar kinds of mental mistakes—errors typically different from those made by younger or older children. Could these age-related differences in error patterns reflect developmental steps, or stages, in intellectual growth? Piaget thought so, and he devoted his life to studying *how* children think, not just *what* they know (Flavell, 1963). Although many of Piaget's ideas were initially formulated in the 1920s, there was little knowledge of his work in North America until the 1960s, when John Flavell's (1963) summary of Piaget's theory appeared in English.

Interested in basic questions of philosophy, Piaget defined his field of interest as **genetic epistemology**—the study of how humans come to know reality and basic dimensions of it such as space, time, and causality. Epistemology is the branch of philosophy that studies knowledge of reality, and *genetic* can be translated as *emergence* or *development*. In other words, Piaget

sought to shed new light on the nature of human knowledge by studying how children come to know the world.

His studies began with close observation of his own three children as infants: how they explored new toys, solved simple problems that he arranged for them, and generally came to understand themselves and their world. Later, Piaget studied larger samples of children through what has become known as his **clinical method,** a flexible question-and-answer technique used to discover how children think about problems. Consider the following exchange between Piaget and 6-year-old Van (Piaget, 1926, p. 293):

> Piaget: Why is it dark at night?
> Van: Because we sleep better, and so that it shall be dark in the rooms.
> Piaget: Where does the darkness come from?
> Van: Because the sky becomes grey.
> Piaget: What makes the sky become grey?
> Van: The clouds become dark.
> Piaget: How is that?
> Van: God makes the clouds become dark.

Many contemporary researchers consider the method imprecise because it does not involve asking standardized questions of all children tested, but Piaget (1926) believed that the investigator should have the flexibility to pursue an individual child's line of reasoning to fully understand that child's mind. Using his naturalistic observations of his own children and the clinical method to explore how children understand everything from the rules of games to the concepts of space and time, Piaget formulated his view of the development of intelligence.

What Is Intelligence?

Piaget's definition of intelligence reflects his background in biology: *intelligence is a basic life function that helps an organism adapt to its environment.* You can see adaptation when you watch a toddler figuring out how to work a jack-in-the-box, a school-age child figuring out how to divide treats among friends, or an adult figuring out how to operate a new digital camera. The newborn enters an unfamiliar world with few means of adapting to it other than working senses and reflexes. But Piaget viewed infants as active agents in their own development, learning about the world of people and things by observing, investigating, and experimenting.

Knowledge gained through active exploration takes the form of a scheme (sometimes called *schema* in the singular and

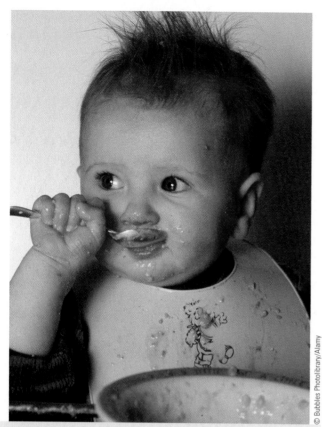

The grasping scheme. Infants have a range of behavioral schemes that allow them to explore new objects. Each scheme is a general pattern of behavior that can be adjusted to fit specific objects.

schemata in the plural). **Schemes** are cognitive structures—organized patterns of action or thought that people construct to interpret their experiences (Piaget, 1952, 1977). Schemes are like having a set of rules or procedures that structure our cognition (Meadows, 2006). For example, the infant's grasping actions and sucking responses are early behavioral schemes, patterns of action used to adapt to different objects. During their second year, children develop symbolic schemes, or concepts. They use internal mental symbols such as images and words to represent or stand for aspects of experience, such as when a young child sees a funny dance and carries away a mental model of how it was done. Older children become able to manipulate symbols in their heads to help them solve problems, such as when they add two numbers together in their heads rather than on paper or with the aid of their fingers.

As children develop more sophisticated schemes, or cognitive structures, they become increasingly able to adapt to their environments. Because they gain new schemes as they develop, children of different ages will respond to the same stimuli differently. The infant may get to know a shoe mainly as something to chew, the preschooler may decide to let the shoe symbolize or represent a telephone and put it to her ear, and the school-age child may mentally count its shoelace eyelets.

How Does Intelligence Develop?

Piaget took an interactionist position on the nature–nurture issue: Children are neither born with innate ideas nor programmed with knowledge by adults. Instead, Piaget viewed humans as active creators of their own intellectual development. As we noted in Chapter 2, Piaget took a position called *constructivism*, maintaining that children "construct reality," or actively create knowledge of the world, from their experiences (Siegler & Ellis, 1996). Their knowledge of the world takes the form of cognitive structures or schemes, which change as children organize and reorganize their existing knowledge and adapt to new experiences.

Piaget believed that all schemes—all forms of understanding—are created through the operation of two inborn intellectual functions, which he called organization and adaptation. These processes operate throughout the life span. Through **organization,** children systematically combine existing schemes into new and more complex ones. Thus, their minds are not cluttered with an endless number of independent facts; they contain instead logically ordered and interrelated actions and ideas. For example, the infant who gazes, reaches, and grasps will organize these simple schemes into the complex structure of visually directed reaching. Complex cognitive structures in older children grow out of reorganizations of simpler structures.

Adaptation is the process of adjusting to the demands of environment (Piaget, 1971). It occurs through two complementary processes, assimilation and accommodation. Imagine that you are a 2-year-old, that the world is still new, and that you see your first horse. What will you make of it? You likely will try to relate it to something familiar. **Assimilation** is the process by which we interpret new experiences in terms of existing schemes or cognitive structures. Thus, if you already have a scheme that mentally represents your knowledge of dogs, you may label this new beast "doggie." Through assimilation, we deal with our environment in our own terms, sometimes bending the world to squeeze it into our existing categories. Throughout the life span, we rely on our existing cognitive structures to understand new events.

But if you notice that this "doggie" is bigger than most dogs and that it has a mane and an awfully strange "bark," you may be prompted to change your understanding of the world of four-legged animals. **Accommodation** is the process of modifying existing schemes to better fit new experiences. Perhaps you will need to invent a new name for this animal or ask what it is and revise your concept of four-legged animals accordingly.

If we always assimilated new experiences, our understandings would never advance. Piaget believed that all new experiences are greeted with a mix of assimilation and accommodation. Once we have schemes, we apply them to make sense of the world, but we also encounter puzzles that force us to modify our understandings through accommodation. According to Piaget, when new events seriously challenge old schemes, or prove our existing understandings to be inadequate, we experience cognitive conflict. This cognitive conflict, or disequilibrium, then stimulates cognitive growth and the formation of more adequate understandings (Piaget, 1985; see ■ Figure 7.1). This occurs because mental conflict is not pleasant; we are motivated to reduce conflict through what Piaget called **equilibration,** the process of achieving mental stability where our internal thoughts are consistent with the evidence we are receiving from the external world (Piaget, 1978).

Intelligence, then, in Piaget's view, develops through the interaction of the individual with the environment. Nature provides the complementary processes of assimilation and accommodation that make adaptation to environments possible. The processes of adaptation and organization are driven by an innate tendency to maintain equilibration. As a result of the interaction of biological maturation and experience, humans progress through four distinct stages of cognitive development:

1. The sensorimotor stage (birth to roughly 2 years)
2. The preoperational stage (roughly 2 to 7 years)
3. The concrete operations stage (roughly 7 to 11 years)
4. The formal operations stage (roughly 11 years and beyond)

These stages represent qualitatively different ways of thinking and occur in an invariant sequence—that is, in the same order in all children. However, depending on their experiences, children may progress through the stages at different rates, with some moving more rapidly or more slowly than others. Thus, the age ranges associated with the stages are only averages. A child's stage of development is determined by his reasoning processes, not his age.

Equilibrium

Current understanding of the world (internal data) is consistent with external data.

Small furry animals with fluffy tails are called cats. They meow and smell nice.

Disequilibrium

Along comes a new piece of information that does not fit with current understanding of the world, leading to disequilibrium—an uncomfortable state of mind that the child seeks to resolve.

That's strange—this small furry creature has a fluffy tail but it doesn't meow and it certainly doesn't smell nice!

Assimilation and Accommodation

This unbalanced (confused) state can be resolved through the processes of organization and adaptation (assimilation and accommodation).

This can't be a cat. Mommy called it a skunk, which must be a different kind of animal.

Equilibrium

These lead to a new way of understanding the world— a new state of equilibrium.

I'll have to remember that skunks and cats are different types of animals.

■ **FIGURE 7.1** Process of change in Jean Piaget's theory.

SOURCE: From T. Brown & K.J. Thampy, *Translators, the equilibration of cognitive structures: The central problem of intellectual development.* Copyright © 1985 University of Chicago Press. Reprinted with permission.

- Piaget's theory focuses on how children acquire knowledge and solve problems. He used the clinical method, a flexible question-and-answer technique to uncover how children think about problems.

- According to Piaget, intelligence is a basic life function that helps an organism adapt to its environment.

- Piaget believed that children progress through four stages of cognitive development, creating more complex schemes or cognitive structures for understanding their world.

- Along with maturation and experience, two innate processes, organization and adaptation, drive children's new understandings. Adaptation involves the complementary processes of assimilating new experiences into existing understandings and accommodating existing understandings to new experiences.

CRITICAL THINKING

1. In Piaget's theory, how do children advance to higher levels of thinking and problem solving? What specific processes does Piaget propose for cognitive growth?

2. Provide a unique example from your experiences of how the inborn processes of organization and adaptation operate.

7.2 | THE INFANT

Piaget's sensorimotor stage, spanning the 2 years of infancy, involves coming to know the world through senses and actions. The dominant cognitive structures are behavioral schemes— patterns of action that evolve as infants begin to coordinate sensory input (seeing and mouthing an object) and motor responses (grasping it). Because infants solve problems through their actions rather than with their minds, their mode of thought is qualitatively different from that of older children.

Substages of the Sensorimotor Stage

The six substages of the sensorimotor stage are outlined in
● **Table 7.1.** At the start of the sensorimotor period, infants may not seem highly intelligent, but they are already active explorers of the world around them. Researchers see increasing signs of intelligent behavior as infants pass through the substages, because they are gradually learning about the world and about cause and effect by observing the effects of their actions. They are transformed from reflexive creatures who adapt to their environment using their innate reflexes to reflective ones who can solve simple problems in their heads.

The advances in problem-solving ability captured in the six substages of the sensorimotor period bring many important changes. Consider changes in the quality of infants' play activities. During the first month, young infants react reflexively to internal and external stimulation. In the primary circular reactions substage (1–4 months), they are more interested in their own bodies than in manipulating toys. Moving their tongues or fingers around is entertainment enough at this age. Piaget named this substage **primary circular reactions** because he observed infants repeating (hence, the term *circular*) actions relating to their own bodies (i.e., primary to themselves) that had initially happened by chance. Piaget reports the example of his son, Laurent, at just over 1 month accidentally getting

● TABLE 7.1   THE SUBSTAGES AND INTELLECTUAL ACCOMPLISHMENTS OF THE SENSORIMOTOR PERIOD

SUBSTAGE	DESCRIPTION
1. Reflex activity (birth to 1 month)	Active exercise and refinement of inborn reflexes (e.g., accommodate sucking to fit the shapes of different objects)
2. Primary circular reactions (1–4 months)	Repetition of interesting acts centered on the child's own body (e.g., repeatedly suck a thumb, kick legs, or blow bubbles)
3. Secondary circular reactions (4–8 months)	Repetition of interesting acts on objects (e.g., repeatedly shake a rattle to make an interesting noise or bat a mobile to make it wiggle)
4. Coordination of secondary schemes (8–12 months)	Combination of actions to solve simple problems (e.g., bat aside a barrier to grasp an object, using the scheme as a means to an end); first evidence of intentionality
5. Tertiary circular reactions (12–18 months)	Experimentation to find new ways to solve problems or produce interesting outcomes (e.g., explore bath-water by gently patting it then hitting it vigorously and watching the results, or stroke, pinch, squeeze, and pat a cat to see how it responds to varied actions)
6. Beginning of thought (18–24 months)	First evidence of insight; solve problems mentally, using symbols to stand for objects and actions; visualize how a stick could be used (e.g., move an out-of-reach toy closer); no longer limited to thinking by doing

his thumb in his mouth. It falls out. This happens again on another day. Indeed, since the first accidental occurrence, Piaget observes it happening over and over again. Increasingly, a finger or thumb successfully makes it into the mouth, which pleases Laurent. He seeks opportunities to repeat this pleasant action involving his body (alas, Laurent was not to be a thumb-sucker for very long—by 2 or 3 months of age, Piaget had bandaged his son's hands to bring this habit to an end).

By the third substage of secondary circular reactions (4–8 months), infants derive pleasure from repeatedly performing an action, such as sucking or banging a toy. Now the repetitive actions are called **secondary circular reactions** because they involve something in the infant's external environment (i.e., secondary to the self). In the fourth substage (8–12 months), called **coordination of secondary schemes**, infants combine (i.e., coordinate) secondary actions to achieve simple goals such as pushing an obstacle out of the way of reaching a desired object.

Later, when they reach the substage of tertiary circular reactions (12–18 months), infants experiment in varied ways with toys, exploring them thoroughly and learning all about their properties. In this stage, a true sense of curiosity and interest in novel actions appears. Piaget defined a **tertiary circular reaction** as "interest in novelty for its own sake" (Ginsburg & Opper, 1988, p. 57). Now it is interesting to the baby to repeat an action with variations, for example, the infant who experiments with all the many ways that oatmeal can land on the floor and walls when launched from a highchair in different directions and at different velocities.

With the final substage, the beginning of thought (about 18 months), comes the possibility of letting one object repre-

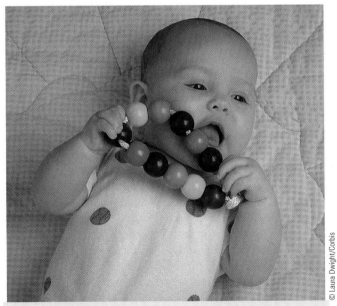

At 5 months, almost everything ends up in Eleanor's mouth. According to Jean Piaget, infants in the sensorimotor stage of development learn a great deal about their world by investigating it with their senses and acting motorically on this information.

sent another so that a cooking pot becomes a hat or a shoe becomes a telephone—a simple form of pretend play made possible by the capacity for symbolic thought. It is also in this stage, according to Piaget, that infants can imitate models no longer present, because they can now create and later recall mental representations of what they have seen.

The Development of Object Permanence

Another important change during the sensorimotor period concerns the infant's understanding of the existence of objects. According to Piaget, newborns lack an understanding of **object permanence** (also called *object concept*). This is the fundamental understanding that objects continue to exist—they are permanent—when they are no longer visible or otherwise detectable to the senses. It probably does not occur to you to wonder whether your coat is still in the closet after you shut the closet door (unless perhaps you have taken a philosophy course). But very young infants, because they rely so heavily on their senses, seem to operate as though objects exist only when they are perceived or acted on. According to Piaget, infants must construct the notion that reality exists apart from their experience of it.

Piaget believed that the concept of object permanence develops gradually over the sensorimotor period. Up through roughly 4 to 8 months, it is "out of sight, out of mind"; infants will not search for a toy if it is covered with a cloth or screen. By substage 4 (8–12 months), they master that trick but still rely on their perceptions and actions to "know" an object (Piaget, 1954). After his 10-month-old daughter, Jacqueline, had repeatedly retrieved a toy parrot from one hiding place, Piaget put it in a new spot while she watched him. Amazingly, she looked in the original hiding place. She seemed to assume that her behavior determined where the object would appear; she did not treat the object as if it existed apart from her actions or from its initial location. The surprising tendency of 8- to 12-month-olds to search for an object in the place where they last found it (A) rather than in its new hiding place (B) is called the **A-not-B error.** The likelihood of infants making the A-not-B error increases with lengthier delays between hiding and searching and with the number of trials in which the object is found in spot A (Marcovitch & Zelazo, 1999).

Some research suggests that task demands and physical limitations of infants influence performance on the A-not-B task (Lew et al., 2007). To evaluate this, Ted Ruffman and his colleagues (2005) conducted a series of studies and concluded that multiple factors do influence performance, but infants do indeed have a conceptual problem when it comes to understanding that the object is located at B and not at A.

In substage 5, the 1-year-old overcomes the A-not-B error but continues to have trouble with invisible displacements—as when you hide a toy in your hand, move your hand under a pillow, and then remove your hand, leaving the toy under the pillow. The infant will search where the object was last seen, seeming confused when it is not in your hand and failing to look under the pillow, where it was deposited. Finally, by 18

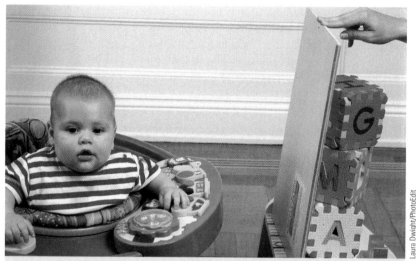

Until an infant masters the concept of object permanence, objects that are outside of his visual sight are "out of mind."

months or so, the infant is capable of mentally representing such invisible moves and conceiving of the object in its final location. According to Piaget, the concept of object permanence is fully mastered at this point.

Does research support Piaget? Recent studies suggest that infants may develop at least some understanding of object permanence far earlier than Piaget claimed (Baillargeon, 2002; Ruffman, Slade, & Redman, 2005). For example, Renee Baillargeon and her colleagues have used a method of testing for object concept that does not require reaching for a hidden object, only looking toward where it should be. In one study, infants as young as 2½ months seemed surprised (as demonstrated by looking longer) when a toy that had disappeared behind one screen (left side of ■Figure 7.2) reappeared from

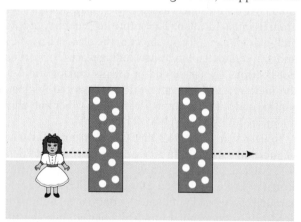

■ **FIGURE 7.2** Test stimuli used by Aguiar and Baillargeon (1999, 2002). The doll moves behind the screen on the left and reappears on the right side of the second screen without appearing in the space between the screens.
SOURCE: Aguiar & Baillargeon (2002), p. 271, part of Figure 1. Reprinted from *Cognitive Psychology, 45,* Developments of young infant's reasoning about occluded objects, Aguilar & Baillargeon, 267–336 © 2002 with permission from Elsevier.

behind a second screen (right side of Figure 7.2) *without* appearing in the open space between the two screens (Aguiar & Baillargeon, 1999).

At this young age, however, understanding of hidden objects is still limited. Consider the scenario shown in ■ **Figure 7.3.** In the high-window condition, a toy is hidden as it moves along a track behind a block that has a window located at its top. There is nothing odd about this condition. In the low-window condition, a toy *should* be visible as it moves along a track behind a block that has a window located at its bottom, but it is not. To someone who understands the properties of object permanence, this should strike them as odd. At 2½ months, infants do not show signs that they detect a difference between an object moving along a track under the high-window and low-window conditions. But, just 2 weeks later, 3-month-olds look longer at the low-window event compared with the high-window event (Aguiar & Baillargeon, 2002). Thus, by 3 months, infants have gained an understanding that objects have qualities that should permit them to be visible when nothing is obstructing them.

In an unusual study of toddlers' advanced understanding of object permanence, researchers compared healthy 2-year-olds with 2-year-olds with spinal muscular atrophy (SMA), which is characterized by normal IQ but severe muscle problems limiting children's movement (Riviere & Lecuyer, 2003). Based on Piaget's original reaching task, infants watch as a hand picks up a toy and then "visits" three separate cloths, depositing the toy under the second location before moving to the last cloth. Healthy toddlers incorrectly searched under the third cloth for the toy, whereas the SMA toddlers correctly searched under the second cloth. In a second study, researchers made healthy toddlers wait before they were allowed to search, and with this delay, they too responded correctly by searching under the second cloth. What explains this? Healthy toddlers may quickly and impulsively search at the location where an object is likely to be hidden (where the hand was last seen), but when given more time to think about it, they can go beyond their first impulsive response to search successfully. SMA toddlers have this extra time "built in." Because of their muscle problems, SMA toddlers are slower at searching and have less experience with manual searches than other children. They are less likely to make an impulsive reach in the wrong direction because of the time and effort required to reach. This research suggests that success at object permanence tasks may depend on more than a cognitive awareness of the properties of objects: success also could be influenced by task conditions such as the time interval between seeing something hidden and being able to search for it.

In general, then, it seems that babies sometimes know a good deal more about object permanence than they reveal through their actions when they are given the kinds of search tasks originally devised by Piaget (Baillargeon, 2002). Such findings, however, are not necessarily inconsistent with Piaget's

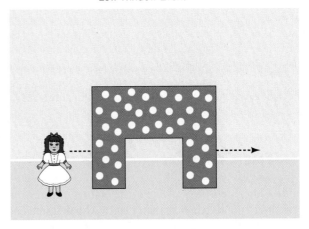

■ **FIGURE 7.3** There is nothing to be surprised about in the high-window event, but in the low-window event, the doll should (but does not) appear in middle space as it moves along the track.
SOURCE: Aguiar & Baillargeon (2002), p. 272, part of Figure 2.

findings (Haith & Benson, 1998). Indeed, Piaget contended that looking behaviors were developmental precursors to the reaching behaviors that he assessed. He did not believe, however, that looking represented complete understanding of object permanence (Fischer & Bidell, 1991; Haith & Benson, 1998). An analysis of infants' looking behaviors by Carolyn Rovee-Collier (2001) suggests that Piaget was wise to distinguish between infants' looking and reaching. In some situations, looking may developmentally precede reaching for an object, as Piaget suggested. In other situations, however, infants' actions may reveal a more sophisticated understanding of the world than looking would indicate. Regardless of the specific measure researchers use, infants gradually become more skilled at acting on their knowledge by searching in the right spot. They improve their looking and reaching skills between 8 and 12 months, and by the end of the sensorimotor period, they are masters of even very complex hide-and-seek games (Moore & Meltzoff, 1999; Newman, Atkinson, & Braddick, 2001).

The Emergence of Symbols

The crowning achievement of the sensorimotor stage is internalizing behavioral schemes to construct mental symbols that can guide future behavior. Now the toddler can experiment mentally and can therefore show a kind of insight into how to solve a problem. This new **symbolic capacity**—the ability to use images, words, or gestures to represent or stand for objects and experiences—enables more sophisticated problem solving. To illustrate, consider young Lucienne's actions after she watches her father—Piaget—place an interesting chain inside a matchbox (Piaget, 1952, pp. 337–338):

> [To open the box], she only possesses two preceding schemes: turning the box over in order to empty it of its contents, and sliding her fingers into the slit to make the chain come out. It is of course this last procedure that she tries first: she puts her finger

inside and gropes to reach the chain, but fails completely. A pause follows during which Lucienne manifests a very curious reaction. . . . She looks at the slit with great attention; then several times in succession, she opens and shuts her mouth, at first slightly, then wider and wider! [Then]. . . . Lucienne unhesitatingly puts her finger in the slit, and instead of trying as before to reach the chain, she pulls so as to enlarge the opening. She succeeds and grasps the chain.

Lucienne uses the symbol of opening and closing her mouth to "think" through the problem. In addition to permitting mental problem solving, the symbolic capacity will appear in the language explosion and pretend play so evident in the preschool years.

In all, children's intellectual achievements during the six substages of the sensorimotor period are remarkable. By its end, they have become deliberate thinkers with a symbolic capacity that allows them to solve some problems in their heads, and they have a grasp of object permanence and many other concepts.

SUMMING UP

❚ According to Piaget, infants progress through six substages of the sensorimotor period by perceiving and acting on the world; they progress from using their reflexes to adapt to their environment to using symbolic or representational thought to solve problems in their heads.

❚ The symbolic capacity that emerges during infancy permits full mastery of object permanence, or the understanding that objects continue to exist even when not perceived by the child.

❚ Basic object permanence emerges in substage 4 (8–12 months) although infants are limited by making the A-not-B error, which they usually overcome in substage 5 at around 1 year of age.

1. Suppose an infant fails to develop an understanding of object permanence. How would this deficit influence his or her behavior and knowledge of the world?

2. Trace the emergence of a behavior, such as producing a goal-directed behavior, through the six sensorimotor substages.

7.3 | THE CHILD

No one has done more to make us aware of the surprising turns that children's minds can take than Piaget, who described how children enter the preoperational stage of cognitive development in their preschool years and progress to the stage of concrete operations as they enter their elementary school years.

The Preoperational Stage

The preoperational stage of cognitive development extends from roughly 2 to 7 years of age. The symbolic capacity that emerged at the end of the sensorimotor stage runs wild in the preschool years and is the greatest cognitive strength of the preschooler. Imagine the possibilities: The child can now use words to refer to things, people, and events that are not physically present. Instead of being trapped in the immediate present, the child can refer to past and future. Pretend or fantasy play flourishes at this age: blocks can stand for telephones, cardboard boxes for trains. Some children—especially firstborns and only children who do not have ready access to play companions—even invent **imaginary companions** (Hoff, 2005a). Some of these imaginary companions are humans, and some are animals; they come with names like Zippy, Simply, Fake Rachel, and Sargeant Savage (Taylor et al., 2004). Their inventors know their companions are not real. Although par-

ents may worry about such flights of fancy, they are normal. In fact, imaginative uses of the symbolic capacity are associated with advanced cognitive and social development, as well as higher levels of creativity and imagery (Bouldin, 2006; Hoff, 2005b).

Yet the young child's mind is limited compared with that of an older child, and it was the limitations of preoperational thinking that Piaget explored most thoroughly. Although less so than infants, preschoolers are highly influenced by their immediate perceptions. They often respond as if they have been captured by, or cannot go beyond, the most perceptually salient aspects of a situation. This focus on **perceptual salience,** or the most obvious features of an object or situation, means that preschoolers can be fooled by appearances. They have difficulty with tasks that require them to use logic to arrive at the right answer. We can best illustrate this reliance on perceptions and lack of logical thought by considering Piaget's classic tests of conservation (also see the Explorations box).

Lack of Conservation

One of the many lessons about the physical world that children must master is the concept of **conservation**—the idea that certain properties of an object or substance do not change when its appearance is altered in some superficial way (see ■ **Figure 7.4**). So, find a 4- or 5-year-old and try Piaget's conservation-of-liquid-quantity task. Pour equal amounts of water into two identical glasses, and get the child to agree that she has the same amount of water. Then, as the child watches, pour the water from one glass into a shorter, wider glass. Now ask whether the two containers—the tall, narrow glass or the shorter, broader one—have the same amount of water to drink or whether one has more water. Children younger than 6 or 7 will usually say that the taller glass has more water than the shorter one. They lack the understanding that the volume of liquid is conserved despite the change in the shape it takes in different containers.

In this conservation-of-area-task, Rachel first determines that the yellow boards have the same amount of space covered by blocks. But after the blocks are rearranged on one of the boards, she fails to conserve area, indicating that one board now has more open space.

CAN THERE REALLY BE A SANTA CLAUS?

Many young children around the world believe in Santa Claus, St. Nicholas, the Tooth Fairy, or a similar magical being. Children whose parents endorse and promote Santa or another mythical being are more likely to believe than children whose parents do not (Harris et al., 2006; Woolley et al., 2004). After all, children normally trust their parents and accept their statements about Santa at face value.

At what point, and why, do their beliefs in these figures begin to waiver? Research with 5- and 6-year-old children shows that they are already somewhat less confident about the existence of Santa and the Tooth Fairy than they are about two invisible but scientifically proven entities—germs and oxygen (Harris et al., 2006). According to Piaget's theory, children would begin to seriously question the existence of Santa Claus when they acquire concrete-operational thought. With their ability to reason logically, they may begin to ask questions such as, "How can Santa Claus get around to all those houses in one night?" "How can one sleigh hold all those gifts?" "Why haven't I ever seen a reindeer fly?" and "How does Santa get into houses without chimneys?" What made sense to the preoperational child no longer

adds up to the logical, concrete-operational thinker. With their focus on static endpoints, preschool-age children may not have a problem imagining presents for all the children in the world (or at least, those on the "nice" list) sitting at the North Pole waiting to be delivered and then sitting under decorated trees Christmas morning. But once children understand transformations, they are confronted with the problem of how all those presents get from the North Pole to the individual houses in record time. The logical thinker notes that the gifts under the tree are wrapped in the same paper that Mom has in her closet. Some children question why gifts sport certain brand labels if Santa and his elves spent the year making gifts in their workshop.

As adults, we can resolve some of these inconsistencies for children to help maintain children's beliefs in Santa Claus. We can, for example, point out that Santa has many helpers and that reindeer native to the North Pole are unlike those ever seen in the wild or in a zoo. Some parents who want to perpetuate the Santa myth get tough and simply tell their children that nonbelievers will not get any presents. So the level of cognitive development and the surrounding culture play roles in whether or not children believe in Santa Claus and for how long.

How can young children be so easily fooled by their perceptions? According to Piaget, the preschooler is unable to engage in **decentration**—the ability to focus on two or more dimensions of a problem at once. Consider the conservation task: the child must focus on height and width simultaneously and recognize that the increased width of the short, broad container compensates for its lesser height. Preoperational thinkers engage in **centration**—the tendency to center attention on a single aspect of the problem. They focus on height alone and conclude that the taller glass has more liquid; or, alternatively, they focus on width and conclude that the short, wide glass has more. In this and other ways, preschoolers seem to have one-track minds.

A second contributor to success on conservation tasks is **reversibility**—the process of mentally undoing or reversing an action. Older children often display mastery of reversibility by suggesting that the water be poured back into its original container to prove that it is still the same amount. The young child shows irreversibility of thinking and may insist that the water

would overflow the glass if it were poured back. Indeed, one young child tested by a college student shrieked, "Do it again!" as though pouring the water back without causing the glass to overflow were some unparalleled feat of magic.

Finally, preoperational thinkers fail to demonstrate conservation because of limitations in **transformational thought**—the ability to conceptualize transformations, or processes of change from one state to another, as when water is poured from one glass to another (see Figure 7.4). Preoperational thinkers engage in **static thought,** or thought that is fixed on end states rather than the changes that transform one state into another, as when the water is sitting in the two glasses not being poured or manipulated.

Preoperational children do not understand the concept of conservation, then, because they engage in centration, irreversible thought, and static thought. The older child, in the stage of concrete operations, has mastered decentration, reversibility, and transformational thought. The correct answer to the

Liquids:

Two identical beakers are filled to the same level, and the child agrees that they have the same amount to drink.

Contents of one beaker are poured into a different-shaped beaker so that the two columns of water are of unequal height.

Conserving child recognizes that each beaker has the same amount to drink (on average, conservation of liquids is attained at age 6–7 years).

Mass (continuous substance):

Two identical balls of playdough are presented. The child agrees that they have equal amounts of dough.

One ball is rolled into the shape of a sausage.

Conserving child recognizes that each object contains the same amount of dough (average age, 6–7).

Number:

Child sees two rows of beads and agrees that each row has the same number.

One row of beads is increased in length.

Conserving child recognizes that each row still contains the same number of beads (average age, 6–7).

Area:

The child sees two identical sheets, each covered by the same number of blocks. The child agrees that each sheet has the same amount of uncovered area.

The blocks on one sheet are scattered.

Conserving child recognizes that the amount of uncovered area remains the same for each sheet (average age, 9–10).

Volume (water displacement):

Two identical balls of clay are placed in two identical beakers that had been judged to have the same amount to drink. The child sees the water level rise to the same point in each beaker.

One ball of clay is taken from the water, molded into a different shape, and placed above the beaker. Child is asked whether the water level will be higher than, lower than, or the same as in the other beaker when the clay is reinserted into the water.

Conserving child recognizes that the water levels will be the same because nothing except the shape of the clay has changed — that is, the pieces of clay displace the same amount of water (average age, 9–12).

■ **FIGURE 7.4** Some common tests of the child's ability to conserve.

SOURCE: From R. Gelman, The nature and development of early number concepts, H.W. Reese (ED.), *Advances in Child Development and Behavior,* 7. Copyright © 1972 by Academic Press. Reprinted with permission of Elsevier.

conservation task is a matter of logic to the older child; there is no longer a need to rely on perception as a guide. Indeed, a 9-year-old tested by another of our students grasped the logic so well and thought the question of which glass had more water so stupid that she asked, "Is this what you do in college?"

Egocentrism

Piaget believed that preoperational thought also involves **egocentrism**—a tendency to view the world solely from one's own perspective and to have difficulty recognizing other points of view. For example, he asked children to choose the drawing that shows what a display of three mountains would look like from a particular vantage point. Young children often chose the view that corresponded to their own position (Piaget & Inhelder, 1956). Similarly, young children often assume that if they know something, other people do, too (Ruffman & Olson, 1989). The same holds for desires: the 4-year-old who wants to go to McDonald's for dinner may say that Mom and Dad want to go to McDonald's, too, even if Mom does not like burgers or chicken nuggets and Dad would rather order Chinese takeout.

Difficulty with Classification

The limitations of relying on perceptions and intuitions are also apparent when preoperational children are asked to classify objects and think about classification systems. When 2- or 3-year-old children are asked to sort objects on the basis of similarities, they make interesting designs or change their sorting criteria from moment to moment. Older preoperational children can group objects systematically on the basis of shape, color, function, or some other dimension of similarity (Inhelder & Piaget, 1964). However, even children ages 4 to 7 have trouble thinking about relations between classes and subclasses or between

wholes and parts (Siegler & Svetina, 2006). ■ **Figure 7.5** illustrates the class inclusion problem. Given a set of furry animals, most of which are dogs but some of which are cats, preoperational children do fine when they are asked whether all the animals are furry and whether there are more dogs than cats. That is, they can conceive of the whole class (furry animals) or of the two subclasses (dogs and cats). However, when the question is, "Which group would have more—the dogs or the animals?" many 5-year-olds say, "dogs." They cannot simultaneously relate the whole class to its parts; they lack what Piaget termed the concept of **class inclusion**—the logical understanding that the parts are included within the whole. Notice that the child centers on the most striking perceptual feature of the problem—dogs are more numerous than cats—and is again fooled by appearances. Performance on class inclusion tasks increases steadily throughout childhood, as shown in ■ **Figure 7.6**.

Did Piaget Underestimate the Preschool Child?

Are preschool children really as bound to perceptions and as egocentric as Piaget believed? Many developmentalists believe that Piaget underestimated the competencies of preschool children by giving them very complex tasks to perform (Bjorklund, 1995). Consider a few examples of the strengths uncovered by researchers using simpler tasks.

Rochel Gelman (1972) simplified Piaget's conservation-of-number task (refer back to Figure 7.4) and discovered that children as young as 3 have some grasp of the concept that number remains the same even when items are rearranged spatially. She first got children to focus their attention on number by playing a game in which two plates, one holding two toy mice and one with three toy mice, were presented; and the plate with the larger number was always declared the winner. Then Gelman started introducing changes, sometimes adding

■ **FIGURE 7.5** A typical class inclusion problem in which children are asked whether there are more dogs or more animals in the picture.
SOURCE: From R.S. Siegler & J. Svetina, What leads children to adopt new strategies? A microgenetic/cross-sectional study of class inclusion, *Child Development, 77,* pp. 997–1015. Copyright © 2006, Blackwell Publishing. Reprinted with permission.

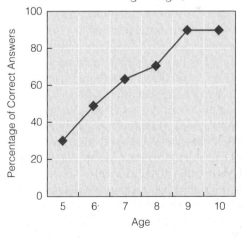

■ **FIGURE 7.6** Between the ages of 5 and 10, children steadily improve on class inclusion problems. At age 5, only 30% of children answer correctly, but by age 9 and 10, nearly all the children "get" the class inclusion problem.
SOURCE: Siegler, R. S. and Svetina, J. (2006). What leads children to adopt new strategies? A microgenetic/cross-sectional study of class inclusion, *Child Development, 77,* 997–1015.

or subtracting mice but sometimes just bunching up or spreading out the mice. Young children were not fooled by spatial rearrangements; they seemed to understand that number remained the same. However, they showed their limitations when given larger sets of numbers they could not count.

Similarly, by reducing tasks to the bare essentials, several researchers have demonstrated that preschool children are not as egocentric as Piaget claimed. In one study, 3-year-olds were shown a card with a dog on one side and a cat on the other (Flavell et al., 1981). The card was held vertically between the child (who could see the dog) and the experimenter (who could see the cat). When children were asked what the experimenter could see, these 3-year-olds performed flawlessly.

Finally, preschool children seem to have a good deal more understanding of classification systems than Piaget believed. Sandra Waxman and Thomas Hatch (1992) asked 3- and 4-year-olds to teach a puppet all the different names they could think of for certain animals, plants, articles of clothing, and pieces of furniture. The goal was to see whether children knew terms associated with familiar classification hierarchies—for example, if they knew that a rose is a type of flower and is a member of the larger category of plants. Children performed well, largely because a clever method of prompting responses was used. Depending on which term or terms the children forgot to mention (rose, flower, or plant), they were asked about the rose: "Is this a dandelion?" "Is this a tree?" "Is this an animal?" Often, children came up with the correct terms in response (for example, "No, silly, [it's not an animal] it's a plant!"). Even though young children typically fail the tests of class inclusion that Piaget devised, then, they appear to have a fairly good grasp of familiar classification hierarchies.

Studies such as these have raised important questions about the adequacy of Piaget's theory and have led to a more careful consideration of the demands placed on children by cognitive assessment tasks. Simplified tasks that focus youngsters' attention on relevant aspects of the task and do not place heavy demands on their memories or verbal skills tend to reveal that young children develop sound understandings of the physical world earlier than Piaget thought. Yet Piaget was right in arguing that preschool children, although they have several sound intuitions about the world, are more perception-bound and egocentric thinkers than elementary school children are. Preschool children still depend on their perceptions to guide their thinking, and they fail to grasp the logic behind concepts such as conservation. They also have difficulty applying their emerging understanding to complex tasks that involve coordinating two or more dimensions.

The Concrete Operations Stage

About the time children start elementary school, their minds undergo another transformation. Piaget's third stage of cognitive development extends from roughly 7 to 11 years of age. The concrete operations stage involves mastering the logical operations missing in the preoperational stage—becoming able to perform mental actions on objects, such as adding and subtracting Halloween candies, classifying dinosaurs, or arranging objects from largest to smallest. This allows school-age children to think effectively about the objects and events they experience in everyday life. For every limitation of the preoperational child, there is a corresponding strength of the concrete-operational child. These contrasts are summarized in ● Table 7.2.

Conservation

Given the conservation-of-liquid task (refer again to Figure 7.4), the preoperational child centers on either the height or the width of the glasses, ignoring the other dimension. The concrete-operational child can decenter and juggle two dimensions at once. Reversibility allows the child to mentally reverse the pouring process and imagine the water in its original container. Transformational thought allows the child to better understand the process of change involved in pouring the water. Overall, armed with logical operations, the child now knows that there must be the same amount of water after it is poured into a different container; the child has logic, not just appearance, as a guide.

Looking back at the conservation tasks in Figure 7.4, you will notice that some forms of conservation (for example, mass and number) are understood years earlier than others (area or volume). Piaget maintained that operational abilities evolve in a predictable order as simple skills that appear early are reorganized into increasingly complex skills. He used the term **horizontal décalage** for the idea that different cognitive skills related to the same stage of cognitive development emerge at different times.

Seriation and Transitivity

To appreciate the nature and power of logical operations, consider the child's ability to think about relative size. A preoperational child given a set of sticks of different lengths and asked to arrange them from biggest to smallest is likely to struggle, awkwardly comparing one pair of sticks at a time. Concrete-operational children are capable of the logical operation of **seriation**, which enables them to arrange items mentally along a quantifiable dimension such as length or weight. Thus they perform this seriating task quickly and correctly.

Concrete-operational thinkers also master the related concept of **transitivity**, which describes the necessary relations among elements in a series. If, for example, John is taller than Mark, and Mark is taller than Sam, who is taller—John or Sam? It follows logically that John must be taller than Sam, and the concrete operator grasps the transitivity of these size relationships. Lacking the concept of transitivity, the preoperational child will need to rely on perceptions to answer the question; she may insist that John and Sam stand next to each other to determine who is taller. Preoperational children probably

TABLE 7.2 COMPARISON OF PREOPERATIONAL AND CONCRETE-OPERATIONAL THINKING

PREOPERATIONAL THINKERS	CONCRETE-OPERATIONAL THINKERS
Fail conservation tasks because they have:	Solve conservation tasks because they have:
• *Irreversible thought*—Cannot mentally undo an action	• *Reversibility of thought*—Can mentally reverse or undo an action
• *Centration*—Center on a single aspect of a problem rather than two or more dimensions at once	• *Decentration*—Can focus on two or more dimensions of a problem at once
• *Static thought*—Fail to understand transformations or processes of change from one state to another	• *Transformational thought*—Can understand the process of change from one state to another
Perceptual salience. Understanding is driven by how things look rather than derived from logical reasoning.	*Logical reasoning.* Children acquire a set of internal operations that can be applied to a variety of problems.
Transductive reasoning. Children combine unrelated facts, often leading them to draw faulty cause–effect conclusions simply because two events occur close together in time or space.	*Deductive reasoning.* Children draw cause–effect conclusions logically, based on factual information presented to them.
Egocentrism. Children have difficulty seeing things from other perspectives and assume that what is in their mind is also what others are thinking.	*Less egocentrism.* Children understand that other people may have thoughts different from their own.
Single classification. Children classify objects by a single dimension at one time.	*Multiple classification.* Children can classify objects by multiple dimensions and can grasp class inclusion.

have a better understanding of such transitive relations than Piaget gave them credit for (Gelman, 1978; Trabasso, 1975), but they still have difficulty grasping the logical necessity of transitivity (Chapman & Lindenberger, 1988).

Other Advances

The school-age child overcomes much of the egocentrism of the preoperational period, becoming increasingly better at recognizing other people's perspectives. Classification abilities improve as the child comes to grasp the concept of class inclusion and can bear in mind that subclasses (brown beads and white beads) are included in a whole class (wooden beads). Mastery of mathematical operations improves the child's ability to solve arithmetic problems and results in an interest in measuring and counting things precisely (and sometimes in fury if companions do not keep accurate score in games). Overall, school-age children appear more logical than preschoolers because they possess a powerful arsenal of "actions in the head."

But surely, if Piaget proposed a fourth stage of cognitive development, there must be some limitations to concrete operations. Indeed, there are. This mode of thought is applied to objects, situations, and events that are real or readily imaginable (thus the term *concrete operations*). As you will see in the next section, concrete operators have difficulty thinking about abstract ideas and unrealistic hypothetical propositions.

SUMMING UP

▌ In Piaget's preoperational stage (ages 2–7), children make many uses of their symbolic capacity but are limited by their dependence on appearances, lack of logical mental operations, and egocentrism. They fail to grasp the concept of conservation because they engage in centration, irreversible thinking, and static thought, although recent research suggests that preschool children's capacities are greater than Piaget supposed.

▌ School-age children enter the stage of concrete operations (ages 7–11) and begin to master conservation tasks by using their newly acquired mental abilities of decentration, reversibility, and transformational thought. They can think about relations, grasping seriation and transitivity, and they understand the concept of class inclusion.

CRITICAL THINKING

1. Compare the concrete-operational thinker to the preoperational thinker. What tasks can the concrete-operational child do that the preoperational child cannot solve? What cognitive skills account for these differences?

Although tremendous advances in cognition occur from infancy to the end of childhood, other transformations of the mind are in store for the adolescent. If teenagers become introspective, question their parents' authority, dream of perfect worlds, and contemplate their futures, cognitive development may help explain why.

The Formal Operations Stage

Piaget set the beginning of the formal operations stage of cognitive development around age 11 or 12 and possibly later. If concrete operations are mental actions on objects (tangible things and events), formal operations are mental actions on ideas. Thus the adolescent who acquires formal operations can mentally juggle and think logically about ideas, which cannot be seen, heard, tasted, smelled, or touched. In other words, formal-operational thought is more hypothetical and abstract than concrete-operational thought; it also involves adopting a more systematic and scientific approach to problem solving (Inhelder & Piaget, 1964).

Hypothetical and Abstract Thinking

If you could have a third eye and put it anywhere on your body, where would you put it, and why? That question was posed to 9-year-old fourth-graders (concrete operators) and to 11- to 12-year-old sixth-graders (the age when the first signs of formal operations often appear). In their drawings, all the 9-year-olds placed the third eye on their foreheads between their existing eyes; many thought the exercise was stupid. The 11- and 12-year-olds were not as bound by the realities of eye location. They could invent ideas contrary to fact (for example, the idea of an eye in a palm) and think logically about the implications of such ideas (see ■ **Figure 7.7**). Thus, concrete operators deal with realities, whereas formal operators can deal with possibilities, including those that contradict known reality.

Formal-operational thought is also more abstract than concrete-operational thought. The school-age child may define the justice system in terms of police and judges; the adolescent may define it more abstractly as a branch of government concerned with balancing the rights of different interests in society. Also, the school-age child may be able to think logically about concrete and factually true statements, as in this syllogism: If you drink poison, you will die. Fred drank poison. Therefore, Fred will die. The adolescent can do this but also engage in such if–then thinking about contrary-to-fact statements ("If you drink milk, you will die") or symbols (If P, then Q. P, therefore, Q).

Problem Solving

Formal operations also permit systematic and scientific thinking about problems. One of Piaget's famous tests for formal-operational thinking is the pendulum task (see ■ **Figure 7.8**). The child is given several weights that can be tied to a string to make a pendulum and is told that he may vary the length of the string, the amount of weight attached to it, and the height from which the weight is released to find out which of these factors,

■ **FIGURE 7.7** Where would you put a third eye? Tanya (age 9) did not show much inventiveness in drawing her "third eye." But Ken (age 11) said of his eye on top of a tuft of hair, "I could revolve the eye to look in all directions." John (also 11) wanted a third eye in his palm: "I could see around corners and see what kind of cookie I'd get out of the cookie jar." Ken and John show early signs of formal-operational thoughts.

The child is shown how four factors can be varied.

A pendulum is made by hanging a weight at the end of a string fixed at the other end. If released from A, it swings at a regular rate.

Length of string

Weight

Point of release

Amount of impetus

Find out which of these factors makes the pendulum go faster or slower.

■ **FIGURE 7.8** The pendulum problem.

SOURCE: From E. Labinowicz, The pendulum problem, *The Piaget primer*, p. 83. Copyright © 1980 Pearson Education. Reprinted with permission.

alone or in combination, determines how quickly the pendulum makes its arc. How would you go about solving this problem?

The concrete operator is likely to jump right in without much advanced planning, using a trial-and-error approach. That is, the child may try a variety of things but fail to test different hypotheses systematically—for example, the hypothesis that the shorter the string is, the faster the pendulum swings, all other factors remaining constant. Concrete operators are therefore unlikely to solve the problem. They can draw proper conclusions from their observations—for example, from watching as someone else demonstrates what happens if a pendulum with a short string is compared with a pendulum with a long string.

What will the formal-operational individual do? In all likelihood, the child will first sit and think, planning an overall strategy for solving the problem. All the possible hypotheses should be generated; after all, the one overlooked may be the right one. Then it must be determined how each hypothesis can be tested. This is a matter of **hypothetical-deductive reasoning,** or reasoning from general ideas to their specific implications. In the pendulum problem, it means starting with a hypothesis and tracing the specific implications of this idea in an if–then fashion: "If the length of the string matters, then I should see a difference when I compare a long string with a short string while holding other factors constant." The trick in hypothesis testing is to vary each factor (for example, the length of the string) while holding all others constant (the weight, the height from which the weight is dropped, and so on). (It is, by the way, the length of the string that matters; the shorter the string, the faster the swing.)

In sum, formal-operational thought involves being able to think systematically about hypothetical ideas and abstract concepts. It also involves mastering the hypothetical-deductive approach that scientists use—forming many hypotheses and systematically testing them through an experimental method.

Progress toward Mastery

Are 11- and 12-year-olds really capable of all these sophisticated mental activities? Anyone who has had dealings with this age group will know that the answer to this question is usually not. Piaget (1970) described the transition from concrete operations

to formal operations as taking place gradually over years. Many researchers have found it useful to distinguish between early and late formal operations. For example, 11- to 13-year-olds just entering the formal operations stage are able to consider simple hypothetical propositions such as the three-eye problem. But most are not yet able to devise an overall game plan for solving a problem or to systematically generate and test hypotheses. These achievements are more likely later in adolescence.

Consider the findings of Suzanne Martorano (1977), who gave 80 girls in grades 6, 8, 10, and 12 a battery of 10 Piagetian tasks. Among them were the pendulum problem; a task requiring students to identify all the possible combinations of chemicals that could produce a particular chemical reaction; and analyzing how the behavior of a balance beam is affected by the heaviness of weights on the beam and their distances from the fulcrum, or center. The 6th- and 8th-graders (ages 11–12 and 13–14) accomplished only 2 or 3 of the 10 tasks on the average; the 10th- and 12th-graders (ages 15–16 and 17–18) accomplished an average of 5 or 6. Similarly, 10th- and 11th-graders (ages 16–17) demonstrate more advanced scientific reasoning than 7th- and 8th-graders (ages 13–14) when asked to consider evidence and evaluate theories regarding religion and social class (Klaczynski, 2000). Still, the responses of older adolescents contain biases similar to those shown by younger adolescents. Both age groups more readily accept evidence consistent with their preexisting beliefs than evidence inconsistent with these beliefs (Klaczynski & Gordon, 1996a, 1996b; Kuhn, 1993). Thus, although reasoning skills improve over the adolescent years, adolescents do not consistently show formal operations and logical scientific reasoning skills on all tasks (Klaczynski & Narasimham, 1998).

Contrary to Piaget's claim that intuitive reasoning is replaced by scientific reasoning as children age, the two forms of reasoning—intuitive and scientific—seem to coexist in older thinkers (Klaczynski, 2000, 2001). Being able to shift between intuitive and scientific reasoning provides flexibility in problem-solving situations as long as the thinker can effectively select the appropriate strategy. However, like children (and adults), adolescents often seem to adopt an intuitive strategy, leading them to conclusions inconsistent with scientific judgment (Klaczynski, 2001). With age, however, adolescents are

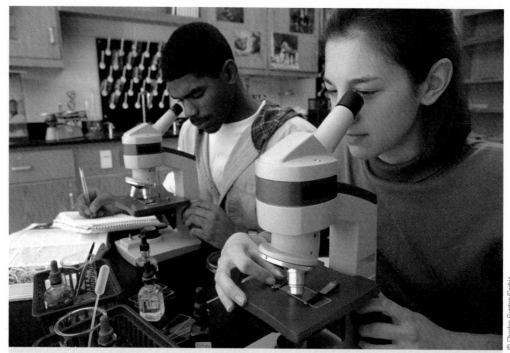

Adolescents are more likely than children to benefit from some types of science instruction because formal-operational thought opens the door for reasoning about abstract and hypothetical material.

increasingly able to **decontextualize,** or separate prior knowledge and beliefs from the demands of the task at hand (Klaczynski, 2000; Stanovich & West, 1997). For example, someone who believes that males are better at math than females may find it difficult to accept new evidence that girls attain higher classroom math grades than boys if their prior beliefs (their intuitions) do not allow them to scientifically process the new information. Decontextualizing increases the likelihood of using reasoning to analyze a problem logically rather than relying on intuition or faulty existing knowledge.

There is some evidence that today's teens (ages 13–15) are better able than earlier cohorts to solve formal-operational tasks. For example, 66% of teens tested in 1996 showed formal-operational thought on a probability test, whereas 49% of teens tested in 1967 showed such skills (Flieller, 1999). Why might formal-operational skills improve over time? Changes in school curricula are the likely explanation. Notably, science curriculums were revised in the 1960s and have increasingly incorporated more hands-on discovery learning activities (Bybee, 1995). The achievement of formal-operational thinking depends on specific experiences, such as exposure to math and science education (Karpov, 2005). The more hands-on the learning, the greater the benefit on traditional hands-on formal-operational tasks.

Several cross-cultural studies have taken advantage of naturally occurring groups that differ in whether or not adults have had structured schooling. The results of such research shows that both age and education level influence performance on formal-operational tasks. For instance, adults with some formal education are able to solve logic problems whereas those adults in the same culture with no formal education are not able to do so (Luria, 1974/1976). Similarly, college and university students outperform adults with no advanced education in solving certain types of formal logic problems, who in turn outperform adolescents who have not yet acquired as much education (Mwamwenda & Mwamwenda, 1989; Mwamwenda, 1999).

Progress toward the mastery of formal operations is slow, at least as measured by Piaget's scientific tasks. These findings have major implications for secondary-school teachers, who are often trying to teach abstract material to students with a range of thinking patterns. Teachers may need to give concrete thinkers extra assistance by using specific examples and demonstrations to help clarify general principles.

Implications of Formal Thought

Formal-operational thought contributes to other changes in adolescence—some good, some not so good. First, the good news: As you will see in upcoming chapters, formal-operational thought may prepare the individual to gain a sense of identity, think in more complex ways about moral issues, and understand other people. Advances in cognitive development help lay the groundwork for advances in many other areas of development, including their appreciation of humor as shown in the Explorations Box on page 204.

Now, the bad news: Formal operations may also be related to some of the more painful aspects of the adolescent experience. Children tend to accept the world as it is and to heed the words of authority figures. The adolescent armed with formal operations can think more independently, imagine alternatives to present realities, and raise questions about everything from why parents set certain rules to why there is injustice in the world. Questioning can lead to confusion and sometimes to rebellion against ideas that do not seem logical enough. Some adolescents become idealists, inventing perfect worlds and envisioning logical solutions to problems they detect in the imperfect world around them, sometimes losing sight of practical considerations and real barriers to social change. Just as infants flaunt the new schemes they develop, adolescents may go overboard with their new cognitive skills, irritate their parents, and become frustrated when the world does not respond to their flawless logic.

Some years ago, David Elkind (1967) proposed that formal-operational thought also leads to **adolescent egocentrism**—difficulty differentiating one's own thoughts and feelings from those of other people. The young child's egocentrism is rooted in ignorance that different people have different perspectives, but the adolescent's reflects an enhanced ability to reflect about one's own and others' thoughts. Elkind identified two types of adolescent egocentrism: the imaginary audience and the personal fable.

The **imaginary audience** phenomenon involves confusing your own thoughts with those of a hypothesized audience for your behavior. Thus, the teenage girl who ends up with pizza sauce on the front of her shirt at a party may feel extremely self-conscious: "They're all thinking what a slob I am! I wish I could crawl into a hole." She assumes that everyone in the room is as preoccupied with the blunder as she is. Or a teenage boy may spend hours in front of the mirror getting ready for a date then may be so concerned with how he imagines his date is reacting to him that he hardly notices her: "Why

did I say that? She looks bored. Did she notice my pimple?" (She, of course, is equally preoccupied with how she is playing to her audience. No wonder teenagers are often awkward and painfully aware of their every slip on first dates.)

The second form of adolescent egocentrism is the **personal fable**—a tendency to think that you and your thoughts and feelings are unique (Elkind, 1967). If the imaginary audience is a product of the inability to differentiate between self and other, the personal fable is a product of differentiating too much. Thus, the adolescent in love for the first time imagines that no one in the history of the human race has ever felt such heights of emotion. When the relationship breaks up, no one—least of all a parent—could possibly understand the crushing agony. The personal fable may also lead adolescents to feel that rules that apply to others do not apply to them. Thus, they will not be hurt if they speed down the highway without wearing a seat belt or drive under the influence of alcohol. And they will not become pregnant if they engage in sex without contraception, so they do not need to bother with contraception. As it turns out, high scores on measures of adolescent egocentrism are associated with behaving in risky ways (Greene et al., 1996; Holmbeck et al., 1994).

Elkind hypothesized that the imaginary audience and personal fable phenomena should increase when formal operations are first being acquired and then decrease as adolescents get older, gain fuller control of formal operations, and assume adult roles that require fuller consideration of others' perspectives. Indeed, both the self-consciousness associated with the imaginary audience and the sense of specialness associated with the personal fable are most evident in early adolescence and decline by late high school (Elkind & Bowen, 1979;

A teenage girl may feel that everyone is as preoccupied with her appearance as she is, a form of adolescent egocentrism known as the imaginary audience phenomenon.

HUMOR AND COGNITIVE DEVELOPMENT

EXPLORATIONS

At age 5, John repeatedly tells his mother the following joke: Why did the football coach go to the bank? Answer: To get his quarter back. When his mom asks him why this is funny, he replies that the coach lost his quarter and needed to get it back. He misses the whole idea that the humor of the joke depends on the double meaning of "quarter back." He repeats it only because of the chuckles it elicits from his listeners, who are amused not by the joke itself but because he is so earnest in his attempt to tell a joke. What really tickles John's funny bone is anything that looks or sounds silly—calling a "shoe" a "floo" or a "poo," for example. At 5 years of age, John is likely to laugh at a variety of verbal behaviors such as silly songs, comments, or words. In comparison, his 3-year-old sister is likely to dissolve into laughter at the sight of a silly face or the repetition of "potty words" (Martin, 2007).

With the onset of concrete-operational

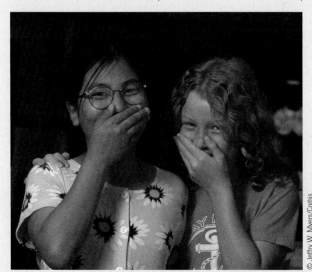

© Jeffry W. Myers/Corbis

thought and advances in awareness of the nature of language, children come to appreciate jokes and riddles that involve linguistic ambiguities. The "quarter back" joke boils down to a classification task. School-age children who have mastered the concept of class inclusion can keep the class and subclasses in mind at once and move mentally between the two meanings of "quarter back." Appreciation of such puns is high among second-graders (7- to 8-year-olds) and continues to grow until fourth or fifth grade (Martin, 2007; McGhee, 1979). With their newfound appreciation of linguistic double meanings, a 7- to 8-year-old is likely to find the following riddle fairly amusing (McGhee, 1979, p. 77):

"Why did the old man tiptoe past the medicine cabinet?
Because he did not want to wake up the sleeping pills."

The ability to appreciate such riddles may also signal greater cognitive competence. Children who are better at solving riddles are also better at reading and other language tasks (Ely, 1997).

As their language and social skills expand, children also become more able to understand sarcasm, irony, and other discrepancies between what is said and what is meant, such as when a teacher says to a noisy 8-year-old, "My, but you're quiet today" (Martin, 2007). To appreciate irony, children need the cogni-

tive ability to infer the speaker's intentions, something called "theory of mind," which we will discuss further in Chapter 13. Children first develop an understanding that irony can be used to "soften" a criticism, but appreciating the humor in ironic criticism is slower to develop (Creusere, 1999; Martin, 2007). Further, understanding ironic criticisms (e.g., "Well, aren't you in a pleasant mood today" to a grumpy sibling) emerges earlier than understanding ironic compliments (e.g., "What a bad play," following a great soccer kick).

Children's tastes in humor change again when they enter the stage of formal operations around age 11 or 12. Simple riddles and puns are no longer cognitively challenging enough, it seems, and are likely to elicit loud groans (McGhee, 1979). Adolescents and adults are more amused by subtle forms of irony rather than obvious irony that is understood by the child (Dews et al., 1996). Adolescents also appreciate jokes that involve an absurd or contrary-to-fact premise and a punch line that is logical if the absurd premise is accepted. The humor in "How do you fit six elephants into a Volkswagen?" depends on appreciating that "three in the front and three in the back" is a perfectly logical answer only if you accept the hypothetical premise that multiple elephants could fit into a small car. Reality-oriented school-age children may simply consider this joke stupid; after all, elephants cannot fit into cars. Clearly, then, children cannot appreciate certain forms of humor until they have the required cognitive abilities. Research on children's humor suggests that children and adolescents are most attracted to jokes that challenge them intellectually and that contain content relevant to their developmental stage (Martin, 2007; McGhee, 1979).

Enright, Lapsley, & Shukla, 1979). Adolescent egocentrism may persist, however, when adolescents have insecure relationships with their parents. Insecure relationships exist when adolescents do not feel that their parents are supportive of them or reliable sources of security (see Chapter 14). Such parent–adolescent relationships may make teens self-conscious and may make them appear to lack self-confidence even as older adolescents (Ryan & Kuczkowski, 1994).

Contrary to what Piaget and Elkind hypothesized, however, researchers have been unable to link the onset of the formal operations stage to the rise of adolescent egocentrism (Gray & Hudson, 1984; O'Connor & Nikolic, 1990). It seems

that adolescent egocentrism may arise when adolescents acquire advanced social perspective-taking abilities and contemplate how other people might perceive them and react to their behavior (Lapsley et al., 1986; Vartanian & Powlishta, 1996).

Furthermore, recent research by Joanna Bell and Rachel Bromnick (2003) suggests that adolescents are preoccupied with how they present themselves in public not because of an imaginary audience but because of a real audience. That is, research indicates that adolescents are aware that there are real consequences to how they present themselves. Their popularity and peer approval, as well as their self-confidence and self-esteem, are often influenced by how others (the real audience) perceive them. Adults, too, are aware that their actions and appearance are often judged by others, but although these adult concerns are usually assumed to be realistic, similar concerns by adolescents are sometimes viewed, perhaps unfairly, as trivial (Bell & Bromnick, 2003).

SUMMING UP

- Adolescents often show the first signs of formal operations at age 11 or 12 and gradually master the hypothetical-deductive reasoning skills required to solve scientific problems.

- Cognitive changes result in other developmental advances and may contribute to confusion, rebellion, idealism, and adolescent egocentrism (the imaginary audience and the personal fable).

CRITICAL THINKING

1. How does the formal-operational thinker differ from the concrete-operational thinker? What tasks might an adolescent with formal-operational thought be able to solve that one without formal-operational thought might struggle with?

2. What type of educational opportunities or programs would help foster formal-operational thought?

7.5 THE ADULT

Do adults think differently than adolescents do? Does cognition change over the adult years? Until fairly recently, developmentalists have not asked such questions. Piaget indicated that the highest stage of cognitive development, formal operations, was fully mastered by most people between age 15 and age 18. Why bother studying cognitive development in adulthood? As it turns out, it has been worth the effort. Research has revealed limitations in adult performance that must be explained, and it suggests that at least some adults progress beyond formal operations to more advanced forms of thought (Jacobs & Klaczynski, 2002).

Limitations in Adult Cognitive Performance

If many high school students are shaky in their command of formal operations, do most of them gain fuller mastery after the high school years? Gains are indeed made between adolescence and adulthood (Blackburn & Papalia, 1992). However, only about half of all college students show firm and consistent mastery of formal operations on Piaget's scientific reasoning tasks (Neimark, 1975). Similarly, sizable percentages of American adults do not solve scientific problems at the formal level, and there are some societies in which no adults solve formal-operational problems (Neimark, 1975).

Why do more adults not do well on Piagetian tasks? An average level of performance on standardized intelligence tests seems to be necessary for a person to achieve formal-operational thought (Inhelder, 1966). What seems more important than basic intelligence, however, is formal education (Neimark, 1979). In cultures in which virtually no one solves Piaget's problems, people do not receive advanced schooling. If achieving formal-operational thought requires education, Piaget's theory may be culturally biased, and his stages may not be as universal as he believed.

But neither lack of intelligence nor lack of formal education is a problem for most college students. Instead, they have difficulty with tests of formal operations when they lack expertise in a domain of knowledge. Piaget (1972) suggested that adults are likely to use formal operations in a field of expertise but to use concrete operations in less familiar areas. This is precisely what seems to happen. For example, Richard De Lisi and Joanne Staudt (1980) gave three kinds of formal-operational tasks—the pendulum problem, a political problem, and a literary criticism problem—to college students majoring in physics, political science, and English. As ■ **Figure 7.9** illustrates, each group of students did well on the problem relevant to that group's field of expertise. On problems outside their fields, however, about half the students failed. Possibly, then, many adolescents and adults fail to use formal reasoning on Piaget's scientific problems simply because these problems are unfamiliar to them and they lack expertise.

As Kurt Fischer (1980; Fischer, Kenny, & Pipp, 1990) maintains, each person may have an optimal level of cognitive performance that will show itself in familiar and well-trained content domains. However, performance is likely to be highly inconsistent across content areas unless the person has had a chance to build knowledge and skills in all these domains. More often, adults may use and strengthen formal modes of thinking only in their areas of expertise. By adopting a contextual perspective on cognitive development, you can appreciate that the individual's experience and the nature of the tasks she is asked to perform influence cognitive performance across the life span (Salthouse, 1990).

Growth Beyond Formal Operations?

Some researchers have been asking why adults sometimes perform so poorly on cognitive tasks; others have been asking why they sometimes perform so well. Take Piaget. Was his ability to generate a complex theory of development no more than the application of formal-operational thought? Or are there advances in cognitive development during adulthood that would better explain the remarkable cognitive achievements of some adults?

Several intriguing ideas have been proposed about stages of cognitive development that may lie beyond formal operations—that is, about **postformal thought** (Commons, Richards, & Armon, 1984; Labouvie-Vief, 1992; Sinnott, 1996; Yan & Arlin, 1995). As noted earlier, adolescents who have attained formal operations sometimes get carried away with their new powers of logical thinking. They insist that there is a logically

■ FIGURE 7.9 Expertise and formal operations. College students show the greatest command of formal-operational thought in the subject area most related to their major.

SOURCE: Data reprinted from *Journal of Applied Developmental Psychology, 1,* pp. 206–208, R. Di Lisi & J. Staudt, Individual differences in college students' performance on formal operations task. Copyright © 1980 with permission from Elsevier Press.

correct answer for every question—that if you simply apply logic, you will arrive at the right answer, at some absolute truth. Perhaps formal-operational adolescents need a more complex way of thinking to adapt to the kinds of problems adults face every day—problems in which there are many ways to look at an issue, no one right answer, and yet a need to make a decision (Sinnott, 1996).

How might thought be qualitatively different in adulthood than it is in adolescence? What might a truly adult stage of cognitive development be like? Several researchers have suggested that adults are more likely than adolescents to see knowledge as relative rather than absolute (Kitchener et al., 1989; Labouvie-Vief, 1992). **Relativistic thinking,** in this sense, means understanding that knowledge depends on the subjective perspective of the knower. An absolutist assumes that truth lies in the nature of reality and that there is only one truth; a relativist assumes that his starting assumptions influence the "truth" discovered and that a problem can be viewed in multiple ways.

Consider this logic problem: "A grows 1 cm per month. B grows 2 cm per month. Who is taller?" (Yan & Arlin, 1995, p. 230). The absolutist might say, "B," based on the information given, but the relativist would be more likely to say, "It depends." It depends on how tall A and B were to begin with and on how much time passes before their heights are measured. The relativistic thinker will recognize that the problem is ill defined and that further information is needed, and he will be able to think flexibly about what the answer would be if he made certain assumptions rather than others.

Or consider this problem, given to preadolescents, adolescents, and adults by Gisela Labouvie-Vief and her colleagues (1983, p. 5):

John is known to be a heavy drinker, especially when he goes to parties. Mary, John's wife, warns him that if he gets drunk one more time she will leave him and take the children. Tonight John is out late at an office party. John comes home drunk.

Does Mary leave John? Most preadolescents and many adolescents quickly and confidently said, "Yes." They did not question the assumption that Mary would stand by her word; they simply applied logic to the information they were given. Adults were more likely to realize that different starting assumptions were possible and that the answer depended on which assumptions were chosen. One woman, for example, noted that if Mary had stayed with John for years, she would be unlikely to leave him now. This same woman said, "There was no right or wrong answer. You could get logically to both answers" (p. 12). Postformal thinkers seem able to devise more than one logical solution to a problem (Sinnott, 1996).

In a fascinating study of cognitive growth over the college years, William Perry (1970) found that beginning college students often assumed that there were absolute, objective truths to be found by consulting their textbooks or their professors. They looked to what they believed were authoritative sources for *the* answer to a question, as if all problems have a single, correct answer. As their college careers progressed, they often became frustrated in their search for absolute truths. They saw that many questions seemed to have several answers, depending on the perspective of the respondent. Taking the extremely relativistic view that any opinion was as good as any other, several of these students said they were not sure how they could ever decide what to believe. Eventually, many understood that some opinions can be better supported than others; they were then able to commit themselves to specific positions, fully aware that they were choosing among relative perspectives.

Between adolescence and adulthood, then, many people start as absolutists, become relativists, and finally make commitments to positions despite their more sophisticated awareness of the nature and limits of knowledge (Sinnott, 1996). Not surprisingly, students at the absolute level of thinking use fewer thinking styles; they stick mainly with traditional modes of thinking (Zhang, 2002). Students who are relativistic thinkers use a greater variety of thinking styles, including ones that promote creativity and greater cognitive complexity.

It has also been suggested that advanced thinkers thrive on detecting paradoxes and inconsistencies among ideas and trying to reconcile them—only to repeatedly challenge and change their understandings (Basseches, 1984; Riegel, 1973). Advanced thinkers also seem to be able to think systematically and logically about abstract systems of knowledge (Fischer, Kenny, & Pipp, 1990; Richards & Commons, 1990). Where the concrete-operational thinker performs mental actions (such as addition) on concrete objects, and the formal-operational thinker performs mental actions on ideas (such as imagining possibilities—what *could* happen), the postformal thinker seems able to manipulate systems of ideas—for example, by comparing and contrasting psychological theories or analyzing abstract similarities and differences between mathematical operations such as addition and division.

It is not yet clear whether relativistic thinking or other forms of advanced thinking might qualify as a new, postformal stage of cognitive development. It is clear, however, that these types of thinking are shown by only a minority of adults, particularly those who have received advanced education, who are open to rethinking issues, and who live in a culture that nourishes their efforts to entertain new ideas (Irwin, 1991; Sinnott, 1996). It is also clear that cognitive growth does not end in adolescence. Yet age does not tell us much about how adults think; life circumstances and the demands placed on people to think at work, in the home, and in the community often tell us more.

Aging and Cognitive Skills

What becomes of cognitive capacities in later adulthood? Some mental abilities decline as the average person ages, and it appears that older adults often have trouble solving Piagetian tests of formal-operational thinking (Blackburn & Papalia, 1992). Indeed, elderly adults sometimes perform poorly relative to young and middle-aged adults even on concrete-operational tasks assessing conservation and classification skills.

This does not mean that elderly adults regress to immature modes of thought. For one thing, these studies have involved cross-sectional comparisons of different age groups. The poorer performance of older groups does not necessarily mean that cognitive abilities are lost as people age. It could be caused by a cohort effect, because the average older adult today has had less formal schooling than the average younger adult

has had. Older adults attending college tend to perform as well as younger college students on tests of formal operations (Blackburn, 1984; Hooper, Hooper, & Colbert, 1985). Moreover, brief training can quickly improve the performance of older adults long out of school, which suggests that the necessary cognitive abilities are there but merely need to be reactivated (Blackburn & Papalia, 1992).

Questions have also been raised about the relevance of the skills assessed in Piagetian tasks to the lives of older adults (Labouvie-Vief, 1985). Not only are these problems unfamiliar to many older adults, but they also resemble the intellectual challenges that children confront in school, not those that most adults encounter in everyday contexts. Thus, older people may not be motivated to solve them. Also, older adults may rely on modes of cognition that have proved useful to them in daily life but that make them look cognitively deficient in the laboratory (Salthouse, 1990).

Consider this example: Kathy Pearce and Nancy Denney (1984) found that elderly adults, like young children but unlike other age groups, often group two objects on the basis of some functional relationship between them (for example, putting a pipe and matches together because matches are used to light pipes) rather than on the basis of similarity (for example, putting a pipe and a cigar together because they are both ways of smoking tobacco). In school and in some job situations, Pearce and Denney suggest, people are asked to group objects on the basis of similarity, but in everyday life it may make more sense to associate objects commonly used together.

Such findings suggest that what appear to be deficits in older people may merely be differences in style. Similar stylis-

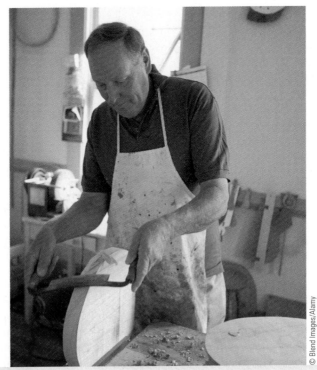

Adults think efficiently once they gain expertise on the job.

tic differences in classification skills have been observed cross-culturally and can, if researchers are not careful, lead to the incorrect conclusion that uneducated adults from non-Western cultures lack basic cognitive skills. A case in point: Kpelle adults in Africa, when asked to sort foods, clothing, tools, and cooking utensils into groups, sorted them into pairs based on functional relationships. "When an exasperated experimenter finally asked, 'How would a fool do it?' he was given sorts of the type that were initially expected—four neat piles with foods in one, tools in another, and so on" (Glick, 1975, p. 636).

So, today's older adults appear not to perform concrete-operational and formal-operational tasks as well as their younger contemporaries do. Planners of adult education for senior citizens might bear in mind that some (although by no means all) of their students may benefit from more concrete forms of instruction. However, these differences may be related to factors other than age, such as education and motivation; an age-related decline in operational abilities has not been firmly established. Most importantly, older adults who perform poorly on unfamiliar problems in laboratory situations often perform far more capably on the sorts of problems that they encounter in everyday contexts (Cornelius & Caspi, 1987; Salthouse, 1990).

SUMMING UP

▌ Adults are most likely to display formal-operational skills in their areas of expertise. Some adults, especially well-educated ones, may advance to postformal modes of thought such as relativistic thinking. Although aging adults often perform less well than younger adults on Piagetian tasks, factors other than biological aging may explain this.

CRITICAL THINKING

1. How important is it to achieve formal-operational thought? What limitations would you experience at work and school if you operated at a concrete-operational level all the time and never progressed to formal-operational thought?

7.6 | PIAGET IN PERSPECTIVE

Now that you have examined Piaget's theory of cognitive development, it is time to evaluate it. We start by giving credit where credit is due, then we consider challenges to Piaget's version of things.

Piaget's Contributions

Piaget is a giant in the field of human development. As one scholar quoted by Harry Beilin (1992) put it, "assessing the impact of Piaget on developmental psychology is like assessing the impact of Shakespeare on English literature or Aristotle on philosophy—impossible" (p. 191). It is hard to imagine that researchers would know even a fraction of what they know about intellectual development without his groundbreaking work.

One sign of a good theory is that it stimulates research. Piaget asked fundamentally important questions about how humans come to know the world and showed that we can answer them "by paying attention to the small details of the daily lives of our children" (Gopnik, 1996, p. 225). His cognitive developmental perspective has been applied to almost every aspect of human development, and the important questions he raised continue to guide the study of cognitive development.

We can credit Piaget with some lasting insights (Flavell, 1996). He showed us that infants are active in their own development—that from the start they seek to master problems and to understand the incomprehensible by using the processes of assimilation and accommodation to deal with cognitive disequilibrium. He taught us that young people think differently than older people do—and often in ways we never would have suspected. The reasoning of preschoolers, for example, often defies adult logic, but it makes sense in light of Piaget's insights about their egocentrism and reliance on the perceptual salience of situations. School-age children have the logical thought processes that allow them to excel at many tasks, but they draw a blank when presented with hypothetical or abstract problems. And adolescents are impressive with their scientific reasoning skills and their ability to wrestle with abstract problems, but they may think so much about events that they get tangled with new forms of egocentrism.

Finally, Piaget was largely right in his basic description of cognitive development. The sequence he proposed—sensorimotor to preoperational to concrete operations to formal operations—seems to describe the course and content of intellectual development for children and adolescents from the hundreds of cultures and subcultures that have been studied (Flavell, Miller, & Miller, 1993). Although cultural factors influence the rate of cognitive growth, the direction of development is always from sensorimotor thinking to preoperational thinking to concrete operations to, for many, formal operations (or even postformal operations).

Challenges to Piaget

Partly because Piaget's theory has been so enormously influential, it has had more than its share of criticism (Lourenco & Machado, 1996). We focus on five major criticisms:

1. *Underestimating young minds.* Piaget seems to have underestimated the cognitive abilities of infants and young children, although he emphasized that he was more interested in understanding the sequences of changes than the specific ages at which they occur (Lourenco & Machado, 1996). When researchers use more familiar problems than Piaget's and reduce tasks to their essentials, hidden competencies of young children—and of adolescents and adults—are sometimes revealed.

2. *Failing to distinguish between competence and performance.* Piaget sought to identify underlying cognitive competencies that guide performance on cognitive tasks. But there is

an important difference between understanding a concept and passing a test designed to measure it. The age ranges Piaget proposed for some stages may have been off target partly because he tended to ignore the many factors besides competence that can influence task performance—everything from the individual's motivation, verbal abilities, and memory capacity to the nature, complexity, and familiarity of the task used to assess mastery. Piaget may have been too quick to assume that children who failed one of his tests lacked competence; they may only have failed to demonstrate their competence in a particular situation.

Perhaps more importantly, Piaget may have overemphasized the idea that knowledge is an all-or-nothing concept (Schwitzgebel, 1999). Instead of having or not having a particular competence, children probably gain competence gradually and experience long periods between understanding and not understanding. Many of the seemingly contradictory results of studies using Piagetian tasks can be accounted for with this idea of gradual change in understanding. For instance, Piaget argued that infants do not show understanding of object permanence until 9 months, but other research indicates that at least some understanding of object permanence is present at 4 months (Ruffman et al., 2005). If researchers accept that conceptual change is gradual, then they can stop debating whether competence is present or not present at a particular age.

3. *Wrongly claiming that broad stages of development exist.* According to Piaget, each new stage of cognitive development is a coherent mode of thinking applied across a range of problems. Piaget emphasized the consistency of thinking *within* a stage and the difference *between* stages (Meadows, 2006). Yet individuals are often inconsistent in their performance on different tasks that presumably measure the abilities defining a given stage. For example, conservation of liquid is acquired earlier than conservation of volume. Researchers increasingly are arguing that cognitive development is domain specific—that is, it is a matter of building skills in particular content areas—and that growth in one domain may proceed much faster than growth in another (Fischer, Kenny, & Pipp, 1990). In addition, the transition between stages is not as swift and abrupt as most of Piaget's writings suggest. Instead the transitions between stages are often lengthy (over several years) and subtle (see Meadows, 2006). It is not always clear when a child has made the shift from one set of structures to a more advanced set of structures, particularly when we consider the two stages based on logical structures—concrete and formal operations.

4. *Failing to adequately explain development.* Several critics suggest that Piaget did a better job of describing development than of explaining how it comes about (Bruner, 1997; Meadows, 2006). To be sure, Piaget wrote extensively about his interactionist position on the nature–nurture issue and did as much as any developmental theorist to tackle the question of how development comes about. Presumably, humans are always assimilating new experiences in ways that their level of maturation allows, accommodating their thinking to those experiences, and reorganizing their cognitive structures into increasingly complex modes of thought. Yet this explanation is vague. Researchers need to know far more about how specific maturational changes in the brain and specific kinds of experiences contribute to important cognitive advances.

5. *Giving limited attention to social influences on cognitive development.* Some critics say Piaget paid too little attention to how children's minds develop through their social interactions with more competent individuals and how they develop differently in different cultures (Karpov, 2005). Piaget's child often resembles an isolated scientist exploring the world alone, but children develop their minds through interactions with parents, teachers, peers, and siblings. True, Piaget had interesting ideas about the role of *peers* in helping children adopt other perspectives and reach new conclusions (see Chapter 13 on moral development). But he did not believe that children learned from their interactions with *adults*. This may seem counter-intuitive, but Piaget believed that children see other children, but not adults, as "like themselves." Hearing a different perspective from someone like oneself can trigger internal conflict but hearing a perspective from someone different from oneself may not be viewed as a challenge to one's current way of thinking because the person—and their views—are simply too different. Thus, in Piaget's model, no notable cognitive conflict, and therefore no cognitive growth, occurs from children interacting with adults. As you will see shortly, the significance of social interaction and culture for cognitive development is the basis of the perspective on cognitive development offered by one of Piaget's early critics, Lev Vygotsky.

SUMMING UP

▌ Piaget's theory of cognitive development has been criticized for several reasons. It has been argued that the tasks he used did not adequately reveal the competencies of infants and young children; thus, the tasks could be improved.

▌ Some critics believe that Piaget should have explored the many factors besides underlying competence that influence performance.

▌ Others believe that he should have provided more convincing evidence that the cognitive stages are coherent and qualitatively distinct from one another, and should have been more specific about why development proceeds as it does.

▌ Finally, Piaget has been criticized for not assigning greater importance to social and cultural influences on the development of thought. It may be unfair, however, to demand of an innovator who accomplished so much that he achieve everything.

CRITICAL THINKING

1. How might Piaget's theory be updated to accommodate the research findings that have emerged since he constructed his theory?

2. Considering the differences between preoperational thought, concrete-operational thought, and formal-operational thought, what should parents keep in mind as they interact with their 4-year-old, 8-year-old, and 17-year-old children?

VYGOTSKY'S SOCIOCULTURAL PERSPECTIVE

You can gain additional insight into Piaget's view of cognitive development by considering the quite different sociocultural perspective of Lev Vygotsky (1962, 1978; see also Karpov, 2005). This Russian psychologist was born in 1896, the same year as Piaget, and was an active scholar in the 1920s and 1930s when Piaget was formulating his theory. For many years, Vygotsky's work was banned for political reasons in the former Soviet Union, and North American scholars lacked English translations of his work, which limited consideration of Vygotsky's ideas until recent decades. In addition, Vygotsky died of tuberculosis at age 38 before his theory was fully developed. However, his main theme is clear: cognitive growth occurs in a sociocultural context and evolves out of the child's social interactions.

Culture and Thought

Culture and society play a pivotal role in Vygotsky's theory. Indeed, intelligence in the Vygotskian model is held by the group, not the individual, and is closely tied to the language system and tools the group has developed over time (Case, 1998). Culture and social experiences affect how we think, not just what we think.

Consider some research by Vygotsky's colleague, Alexander Luria, who tested groups of 9- to 12-year-old children growing up in different social environments. Children were given target words and asked to name the first thing that came to mind when they heard each word. Luria found that children growing up in a remote rural village with limited social experiences gave remarkably similar responses, whereas children growing up in a large city gave more distinctly individual answers. Vygotsky and Luria believed that this difference reflected the city

According to Lev Vygotsky's theory, cognitive development is shaped by the culture in which children live and the kinds of problem-solving strategies that adults and other knowledgeable guides pass on to them.

children's broader exposure to various aspects of culture. On their own, the rural children were unable to develop certain types of knowledge. Knowledge, then, depends on social experiences.

Vygotsky would not be surprised to learn that formal-operational thought is rarely used in some cultures; he expected cognitive development to vary from society to society depending on the mental tools such as the language that the culture values and makes available. How do children acquire their society's mental tools? They acquire them by interacting with parents and other more experienced members of the culture and by adopting their language and knowledge (Frawley, 1997).

Social Interaction and Thought

Consider this scenario: Annie, a 4-year-old, receives a jigsaw puzzle, her first, for her birthday. She attempts to work the puzzle but gets nowhere until her father sits down beside her and gives her some tips. He suggests that it would be a good idea to put the corners together first. He points to the pink area at the edge of one corner piece and says, "Let's look for another pink piece." When Annie seems frustrated, he places two interlocking pieces near each other so that she will notice them. And when she succeeds, he offers words of encouragement. As Annie gets the hang of it, he steps back and lets her work more independently. This kind of social interaction, said Vygotsky, fosters cognitive growth.

How? First, Annie and her father are operating in what Vygotsky called the **zone of proximal development**—the gap between what a learner can accomplish independently and what she can accomplish with the guidance and encouragement of a more skilled partner. Skills within the zone are ripe for development and are the skills at which instruction should be aimed. Skills outside the zone are either well mastered already or still too difficult. In this example, Annie obviously becomes a more competent puzzle-solver with her father's help than without it. More importantly, she will internalize the problem-solving techniques that she discovered in collaboration with her father, working together in her zone of proximal development, and will use them on her own, rising to a new level of independent mastery. What began as a social process involving two people becomes a cognitive process within one.

An important implication of the zone of proximal development is that knowledge is not a fixed state and no single test or score can adequately reflect the range of a person's knowledge. The mind has potential for unlimited growth. Development consists of moving toward the upper range of the zone using the tools of society such as the language and the inventions that have been created. The upper limit continues to move upward in response to cultural changes (Smagorinsky, 1995). Support for Vygotsky's idea of the zone of proximal development comes from various sources, including research showing

By working with a more knowledgeable partner, this child is able to accomplish more than would be possible on his own. According to Lev Vygotsky, the difference between what a child can accomplish alone and with a partner is the zone of proximal development.

with an array of tools—shovel, rake, gloves, fertilizer, seeds, etc.—that have already been proven useful for accomplishing this task. Further, we would probably show her how to best use these tools to accomplish the desired task. We might show the child how to poke holes in the soil and drop seeds inside and then watch while the child attempted this and maybe correct her if it looks like she is pushing the seeds in too deep. As the child practices and masters the use of the tools presented by the adult, the child adopts the tools as her own. The same process occurs for passing along culturally derived tools for mental activity.

In Vygotsky's view, adults use a variety of tools to pass culturally valued modes of thinking and problem solving to their children. Spoken language is the most important tool, but writing, using numbers, and applying problem-solving and memory strategies also convey information and enable thinking (Vygotsky, 1978). The type of tool used to perform a task influences performance on the task. Consider a study by Dorothy Faulkner and her colleagues (2000) with 9- and 10-year-old children. Children worked in pairs on a science project (Inhelder and Piaget's chemical combination task), using either a computer simulation of the task or the actual physical materials. The children who worked with the computerized version talked more, tested more possible chemical combinations, and completed the task more quickly than children who worked with the physical materials. The computer, then, was a tool that changed the nature of the problem-solving activity and influenced performance, as Vygotsky would have predicted.

Look more closely at Vygotsky's notion of how tools—especially language—influence thought. Whereas Piaget maintained that cognitive development influences language development, Vygotsky argued that language shapes thought in important ways and that thought changes fundamentally once we begin to think in words (Bodrova & Leong, 1996). Piaget and Vygotsky both noticed that preschool children often talk to themselves as they go about their daily activities, almost as if they were play-by-play sports announcers. ("I'm putting the big piece in the corner. I need a pink one. Not that one—this one.") Two preschool children playing next to each other sometimes carry on separate monologues rather than conversing. Piaget (1926) regarded such speech as egocentric—further evidence that preoperational thinkers cannot yet take the perspectives of other people (in this case, their conversation partners) and therefore have not mastered the art of social speech. He did not believe that egocentric speech played a useful role in cognitive development.

In contrast, Vygotsky called children's recitations **private speech**—speech to oneself that guides one's thought and behavior. Rather than viewing it as a sign of cognitive immaturity, he saw it as a critical step in the development of mature thought and as the forerunner of the silent thinking-in-words that adults engage in every day. Adults guide children's behavior with speech, a tool that children appropriate and initially use exter-

that children's performance on assisted learning tasks is a good predictor of their future achievement (Meijer & Elshout, 2001). And research on pairing less-skilled readers with more-skilled ones shows that reading fluency increases substantially when the less-skilled readers are provided with a model of good reading and encouragement (Nes, 2003).

In many cultures, children do not go to school with other children to learn, nor do their parents explicitly teach them tasks such as weaving and hunting. Instead, they learn through **guided participation**—by actively participating in culturally relevant activities with the aid and support of their parents and other knowledgeable guides (Rogoff, 1998). Jerome Bruner (1983) had a similar concept in mind when he wrote of the many ways in which parents provide "scaffolding" for their children's development, structuring learning situations so that learning becomes easier. By calling attention to guided participation processes, in the zone of proximal development, Vygotsky was rejecting Piaget's view of children as independent explorers in favor of the view that they learn more sophisticated cognitive strategies through their interactions with more mature thinkers. To Piaget, the child's level of cognitive development determines what he can learn; to Vygotsky, learning in collaboration with more knowledgeable companions drives cognitive development.

The Tools of Thought

Vygotsky believed that mental activity, like physical activity, is mediated by tools (Karpov, 2005). If a child wants to start a garden, we wouldn't send her outside empty handed and say, "go ahead and make a garden." We would, instead, equip her

IMPROVING COGNITIVE FUNCTIONING

What do the theories of Piaget and Vygotsky have to contribute to the goal of optimizing mental functioning? As Piaget's views first became popular in the United States and Canada, psychologists and educators designed studies to determine whether they could speed cognitive development and help children and adults solve problems more effectively. Some researchers had a different motive: to challenge Piaget's view that concepts such as conservation cannot be mastered until the child is intellectually ready.

What has been learned from these training studies? Generally, they suggest that many Piagetian concepts can be taught to children who are slightly younger than the age at which the concepts would naturally emerge. Training is sometimes difficult, and it does not always generalize well to new problems, but progress can be achieved. Dorothy Field (1981), for example, demonstrated that 4-year-olds could be trained to recognize the identity of a substance such as a ball of clay before and after its appearance is altered—that is, to understand that although the clay looks different, it is still the same clay and has to be the same amount of clay. Field found that nearly 75% of the children given this identity training could solve at least three of five conservation problems 2 to 5 months after training.

Similar training studies have demonstrated that children who function at the late concrete operations stage can be taught formal operations (Adey & Shayer, 1992). Researchers have had even more luck improving the cognitive performance of older adults, sometimes with simple interventions (Blackburn & Papalia, 1992). Such studies suggest that many elderly individuals who perform poorly on Piagetian problem-solving tasks simply need a quick refresher course to demonstrate their underlying competence. Make no mistake: no one has demonstrated that 2-year-olds can be taught formal operations. But at least these studies establish that specific training experiences can somewhat speed a child's progress through Piaget's stages or bring out more advanced capacities in an adult performing at a less advanced level.

Piaget disapproved of attempts by Americans to speed children's progress through his stages (Piaget, 1970). He believed that parents should simply provide young children with opportunities to explore their world and that teachers should use a discovery approach in the classroom that allows children to learn by doing. Given their natural curiosity and normal opportunities to try their hand at solving problems, children would construct ever more complex understandings on their own. Many educators began building Piaget's ideas about discovery-based education into school curricula, especially in science classes (Gallagher & Easley, 1978). Teachers have also taken seriously Piaget's notion that children understand material best if they can assimilate it into their existing understandings. So, for example, they have designed curricula to guide severely mentally retarded adults through the substages of the sensorimotor period (Williams, 1996). Finding out what the learner already knows or can do and providing instruction matched to the child's level of development are in the spirit of Piaget.

What would Vygotsky recommend to teachers who want to stimulate cognitive growth? As you might guess, Vygotsky's theoretical orientation leads to a different approach to education than Piaget's does—a more social one. Whereas students in Piaget's classroom would most likely be engaged in independent exploration, students in Vygotsky's classroom would be involved in guided participation, "co-constructing" knowledge during interactions with teachers and more knowledgeable peers. The roles of teachers and other more skillful collaborators would be to organize the learning activity, break it into steps, provide hints and suggestions carefully tailored to the student's abilities, and gradually turn over more of the mental work to the student. According to Vygotsky's sociocultural perspective, the guidance provided by a skilled partner will then be internalized by the learner, first as private speech and eventually as silent inner speech.

Education ends up being a matter of providing children with tools of the mind important in their culture, whether hunting strategies or computer skills (Bodrova & Leong, 1996; Berk & Winsler, 1995).

Is there evidence that Vygotsky's guided participation approach might be superior to Piaget's discovery approach? Consider what Lisa Freund (1990) found when she had 3- to 5-year-old children help a puppet with a sorting task: deciding which furnishings (sofas, beds, bathtubs, stoves, and so on) should be placed in each of six rooms of a dollhouse that the puppet was moving into. First, the children were tested to determine what they already knew about proper furniture placement. Then, each child worked at a similar task, either alone (as might be the case in Piaget's discovery-based education, although here children were provided with corrective feedback by the experimenter) or with his or her mother (Vygotsky's guided learning). Finally, to assess what they had learned, Freund asked the children to perform a final, rather complex, furniture-sorting task. The results were clear: Children who had sorted furniture with help from their mothers showed dramatic improvements in sorting ability, whereas those who had practiced on their own showed little improvement. Moreover, the children who gained the most from guided participation with their mothers were those whose mothers talked the most about how to tackle the task. Collaborating with a competent peer can also produce cognitive gains that a child might not achieve working alone (Azmitia, 1992; Gauvain & Rogoff, 1989).

So, children do not always learn the most when they function as solitary scientists, seeking discoveries on their own; often, conceptual growth springs more readily from children's interactions with other people—particularly with competent people who provide an optimal amount of guidance. Yet it would seem that many children might benefit most from the best of both worlds: opportunities to explore on their own and supportive companions to offer help when needed.

nally, just as adults did with them. Gradually, this regulatory speech is internalized.

Studies conducted by Vygotsky and other researchers support his claim. For example, in one set of studies, Vygotsky (1934/1962) measured children's private speech first as they worked unimpeded on a task then as they worked to overcome an obstacle placed in their path. Their use of private speech increased dramatically when they confronted an interruption of their work—a problem to solve. Thus, young children rely most heavily on private speech when they are struggling to solve difficult problems (Berk, 1992). Even adults sometimes revert to thinking aloud when they are stumped by a problem (John-Steiner, 1992).

The incidence of private speech varies with age and task demands. Both 3- and 4-year-olds use private speech, but 4-year-olds are more likely to use it systematically when engaged in a sustained activity. Four-year-olds are presumably more goal oriented than 3-year-olds and use private speech to regulate their behavior and achieve their goals (Winsler, Carlton, & Barry, 2000). As the task becomes familiar and children gain competence, the use of private speech decreases (Duncan & Pratt, 1997). Private speech is also more frequent during open-ended activities (such as pretend play) that have several possible outcomes than during closed-ended tasks that have a single outcome (Krafft & Berk, 1998). Open-ended activities tend to be directed more by the child than by an adult; they allow children to alter the difficulty level of the task so that it is appropriately challenging. In contrast, adult-directed activities provide fewer opportunities for children to regulate their own behavior.

Intellectually capable children rely more heavily on private speech in the preschool years and make the transition to inner speech earlier in the elementary school years than their less academically capable peers do (Berk & Landau, 1993). This suggests that the preschool child's self-talk is indeed a sign of cognitive maturity, as Vygotsky claimed, rather than a sign of immature egocentrism, as Piaget claimed.

In addition, heavy use of private speech contributes to effective problem-solving performance—if not immediately, then when children encounter similar problems in the future (Behrend, Rosengren, & Perlmutter, 1989; Bivens & Berk, 1990). The amount of private speech and the nature of what the child says are both related to performance (Chiu & Alexander, 2000). In particular, children who use metacognitive private speech ("No, I need to change this. Try it over here. Yes, that's good.") show greater motivation toward mastery; that is, they are more likely to persist on a task without adult intervention (Chiu & Alexander, 2000). Thus, private speech not only helps children think their way through challenging problems but also allows them to incorporate into their own thinking the problem-solving strategies they learned during their collaborations with adults. Notice that, as in guided participation, what is at first a social process becomes an individual psychological process. In other words, social speech (for example, the conver-

● TABLE 7.3   A COMPARISON OF VYGOTSKY AND PIAGET

VYGOTSKY'S SOCIOCULTURAL VIEW	PIAGET'S COGNITIVE DEVELOPMENTAL VIEW
Processes of animal and human development are fundamentally different.	Processes of animal and human development are fundamentally the same.
Cognitive development is different in different social and historical contexts.	Cognitive development is mostly the same universally.
Appropriate unit of analysis is the social, cultural, and historical context in which the individual develops.	Appropriate unit of analysis is the individual.
Cognitive growth results from social interactions (guided participation in the zone of proximal development).	Cognitive growth results from the child's independent explorations of the world.
Children and their partners "co-construct" knowledge.	Children construct knowledge on their own.
Social processes become individual psychological ones (e.g., social speech becomes inner speech).	Individual, egocentric processes become more social (e.g., egocentric speech becomes social speech).
Adults are especially important because they know the culture's tools of thinking.	Peers are especially important because the cognitive conflict triggered by different perspectives of other children is not so overwhelming that it cannot be resolved.
Learning precedes development (tools learned with adult help become internalized).	Development precedes learning (children cannot master certain things until they have the requisite cognitive structures).
Training can help mediate development.	Training is largely ineffective in "speeding up" development.

sation between Annie and her father as they jointly worked a puzzle) gives rise to private speech (Annie talking aloud, much as her father talked to her, as she then tries to work the puzzle on her own), which in turn goes "underground" to become first mutterings and lip movements and then inner speech (Annie's silent verbal thought).

Evaluation of Vygotsky

Although many scholars find Vygotsky's ideas a refreshing addition to Piaget's, some concerns should be noted. Piaget has been criticized for placing too much emphasis on the individual and not enough on the social environment; Vygotsky has been criticized for placing too much emphasis on social interaction (Feldman & Fowler, 1997). Vygotsky seemed to assume that all knowledge and understanding of the world is transmitted through social interaction. But at least some understanding is individually constructed, as Piaget proposed. Vygotsky and Piaget are often presented as opposites on a continuum representing the extent to which cognitive development derives from social experience. However, a careful reading of the two theorists reveals that they are not as dissimilar as they are often presented to be (DeVries, 2000; Matusov & Hayes, 2000). Both Piaget and Vygotsky acknowledge the importance of the social context of development. Still, there are differences in their emphasis. ● Table 7.3 summarizes some of the differences between Vygotsky's sociocultural perspective and Piaget's cognitive developmental view. The Applications box on page 212 explains their views on improving cognitive functioning.

Pause for a moment and consider the remarkable developmental accomplishments we described in this chapter. The capacity of the human mind for thought is awesome. Because the human mind is so complex, you should not be surprised that it is not yet understood. Piaget attacked only part of the puzzle, and he only partially succeeded. Vygotsky alerted us to sociocultural influences on cognitive development but died before he could formalize his theory. As you will see in Chapters 8 and 9, other ways to think about mental development are needed.

Summing Up

▪ Vygotsky's sociocultural perspective stresses social influences on cognitive development that Piaget largely ignored.

▪ According to Vygotsky's perspective, children's minds develop (1) in response to cultural influences; (2) in collaborative interactions with skilled partners, or guided participation, on tasks within their zone of proximal development; and (3) as they incorporate what skilled partners say to them into what they say to themselves.

▪ As social speech is transformed into private speech and then into inner speech, the culture's preferred tools of problem solving work their way from the language of competent guides into the thinking of the individual.

1. Create descriptions of a Piagetian preschool and a Vygotskian preschool. What are the main differences in how children will be assessed, what they will be taught, and how they will be taught?

2. Piaget and Vygotsky differed in their views of the importance of the individual versus society. Compare their positions on individual versus society in terms of cognitive development.

CHAPTER SUMMARY

7.1 PIAGET'S CONSTRUCTIVIST APPROACH

● Jean Piaget developed a theory of how children come to know their world by constructing their own schemes or cognitive structures through active exploration. Studying children using the clinical method, Piaget formulated four stages of cognitive development in which children construct increasingly complex schemes through an interaction of maturation and experience.

● Intelligence is a basic life function that allows organisms (including humans) to adapt to the demands of their environment.

● Children adapt to the world through the processes of organization and adaptation (assimilating new experiences to existing understandings and accommodating existing understandings to new experiences).

7.2 THE INFANT

● Infants are in the sensorimotor stage, during which they construct simple schemes by taking in information through their senses and acting motorically on it.

● Major accomplishments of the sensorimotor stage include the development of object permanence, or the realization that objects continue to exist even when they are not directly experienced, and the symbolic capacity, or the ability to allow one thing to represent something else. The emergence of the symbolic capacity paves the way for language and pretend play.

7.3 THE CHILD

● In the preoperational stage, preschool-age children do not yet reason logically; instead they rely on perceptually salient features of a task or object. Their pre-logical set of cognitive structures leads them to have trouble with conservation and classification tasks. In particular, preoperational children lack the abilities to decentrate, reverse thought, and transform ideas. In addition, they tend to be egocentric—viewing the world from their own perspective and not recognizing others' points of views.

● Concrete-operational thinkers can reason logically about concrete information, which allows them to solve conservation and classification tasks. Concrete-operational children have acquired the abilities of decentration, reversibility of thought, and transformational thought.

7.4 THE ADOLESCENT

● Adolescents may advance to Piaget's last stage of cognitive development—formal-operational thought, in which they apply their logical reasoning to hypothetical problems. Formal-operational thinkers can simultaneously consider multiple task components.

- Formal-operational thought may give rise to special forms of egocentrism, namely, the imaginary audience and personal fable.

7.5 THE ADULT

- Many adults seem to function at the concrete-operational level, rather than at Piaget's highest level of formal-operational thought. Formal-operational thought appears to be highly dependent on formal education. It is also influenced by culture and area of expertise.
- Some adults may acquire advanced levels of thought not considered by Piaget, such as relativistic thinking, or understanding that knowledge is dependent on the knower's subjective perspective.

7.6 PIAGET IN PERSPECTIVE

- Piaget has made huge contributions to the field of human development but has been criticized for underestimating the capacities of infants and young children, not considering factors besides competence that influence performance, failing to demonstrate that his stages have coherence, offering vague explanations of development, and underestimating the role of language and social interaction in cognitive development.

7.7 VYGOTSKY'S SOCIOCULTURAL PERSPECTIVE

- Lev Vygotsky's sociocultural perspective emphasizes cultural and social influences on cognitive development more than Piaget's theory does.
- Through guided participation in culturally important activities, children learn problem-solving techniques from knowledgeable partners sensitive to their zone of proximal development.
- Language is the most important tool that adults use to pass culturally valued thinking and problem solving to their children. Language shapes their thought and moves from social speech to private speech and later to inner speech.

KEY TERMS

MEDIA RESOURCES

BOOK COMPANION WEBSITE

academic.cengage.com/psychology/sigelman
Find online quizzes, flash cards, animations, video clips, experiments, interactive assessments, and other helpful study aids for this text at **academic.cengage.com/psychology/sigelman.** You can also connect directly to the following sites:

CONSTRUCTIVISM

This site is a one-stop shop for anyone interested in constructivism and includes links to the works of many constructivist theorists (e.g., Piaget, Vygotsky, Bruner).

JEAN PIAGET'S GENETIC EPISTEMOLOGY: APPRECIATION AND CRITIQUE

This site, maintained by Robert Campbell of Clemson University, offers the visitor a highly detailed biography of Piaget's life, works, as well as a detailed critique of Piaget's theory.

LEV VYGOTSKY ARCHIVES

The Lev Vygotsky Archives is a tremendous resource for anyone seeking information on the life and work of this famous Soviet theorist. Highlights include direct access to several important written works and an image gallery.

VYGOTSKY RESOURCES

A great site at which to become familiar with life and works of Lev Vygotsky. Includes a photo archive, biography section, and links to many articles by or about Vygotsky.

UNDERSTANDING THE DATA: EXERCISES ON THE WEB

academic.cengage.com/psychology/sigelman
For additional insight on the data presented in this chapter, try out the exercise for this figure at **academic.cengage.com/psychology/sigelman:**

  Figure 7.9 Expertise and formal operations

CENGAGENOW

academic.cengage.com/login
Go to **academic.cengage.com/login** to link to CengageNOW, your online study tool. First take the Pre-Test for this chapter to get your Personalized Study Plan, which will identify topics you need to review and direct you to online resources. Then take the Post-Test to determine what concepts you have mastered and what you still need work on.

8

Memory and Information Processing

▪▪▪

In this chapter, we consider how memory develops and changes over the life span. We also continue examining cognitive development by looking at a view different from Jean Piaget's and Lev Vygotsky's approaches, described in the last chapter. Cognitive psychologists, influenced by the rise of computer technology, began to think of the brain as a computer that processes input and converts it to output (correct answers on tests, for example). This information-processing perspective has revealed much about how the capacities to acquire, remember, and use information change over the life span.

8.1 | THE INFORMATION-PROCESSING APPROACH

According to Howard Gardner (1985), the "cognitive revolution" in psychology that generated the information-processing approach could not have occurred without a demonstration of the inadequacies of the behaviorist approach and the rise of computer technology. Showing deficiencies in the behaviorist approach was easiest in relation to complex learning and memory tasks. Consider learning from this textbook. Obviously, some complex processes occur between when you register the pattern of print on this page and when you write an essay about it. To account for these processes, behaviorists such as John B. Watson and B. F. Skinner (see Chapter 2) would have to describe chains of mental stimuli and responses between an external stimulus (for instance, the printed page) and an overt response (for example writing an essay). This approach proved cumbersome at best, as more cognitively oriented learning theorists, such as Albert Bandura, recognized.

Then came computers with their capacity for systematically converting input to output. The computer seemed to provide a good analogy to the human mind, and efforts to program computers to play chess and solve other problems as well as human experts have revealed a great deal about the strengths and limitations of human cognition (Newell & Simon, 1961; Simon, 1995).

Any computer has a limited capacity, associated with its hardware and software, for processing information. The computer's hardware is the machine itself—its keyboard (or input system), its storage capacity, and so on. The mind's "hardware" is the nervous system, including the brain, the sensory receptors, and their neural connections. The computer's software consists of the programs used to manipulate stored and received information: word processing, statistics programs, and the like. The mind, too, has its "software"—rules, strategies, and other mental "programs" that specify how information is to be registered, interpreted, stored, retrieved, and analyzed.

The computer, then, was the model for the **information-processing approach** to human cognition, which emphasizes the basic mental processes involved in attention, perception, memory, and decision making. When the information-processing approach began to guide studies of development, the challenge became one of determining how the hardware and software of the mind change over the life span. Just as today's more highly developed computers have greater capacity than those of the past, maturation of the nervous system plus experience presumably enables adults to remember more than young children can and to perform more complex cognitive feats with greater accuracy (Kail & Bisanz, 1992).

Memory Systems

▪ **Figure 8.1** presents an early and influential conception of the human information-processing system offered by Richard Atkinson and Richard Shiffrin (1968). If your history professor says that the U.S. Constitution was ratified in 1789, this statement is an environmental stimulus. Assuming that you are not lost in a daydream, your **sensory register** will log it, holding it for a fraction of a second as a kind of afterimage (or, in this example, a kind of echo). Much that strikes the sensory register quickly disappears without further processing. Attentional processes (see Chapter 6) have a good deal to do with which sensory stimuli enter the sensory register and which are processed further. If you think you may need to remember 1789, it will be moved into **short-term memory,** which can hold a limited amount of information (about seven items or chunks of information) for several seconds. For example, short-term memory can hold onto a telephone number while you dial it. Today, cognitive researchers distinguish between passive and active forms of short-term memory and use the term **working memory** to refer to a mental "scratch pad" that temporarily stores information while actively operating on it (Baddeley, 1986, 1992). It is what is "on one's mind," or in one's consciousness, at any moment. As you know, people can juggle only so much information at once without some of it slipping away.

■ **FIGURE 8.1** A model of information processing.
SOURCE: Adapted from Atkinson & Shiffrin (1968).

To illustrate working memory, look at the following seven numbers. Then look away and add the numbers in your head while trying to remember them:

7 2 5 6 1 4 7

Most likely, having to actively manipulate the numbers in working memory to add them disrupted your ability to rehearse them to remember them. People who are fast at adding numbers would have better luck than most people, because they would have more working-memory space left for remembering the items (Byrnes, 1996).

To be remembered for any length of time, information must be moved from short-term memory into **long-term memory,** a relatively permanent store of information that represents what most people mean by memory. More than likely, you will hold the professor's statement in short-term memory just long enough to record it in your notes. Later, as you study your notes, you will rehearse the information in working memory to move it into long-term memory so that you can retrieve it the next day or week when you are taking the test.

This simplified model shows what you must do to learn and remember something. The first step is **encoding** the information: getting it into the system. If it never gets in, it cannot be remembered. Second, information undergoes **consolidation,** during which it is processed and organized in a form suitable for long-term storage. Consolidation transforms the immediate sensory-perceptual experience of an event into a long-lasting memory trace, a process that is facilitated by sleep (Backhaus et al., 2006; Born, Rusch & Gais, 2006; Gais & Born, 2004). In the absence of consolidation, the information would not make the leap from the first step of encoding to the third step of storage. **Storage,** of course, refers to holding information in a long-term memory store. Memories fade over time unless they are appropriately stored in long-term memory. Finally, there is **retrieval**—the process of getting information out

when it is needed. People say they have successfully remembered something when they can retrieve it from long-term memory.

Retrieval can be accomplished in several ways. If you are asked a multiple-choice question about when the Constitution was ratified, you need not actively retrieve the correct date; you merely need to recognize it among the options. This is an example of **recognition memory.** If, instead, you are asked, "When was the Constitution ratified?" this is a test of **recall memory;** it requires active retrieval without the aid of cues. Between recognition and recall memory is **cued recall memory,** in which you would be given a hint or cue to facilitate retrieval (for example, "When was the Constitution ratified? It is the year the French Revolution began and rhymes with *wine.*"). Most people find questions requiring recognition memory easier to answer than those requiring cued recall, and those requiring cued recall easier than those requiring pure recall. This holds true across the life span, which suggests that many things people have apparently encoded or learned are "in there someplace" even though they may be difficult to retrieve without cues. Breakdowns in remembering may involve difficulties in initial encoding, storage, or retrieval.

Implicit and Explicit Memory

Memory researchers have concluded that the long-term memory store responds differently depending on the nature of the task. They distinguish between **implicit memory** (sometimes called nondeclarative memory), which occurs unintentionally, automatically, and without awareness, and **explicit memory** (also called declarative memory), which involves deliberate, effortful recollection of events (see ■ Figure 8.2). Explicit memory is tested through traditional recognition and recall tests (such as a course's final exam with multiple choice and essay

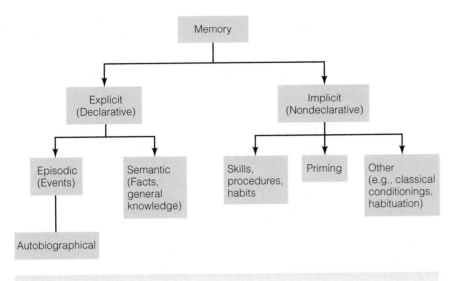

■ FIGURE 8.2 Types of memory.
Based on Squire (2004).

questions) and typically involves information that can be described with language. In contrast, when implicit memory is tested, learners do not even know their memory is being assessed. For example, individuals might be exposed to a list of words (*orange*, *tablet*, *forest*, and so on) to be rated for likeability, not to be memorized. In a second task, they are given word stems such as *tab___* and asked to complete them with the first word that comes to mind. People who are exposed to the word *tablet* in the initial task are more likely than people who are not exposed to the word to come up with *tablet* rather than *table* or *tabby* to complete the word stem, demonstrating that they learned something from their earlier exposure to the words even though they were not trying to learn. Adults with amnesia do poorly on tests of explicit memory in which they study words and then are asked to finish word stems such as *tab___* with a word they studied earlier. Amazingly, however, if they are merely exposed to a list of words and then given an implicit memory test that asks them to write the first word that comes to mind, they do fine (Graf, Squire, & Mandler, 1984). Many forms of amnesia destroy explicit memory but leave implicit memory undamaged (Schacter, 1996). As Patricia Bauer (2007) describes it, explicit memory is fallible—subject to forgetting—whereas implicit memory is largely infallible—it remains intact.

Research makes it clear that implicit and explicit memories are two distinct components of long-term memory that operate independently. It is not surprising, then, that recent research on the neural basis of memory shows that different parts of the brain are involved in the different forms of memory. Procedural memories (such as riding a bike), which are a type of implicit memory, are mediated by the striatum. Explicit memory is largely localized in the medial temporal lobe of the brain (medial refers to the middle of the brain and the temporal lobe is located at the base of the brain). In particular, the medial temporal structures are thought to be crucial to consolidating information into a memory trace for long-term storage (Bauer,

2007). Damage to a specific region of the medial temporal lobe—the hippocampus—leads to significant impairments in creating new episodic memories (such as recalling that you went to the dentist on Monday morning; Vargha-Khadem et al., 1997). The actual storage and retrieval of the information take place in whichever cortex originally encoded or was activated by the information. For example, vocabulary seems to be stored in the limbic-temporal cortex, as evidenced by the vocabulary impairment experienced by individuals with damage to this part of the brain (Bauer, 2007). Thus, sensory information initially activates one of the cortical association areas distributed throughout the brain. This information then passes to the medial temporal lobe for consolidation. If and when this consolidation occurs, the resulting memory trace is stored in the cortical association area of the brain that first registered the information, and it is from this area that the information must be retrieved.

Some researchers believe that implicit memory develops earlier in infancy than explicit memory (Schneider, 2004). Others believe that both forms of memory are evident early in infancy (Rovee-Collier, 1997). All agree that the two types of memory follow different developmental paths. Explicit memory capacity increases from infancy to adulthood then declines in later adulthood. By contrast, implicit memory capacity changes little; young children often do no worse than older children and elderly adults often do no worse than younger adults on tests of implicit memory (Schneider, 2004; Schneider & Bjorklund, 1998). Research on implicit memory shows that young and old alike learn and retain a tremendous amount of information from their everyday experiences without any effort.

Problem Solving

Now imagine that you are asked how many years passed between the signing of the Declaration of Independence (1776, remember?) and the ratification of the Constitution. This is a simple example of **problem solving**, or use of the information-processing system to achieve a goal or arrive at a decision (in this case, to answer the question). Here, too, the information-processing model describes what happens between stimulus and response. The question will move through the memory system. You will need to draw on your long-term memory to understand the question, then you will have to search long-term memory for the two relevant dates. Moreover, you will need to locate your stored knowledge of the mathematical operation of subtraction. You will then transfer this stored information to working memory so that you can use your subtraction "program" (1789 minus 1776) to derive the correct answer.

Notice that processing information successfully requires both knowing what you are doing and making decisions. This is why the information-processing model (see Figure 8.1) includes **executive control processes** involved in planning and monitoring what is done. These control processes run the show, guiding the selection, organization, manipulation, and interpretation of information throughout. Stored knowledge about the world and about information processing guides what is done with new information.

Cognitive psychologists now recognize that information processing is more complex than this model or similar models suggest (Bjorklund, 1997). For example, they appreciate that people, like computers, engage in "parallel processing," carrying out many cognitive activities simultaneously (for example, listening to a lecture and taking notes at the same time) rather than performing operations in a sequence (such as solving a math problem by carrying out a series of ordered steps). They also appreciate that different processing approaches are used in different domains of knowledge. Still, the information-processing approach to cognition has the advantage of focusing attention on how people remember things or solve problems, not just on what they recall or what answer they give. A young child's performance on a problem could break down in any number of ways: The child might not be paying attention to the relevant aspects of the problem, might be unable to hold all the relevant pieces of information in working memory long enough to do anything with them, might lack the strategies for transferring new information into long-term memory or retrieving information from long-term memory as needed, might simply not have enough stored knowledge to understand the problem, or might not have the executive control processes needed to manage the steps for solving problems. If researchers can identify how information processes in the younger individual differ from those in the older person, they will gain much insight into cognitive development.

Many processes involved in memory and problem solving improve between infancy and adulthood then decline somewhat in old age, although this pattern is not uniform for all processes or all people. Our task in this chapter is to describe these age trends and, of greater interest, to try to determine why they occur.

SUMMING UP

- The information-processing approach uses a computer analogy to illustrate how the mind processes information. The human "computer" takes in information through the sensory registers, which hold the information for a very brief period of time.

- If the person pays attention to the information that "hits" the sensory register, then it is further processed in short-term, or working, memory.

- Eventually, information may be stored in long-term memory, which seems to be unlimited in terms of size and permanency. In order for something to move into the long-term memory

store, it must undergo a process of consolidation in which a memory trace of the event is created.

- Encoding and retrieval strategies influence memory performance. Types of retrieval include recognition, recall, and cued recall.

- Explicit memory is deliberate and effortful and changes over the life span, whereas implicit memory is automatic and relatively stable over the life span. Explicit and implicit memories are separate components of long-term memory and are localized in different parts of the brain.

- Stored memories are instrumental to success at problem solving, or using stored information to achieve a goal. Executive control processes select, organize, manipulate, and interpret what is going on in the context of problem solving.

CRITICAL THINKING

1. Consider your own memory profile. On what types of memory tasks and under what conditions is your memory good, and conversely, which types of tasks and conditions challenge your memory?

2. What features distinguish implicit memory from explicit memory?

8.2 | THE INFANT

You have already seen that infants explore the world thoroughly through their senses. But are they remembering anything of their experiences? First, look at what research on information processing has taught developmentalists about early memory; then, consider whether infants demonstrate problem-solving skills.

Memory

Assessing infant memory requires some ingenuity because infants cannot tell researchers what they remember (Bauer, 2007; Rovee-Collier & Barr, 2004). Several methods have been used to uncover infants' memory capabilities. Here we consider imitation, habituation, and operant conditioning techniques before examining infants' abilities to recall previously presented information.

Imitation

Researchers can learn something about memory by noting whether or not infants can imitate an action performed by a model. Some studies suggest that young infants, even newborns, can imitate certain actions, such as sticking out the tongue or opening the mouth (see Meltzoff, 2004). These findings are exciting because they challenge Piaget's claim that infants cannot imitate actions until about 1 year, when they have some ability to represent mentally what they have seen.

At first, such findings were viewed with skepticism by some, who believed that early tongue protrusions did not dem-

Andrew Meltzoff is one researcher who has demonstrated imitation of facial expressions in newborns. These sample photographs are from videotaped recordings of 2- to 3-week-old infants imitating tongue protrusion, mouth opening, and lip protrusion. Of the three responses shown here, tongue protrusion is the most reliably observed.

From A. N. Meltzoff & M. K. Moore (1977). "Imitation of facial and manual gestures by human neonates." *Science, 198, 75–78.*

onstrate true imitation but instead reflected reflexive responses to specific stimuli or attempts to "explore" interesting sights (for example, Bjorklund, 1995; Jones, 1996). However, observations of infants sticking out their tongues and moving their mouths in ways consistent with a model have now been replicated with different populations (Meltzoff & Moore, 1997). In addition, infants as young as 6 months display **deferred imitation,** the ability to imitate a novel act after a delay, which clearly requires memory ability (see Bauer, 2007; Jones & Herbert, 2006). Deferred imitation may represent an early form of explicit memory (Jones & Herbert, 2006).

Habituation

Another method to assess memory uses habituation, a simple and often overlooked form of learning introduced in Chapter 6. Habituation—learning *not* to respond to a repeated stimulus—might be thought of as learning to be bored by the familiar (for example, eventually not hearing the continual ticking of a clock) and is evidence that a stimulus is recognized as familiar. From birth, humans habituate to repeatedly presented lights, sounds, and smells; such stimuli are recognized as "old hat" (Bauer, 2004; Rovee-Collier & Barr, 2004). In other words, newborns are capable of recognition memory and prefer a new sight to something they have seen many times. As they age, infants need less "study time" before a stimulus be-

comes old hat, and they can retain what they have learned for days or even weeks (Bahrick & Pickens, 1995).

Operant Conditioning

To test long-term memory of young infants, Carolyn Rovee-Collier and her colleagues devised a clever task that relies on the operant conditioning techniques introduced in Chapter 2 (Rovee-Collier & Barr, 2004). When a ribbon is tied to a baby's ankle and connected to an attractive mobile, the infant will shake a leg now and then and learn in minutes that leg kicking brings about a positively reinforcing consequence: the jiggling of the mobile.

To test infant memory, the mobile is presented at a later time to see whether the infant will kick again. To succeed at this task, the infant must not only recognize the mobile but also recall that the thing to do is to kick. When given two 9-minute training sessions, 2-month-olds remember how to make the mobile move for up to 2 days, 3-month-olds for about 1 week, and 6-month-olds for about 2 weeks (Rovee-Collier & Boller, 1995). By 18 months, infants can remember for at least 3 months (Rovee-Collier & Barr, 2004). The researchers could enhance young infants' memory by giving them three 6-minute learning sessions rather than two 9-minute sessions (Rovee-Collier, 1999). Although the total training time is the same in the two conditions, the distributed, or spread out, training is more effective. As it turns out, distributed practice is beneficial across the life span (Son, 2004).

What if stronger cues to aid recall are provided? Carolyn Rovee-Collier and Rachel Barr (2004) report that 2 to 4 weeks after their original learning experience, 3-month-old infants who were reminded of their previous learning by seeing the mobile move, kicked up a storm as soon as the ribbon was attached to their ankles, whereas infants who were not reminded showed no sign of remembering to kick. It seems, then, that cued recall (in this case, memory cued by the presence of the mobile or, better yet, its rotation by the experimenter) emerges during the first couple of months of life and that infants remember best when they are reminded of what they have learned. Other research shows that verbal reminders are also effective with 15-month-olds and can help them remember an event after a month as well as they did after a week (Bauer, Hertsgaard, & Wewerka, 1995; Bauer et al., 2000).

However, this research also suggests that young infants have difficulty recalling what they have learned if cues are insufficient or different. They have trouble remembering when the mobile (for example, the specific animals hanging from it) or the context in which they encountered it (for example, the design on the playpen liner) is even slightly different from the

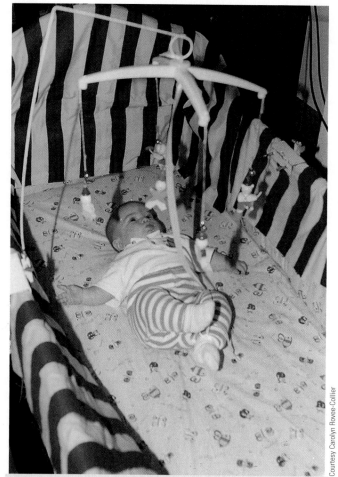

When ribbons are tied to their ankles, young infants soon learn to make a mobile move by kicking their legs. Carolyn Rovee-Collier has made use of this operant conditioning paradigm to find out how long infants will remember the trick for making the mobile move.

context in which they learned. In short, early memories are *cue-dependent* and *context-specific*.

Recall

When are infants capable of pure recall—of actively retrieving information from memory when no cues are available? As noted earlier, infants as young as 6 months, given repeated exposure to a model's actions, can imitate novel behaviors (for example, pushing a button on a box to produce a beep) after a 24-hour delay (Barr, Dowden, & Hayne, 1996; Meltzoff, 1988). As infants age, they demonstrate recall or deferred imitation over longer periods. By 9 months, infants can defer their imitation of an action over a longer delay—up to 1 month—and can recall the order of a simple sequence of events (Bauer, 2007). Fourteen- to sixteen-month-olds show deferred imitation after delays of 4 months (Meltzoff, 1995). By age 2, events can be recalled for as long as 1 year and recall is more flexible—less bound by the specific cues present at the time of learning (Herbert & Hayne, 2000; Klein & Meltzoff, 1999).

Patricia Bauer (1996, 2000) and her colleagues have shown sequences of actions to infants of different ages and then asked them to imitate what they saw—for example, putting a teddy bear in bed, covering him with a blanket, and reading him a story. Infants as young as 13 months can reconstruct a sequence of actions for as long as 3 months afterward. Older infants (16 months and 20 months) can store and retrieve events for 12 months after exposure (Bauer et al., 2000). Much like children and adults, infants remember best when they have repeated exposures to what they are to remember, when they are given plenty of cues to help them remember, and when the events they must remember occur in a meaningful or logical order.

By age 2, infants have become verbal and can use words to reconstruct events that happened months earlier. In one study, for example, researchers interviewed young children about emergency room visits for accidents the children had between about 1 and 3 years of age (Peterson & Rideout, 1998). Interviews were conducted soon after the ER visits and 6, 12, 18, or 24 months later. Children who were 18 months or younger at the time of their ER visit were unable to verbally recall aspects of their visits after a 6-month delay, but children 20 months or older were able to do so. Children who were at least 26 months old at the time of their ER visit could retain information and answer verbal questions about their experiences for at least 2 years following the event.

Problem Solving

Infants, like children and adults, face problem-solving tasks every day. For example, they may want to obtain an object beyond their reach or to make a toy repeat the interesting sound it produced earlier. Can infants overcome obstacles to achieve desired goals? It appears they can. In one study, infants were presented with an object out of their reach; however, by pulling on a cloth, they could drag the object to within reach (Willats, 1990). Although 6-month-olds did not retrieve the object, 9-month-olds solved this problem. Even the younger infants were successful when given

Infants begin to learn problem-solving strategies around 6 months of age.

hints about how they might retrieve the object (Kolstad & Aguiar, 1995). By 14 months of age, infants have figured out that adults are often useful sources of information in problem-solving situations (Goubert et al., 2006). As they get older, infants increasingly pay attention to the cues provided by adults and they increasingly solicit help by pointing, reaching, or otherwise letting the adult know that assistance is needed. Simple problem-solving behaviors improve considerably over the first 2 years of life and then, as you will see shortly, flourish during childhood.

SUMMING UP

- Using imitation, habituation, and operant conditioning techniques, researchers have gone from believing that infants have no memory beyond a few seconds to appreciating that even young 1-year-olds can recall experiences for weeks and even months under certain conditions.

- Infants clearly show recognition memory for familiar stimuli at birth and cued recall memory by about 2 months. More explicit memory, which requires actively retrieving an image of an object or event no longer present, appears to emerge toward the end of the first year. By age 2, it is even clearer that infants can recall events that happened long ago, for they, like adults, use language to represent and describe what happened.

- Simple problem solving improves throughout infancy and infants realize that they can get adults to help them solve problems.

CRITICAL THINKING

1. Uncle Jed says there is no way a baby can learn or remember anything. His position is that babies just eat, sleep, cry, and poop. What three key pieces of evidence might you use to convince Uncle Jed that there is something going on inside the infant's head in terms of learning and memory?

2. Would you characterize infants' memory as robust or fragile? What factors influence the robustness of infants' memory?

8.3 THE CHILD

The 2-year-old is already a highly capable information processor, as evidenced by the rapid language learning that takes place at this age. But dramatic improvements in learning, memory, and problem solving occur throughout the childhood years as children learn everything from how to flush toilets to how to work advanced math problems.

Explaining Memory Development

In countless situations, older children learn faster and remember more than younger children do. For example, 2-year-olds can repeat back about two digits immediately after hearing them, 5-year-olds about four digits, and 10-year-olds about six digits. And second-graders not only are faster learners than kindergartners but also retain information longer (Howe, 2000).

Why is this? Here are four major hypotheses about why learning and memory improve, patterned after those formulated by John Flavell and Henry Wellman (1977):

1. *Changes in basic capacities.* Older children have higher-powered "hardware" than younger children do; neural advances in their brains have contributed to more working-memory space for manipulating information and an ability to process information faster.

2. *Changes in memory strategies.* Older children have better "software"; they have learned and consistently use effective methods for putting information into long-term memory and retrieving it when they need it.

3. *Increased knowledge about memory.* Older children know more about memory (for example, how long they must study to learn things thoroughly, which kinds of memory tasks take more effort, and which strategies best fit each task).

4. *Increased knowledge about the world.* Older children know more than younger children about the world in general. This knowledge, or expertise, makes material to be learned more familiar, and familiar material is easier to learn and remember than unfamiliar material.

Do Basic Capacities Change?

Because the nervous system continues to develop in the years after birth, it seems plausible that older children remember more than younger children do because they have a better "computer"—a larger or more efficient information-processing system. However, we can quickly rule out the idea that the storage capacity of long-term memory enlarges. There is no consistent evidence that it changes after the first month of life (Perlmutter, 1986). In fact, young and old alike have more room for storage than they could ever use. Nor does the capacity of the sensory register to take in stimuli seem to change much (Schneider & Bjorklund, 1998).

So we can rule out improvements in the sensory register and long-term memory capacity as causes of developmental memory changes, but what about changes in short-term, or working, memory?

To test the capacity of short-term memory, researchers quickly present a list of items (such as numbers) then count the number of items that a person can recall in order. Measured this way, the basic features of working memory are in place by age 4 (Alloway, Gathercole, & Pickering, 2006) but improvements on a variety of working-memory tasks are evident across childhood and into adolescence (Conklin et al., 2007). The capacity of short-term memory improves from just over two items in early childhood to close to seven items in adulthood (Rose et al., 1997). In addition, the speed of mental processes improves with age and this allows older children and adults to simultaneously perform more mental operations in working memory than young children can (Halford, 2004; Kail & Salthouse, 1994). As basic mental processes become automatic, they can also be performed with little mental effort. This, in turn, frees space in working memory for other purposes, such as storing the information needed to solve a problem.

This focus on changes in working memory has been featured in revisions of Piaget's theory of cognitive development proposed by neo-Piagetian theorists who retain Piaget's original emphasis on stages and qualitative change, but try to articulate the processes of change more concretely. One such theorist is Robbie Case (1985; Marini & Case, 1994), who has been strongly influenced by the information-processing approach. Case proposes that more advanced stages of cognitive development are made possible because children make better use of the available space in their working memory. For example, Piaget stressed the preschooler's tendency to *center* on one aspect of a problem and lose sight of another (for example, to attend to the height of a glass but ignore its width, or vice versa). Perhaps, say the neo-Piagetians, this is not a matter of lacking certain cognitive structures; perhaps young children simply do not have enough working-memory capacity to keep both pieces of information in mind at once and to coordinate them. Similarly, young children may do poorly on memory tasks because they cannot keep the first items on a list in mind while processing later ones. And they may fail to solve mathematical problems correctly because they cannot keep the facts of the problem in mind while they are performing the calculations.

Some research suggests that the degree of improvement in short-term memory capacity that is evident as children age depends on what is tested or how it is tested. That is, short-term memory capacity is domain-specific — it varies with background knowledge and type of task (Conklin et al., 2007; Schneider, 2004). Greater knowledge in a domain or area of study increases the speed with which new, related information can be processed. In other words, the more you know about a subject, the faster you can process information related to this subject. In addition, more complex tasks consume more working-memory resources than less complex tasks (Luciano et al., 2005).

In sum, the basic capacities of the sensory register and long-term memory do not change with age. There are, however, improvements with age in operating speed and working-memory efficiency. These changes correspond to maturational changes in the brain. During infancy, brain activity during working-memory tasks is scattered and general (Bell & Wolfe, 2007). By age 4 or 5, working memory has found its "home" in the frontal lobes of the brain. Maturation of the frontal lobes continues throughout childhood and adolescence, bringing further improvements in working memory (Bell & Wolfe, 2007; Conklin et al., 2007).

Do Memory Strategies Change?

If shown the 12 items in ■ **Figure 8.3,** 4-year-olds might recall only 2 to 4 of them, 8-year-olds would recall 7 to 9 items, and adults might recall 10 to 11 of the items after a delay of several minutes. Are there specific memory strategies that evolve during childhood to permit this dramatic improvement in performance?

Children as young as 2 years can deliberately remember to do "important" things, such as reminding Mom to buy candy at the grocery store (Somerville, Wellman, & Cultice, 1983).

■ **FIGURE 8.3** A memory task. Imagine that you have 120 seconds to learn the 12 objects pictured here. What tricks or strategies might you devise to make your task easier?

They are more likely to use external memory aids (for example, pointing at or holding a toy pig when asked to remember where it was hidden) if they are instructed to remember than if they are not (Fletcher & Bray, 1996). However, children younger than 4 show little flexibility in switching from an ineffective strategy to an effective one, and they typically do not generate new strategies even as they gain experience with a task (Chen, 2007). In contrast, many 4- and 5-year-olds will flexibly switch strategies and generate new strategies, making them more effective on memory tasks than younger children. Younger children also have a tendency to make **perseveration errors:** they continue to use the same strategy that was successful in the *past* despite the strategy's *current* lack of success. Thus, if they previously found their favorite toy under the sofa, they search this location on future occasions when the toy is lost (Chen, 2007). They seem to be unable to get the old strategy — ineffective in the new situation — out of their mind and move on to a different strategy that could potentially be successful. By age 4, we see a decline in these perseveration errors.

Yet even 4-year-olds have not mastered many of the effective strategies for moving information into long-term memory. For example, when instructed to remember toys they have been shown, 3- and 4-year-olds will look carefully at the objects and will often label them once, but they only rarely use the memory strategy called **rehearsal** — the repeating of items they are trying to learn and remember (Baker-Ward, Ornstein, & Holden, 1984). To rehearse the objects in Figure 8.3, you might simply say, "apple, truck, grapes. . . ." repeatedly. John Flavell and his associates found that only 10% of 5-year-olds repeated the names of pictures they were asked to recall, but more than half of 7-year-olds and 85% of 10-year-olds used this strategy (Flavell, Beach, & Chinsky, 1966).

Another important memory strategy is **organization,** or classifying items into meaningful groups. You might lump the apple, the grapes, and the hamburger in Figure 8.3 into a category of foods and form other categories for animals, vehicles, and baseball equipment. You would then rehearse each category and recall it as a cluster. Another organizational strategy, *chunking,* is used to break a long number (6065551843) into manageable subunits (606-555-1843, a phone number). Organization is mastered later in childhood than rehearsal. Until about age 9 or 10, children are not much better at recalling lists of items that lend themselves readily to grouping than they are at recalling lists of unrelated words (Flavell & Wellman, 1977).

Finally, the strategy of **elaboration** involves actively creating meaningful links between items to be remembered. Elaboration is achieved by adding something to the items, in the form of either words or images. Creating and using a sentence such as "the apple fell on the horse's nose" could help you remember two of the items in Figure 8.3. Elaboration is especially helpful in learning foreign languages. For example, you might link the Spanish word *pato* (pronounced pot-o) to the English equivalent *duck* by imagining a duck in a pot of boiling water. Children who can elaborate on the relationship between two items (e.g., generating similar and different features of the items) have improved retention of these items (Howe, 2006).

Memory or encoding strategies develop in a fairly predictable order, with rehearsal emerging first, followed by organization, and then by elaboration. Children do not suddenly start using strategies, however. According to Patricia Miller (1990, 1994; Miller & Seier, 1994), they typically progress through four phases on their way to successful strategy use. Initially, children have a **mediation deficiency,** which means they cannot spontaneously use or benefit from strategies, even if they are taught how to use them. This gives way to a different kind of problem, a **production deficiency,** in which children can use strategies they are taught but do not produce them on their own. The third phase is a **utilization deficiency,** in which children spontaneously produce a strategy but their task performance does not yet benefit from using the strategy. Finally, children exhibit effective strategy use by both producing and benefiting from a memory strategy.

There is ample evidence of utilization deficiencies across various age groups and for different types of strategies (see, for example, Coyle & Bjorklund, 1996; Miller & Seier, 1994; Pressley & Hilden, 2006). Why would children who use a strategy fail to benefit from it? One possibility is that using a new strategy is mentally taxing and leaves no free cognitive resources for other aspects of the task (Pressley & Hilden, 2006). Once using the strategy becomes routine, then other components of the task can be addressed simultaneously. Whatever the reason for utilization deficiencies, they reflect a child–task interaction; that is, they depend on how difficult a task is for a particular child rather than on task difficulty per se (Bjorklund et al., 1997).

Using effective storage strategies to learn material is only half the battle; retrieval strategies can also influence how much is recalled. Indeed, retrieving something from memory can often be a complex adventure when solving problems, such as when you try to remember when you went on a trip by searching for cues that might trigger your memory ("Well, I still had long hair then, but it was after Muffy's wedding, and. . . .").

Strange as it may seem, even when young schoolchildren are shown how to use the memory strategy of elaboration, they may not do as well as older children on memory tests because it does not occur to them to use the images they worked so hard to create to help them retrieve what they have learned (Pressley & Levin, 1980). In general, young children rely more on external cues for both encoding and retrieving information than do older children (Schneider & Pressley, 1997). Thus, young children may need to put their toothbrushes next to their pajamas so that they have a physical reminder to brush their teeth before they go to bed. Older children are less likely to need such external cues but may continue to use them throughout elementary school (Eskritt & Lee, 2002). In many ways, then, command of memory strategies increases over the childhood years, but the path to effective strategy use is characterized more by ups and downs than by steady increases (Schneider, 2004).

Does Knowledge about Memory Change?

The term **metamemory** refers to knowledge of memory and to monitoring and regulating memory processes. It is knowing, for example, what your memory limits are, which memory strategies are more or less effective, and which memory tasks are more or less difficult (Flavell, Miller, & Miller, 1993). It is also noting that your efforts to remember something are not working and that you need to try something different (Schneider, 2004). Metamemory is one aspect of **metacognition,** or knowledge of the human mind and of the range of cognitive processes. Your store of metacognitive knowledge might include an understanding that you are better at learning language than at learning algebra, that it is harder to pay attention to a task when there is distracting noise in the background than when it is quiet, and that it is wise to check a proposed solution to a problem before concluding that it is correct.

When do children first show evidence of metacognition? If instructed to remember where the *Sesame Street* character Big Bird has been hidden so that they can later wake him up, even 2- and 3-year-olds will go stand near the hiding spot, or at least look or point at that spot; they do not do these things as often if Big Bird is visible and they do not need to remember where he is (DeLoache, Cassidy, & Brown, 1985). By age 2, then, children understand that to remember something, you have to work at it. Researchers have found that 3-year-olds understand the difference between thinking about an object in their heads and experiencing it in reality and that 4-year-olds realize behavior is guided by beliefs (Flavell, 1999). These findings indicate that metacognitive awareness is present at least in a rudimentary form at a young age (Kuhn, 2000).

In another study (Ghetti & Alexander, 2004), children and adults were asked to rate the importance and memorability of past events. Even 5-year-olds detected differences in the importance of events and expected that more prominent events would be easier to remember. These findings contrast with earlier ones in which children were asked to predict how many items they would be able to remember (for example, Yussen &

Levy, 1975). Under these conditions, preschoolers' estimates were highly unrealistic—as if they believed they could perform any memory feat imaginable—and they were unfazed by information about how another child had done on the task. But if researchers gave children more time before asking them to estimate how much they would be able to recall of what they had just studied, accuracy was good among children as young as age 6 (Schneider, Roth, & Ennemoser, 2000). When asked immediately after the learning task, children (and adults) overestimated their future ability to remember, presumably based on what was still in their short-term memory. After a few minutes, this information is typically lost from short-term memory, and children base their estimates on what has made it into long-term memory.

Are increases in metamemory a major contributor to improved memory performance over the childhood years? Children with greater metamemory awareness demonstrate better memory ability, but several factors influence the strength of this relationship (Bjork & Bjork, 1998; Schneider, 2004). Researchers are most likely to see a connection between metamemory and memory performance among older children and among children who have been in situations in which they must remember something (DeMarie & Ferron, 2003; Schneider & Bjorklund, 1998). Not only is task experience important, but the nature of the task is also relevant. Awareness of memory processes benefits even young children on tasks that are simple and familiar and where connections between metamemory knowledge and memory performance are fairly obvious (Schneider & Sodian, 1988). Yet children who know what to do may not always do it, so good metamemory is no guarantee of good recall (Schneider & Pressley, 1997). It seems that children not only must know that a strategy is useful but also must know why it is useful in order to be motivated to use it and to benefit from its use (Justice et al., 1997). Metamemory is also influenced by children's language skills and by their general knowledge about mental states and their roles—what is known as theory of mind (Lockl & Schneider, 2007; see Chapter 13 for definition and discussion). The links between metamemory and memory performance, although not perfect, are strong enough to suggest the merits of teaching children more about how memory works and how they can make it work more effectively for them.

Does Knowledge of the World Change?

Ten-year-olds know considerably more about the world in general than two-year-olds do. The individual's knowledge of a content area to be learned, or **knowledge base,** as it has come to be called, clearly affects learning and memory performance. Think about the difference between reading about a topic that you already know well and reading about a new topic. In the first case, you can read quickly because you are able to link the information to the knowledge you have already stored. All you really need to do is check for any new information or information that contradicts what you already know. Learning about a highly unfamiliar topic is more difficult ("It's Greek to me").

Perhaps the most dramatic illustration of the powerful influence of knowledge base on memory was provided by Michelene Chi (1978). She demonstrated that even though adults typically outperform children on tests of memory, this age difference could be reversed if children have more expertise than adults. Chi recruited children who were expert chess players and compared their memory skills with those of adults who were familiar with the game but lacked expertise. On a test of memory for sequences of digits, the children recalled fewer than the adults did, demonstrating their usual deficiencies. But on a test of memory for the locations of chess pieces, the children clearly beat the adults (see ■ Figure 8.4). Because they were experts, these children were able to form more and larger mental chunks, or meaningful groups, of chess pieces, which allowed them to remember more. When child experts were compared with adult experts, there were no differences in performance (Schneider et al., 1993).

Pause to consider the implications: On most tasks, young children are the novices and older children or adults are the experts. Perhaps older children and adults recall longer strings of digits because they are more familiar with numbers than young children are, not because they have better basic learning capacities. Perhaps they recall more words in word lists simply because they have more familiarity with language. Perhaps memory improves over childhood simply because older children know more about all kinds of things than younger children do (Bjorklund, 1995).

In their areas of expertise—whether baseball, dinosaurs, Pokémon cards, or *Harry Potter* trivia—children appear to develop highly specialized and effective strategies of information processing, just as the young chess players studied by Chi apparently had (see Schneider & Bjorklund, 1998, for review). Indeed, children with low general intellectual ability but high expertise sometimes understand and remember more about stories in their area of expertise than do children with higher intellectual ability but less expertise (Schneider, Bjorklund, & Maier-Bruckner, 1996). It seems that the more you know, the more you *can* know. It also seems that how well a child does on a memory task depends not only on age but also on familiarity with the specific task.

Revisiting the Explanations

We can now draw four conclusions about the development of learning and memory:

1. Older children are faster information processors and can juggle more information in working memory. Older and younger children, however, do not differ in terms of sensory register or long-term memory capacity.

2. Older children use more effective *memory strategies* in encoding and retrieving information.

3. Older children know more about memory, and good *metamemory* may help children choose more appropriate strategies and control and monitor their learning more effectively.

4. Older children know more in general, and their larger *knowledge base* improves their ability to learn and remember.

■ **FIGURE 8.4** Effects of expertise on memory. Michelene Chi found that child chess experts outperformed adult chess novices on a test of recall for the location of chess pieces (although, in keeping with the usual developmental trend, these children could not recall strings of numbers as well as adults could).
Adapted from Chi in Siegler (1978).

Is one of these explanations of memory development better than the others? Darlene DeMarie and John Ferron (2003) tested whether a model that includes three of these factors—basic capacities, strategies, and metamemory—could explain recall memory better than a single factor. For both younger (5–8 years) and older (8–11 years) children, the three-factor model predicted memory performance better than a single-factor model. Use of memory strategies was an especially strong direct predictor of recall. Importantly, there were also correlations among factors. Having good basic capacities, for example, was related to advanced metamemory and to command of strategies and had both direct and indirect influences on recall. So all these phenomena may contribute something to the dramatic improvements in learning and memory that occur over the childhood years. We return to these four hypotheses when we consider changes in learning and memory in adulthood.

Autobiographical Memory

Children effortlessly remember all sorts of things: a birthday party last week, where they left their favorite toy, what to do when they go to a fast-food restaurant. Much of what children remember and talk about consists of events that have happened to them at a particular time and place. Such **autobiographical memories** are essential ingredients of present and future experiences. Here we look at how autobiographical memories are stored and organized and at factors that influence their accuracy.

When Do Autobiographical Memories Begin?

You learned earlier in this chapter that infants and toddlers are able to store memories. You also know that children and adults have many specific autobiographical events stored in long-term memory. Yet research shows that older children and adults exhibit **childhood** (or infantile) **amnesia;** that is, they have few

autobiographical memories of events that occurred before about age 2 or 3 (Bauer, 2007; Hayne, 2004). As Patricia Bauer (2007) notes, memories for the first few years of life seem to fall into a large black hole from which there is no return.

To determine how old we have to be when we experience significant life events to remember them, JoNell Usher and Ulric Neisser (1993) asked college students who had experienced the birth of a younger sibling, a hospitalization, the death of a family member, or a family move early in life to answer questions about those experiences (for example, who told them their mothers were going to the hospital to give birth, what they were doing when she left, and where they were when they first saw the new baby). As ■ **Figure 8.5** shows, the proportion of memory questions students were able to answer increased dramatically as age at the time of the experience increased. Overall, children had to be at least age 2 to recall the birth of a sibling or hospitalization and age 3 to recall the death of a family member or a move.

Why do we remember little about our early years? As you have seen, infants and toddlers are certainly capable of encoding their experiences (Fivush, 2002; Howe, 2000). Also, young preschool children seem able to remember a good deal about events that occurred when they were infants even though older children and adults cannot (Bauer, 1996; Fivush, Gray, & Fromhoff, 1987). One explanation of childhood amnesia is that infants and toddlers may not have enough space in working memory to hold the multiple pieces of information about actor, action, and setting needed to encode a coherent memory of an event (White & Pillemer, 1979). As you learned earlier in this chapter, functional working-memory capacity increases with age as the brain, particularly the frontal lobe, matures.

Also, infants do not use language, and adults do. Because autobiographical memory seems to rely heavily on language skills, we would expect such memories to increase with increased language skills (Marian & Neisser, 2000). Gabrielle Simcock and Harlene Hayne (2002, 2003) assessed the verbal

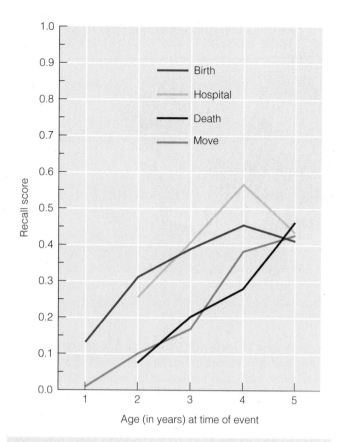

■ FIGURE 8.5 College students' recall of early life events increases as a function of how old they were at the time of the event.

SOURCE: From J.A. Usher & U. Neisser, Childhood amnesia and the beginnings of memory for four early life events, *Journal of Experimental Psychology: General, Vol. 122*, pp. 155–165. Copyright © 1993 American Psychological Association. Reprinted with permission from the American Psychological Association.

skills of young children (27, 33, and 39 months old) who participated in a unique event involving a "magic shrinking machine" that seemingly made items smaller in a matter of seconds. After a 6- or 12-month delay, children were tested for both verbal recall (answers to open-ended questions) and nonverbal recall (identification of photos of the items used in the activity) of the unique event. Their nonverbal recall improved across the age groups but was good at all ages. Verbal recall was poor and depended on the simpler verbal skills present at the time of encoding rather than the more developed verbal skills present at the time of recall. In other words, "children's verbal reports of the event were frozen in time" (p. 229). So a relative lack of verbal skills during the first few years of life may limit what we are able to recall from this period. However, this language explanation does not account for why children cannot remember nonverbal information such as the faces of preschool classmates (Lie & Newcombe, 1999).

Alternatively, perhaps memories no longer useful once we reach new developmental levels and face new developmental tasks are no longer retrieved and are therefore lost (Rovee-Collier & Boller, 1995). Or maybe what

is lacking is a sense of self around which memories of personally experienced events can be organized as "events that happened to *me*" (Howe & Courage, 1993, 1997). Indeed, young children's ability to recognize themselves in a mirror is a good predictor of children's ability to talk about their past (Harley & Reese, 1999).

Some researchers have also tried to explain childhood amnesia in terms of **fuzzy-trace theory** (Howe, 2000). According to this explanation, children store verbatim and general accounts of an event separately. Verbatim information (such as word-for-word recall of a biology class lecture) is unstable and likely to be lost over long periods (Leichtman & Ceci, 1993); it is easier to remember the gist (for example, recall of the general points covered in a biology lecture) of an event than the details (Brainerd & Reyna, 1993; Koriat, Goldsmith, & Pansky, 2000). With age, we are increasingly likely to rely on gist memory traces, which are less likely to be forgotten and are more efficient than verbatim memory traces in the sense that they take less space in memory (Brainerd & Gordon, 1994; Klaczynski, 2001). Children pass through a transition period from storing largely verbatim memories to storing more gist memories, and the earlier verbatim memories are unlikely to be retained over time (Howe, 2000).

Finally, there is evidence that although children may lose explicit recall of early experiences, they retain some implicit memories, at least for nonverbal information (such as classmates' faces; see Lie & Newcombe, 1999). As you can see, there are plenty of ideas about the causes of childhood amnesia but still no firm explanation of why a period of life that is highly important to later development is a blank for most of us.

Scripts

As children engage in routine daily activities such as getting ready for bed or eating at a fast-food restaurant, they construct **scripts** of these activities (Nelson, 1986). Scripts represent the

Children develop scripts in memory for routine activities, such as visiting a fast-food restaurant, that guide their behavior in these situations.

typical sequence of actions related to an event and guide future behaviors in similar settings (Schank & Abelson, 1977). For instance, children who have been to a fast-food restaurant might have a script like this: Wait in line, tell the person behind the counter what you want, pay for the food, carry the tray of food to a table, open the packages and eat the food, gather the trash, and throw it away before leaving. With this script in mind, children can act effectively in similar settings. Children as young as 3 years use scripts when reporting familiar events (Nelson, 1997). When asked about their visit to a fast-food restaurant the day before, children report generally what happens when they go to the restaurant rather than what specifically happened during yesterday's visit (Kuebli & Fivush, 1994). As children age, their scripts become more detailed. Perhaps more important than age, however, is experience: Children with greater experience of an event develop richer scripts than children with less experience (DeMarie, Norman, & Abshier, 2000).

Eyewitness Memory

Children's scripts affect their memory. For example, when presented with information inconsistent with their scripts, preschoolers may misremember the information so that it better fits their script (Nelson & Hudson, 1988). Four-year-old Damian may have a script for birthdays that includes blowing out candles, eating cake, and opening presents. Although his brother is sick on his birthday and eats Jell-O instead of cake, Damian later recalls that they all ate cake before opening presents. This indicates that memory is a reconstruction, not an exact replication (Koriat, Goldsmith, & Pansky, 2000). This, in turn, has significant implications for **eyewitness memory** (or testimony), or the reporting of events witnessed or experienced—for example, a child's reporting that she saw her little brother snitch some candy before dinner. Children are increasingly asked to report events that have happened in the context of abuse cases or custody hearings (Bruck & Ceci, 1999; Ceci & Bruck, 1998). To what extent can you "trust" a child's memory in these situations? What factors influence the accuracy of children's eyewitness memory?

When asked generally about events ("Tell me what happened at Uncle Joe's house"), preschoolers recall less information than older children, but the recall of both groups is accurate (Fivush & Hammond, 1989; Howe, Courage, & Peterson, 1994). Specific questions ("Was Uncle Joe wearing a red shirt?") elicit more information, but accuracy of recall begins to slip (Hilgard & Loftus, 1979). This is especially true as the questions become more directed or leading ("Uncle Joe touched you here, didn't he?"). Preschool-age children, more so than older children and adults, are suggestible; they can be influenced by information implied in direct questioning and by relevant information introduced after the event (Bjorklund, Brown, & Bjorklund, 2002).

Perhaps it is unfortunate, then, that preschoolers, because they initially offer less information in response to open-ended questions, are asked a larger number of directed questions than

older children (Baker-Ward et al., 1993; Price & Goodman, 1990). They are also frequently subjected to repeated questioning, which increases errors in reporting among children (Bjorklund, Brown, & Bjorklund, 2002). Although repeated questioning with general, open-ended questions can increase accuracy, repeated questioning with directed or closed questions can decrease accuracy (Memon & Vartoukian, 1996). For example, in a study with 5- and 6-year-olds, researchers "cross-examined" children about events that occurred on a field trip to a police station during which the children saw a jail cell and police car and were fingerprinted and photographed (Zajac & Hayne, 2003). After a delay of 8 months, children's memories were probed using irrelevant, leading, and ambiguous questions like those you might hear in a courtroom. Many children "cracked" under the pressure as evidenced by backing down and changing their answers in response to the questioning. Fully one out of three children changed *all* their answers, and most changed at least one answer. So although children can demonstrate accurate recall when asked clear and unbiased questions, this study shows that young children's memory for past events can quickly become muddied when the questioning becomes tough.

Problem Solving

Memories are vital to problem-solving skills. To solve any problem, a person must process information about the task, as well as use stored information, to achieve a goal. How do problem-solving capacities change during childhood? Piaget provided one answer to this question by proposing that children progress through broad stages of cognitive growth, but information-processing theorists were not satisfied with this explanation. They sought to pinpoint more specific reasons why problem-solving prowess improves so dramatically as children age.

Consider the problem of predicting what will happen to the balance beam in ■ Figure 8.6 when weights are put on each side of the fulcrum, or balancing point. The goal is to decide which way the balance beam will tip when it is released. To judge correctly, you must take into account both the number of weights and their distances from the fulcrum. Piaget believed that concrete operational thinkers can appreciate the significance of either the amount of weight or its distance from the center but will not grasp the inverse relationship between the two factors. Only when they reach the stage of formal operations will new cognitive structures allow them to understand

■ **FIGURE 8.6** The balance beam apparatus used by Robert Siegler to study children's problem-solving abilities. Which way will the balance beam tip?

SOURCE: From R.S. Siegler, Developmental sequences within and between concepts, *Monographs of the Society for Research in Child Development*, 46, (2, Serial No. 189). Copyright © 1981 Blackwell Publishing. Reprinted with permission.

that balance can be maintained by decreasing a weight *and* moving it farther from the fulcrum or by increasing a weight *and* moving it closer to the fulcrum (Piaget & Inhelder, 1969).

Robert Siegler (1981, 2000) proposed that the information-processing perspective could provide a fuller analysis. His **rule assessment approach** determines what information about a problem children take in and what rules they then formulate to account for this information. This approach assumes that children's problem-solving attempts are not hit or miss but are governed by rules; it also assumes that children fail to solve problems because they fail to encode all the critical aspects of the problem and are guided by faulty rules.

Siegler (1981) administered balance beam problems to individuals ages 3 to 20. He detected clear age differences in the extent to which both weight and distance from the fulcrum were taken into account in the rules that guided decisions about which end of the balance beam would drop. Few 3-year-olds used a rule; they guessed. By contrast, 4- and 5-year-olds were governed by rules. More than 80% of these children used a simple rule that said the side of the balance beam with greater weight would drop; they ignored distance from the fulcrum. By age 8, most children had begun to consider distance from the fulcrum and weight under some conditions: when the weight on the two sides was equal, they appreciated that the side of the balance beam with the weights farthest from the fulcrum would drop. By age 12, most children considered both weight and distance on a range of problems, although they still became confused on complex problems in which one side had more weights but the other had its weights farther from the fulcrum. Finally, 30% of 20-year-olds discovered the correct rule—that the pull on each arm is a function of weight times distance. For example, if there are three weights on the second peg to the left and two weights on the fourth peg to the right, the left torque is $3 \times 2 = 6$ and the right torque is $2 \times 4 = 8$, so the right arm will drop.

The increased accuracy of young adults comes with a price—increased time to solve the problem (van der Maas & Jansen, 2003). Although, in general, information-processing time gets faster with age, the complex rules needed to successfully solve all the variations of the balance beam problem demand more time. So on some problems, adults are slower than children because they are using a more sophisticated strategy.

In most important areas of problem solving, Siegler (1996) concluded, children do not simply progress from one way of thinking to another as they age, as his balance beam research suggested. Instead, in working problems in arithmetic, spelling, science, and other school subjects, most children in any age group use multiple rules or problem-solving strategies rather than just one. In working a subtraction problem such as $12 - 3 = 9$, for example, children sometimes count down from 12 until they have counted off 3 and arrive at 9 but other times count from 3 until they reach 12. In one study of second- and fourth-graders, more than 90% of the children used three or more strategies in working subtraction problems (Siegler, 1989).

Similarly, Michael Cohen (1996) found that most preschoolers used all possible strategies when attempting to solve a practical mathematical problem in the context of playing store. He also found that children's selection and use of strategies became more efficient over multiple task trials; that is, they increasingly selected strategies that would allow them to solve the task in fewer steps.

Such results suggest that cognitive development works much as evolution does, through a process of natural selection in which many ways of thinking are available and the most adaptive survive (DeLoache, Miller, & Pierroutsakos, 1998; Siegler, 1996, 2000). Rather than picturing development as a series of stages resembling stairsteps, Siegler argues, we should picture it as overlapping waves, as shown in ■ **Figure 8.7**. Siegler (2006) summarizes the **overlapping waves theory** as a "process of variability, choice, and change" (p. 478). Thus, the development of problem-solving skills is a matter of knowing and using a variety of strategies, becoming increasingly selective with experience about which strategy to use, and changing or adding strategies as needed. At each age, children have multiple problem-solving strategies available to them. As children gain more experience, which typically occurs as they age, they decrease their use of less-adaptive strategies and increase their use of more-adaptive strategies; occasionally, new strategies may appear. Strategies evolve from their initial acquisition in a particular context to their generalization to other contexts, which helps strengthen the fledgling strategies (Siegler, 2006). Gradually, children not only learn to choose the most useful strategy for a problem but also become increasingly effective at executing new strategies. Familiarity with a task and with strategies frees processing space, allowing children to engage in more metacognitive analysis of the strategies at their dis-posal (Whitebread, 1999). Throughout, there is significant variability—both between children and within the same child across time and tasks.

Notice the difference between this information-processing explanation and Piaget's explanation of cognitive change.

■ **FIGURE 8.7** Cognitive development may resemble overlapping waves more than a staircase leading from one stage to another. Children of a particular age typically use multiple thinking strategies rather than just one.

SOURCE: *Emerging minds: The process of change in children's thinking* by Siegler copyright © 1996 by Oxford University Press, Inc. Used by permission of Oxford University Press, Inc.

Piaget argued that change is qualitative, with new, more effective strategies replacing older, less effective strategies all at once as children move from one stage to another. Siegler argues that strategies emerge gradually and become more effective over time, with multiple strategies available any time.

Imagine how effective teachers might be if they, like Siegler, could accurately diagnose the information-processing strategies of their learners to know what each child is noticing (or failing to notice) about a problem and what rules or strategies each child is using when. Like a good car mechanic, the teacher would be able to pinpoint the problem and encourage less use of faulty strategies and rules and more use of adaptive ones. Much remains to be learned about how problem-solving strategies evolve as children age, and why. However, the rule assessment approach and overlapping waves theory give a fairly specific idea of what children are doing (or doing wrong) as they attack problems and illustrate how the information-processing approach to cognitive development provides a different view of development than Piaget's account does.

SUMMING UP

▌ Memory improves during childhood with increased efficiency of basic information-processing capacities, greater use of memory strategies, improvement in metamemory, and growth of general knowledge base.

▌ Much of what we remember is autobiographical. Even though infants and toddlers show evidence of memory, older children and adults often experience childhood amnesia, or lack of memory for events that happened during infancy and early childhood. Such childhood amnesia may occur because of space limitations in working memory or because early events are stored in ways that make later retrieval difficult or because children store more verbatim information and less gist.

▌ By age 3, children store routine daily events as scripts that they can draw on in similar situations. Our scripts influence what we remember about an event, which is also influenced by information related to but coming after the event.

▌ Even young children can use systematic rules to solve problems, but according to Siegler's overlapping wave theory, their problem-solving skills improve as they use faulty rules less and rules that incorporate all the relevant aspects of the problem more.

CRITICAL THINKING

1. You are a first-grade teacher, and one of the first things you notice is that some of your students remember a good deal more than others about the stories you read to them. Based on what you have read in this chapter, what are your main hypotheses about why some children have better memories than other children the same age?

2. You have been called in to interview a young child who may have witnessed a crime. Given the research on children's memory, how will you gather information from your young witness?

8.4 THE ADOLESCENT

Although parents in the midst of reminding their adolescent sons and daughters to do household chores or homework may wonder whether teenagers process any information, learning, memory, and problem solving continue to improve considerably during the adolescent years. Research on episodic memory shows that the performance of young teens (11–12 years) is quite similar to that of children, and both groups are markedly worse than young adults (Brehmer et al., 2007). Clearly, then, there is room for improvement during adolescence. How does this improvement occur?

Strategies

First, new learning and memory strategies emerge. It is during adolescence that the memory strategy of elaboration is mastered (Schneider & Pressley, 1997). Adolescents also develop and refine advanced learning and memory strategies highly relevant to school learning—for example, note-taking and underlining skills. Ann Brown and Sandra Smiley (1978) asked students from 5th to 12th grade (approximately 11–18 years) to read and recall a story. Some learners were asked to recall the story immediately; others were given an additional 5 minutes to study it before they were tested. Amazingly, fifth-graders gained almost nothing from the extra study period except for those few who used the time to underline or take notes. The older junior high school students benefited to an extent, but only senior high school students used underlining and note-taking methods effectively to improve their recall. When some groups of students were told specifically that they could underline or take notes if they wished, fifth-graders still did not improve, largely because they tended to underline everything rather than to highlight the most important points.

Adolescents also make more deliberate use of strategies that younger children use unconsciously (Bjorklund, 1985). For example, they may deliberately organize a list of words instead of simply using the organization or grouping that happens to be there already. And they use existing strategies more selectively. For example, they are adept at using their strategies to memorize the material on which they know they will be tested and at deliberately forgetting anything else (Bray, Hersh, & Turner, 1985; Lorsbach & Reimer, 1997). To illustrate, Patricia Miller and Michael Weiss (1981) asked children to remember the locations of animals that had been hidden behind small doors and to ignore the household objects hidden behind other doors. As ▪ Figure 8.8 shows, 13-year-olds recalled more than 7- and 10-year-olds about where the animals had been hidden, but they remembered less about task-irrelevant information (the locations of the household objects). Apparently, they are better able to push irrelevant information out of working memory so that it does not interfere with task performance (Lorsbach & Reimer, 1997). So, during elementary school, children get better at distinguishing between what is relevant and what is irrelevant, but during adolescence they advance further by selectively using their memory

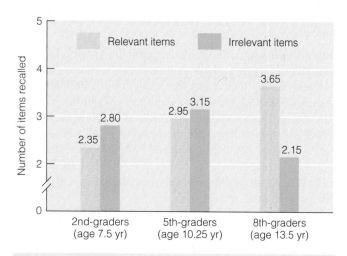

FIGURE 8.8 Adolescents are better able than children to concentrate on learning relevant material and to ignore irrelevant material.
SOURCE: From P.H. Miller & M.G. Weiss, Children's attention allocation, understanding of attention and performance on the incidental learning task, *Child Development*, 52, pp. 1183–1190. Copyright © 1981, Blackwell Publishing. Reprinted with permission.

strategies only on the relevant material. If it is not going to be on the test, forget it!

Basic Capacities

Adolescents make other strides besides these changes in memory strategies. Basic capacities continue to increase; for example, adolescents perform any number of cognitive operations faster than children do (Kail, 1991). As discussed earlier in this chapter, adolescents have greater functional use of their working memory because maturational changes in the brain allow them to process information more quickly and to simultaneously process more chunks of information. Older teens (16–20 years) perform better than younger ones (less than 15 years) on highly complex cognitive tasks that require them to use recalled information to strategically direct their search behavior (Luciana et al., 2005). There is no difference, though, on tasks of low complexity such as face recognition.

Metamemory and Knowledge Base

There is little to say about knowledge base other than it continues to expand during adolescence. So adolescents may do better than children on some tasks simply because they know more about the topic.

Metamemory and metacognition also improve. For example, adolescents become better able to tailor their reading strategies to different purposes (studying versus skimming) and better able to realize when they do not understand something (Baker & Brown, 1984). They can monitor their strategy choice, selecting elaboration over rote repetition when they realize that the former is more effective (Pressley, Levin, & Ghatala, 1984). They

are also fairly accurate at monitoring whether or not they have allocated adequate study time to learn new material (Kelemen, 2000). Teens typically allocate more study time to information judged to be difficult, indicating that they understand this material needs additional processing to be retained (Thiede & Dunlosky, 1999). Interestingly, when pressed for time, college students devote more study time to easy items (Son & Metcalfe, 2000). Apparently, they decide it is futile to work on the difficult material when they do not have adequate time, so they spend their time on what seems most likely to pay off. Hopefully, you can see the implication of this for your own studying: Set aside enough time to study all the material; otherwise, you may end up in a time crunch reviewing only the easy material.

Growth in strategies, basic capacities, knowledge base, and metacognition probably also helps explain the growth in everyday problem-solving ability that occurs during the adolescent years. Teenagers perfect several information-processing skills and become able to apply them deliberately and spontaneously across a variety of tasks.

SUMMING UP

▌ Adolescents are able to use more sophisticated memory strategies such as elaboration, although they often rely on the strategy of rehearsal that served them well during childhood.

▌ Maturational changes in the brain expand the functional use of working memory. Adolescents can simultaneously juggle more information in working memory and can process information more quickly than they could during childhood.

▌ Adolescents' knowledge bases and metamemory skills also improve and contribute to increased memory performance and problem-solving ability.

CRITICAL THINKING

1. Using the information-processing model presented earlier in the chapter (see Figure 8.1), explain why 17-year-old Nathaniel outperforms his 7-year-old sibling when asked to recall a TV program on the Civil War both watched last week.

2. Abigail has a big exam coming up—the results could determine whether or not she earns a scholarship for college. How should she prepare for the exam and what characteristics of the test itself or the testing conditions might affect her performance?

8.5 | THE ADULT

If you are about age 20, you will be pleased to know that the young adult college student has served as the standard of effective information processing against which all other age groups are compared. In other words, information processing is thought to be most efficient—at its peak—in young adults. Still, improvements in cognitive performance continue during the adult years before aging begins to take its toll on some memory and problem-solving capacities.

Developing Expertise

Comparing people new to their chosen fields of study with those more experienced tells researchers that experience pays off in more effective memory and problem-solving skills. In Chapter 7, you saw that people in Piaget's highest stage of cognitive development, formal operations, often perform better in their areas of specialization than in unfamiliar areas. Similarly, information-processing research shows that adults often function best cognitively in domains in which they have achieved expertise (Byrnes, 1996; Ericsson, 1996; Glaser & Chi, 1988). It seems to take about 10 years of training and experience to become a true expert in a field and to build a rich and well-organized knowledge base (Ericsson, 1996). But once this base is achieved, the expert not only knows and remembers more but thinks also more effectively than individuals who lack expertise.

Consider first the effects of knowledge base on memory. How might adults who are baseball experts and adults who care little for baseball perceive and remember the same game? George Spilich and his associates (1979) had baseball experts and novices listen to a tape of a half inning of play. Experts recalled more of the information central to the game—the important plays and the fate of each batter, in proper order—whereas novices were thrown off by irrelevant facts such as the threatening weather conditions and the number of people attending the game. Experts also recalled more details—for example, noting that a double was a line drive down the left-field line rather than just a double. At any age, experts in a field are likely to remember new information in that content domain more fully than novices do (Morrow et al., 1994).

In addition, experts are able to use their elaborately organized and complete knowledge bases to solve problems effec-

Adults who have gained proficiency in their chosen fields can draw from their well-organized knowledge bases to find just the right information to fit the problem at hand. Solving problems is automatic and effortless for experts.

tively and efficiently (Proffitt, Coley, & Medin, 2000). They are able to size up a situation quickly, see what the problem really is, and recognize how the new problem is similar to and different from problems encountered in the past (Glaser & Chi, 1988). They can quickly, surely, and almost automatically call up the right information from their extensive knowledge base to devise effective solutions to problems and to carry them out efficiently.

Are the benefits of expertise content-specific, or does gaining expertise in one domain carry over into other domains and make a person a more generally effective learner or problem solver? This is an interesting and important question. One research team (Ericsson, Chase, & Faloon, 1980) put an average college student to work improving the number of digits he could recall. He practiced for about 1 hour a day, 3 to 5 days a week, for more than 1½ years—more than 200 hours in all. His improvement? He went from a memory span of 7 digits to one of 79 digits. His method involved forming meaningful associations between strings of digits and running times—for example, seeing 3492 as "3 minutes and 49 point 2 seconds, near world-record mile time" (p. 1181). It also involved chunking numbers into groups of three or four then organizing the chunks into large units.

Did all this work pay off in a better memory for information other than numbers? Not really. When he was given letters of the alphabet to recall, this young man's memory span was unexceptional (about six letters). Clearly the memory ability he developed was based on strategies of use only in the subject matter he was trying to remember. Similarly, Rajan Mahadevan, a man with an exceptional memory for arrays of numbers, turns out to possess no special ability for remembering the positions and orientations of objects (Biederman et al., 1992), and Shakuntala Devi, a woman who can solve complex mathematical problems in her head at amazing speeds, is apparently average at performing other cognitive operations (Jensen, 1990). Each expert apparently relies on domain-specific knowledge and domain-specific information-processing strategies to achieve cognitive feats (Ericsson & Kintsch, 1995; Schunn & Anderson, 1999).

Sometimes, domain expertise can be a hindrance. Tax experts typically outperform tax novices on hypothetical tax cases (Marchant et al., 1991). But when primed to think about a general tax principle, experts then had more trouble than novices on a tax case that violated this principle, presumably because they had trouble "overriding" the rich source of information activated in their memory (Lewandowsky & Kirsner, 2000). And although older adults know more about the world than younger adults, they do not always perform better when given an explicit memory task (Foos & Sarno, 1998). In one study, for example, older adults first demonstrated that they had greater knowledge of U.S. presidents than younger adults. Both groups were then given a set of 20 presidents' names to study for as long as they wanted before being tested for recall and recognition of the list (Foos & Sarno, 1998). The younger adults outperformed the older ones. The older adults spent less time studying the list than the younger adults, possibly because they were confident that they already knew this familiar material.

Overall, experts know more than novices do, their knowledge base is more organized, and they are able to use their knowledge and the specialized strategies they have devised to learn, remember, and solve problems efficiently in their areas of expertise—but not in other domains. In effect, experts do not need to think much; they are like experienced drivers who can put themselves on "autopilot" and carry out well-learned routines quickly and accurately. By gaining expertise over the years, adults can often compensate to some extent for age-related losses in information-processing capacities (Jastrzembski, Charness, & Vasyukova, 2006).

Autobiographical Memory

Earlier in this chapter, we examined the emergence of autobiographical memories and you learned that most adults do not remember much about their first few years of life. Yet we also noted that the long-term memory store seems limitless in terms of space and longevity. Is everything we have ever experienced "in there" somewhere? This seems unlikely, given the difficulties most adults have recalling past events. So what determines whether an event is likely to be recalled at a later point in time? We will consider four factors identified by Patricia Bauer (2007) that may influence autobiographical memories: personal significance, distinctiveness, emotional intensity, and life phase of the event.

To begin, most people believe that the personal significance of an event affects our memory for the event—that events of great importance to the self will be remembered better than less important events. As it turns out, the personal significance of an event, as rated at the time the event occurs, has almost no effect on one's ability to later recall the event. It may be that what was once considered important becomes less so with the passage of time and with the broader perspective gained over the years. For example, imagine that at age 17, you break up with your boy/girl friend of 2 years. This is traumatic and of great importance to you as a 17-year-old. You expect you'll never get over it and that the details of the event will be forever etched into your memory. But over the next 10, 20, 30 years or more, so many other events occur that the importance of this youthful breakup fades as you date others, marry, work, raise children, and so on.

In contrast, the distinctiveness or uniqueness of an event has been consistently associated with better recall (Bauer, 2007). The more unique an event is, the more likely it is to be recalled later on, and to be recalled as a distinct event with relevant details. Common events and experiences are often recalled, if at all, as multiple events lumped together as one (Burt, Kemp, & Conway, 2003). Thus, if you attended the same camp every summer throughout your childhood, you may retain fond memories of your experiences at the camp. But the chances are good that you have integrated in your memory many of the common and similar camp experiences: you re-

member singing songs around the campfire, but because you did this every year of the camp, you don't recall the experience of this one year as separate from your experience of this other years. On the other hand, if one year a camper did something highly unusual during one of these campfire sing-alongs (e.g., streaked through the fire), you may indeed remember this particular event for many years to come because of its uniqueness.

Bauer (2007) notes that the affective or emotional intensity of an event also influences later recall. Events associated with either highly negative or highly positive emotions are recalled better than events that were experienced in the context of more neutral emotions. This enhanced memory for emotion-arousing events occurs even though the emotion associated with the event tends to dissipate with time, especially if it is a negative emotion (Walker, Skowronski, & Thompson, 2003). It is likely that strong emotions activate the body's arousal system and the neural components associated with arousal enhance encoding and consolidation of events.

Finally, research on autobiographical memory has revealed that people recall more information from their teens and 20s than from any other time frame except for the near present (Fitzgerald, 1999; Rubin, 2002; Rybash, 1999). ■ **Figure 8.9** shows the number of memories recalled by 70-year-old adults. Not surprisingly, they recalled a lot from their recent past (for example, age 65). But the number of memories recalled from about ages 15 to 25 was higher than the number recalled from other points of the life span. Why? Possibly, this

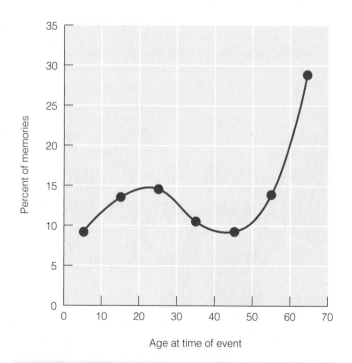

■ **FIGURE 8.9** The distribution of autobiographical memories over the life span of older adults (70 years).

SOURCE: From D.C. Rubin, S.E. Wetzler, & R.D. Nebes, Autobiographical memory across the adult lifespan. In D.C. Rubin (ED.), *Autobiographical memory*. Copyright © 1986 Cambridge University Press. Reprinted with permission.

phase of life is more memorable because it is instrumental in shaping who people are as adults—their identity—and is often full of significant life changes (Fitzgerald, 1999). David Rubin (2002) suggests that the *bump*, as he calls it, occurs because memories from adolescence and early adulthood are more easily accessible than memories from other periods of the life span. They are more accessible because of their distinctiveness and the effort applied by adolescents and young adults to understanding the meaning of the events (Rubin, Rahhal, & Poon, 1998).

Memory and Aging

No less an expert on learning than B. F. Skinner complained about memory problems: "One of the more disheartening experiences of old age is discovering that a point you have just made—so significant, so beautifully expressed—was made by you in something you published a long time ago" (Skinner, 1983, p. 242). Most elderly adults report that they have at least minor difficulties remembering things (Smith et al., 1996). They are especially likely to have trouble remembering names and items they will need later; they are also more upset than young adults by memory lapses, perhaps because they view them as signs of aging (Cavanaugh, Grady, & Perlmutter, 1983). The Explorations box on page 236 describes when forgetfulness is normal and when it is indicative of a more serious problem.

Areas of Strength and Weakness

Much research indicates that, on average, older adults learn new material more slowly and sometimes learn it less well than young and middle-aged adults do and that they remember what they have learned less well. However, the following qualifications are important and will be expanded on in the following sections:

- Most of the research is based on cross-sectional studies that compare age groups, which suggests that the age differences detected could be related to factors other than age. (If needed, you can refresh your memory of the strengths and weaknesses of cross-sectional designs by referring back to Chapter 1.)
- Declines, when observed, typically do not become noticeable until we hit our 70s.
- Difficulties in remembering affect elderly people more noticeably as they continue to age and are most severe among the oldest elderly people.
- Not all older people experience these difficulties.
- Not all kinds of memory tasks cause older people difficulty.

Studies of memory skills in adulthood suggest that the aspects of learning and memory in which older adults look most deficient in comparison with young and middle-aged adults are some of the same areas in which young children compare unfavorably with older children (see Bauer, 2007). The following sections describe some of the major weaknesses—and, by implication, strengths—of older adults' memory skills.

Timed Tasks. On average, older adults are slower than younger adults are to learn and retrieve information; they may need to go through the material more times to learn it equally well and may need more time to respond when their memory is tested. Thus, they are hurt by time limits (Finkel et al., 2003b).

Unfamiliar Content. Older adults fare especially poorly compared with younger adults when the material to be learned is unfamiliar or meaningless—when they cannot tie it to their existing knowledge. In a convincing demonstration of how familiarity influences memory, researchers had young and elderly adults examine words likely to be more familiar to the young adults at the time of the testing (for example, *dude, disco,* and *bummer*) and words from the past likely to be more familiar to the older adults (for example, *pompadour, gramophone,* and *vamp*). Young adults outperformed older adults on the "new" words, but older adults outperformed young adults on the "old" words (Barrett & Wright, 1981). Many memory tasks involve learning unfamiliar material and thus do not allow older adults to use their knowledge base.

Artificial Tasks. Memory is often assessed in the artificial context of the laboratory, which may be more detrimental to older adults than to young ones. In a recent meta-analysis of prospective memory, or memory for future events (for example, remembering that you must take your medicine at bedtime), Julie Henry and her colleagues (2004) reported that older adults performed significantly worse in laboratory contexts. In naturalistic contexts, however, the older adults outperformed the younger adults. So when the task is meaningful, older adults may be able to draw on their greater experience or knowledge bases to enhance their memory performance.

Unexercised Skills. Older adults are also likely to be at a disadvantage when they are required to use learning and memory skills that they rarely use in daily life; they hold their own when they can rely on well-practiced skills that have become effortless and automatic with practice. For example, Lynne Reder, Cynthia Wible, and John Martin (1986) found that elderly adults were just as good as young adults at judging whether sentences presented to them were plausible based on a story they had read. Judging whether something makes sense in the context of what has been read is a well-exercised ability. However, older adults were deficient when it came to judging whether specific sentences had or had not appeared in the story—a skill seldom used outside school. It seems that older adults read to get the gist or significance of a story and do not bother with the details, a strategy that may be adaptive if they have no need to memorize details and if their ability to do so has fallen off with age (Adams, 1991; Stine-Morrow, Loveless, & Soederberg, 1996). In other ways, age differences are smaller when well-practiced skills are assessed than when less-practiced skills are assessed (Denney, 1982).

Recall versus Recognition. Older adults are likely to be more deficient on tasks requiring recall memory than on tasks re-

FORGETTING: WHAT IS NORMAL AND WHAT IS NOT?

As we age, or watch parents and grandparents age, how can we distinguish between normal forgetfulness and abnormal memory changes? Many older adults worry that forgetting an appointment or where they put their reading glasses is a precursor to the devastating memory loss associated with Alzheimer's disease (see Chapter 16). Fortunately, most of us will not develop Alzheimer's disease (AD) and the atypical memory changes that accompany it. Most will, however, exhibit some changes in memory and information-processing skills. So how can we discriminate between normal memory changes and those associated with disease?

Giovanni Carlesimo and his colleagues (1998) compared the memory performance of healthy younger, elderly, and very old adults with that of adults with Alzheimer's disease. The table in this Explorations box shows how the four groups compared on several memory evaluations: a digit-span test assessing how many pieces of information can be held in short-term memory, immediate recall of semantically related items, and delayed recall of semantically related items. The digit span or short-term memory capacity of Alzheimer's disease patients was worse than that of their healthy age-mates, although it was not markedly different from that of very old adults. However, recall was clearly deficient in Alzheimer's disease patients compared not only with their age-mates but also with very old healthy adults. Even more striking was the difference in the extent to which the groups took advantage of the semantic relatedness of items (how closely related the items are in terms of their meaning) to help their memory. The last column

AGE, MEMORY PERFORMANCE, AND CLUSTERING SCORES OF HEALTHY ADULTS AND ADULTS WITH ALZHEIMER'S DISEASE

	AVERAGE AGE (IN YEARS)	SHORT-TERM MEMORY CAPACITY	IMMEDIATE RECALL	DELAYED RECALL	CLUSTERING INDEX—CATEGORIZING ITEMS RELATIVE TO CHANCE (0.00)
Young Adults	29	6.4	51	12	+0.25
Elderly Adults	67	5.5	39	9	+0.24
Very Old Adults	83	4.6	34	7	+0.30
Alzheimer's Patients	67	4.3	18	2	−0.13

quiring only recognition of what was learned (Charles, Mather, & Carstensen, 2003). In one study of memory for high school classmates (Bahrick, Bahrick, & Wittlinger, 1975), even adults who were almost 35 years past graduation could recognize which of five names matched a picture in their yearbook about 90% of the time. However, the ability to actively recall names of classmates when given only their photos as cues dropped considerably as the age of the remember increased. A large gap between recognition and recall shows that older people have encoded and stored the information but cannot retrieve it without the help of cues. Sometimes older adults fail to retrieve information because they never thoroughly encoded or learned it, but at other times they simply cannot retrieve information that is "in there."

Explicit Memory Tasks. Finally, older adults seem to have more trouble with explicit memory tasks that require mental effort than with implicit memory tasks that involve more automatic mental processes (Hoyer & Verhaeghen, 2006). Older adults, then, have little trouble with skills and procedures that have been routinized over the years—established as habits. But even though explicit memory declines, the magnitude of the decline varies with the type of explicit memory. Older adults

retain fairly good semantic memory (general factual knowledge accumulated over time) but show steady declines in episodic memory (recall of specific events that are tied to a specific time and place).

Overall, these findings suggest that older adults, like young children, have difficulty with tasks that are cognitively demanding—that require speed, the learning of unfamiliar material, the use of unexercised abilities, recall rather than recognition, or explicit and effortful rather than implicit and automatic memory. Yet older adults and young children have difficulty for different reasons, as you will now see.

Explaining Declines in Old Age

In asking why some older adults struggle with some learning and memory tasks, we will first return to the hypotheses used to explain childhood improvements in performance: knowledge base, metamemory, strategy use, and basic processing capacities. Then we will consider some additional possibilities.

Knowledge Base. If you start with the hypothesis that differences in knowledge base explain memory differences between older and younger adults, you immediately encounter a probshows that the three healthy groups of adults performed at above-chance levels in categorizing or clustering items, whereas the Alzheimer's disease patients were below chance and sharply different from all the healthy groups on the clustering index. Clearly, normal aging does not take nearly the toll on memory skills that Alzheimer's disease does.

How, then, can family members and professionals recognize the difference between normal and unhealthy memory deficits? Cynthia Green (2001) suggests three criteria that can be used to alert us to atypical memory problems:

- Has memory gotten noticeably worse over the past 6 months?
- Do memory problems interfere with everyday activities at home or work?
- Are family and friends concerned about an individual's memory problems?

Answering "yes" to these questions may indicate unusual memory loss that should be evaluated by a professional.

In practical terms, it is normal to forget where you put something but abnormal to forget how to use it (Cherry & Smith, 1998). Thus, do not worry when Grandpa cannot find his car keys, but be alert if he cannot remember how to use them when they are in his hand. Similarly, it is normal to forget a new phone number you recently looked up in the phone book but abnormal to forget phone numbers you have known and used for years.

Researchers who study memory now believe there is a third type of memory loss that distinguishes normal loss with age from unhealthy disease-related loss (Petersen et al., 1997, 2001). Individuals with **mild cognitive impairment** experience significant memory problems—forgetting important appointments, trouble learning new names, and repeating themselves to the same person—but otherwise do not appear to be suffering from dementia. At least not yet. Some research suggests that a majority of those with mild cognitive impairment will eventually develop forms of dementia such as Alzheimer's disease (Maioli et al., 2007; Fischer et al., 2007). Research also suggests that patients with mild cognitive impairment experience deficits on other cognitive tasks as well, which could mean the problem is more general than memory impairment (Ribeiro, de Mendonca, & Guerreiro, 2006).

The good news is that age-related memory loss may be preventable, and some losses may be reversible. Reducing stress, for example, is one way to improve memory performance (Bremner & Narayan, 1998). Chronic stress elevates levels of cortisol in the brain, which impedes memory. A study by the MacArthur Foundation found that three things predicted good memory over time: physical fitness and activity, mental activity, and a sense of control over life events (Rowe & Kahn, 1998). Mental activity—working crossword puzzles, reading, playing musical instruments—increases connections among neurons. Physical activity seems to release chemicals that protect neurons involved in cognitive function. Thus, remaining physically and mentally active can help protect against memory loss associated with aging. Having a sense of control over memory can boost both confidence and memory performance.

In sum, significant memory loss is not likely among healthy older adults. It is true that, relative to young adults, older adults exhibit poorer memory performance in some situations. But these changes are minor and can often be avoided by remaining physically and mentally active. Families and professionals should be on the lookout for older adults who show marked declines in their memory performance. They may be experiencing mild cognitive impairment and may eventually develop Alzheimer's disease and impaired memory.

lem: Young children may lack knowledge, but elderly adults do not. Indeed, older adults are generally at least as knowledgeable as young adults: Semantic memory *increases* until about age 65 (Rönnlund et al., 2005). Verbal knowledge shows no decrease throughout mid and older adulthood and may not decline until we are pushing 90! (Park et al., 2002; Singer et al., 2003; Rönnlund et al., 2005). Older adults clearly know a lot about the world. For example, they know more than younger adults about real-world categories of information such as U.S. presidents, countries, international cities, and bodies of water (Foos & Sarno, 1998). So, deficiencies in knowledge base are probably not the source of most memory problems that many older adults display. On the contrary, gains in knowledge probably help older adults compensate for losses in information-processing efficiency (Salthouse, 1993). Thus, older pilots are as adept as younger pilots and better than nonpilots at repeating back flight commands, but they show the usual effects of aging if they are given tasks less relevant to their work (Morrow et al., 1994). Older adults also perform better than younger adults on memory tasks in which they can spontaneously use analogies, another indication that a rich knowledge base can aid memory (Caplan & Schooler, 2001). Knowledge enhances learning (Kaplan & Murphy, 2000). Indeed, as Paul Baltes has put it, "Knowledge is power!" (Baltes, Smith, & Staudinger, 1992, p. 143).

Metamemory. Could elderly adults, like young children, be deficient in the specific knowledge called metamemory? Is their knowledge of some of the strategies that prove useful in school learning—and in laboratory memory tasks—rusty? This theory sounds plausible, but research shows that older adults seem to know as much as younger adults about such things as which memory strategies are best and which memory tasks are hardest (Light, 1991). Still, older adults are more likely than younger ones to misjudge the accuracy of some aspects of their memory such as the source of the memories (Dodson, Bawa, & Krueger, 2007).

So whereas metamemory seems largely intact across the lifespan, there may be some isolated areas of weakness. Moreover, although older adults know a lot about memory, they express more negative beliefs about their memory skills than do younger adults (Cavanaugh, 1996). Memory loss may contribute to a drop in confidence in memory skills, but negative beliefs about memory skills also appear to hurt memory performance (Hess, 2006). Therefore, it's not clear whether declines in actual memory performance lead to the development of

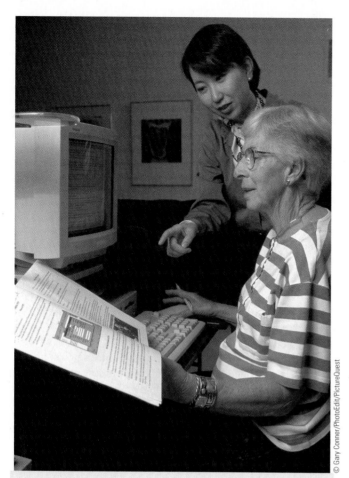

Many adults continue to expand their knowledge bases well into old age.

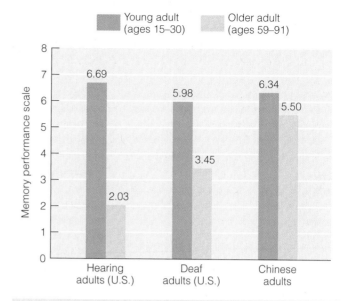

Young adult (ages 15–30)   Older adult (ages 59–91)

■ **FIGURE 8.10** Declines in memory skills in old age are not universal. In deaf culture and in Chinese culture, elderly people are not stereotyped as forgetful or senile. Perhaps as a result, Chinese elders perform almost as well as young Chinese adults on memory tasks, whereas in the United States, elders, especially in the hearing population, perform poorly.
SOURCE: Adapted from Levy & Langer (1994).

negative beliefs about memory, or whether negative beliefs—either your own or those of the surrounding culture—affect memory performance (Hess, 2006).

To understand the connection between memory performance and stereotypes, Becca Levy and Ellen Langer (1994) tested the memory of young and elderly adults (ages 59–91) in three groups: hearing Americans, deaf Americans, and hearing Chinese. In both the American deaf and Chinese cultures, elders are respected and negative stereotypes of intellectual aging are not as prevalent as they are among hearing Americans. As ■ Figure 8.10 shows, young adults in the three groups performed about equally well on a set of recall tasks, but Chinese elders clearly outperformed both deaf American elders (who were second best) and hearing American elders. Elderly Chinese adults scored only a little lower than young Chinese adults despite having less education. In addition, those older people in the study who believed that aging brings about memory loss performed more poorly than those who did not hold this belief. Levy (1996) has also shown that activating negative stereotypes in the minds of elderly adults (through rapid, subliminal presentation of words such as *Alzheimer's* and *senile* on a computer screen) causes them to perform worse on memory tests and to express less confidence in their memory skills than when

positive stereotypes of old age are planted in their minds (through words such as *wise* and *sage*). Findings such as these clearly call into question the idea of a universal decline in memory skills in later life and point to the influence of culture and its views of aging on performance.

Memory Strategies. What about the hypothesis that failure to use effective memory strategies accounts for deficits in old age? Many older adults do not spontaneously use strategies such as organization and elaboration even though they know them and are capable of using them (Light, 1991; Smith & Earles, 1996). This may be an important part of the problem when older adults are asked to deliberately memorize something. Older adults' biggest problem, though, seems to be with effective *retrieval* of details of an event and not with the original *encoding* of the event (Thomas & Bulevich, 2006). Thus, retrieval strategies may be more susceptible to aging than encoding strategies. But why do many older adults fail to use effective memory and retrieval strategies?

Basic Processing Capacities. The answer may lie in the fourth hypothesis—the notion that basic processing capacities change with age. Which capacities? Much attention has focused on declines in the capacity to use working memory to operate actively on a lot of information simultaneously. Working-memory capacity increases during childhood and adolescence, peaks around age 45, then begins to decline (Swanson, 1999). Moreover, working-memory capacity predicts how well adults will perform on a range of cognitive tasks

(Hoyer & Verhaeghen, 2006). Older adults do fine on short-term memory tasks that require them to juggle just a few pieces of information in working memory. However, when the amount of information that they are to "operate on" increases, they begin to show deficits. Older adults may have more trouble than younger ones ignoring irrelevant task information. For instance, trying to memorize a list of words while walking is more problematic for older adults than for middle-aged or younger adults (Li et al., 2001; Lindenberger, Marsiske, & Baltes, 2000). Thus, their working-memory space may become cluttered with unnecessary information, limiting the space available for the task at hand (Hoyer & Verhaeghen, 2006).

Limitations in working-memory capacity are most likely rooted in slower functioning of the nervous system both early and late in life (see Hartley, 2006; also see Chapter 5). Much research shows that speed of processing increases during childhood and adolescence, peaks in early adulthood, then declines slowly over the adult years (Hartley, 2006). Much research also shows that age differences in performance on cognitive tasks often shrink when age differences in speed of information processing are taken into account and controlled. Experience in a domain of learning can certainly enhance performance, but if children and older adults generally have sluggish "computers," they simply may not be able to keep up with the processing demands of complex learning and memory tasks (Hartley, 2006). Slow neural transmission, then, may be behind limitations in working memory in both childhood and old age. Limitations in working memory, in turn, may contribute not only to limitations in long-term memory but also to difficulties performing a range of cognitive tasks, including problem-solving tasks and tests of intelligence, even those that have no time limits (Hartley, 2006; Salthouse, 2000).

To this point, then, you might conclude that many older adults, although they have a vast knowledge base and a good deal of knowledge about learning and memory, experience declines in basic processing capacity that make it difficult for them to carry out memory strategies that will drain their limited working-memory capacity. But the basic processing capacity hypothesis cannot explain everything about age differences in memory (Light, 1991). You must consider some additional hypotheses, including sensory changes and a variety of contextual factors.

Sensory Changes. As you learned in Chapter 6, older adults experience declines in sensory abilities. Might these affect memory performance? Yes indeed. Research shows that visual and auditory skills are often better predictors than processing speed of cognitive performance among older adults (Anstey, Hofer, & Luszcz, 2003; Baltes & Lindenberger, 1997). As noted in Chapter 6, many older adults experience some hearing loss. Even young adults, when tested under moderately noisy conditions, show short-term memory performance decreases (Murphy et al., 2000). Sensory loss at any age may tax available processing resources, leading to memory deficits.

Contextual Contributors. Many researchers have adopted a contextual perspective on learning and memory, emphasizing both biological and genetic factors and environmental and situational factors (Blanchard-Fields, Chen, & Norris, 1997; Dixon, 1992). They emphasize that performance on learning and memory tasks is the product of an interaction among (1) characteristics of the learner, such as goals, motivations, abilities, and health; (2) characteristics of the task or situation; and (3) characteristics of the broader environment, including the cultural context, in which a task is performed. They are not convinced that there is a universal biological decline in basic learning and memory capacities because older individuals often perform capably in certain contexts.

First, cohort differences in education and IQ can explain age differences in some learning and memory skills. Elderly people today are less educated, on average, than younger adults are, and they are further removed from their school days. When education level is controlled for, age differences shrink, although they do not disappear (Nilsson et al., 2002; Rönnlund et al., 2005). Thus, to some extent, education can compensate for aging. Older adults who are highly educated or who have high levels of intellectual ability often perform as well as younger adults (Cherry & LeCompte, 1999; Haught et al., 2000).

Similarly, health and lifestyle differences between cohorts may contribute to age differences in learning and memory. Older adults are more likely than younger adults to have chronic or degenerative diseases, and even mild diseases can impair memory performance (Houx, Vreeling, & Jolles, 1991; Hultsch, Hammer, & Small, 1993). Older adults also lead less active lifestyles and perform fewer cognitively demanding activities than younger adults do, on average. These age group differences in lifestyle also contribute to age differences in cognitive performance. Older adults who engage in fitness training show enhanced cognitive ability, possibly because physical activity increases blood flow to the brain (Colcombe et al., 2004). Similarly, older adults who remain *mentally* active outperform other older adults and perform similarly to young professors on some tests of recall (Shimamura et al., 1995).

The implications of such research are clear: Declines in information-processing skills are not inevitable or universal. Nature may place some boundaries on the information-processing system, but nurture plays a significant role in sustaining memory and problem-solving skills. Older adults may be able to maintain their memory skills if they are relatively well educated, stay healthy, and exercise their minds. Simply reviewing material after its presentation can help them improve their memory performance (Koutstaal et al., 1998; see the Applications box on page 240 for more ways to improve memory across the life span). Still, factors such as education and health cannot account completely for age differences in cognitive performance.

Perhaps the truth lies somewhere between the basic processing capacity view, which emphasizes nature by pointing to a universal decline in cognitive resources such as speed and working memory that affect performance on many cognitive tasks, and the contextual view, which emphasizes nurture. Contextual theorists stress variability from person to person and situation to situation based on cohort differences, motivational fac-

IMPROVING MEMORY AND STUDY SKILLS

Have you noticed that the material in this chapter has great potential value to teachers? The information-processing perspective has yielded improved methods for diagnosing learning problems and improving instruction. Here we focus on interventions aimed at boosting the memory skills of young children and older adults. Just how much can be achieved through training?

Garrett Lange and Sarah Pierce (1992) took on the challenge of teaching the memory strategy of organization (grouping) to 4- and 5-year-olds. Using pictures of objects and animals as the stimuli, they taught these preschoolers a "group-and-name trick" that involved sorting items to be learned into groups based on similarity, naming the group, naming the items within the group, and, at recall, naming the group before calling out the items within that group. Because such memory-training programs have not always been successful, these researchers attempted to increase motivation through encouragement and praise. They even included training in metamemory: They made sure children understood the rationale for the sorting strategy, knew when it could be used, and could see firsthand that it could improve their performance.

How successful was the training? These children did virtually no sorting of items to be learned before they were trained, but they did a good deal of it after training, even 7 days later. They clearly learned to use the organization strategy they were taught. They also outperformed untrained control children on measures of recall, but the gains in recall were fairly small compared with the much larger gains in strategy use. This discrepancy between gains in strategy use and gains in recall performance shows that these young children experienced utilization deficiencies: They could not derive full benefit from the memory strategy they were taught, possibly because they did not have the working-memory capacity to carry out the strategy.

Other programs that teach memory strategies and metacognitive skills to elementary school children often work much better, especially with children who are underachievers and who may be capable of executing strategies

but fail to do so on their own (Hattie, Biggs, & Purdie, 1996). Still, the benefits of training are often domain-specific; they do not generalize to learning tasks different from those that were the focus of training. Perhaps this makes sense if you realize that the strategies that work best in learning math skills may be different from the strategies that work best in learning historical facts or basketball skills.

In an important study of cognitive training effects, Sherry Willis and her colleagues for the ACTIVE Study Group (2006) followed four groups of older adults (average age of 74 years) over a period of 5 years. The groups differed in the type of cognitive training they received at the beginning of the study:

- Memory training—participants were taught strategies of organization, visualization, and association to remember verbal material.
- Reasoning training—participants were taught strategies for detecting a pattern in a series of letters or words.
- Speed training—participants learned to complete visual search tasks in increasingly less time and they were trained to divide their attention between two tasks.
- No training—these participants served as a control group.

How did the groups fare after 5 years? Compared with the control group, the adults who received memory training still did better on memory tasks; those who received reasoning training performed better on reasoning tasks; and those who received speed training were much faster. Importantly, the benefits of training were evident not just on laboratory tasks but on activities important to daily living such as driving or understanding the interaction and side effects of prescription drugs.

This study and others show that older adults can profit from mental exercise that increasingly challenges them. Just as physical exercise contributes to overall physical well-being, mental exercise contributes to overall mental well-being. And just as your physical workouts need to increasingly challenge you (if you start out walking a half-mile at a slow pace, you need to increase your distance and/or your pace to reap the most benefits), your mental workouts

must become more rigorous. If you start out solving easy Sudoku puzzles, you need to push yourself to move on to more difficult ones.

Finally, it sometimes makes more sense to change the learning environment than to change the learner (Pressley, 1983). If, for example, young children and some older adults do not spontaneously organize the material they are learning to make it more meaningful, it can be organized for them. Giving children practice at learning highly organized material can help them master the grouping strategy on their own (Best, 1993). Similarly, if the material to be learned is unfamiliar, you can use examples or analogies that will help learners relate it to something that is familiar (for example, teaching a senior citizens' group about the federal budget by likening it to their personal budgets). If young children and older adults need more time, let them set their own pace.

To use a real-world example, older adults have more trouble understanding and remembering information about their drug prescriptions than young adults do (Morrell, Park, & Poon, 1989). Yet by writing clear, organized instructions and spending time explaining to older patients what they are to do, health-care professionals can simplify the learning task (Morrell, Park, & Poon, 1989). Alternatively, older adults can be given external memory aids. Denise Park and her colleagues (1992) explored the benefits of two such aids: an organization chart (a poster or pocket-sized table giving an hour-by-hour account of when drugs should be taken) and a medication organizer (a dispenser with columns for different days of the week and pill compartments for times of the day). Adults over 70 more often took their pills correctly when they were given both the chart and the organizer than when they were given one or neither. Because researchers know that poor health is one contributor to poor memory functioning, it makes especially good sense to reduce the cognitive demands on old and ailing patients by letting external memory aids do the mental work for them. Surely the best of all possible worlds for the learner would be one in which materials and teaching techniques are tailored to the learner's information-processing capacities and in which training is offered in how to stretch those capacities.

tors, and task demands. Most adults, at least if they live to an advanced old age, may experience some loss of basic processing resources. However, they may also have developed specialized knowledge and strategies that allow them to compensate for these losses as they carry out the everyday cognitive activities most important to them (Baltes, Smith, & Staudinger, 1992).

Problem Solving and Aging

You know that problem-solving skills improve steadily from early childhood through adolescence, but what becomes of them in adulthood? On the one hand, you might expect to see a decline in problem-solving prowess paralleling declines in learning and memory performance. On the other hand, if adults increase their knowledge bases and develop expertise as they age, might not older adults outwit younger novices on many problem-solving tasks?

Familiar versus Unfamiliar Tasks

When given traditional problem-solving tasks to perform in the laboratory, young adults typically perform better than middle-aged adults, who in turn outperform older adults (Denney, 1989). However, consider research using the Twenty Questions task. Subjects are given an array of items and asked to find out, using as few questions as possible, which item the experimenter has in mind (see ■ Figure 8.11). The soundest problem-solving

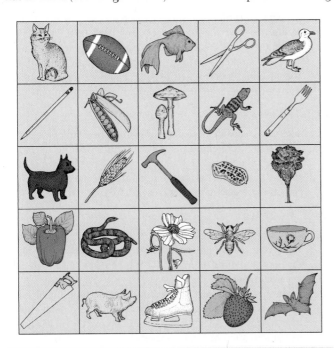

■ **FIGURE 8.11** A Twenty Questions game. You can try it on a young child or a friend by thinking of one item in the group and asking your testee to find out which it is by asking you yes–no questions. Look for the constraint-seeking questions (for example, "Is it animate?"), and note the total number of questions required to identify the correct item.

strategy is to ask **constraint-seeking questions**—ones that rule out more than one item (for example, "Is it an animal?"). Young children and older adults tend to pursue specific hypotheses instead ("Is it a pig?" "Is it a pencil?"). Consequently, they must ask more questions to identify the right object. However, if the task is altered to make it more familiar (for example, through the use of playing cards as stimuli), then older adults do far better. The familiarity of the material allows them to draw on their knowledge base to solve the problem. Thus, older adults are capable of using effective problem-solving strategies but do not use them in some contexts, especially when given unfamiliar tasks in a laboratory.

What if adults are asked to deal with real-life problems such as grease fires in the kitchen, family squabbles, or refrigerators that break down in the middle of the night? Nancy Denney and Kathy Pearce (1989) asked elderly adults to help them devise everyday problems that would be meaningful and familiar to older individuals. One problem was to generate ideas about how a 65-year-old recently widowed woman could improve her social life; another was to advise an elderly couple living on Social Security what to do when they were unable to pay their heating bill one winter. On these everyday problems, performance increased from early adulthood to middle age and declined in old age.

Other findings echo this one: When given everyday problems to which they can apply the expertise they have gained through experience, middle-aged adults often outperform young adults. Elderly adults sometimes equal and sometimes do worse than young and middle-aged adults; either way, they show smaller deficits on the everyday problems than they do on unfamiliar problems in the laboratory (Berg & Klaczynski, 1996; Marsiske & Willis, 1995). Ultimately, declines in basic capacities may limit the problem-solving skills of many elderly adults, not only in the laboratory but also in real life (Denney, 1989; Kasworm & Medina, 1990). You should bear in mind, however, that cognitive competence among older adults varies widely because of differences in health, education, experience, and so on.

Selection, Optimization, and Compensation

Some cognitive researchers believe that older adults may approach problem solving differently than younger adults. It's true that younger adults generate more possible solutions to a problem than do older adults. But the solutions generated by older adults tend to be more goal-focused and selective, emphasizing quality over quantity (Marsiske & Margrett, 2006). When faced with a broken water pipe in the middle of the night, an older couple may generate one solution—call their grown son who lives down the street. Although this may not seem like an ideal solution to the son, the older adults may realize that this is the easiest and fastest solution.

In addition, researchers have proposed a selection, optimization, and compensation (SOC) framework to understand how older adults may cope with and compensate for their diminishing cognitive resources (Riediger, Li, & Lindenberger,

2006; and see Chapter 11). Older adults may adapt to changes in their problem-solving skills by letting little-needed cognitive skills grow rusty (compensation) so that they can maintain and strengthen those skills most useful to them in everyday life (selection and optimization). If your resources are limited or unstable, then you can't take on everything; you need to be selective. Choose those tasks that are most important or have to be done. For example, prepare dinner (after all, you have to eat), but don't worry about getting every surface of the house dusted. Focus on what you do well—optimize your strengths and minimize weaknesses. If you still have the skills to balance a checkbook and this is something your partner struggles with, then you should take over managing the checkbook. If your vision is so bad that you cannot tell that your "clean" dishes have chunks of food remaining on them, then offload this task to a dishwasher or partner.

Researchers have investigated whether this selection, optimization, and compensation model can be applied to help older adults overcome weaknesses in explicit memory by taking advantage of their relative strength of implicit memory. For instance, Cameron Camp and his colleagues (Camp et al., 1996; Camp & McKitrick, 1992) have tried to help patients with dementia caused by Alzheimer's disease use the implicit memory capacities that they, like people with amnesia, retain even though they have serious deficits in explicit memory. For example, they have taught patients with Alzheimer's disease to remember the names of staff members by having the patients name photos of staff members repeatedly and at ever longer intervals between trials. People who could not retain names for more than a minute were able to recall the names weeks later after training. The technique appears to work because it uses implicit memory processes; adults learn effortlessly when they repeatedly encounter the material to be learned. By selecting and optimizing, older adults can often compensate for their diminishing explicit memory, allowing them to maintain independence for a longer period of time (Riediger, Li, & Lindenberger, 2006).

SUMMING UP

▌ Adults increasingly develop larger and more organized knowledge bases that aid memory and problem solving.

▌ Some older adults may begin to experience problems on tasks that require speed or working with unfamiliar material or unexercised skills. Declines in basic processing capacity can tax memory and retrieval strategies, and contextual factors such as motivation, cohort, and the nature of the task also influence memory.

▌ The message about problem-solving skills is similar to that about memory capacities. Although performance on unfamiliar, meaningless laboratory tasks often appears to decline after early adulthood, the ability to perform more-familiar, everyday information-processing tasks often improves through middle age and is maintained until late in life.

▌ Older adults may be able to minimize the effects of shrinking resources by selecting, optimizing, and compensating so that they maximize their strengths and minimize their weaknesses.

CRITICAL THINKING

1. As a teacher in an Elderhostel program for older adults, you want to base your teaching methods on knowledge of the information-processing capacities of elderly adults. What practical recommendations would you derive from (a) the view that there is a universal decline with age in basic processing capacities and (b) the contextual perspective on cognitive aging?

2. Revisit Figure 8.9 showing the distribution of autobiographical memories over the life span. What factors might account for the rise and fall of autobiographical memories at different phases of the life span?

3. Every time your mother and grandmother forget something, they express concerns about "losing it" and "getting senile." Knowing that you have taken a course in life-span human development, they seek you out for reassurance. What can you tell them about memory and aging that might alleviate their concerns?

CHAPTER SUMMARY

8.1 THE INFORMATION-PROCESSING APPROACH

• The information-processing approach uses a computer analogy to illustrate how the mind processes information. The human "computer" puts information into a sensory register, into short-term and working memory, then into long-term memory during encoding; stores it; retrieves it (demonstrating recognition, cued recall, or recall memory); and uses it to solve problems.

8.2 THE INFANT

• Infants are capable of remembering from the start of life.
• They show recognition memory at birth, simple recall in the presence of cues at 2 or 3 months, recall in the absence of cues toward the end of the first year, and deliberate, conscious attempts to retrieve memories by age 2.

8.3 THE CHILD

• Learning and memory continue to improve during childhood.
• Basic information-processing capacity increases as the brain matures and fundamental processes are automated to free working-memory space.
• Memory strategies such as rehearsal, organization, and elaboration improve. Metamemory improves and the general knowledge base grows. All of these changes improve the processing of new information in areas of expertise.
• According to Robert Siegler, even young children use systematic rules to solve problems, but their problem-solving skills improve as they replace faulty rules with ones that incorporate all the relevant aspects of the problem. Multiple strategies are used at any age so that development proceeds through a natural selection process and resembles overlapping waves more than a set of stairsteps leading from one way of thinking to the next.

8.4 THE ADOLESCENT

- Adolescents master advanced learning strategies such as elaboration, note taking, and underlining; use their strategies more deliberately and selectively; and use their increased metacognitive abilities to guide learning and remembering.

8.5 THE ADULT

- As adults gain expertise in a domain, they develop large and organized knowledge bases and highly effective, specialized, and automated ways of retrieving and using their knowledge.
- Many older adults perform less well than young adults on memory tasks that require speed, the learning of unfamiliar or meaningless material, the use of unexercised abilities, recall rather than recognition memory, and explicit rather than implicit memory.
- Declines in basic processing capacity and difficulty using strategies, plus contextual factors such as cohort differences and the irrelevance of many laboratory tasks to everyday life, contribute to age differences in memory.
- On average, older adults also perform less well than younger adults on laboratory problem-solving tasks, but everyday problem-solving skills are likely to improve from early adulthood to middle adulthood and to be maintained in old age.

KEY TERMS

information-processing
    approach 217
sensory register 217
short-term memory 217
working memory 217
long-term memory 218
encoding 218
consolidation 218
storage 218
retrieval 218
recognition memory 218
recall memory 218
cued recall memory 218
implicit memory 218
explicit memory 218
problem solving 219
executive control processes 220
deferred imitation 221
perseveration error 224

rehearsal 224
organization (as memory
    strategy) 224
elaboration 225
mediation deficiency 225
production deficiency 225
utilization deficiency 225
metamemory 225
metacognition 225
knowledge base 226
autobiographical memories 227
childhood amnesia 227
fuzzy-trace theory 228
script 228
eyewitness memory 229
rule assessment approach 230
overlapping waves theory 230
mild cognitive impairment 237
constraint-seeking questions 241

MEDIA RESOURCES

BOOK COMPANION WEBSITE

academic.cengage.com/psychology/sigelman
Find online quizzes, flash cards, animations, video clips, experiments, interactive assessments, and other helpful study aids for this text at **academic.cengage.com/psychology/sigelman.** You can also connect directly to the following sites:

MEMORY AND AGING: IMPROVING YOUR MEMORY

This colorful and informative site provides an interesting discussion of memory and the aging process. It includes a great list of general guidelines for improving memory including discussions of mnemonic devices and brain exercises. Be sure to check out the great set of external links to other sites at the bottom of the welcome page.

MEMORY AND AGING RESOURCE CENTER

The website of the Memory and Aging Research Center at the University of California at Los Angeles contains links to scholarly information.

MEMORY TECHNIQUES AND MNEMONICS

This Mind Tools sponsored site offers an extensive list of articles on methods of improving memory. It also contains links to several articles that explain how specific memory strategies work.

PSI CAFÉ: COGNITIVE DEVELOPMENT & PSI CAFÉ: INFORMATION-PROCESSING

These companion sites hosted by the Psi Café (a psychological resource group) provide the visitor access to a plethora of articles on the topics of cognitive development and information-processing. Each site includes both basic definitions as well as more in depth articles.

UNDERSTANDING THE DATA: EXERCISES ON THE WEB

academic.cengage.com/psychology/sigelman
For additional insight on the data presented in this chapter, try out the exercises for these figures at **academic.cengage.com/psychology/sigelman:**

    Figure 8.4 Effects of expertise on memory

    Figure 8.8 Adolescents are better able than children to concentrate on learning relevant material and to ignore irrelevant material

CENGAGENOW

academic.cengage.com/login
Go to **academic.cengage.com/login** to link to CengageNOW, your online study tool. First take the Pre-Test for this chapter to get your Personalized Study Plan, which will identify topics you need to review and direct you to online resources. Then take the Post-Test to determine what concepts you have mastered and what you still need work on.

© William Taufic/Corbis

9

CHAPTER

Intelligence and Creativity

SHO YANO WAS BORN in Oregon, USA, and started writing at age 2, reading at age 3, playing music at age 4, and composing music at age 4. By age 7, when most children are starting first grade, Sho was doing high school work under the tutelage of his mother because the gifted school he attended seemed unable to keep pace with his learning needs. He started college at age 9, and at age 12 he became the youngest person to enter the University of Chicago's joint MD/PhD program. He purportedly has an IQ of over 200. (*60 Minutes*, December 27, 2006).

At age 35, Michael lives in an institution for the mentally retarded. He has been labeled profoundly retarded and has an IQ score of 17, as nearly as it can be estimated. Michael responds to people with grins and is able to walk haltingly, but he cannot feed or dress himself and does not use language.

■ ■ ■

As these examples indicate, the range of human intellectual abilities is immense. So far, much of the material on cognitive development in this book has focused on what human minds have in common, not on how they differ. Piaget, after all, was interested in identifying universal stages of cognitive development. And the information-processing approach has been used mainly to understand the basic cognitive processes all people rely on to learn, remember, and solve problems.

This chapter continues the exploration of how the human mind normally changes over the life span. Here we introduce still another approach to the study of the mind: the psychometric, or testing, approach to intelligence, which led to the creation of intelligence tests. Many people find it hard to say anything nice about IQ tests. These measures have their limitations and they have been misused. Yet they have also provided researchers with a good deal of information about intellectual development and about variations in intellectual performance. This chapter examines how performance on intelligence tests typically changes and stays the same over the life span, what IQ tests reveal about a person, and why people's IQ scores differ. It also looks at both gifted and mentally retarded individuals from a life-span perspective. We will also discuss creativity, a type of intellectual ability not measured by traditional intelligence tests. Before going further, take the quiz in ● **Table 9.1** to see

Some gifted children thrive as college students, such as Sho Yano shown here, who entered college at age 9.

Associated Press

● TABLE 9.1   WHAT DO YOU KNOW ABOUT INTELLIGENCE AND CREATIVITY?

Answer each question true or false:

1. On the leading tests of intelligence, a score of 100 is average.

2. Most scholars now conclude that there is no such thing as general intelligence; there are only separate mental abilities.

3. Individuals who are intellectually gifted are typically gifted in all mental abilities.

4. Intellectually gifted children do well in school but are more likely than most children to have social and emotional problems.

5. IQ predicts both a person's occupational status and his success compared with others in the same occupation.

6. On average, performance on IQ tests declines for people in their 70s and 80s.

7. Qualities associated with wisdom are as common among young and middle-aged adults as among elderly adults.

8. It has been established that children's IQs are far more influenced by their environments than by their genes.

9. How well a child does on a test of creativity cannot be predicted well from her IQ score.

10. Creative achievers (great musicians, mathematicians, writers, and so on) typically do all their great works before about age 40 or 45 and produce only lesser works from then on.

Answers: 1-T, 2-F, 3-F, 4-F, 5-T, 6-T, 7-T, 8-F, 9-T, 10-F

9.1 WHAT IS INTELLIGENCE?

There is no clear consensus on the definition of intelligence. As noted in Chapter 7, Piaget defined intelligence as thinking or behavior that is adaptive. Other experts have offered different definitions, many of them centering on the ability to think abstractly or to solve problems effectively (Sternberg, 2000). Early definitions of intelligence tended to reflect the assumption that intelligence reflects innate ability; genetically determined and thus fixed at conception. But it has become clear that intelligence is not fixed, that it is changeable and subject to environmental influence (Perkins, 1996). As a result, an individual's intelligence test scores sometimes vary considerably over a lifetime. Bear in mind that understanding of this complex human quality has changed since the first intelligence tests were created at the turn of the last century—and that there is still no single, universally accepted definition of intelligence.

The Psychometric Approach

The research tradition that spawned the development of standardized tests of intelligence is the **psychometric approach.** According to psychometric theorists, intelligence is a trait or a set of traits that characterizes some people to a greater extent than others. The goals, then, are to identify these traits precisely and to measure them so that differences among individuals can be described. But from the start, experts could not agree on whether intelligence is one general cognitive ability or many specific abilities.

Early on, Charles Spearman (1927) proposed a two-factor theory of intelligence consisting of a general mental ability (called *g*) that contributes to performance on many different kinds of tasks. This *g* factor is what accounts for Spearman's observation that people were often consistent across a range of tasks. In a recent study, for example, general intelligence was found to correlate with performance on exams in 25 different academic subjects (Deary et al., 2007). However, Spearman also noticed that a student who excelled at most tasks might score low on a particular measure (for example, memory for words). So he proposed a second aspect of intelligence: *s*, or special abilities, each of which is specific to a particular kind of task. Some research suggests that *g* may play a greater role in IQ test performance during childhood than adolescence (Kane & Brand, 2006). By adolescence, many effortful processes that underlie expression of *g* have become automated, freeing up cognitive resources to hone certain specific abilities.

Louis Thurstone (1938; Thurstone & Thurstone, 1941) later analyzed test scores obtained by eighth-graders and college students and identified seven fairly distinct factors that he called *primary mental abilities*: spatial ability, perceptual speed (the quick noting of visual detail), numerical reasoning (arithmetic skills), verbal meaning (the defining of words), word fluency (speed in recognizing words), memory, and inductive reasoning (creating a general rule to describe a specific set of observations, such as noticing that it always seems to rain when there are dark clouds in the sky and concluding from these observations that clouds bring rain). Thus, Thurstone concluded that Spearman's general ability factor should be broken into several distinct mental abilities.

Raymond Cattell and John Horn have greatly influenced current thinking concerning intelligence by focusing attention on two broad dimensions of intellect: fluid intelligence and crystallized intelligence (Cattell, 1963; Horn & Cattell, 1967; Horn & Noll, 1997). **Fluid intelligence** is the ability to use your mind actively to solve novel problems—for example, to solve verbal analogies, remember unrelated pairs of words, or recognize relationships among geometric figures. The skills involved—reasoning, seeing relationships among stimuli, and drawing inferences—are usually not taught and are believed to be relatively free of cultural influences (see ▪ Figure 9.1). **Crystallized intelligence,** in contrast, is the use of knowledge acquired through schooling and other life experiences. Tests of general information (At what temperature does water boil?), word comprehension (What is the meaning of *duplicate?*), and numerical abilities (What is 23 × 3?) are all measures of crystallized intelligence. Thus, fluid intelligence involves using your mind in new and flexible ways, whereas crystallized intelligence involves using what you have already learned through experience.

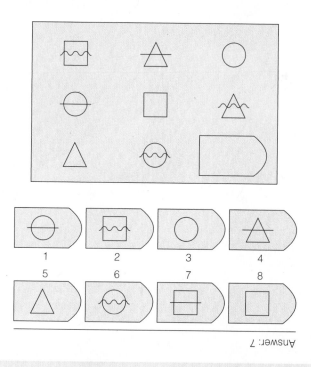

Answer: 7

▪ **FIGURE 9.1** An item assessing fluid intelligence (similar to those in a test called the Raven Progressive Matrices Test). Which of the numbered pieces completes the design?

Obviously, there is no single answer to the question, what is intelligence? Nonetheless, some consensus is emerging. Intelligence is most often viewed as a hierarchy that includes (1) a general ability factor at the top that influences how well people do on a range of cognitive tasks; (2) a few broad dimensions of ability that are distinguishable in factor analyses (for example, fluid intelligence, crystallized intelligence, memory capacity, perceptual skills, and processing speed); and (3) at the bottom, many specific abilities such as numerical reasoning, spatial discrimination, and word comprehension that also influence how well a person performs cognitive tasks that tap these specific abilities (Carroll, 1993; Horn & Noll, 1997).

In the end, the intelligence tests guided by psychometric theories have emphasized general intellectual ability by summarizing performance in a single IQ score, and they have assessed only some of the specialized abilities humans possess. Critics believe traditional psychometric tests have not fully described what it means to be an intelligent person and some have offered alternative ways of thinking about intelligence that represent challenges to the traditional view. Reading about these approaches in the following sections will help you capture the nature of intelligence and appreciate the limitations of the tests used to measure it. In addition, the Explorations box on page 248 examines two traditional psychometric tests and two modern alternatives.

Gardner's Theory of Multiple Intelligences

Howard Gardner (1993, 1999/2000; Chen & Gardner, 1997) rejects the idea that a single IQ score is a meaningful measure of human intelligence. He argues that there are many intelligences, most of which have been ignored by the developers of standardized intelligence tests. Instead of asking, "How smart are you?" researchers should be asking, "How are you smart?" and identifying people's strengths and weaknesses across the full range of human mental faculties (Chen & Gardner, 1997). Gardner (1993, 2000) argues that there are at least eight distinct intellectual abilities:

1. *Linguistic intelligence.* Language skills, such as those seen in the poet's facility with words.
2. *Logical–mathematical intelligence.* The abstract thinking and problem solving shown by mathematicians and computer scientists and emphasized by Piaget.
3. *Musical intelligence.* Based on an acute sensitivity to sound patterns.
4. *Spatial intelligence.* Most obvious in great artists who can perceive things accurately and transform what they see.
5. *Bodily-kinesthetic intelligence.* The skillful use of the body to create crafts, perform, or fix things; shown, for example, by dancers, athletes, and surgeons.
6. *Interpersonal intelligence.* Social intelligence, social skill, exceptional sensitivity to other people's motivations and moods; demonstrated by salespeople and psychologists.
7. *Intrapersonal intelligence.* Understanding of one's own feelings and inner life.

8. *Naturalist intelligence.* Expertise in the natural world of plants and animals.

Traditional IQ tests emphasize linguistic and logical–mathematical intelligence and to some extent test spatial intelligence, perhaps because those are the forms of intelligence Western societies value most highly and work the hardest to nurture in school. But IQ tests can be faulted for ignoring most of the other forms of intelligence. Although Gardner does not claim that his is the definitive list of intelligences, he presents evidence suggesting that each of these eight abilities is distinct. For example, it is clear that a person can be exceptional in one ability but poor in others—witness **savant syndrome,** the phenomenon in which extraordinary talent in a particular area is displayed by a person otherwise mentally retarded (Treffert, 2000). Leslie Lemke, one such individual, is blind, has cerebral palsy, is mentally retarded, and could not talk until he was an adult (Treffert, 2000). Yet he can hear a musical piece once and play it flawlessly on the piano or imitate songs in perfect German or Italian even though his own speech is still primitive. He apparently has a high level of musical intelligence. Other savants, despite IQs below 70, can draw well enough to gain admittance to art school or can calculate on the spot what day of the week it was January 16, 1909 (Hermelin & Rutter, 2001). Some scholars think that the skills shown by savants are so specific and depend so much on memory that they do not qualify as separate "intelligences" (Nettelbeck & Young, 1996). However, Gardner insists that savant syndrome simply cannot be explained by theories that emphasize a general intelligence factor, g.

Gardner also marshals evidence to show that each intelligence has its own distinctive developmental course. Many great musical composers and athletes, for example, revealed their genius in childhood, whereas exceptional logical–mathematical intelligence typically shows up later, after the individual has gained the capacity for abstract thought and has mastered an area of science. Finally, Gardner links his distinct intelligences to distinct structures in the brain, arguing that the eight intelligences are neurologically distinct.

Sternberg's Triarchic Theory

Agreeing with Gardner that traditional IQ tests do not capture all that it means to be an intelligent person, Robert Sternberg (1985, 1988, 2003) has proposed a **triarchic theory of intelligence** that emphasizes three aspects of intelligent behavior: contextual, experiential, and information-processing components (see ■ **Figure 9.2**).

First, according to the practical or **contextual subtheory,** what is defined as intelligent behavior depends on the sociocultural context in which it is displayed. This perspective views intelligent behavior as varying from one culture or subculture to another, from one period in history to another, and from one period of the life span to another. Sternberg (1999a, b) reports a study in which he and a colleague tested the reasoning skills of second-graders in a school where instruction was conducted in English in the morning and in Hebrew in the afternoon. Some

MEASURING INTELLIGENCE

At the turn of the last century, Alfred Binet and Theodore Simon produced the forerunner of modern intelligence tests. In 1904, they were commissioned by the French government to devise a test that would identify "dull" children who might need special instruction. Binet and Simon devised a large battery of tasks measuring the skills believed to be necessary for classroom learning: attention, perception, memory, reasoning, verbal comprehension, and so on. Items that discriminated between normal children and those described by their teachers as slow were kept in the final test.

The test was soon revised so that the items were age-graded. For example, a set of "6-year-old" items could be passed by most 6-year-olds but by few 5-year-olds; "12-year-old" items could be handled by most 12-year-olds but not by younger children. This approach permitted the testers to describe a child's **mental age**—the level of age-graded problems that the child is able to solve. Thus, a child who passes all items at the 5-year-old level but does poorly on more advanced items—regardless of the child's actual age—is said to have a mental age of 5.

Binet's test became known as the Stanford-Binet Intelligence Scale after Lewis Terman of Stanford University translated and published a revised version of the test for use with American children. Terman developed a procedure for comparing a child's mental age (MA) with his chronological age (CA) by calculating an **intelligence quotient (IQ),** which consisted of MA divided by CA and then multiplied by 100 ($IQ = MA/CA \times 100$). An IQ score of 100 indicates average intelligence, regardless of a child's age: The normal child passes just the items that age-mates typically pass; mental age increases each year, but so does chronological age. The child of 8 with a mental age of 10 has experienced rapid intellectual growth and has a high IQ (specifically, 125); if she still has a mental age of 10 when she is 15 years old, then she has an IQ of only 67 and is clearly below average compared with children of the same age.

The Stanford-Binet, now in its fifth edition, is still in use (Roid, 2003). Its **test norms**—standards of normal performance expressed as average scores and the range of scores around the average—are based on the performance of a large, representative sample of people (2-year-olds through adults) from many socioeconomic and racial backgrounds. The concept of mental age is no longer used to calculate IQ; instead, individuals receive scores that reflect how well or how poorly they do compared with others of the same age. An IQ of 100 is still average, and the higher the IQ score an individual attains, the better the performance is in comparison with that of age-mates.

David Wechsler constructed a set of intelligence tests also in wide use. The Wechsler Preschool and Primary Scale of Intelligence is for children between ages 3 and 8 (Wechsler, 2002). The Wechsler Intelligence Scale for Children (WISC-IV) is appropriate for school-children ages 6 to 16 (Wechsler, 2003), and the Wechsler Adult Intelligence Scale is used with adults (Wechsler, 1997). The Wechsler tests yield a verbal IQ score based on items measuring vocabulary, general knowledge, arithmetic reasoning, and the like and a performance IQ based on such nonverbal skills as the ability to assemble puzzles, solve mazes, reproduce geometric designs with colored blocks, and rearrange pictures to tell a meaningful story. As with the Stanford-Binet, a score of 100 is defined as average performance for the person's age. A person's full-scale IQ is a combination of the verbal and performance scores.

Scores on both the Stanford-Binet and Wechsler Scales form a **normal distribution,** or a symmetrical, bell-shaped spread around the average score of 100 (see the graph in this box). Scores around the average are common; very high and very low scores are rare. About two-thirds of people taking one of these IQ tests have scores between 85 and 115, which corresponds to the spread or range of scores

children got all of the problems wrong, suggesting they were not bright. However, this group of children had been tested with English problems in the afternoon when they normally would have received problems in Hebrew; consequently, the children read the problems from right to left. In their normal classroom context, this would have been a smart thing to do.

Just as intelligent behavior varies from one culture to another, contextual subtheory predicts that it changes over time. Numerical abilities may not play as important a role in intelligent behavior now that calculators and computers are widely used, for example, whereas analytical skills may be more important than ever in a complex, urban world. And certainly the infant learning how to master new toys shows a different kind of intelligence than the adult mastering a college curriculum. Thus, the definition of the intelligent infant must differ from the definition of the intelligent adult.

Contextual subtheory, then, defines intelligent behavior differently depending on the sociocultural context in which it is displayed. Intelligent people adapt to the environment they are in (for example, a job setting), shape that environment to

How would you define an intelligent child? Mexican American parents, like Cambodian, Filipino, and Vietnamese parents, say that intelligent children are motivated, socially skilled, and able to manage their own behavior. European American parents place less emphasis on these noncognitive aspects of intelligence (Okagaki & Sternberg, 1993). Each cultural group defines intelligence in its own way.

© Dean Berry/Index Stock Imagery

within one **standard deviation** above and below the average score. Fewer than 3% have scores of 130 or above, a score often used as one criterion of giftedness. Similarly, fewer than 3% have IQs below 70, a cutoff commonly used to define mental retardation.

Several alternatives to these traditional tests have been proposed. Alan Kaufman and Nadeen Kaufman, for example, designed the Kaufman Assessment Battery for Children (K-ABC-II; Kaufman & Kaufman, 2003). This test, based on information-processing theory, focuses on *how* children solve problems rather than on *what* problems they solve (Kaufman, 2001; Sparrow & Davis, 2000). The K-ABC-II, which is appropriate for children ages 3 through 18, has two subscales. One measures a child's ability to process information sequentially; the other measures the ability to integrate several pieces of information. The test also has a separate section of questions to assess children's achievement or acquired knowledge.

Another promising approach, called **dynamic assessment,** attempts to evaluate how well children learn new material when an examiner provides them with competent instruction (Haywood & Tzuriel, 2002; Lidz & Elliott, 2001). Dynamic assessment involves interactions between the child being assessed and the adult doing the assessment. During an assessment, children are tested to identify gaps in their knowledge; they receive instruction to remediate the gaps; then they are retested to

see if the instruction was effective.

Reuven Feuerstein and his colleagues have argued that even though intelligence is often defined as the potential to learn from experience, IQ tests typically assess what *has been* learned, not what *can be* learned (Feuerstein, Feuerstein, & Gross, 1997). The traditional IQ tests may be biased against children from culturally different or disadvantaged backgrounds who lack opportunities to learn what the tests measure. Feuerstein developed the Learning Potential Assessment Device to assess children's ability to learn new things with the guidance of an adult who provides increasingly helpful cues. This test interprets intelligence as the ability to learn quickly with minimal guidance. Feuerstein believes that learners first need a "mediator," a guide who structures and interprets the environment for them; then, they are able to learn more from their experiences on their own. This approach should remind you of Lev Vygotsky's theory, described in Chapter 7, that children acquire new ways of thinking through their social interactions with more experienced problem solvers; it is based partly on Vygotsky's work.

The approximate distribution of IQ scores.

The dynamic assessment of learning capacity provides information beyond what traditional IQ tests provide about a child's intellectual competence and likely achievement (Haywood & Tzuriel, 2002; Lidz, 1997).

Trying to boil down a person's intelligence to a single score is a formidable task. A single score derived from a test that assesses only some of the many intelligences that humans can display does not do justice to the complexity of human mental functioning. Moreover, it is a measure of the individual's performance at one point—an estimate that is not always a good indicator of the person's underlying intellectual competence.

make it suit them better, or find a better environment. Such people have "street smarts." They can walk into a new situation, quickly evaluate it, and adapt their behavior to be successful in this new context. Although recognized by many people as an important form of intelligence, this real-world adaptability is not assessed by traditional intelligence tests.

The second aspect of the triarchic theory focuses on the role of experience in intelligence. According to this **experiential subtheory,** what is intelligent when a person first encounters a new task is not the same as what is intelligent after extensive experience with that task. The first kind of intelligence, *response to novelty*, requires active and conscious information processing. Sternberg believes that relatively novel tasks provide the best measures of intelligence because they tap the individual's ability to come up with creative ideas or fresh insights.

In daily life, however, people also perform more or less intelligently on familiar and repetitive tasks (preparing breakfast, for example). This second kind of intelligence reflects **au-**

tomatization, or an increased efficiency of information processing with practice. It is intelligent to develop little "programs in the mind" for performing common, everyday activities efficiently and unthinkingly. Thus, according to Sternberg, it is crucial to know how familiar a task is to a person before assessing that person's behavior. For example, giving people of two different cultural groups an intelligence test whose items are familiar to one group and novel to the other introduces culture bias into the testing process, making it difficult to obtain a fair assessment of the groups' relative abilities.

The third aspect of the triarchic theory, the **componential subtheory,** focuses on information-processing components. These include the *metacomponents* or decision-making processes that specify how to solve problems and the *performance components* that carry out the actions dictated by the metacomponents. The information-processing components also include *knowledge-acquisition components* that are involved in acquiring new information and sorting relevant from irrelevant information.

Experiential subtheory

How experiences affect intelligence and how intelligence affects a person's experiences. Includes:
1. Ability to deal with novelty
2. Ability to automatize processing

Intelligence

Contextual subtheory

Behaviors considered intelligent in a particular culture. Includes:
1. Adaptation
2. Selection
3. Shaping

Componential (information-processing) subtheory

Cognitive processes that underlie intelligent behavior. Includes:
1. Metacomponents (e.g., strategy construction, strategy selection, and solution monitoring)
2. Performance components (e.g., encoding and comparing)
3. Knowledge acquisition components (e.g., selective encoding, selective combination, and selective comparison)

■ **FIGURE 9.2** Robert Sternberg's triarchic theory of intelligence.
SOURCE: From F.E. Weinert & E.A. Haney, The stability of individual differences in intellectual development: Empirical evidence, theoretical problems, and new research questions, in R.J. Sternberg, J. Lautrey, & T.I. Lubart, EDs. *Models of intelligence: International perspective.* Copyright © 2003, American Psychological Association. Reprinted with permission from the American Psychological Association.

As an information-processing theorist, Sternberg believes that the theories of intelligence underlying the development of traditional IQ tests ignore *how* people produce intelligent answers—that a full picture of intelligence includes not only the number of answers people get right but also the processes they use to arrive at their answers and the efficiency with which they use those processes. So, to fully assess how intelligent people are, researchers must consider the *context* in which they perform (their age, culture, and historical period), their previous *experience* with a task (whether their behavior reflects response to novelty or automatized processes), and their *information-processing* strategies. Individuals who are intelligent, according to this triarchic model, are able to carry out logical thought processes efficiently and effectively to solve both novel and familiar problems and to adapt to their environment.

Sternberg (1999a; 2003) expanded his triarchic theory of intelligence to include what he calls the theory of **successful intelligence.** According to this view, people are intelligent "to the extent that they have the abilities needed to succeed in life, according to their own definition of success within their sociocultural context" (2003, p. xvi). These individuals are strong in all three areas—contextual, experiential, and componential. Thus, intelligence is not just the ability to do well in school, something measured by traditional intelligence tests, but also the ability to do well in life (Sternberg, 2004). Smart people find ways to optimize their strengths and minimize their weak-

nesses so that they can succeed. They select environments (including occupations) that suit their profile of abilities, or, to the extent possible, they modify their abilities or environments. Unfortunately, today's widely used tests of intelligence do not reflect this sophisticated view of intelligence.

How Intelligence Relates to Creativity

Now that you know how the experts define and measure intelligence, we can consider how this construct is related to creativity. **Creativity** is often defined as the ability to produce novel responses appropriate in context and valued by others—products both original and meaningful (Simon, 2001; Simonton, 1999; Sternberg, 2003). Thus, someone who comes up with a novel and useful idea is considered creative, whereas someone who comes up with a novel idea that has no apparent value may not be considered creative. Some researchers who study creativity, however, have concerns about defining as creative only those ideas that are deemed useful (see Smith, 2005). After all, who decides what is useful, and who is to say whether something will be valued by someone at some time? Consequently, some researchers examine all novel outputs and not just those that are deemed useful or valuable. Before reading further, you may want to test your creativity with the problems in ■ **Figure 9.3.**

The study of creativity emerged from the study of intelligence; indeed, creativity was once thought to be entirely en-

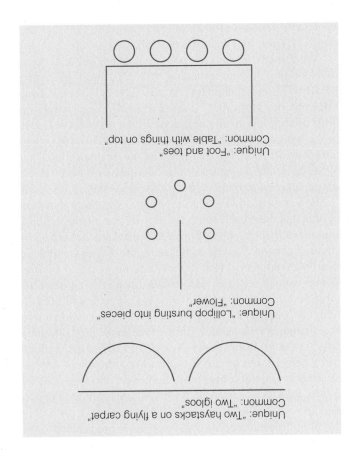

The figure contains three drawings with rotated text beneath each:

Common: "Table with things on top."
Unique: "Foot and toes."

Common: "Flower."
Unique: "Lollipop bursting into pieces."

Common: "Two igloos."
Unique: "Two haystacks on a flying carpet."

■ **FIGURE 9.3** Are you creative? Indicate what you see in each of the three drawings. Below each drawing you will find examples of unique and common responses, drawn from a study of creativity in children.
SOURCE: Wallach & Kogan (1965).

of different (including novel) ideas that a person can generate—is most often used to assess creativity because it is easy to score. Quick—list all the uses you can think of for a pencil. An uncreative person might say you could write letters, notes, postcards, and so forth; by contrast, one creative person envisioned a pencil as "a backscratcher, a potting stake, kindling for a fire, a rolling pin for baking, a toy for a woodpecker, or a small boat for a cricket" (Richards, 1996, p. 73).

As you can see, although the two constructs are related, intelligence, with its focus on convergent thinking, and creativity, with its focus on divergent thinking, are distinct. In subsequent sections, as we discuss the intellectual profiles of children, adolescents, and adults, we will also consider the development of their creative selves. Note, however, that the infant is not included in our discussion of creativity because, to date, researchers have not developed a method for uncovering signs of creativity at this young age.

SUMMING UP

- The psychometric or testing approach to cognition defines intelligence as a set of traits that allows some people to think and solve problems more effectively than others. It can be viewed as a hierarchy consisting of a general factor *(g)*, broad abilities such as fluid and crystallized intelligence, and many specific abilities.

- Gardner's theory of multiple intelligences, with its focus on eight distinct forms of intelligence, offers an alternative view. His theory includes these types of intelligence: linguistic, logical–mathematical, musical intelligence, spatial, bodily-kinesthetic, interpersonal, intrapersonal, and naturalist.

- Sternberg's triarchic theory of intelligence proposes three components to intelligence. The contextual component predicts that intelligent behavior will vary across different sociocultural contexts. According to the experiential component, intelligent responses will vary depending on whether problems are novel or routine (automated). Finally, the componential aspect of intelligence includes the information-processing skills that a person brings to a problem-solving situation.

- Creativity is the ability to produce novel and socially valuable work. It involves divergent rather than convergent thinking and is often measured in terms of ideational fluency, the sheer number of different (including novel) ideas that a person can generate.

CRITICAL THINKING

1. Imagine that you are chosen to head a presidential commission on intelligence testing whose task it is to devise an IQ test for use in the schools that is better than any that currently exists. Sketch out the features of your model IQ test. What would be included and excluded from your definition of intelligence? How would you measure intelligence? In what ways would your test improve upon the tests that are currently used?

2. Traditional IQ tests assess convergent thinking. Should they also assess divergent thinking? Why or why not?

twined with intelligence (Runco, 2007). But in a now classic study, Wallach and Kogan (1965) demonstrated that creative thinking was distinct from IQ and from grades earned in the classroom. Correlations between scores on creativity measures and scores on IQ tests are low to moderate, depending on the area of creativity measured (Sternberg, 2003). Creativity and general intelligence are related only in the sense that highly creative people rarely have below-average IQs. Thus, a minimum of intelligence is probably required for creativity (Runco, 2007; Simonton, 1999). However, among people who have average or above-average IQs, an individual's IQ score is essentially unrelated to her level of creativity.

IQ scores and creativity scores do not correlate very well because they measure two different types of thinking. IQ tests measure **convergent thinking,** which involves "converging" on the best answer to a problem. In contrast, creativity involves **divergent thinking,** or coming up with a variety of ideas or solutions to a problem when there is no single correct answer. Responses on divergent thinking tasks can be analyzed along three dimensions: the originality or uniqueness of the generated ideas, the flexibility of or number of different categories expressed by the ideas, and the fluency of the ideas (Runco, 2007). This last one—ideational fluency, or the sheer number

As you saw in Chapters 7 and 8, the mind develops rapidly in infancy. But how can an infant's intellectual growth be measured? Is it possible to identify infants who are more or less intelligent than their age-mates? And how well does high (or low) intelligence in infancy predict high (or low) intelligence in childhood and adulthood?

Developmental Quotients

None of the standard intelligence tests can be used with children much younger than 3, because the test items require verbal skills and attention spans that infants do not have. Some developmentalists have tried to measure infant intelligence by assessing the rate at which infants achieve important developmental milestones. Perhaps the best known and most widely used of the infant tests is the Bayley Scales of Infant Development (Bayley, 1993). This test, designed for infants ages 1 month to 42 months, has the following three parts:

- The *motor scale*, which measures the infant's ability to do such things as grasp a cube and throw a ball
- The *mental scale*, which includes adaptive behaviors such as reaching for a desirable object, searching for a hidden toy, and following directions
- The *behavior rating scale*, a rating of the child's behavior on dimensions such as goal-directedness, emotional regulation, and social responsivity

On the basis of the first two scores, the infant is given a **developmental quotient (DQ)** rather than an IQ. The DQ summarizes how well or how poorly the infant performs in comparison with a large norm group of infants the same age.

Infant Intelligence and Later Intelligence

As they age, infants progress through many developmental milestones of the kind assessed by the Bayley scales, so such scales are useful in charting infants' developmental progress. They are also useful in diagnosing neurological problems and mental retardation—even when these conditions are mild and difficult to detect through standard pediatric or neurological examinations (Escalona, 1968; Honzik, 1983). But developmentalists have also been interested in the larger issue of continuity versus discontinuity in intellectual development: Is it possible to predict which infants are likely to be gifted, average, or mentally retarded during the school years?

Not from their DQ Scores. Correlations between infant DQ and child IQ are low, sometimes close to zero. The infant who does well on the Bayley scales or other infant tests may or may not obtain a high IQ score later in life (Honzik, 1983; Rose et al., 1989). True, the infant who scores low on an infant test often turns out to be mentally retarded, but otherwise there seems to be a good deal of discontinuity between early and later scores—at least until a child is 4 or older.

What might explain the poor connection between scores on infant development scales and children's later IQs? Perhaps the main reason is that infant tests and IQ tests tap qualitatively different kinds of abilities (Columbo, 1993). Piaget would undoubtedly approve of this argument. Infant scales focus heavily on the sensory and motor skills that Piaget believed are so important in infancy; IQ tests such as the Stanford-Binet and WISC-III emphasize more abstract abilities, such as verbal reasoning, concept formation, and problem solving.

Robert McCall (1981, 1983) offers a second explanation, arguing that the growth of intelligence during infancy is highly influenced by powerful and universal maturational processes. Maturational forces (such as the unfolding of the genetic blueprint for intelligence) pull infants back on course if environmental influences (such as growing up in an impoverished home and neighborhood) cause them to stray. For this reason, higher or lower infant test scores are likely to be nothing more than temporary deviations from a universal developmental path. As the child nears age 2, McCall argues, maturational forces become less strong, so individual differences become larger and more stable over time. Consistent differences related to both individual genetic makeup and environment begin to emerge.

Should researchers give up on trying to predict later IQ on the basis of development in infancy? Perhaps not yet. The information-processing approach has given new life to the idea that there is continuity in intelligence from infancy to childhood. Several researchers have found that certain measures of infant attention predict later IQ better than infant intelligence tests do. For example, speed of habituation (how fast or slow the infant loses interest in a repeatedly presented stimulus) and preference for novelty (the degree to which an infant prefers a novel stimulus to a familiar one), assessed in the first year of life, have an average correlation of about +0.45 with IQ in childhood, particularly with verbal IQ and memory skills (McCall & Carriger, 1993; Rose & Feldman, 1997; Rose, Feldman, & Jankowski, 2003). Thus, the infant who quickly becomes bored and likes novelty over familiarity is likely to be brighter in childhood than the infant who is slow to habituate and does not like novelty. In addition, fast reaction time in infancy (time taken to look in the direction of a visual stimulus as soon as it appears) predicts later IQ about as well as speed of habituation and novelty preferences scores (Dougherty & Haith, 1997).

From this, we can characterize the "smart" infant as the speedy information processor—the infant who quickly becomes bored by the same old thing, seeks novel experiences, and soaks up information rapidly. There seems to be some continuity between infant intelligence and childhood intelligence after all. Such Bayley scale accomplishments as throwing a ball are unlikely to carry over into vocabulary-learning or problem-solving skills in childhood. However, the extent to which the young infant processes information quickly can predict the extent to which he will learn quickly and solve problems efficiently later in childhood.

- The Bayley scales include motor, mental, and behavior ratings to assess infant development. Although traditionally used as a measure of infant intelligence, they do not correlate well with later IQ scores.

- Infant measures that capture speed of information processing and preference for novelty are better at predicting later intelligence. Infants who can quickly process information are able to take in more information than those who are slower.

CRITICAL THINKING

1. What characteristics or behaviors of infants are associated with later intelligence?

2. Are there specific activities that parents should be doing with their infants to ensure that they develop to their intellectual potential? What might some of these activities be?

9.3 THE CHILD

Over the childhood years, children generally become able to answer more questions, and more difficult questions, on IQ tests. That is, their mental ages increase. But what happens to the IQ scores of individual children, which reflect how they compare with peers?

How Stable Are IQ Scores during Childhood?

It was once assumed that a person's IQ reflected her genetically determined intellectual capacity and therefore would remain stable over time. In other words, a child with an IQ of 120 at age 5 was expected to obtain a similar IQ at age 10, 15, or 20. Is this idea supported by research? As you have seen, infant DQs do not predict later IQs well. However, starting around age 4 there is a fairly strong relationship between early and later IQ, and the relationship grows even stronger by middle childhood. ● **Table 9.2** summarizes the results of a longitudinal study of 220 children from ages 4 to 12 (Weinert & Hany, 2003; Weinert & Schneider, 1999). The shorter the interval between two testings, the higher the correlation between children's IQ scores on the two occasions. Even when several years have passed, however, IQ seems to be a stable attribute: the scores that children obtain at age 7 are clearly related to those they obtain 5 years later, at age 12.

These correlations do not reveal everything, however. They are based on a large group of children, and they do not necessarily mean that the IQs of individual children will remain stable over the years. As it turns out, many children show sizable ups and downs in their IQ scores over the course of childhood. Patterns of change differ considerably from child to child, as though each were on a private developmental trajec-

● **TABLE 9.2 CORRELATIONS OF IQS MEASURED AT VARIOUS AGES**

AGE OF CHILD	CORRELATION WITH IQ AT AGE 9	CORRELATION WITH IQ AT AGE 12
4	0.46	0.42
5	0.47	0.49
7	0.81	0.69
9	—	0.80

SOURCE: Adapted from Weinert & Hany, 2003, p. 171, Table 10.1.

tory (Gottfried et al., 1994). One team of researchers looked at the IQ scores of 140 children who had taken intelligence tests at regular intervals from age 2 to age 17 (McCall, Applebaum, & Hogarty, 1973). The average difference between a child's highest and lowest scores was a whopping 28.5 points. About one-third showed changes of more than 30 points, and one child changed by 74 IQ points.

How do researchers reconcile the conclusion that IQ is relatively stable with this clear evidence of instability? They can still conclude that, within a group, children's standings (high or low) in comparison with peers stay stable from one point to another during the childhood years (Sternberg, Grigorenko, & Bundy, 2001). But many individual children experience drops or gains in IQ scores over the years. Remember, however, that this relates to performance on IQ tests rather than underlying intellectual competence. IQ scores are influenced not only by people's intelligence but also by their motivation, testing procedures and conditions, and many other factors that we will discuss in this chapter. As a result, IQ may be more changeable over the years than intellectual ability.

Causes of Gain and Loss

Some wandering of IQ scores upward or downward over time is just random fluctuation—a good day at one testing, a bad day at the next. Yet there are patterns. Children whose scores fluctuate the most tend to live in unstable home environments; their life experiences fluctuate between periods of happiness and turmoil.

In addition, some children gain IQ points over childhood and others lose them. Who are the gainers, and who are the losers? Gainers seem to have parents who foster achievement and who are neither too strict nor too lax in child rearing (McCall, Applebaum, & Hogarty, 1973). Noticeable drops in IQ with age often occur among children who live in poverty. Otto Klineberg (1963) proposed a **cumulative-deficit hypothesis** to explain this: impoverished environments inhibit intellectual growth, and these negative effects accumulate over time. There is some support for the cumulative-deficit hypothesis, especially when a child's parents are not only poor but also

EARLY INTERVENTION FOR PRESCHOOL CHILDREN

During the 1960s, several programs were launched to enrich the early learning experiences of disadvantaged preschoolers. Project Head Start is perhaps the best known of these interventions. The idea was to provide a variety of social and intellectual experiences that might better prepare these children for school. High-quality Head Start programs provide the nutrition, health care, parent training, and intellectual stimulation that can get disadvantaged children off to a good start. At first, Head Start and similar programs seemed to be a smashing success; children in the programs were posting average gains of about 10 points on IQ tests. But then discouragement set in: By the time children reached the middle years of grade school, their IQs were no higher than those of control-group children (Gray, Ramsey, & Klaus, 1982). Such findings led Arthur Jensen (1969) to conclude that "compensatory education has been tried and it apparently has failed" (p. 2).

But that was not the end of the story. Children in some of these programs have been followed into their teens, 20s, and beyond. Irving Lazar and Richard Darlington (1982) reported on the long-term effects of 11 early intervention programs in several areas of the United States. Other follow-up studies of Head Start and similar early education programs for disadvantaged children have been conducted since then (Campbell & Ramey, 1995; Guralnick, 1997).

These long-term studies indicate the following:

- Children who participate in early intervention programs show immediate gains on IQ and school achievement tests, whereas nonparticipants do not. However, the gains

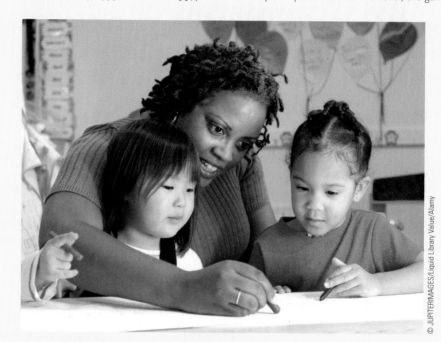

High-quality Head Start programs provide the nutrition, health care, parent training, and intellectual stimulation that can get disadvantaged children off to a good start.

low in intellectual functioning themselves (Jensen, 1977; Ramey & Ramey, 1992). The Applications box examines the success of early intervention programs designed to raise the IQ scores and academic success of children living in poverty.

The Emergence of Creativity

We often hear young children's play activities and artwork described as "creative." When does creativity emerge and what is the child who scores high on tests of creativity like? To answer the first question, researchers have measured divergent thinking at different ages throughout childhood. Early on, it became apparent that preschool-aged children display fairly high levels of divergent thought—generating many original ideas. But creative output begins to decline somewhat as children enter kindergarten and first grade, and drops even further by fourth grade (e.g., Gardner, 1982; Torrance, 1968). Following this fourth-grade slump, as it is called among creativity researchers, levels of divergent thinking rise again after the age of 12 (Runco, 2007; Smith & Carlsson, 1990).

More recent research suggests that the peaks and valleys of creative thought during childhood are not as large as originally reported, although there is some drop-off during elementary school (Claxton, Pannells, & Rhoads, 2005). This may reflect the demands of school and peers to conform to the group rather than to be a "free spirit" (Gardner, 1982).

To address the second question of what the creative child is like, one group of researchers compared children who had high creativity scores but normal-range IQ scores with children who scored high in IQ but not in creativity (Getzels & Jackson, 1962). Personality measures suggested that the creative children showed more freedom, originality, humor, aggression, and playfulness than the high-IQ children. Perhaps as a result, the high-IQ children were more success-oriented and received more approval from teachers. The unconventional responses of highly creative children are not always appreciated in the conventional classroom (Runco, 2007). Compared with their less creative peers, creative children also engage in more fantasy or pretend play, often inventing new uses for familiar objects and new roles for themselves (Kogan, 1983). They have active imaginations and their parents are often tolerant of their sometimes unconventional ideas (Runco, 2007). Finally, creative children are more likely to be open to new experiences and ideas, as are their parents (Simonton, 1999).

rarely last more than 3 or 4 years after the program has ended. Effects on measures other than IQ are more encouraging.

- Compensatory education improves both children's and mothers' attitudes about achievement. When asked to describe something that has made them feel proud of themselves, program participants are more likely than nonparticipants to mention scholastic achievements or (in the case of 15- to 18-year-olds) job-related successes. Mothers of program participants tend to be more satisfied with their children's school performance and to hold higher occupational aspirations for their children.

- Program participants are more likely to meet their school's basic requirements than nonparticipants are. They are less likely to be assigned to special education classes, to be retained in a grade, or to drop out of high school.

- There is even some evidence (although not in all studies) that teenagers who have participated in early compensatory education are less likely than nonparticipants to become pregnant, to require welfare assistance, and to be involved in delinquent behavior.

In sum, longitudinal evaluations suggest that compensatory education does work. Programs seem most effective if they start early, last long, and involve several components. For example, Craig Ramey and his colleagues (Campbell et al., 2001; Campbell, Shirley, & Caygill, 2002; Campbell & Ramey, 1995) have reported outstanding success with the Abecedarian Project, an early intervention for extremely disadvantaged, primarily African American, children that involved an intellectually stimulating day care program, home visits and efforts to involve parents in their children's development, and medical and nutritional care from early infancy to kindergarten entry. Program participants outperformed nonparticipants throughout childhood and into adolescence. By age 15, the impressive IQ advantage they had shown as young children had narrowed to less than 5 points, but they continued to perform better on math and reading achievement tests, were less likely to have been held back a grade, and were less in need of special education services. Some children in the study were randomly assigned to a group whose intervention did not begin until school age, when a teacher worked with their regular teachers and their parents over a 3-year period.

These children did not show as many gains as those who received the preschool intervention, suggesting that it is best to intervene early in children's lives (Campbell & Ramey, 1995).

The success of early compensatory education for at-risk preschoolers has led some experts in the field to call for mandatory preschool education for all children (Barnett et al., 2007). Although many young children do attend some sort of program prior to entering kindergarten, the programs are quite varied in their quality and focus. Some focus on preparing children for the academic life that they will encounter when they begin kindergarten, others focus on developing social skills, and still others really have no particular focus. A universal preschool system would aim to reduce these inequalities. Not all experts, though, agree that universal preschool should be the goal (Stipek & Hakuta, 2007). Instead, they believe that improving the existing preschool programs that target at-risk children, such as Head Start and the Abecedarian Project, will help ensure that "no child starts from behind," struggling to catch up to peers on cognitive and social skills that they did not have the opportunity to develop at home (Stipek & Kahuta, 2007, p. 129).

As you will see later in this chapter, average IQ scores differ across racial and socioeconomic groups, but scores on creativity tests usually do not (Kogan, 1983). Moreover, genetic influences (a source of individual differences in IQ) have little to do with performance on tests of creativity; twins are similar in the degree of creativity they display, but identical twins are no more similar than fraternal twins (Plomin, 1990; Reznikoff et al., 1973). This suggests that certain qualities of the home environment tend to make brothers and sisters alike in their degree of creativity. What qualities? Although there is little research to go on, parents of creative children and adolescents tend to value nonconformity and independence, accept their children as they are, encourage their curiosity and playfulness, and grant them a good deal of freedom to explore new possibilities on their own (Harrington, Block, & Block, 1987; Runco, 1992). In some cases, the parent–child relationship is even distant; a surprising number of eminent creators seem to have experienced rather lonely, insecure, and unhappy childhoods (Ochse, 1990; Simonton, 1999). Out of their adversity may have come an active imagination and a strong desire to develop their talents. Indeed, several early studies suggested that childhood adversity was a common theme among highly creative individuals—that adversity was the driving force behind their creativity (e.g., Goertzel & Goertzel,

1962). Although this may be true for some creative individuals, it is certainly not true for all creative individuals. Overall, then, creative abilities are influenced by factors distinct from those that influence the cognitive abilities measured on IQ tests.

SUMMING UP

- During childhood, IQ scores become more stable so that scores at one point in time are generally consistent with scores obtained at a second point.

- Despite group stability, the scores of individuals can fluctuate over time. Greater changes are evident when children grow up in unstable environments.

- Overall, there is both continuity and change in IQ scores during childhood; IQ scores remain stable for many children, and mental ages rise.

- Creativity increases throughout early childhood but dips during elementary school, possibly in response to societal expectations to conform. Creativity is associated with playfulness, openness to new experiences, and originality, but is largely independent of intelligence.

9.4 THE ADOLESCENT

Intellectual growth is rapid during infancy and childhood. What happens during adolescence, and how well does IQ predict school performance?

Continuity between Childhood and Adulthood

Intellectual growth continues its rapid pace in early adolescence then slows and levels off in later adolescence (Thorndike, 1997). As noted in Chapter 5, a spurt in brain development occurs around age 11 or age 12, when children are believed to enter Piaget's formal operational stage. Brain development may give children the information-processing speed and working-memory capacity they need to perform at adult-like levels on IQ tests (Kail & Salthouse, 1994). Thus, basic changes in the brain in early adolescence may underlie a variety of cognitive advances—the achievement of formal operations, improved memory and information-processing skills, and better performance on tests of intelligence.

Although adolescence is a time of impressive mental growth, it is also a time of increased stability of individual differences in intellectual performance. During the teen years, IQ scores become even more stable than they were in childhood and predict IQ in middle age well (Deary et al., 2004). Even while adolescents as a group are experiencing cognitive growth, then, each adolescent is establishing a characteristic level of intellectual performance that will most likely be carried into adult life unless the individual's environment changes dramatically.

IQ and School Achievement

The original purpose of IQ tests was to estimate how well children would do in school and they do this fairly well. Correlations between children's and adolescents' IQ scores and their grades range from +0.50 to 0.86, making general intellectual ability one of the best predictors of school achievement available (Deary et al., 2007; Neisser et al., 1996). Adolescents with high IQs are also less likely to drop out of high school and more likely to go on to college than their peers with lower IQs; the correlation between IQ and years of education obtained averages +0.55 (Neisser et al., 1996). However, IQ scores do not predict college grades as well as they predict high school grades (Brody & Brody, 1976). Most college students probably have at least the average intellectual ability needed to succeed in college; success is therefore more influenced by personal qualities such as motivation. Overall, an IQ score is a good predictor of academic achievement, but it does not reveal everything about a student. Factors such as work habits, interests, and motivation to succeed also affect academic achievement.

Fostering Creativity

We noted earlier that there is some dip in creativity during elementary school. What happens during adolescence? According to Howard Gardner (1990), adolescents often regain the innovativeness and freedom of expression they had as preschoolers and put it to use, with the technical skills they gained as children, to produce highly creative works. The ages at which creativity flourishes or is stifled seem to vary from culture to culture depending on when children are pressured to conform (Torrance, 1975). Overall, the developmental course of creativity is not so predictable or steady as the increase in mental age seen on measures of IQ. Instead, creativity seems to wax and wane with age in response to developmental needs and task demands. For example, in one study, researchers found that sixth-graders demonstrated greater creativity than college students on one type of task, but the college students outperformed the sixth-graders on a different task of creativity (Wu et al., 2005; see also Runco, 2006). In other research (Claxton, Pannells, & Rhoads, 2005), creative thinking remained fairly stable from fourth to ninth grade, but creative *feelings* increased significantly throughout adolescence. Creative feelings include curiosity, imagination, and willingness to take calculated risks. So teens may be feeling more creative than children even if they are not expressing creativity in their actions.

Is it possible to foster creativity? Researchers have looked at individuals who demonstrate creativity in a particular field to try to identify the factors that contribute to their accomplishments. David Feldman (1982, 1986), for example, has studied children and adolescents who are prodigies in such areas as chess, music, and mathematics. These individuals were generally similar to their peers in areas outside their fields of expertise. What contributed to their special achievements? On the nature side, they had *talent* as well as a powerful *motivation* to develop their special talents—a real passion for what they were doing. Olympic gymnast Olga Korbut put it well: "If gymnastics did not exist, I would have invented it" (Feldman, 1982, p. 35). Other research confirms that internal motivation and a thirst for challenge are crucial elements of creative productivity (Sternberg, 2006; Yeh & Wu, 2006). Individuals with a posi-

FOSTERING CREATIVITY

Creativity is not a fixed trait. As noted in the text, levels of creativity vary depending on both personal characteristics and environmental conditions. Researchers have identified several ways to foster creativity. But first, why should we be concerned with fostering creativity? According to Richard Florida (2002), author of *The Rise of the Creative Class,* "human creativity is the ultimate economic resource. The ability to come up with new ideas and better ways of doing things is ultimately what raises productivity and thus living conditions" (p. xiii).

So how can this resource be fostered? Mark Runco (2007) provides several suggestions:

1. Change your perspective on a problem. Sometimes, we need to approach a problem from a fresh angle in order to generate new and potentially useful solutions. Runco notes that mentally readjusting your thoughts as well as physically relocating yourself can both be productive. Many people report that some of their most innovative ideas have been generated after they have taken a break from their task and moved on to some other activity. Indeed, Robert Epstein (1995) claims that the best ideas come to us in bed, the bath, or on a bus.

2. Generate analogies to help place the current problem in another context that may yield a solution. The inventor of Velcro is said to have been struck by how burrs from the field stuck to his clothes and his dog's fur. He examined one of the burrs under a microscope and saw that the surface of the burr consisted of many small hooks. He realized that these hooks were catching on the loops of his pants' fabric and that he could apply this same hook-loop principle to creating a new type of fastener that could rival buttons, zippers, and tape.

3. Borrow or extend existing ideas. You may have heard the expression "don't reinvent the wheel." If a great idea already exists, consider how it might be adapted or extended to help solve other problems rather than starting from scratch. Piaget applied ideas from his training in biology to help frame his theory of cognitive development. Although it may have been creative to talk about children adapting their cognitive structures in order to make sense of their world, adapting to the demands of the environment was not a new concept.

4. Experiment with the materials of your field, whether these are words, musical instruments, or chemical substances. Some of the best chefs have come up with their signature dishes by experimenting with ingredients, cooking techniques, and new presentation styles.

5. Be persistent if at first you don't succeed. Milton Hershey, of Hershey chocolate fame, started out making caramels and experimented over and over again with the relative quantities of his ingredients before finding just the right combination that yielded a smooth, creamy caramel that didn't stick to customers' teeth (D'Antonio, 2006). Once he turned his attention to making chocolate, Hershey spent years testing different methods of combining and heating ingredients to create the milk chocolate that is popular today.

6. Question conventional wisdom—the assumptions held by many people with little thought regarding the source or accuracy of the assumptions. People are often remarkably resistant to change, commenting "this is the way it's always been done." Why is it done this way? Does it make sense to continue this practice? Might there be other, better ways to do it?

Clearly, there are many ways to foster creativity, but do any of them actually work? In a word, yes. In two separate analyses of creativity-training programs, researchers found effect sizes ranging from 0.68 to 0.77 (Ma, 2006; Scott et al., 2004). Effect size is an estimate, averaged over many studies, of the size of the difference in post-test creativity scores between the treatment group—in this case the creativity-training group—and a control group. Effect sizes around 0.50 are considered moderate and effect sizes of 0.80 or higher are considered large. Thus, the analyses of creativity-training programs show that people can learn techniques to improve their creativeness. But individual training will be constrained if the surrounding culture does not value, reward, or model creativity (Runco, 2007). Characteristics of the individual—some of which can be enhanced by training—and characteristics of society operate in conjunction to produce creativity.

---

tive outlook also seem more likely to display creativity, perhaps because they are more open to challenges and derive more pleasure from challenges (see Yeh & Wu, 2006). Creative thinkers have other personal qualities as well—they display a willingness to take risks and are able to put up with some ambiguity without becoming frustrated (Proctor & Burnett, 2004; Sternberg, 2006).

On the nurture side, creative individuals seem to be blessed with *environments* that recognize, value, and nurture their creative endeavors (Sternberg, 2006). Their environments allow them a certain degree of independence to explore different fields and acquire knowledge of their chosen field. According to Feldman (1982), the child with creative potential in a specific field must become intimately familiar with the state of the field if he is to advance or transform it, as the groundbreaking artist or musician does. Thus, building a knowledge base is a necessary, although not sufficient, component of creativity (Sternberg, 2006). So parents can help foster creativity by giving their children freedom to explore and opportunities to experiment with ideas and activities. But talent and creativity can be squashed if parents and trainers are too pushy. For example, David Helfgott, the Australian pianist who was the subject of the movie *Shine*, was nearly destroyed by an abusive father who pushed him unmercifully to master difficult pieces (Page, 1996). Cellist Yo-Yo Ma, a prodigy himself, says this about nurturing young musicians:

If you lead them toward music, teach them that it is beautiful, and help them learn—say, "Oh, you love music, well, let's work on this piece together, and I'll show you something. . . ." That's a *creative* nurturing. But if you just push them to be stars, and tell them they'll become rich and famous—or, worse, if you try to live through them—that is damaging (Page, 1996, p. G10).

The Applications box on page 257 provides additional suggestions for fostering creativity.

Finally, we should ask whether performance on the tests of creativity used in studies of creative development predict actual creative accomplishments, such as original artwork or outstanding science projects. Some researchers have found that scores on creativity tests administered in either elementary or secondary school predict creative achievements, such as inventions and writing novels, in adulthood (Howieson, 1981; Runco, 1992; Torrance, 1988). However, just as it is a mistake to expect IQ to predict accomplishments, it may also be a mistake to expect tests of creativity to do so with any great accuracy (Albert, 1996). Why? First, creativity is expressed in different ways at different points in the life span; engaging in imaginative play as a child is correlated with high scores on tests of creativity (Russ, 1996) but may have little to do with being a creative scientist or musician as an adult. Also, creativity tests, like IQ tests, attempt to measure a general cognitive ability when many specific talents exist, and each (artistic, mathematical, musical, and so on) requires distinct skills and experiences, as suggested by Gardner's theory of multiple intelligences.

Finally, scores on tests of creativity, but not IQ scores, correlate with out-of-class achievements of students (Runco, 2007;

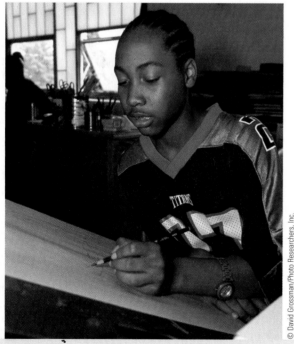

Creativity often increases during adolescence as talents emerge and are fostered by a supportive environment.

Wallach & Wing, 1969). Thus, if you want to know how well someone will do in the classroom, an IQ test will likely be your best bet, but if you want to know how well someone will do in extracurricular activities outside the classroom, measures of creativity—divergent thinking—may prove more useful.

SUMMING UP

- During adolescence, IQ scores continue to stabilize as intellectual performance reaches near-adult level. IQ scores are useful at predicting academic achievement of adolescents.
- Levels of creativity vary considerably, with some adolescents conforming to societal norms and expressing little creativity and others showing a great deal of innovation.
- Adolescents with exceptional talents or creativity have both talent and motivation on the nature side, and environments that foster their talents on the nurture side.
- Tests of creativity do not always do a good job of predicting creative accomplishment in a specific field.

CRITICAL THINKING

1. To what extent have your schools fostered creativity? Is this something that *can* be fostered in schools and *should* it be fostered in schools?

2. IQ scores stabilize in adolescence and are highly correlated with adult IQ scores. Given this stability, should greater use be made of IQ scores? If so, what would be one or two meaningful uses of IQ scores during adolescence?

9.5 | THE ADULT

Do IQ scores predict achievement and success after people have left school? Does performance on IQ tests change during the adult years? And do IQ scores decline in old age, as performance on Piagetian cognitive tasks and some memory tasks does?

IQ and Occupational Success

There is a relationship between IQ and occupational status. Professional and technical workers (such as scientists and engineers in the pharmaceutical industry) score higher on IQ tests than white-collar workers (such as bank managers), who in turn score higher than blue-collar, or manual, workers (such as construction workers) (Schmidt & Hunter, 2004). As shown in ■ **Figure 9.4,** the average IQ score of workers increases as the prestige of the occupation increases (Nyborg & Jensen, 2001). This is true for both African American and European American workers, although the relationship is stronger among African American samples. The reason for this relationship is clear: It undoubtedly takes more intellectual ability to complete law

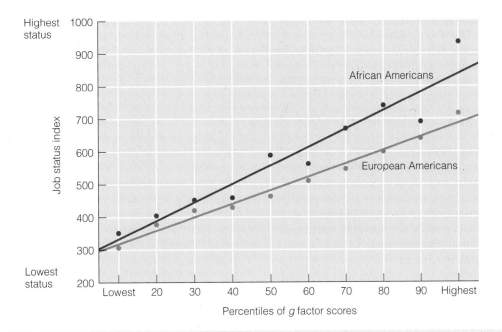

FIGURE 9.4 Job status in relation to intelligence test performance for African Americans and European Americans.
SOURCE: Reprinted from *Intelligence, 29*, H. Nyborg & A. R. Jensen, Fig 1, p. 15, copyright © 2001, with permission from Elsevier Science.

school and become a lawyer (a high-status occupation) than it does to be a farmhand (a low-status occupation). However, the prestige or status of the occupation is not as important as the complexity of the work (Gottfredson, 1997; Kuncel, Hezlett, & Ones, 2004). Greater intelligence is required to handle more complex or cognitively challenging work. Still, IQs vary considerably in every occupational group, so many people in low-status jobs have high IQs.

Now a second question: Are bright lawyers, electricians, or farmhands more successful or productive than their less intelligent colleagues? The answer here is also yes. The correlation between scores on tests of intellectual ability and such measures of job performance as supervisor ratings averages +0.30 to +0.50 (Neisser et al., 1996). General intellectual ability seems to predict job performance in a range of occupations better than any other indicator, and it predicts likelihood of success as accurately for members of racial and ethnic minority groups as for whites (Gottfredson, 2002; Schmidt & Hunter, 1998, 2004). More intellectually capable adults are better able to learn what they need to know about their occupations and to solve the problems that arise. This literally pays off, as shown in ■ **Figure 9.5**: Individuals with greater cognitive ability earn more money that those with lower cognitive ability (Ceci & Williams, 1997).

IQ and Health

People who score higher on measures of intelligence tend to be healthier and live longer than those who score lower (Gottfredson, 2004). Research in Scotland has investigated the relationship between intelligence and health. In a rather amazing study, nearly everyone in the country born in 1921 completed an intelligence test in 1932 when they were 11 years old.

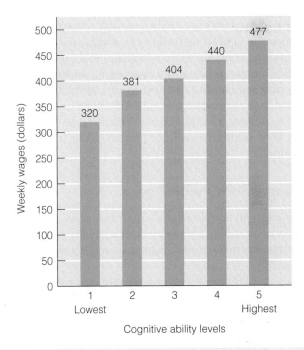

FIGURE 9.5 Weekly wages by level of cognitive ability.
SOURCE: From S.J. Ceci & W.M. Williams, Schooling, intelligence and income, in *American Psychologist, 52*, pp. 1051–1058. Copyright © 1997 by American Psychological Association. Reprinted with permission from the American Psychological Association.

Following up on health and death records decades later, researchers found that individuals who scored one standard deviation (15 points) below other individuals (see the Explorations box on measuring intelligence) were less likely to be alive at age 76 and more likely to have experienced stomach or lung cancers and cardiovascular or coronary heart disease (Deary, Whalley, & Starr, 2003; Deary et al., 2004).

A common explanation for this connection between IQ and health is socioeconomic status: Smart people may have better jobs, giving them the resources to obtain better health care. But when living conditions are statistically controlled (that is, held constant), there is still a connection between intelligence and health (Gottfredson & Deary, 2004). Similarly, providing equal access to health care reduces but does not eliminate the social-class differences in health (Steenland, Henley, & Thun, 2002).

So what else could be going on? Linda Gottfredson (2004) argues that good health takes more than access to material resources. It requires some of the abilities measured by intelligence tests, such as efficient learning and problem solving. In other words, successfully monitoring health and properly applying treatment protocols require a certain amount of intelligence. Consider the chronic illness diabetes. Successful management requires acquiring knowledge of the disease symptoms and course, identifying signs of inappropriate blood sugar levels, and making judgments about how to respond to blood sugar fluctuations. A patient's IQ predicts how much knowledge of diabetes he or she acquires during the year following diagnosis (Taylor et al., 2003). Other research shows that many people with diabetes who have limited literacy, which correlates with intelligence, do not know the signs of high or low blood sugar and do not know how to correct unhealthy levels (Williams et al., 1998).

Research on relationships between IQ and health is relatively new and ongoing. But it suggests that IQ influences socioeconomic status, which in turn influences health, but that IQ also influences health directly. Smarter people are able to apply their intellectual skills to understanding and managing their health.

Changes in IQ with Age

Perhaps no question about adult development has been studied as thoroughly as that of how intellectual abilities change with age. Alan Kaufman (2001) examined cross sections of adults ranging in age from 16 to 89 who were tested with the Wechsler Adult Intelligence Scale. As ■ **Figure 9.6** shows, IQs rise slightly until the mid-40s and then decline, with the steepest declines starting around age 80. But recall the description of cross-sectional designs in Chapter 1. Cross-sectional studies compare people of different cohorts who have had different levels of education and life experiences because they were born at different times. Could the apparent declines in IQ with age reflect cohort differences?

Kaufman (2001) also studied the longitudinal performance of several cohorts of adults over a 17-year period. The results of this longitudinal study were similar to those obtained cross-sectionally. Over the 17-year period, there was a loss of about 5 IQ points among the 40-year-old cohort; losses of 7 to 8 points among the 50- and 60-year-old cohorts; and losses of about 10 points among the two oldest cohorts who were 67 and 72 at the start of the study. Thus, the youngest cohort lost about 5 IQ points over a 17-year period and the oldest cohorts lost twice this—about 10 IQ points over the same period. Do intellectual abilities decline with age, as these data suggest? It depends on which abilities are examined. In both the cross-sectional and longitudinal studies, verbal IQ was essentially unchanged with age, at least until the person's 80s. In contrast, performance IQ peaked by ages 20 to 24 then steadily declined.

More data on changes in IQ with age come from a comprehensive sequential study directed by K. Warner Schaie (1996, 2005). Schaie's study began in 1956 with a sample of members of a health maintenance organization ranging in age from 22 to 70. They were given a revised test of primary mental abilities that yielded scores for five separate mental abilities: verbal meaning, spatial ability, reasoning, numerical ability, and word fluency. Seven years later, as many of them as could be found were retested. In addition, a new sample of adults ranging from their 20s to their 70s was tested. This design made it possible to determine how the performance of the same individuals changed over 7 years and to compare the performance of people who were 20 years old in 1956 with that of people who were 20 years old in 1963. This same strategy was repeated at regular intervals, giving the researchers a wealth of informa-

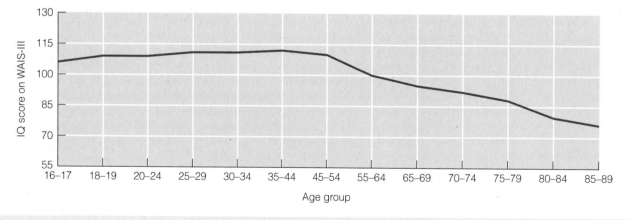

■ **FIGURE 9.6** IQ scores by age, showing a slow decline starting at about age 55.
SOURCE: Based on data from Kaufman (2001).

tion about different cohorts including longitudinal data on some people over a 45-year period.

Several findings have emerged from this important study. First, it seems that *when a person was born* has at least as much influence on intellectual functioning as age does. In other words, cohort or generational effects on performance exist. This evidence confirms the suspicion that cross-sectional comparisons of different age groups have usually yielded too grim a picture of declines in intellectual abilities during adulthood. Specifically, recently born cohorts (the youngest people in the study were born in 1973) tended to outperform earlier generations (the oldest were born in 1889) on most tests. Yet on the test of numerical ability, people born between 1903 and 1924 performed better than both earlier and later generations. Inductive reasoning scores have increased with every cohort tested since 1889. Scores on verbal meanings increased until 1952 but dropped off in the three most recently born cohorts (Schaie & Zanjani, 2006). So different generations may have a special edge in different areas of intellectual performance. Overall, though, judging from Schaie's findings, young and middle-aged adults today can look forward to better intellectual functioning in old age than their grandparents experienced.

Another important message of Schaie's study, and of other research, is that patterns of aging differ for different abilities. Fluid intelligence (those abilities requiring active thinking and reasoning applied to novel problems, as measured by tests such as the primary mental abilities tests of reasoning and space) usually declines earlier and more steeply than crystallized intelligence (those abilities involving the use of knowledge acquired through experience, such as in answering the verbal meaning test used by Schaie). Consistently, adults lose some of their ability to grapple with new problems starting in middle age, but their crystallized general knowledge and vocabulary stay steady throughout middle and older adulthood (Rabbitt, Chetwynd, & McInnes, 2003; Singer et al., 2003). Some research even shows that knowledge, such as vocabulary, is higher among older adults than among younger adults (Field & Gueldner, 2001; Verhaeghen, 2003).

Why is this? Tests of performance and fluid IQ are often timed, and, as noted in Chapter 8, performance on timed tests declines more in old age than performance on untimed tests does. This may be linked to the slowing of central nervous system functioning that most people experience as they age (Salthouse, 1996; Sliwinski & Buschke, 1999; Zimprich & Martin, 2002). Performance, fluid, and speeded IQ test items may also be less familiar to older adults who have been out of school for years than to younger adults; in this sense, the tests may be subtly biased against older adults (Berg, 2000).

A clear message here is that speed of information processing is related to intellectual functioning across the life span. Not only is rapid information processing in infancy associated with high IQ scores in childhood, but young adults with quick reaction times also outperform their more sluggish age-mates on IQ tests and adults who lose information-processing speed in later life lose some of their ability to think through complex and novel problems (Jensen, 1993). It is not just that older

adults cannot finish tests that have time limits; declines in performance intelligence occur in later life even on untimed tests (Kaufman & Kaufman, 1997). The problem is that the slower information processor cannot keep in mind and process simultaneously all relevant aspects of a complex problem.

You now have an overall picture of intellectual functioning in adulthood. Age group differences in performance suggest that older adults today are at a disadvantage on many tests compared with younger adults, partly because of deficiencies in the amount and quality of education they received early in life. But actual declines in intellectual abilities associated with aging are generally minor until people reach their late 60s or 70s. Even in old age, declines in fluid intelligence, performance intelligence, and performance on timed tests are more apparent than declines in crystallized intelligence, verbal intelligence, and performance on untimed tests. As you will soon see, declines in fluid intelligence can be reduced when adults remain cognitively stimulated through work or other activities (Weinert & Hany, 2003).

One last message of this research is worth special emphasis: Declines in intellectual abilities are not universal. Even among the 81-year-olds in Schaie's study, only about 30 to 40% had experienced a significant decline in intellectual ability in the previous 7 years (Schaie, 2005). Moreover, although few 81-year-olds maintained all five mental abilities, almost all retained at least one ability from testing to testing and about half retained four out of five (Schaie & Zanjani, 2006). The range of differences in intellectual functioning in a group of older adults is extremely large (Dixon, 2003). Anyone who stereotypes all elderly adults as intellectually limited is likely to be wrong most of the time.

Predictors of Decline

What is most likely to affect whether or not a person experiences declines in intellectual performance in old age? *Poor health*, not surprisingly, is one risk factor. People who have cardiovascular diseases or other chronic illnesses show steeper declines in mental abilities than their healthier peers (Schaie, 2005). Diseases (and most likely the drugs used to treat them) also contribute to a rapid decline in intellectual abilities within a few years of death (Johansson, Zarit, & Berg, 1992; Singer et al., 2003). This phenomenon has been given the depressing label **terminal drop**. Perhaps there is something, then, to the saying "Sound body, sound mind."

A second factor in decline is an *unstimulating lifestyle*. Schaie and his colleagues found that the biggest intellectual declines were shown by elderly widows who had low social status, engaged in few activities, and were dissatisfied with their lives (Schaie, 1996). These women lived alone and seemed disengaged from life. Individuals who maintain their performance or even show gains tend to have above-average socioeconomic status, advanced education, intact marriages, intellectually capable spouses, and physically and mentally active lifestyles. Interestingly, married adults are affected by the intellectual environment they provide for each other. Their IQ test

IQ TRAINING FOR AGING ADULTS

Can you teach old dogs new tricks? And can you reteach old dogs who have suffered declines in mental abilities the old tricks they have lost? K. Warner Schaie and Sherry Willis (1986; Willis & Schaie, 1986) sought to find out by training elderly adults in spatial ability and reasoning, two of the fluid mental abilities most likely to decline in old age. Within a group of older people ranging in age from 64 to 95 who participated in Schaie's longitudinal study of intelligence, they first identified individuals whose scores on one of the two abilities had declined over a 14-year period and individuals who had remained stable over the same period. The goal with the decliners would be to restore lost ability; the goal with those who had maintained their ability would be to improve it. Participants took pretests measuring both abilities, received 5 hours of training in either

spatial ability or reasoning, and then were given post-tests on both abilities. The spatial training involved learning how to rotate objects in space, at first physically and then mentally. Training in reasoning involved learning how to detect a recurring pattern in a series of stimuli (for example, musical notes) and to identify what the next stimulus in the sequence should be.

The training worked. Both those who had suffered ability declines and those who had maintained their abilities before the study improved, although decliners showed significantly more improvement in spatial ability than nondecliners did. Schaie and Willis estimated that 40% of the decliners gained enough through training to bring them back to the level of performance they had achieved 14 years earlier, before decline set in. What is more, effects of the training among those who had experienced declines in performance were

still evident 7 years later (Schaie, 1996). And, as noted in Chapter 8, the benefits of cognitive training with older adults extends beyond improving their performance on laboratory-type tests; their daily functioning improved as well (Willis et al., 2006).

The larger messages? You can teach old dogs new tricks—and reteach them old tricks—in a short amount of time. This research does not mean that cognitive abilities can be restored in elderly people who have Alzheimer's disease or other brain disorders and have experienced significant neural loss. Instead, it suggests that many intellectual skills decline in later life because they are not used—and that these skills can be revived with a little coaching and practice. This research, combined with research on children, provides convincing evidence of the plasticity of cognitive abilities over the entire life span.

---

scores become more similar over the years, largely because the lower-functioning partner's scores rise closer to those of the higher-functioning partner (Gruber-Baldini, Schaie, & Willis, 1995; Weinert & Hany, 2003).

The moral is "Use it or lose it." This rule, applicable to muscular strength and sexual functioning, also pertains to intellectual functioning in later life. The plasticity of the nervous system throughout the life span enables elderly individuals to benefit from intellectual stimulation and training, to maintain the intellectual skills most relevant to their activities, and to compensate for the loss of less-exercised abilities (Dixon, 2003; Weinert & Hany, 2003; see also the Applications box). There is still much to learn about how health, lifestyle, and other factors shape the individual's intellectual growth and decline. What is certain is that most people can look forward to many years of optimal intellectual functioning before some of them experience losses of some mental abilities in later life.

Potential for Wisdom

Many people believe, incorrectly, as you have seen, that intellectual decline is an inevitable part of aging—yet many people also believe that old people are wise. Indeed, this belief has been expressed in many cultures throughout history. It is also featured in Erik Erikson's influential theory of life-span development. Erikson says that older adults often gain wisdom as they face the prospect of death and attempt to find meaning in their lives (see Chapter 11). Notice, too, that the word *wise* is rarely used to describe children, adolescents, or even young adults (unless perhaps it is to call one of them a *wise guy*). Is the

association between wisdom and old age just a stereotype, or is there some truth to it?

People tend to believe that age brings wisdom. It can—but wisdom is rare even in later life. But first, what is wisdom, and how can researchers assess it? There is no consensus on these questions, and, until recently, little research (Sternberg, 2003). Researchers do know that wisdom is not the same as high intelligence: There are many highly intelligent people who are not wise. Paul Baltes and his colleagues offer this definition of wisdom: "expert knowledge in the fundamental pragmatics of life that permits exceptional insight, judgment, and advice about complex and uncertain matters" (Pasupathi, Staudinger, & Baltes, 2001, p. 351). Similarly, Robert Sternberg (2003) defines a wise person as someone who can combine successful intelligence with creativity to solve problems that require balancing multiple interests or perspectives. In addition, the wise person has the following five qualities (Baltes & Staudinger, 2000; Pasupathi, Staudinger, & Baltes, 2001):

- Rich factual knowledge about life (a knowledge base regarding such areas as human nature, interpersonal relations, and critical events in life)
- Rich procedural knowledge (such as strategies for giving advice and handling conflicts)
- A life-span contextual perspective (consideration of the contexts of life—family, education, work, and others)
- Relativism of values and life priorities (acknowledgment and tolerance of different values)
- Recognition and management of uncertainty (understanding that knowledge of the world is limited and the future is unknown)

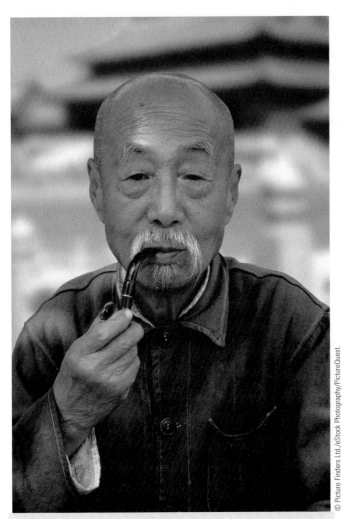

People tend to believe that age brings wisdom. It can—but wisdom is rare even in later life.

ment of wisdom. That is, clinical psychologists, whether young or old, displayed more signs of wisdom than other women did. Older women were generally no wiser—or less wise—than younger women.

Age, then, does not predict wisdom. Yet the knowledge base that contributes to wisdom, like other crystallized intellectual abilities, holds up well later in life (Baltes et al., 1995). Older adults, like younger adults, are more likely to display wisdom if they have life experiences (such as work as a clinical psychologist) that sharpen their insights into the human condition. The immediate social context also influences the degree to which wisdom is expressed; wiser solutions to problems are generated when adults have an opportunity to discuss problems with someone whose judgment they value and when they are encouraged to reflect after such discussions (Staudinger & Baltes, 1996). Thus, consulting with your fellow students and work colleagues and thinking about their advice may be the beginning of wisdom.

Finally, wisdom seems to reflect a particular combination of intelligence, personality, and cognitive style (Baltes & Staudinger, 2000). For example, individuals who have a cognitive style of comparing and evaluating relevant issues and who show tolerance of ambiguity are more likely to demonstrate wisdom than individuals without these characteristics. In addition, external factors influence the development of wisdom. Monika Ardelt (2000) found that a supportive social environment (loving family, good friends) during early adulthood was positively associated with wisdom 40 years later.

At this early stage in the study of wisdom, there is much disagreement about what it is, how it develops, and how it is related to other mental abilities. However, research on wisdom provides further evidence that different mental faculties develop and age differently over the adult years.

Creative Endeavors

Many studies of creativity during the adult years have focused on a small number of so-called eminent creators in such fields as art, music, science, and philosophy. The big question has been this: When in adulthood are such individuals most productive and most likely to create their best works? Is it early in adulthood, when they can benefit from youth's enthusiasm and freshness of approach? Or is it later in adulthood, when they have fully mastered their field and have the experience and knowledge necessary to make a breakthrough in it? And what becomes of the careers of eminent creators in old age?

Early studies by Harvey Lehman (1953) and Wayne Dennis (1966) provided a fairly clear picture of how creative careers unfold (see also Runco, 2007; Sternberg, 1999b). In most fields, creative production increases steeply from the 20s to the late 30s and early 40s then gradually declines thereafter, although not to the same low levels that characterized early adulthood. Peak times of creative achievement also vary from field to field (Csikszentmihalyi & Nakamura, 2006). As ▪ **Figure 9.7** shows, the productivity of scholars in the humanities

Does wisdom typically increase with age, or are life experiences more important than age in determining whether or not a person is wise? Ursula Staudinger, Jacqui Smith, and Paul Baltes (1992) attempted to find out by interviewing young (ages 25–35) and elderly (ages 65–82) women who were clinical psychologists or similarly well-educated professionals in other fields. The goal was to assess the relative contributions of age and specialized experience to wisdom, based on the assumption that clinical psychologists gain special sensitivity to human problems from their professional training and practice.

These women were interviewed about a person named Martha, who had chosen to have a family but no career and who met an old friend who had chosen to have a career but no family. The women were asked to talk about how Martha might review and evaluate her life after this encounter. Answers were scored for the five qualities listed earlier that were judged to be indicators of wisdom.

What was found? First, wisdom proved to be rare; it seems that only about 5% of the answers given by adults to problems such as these qualify as wise (Smith & Baltes, 1990). Second, expertise proved to be more relevant than age to the develop-

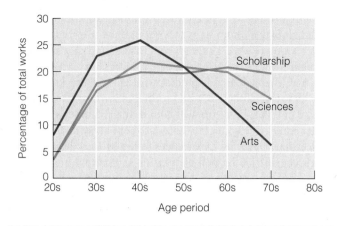

■ **FIGURE 9.7** Percentage of total works produced in each decade of the lives of eminent creators. The "scholarship" group includes historians and philosophers; the "sciences" category includes natural and physical scientists, inventors, and mathematicians; the "arts" creators include architects, musicians, dramatists, poets, and the like.
SOURCE: Data from Creative productivity between the ages of 20 and 80 years by W. Dennis, 1966, *Journal of Gerontology, 21,* p. 2. Reprinted by permission.

(for example, historians and philosophers) continues well into old age and peaks in the 60s, possibly because creative work in these fields often involves integrating knowledge that has crystallized over years. By contrast, productivity in the arts (for example, music or drama) peaks in the 30s and 40s and declines steeply thereafter, perhaps because artistic creativity depends on a more fluid or innovative kind of thinking. Scientists seem to be intermediate, peaking in their 40s and declining only in their 70s. Even within the same general field, differences in peak times have been noted. For example, poets reach their peak before novelists do, and mathematicians peak before other scientists do (Dennis, 1966; Lehman, 1953).

Still, in many fields (including psychology), creative production rises to a peak in the late 30s or early 40s, and both the total number of works and the number of high-quality works decline thereafter (Simonton, 1990). This same pattern can be detected across different cultures and historical periods. Even so, the percentage of a creator's works that are major, significant ones changes little over the years (Simonton, 1999). This means that many creators are still producing outstanding works in old age— sometimes their greatest works—not just rehashes of earlier triumphs. Michelangelo, for instance, was in his 70s and 80s when he worked on St. Peter's Cathedral, and Frank Lloyd Wright was 91 when he finished the blueprint for the Guggenheim Museum in New York City. Indeed, the most eminent among the eminent seem to start early and finish late (Simonton, 1999).

How can researchers account for changes in creative production over the adult years? One explanation, proposed long ago (Beard, 1874, in Simonton, 1984), is that creative achievement requires both enthusiasm and experience. In early adulthood, the enthusiasm is there, but the experience is not; in later adulthood, the experience is there, but the enthusiasm or vigor has fallen off. People in their 30s and 40s have it all.

Dean Simonton (1999) has offered another theory: Each creator may have a certain potential to create that is realized over the adult years; as the potential is realized, less is left to express. According to Simonton, creative activity involves two processes: ideation (generating creative ideas) and elaboration (executing ideas to produce poems, paintings, or scientific publications). After a career is launched, some time elapses before any ideas are generated or any works are completed. This would explain the rise in creative achievement between the 20s and 30s. Also, some kinds of work take longer to formulate or complete than others, which helps explain why a poet (who can generate and carry out ideas quickly) might reach a creative peak earlier in life than, say, a historian (who may need to devote years to the research and writing necessary to complete a book once the idea for it is hatched).

Why does creative production begin to taper off? Simonton (1999) suggests that older creators may simply have used up much of their stock of potential ideas. They never exhaust their creative potential, but they have less of it left to realize. Simonton argues, then, that changes in creative production over the adult years have more to do with the nature of the creative process than with a loss of mental ability in later life. Creators who start their careers late are likely to experience the same rise and fall of creative output that others do, only later in life. And those lucky creators with immense creative potential to realize will not burn out; they will keep producing great works until they die.

What about mere mortals? Here, researchers have fallen back on tests designed to measure creativity. In one study, scores on a test of divergent thinking abilities decreased at least modestly after about age 40 and decreased more steeply starting around 70 (McCrae, Arenberg, & Costa, 1987). It seems that elderly adults do not differ much from younger adults in the originality of their ideas; the main difference is that they generate fewer of them (Jaquish & Ripple, 1981). Generally, then, these studies agree with the studies of eminent achievers: Creative behavior becomes less frequent in later life, but it remains possible throughout the adult years.

SUMMING UP

▌ IQ is related to the status or prestige of an adult's occupation and to his success within that occupation. Intelligence also affects health and longevity.

▌ Both cross-sectional studies and longitudinal studies tend to show age-related decreases in IQ. Schaie's sequential study suggests that (1) date of birth (cohort) influences test performance, (2) no major declines in mental abilities occur until the late 60s or 70s, (3) some abilities (especially fluid ones) decline more than others (especially crystallized ones), and (4) not all people's abilities decline.

▌ Declines in IQ are most likely in those who have poor health and unstimulating lifestyles.

- A few adults display wisdom, which requires a rich knowledge base along with particular personality traits and cognitive styles and is influenced more by experience than age.

- Creative output increases sharply from early to middle adulthood and although it then drops somewhat, it remains above the level where it started in young adulthood. Creativity varies from one field to another. Creative output may drop off in older adulthood because people have already generated and expressed their creative potential.

CRITICAL THINKING

1. As the administrator of a large health maintenance organization, would it be useful to collect information on intelligence from your clients? Why or why not?

2. In what ways are you smarter than your parents and grandparents and in what ways are these two older generations smarter or wiser than you? What are some factors that contribute to generational differences in intelligence and age differences in wisdom?

9.6 | FACTORS THAT INFLUENCE IQ SCORES

Now that we have surveyed changes in intellectual functioning over the life span, we will address a different question: Why do children or adults who are the same age differ in IQ? Part of the answer is that they differ in the kinds of motivational and situational factors that can affect performance on a given day. Yet there are real differences in underlying intellectual ability that need to be explained. As usual, the best explanation is that genetic and environmental factors interact to make us what we are.

Flynn Effect

Over the 20th century, average IQ scores have increased in all countries studied, a phenomenon called the **Flynn effect** after its discoverer, James Flynn (1987, 1998, 1999). In the United States, the increase has amounted to 3 to 4 IQ points per decade. So a group of adults born in, say, 1970 will score, on average, 3 to 4 points higher than a similar group of adults born in 1960 and 6 to 8 points higher than those born in 1950. Most researchers argue that increases of this size cannot be caused by genetic evolution and therefore must have environmental causes (but see Mingroni, 2004). Flynn has suggested that improved nutrition and living conditions over the course of the 20th century have contributed to the rise in intellectual functioning. In addition, today's children grow up in smaller families where they have the opportunity to receive more focused attention from their parents than previous generations of children. Children today are also better educated than earlier generations; 85% today complete high school compared to just 5% in 1895 (Greve, 2006).

Interestingly, the Flynn effect is clearer for some measures of intelligence than for other measures of intelligence. Joel Bradmetz and Fabien Mathy (2006) compared children tested in 1965 to others tested more than 20 years later and found that performance on spatial and visual portions of the tests had improved, whereas performance on verbal portions had actually declined somewhat. What might explain these findings? The researchers believe that the later-born cohort of children spent considerably more time watching television and playing video games and less time reading than the earlier-born cohort. Consequently, they sharpened their visual and spatial skills at the expense of their verbal skills. Overall, though, they still score higher than their parent's generation. Although this does not entirely explain the overall rise in IQ scores, it does help us understand which intellectual skills are improving the most over time.

Genes

The pioneers of the IQ testing movement believed that individual differences in IQ exist simply because some people inherit better genes at conception than others do. Even though IQ scores are now known not to be determined entirely by genes, heredity helps explain individual differences in intellectual performance. As you saw in Chapter 3, identical twins obtain more similar IQ scores than fraternal twins do even when they have been raised apart (you might want to look again at Table 3.5). Moreover, the IQs of adopted children, once they reach adolescence, are more strongly correlated with those of their biological parents than with those of their adoptive parents. Overall, most researchers find that about half of the variation in IQ scores within a group of individuals is associated with genetic differences among them (Plomin & Spinath, 2004). Some researchers report that genetic influences on IQ differences are somewhat greater than environmental influences (Rowe, Vesterdal, & Rodgers, 1999). In either case, as much as half of the variation in scores is attributable to differences in the environments in which people develop. Children growing up in the same home show family resemblance in IQ scores (an effect of shared environment) when they are young children but not by the time they reach adolescence and adulthood (Bartels et al., 2002; Loehlin, Horn, & Willerman, 1997; McGue et al., 1993). Most effects of environment on IQ are unique to the individual and are not shared by siblings (Maccoby, 2000).

Although differences in IQ are linked to differences in genetic makeup, this says nothing about the extent to which IQ can be increased. Height, for example, is even more strongly associated with genetic endowment than IQ. Yet it can clearly be decreased by poor nutrition or increased by good nutrition, and it has increased over several generations as nutrition has improved (Sternberg, 1997). So we must look further at aspects of the environment in infancy and early childhood that can stimulate or inhibit intellectual growth. Then it will become clear how far this information can go in explaining differences in IQ scores associated with socioeconomic status and race or ethnicity.

Home Environment

Research by Arnold Sameroff and his colleagues (1993) provides a broad overview of some of the environmental factors that put children at risk for having low IQ scores—and, by implication, some of the factors associated with higher IQs. These researchers assessed the 10 risk factors shown in ● Table 9.3 at age 4 and again at age 13. Every factor was related to IQ at age 4, and most predicted IQ at age 13. In addition, the greater the number of these risk factors affecting a child, the lower his IQ. Which risk factors the child experienced was less important than how many he experienced. Clearly, it is not good for intellectual development to grow up in a disadvantaged home with an adult unable to provide much intellectual nurturance.

In what ways do parents and the home influence children's intellectual development? A widely used assessment of the intellectual stimulation of the home environment is the **Home Observation for Measurement of the Environment (HOME) inventory** (Bradley et al., 2001). Sample items from the preschool version of a HOME inventory are shown in ● Table 9.4 (Caldwell & Bradley, 1984). Bradley and his colleagues (1989) have found that scores on the HOME can predict the IQs of African American and European American children at age 3, with correlations of about 0.50 (see also Cleveland et al., 2000). HOME scores continue to predict IQ scores between ages 3 and 6 (Espy, Molfese, & DiLalla, 2001). Gains in IQ from age

1 to age 3, as measured by habituation and speed of processing, are likely to occur among children from stimulating homes, whereas children from families with low HOME scores often experience drops in IQ over the same period. The early IQ scores of Mexican American children are not closely related to their families' HOME scores, however, so researchers know less about how the home environments provided by Hispanic parents influence their children's intellectual development (Bradley et al., 1989).

What aspects of the home environment best predict high IQs? Studies using the HOME inventory indicate that the most important factors are parental involvement with the child and opportunities for stimulation (Gottfried et al., 1994). However, the amount of stimulation parents provide to their young children may not be as important as whether that stimulation is responsive to the child's behavior (a smile in return for a smile) and matched to the child's competencies so that it is neither too simple nor too challenging (Miller, 1986; Smith, Landry, & Swank, 2000). In short, an intellectually stimulating home is one in which parents are eager to be involved with their children and are responsive to their developmental needs and behavior. This may help explain why some research on intelligence finds a connection to family size and birth order, with first borns and children from small families scoring just slightly higher (about 2 points) on IQ tests than later borns and children from large families (e.g., Zajonc, 2001a, b; see also Sulloway, 2007).

Do differences in stimulation in the home really cause individual differences in IQ? More intelligent parents are more likely than less intelligent parents to provide intellectually stim-

● TABLE 9.3 HOW 10 ENVIRONMENTAL RISK FACTORS ASSOCIATED WITH LOW IQ AFFECT CHILDREN

	MEAN IQ AT AGE 4	
RISK FACTOR	CHILD EXPERIENCED RISK FACTOR	CHILD DID NOT EXPERIENCE RISK FACTOR
Child is member of minority group	90	110
Head of household is unemployed or low-skilled worker	90	108
Mother did not complete high school	92	109
Family has four or more children	94	105
Father is absent from family	95	106
Family experienced many stressful life events	97	105
Parents have rigid child-rearing values	92	107
Mother is highly anxious or distressed	97	105
Mother has poor mental health or diagnosed disorder	99	107
Mother shows little positive affect toward child	88	107

SOURCE: Based on A.J. Sameroff, R. Seifer, A. Baldwin, & C. Baldwin, Stability of intelligence from pre-school to adolescence: The influence of social and family risk factors, *Child Development*, 64, pp. 80–97. Copyright © 1993 Blackwell Publishing. Reprinted with permission.

SUBSCALE 1: EMOTIONAL AND VERBAL RESPONSIVITY OF PARENT (11 ITEMS)

SAMPLE ITEMS:	Parent responds verbally to child's vocalization or verbalizations.
	Parent's speech is distinct, clear, and audible.
	Parent caresses or kisses child at least once.

SUBSCALE 2: AVOIDANCE OF RESTRICTION AND PUNISHMENT (8 ITEMS)

SAMPLE ITEMS:	Parent neither slaps nor spanks child during visit.
	Parent does not scold or criticize child during visit.
	Parent does not interfere with or restrict child more than three times during visit.

SUBSCALE 3: ORGANIZATION OF PHYSICAL AND TEMPORAL ENVIRONMENT (6 ITEMS)

| SAMPLE ITEMS: | Child gets out of house at least four times a week. |
| | Child's play environment is safe. |

SUBSCALE 4: PROVISION OF APPROPRIATE PLAY MATERIALS (9 ITEMS)

SAMPLE ITEMS:	Child has a push or pull toy.
	Parent provides learning facilitators appropriate to age—mobile, table and chairs, highchair, playpen, and so on.
	Parent provides toys for child to play with during visit.

SUBSCALE 5: PARENTAL INVOLVEMENT WITH CHILD (6 ITEMS)

| SAMPLE ITEMS: | Parent talks to child while doing household work. |
| | Parent structures child's play periods. |

SUBSCALE 6: OPPORTUNITIES FOR VARIETY IN DAILY STIMULATION (5 ITEMS)

| SAMPLE ITEMS: | Father provides some care daily. |
| | Child has three or more books of his or her own. |

SOURCE: Adapted from Caldwell & Bradley, 1984.

ulating home environments for their children and to pass on to their children genes that contribute to high intelligence; that is, there is evidence of the gene–environment correlations described in Chapter 3. Maternal IQ, for example, is correlated with a child's IQ at 3 years and it is also correlated with family income and quality of home environment (Bacharach & Baumeister, 1998). Although a mother's IQ is reliably associated with her children's IQ, a father's IQ is a less reliable predictor of his children's IQ.

So, are bright children bright because of the genes they inherited or because of the home environment their bright parents provided? Keith Yeates and his colleagues (1983) evaluated these alternative hypotheses in a longitudinal study of 112 mothers and their children, ages 2 to 4. They measured the mothers' IQs, the children's IQs from age 2 to age 4, and the families' home environments. The best predictor of a child's IQ at age 2 was the mother's IQ, just as a genetic hypothesis would suggest; home environment had little effect. But the pic-

ture changed by the time children were 4 years old, when the mother's IQ and the quality of the home environment were about equally important predictors of a child's IQ. Moreover, the researchers established statistically that differences in the quality of the home environment influenced children's IQs beyond the effects of their mothers' IQs, and that much of the effect of a mother's IQ could be attributed to high-IQ mothers providing more stimulating home environments than low-IQ mothers (Bacharach & Baumeister, 1998). In addition, adopted children's IQ scores rise considerably when they are moved from less stimulating to more stimulating homes (Turkheimer, 1991), and the quality of day care children receive predicts their verbal IQ scores (Broberg et al., 1997).

Thus, the argument that genetic influences can fully explain the apparent effects of home environment on IQ does not hold up. Yet researchers cannot ignore genetic influences; gifted children are more likely than their less gifted peers to seek intellectual stimulation (Gottfried et al., 1994). Overall, intellectual development seems to go best when a motivated, intellectually capable child begging for intellectual nourishment is fortunate enough to get it from involved and responsive parents.

Social Class

Children from lower-class homes average some 10 to 20 points below their middle-class age-mates on IQ tests. This is true in all racial and ethnic groups (Helms, 1997). Socioeconomic status affects IQ scores as well as children's rate of intellectual growth (Espy, Molfese, & DiLalla, 2001). What if socioeconomic conditions were to improve?

Research shows that improving the economic conditions of children's homes can improve their IQs. For example, Sandra Scarr and Richard Weinberg charted the intellectual growth of African American and European American children adopted before their first birthday (Scarr & Weinberg, 1983; Weinberg, Scarr, & Waldman, 1992). Many of these children came from disadvantaged family backgrounds and had biological parents who were poorly educated and somewhat below average in IQ. They were placed in middle-class homes with adoptive parents who were highly educated and above average in intelligence. Throughout childhood and adolescence, these adoptees posted average or above average scores on standardized IQ tests—higher scores than they would have obtained if they had stayed in the disadvantaged environments offered by their natural parents. Research with French children who were adopted later—around age 5—indicates that increases in IQ are much larger among children adopted into affluent homes with highly educated parents than among those adopted into disadvantaged homes (Duyme, Dumaret, & Tomkiewicz, 1999).

Could social-class differences in IQ be caused by differences in the quality of the home environment that parents of different socioeconomic levels provide? Yes, at least partially. Scores on the HOME inventory are higher in middle-class homes than in lower-class homes, indicating that middle-class homes are more intellectually stimulating on average (Bradley et al., 1989; Gottfried, 1984). Poor nutrition, drug abuse, disruptive family experiences, and other factors associated with poverty may also contribute to the social-class gap in IQ (Gottfried & Gottfried, 1984).

Race and Ethnicity

Most studies find racial and ethnic differences in IQ scores and this has sparked much controversy. In the United States, for example, Asian American and European American children tend to score higher, on average, on IQ tests than African American, Native American, and Hispanic American children (Neisser et al., 1996). Although some research suggests that racial differences on IQ tests have been shrinking in recent decades, other research shows little narrowing of the gap between, for example, black and white children on IQ tests (Dickens &

Flynn, 2006; Murray, 2006). Different subcultural groups sometimes show distinctive profiles of mental abilities; for example, black children often do well on verbal tasks, whereas Hispanic children, perhaps because of language differences, tend to excel on nonverbal items (Neisser et al., 1996; Taylor & Richards, 1991). It is essential to keep in mind that we are talking about *group averages*. Like the IQ scores of white children, those of minority children run the range from the mentally retarded to the gifted. Researchers certainly cannot predict an individual's IQ merely on the basis of racial or ethnic identity. Having said that, why do these average group differences exist? Consider the following hypotheses: bias in the tests, motivational factors, genetic differences among groups, and environmental differences among groups.

Culture Bias

Racial differences in IQ tests may be attributable to **culture bias** in testing; that is, IQ tests may be more appropriate for children from white middle-class backgrounds than for those from other subcultural groups (Helms, 1992; Lopez, 1997). Low-income African American children who speak a dialect of English (i.e., Ebonics or Black English) different from that spoken by middle-class European American children, as well as Hispanic children who hear Spanish rather than English at home, may not understand some test instructions or items. What is more, their experiences may not allow them to become familiar with some of the information called for on the tests (for example, What is a 747? Who wrote *Hamlet?*).

Minority-group children often do not have as much exposure to the culture reflected in the tests as nonminority children do. If IQ tests assess "proficiency in European American culture," minority children are bound to look deficient (Helms, 1992). Using IQ tests designed to be fair to all ethnic groups and introducing procedures to help minority children feel more

Differences in intellectual functioning within any racial or ethnic group are far greater than differences among groups.

comfortable and motivated can cut the usual IQ gap between African American and European American children in half (Kaufman, Kamphaus, & Kaufman, 1985). But, even though standardized IQ test items sometimes have a white middle-class flavor, group differences in IQ probably cannot be traced solely to test bias. Culture-fair IQ tests include items that should be equally unfamiliar (or familiar) to people from all ethnic groups and social classes—for example, items that require completing a geometric design with a piece that matches the rest of the design. Still, racial and ethnic differences emerge on such tests (Jensen, 1980). In addition, IQ tests predict future school achievement as well for African Americans and other minorities as they do for European Americans (Neisser et al., 1996).

Motivational Factors

Another possibility is that minority individuals are not motivated to do their best in testing situations because they are anxious or resist being judged by an examiner who is often of a different racial/ethnic background (Moore, 1986; Ogbu, 1994; Steele, 1997). They may be wary of strange examiners, may see little point in trying to do well, and may shake their heads before the question is completed as if to say they do not know the answer. Disadvantaged children score some 7 to 10 points better when they are given time to get to know a friendly examiner or are given a mix of easy and hard items so that they do not become discouraged by a long string of difficult items (Zigler et al., 1982). Even though most children do better with a friendly examiner, it seems that African American children, even those from middle-class homes, are often less comfortable in testing situations than white middle-class children are (Moore, 1986).

Claude Steele and his colleagues have argued that the performance of African Americans is especially likely to suffer whenever negative stereotypes of their group come into play (Steele, 1997, 1999; Steele & Aronson, 1995; see also Sackett, Hardison, & Cullen, 2004). In one study, female students at Stanford University were given difficult test items. Some students were told that they were taking a test of verbal abilities and would get feedback about their strengths and weaknesses; others were told that they were going to do some verbal problems but that their ability would not be evaluated. As ■ Figure 9.8 shows, African American students performed poorly when they were led to believe that the test would reveal their level of intellectual ability, but performed more like European American students when they did not think their ability would be judged. Even being asked to identify their race in a personal information section at the start of a test of intellectual ability can undermine the performance of African American college students (Steele & Aronson, 1995).

Why? Steele concluded that African Americans perform poorly on IQ tests partly because of **stereotype threat**—fear that they will be judged to have the qualities associated with negative stereotypes of African Americans (see also Aronson et al., 1999). It is not that African Americans have internalized stereotypes and believe they are intellectually inferior, according to Steele. Instead, they become anxious and unable to per-

■ **FIGURE 9.8** African American students perform poorly on tests of mental abilities when they think they are taking a test that may result in their being stereotyped as unintelligent.

SOURCE: From Stereotype threat and the intellectual test performance of African Americans by C. M. Steele and J. Aronson, *Journal of Personality and Social Psychology, 69,* 1995. Copyright © 1995 by the American Psychological Association. Reprinted by permission from the American Psychological Association.

form well in testing situations that arouse concerns about being negatively stereotyped.

Other research has demonstrated that positive stereotypes about a group can increase the performance of members of that group. Margaret Shih and her colleagues (Shih, Pittinsky, & Ambady, 1999) gave Asian American women a math test under one of three conditions. In one, their identity as women was made noticeable; in another, their Asian American identity was made evident; and in a third condition, no identity was emphasized. Consistent with stereotypes, these women performed worse when their gender was emphasized and better when their ethnic background was emphasized, relative to the group that was not primed to think about either identity. So, stereotypes can either hinder or enhance performance, depending on whether a person identifies with a group that is viewed negatively or positively on the dimension measured.

The effects of stereotype threat can be reduced by providing students with a mentor. Catherine Good, Joshua Aronson, and Michael Inzlicht (2003) had college students serve as mentors to seventh-graders likely to experience stereotype threat as a result of being female, impoverished, and a member of a minority group. The mentors encouraged students to interpret their academic troubles as a result of the transition to a new school for seventh grade. In addition, they talked about intelligence being flexible and responsive to new learning. Following such mentoring, the students performed better on standardized tests than students who did not receive mentoring. These findings provide a practical means for eliminating or reducing the negative influence of stereotype threat.

Genetic Influences

Perhaps no idea in psychology has sparked more heated debate than the suggestion that racial and ethnic differences in IQ scores could be caused by group differences in genetic makeup.

Differences in genetic makeup contribute, with differences in environment, to IQ differences *within* either the European American or the African American population, but whether or how they contribute to differences *between* racial/ethnic groups is highly controversial. Scholars such as Arthur Jensen (1969) and Herrnstein and Murray (1994) have gone a step further to suggest that IQ differences between European Americans and African Americans may be because of genetic differences between the races.

However, most psychologists do not think the evidence that heredity contributes to within-group differences says much about the reasons for between-group differences. Richard Lewontin (1976) makes this point with an analogy. Suppose that corn seeds with different genetic makeups are randomly drawn from a bag and planted in two fields—one that is barren and one that has fertile soil. Because all the plants within each field were grown in the same soil, their differences in height would have to be because of differences in genetic makeup. A genetic explanation of differences would fit. But, if the plants in the fertile field are generally taller than those in the barren field, this between-field variation must be entirely because of environment. Similarly, even though genes partially explain individual differences in IQ within African American and European American groups, the average difference between the racial groups may still reflect nothing more than differences in the environments they typically experience. There is no direct evidence that differences in genetic makeup between the races account for average group differences in IQ (Neisser et al., 1996).

Environmental Influences

It is time to return to an environmental hypothesis about racial and ethnic differences in IQ. Many of the intellectual and academic differences attributed to race or ethnicity probably reflect racial and ethnic differences in socioeconomic status instead (Patterson, Kupersmidt, & Vaden, 1990). As noted earlier, placement in more advantaged homes has allowed lower-income African American children to equal or exceed the average IQ in the general population and to exceed the IQs of comparable African American children raised in more disadvantaged environments by 20 points (Moore, 1986; Scarr & Weinberg, 1983; Weinberg, Scarr, & Waldman, 1992). This could not have happened if African American children were genetically deficient.

The major message of this research is that children, whatever their racial background, perform better on IQ tests when they grow up in intellectually stimulating environments with involved, responsive parents and are exposed to the "culture of the tests and the schools" (Scarr & Weinberg, 1983, p. 261). How much of the racial gap in IQ can be explained by racial differences in neighborhood and family socioeconomic conditions, mother's education, and qualities of the home environment? Jeanne Brooks-Gunn, Pamela Klebanov, and Greg Duncan (1996) used statistical procedures to correct for these environmental differences between African American and Eu-

ropean American children so that they could estimate what the IQ difference would be if the two racial groups had been raised in similar environments. Without any controls for environmental differences, there was an IQ gap of 18 points. The gap narrowed to 8 points when family and neighborhood income levels were controlled and was reduced to 3 points, a trivial difference, when racial differences in the provision of a stimulating home environment (HOME scores) were also controlled. In short, that more African American than European American children live in poverty and have limited learning opportunities at home has a lot to do with racial difference in average IQ scores.

SUMMING UP

▌ Individual differences in IQ scores are related to both genetic and home environmental factors.

▌ The lower average IQ scores of some minority groups may be better explained by culture bias in testing, low motivation (including anxiety caused by negative group stereotypes), and low socioeconomic status than by genetic differences. Minority children perform better when they grow up in intellectually stimulating homes.

CRITICAL THINKING

1. The Maori are a socioeconomically disadvantaged group in New Zealand, a country colonized by the British long ago. Maori children typically score lower on IQ tests than children of British background. Knowing what you know about minorities in the United States, what are your top two hypotheses about why Maori children perform relatively poorly, and how might you test these hypotheses?

2. Considering material from this chapter as well as material from Chapter 3 on genetic influences, evaluate the relative contributions of nature and nurture to intelligence. Does one or the other have a greater contribution to intelligence? What evidence supports your position?

9.7 THE EXTREMES OF INTELLIGENCE

Although we have identified some of the factors that contribute to individual differences in intellectual performance, you cannot fully appreciate the magnitude of these differences without considering people at the extremes of the IQ continuum. Just how different are mentally retarded and gifted individuals? And how different are their lives?

Mental Retardation

Mental retardation, or intellectual disability as it is increasingly called, is defined by the American Association on Intellectual and Developmental Disabilities (AAIDD, 2007) as significantly below-average intellectual functioning with limitations in areas of adaptive behavior such as self-care and social skills, originating before age 18. To be diagnosed as mentally retarded, an individual must obtain an IQ score of 70 or lower and have difficulties meeting age-appropriate expectations in important areas of everyday functioning. According to this definition, mental retardation is not merely a deficiency within the person; rather, it is the product of the interaction between person and environment, strongly influenced by the type and level of supportive help the individual receives (Reiss, 1994). Thus, a person with an IQ score of 60 in a supportive environment that is structured in ways that allow the individual to fit in and flourish may not be considered retarded in this environment. However, in an environment with different expectations and support, this same individual may be viewed as retarded.

Individuals with mental retardation differ greatly in their levels of functioning (see ● Table 9.5). An adult with an IQ in the range of about 55 to 70 is likely to have a mental age comparable to that of an 8- to 12-year-old child. Individuals with mild mental retardation can learn both academic and practical skills in school, and they can potentially work and live independently as adults. Many of these individuals are integrated into regular classrooms, where they excel academically and socially relative to comparable individuals who are segregated into special classrooms (Freeman, 2000). At the other end of the continuum, individuals with IQs below 20 to 25 and mental ages below 3 years ("profoundly retarded") show major delays in all areas of development and require basic care, sometimes in institutional settings. However, they, too, can benefit considerably from training.

Mental retardation has many causes. Severely and profoundly retarded people are often affected by **organic retardation,** meaning that their retardation is because of some identifiable biological cause associated with hereditary factors, diseases, or injuries. Down syndrome, the condition associated with an extra 21st chromosome, and phenylketonuria (PKU) are familiar examples of organic retardation associated with genetic factors (Lovering & Percy, 2007; see also Chapter 3). Other forms of organic retardation are associated with prenatal risk factors—an alcoholic mother, exposure to rubella, and so on (Nulman et al., 2007; see also Chapter 4). Because many organically retarded children are seriously delayed or have physical defects, they can often be identified at birth or during infancy. However, the most common form of mental retardation, **cultural–familial retardation,** is typically milder and appears to be caused by a combination of a low genetic potential and a poor, unstimulating environment (Simonoff, Bolton, & Rutter, 1996). Whereas children with organic retardation come from all socioeconomic levels, children with cultural–familial retardation often come from poverty areas and have a parent or sibling who is also retarded (Zigler, 1995).

Historically, about 3% of school-age children have been classified as mentally retarded, although this rate is decreasing because fewer children are diagnosed as mildly retarded today (Patton, 2000). What becomes of these children as they grow up? Generally, they proceed along the same paths and through the same sequences of developmental milestones as other children do (Zigler & Hodapp, 1991). Their IQs remain low because they do not achieve the same level of growth that others do. They, like nonretarded people, show signs of intellectual aging in later life, especially on tests that require speed (Devenny et al., 1996). Individuals with Down syndrome may experience even greater intellectual deterioration later in life because they are at risk for premature Alzheimer's disease (Lovering & Percy, 2007).

As for their outcomes in life, consider a follow-up study of individuals with mild and borderline mental retardation who had been placed in segregated special education classes during the 1920s and 1930s (Ross et al., 1985). The individuals studied had a mean IQ of 67. They were compared with their siblings and with nonretarded peers about 35 years later. Generally, these mentally retarded adults had poor life outcomes in mid-

● TABLE 9.5 LEVELS AND CHARACTERISTICS OF MENTAL RETARDATION

	LEVEL			
	MILD	MODERATE	SEVERE	PROFOUND
APPROXIMATE RANGE OF IQ SCORES	52 to 70	35 to 51	20 to 34	Below 19
DEGREE OF INDEPENDENCE	Usually independent	Some independence; needs some supervision	May be semi-independent with close supervision	Dependent; needs constant supervision
EDUCATIONAL ACHIEVEMENT	Can do some academic work—usually to sixth-grade level; focus is on career	Focus is on daily living skills rather than academics; some career training	Focus is on self-care (toileting, dressing, eating) and communication skills	Focus is on self-care, mobility, and basic communication education

SOURCE: From J.A. Barack, R.M. Hodapp, & E Zigler (EDs.), *Handbook of mental retardation and development.* Copyright © 1998 Cambridge University Press. Reprinted with permission.

dle age in comparison with nonretarded groups (see also Schalock et al., 1992). About 80% of the men with retardation were employed, but they usually held semiskilled or unskilled jobs that required little education or intellectual ability. The women often married and became homemakers. Compared with nonretarded peers, men and women with retardation also fared worse on other counts. For example, they had lower incomes, less adequate housing, poorer adjustment in social relationships, and greater dependency on others.

Yet the authors of the study found grounds for optimism. These individuals had done much better during adulthood than stereotyped expectations of people with mental retardation would predict. Most of them worked and had married, and about 80% reported having had no need for public assistance in the 10 years before they were interviewed. This study, like others before it, suggests that many children labeled mentally retarded by the schools—and who have difficulty with the tasks demanded of them in school—"vanish" into the general population after they leave school. Apparently they can adapt to the demands of adult life. As the authors put it, "It does not take as many IQ points as most people believe to be productive, to get along with others, and to be self-fulfilled" (Ross et al., 1985, p. 149).

Giftedness

The gifted child used to be identified solely by an IQ score—one that was at least 130. Programs for gifted children still focus mainly on those with very high IQs, but there is increased recognition that some children are gifted because they have special abilities rather than because they have high general intelligence. Even high-IQ children are usually not equally talented in all areas; contrary to myth, they cannot just become

Gifted children have either high IQ scores or special abilities. This young girl is performing with the Pacific Symphony of Orange County, California.

anything they choose (Winner, 1996). More often, high-IQ children have exceptional talent in an area or two and otherwise are good, but not exceptional, performers (Achter, Benbow, & Lubinski, 1997). So, today's definitions emphasize that **giftedness** involves having a high IQ or showing special abilities in areas valued in society, such as mathematics, the performing and visual arts, or even leadership.

Joseph Renzulli (1998) has long argued that giftedness emerges from a combination of above-average ability, creativity, and task commitment. According to this view, someone might have a high IQ and even creative ability, but Renzulli questions whether they are truly gifted if they are not motivated to use this intelligence. Here we focus on individuals with exceptional IQs.

How early can intellectually gifted children be identified? Giftedness is apparent by toddlerhood, according to a longitudinal study by Allen Gottfried and his colleagues (1994). They tracked a large sample of children from age 1 to age 8, determined which children had IQs of 130 or above at age 8, and then looked for differences between these gifted children and other children earlier in life. The gifted children turned out to be identifiable as early as 18 months, primarily by their advanced language skills. They were also highly curious and motivated to learn; they even enjoyed the challenge of taking IQ tests more than most children. Linda Silverman and her colleagues at the Gifted Development Center have used the Characteristics of Giftedness Scale to identify gifted children (Rogers, 1986; Silverman, Chitwood, & Waters, 1986). They have found that gifted children can be distinguished from average children in terms of: rapid learning, extensive vocabulary, good memory, long attention span, perfectionism, preference for older companions, excellent sense of humor, early interest in reading, strong ability with puzzles and mazes, maturity, and perseverance on tasks.

The rest of the story of the development of high-IQ children is told by a major longitudinal study launched in 1921 by Lewis Terman, developer of the Stanford-Binet test (Holahan & Sears, 1995; Oden, 1968; Terman, 1954). The participants were more than 1500 California schoolchildren who were nominated by their teachers as gifted and who had IQs of 140 or higher. It soon became apparent that these high-IQ children (who came to be called *Termites*) were exceptional in many other ways. For example, they had weighed more at birth and had learned to walk and talk sooner than most toddlers. They reached puberty somewhat earlier than average and had better-than-average health. Their teachers rated them as better adjusted and more morally mature than their less intelligent peers. And, although they were no more popular than their classmates, they were quick to take on leadership responsibilities. Taken together, these findings destroy the stereotype that most gifted children are frail, sickly youngsters who are socially inadequate and emotionally immature.

Another demonstration of the personal and social maturity of most gifted children comes from a study of high-IQ children who skipped high school and entered the University of Washington as part of a special program to accelerate their education

(Robinson & Janos, 1986). Contrary to the common wisdom that gifted children will suffer socially and emotionally if they skip grades and are forced to fit in with much older students, these youngsters showed no signs of maladjustment (see also Kulik & Kulik, 1992). On several measures of psychological and social maturity and adjustment, they equaled their much older college classmates and similarly gifted students who attended high school. Many of them thrived in college, for the first time finding friends like themselves—friends who were like-minded rather than like-aged (Boothe, Sethna, & Stanley, 2000).

Most of Terman's gifted children remained as remarkable in adulthood as they had been in childhood. Fewer than 5% were rated as seriously maladjusted. Their rates of such problems as ill health, mental illness, alcoholism, and delinquent behavior were but a fraction of those observed in the general population (Terman, 1954), although they were no less likely to divorce (Holahan & Sears, 1995).

The occupational achievements of the men in the sample were impressive. In middle age, 88% were employed in professional or high-level business jobs, compared with 20% of men in the general population (Oden, 1968). As a group, they had taken out more than 200 patents and written some 2000 scientific reports, 100 books, 375 plays or short stories, and more than 300 essays, sketches, magazine articles, and critiques. And gifted women? Because of the influence of gender-role expectations during the period covered by the study, gifted women achieved less than gifted men vocationally, often interrupting their careers or sacrificing their career goals to raise families. Still, they were more likely to have careers, and distinguished ones, than most women of their generation.

Finally, the Termites aged well. In their 60s and 70s, most of the men and women in the Terman study were highly active, involved, healthy, and happy people (Holahan & Sears, 1995). The men kept working longer than most men do and stayed involved in work even after they retired. The women too led exceptionally active lives. Contrary to the stereotype that gifted individuals burn out early, the Termites continued to burn bright throughout their lives.

Yet, just as it is wrong to view intellectually gifted children as emotionally disturbed misfits, it is inaccurate to conclude that intellectually gifted children are models of good adjustment, perfect in every way. Some research suggests that children with IQs closer to 180 than 130 are often unhappy and socially isolated, perhaps because they are so out of step with their peers, and sometimes even have serious problems (Winner, 1996). In *Terman's Kids*, Joel Shurkin (1992) describes several less-than-happy life stories of some of Terman's Termites. A woman who graduated from Stanford at age 17 and was headed for success as a writer became a landlady; an emotionally disturbed boy took cyanide at age 18 after being rejected in love.

These are exceptions, however. Overall, most of Terman's gifted children moved through adulthood as healthy, happy, and highly productive individuals. Yet some fared better than others. Even within this elite group, for example, the quality of the individual's home environment was important. The most well-adjusted and successful adults had highly educated parents who offered them both love and intellectual stimulation (Tomlinson-Keasey & Little, 1990).

SUMMING UP

- The extremes of intelligence are represented by mental retardation at one end of the continuum and giftedness at the other end.

- Mental retardation is defined by deficits in adaptive behavior with low IQ scores. Functioning varies by level of retardation, but is often better than expected during adulthood.

- Giftedness has most often been defined by high IQ scores, although more recent definitions recognize special talents not measured by traditional IQ tests. Life outcomes for gifted people are generally above average.

CRITICAL THINKING

1. Should gifted, "regular," and mentally retarded children be educated in the same classroom? What are some of the pros and cons of such integrated education for each of the three groups of children?

9.8 | INTEGRATING COGNITIVE PERSPECTIVES

Our account of cognitive development over the life span is now complete. We hope you appreciate that each of the four major approaches to the mind that we have considered—the Piagetian cognitive-developmental approach and Vygotsky's sociocultural theory described in Chapter 7, the information-processing approach explained in Chapter 8, and the psychometric, or testing, approach covered here—offers something of value. ● **Table 9.6** lists how these four approaches compare on their views of intelligence.

We can summarize the four approaches to cognitive development this way: Piaget has shown that comparing the thought of a preschooler with the thought of an adult is like comparing a caterpillar with a butterfly. Modes of thought change qualitatively with age. Vygotsky has highlighted the importance of culturally transmitted modes of thinking and interactions with others. The information-processing approach has helped researchers understand thinking processes and explain why the young child cannot remember as much information or solve problems as effectively as the adult can. Finally, the psychometric approach has told researchers that, if they look at the range of tasks to which the mind can be applied, they can recognize distinct mental abilities that each person consistently displays in greater or lesser amounts.

You need not choose one approach and reject the others. Your understanding of the mind is likely to be richer if all four

	PIAGETIAN COGNITIVE-DEVELOPMENTAL THEORY	VYGOTSKIAN SOCIOCULTURAL THEORY	INFORMATION-PROCESSING APPROACH	PSYCHOMETRIC APPROACH
WHAT IS INTELLIGENCE?	Cognitive structures that help people adapt	Tools of culture	Attention, memory, and other mental processes	Mental abilities and scores on IQ tests
WHAT CHANGES WITH AGE?	Stage of cognitive development	Ability to solve problems without assistance of others and with use of inner speech	Hardware (speed) and software (strategies) of the mind	Mental age (difficulty of problems solved)
WHAT IS OF MOST INTEREST?	Universal changes	Culturally influenced changes and processes	Universal processes	Individual differences

approaches continue to thrive. There are truly many intelligences, and it is foolish to think that a single IQ score can describe the complexities of human cognitive development.

SUMMING UP

▮ Four major approaches to cognitive development have been presented in Chapters 7, 8, and 9. These include Piaget's focus on qualitatively different stages of thought and Vygotsky's emphasis on culturally transmitted modes of thought. The information-processing approach reveals how memory and problem solving are influenced by characteristics of the person such as age and task factors such as complexity. The psychometric approach defines cognitive abilities in measurable ways, illustrating that people have more or less of distinct mental abilities.

CRITICAL THINKING

1. Putting together material from Chapters 7, 8, and 9, how would you describe the cognitive functioning of a typical 70-year-old person? What are the greatest cognitive strengths of older adults, what are their greatest limitations, and how much can an individual do to optimize her functioning?

CHAPTER SUMMARY

9.1   WHAT IS INTELLIGENCE?

- Most modern intelligence tests are based on the psychometric approach, which assumes that intelligence consists of a set of traits that can be measured.
- The Stanford-Binet and Wechsler scales are the most common intelligence tests and compare an individual's performance on a variety of cognitive tasks with the average performance of age-mates.
- Creativity—the ability to produce novel and socially valued works—is a distinct mental ability that demands divergent

rather than convergent thinking; it is largely independent of IQ (above a certain minimum level).

9.2   THE INFANT

- In infancy, mental growth is rapid and is measured by DQs derived from tests such as the Bayley scales. However, infant scores do not predict later IQ as well as measures of speed of information processing such as rapid habituation and preference for novelty do.

9.3   THE CHILD

- During childhood, mental growth continues, and IQs at one age can predict IQs at later ages.
- Many individuals show wide variations in their IQ scores over time. Those who gain IQ points often have favorable home environments, whereas disadvantaged children often show a cumulative deficit.

9.4   THE ADOLESCENT

- IQ is relatively stable throughout adolescence. IQ scores predict school achievement and years of education obtained.
- After decreasing somewhat during elementary school, creativity levels rise during adolescence. Creative thinking is fostered in homes where independence is valued.

9.5   THE ADULT

- IQ scores remain very stable throughout adulthood. They are correlated with occupational status as well as health in adulthood. Among older adults, fluid intelligence is more likely to show declines than crystallized intelligence.
- Adults in their 30s and 40s often demonstrate high levels of creativity, especially in fields where they have a large knowledge base. Performance on creativity tests declines in later life, but creative capacities clearly survive into old age, particularly for adults in some fields.

9.6   FACTORS THAT INFLUENCE IQ SCORES

- The Flynn effect describes a global increase in IQ scores over the past century that is likely the result of better nutrition, living conditions, and education.
- Individual differences in IQ at a given age are linked to genetic factors and to intellectually stimulating qualities of the home

environment such as parental involvement and responsive stimulation.

- Social class impacts IQ scores, raising the issue of middle-class testing bias. Children who are moved from low to higher socio-economic status homes show an increase in IQ scores.
- Race and ethnicity also affect IQ scores, with African American and Hispanic children typically scoring, on average, lower than European American children. There may be motivational differences, stereotype threat, and genetic factors that influence the pattern of scores associated with children's race and ethnicity.

9.7 THE EXTREMES OF INTELLIGENCE

- Mentally retarded individuals show varied levels of functioning, depending on their IQs and the causes (organic or cultural–familial) of their retardation.
- Children identified as gifted on the basis of high IQ scores have been found above average in life outcomes.

9.8 INTEGRATING COGNITIVE PERSPECTIVES

- Chapters 7, 8, and 9 have presented four major approaches to cognitive development: Piaget's qualitatively different stages, Vygotsky's socioculturally transmitted modes of thought, the information-processing view of memory and problem solving, and the psychometric approach to measuring individual differences.

KEY TERMS

psychometric approach 246
fluid intelligence 246
crystallized intelligence 246
savant syndrome 247
triarchic theory of
    intelligence 247
contextual subtheory 247
mental age 248
intelligence quotient (IQ) 248
test norms 248
normal distribution 248
standard deviation 249
dynamic assessment 249
experiential subtheory 249
automatization 249
componential subtheory 249
successful intelligence 250
creativity 250

convergent thinking 251
divergent thinking 251
developmental quotient
    (DQ) 252
cumulative-deficit
    hypothesis 253
terminal drop 261
Flynn effect 265
Home Observation for Measure-
    ment of the Environment
    (HOME) inventory 266
culture bias 268
stereotype threat 269
mental retardation 270
organic retardation 271
cultural–familial
    retardation 271
giftedness 272

MEDIA RESOURCES

BOOK COMPANION WEBSITE

academic.cengage.com/psychology/sigelman
Find online quizzes, flash cards, animations, video clips, experiments, interactive assessments, and other helpful study aids for this text at **academic.cengage.com/psychology/sigelman.** You can also connect directly to the following sites:

AMERICAN ASSOCIATION ON INTELLECTUAL AND DEVELOPMENTAL DISABILITIES

This homepage of the American Association on Intellectual and Developmental Disabilities (formerly known as the American Association on Mental Retardation) offers a wide range of materials on special needs individuals. Be sure to check out the link to additional resources and the special initiatives section.

BARBARIAN'S ONLINE TESTS PAGE: INTELLIGENCE TESTS

This site allows visitors to access a wide variety of online intelligence tests (including a set of lateral thinking puzzles and a MENSA workout test.)

INTELLIGENCE

This site offers the visitor an excellent overview of nine theories of intelligence. It also contains an outstanding list of links to other websites focusing on the issues of intelligence and intelligence testing.

NATIONAL ASSOCIATION FOR GIFTED CHILDREN

The National Association for Gifted Children website is dedicated to offering support for the needs of "high potential learners." This site contains information for parents and educators and has an outstanding "information and resources section."

UNDERSTANDING THE DATA: EXERCISES ON THE WEB

academic.cengage.com/psychology/sigelman
For additional insight on the data presented in this chapter, try out the exercises for these figures at **academic.cengage.com/psychology/sigelman:**

> **Unnumbered figure** in Explorations box titled "Measuring Intelligence"
>
> **Figure 9.5** Weekly wages by level of cognitive ability
>
> **Figure 9.7** Percentage of total works produced in each decade of the lives of eminent creators
>
> **Figure 9.8** African American students perform poorly on tests of mental abilities when they think they are taking a test that may result in their being stereotyped as unintelligent

CENGAGENOW

academic.cengage.com/login
Go to **academic.cengage.com/login** to link to CengageNOW, your online study tool. First take the Pre-Test for this chapter to get your Personalized Study Plan, which will identify topics you need to review and direct you to online resources. Then take the Post-Test to determine what concepts you have mastered and what you still need work on.

© SuperStock/Alamy

10 Language and Education

CHAPTER

AS THE COOL STREAM gushed over one hand, she [Annie] spelled into the other the word water, first slowly, then rapidly. I stood still, my whole attention fixed upon the motions of her fingers. Suddenly I felt a misty consciousness as of something forgotten— a thrill of returning thought; and somehow the mystery of language was revealed to me. I knew then that W-A-T-E-R meant the wonderful cool something that was flowing over my hand. . . . I left the well-house eager to learn. Everything had a name, and each name gave birth to a new thought. As we returned to the house every object which I touched seemed to quiver with life. (Keller, 1954, p. 15)

■ ■ ■

Perhaps the most important milestone in development is mastering some type of language. Consider how the world changed for Helen Keller, deaf and blind from a young age, when she finally realized that every object, every person, every concept could be represented with a symbol. From this point on, she was able to communicate with the people around her and participate in the world in ways that were not available without a tool such as sign or spoken language. As you learned in Chapter 7, psychologist Lev Vygotsky argued that language is the primary vehicle through which adults pass culturally valued modes of thinking and problem solving to their children. He also believed that language is our most important tool of thinking.

In this chapter, we begin by examining how and when language is acquired. Basic language skills become established largely through an informal education system consisting of parents, other grown-ups, peers, and even the media. We then consider formal education, which uses basic language skills to cultivate the reading, writing, thinking, and problem-solving skills that allow individuals to become fully functioning members of society. Getting the most out of education requires more than acquiring language and literacy skills, however. As Terrel Bell, former secretary of education, asserted: "There are three things to remember about education. The first one is motivation. The second one is motivation. The third one is motivation" (quoted in Maehr & Meyer, 1997, p. 372). Thus, we also examine achievement motivation and its relationship to education and educational outcomes.

10.1 MASTERING LANGUAGE

Although language is one of the most intricate forms of knowledge we will ever acquire, all normal children master a language early in life. Indeed, many infants are talking before they can walk. Can language be complex, then? It certainly can be. Linguists (scholars who study language) have yet to fully describe the rules of English (or of any other language), and so far computers cannot understand speech as well as most 5-year-olds can.

Linguists define **language** as a communication system in which a limited number of signals—sounds or letters (or gestures, in the case of the sign language used by deaf people)—can be combined according to agreed-upon rules to produce an infinite number of messages. To master a spoken language such as English, a child must learn basic sounds, how sounds are combined to form words, how words are combined to form meaningful statements, what words and sentences mean, and how to use language effectively in social interactions. How does this remarkable accomplishment unfold and what are the contributions of nature and nurture to language?

The Course of Language Development

For the first 10 to 13 months of life, infants are not yet capable of speaking meaningful words. But they are building up to that achievement by listening to the speech around them and by cooing and babbling.

Before the First Words

As you learned in Chapter 6, newborns seem to tune in to human speech immediately and show a preference for speech over nonspeech sounds (Saffran, Werker, & Werner, 2006; Vouloumanos & Werker, 2007). Very young infants can distinguish between phonemes such as *b* and *p* or *d* and *t* (Eimas, 1975a). **Phonemes** are the basic units of sound in any given language. Infants are also sensitive to the rhythm and **intonation** of language—the variations in pitch, loudness, and timing used when saying words or sentences, and often considered the "melody" of speech (Saffran, Werker, & Werner, 2006). Two-month-olds, for example, can distinguish between two languages based on their rhythms. Before they ever speak a word, infants are also becoming sensitive to the fact that pauses in speech fall between clauses, phrases, and words rather than in the middle of these important language units (Fisher & Tokura, 1996; Myers et al., 1996). By 7½ months, infants demonstrate **word segmentation** ability when they detect a target word in a stream of speech (Jusczyk & Aslin, 1995; Seidl & Johnson, 2006). Thus, when they hear the sentence, "the cat scratched the dog's nose," they understand that this is not one long word, but a string of six words. Word segmentation is a formidable task, but infants seem to be sensitive to a number of cues marking the boundaries between words and this skill improves throughout the first 2 years of life (Saffran, Werker, & Werner, 2006). Among English-learning infants, for example, 7-month-olds have figured out that many two-syllable words (especially nouns and adjectives) are stressed on their first syllable (e.g., <u>kitch</u>-en). But with brief exposure to words stressed on the second syllable (e.g., be-<u>gin</u>), these infants quickly switch their word segmentation strategies so that they correctly segment

A mother draws her 3-month-old infant into a "conversation."

both types of words (Thiessen & Saffran, 2007). Infants who are more skilled at word segmentation tend to have higher vocabulary scores as toddlers than those less skilled at word segmentation (Newman et al., 2006).

What about producing sounds? From birth, infants produce sounds—cries, burps, grunts, and sneezes. These sounds help exercise the vocal cords and give infants an opportunity to learn how airflow and different mouth and tongue positions affect sounds. Furthermore, parents typically respond to these prelinguistic sounds as if they were genuine efforts to communicate (McCune et al., 1996). For instance, in response to her 3-month-old's hiccup sound, a mother replies, "My goodness! What's going on in there? Huh? Tell Mommy." The mother draws her infant into a sort of dialogue. Such prelinguistic sounds, and the feedback infants receive, will eventually be incorporated into meaningful speech sounds (Hoff, 2005). Perhaps most impressive about this early verbal and nonverbal "dance" between infants and their caregivers is that it relates positively to later attachment between them and to the cognitive development of the infant (Jaffe et al., 2001).

The next milestone in vocalization, around 6 to 8 weeks of age, is **cooing**—repeating vowel-like sounds such as "oooooh" and "aaaaah." Babies coo when they are content and often in response to being spoken to in a happy voice. Do infants this age understand the words spoken to them? Not likely—they primarily respond to the intonation or "melody" of speech. Parents can say some rather nasty things to their young infants ("You're driving me nuts today!") as long as they say them with a happy voice (Hirsh-Pasek, Golinkoff, & Hollich, 1999).

Around 3 to 4 months, infants expand their vocal range considerably as they begin to produce consonant sounds. They enter a period of **babbling** between about 4 and 6 months, repeating consonant–vowel combinations such as "baba" or "dadadada," which is what Jean Piaget would call a primary circular reaction—the repeating of an interesting noise for the pleasure of making it.

Up to about 6 months, infants all over the world, even deaf ones, sound pretty much alike, but the effects of experience soon become apparent. Without auditory feedback, deaf infants fall behind hearing infants in their ability to produce well-formed syllables (Koopmans-van Beinum, Clement, & van den Dikkenberg-Pot, 2001). By the time infants are about 8 months old, they babble with something of an accent; adults can often tell which language infants have been listening to from the sound of their babbling (Poulin-Dubois & Goodz, 2001). These advanced babblers increasingly restrict their sounds to phonemes in the language they are hearing, and they pick up the intonation patterns of that language (Hoff, 2005; Snow, 2006). Once these intonation patterns are added to an infant's babbles, the utterances sound much like real speech until, as Erika Hoff (2005) puts it, "you listen closely and realize that the infant is producing the melody of language without the words" (p. 103).

As they attempt to master the **semantics,** or meaning, of language, infants come to understand many words before they can produce them. That is, *comprehension* (or reception) is ahead of *production* (or expression) in language development. Ten-month-olds can comprehend, on average, about 50 words but do not yet produce any of these (Golinkoff & Hirsh-Pasek, 2006). This early understanding of words is related to academic achievement in elementary school: 10-month-olds who understand more words are later the children who get better grades (Hohm et al., 2007).

Shortly before speaking their first true words, as they approach 1 year, infants really seem to understand familiar words. How do they figure out what words mean? When Mom points to a small, four-legged furry animal and says "Furrball," how do infants learn that this refers to the cat and not to its movement or to its tail or to the animal next door? It turns out that infants use a variety of cues in learning to connect words with their referents—the objects, people, or ideas represented by a name (Golinkoff & Hirsh-Pasek, 2006). At first, 10-month-old infants rely on attentional cues such as how important an object seems to be from their perspective (Pruden et al., 2006). Thus, if their attention is captured by the ball in front of them, they may assume that mom's verbalizations refer to this ball. By 12 months of age, though, their reliance on personal relevance is decreasing and infants begin to use social and linguistic cues to learn words. One important social cue is **joint attention,** or social eye gaze—two people looking at the same thing (Carpenter, Nagell, & Tomasello, 1998; Woodward & Markman, 1998). Infants listen to parents repeatedly labeling and pointing at objects, directing their gaze, and otherwise making clear the connection between words and their referents (Hollich, Hirsh-Pasek, & Golinkoff, 2000). If Mom says "cat" when both she and her child are looking at the furry animal, then this likely is the referent for the label. Infants also tend to assume that a word refers to a whole object rather than to some part of the object (Pan, 2005; Woodward & Markman, 1998). Thus, infants realize that Furrball refers to the family's whole cat and not to individual properties of the cat.

The First Words

An infant's first meaningful word, spoken around 1 year, is a special event for parents. First words have been called **holophrases** because a single word often conveys an entire sentence's worth of meaning. These single-word "sentences" can serve different communication functions depending on the way they are said and the context in which they are said (Tomasello, 2006). For example, 17-month-old Shelley used the word *ghetti (spaghetti)* in three different ways over a 5-minute period. First, she pointed to the pan on the stove and seemed to be asking, "Is that spaghetti?" Later, the function of her holophrase was to name the spaghetti when shown the contents of the pan, as in "It's spaghetti." Finally, there was little question that she was requesting spaghetti when she tugged at her companion's sleeve as he was eating and used the word in a whining tone.

Although there are limits to the meaning that can be packed into a single word and its accompanying intonation pattern and gestures, 1-year-olds in the holophrastic stage of language development seem to have mastered such basic language functions as naming, questioning, requesting, and demanding. When they begin to use words as symbols, they also begin to use nonverbal symbols—gestures such as pointing, raising their arms to signal "up," or panting heavily to say "dog" (Acredolo & Goodwyn, 1988; Camaioni, 2004; Lock, 2004).

What do 1-year-olds talk about? They talk mainly about familiar objects and actions (Nelson, Hampson, & Shaw, 1993; Pan, 2005; and see ● Table 10.1). Katherine Nelson (1973) studied 18 infants as they learned their first 50 English words and found that nearly two-thirds of these early words were common nouns representing objects and people that the children interacted with daily (*mommy, kitty*). These objects were nearly all things that the children could manipulate (*bottles, shoes*) or that were capable of moving on their own (*animals, trucks*). Children also acquire words that facilitate social interactions (*hello, bye-bye, no*).

Initial language acquisition proceeds literally one word at a time. Three or four months may pass before the child has a vocabulary of 10 words, slowly acquired one by one (Nelson, 1973). Then, in what is called the **vocabulary spurt,** around 18 months when the child has mastered about 30 to 50 words, the pace of word learning quickens dramatically (Bloom, 1998; Carroll, 2008). At 20 months, children are producing an average of 150 words, and just 4 months later, this has doubled to 300 words (Camaioni, 2004). What changes? During the vocabulary spurt, toddlers seem to arrive at the critical realization, as Helen Keller did, that everything has a name and by learning the names of things, they can share what they are thinking with someone else and vice versa (Bloom & Tinker, 2001). The vocabulary spurt also seems to follow the switch from reliance on attentional cues to the more effective use of social cues such as joint attention (Golinkoff & Hirsh-Pasek, 2006).

With such a rapidly increasing vocabulary, it should come as no surprise that children sometimes make mistakes. Al-

● **TABLE 10.1   EXAMPLES OF WORDS USED BY CHILDREN YOUNGER THAN 20 MONTHS**

CATEGORY	WORDS
Sound effects	*baa baa, meow, moo, ouch, uh-oh, woof, yum-yum*
Food and drink	*apple, banana, cookie, cheese, cracker, juice, milk, water*
Animals	*bear, bird, bunny, dog, cat, cow, duck, fish, kitty, horse, pig, puppy*
Body parts and clothing	*diaper, ear, eye, foot, hair, hand, hat, mouth, nose, toe, tooth, shoe*
House and outdoors	*blanket, chair, cup, door, flower, keys, outside, spoon, tree, TV*
People	*baby, daddy, gramma, grampa, mommy, [child's own name]*
Toys and vehicles	*ball, balloon, bike, boat, book, bubbles, plane, truck, toy*
Actions	*down, eat, go, sit, up*
Games and routines	*bath, bye, hi, night-night, no, peek-a-boo, please, shhh, thank you, yes*
Adjectives and descriptors	*all gone, cold, dirty, hot*

SOURCE: From Jean Berko Gleason, *The development of language 6/e.* Published by Allyn and Bacon, Boston, MA. Copyright © 2005 by Pearson Education. Reprinted by permission of the publisher.

though they rarely get the meaning entirely wrong, they often use a word too broadly or too narrowly (Pan, 2005). One error is **overextension,** or using a word to refer to too wide a range of objects or events, as when a 2-year-old calls all furry, four-legged animals "doggie." The second, and opposite, error is **underextension,** as when a child initially uses the word *doggie* to refer only to basset hounds like the family pet. Notice that both overextension and underextension are examples of Piaget's concept of assimilation, using existing concepts to interpret new experiences. Getting semantics right seems to be mainly a matter of discriminating similarities and differences—for example, categorizing animals on the basis of size, shape, the sounds they make, and other perceptual features (Clark & Clark, 1977).

But might children know more about the world than their semantic errors suggest? Yes, 2-year-olds who say "doggie" when they see a cow will point to the cow rather than the dog when asked to find the cow (Naigles & Gelman, 1995; Thompson & Chapman, 1977). Children may overextend the meaning of certain words such as *doggie* not because they misunderstand word meanings but because they want to communicate, have only a small vocabulary with which to do so, and have not yet learned to call something a "whatchamacallit" when they cannot come up with the word for it (Naigles & Gelman, 1995).

You must be careful about applying these generalizations about early language acquisition to all children because they mask large individual differences in speaking style (Nelson, 2007). As ■ **Figure 10.1** shows, one 24-month-old may have a vocabulary of approximately 50 words, and another may be able to produce more than 500 words (Fenson et al., 1994). Some children use a referential style—lots of nouns referring to objects such as ball and truck. Others seem to treat language as a social tool; they use an expressive style of speaking with more personal pronouns and memorized social routines such as "bye-bye" and "I want it" (Nelson, 2007). Culture exerts some influence: Infants learning English use many nouns and few verbs in their early speech, whereas infants learning Korean use more verbs (Gopnik & Choi, 1995). More important, differences in the daily language experiences of children contribute to the differences in their speech. Both quantity of speech (how many words the child hears in the home) and quality of speech (how sophisticated the speech is) affect young children's vocabularies (Hoff, 2005; Weizman & Snow, 2001). So, individual differences in language acquisition are the norm rather than the exception.

Telegraphic Speech

The next step in language development, normally taken about 18 to 24 months of age, is combining two words into a simple sentence. Toddlers all over the world use two-word sentences to express the same basic ideas (see ● **Table 10.2**). Early combinations of two, three, or more words are sometimes called **telegraphic speech** because, like telegrams, these sentences contain critical content words and omit frills such as articles, prepositions, and auxiliary verbs.

It is ungrammatical in adult English to say "No want" or "Where ball." However, these two-word sentences are not just random word combinations or mistakes; they reflect children's developing understanding of **syntax,** the systematic rules for forming sentences. Consider these three sentences: (1) Fang Fred bit. (2) Fang bit Fred. (3) Fred bit Fang. The first, as even young children recognize, violates the rules of English sentence structure or syntax, although this word order would be acceptable in German. The second and third are both grammatical English sentences, but their different word orders convey different meanings.

Psycholinguists such as Lois Bloom (1998) believe it is appropriate to describe children's early sentences in terms of a **functional grammar**—one that emphasizes the semantic relationships among words, the meanings being expressed, and the functions served by sentences (such as naming, questioning, or commanding). For example, young children often use the same word order to convey different meanings. "Mommy nose" might mean "That's Mommy's nose" in one context, but for one 22-month-old girl one afternoon it meant "Mommy, I've just wiped my runny nose the length of the living room couch." Word order sometimes does matter: "Billy hit" and "Hit Billy" may mean different things. Body language and tone of voice also communicate meanings, such as when a child points and whines to request ice cream, not merely to note its existence.

Between ages 2 and 5, children learn to speak sentences that are remarkably complex and adultlike. ● **Table 10.3** gives an inkling of how fast things move in the particularly important period from age 2 to age 3. From the two-word stage of language acquisition, children progress to three-word telegraphic sentences then to longer sentences, beginning to add the little function words such as articles and prepositions that were often missing in their early telegraphic sentences (Hoff, 2005). They increasingly infer the rules of adult language.

How do people know when children are mastering new rules? Oddly enough, their progress sometimes reveals itself in new "mistakes." Consider the task of acquiring **morphology**— the rules for forming words from sounds, such as forming plurals and past tenses. Typically this happens sometime during the third year (Hoff, 2005). A child who has been saying "feet" and "went" may suddenly start to say "foots" and "goed." Does this represent a step backward? Not at all. The child was probably using the correct irregular forms at first by imitating adult speech without understanding the meaning of

■ **FIGURE 10.1** The range of individual differences in vocabulary size from 16 to 30 months.
SOURCE: From L. Fenson, P.S. Dale, J.S. Reznick, E. Bates, D.J. Thal, S.J. Pethick, Variability in early communicative development: *Monographs of the Society for Research in Child Development, 59,* (Serial No. 242). Copyright © 1994 Blackwell Publishing. Reprinted with permission.

TABLE 10.2 TWO-WORD SENTENCES SERVE SIMILAR FUNCTIONS IN DIFFERENT LANGUAGES

LANGUAGE		
FUNCTION OF SENTENCE	ENGLISH	GERMAN
To locate or name	*There book*	*Buch da (book there)*
To demand	*More milk*	*Mehr milch (more milk)*
To negate	*No wet*	*Nicht blasen (not blow)*
To indicate possession	*My shoe*	*Mein ball (my ball)*
To modify or qualify	*Pretty dress*	*Armer wauwau (poor doggie)*
To question	*Where ball*	*Wo ball (where ball)*

SOURCE: Adapted from Slobin, 1979.

TABLE 10.3 SAMPLES OF KYLE'S SPEECH AT 24 MONTHS AND 35 MONTHS

AT 24 MONTHS (HIS SECOND BIRTHDAY PARTY)	AT 35 MONTHS (PLAYING WITH A POTATO BUG)
Want cake now. Boons! Boons! [pointing to balloons] They mine! [referring to colors] I wan' see. See sky now. Ow-ee [pointing to knee].	*Mother:* Kyle, why don't you take the bug back to his friends? *Kyle:* After I hold him, then I'll take the bug back to his friends. Mommy, where did the bug go? Mommy, I didn't know where the bug go. Find it. Maybe Winston's on it [the family dog]. Winston, get off the bug! [Kyle spots the bug and picks it up.] *Mother:* Kyle, *please* let the bug go back to his friends. *Kyle:* He does not want to go to his friends. [He drops the bug and squashes it, much to his mother's horror.] I stepped on it and it will not go to his friends.

At 24 months, Kyle speaks in telegraphic sentences no more than three words long; by 35 months, his sentences are much longer and more grammatically complex, although not free of errors, and he is better able to participate in the give-and-take of conversation (despite not heeding his mother and respecting the dignity of potato bugs).

plurality or verb tense. The use of "foots" and "goed" is a breakthrough: The child has inferred the morphological rules of adding *-s* to pluralize nouns and adding *-ed* to signal past tense. At first, however, the youngster engages in **overregularization,** overapplying the rules to cases in which the proper form is irregular. When the child masters exceptions to the rules, she will say "feet" and "went" once more.

Children must also master rules for creating variations of the basic declarative sentence; that is, they must learn the rules for converting a basic idea such as "I am eating pizza" into such forms as questions ("Am I eating pizza?"), negative sentences ("I am not eating pizza"), and imperatives ("Eat the pizza!"). The prominent linguist Noam Chomsky (1968, 1975) drew attention to the child's learning of these rules by proposing that language be described in terms of a **transformational grammar,** or rules of syntax for transforming basic underlying thoughts into a variety of sentence forms.

How do young children learn to phrase the questions that they so frequently ask to fuel their cognitive growth? The earliest questions often consist of nothing more than two- or three-word sentences with rising intonation ("See kitty?"). Sometimes *wh-* words such as *what* or *where* appear ("Where kitty?"). During the second stage of question asking, children begin to use auxiliary, or helping, verbs, but their questions are of this form: "What Daddy is eating?" "Where the kitty is going?" Their understanding of transformation rules is still incomplete (Tager-Flusberg, 2005). Finally, they learn the transformation rule that calls for moving the auxiliary verb ahead of the subject (as in the adultlike sentence "What is Daddy eating?").

By the end of the preschool period (ages 5–6), children's sentences are much like those of adults even though they have never had a formal lesson in grammar. It is an amazing accomplishment. Yet there is more growth that needs to occur.

Later Language Development

School-age children improve their pronunciation skills, produce longer and more complex sentences, and continue to expand their vocabularies. The average first-grader starts school with a vocabulary of about 10,000 words and adds somewhere between 5 and 13 new words a day throughout the elementary-school years (Anglin, 1993; Bloom, 1998). During adolescence, with the help of formal operational thought, teens become better able to understand and define abstract terms such as ethics (McGhee-Bidlack, 1991). They also become better able to infer meanings that are not explicitly stated (Beal, 1990).

School-age children also begin to think about and manipulate language in ways previously impossible (Ely, 2005; Klein, 1996). They can, for example, interpret passive sentences such as "Goofy was liked by Donald" and conditional sentences such as "If Goofy had come, Donald would have been delighted" (Boloh & Champaud, 1993; Sudhalter & Braine, 1985). Command of grammar continues to improve through adolescence; teenagers' spoken and written sentences become increasingly long and complex (Christie, 2002).

Children are also mastering the **pragmatics** of language—rules for specifying how language is used appropriately in different social contexts. That is, children have to learn when to say what to whom. They must learn to communicate effectively by taking into account who the listener is, what the listener already knows, and what the listener needs or wants to hear. "Give me that cookie" may be grammatical English, but the child is far more likely to win Grandma's heart (not to mention a cookie) with a polite "May I please try one of your yummy cookies, Grandma?" Children also increasingly use **decontextualized language** as they move from talking about the immediate conversational context ("I see a dog over there") to talking about past or remote events ("I saw a dog while on vacation last week"; Ely, 2005). They can tell stories about events that happened in the past or are not part of the current context. By adolescence, these narratives are often detailed and lengthy.

Throughout childhood and adolescence, advances in cognitive development are accompanied by advances in language and communication skills. For example, as children become less cognitively egocentric, they are more able to take the perspective of their listeners (Hoff, 2005). Middle childhood and adolescence also bring increased **metalinguistic awareness,** or knowledge of language as a system (Ely, 2005). Children with metalinguistic awareness understand the concept of words and can define words (semantics). Adolescents are increasingly able to define abstract words (such as *courage* or *pride*) but are still outperformed by adults on difficult words (such as *idleness* or *goodness*; Nippold et al., 1999). Development of metalinguistic awareness also means that children and adolescents can distinguish between grammatically correct and grammatically incorrect sentences (syntax) and can understand how language can be altered to fit the needs of the specific social context in which it is used (pragmatics).

What happens to language skills during adulthood? Adults simply hold onto the knowledge of the phonology they gained as children, although elders can have difficulty distinguishing speech sounds (such as *b* from *p*) if they have hearing impairments or deficits in the cognitive abilities required to make out what they hear (Thornton & Light, 2006). Adults also retain their knowledge of grammar or syntax. Older adults tend to use less complex sentences than younger adults do, however. Also, those with memory difficulties may have trouble understanding sentences that are highly complex syntactically (for example, "The children warned about road hazards refused to fix the bicycle of the boy who crashed"); they may not be able to remember the beginning of the sentence by the time they get to the end (Kemtes & Kemper, 1997; Stine, Soederberg, & Morrow, 1996).

Meanwhile, knowledge of the semantics of language, of word meanings, often expands during adulthood, at least until people are in their 70s or 80s (Obler, 2005; Schaie, 1996). After all, adults gain experience with the world from year to year, so it is not surprising that their vocabularies continue to grow and that they enrich their understandings of the meanings of words. However, older adults more often have the "tip-of-the-tongue" experience of not being able to recall the name of an object (or especially a person's name) when they need it (Thornton & Light, 2006). This problem is a matter of not being able to retrieve information stored in memory rather than a matter of no

longer knowing the words. In order to maintain fluency in the face of these retrieval problems, older adults speak a little more slowly and plan their choice of words further in advance than when they were younger (Spieler & Griffin, 2006).

Adults also refine their pragmatic use of language—adjusting it to different social and professional contexts (Obler, 2005). Physicians, for example, must develop a communication style that is effective with their patients. Partners who have been together for years often develop a unique way of communicating with one another that is distinctly different from how they communicate with others. Overall, command of language holds up well in later life unless the individual experiences major declines in cognitive functioning (Kemper & Mitzner, 2001; Stine, Soederberg, & Morrow, 1996).

How Language Develops

We cannot help but be awed by the pace at which children master the fundamentals of language during their first 5 years of life, but we must also appreciate the continued growth that occurs in childhood and adolescence and the maintenance of language skills throughout the life span. How are these remarkable skills acquired? Theorists attempting to explain language acquisition have differed considerably in their positions on the nature–nurture issue, as illustrated by the learning, nativist, and interactionist perspectives on language development (Bohannon & Bonvillian, 2005).

The Learning Perspective

How do children learn language? To answer this, you have another opportunity to examine the role of nature and nurture. Intuitively, many people believe that language learning is a matter of nurture: Children imitate what they hear, receiving praise when they get it right and being corrected when they get it wrong. Different learning theorists emphasize different aspects of this broad process. Social learning theorist Albert Bandura (1971) and others emphasize observational learning—learning by listening to and then imitating older companions. Behaviorist B. F. Skinner (1957) and others have emphasized the role of reinforcement. As children achieve better approximations of adult language, parents and other adults praise meaningful speech and correct errors. Children are also reinforced by getting what they want when they speak correctly. In general, learning theorists consider the child's social environment to be critical to what and how much she learns.

How well does the learning perspective account for language development? It is no accident that children learn the language their parents speak, down to the regional accent. Children learn the words they hear spoken by others—even when the words are not spoken directly to them (Floor & Akhtar, 2006). For example, 18-month-olds can learn object labels and verbs by "eavesdropping" on a conversation between two adults (so be careful about what you say within earshot of toddlers). In addition, young children are more likely to start using new words if they are reinforced for doing so than if they are not (Whitehurst & Valdez-Menchaca, 1988). Finally, children whose caregivers frequently encourage them to converse by asking questions, making requests, and the like are more advanced in early language development than those whose parents are less conversational (Bohannon & Bonvillian, 2005).

However, learning theorists have had an easier time explaining the development of phonology and semantics than accounting for how syntactical rules are acquired. For example, after analyzing conversations between mothers and young children, Roger Brown, Courtney Cazden, and Ursula Bellugi (1969) discovered that a mother's approval or disapproval depended on the truth value or semantics of what was said, not on the grammatical correctness of the statement. Thus, when a child looking at a cow says, "Her cow" (accurate but grammatically incorrect), Mom is likely to provide reinforcement ("That's right, darling"), whereas if the child were to say, "There's a dog, Mommy" (grammatically correct but untruthful), Mom would probably correct the child ("No, sweetie—that's a cow"). Similarly, parents seem just as likely to reward a grammatically primitive request ("Want milk") as a well-formed version of the same idea (Brown & Hanlon, 1970). Such evidence casts doubt on the idea that the major mechanism behind syntactic development is reinforcement.

Could imitation of adults account for the acquisition of syntax? You have already seen that young children produce many sentences they are unlikely to have heard adults using ("All gone cookie," overregularizations such as "It swimmed," and so on). These kinds of sentences are not imitations. Also, an adult is likely to get nowhere in teaching syntax by saying "Repeat after me" unless the child already has at least some knowledge of the grammatical form to be learned (Baron, 1992; McNeill, 1970). Young children frequently imitate other people's speech, and this may help them get to the point of producing new structures. But it is hard to see how imitation and reinforcement alone can account for the learning of grammatical rules.

The Nativist Perspective

In contrast to the learning theorists who adopt a nurture perspective, nativists minimize the role of the language environment and maximize the role of the child's biologically programmed capacities in explaining language development (see,

A is for *apple*. The learning perspective helps explain how young children learn the meaning of words.

for example, Chomsky, 1995; Pinker, 1999; see also Tomasello, 2006). Chomsky (1968, 1975, 1995) proposed that humans have an inborn mechanism for mastering language called the **language acquisition device (LAD).** The LAD was conceived as an area in the brain equipped to identify certain universal features of language and to figure out the specific rules of any particular language. To learn to speak, children need only to hear other humans speak; using the LAD, they quickly grasp the rules of whatever language they hear (see ■ **Figure 10.2**).

What evidence supports a nativist perspective on language development? First, there are areas of the brain that specialize in language functions; Broca's area in the frontal lobe controls speaking, for example, whereas Wernicke's area controls speech recognition (Bear, Connors, & Paradiso, 2001). Second, children acquire an incredibly complex communication system rapidly and without formal instruction. For example, 18-month-olds show an understanding of syntax that they could not have acquired solely from information provided by the researchers; they must have inferred rules of syntax on their own (Lidz, Waxman, & Freedman, 2003). Third, children all progress through the same sequences at roughly similar ages, and they even make the same kinds of errors, which suggests that language development is guided by a species-wide maturational plan. Fourth, these universal aspects of early language development occur despite cultural differences in the styles of speech

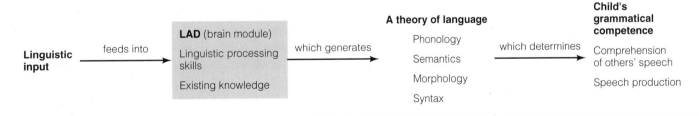

■ **FIGURE 10.2** The language acquisition device (LAD).
SOURCE: Chomsky, 1965.

that adults use in talking to young children. In some cultures, for example, parents believe that babies are incapable of understanding speech and do not even talk directly to them (Crago, Allen, & Hough-Eyamir, 1997).

Finally, there is evidence that the capacity for acquiring language has a genetic basis. Some of our linguistic competencies, including the ability to combine symbols to form short sentences, are shared with chimpanzees and other primates, suggesting that they arose during the course of evolution and are part of our genetic endowment as humans (Greenfield & Savage-Rumbaugh, 1993; Pinker, 1994). Identical twins score more similarly than fraternal twins on measures of verbal skills, and certain speech, language, and reading disorders run in families, indicating that individual heredity influences the course of language development (Lewis & Thompson, 1992; Plomin, 1990).

Although nativists are correct to emphasize the importance of biologically based capacities in language acquisition, the nativist perspective has two major limitations. First, attributing language development to a built-in LAD may describe development but does not really explain it (Moerk, 1989). Second, nativists, in focusing on the defects of learning theories of language development, tend to underestimate the contributions of children's language environment. The nativists base much of their argument on three assumptions: (1) that the only thing children need to develop language is exposure to speech, (2) that the speech children hear is so incredibly complex that only a highly powerful brain could detect regularities in it, and (3) that adults give children little useful feedback about whether their sentences are grammatically correct. These assumptions now seem to be largely inaccurate, and most researchers currently believe that language development depends on both nature and nurture.

The Interactionist Perspective

Interactionists believe that both learning theorists (nurture) and nativists (nature) are correct: Children's biologically based competencies and their language environment interact to shape the course of language development (Bloom, 1998; Bohannon & Bonvillian, 2005). They emphasize that acquisition of language skills depends on and is related to the acquisition of many other capacities: perceptual, cognitive, motor, social, and emotional. They point out that the capacity for acquiring language is not unique, as nativists who speak of the LAD claim (Bates, O'Connell, & Shore, 1987). It is, instead, interrelated to other developments that are taking place concurrently with language acquisition. For example, young children first begin to use words as meaningful symbols when they begin to display nonlinguistic symbolic capacities, such as the ability to use gestures (waving bye-bye), and begin to engage in pretend play (treating a bowl as if it were a hat).

The interactionists' position is not unlike that taken by Piaget (1970). He believed that milestones in cognitive development pave the way for progress in language development and that maturation and environment interact to guide both cogni-

tive development and language development. Like Piaget (but unlike learning theorists), many interactionists argue that language development depends on the maturation of cognitive abilities such as the capacity for symbolic thought. However, the interactionist position also emphasizes—as Vygotsky did but Piaget did not—ways in which social interactions with adults contribute to cognitive and linguistic development. Language is primarily a means of communicating—one that develops in the context of social interactions as children and their companions strive to get their messages across (Tomasello, 2006).

Long before infants use words, Jerome Bruner (1983) says, their caregivers show them how to take turns in conversations—even if the most these young infants can contribute when their turn comes is a laugh or a bit of babbling. As adults converse with young children, they create a supportive learning environment—a scaffold in Bruner's terms, a zone of proximal development in Vygotsky's—that helps the children grasp the regularities of language (Bruner, 1983; Harris, 1992). For example, parents may go through their children's favorite picture books at bedtime and ask "What's this?" and "What's that?" This gives their children repeated opportunities to learn that conversing involves taking turns, that things have names, and that there are proper ways to pose questions and give answers. Soon the children are asking "What's this?" and "What's that?"

Adults are not the only ones who use child-directed speech. Children also adjust their speech to their listener.

On a daily basis, toddlers in English-speaking homes hear between 5,000 and 7,000 utterances (Tomasello, 2006). As they gain new language skills, adults adjust their styles of communication accordingly. Language researchers use the term **child-directed speech** to describe the speech adults use with young children: short, simple sentences spoken slowly, in a high-pitched voice, often with much repetition, and with exaggerated emphasis on key words (usually words for objects and activities). For example, the mother trying to get her son to eat his peas might say, "Eat your *peas* now. Not the cracker. See those *peas*? Yes, eat the *peas*. Oh, such a good boy for eating your *peas*." Mothers also convey more exaggerated emotions (positive and negative) when speaking to their infants than when speaking to other adults (Kitamura & Burnham, 2003). From the earliest days of life, toddlers seem to pay more attention to the high-pitched sounds and varied intonational patterns of child-directed speech than to the speech adults use when communicating with one another (Cooper et al., 1997; Pegg, Werker, & McLeod, 1992). Finally, it is important to note that caregivers' child-directed speech is dynamic—constantly changing in response to the child's utterances (Gros-Louis et al., 2006).

Would children learn language just as well if adults talked to them in an adultlike style? Perhaps not. The nativists seem to have underestimated the contributions of environment to language development. Mere exposure to speech is not enough; children must be actively involved in using language (Locke, 1997). Catherine Snow and her associates, for example, found that a group of Dutch-speaking children, although they watched a great deal of German television, did not acquire German words or grammar (Snow et al., 1976). True, there are cultural groups (the Kaluli of New Guinea, the natives of American Samoa, and the Trackton people of the Piedmont Carolinas) in which child-directed speech does not seem to be used. Children in these societies still seem to acquire their native language without noticeable delays (Gordon, 1990; Ochs, 1982; Schieffelin, 1986). Yet even these children overhear speech and participate in social interactions in which language is used, and that is what seems to be required to master a human language (Lieven, 1994). Those parents who use child-directed speech further simplify the child's task of figuring out the rules of language (Harris, 1992; Kemler Nelson et al., 1989). They converse with children daily in attention-getting and understandable ways about the objects and events that have captured the youngsters' attention.

Adults speaking to young children also use certain communication strategies that foster language development. For example, if a child says, "Kitty goed," an adult may respond with an **expansion**—a more grammatically complete expression of the same thought ("Yes, the cat went in the car"). Adults use conversational techniques such as expansions mainly to improve communication, not to teach grammar (Penner, 1987). However, these techniques also serve as a subtle form of correction after children produce grammatically incorrect sentences and show children more grammatical ways to express the same ideas (Bohannon & Stanowicz, 1988; Saxton, 1997).

It is not quite true, then, that adults provide no corrective feedback concerning children's grammatical errors, as nativists claim. True, they rarely say, "No, that's wrong; say it this way." Nevertheless, they provide subtle corrective feedback through their responses to children, and this feedback helps children grow linguistically (Bohannon & Bonvillian, 2005).

How can adults best facilitate young children's language learning? What cognitive capacities enable children to learn how language works? Much remains to be learned about language development, but it does seem to require the interaction of a biologically prepared child with at least one conversational partner, ideally one who tailors her own speech to the child's level of understanding.

A Critical Period for Language?

Young children are so adept at learning languages that some scholars have wondered whether a critical (or at least sensitive) period for language acquisition may exist. Some years ago, Eric Lenneberg (1967) said that there is such a critical period and that it lasts until puberty, when the development of lateralization of language functions in the left hemisphere of the brain is completed. Although researchers now know that lateralization of the brain occurs more rapidly than Lenneberg thought (see Chapter 5), they continue to be interested in determining whether young children are uniquely capable of language learning.

What evidence supports the critical period hypothesis of language acquisition? Some comes from studies of deaf children, some of whom (especially those with hearing parents) do not have an opportunity to learn any language, oral or signed, in their early years. Rachel Mayberry (1994) studied language mastery in deaf college students exposed to American Sign Language (ASL) at different ages and found that the rule "the earlier, the better" applies (see also Mayberry, Lock, & Kazmi, 2002). Mastery of the morphology, syntax, and semantics of sign language was greatest among students exposed to it in infancy or early childhood. Those who learned sign later in their development (ages 9–16) mastered it better if they had had some exposure to English early in life than if they had not been exposed to any language system before they encountered sign language. The Explorations box on page 286 provides more details on how the language development of deaf children compares with that of hearing children.

Elissa Newport and her colleagues (Newport, 1991) uncovered similar evidence of a critical period for second-language learning. In one study (Johnson & Newport, 1989), native speakers of Korean or Chinese who had come to the United States between age 3 and age 39 were tested for mastery of English grammar. Among those who began learning English before puberty, those who learned it earliest knew it best. Among those who arrived in the United States after puberty, performance was generally poor regardless of age of arrival or number of years using English. Such findings have been used to argue that there is a critical period for language acquisition that ends around puberty. But other research shows that, even beyond puberty, age of arrival in the United States is related to proficiency in English as

LANGUAGE ACQUISITION AMONG DEAF CHILDREN

Many deaf children gain their first exposure to language by learning ASL (American Sign Language). This is a true language. For example, signs are arbitrary symbols, not attempts to mimic objects and events, and they are used according to a system of grammatical rules that determines their ordering. You ought to be able to learn some interesting lessons about language acquisition in general, then, by studying language acquisition among deaf children.

On average, deaf children acquire sign language in much the same sequence and at much the same rate as hearing children acquire spoken language, and they make many of the same kinds of errors along the way (Bellugi, 1988; Masataka, 2000). Interestingly, deaf infants whose parents are deaf "babble" in sign language. They experiment with gestures in much the same way that hearing infants experiment with sounds in preparation for their first meaningful communications (Petitto & Marentette, 1991). They then sign their first meaningful single words around 12 months, use their first syntax (combinations of two signs) between 18 and 24 months, and master many rules of morphology, such as past tense formation, between 2 and 3 years (Meier, 1991). Just as hearing children have difficulty with the pronunciation of certain words and overgeneralize certain rules, deaf children make predictable errors in their signing (Meier, 1991). Moreover, for both deaf and hearing children, advances in language development are linked closely to advances in cognitive development; for example, putting signs or words together in sentences happens around the same age that children put sequences of actions together in their play (Spencer, 1996).

The language environment experienced by deaf infants is also far more similar to that of hearing infants than you would imagine. For example, deaf mothers sign in child-directed speech; they present signs at a slower pace, repeat signs more, and exaggerate their signing motions more when they talk to their infants than when they talk to their deaf friends (Holzrichter & Meier, 2000). Moreover, just as hearing babies prefer the exaggerated intonations of child-directed speech, deaf infants pay more attention and give more emotional response when they are shown videos of infant-directed signing than tapes of adult-directed signing.

Finally, it turns out that language areas of the brain develop much the same in deaf children exposed to sign as in hearing children exposed to speech. For example, Helen Neville and her colleagues (1997) examined brain activity during the processing of sentences by deaf and hearing ASL users, hearing individuals (interpreters) who acquired sign late in life, and hearing individuals who did not know ASL. Mostly, reliance on areas of the left hemisphere of the cortex to process sentences was as evident among those who acquired ASL early in life as among hearing individuals who acquired English early in life. Reliance on the left hemisphere to process syntax was not as clear among individuals who acquired a language later in life. Early learners of ASL used their right hemispheres more in responding to sentences, perhaps because spatial skills based in the right hemisphere come into play in interpreting the gestures of someone who is signing.

As you have seen, language development is sometimes delayed among deaf children of hearing parents if they cannot hear well enough to understand spoken language but are not exposed to sign language (Mayberry, 1994). Overall, then, studies of language acquisition among deaf children suggest that young humans are biologically prepared to master language and will do so if given the opportunity, whether that language is signed or spoken and whether it involves visual–spatial skills or auditory ones (see Goldin-Meadow, 2003, 2005).

© Stephen McBrady/PhotoEdit

a second language (Birdsong, 1999, 2005). Thus, adults relocating at age 25 develop greater proficiency than adults relocating at age 30, an advantage related more to age than to length of residence in the United States (Stevens, 1999). And although adults are generally less likely than children to ever attain nativelike proficiency in a second language—suggesting a critical period—some adults achieve such proficiency (Birdsong, 1999).

Young children may have advantages over adults when learning a second language. This does not necessarily mean that there is a critical period for language acquisition. Children are generally immersed in their second language through school and peer-group activities. This greater exposure may facilitate second-language acquisition partly by making the new language dominant in their lives. Adults, by contrast, may be more likely to continue using their native language as their dominant mode of communication, making second-language acquisition more difficult (Jia & Aaronson, 1999).

It is possible that the language-processing areas of the brain are shaped for a lifetime by early experience with language in ways that limit later learning of other languages. But it seems unlikely that there is a hard-and-fast critical period for language acquisition. Janet Werker and Richard Tees (2005) suggest that it is more accurate to say there is an "optimal period" during which languages are most easily and flawlessly acquired. Perhaps the main message is that young children are supremely capable of learning languages and advancing their cognitive development in the process. Meanwhile, college students learning a foreign language for the first time must appreciate that they may never speak it as well as someone who learned it as a young child.

Developing language competence may be our earliest and greatest learning challenge, but it is only the beginning. There is much more to be mastered during the school years and beyond. Language lays the foundation for acquiring reading, writing, and countless other skills. But unlike language, which seems to develop effortlessly in the absence of formal education, these other skills typically require directed education. In the following sections, we look at education across the life span, examining changes in motivation for learning and changes in educational environments as learners get older.

SUMMING UP

▌ To acquire language, children must master phonology (sound), semantics (meaning), morphology (word structure), and syntax (sentence structure). They must also learn how to use language appropriately (pragmatics) and how to understand nonverbal communication.

▌ Infants are able to discriminate speech sounds and progress from crying, cooing, and babbling to one-word holophrases (at 12 months) and then to telegraphic speech (at 18 months).

▌ During the preschool years, language abilities improve dramatically, as illustrated by overregularizations and new transformation rules.

▌ School-age children and adolescents refine their language skills and become less egocentric communicators.

▌ Theories of language development include learning theories, nativist theories, and interactionist theories. These emphasize the child's biologically based capacities and experience conversing with adults who use child-directed speech and strategies such as expansion that simplify the language-learning task.

CRITICAL THINKING

1. What should parents and early childhood educators look for (or listen for) to confirm that infants and toddlers are progressing typically with regard to their language acquisition at ages 1, 2, and 3?

2. Describe a characteristic of children's language that supports each of the three theories of language development—learning, nativist, and interactionist.

10.2 THE INFANT

Before children begin their formal education, they are learning a great deal from the informal curriculum of their lives. Above all, they are learning to master their environments.

Mastery Motivation

Infants seem to be intrinsically motivated to master their environment (Morgan, MacTurk, & Hrncir, 1995). This **mastery motivation** can be seen clearly when infants struggle to open kitchen cabinets, take their first steps, or figure out how new toys work—and derive great pleasure from their efforts (Jennings & Dietz, 2003; Masten & Reed, 2002).

Much evidence supports the claim that infants are curious, active explorers constantly striving to understand and to exert control over the world around them. This, you should recall, was one of Piaget's major themes. A striving for mastery or competence appears to be inborn and universal and will display itself in the behavior of all normal infants without prompting from parents. Even so, some infants appear to be more mastery oriented than others. Given a new push toy, one baby may simply look at it, but another may mouth it, bang it, and push it across the floor (Jennings & Dietz, 2003). Why might some infants have a stronger mastery motive than others?

Mastery motivation seems higher when parents frequently provide sensory stimulation designed to arouse and amuse their babies—tickling them, bouncing them, playing games of pat-a-cake, giving them stimulating toys, and so on (Busch-Rossnagel, 1997). Mastery motivation also flourishes when infants grow up in a responsive environment that provides plenty of opportunities to see for themselves that they can control their environments and experience successes (Maddux, 2002; Masten & Reed, 2002). Consider the toddler who, faced with the challenge of retrieving a cookie from the kitchen counter,

Every day, infants and young children display their innate mastery motive.

struggles to maneuver a chair across the room and to climb up without tipping the chair or falling off. When Mom offers to help him, he shrieks, "Me do it!" And when he does it, he feels a sense of accomplishment that will increase the likelihood he will tackle future challenges. Parents who return smiles and coos or respond promptly to cries show infants they can affect people around them. By contrast, the children of parents who are depressed show less interest in and persistence on challenging tasks, perhaps because their parents are not responsive to them (Redding, Harmon, & Morgan, 1990).

An infant's level of mastery motivation affects her later achievement behavior. Babies who actively attempt to master challenges at 6 and 12 months score higher on tests of mental development at 2 and 3 years than their less mastery-oriented peers (Jennings & Dietz, 2003; Messer et al., 1986). In short, infants are intrinsically motivated to master challenges, but parents may help strengthen this inborn motive by stimulating their infants appropriately and responding to their actions. What about infants and toddlers who spend considerable amounts of time away from their parents? Is their motivation influenced by time spent in preschool?

Early Education

As you have seen in previous chapters, babies learn a great deal in the first few years of life. But do infants and toddlers need specific educational experiences? Manufacturers of products such as "Baby Einstein" videos and "Baby Mozart" compact discs hope that parents will buy into the idea that early stimulation is critical to infants' intellectual development (McCormick, 1998). Formal programs such as Bookstart, which promotes literacy early by providing 6- to 9-month-old infants and their parents with books and literacy information, have even been developed (Hall, 2001; Wade & Moore, 1998).

Despite its popular appeal, most experts dispute the idea that children need special educational experiences during their first 3 years (Bruer, 1999; Kagan, 1998). And some, such as David Elkind (1987), author of *Miseducation: Preschoolers at Risk*, fear that the push for earlier education may be going too far and that young children today are not given enough time simply to be children—to play and socialize as they choose. Elkind even worries that children may lose their self-initiative and intrinsic motivation to learn when their lives are orchestrated by parents who pressure them to achieve at early ages. Is there anything to these concerns?

Some research seems to confirm Elkind's fears. In one study (Hyson, Hirsh-Pasek, & Rescorla, 1989), 4-year-

olds in preschools with strong academic thrusts gained an initial advantage in basic academic skills such as knowledge of letters and numbers but lost it by the end of kindergarten. What is more, they proved to be less creative, more anxious in testing situations, and more negative toward school than children who attended preschool programs with a social rather than academic emphasis. Similarly, Deborah Stipek and her colleagues (1995) have found that highly academic preschool programs raise children's academic achievement test scores but decrease their expectancies of success and pride in accomplishment. So, it may be possible to undermine achievement motivation by overemphasizing academics in the preschool years (Garner, 1999).

However, preschool programs that offer a healthy mix of play and academic skill-building activities can be beneficial to young children, especially disadvantaged ones (Barnett, 2002; Gottlieb & Blair, 2004). Although many children who attend preschool programs are no more or less intellectually advanced than those who remain at home, disadvantaged children who attend programs specially designed to prepare them for school experience more cognitive growth and achieve more success in school than disadvantaged children who do not attend such programs (Barnett, 2002). Consider again the Abecedarian Project, a full-time educational program from infancy (starting around 4–5 months) to age 5 for children from low-income families (Campbell et al., 2001; and see Chapter 9). Compared with children who did not participate, Abecedarian children showed impressive cognitive gains during and immediately after the program (see ■ **Figure 10.3**). Although their performance level compared with test norms decreased over the subsequent years, these children continued to show an advantage over children who did not receive this intensive early educational experience (Nelson, Westhues, & MacLeod, 2003).

Thus, early education can provide disadvantaged children with a boost that has lasting consequences, lending support to the basic idea of Head Start. Positive effects on later school

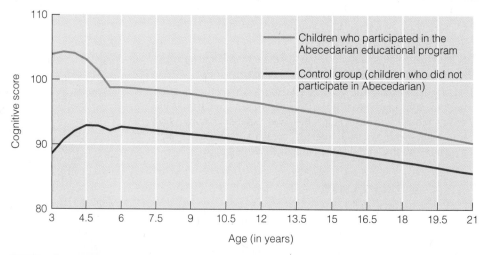

■ **FIGURE 10.3** Cognitive growth curves as a function of preschool treatment.
SOURCE: From F.A. Campbell, E.P. Pungello, S. Miller-Johnson, M. Burchinal, & C.T. Ramey, The development of cognitive and academic abilities: Growth curves from an early childhood educational experience, *Developmental Psychology*, 37, pp. 231–242. Copyright © 2001, American Psychological Association. Reprinted with permission from the American Psychological Association.

Preschools that offer a healthy combination of preacademic and social activities can help children prepare for school.

© ClassicStock/Alamy

With infancy behind them, children begin to show true achievement motivation. Even by age 2, they seem capable of appraising their performances as successes or failures and look to others for approval when they succeed and for disapproval when they fail (Stipek, Recchia, & McClintic, 1992). By age 3, children have clearly internalized standards of performance and experience true pride or shame, depending on how successfully they meet those standards (Stipek, Recchia, & McClintic, 1992). Some children are clearly more achievement oriented and high achieving than others, however, and it is these differences we now seek to explain.

Achievement Motivation

All children occasionally experience failure in their efforts to master challenges and meet achievement standards. What are the differences between children who persist and triumph in the face of failure and those who give up? Carol Dweck (2002; Heyman, Dweck, & Cain, 1992) finds that high achievers tend to attribute their successes to internal and stable causes such as high ability. However, they blame their failures either on external factors beyond their control ("That test was impossibly hard," "That teacher's grading is biased") or—and this is even more adaptive—on internal causes that they can overcome (particularly insufficient effort). They do not blame the internal but stable factor of low ability ("I'm terrible at this and will never do any better"). Students with this healthy attributional style are said to have a **mastery orientation;** they thrive on challenges and persist in the face of failure, believing that their increased effort will pay off.

By contrast, children who tend to be low achievers often attribute their successes either to the internal cause of hard work or to external causes such as luck or the easiness of the task. Thus, they do not experience the pride and self-esteem that come from viewing themselves as highly capable. Yet they often attribute their failures to an internal and stable cause—namely, lack of ability. As a result, they have low expectancies of success and tend to give up. Dweck describes children with this attributional style as having a **learned helplessness orientation**—a tendency to avoid challenges and to cease trying when they experience failure, based on the belief that they can do little to improve.

Child Contributions

Several characteristics of the child contribute to achievement levels and motivation to succeed. First is the child's age or developmental level. Before age 7 or so, children tend to be un-

achievement are especially likely if the preschool experience not only stimulates children's cognitive growth but also gets parents more involved with their children's education and includes follow-up during elementary school (Nelson et al., 2003). More generally, preschool programs that build school readiness skills but also allow plenty of time for play and social interaction can help all children make a smooth transition to kindergarten and elementary school (Parker et al., 1999).

SUMMING UP

▌ Mastery motivation, the forerunner of achievement motivation, is an urge for mastery evident in infancy and is nurtured by sensory stimulation, a responsive environment, and a secure attachment.

▌ Early education can help prepare disadvantaged children for formal schooling, but an overemphasis on academics at the expense of other activities may hinder young children's development.

CRITICAL THINKING

1. Should preschool education be mandatory? At what age should formal education begin? Provide some evidence to support your answer.

2. How can parents and early childhood teachers foster mastery motivation in their youngsters?

LEARNING GOALS	PERFORMANCE GOALS
· Ability as a changeable trait	· Ability as a fixed trait
· Ability to focus on increasing competence or knowledge ("I understand this material better than I did before")	· Ability to focus on increasing status relative to others ("I did better on this than the other students did")
· Self-regulated learning; ability to monitor understanding of material and adjust behavior (for example, effort) accordingly	· Other-regulated learning; ability to monitor performance relative to peers and increase effort (approach) to outperform them or decrease effort (avoidance) to save face (to say that failures are because of a lack of effort, not incompetence)
· Deep-level processing of material (for example, learning to understand)	· Superficial-level processing of material (for example, memorizing for a test)
· Feelings of pride and satisfaction associated with success, with failures indicating a need for more effort or different learning strategies	· Feelings of anxiety and shame associated with failure; boastful feelings associated with success

SOURCES: Based on Covington, 2000; Elliot & Church, 1997.

realistic optimists who think they can succeed on almost any task (Stipek & Mac Iver, 1989). With age, children's perceptions of their academic abilities become more accurate (Wigfield et al., 1997). Even after repeated poor performances, young children often continue to think they have high ability and will do well, whereas older children tend to become helpless (Miller, 1985; Ruble, Eisenberg, & Higgins, 1994). Young children can be made to feel helpless if their failures are clearcut and they conclude they have been bad (Burhans & Dweck, 1995), but they are clearly less susceptible than older children to learned helplessness.

Why is this? Young children are protected from damaging self-perceptions partly because they do not yet fully understand the concept of ability as a stable capacity (Nicholls & Miller, 1984; Pomerantz & Ruble, 1997). They believe that ability is a changeable quality and that they can become smarter and improve their ability if they work hard (Freedman-Doan et al., 2000). This view of ability encourages them to adopt mastery or **learning goals** in achievement situations, aiming to learn new things so that they can improve their abilities (Covington, 2000; Dweck & Leggett, 1988).

As children age, they begin to see ability as a fixed trait that does not change much with effort. As a result, more of them adopt **performance goals** in school; they aim to *prove* their ability rather than to *improve* it and seek to be judged smart rather than dumb (Dweck & Leggett, 1988; Erdley et al., 1997; and see ● **Table 10.4**). These changes in the understanding of ability are probably caused both by cognitive development—especially an increased ability to analyze the causes of successes and failures and to infer enduring traits from behavior—and by an accumulation of feedback in school (Stipek, 1984).

Importantly, children who continue to focus on learning goals tend to do better in school than those who switch to performance goals (Butler, 1999; Covington, 2000; Stipek &

Gralinski, 1996). As Table 10.4 illustrates, when students believe that ability is a fixed entity that they either have or do not have and conclude that they lack it, they set performance goals rather than learning goals; figuring that hard work will not pay off, they run the risk of becoming helpless in the classroom (Dweck & Leggett, 1988). Even gifted students can fall into this trap (Ablard & Mills, 1996).

In addition to their age, children's overall level of intelligence, not surprisingly, contributes to their success in academics (Spinath et al., 2006). But, clearly, level of intelligence is just a piece of the puzzle because some students with above average intelligence do not do particularly well in school and others exceed expectations based solely on their IQ scores. It turns out that both motivation and achievement levels are higher when children value a subject—when they believe that it is important (Spinath et al., 2006).

Parent Contributions

As you saw earlier, parents can foster mastery motivation in infancy by providing their babies with appropriate sensory stimulation, being responsive, and (as you will see in Chapter 14) building a secure attachment relationship. Parents can then strengthen their children's achievement motivation by stressing and reinforcing independence and self-reliance at an early age, encouraging children to do things on their own (Peterson & Steen, 2002). They can also emphasize the importance of doing things well, or meeting high standards of performance (Deci & Ryan, 1992). As children begin formal schooling, parents can help foster high levels of achievement motivation by getting involved with their child's education (Stevenson & Stigler, 1994).

Finally, parents can provide a cognitively stimulating home environment (Gottfried, Fleming, & Gottfried, 1998). This includes having reading material in the home, engaging in intellectual discussions, attending lectures or cultural events, visiting museums, and holding high expectations for children's education. By doing these things, parents stimulate intellectual curiosity and a desire to learn. Children who are encouraged and supported in a positive manner are likely to enjoy new challenges and feel confident about mastering them. They are also unlikely to make the kinds of counterproductive attributions ("I'm dumb") that can cause them to lose interest in schoolwork (Glasgow et al., 1997). Children typically feel competent when their parents are satisfied with their performance (McGrath & Repetti, 2000). By contrast, parents can undermine a child's school performance and intrinsic motivation to learn if they are uninvolved and offer little guidance or if they are highly controlling, nag continually about homework, offer bribes for good grades, and criticize bad grades (Ginsburg & Bronstein, 1993). Thus, parents need to strike a healthy balance between being supportive and being controlling.

School Contributions

How do schools affect achievement? Nearly every school asserts that the major goal of classroom instruction is improvement of children's learning. Many of these same schools, however, are structured in ways that focus on the external rewards that students can earn (such as grades or stickers). As a result, they may encourage children to set performance goals rather than learning goals (Covington, 2000). Many classrooms are competitive places where students try to outdo each other to earn the best grades and gain teacher recognition. Students receive a grade (good or bad), indicating their performance on a test or project, and that is the end of it. If they did not fully learn the material, they are given no opportunity to do so: They learn that the grade, not learning, is the goal.

Martin Covington (2000, 1998) believes that schools can foster children's academic motivation by downplaying the competitive race for the best grades in class. How might this work? Consider some research by Elaine Elliott and Carol Dweck (1988). They asked fifth-graders to perform a novel task. The students were led to believe that they had either low or high ability and were warned that they would soon be performing similar tasks that would prove difficult. Half the children worked under a performance goal (not unlike the goals emphasized in many classrooms): They were told that their performance would be compared with that of other children and evaluated by an expert. The remaining children were induced to adopt a learning goal: Although they would make some mistakes, they were told, working at the tasks would "sharpen the mind" and help them at school.

As expected, the only children who displayed the telltale signs of helplessness (that is, deteriorating performance and attribution of failure to low ability) were those who believed they had low ability and were pursuing a performance goal. For them, continuing to work on the difficult task meant demonstrating again that they were stupid. By contrast, even "low ability" students who pursued a learning goal persisted despite their failures and showed remarkably little frustration, probably because they

believed they could grow from their experience. Perhaps, then, teachers undermine achievement motivation by distributing gold stars and grades and frequently calling attention to how students compare with one another (Deci, Koestner, & Ryan, 1999). Children might be better off if teachers nurtured their intrinsic motivation to master challenges (Boggiano & Katz, 1991; Butler, 1990). Then, slow learners could view their mistakes as a sign that they should change strategies to improve their competencies rather than as further proof that they lack ability.

Finally, the school climate can influence achievement. Academic achievement is greater when schools encourage family involvement and regular parent–teacher communication and when they develop a system that makes family involvement possible (Rimm-Kaufman & Pianta, 1999). Schools can also try to capture students' enthusiasm for learning from the start of schooling. Students who start out liking school are typically the ones who like school later; they also participate more in the classroom, which leads to higher levels of achievement (Ladd, Buhs, & Seid, 2000).

To recap what you have learned so far, children approach achievement tasks with either a mastery orientation or a learned helplessness orientation, based on how they view their academic triumphs and disasters. As they age, children understand the concept of ability as a stable trait and shift from focusing on learning goals to focusing on performance goals. These changes, brought about by both cognitive development and feedback in school, give them a more realistic picture of their own strengths and weaknesses but also make them more vulnerable to learned helplessness. Yet some children remain far more motivated to succeed in school than others, and parents and schools have a lot to do with that.

Learning to Read

Perhaps the most important achievement in school is acquiring the ability to read. Mastery of reading paves the way for mastering other academic skills. Skilled readers consume more printed material than unskilled readers or nonreaders, giving them an advantage in other academic areas that increasingly rely on reading skills over the school years (Stanovich, 1986). Unlike language acquisition, a natural learning task that typically requires no formal education, reading acquisition is an "unnatural" task (Stanovich & Stanovich, 1999). Learning to read almost always requires direct instruction. How do children master this complex and important skill?

Mastering the Alphabetic Principle

Before children can read, they must understand the **alphabetic principle**—the idea that the letters in printed words represent the sounds in spoken words in a systematic way (Byrne, 1998; Treiman, 2000). According to Linnea Ehri (1999), this is a four-step process. First, children in the prealphabetic phase memorize selected visual cues to remember words. They can "read" text that they have memorized during previous readings. For instance, seeing a picture of a dinosaur on a page in a favorite book cues a child to recall the words she has often heard her mother read when they turned to this page. Or, a child in the prealphabetic phase might recognize a word by its shape (physically, the printed word *bed* looks different than the word *egg*).

In the partial alphabetic phase, children learn the shapes and sounds of letters. For example, they recognize the curved shape of the letter *C* and begin to associate this with a particular sound. These children begin to connect at least one letter in a word—usually the first—to its corresponding sound. Not surprisingly, children typically recognize the initial letter of their first name before other letters (Treiman & Broderick, 1998).

Complete connections between written letters and their corresponding sounds are acquired during the full alphabetic phase. In this phase, children apply to the challenge of reading their full **phonological awareness**—the sensitivity to the sound system of language that enables them to segment spoken words into sounds or phonemes (Carroll et al., 2003). Children who have phonological awareness can recognize that *cat* and *trouble* both have the phoneme *t* in them, can tell you how many distinct sounds there are in the word *bark*, and can tell you what will be left if you take the *f* sound out of *fat*. Children can decode words never before seen by applying their knowledge of phonetics. They can decipher the new word *mat* from their previous understanding of the word *cat* and the letter *m*.

In addition to decoding unfamiliar words, children in the full alphabetic phase use sight reading for familiar words. Sight reading is fast and works well for words that are hard to decode (such as those with unusual spellings) or frequently encountered. If you regularly run across the word *alligator* in your readings, you may initially read this by decoding it, or "unpacking" each sound then putting the sounds together. But after many encounters with this word, you can sight-read it, or recall it from memory, without having to decode every sound.

Finally, in the consolidated alphabetic phase, letters that regularly occur together are grouped as a unit. For instance, the letter sequence *ing*, which frequently appears at the end of verbs, is perceived as a single unit rather than as three separate letters. This grouping speeds the processing of the multisyllabic words that older children are increasingly exposed to in their books.

Thus, the basic components of literacy include mastering a language system, understanding connections between sounds and their printed symbols (the alphabetic principle), and discriminating phonemes that make up words (phonological awareness). How does the child pull all this together into reading?

Emergent Literacy

Several activities help promote **emergent literacy**—the developmental precursors of reading skills in young children (Whitehurst & Lonigan, 1998). Emergent literacy includes knowledge, skills, and attitudes that will facilitate the acquisition of reading ability. For instance, reading storybooks to preschoolers positively influences their later literacy (Roskos, Christie, & Richgels, 2003). Repetitious storybook reading enhances children's vocabulary and allows them to see the connection between printed and spoken words (Whitehurst & Lonigan, 1998). With each successive reading, parents ask in-

creasingly complex questions about the text, moving the child from a superficial to a deeper understanding (van Kleeck et al., 1997). Even older children benefit from reading the same book on multiple occasions (Faust & Glenzer, 2000) and from shared reading with a parent (Clarke-Stewart, 1998). Parents, with their greater mastery of reading, can help their fledgling readers develop an understanding of printed words. If you think of this in Vygotsky's framework, it is an example of parent and child operating in the zone of proximal development.

Rhyming stories and games can help foster phonological awareness. For this reason, listening to books with a rhyming structure (for example, Dr. Seuss's *The Cat in the Hat*) can benefit children. Young children's sensitivity to rhyme (for example, *cat–sat*) helps predict their later reading success (Bryant, 1998; Goswami, 1999).

By assessing preschool children's emergent literacy skills, parents can develop a fairly accurate idea of what their later reading skills will be (Lonigan, Burgess, & Anthony, 2000). In particular, differences among children in knowledge of letters (for example, knowing the alphabet) and phonological awareness predict later differences in their reading ability (Carroll et al., 2003). In addition, semantic knowledge, reflected in children's ability to retrieve words and provide word definitions, can predict later reading ability (Roth, Speece, & Cooper, 2002). This suggests that parents can help children get a head start on reading by encouraging activities such as rhyming, repeating the ABCs, and defining words.

Skilled and Unskilled Readers

After children have received reading instruction, why are some children quick, advanced readers but others struggle to master the most basic reading material? For starters, skilled readers

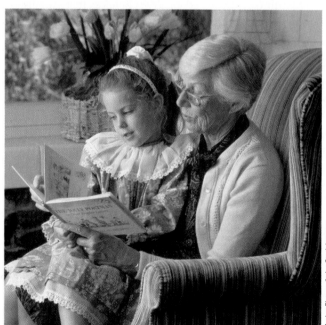

Repeatedly reading the same story fosters vocabulary and deepens children's understanding of the story content.

have a solid understanding of the alphabetic principle—the notion that letters must be associated with phonemes. Thus, when they see the letter *b*, they know the sound that it represents. A large body of research also confirms that reading ability is influenced by a child's level of phonological awareness (Adams, Treiman, & Pressley, 1998; Bus & van Ijzendoorn, 1999). Children with higher levels of phonological awareness usually become better readers than children with lower levels of phonological awareness (Schneider, Roth, & Ennemoser, 2000).

But there is more to being a skilled reader than connecting letters with sounds. Analyses of eye movement patterns show that unskilled readers skip words or parts of words, whereas skilled readers' eyes hit all the words (Perfetti, 1999). Skilled readers do not use context to help them identify words, although they may use context to help with comprehension. As noted previously, they rely on phonology to identify words, something most unskilled readers have trouble with.

Some children have serious difficulties learning to read, even though they have normal intellectual ability and no sensory impairments or emotional difficulties that could account for their problems. These children have **dyslexia,** or a reading disability. A minority have the kind of visual perception problem that used to be seen as the heart of dyslexia; they cannot distinguish between letters with similar appearances, or they read words backward (*top* might become *pot*). However, it is now clear that the difficulties of most dyslexic children involve auditory perception more than visual perception (see, for example, Temple et al., 2000).

Specifically, children who become dyslexic readers often show deficiencies in phonological awareness well before they enter school (Bruck, 1992; Vellutino et al., 1996). There is even evidence that the brains of dyslexic children respond differently to speech sounds soon after birth (Molfese, 2000). This suggests that a perceptual deficit may develop during the prenatal period of brain development. Because dyslexic children have difficulty analyzing the sounds in speech, they also have trouble detecting sound–letter correspondences, which in turn impairs their ability to recognize printed words automatically and effortlessly (Bruck, 1990; Vellutino, 1991). They must then devote so much effort to decoding the words on the page that they have little attention to spare for interpreting and remembering what they

have read. Dyslexic children continue to perform poorly on tests of phonological awareness and tests of word recognition as adolescents and adults, even if they have become decent readers (Bruck, 1990, 1992; Shaywitz et al., 1999). It is now clear that dyslexia is a lifelong disability, not just a developmental delay that is eventually overcome (Shaywitz et al., 1999).

How Should Reading Be Taught?

What does all this suggest about teaching children to read? For years a debate has raged over the merits of two broad approaches to reading instruction: the phonics approach and the whole-language approach (see, for example, Chall, 1967; Lemann, 1997). The phonics (or code-oriented) approach teaches children to analyze words into their component sounds; that is, it systematically teaches them letter–sound correspondence rules (Vellutino, 1991). By contrast, the whole-language (or look–say) approach emphasizes reading for meaning and teaches children to recognize specific words by sight or to figure out what they mean using clues in the surrounding context. It assumes that the parts of printed words (the letters) are not as meaningful as the whole words and that by focusing on whole words children can learn to read as effortlessly and naturally as they learn to understand speech.

Research strongly supports the phonics approach. To read well, children must somehow learn that spoken words are made up of sounds and that the letters of the alphabet correspond to these sounds (Foorman, 1995). Teaching phonological awareness skills can pay off in better reading skills (National Reading Panel, 1999). ● **Table 10.5** shows what happened when a third-grade boy with poor phonological awareness tried to read by the look–say method. He ended up with an incorrect interpretation and lost the intended meaning of the sentence. Better decoding skills (phonics) might have enabled him to read the sentence accurately.

With this in mind, several programs have been developed for at-risk and dyslexic children who have special difficulty discriminating speech sounds that are made rapidly, such as *b*, *d*, and *t*. By playing an entertaining computer game, children are able to practice discriminating pairs of these hard-to-distinguish sounds, which are altered so that they are stretched in time and

● **TABLE 10.5   ONE BOY'S MISREADING OF THE SENTENCE "A BOY SAID, 'RUN, LITTLE GIRL.'"**

WORDS IN TARGET SENTENCE	STRATEGIES EMPLOYED BY READER	WORDS "READ"
A	Sight word known to reader	A
boy	Unknown; uses beginning *b* to guess *baby*	baby
said, "Run,	*Said* unknown; jumps to the next word *(run)*, which he recognizes, then uses the *s* in *said* and his knowledge of syntax to generate *is running*	is running
little	Sight word known to reader	little
girl."	Unknown; uses beginning *g* to guess *go*	go

SOURCE: Adapted from Ely, 2001.

thereby made easier to perceive (Merzenich et al., 1996; Tallal et al., 1996). After only a month of such game playing, children's ability to recognize fast sequences of speech sounds and to understand language improves dramatically. These gains eventually pay off in improved reading performance as children become more able to sound out words on the page (Foorman et al., 1998). Despite the importance of phonological awareness, however, children must also make sense of what they are reading—they must be able to read for meaning. Thus, reading programs should use both phonics and whole-language instruction, teaching letter–sound correspondences but also helping children find meaning and enjoyment in what they read (Adams, 1990).

The debate over reading instruction and its effectiveness raises a broader question about just how well schools are doing at educating children. What factors contribute—or do not contribute—to effective schools?

Effective Schools

As a result of the federal No Child Left Behind Act in the United States (NCLB, 2002), schools are under increasing pressure to demonstrate their effectiveness with annual increases in the percentage of children scoring at or above the proficient level in reading/language arts and mathematics. Clearly, some schools seem to do a better job than others—they graduate a higher percentage of students or have a higher percentage of students at or above the proficient level in one or more subjects. Why? Is it something the schools are doing differently or does it simply reflect the different qualifications of the entering students? After all, families select schools by selecting neighborhoods, and neighborhood selection is based on numerous variables including socioeconomic status. Some schools may take in more successful students from the start. We'll keep this in mind as we review, first, the school factors that do not seem to matter a great deal, and then, the school factors that do influence students' performance.

Less Important Factors

Many people assume that pouring financial resources into schools will automatically increase school effectiveness. But the relationship between funding and student outcome is complex. Some research shows that as long as schools have reasonable resources, the precise amount of money spent per pupil plays only a minor role in determining student outcomes (Hanushek, 1997; Rutter, 1983). Other research suggests that increased resources, if applied directly to classroom instruction, can increase student achievement in the earlier grades (Wenglinsky, 1998). Thus, simply adding money to school budgets is unlikely to improve school effectiveness unless schools invest this money wisely.

Another factor that has relatively little to do with a school's effectiveness is average class size (Ehrenberg et al., 2001; Rutter & Maughan, 2002). Within a range of 18 to 40 students per class, reducing class sizes (from, say, 36 to 24 students) is unlikely to increase student achievement (Hanushek, 1997,

1998). Instead, tutoring students in the early grades (kindergarten through third), especially disadvantaged and low-ability ones, one-on-one or in small groups makes a big difference in their learning of reading and mathematics (Blatchford et al., 2002; Finn, 2002). However, more modest reductions in the student–teacher ratio do not seem to be worth the large amount of money they cost.

What about the amount of time spent in school? Most children go to school for 6 hours on about 180 days of each school year. Many people assume that schools could improve student outcomes if they lengthened the school day or year. But research shows that the modest increases in time that some schools have implemented have only minimal effects on achievement (Glass, 2002c). Thus, adding 30 minutes to each school day or lengthening the school year by 15, 20, or even 25 days has negligible effects on student outcomes. Similarly, redistributing school days so that they are evenly spread across the year (called *year-round schools*) rather than bunched between September and May does not improve student achievement.

Finally, it matters little whether or not a school uses **ability grouping,** in which students are grouped according to ability then taught in classes or work groups with others of similar academic or intellectual standing. Grouping by ability has no clear advantage over mixed-ability grouping for most students (Glass, 2002a). It *can* be beneficial, especially to higher ability students, if it results in a curriculum more appropriate to students' learning needs (Glass, 2002a; Kulik & Kulik, 1992). Research with gifted students shows that they can benefit from being grouped with their gifted peers for a substantial part of the school day (Cornell & Delcourt, 1992; Kulik & Kulik, 1987). Such high-ability grouping allows these students to move through the curriculum at a faster rate and/or deeper levels. In contrast, low-ability students are unlikely to benefit from being grouped with like-ability peers and may suffer if they are denied access to the most effective teachers, taught less material than other children, and stigmatized as "dummies" (Mac Iver, Reuman, & Main, 1995; Mehan et al., 1996). Too often, this is what happens. As Hugh Mehan and his colleagues (1996) put it, "It is not that dumb kids are placed in slow groups or low tracks; it is that kids are made dumb by being placed in slow groups or low tracks" (p. 230). The Explorations box on page 296 takes a closer look at mixing students with different abilities and backgrounds.

These, then, are examples of school characteristics that do not seem to contribute a great deal to effective education. A school that has limited financial support (assuming it exceeds a basic minimum), places most students (except perhaps beginning readers) in relatively large classes, and combines students in mixed-ability learning groups or classes is often just as effective as a school that has ample financial resources, small classes, and ability grouping.

Factors That Matter

So what does influence how well children perform? To understand why some schools are more effective than others, you must consider characteristics of the students, characteristics of the teachers, characteristics of the learning environment, and the interaction between student and environment.

First, as noted earlier, a school's effectiveness is a function of what it has to work with—the students it takes in and the teachers who provide the instruction. With respect to the children, genetic differences among children contribute to differences in aptitude among them (Rutter & Maughan, 2002). As you learned in Chapters 3 and 9, IQ scores have a genetic component, and children with higher IQs attain higher grades throughout their 12 years of school (Gutman, Sameroff, & Cole, 2003). Schools cannot eliminate these genetic differences among children but they can influence (that is, raise) overall levels of academic achievement (Zvoch & Stevens, 2006). In addition, academic achievement, on average, tends to be higher in schools with a preponderance of economically advantaged students; children are better able to make academic progress in school when they come from homes that are stocked with computers, books, and intellectually stimulating toys (Portes & MacLeod, 1996). However, this does not mean that schools are only as good as the students they serve. Many schools that serve disadvantaged populations are highly effective at motivating students and preparing them for jobs or further education. To really determine a school's effectiveness, researchers need to look at how students change from before to after they receive instruction (Zvoch & Stevens, 2006). This is, in large part, the goal of *No Child Left Behind* (NCLB)—to show that children, regardless of how high or low they score at the start, improve their performance after each year of instruction.

Finally, studies of the effects of schools provide another illustration of the interaction of nature and nurture. High-achieving parents pass their genes to their children, providing genetic potential for high achievement to their children (Rutter & Maughan, 2002). These same high-achieving parents are likely to select schools that have strong academic reputations, often by choosing to live in a neighborhood served by a "good" school district (Rutter & Maughan, 2002). This is an example of a passive gene–environment correlation, described in Chapter 3, in which children are influenced by their parent's genes directly through genetic transmission and indirectly through the environments their parents create for them.

As for the effects of teachers on school achievement, Andrew Wayne and Peter Youngs (2003) reviewed research on the relationship between teacher characteristics and student achievement. They found that student achievement scores rose with increases in the quality of their teachers' undergraduate institutions and their teachers' licensure examination scores. There was also a connection between teachers' coursework and student achievement, but only in high school mathematics (see also Zvoch & Stevens, 2006). Thus, high school math teachers are more effective, as measured by student achievement gains, when they have completed more math courses as part of their teacher training. Similarly, in a review of teacher characteristics, Gene Glass (2002b) concluded that student achievement is enhanced when students are taught by regularly licensed teachers who have more experience. It should be noted that not all research shows a connection between teach-

ers' education and students' achievement. At the preschool level, it does not seem to matter what level of education was attained (e.g., Associate versus Bachelor's degree) or what major was pursued by teachers (Early et al., 2007).

Third, the learning environment of some schools allows them to nurture achievement. Basically, the effective school environment is a comfortable but businesslike setting in which teachers are involved with students, students are motivated to learn, and serious teaching takes place (Mac Iver, Reuman, & Main, 1995; Phillips, 1997; Rutter, 1983). More specifically, in effective schools and classrooms, teachers:

- Strongly emphasize academics. They demand a lot from their students, expect them to succeed, regularly assign homework, and work hard to achieve their objectives in the classroom.
- Create a task-oriented but comfortable atmosphere. For example, they waste little time starting activities or dealing with distracting discipline problems, provide clear instructions and feedback, and encourage and reward good work.
- Manage discipline problems effectively. For example, they enforce the rules on the spot rather than sending offenders to the principal's office, and they avoid the use of physical punishment.

Effective schools also have supportive parents and supportive communities behind them (Comer, 1997). Students achieve more when their parents are interested in and value school and school achievement; participate in parent–teacher conferences, PTA meetings, and other school events; and participate in homework and other school-related activities at home (Hill & Craft, 2003; Hill & Taylor, 2004). Parents' involvement in school is also associated with better social skills and fewer behavioral problems among their children (Kohl et al., 2000; Marcon, 1999). Parents with less education are typically less involved in their children's education than highly educated parents are, yet they can have a greater effect on their children's grades if they become involved (Bogenschneider, 1997; Downey, 2002).

In a comfortable and task-oriented classroom, children are motivated to learn.

MAKING INTEGRATION AND INCLUSION WORK

For many minority students of the past, especially African Americans, additional barriers to school success were created by school segregation. Black children in many states were forced to attend "black schools" that were clearly inferior to "white schools." In its landmark decision in the case of *Brown v. Board of Education of Topeka* in 1954, the Supreme Court ruled that segregated schools were "inherently unequal" and declared that they must be desegregated. More than 50 years have passed since this ruling. What has been learned about desegregation during this time?

In general, the effects of school integration on children's racial attitudes, self-esteem, and school achievement have been mixed (Gray-Little & Carels, 1997; Rumberger & Palardy, 2005). Some studies suggest that both African American and European American children tend to have higher self-esteem and higher achievement when they attend racially mixed schools, but the effects are often small (Gray-Little & Carels, 1997). White prejudice toward black students often does not decrease much. The self-esteem of black children in integrated schools is only sometimes higher than that of black children in racially homogeneous schools (Gray-Little & Carels, 1997). And although minority students sometimes achieve more in integrated schools, especially if they begin to attend them early in their academic careers, school integration often has little effect on achievement (Rossell, Armor, & Walberg, 2002).

What seems to be more important than a school's racial composition is the socioeconomic status of its students. Russell Rumberger and Gregory Palardy (2005) examined over 14,000 students attending 913 different high schools to determine the school factors that affect students' academic achievement. They found that, regardless of a student's race or the ratio of different racial groups attending the school, students achieved at higher levels when they attended schools with students from higher socioeconomic backgrounds than when they attended with students from low socioeconomic backgrounds (see also Ryabov & van Hook, 2007). Importantly, it didn't matter whether the individual student's background was poor or affluent: attending a school with affluent peers benefited students from all economic backgrounds. In particular, the connection between socioeconomic status of the students attending a school and achievement levels of the students was determined by four school practices: (1) teachers' expectations about students' abilities to learn; (2) average amount of homework that was assigned; (3) average number of advanced courses taken by students; and (4)

percentage of students who reported feeling unsafe at school (p. 2016).

The message from this research is not that integration has been unsuccessful. The message is that desegregation alone will not improve academic achievement if other school factors are not addressed. School safety, availability of advanced courses, homework assignment, and teacher expectations need to be addressed regardless of what is done to continue the 50-year-old struggle to desegregate schools.

© Richard Hutchings/PhotoEdit

Finally, characteristics of the student and characteristics of the school environment often interact to affect student outcome. This is an example of the concept of goodness of fit—an appropriate match between the person's characteristics and her environment (see Chapter 11). Much educational research has been based on the assumption that one teaching method, organizational system, or philosophy of education will prove superior for all students, regardless of their ability levels, learning styles, personalities, and cultural backgrounds. This assumption is often wrong. Instead, many educational practices are highly effective with some kinds of students but ineffective with other students. The secret is to find an appropriate match between the learner and the teaching method.

In a good illustration of goodness of fit between learners and environments, highly achievement-oriented students adapt well to unstructured classrooms in which they have a

good deal of choice, whereas less achievement-oriented students often do better with more structure (Peterson, 1977). Sometimes an alternative teaching method works as well as a traditional one for highly capable students but only one of these methods suits less capable students. In one study, for example, highly distractible students got more from computer-assisted instruction than from a teacher's presentation of the same material, whereas more attentive students benefited equally from both methods (Orth & Martin, 1994). Finally, students tend to have more positive outcomes when they and their teacher share similar backgrounds (Goldwater & Nutt, 1999). Evidence of the importance of the fit between student and classroom environment implies that educational programs are likely to be most effective when they are highly individualized—tailored to suit each student's developmental competencies and needs.

Children with developmental disabilities (mental retardation, learning disabilities, physical and sensory handicaps, and other special learning needs) have had a similar history (Ferri & Connor, 2005). They used to be placed in separate schools or classrooms—or, in some cases, rejected as unteachable by the public schools. But the Individuals with Disabilities Education Act (an extension of the 1975 Education for All Handicapped Children Act) requires schools to provide such children with a free and appropriate education that occurs "to the maximum extent appropriate. . . . with children who are not disabled."

What has been achieved? Studies of developmentally disabled children integrated into regular classrooms through a practice called **inclusion** (formerly called *mainstreaming*)—to emphasize the philosophy that children with special learning needs should spend the entire school day rather than only parts of it in a regular classroom and truly be included in the normal educational process—have yielded mixed results. Compared with similar students who attend segregated special education classes, these mainstreamed youngsters sometimes fare better in terms of academic performance, self-esteem, and social adjustment but sometimes do not (Buysse & Bailey, 1993; Hunt & Goetz, 1997; Manset & Semmel, 1997). The outcome depends partly on the severity of the child's disability. The performance of higher-functioning disabled children often benefits from inclusion in the regular classroom, whereas the performance of lower-functioning children is similar in integrated and segregated classrooms (Holahan & Costenbader, 2000).

In terms of peer acceptance, children with severe disabilities are better accepted by their normally developing peers than are children with mild disabilities in regular classrooms, where those with more severe disabilities presumably stand out as different, prompting other students to adjust their expectations (Cook & Semmel, 1999). Children with mild disabilities may not stand out in the regular classroom and therefore do not achieve "special" status; these children are better accepted in heterogeneous classrooms that include a wide range of abilities including children with mild and moderate disabilities (Cook & Semmel, 1999). Overall, though, children with disabilities often remain stigmatized and invisible in the regular classroom (Books, 2007).

What researchers seem to be learning about both racial integration and inclusion is that simply putting diverse students into the same schools and classrooms accomplishes little. Instead, something special must be done to ensure that students of different ethnic backgrounds and ability levels interact in positive ways and learn what they are supposed to be learning.

One promising model uses **cooperative learning,** in which diverse students are assigned to work teams and are reinforced for performing well as a team (Salend, 1999; Slavin, 1986; Stevens & Slavin; 1995). Consider research conducted by Uri Treisman at the University of California at Berkeley in the 1970s (Fullilove & Treisman, 1990). Treisman studied African Americans and Asian Americans enrolled in first-year calculus. The Asian Americans did well in the class, whereas the

African Americans performed poorly. But this was not the only difference between the two groups of students. The African American students worked independently on work related to the class; the Asian Americans worked in small study groups and often combined studying with socializing, something the African American students rarely did. Treisman decided to see whether working together and receiving support from peers could boost the African American students' performance—it did (see also Duncan & Dick, 2000).

In cooperative learning classrooms, children of different races and ability levels interact in a context where, ideally, the efforts of even the least capable team members are important to the group's success. Typically developing elementary-school students like school better and learn more when they participate in cooperative learning groups than when they receive traditional instruction, although the brightest children may sometimes experience frustration if the ability range of the group is quite large (Johnson, Johnson, & Maruyama, 1983; O'Donnell & O'Kelly, 1994; Stevens & Slavin, 1995). Moreover, team members gain self-esteem from their successes, and minority students and students with developmental disabilities are more fully accepted by their peers. In short, racial integration and inclusion can succeed if educators deliberately design learning experiences that encourage students from different backgrounds to pool their efforts to achieve common goals. Interventions such as this are important if children are to be ready for the challenges of secondary school.

SUMMING UP

▌ During childhood, some children develop higher levels of achievement motivation than others; they tend to have mastery-oriented rather than helpless attribution styles, and they set learning goals rather than performance goals in the classroom.

▌ To read, children must master the alphabetic principle and develop phonological awareness so that they can grasp letter–sound correspondence rules. Emergent literacy activities such as listening to storybooks facilitate later reading. Compared with unskilled readers, skilled readers have better understanding of the alphabetic principle and greater phonological awareness.

▌ A school's effectiveness is not influenced much by financial support, class size, time spent in school, or use of ability grouping. Instead, students perform best when (1) they are intellectually

capable and motivated; (2) their teachers create an effective learning environment; and (3) there is a good fit between children's characteristics and the kind of instruction they receive.

CRITICAL THINKING

1. Using the material on effective schools, evaluate your high school and indicate ways it could improve to become a highly effective school.

2. What are the advantages and disadvantages of grouping children by ability versus grouping them by age in the classroom?

3. Unlike most of his peers, Johnny, age 7, is not yet reading despite having the usual classroom instruction. What might account for Johnny's trouble with reading?

Adolescents make critical decisions about such matters as how much time to devote to studying, whether to work part-time after school, whether to go to college, and what to be when they grow up. They become more capable of making these educational and vocational choices as their cognitive and social skills expand; in turn, the choices they make shape their development. But many of them lose interest in school when they leave elementary school.

Declining Levels of Achievement

You might think that adolescents would become more dedicated to academic success once they begin to realize that they need a good education to succeed in life. But consider what Deborah Stipek (1984, p. 153) concluded after reviewing studies on the development of achievement motivation from early childhood to adolescence:

> On the average, children value academic achievement more as they progress through school, but their expectations for success and self-perceptions of competence decline, and their affect toward school becomes more negative. Children also become increasingly concerned about achievement outcomes and reinforcement (e.g., high grades) associated with positive outcomes and less concerned about intrinsic satisfaction in achieving greater competence.

Many of the negative trends Stipek describes become especially apparent as young adolescents make the transition from elementary school to middle school (typically grades 6 to 8) or junior high school (grades 7 to 9). At this critical juncture, achievement motivation, self-esteem, and grades may all decline.
■ **Figure 10.4** shows the academic trajectories for four groups of students studied by Leslie Gutman and his colleagues: those with high and low IQ scores who had either many or few risk factors (Gutman, Sameroff, & Cole, 2003). Risk factors included minority group status, low maternal education and mental health, stressful life events, family size, and father absence. Students with more risk factors showed a steady decline in academic achievement throughout their schooling, regardless of whether they had high or low IQ scores to begin with. Students with few risk factors showed a slight increase in achievement until around grade 6 or 7, at which time achievement began to drop slowly.

What might explain these discouraging trends? To answer this question, we'll first examine what is going on at the individual level, and then consider family and peer influences before ending with a look at the wider context of school and society.

At this individual level, children become increasingly capable of analyzing the causes of events, interpreting feedback from teachers, and inferring enduring traits such as high or low ability from their behavior (Stipek & Mac Iver, 1989). The result is that they view their strengths and weaknesses more realistically—and lose some of their high academic self-esteem and high expectancies of success (Stipek & Mac Iver, 1989; Wigfield et al., 1997). Those who manage to maintain an emphasis on mastery or learning goals attain higher grades in high school than those who do not (Gutman, 2006). Students who believe that success is a matter of luck have lower grades than students without this attributional style (House, 2006).

By adolescence, some students have little motivation to achieve in the classroom.

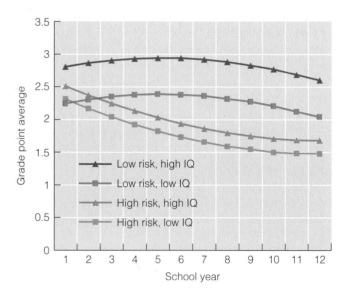

■ **FIGURE 10.4** Grade point average from 1st grade to 12th grade for students with high and low risk and IQ.
SOURCE: From L.M. Gutman, A.J. Samereroff, & R. Cole, Academic growth curve trajectories from 1st grade to 12th grade: Effects of multiple social risk factors and preschool child factors, *Developmental Psychology, 39*, pp. 777–790. Copyright © 2003 by the American Psychological Association. Reprinted with permission from the American Psychological Association.

At the family level, several characteristics are associated with lower achievement and greater absences from school. Being a member of a minority group, growing up in a single-parent family, and having a mother with less education or with mental health problems are potential academic risk factors (Gutman, Sameroff, & Eccles, 2002; Gutman, Sameroff, & Cole, 2003). In contrast, living in a small, caring family with a stable parent who uses consistent discipline can bolster school performance (Gutman, Sameroff, & Eccles, 2002). Mothers who talk to their middle-school children about assuming responsibility and making decisions have teens who are more likely to complete high school and continue their education (Tenenbaum et al., 2007). Adolescents who believe their parents are more involved in their schooling are generally more motivated toward school than adolescents who believe their parents are less involved (Spera, 2006). Importantly, it is the students' *perceptions* of parental involvement and not actual involvement that is related to motivation levels.

The adolescent's achievement motivation is also affected by the increasing importance of the peer group, which at times can undermine parents' and teachers' efforts to encourage school achievement. Many years ago, when James Coleman (1961) asked high school students how they would like to be remembered, only 31% of the boys and 28% of the girls wanted to be remembered as bright students. They were more concerned with having the athletic and social skills that lead to popularity. Not much has changed. Tim Urdan and Miranda Mestas (2006) interviewed high school seniors about their reasons for pursuing performance goals. Many of the responses indicated that teens were motivated by a desire to avoid looking dumb or to look competent and make their parents proud. But some of the students specifically noted that they wanted to be average and not appear to be too smart. As one student said, "I just want to be normal, not the best. I don't want to be the worst but I just want to be normal" (p. 361).

Peer pressures that undermine achievement motivation tend to be especially strong for many lower-income minority students. In particular, African American and Hispanic peer cultures in many low-income areas actively discourage academic achievement, whereas European American and especially Asian American peer groups tend to value and encourage it (Steinberg, Dornbusch, & Brown, 1992). High-achieving African American students in some inner-city schools risk being rejected by their African American peers if their academic accomplishments cause them to be perceived as "acting white" (Fordham & Ogbu, 1986). They may feel that they have to abandon their cultural group and racial identity to succeed in school, and this takes a psychological toll (Arroyo & Zigler, 1995; Ogbu, 2003). Alternatively, some may disengage from academics to preserve their cultural identity with a group that has historically placed less emphasis on academics (Ogbu, 2003). Although African American parents are as likely as European American parents to value education and to provide the kind of authoritative parenting that encourages school achievement, their positive influences are sometimes canceled out by negative peer influences (Steinberg, Dornbusch, & Brown, 1992).

For those African American teens who belong to a supportive peer group, academic achievement is strengthened (Gutman, Sameroff, & Eccles, 2002). In addition, African American teens who strongly value their ethnic group membership and have positive beliefs about how society views African Americans tend to have more positive beliefs about education (Chavous et al., 2003).

Finally, we must consider that some of the decline in the achievement motivation of adolescents may reflect a poor fit between person and environment. Adopting a goodness-of-fit explanation, Jacquelynne Eccles and her colleagues (Eccles, Lord, & Midgley, 1991; Eccles, Midgley, et al., 1993) argue that the transition to middle school or junior high school is likely to be especially difficult because young adolescents are often experiencing major physical and psychological changes at the time they are switching schools. For example, girls who were reaching puberty when they were moving from sixth grade in an elementary school to seventh grade in a junior high school were more likely to experience drops in self-esteem and other negative changes than girls who remained in a K–8 school during this vulnerable period (Simmons & Blyth, 1987).

Could it be that more adolescents would remain interested in school if they did not have to change schools when they are experiencing pubertal changes? This idea became an important part of the rationale for middle schools (grades 6 to 8), which were developed to make the transition from elementary school to high school easier for early adolescents (Braddock & McPartland, 1993). Yet Eccles and her colleagues (1991, 1993) have shown that students do not necessarily find the transition to middle school any easier than the transition to junior high school. These researchers suspect that when adolescents make a school change is less important than what their new school is like.

The transition to middle school or junior high school often involves going from a small school with close student–teacher relationships, a good deal of choice regarding learning activities, and reasonable discipline to a larger, more bureaucratized environment in which student–teacher relationships are impersonal, good grades are more emphasized but harder to come by, opportunities for choice are limited, assignments are not as intellectually stimulating, and discipline is rigid—all when adolescents are seeking more rather than less autonomy and are becoming more rather than less intellectually capable. Students who had what Carol Dweck calls learning goals in elementary school perceive an increased emphasis on performance goals when they move to middle school (Anderman & Midgley, 1997).

Eccles and her colleagues have demonstrated that the fit between developmental needs and school environment is an important influence on adolescent adjustment to school. In one study (Mac Iver & Reuman, 1988), the transition to junior high school brought about a decline in intrinsic motivation to learn mainly among students who wanted more involvement in classroom decisions but ended up with fewer such opportunities than they had in elementary school. In another study (Midgley, Feldlaufer, & Eccles, 1989), students experienced negative changes in their attitudes toward mathematics only when their move from elementary school to junior high resulted in less personal and supportive relationships with math teachers. For those few students whose junior high school teachers were more supportive than those they had in elementary school, interest in academics increased.

The message? Declines in academic motivation and performance are not inevitable during early adolescence. Students may indeed form more realistic expectancies of success as their growing cognitive abilities allow them to use the increasingly informative feedback they receive from teachers. Experiencing pubertal changes at the same time as other stressful changes and needing to downplay academics to gain popularity may also hurt school achievement. However, educators can help keep adolescents engaged in school by creating school environments that provide a better fit to the developmental needs and interests of adolescents. Whether they are called middle schools or junior high schools, such schools should provide warm, supportive relationships with teachers, intellectual challenges, and increased opportunities for self-direction (Eccles, Midgley, et al., 1993). Specially designed school transition programs can help students adjust to high school and reduce the risk that they will drop out (Smith, 1997).

Science and Mathematics Education

Elementary schools necessarily spend much time on reading and writing skills. But secondary-school teachers take these skills largely for granted and focus energy on other academic areas. More advanced skills of concrete-operational and then formal-operational thought enable children to tackle more challenging academic tasks. Much attention has been focused on mathematics and science, skills important for success in many industrialized nations. How well do secondary-school students perform in science and math? And how might achievement in these areas be optimized?

● **Table 10.6** shows average mathematics and science achievement test scores of eighth-grade students in various countries. Students in the United States score above the international average but significantly below achievement levels in nations such as Singapore, Japan, and Korea. When researchers looked at the best students—those in the top 10% of all eighth-graders surveyed in the 38 nations—only 9% of U.S. students met the criteria in math and only 15% met it in science. In comparison, the nation with the largest percentage of students in the top 10% was Singapore, with 46% in math and 32% in science. What might account for these international differences in math and science achievement? Are students in some nations simply more intelligent than students in other nations?

Cross-cultural research conducted by Harold Stevenson and his colleagues (Chen & Stevenson, 1995; Stevenson & Lee, 1990; Stevenson, Chen, & Lee, 1993) shows that American schoolchildren perform about as well on IQ tests as their Asian counterparts when they enter school (Stevenson et al., 1985). They score at least as well as Japanese and Chinese students on tests of general information not typically covered in

school (Stevenson, Chen, & Lee, 1993). Instead, the achievement gap between American and Asian students seems to be rooted in cultural differences in attitudes concerning education and educational practices. Here is what some of this cross-cultural research on education and achievement shows:

- Asian students spend more time being educated. Elementary-school teachers in Asian countries devote more class time to academics. The classroom is a business-like place where little time is wasted; Asian students spend about 95% of their time "on task" (in activities such as listening to the teacher and completing assignments), whereas American students spend only about 80% of their time "on task" (Stigler, Lee, & Stevenson, 1987). Asian students also attend school for more hours per day and more days per year (Stevenson, Lee, & Stigler, 1986).
- Teachers have different approaches to instruction. For instance, in China, more time in the math classroom is spent on extended discourse in which the teacher continues to question and discuss students' correct answers (Schleppenbach et al., 2007). In contrast, teachers in U.S. math classrooms tend to move on to the next problem once a student has given a correct answer.
- Asian students, especially Japanese students, are assigned and complete considerably more homework than American students (Verma & Larson, 2003). When American students are working or socializing with friends, Asian students are hitting the books (Fuligni & Stevenson, 1995).
- Asian parents are strongly committed to the educational process. About 40% think their children should have 3 hours or more of homework each day (Ebbeck, 1996). Asian parents are rarely satisfied with how their children are doing in school or with the quality of education their children are receiving; American parents seem to settle for less (Mathews, 2003). Asian parents also receive frequent communications from their children's teachers in notebooks children carry to and from school each day. They find out how their children are progressing and follow teachers' suggestions for encouraging and assisting their children at home (Stevenson & Lee, 1990).
- Asian peers also value school achievement and have high standards; time spent with peers often involves doing homework rather than engaging in activities that interfere with homework (Chen & Stevenson, 1995). Asian high school students report doing about a half hour more homework each night than high school students from other racial/ethnic groups (Ferguson, 2002).
- Asian parents, teachers, and students all share a strong belief that hard work or effort will pay off in better academic performance (that is, they set what Dweck calls learning goals), whereas Americans tend to put more emphasis on ability as a cause of good or poor performance. The result may be that Americans give up too quickly on a child who appears to have low intellectual ability. In doing so, they may help create a case of learned helplessness.

● TABLE 10.6   AVERAGE MATHEMATICS AND SCIENCE ACHIEVEMENT OF EIGHTH-GRADE STUDENTS IN VARIOUS NATIONS (2003 SCORES)

MATHEMATICS		SCIENCE	
Singapore	605	Singapore	578
Republic of Korea	589	Chinese Taipei	571
Hong Kong SAR	586	Republic of Korea	558
Chinese Taipei	585	Hong Kong SAR	556
Japan	570	Japan	552
Canada (Quebec Province)	543	England	544
Russian Federation	508	Netherlands	536
Australia	505	Canada (Quebec Province)	531
United States	504	Australia	527
Lithuania	502	United States	527
England	498	Slovenia	520
New Zealand	494	New Zealand	520
Italy	484	Russian Federation	514
Serbia	477	Italy	491
Romania	475	INTERNATIONAL AVERAGE FOR SCIENCE	474
INTERNATIONAL AVERAGE FOR MATH	467	Romania	470
Egypt	406	Chile	413
Chile	387	Philippines	377
South Africa	264	South Africa	244

☐ Average is significantly higher than the U.S. average

▨ Average does not differ significantly from the U.S. average

▨ Average is significantly lower than the U.S. average

SOURCE: From Martin, et al. (2004). *TIMSS 2003 international science report: Findings from IEA's repeat of the third international mathematics and science study at the eighth grade.* Exhibit 1.1. Chestnut Hill, MA: Boston College, Figure 2. Reprinted with permission.

This cross-cultural research carries an important message: The secret of effective education is to get teachers, students, and parents working together to make education the top priority for youth, to set high achievement goals, and to invest the day-by-day effort required to attain those goals. Many states and local school districts have begun to respond to evidence that American schools are being outclassed by schools in other countries by strengthening curricula, tightening standards for teacher certification, and raising standards for graduation and promotion from grade to grade.

Integrating Work and School

Unlike teens in many other industrialized nations, a sizable number (between one-third and one-half) of teens in the United States and Canada work part-time during their high school careers (Bachman et al., 2003; Thomas, 1998). How do these early work experiences affect their development and, in particular, their school achievement?

Laurence Steinberg and his associates have compared working and nonworking high school students in terms of such outcomes as autonomy from parents, self-reliance, self-esteem, sense of investment in school, academic performance, delinquency, and drug and alcohol use (Greenberger & Steinberg, 1986; Steinberg & Dornbusch, 1991; Steinberg, Fegley, & Dornbusch, 1993). Overall, this research offers more bad news than good. The good news is that working students seem to gain knowledge about work, consumer issues, and financial management and sometimes about greater self-reliance. However, high school students who worked 20 or more hours a week had lower grade-point averages than those of students who did not work or who worked only 10 or fewer hours per week (Steinberg & Dornbusch, 1991). Working students were also more likely than nonworkers to be disengaged from school—bored and uninvolved in class and prone to cut class and spend little time on homework.

In addition, the more adolescents worked, the more independent they were of parental control, the more likely they were to be experiencing psychological distress (anxiety, depression, and physical symptoms such as headaches), and the more frequently they used alcohol and drugs and engaged in delinquent acts. These negative effects of work generally increased as the number of hours a student worked increased.

Jerald Bachman and his colleagues (2003) have found that not-yet-employed students who want to work long hours tend to be disenchanted with school, have low grades, and are more likely to use alcohol and cigarettes. Once they start working, the disenchantment and problem behaviors are exacerbated (Bachman et al., 2003; Steinberg, Fegley, & Dornbusch, 1993). Similarly, longitudinal research on adolescents and work confirms that academically struggling students are the ones likely to work more hours (Warren, LePore, & Marc, 2000). Kusum Singh and Mehmet Ozturk (2000) reached a similar conclusion from their research on employment during high school and performance in mathematics and science courses. They found that students with low achievement in science and math were more likely to work part-time than students with high achievement in these courses. Working reduced the number of math and science courses that students enrolled in. Ultimately, students who work during high school may limit their future educational and vocational prospects by limiting their exposure to potentially important coursework.

Not all research findings are this discouraging. Jeylen Mortimer and his colleagues (1996) also conducted a longitudinal study of high school students but controlled for differences between working and nonworking students on factors such as family background and prior academic performance. In their study, working 20 hours or more a week did not hurt academic achievement, self-esteem, or psychological adjustment once other factors were controlled. Students who worked 1 to 20 hours a week actually earned better grades than either nonworkers or students who worked more than 20 hours a week. As in Steinberg's study, however, students who worked more than 20 hours used alcohol more frequently than students who were not employed.

When all the research is examined as a package, the findings suggest that working while attending high school is often more damaging than beneficial (Marsh & Kleitman, 2005). Much depends on the nature of the work adolescents do. Many teenagers work in food service jobs (pouring soft drinks behind the counter at fast-food restaurants, scooping ice cream, and the like) or perform manual labor (especially cleaning or janitorial work). These routine and repetitive jobs offer few opportunities for self-direction or decision making and only rarely call on academic skills such as reading and mathematics (Greenberger & Steinberg, 1986). They are not the kinds of jobs that build character or teach new skills. Adolescents experience gains in mastery motivation and become less depressed over time when the work they do provides opportunities for advancement and teaches useful skills, but they lose mastery motivation and become more depressed when they hold menial job that interfere with their schooling (Call, Mortimer, & Shanahan, 1995; Shanahan et al., 1991). Thus, many adolescents who are flipping hamburgers might be better off postponing work or working only a limited number of hours so that they can concentrate on obtaining a solid education and exploring their career options (Greenberger & Steinberg, 1986).

Working in fast-food restaurants is not the kind of intellectually challenging work that can contribute positively to adolescent development.

Pathways to Adulthood

The educational paths and attainments of adolescents are partially set long before they enter adolescence. Because many individuals' IQ test scores remain stable from childhood on, some children enter adolescence with more aptitude for schoolwork than others do (see Chapter 9). Moreover, some students have more achievement motivation than others. Clearly, a bright and achievement-oriented student is more likely to obtain good grades and go on to college and is less likely to drop out of school than a student with less ability and less need to achieve. By early elementary school, and sometimes even before they enter school, future dropouts are often identifiable by such warning signs as low IQ and achievement test scores, poor grades, aggressive behavior, low socioeconomic status, and troubled homes (Ensminger & Slusarcick, 1992; Gamoran et al., 1997).

This does not mean that adolescents' fates are sealed in childhood, however; experiences during adolescence clearly make a difference. Some teenagers make the most of their intellectual abilities, whereas others who have the ability to do well in school drop out or get poor grades. The quality of an adolescent's school, the extent to which her parents are authoritative and encourage school achievement, and the extent to which her peers value school can make a big difference (Brown et al., 1993; Rutter et al., 1979; Steinberg, Dornbusch, & Brown, 1992).

The stakes are high. Students who achieve good grades are more likely to complete high school; recently, 92% of European American students, 86% of African American students, 85% of Asian Americans, and an alarmingly low 70% of Hispanic students achieved this milestone (National Center for Education Statistics, 2007). They then stand a chance of being among the 30% of European American, 17% of African American, 49% of Asian Americans, and 11% of Hispanics who complete 4 years of college or more (U.S. Census Bureau, 2007). These youth, in turn, are likely to have higher career aspirations and to end up in higher status occupations than their peers who do not attend college or do not even finish high school (McCaul et al., 1992). If their grades are good, they are likely to perform well in those jobs and advance far in their careers (Roth et al., 1996). In a real sense, then, individuals are steered along "high success" or "low success" routes starting in childhood. Depending on their own decisions and family, peer, and school influences, adolescents are more distinctly "sorted" in ways that will affect their adult lifestyles, income levels, and adjustment. Meanwhile, high school dropouts not only have less successful careers but also miss out on the beneficial effects that every year of schooling has on intellectual functioning (Ceci & Williams, 1997). In addition, they experience more psychological problems than those who stay in school (Kaplan, Damphousse, & Kaplan, 1994).

SUMMING UP

▪ Achievement motivation tends to decline as children move into middle school and high school. Various factors may account for this, including family characteristics, cognitive development, more negative teacher feedback, peer pressures, puberty, and poor person–environment fit.

▪ Middle school and high school include a greater focus on science and mathematics education. U.S. students score close to the international average but below several other countries in math and science. Cross-cultural research suggests that the success of Asian schools is rooted in more class time spent on academics, more homework, more parent involvement, more peer support, and a stronger belief that hard work pays off.

CRITICAL THINKING

1. Research shows that achievement motivation and grades often drop as students move through middle school and high school. Develop a program to combat this trend, keeping in mind that students of different backgrounds may lose motivation for different reasons.

2. After finishing up ninth grade, your teenager says he wants to work for the next 3 years while in high school. What advice will you give him?

10.5 | THE ADULT

The lives of adults are dominated by work—paid or unpaid, outside the home or within the home. What becomes of achievement motivation and literacy during the adult years? What educational options are available to adults, and what are the benefits of lifelong education?

Achievement Motivation

The level of achievement motivation that we acquire in childhood and adolescence carries into adulthood to influence our decisions and life outcomes (Wlodkowski, 1999). For instance, women who have a strong need to achieve are more likely than less achievement-oriented women to work outside the home (Krogh, 1985). Adults with strong achievement needs are also likely to be more competent workers than adults who have little concern with mastering challenges (Helmreich, Sawin, & Carsrud, 1986; Spence, 1985).

What happens to achievement motivation in later life? Is there any support for the common belief that older adults lose some of their drive to excel? Joseph Veroff, David Reuman, and Sheila Feld (1984) explored this question by analyzing motivational themes in stories that American adults told in response to pictures. Older men displayed only slightly lower levels of achievement motivation than young or middle-aged men did. Here, then, there is no support for the stereotyped idea that older adults are "unmotivated" or have ceased to pursue goals (Filipp, 1996; McAdams, de St. Aubin, & Logan, 1993).

Veroff and his associates (1984) did find that women's achievement motivation declined fairly steeply with age (see also Mellinger & Erdwins, 1985). However, this age trend pertained mainly to career-related motivation and an interest in striving for success in competitive situations. Women's motivation in other areas remains high. Many women set aside career-achievement goals after they have children and make nurturing those children their priority (Krogh, 1985). However, highly educated women often regain a strong motive to achieve outside the home once their children are older and they can invest more energy in outside work. Apparently, then, women are especially likely to be motivated to achieve career success when they have the educational background that would allow them

Many older adults remain motivated to learn and seek challenging experiences.

© Ian Shaw/Alamy

to pursue attractive career goals and when they are not pursuing family-related goals.

Overall, adults' achievement-related motives are far more affected by changes in work and family contexts than by the aging process (Filipp, 1996). Adults of different ages are often more alike than they are different, and different people tend to retain their characteristic levels of achievement motivation over the years, much as they retain many personality traits (Stevens & Truss, 1985). There is little evidence that elderly adults inevitably lose their motivation to pursue important goals. Moreover, those elders who have a strong sense of purpose and direction and feel they are achieving their goals enjoy greater physical and psychological well-being than those who do not (Hooker & Siegler, 1993; Rapkin & Fischer, 1992; Reker, Peacock, & Wong, 1987). Throughout the life span, then, setting and achieving goals are important.

Literacy

Literacy is the ability to use printed information to function in society, achieve goals, and develop one's potential (National Center for Education Statistics, 2007). Few adults are completely illiterate, but many adults do not have functional literacy skills despite years of formal education. The National Adult Literacy Survey reports that about 14% of adults in the United States demonstrate the lowest level of literacy skills, which is roughly equivalent to a third-grade or lower reading ability. Such an adult could probably find an expiration date on a driver's license and sign a form but would have trouble filling out an application or reading a simple book to a child. Al-

though one-quarter of this group consists of immigrants learning English as a second language, most individuals in this group are U.S.-born citizens and nearly two-thirds did not finish high school. Another 29% of adults have just rudimentary, or basic, literacy skills, allowing them to perform simple literacy tasks such as using a television guide or comparing prices on two receipts, but limiting their abilities to consult reference information online or in texts (National Center for Education Statistics, 2007). Only 13% of adults demonstrate proficient levels of literacy. When the U.S. literacy rate is compared with rates in other countries, researchers find that the United States has one of the largest pockets of illiterate adults but also has some of the most highly literate adults (U.S. Department of Education, 1997). Thus, literacy in the United States is unevenly distributed.

Literacy contributes to economic security through occupational advancement. Nearly half of the adults with the lowest literacy scores live in poverty, whereas few adults with the highest literacy scores do (Bowen, 1999). Improving the literacy skills of impoverished adults, however, does not automatically raise them out of poverty. For many low-income and functionally illiterate adults, other obstacles must be overcome, including addiction, discrimination, and disabilities (Bowen, 1999).

Programs to raise the literacy level of adults are rarely successful. Several factors limit the success of such programs. For one thing, despite having limited literacy skills, many of these adults (75%) reported that they could read or write "well" or "very well"—attitudes that must make it difficult to motivate them to improve their literacy skills. Second, adults do not stay in literacy programs long enough to make improvements (Amstutz & Sheared, 2000). The dropout rate is as high as 70 to 80%, and many leave in the first weeks of the program (Quigley & Uhland, 2000). Adults who do not persist report that the programs are boring and do not meet their needs (Imel, 1996; Kerka, 1995; Quigley, 1997). Materials, for example, are often geared toward children, not adults who often have families, jobs, and different interests than children do.

Continuing Education

Increasingly, adults are seeking education beyond basic literacy skills. Nearly 40% of college students are 25 years or older, representing 15 million adults enrolled in college (National Center for Education Statistics, 1998). The number of "older" adults attending college is expected to increase as the overall population ages. Whether we call them adult learners, nontraditionals, returning students, mature students, or lifelong learners, these adults represent a diverse group. They bring different work and life experiences to the classroom, and they report a variety of reasons for enrolling in postsecondary education (Kopka & Peng, 1993).

Many "traditional" students (17- to 24-year-olds) are motivated to attend college by external expectations, but older stu-

WHAT CAN THEORY AND RESEARCH CONTRIBUTE TO EDUCATION?

To help you appreciate the practical implications for school reform and school achievement of the material in Chapters 6 through 9, we provide the following recommendations based on the research and theories discussed in these chapters.

Piaget

- Provide opportunities for independent, hands-on interaction with the physical environment, especially for younger children. Children need to "see" for themselves how things work and from this construct their own understanding of the world.
- Be aware of children's cognitive strengths and limitations (their stage of development). For example, teachers and parents should recognize that a preoperational child is cognitively unable to master multi-dimensional or abstract tasks.
- With the child's current level of understanding in mind, create some disequilibrium by presenting new information slightly above the child's current level. Children who experience disequilibrium—cognitive discomfort with their understanding (or lack of understanding)—will work to resolve it, achieving a higher level of mastery of the material.
- Encourage interaction with peers, which will expose children to other perspectives and give them an opportunity to reevaluate and revise their own view.
- Connect abstract ideas to concrete information as much as possible.

Vygotsky

- Provide opportunities for children to interact with others who have greater mastery of the material—an older peer, teacher, or parent. These more advanced thinkers can help "pull" children to a level of understanding they would be unable to achieve on their own.
- Encourage students, especially young ones, to talk to themselves as they work on difficult tasks. Such private speech can guide behavior and facilitate thought.
- Present challenging tasks, but do not expect students to complete such tasks successfully without guidance. With support, students can accomplish more difficult tasks than those they would be able to achieve independently.
- Help children master the cognitive tools of their culture—writing, computers, and so on—so that they can function successfully in the culture.

Research on Information Processing

- Provide opportunities for rehearsal and other memory strategies to move information into long-term memory. Realize that young children do not spontaneously use memory strategies but can use them when prompted.
- Structure assignments so that retrieval cues are consistent with cues present at acquisition to facilitate retrieval of information from long-term memory.
- Enable learners to develop some knowledge base and expertise in domains of study. This means presenting "facts and figures" through readings, lectures, observations, and other appropriate methods. When beginning a new lesson, start with and build on what students already know.
- Assess the knowledge and strategies required to solve assigned problems; then determine which aspects of a task pose difficulties for learners and target these for further instruction.

- Be aware that well-learned and frequently repeated tasks become automatized over time, freeing information-processing capacity for other tasks. For example, reading is labor intensive for those new to the task, but with practice, the process of reading becomes "invisible" and learners focus their processing resources on other aspects of the task.

Research on Intelligence

- Realize that individual differences in intelligence have implications for the classroom. Students at both ends of the continuum may need special educational services to optimize their learning.
- Recognize that although IQ scores do a reasonably good job of predicting achievement in the classroom, such tests have weaknesses that limit their usefulness, especially in assessing members of minority groups.

Research on Sensory and Perceptual Abilities

- Test all children early and regularly for sensory and perceptual problems that might limit their ability to benefit from regular classroom instruction.
- Be aware of developmental differences in attention span. Clearly, a young child will not be able to attend to a task for as long as a teenager. Determine what "captures" students' attention at different ages.
- Minimize distractions in the learning environment. Younger students have trouble "tuning out" background noise and focusing on the task at hand.

dents are often motivated by internal factors (Dinmore, 1997). Women are more likely to return to the classroom for personal enrichment or interest, whereas men are more likely to take classes required or recommended for their work (Sargant et al., 1997). The internal motivation of adult students often leads to deeper levels of processing information (Harper & Kember, 1986). In other words, returning students may put forth greater effort to truly understand material because they want to learn and want (or need) to use the material. Traditional students who do not have the benefit of experience may learn the material necessary to do well on an examination but may not process the material in ways that will lead to long-term retention.

Continued or lifelong education has its drawbacks. Mainly, it is often difficult for adults already busy with jobs and family to find the time to take classes. Successful continuing education programs must devise ways to schedule classes at convenient times and must be responsive to the lifestyles of their adult learners (Parnham, 2001). Yet the benefits of lifelong education typically outweigh drawbacks. For instance, continued education allows adults to remain knowledgeable and competitive in fields that change rapidly. Adults who return to school for bachelor's or master's degrees can also advance their careers, particularly if their education and work are closely related (Senter & Senter, 1997). Finally, higher education is associated with maintaining or improving physical and mental health (Fischer, Blazey, & Lipman, 1992).

In this and previous chapters, you have examined a great deal of material on thinking and learning across the life span. How can principles of cognitive development be used to improve education for all ages? Before closing this chapter, we summarize, in the Applications box on page 305, what theorists Piaget and Vygotsky contribute to education and what research on information processing, intelligence, and perception suggests about optimal learning environments.

SUMMING UP

▍ Adults of different ages are similar in their levels of achievement motivation, although women who turn their attention to child rearing may lose some of their career-oriented achievement motivation.

▍ Some adults, despite years of education, have not acquired the skills of functional literacy. Literacy programs have had minimal success in improving literacy rates. Adults increasingly are seeking continued educational opportunities for both personal and work-related reasons.

CRITICAL THINKING

1. What are the advantages of maintaining high levels of achievement motivation throughout adulthood?

2. Based on what you have learned in this and previous chapters about memory, thinking, problem solving, and language skills, how would you teach older adult students versus students of traditional high school or college age?

CHAPTER SUMMARY

10.1 Mastering Language

- The complex process of language acquisition appears to occur effortlessly through an interaction of inborn readiness and a normal language environment.

- Over the first few years of life, children master many elements of language, including phonology, semantics, morphology, syntax, and pragmatics. Language skills are refined throughout childhood and adolescence. Most language abilities remain strong throughout adulthood.

10.2 The Infant

- Precursors of achievement motivation can be seen among infants who strive to master their environments. Opportunities to succeed are important for children of all ages. Without such opportunities, children are at risk for developing a learned helplessness orientation.

10.3 The Child

- Learning to read is typically an effortful process that relies on understanding the alphabetic principle and acquiring phonological awareness. There is a great deal of variability in reading ability among children and among adults.

- Effective schools are characterized by a focus on academics and a good fit between the learners and the instruction they receive. Student achievement is not strongly influenced by spending, class size, ability grouping, or length of the school day or year.

- Some students (for example, those from advantaged homes) typically outperform others, and some learning environments (especially those in which teachers create a motivating, comfortable, and task-oriented setting and involve parents in their children's schooling) are generally more conducive to learning than others. Still, what works best for one kind of student may not work as well for another kind of student.

10.4 The Adolescent

- Achievement motivation and grades tend to drop during adolescence for a variety of reasons, including cognitive growth, family characteristics, peer pressure, and a poor fit between the student and the school.

- Students from Asian cultures often outperform U.S. adolescents in mathematics and science, partly because they spend many more hours a week on homework and have parents and peers who highly value academics.

10.5 The Adult

- Level of achievement carries over from adolescence into adulthood. There may be some decline in achievement motivation among women who set aside career goals to raise children, but career goals reemerge as their children age, especially among women with higher levels of education.

- Some adults struggle with literacy, and some return to school.

KEY TERMS

language 277
phonemes 277
intonation 277
word segmentation 277
cooing 278
babbling 278
semantics 278
joint attention 278
holophrase 279
vocabulary spurt 279
overextension 279
underextension 279
telegraphic speech 280
syntax 280
functional grammar 280
morphology 280
overregularization 281
transformational grammar 281
pragmatics 281
decontextualized language 282

metalinguistic awareness 282
language acquisition device (LAD) 283
child-directed speech 285
expansion 285
mastery motivation 287
mastery orientation 289
learned helplessness orientation 289
learning goal 290
performance goal 290
alphabetic principle 291
phonological awareness 292
emergent literacy 292
dyslexia 293
ability grouping 294
inclusion 297
cooperative learning 297
literacy 304

MEDIA RESOURCES

BOOK COMPANION WEBSITE

academic.cengage.com/psychology/sigelman
Find online quizzes, flash cards, animations, video clips, experiments, interactive assessments, and other helpful study aids for this text at academic.cengage.com/psychology/sigelman. You can also connect directly to the following sites:

LANGUAGE DEVELOPMENT IN CHILDREN

A superb website for anyone interested in the pattern of language acquisition in childhood. Highlights include a great language development chart (age 6 months to 8 years) and an excellent set of links to other resources.

LITERACY RESOURCE GUIDE FOR FAMILIES AND EDUCATORS

This links to a pdf version of *Literacy Resource Guide for Families and Educators* (a publication of the Federation for Children with Special Needs Boston, Massachusetts). This 50-page publication contains an expansive amount of information and advice on reading and literacy.

PSI CAFÉ: LANGUAGE DEVELOPMENT AND READING

This Psi Café hosted site provides the visitor access to a wide variety of theoretical and practical information concerning the topics of language development and reading. Interesting links include one on second/multiple languages and an online test of reading.

READING AND YOUR CHILD

This University of Michigan Health Systems-hosted site does an amazing job of including both research findings and practical advice for improving reading in one place. This is a great place for parents or professionals to pick up tips on improving the reading skills in children. It also includes information on improving adult literacy.

UNDERSTANDING THE DATA: EXERCISES ON THE WEB

academic.cengage.com/psychology/sigelman
For additional insight on the data presented in this chapter, try out the exercises for these figures at academic.cengage.com/psychology/sigelman:

Figure 10.1 The range of individual differences in vocabulary size from 16 to 30 months

Figure 10.4 Grade point average from 1st grade to 12th grade for students with high and low risk and IQ

CENGAGENOW

academic.cengage.com/login
Go to academic.cengage.com/login to link to CengageNOW, your online study tool. First take the Pre-Test for this chapter to get your Personalized Study Plan, which will identify topics you need to review and direct you to online resources. Then take the Post-Test to determine what concepts you have mastered and what you still need work on.

Cary Wolinsky/Aurora Photos

11 Self and Personality

CHAPTER

FOR TOM CRUISE, childhood was a painful period; he was abused by his father, diagnosed as dyslexic, regularly beaten up by bullies. A turning point in his life came when his mother finally stood up to his father and divorced him, teaching Cruise this lesson: "People can create their own lives," he said. "I saw how my mother created hers and so made it possible for us to survive. . . . And I decided that I'm going to create, for myself, who I am, not what other people say I should be" (Rader, 2006, p. 7). After contemplating the priesthood, Cruise took a role in a student production at his high school, set off for New York, and in 2 years, at age 21, became a star when the film *Risky Business* became a big success. Now a father and happy with Katie Holmes after two failed marriages, Cruise says he defines happiness this way: "It's being able to confront and overcome problems. It's not running away but trying to see life in its full glory" (Rader, 2006, p. 8).

■ ■ ■

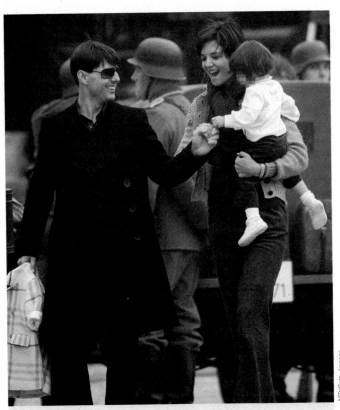

Tom Cruise and Katie Holmes.

AFP/Getty Images

11.1 | CONCEPTUALIZING THE SELF AND PERSONALITY

Personality is often defined as an organized combination of attributes, motives, values, and behaviors unique to each individual. Most people describe personalities in terms of relatively enduring personality traits such as sociability, independence, dominance, and so on. As you will see, though, there is more to personality than traits.

When you describe yourself, you may not be describing your personality so much as revealing your **self-concept**—your perceptions, positive or negative, of your unique attributes and traits as a person. We all know people who seem to have unrealistic self-conceptions—the fellow who thinks he is "God's gift to women" (who do not agree) or the woman who believes she is a dull plodder (but is actually brilliant). A closely related aspect of self-perception is **self-esteem**—your overall evaluation of your worth as a person, high or low, based on all the positive and negative self-perceptions that make up your self-concept. Self-concept is about "what I am," whereas self-esteem concerns "how good I am" (Harter, 1999). This chapter examines how self-concept and self-esteem change and remain the same over the life span. It also takes up the question of how adolescents pull together their various self-perceptions to form an **identity**—an overall sense of who they are, where they are heading, and where they fit into society.

Here is one human, Tom Cruise, putting together the life story that defines him as a unique person who overcame challenges to find out who he was. How would you tell your life story? Who are you, how have you changed over the years, and what do you think you will be like 20 years from now?

This chapter is about the self and the personality and the ways in which personalities, and perceptions of those personalities, change—and remain the same—over the life span. It is, in other words, about the issue of continuity (stability) and discontinuity (change) in human development (see Chapter 2). It is also about influences on and implications of our self-concepts and personalities. We begin by clarifying some terms and laying out key theoretical perspectives.

Principles of Personality Development

Dan McAdams and Jennifer Pals (2006) have outlined five principles that they believe define personality. They start with the assumption that each of us is in some ways like all other humans, in some ways like only some other humans (for example, the extraverts or the introverts), and in some ways unique. They suggest that to understand personality we must understand the following:

1. We all share a *human nature* that has been shaped by evolution and has helped humans adapt to their environments.

2. We differ from each other in **dispositional traits,** broad and relatively stable dimensions of personality such as extraversion–introversion along which humans differ in their thinking, feeling, and behavior.

3. We also differ in **characteristic adaptations,** more situation-specific and changeable ways in which people adapt to their roles and environments, including motives, goals, plans, schemas, self-conceptions, stage-specific concerns, and coping mechanisms.

4. We differ too in **narrative identities,** unique and integrative "life stories" that we construct about our pasts and futures to give ourselves an identity and our lives meaning.

5. *Cultural and situational influences* help shape all of these aspects of personality; they have their weakest effects on dispositional traits and strongest effects on narrative identities or life stories.

Personality, then, includes ways in which we are like all other people (human nature), like some other people (those with similar dispositional traits and characteristic adaptations), and like no one else on the planet (with our unique life stories), as influenced by cultural and situational factors. As McAdams and Pals sum it up, "Personality is an individual's unique variation on the general evolutionary design for human nature, expressed as a developing pattern of dispositional traits, characteristic adaptations, and integrative life stories complexly and differentially situated in culture (2006, p. 212).

Theories of Personality

Although these five principles give us a starting point, there are different perspectives on the nature of personality development and how to study it. Consider some striking differences among these three major theoretical perspectives: psychoanalytic theory, trait theory, and social learning theory.

Psychoanalytic Theory

Psychoanalytic theorists generally use in-depth interviews, dream analysis, and similar techniques to get below the surface of the person and her behavior and to understand the inner dynamics of personality. As you will recall from Chapter 2, Sigmund Freud believed that biological urges residing within the id push all children through universal stages of psychosexual development, starting with the oral stage of infancy and ending with the genital stage of adolescence. Freud did not see psychosexual growth continuing during adulthood. Indeed he believed that the personality was formed during the first 5 years of life and showed considerable continuity thereafter. Anxieties arising from harsh parenting, overindulgence, or other unfavorable early experiences, he said, would leave a permanent mark on the personality and reveal themselves in adult personality traits.

The psychosocial theory of personality development formulated by neo-Freudian Erik Erikson was also introduced in Chapter 2 and will be highlighted in this chapter. Like Freud, Erikson concerned himself with the inner dynamics of personality and proposed that the personality evolves through systematic stages that confront people with different challenges (Erikson 1963, 1968, 1982). Compared with Freud, however, Erikson placed more emphasis on social influences such as

peers, teachers, and cultures; the rational ego and its adaptive powers; possibilities for overcoming the effects of harmful early experiences; and the potential for growth during the adult years.

Erikson clearly did not agree with Freud that the personality is largely formed by the end of early childhood; he appreciated possibilities for personality change and development throughout the life span. Yet Freud, Erikson, and other psychoanalytic theorists agreed on this: *People everywhere progress through the same stages of personality development, undergoing similar personality changes at similar ages.*

Trait Theory

The approach to personality that has most strongly influenced efforts to study it is trait theory, based on the psychometric approach that guided the development of intelligence tests (see Chapter 9). According to trait theorists, personality is a set of trait dimensions or continua along which people can differ (for example, sociable–unsociable, responsible–irresponsible). (You may want to complete the brief personality scale in the Explorations box before reading further.) To identify distinct trait dimensions, researchers construct personality scales and use the statistical technique of factor analysis to identify groupings of personality scale items that are correlated with each other but not with other groupings of items. Trait theorists assume that personality traits are relatively enduring; like psychoanalytic theorists, they expect to see carryover in personality over the years. Unlike psychoanalytic theorists, however, they do not believe that the personality unfolds in a series of stages.

How many personality trait dimensions are there? Just as scholars have disagreed about how many distinct mental abilities exist, they have disagreed about how many personality dimensions exist. However, a consensus has been forming around the idea that human personalities can be described in terms of a five-factor model, with five major dimensions of personality that have come to be called the **Big Five** (Digman, 1990; McCrae & Costa, 2003). These five personality dimensions— openness to experience, conscientiousness, extraversion, agreeableness, and neuroticism—are described in ● **Table 11.1.** If you score the personality scale in the Explorations box, you will get a rough sense of where you fall on the Big Five trait dimensions.

Evidence suggests that all five of the Big Five trait dimensions are genetically influenced and emerge early in life, as we will see (McCrae & Costa, 2003; Krueger, Johnson, & Kling, 2006). The Big Five also seem to be universal; they capture personality differences in a variety of cultures (McCrae, 2004; McCrae et al., 2000). This is true even though levels of Big Five traits differ from culture to culture (for example, Europeans appear to be more extroverted on average than Asians or Africans) and even though traits may be expressed differently in different cultures (as when a Chinese extravert smiles to convey happiness but an American one like Tom Cruise jumps up and down). You will soon see what happens to these trait dimensions as we age.

A BRIEF PERSONALITY SCALE

Here are several personality traits that may or may not apply to you. Write a number from 1 to 7 next to each statement to indicate the extent to which you agree or disagree with that statement. You should rate the extent to which the pair of traits applies to you, even if one characteristic applies more strongly than the other.

1 = Disagree strongly
2 = Disagree moderately
3 = Disagree a little
4 = Neither agree nor disagree

5 = Agree a little
6 = Agree moderately
7 = Agree strongly

I see myself as:

1. _____ Extraverted, enthusiastic
2. _____ Critical, quarrelsome
3. _____ Dependable, self-disciplined
4. _____ Anxious, easily upset
5. _____ Open to new experiences, complex
6. _____ Reserved, quiet
7. _____ Sympathetic, warm
8. _____ Disorganized, careless
9. _____ Calm, emotionally stable
10. _____ Conventional, uncreative

To score yourself, reverse the scoring of items marked below with *R* so that a score of 1 becomes 7, 2 becomes 6, 3 becomes 5, 4 stays 4, 5 becomes 3, 6 becomes 2, and 7 becomes 1. Then add the pair of scores listed here for each of the Big Five personality dimensions:

Extraversion	Item 1 + item 6R =
Agreeableness	Item 2R + item 7 =
Conscientiousness	Item 3 + item 8R =
Low neuroticism (high emotional stability)	Item 4R + item 9 =
Openness to experience	Item 5 + item 10R =

To help you see roughly where you stand, mean scores for a sample of 1813 individuals tested by Samuel Gosling and colleagues (2003) were 4.44 for extraversion, 5.23 for agreeableness, 5.40 for conscientiousness, 4.83 for low neuroticism (high emotional stability), and 5.38 for openness to experience.

SOURCE: Reprinted from *Journal of Research in Personality*, Vol. 37, Gosling/Rentfrow/Swann, "A Brief Personality Scale," p. 525, Copyright 2003, with permission from Elsevier.

● TABLE 11.1   THE BIG FIVE PERSONALITY DIMENSIONS

DIMENSION	BASIC DEFINITION	KEY CHARACTERISTICS
Openness to experience	Curiosity and interest in variety vs. preference for sameness	Openness to fantasy, esthetics, feelings, actions, ideas, values
Conscientiousness	Discipline and organization vs. lack of seriousness	Competence, order, dutifulness, striving for achievement, self-discipline, deliberation
Extraversion	Sociability and outgoingness vs. introversion	Warmth, gregariousness, assertiveness, activity, excitement seeking, positive emotions
Agreeableness	Compliance and cooperativeness vs. suspiciousness	Trust, straightforwardness, altruism, compliance, modesty, tender-mindedness
Neuroticism	Emotional instability vs. stability	Anxiety, hostility, depression, self-consciousness, impulsiveness, vulnerability

As a mnemonic device, notice that the first letters of the five dimensions spell *ocean*.
SOURCE: Adapted from Costa & McCrae (1992).

Social Learning Theory

Finally, social learning (or social cognitive) theorists such as Albert Bandura (1986; and see Chapter 2) and Walter Mischel (1973; Shoda & Mischel, 2000) not only reject the notion of universal stages of personality development but also have questioned the existence of enduring personality traits that show themselves in a variety of situations and over long stretches of the life span. Instead, they emphasize that people change if their environments change. An aggressive boy can become a warm and caring man if his aggression is no longer reinforced; a woman who has been socially withdrawn can become more outgoing if she begins to socialize with friends who serve as models of outgoing, sociable behavior. From this perspective, personality is a set of behavioral tendencies shaped by interactions with other people in specific social situations.

Social learning theorists believe strongly in situational influences on behavior (Shoda & Mischel, 2000). They argue that consistency over time in personality is most likely if the social environment remains the same. Thus, if Rick the rancher continues to run the same ranch in the same small town for a lifetime, he might stay the "same old Rick." However, most of us experience changes in our social environments as we become older. Just as we behave differently when we are in a library than when we are in a bar, we become "different people" as we take on new roles, develop new relationships, or move to new locations.

An excellent example of this principle comes from research on the relationship between birth order and personality. How would you characterize firstborns? Second-borns? Last-borns? Many of us have strong beliefs about the differences; we think of firstborns as bossy and dominant, for example, and last-borns as rebellious and spoiled. Yet most research reveals few consistent differences between the personalities of firstborns and later-borns (Harris, 2000b). Why might we be misled into thinking such differences exist? Judith Rich Harris (2000b, 2006) notes that we see members of our families in a family context and observe real differences in personality *in that context*. Firstborns often *are* bossy and younger siblings may be rebellious when firstborns baby-sit younger siblings, for example. However, the differences in personality are created by the family context and do not necessarily carry over into other situations. The same firstborn may not be bossy in interactions with peers who are similar in age and competence and cannot be pushed around as easily as younger brothers and sisters. Different context, different personality.

This chapter explores continuity and discontinuity in self-conceptions and personality traits across the life span. When do infants become aware of themselves as unique individuals, and when do they begin to display unique personalities? What influences how children perceive and evaluate themselves, and to what extent can we detect in them the personalities they will have as adults? How do adolescents go about finding their identities as individuals? Finally, do people's personalities and self-perceptions change systematically over the adult years, or do they remain essentially the same, and what does it all mean for their career development and adjustment?

SUMMING UP

- Personality is an organized combination of attributes unique to the individual; self-concept is an individual's perception of those attributes; self-esteem is an overall evaluation of self worth; and identity is an overall sense of who one is and how one fits with others.

- The five principles of personality of McAdams and Pals call attention to evolved human nature, dispositional traits, characteristic adaptations, unique narrative identities or life stories, and cultural and situational influences on personality.

- Psychoanalytic theorists explore inner dynamics of personality and universal, age-related personality changes, with Freud believing that the personality emerges in the first 5 years of life but Erikson seeing stagelike changes throughout the life span.

- Trait theorists emphasize the continuity of major dimensions of personality such as the Big Five, whereas social learning theorists question the existence of traits and call attention to the potential for discontinuity in personality caused by environmental change.

CRITICAL THINKING

1. Sketch out a few major characteristics of your own personality in terms of these three components: dispositional traits, characteristic adaptations, and life story or narrative identity.

2. What might a psychoanalytic theorist and a social learning theorist have to say about how you got to be the way you are and what your personality will be like 20 years from now?

11.2 THE INFANT

When do infants display an awareness that they exist and a sense of themselves as distinct individuals? We will explore this issue and then look at infants' unique "personalities."

The Emerging Self

Infants may be born without a sense of self, but they quickly develop an implicit, if not conscious, sense of self through their perceptions of their bodies and actions (Rochat & Striano, 2000). The capacity to differentiate self from world becomes even more apparent in the first 2 or 3 months of life as infants discover that they can cause things to happen. For example, 2-month-old infants whose arms are connected by strings to audiovisual equipment delight in producing the sight of a smiling infant's face and the theme from *Sesame Street* by pulling the strings (Lewis, Alessandri, & Sullivan, 1990). When the strings are disconnected and they can no longer produce such effects, they pull harder and become frustrated and angry. Over the first 6 months of life, then, infants discover properties of their physical selves, distinguish between the self and the rest of the world, and appreciate that they can act upon other people and objects (Thompson, 1998).

In the second half of their first year, infants realize that they and their companions are separate beings with different perspectives, ones that can be shared (Thompson, 1998). This is illustrated by the phenomenon of *joint attention*, in which infants about 9 months or older and their caregivers share perceptual experiences by looking at the same object at the same time (Mitchell, 1997; Mundy & Acra, 2006). When an infant points at an object and looks toward her companions in an effort to focus their attention on the object, she shows awareness that self and other do not always share the same perceptions.

Around 18 months, infants recognize themselves visually as distinct individuals. To establish this, Michael Lewis and Jeanne Brooks-Gunn (1979) used an ingenious technique first used with chimpanzees to study **self-recognition**—the ability to recognize oneself in a mirror or photograph. Mother daubs a spot of blush or rouge on an infant's nose and then places the infant in front of a mirror. If the infant has some mental image of his own face and recognizes his mirror image as himself, he should soon notice the red spot and reach for or wipe his own nose rather than the nose of the mirror image.

When infants 9 to 24 months old were given this mirror test, the youngest infants showed no self-recognition: they seemed to treat the image in the mirror as if it were "some other kid." Some 15-month-olds recognized themselves, but only among 18- to 24-month-olds did most infants show clear evidence of self-recognition. They touched their noses rather than the mirror, apparently realizing that they had a strange mark on their faces that warranted investigation. They knew exactly who that kid in the mirror was. At the time they first pass the "mirror test" of self-recognition, infants also take more interest in watching a video of themselves than in watching a video of another infant (Nielsen, Dissanayake, & Kashima, 2003).

As babies develop, they also form a **categorical self;** that is, they classify themselves into social categories based on age, sex, and other visible characteristics, figuring out what is "like me" and what is "not like me." Before they are 18 months old, toddlers can tell themselves apart from toddlers of the other sex or from older individuals but are less able to distinguish between photos of themselves and photos of other infants of the same sex. As they approach age 2, they also master this task (Brooks-Gunn & Lewis, 1981; Lewis & Brooks-Gunn, 1979). By 18 to 24 months, then, most infants have an awareness of who they

are—at least as a physical self with a unique appearance and as a categorical self belonging to specific age and gender categories. They even begin to use their emerging language skills to talk about themselves and to construct stories about events in their lives, past and present (Thompson, 1998).

What contributes to self-awareness in infancy? First, the ability to recognize the self depends on *cognitive development* (Bertenthal & Fischer, 1978). Mentally retarded children are slow to recognize themselves in a mirror but can do so once they have attained a mental age of at least 18 months (Hill & Tomlin, 1981). Second, self-awareness depends on *social experiences.* Chimpanzees who have been raised without contact with other chimps fail to recognize themselves in a mirror as normal chimps do (Gallup, 1979). Moreover, human toddlers who have formed secure attachments to their parents are better able to recognize themselves in a mirror and know more about their names and genders than do toddlers whose relationships are less secure, further evidence that a sense of self grows out of social relationships (Pipp, Easterbrooks, & Harmon, 1992).

The critical role of social interaction in the development of the self was appreciated long ago by Charles Cooley (1902) and George Herbert Mead (1934). Cooley used the term **looking-glass self** to emphasize that our understanding of self is a reflection of how other people view and respond to us; that is, our self-concepts are the images cast by a social mirror.

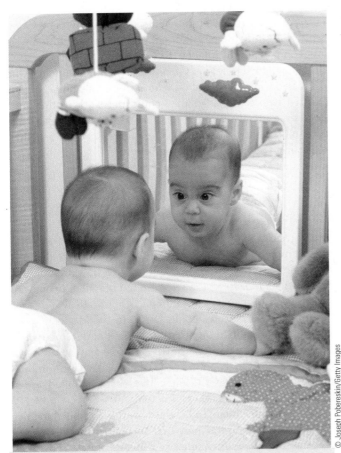

Does this boy know that he is the fascinating tot in the mirror? Probably not if he is younger than 18 months, which is about when self-recognition is mastered by most toddlers.

Humans, apes, dolphins, and elephants are all known to be capable of empathy and altruistic behavior when a companion needs help, attributes which are believed to require some degree of self-awareness and an ability to draw on knowledge of self to make inferences about companions. Because all but elephants had been shown to be self-aware, as judged by the ability to recognize themselves in a mirror, Joshua Plotnik, Frans de Waal, and Diana Reiss (2006) tried the mirror self-recognition task on elephants by installing a huge mirror at the Bronx Zoo. The result? The three elephants tested all took good looks inside their mouths in front of the mirror and one touched her trunk repeatedly to a white X planted on her cheek—evidence of mirror self-recognition in at least one elephant.

Through their actions and words, parents and other companions communicate to infants that they are babies and are either girls or boys. Later, social feedback helps children determine what they are like and what they can and cannot do well. Throughout life, we forge new self-concepts from the social feedback we receive, good and bad (Harter, 1999). Thus the development of the self is closely related to both cognitive development and social interaction, beginning in infancy.

Awareness of the self paves the way for many important emotional and social developments. Toddlers who recognize themselves in the mirror are more able than those who do not to talk about themselves and to assert their wills (DesRosiers et al., 1999). They are more likely to experience self-conscious emotions such as embarrassment—for example, if asked to show off by dancing in front of strangers (Lewis et al., 1989). Toddlers who have gained self-awareness are also more able to coordinate their own perspectives with those of other individuals—for example, to communicate with their playmates by imitating their actions (Asendorpf, Warkentin, & Baudonnière, 1996), to cooperate with peers to achieve common goals such as retrieving toys from containers (Brownell & Carriger, 1990), and to empathize with peers in distress (Eisenberg, Spinrad, & Sadovsky, 2006).

Temperament

Even though it takes infants some time to become aware of themselves as individuals, they are individuals with distinctive personalities from the first weeks of life. The study of infant personality has centered on dimensions of **temperament**—early, genetically based tendencies to respond in predictable ways to events that serve as the building blocks of personality (see Rothbart & Bates, 2006). Learning theorists have tended to view babies as "blank slates" who can be shaped in any number of directions by their experiences. However, it is now clear that babies differ from the start in basic response tendencies. Temperament has been defined and measured in several ways, each of which gives us insights into baby personality (Rothbart & Bates, 2006).

Easiness and Difficultness

One of the first attempts to characterize infant temperaments was the influential work of Alexander Thomas, Stella Chess, and their colleagues (Chess & Thomas, 1999; Thomas & Chess, 1986). These researchers gathered information about nine dimensions of infant behavior, including typical mood, regularity or predictability of biological functions such as feeding and sleeping habits, tendency to approach or withdraw from new stimuli, intensity of emotional reactions, and adaptability to new experiences and changes in routine. Based on the overall patterning of these temperamental qualities, most infants could be placed into one of three categories:

- **Easy temperament.** Easy infants are even tempered, typically content or happy, and open and adaptable to new experiences such as the approach of a stranger or their first taste of strained plums. They have regular feeding and sleeping habits, and they tolerate frustrations and discomforts.

- **Difficult temperament.** Difficult infants are active, irritable, and irregular in their habits. They often react negatively (and vigorously) to changes in routine and are slow to adapt to new people or situations. They cry frequently and loudly and often have tantrums when they are frustrated by such events as being restrained or having to live with a dirty diaper.

- **Slow-to-warm-up temperament.** Slow-to-warm-up infants are relatively inactive, somewhat moody, and only moderately regular in their daily schedules. Like difficult infants, they are slow to adapt to new people and situations, but they typically respond in mildly, rather than intensely, negative ways. For example, they may resist cuddling by looking away from the cuddler rather than by kicking or screaming. They eventually adjust, showing a quiet interest in new foods, people, or places.

Of the infants in Thomas and Chess's longitudinal study of temperament, 40% were easy infants, 10% were difficult infants, and 15% were slow-to-warm-up infants. The remaining third could not be clearly placed in one category because they shared qualities of two or more categories. Thomas and Chess went on to study the extent of continuity and discontinuity in temperament from infancy to early adulthood (Chess & Thomas, 1984; Thomas & Chess, 1986). Difficult infants who had fussed when they could not have more milk often became children who fell apart if they could not work mathematics problems correctly. By adulthood, however, an individual's adjustment had little to do with her temperament during infancy, suggesting a good deal of discontinuity over this long time span (Guerin et al., 2003).

Behavioral Inhibition

Jerome Kagan and his colleagues identified another aspect of early temperament that they believe is highly significant—**behavioral inhibition,** or the tendency to be extremely shy, restrained, and distressed in response to unfamiliar people and situations as opposed to uninhibited (Kagan, 1994; Kagan & Snidman, 2004; Reznick et al., 1986). In the language of the Big Five personality dimensions, inhibited children could be considered high in neuroticism and low in extraversion. Kagan (1989) estimates that about 15% of toddlers have this inhibited temperament, whereas 10% are extremely uninhibited, exceptionally eager to jump into new situations.

At 4 months, infants who will turn into inhibited toddlers wriggle and fuss and fret more than most infants in response to new sights and sounds such as a moving mobile (Fox et al., 2001). At 21 months, they take a long time to warm up to a strange examiner, retreat from unfamiliar objects such as a large robot, and fret and cling to their mothers, whereas uninhibited toddlers readily and enthusiastically engage with strangers, robots, and all manner of new experiences (Kagan, 1994). As children, uninhibited youngsters are shy in a group of strange peers and afraid to try a balance beam. And of the children who had maintained the same temperament from age 2 to age 7, about half still had the same temperament as young adolescents, suggesting a fair amount of continuity in this dimension of temperament (Kagan, 1994).

Kagan and his colleagues have concluded that behavioral inhibition is biologically rooted. They have found that youngsters with an inhibited temperament show distinctive physiological reactions to novel events; for example, they become highly aroused (as indicated by high heart rates) in situations that barely faze other children (Kagan, 1994). Even as adults, individuals who were inhibited toddlers show stronger responses to novel faces in the part of the brain called the amygdala than do adults who were uninhibited early in life, whereas they respond no differently to familiar faces (Schwartz et al., 2003). The excitability of behaviorally inhibited children in response to novelty is probably genetically influenced. In one study (DiLalla, Kagan, & Reznick, 1994), the correlation between the inhibition scores of identical twins was strong (+0.82), and that for fraternal twins only moderate (+0.47). Possibly then, genes affect temperament by influencing the development of the nervous system and the way it responds to stimuli.

Behavioral inhibition is a risk factor for later anxiety disorders (Fox et al., 2005), but genes and environment interact to determine outcomes. If the parents of inhibited children overprotect their sensitive children from stress, or if they become angry and impatient with their timid children's behavior, these children do not learn to control their inhibition as they develop and they remain inhibited (Kagan, 1994). By contrast, when parents prepare inhibited youngsters for potentially upsetting experiences, then make reasonable but firm demands that they cope, early inhibition may be overcome.

Surgency, Negative Affect, and Effortful Control

Finally, Mary Rothbart and her colleagues (Rothbart, Ahadi, & Evans, 2000; Rothbart & Derryberry, 2002; Putnam, Gartstein, & Rothbart, 2006) have defined infant temperament in terms of emotional reactions and the control or regulation of such reactions. They have identified three dimensions of temperament, the first two evident from infancy, the last emerging more clearly in toddlerhood or early childhood:

- **Surgency/extraversion**—the tendency to actively and energetically approach new experiences in an emotionally positive way (rather than to be inhibited and withdrawn)
- **Negative affectivity**—the tendency to be sad, fearful, easily frustrated, and irritable (as opposed to laid back and adaptable)
- **Effortful control**—the ability to sustain attention, control one's behavior, and regulate one's emotions (as opposed to an inability to regulate one's arousal and stay calm and focused)

● **Table 11.2** shows the different ways of describing infant temperaments we have described. There are some clear similarities. Today, Rothbart's dimensions of temperament have become especially influential, probably because research suggests they share similarities with the Big Five dimensions used to describe adult personality. Surgency/extraversion clearly matches up with extraversion (and perhaps agreeableness too), negative affectivity with neuroticism, and effortful control with conscientiousness. Researchers have had difficulty confirming the dimensions of temperament (easy, difficult, slow to warm up) identified by Thomas and Chess, but accumulating evidence suggests that Rothbart and her colleagues are on the right track and that there are meaningful connections between temperament in infancy and early childhood and personality later in life (Saucier & Simonds, 2006; Shiner, 2006).

Goodness of Fit

Differences in temperament appear to be rooted in genetically based differences in levels of certain neurotransmitters and in the functioning of the brain (Ebstein, Benjamin, & Belmaker, 2003). However, environment helps determine how adaptive particular temperamental qualities are and whether they persist (Rothbart & Bates, 2006). Much may depend on what Thomas and Chess call the **goodness of fit** between child and environment—the extent to which the child's temperament is compatible with the demands and expectations of the social world to which she must adapt.

A good example comes from observations of the Masai of East Africa (DeVries, 1984). In most settings, an easy temperament is likely to be more adaptive than a difficult one, but among the Masai during famine, babies with difficult temperaments outlived easy babies. Why? Perhaps because Masai parents believe that difficult babies are future warriors or perhaps because babies who cry loud and long get noticed and fed. As this example suggests, a particular temperament may be a good fit to the demands of one environment but maladaptive under other circumstances. The goodness-of-fit concept is an excellent example of the theme that individual predispositions and the environment interact to influence developmental outcomes.

● **TABLE 11.2 SUMMARY OF TEMPERAMENT CATEGORIES**

RESEARCHERS	DIMENSIONS OF TEMPERAMENT
THOMAS AND CHESS	Easy temperament Difficult temperament Slow-to-warm-up temperament
KAGAN	Behaviorally inhibited Uninhibited
ROTHBART	Surgency/extraversion Negative affectivity Effortful control

The case of Carl, one of the children studied by Thomas and Chess, also illustrates the significance for later personality development of the match between a child's temperament and his social environment. Early in life, Carl was clearly a difficult child: "Whether it was the first bath or the first solid foods in infancy, the beginning of nursery and elementary school, or the first birthday parties or shopping trips, each experience evoked stormy responses, with loud crying and struggling to get away" (1984, p. 188). Carl's mother became convinced that she was a bad parent, but his father accepted and even delighted in Carl's "lusty" behavior. He patiently and supportively waited for Carl to adapt to new situations. As a result, Carl did not develop serious behavioral problems as a child and became a well-adjusted adult after weathering some adjustment problems when he started college.

If the fit between his difficult temperament and his parents' demands and expectations had been poor—for example if his parents had been impatient, angry, and overly demanding—research suggests Carl might have been headed for serious behavioral problems and poor adjustment (Guerin et al., 2003; Shiner, 2006). Recall Kagan's (1994) finding that behaviorally inhibited children remain inhibited if their parents are either overprotective or impatient but that they overcome their inhibition if their parents prepared them for potentially upsetting experiences and make reasonable but firm demands that they cope.

The moral for parents is clear: get to know your baby as an individual, and allow for his personality quirks. Infants' temperaments and their parents' parenting behaviors reciprocally influence one another and interact over time to steer the direction of later personality development (Sanson, Hemphill, & Smart, 2004). Teaching parents of irritable babies how to interpret their infants' cues and respond sensitively and appropriately to them can produce calmer infants who cry less and become less irritable preschoolers than temperamentally similar

Difficult or behaviorally inhibited children may remain so if there is a "bad fit" between them and an impatient parent.

children whose parents do not receive training (van den Boom, 1995; Crockenberg & Leerkes, 2003).

SUMMING UP

▌ Two- to three-month-olds discover they are physically distinct from the world around them and can act upon it, and by 18 to 24 months, toddlers show self-awareness and form a categorical self, thanks to both cognitive development and social experience.

▌ Each infant has distinct temperamental qualities sketched in the genetic code and expressed from the first days of life—qualities such as an easy, difficult, or slow-to-warm-up temperament; behavioral inhibition; or surgency/extraversion, negative affectivity, and effortful control.

▌ Early temperamental qualities may or may not be elaborated into later personality traits depending on the goodness of fit between the individual's predispositions and his social environment.

CRITICAL THINKING

1. Gracie the toddler tends to become stressed when her routines are changed, a stranger comes to visit, or she is asked to try something she has never tried before. Using three different systems for analyzing temperament, help her parents understand her temperament.

2. The mirror test has become the main way of assessing self-awareness in infants. What do you see as the strengths and limitations of this approach? Can you think of any other way to assess infant self-awareness?

11.3 THE CHILD

Children's personalities continue to form, and children acquire much richer understandings of themselves as individuals, as they continue to experience cognitive growth and interact with other people. Ask children of different ages to tell you about themselves. You will find their responses amusing, and you will learn something about how children come to think about themselves as individuals.

Elaborating on a Sense of Self

Once toddlers begin to talk, they can and do tell us about their emerging self-concepts. By age 2, some toddlers are already using the personal pronouns *I, me, my,* and *mine* (or their names) when referring to the self and *you* when addressing a companion (Lewis & Brooks-Gunn, 1979; Stipek, Gralinski, & Kopp, 1990). Toddlers also show their emerging categorical selves when they describe themselves in terms of age and sex ("Katie big girl"). Parent–child conversations that focus on past experiences and the emotions associated with them help young children pull together what they know of themselves into a consistent self-concept (Bird & Reese, 2006).

The preschool child's self-concept is concrete and physical (Damon & Hart, 1988; Harter, 2006). Asked to describe themselves, preschoolers dwell on their physical characteristics, their possessions, their physical activities and accomplishments, and their preferences. One exuberant 3-year-old described herself this way:

> I'm 3 years old and I live in a big house with my mother and father and my brother, Jason, and my sister, Lisa. I have blue eyes and a kitty that is orange and a television in my own room. I know all of my ABC's, listen: A, B, C, D, E, F, G, H, J, L, K, O, M, P, Q, X, Z. I can run real fast. I like pizza and I have a nice teacher at preschool. I can count up to 100, want to hear me? I love my dog Skipper. (Harter, 1999, p. 37)

Few young children mention their psychological traits or inner qualities. At most, young children use global terms such as *nice* or *mean* and *good* or *bad* to describe themselves and others (Livesley & Bromley, 1973). However, their descriptions of their characteristic behavioral patterns and preferences ("I like to play by myself at school") may provide the foundation for their later personality trait descriptions ("I'm shy"; Eder, 1989).

Self-conceptions become more sophisticated around age 8, partly because of cognitive development (Harter, 2003, 2006). First, children begin to form social identities, defining themselves as part of social units ("I'm a Kimball, a second-grader at Brookside School, a Brownie Scout"; Damon & Hart, 1988). Second, they begin to describe their enduring qualities using personality trait terms such as *funny* and *smart* (Harter, 1999; Livesley & Bromley, 1973). Third, they are now capable of **social comparison**—of using information about how they compare with other individuals to characterize and evaluate themselves (Frey & Ruble, 1985; Pomerantz et al., 1995). The preschooler who said she could hit a baseball becomes the elementary-school child who says she is a better batter than her teammates.

Preschool children emphasize the "active self" in their self-descriptions, noting things they can do but saying little about their psychological traits.

Young children often seem oblivious to information about how they compare with others and seem to have difficulty interpreting and acting on such information when they receive it (Butler, 1990). They tend to believe that they are the greatest, even in the face of compelling evidence that they have been outclassed. By contrast, first-grade children glance at each other's papers, ask "How many did you miss?," and say things like "I got more right than you did" (Frey & Ruble, 1985; Pomerantz et al., 1995).

Self-Esteem

As children amass a range of perceptions of themselves and engage in social comparisons, they begin to evaluate their worth. Susan Harter (1999, 2003, 2006) has developed self-perception scales for use across the life span and has found that self-concepts become more differentiated or multidimensional with age. Preschool children distinguish only two broad aspects of self-esteem: their competence (both physical and cognitive) and their personal and social adequacy (for example, their social acceptance). By mid–elementary school, children differentiate among five aspects of self-worth: scholastic competence (feeling smart or doing well in school); social acceptance (being popular or feeling liked); behavioral conduct (staying out of trouble); athletic competence (being good at sports); and physical appearance (feeling good-looking). When Harter's scale was given to third- through ninth-graders, even third-graders showed that they had well-defined positive or negative feelings about themselves. Moreover, children made clear distinctions between their competency in one area and their competency in another. They did not just have generally high or generally low self-esteem.

Thus self-esteem is *multidimensional* rather than unidimensional. As children organize their perceptions of themselves over the elementary-school years, they differentiate more sharply among distinct aspects of the self-concept. But self-esteem is also *hierarchical* in nature: children integrate self-perceptions in distinct domains to form an overall, abstract sense of self-worth (Harter, 1999; Marsh & Ayotte, 2003). ■ **Figure 11.1** shows the kind of self-esteem hierarchy that results, with global self-worth at the top and specific dimensions of self-concept below it.

The accuracy of children's self-evaluations increases steadily over the elementary-school years (Harter, 1999; Marsh, Craven, & Debus, 1999). Children as young as 5 already have some sense of whether they are worthy and lovable (Verschueren, Buyck, & Marcoen, 2001). However, the self-esteem scores of young children (4- to 7-year-olds) sometimes reflect their desires to be liked or to be good at various activities more than their true competencies (Harter, 2006). Overall, young children tend to have unrealistically positive views of themselves. Starting about age 8, partly because of cognitive development, children's self-evaluations become more accurate. For example, those with high scholastic self-esteem are more likely than those with low scholastic self-esteem to be rated as intellectually competent by their teachers, and those

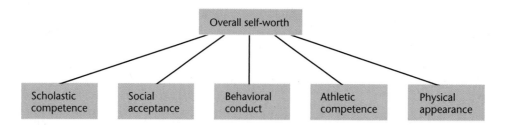

FIGURE 11.1 The multidimensional and hierarchical nature of self-esteem.
SOURCE: From S. Harter, Historical roots of contemporary issues involving self-concepts. In B. A. Bracken (Ed.), *Handbook of self-concept: Developmental, social, and clinical considerations.* Copyright © 1996 by Wiley. Reprinted with permission.

with high athletic self-esteem are frequently chosen by peers in sporting events (Harter, 1999).

At the same time, children are forming an ever grander sense of what they "should" be like—an **ideal self.** With age, the gap between the real self and the ideal self increases; older children therefore run a greater risk than younger children do of thinking that they fall short of what they should be (Glick & Zigler, 1985; Oosterwegel & Oppenheimer, 1993). Social comparisons that do not always come out well, a widening gap between the real self and the ideal self, and a tendency for parents and teachers to "raise the bar" and give older children more critical feedback than they give younger children contribute to both a decrease in self-esteem from early to middle childhood and wider differences among children in their levels of self-esteem (Harter, 2006).

Influences on Self-Esteem

Why do some children develop higher self-esteem than others? Part of the answer lies in genes; like so most human characteristics, self-esteem is a heritable trait (Kamakura, Ando, & Ono, 2007). Unique experiences also influence self-esteem: some children discover that they are more competent than other children, and, apart from their competence, some children receive more positive social feedback (Harter, 1999).

Children who are more capable and socially attractive than other children experience more success in areas important to them and come out better in social comparisons. Thus, for example, achievement in school has a positive effect on academic self-concept; a positive academic self-concept, in turn, contributes to future academic achievement (Guay, Marsh, & Boivin, 2003; Marsh & Craven, 2006).

Even when two children are equally competent and do equally well in social comparisons, social feedback from parents, teachers, and peers can make a big difference in their self-perceptions. Most notably, children with high self-esteem tend to be securely attached to parents who are warm and democratic (Arbona & Power, 2003; Coopersmith, 1967). Parents who are loving, form secure attachments with their children, and frequently communicate approval and acceptance help their children think positively about themselves (Doyle, Markiewicz, et al., 2000). Saying, through words, looks, or actions, "You're not important" or "Why can't you be more like your older brother?" is likely to have the opposite effect. Need-

less to say, children who are mistreated or abused by their parents often have low self-esteem (Burack et al., 2006). This is the concept of the looking-glass self in action: children will form self-concepts that reflect the evaluations of significant people in their lives.

Parents whose children have high self-esteem also enforce clearly stated rules of behavior and allow their children to express their opinions and participate in decision making. This democratic parenting style most likely gives children a firm basis for evaluating their behavior and sends them the message that their opinions are respected. The relationship between high self-esteem and a warm, democratic parenting style has been observed in most ethnic groups in the United States and in other countries (Scott, Scott, & McCabe, 1991; Steinberg, Dornbusch, & Brown, 1992).

Once a child's level of self-esteem has been established, it tends to remain surprisingly stable over the elementary-school years. Moreover, high self-esteem is positively correlated with a variety of measures of good adjustment (Coopersmith, 1967; Harter, 1999). Finally, interventions that focus on specific aspects of self-esteem such as self-esteem in mathematics can be effective in raising the self-esteem of children who are low in it (O'Mara et al., 2006). Despite evidence of the importance of self-esteem, though, William Damon (1994) and other observers believe that Americans go overboard in trying to make all children feel good about themselves. Self-esteem, Damon maintains, means nothing unless it grows out of one's real achievements. Moreover, he argues, children need opportunities to learn not only about their strengths but about their limitations as they progress through school; giving them an inflated and unrealistic sense of their worth will do more harm than good in the end. Perhaps it is best to appreciate that self-esteem and performance influence one another reciprocally (Marsh & Craven, 2006). From this perspective, it will not work in the long run to tell children they are the greatest when they can see for themselves that they are not, but one can expect high achievement and high self-esteem to fuel one another.

The Developing Personality

The biologically based response tendencies called temperament are increasingly shaped, with the help of the individual's social experiences, into a predictable personality during childhood. Links between temperament in infancy and early child-hood and later personality are increasingly being identified after many years in which temperament researchers and personality researchers went their separate ways (Halverson et al., 2003; Sanson, Hemphill, & Smart, 2004; Shiner, 2006).

For example, in a longitudinal study of 1000 children in New Zealand, Avshalom Caspi and his colleagues (Caspi, 2000; Caspi, Harrington, et al., 2003) found that inhibited 3-year-olds who are shy and fearful tend to become teenagers who are cautious and unassertive, and later become young adults who have little social support, tend to be depressed, and are barely engaged in life. By contrast, 3-year-olds who are difficult to control, irritable, and highly emotional tend to be difficult to manage later in childhood and end up as impulsive adolescents and adults who do not get along well with other people at home and on the job, are easily upset, get into scrapes with the law, and abuse alcohol. Finally, well-adjusted ("easy") 3-year-olds tend to remain well adjusted. Interestingly, the assessments of personality at age 3 that proved predictive of later personality and adjustment were made on the basis of only 90 minutes of observation by an adult examiner who did not know the child (see Pesonen et al., 2003).

Links between dimensions of temperament and Big Five personality trait dimensions are becoming clearer all the time. For example, behavioral inhibition in the preschool period is predictive of low extraversion (introversion) in middle childhood, and negative affectivity is related to later neuroticism (Hagekull & Bohlin, 1998; and see Shiner, 2006). An uninhibited temperament that embraces novelty may relate to later openness to experience, and the ability of infants to exert effortful control over their attention and arousal (for example, to calm themselves) appears to be linked to later conscientiousness (Rothbart, Ahadi, & Evans, 2000; Sanson, Hemphill, & Smart, 2004).

Researchers are finding that children as young as 5 to 7 can, if asked simple questions by a puppet, provide meaningful reports of their Big Five traits—reports that correlate in expected ways with ratings of their traits provided by parents and teachers and with their own behavior (Measelle et al., 2005). Moreover, Charles Halverson and his colleagues (2003) found that parents in all seven countries they studied describe children as young as age 3 in Big Five terms, also suggesting that these adult personality dimensions begin to show themselves in early childhood. Indeed, mothers' ratings of Big Five traits in their 3½-year-olds predict their behavior during childhood and self-ratings during adolescence in expected ways (Abe, 2005).

Despite this evidence, we cannot accept Freud's view that the personality is mostly formed by age 5. Correlations between early childhood traits and adult traits are usually quite small. Some dimensions of personality do not seem to "gel" until the elementary-school years, when they begin to predict adult personality and adjustment much better. Other aspects of personality do not seem to stabilize until adolescence or even early adulthood (Caspi & Roberts, 2001; McCrae & Costa, 2003). The older the individual, the more accurately personality traits predict later personality and adjustment.

SUMMING UP

▪ Major changes in self-conceptions occur at about age 8 as children shift from describing their physical and active selves to talking about their psychological and social qualities. Other changes include increased social comparison, formation of a multidimensional and hierarchically organized self-concept with an overall sense of self-worth at the top, more accurate self-evaluations, and a widening ideal self–real self gap.

▪ Competence, positive social feedback from warm, democratic parents, and favorable social comparisons contribute to high self-esteem.

▪ Some aspects of temperament translate into Big Five personality traits and carry over into adulthood, but other aspects of personality do not gel until middle childhood or beyond.

CRITICAL THINKING

1. Todd, age 5, has low self-esteem, his preschool teacher has concluded. What do you think he says about himself at this age that makes the teacher think so, and what do you hypothesize might have caused his low self-esteem?

11.4 | THE ADOLESCENT

Perhaps no period of the life span is more important to the development of the self than adolescence. Adolescence is truly a time for "finding oneself," as research on adolescent self-conceptions, self-esteem, and identity formation illustrates.

Self-Conceptions

Raymond Montemayor and Marvin Eisen (1977) learned a great deal about the self-concepts of children and adolescents from grades 4 to 12 by asking students to write 20 different answers to the question "Who am I?" How would you describe the age differences evident in these answers given by a 9-year-old, an 11½-year-old, and a 17-year-old (pp. 317–318)?

9-year-old: My name is Bruce C. I have brown eyes. I have brown hair. I love! sports. I have seven people in my family. I have great! eye sight. I have lots! of friends. I live at. . . . I have an uncle who is almost 7 feet tall. My teacher is Mrs. V. I play hockey! I'm almost the smartest boy in the class. I love! food. . . . I love! school.

11½-year-old: My name is A. I'm a human being. . . . a girl. . . . a truthful person. I'm not pretty. I do so-so in my studies. I'm a very good cellist. I'm a little tall for my age. I like several boys. . . . I'm old fashioned. I am a very good swimmer. . . . I try to be helpful. . . . Mostly I'm good, but I lose my temper. I'm not well liked by some girls and boys. I don't know if boys like me. . . .

17-year-old: I am a human being. . . . a girl. . . . an individual. . . . I am a Pisces. I am a moody person. . . . an indecisive person. . . . an ambitious person. I am a big curious person. . . .

I am lonely. I am an American (God help me). I am a Democrat. I am a liberal person. I am a radical. I am conservative. I am a pseudoliberal. I am an Atheist. I am not a classifiable person (i.e., I don't want to be).

There are remarkable differences between the self-descriptions of children and adolescents (Damon & Hart, 1988; Harter, 1999, 2003). First, self-descriptions become *less physical and more psychological* as children age (contrast "I have brown eyes," "I play hockey" with "I am lonely"). Second, self-portraits become *less concrete and more abstract.* Recall Piaget's theory that children begin to shift from concrete operational to formal operational thinking at about age 11 or 12. Children entering adolescence (11- to 12-year-olds) go beyond describing their traits in largely concrete terms ("I love! food") and more often generalize about their broader personality traits ("I am a truthful person"). High-school students' self-descriptions are even more abstract, focusing not only on personality traits but also on important values and ideologies or beliefs ("I am a pseudoliberal").

Third, adolescents reflect more about what they are like; they are *more self-aware* than children are (Selman, 1980). Indeed, their new ability to think about their own and other people's thoughts and feelings can make them painfully self-conscious. Fourth, adolescents have a *more differentiated* self-concept than children. For example, the child's "social self," which reflects perceived acceptance by peers, splits into distinct aspects such as acceptance by the larger peer group, acceptance by close friends, and acceptance by romantic partners (Harter, 1999). Finally, older adolescents gain the ability to combine their differentiated self-perceptions into a *more integrated, coherent self-portrait.* Instead of merely listing traits, they organize their self-perceptions, including those that seem contradictory, into a coherent picture—a theory of what makes them tick. Adolescents who at first do not recognize inconsistencies in their behavior—for example, being cheerful in some situations, irritable in others—become bothered by such inconsistencies and then, in their later teens, are able to integrate these discrepant self-perceptions using concepts such as moodiness (Harter & Monsour, 1992).

In sum, from childhood to adolescence and over the course of adolescence, self-understandings become more psychological, abstract, differentiated, and integrated, and self-awareness increases. Many adolescents even become sophisticated personality theorists who reflect upon the workings of their own personalities and those of their companions.

Self-Esteem

Self-esteem tends to decrease from childhood to early adolescence, partly because adolescents are more knowledgeable and realistic about their strengths and weaknesses (Jacobs et al., 2002; Robins et al., 2002), partly because they sometimes become temporarily unsure of themselves when they move from elementary school to middle school or junior high school (Cole et al., 2001), and partly because they become unhappy with their changing bodies (Paxton et al., 2006). This

dip in self-esteem affects only some teens, though. It is common among white females, especially those facing multiple stressors—for example, making the transition from elementary school to middle school, coping with pubertal changes, beginning to date, and perhaps dealing with a family move all at the same time (Gray-Little & Hafdahl, 2000; Simmons et al., 1987). Changes in body image may explain a lot, especially for girls who think they must look like ultra thin movie stars or models; the dip in self-esteem has been observed among both girls and boys who are dissatisfied with their changing bodies (Paxton et al., 2006).

Self-esteem can also be affected by the social context and the social comparisons an adolescent therefore makes. For example, Herbert Marsh and Kit-Tai Hau (2003) studied more than 100,000 15-year-olds in 26 countries to better understand the **big-fish–little-pond effect.** Holding factors such as academic competence equal, a student's academic self-concept tends to be less positive when the average academic achievement level of her classmates is high (when she is a small fish in a big pond) than when her school's average academic achievement level is low (when she is a big fish in a little pond).

The big-fish–little-pond effect suggests that making the transition from regular classes to classes for gifted students, or from an unselective high school to a selective college or university, could threaten an adolescent's self-esteem. Indeed, gifted children moved from regular classes into gifted programs sometimes do lose academic self-esteem (Marsh et al., 1995). Similarly, special education students tend to have higher academic self-esteem when they are placed in homogeneous special education classes than when they are placed in regular classes with higher-achieving classmates, despite other benefits that may come from including students with learning problems in the mainstream (Manning, Bear, & Minke, 2006; Marsh & Hau, 2003).

Overall, though, adolescence is not as hazardous to self-esteem as most people believe. Although some adolescents do experience drops in self-esteem in early adolescence, most emerge from this developmental period with higher self-esteem than they had at the onset (Donnellan, Trzesniewski, &

Adolescents sometimes experiment with a variety of looks in their search for a sense of identity.

© Mark Azavedo/Alamy

Robins, 2006; Robins et al., 2002). Apparently they are able to revise their self-concepts in fairly minor ways as they experience the physical, cognitive, and social changes of adolescence. Assuming that they have opportunities to feel competent in areas important to them and to experience the approval and support of parents, peers, and other important people in their lives, they are likely to feel good about themselves (Harter, 1999). It matters: As adults, adolescents with low self-esteem tend to have poorer physical and mental health, poorer career and financial prospects, and higher levels of criminal behavior than adolescents with high self-esteem (Trzesniewski et al., 2006).

Forging a Sense of Identity

Erikson (1968) characterized adolescence as a critical period in the lifelong process of forming an identity as a person and proposed that adolescents experience the psychosocial conflict of **identity versus role confusion.** The concept of identity, explained at the start of the chapter, refers to a definition of who you are, where you are going, and where you fit into society. To achieve a sense of identity, the adolescent must somehow integrate the many separate perceptions that are part of the self-concept into a coherent sense of self and must feel that she is, deep down, the same person yesterday, today, and tomorrow—at home, at school, or at work (van Hoof, 1999). The search for identity involves grappling with many important questions: What kind of career do I want? What religious, moral, and political values can I really call my own? Who am I as a man or woman and as a sexual being? Where do I fit into the world? What do I really want out of my life?

If you have struggled with such issues, you can appreciate the uncomfortable feelings that adolescents may experience when they cannot seem to work out a clear sense of who they are. Erikson believed that many young people in complex societies such as that of the United States experience a full-blown and painful "identity crisis." There are many reasons they might do so. First, their bodies are changing and they must revise their body images (a part of their self-concepts) and adjust to being sexual beings. Second, cognitive growth allows adolescents to think systematically about hypothetical possibilities, including possible future selves. Third, social demands are placed on them to "grow up"—to decide what they want to do in life and to get on with it. According to Erikson (1968), our society supports youths by allowing them a **moratorium period**—a time during the high school and college years when they are relatively free of responsibilities and can experiment with different roles to find themselves (see Arnett, 2006). But our society also makes establishing an identity hard by giving youths a huge number of options and encouraging them to believe they can be anything they want to be.

Developmental Trends

James Marcia (1966) expanded on Erikson's theory and stimulated much research on identity formation by developing an interview procedure to assess where an adolescent is in the process of identity formation. Adolescents are classified into one of four identity statuses based on their progress toward an identity in each of several domains (for example, occupational, religious, and political–ideological). The key questions are whether an individual has experienced a *crisis* (or has seriously grappled with identity issues and explored alternatives) and whether he has achieved a *commitment* (that is, resolved the questions raised). On the basis of crisis and commitment, the individual is classified into one of the four identity statuses shown in ■ Figure 11.2.

	Commitment?	
	No Commitment Made	**Commitment Made**
No Crisis Experienced	**Diffusion Status** The individual has not yet thought about or resolved identity issues and has failed to chart directions in life. Example: "I haven't really thought much about religion, and I guess I don't know what I believe exactly."	**Foreclosure Status** The individual seems to know who he or she is but has latched onto an identify prematurely with little thought. Example: "My parents are Baptists, and I'm a Baptist; it's just the way I grew up."
Crisis Experienced	**Moratorium Status** The individual is experiencing an identity crisis, actively raising questions, and seeking answers. Example: "I'm in the middle of evaluating my beliefs and hope that I'll be able to figure out what's right for me. I've become skeptical about some of what I have been taught and am looking into other faiths for answers."	**Identity Achievement Status** The individual has resolved his/her identify crisis and made commitments to particular goals, beliefs, and values. Example: "I really did some soul-searching about my religion and other religions, too, and finally know what I believe and what I don't."

Crisis? (row axis label)

■ **FIGURE 11.2** The four identity statuses as they apply to religious identity.

How long does it take to achieve a sense of identity? Philip Meilman's (1979) study of college-bound boys between 12 and 18, 21-year-old college males, and 24-year-old young men provides an answer (see ■ **Figure 11.3**). Most of the 12- and 15-year-olds were in either the identity diffusion status or the identity foreclosure status. At these ages, many adolescents simply have not yet thought about who they are—either they have no idea or they know that any ideas they do have are likely to change (the **diffusion status,** with no crisis and no commitment). Other adolescents have made commitments, may say things like "I'm going to be a doctor like my dad," and appear to have their acts together. However, it becomes apparent that they have never thought through on their own what suits them best and have simply accepted identities suggested to them by their parents or other people (the **foreclosure status,** involving a commitment without a crisis).

As Figure 11.3 indicates, progress toward identity achievement becomes more evident starting at age 18. Notice that diffusion drops off steeply and more individuals begin to fall into the **moratorium status.** Now they are experiencing a crisis or actively exploring identity issues; now they may be questioning their religious upbringing, experimenting with drugs, changing majors or relationships, or putting outrageous postings in Facebook or MySpace, all to find themselves. Presumably, en-

tering the moratorium status is a good sign; if the individual can not only raise questions but answer them, he will move to the **identity achievement status.** About 20% of the 18-year-olds, 40% of the college students, and slightly more than half of the 24-year-olds in Meilman's study had achieved a firm identity based on a careful weighing of alternatives.

Females progress toward achieving a clear sense of identity at about the same rate that males do. However, one reliable sex difference has been observed: Although college women are just as concerned about establishing a career identity as men are, they attach greater importance to and think more about the aspects of identity that center on sexuality, interpersonal relations, and balancing career and family goals (S. L. Archer, 1992; Kroger, 1997; Meeus et al., 1999). These concerns probably reflect the influence of traditional gender roles.

Judging from such research, identity formation *takes a long time.* Many young men and women move from the diffusion or the foreclosure status to the moratorium status and then achieve a sense of identity in their late teens or early 20s during the period of emerging adulthood (Waterman, 1982). But this is by no means the end of the identity formation process. Some adults continue in a moratorium status for years; others reopen the question of who they are after thinking they had all the answers earlier in life (Anthis & LaVoie, 2006; Kroger, 1996). Even in their 60s, some adults are reworking and strengthening their sense of identity (Zucker, Ostrove, & Stewart, 2002).

Identity formation not only takes a long time but *occurs at different rates in different domains of identity* (Kroger, 1996). For example, Sally Archer (1982) assessed the identity statuses of 6th- to 12th-graders in four domains: occupational choice, gender-role attitudes, religious beliefs, and political ideologies. Only 5% of the adolescents were in the same identity status in all four areas, and more than 90% were in two or three statuses across the four areas. Generally adolescents seem to make greater progress in sorting out their vocational identity than in exploring their religious or political identities (Coté, 2006).

Finally, the patterns of identity development discovered in longitudinal studies *are not always consistent with theory* (Meeus et al., 1999; van Hoof, 1999). For example, some youth slide backward before they move forward again (Reis & Youniss, 2004). In short, identity development is complex. It takes a long time, occurs at different rates in different domains, and does not always unfold in the theoretically expected way from diffusion or foreclosure to moratorium to identity achievement. In the Explorations box, we look at an alternative approach to studying identity—the life story, or narrative identity, approach.

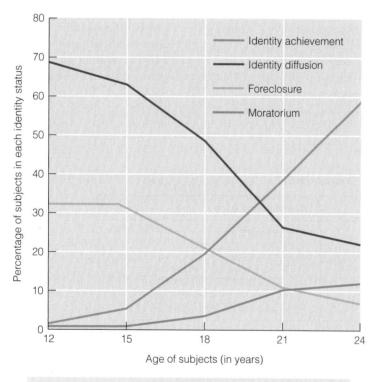

■ **FIGURE 11.3** Percentage of subjects in each of James Marcia's four identity statuses as a function of age. Note that only 4% of the 15-year-olds and 20% of the 18-year-olds had achieved a stable identity.

SOURCE: From P. W. Meilman, Cross-sectional age changes in ego identity status during adolescence, *Developmental Psychology, 15,* pp. 230–231. Copyright 1997 American Psychological Association. Reprinted with permission from the American Psychological Association.

Developing a Positive Ethnic Identity

The process of identity development includes forging an **ethnic identity**—a sense of personal identification with an ethnic group and its values and cultural traditions (Phinney, 1996, 2006; Umana-Taylor & Alfaro, 2006). Everyone has an ethnic and racial background, but members of minority groups tend to put more emphasis than white adolescents on defining who they are ethnically or racially. This is probably because major-

THE NARRATIVE IDENTITY APPROACH TO PERSONALITY: LIFE STORIES

Picture your life as a book that tells your life story from your birth to your death. Outline the major scenes, describing the high and low points, the turning points that really defined who you are, and your dreams and fears for the future.

One of the principles of personality introduced at the start of this chapter is that people construct narrative identities, or life stories, that reconstruct their personal histories and imagine their futures. These coherent, integrative stories give their lives meaning and purpose (McAdams & Pals, 2006). What do these life stories look like, and how does the process of constructing a life story relate to the process of forming an identity in Erik Erikson's sense?

According to Dan McAdams (2005), a life story says "who I am, how I came to be, and where my life is going in the future" (p. 241). (Sounds like identity so far, doesn't it?) We start narrating our experiences at about age 2 and learn how to structure a story better as we get older. Emerging adulthood (roughly age 18–25) appears to be the prime time, though, for creating a life story that gives life purpose and direction—as well as for achieving a sense of identity. Life stories are then revised over the years and reflected upon in old age, and they become an important element of our unique personalities. In the chapter opener, you heard snippets from Tom Cruise's life story.

To study life stories, McAdams and other researchers ask people to do what you were asked to do at the start of this Explorations box—to talk or write about your past, present, and future. Stories are then coded for such qualities as their coherence, tone, and themes. McAdams has found that adults who tell "redemptive life stories" in which they overcome difficulties and go on to a better life (like Tom Cruise at the start of the chapter going from abused child to successful movie star and father) tend to be more satisfied with their lives and to have a stronger sense of generativity or caring in Erikson's sense than other adults.

Kate McLean and Michael Pratt (2006) directly compared James Marcia's identity status approach and the narrative identity–life story approach by asking young people to write about turning points in their lives and to answer questions aimed at establishing their identity statuses. The same questions were asked periodically beginning when the participants were 17-year-old high school students and concluding when they were age 23. The researchers coded the extent of "meaning making" in the life narratives—the extent to which individuals derived personal meaning from turning points such as the death of a loved one, falling in love, or landing a job and came to think differently about themselves as a result.

The study revealed clear connections between meaning making and identity statuses. Specifically, sophisticated meaning making in narratives was negatively correlated with being in the diffusion or foreclosure statuses and positively correlated with an index of overall identity achievement, as well as with optimism and a measure of Erikson's concept of generativity. Moreover, individuals who made progress in exploring identity at age 19 told more reflective turning point narratives at age 23, suggesting that forming an identity and constructing a meaningful life story are related.

In a review of research on narrative identity, James Birren and Johannes Schroots (2006) conclude that most people tell more positive than negative stories about themselves and that men focus more on work whereas women focus more on family and health themes. An interesting age difference also emerges: Older adults recall their pasts more positively and envision their futures more negatively than young adults do. Possibly they have come to terms with some of the bad things that happened to them years ago and, realistically, anticipate health-related problems as they age. How people construct their life stories probably influences not only their sense of well-being but, by incorporating their aspirations, the choices they make and their later life outcomes (Birren & Schroots, 2006). We are just beginning to learn how to decipher the stories people tell about themselves.

---

ity group members often do not think of themselves as having an ethnicity whereas minority group members become very aware of theirs (Bracey, Bamaca, & Umana-Taylor, 2004; Laursen & Williams, 2002).

The process begins in infancy as babies notice differences among people; in one study, 3-month-old Caucasian infants already showed a preference for looking at other Caucasian babies rather than at babies from other ethnic backgrounds (Kelly et al., 2005). African babies living in Israel show a similar preference for African faces, though not if they grow up among Caucasians, suggesting that babies form these preferences based on the faces they see most often (Bar-Haim et al., 2006).

During the preschool years, children learn more about different racial and ethnic categories and gradually become able to classify themselves correctly into one (Spencer & Markstrom-Adams, 1990). For example, Mexican American preschool children learn behaviors associated with their culture, such as how to give a Chicano handshake, but they often

do not know until about age 8 what ethnic labels apply to them, what they mean, or that their ethnicity will last a lifetime (Bernal & Knight, 1997).

In forming a positive ethnic identity, adolescents seem to proceed through the same identity statuses as they do in forming a vocational or religious identity (Phinney, 1993; Seaton, Scottham, & Sellers, 2006). School-age children and young adolescents say either that they identify with their racial or ethnic group because their parents and others in their ethnic group influenced them to do so (foreclosure status) or that they have not given the matter much thought (diffusion status). In their mid to late teens, many minority youths move into the moratorium and achievement statuses with respect to ethnic identity, although some regress backward too (Seaton, Scottham, & Sellers, 2006). Others do not reflect on their ethnic identity until their 20s, especially if they have grown up in a homogenous environment and have had little interaction with other ethnic and racial groups (Phinney, 2006).

Youth are most likely to explore ethnic identity issues, establish a positive ethnic identity, and enjoy high self-esteem when their parents socialize them regarding their ethnicity by teaching them about their group's cultural traditions, preparing them to live in a culturally diverse society, and even preparing them to deal with prejudice, at least as long as it does not make them overly angry and mistrustful (Hughes et al., 2006; Umana-Taylor, Bhanot, & Shin, 2006). By contrast, minority youth may have difficulty feeling good about themselves if they must deal with prejudice—if, for example, they are called racist names or treated by teachers as if they were incompetent (Nyborg & Curry, 2003).

Once formed, a positive ethnic identity can protect adolescents' self-concepts from the damaging effects of racial discrimination (Wong, Eccles, & Sameroff, 2003), breed high self-esteem (Bracey et al., 2004), and promote academic achievement and good adjustment (Laursen & Williams, 2002). Most minority adolescents cope well with the special challenges they face in identity formation. They settle their questions of ethnic identity, they resolve other identity issues around the same ages that European American youth do (Markstrom-Adams & Adams, 1995), and they wind up feeling at least as good about themselves (Gray-Little & Hafdahl, 2000). Even multiracial youth, who must figure out what it means to have a mixed heritage, appear to be as well-adjusted in most respects as other youth (Shih & Sanchez, 2005).

Vocational Identity and Choice

I wanted to be a firefighter, then I touched a spark. I'm too afraid. I wanted to be a teacher, then I babysat for a 4-year-old. I'm too impatient. I wanted to be a model, then I looked in the mirror. I'm too short.

I know, I know—I can be anything I want when I am all grown up. But I am rapidly approaching all grown up and I see less of what I can be and more of what I cannot be. (Kelly Witte, *The Washington Post*, April 2, 2006, p. D1)

Vocational identity is a central aspect of identity with major implications for adult development. How do adolescents choose careers that express their sense of self as they prepare for adulthood? Children under about age 10 actively explore vocational possibilities but are not very realistic in their choices; they may want to be zookeepers, professional basketball players, firefighters, rock stars, or whatever else strikes them as glamorous and exciting (Ginzberg, 1972, 1984; Hartung, Porfeli, & Vondracek, 2005). As Linda Gottfredson (1996) emphasizes, children make important progress, though, beginning to narrow their ideas about future careers to those consistent with their emerging self-concepts—as humans rather than as bunnies or ninja turtles, as males rather than as females, and so on. As early as kindergarten, for instance, boys choose traditionally masculine occupations, and girls choose traditionally female occupations, although more girls today are daring to express interest in traditionally male jobs (Etaugh & Liss, 1992; Hartung et al., 2005). Children also learn a lot about and are guided by the social status associated with different careers; they begin to prefer the idea of being a surgeon to the idea of being a butcher.

Like teenager Kelly Witte, quoted above, adolescents age 11 to age 18 become more realistic, begin to weigh factors other than their wishes, and make preliminary vocational choices (Ginzberg, 1972, 1984). They consider their interests ("Would I enjoy counseling people?"), their capacities ("Am I skilled at relating to people?"), and their values ("Is it really important to me to help people, or do I value power or money more?"). By early adolescence, expressed vocational interests become quite stable, at least as stable as personality traits, and begin to predict vocational interests in early adulthood and middle age quite well (Low et al., 2005).

As they get still older, adolescents begin to take into account the realities of the job market and the physical and intellectual requirements for different occupations, and they begin serious preparation for their chosen occupations (Ginzberg, 1972, 1984; Walls, 2000). By late adolescence or emerging adulthood, they are in a good position to consider the availability of job openings in a field such as school counseling, the years of education required, the work conditions, and other relevant factors.

The main developmental trend evident in vocational choice is *increasing realism with age*. As adolescents narrow career choices in terms of both personal factors (their own interests, capacities, and values) and environmental factors (the opportunities available and the realities of the job market), they seek the vocation that best suits them. According to vocational theorists such as John Holland (1985), vocational choice is just this: a search for an optimal fit between one's self-concept and personality and an occupation (see also Super, Savickas, &

Establishing a positive ethnic identity is more central for minority adolescents than for white ones.

Mike Watson Images Limited/First Light

Super, 1996). People do indeed tend to enter occupations that match up well with their personalities (Ozer & Benet-Martinez, 2006).

Adolescents from lower income families, especially minority group members living in poverty and facing limited opportunities, stigmatization, and stress, may have difficulty forming a positive vocational identity (Phillips & Pittman, 2003). They may aim high at first but lower their career aspirations and aim toward the jobs they think they are likely to get rather than the jobs they most want (Armstrong & Crombie, 2000; Hartung et al., 2005). Similarly, the vocational choices of females have been and continue to be constrained by traditional gender norms. Young women who have adopted traditional gender-role attitudes and expect to marry and start families early in adulthood sometimes set their educational and vocational sights low, figuring that they cannot "have it all" (Mahaffy & Ward, 2002). Although more young women aspire toward high-status jobs now, many others, influenced by gender norms, do not seriously consider traditionally male-dominated jobs, doubt their ability to attain such jobs, and aim instead toward feminine-stereotyped, and often lower-status and lower-paying, occupations (Armstrong & Crombie, 2000; Hartung et al., 2005).

Moreover, many teenagers, male and female, simply do not do as Erikson and vocational theorists would advise—explore a range of possible occupations, then make a choice. Fully 69% of the high school and university students in one study acknowledged that chance events had a lot to do with their career decisions (Bright, Pryor, & Harpham, 2005). Those adolescents who *do* investigate a range of options are more likely than those who do not to choose careers that fit their personalities (Grotevant & Cooper, 1986). A good fit between person and vocation, in turn, predicts greater job satisfaction and success (Spokane, Meir, & Catalano, 2000; Verquer, Beehr, & Wagner, 2003). The saving grace is that those who do not explore thoroughly as adolescents have plenty of opportunities to change their minds as adults.

Influences on Identity Formation

The adolescent's progress toward achieving identity in various domains is a product of at least five factors: (1) cognitive growth, (2) personality, (3) relationships with parents, (4) opportunities to explore, and (5) cultural context. *Cognitive development* enables adolescents to imagine and contemplate possible future identities. Adolescents who have achieved solid mastery of formal-operational thought, who think in complex and abstract ways, and who are self-directed and actively seek relevant information when they face decisions are more likely to raise and resolve identity issues than less cognitively advanced adolescents (Berzonsky & Kuk, 2000; Waterman, 1992). Second, *personality* is a factor; adolescents who explore and achieve identity have been found to be low in neuroticism and high in openness to experience and conscientiousness (Ozer & Benet-Martinez, 2006). That is, they are well-adjusted, curious, and responsible.

Third, adolescents' *relationships with parents* affect their progress in forging an identity (Markstrom-Adams, 1992; Waterman, 1982). Youths who get stuck in the diffusion status of identity formation are more likely than those in the other categories to be neglected or rejected by their parents and to be distant from them. It can be difficult to forge an identity without first having the opportunity to identify with respected parental figures and to take on some of their desirable qualities. At the other extreme, adolescents in the foreclosure status appear to be extremely close—sometimes too close—to parents who are loving but overly protective and controlling. Because foreclosed adolescents love their parents and have little opportunity to make decisions on their own, they may never question parental authority or feel a need to forge a separate identity.

By comparison, students classified in the moratorium and identity achievement statuses appear to have a solid base of affection at home combined with freedom to be individuals. Adolescents who make good progress in identity formation tend to be securely attached to their parents (Samuolis, Layburn, & Schiaffino, 2001). In addition, their parents set rules and monitor their activities (Sartor & Youniss, 2002). In family discussions, these adolescents experience a sense of closeness and mutual respect but also feel free to disagree with their parents (Grotevant & Cooper, 1986). Notice that this is the same warm and democratic parenting style that seems to help younger children gain a strong sense of self-esteem.

Opportunities to explore are a fourth influence on identity formation. For example, adolescents who attend college are exposed to diverse ideas and encouraged to think through issues independently. Although college students may be more confused for a time about their identities than peers who begin working after high school (Munro & Adams, 1977), going to college provides the kind of moratorium period with freedom to explore that Erikson felt was essential to identity formation.

Finally, identity formation is influenced by the broader *cultural context* in which it occurs—a point Erikson also emphasized. The notion that adolescents should forge a personal identity after carefully exploring many options may well be peculiar to modern industrialized Western societies (Coté & Levine, 1988; Flum & Blustein, 2000). As was true of adolescents in earlier eras, adolescents in many traditional societies today simply adopt the adult roles they are expected to adopt in their culture, without much soul-searching or experimentation. For many adolescents in traditional societies, what Marcia calls identity foreclosure may be the most adaptive path to adulthood (Coté & Levine, 1988).

In Western industrialized societies, however, the adolescent who is able to raise serious questions about the self and answer them—that is, the individual who achieves identity—is likely to be better off for it. Identity achievement is associated with psychological well-being and high self-esteem, complex thinking about moral issues and other matters, a willingness to accept and cooperate with other people, and a variety of other psychological strengths (Waterman, 1992).

Summing Up

- During adolescence, self-awareness increases, self-concepts become more psychological, abstract, and integrated, and self-esteem may dip early but rebounds.

- Resolving Erikson's crisis of identity versus role confusion means progressing from Marcia's diffusion and foreclosure identity statuses to the moratorium and identity achievement statuses, a process that is uneven across domains of identity and extends into late adolescence and early adulthood.

- Establishing an ethnic identity begins in infancy and childhood and is generally more important to minority youths than to majority youths.

- In establishing vocational identities, adolescents become more realistic with age and seek a good fit between self and occupation.

- Identity achievement is facilitated by cognitive development, personality traits such as openness to experience, warm and democratic parenting, opportunities to explore, and a culture that encourages experimentation.

Critical Thinking

1. Write three brief descriptions of yourself to show how you might have answered the question "Who am I?" at age 4, age 9, and age 18. What developmental changes in self-conceptions do your self-descriptions illustrate?

2. Aaron is having a terrible time achieving a sense of identity; he has been drifting aimlessly through various jobs and relationships for years. Drawing on the material in this chapter, explain why this may be the case.

11.5 | The Adult

We enter adulthood having gained a great deal of understanding of what we are like as individuals—but we are not done developing. How do self-conceptions change and stay the same over the adult years, and to what extent are they shaped by the culture in which the individual develops? How do personalities change and remain the same, and how are both self-concepts and personalities related to the psychological changes adults experience as their careers unfold?

Self-Conceptions

It is clear that adults differ from one another in their self-perceptions and levels of self-esteem. We now discuss how both age and cultural context help explain that variation.

Age Differences

In Western society, it is commonly believed that adults gain self-esteem as they cope successfully with the challenges of adult life but then lose it as aging, disease, and losses of roles and relationships take their toll in later life. Is there truth to this view? A large survey over the Internet of more than 300,000 people ages 9 to 90 conducted by Richard Robins and his colleagues (2002) suggests there is. Self-esteem tends to be relatively high in childhood, to drop in adolescence, to rise gradually through the adult years until the mid-60s, then to drop in late old age, as shown in ■ Figure 11.4. The same analysis showed that males generally have higher self-esteem than females except in childhood and very old age.

So there is some support for the idea that self-esteem increases during the adult years and drops in late adulthood, although only in the 70s and 80s. Some other work suggests that elderly adults are more like young- and middle-aged adults than different in both levels of self-esteem and in the ways in which they describe themselves (Helgeson & Mickelson, 2000; Ruth & Coleman, 1996). Moreover, self-esteem at one age and self-esteem at a subsequent age are generally consistent (Trzesniewski, Donnellan, & Robins, 2003). There is little truth, then, to the stereotyped view that most older adults suffer from a poor self-image, even though self-esteem drops for some adults in very old age. How, then, do most elderly people manage to maintain positive self-images for so long, even as they experience some of the disabilities and losses that come with aging?

First, *older people adjust their ideal selves to be more in line with their real selves.* Carol Ryff (1991) asked young, middle-

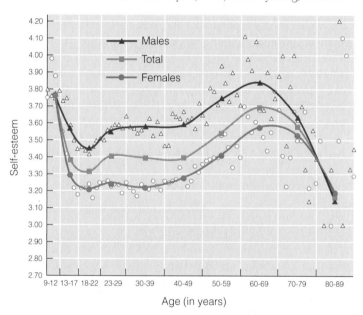

■ **FIGURE 11.4** Self-esteem dips in early adolescence and rises during the adult years until it declines in very old age. Males have higher scores than females except in childhood and late old age. The lines graph mean self-esteem for the various age groups shown; the triangles (for males) and circles (for females) plot mean self-esteem at particular ages in the many studies summarized in this meta-analysis.
SOURCE: From R. W. Robins, K. H. Trzesniewski, J. L. Tracy, S. D. Gosling, & J. Potter, Global self-esteem across the life span. *Psychology and Aging, 17,* pp. 423–434. Copyright © 2002 American Psychological Association. Reprinted with permission from the American Psychological Association.

aged, and elderly adults to assess their ideal, likely future, present, and past selves with respect to various dimensions of well-being, including self-acceptance. ■ Figure 11.5 shows the average scores on the self-acceptance scale. Ratings of the present self changed little across the adult years. However, older adults scaled down their visions of what they could ideally be and what they likely will be, possibly because they recognized that aging brings with it a loss of capacities. They also judged more positively what they had been. As a result, their ideal, future, present, and past selves converged. Notice, then, that the gap between the ideal self and the real self that widens during childhood and adolescence, and that gives us a sense of falling short, apparently closes again in later life, helping us maintain self-esteem.

Second, *people's goals and standards change with age* so that what seem like losses or failures to a younger person may not be perceived as such by the older adult (Carstensen & Freund, 1994; Helgeson & Mickelson, 2000). A 40-year-old may be devastated at being passed over for a promotion, whereas a 60-year-old nearing retirement may not be bothered at all (Carstensen & Freund, 1994, p. 87). For the older adult with

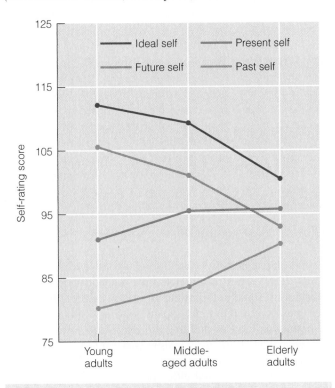

■ FIGURE 11.5 Favorability of ratings of their ideal, likely future, present (real), and past selves by young, middle-aged, and elderly adults. The gap between the ideal and the real self that widens during childhood and adolescence shrinks during adulthood, as indicated by the converging lines in the graph. As they age, adults become more comfortable with the idea of remaining as they are and as they have been.

SOURCE: From C. D. Ryff, Possible selves in adulthood and old age: A tale of shifting horizons, *Psychology and Aging, 6*, p. 286–295. Copyright © 1991 American Psychological Association. Reprinted with permission from the American Psychological Association.

a disability, walking a mile may be as much a triumph as running a mile might have been earlier in life (Rothermund & Brandtstädter, 2003b). As our goals and standards change over the life span, we apply different measuring sticks in evaluating ourselves and do not mind failing to achieve goals that are no longer important.

Third, older adults maintain self-esteem because *the people to whom they compare themselves are also old* (Brandtstädter & Greve, 1994; Helgeson & Mickelson, 2000). Older adults generally do not compare themselves with young adults but with people who have the same kinds of chronic diseases and impairments they have—or worse ones. If they want to feel good about themselves, they may even strategically select worse-off peers for social comparison (Frieswijk et al., 2004; Rothermund & Brandtstädter, 2003a), as in, "I'm getting around much better than poor Bessie is." Indeed, some observers argue that stereotypes of aging in our society are so bleak that older adults can feel better about their own aging simply by conjuring up an image of the typical "old person" (Brandtstädter & Greve, 1994). On balance, however, negative stereotypes of old age probably have more damaging than beneficial effects on the self-perceptions of elderly people, as shown in the Applications box on page 328.

Overall, then, adults of different ages generally describe themselves in similar ways, but self-esteem appears to rise in early and middle adulthood and to drop off in late old age. Many older adults are able to maintain self-esteem by perceiving a smaller gap than younger adults do between their real and ideal selves, changing the standards by which they evaluate their self-worth, and making social comparisons with other older people.

Cultural Differences

Self-conceptions show the imprint not only of individual experiences such as positive or negative feedback from parents and bosses but also of broader cultural influences. In an **individualistic culture,** individuals define themselves primarily as individuals and put their own goals ahead of their social group's goals, whereas in a **collectivist culture,** people define themselves in terms of group memberships and give group goals higher priority than personal goals (Triandis, 1989, 1995). Individualistic cultures socialize children to be independent and self-reliant, whereas collectivist ones teach interdependence with others, social harmony, and subordination of self-interest to the interests of the group. North American and Western European societies typically have an individualistic orientation, whereas many societies in Latin America, Africa, and Asia are primarily collectivist.

How do self-conceptions differ in individualistic and collectivist cultures? Hazel Markus and her colleagues have carefully studied the meanings of self in the United States and Japan (Cross, 2000; Markus, 2004; Markus, Mullally, & Kitayama, 1997). They have found that being a person in the United States (an individualistic culture) means being your own person—independent, unique, and differentiated from the rest of the social world, whereas being a person in Japan (a collec-

STEREOTYPES OF AGING AND SELF-PERCEPTIONS IN OLD AGE

Are the self-perceptions of elderly adults affected by the negative stereotypes of aging rampant in our society and, if so, can anything be done about it? Becca Levy (2003) argues that stereotypes of old people learned in childhood often become self-stereotypes when people reach old age. She cites studies indicating that children learn early to take a dim view of elderly people, to stereotype them as sick, weak, forgetful, and incompetent (and see Hess, 2006). These negative stereotypes are reinforced over the years and are available to be applied to the self once people begin to think of themselves as "old." True, aging adults often go to great lengths to deny that they are old—a sign in itself that old age is negatively perceived in our society. But eventually they can deny no longer, apply the "old" label to themselves, and run the risk of negatively stereotyping themselves.

To demonstrate that aging self-stereotypes can negatively affect the behavior of elderly adults, Levy and her associates (Hausdorff, Levy, & Wei, 1999) used a priming technique. Words reflecting either negative stereotypes of aging or positive stereotypes of aging were flashed rapidly on a computer screen to elderly participants in the study so that the words were perceived but were below the level of awareness. After the priming experience, these adults were asked to walk down a hall

wearing measuring devices on their feet that registered how rapidly they walked and how lightly they stepped (how long their feet were off the ground). Most people assume that a slow, shuffling gait in old age is caused by either biological aging or illness. This study demonstrated that social stereotypes can also slow people down. Older adults primed with positive stereotypes of aging clocked faster speeds and more foot-off-the-floor time than older adults who were exposed to negative stereotypes and shuffled along like old people. As Chapter 8 revealed, Levy (1996) has also found that priming older adults with words such as *senile* results in poorer memory performance than priming them with words such as *wise*.

Levy and her colleagues (2002) have even found that middle-aged adults who have positive perceptions of their own aging (for example, who disagree with statements such as "Things keep getting worse as I get older") end up not only in better health in old age but live more than 7 years longer than adults who have less positive self-perceptions of aging. This was the case even when age, health, socioeconomic status, and other relevant variables were controlled.

Are ageist stereotypes a hazard to old people, then? Klaus Rothermund and Jochen Brandtstädter (2003a) wanted to find out. They tested three competing hypotheses about the

relationship between aging stereotypes and self-perceptions in later life:

- Do aging stereotypes contaminate self-perceptions, as Levy (2003) argues?
- Alternatively, do aging stereotypes offer such a dismal view of old age that they give the self-concepts of aging adults a boost by allowing them to compare themselves with worse-off others?
- Instead, might aging stereotypes reflect self-perceptions rather than shape them? That is, might adults experiencing the negative effects of aging begin to take a dim view of old people in general?

These researchers asked German adults ages 54 to 77 at the start of the study to rate a "typical old person" and to rate themselves on the same scale. The sample was then studied over 8 years so that relationships between earlier and later stereotyped beliefs and self-perceptions could be assessed.

The adults in this study clearly had a more positive view of themselves than they had of the typical old person. They also became more charitable in their evaluations of old people as they aged. Otherwise, the results supported Levy's view that aging stereotypes damage self-perceptions. Holding negative aging stereotypes at the outset of the study led to negative self-perceptions later, whereas

---

tivist culture) means being interdependent, connected to others in social groups, and embedded in society. Thus, when asked to describe themselves, American adults talk about their unique personal qualities but Japanese adults more often refer to their social roles and identities and mention other people (for example, "I try to make my parents happy").

In addition, Americans describe their generalizable personality traits—traits they believe they display in most situations and relationships. By contrast, Japanese adults describe their behavior in specific contexts such as home, school, or work and may describe themselves differently depending on the social situation or context they are talking about. Indeed, the Japanese language has no word to refer to *I* apart from social context (Cross, 2000). In short, Americans think like trait theorists, whereas Japanese people seem to adopt a social learning theory on personality. The result is that Westerners are more likely than Easterners to feel that they have an inner self consistent across situations and over time (Tafarodi et al., 2004).

Finally, Americans are obsessed with maintaining high self-esteem; most believe that they are above average in most

respects. Japanese adults are more modest and self-critical (Cross, 2000). They readily note their inadequacies and seem reluctant to "stand out from the crowd" by calling attention to their positive qualities. In Japan, making a point of your strengths would mean slighting the importance of your group (Shweder et al., 1998, p. 907; also see ● **Table 11.3** for a summary of these differences).

Interestingly, cultural differences in self-descriptions can be detected as early as age 3 or 4 by asking children to talk about themselves and their experiences (Wang, 2004, 2006). American children talk about their roles, preferences, characteristics, and feelings, whereas Chinese children describe themselves in terms of social roles and social routines such as family dinners. They are a good deal more modest, too, saying things like "I sometimes forget my manners." Parents probably contribute to these cultural differences through everyday conversations with their children; for example, American mothers tell stories in which their children are the stars, whereas Chinese mothers talk about the experiences of the family as a group (Wang, 2004).

early self-perceptions did not affect later aging stereotypes. Moreover, the link between negative stereotypes of old age and negative self views was especially strong among the oldest adults in the study, perhaps helping explain the tendency for self-esteem to drop in late old age. In some studies, feeling healthier and more capable than other old people makes older people feel better rather than worse about themselves (Rothermund, 2005). On balance, though, this study and others suggest that ageist stereotypes do more harm than good, especially among people who have come to identify themselves as "old" and therefore apply ageist stereotypes to themselves (Hess, 2006; O'Brien & Hummert, 2006).

How might we combat ageist stereotypes and call attention to positive aspects of old age and aging? Intervention might best begin in childhood. For example, intergenerational programs in which elderly adults work with children in the schools not only help children learn but also improve their attitudes toward old people (Cummings, Williams, & Ellis, 2003). Interventions to combat ageism also need to be aimed at elderly people. For example, Levy's (2003) work suggests that activating positive stereotypes of aging before elderly people perform cognitive tasks may boost their performance, at least temporarily.

Some years ago, Judith Rodin and Ellen Langer (1980) set out to boost the self-esteem of elderly nursing home residents after discovering that 80% blamed physical aging for many of their difficulties in functioning and did not consider that the nursing home environment could be a source of their problems. In an experiment, Rodin and Langer exposed one group of nursing home residents to a new theory highlighting environmental causes of their limitations in functioning: That they had difficulty walking, for example, was attributed to the nursing home floors, which were tiled and therefore slippery for people of any age. Compared with an untreated control group and a group that received medical information that physical aging was not the major source of their difficulties, the group that learned to attribute everyday problems in functioning to the nursing home environment rather than to old age became more active, more sociable, and even more healthy.

Ultimately, societal-level change may be needed. Some countries (China, for example) clearly have more positive views of old age than the United States does (Levy & Langer, 1994). Possibly our ageist society can reduce ageism and promote more positive views of aging across the life span by instituting new social policies and programs (Braithwaite, 2002). Meanwhile, it seems that elderly people who can avoid taking negative stereotypes of old people to heart and who can avoid blaming the difficulties they encounter on the ravages of old age—that is, older adults who can avoid thinking like ageists—stand a good chance of feeling good about themselves.

What stereotypes do we have of elderly women?

Cross-cultural studies of individualistic and collectivist cultures challenge the Western assumption that a person cannot develop normally without individuating himself from others and coming to know his identity as an individual. In much of the world, it's about "self-in-relation-to-others," not about individuals with their own unique identities (Shweder et al., 2006). These studies also suggest that our methods for studying the self—asking people who they are, having them respond to personality scale items about how they generally behave across social contexts—may be culturally biased. Many of the world's people seem to get on quite nicely by not thinking much about how they differ from other group members and by describing themselves in specific social contexts. It is wise to bear in mind, then, that self-conceptions are culturally defined.

Continuity and Discontinuity in Personality

Apart from how we conceive of ourselves, how do our personalities change or remain the same over the years? To address questions of continuity and change in adult personality, we must ask two questions: Do *individual* adults retain their rankings on trait dimensions compared with others in a group over the years? Do *average* scores on personality trait measures increase, decrease, or remain the same as age increases?

Do People Retain Their Rankings?

Paul Costa, Robert McCrae, and their colleagues have closely studied personality change and continuity by giving adults from their 20s to their 90s personality tests and administering these tests repeatedly over the years (McCrae & Costa, 2003). Focusing on the Big Five dimensions of personality listed in Table 11.1, they have found a good deal of *stability in rankings within a group*, as indicated by high correlations between scores on the same trait dimensions at different ages. In other words, the person who tends to be extraverted as a young adult is likely to be extraverted as an elderly adult, and the introvert is likely to remain introverted over the years. Similarly, the adult who shows high or low levels of neuroticism, conscientiousness, agreeableness, or openness to new experiences is likely to retain that rank-

TABLE 11.3 VIEWS OF THE SELF IN INDIVIDUALISTIC AND COLLECTIVIST CULTURES

INDIVIDUALISTIC (E.G., UNITED STATES)	COLLECTIVIST (E.G., JAPAN)
Separate	Connected
Independent	Interdependent
Traitlike, personal qualities transcend specific situations and relationships	Flexible, different in different social contexts
Need for self-esteem results in seeing self as above average	Self-critical, aware of inadequacies
Emphasis on uniqueness	Emphasis on group memberships and similarities to others

SOURCE: From H. R. Markus, P. R. Mullally, & S. Kitayama, Diversity in modes of cultural participation, in U. Neisser & D. A. Jopling (EDs.), *The conceptual self in context. Culture, experience, self-understanding.* Copyright © 1997 Cambridge University Press. Reprinted with permission.

ing compared with that of peers years later. Correlations between personality trait scores on two occasions 20 to 30 years apart average about 0.60 across the five personality dimensions. Correlations of this size suggest consistency in personality over time but also room for change in response to life events (McCrae & Costa, 2003; Morizot & Le Blanc, 2003).

The tendency to be consistent increases with age. In a meta-analysis of 152 studies in which personality was assessed on two or more occasions, Brent Roberts and Wendy DelVecchio (2000) found that the average correlation between scores at two testings 6 to 7 years apart was 0.31 in infancy and early childhood, 0.54 in the college years, 0.64 at age 30, and 0.74 from age 50 on. Because they are still forming, personalities are unsettled in childhood and even in a person's teens and 20s. McCrae and Costa (2003) concluded that rankings on the Big Five are very stable by the time adults are in their 30s, but Roberts and DelVecchio (2000) and others have shown that personalities are still stabilizing as late as ages 50 to 60.

Do Mean Personality Scores Change?

Do most people change systematically in common directions over the years? You may be consistently more extraverted than your best friend over the years, and yet both of you could become less extraverted at age 70 than you were at age 20. This second major type of continuity in personality, *stability in the average level of a trait,* is relevant when we ask whether there is truth to stereotypes of older adults—for example, that they are more rigid, grumpy, depressed, and passive than younger adults.

Early cross-sectional studies suggested that younger and older adults have different personalities on average. However, some age-group differences have turned out to be generational,

or cohort, differences rather than true maturational changes. That is, people's personalities are affected by when they were born and by the experiences they had in their formative years (Roberts, Walton, & Viechtbauer, 2006; Schaie & Parham, 1976). For example, Jean Twenge (2000) has shown that recent cohorts of children and adults have scored higher on measures of anxiety and neuroticism than earlier generations did, possibly because the world has become more complex and frightening.

When age-group differences appear consistently in different cultures undergoing different social changes at different times, they are not likely to be because of cohort effects. McCrae, Costa, and their colleagues (2000) have examined age-group differences in scores on the Big Five personality dimensions in countries as diverse as Turkey, the Czech Republic, and Japan. They find that extraversion (especially excitement-seeking) and openness to experience decline modestly from adolescence to middle age, whereas emotional stability (the opposite of neuroticism), agreeableness, and conscientiousness increase over this same age range. From adolescence to middle adulthood, then, we become less in need of stimulation and less open to new experiences but more psychologically mature—more emotionally stable, more cooperative and easy to get along with, and more disciplined and responsible. A major meta-analysis combining the results of longitudinal studies largely reinforced these findings, especially the decrease in openness to experience and the increase in emotional stability and conscientiousness (Roberts et al., 2006). Although personality change was most evident in early adulthood, several modest changes were detected in middle age, contradicting McCrae and Costa's view (which they have now softened), that the personality is largely set by age 30.

Middle-aged adults tend to be less neurotic and open to new experiences but more agreeable and conscientious than adolescents.

What personality changes can people expect from middle age to old age? Activity level—the tendency to be energetic and action oriented, an aspect of extraversion—begins to decline in people's 50s and continues declining through the 80s and 90s (McCrae & Costa, 2003). Otherwise, most of us will not undergo similar personality changes as part of the aging experience. Either we will remain much the same or we will change in response to life experiences in our own ways and at our own times (Helson, Jones, & Kwan, 2002).

Evidence of similar age differences in personality in different cultures, coupled with evidence that the Big Five personality trait dimensions are genetically influenced (Krueger et al., 2006; Yamagata et al., 2006), has led McCrae and Costa (2003) to conclude that the Big Five:

- Are biologically based temperaments
- Are relatively resistant to environmental influences
- Undergo a universal process of maturational change

McCrae and Costa go on to theorize that evolution is behind maturational changes in personality. For our ancestors, they argue, a good deal of extraversion and openness to new experiences during adolescence might have proved useful in exploring the environment and, in the process, finding mates and other valued resources. For adults raising children, though, emotional stability, conscientiousness, and agreeableness may have proved more adaptive.

Although they are convinced that age-related changes in Big Five personality dimensions are universal and biologically based, McCrae and Costa acknowledge that cultural and social influences more strongly shape what McAdams and Pals (2006) call *characteristic adaptations*—the specific ways in which people adjust to their environments and learn habits, social roles, and attitudes.

So most evidence points to (1) a good deal of cross-age consistency in people's rankings compared with other people on Big Five personality trait dimensions; (2) cohort effects suggesting that the historical context in which people grow up affects their personality development; (3) personality growth from adolescence to middle adulthood highlighted by less openness to experience but more emotional stability and conscientiousness; and (4) little personality change from middle adulthood to later adulthood except for decreased activity level. In short, there is both continuity and discontinuity in personality during adulthood.

Why Do People Change or Remain the Same?

Having figured out that personality exhibits both stability and change over the life span, developmentalists naturally want to know why people stay the same and why they change. What makes a personality stable? First, *heredity* is at work. As we have noted, genes contribute to individual differences in all five of the Big Five personality factors (Borkenau et al., 2001; Krueger et al., 2006). Second, *lasting effects of childhood experiences* may contribute; you have seen, for example, that parents can either help a child overcome a difficult temperament or con-

tribute to its becoming an enduring pattern of response. Third, traits may remain stable because people's *environments remain stable*. Fourth, *gene–environment correlations* may promote continuity. That is, genetic endowment may influence the kinds of experiences we have, and those experiences, in turn, may strengthen our genetically based predispositions (Roberts & Caspi, 2003; also see Chapter 3). Thus, an extravert's early sociability will elicit friendly responses from others, cause her to seek out social activities, and in the process strengthen her initial tendency to be extraverted. By contrast, the person genetically predisposed to be introvert may avoid crowds, keep to himself, and therefore remain an introverted individual, comfortable with himself and his lifestyle. In a kind of snowball effect involving correlated genes and environments, the consequences of having one early temperament rather than another will cumulate over the years (Caspi, 1998; Donnellan et al., 2006).

What, then, might cause the significant changes in personality that some adults experience? *Biological factors* such as disease could contribute. The nervous system deterioration associated with Huntington's disease or Alzheimer's disease, for example, can cause victims to become moody, irritable, and irresponsible (McCrae & Costa, 2003). Adults also change in response to *changes in the environment*, including major life events (Caspi, 1998; Maiden et al., 2003). For example, young adults who land good jobs after college tend to gain confidence, whereas those who face job insecurity and unemployment in their early careers lose it (Mortimer, Finch, & Kumka, 1982), and marriage decreases neuroticism whereas the death of a spouse increases it for a time (Mroczek & Spiro, 2003). In this way, life events and learning experiences help shape personality development, much as social learning theorists claim.

Finally, change is more likely when there is *a poor fit between person and environment* (Roberts & Robins, 2004). For example, Florine Livson (1976) discovered that independent women who did not have traditionally feminine traits experienced more personality change during midlife than traditional women who fit the stereotypically feminine roles of wife and mother better. Bothered by the mismatch between their personalities and their traditionally feminine roles, the nontraditional women redirected their lives in their 40s, expressed their masculine sides, and experienced better psychological health by their 50s. Similarly, men who fit the traditional male role changed less over the years than nontraditional men who felt cramped by this role and who, after a crisis in their 40s, began to express their more feminine, emotional sides (Livson, 1981). For both men and women, then, a poor person–environment fit prompted personality change.

Thus, genes, lasting effects of early childhood experiences, stable environments, and gene–environment correlations all contribute to the considerable continuity seen in adult personality. Change in personality becomes more likely if people's biologies or environments change or if there is a poor fit between their personalities and their lifestyles.

To the extent that there is continuity in personality, people can predict what they and other people will be like in the future or how they will respond to life events. For example, individuals who score high on measures of neuroticism and low on measures of extraversion are likely to experience more negative and fewer positive life events than other people (Magnus et al., 1993) and to have more difficulty coping with negative life events when they occur (Hoffman, Levy-Shiff, & Malinski, 1996), whereas older adults who are extraverted and open to experience adapt well to potential stressors (Kling et al., 2003).

Eriksonian Psychosocial Growth

Researchers like Costa and McCrae who conclude that adults change little over the years typically study personality by administering standardized personality scales. These tests were designed to assess enduring traits and probably reveal the most stable aspects of personality. Researchers who interview people in depth about their lives often detect considerably more change and growth (McCrae & Costa, 2003).

This is clear in research on Erikson's theory of psychosocial development through the life span. Erikson's eight stages of psychosocial development, listed in ● **Table 11.4,** will be reviewed briefly here, with emphasis on their implications for development during adulthood (see also Chapter 2). Both maturational forces and social demands, Erikson believed, push humans everywhere through these eight psychosocial crises. Later conflicts may prove difficult to resolve if early conflicts were not resolved successfully. For development to proceed optimally, a healthy balance between the terms of each conflict must be struck; if this happens, the individual gains a particular "virtue," or psychosocial strength.

The Path to Adulthood

During Erikson's first psychosocial conflict, **trust versus mistrust,** infants learn to trust other people if their caregivers are responsive to their needs; otherwise, the balance of trust versus

mistrust will tip in the direction of mistrust. Erikson believed that infants, in resolving the psychosocial conflict of basic trust versus mistrust, begin to recognize that they are separate from the caregivers who respond to their needs. Indeed, as you saw earlier in this chapter, infants begin to distinguish self from other (typically the mother) during the first 2 or 3 months of life.

Toddlers acquire an even clearer sense of themselves as individuals as they struggle with the psychosocial conflict of **autonomy versus shame and doubt.** According to Erikson, they develop a sense of themselves and assert that they have wills of their own. Consistent with this view, toddlers recognize themselves in a mirror and lace their speech with "me" and "no" around 18 months of age. Four- and five-year-olds who have achieved a sense of autonomy then enter Erikson's stage of **initiative versus guilt.** They develop a sense of purpose by devising bold plans and taking great pride in accomplishing the goals they set. As you have seen, preschoolers define themselves primarily in terms of their physical activities and accomplishments.

A sense of initiative, Erikson believed, paves the way for success when elementary-school children face the conflict of **industry versus inferiority** and focus on mastering important cognitive and social skills. As you have seen, elementary-school children seem intent on evaluating their competencies; they engage in more social comparison than younger children and are likely to acquire a sense of industry rather than one of inferiority if those comparisons turn out favorably.

According to Erikson, children who successfully master each of these childhood psychosocial conflicts gain new ego strengths. Moreover, they learn a good deal about themselves and position themselves to resolve the adolescent crisis of *identity versus role confusion,* Erikson's fifth stage. As you saw in some detail earlier in this chapter, adolescence is a time for raising and answering identity questions. But what happens to adolescents with newfound identities during the adult years? Erikson thought that stagelike changes in personality—and ex-

● TABLE 11.4 THE EIGHT STAGES OF ERIKSON'S PSYCHOSOCIAL THEORY

STAGE	AGE RANGE	CENTRAL ISSUE	VIRTUE OR STRENGTH
1. Trust vs. mistrust	Birth to 1 year	Can I trust others?	Hope
2. Autonomy vs. shame and doubt	1 to 3 years	Can I act on my own?	Will
3. Initiative vs. guilt	3 to 6 years	Can I carry out my plans successfully?	Purpose
4. Industry vs. inferiority	6 to 12 years	Am I competent compared with others?	Competence
5. Identity vs. role confusion	12 to 20 years	Who am I?	Fidelity
6. Intimacy vs. isolation	20 to 40 years	Am I ready for a relationship?	Love
7. Generativity vs. stagnation	40 to 65 years	Have I left my mark?	Care
8. Integrity vs. despair	65 years and older	Has my life been meaningful?	Wisdom

citing possibilities for personal growth—continue during adulthood through psychosocial crises focused on intimacy versus isolation, generativity versus stagnation, and integrity versus despair.

Early Adult Intimacy

As Erikson saw it, early adulthood is a time for dealing with the psychosocial conflict of **intimacy versus isolation.** He theorized that a person must achieve a sense of individual identity before becoming able to commit himself to a shared identity with another person—that is, you must know yourself before you can love someone else. The young adult who has no clear sense of self may be threatened by the idea of entering a committed, long-term relationship and being "tied down," or he may become overdependent on a romantic partner (or possibly a close friend) as a source of identity.

Does identity indeed pave the way for genuine intimacy? To find out, Susan Whitbourne and Stephanie Tesch (1985) measured identity status and intimacy status among college seniors and 24- to 27-year-old alumni from the same university. The researchers interviewed people about their closest relationships and placed each person in one of six "intimacy statuses." These included being a social isolate with no close relationships, being in a shallow relationship with little communication or involvement, being in a deep relationship but not yet being ready to make a long-term commitment to a partner, and being in a genuinely intimate relationship that has it all—involvement, open communication, and a long-term commitment. College graduates had progressed farther than college seniors in resolving intimacy issues; more of them were in long-term, committed relationships. In addition, the college gradu-

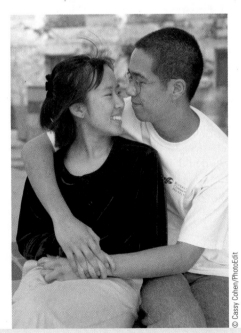

Early adulthood is the time, according to Erik Erikson, for deciding whether to commit to a shared identity with another person.

ates who had well-formed identities were more likely than those who did not to be capable of genuine and lasting intimacy.

As Erikson theorized, then, we must know ourselves before we can truly love another person (see also Montgomery, 2005). Yet Erikson believed that women resolve identity questions when they choose a mate and fashion an identity around their roles as wife and mother-to-be. Is this rather sexist view correct? Only for some women. Influenced by traditional sex-role expectations, some women resolve intimacy issues before identity issues: they marry, raise children, and only after the children are more self-sufficient ask who they are as individuals (Hodgson & Fischer, 1979). Other women with feminine gender-role orientations tackle identity and intimacy issues simultaneously, perhaps forging a personal identity that centers on caring for other people or defining themselves in the context of a love relationship (Dyk & Adams, 1990).

However, still other women with more masculine gender-role orientations tend to follow the identity-before-intimacy route that characterizes men, settling on a career first, thinking about a serious relationship next (Dyk & Adams, 1990). Overall, then, Erikson's theory seems to fit men better than it fits women because fewer women follow the hypothesized identity-then-intimacy path. Sex differences in routes to identity and intimacy are likely to diminish, however, as more women postpone marriage to pursue careers.

Midlife Generativity

Does psychosocial growth continue in middle age? George Vaillant (1977), a psychoanalytic theorist, conducted an in-depth longitudinal study of mentally healthy Harvard men from college to middle age and a similar longitudinal study of blue-collar workers (Vaillant, 1983; Vaillant & Milofsky, 1980). Vaillant found support for Erikson's view that the 20s are a time for intimacy issues. He found that in their 30s, men shifted their energies to advancing their careers and were seldom reflective or concerned about others. Finally, in their 40s, many men became concerned with Erikson's issue of **generativity versus stagnation,** which involves gaining the capacity to generate or produce something that outlives you and to care about the welfare of future generations through such activities as parenting, teaching, mentoring, and leading (de St. Aubin, McAdams, & Kim, 2004; Slater, 2003). Vaillant's 40-something men expressed more interest in passing on something of value, either to their own children or to younger people at work. Few experienced a full-blown and turbulent midlife crisis, just as few had experienced a severe identity crisis as college students. Nonetheless, they were growing as individuals, often becoming more caring and self-aware as they entered their 50s. One of these men expressed the developmental progression Vaillant detected perfectly: "At 20 to 30, I think I learned how to get along with my wife. From 30 to 40, I learned how to be a success in my job. And at 40 to 50, I worried less about myself and more about the children" (1977, p. 195).

Dan McAdams and others have been studying midlife generativity in more depth (de St. Aubin, McAdams, & Kim,

2004). Their studies show, first, that middle-aged men and women are more likely than young adults to have achieved a sense of generativity (McAdams, Hart, & Maruna, 1998; Timmer, Bode, & Dittmann-Kohli, 2003). Moreover, those adults who have achieved a sense of identity and intimacy are more likely than other adults to achieve generativity, as Erikson predicted (Christiansen & Palkovitz, 1998). Adults who score high on measures of generativity are caring people, committed parents, productive workers and mentors, and community leaders. In Big Five terms, generative adults tend to be agreeable, emotionally stable (low in neuroticism), and open to experience (McAdams et al.,1998), and they are more satisfied with their lives (McAdams & Logan, 2004). Overall, research on generativity supports Erikson's view that both women and men are capable of impressive psychosocial growth during middle adulthood.

Old Age Integrity

Elderly adults, according to Erikson, confront the psychosocial issue of **integrity versus despair.** They try to find a sense of meaning in their lives that will help them face the inevitability of death. If they constructed a life story or narrative identity during their early adult years, they work on accepting it in old age as the only life they could have led (McAdams & Adler, 2006).

A sense of identity in early adulthood predicts both generativity and integrity in later life, and a sense of integrity is in turn related to a high sense of psychological well-being and low depression or despair (James & Zarrett, 2005). Ultimately, most older adults seem to attain a sense of integrity; when asked what they would do differently if they had their lives to live over, they say there is little, if anything, they would change (Erikson, Erikson, & Kivnick, 1986).

Some years ago, gerontologist Robert Butler (1963) proposed that elderly adults engage in a process called **life review,** in which they reflect on unresolved conflicts of the past to come to terms with themselves, find new meaning and coher-

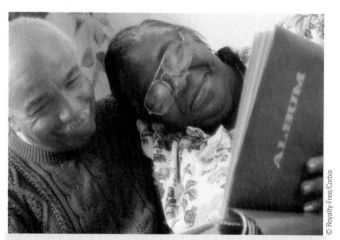

Reminiscence and life review can help older adults achieve a sense of integrity.

ence in their lives, and prepare for death (see also Haber, 2006; Webster & Haight, 2002). Do older adults engage in life review, and does it help them achieve a healthy sense of integrity? Elders who use the life review process display a stronger sense of ego integrity and better overall adjustment and well-being than those who do not reminisce and those who mainly stew about how poorly life has treated them or who have unresolved regrets (Taft & Nehrke, 1990; Wong & Watt, 1991; Wrosch, Bauer, & Scheier, 2005). Elderly adults are more likely than younger adults to focus on positive experiences and the positive emotions associated with them when they reminisce, which may help them accept their lives and feel good about themselves (Pasupathi & Carstensen, 2003). Believing that life review can be beneficial in later life, Butler and other gerontologists have used it as a form of therapy, asking elderly adults to reconstruct and reflect on their lives with the help of photo albums and other memorabilia. Participation in life review therapy can indeed benefit elderly adults (Molinari, 1999; Webster & Haight, 2002).

On balance, Erikson's view that humans experience psychosocial growth throughout the life span has gained support from research. Although few studies have directly tested Erikson's ideas about psychosocial development during childhood, his theorizing about the adolescent stage of identity versus role confusion has been tested extensively and is well supported. In addition, achieving a sense of identity in adolescence paves the way for forming a truly intimate relationship as a young adult, many middle-aged adults go on to attain a sense of generativity, and many older adults work toward a sense of integrity through the process of life review.

Midlife Crisis?

Where in all this evidence of stability in personality traits such as extraversion and neuroticism and of Eriksonian psychosocial growth is the midlife crisis that many people believe is a standard feature of personality development in middle age? Although Erikson saw few signs of a midlife crisis, another psychoanalytic theorist, Daniel Levinson (1986, 1996; Levinson et al., 1978), did. He proposed an influential stage theory of adult development based on intensive interviews with 40 men and later reported that it fit women as well (Levinson, 1996).

Levinson's stages, which he believed to be universal, describe the unfolding of what he calls an individual's "life structure," an overall pattern to a person's activities that reflects the person's priorities and relationships with other people and the larger society. Levinson proposed that adults go through a repeated process of first building a life structure and then questioning and altering it during transition periods (see ● **Table 11.5**).

Levinson believed that the transition period from age 40 to age 45 is an especially significant time developmentally, a time of **midlife crisis**—of a person questioning his entire life structure and raising unsettling issues about where he has been and where he is heading. Most middle-aged men Levinson studied

● TABLE 11.5 LEVINSON'S STAGES OF ADULT DEVELOPMENT

STAGE	AGE	CHARACTERISTICS
Early adult transition	17–21	Period of questioning. Young people make the transition from adolescence to early adulthood and explore possibilities for an adult identity. They form "the dream," a vision of their life goals.
Entering the adult world	22–28	Adults build their first life structure, often by making and testing a career choice and by getting married. They work to succeed; find a supportive spouse, mentor, or both if possible; and do not question their lives much.
Age 30 transition	28–33	Period of questioning. Adults ask whether their career choices and marriages are what they want. If not, they may make small adjustments in their life structure or plan major life changes (e.g., a job change, a divorce, or a decision to return to school).
Settling down	33–40	This is a time for building and living a new, and often different, life structure and for "making it," or realizing one's dream. An adult may outgrow his need for a mentor and become his own person. As in the structure-building period of entering the adult world, adults tend to be ambitious, task oriented, and unreflective.
Midlife transition	40–45	In this major period of questioning, successful adults ask whether the dreams they formulated as young adults were worth achieving. If they have not achieved their dreams, they face the reality that they may never achieve them and may again make major changes in their life structures.

did not seek divorces, quit their jobs, buy red sports cars, or behave like lovesick adolescents, as popular images of the midlife crisis would have it. However, Levinson characterized 80% of the men in his study as having experienced a bona fide crisis—a period of intense inner struggles and disturbing realizations—in their early 40s. And, in his in-depth study of 45 women between age 35 and age 45, Levinson (1996) concluded that women experience significant crises during both the age 30 transition (28 to 33) and the midlife transition (40 to 45), often centered on the balancing of career and family.

Many researchers agree that middle age is often a time when important issues arise, self-evaluations are made, and goals may change (Hermans & Oles, 1999; McAdams & Adler, 2006; Rosenberg, Rosenberg, & Farrell, 1999). What's more, some people experience midlife changes in personality in response to life events such as divorce, a job change, or the death of a parent. Still, there is not much support for Levinson's claim that most adults experience a genuine "crisis" in their early 40s (Hedlund & Ebersole, 1983; Vaillant, 1977). In sum, Levinson may have overestimated the extent to which midlife crisis occurs. It seems sounder to call the phenomenon midlife *questioning*, to recognize that it can occur in response to life events at a variety of ages, and to appreciate that it is usually not a true psychological crisis.

Vocational Development and Adjustment

Although Levinson's concept of midlife crisis is not well supported, he was right to emphasize that adults revise important life decisions as they develop. To illustrate, consider vocational development during adulthood, a reflection of self-concept

and personality (Judge & Bono, 2001). After much experimenting in early adulthood, people settle into chosen occupations in their 30s and strive for success. Ultimately, they prepare for the end of their careers, make the transition into retirement, and attempt to establish a satisfying lifestyle during their "golden years."

Establishing a Career

Levinson was right that early adulthood is a time for exploring vocational possibilities, launching careers, making tentative commitments, revising them if necessary, seeking advancement, and establishing yourself firmly in what you hope is a suitable occupation. Using data from a longitudinal study of males tracked from adolescence to age 36 (see Super, Savickas, & Super, 1996), Susan Phillips (1982) examined whether men's decisions about jobs at different ages were tentative and exploratory (for example, "to see if I really liked that kind of work") or more final (for example, "to get started in a field I wanted [to enter]"). The proportions of decisions that were predominantly exploratory were 80% at age 21, 50% at age 25, and 37% at age 36. From age 21 to age 36, then, young adults progressed from wide-open exploration of different career possibilities to tentative or trial commitments to a stabilization of their choices. Even in their mid-30s, however, about a third of adults were still exploring what they wanted to be when they grew up! The average man held *seven* full-time jobs or training positions between age 18 and age 36 (Phillips, 1982). The picture for women is similar (Jenkins, 1989).

After their relatively unsettled 20s and decision-making 30s, adults often reach the peaks of their careers in their 40s (Simonton, 1990). They often have major responsibilities and define themselves in terms of their work. Personality is an important influence on how it goes. Job performance is consistently correlated with the Big Five dimension of conscientiousness; extraversion and emotional stability also contribute to career success (Ozer & Benet-Martinez, 2006). Person–environment fit can be critical, too: people tend to perform poorly and become open to changing jobs when the fit between their personality and aptitudes and the demands of their job or workplace is poor (Hoffman & Woehr, 2006).

Gender is another significant influence on vocational development. Although women are entering a much wider range of fields today than they were a few decades ago, most administrative assistants, teachers, and nurses are still women. Partly because they are clustered in traditionally feminine-stereotyped occupations, U.S. women earn about 80 cents for every dollar men earn (Associated Press, 2003). Why the gap? It is probably caused by the influence of gender-role norms on the choices women make and discrimination in the workplace.

Traditional gender-role norms have prompted many women to subordinate career goals to family goals. Women often interrupt their careers, drop down to part-time work, take less demanding jobs, and decline promotions that would involve transferring to a new location so that they can bear and raise children (Kirchmeyer, 2006; Moen, 1992). In the process, they hurt their chances of rising to higher paid, more responsible positions. Meanwhile, the women who make it to the top of the career ladder, especially in male-dominated fields, sometimes achieve this success by remaining single, divorcing, or limiting their childbearing (Jenkins, 1989). Overall, women without children achieve more in their careers than women with children (Carr et al., 1998; Wilson, 2003). Each additional child reduces a woman's earnings further, and that leaves her in worse financial shape than a man when she retires (Avellar & Smock, 2003). Women are also less likely than men to enjoy the career boost that comes from having a nonworking partner supporting one's career (Kirchmeyer, 2006).

In addition to family taking priority over career, discrimination can limit women's vocational development. For example:

- Traditionally "female" jobs pay less than "male" jobs even when the intellectual demands of the work are similar (England, Reid, & Kilbourne, 1996).
- Women who enter jobs with the same management degrees and salaries as men, and receive equal performance ratings, still do not rise as far in the organization or earn as much as men (Cox & Harquail, 1991).
- Women earn about 20% less than men even controlling for the tendency of women to work less, step out of the work force more, and enter lower-paying occupations (Associated Press, 2003).

In sum, although we make preliminary vocational choices as adolescents, we remain open to making new choices as young adults and take some time to settle on careers that fit our personalities and gender roles. People's personalities affect their vocational choices and adjustment; in turn, people whose work is complex and intellectually challenging grow as a result of the intellectual stimulation they receive, becoming more able to handle intellectual problems adeptly and more self-confident (Kohn & Schooler, 1982; Schooler, Mulatu, & Oates, 1999).

The Aging Worker

Many people believe that adults become less able or less motivated to perform well on the job as they approach retirement. As it turns out, the job performance of workers in their 50s and 60s is similar overall to that of younger workers (Avolio & Sosik, 1999; Hansson et al., 1997). Not only are older workers generally as competent as younger workers, but they tend to be more satisfied with their jobs, more involved in their work, and less interested in landing new jobs than younger workers are (Rhodes, 1983).

Why is the performance of older workers not hurt by some of the age-related physical and cognitive declines described in this book? First, these declines typically do not become significant until people are in their 70s and 80s, long after they have retired. Second, many older workers have accumulated a good

Gender roles and career choices illustrated in *Doonesbury*.

Older workers generally perform as well as younger ones, possibly because they use selective optimization with compensation to cope with aging.

deal of on-the-job expertise that helps them continue to perform well (Hansson et al., 1997). Finally, the answer may lie in the strategies that aging adults use to cope with aging.

Gerontologists Paul and Margaret Baltes (1990) have theorized that older people can best cope with aging, and people in general can best cope with living, through the strategy they call **selective optimization with compensation,** or **SOC** (Baltes & Baltes, 1990; Baltes & Freund, 2003; Freund & Riediger, 2006; and see Chapter 8). Three processes are involved: *selection* (focus on a limited set of goals and the skills most needed to achieve them), *optimization* (practice those skills to keep them sharp), and *compensation* (develop ways to get around the need for other skills). Using selective optimization with compensation, an overworked 60-year-old lawyer might, for example, avoid spreading herself too thin by focusing on her strongest specialty area and delegating other types of assignments to younger workers (selection), putting a lot of time into staying up-to-date in her main area of specialization (optimization), and making up for her failing memory by taking more notes at meetings (compensation). For pianist Arthur Rubenstein, maintaining excellence in old age meant playing fewer different pieces (selection), practicing them more (optimization), and compensating for loss of speed by increasing the contrast between the slower and faster parts of a piece to make the faster parts sound faster (Baltes, Lindenberger, & Staudinger, 2006). Thinking about the gains and losses that come with aging, the idea of selective optimization with compensation is to prioritize, maximize gains, and minimize losses (Riediger, Li, & Lindenberger, 2006).

In one study of this coping strategy (Abraham & Hansson, 1995), workers age 40 to age 69 completed scales measuring their reliance on selection, optimization, and compensation strategies. Among older adults in the sample, especially those with highly stressful jobs, heavy reliance on selective optimization with compensation helped workers maintain a high level of performance and achieve their goals at work. There is now evidence that this strategy helps both middle-aged and older adults to function effectively (Freund & Riediger, 2006). The federal government seemed to have recognized that older workers are typically effective workers when it raised or eliminated mandatory retirement ages, increased the age of eligibility for receiving Social Security, and, through the Age Discrimination in Employment Act, protected older workers from age discrimination in hiring and retention (Hansson et al., 1997). But there is work left to do in our society to understand true strengths and limitations of older workers and to meet the needs of those who want to continue working well into old age (see Hedge, Borman, & Lammlein, 2006).

Retirement

A century ago, most adults continued working as long as they were able. As late as 1930, more than half of all men age 65 or older were still working (Palmore et al., 1985). The introduction of Social Security in 1934, affluence, and increased availability of private pension plans changed that, making it financially possible for more men and women to retire and to do so earlier. In 1960, for example, 78% of men age 60 to age 64 were still in the labor force; by 2000, only 55% were (Samuelson, 2002). Over this period, the average age of retirement dropped from over 67 to 62, although it may be inching up again as retiring baby boomers find that they need to continue earning money (Wilmoth & Longino, 2006).

How do people adjust to the final chapter of the work life cycle? Robert Atchley (1976) proposed that adults progress through a series of phases as they make the transition from worker to retiree. The process of adjustment begins with a *preretirement phase* in which workers nearing retirement gather information, talk about retirement, and plan for the future (Ekerdt, Kosloski, & DeViney, 2000). Deciding when to retire is an important part of the process. Some workers are forced to retire early because of poor health or because they are pushed out of their jobs, but others choose to retire early because they have enough money to do so, do not feel attached to their jobs, or simply like the idea (Beehr et al., 2000; Hansson et al., 1997).

Just after they retire, workers often experience a *honeymoon phase* in which they relish their newfound freedom; they head for the beach, golf course, or camp grounds and do all the projects they never had time to do while they worked. Then, according to Atchley, many enter a *disenchantment phase* as the novelty wears off; they feel aimless and sometimes unhappy. Finally, they move to a *reorientation phase* in which they begin to put together a realistic and satisfying lifestyle. Research supports this view. For example, David Ekerdt and his colleagues (Ekerdt, Bossé, & Levkoff, 1985) found that (1) men who had been retired only a few months were in a honeymoon period in which they were highly satisfied with life and optimistic about the future, (2) men who had been retired 13 to 18 months were rather disenchanted, and (3) men who had been retired for longer periods were relatively satisfied (see also Gall, Evans, & Howard, 1997).

Clearly, retirement takes getting used to. After retirees have adjusted, however, are they worse off than they were before they retired? Negative images of the retired person abound in our society; the retiree supposedly ends up feeling useless, old, bored, sickly, and dissatisfied with life. Yet research shows that retirement has few effects on adults (Gall et al.,1997; Hansson et al., 1997; Palmore et al., 1985). Retirement's most consistent effect is to reduce the individual's income (Palmore et al., 1985). Retired people generally do not experience a decline in health simply because they retire. Poor health more often causes retirement than retirement causes poor health. Retirees' activity patterns and social lives do not change much either (Palmore et al., 1985). Retirement typically has no noticeable effect on the size of people's social networks, the frequency of their social contacts, or their satisfaction with the social support they receive. Finally, retirement generally does not disrupt marriages or reduce life satisfaction or mental health.

Overall, then, retirees are likely to experience an adjustment process involving preretirement then honeymoon, disenchantment, and reorientation phases. They end up adapting successfully to retirement and to the drop in income that it typically involves. Yet there are huge individual differences in adjustment. What makes for a favorable adjustment? Adults who retire voluntarily rather than involuntarily, enjoy good health, have the financial resources to live comfortably, and are married or otherwise have strong social support typically fare better than those forced to retire because of poor health or those who find themselves with inadequate incomes and few social ties (Fouquereau et al., 2005; Gall et al., 1997; Palmore et al., 1985). Attitudes matter too: Positive adjustment to retirement is more likely when the individual goes into it with positive expectations (van Solinge & Henkens, 2005).

We also need to consider retirement in a family context. For example, retirement seems to go most smoothly when partners retire together; neither retired husbands nor retired wives are happy if their spouse continues to work and they end up losing power in the relationship as a result (Szinovacz & Davey, 2005). Finally, cultural context is important: For example, Scandinavian countries generally have generous social welfare systems, but because the Chinese government has restricted families to one child, an increasing number of elders in China find themselves with no son to support them and no pension either (Eberstadt, 2006).

Personality and Successful Aging

What lifestyle decisions make not only for a successful transition to retirement but also for a happy and fulfilling old age? Theories of successful aging have been offered to answer that question. **Activity theory** holds that aging adults will find their lives satisfying to the extent that they can maintain their previous lifestyles and activity levels, either by continuing old activities or by finding substitutes—for example, by replacing work with hobbies, volunteer work, or other stimulating pursuits (Fry, 1992; Havighurst, Neugarten, & Tobin, 1968). According to this view, psychological needs do not really change as people enter old age: most aging individuals continue to want an active lifestyle.

By contrast, **disengagement theory** says that successful aging involves a withdrawal of the aging individual from society that is satisfying to both (Achenbaum & Bengtson, 1994; Cumming & Henry, 1961). The aging individual is said to have needs different from those he once had and to seek to leave old roles behind and reduce activity. Meanwhile, society both encourages and benefits from the older person's disengagement, which makes room for the younger generation.

Which is it? Throughout this text, you have seen evidence that individuals who remain active in old age benefit from their activity. Those who are physically active maintain their health longer (see Chapter 5), those who are intellectually active maintain their cognitive functions longer (see Chapter 9), and those who remain involved in meaningful social relationships are likely to be more satisfied with their lives (see Chapter 14). In other words, there is more support for activity theory than for disengagement theory.

Many older adults subscribe to the activity theory of aging, attempting to find substitutes for lost roles and activities. Others find happiness through disengagement and prefer to sit and watch.

© Homer Sykes/Alamy

But before you conclude that activity theory explains all you need to know about successful aging, add three qualifications. First, the relationship between level of activity and life satisfaction or well-being is surprisingly weak (Fry, 1992). Apparently, many inactive individuals are nonetheless satisfied with their lives, and many busy individuals are nonetheless miserable. This suggests that quality of activity is probably more important than its quantity (Pinquart & Sorensen, 2000).

Second, some messages of disengagement theory have merit (Achenbaum & Bengtson, 1994). As you saw earlier in this chapter, for example, older adults sometimes become less active than they were earlier in life. This can be viewed as a sign of disengagement. Moreover, most older people today do indeed withdraw voluntarily from certain roles and activities. Most notably, they choose to retire from work, and society generally supports their doing so.

But third, neither activity theory nor disengagement theory emphasizes that the personality traits people carry with them from childhood influence their well-being in old age. Generally, for example, people who are highly extraverted and conscientious and score low in neuroticism have a greater sense of well-being than other adults (Siegler & Brummett, 2000). Even more important, a good fit between the individual's lifestyle and the individual's needs, preferences, and personality may be the real secret to successful aging (Fry, 1992; Seleen, 1982). An energetic and outgoing person may want to maintain her active lifestyle in old age, whereas a person who always found work to be a hassle may like nothing better than to disengage and might be miserable if forced to continue working or to participate in a retirement community's sing-alongs, dances, and skits.

Still other older adults may find satisfaction in focusing on a few highly important roles, relationships, and personally meaningful projects, optimizing their competencies in those areas, and compensating for performance declines in other areas (Lawton et al., 2002; Turk-Charles & Carstensen, 1999). That is, *selective optimization with compensation*, which as you saw helps aging workers maintain good job performance, may also work as a strategy for maintaining a sense of well-being in old age (Baltes & Carstensen, 2003; Freund & Riediger, 2006). In short, you cannot assume, as both activity theory and disengagement theory do, that what suits one suits all. Rather, you should again adopt an interactionist model of development that emphasizes the goodness of fit between person and environment. In the next chapter, we explore some fascinating interactions between biology and environment that contribute to differences between males and females.

SUMMING UP

■ Older adults are able to maintain self-esteem by closing the gap between ideal and real self, altering goals and standards, and comparing themselves with other aging people, until some lose self-esteem in late old age.

■ Self-conceptions differ in individualistic and collectivist cultures.

■ There is both continuity and discontinuity in personality, as suggested by stable individual rankings and changes in some Big Five mean scores.

■ Stability of personality may be caused by genes, early experience, stable environments, and gene–environment correlations.

■ As Erikson theorized, resolution of childhood conflicts paves the way for identity achievement in adolescence, intimacy in early adulthood, generativity in middle age, and integrity (through life review) in late adulthood.

■ Levinson's theory of adult development, featuring a midlife crisis in a person's early 40s, is not well supported, but adults do engage in much career exploration before they settle down in their 30s and achieve peak success in their 40s. Older workers remain productive and satisfied, perhaps partly through selective optimization with compensation.

■ Retiring workers experience preretirement, honeymoon, disenchantment, and reorientation phases and little change except a drop in income. Neither activity theory nor disengagement theory adequately accounts for successful aging.

CRITICAL THINKING

1. Costa and McCrae have argued that people's personalities are very stable by age 30 and hardly change thereafter. What evidence would you cite to refute them?

2. Aunt Rosalia is about to retire and wants to establish a satisfying lifestyle for her old age. What would an activity theorist, a disengagement theorist, and a selective optimization with compensation theorist recommend that she do and why?

3. How is vocational development similar and different for men and women?

CHAPTER SUMMARY

11.1 CONCEPTUALIZING THE SELF AND PERSONALITY

- Personality is an organized combination of attributes unique to the individual; self-concept an individual's perceptions of those attributes; self-esteem an overall evaluation of self-worth; and identity a coherent self-definition.

- In their five principles of personality, McAdams and Pals emphasize that we (1) are alike due to our evolved human nature, (2) differ in dispositional traits, (3) differ in more changeable characteristic adaptations, (4) construct unique narrative identities, and (5) are shaped by cultural and situational factors.

- Freudian psychoanalytic theorists such as Erikson maintain that we all experience stagelike personality changes at similar ages; trait theorists believe that aspects of personality such as the Big Five trait dimensions are enduring, and social learning theorists maintain that people can change in any number of directions at any time if their social environments change.

11.2 THE INFANT

- Early in their first year, infants sense that they are separate from the world around them and can affect it; by 18 to 24 months, they display self-recognition and form a categorical self based on age and sex.

- Infants differ in temperament: in easy, difficult, and slow-to-warm-up temperaments (Thomas and Chess); behavioral inhibition (Kagan); and surgency/extraversion, negative affectivity, and effortful control (Rothbart). Temperament is influenced by genes and goodness of fit with the environment, and is only moderately related to later personality.

11.3 THE CHILD

- Whereas the self-concepts of preschool children are focused on physical characteristics and activities, 8-year-olds describe their inner psychological traits and evaluate their competencies through social comparison.

- Children are most likely to develop high self-esteem when they are competent, fare well in social comparisons, and have warm, democratic parents.

- Links between early temperament and Big Five personality traits are evident, and personality traits become more consistent and enduring with age.

11.4 THE ADOLESCENT

- During adolescence, self-concepts become more psychological, abstract, and integrated, and self-awareness increases; self-esteem dips for some but mainly increases.

- In resolving Erikson's conflict of identity versus role confusion, many college-age youths progress from diffusion or foreclosure to moratorium to identity achievement status, at different rates in different domains. Analyzing life stories, or narrative identities, is another approach to studying identity.

- Developing a positive ethnic identity is more central to minority than to majority group adolescents. Adolescents' vocational choices become increasingly realistic with age; the choices made by females and by low-income youth are sometimes constrained.

- Cognitive development, personality, parenting, opportunities to explore, and culture influence identity development.

11.5 THE ADULT

- Older adults maintain self-esteem until late old age by converging their ideal and real selves, changing standards of self-evaluation, and comparing themselves with other aging adults. Self-conceptions differ in individualistic cultures and collectivist cultures.

- Individuals' rankings on Big Five dimensions of personality become more stable with age; openness to experience and activity level typically decline while emotional stability and conscientiousness increase during adulthood.

- Stability of personality may be caused by genes, early experience, stable environments, and gene–environment correlations; personality change may result from biological or environmental changes or a poor person–environment fit.

- Erikson's psychosocial theory is supported by evidence that resolution of conflicts centering on trust, autonomy, initiative, and industry paves the way for achieving a sense of identity in adolescence, intimacy in early adulthood, generativity in middle age, and integrity through life review in old age.

- Daniel Levinson's theory that adults build and question life structures and experience a midlife crisis is only partly supported, but young adults do engage in much career exploration and questioning before they settle down in their 30s and

achieve peak success in their 40s. Older workers are as productive as and more satisfied than younger workers, possibly because they use selective optimization with compensation to cope with aging.

- Retiring workers experience preretirement, honeymoon, disenchantment, and reorientation phases, and a drop in income, but little change in health or psychological well-being. In accounting for successful aging, neither activity theory nor disengagement theory places enough emphasis on person–environment fit and selective optimization with compensation.

KEY TERMS

personality 309
self-concept 309
self-esteem 309
identity 309
dispositional traits 309
characteristic adaptations 310
narrative identities 310
Big Five 310
self-recognition 312
categorical self 313
looking-glass self 313
temperament 314
easy temperament 314
difficult temperament 314
slow-to-warm-up
    temperament 314
behavioral inhibition 314
surgency/extraversion 315
negative affectivity 315
effortful control 315
goodness of fit 315
social comparison 317
ideal self 318
big-fish–little-pond effect 320

identity versus role
    confusion 321
moratorium period 321
diffusion status 322
foreclosure status 322
moratorium status 322
identity achievement status 322
ethnic identity 322
individualistic culture 327
collectivist culture 327
trust versus mistrust 332
autonomy versus shame and
    doubt 332
initiative versus guilt 332
industry versus inferiority 332
intimacy versus isolation 333
generativity versus
    stagnation 333
integrity versus despair 334
life review 334
midlife crisis 334
selective optimization with
    compensation (SOC) 337
activity theory 338
disengagement theory 338

MEDIA RESOURCES

BOOK COMPANION WEBSITE

academic.cengage.com/psychology/sigelman
Find online quizzes, flash cards, animations, video clips, experiments, interactive assessments, and other helpful study aids for this text at **academic.cengage.com/psychology/sigelman.** You can also connect directly to the following sites:

BIG FIVE QUICKSTART: INTRODUCTION TO THE FIVE-FACTOR MODEL OF PERSONALITY

This site provides a very detailed description of the Big Five trait theory and discusses ways of using the theory in business settings with individuals and teams.

BETTER SELF-ESTEEM

This University of Texas at Austin-based site not only provides a nice description of self-esteem but also includes specific steps that students can take to improve their own self-esteem.

Career Developmental Activities and Vocational Lesson Plans

The amazing Vocational Information Center site contains literally hundreds of links to interactive lesson plans focusing on career selection, career decision-making, and career guidance.

Great Ideas in Personality

This site could be subtitled, "Everything you wanted to know about personality theory, personality research, and more!" Covering most of the major personality theories, this site allows the visitor access to the historical development of each approach, a general overview of each approach, and most importantly links to other sites focusing on each theory.

Understanding the Data: Exercises on the Web

academic.cengage.com/psychology/sigelman

For additional insight on the data presented in this chapter, try out the exercises for these figures at **academic.cengage.com/psychology/sigelman**:

Figure 11.3 Percentage of subjects in each of James Marcia's four identity statuses as a function of age

Figure 11.5 Favorability of ratings of their ideal, likely future, present (real), and past selves by young, middle-aged, and elderly adults

CengageNOW

academic.cengage.com/login

Go to **academic.cengage.com/login** to link to CengageNOW, your online study tool. First take the Pre-Test for this chapter to get your Personalized Study Plan, which will identify topics you need to review and direct you to online resources. Then take the Post-Test to determine what concepts you have mastered and what you still need work on.

Elyse Lewin Studio Inc./Getty Images

12 CHAPTER
Gender Roles and Sexuality

DEVELOPMENTAL PSYCHOLOGIST Carole Beal (1994) learned an interesting lesson about the significance of being a girl or a boy when she was interviewing 9-year-olds:

> I had just finished one interview and was making some quick notes when the next child came into the office. I looked up, and an odd thing happened: I could not tell whether the child was a boy or a girl. The usual cues were not there: The child's hair was trimmed in a sort of pudding-bowl style, not really long but not definitively short either. The child was dressed in a gender-neutral outfit of jeans, sneakers, and a loose T-shirt, like most of the children at the school. The name on the interview permission slip was "Cory," which did not clarify matters much as it could be either a boy's or a girl's name. Still puzzled, I began the interview and found myself becoming increasingly frustrated at not knowing Cory's sex. I quickly realized how many unconscious assumptions I usually made about boys and girls; for example, that a girl would probably like a particular story about a horse and be willing to answer a few extra questions about it, or that a boy would probably start to get restless after a certain point and I would have to work a bit harder to keep his attention. (p. 3)

■ ■ ■

Unlike Cory, most children are readily identified as girls or boys and treated accordingly. How much does it matter, in terms of development, whether a child is perceived and treated as a girl or as a boy? How much does it matter whether a child is a girl or a boy biologically? These are the kinds of questions we tackle in this chapter.

Gender matters. It used to be that the first question following a birth was whether the baby was a boy or girl. With today's technology, this question is often posed as soon as a pregnancy is announced. As children develop, girls discover that they are girls, and many acquire a taste for frilly dresses and dolls, and boys discover that they are boys and often wrestle each other on the lawn. As an adult, you are probably keenly aware of being either a man or a woman and may define yourself partly in terms of your "feminine" or "masculine" qualities. In short, being female or male is a highly important aspect of the self throughout the life span. Before you read any further, try the quiz in ● **Table 12.1** to see if you know which of the many ideas about male–female differences have some truth to them.

12.1 MALE AND FEMALE

What difference does it make whether a person is a male or a female? It matters in terms of physical differences, psychological differences, and differences in roles played in society. The physical differences are undeniable. A zygote that receives an X chromosome from each parent is a genetic (XX) female, whereas a zygote that receives a Y chromosome from the father is a genetic (XY) male. In rare cases of gender chromosome abnormalities (see Chapter 3), this is not the case; a girl may have only one X chromosome or a boy may have three chromosomes (XYY or XXY). Chromosomal differences result in different prenatal hormone balances in males and females, and hormone balances before and after birth are responsible for the facts that the genitals of males and females differ and that only females can bear children. Moreover, males typically grow to be taller, heavier, and more muscular than females, although females may be the hardier sex in that they live longer and are

● **TABLE 12.1   WHICH OF THESE SEX DIFFERENCES IS REAL?**

Which of the following do you think are consistent sex differences that have been demonstrated in studies comparing males and females? Mark each statement *T* (true) or *F* (false). Answers are printed upside down; they will be clarified in the main text.

____ 1. Males are more aggressive than females.

____ 2. Males are more active than females.

____ 3. Females are more social than males.

____ 4. Females have stronger verbal abilities than males.

____ 5. Males have greater achievement motivation than females.

____ 6. Males are more analytical than females.

____ 7. Females are more suggestible and prone to conform than males.

____ 8. Females are more emotionally unstable than males.

____ 9. Males are more rational and logical than females.

____ 10. Males have greater spatial and mathematical abilities than females.

Answers: 1-T, 2-T, 3-F, 4-T, 5-F, 6-F, 7-F, 8-F, 9-F, 10-T.

less susceptible to many physical disorders (Giampaoli, 2000). As you will see later in the chapter, some theorists argue that biological differences between males and females are responsible for psychological and social differences.

However, there is much more to being male or female than biology. Virtually all societies expect the two sexes to adopt different **gender roles**—the patterns of behavior that females and males should adopt in a particular society (for example, the roles of wife, mother, and woman or of husband, father, and man). Characteristics and behaviors viewed as desirable for males or females are specified in **gender-role norms**—society's expectations or standards concerning what males and females *should be* like. Each society's norms generate **gender-role stereotypes,** overgeneralized and largely inaccurate beliefs about what males and females *are* like.

Through the process of **gender typing,** children not only become aware that they are biological males or females but also acquire the motives, values, and patterns of behavior that their culture considers appropriate for members of their biological sex. Through the gender-typing process, for example, Susie may learn a gender-role norm stating that women should strive to be good mothers and gender-role stereotypes indicating that women are more skilled at nurturing children than men are. As an adult, Susan may then adopt the traditional feminine role by switching from full-time to part-time work when her first child is born and devoting herself to the task of mothering.

It would be a mistake, then, to attribute any differences that we observe between girls and boys (or women and men) solely to biological causes. They could just as easily be caused by differences in the ways males and females are perceived and raised. But before we try to explain sex differences, perhaps we should describe what these differences are believed to be and what they actually are.

Gender Norms and Stereotypes

Which sex is more likely to express emotions? To be neat and organized? To be competitive? To use harsh language? If you are like most people, you undoubtedly have ideas about how men and women differ psychologically and can offer some answers to these questions.

The female's role as childbearer has shaped the gender-role norms that prevail in many societies, including our own. At the heart of the feminine gender role is **communality,** an orientation that emphasizes connectedness to others and includes traits of emotionality and sensitivity to others (Best & Williams, 1993; Conway & Vartanian, 2000). Simon Baron-Cohen (2003) goes so far as to argue that the female brain is "hard-wired for empathy," which is a significant component of communality (p. 1). Girls who adopt communal traits will presumably be prepared to play the roles of wife and mother—to keep the family functioning and to raise children successfully. By contrast, the central aspect of the masculine gender role is **agency,** an orientation toward individual action and achievement that emphasizes traits of dominance, independence, assertiveness, and competitiveness. Boys have been encouraged to adopt agentic traits to fulfill the traditionally defined roles of husband and father, which involve providing for the family and protecting it from harm. Taking this one step further, Baron-Cohen (2003) claims that men's focus on work, achievement, and independence stems from the male brain's tendency to **systemize,** or analyze and explore how things work.

Norms in many cultures mandate that females play a communal role and males play an agentic role, which leads us to stereotypes saying that females possess communal traits and males possess agentic traits (Williams & Best, 1990). If you are thinking that these stereotypes have disappeared as attention to women's rights has increased and as more women have entered the labor force, think again. Although some change has occurred, adolescents and young adults still endorse many traditional stereotypes about men and women (Botkin, Weeks, & Morris, 2000; Lueptow, Garovich-Szabo, & Lueptow, 2001; Oswald & Lindstedt, 2006). Boys are more likely than girls to endorse traditional stereotypes, perhaps because stereotypes about males (e.g., independent) tend to be more positive than the stereotypes about females (e.g., dependent) (Rowley et al., 2007).

Moreover, males and females continue to describe themselves differently. When Jean Twenge (1997) analyzed studies conducted from 1970 to 1995 in which standard scales assessing gender-relevant traits had been administered, she found that men and women in the mid-1990s described themselves more similarly than men and women did 20 years previously, largely because modern women saw themselves as having more masculine traits. However, male and female personality profiles continued to differ in ways consistent with gender stereotypes. Might beliefs about sex differences, then, have a basis in fact?

Are There Gender Differences?

Much research has attempted to answer the question of whether there are sex or gender differences in behavior. Although differences in some areas have been identified, other areas show no gender differences. As you review the areas in which there are some differences, keep in mind that these are often small, group differences. That is, even when research shows that women score higher (or lower) than men on average, there will be individual women who score lower (or higher) than individual men. With this in mind, here is what the research shows:

- *Females sometimes display greater verbal abilities than males, but the difference is small.* According to Eleanor Maccoby and Carol Jacklin's (1974) classic review of more than 1500 studies, girls tend to develop verbal skills at an earlier age than boys and show a small but consistent advantage on tests of vocabulary, reading comprehension, and speech fluency. Sex differences in verbal ability have all but disappeared in more recent studies, although some continue to show a female advantage on some measures of verbal ability at some ages (e.g., Arden & Plomin, 2006; Galsworthy et al., 2000).
- *Males outperform females on tests of spatial ability* (for example, arranging blocks in patterns or identifying the same figure from different angles; see ■ **Figure 12.1**). Although Maccoby and Jacklin concluded in their 1974 review that these differences emerge only in adolescence, differences on some tests—especially mental rotations— can be detected in childhood and persist across the life span (Choi & Silverman, 2003; Kaufman, 2007; Johnson & Bouchard, 2007; Nordvik & Amponsah, 1998).

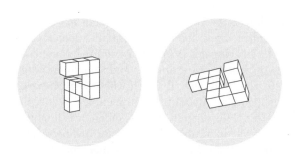

■ FIGURE 12.1 A spatial ability task. Are the two figures alike or different? The task assesses the ability to mentally rotate visual information and is a task on which average differences between males and females are large.

SOURCE: From Mental rotation of three-dimensional objects, by R. N. Shepard and J. Metzler, 1971, *Science, 17,* p. 701–703. Copyright 1971 by the American Association for the Advancement of Science. Reprinted with permission.

- Historically, males outperformed females on standardized tests of mathematical ability, but this male advantage has all but disappeared: *females and males perform similarly on most standardized math tests and females obtain slightly higher math grades in the classroom than males* (Hyde, Fennema, & Lamon, 1990; Kenney-Benson et al., 2006; Lachance & Mazzocco, 2006; U.S. Department of Education, 2005). There is a male advantage in mathematical problem-solving skills when we look at the top performing math students; that is, more males than females are mathematically talented (Stumpf & Stanley, 1996). Some research shows that this male advantage is evident in the earliest grades (Nowell & Hedges, 1998; Robinson et al., 1996). As it turns out, more males than females are also low math achievers; on several cognitive ability tests, more males than females show up at both the top and the bottom of the scale (Feingold, 1992).

- *Girls display greater memory ability than boys.* Some studies show that this is a general or overall advantage (Johnson & Bouchard, 2007), whereas other research suggests that female's memory advantage is in specific areas such as memory for object locations (e.g., Voyer et al., 2007).

- *Males engage in more physical and verbal aggression than females, starting as early as 17 months* (Baillargeon et al., 2007; Burton, Hafetz, & Henninger, 2007; Buss & Perry, 1992). Across 21 diverse countries, teachers in nearly all the countries report that boys are more aggressive than girls (Rescorla et al., 2007). Sex differences are more obvious for physical aggression than for other forms of aggression. For example, at 17 months, for every girl who is physically aggressive, there are five boys who display frequent physical aggression (Baillargeon et al., 2007). Males also commit more serious, and physically violent, crimes (Barash, 2002). Some research shows that females tend to specialize in subtle, indirect, and relational forms of aggression such as gossiping about and excluding others (Crick & Bigbee, 1998; Murray-Close, Ostrov, & Crick, 2007), but other research shows that males are as likely as females to use relational aggression (Basow et al., 2007).

- Even before birth and throughout childhood, *boys are more physically active* than girls (Almli, Ball, & Wheeler, 2001); they fidget and squirm more as infants and run around more as children. In 19 out of 21 countries studied by Leslie Rescorla and colleagues (2007), teachers report that boys are more hyperactive than girls.

- *Boys are more developmentally vulnerable*, not only to prenatal and perinatal (birth-related) stress (for example, they die more often before birth) but also to several diseases and to disorders such as reading disabilities, speech defects, hyperactivity, emotional problems, and mental retardation (Henker & Whalen, 1989; Jacklin, 1989; Raz et al., 1994).

- *Girls are more tactful and cooperative, as opposed to being forceful and demanding, and are more compliant with requests from adults,* although they are no more likely than boys to give in to peers (Baron-Cohen, 2003; Maccoby, 1998).

- *Both males and females report that females are more nurturant and empathic; sex differences in behaviors are small but show females empathizing more than males* (Baron-Cohen, 2003; Deutsch, 1999; Feingold, 1994b). Females also take more interest in and are more responsive to infants (Reid & Trotter, 1993).

- *Females are somewhat more anxious, cautious, and fearful,* although not in social situations (Feingold, 1994b). *Females are also more prone to develop anxiety disorders, depression, and phobias* (Pigott, 2002). In contrast, *males are more likely to display antisocial behaviors and drug and alcohol abuse* (Hicks et al., 2007).

- *Males use computers more than females and express greater confidence in their computer abilities* (Li & Kurkup, 2007). These findings do not tell us, though, whether there are gender differences in computer ability.

Despite such evidence of gender differences from some researchers, others take the contrasting view that even the largest of the "real" psychological differences between the sexes are trivial. For example, if you imagine all the differences in aggressiveness among individuals, from the most aggressive to the least aggressive person in a group, it turns out that only 5% of that variation can be traced directly to whether a person is male or female (Hyde, 1984); apparently, the remaining 95% of the variation is caused by other differences among people. It is worth reiterating the point we made at the beginning of this section: *Average* levels of a behavior such as aggression may be noticeably different for males and females, but within each sex there are both extremely aggressive and extremely nonaggressive individuals. Thus, it is impossible to predict accurately how aggressive a person is simply by knowing his or her gender. Sex differences in most other abilities and personality traits are similarly small. Moreover, some sex differences are smaller today than they used to be (Hyde et al., 1990; Stumpf & Stanley, 1996).

As it turns out, many of our stereotypes of males and females are just that—overgeneralizations unsupported by fact.

Despite some differences, females and males are more psychologically similar than different. So why do unfounded stereotypes persist? Partly because we, as the holders of male–female stereotypes, are biased in our perceptions. We are more likely to notice and remember behaviors that confirm our beliefs than to notice and remember exceptions, such as independent behavior in a woman or emotional sensitivity in a man (Martin & Halverson, 1981).

We also perpetuate gender stereotypic thinking by applying the positive aspects of the stereotypes to ourselves and the negative aspects to others (Oswald & Lindstedt, 2006). For example, college students describe the "masculine personality" as aggressive, insensitive, and competitive, and view the first two traits as negative and the third as positive. Whereas they believe that the negative traits may characterize masculine men in general, they believe that only the positive trait applies to them. The same is true of the feminine gender stereotype of sensitive, nurturant, and dependent. This positive self-bias may help continue negative gender stereotypes in general while preserving self-esteem about one's own gender identity (Oswald & Lindstedt, 2006).

In addition, Alice Eagly's (1987) **social-role hypothesis** suggests that differences in the roles that women and men play in society do a lot to create and maintain gender-role stereotypes (see also Eagly & Steffen, 2000). For example, men have traditionally occupied powerful roles in business and industry that require them to be dominant and forceful. Women have more often filled the role of homemaker and therefore have been called upon to be nurturant and sensitive to their children's needs. As a result, we begin to see men as dominant or agentic by nature and women as nurturant or communal by nature. We lose sight that it is differences in the social roles they play that cause men and women to behave differently. It could be that sex differences in behavior might be reversed if women ran companies and men raised children.

As Eagly's social-role hypothesis suggests, we must adopt a contextual perspective on psychological differences between males and females. Sex differences evident in one culture or social context often are not evident in another (Deaux & Major, 1990; Feingold, 1994a). For example, women do better on tests of mathematical ability—and sometimes outperform men—in countries such as Israel, where women have excellent occupational opportunities in technical fields (Baker & Jones, 1992). This suggests that sex differences in abilities are not biologically inevitable. From a contextual perspective, it is silly to speak about the "nature of women" or the "nature of men." Differences between males and females can be large or small depending on the social contexts in which they find themselves.

Although psychological sex differences are often small, it makes a difference in society whether a person is male or female. First, gender norms and stereotypes, even when they are unfounded, affect how we perceive ourselves and other people. As long as people expect females to be less competent in math than males, for example, females may lack confidence in their abilities and perform less competently (Eccles, Jacobs, & Harold, 1990). That many stereotypes are unfounded does not make them less potent.

In addition, even though males and females are similar psychologically, they are steered toward different roles in society. In childhood, girls and boys conform to their gender roles by segregating themselves by sex and developing different interests and play activities (Maccoby, 1998). As adolescents and adults, males and females pursue different vocations and lifestyles. Although more women are entering male-dominated fields today than in the past, they are underrepresented in many traditionally male-dominated fields, and men rarely enter female-dominated fields (U.S. Department of Labor, 2001). If you go to a college graduation ceremony today, you will still see relatively few women among the engineers and few men among the nursing graduates. More men are sharing child-rearing and household responsibilities with their partners, but many couples still divide the labor along traditional lines, so that the woman is primarily responsible for child care and housework and the man is primarily responsible for income and money management (Bianchi et al., 2000; Perkins & DeMeis, 1996; Sayer, 2005). When we think about who asks whom out on a date, who stays home from work when a child has an ear infection, or who sews the buttons back on shirts, we must conclude that, despite significant social change, traditional gender roles are alive and well.

According to Alice Eagly's social-role hypothesis, this man would be perceived as nurturant, warm, and caring because he has assumed the role of caregiver.

© Michael Newman/PhotoEdit

SUMMING UP

▌ We continue to live in a society where, for better or worse, being male or female matters.

▌ There are a few small psychological differences between the sexes, but males and females are more similar than different in terms of psychological traits. There is far more variation within a group of males than there is between groups of males and females.

- There are clear physical differences between males and females, and the roles that most men and women play in society continue to differ.

CRITICAL THINKING

1. What roles do you play as a result of your biological sex? For example, are you a son or a daughter? How do these roles influence your behavior? Would you, for instance, behave any differently if you were a son rather than a daughter (or vice versa)?

2. Your grandmother strongly believes that boys and girls, men and women, are quite different from one another. Sometimes, she is even bothered by some of your behaviors because she doesn't believe you are behaving like a "proper" young woman/man. How did her thinking about gender become so entrenched and what could be done to soften her views?

12.2 THE INFANT

At birth there are few differences, other than the obvious anatomical ones, between males and females. Male newborns tend to be somewhat more irritable than females and female newborns are more alert than males (Boatella-Costa et al., 2007). But overall, differences between males and females at birth are small and inconsistent. Nonetheless, it does not take long after newborns are labeled as girls or boys for gender stereotypes to affect how they are perceived and treated—and for infants to notice that males and females are different.

Differential Treatment

When the baby is still in the hospital delivery room or nursery, parents tend to use masculine terms when talking to or about their infant son (such as "big guy" or "tiger") and to comment on the strength of his cries, kicks, and grasps. Girl infants are more likely to be labeled "sugar" or "sweetie" and to be described as soft, cuddly, and adorable (Maccoby, 1980). Even when objective examinations reveal no such differences between boys and girls at birth, adults perceive boys as strong, large featured, and coordinated and view girls as weaker, finer featured, and more awkward (Rubin, Provenzano, & Luria, 1974; see also Karraker, Vogel, & Lake, 1995). Soon boys and girls are decked out in either blue or pink and provided with "sex-appropriate" hairstyles, toys, and room furnishings (Pomerleau et al., 1990).

In an early study of the effects of gender stereotyping, college students watched a videotape of a 9-month-old infant who was introduced as either a girl ("Dana") or a boy ("David"; Condry & Condry, 1976). Students who saw "David" interpreted his strong reaction to a jack-in-the-box as anger, whereas students who watched "Dana" concluded that the same behavior was fear. Although stereotyping of boys and girls from birth could be partly the effect of differences between the sexes (Benenson, Philippoussis, & Leeb, 1999), it may also be a cause of such differences.

Early Learning

Yet infants are not merely the passive targets of other people's reactions to them; they are actively trying to get to know the social world around them and to get to know themselves. By the end of the first year, babies can already distinguish women from men in photographs, and they look longer at a male (or female) face when they hear a male (or female) voice than when they hear a voice that does not match the gender of the face (Fagot & Leinbach, 1993; Poulin-Dubois & Serbin, 2006). By 24 months, they look longer at males and females performing gender inconsistent activities (e.g., a man putting on makeup) than those performing activities consistent with gender stereotypes (e.g., a man mowing the grass; Hill & Flom, 2007). Their response shows that they recognize something incongruent or odd about males and females engaged in activities inconsistent with gender stereotypes.

As they begin to categorize other people as males and females, they also figure out which of these two significant social categories they belong to. By 18 months, most toddlers seem to have an emerging understanding that they are either like other males or like other females, even if they cannot verbalize it (Lewis & Weinraub, 1979). Almost all children give verbal proof that they have acquired a basic sense of **gender identity,** or an awareness that they are either a boy or a girl, by age 2½ to age 3 (Levy, 1999; Warin, 2000).

As they acquire their gender identities, boys and girls are also beginning to behave differently. By the end of their second year, boys usually prefer trucks and cars to other playthings, whereas girls of this age would rather play with dolls and soft toys (Smith & Daglish, 1977; Wood, Desmarais, & Gugala, 2002). Many 18- to 24-month-old toddlers are not interested in playing with toys regarded as appropriate for the opposite sex—even when there are no other toys to play with (Caldera, Huston, & O'Brien, 1989). As they approach age 2, then, infants are already beginning to behave in ways considered gender appropriate in our society.

SUMMING UP

- The 2 years of infancy lay the groundwork for later gender-role development.

- Because their sex is important to those around them, and because they see that males and females differ, infants begin to form categories of "male" and "female," establish a basic gender identity, and pursue "gender-appropriate" activities.

CRITICAL THINKING

1. Think of someone who recently became a new parent. In what ways has this person's thinking, and the thinking of his/her surrounding social network, already been shaped by knowing the biological sex of the baby? What is the baby's world like—can you tell by looking at its room or clothes whether it is a boy or girl?

Much of the action in gender-role development takes place during the toddler and preschool years. Having already come to understand their basic gender identity, young children rapidly acquire gender stereotypes, or ideas about what males and females are supposedly like, and gender-typed behavioral patterns, or tendencies to favor "gender-appropriate" activities and behaviors over those typically associated with the other sex.

Acquiring Gender Stereotypes

Remarkably, young children begin to learn society's gender stereotypes around the time they become aware of their basic gender identities. Judith Blakemore (2003) showed pictures of toys to 3- to 11-year-olds and asked them whether boys or girls would usually play with each toy. Toys included masculine-stereotyped ones (for example, GI Joe dolls) and feminine-stereotyped ones (for example, Barbie dolls). Even the youngest children (3 years) knew that girls, but not boys, play with Barbie dolls and vice versa for GI Joes. They also recognized that boys and girls differ in clothes and hairstyles. By age 5, boys hold more gender stereotypical toy preferences than girls (Cherney, Harper, & Winter, 2006).

In other research, girls as young as 24 months understood which activities were masculine and which ones were feminine (Poulin-Dubois et al., 2002; see also Serbin, Poulin-Dubois, & Eichstedt, 2002). Boys, however, did not show the same understanding until at least 6 months later. Even by 18 months of age, girls can match photos of gender-stereotypic toys with faces of boys or girls (Serbin et al., 2001). So children, at least girls, are aware of gender stereotypes at an early age.

Over the next several years, children acquire considerably more "knowledge" about the toys and activities considered appropriate for girls or boys (Blakemore, 2003; Serbin, Powlishta, & Gulko, 1993). For instance, Gary Levy and his associates (2000) asked 4- and 6-year-olds whether men or women would be better in two masculine-stereotyped occupations (car mechanic and airplane pilot) and two feminine-stereotyped occupations (clothes designer and secretary). Children believed that men would be more competent than women as mechanics and pilots whereas women would make better designers and secretaries. Boys and girls also expressed positive emotions at the thought of growing up and holding gender-stereotypic occupations. They reacted negatively, however, when asked to consider holding gender-counterstereotypic occupations.

How seriously do children take the gender-role norms and stereotypes that they are rapidly learning? It depends on how old they are. Robin Banerjee and Vicki Lintern (2000) tested the rigidity of 4- to 9-year-olds' gender-stereotypic beliefs with four brief stories in which characters had either gender-stereotypic interests (for example, a boy named Tom who was best friends with another boy and liked playing with airplanes) or gender-counterstereotypic interests (for example, a boy named John who was best friends with a girl and liked playing with doll carriages). Children were then asked whether the target child

would like to play with dolls, play football, skip, or play with toy guns. Younger children (4- and 6-year-olds) were considerably more rigid in their beliefs than older children; they did not believe that boys would want to play with dolls or skip (stereotypic girl activities) or that girls would want to play with footballs or toy guns (stereotypic boy activities). Consistent with earlier research (Damon, 1977), rigidity about gender stereotypes increased from 4 to 6 years of age and then decreased significantly from age 6 to age 8 or 9. Similar findings emerged from a longitudinal study of gender stereotypes. Hanns Trautner and his colleagues (2005) followed the same group of children from age 5 through age 10 to see if children who held rigid beliefs about gender stereotypes at age 5 remained unshakable in these beliefs over the next 5 years. As ■ Figure 12.2 shows, peak levels of rigidity occurred between ages 5 and 7, followed by significant relaxation of beliefs from age 7 to age 10.

Why? The younger children are in the process of acquiring a clear understanding that their sex will remain constant, making them intolerant of anyone who violates traditional

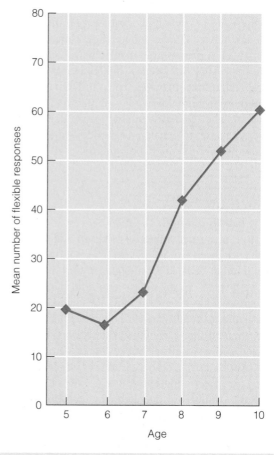

■ **FIGURE 12.2** Once gender identities are clearly established, usually by age 7, children become much more open about gender behaviors, as illustrated by the sharp increase in number of flexible responses after the age of 7.
SOURCE: From H. M. Trautner, D. N. Ruble, L. Cyphers, B. Kirsten, R. Behrendt, & P. Hartman, Rigidity and flexibility of gender stereotypes in childhood: Developmental or differential? *Infant and Child Development*, 14, p. 370. Copyright © 2005 Wiley. Reprinted with permission.

gender-role standards. These norms now have the force of absolute moral laws and must be obeyed: boys must not play with dolls. Eleanor Maccoby (1998) suggests that young children may exaggerate gender roles to cognitively clarify these roles. However, once their gender identities are more firmly established, children can afford to be more flexible in their thinking about what is "for boys" and what is "for girls." They still know the stereotypes, but no longer believe the stereotypes are "written in stone" (Martin, Ruble, & Szkrybalo, 2002). Other research suggests that children's rigidity about gender-role violations depends on how essential a behavior is to children's understanding of gender identity (Blakemore, 2003). Thus, children believe it would be bad for boys to wear dresses because dresses are strongly associated with the feminine gender role. But if boys wanted to play with a toy kitchen, this would not be too bad because, although the toy kitchen may be associated with the feminine gender role, it is not considered an essential aspect of the feminine gender role (Blakemore, 2003).

Gender-Typed Behavior

Finally, children rapidly come to behave in "gender-appropriate" ways. As you have seen, preferences for gender-appropriate toys are detectable in infancy. Apparently, babies

Boys and girls may segregate themselves into same-sex play groups because they have different play styles.

establish preferences for "boys' toys" (such as action figures and building toys) or "girls' toys" (such as dolls and stuffed animals) even before they have established clear identities as males or females or can correctly label toys as "boy things" or "girl things" (Cherney & London, 2006; Fagot, Leinbach, & Hagan, 1986). In childhood, preference for same-sex toys is still evident, although occasionally both boys and girls choose "boys' toys" more than "girls' toys" (Cherney, 2005; Klinger, Hamilton, & Cantrell, 2001). Their leisure activities also differ, with boys spending more time playing sports and video/computer games than girls (Cherney & London, 2006).

Children begin to favor same-sex playmates as early as 30 to 36 months of age (see, for example, Howes, 1988; Martin & Fabes, 2001). During the elementary-school years, boys and girls develop even stronger preferences for peers of their own sex and show increased **gender segregation,** separating themselves into boys' and girls' peer groups and interacting far more often with their own sex than with the other sex (Maccoby, 1998; Pellegrini et al., 2007). Gender segregation occurs in a variety of cultures, including Botswana, Kenya, India, and the Philippines, and it increases with age (Bock, 2005; Leaper, 1994; Whiting & Edwards, 1988). At age 4½, children in the United States spend 3 times more time with same-sex peers than with peers of the other sex; by age 6½, they spend 11 times more time (see ■ Figure 12.3; Maccoby & Jacklin, 1987). This is partly because of incompatibilities between boys' and girls' play styles. Boys are too rowdy, domineering, and unresponsive to suit the tastes of many girls, so girls gravitate toward other girls and develop a style of interacting among themselves different from the rather timid style they adopt in the company of boys (Maccoby, 1998; Pellegrini et al., 2007).

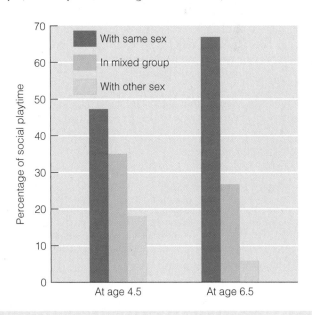

■ **FIGURE 12.3** Do children prefer playmates of their own sex? Apparently so. Both boys and girls spend more time playing with same-sex peers, especially at age 6.
SOURCE: Reprinted from *Advances in child development and behavior*, Volume 20, edited by H. Reese, Copyright © 1987 with permission from Elsevier.

But there is more to gender segregation than different activity levels of boys and girls. Preschool girls who are just as active as boys often start the school year playing with boys but end up in gender-segregated groups as they progress through the year in preschool (Pellegrini et al., 2007). Socialization pressures seem to encourage the girls to drift away from the boys and create their own play group, separate from the active boys and the less-active girls. Preschool boys also seem to experience some pressure to exclude girls from their group; thus, even boys and girls who might be good playmates are discouraged from mingling, at least in the presence of other children.

As it turns out, children who insist most strongly on clear boundaries between the sexes and avoid consorting with the opposite sex tend to be socially competent and popular, whereas children who violate gender segregation rules tend to be less well adjusted and run the risk of being rejected by their peers (Kovacs, Parker, & Hoffman, 1996; Sroufe et al., 1993). Boys face stronger pressures to adhere to gender-role expectations than girls do. This may be why they develop stronger gender-typed preferences at earlier ages (Banerjee & Lintern, 2000; O'Brien et al., 2000). Just ask your female classmates if they were tomboys when they were young; you are likely to find that about half were (Bailey, Bechtold, & Berenbaum, 2002). But we challenge you to find many male classmates who willingly admit they were "sissies" in their youth. The masculine role is clearly defined in our society, and boys are ridiculed and rejected if they do not conform to it (Martin, 1990).

SUMMING UP

▌ Gender-role development proceeds with remarkable speed. By the time they enter school, children have long been aware of their basic gender identities, have acquired many stereotypes about how the sexes differ, and have come to prefer gender-appropriate activities and same-sex playmates.

▌ During middle childhood, their knowledge continues to expand as they learn more about gender-stereotyped psychological traits, but they also become more flexible in their thinking about gender roles. Their behavior, especially if they are boys, becomes even more gender typed, and they segregate themselves even more from the other sex.

CRITICAL THINKING

1. Boys and girls have sometimes been characterized as living in two different worlds. Thinking about your own childhood, how was your world similar or different from that of your other-sexed siblings (if any) and friends?

12.4 | THE ADOLESCENT

After going their separate ways in childhood, boys and girls come together in the most intimate ways during adolescence. How do they prepare for the masculine or feminine gender roles they will be asked to play in adulthood?

Adhering to Gender Roles

As you have just seen, young elementary-school children are highly rigid in their thinking about gender roles, whereas older children think more flexibly, recognizing that gender norms are not absolute, inviolable laws. Curiously, adolescents again seem to become highly intolerant of certain role violations and to become stereotyped in their thinking about the proper roles of males and females in adolescence. They are more likely than somewhat younger children to make negative judgments about peers who violate expectations by engaging in cross-sex behavior or expressing cross-sex interests (Alfieri, Ruble, & Higgins, 1996; Sigelman, Carr, & Begley, 1986).

Consider what Trish Stoddart and Elliot Turiel (1985) found when they asked children ages 5 to 13 questions about boys who wear a barrette in their hair or put on nail polish and about girls who sport a crew haircut or wear a boy's suit. Both the kindergartners and the adolescents judged these behaviors to be wrong, whereas third-graders and fifth-graders viewed them far more tolerantly. Like the elementary-school children, eighth-graders clearly understood that gender-role expectations are just social conventions that can easily be changed and do not necessarily apply in all societies. However, these adolescents had also begun to conceptualize gender-role violations as a sign of psychological abnormality and could not tolerate them.

Increased intolerance of deviance from gender-role expectations is tied to a larger process of **gender intensification,** in which sex differences may be magnified by hormonal changes associated with puberty and increased pressure to conform to gender roles (Boldizar, 1991; Galambos, Almeida, & Petersen, 1990). Boys begin to see themselves as more masculine; girls emphasize their feminine side. Girls often become more involved with their mothers, and boys spend more time with their fathers (Crouter, Manke, & McHale, 1995). Why might this gender intensification occur? Hormonal influences may be at work, or adolescents may emphasize gender more once they mature physically and begin to look like either a man or a woman. Parents may also contribute: as children enter adolescence, mothers do more with their daughters and fathers do more with their sons (Crouter et al., 1995).

Peers may be even more important. Adolescents increasingly find that they must conform to traditional gender norms to appeal to the other sex. A girl who was a tomboy and thought nothing of it may find, as a teenager, that she must dress and behave in more "feminine" ways to attract boys and must give up her tomboyish ways (Burn, O'Neil, & Nederend, 1996; Carr, 2007). A boy may find that he is more popular if he projects a more sharply "masculine" image. Social pressures on adolescents to conform to traditional roles may even help explain why sex differences in cognitive abilities sometimes become more noticeable as children enter adolescence (Hill & Lynch, 1983; Roberts et al., 1990). It should be noted that the social pressure to conform to gender stereotypes does not need to be real—adolescents' *perceptions* of their peers' thoughts and expectations can affect behaviors and lead to gender intensification (Pettitt, 2004). Later in adolescence, teenagers again become more comfortable with their identities as men and women and more flexible in their thinking.

We have now surveyed some major milestones in gender-role development from infancy to adolescence—the development of basic gender identity in toddlerhood, gender segregation in childhood, and a return to rigid thinking about gender as part of gender intensification during adolescence. Now comes the most intriguing question about gender-role development in childhood and adolescence: How can it be explained?

Explaining Gender-Role Development

"Once there was a baby named Chris. . . . [who] went to live on a beautiful island. . . . [where] there were only boys and men; Chris was the only girl. Chris lived a very happy life on this island, but she never saw another girl or woman" (Taylor, 1996, p. 1559). Do you think Chris developed traditionally masculine or traditionally feminine characteristics? When Marianne Taylor (1996) asked children about Chris's toy preferences, occupational aspirations, and personality traits, she found that 4- to 8-year-olds took the nature side of the nature–nurture controversy: They expected Chris's biological status as a girl to determine her development. The 9- and 10-year-olds in the study emphasized the role of nurture in Chris's development, expecting her to be influenced by the masculinizing environment in which she was raised. Where do you come down in this debate, and why?

Several theories about the development of gender roles have been proposed. Some theories emphasize the role of biological differences between the sexes, whereas others emphasize social influences on children. Some emphasize what society does to children; others focus on what children do to themselves as they try to understand gender and all its implications. We will briefly examine a biologically oriented theory then consider the more "social" approaches offered by psychoanalytic theory, social learning theory, cognitive developmental theory, and gender schema theory.

Biosocial Theory

The biosocial theory of gender-role development proposed by John Money and Anke Ehrhardt (1972) calls attention to the ways in which biological events influence the development of boys and girls. But it also focuses on ways in which early biological developments influence how people react to a child and suggests that these social reactions have much to do with children's assuming gender roles.

Chromosomes, Hormones, and Social Labeling. Money and Ehrhardt stress that the male (XY) or female (XX) chromosomes most of us receive at conception are merely a starting point in biological differentiation of the sexes. Several critical events affect a person's eventual preference for the masculine or feminine role (see also Breedlove, 1994):

1. If certain genes on the Y chromosome are present, a previously undifferentiated tissue develops into testes as the embryo develops; otherwise, it develops into ovaries.
2. The testes of a male embryo normally secrete more of the male hormone testosterone, which stimulates the development of a male internal reproductive system, and another hormone that inhibits the development of female organs. Without these hormones, the internal reproductive system of a female will develop from the same tissues.
3. Three to four months after conception, secretion of additional testosterone by the testes normally leads to the growth of a penis and scrotum. If testosterone is absent (as in normal females), or if a male fetus's cells are insensitive to the male sex hormones he produces, female external genitalia (labia and clitoris) will form.
4. The relative amount of testosterone alters the development of the brain and nervous system. For example, it signals the male brain to stop secreting hormones in a cyclical pattern so that males do not experience menstrual cycles at puberty.

Thus, fertilized eggs have the potential to acquire the anatomical and physiological features of either sex. Events at each critical step in the sexual differentiation process determine the outcome.

Once a biological male or female is born, social labeling and differential treatment of girls and boys interact with biological factors to steer development. Parents and other people label and begin to react to children on the basis of the appearance of their genitalia. If children's genitals are abnormal and they are mislabeled as members of the other sex, this incorrect label will affect their future development. For example, if a biological male were consistently labeled and treated as a girl, he would, by about age 3, acquire the gender identity of a girl. Finally, biological factors reenter the scene at puberty when large quantities of hormones are released, stimulating the growth of the reproductive system and the appearance of secondary sex characteristics. These events, with a person's earlier self-concept as a male or female, provide the basis for adult gender identity and role behavior. The complex series of critical points in biological maturation and social reactions to biological changes that Money and Ehrhardt (1972) propose is diagrammed in ■ Figure 12.4. But how much is nature, and how much is nurture?

Evidence of Biological Influences. Much evidence suggests that biological factors influence the development of males and females in many species of animals (Breedlove, 1994). Evolutionary psychologists notice that most societies socialize males to have agentic traits and females to have communal ones; they conclude that traditional gender roles may be a reflection of species heredity (Archer, 1996; Buss, 1995). In addition, individual differences in masculinity and femininity may be partly genetic. Twin studies suggest that individual heredity

accounts for 20 to 50% of the variation in the extent to which people describe themselves as having masculine and feminine psychological traits (Iervolino et al., 2005; Loehlin, 1992). In other words, experience does not explain everything.

Biological influences on development are also evident in studies of children exposed to the "wrong" hormones prenatally (Ehrhardt & Baker, 1974; Money & Ehrhardt, 1972). Before the consequences were known, some mothers who previously had problems carrying pregnancies to term were given drugs containing progestins, which are converted by the body into the male hormone testosterone. These drugs had the effect of masculinizing female fetuses so that, despite their XX genetic endowment and female internal organs, they were born with external organs that resembled those of a boy (for example, a large clitoris that looked like a penis and fused labia that resembled a scrotum). Several of these **androgenized females** (girls prenatally exposed to excess androgens) were recognized as genetic females, underwent surgery to alter their genitals, and were then raised as girls. When Money and Ehrhardt compared them with their sisters and other girls, it became apparent that many more androgenized girls were tomboys and preferred boys' toys and vigorous activities to traditionally feminine pursuits (see also Meyer-Bahlburg et al., 2006). As adolescents, they began dating somewhat later than other girls and felt that marriage should be delayed until they had established their careers. A high proportion (37%) described themselves as homosexual or bisexual (Money, 1985; see also Dittman, Kappes, & Kappes, 1992). Androgenized females may also perform better than most other females on tests

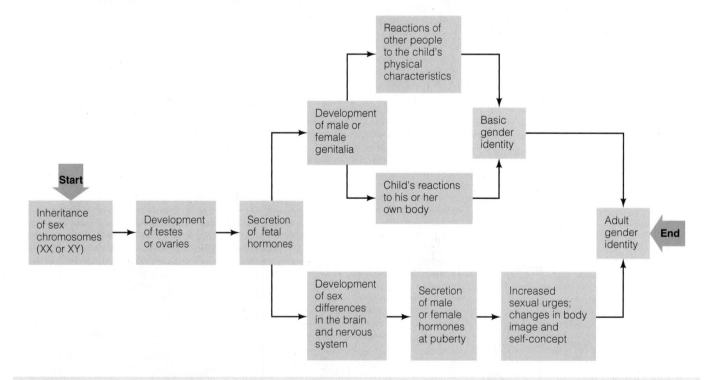

■ **FIGURE 12.4** Critical events in John Money and Anke Ehrhardt's biosocial theory of gender typing.
SOURCE: From *Man and woman, boy and girls,* by J. Money and A. Ehrhardt, 1972, Johns Hopkins University Press. Reprinted by permission.

of spatial ability, further evidence that early exposure to male hormones has "masculinizing" effects on a female fetus (Kimura, 1992; Resnick et al., 1986; but see Malouf et al., 2006).

In addition, male exposure to testosterone and other male hormones may be part of the reason males are more likely than females to commit violent acts (Rubinow & Schmidt, 1996). Evidence from experiments conducted with animals is quite convincing. For example, female rhesus monkeys exposed prenatally to the male hormone testosterone often threaten other monkeys, engage in rough-and-tumble play, and try to "mount" a partner as males do at the beginning of a sexual encounter (Young, Goy, & Phoenix, 1964; Wallen, 1996). Men with high testosterone levels tend to have high rates of delinquency, drug abuse, abusiveness, and violence, although nature interacts with nurture so that these links between testosterone and antisocial behavior are not nearly as evident among men high in socioeconomic status as among men low in socioeconomic status (Dabbs & Morris, 1990).

Because testosterone levels rise as a result of aggressive and competitive activities, it has been difficult to establish unambiguously that high concentrations of male hormones cause aggressive behavior in humans (Archer, 1991). Still, animal studies show that early experiences can alter the developing nervous systems of males and females and, in turn, their behavior (Breedlove, 1994). Much evidence suggests that prenatal exposure to male or female hormones has lasting effects on the organization of the brain and, in turn, on sexual behavior, aggression, cognitive abilities, and other aspects of development (Rubinow & Schmidt, 1996). Yet biology does not dictate gender-role development. Instead, gender-role development evolves from the complex interaction of biology, social experience, and the individual's behavior.

Evidence of Social-Labeling Influences. We must also take seriously the social aspect of Money and Ehrhardt's biosocial theory. How a child is labeled and treated can considerably affect gender development. For instance, some androgenized females were labeled as boys at birth and raised as such until their abnormalities were detected. Money and Ehrhardt (1972) report that the discovery and correction of this condition (by surgery and relabeling as a girl) caused few adjustment problems if the sex change took place before 18 months. After age 3, sexual reassignment was exceedingly difficult because these genetic females had experienced prolonged masculine gender typing and had already labeled themselves as boys. These findings led Money and Ehrhardt to conclude that there is a critical period (between 18 months and 3 years) for the establishment of gender identity when the label society attaches to the child is likely to stick. Yet some studies in which infants are presented to some people as boys but to others as girls indicate that labeling has little effect on how people perceive and treat these infants (Stern & Karraker, 1989). And, as the Explorations box on page 354 on social labeling and biological destiny shows, biological males who are labeled as girls during the so-called critical period sometimes adopt a male gender identity

later in life despite their early labeling and socialization, suggesting that we should refer to a sensitive rather than a critical period. Once again, then, we see both nature and nurture at work in development.

Psychoanalytic Theory

As is true of thinking about most areas of development, thinking about gender-role development was shaped early on by Sigmund Freud's psychosexual theory. The 3- to 6-year-old child in Freud's phallic stage is said to harbor a strong, biologically based love for the parent of the other sex, experience internal conflict and anxiety as a result of this incestuous desire, and resolve the conflict through a process of **identification** with the same-sex parent. According to Freud, a boy experiencing his **Oedipus complex** loves his mother, fears that his father will retaliate by castrating him, and is forced to identify with his father, thereby emulating his father and adopting his father's attitudes and behaviors. Freud believed that a boy would show weak masculinity later in life if his father was inadequate as a masculine model, was often absent from the home, or was not dominant or threatening enough to foster a strong identification based on fear.

Meanwhile, a preschool-age girl is said to experience an **Electra complex** involving a desire for her father (and envy him for the penis she lacks) and a rivalry with her mother. To resolve her unconscious conflict, she identifies with her mother. Her father also contributes to gender-role development by reinforcing her for "feminine" behavior resembling that of her mother. Thus, Freud emphasized the role of emotions (love, fear, and so on) in motivating gender-role development and argued that children adopt their roles by patterning themselves after their same-sex parents.

We can applaud Freud for identifying the preschool years as a critical time for gender-role development. In addition, his view that boys, because of fear of castration, have a more powerful motivation than girls to adopt their gender role is consistent with the finding that boys seem to learn gender-typed behaviors faster and more completely than girls do. It is also true that boys whose fathers are absent from the home tend to be less traditionally sex-typed than other boys (Stevenson & Black, 1988). Finally, Freud's notion that fathers play an important role in the gender typing of their daughters and of their sons has been confirmed (Parke, 1996).

On other counts, however, psychoanalytic theory has not fared well. Many preschool children are so ignorant of male and female anatomy that it is hard to see how most boys could fear castration or most girls could experience penis envy (Bem, 1989). Moreover, Freud assumed that a boy's identification with his father is based on fear, but most researchers find that boys identify most strongly with fathers who are warm and nurturant rather than overly punitive and threatening (Hetherington & Frankie, 1967; Mussen & Rutherford, 1963). Finally, children are not especially similar psychologically to their same-sex parents (Maccoby & Jacklin, 1974). Apparently, other individuals besides parents influence a child's gender-related characteris-

IS THE SOCIAL LABEL EVERYTHING, OR IS BIOLOGY DESTINY?

When biological sex and social labeling conflict, which wins out? Consider the tragic case of a male identical twin, named Bruce at birth, whose penis was damaged beyond repair during a botched circumcision (Money & Tucker, 1975). On the advice of John Money, who at the time was considered the world's leading authority on gender identity, the parents agreed to a surgical procedure that removed what was left of the damaged penis and altered their 21-month-old boy's external genitals to appear feminine. From then on, they treated him like a girl. By age 5, Money reported that this boy-turned-girl, now named Brenda, was reportedly different from her genetically identical brother. According to Money and the team in charge of her treatment, Brenda clearly knew she was a girl; had developed strong preferences for feminine toys, activities, and apparel; and was far neater and daintier than her brother. This, then, was supposedly a vivid demonstration that the most decisive influence on gender-role development is how a child is labeled and treated during the critical period for such development. But there is much more to the story.

Bruce/Brenda/David

Milton Diamond and H. Keith Sigmundson (1997) followed up on this twin and found that the story had a very different and ultimately disastrous ending from what Money reported (see also Colapinto, 1997, 2000, 2004). Brenda was never comfortable with doll play and other traditionally feminine pursuits; she preferred to dress up in men's clothing, play with her

tics. It seems we must look elsewhere for more complete explanations of gender-role development.

Social Learning Theory

According to social learning theorists, children learn masculine or feminine identities, preferences, and behaviors in two ways. First, through *differential reinforcement*, children are rewarded for sex-appropriate behaviors and are punished for behaviors considered more appropriate for members of the other sex. Second, through *observational learning*, children adopt the attitudes and behaviors of same-sex models. In this view, children's gender-role development depends on which of their behaviors people reinforce or punish and on what sorts of social models are available. Change the social environment, and you change the course of gender-role development.

Differential Reinforcement. Parents use differential reinforcement to teach boys how to be boys and girls how to be girls (Lytton & Romney, 1991). By the second year of life, parents are already encouraging sex-appropriate play and discouraging cross-sex play, before children have acquired their basic gender

identities or display clear preferences for male or female activities (Fagot & Leinbach, 1989). By 20 to 24 months, daughters are reinforced for dancing, dressing up (as women), following their parents around, asking for help, and playing with dolls; they are discouraged from manipulating objects, running, jumping, and climbing. By contrast, sons are not encouraged to pursue such "feminine" behavior as playing with dolls or seeking help and they receive more positive responses from their parents when they play with "masculine" toys such as blocks, trucks, and push-and-pull toys (Blakemore, 2003; Fagot, 1978; Fagot, Leinbach, & O'Boyle, 1992). Mothers and fathers may also discipline their sons and daughters differently, with fathers more likely to use physical forms of discipline (such as spanking) than mothers and mothers more likely to use reasoning to explain rules and consequences (Conrade & Ho, 2001; Russell et al., 1998). In addition, boys end up on the receiving end of a spanking more often than girls do (Day & Peterson, 1998).

In research by Barbara Morrongiello and Kerri Hogg (2004), mothers were asked to imagine how they would react if their 6- to 10-year-old son or daughter misbehaved in some way that might be dangerous (for example, bicycling fast down a twin brother's toys, and take things apart to see how they worked. She used the jumping rope she was given to whip people and tie them up; she was miserable when she was forced to make daisy chains and become a Girl Scout rather than a Boy Scout (Colapinto, 1997). Somewhere around age 10, she had the distinct feeling that she was not a girl: "I began to see how different I felt and was. . . . I thought I was a freak or something. . . . but I didn't want to admit it. I figured I didn't want to wind up opening a can of worms" (Colapinto, 2000, pp. 299–300). Being rejected by other children because of her masculine looks and feminine dress and being called "cavewoman" and "gorilla" also took their toll, as did continued pressure from psychiatrists to behave in a more feminine manner. Finally, at age 14 and after years of inner turmoil and suicidal thinking, Brenda had had it and simply refused to take the female hormones prescribed for her and pretend to be a girl any longer. When finally told that she was a chromosomal male and had started life as a normal baby boy, Brenda was relieved: "Suddenly it all made sense why I felt the way I did. I *wasn't* some sort of weirdo" (Colapinto, 1997, p. 92). She then received male hormone shots, a double mastectomy, and surgery to construct a penis and emerged as a nice young man who eventually dated girls, married at age 25, and for a time, seemed to settle into his hard-won identity as an adult male with the name David.

When he realized that his case was being used to justify sex change operations on other infants with injured or ambiguous genitals, he went public with his story and spoke out against this practice. David and his family struggled for years with the aftermath of the attempt to change his sex. His twin brother died of a drug overdose at age 36 and, 2 years later, David committed suicide.

This disturbing case study shows that we must back off from the conclusion that social learning is all that matters. Clearly, for Bruce/Brenda/David, gender identity was not as pliable as Money believed. And this is not the only case that illustrates that biology, along with social environment, matters when it comes to gender identity. Researchers studied a group of 18 biological males in the Dominican Republic who had a genetic condition that made their cells insensitive to the effects of male hormones (Imperato-McGinley et al., 1979; see also Herdt & Davidson, 1988). They had begun life with ambiguous genitals, were mistaken for girls, and so were labeled and raised as girls. However, under the influence of male hormones produced at puberty, they sprouted beards and became entirely masculine in appearance. How, in light of Money and Ehrhardt's critical-period hypothesis, could a person possibly adjust to becoming a man after leading an entire childhood as a girl?

Amazingly, 16 of these 18 individuals seemed able to accept their late conversion from female to male and to adopt masculine lifestyles, including the establishment of heterosexual relationships. One retained a female identity and gender role, and the remaining individual switched to a male gender identity but still dressed as a female. This study also casts doubt on the notion that socialization during the first 3 years is critical to later gender-role development. Instead, it suggests that hormonal influences may be more important than social influences. It is possible, however, that Dominican adults, knowing that this genetic disorder was common in their society, treated these girls-turned-boys differently from other girls when they were young or that these youngsters recognized on their own that their genitals were not normal (Ehrhardt, 1985). As a result, these "girls" may never have fully committed themselves to being girls.

What studies such as these of individuals with genital abnormalities appear to teach us is this: We are predisposed by our biology to develop as males or females; the first 3 years of life are a sensitive period perhaps, but not a critical period, for gender-role development; and both biology and social labeling contribute to gender-role development.

hill they had been told to avoid). Mothers reported that they would be angry with their sons but disappointed and concerned with their daughters for misbehaving and putting themselves in harm's way. Boys will be boys, they reasoned, but girls should know better. To prevent future risky behaviors, mothers said they would be more rule-bound with their daughters but would not do anything different with their sons. After all, they reasoned, there is no point in trying to prevent these risky behaviors in boys because it is "in their nature." Girls' behavior, on the other hand, can be influenced, so mothers may believe that it is worth enforcing an existing rule or instituting a new one. It's not just mothers: other research shows that fathers are more protective of their preschool-aged daughters than their preschool-aged sons (Hagan & Kuebli, 2007).

Does this "gender curriculum" in the home influence children? It certainly does. Parents who show the clearest patterns of differential reinforcement have children who are relatively quick to label themselves as girls or boys and to develop strongly sextyped toy and activity preferences (Fagot & Leinbach, 1989; Fagot, Leinbach, & O'Boyle, 1992). Fathers play a central role in gender socialization; they are more likely than mothers to reward children's gender-appropriate behavior and to discourage behavior considered more appropriate for the other sex (Leve & Fagot, 1997; Lytton & Romney, 1991). Women who choose nontraditional professions are more likely than women in traditionally female fields to have had fathers who encouraged them to be assertive and competitive (Coats & Overman, 1992). Fathers, then, seem to be an especially important influence on the gender-role development of both sons and daughters.

Could differential treatment of boys and girls by parents also contribute to sex differences in ability? Possibly so. Jacquelynne Eccles and her colleagues (1990) have conducted several studies to determine why girls tend to shy away from math and science courses and are underrepresented in occupations that involve math and science (see also Benbow & Arjmand, 1990). They suggest that parental expectations about sex differences in mathematical ability become self-fulfilling prophecies. The plot goes something like this:

1. Parents, influenced by societal stereotypes about sex differences in ability, expect their sons to outperform their daughters in math and expect their sons will be more interested in math and science than their daughters (Tenenbaum & Leaper, 2003).

According to psychoanalytic theory, children become appropriately "masculine" or "feminine" through identification with the same-sex parent. Social learning theorists call this process observational learning.

2. Parents attribute their sons' successes in math to ability but credit their daughters' successes to hard work. Perhaps as a result of this, fathers talk differently to their sons and daughters when discussing science with them (Tenenbaum & Leaper, 2003). With their sons, they use more scientific terms, provide more detailed explanations, and ask more abstract questions than with their daughters. These differences reinforce the belief that girls lack mathematical talent and turn in respectable performances only through plodding effort.

3. Children begin to internalize their parents' views, so girls come to believe that they are "no good" in math. Girls report that they are less competent and more anxious about their performance than boys (Pomerantz, Altermatt, & Saxon, 2002).

4. Thinking they lack ability, girls become less interested in math, less likely to take math courses, and less likely to pursue career possibilities that involve math after high school.

In short, parents who expect their daughters to have trouble with numbers may get what they expect. The negative effects of low parental expectancies on girls' self-perceptions are evident regardless of their performance. Indeed, girls feel less competent than do boys about math and science even when they outperform the boys (Pomerantz et al., 2002). Girls whose parents are nontraditional in their gender-role attitudes and behaviors do not show the declines in math and science achievement in early adolescence that girls from more traditional families display, so apparently the chain of events Eccles describes can be broken (Updegraff, McHale, & Crouter, 1996).

Peers, like parents, reinforce boys and girls differentially. As Beverly Fagot (1985) discovered, boys only 21 to 25 months of age belittle and disrupt each other for playing with "feminine" toys or with girls, and girls express their disapproval of other girls who choose to play with boys (see also Blakemore, 2003). Similarly, on the playground, preschoolers who engage in same-sex play are better liked by their peers than those who engage in play with the opposite sex (Colwell & Lindsey, 2005).

Observational Learning. Social learning theorists call attention to differential treatment of girls and boys by parents, peers, and teachers; they also emphasize that observational learning contributes in important ways to gender typing. Children see which toys and activities are "for girls" and which are "for boys" and imitate individuals of their own sex. Around age 6 or 7, children begin to pay much closer attention to same-sex models than to other-sex models; for example, they will choose toys that members of their own sex prefer even if it means passing up more attractive toys (Frey & Ruble, 1992). Children who see their mothers perform so-called masculine tasks and their fathers perform household and child care tasks tend to be less aware of gender stereotypes and less gender typed than children exposed to traditional gender-role models at home (Sabattini & Leaper, 2004; Turner & Gervai, 1995). Similarly, boys with sisters and girls with brothers have less gender-typed activity preferences than children who grow up with same-sex siblings (Colley et al., 1996; Rust et al., 2000).

Not only do children learn by watching the children and adults with whom they interact, but they also learn from the media—radio, television, movies, video games—and even from their picture books and elementary-school texts. Although sexism in children's books has decreased over the past 50 years, male characters are still more likely than female characters to engage in active, independent activities such as climbing, riding bikes, and making things, whereas female characters are more often depicted as passive, dependent, and helpless, spending their time picking flowers, playing quietly indoors, and "creating problems that require masculine solutions" (Diekman & Murnen, 2004; Kortenhaus & Demarest, 1993). In a recent analysis of 200 popular children's picture books, David Anderson and Mykol Hamilton (2007) found that portrayals of fathers, but not mothers, were largely absent. In the few instances where fathers were portrayed, they were not engaged with their children, which conveys the message that it is still mothers who are the primary caretakers of children.

In recent decades, blatant gender stereotyping of television characters has decreased, but not disappeared. Male char-

© Mark Adams/Getty Images

acters still dominate on many children's programs, prime-time programs, and advertisements (Ganahl, Prinsen, & Netzley, 2003; Glascock, 2001; Oppliger, 2007). Even on shows with an equal number of male and female characters, the male characters assume more prominent roles (Ogletree et al., 2004). Typically, men are influential individuals who work at a profession, whereas many women—especially those portrayed as married—are passive, emotional creatures who manage a home or work at "feminine" occupations such as nursing (Signorielli & Kahlenberg, 2001). Women portrayed as single are often cast in traditionally male occupations. The message children receive is that men work regardless of their marital status and they do important business, but women only work at important jobs if they are single (Signorielli & Kahlenberg, 2001). Children who watch a large amount of television are more likely to choose gender-appropriate toys and to hold stereotyped views of males and females than their classmates who watch little television (Oppliger, 2007; Signorielli & Lears, 1992).

Perhaps the strongest traditional gender stereotypes are found in today's video games, which males play at a much higher rate than females (Ogletree & Drake, 2007). College students, both male and female, report that female video game characters are portrayed as helpless and sexually provocative in contrast to male characters who are portrayed as strong and aggressive (Ogletree & Drake, 2007). Men do not find these stereotypes as offensive as do women, perhaps because men already hold more traditional gender stereotypes than women (Brenick et al., 2007).

To recap, there is much evidence that both differential reinforcement and observational learning contribute to gender-role development. However, social learning theorists often portray children as the passive recipients of external influences: parents, peers, television and video game characters, and others show them what to do and reinforce them for doing it. Perhaps this perspective does not put enough emphasis on what children contribute to their own gender socialization. Youngsters do not receive gender-stereotyped birthday presents simply because their parents choose these toys for them. Instead, parents tend to select gender-neutral and often educational toys for their children, but their boys ask for trucks and their girls request tea sets (Alexander, 2003; Robinson & Morris, 1986; Servin, Bohlin, & Berlin, 1999).

Cognitive Theories

Some theorists have emphasized cognitive aspects of gender-role development, noting that as children acquire understanding of gender, they actively teach themselves to be girls or boys. Lawrence Kohlberg based his cognitive theory on Jean Piaget's cognitive developmental theory, whereas Carol Martin and Charles Halverson Jr. based their theory on an information-processing approach to cognitive development.

Cognitive Developmental Theory. Kohlberg (1966a) proposed a cognitive theory of gender typing that is different from the other theories you have considered and that helps explain why boys and girls adopt traditional gender roles even when their parents do not want them to do so. Among Kohlberg's major themes are the following:

- Gender-role development depends on stagelike changes in cognitive development; children must acquire certain understandings about gender before they will be influenced by their social experiences.
- Children engage in self-socialization; instead of being the passive targets of social influence, they actively socialize themselves.

According to both psychoanalytic theory and social learning theory, children are influenced by their companions to adopt male or female roles before they view themselves as girls or boys and identify with (or habitually imitate) same-sex models. Kohlberg suggests that children first understand that they are girls or boys and then actively seek same-sex models and a range of information about how to act like a girl or a boy. To Kohlberg, it is not "I'm treated like a boy; therefore, I must be a boy." It is more like "I'm a boy, so now I'll do everything I can to find out how to behave like one."

What understandings are necessary before children will teach themselves to behave like boys or girls? Kohlberg believes that children everywhere progress through the following three stages as they acquire gender constancy or an understanding of what it means to be a female or a male:

1. Basic gender identity is established by age 2 or 3, when children can recognize and label themselves as males or females (Campbell, Shirley, & Caygill, 2002).

2. Somewhat later, usually by age 4, children acquire **gender stability**—that is, they come to understand that gender identity is stable over time. They know that boys invariably become men, and girls grow up to be women.

3. The gender concept is complete, somewhere between age 5 and age 7, when children achieve **gender consistency** and realize that their sex is also stable across situations. Now, children know that their sex cannot be altered by superficial changes such as dressing up as a member of the other sex or engaging in cross-sex activities.

Children 3 to 5 years of age often do lack the concepts of gender stability and gender consistency; they often say that a boy could become a mommy if he really wanted to or that a girl could become a boy if she cut her hair and wore a hockey uniform (Warin, 2000). This changes over the kindergarten and early grade-school years (Ruble et al., 2007). As children enter Piaget's concrete-operational stage of cognitive development and come to grasp concepts such as conservation of liquids, they also realize that gender is conserved—remains constant—despite changes in appearance. Gender constancy is demonstrated by very few 3- to 5-year-olds, about half of 6- to 7-year-olds, and a majority of 8- to 9-year-olds (Trautner et al., 2003). In support of Kohlberg's theory, Jo Warin (2000) found that children who have achieved the third level of understanding display more gender-stereotypic play preferences than children who have not yet grasped gender consistency.

Criticisms? Children need not reach the concrete operations stage to understand gender stability and consistency if they have sufficient knowledge of male and female anatomy to realize that people's genitals make them male or female (Bem, 1989). Still, knowledge of male–female anatomy alone is no guarantee that children will understand gender stability and consistency (Trautner et al., 2003). The most controversial aspect of Kohlberg's cognitive developmental theory, however, has been his claim that only when children fully grasp that their biological sex is unchangeable, around age 5 to age 7, do they actively seek same-sex models and attempt to acquire values, interests, and behaviors consistent with their cognitive judgments about themselves. Although some evidence supports Kohlberg, this chapter shows that children learn many gender-role stereotypes and develop clear preferences for same-sex activities and playmates long before they master the concepts of gender stability and gender consistency and then, according to Kohlberg, attend more selectively to same-sex models (Martin, Ruble, & Szkrybalo, 2002; Ruble et al., 2007). It seems that only a rudimentary understanding of gender is required before children learn gender stereotypes and preferences.

Gender Schema Theory. Martin and Halverson (1981, 1987) have proposed a somewhat different cognitive theory, an information-processing one, that overcomes the key weakness of Kohlberg's theory. Like Kohlberg, they believe that children are intrinsically motivated to acquire values, interests, and behaviors consistent with their cognitive judgments about the self. However, Martin and Halverson argue that self-socialization begins as soon as children acquire a basic gender identity, around age 2 or 3. According to their schematic-processing model, children acquire **gender schema (plural:** schemata)—organized sets of beliefs and expectations about males and females that influence the kinds of information they will attend to and remember.

First, children acquire a simple in-group–out-group schema that allows them to classify some objects, behaviors, and roles as appropriate for males and others as appropriate for females (cars are for boys, girls can cry but boys should not, and so on). Then, they seek more elaborate information about the role of their own sex, constructing an own-sex schema. Thus, a young girl who knows her basic gender identity might first learn that sewing is for girls and building model airplanes is for boys. Then, because she is a girl and wants to act consistently with her own self-concept, she gathers a great deal of information about sewing to add to her own-sex schema, largely ignoring any information that comes her way about how to build model airplanes (see ■ Figure 12.5).

Consistent with this schema-processing theory, children appear to be especially interested in learning about objects or activities that fit their own-sex schemata. In one study, 4- to 9-year-olds were given boxes of gender-neutral objects (hole punches, burglar alarms, and so on) and were told that some objects were "girl" items and some were "boy" items (Bradbard et al., 1986). Boys explored boy items more than girls did, and girls explored girl items more than boys did. A week later, the children easily recalled which items were for boys and which were for girls; they had apparently sorted the objects according to their in-group–out-group schemata. In addition, boys recalled more in-depth information about boy items than did girls, whereas girls recalled more than boys about these same objects if they had been labeled girl items. If children's information-gathering efforts are guided by their own-sex schemata in this way, you can easily see how boys and girls might acquire different stores of knowledge as they develop.

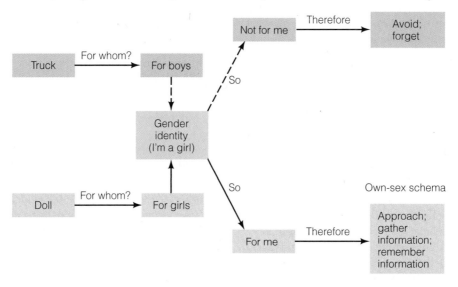

■ **FIGURE 12.5** Gender schema theory in action. A young girl classifies new information according to an in-group–out-group schema as either "for boys" or "for girls." Information about boys' toys and activities is ignored, but information about toys and activities for girls is relevant to the self and is added to an even-larger own-sex schema.
SOURCE: Adapted from Martin & Halverson (1987).

Once gender schemata are in place, children will distort new information in memory so that it is consistent with their schemata (Liben & Signorella, 1993; Martin & Halverson, 1983). For example, Martin and Halverson (1983) showed 5- and 6-year-olds pictures of children performing gender-consistent activities (for example, a boy playing with a truck) and pictures of children performing gender-inconsistent activities (for example, a girl sawing wood). A week later, the children easily recalled the sex of the actor performing gender-consistent activities; when an actor expressed gender-inconsistent behavior, however, children often distorted the scene to reveal gender-consistent behavior (for example, by saying that it was a boy, not a girl, who had sawed wood). This research gives some insight into why inaccurate gender stereotypes persist. The child who believes that women cannot be doctors may be introduced to a female doctor but may remember meeting a nurse instead and continue to state that women cannot be doctors. Even adults have trouble suppressing gender stereotypes and are influenced by their gender stereotypes when reading and interpreting text (Oakhill, Garnham, & Reynolds, 2005).

An Attempt at Integration

The biosocial, social learning, and cognitive perspectives all contribute to our understanding of sex differences and gender-role development. The biosocial model offered by Money and Ehrhardt notes the importance of biological developments that influence how people label and treat a child. Yet socialization agents—not only parents, as noted by Freud, but also siblings, peers, and teachers, as noted by social learning theorists—are teaching children how to be girls or boys well before they understand that they are girls or boys. Differences in social learning experiences may also help explain why, even though virtually all children form gender concepts and schemata, some children are far more gender typed than others in their preferences and activities (Serbin, Powlishta, & Gulko, 1993).

Kohlberg's cognitive developmental theory and Martin and Halverson's gender schema approach convince us that cognitive growth and self-socialization processes also contribute to gender-role development. Once children acquire a basic gender identity as a boy or a girl and form gender schemata, they become highly motivated to learn their appropriate roles. When they finally grasp, from age 5 to age 7, that their sex will never change, they become even more determined to learn their gender roles and pay special attention to same-sex models. Parents who want to avoid socializing their children into traditional gender roles are often amazed to see their children turn into traditional girls and boys on their own.

In short, children have a male or female biological endowment that helps guide their development, are influenced by other people from birth on to become "real boys" or "real girls," and actively socialize themselves to behave in ways that seem consistent with their understandings that they are either boys or girls (see ● Table 12.2). Most developmentalists today would

● **TABLE 12.2 AN INTEGRATIVE OVERVIEW OF THE GENDER-TYPING PROCESS**

DEVELOPMENTAL PERIOD	EVENTS AND OUTCOMES	PERTINENT THEORY OR THEORIES
Prenatal period	The fetus develops male or female genitalia, which others will react to once the child is born.	Biosocial
Birth to 3 years	Parents and other companions label the child as a boy or a girl; they begin to encourage gender-consistent behavior and discourage cross-sex activities. As a result of these social experiences and the development of basic classification skills, the young child acquires some gender-typed behavioral preferences and the knowledge that he or she is a boy or a girl (basic gender identity).	Social learning
3 to 6 years	Once children acquire a basic gender identity, they begin to seek information about sex differences, form gender schemata, and actively try to behave in ways viewed as appropriate for their own sex.	Gender schema
7 to puberty	Children finally acquire the concepts of gender stability and consistency, recognizing that they will be males or females all their lives and in all situations. They begin to look closely at the behavior of same-sex models to acquire attributes consistent with their firm self-categorization as male or female.	Cognitive developmental
Puberty and beyond	The biological changes of adolescence, with social pressures, intensify gender differences and stimulate formation of an adult gender identity.	Biosocial Social learning Gender schema Cognitive developmental

agree that what children learn regarding how to be male or female depends on an interaction between biological factors and social influences. Thus, we must respect the role of genes and hormones in gender-role development but also view this process from a contextual perspective and appreciate that the patterns of male and female development that we observe in society today are not inevitable. In another era, in another culture, the process of gender-role socialization could produce different kinds of boys and girls.

SUMMING UP

▪ Theories of gender-role development include the biosocial theory proposed by Money and Ehrhardt, which emphasizes prenatal biological developments and stresses the importance of how a child is labeled and treated during a critical period for gender identity information.

▪ According to Freud's psychoanalytic perspective, gender-role development results from the child's identification with the same-sex parent.

▪ Social learning theorists focus on differential reinforcement and observational learning. Cognitive perspectives emphasize understanding of gender and active self-socialization:

▪ Kohlberg's cognitive developmental theory emphasizes that children master gender roles once they master the concepts of gender identity, gender stability, and gender consistency.

▪ Martin and Halverson's gender schema theory holds that children socialize themselves as soon as they have a basic gender identity and can construct gender schemata. Each theory has some support, but none is completely right.

CRITICAL THINKING

1. Jen and Ben are fraternal twins whose parents are determined that they should grow up having no gender stereotypic attitudes or behaviors. Nonetheless, when the twins are only 4, Jen wants frilly dresses and loves to play with her Barbie doll, and Ben wants a machine gun and loves to pretend he's a football player and tackle people. Each seems headed for a traditional gender role. Which of the theories in this chapter do you think explains this best, which has the most difficulty explaining it, and why did you reach these conclusions?

2. Fewer women than men become architects. Drawing on the material in this chapter, explain the extent to which nature and nurture may be responsible for this, citing evidence.

12.5 THE ADULT

You might think that once children and adolescents have learned their gender roles, they simply play them out during adulthood. Instead, as people face the challenges of adult life and enter new social contexts, their gender roles and their concepts of themselves as men and women change.

Changes in Gender Roles

Although males and females fill their masculine or feminine roles throughout their lives, the specific content of those roles changes considerably over the life span. The young boy may act out his masculine role by playing with trucks or wrestling with his buddies; the grown man may play his role by holding down a job. Moreover, the degree of difference between male and female roles also changes. Children and adolescents adopt behaviors consistent with their "boy" or "girl" roles, but the two sexes otherwise adopt similar roles in society—namely, those of children and students. Even as they enter adulthood, males' and females' roles differ little because members of both sexes are often single and in school or working.

However, the roles of men and women become more distinct when they marry and, especially, when they have children. In most couples, for example, the wife typically does more housework than her husband, whether or not she is employed—about 17 to 18 hours per week for her compared with 10 hours for him (Bianchi et al., 2000). If this does not seem like a large discrepancy on a weekly basis, consider that over 1 year, wives contribute more than 400 hours to housework beyond the amount their husbands contribute. By their silver wedding anniversary, wives will have logged about 10,000 more hours than husbands have. Furthermore, specific tasks tend to be parceled out along traditional lines—she does the cooking, he takes out the garbage (Bianchi et al., 2000). The birth of a child tends to make even egalitarian couples divide their labors in more traditional ways than they did before the birth (Cowan & Cowan, 2000). She becomes primarily responsible for child care and household tasks; he tends to emphasize his role as breadwinner

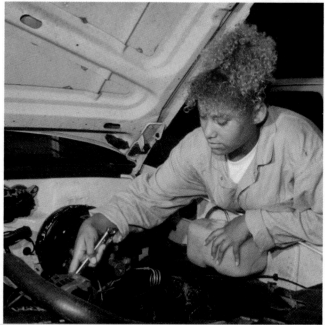

After the androgyny shift, women may feel freer to express their "masculine" side, and men may express "feminine" qualities that they suppressed during their parenting years.

and center his energies on providing for the family. Even as men increase their participation in child care and housework, they tend to play a helper role and spend only two-thirds as much time with their children as women do (Bianchi, 2000).

What happens after the children are grown? The roles played by men and women become more similar again starting in middle age, when the nest empties and child care responsibilities end. The similarity between gender roles continues to increase as adults enter old age; as retirees and grandparents, men and women lead similar lives. It would seem, then, that the roles of men and women are fairly similar before marriage, maximally different during the child-rearing years, and similar again later (Gutmann, 1997).

Masculinity, Femininity, and Androgyny

Do the shifts in the roles played by men and women during adulthood affect them psychologically? For years, psychologists assumed that masculinity and femininity were at opposite ends of a continuum. If a person possessed highly masculine traits, then that person must be very unfeminine; being highly feminine implied being unmasculine. Bem (1974) challenged this assumption by arguing that individuals of either sex can be characterized by psychological **androgyny**—that is, by a balancing or blending of both masculine-stereotyped traits (for example, being assertive, analytical, and independent) and feminine-stereotyped traits (for example, being affectionate, compassionate, and understanding). In Bem's model, then, masculinity and femininity are two separate dimensions of personality. A male or female who has many masculine-stereotyped traits and few feminine ones is defined as a masculine sex-typed person. A person who has many feminine-stereotyped traits and few masculine-stereotyped traits is said to be a feminine sex-typed person. The androgynous person possesses both masculine and feminine traits, whereas the undifferentiated individual lacks both kinds of attributes (see ■ **Figure 12.6**).

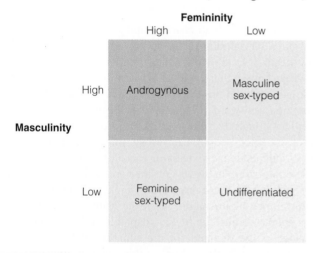

■ **FIGURE 12.6** Categories of gender-role orientation based on viewing masculinity and femininity as separate dimensions of personality.

How many of us are androgynous? Research with college students using self-perception inventories that contain both a masculinity (or instrumentality) scale and a femininity (or expressivity) scale found that roughly 33% of the test takers were "masculine" men or "feminine" women; about 30% were androgynous, and the remaining individuals were either undifferentiated (low on both scales) or sex reversed (masculine sex-typed females or feminine sex-typed males) (Spence & Helmreich, 1978). Around 30% of children can also be classified as androgynous (Boldizar, 1991; Hall & Halberstadt, 1980). But do perceived masculinity, femininity, and androgyny change over the adult years?

Changes with Age

David Gutmann (1987, 1997) has offered the intriguing hypothesis that gender roles and gender-related traits in adulthood are shaped by what he calls the **parental imperative**—the requirement that mothers and fathers adopt different roles to raise children successfully. Drawing on his own cross-cultural research and that of others, he suggests that in many cultures, young and middle-aged men must emphasize their "masculine" qualities to feed and protect their families, whereas young and middle-aged women must express their "feminine" qualities to nurture the young and meet the emotional needs of their families.

According to Gutmann, this changes dramatically starting in midlife, when men and women are freed from the demands of the parental imperative. Men become less active and more passive, take less interest in community affairs, and focus more on religious contemplation and family relationships. They also become more sensitive and emotionally expressive. Women, meanwhile, are changing in the opposite direction. After being passive, submissive, and nurturing in their younger years, they become more active, domineering, and assertive in later life. In many cultures, they take charge of the household after being the underlings of their mothers-in-law and become stronger forces in their communities. In short, Gutmann's parental imperative hypothesis states that, over the course of adulthood, psychologically "masculine" men become "feminine" men and "feminine" women become "masculine" women—that the psychological traits of the two sexes flip-flop.

A similar hypothesis is that adults experience a midlife **androgyny shift.** Instead of giving up traits they had as young adults, men and women retain their gender-typed qualities but add qualities traditionally associated with the other sex; that is, they become more androgynous. Ideas along this line were proposed by the psychoanalytic theorist Carl Jung (1933), who believed that we have masculine and feminine sides all along but learn to integrate them and express both facets of our human nature only in middle age. Now we look at how these ideas have fared.

What age-related differences do researchers find when they administer masculinity and femininity scales to men and women of different cohorts? In one study, Shirley Feldman and her associates (Feldman, Biringen, & Nash, 1981) gave Bem's

Some people believe that the world would be a better place if boys and girls were no longer socialized to adopt traditional masculine or feminine roles, interests, and behaviors. Children of both sexes would then have the freedom to be androgynous; women would no longer suffer from a lack of assertiveness in the world of work, and men would no longer be forced to suppress their emotions. Just how successful are efforts to encourage more flexible gender roles?

In several projects designed to change gender-role behavior, children have been exposed to nonsexist films, encouraged to imitate models of cross-sex behavior, reinforced by teachers for trying cross-sex activities, and provided with nonsexist educational materials (Katz, 1986; Katz & Walsh, 1991). For example, Rebecca Bigler and Lynn Liben (1990) reasoned that if they could alter children's gender stereotypes, they could head off the biased information processing that stereotypes promote. They exposed 6- to 11-year-olds to a series of problem-solving discussions emphasizing that (1) the most important considerations in deciding who could perform well in such traditionally masculine or feminine occupations

as construction worker and beautician are the person's interests and willingness to learn and (2) the person's gender is irrelevant. Compared with children who received no such training, program participants showed a clear decline in occupational stereotyping, especially if they had entered the study with firm ideas about which jobs are for women and which are for men. Moreover, this reduction in stereotyping brought about the predicted decrease in biased information processing: Participants were more likely than nonparticipants to remember counterstereotypic information presented to them in stories (for example, recalling that the garbage collector in a story was a woman).

Yet many efforts at change that work in the short run fail to have lasting effects. Children encouraged to interact in mixed-sex groups revert to their preference for same-sex friends as soon as the program ends (Lockheed, 1986; Serbin, Tonick, & Sternglanz, 1977). Why is it so difficult to change children's thinking? Perhaps because children are groomed for their traditional gender roles from birth and are bombarded with traditional gender-role messages every day. A short-term intervention project may have little chance of succeeding in this larger context.

Other research shows that it is often difficult to change the gender schemata we have constructed. Farah Hughes and Catherine Seta (2003) gave fifth-graders descriptions of men and women behaving in ways inconsistent with traditional gender stereotypes. The children were then asked to rate the likelihood that another man or woman would behave in gender-inconsistent ways. Despite being exposed to a model of inconsistent gender-stereotypic behavior, children believed that the other man (although not the other woman) would behave in a gender-consistent manner. The authors interpret this in terms of gender schema theory and children's desire to maintain their stereotypic gender schemata by countering an inconsistent piece of information with a highly consistent one. It also illustrates that simply exposing children to models of inconsistent gender roles is not going to miraculously lead to changes in the way they think about gender-stereotypic behavior: Men should still behave in masculine ways. Consistent with other research presented in this chapter, Hughes and Seta found that women were given more flexibility to express both their feminine and masculine sides.

androgyny inventory to individuals at eight different stages of the family life cycle. Consistent with Gutmann's notion of a parental imperative, taking on the role of parent seemed to lead men to perceive themselves as more masculine in personality and women to perceive themselves as having predominantly feminine strengths. Among adults beyond their parenting years, especially among grandparents, sex differences in self-perceptions were smaller. Contrary to Gutmann's hypothesis, however, grandfathers did not replace their masculine traits with feminine traits, and grandmothers did not become less feminine and more masculine. Instead, both sexes appeared to experience an androgyny shift: Grandfathers retained their masculine traits and gained feminine attributes; grandmothers retained their feminine traits and took on masculine attributes (see also Wink & Helson, 1993). This finding is particularly interesting because today's older people should, if anything, be more traditionally gender typed than younger adults who have grown up in an era of more flexible gender norms.

Is Androgyny Advantageous?

If a person can be both assertive and sensitive, both independent and understanding, being androgynous sounds psychologically healthy. Is it? Most college students—both males and females—believe that the ideal person is androgynous (Slavkin & Stright, 2000). Bem (1975, 1978) demonstrated that androgynous men and women behave more flexibly than more sextyped individuals. For example, androgynous people, like masculine sex-typed people, can display the "masculine" agentic trait of independence by resisting social pressure to conform to undesirable group activities. Yet they are as likely as feminine sex-typed individuals to display the "feminine" communal trait of nurturance by interacting positively with a baby. Androgynous people seem to be highly adaptable, able to adjust their behavior to the demands of the situation at hand (Shaffer, Pegalis, & Cornell, 1992). Perhaps this is why androgynous parents are viewed as warmer and more supportive than nonandrogynous parents (Witt, 1997). In addition, androgynous individuals appear to enjoy higher self-esteem and are perceived as better adjusted than their traditionally sex-typed peers, although this may be largely because of the masculine qualities they possess (Boldizar, 1991; Lefkowitz & Zeldow, 2006; Spence & Hall, 1996).

Before you jump to the conclusion that androgyny is a thoroughly desirable attribute, can you imagine any disadvantages of androgyny? During childhood, expressing too many of the traits considered more appropriate in the other sex can result in rejection by peers and low self-esteem (Lobel, Slone, & Winch, 1997). In addition, you may need to distinguish between the androgynous individual who possesses *positive* masculine and feminine traits and the one who possesses *negative* masculine and feminine traits (Woodhill & Samuels, 2003, 2004). People with positive androgyny score higher on measures of mental health and well-being than those with negative androgyny (Woodhill & Samuels, 2003). It may be premature, then, to conclude that it is better in all respects to be androgynous rather than either masculine or feminine in orientation. Still, you can at least conclude that it is unlikely to be damaging for men to become a little more feminine or for women to become a little more masculine than they have traditionally been. This chapter's Applications box looks at whether researchers have had any success in changing gender-role attitudes and behavior.

SUMMING UP

▌ Adults are influenced by the changing demands of gender roles. Marriage and parenthood appear to cause men and women to adopt more traditionally sex-typed roles.

▌ Freed from the parental imperative, middle-aged and elderly adults tend to experience a shift toward androgyny, blending desirable masculine-stereotyped and feminine-stereotyped qualities (although not switching personalities). Androgyny tends to be associated with good adjustment and adaptability.

CRITICAL THINKING

1. The extent to which males and females differ changes from infancy to old age. When are gender differences in psychological characteristics and roles played in society most evident, and when are they least evident? How would you account for this pattern?

12.6 SEXUALITY OVER THE LIFE SPAN

A central part of the process of becoming a woman or a man is the process of becoming a sexual being, so it is appropriate that we examine sexual development here. It is a lifelong process that starts in infancy.

Are Infants Sexual Beings?

Sigmund Freud made the seemingly outrageous claim that humans are sexual beings from birth onward. We are born, he said, with a reserve of sexual energy redirected toward different parts of the body as we develop. Freud may have been wrong about some things, but he was right that infants are sexual beings.

Babies are biologically equipped at birth with male or female chromosomes, hormones, and genitals. Moreover, young infants in Freud's oral stage of development appear to derive pleasure from sucking, mouthing, biting, and other oral activities. But the clincher is this: Both male babies and female babies have been observed to touch and manipulate their genital areas, to experience physical arousal, and to undergo what appear to be orgasms (Hyde & DeLamater, 2006; Leung & Robson, 1993).

What should you make of this infant sexuality? Infants feel bodily sensations, but they are hardly aware that their behavior is "sexual" (Crooks & Baur, 2008). Infants are sexual beings primarily in the sense that their genitals are sensitive and their nervous systems allow sexual responses. They are also as curious about their bodies as they are about the rest of the world. They enjoy touching all parts of their body, especially those that produce pleasurable sensations, and are likely to continue touching themselves unless reprimands from parents or other grown-ups discourage this behavior (at least in front of adults). From these early experiences, children begin to learn what human sexuality is about and how the members of their society regard it.

Childhood Sexuality

Although boys and girls spend much of their time in gender-segregated groups, they are nonetheless preparing for the day they will participate in sexual relationships with the other sex.

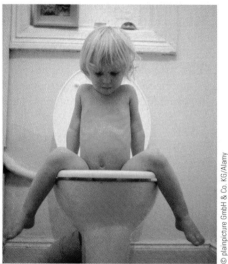

Preschoolers are naturally curious about the human body.

They learn a great deal about sexuality and reproduction, continue to be curious about their bodies, and begin to interact with the other sex in ways that will prepare them for dating in adolescence.

Knowledge of Sex and Reproduction

With age, children learn that sexual anatomy is the key differentiator between males and females, and they acquire a more correct and explicit vocabulary for discussing sexual organs (Brilleslijper-Kater & Baartman, 2000; Gordon, Schroeder, & Abrams, 1990). As Anne Bernstein and Philip Cowan (1975) have shown, children's understandings of where babies come from also change as they develop cognitively. Young children often seem to assume either that babies are just there all along or that they are somehow manufactured, much as toys might be. According to Jane, age 3½, "You find [the baby] at a store that makes it. . . . Well, they get it and then they put it in the tummy and then it goes quickly out" (p. 81). Another preschooler, interpreting what he could of an explanation about reproduction from his mom, created this scenario (author's files):

> The woman has a seed in her tummy that is fertilized by something in the man's penis. (How does this happen?) The fertilizer has to travel down through the man's body into the ground. Then it goes underground to get to the woman's body. It's like in our garden. (Does the fertilizer come out of his penis?) Oh no. Only pee-pee comes out of the penis. It's not big enough for fertilizer.

As these examples illustrate, young children construct their own understandings of reproduction well before they are told the "facts of life." Consistent with Piaget's theory of cognitive development, children construct their understanding of sex by assimilating and accommodating information into their existing cognitive structures. Children as young as age 7 know that sexual intercourse plays a role in the making of babies, but their understanding of just how this works is limited (Cipriani, 2002; Hyde & DeLamater, 2006). By age 12, most children have integrated information about sexual intercourse with information about the biological union of egg and sperm and can provide an accurate description of intercourse and its possible outcomes. Thus, as children mature cognitively and as they gain access to information, they are able to construct ever more accurate understandings of sexuality and reproduction.

Sexual Behavior

According to Freudian theory, preschoolers in the phallic stage of psychosexual development are actively interested in their genitals and seek bodily pleasure through masturbation, but school-age children enter a latency period during which they repress their sexuality and turn their attention instead to schoolwork and friendships with same-sex peers. It turns out that Freud was half right and half wrong.

Freud was correct that preschoolers are highly curious about their bodies, masturbate, and engage in both same-sex and cross-sex sexual play. He was wrong to believe that such activities occur infrequently among school-age children. By age 6, about half of children have engaged in sexual play (playing doctor or house), and sexual exploration (such as looking at and touching genitals) is increasingly common in elementary school (Larsson & Svedin, 2002; Okami, Olmstead, & Abramson, 1997; Simon & Gagnon, 1998). Elementary school–age children in Freud's latency period may be more discreet about their sexual experimentation than preschoolers, but they have by no means lost their sexual curiosity. Surveys show, for example, that about two-thirds of boys and half of girls have masturbated by age 13 (Janus & Janus, 1993; Larsson & Svedin, 2002).

Gilbert Herdt and Martha McClintock (2000) have gathered evidence that age 10 is an important point in sexual development, a time when many boys and girls experience their first sexual attraction (often to a member of the other sex if they later become heterosexual or to a member of their own sex if they later become gay or lesbian). This milestone in development appears to be influenced by the maturation of the adrenal glands (which produce male androgens). It comes well before the maturation of the sex organs during puberty and therefore challenges the view of Freud (and many of the rest of us) that puberty is the critical time in sexual development. As Herdt and McClintock note, our society does little to encourage fourth-graders to have sexual thoughts, especially about members of their own sex, so perhaps a hormonal explanation of early sexual attraction makes more sense than an environmental one (see also Halpern, 2006). The adrenal glands mature around age 6 to age 8 and produce low, but increasing, amounts of androgens (McClintock & Herdt, 1996).

Yet sexual development is also shaped by the social and cultural contexts in which children develop. For example, research shows that teens are less likely to use condoms if their friends report engaging in sex without condoms (Henry et al., 2007). Conversely, teens are more likely to use condoms if they believe their friends are using condoms. In terms of the larger cultural context, Eric Widmer and his colleagues (Widmer, Treas, & Newcomb, 1998) found wide variations in sexual beliefs across 24 countries that they examined. The prevailing cultural beliefs, whether conservative, permissive, or somewhere in the middle, influence how teens construct their individual sexual identities. Teens growing up in cultures that have more permissive attitudes about sexuality are likely to interpret their own behaviors differently than teens growing up in cultures with largely conservative beliefs. Thus, sexual behavior is not driven simply by the surge in hormones that accompanies puberty; it is mediated by social context and by the personal beliefs that are constructed in response to physical changes and surrounding beliefs.

Childhood Sexual Abuse

Every day in this country, children, adolescents, and even infants are sexually abused by the adults closest to them. A typical scenario would be this: A girl age 12 or 13—although it happens to boys, too—is abused repeatedly by her father, stepfather, or another male relative or family friend (Putnam, 2003; Trickett & Putnam, 1993). Estimates of the percentages of girls and boys who are sexually abused vary wildly, perhaps because so many cases go unreported and because definitions vary substantially. Kevin Gorey and Donald Leslie (1997) combined the results from 16 surveys, controlling for differences in definitions. They found that 17% of women (roughly 1 in 6) and 8% of men (roughly 1 in 12) have experienced childhood sexual abuse. Clearly, childhood sexual abuse is a serious and widespread social problem. Unfortunately, only one out of every four abused children tell someone about the abuse within the first 24 hours and one in four remain silent, never telling anyone about their painful experience (Kogan, 2004).

What is the effect of sexual abuse on the victim? Kathleen Kendall-Tackett, Linda Williams, and David Finkelhor (1993) offer a useful account, based on their review of 45 studies. No single distinctive "syndrome" of psychological problems characterizes abuse victims. Instead, they may experience any number of problems commonly seen in emotionally disturbed individuals, including anxiety, depression, low self-esteem, aggression, acting out, withdrawal, and school learning problems. Roughly 20 to 30% experience each of these problems, and boys seem to experience the same types and degrees of disturbance as girls do.

Many of these aftereffects boil down to lack of self-worth and difficulty trusting others (Cole & Putnam, 1992). A college student who had been abused repeatedly by her father and other relatives wrote this about her experience (author's files):

> It was very painful, emotionally, physically, and psychologically. I wanted to die to escape it. I wanted to escape from my body. . . . I developed a "good" self and a "bad" self. This was the only way I could cope with the experiences. . . . I discovered people I trusted caused me harm. . . . It is difficult for me to accept the fact that people can care for me and expect nothing in return. . . . I dislike closeness and despise people touching me.

Two problems seem to be especially linked to being sexually abused. First, about a third of victims engage in sexualized behavior, acting out sexually by putting objects in their vaginas, masturbating in public, behaving seductively, or if they are older, behaving promiscuously (Kendall-Tackett et al., 1993). One theory is that this sexualized behavior helps victims master or control the traumatic events they experienced (Tharinger, 1990). Second, about a third of victims display the symptoms of **posttraumatic stress disorder.** This clinical disorder, involving nightmares, flashbacks to the traumatizing events, and feelings of helplessness and anxiety in the face of danger, affects some soldiers who have experienced combat and other victims of extreme trauma (Kendall-Tackett et al., 1993).

In a few children, sexual abuse may contribute to severe psychological disorders including multiple-personality disorder, the splitting of the psyche into distinct personalities (Cole & Putnam, 1992; Ross et al., 1991). Yet about a third of children seem to experience no psychological symptoms (Kendall-Tackett et al., 1993). Some of these symptomless children may

experience problems in later years. Nevertheless, some children are less severely damaged and more able to cope than others are.

Which children have the most difficulty? The effects of abuse are likely to be most severe when the abuse involved penetration and force and occurred frequently over a long period, when the perpetrator was a close relative such as the father, and when the child's mother did not serve as a reliable source of emotional support (Beitchman et al., 1991; Kendall-Tackett et al., 1993; Trickett & Putnam, 1993). Children are likely to recover better if they have high-quality relationships with their mother and friends (Adams & Bukowski, 2007; Aspelmeier, Elliott, & Smith, 2007). Psychotherapy aimed at treating the anxiety and depression many victims experience and teaching them coping and problem-solving skills so that they will not be revictimized can also contribute to the healing process (Finkelhor & Berliner, 1995). Recovery takes time, but it does take place.

Adolescent Sexuality

Although infants and children are sexual beings, sexuality assumes far greater importance once sexual maturity is achieved. Adolescents must incorporate into their identities as males or females concepts of themselves as sexual males or females. Moreover, they must figure out how to express their sexuality in relationships. As part of their search for identity, teenagers raise questions about their sexual attractiveness, their sexual values, and their goals in close relationships. They also experiment with sexual behavior—sometimes with good outcomes, sometimes with bad ones.

Sexual Orientation

Part of establishing a sexual identity, part of an individual's larger task of resolving Erikson's conflict of identity versus role confusion, is becoming aware of her **sexual orientation**—that is, her preference for sexual partners of the same or other sex, or both. Sexual orientation exists on a continuum; not all cultures categorize sexual preferences as ours does (Paul, 1993), but we commonly describe people as having primarily heterosexual, homosexual, or bisexual orientations. Most adolescents establish a heterosexual sexual orientation without much soul-searching. For youths attracted to members of their own sex, however, the process of accepting that they have a homosexual orientation and establishing a positive identity in the face of negative societal attitudes can be a long and torturous one. Many have an initial awareness of their sexual preference before reaching puberty but do not accept being gay or lesbian, or gather the courage to "come out," until their mid-20s (Savin-Williams, 1995). Among 17- to 25-year-olds with same-sex attractions, fewer than half have told both their parents and about one-third have not told either parent about their sexual orientation (Savin-Williams & Ream, 2003). Those who had disclosed to one or both parents did so around age 19. By this age, most are out of high school and have achieved some independence from their parents, which may give them the confidence to share this information.

Experimentation with homosexual activity is fairly common during adolescence, but few adolescents become part of the estimated 5 to 6% of adults who establish an enduring homosexual or bisexual sexual orientation (Savin-Williams & Ream, 2007). Contrary to societal stereotypes of gay men as effeminate and lesbian women as masculine, gay and lesbian individuals have the same range of psychological and social attributes that heterosexual adults do. Knowing that someone prefers same-sex romantic partners reveals no more about his personality than knowing that someone is heterosexual.

What influences the development of sexual orientation? Part of the answer lies in the genetic code. Twin studies have established that identical twins are more alike in sexual orientation than fraternal twins (Bailey & Pillard, 1991; Bailey et al., 1993). As ● Table 12.3 reveals, however, in about half the identical twin pairs, one twin is homosexual or bisexual but the other is heterosexual. This means that environment contributes at least as much as genes to the development of sexual orientation (Bailey, Dunne, & Martin, 2000).

Research also shows that many gay men and lesbian women expressed strong cross-sex interests when they were young, despite being subjected to the usual pressures to adopt a traditional gender role (Bailey et al., 2000; LeVay, 1996). Richard Green (1987), for example, studied a group of highly feminine boys who did not just engage in cross-sex play now and then but who strongly and consistently preferred female roles, toys, and friends. He found that 75% of these boys (compared with 2% of a control group of gender-typical boys) were exclusively homosexual or bisexual 15 years later. Yet the genetic research by J. Michael Bailey and Richard Pillard suggests that sexual orientation is every bit as heritable among gay men who were typically masculine boys and lesbian women who were typically feminine girls as among those who showed early cross-sex interests (Bailey & Pillard, 1991; Bailey et al., 1993). All that is clear, then, is that many gay and lesbian adults

knew from an early age that traditional gender-role expectations did not suit them.

What environmental factors may help determine whether a genetic predisposition toward homosexuality is actualized? We do not know yet. The old psychoanalytic view that male homosexuality stems from having a domineering mother and a weak father has received little support (LeVay, 1996). Growing up with a gay or lesbian parent also seems to have little effect on later sexual orientation (Patterson, 2004). Nor is there support for the idea that homosexuals were seduced into a homosexual lifestyle by older individuals.

A more promising hypothesis is that hormonal influences during the prenatal period influence sexual orientation (Ellis et al., 1988; Meyer-Bahlburg et al., 1995). For example, androgenized females are more likely than other women to adopt a lesbian or bisexual orientation, suggesting that high prenatal doses of male hormones may predispose at least some females to homosexuality (Dittman et al., 1992; Money, 1988). Later-born males with older brothers may be more prone to a homosexual orientation because, according to one theory, their mother produces anti-male antibodies that accumulate over the course of each pregnancy with a male (e.g., Blanchard & Lippa, 2007), but this does not explain why some firstborn males or males without older brothers develop a homosexual orientation (e.g., Gooren, 2006). Another possibility is that nature and nurture interact. Biological factors may predispose an individual to have certain psychological traits, which in turn influence the kinds of social experiences the person has, which in turn shape her sexual orientation (Byne, 1994). However, no one yet knows which factors in the prenatal or postnatal environment contribute, with genes, to a homosexual orientation (Byne, 1994; LeVay, 1996).

Sexual Morality

Whatever their sexual orientation, adolescents establish attitudes regarding what is and is not appropriate sexual behavior. The sexual attitudes of adolescents changed dramatically during the 20th century, especially during the 1960s and 1970s, yet many of the old values have endured (Caron & Moskey, 2002). Three generalizations emerge from the research on sexual attitudes.

First, many adolescents have come to believe that sex with affection in the context of a committed relationship is acceptable. They no longer buy the traditional view that premarital intercourse is always morally wrong (National Campaign to Prevent Teen Pregnancy, 2005a). However, they do not go so far as to approve of casual sex, although males have somewhat more permissive attitudes about this than females (National Campaign to Prevent Teen Pregnancy, 2003). Most adolescents believe that partners should be in a long-term romantic relationship or feel a close emotional involvement with each other (Caron & Moskey, 2002).

A second finding is that the **double standard** has declined over the years. According to the double standard, sexual behavior that is viewed as appropriate for males is considered inap-

● **TABLE 12.3 PERCENTAGE OF TWINS WHO ARE ALIKE FOR HOMOSEXUAL OR BISEXUAL SEXUAL ORIENTATION**

	IDENTICAL TWINS	FRATERNAL TWINS
Both male twins are gay or bisexual if one is	52%	22%
Both female twins are lesbian or bisexual if one is	48%	16%

SOURCES: From J. M. Bailey & R. C. Pillard, A genetic study of male sexual orientation. *Archives of General Psychiatry, 48*, pp. 1089–1096. Copyright © 1991 American Medical Association. Reprinted with permission.

Note: Higher rates of similarity for identical twin pairs than for fraternal twin pairs provide evidence of genetic influence on homosexuality. Less-than-perfect agreement points to the additional operation of environmental influences.

propriate for females; there is one standard for males, another for females. In the "old days," a young man was expected to sow some wild oats and obtain some sexual experience, and gained respect from peers for his sexual exploits ("he's a stud"). In contrast, a young woman was expected to remain a virgin until she married, and was viewed negatively for engaging in sexual behaviors ("she's a slut"). Although the double standard has declined, it has by no means disappeared (Crawford & Popp, 2003; Marks & Fraley, 2006). For instance, college students still tend to believe that a woman who has many sexual partners is more immoral than an equally promiscuous man (Blumberg, 2003; Crawford & Popp, 2003). In part, the double standard for male–female sexuality may persist because it fits entrenched societal expectations, even though actual sexual behaviors of males and females are more similar than different (Marks & Fraley, 2006).

A third generalization that emerges from research on sexual attitudes is that adolescents are confused about sexual norms. Adolescents continually receive mixed messages about sexuality (Ponton, 2001). They are encouraged to be popular and attractive to the other sex, and they watch countless television programs and movies that glamorize sexual behavior. Yet they are told to value virginity and to fear and avoid pregnancy, bad reputations, and AIDS and other sexually transmitted diseases (STDs). Adults often tell teens that they are too young to engage in sexual activity with a peer, yet they make teens feel ashamed about masturbating (Halpern et al., 2000; Ponton, 2001). The standards for males and females are now more similar, and adolescents tend to agree that sexual intercourse in the context of emotional involvement is acceptable; but teenagers still must forge their own codes of behavior, and they differ widely in what they decide.

Many of today's adolescents become involved in sexual activity early and give little thought to the long-term consequences of their behavior.

Sexual Behavior

If attitudes about sexual behavior have changed over the years, has sexual behavior itself changed? Yes, it has. Today's teenagers are involved in more intimate forms of sexual behavior at earlier ages than adolescents of the past were. Several themes emerge from the research on teens' sexual behavior:

- Rates of sexual activity climbed in the 1960s and continued to climb through the 1980s before leveling off and then declining somewhat from the mid-1990s on (National Campaign to Prevent Teen Pregnancy, 2006).
- The percentages of both males and females who have had intercourse increased steadily over the past century.
- Perhaps reflecting the decline of the double standard, the sexual behavior of females has changed more than that of males, and the difference in experience between the sexes has narrowed (National Campaign to Prevent Teen Pregnancy, 2006). Today, male and female teenagers begin having sex at about the same age.

The percentage of adolescents with sexual experience increases steadily over the adolescent years. Nearly half of all high school students report that they have had sexual intercourse, although as ● Table 12.4 shows, this varies by the students' gender and race/ethnicity. By age 21 to age 24, 85% report having had sexual intercourse (Meschke et al., 2000). Of course, rates of sexual activity depend greatly on how sexual activity is defined. What constitutes "having sex"? Virtually all college students—both male and female—agree that penile–vaginal intercourse is having sex, but only 38% believe that oral sex constitutes having sex (Pitts & Rahman, 2001). Perhaps this is why there are higher rates of **oral sex** than intercourse among today's high school students (Prinstein, Meade, & Cohen, 2003). If their cognitive schema of having sex does not include oral sex (or anal sex for some teens), they can engage in oral sex without feeling they are really having sex. Consequently, as many as 40% of college students who label themselves virgins report giving or receiving oral sex, and some of these have had three or more oral sex partners (Chambers, 2007; National Campaign to Prevent Teen Pregnancy, 2005).

Interestingly, today's teens rate oral sex as less intimate than intercourse, the opposite of what many from their parent's generation believe (Chambers, 2007). This may help explain the rise in oral sex among teenagers. Another reason is teens' inaccurate perception that oral sex is safer than vaginal pene-

● TABLE 12.4 PERCENTAGE OF HIGH SCHOOL STUDENTS WHO HAVE EVER HAD SEXUAL INTERCOURSE

	WHITE	BLACK	HISPANIC
FEMALE	44	61	44
MALE	42	75	58

SOURCE: Eaton et al., 2006.

tration. Although oral sex without intercourse may sharply reduce pregnancy rates, it does not prevent transmission of sexually transmitted infections unless partners consistently use protection. Unfortunately, many teens lack knowledge about how to protect themselves during oral sex (Brady & Halpern-Fisher, 2007; Chambers, 2007). In addition to possible health consequences, there may be emotional consequences for teens who engage in oral sex. Teens who engage only in oral sex (without intercourse) report less positive feelings about themselves and their relationship than other sexually active teens (Brady & Halpern-Fisher, 2007).

Becoming sexually active is a normal part of development, but parents and society often express concerns about teens becoming sexually active when they are too young because early sexual activity is associated with risky behaviors that can lead to unwanted pregnancies and sexually transmitted infections. Jessica Siebenbruner and her colleagues (2007) studied the antecedents of early sexual behavior among three groups of 16-year-olds who had previously been evaluated on a variety of measures at ages 6, 9, 12, and 13. The researchers distinguished among three groups on the basis of self-reported sexual behaviors at age 16: sexual abstainers who had not yet had sexual intercourse, low risk-takers who reported having 5 or fewer sexual partners and always using contraception, and high risk-takers who reported having 6 or more sexual partners and inconsistently using contraception. The researchers wanted to know whether they could predict which of these three groups a teen would end up in at age 16 based on information collected at the earlier ages.

Several findings emerged from this research. High-risk sexual behavior at age 16 seemed to be part of a general pattern of problem behavior that started at birth with a mother who was unmarried (Siebenbruner et al., 2007). Unwed mothers tend to be younger, less educated, and more likely to experience economic hardships. High-risk teens grew up in homes that were characterized as less emotionally responsive and they were rated by teachers as engaging in more externalizing behaviors at ages 9 and 12. In these respects, the high-risk teens were different from both the low-risk teens and the abstainers throughout childhood. In contrast, the low-risk teens and the abstainers were similar to one another throughout childhood, yet began to diverge in early adolescence. At age 13, low-risk teens *looked* more mature than abstainers and were more involved in romantic relationships. They were also somewhat more likely to drink alcohol at age 16 than the abstainers. Their mature appearance may have led others to respond to them differently, leading them to romantic relationships, sexual involvement, and alcohol use at an earlier age than their peers who appeared less mature. These findings suggest that parents who are concerned about early involvement in sex should be on the alert for problem behaviors during childhood, provide an emotionally responsive home environment, and talk to their teens about how their appearance may influence how others perceive and treat them.

Regardless of when teens and young adults become sexually active, males and females feel different about their sexual

encounters. Teenage boys often report that their first sexual intercourse was pleasurable, whereas teenage girls respond more negatively, with some feelings of disappointment (Else-Quest, Hyde, & DeLamater, 2005; Hyde & DeLamater, 2006). Among girls who have been sexually active, many wish they waited longer to start having sex (National Campaign to Prevent Teenage Pregnancy, 2003). Females are more insistent than males that sex and love—physical intimacy and emotional intimacy—go together. In one survey, 61% of college women, but only 29% of college men, agreed with the idea of "no intercourse without love" (Darling, Davidson, & Passarello, 1992; see also de Gaston, Weed, & Jensen, 1996). Females are also more likely than males to have been in a steady relationship with their first sexual partner (Darling et al., 1992). This continuing gap between the sexes can sometimes create misunderstandings and hurt feelings, and it may partly explain why females are more likely than males to wish they had waited to have sex (de Gaston, Jensen, & Weed, 1995).

It is clear that sexual involvement is part of the average adolescent's experience. Although most adolescents seem to adjust successfully to becoming sexually active, there have also been some casualties among those who are psychologically unready for sex or who end up with an unintended pregnancy or an STD. Sexually active adolescent couples often fail to use contraception, partly because they are cognitively immature and do not take seriously the possibility that their behavior could have unwanted long-term consequences (Loewenstein & Furstenberg, 1991). Although condom use has increased over past decades, it is still lower than health-care professionals would like to see. Overall, more than one-third of sexually active teens did not use a condom during their last sexual intercourse (Eaton et al., 2006). Adolescent females report less frequent condom use than males, possibly because their sexual partners are often several years older and because condom use among males declines from mid to late adolescence (Eaton et al., 2006). This may reflect that adolescent couples who are in long-term, monogamous relationships stop using condoms because they no longer fear transmission of HIV or STDs.

For the adolescent who gives birth, the consequences of teenage sexuality can include an interrupted education, a low income, and a difficult start for both her and her child (Furstenberg, Brooks-Gunn, & Chase-Lansdale, 1989). This young mother's life situation and her child's developmental status are likely to improve later, especially if she goes back to school and limits her family size, but she is likely to remain economically disadvantaged compared with her peers who postpone parenthood until their 20s (Furstenberg, Brooks-Gunn, & Morgan, 1987).

What effect has the threat of AIDS had on adolescent sexual behavior? Most studies find change, but perhaps not enough. As noted, teens are more likely to use condoms (at least some of the time) than they used to be, and rates of teenage pregnancy have begun to decline recently as a result (Vobejda & Havemann, 1997). However, few adolescents are doing what they would need to do to protect themselves from HIV infection: abstaining from sex or using a condom *every* time. No wonder many educators are calling for stronger programs of sex education and distribution of free condoms at school. There is little chance of preventing the unwanted consequences of teenage sexuality unless more adolescents either postpone sex or practice safer sex. One encouraging finding is that warmth and connectedness between mothers and their children can delay the age of first intercourse (Sieving, McNeely, & Blum, 2000), as can parent–child communication about sexuality (Blake et al., 2001).

Adult Sexuality

Adults' sexual lifestyles are as varied as their personalities and intellects. Some adults remain single—some of them actively seeking a range of partners, others having one partner at a time, and still others leading celibate lives. More than 9 of 10 Americans marry, and most adults are married at any given time. Men have more sexual partners than women during their adult lives, but most members of both sexes have just one sexual partner at a time (Laumann et al., 1994).

Among married couples, there is a small decline in quality of sex over the course of marriage (Liu, 2003). And married women report somewhat less satisfaction with their sex lives than do married men (Liu, 2003). On average, married middle-aged couples have sex about once a week and report that they would have sex more often if they were not so busy and tired from their jobs and raising kids (Deveny, 2003). Men's sexual satisfaction, more so than women's, is largely determined by the frequency of their sexual activity (McNulty & Fisher, 2007). Middle-aged women report more positive moods and lower stress levels on days following sexual behavior with a partner (Burleson, Trevathan, & Todd, 2007). This benefit may be due to sexual activity alone or in combination with the affection that many women reported with the sexual activity.

What becomes of people's sex lives as they age? Many young people can barely conceive of their parents or—heaven forbid—their grandparents as sexual beings. We tend to stereotype older adults as sexless or asexual. But we are wrong: people continue to be sexual beings throughout the life span.

In a recent survey of over 3000 adults ranging in age from 57 to 85, many adults reported being sexually active (Lindau et al., 2007). Among those 57 to 64 years of age, 75% were sexually active, and about half of the 65- to 74-year-olds were sexually active, as were 25% of the 75- to 85-year-olds. Obviously, people can remain highly interested in sex and sexually active in old age. Older men are more likely to be sexually active than women, and, as you might expect, adults are more likely to be sexually active if they are married (91%) than if they are separated or divorced (74–80%) or widowed (only 14%) (Gott & Hinchliff, 2003; Smith, 1991).

But what about sexual desire—does this also decline with age? ● Table 12.5 shows the percentage of adults who report either low or high sexual desire. Clearly, sexual desire does decrease with age, more so for women than for men. Still, many adults retain sexual desire through their 60s and 70s.

● **TABLE 12.5 PERCENTAGE OF MEN AND WOMEN, BY AGE, REPORTING LOW AND HIGH SEXUAL DESIRE**

	WOMEN		MEN	
AGE	LOW DESIRE	HIGH DESIRE	LOW DESIRE	HIGH DESIRE
45–49 years	3	44	3	33
50–54 years	9	32	4	21
55–59 years	11	25	11	26
60–64 years	23	14	18	5
65–69 years	27	10	21	6
70–74 years	46	8	38	2
75–79 years	49	5	27	2
80–84 years	85	3	50	4
85–89 years	73	0	50	0
90–94 years	100	0	–	–

SOURCE: From J. S. DeLamater & M. Sill, Sexual desire in later life, *Journal of Sex Research*, 42, pp. 138–149. Copyright © 2005 Society for the Scientific Study of Sexuality. Reprinted with permission.
Note: Respondents who reported average levels of desire are not included in this table.

How can we explain declines with age in sexual interest and activity? Consider first the physiological changes in sexual capacity that occur with age, as revealed by the pioneering research of William Masters and Virginia Johnson (1966, 1970). Males are at their peak of sexual responsiveness in their late teens and early 20s and gradually become less responsive thereafter. A young man is easily and quickly aroused; his orgasm is intense; and he may have a refractory, or recovery, period of only minutes before he is capable of sexual activity again. The older man is likely to be slower—slower to arouse, slower to ejaculate after being aroused, and slower to recover afterward. In addition, levels of male sex hormones decline gradually with age in many men. This may contribute to diminished sexual functioning among older men (Schiavi et al., 1991), although most researchers do not believe that hormonal factors fully explain the changes in sexual behavior that most men experience (Kaye, 1993).

Physiological changes in women are less dramatic. Females reach their peak of sexual responsiveness later than men do, often not until their mid-30s. Women are capable of more orgasms in a given time span than men are because they have little or no refractory period after orgasm, and this capacity is retained into old age. As noted in Chapter 5, menopause does not seem to reduce sexual activity or interest for most women. However, like older men, older women typically are slower to

Most older adults continue to be sexual beings who seek love and affection.

become sexually excited. Moreover, some experience discomfort associated with decreased lubrication that occurs as estrogen levels drop with menopause.

The physiological changes that men and women experience do not explain why many of them become less sexually active in middle and old age. Masters and Johnson concluded that both men and women are physiologically capable of sexual behavior well into old age. Women retain this physiological capacity even longer than men, yet they are less sexually active in old age.

Apparently, we must turn to factors other than biological aging to explain changes in sexual behavior. In summarizing these factors, Pauline Robinson (1983) quotes Alex Comfort (1974): "In our experience, old folks stop having sex for the same reason they stop riding a bicycle—general infirmity, thinking it looks ridiculous, and no bicycle" (p. 440).

Under the category of infirmity, diseases and disabilities, as well as the drugs prescribed for them, can limit sexual functioning (DeLamater & Sill, 2005). This is a particular problem for men, who may become impotent if they have high blood pressure, coronary disease, diabetes, or other health problems. Mental health problems are also important: Many cases of impotence among middle-aged and elderly men are attributable to psychological causes such as stress at work and depression rather than to physiological causes (Persson & Svanborg, 1992).

The second source of problems is social attitudes that view sexual activity in old age as ridiculous, or at least inappropriate. Old people are stereotyped as sexually unappealing and sexless (or as "dirty old men") and are discouraged from expressing sexual interests. These negative attitudes may be internalized by elderly people, causing them to suppress their sexual desires

(Kaye, 1993; Purifoy, Grodsky, & Giambra, 1992). Older females may be even further inhibited by the double standard of aging, which regards aging in women more negatively than aging in men (Arber & Ginn, 1991).

Third, there is the "no bicycle" part of Comfort's analogy—the lack of a partner, or at least of a willing and desirable partner. Most older women are widowed, divorced, or single and face the reality that there just are not enough older men to go around. Moreover, most of these men are married: 85% of men compared to 12% of women over the age of 85 (Martinez, Chandra, Abma et al., 2006). Lack of a partner, then, is the major problem for elderly women, many of whom continue to be interested in sex, physiologically capable of sexual behavior, and desirous of love and affection (DeLamater & Sill, 2005).

Perhaps we should add one more element to Comfort's bicycle analogy: lack of cycling experience. Masters and Johnson (1966, 1970) proposed a "use it or lose it" principle of sexual behavior to reflect two findings. First, an individual's level of sexual activity early in adulthood predicts his level of sexual activity in later life. The relationship is not necessarily causal, by the way; it could simply be that some people are more sexually motivated than others throughout adulthood. A second aspect of the use it or lose it rule may be causal, however: Middle-aged and elderly adults who experience a long period of sexual abstinence often have difficulty regaining their sexual capacity.

Summing Up

▌ We are sexual beings from infancy onward. School-age children engage in sex play and appear to experience their first sexual attractions around age 10. In adolescence, forming a positive sexual identity is an important task, one that can be difficult for those with a gay or lesbian sexual orientation.

▌ During the past century, we have witnessed increased endorsement of the view that sex with affection is acceptable, a weakening of the double standard, and increased confusion about sexual norms.

▌ Many older adults continue having sexual intercourse, and many of those who cease having it or have it less frequently continue to be sexually motivated. Elderly people can continue to enjoy an active sex life if they retain their physical and mental health, do not allow negative attitudes surrounding sexuality in later life to stand in their way, have a willing and able partner, and continue to "use" their capacity for sex.

Critical Thinking

1. What factors are likely to influence the age at which young people today become sexually active? If you wanted to delay the age of first intercourse, what would be some ways to do this?

CHAPTER SUMMARY

12.1 MALE AND FEMALE

- Differences between males and females can be detected in the physical, psychological, and social realms; gender differences arise from an interaction of biological influences and socialization into gender roles (including the learning of gender-role norms and stereotypes).

- Research comparing males and females indicates that the two sexes are far more similar than different psychologically. The average male is more aggressive and better at spatial and mathematical problem-solving tasks, but less adept at verbal tasks, than the average female. Males also tend to be more active, assertive, and developmentally vulnerable than females, who tend to be more compliant with adults' requests, tactful, nurturant, and anxious. Most sex differences are small, however, and some are becoming smaller.

12.2 THE INFANT

- During infancy, boys and girls are similar but adults treat them differently. By age 2, infants have often gained knowledge of their basic gender identity and display "gender-appropriate" play preferences.

12.3 THE CHILD

- Gender typing progresses most rapidly during the toddler and preschool years, with 2- and 3-year-olds already learning gender stereotypes; school-age children are at first rigid and then more flexible in their thinking about gender norms, and they segregate themselves by sex.

12.4 THE ADOLESCENT

- Adolescents become intolerant in their thinking about gender-role deviations and, through gender intensification, show increased concern with conforming to gender norms.

- Theories of gender-role development include John Money and Anke Ehrhardt's biosocial theory, Sigmund Freud's psychoanalytic perspective, social learning theory, and the cognitive theories such as Lawrence Kohlberg's cognitive developmental theory and the gender schema theory. Each theory has some support, but none is completely right.

12.5 THE ADULT

- Gender roles become more distinct when adults marry and have children, as men and women fulfill their roles as husband/wife and father/mother. Once children are grown, however, older adults often display greater flexibility in their behavior.

- Some adults display androgyny, a combination of both masculine-stereotypic and feminine-stereotypic traits. Some evidence suggests that androgyny is beneficial, but not at all ages or in all situations.

12.6 SEXUALITY OVER THE LIFE SPAN

- Sexuality is an important component of our development throughout the life span. Infants and children are curious about their bodies and begin experimenting with sexual behaviors. A significant increase in sexual behavior occurs during adolescence.

- Most adults marry and engage in regular sexual activity, with declines evident as they age. Declines in the physiological capacity for sex cannot fully explain declines in sexual activity; poor physical or mental health, lack of a partner, negative societal attitudes, and periods of sexual abstinence also contribute.

KEY TERMS

gender role 343
gender-role norms 344
gender-role stereotypes 344
gender typing 344
communality 344
agency 344
systemize 344
social-role hypothesis 346
gender identity 347
gender segregation 349
gender intensification 350
androgenized female 352
identification 353

Oedipus complex 353
Electra complex 353
gender stability 357
gender consistency 357
gender schema (plural: schemata) 358
androgyny 361
parental imperative 361
androgyny shift 361
posttraumatic stress disorder 365
sexual orientation 365
double standard 366
oral sex 367

MEDIA RESOURCES

BOOK COMPANION WEBSITE

academic.cengage.com/psychology/sigelman
Find online quizzes, flash cards, animations, video clips, experiments, interactive assessments, and other helpful study aids for this text at **academic.cengage.com/psychology/sigelman.** You can also connect directly to the following sites:

APA ONLINE: ANSWERS TO YOUR QUESTIONS ABOUT SEXUAL ORIENTATION AND HOMOSEXUALITY

The American Psychological Association website on sexual orientation offers answers to many questions about sexual orientation.

HOW STUFF WORKS: HOW SEX WORKS

This site is a one-stop-shop for information on all things related to basic human reproduction. Of special interest are animations of various events like egg production and sperm production and delivery (requires Shockwave player which is available for fee via a link to the site).

THE ELECTRONIC JOURNAL OF HUMAN SEXUALITY

Explore cutting edge research on sexuality by reviewing some of the research articles available free at this site.

THE PSI CAFÉ: DEVELOPMENTAL PSYCHOLOGY— GENDER DEVELOPMENT

Visitors to this site can find links to many areas related to sex and gender including theories of gender development, gender stereotypes, and sexual identity and orientation.

UNDERSTANDING THE DATA: EXERCISES ON THE WEB

academic.cengage.com/psychology/sigelman
For additional insight on the data presented in this chapter, try out the exercises for these figures at **academic.cengage.com/psychology/sigelman**:

> **Figure 12.3** Do children prefer playmates of their own sex?

> **Table 12.3** Percentage of Twins Who are Alike for Homosexual or Bisexual Sexual Orientation

CENGAGENOW

academic.cengage.com/login
Go to **academic.cengage.com/login** to link to CengageNOW, your online study tool. First take the Pre-Test for this chapter to get your Personalized Study Plan, which will identify topics you need to review and direct you to online resources. Then take the Post-Test to determine what concepts you have mastered and what you still need work on.

© Digital Vision/Alamy

13 CHAPTER

Social Cognition and Moral Development

In this chapter, we continue our examination of the development of the self by exploring how we come to understand people and think through social issues, especially issues of right and wrong like those raised by the example above, and how our thinking about self and others is related to our behavior. We begin with the broad topic of **social cognition**—thinking about the perceptions, thoughts, emotions, motives, and behaviors of self, other people, groups, and even whole social systems (Flavell, 1985; and see Harris, 2006). We then look closely at a particularly important form of social cognition, thinking about moral issues. We will ask how humans acquire a set of moral standards, how they decide what is right and wrong, how their thoughts and emotions influence what they do, and how their moral decision making changes over the life span.

13.1 | SOCIAL COGNITION

We have already touched on some important aspects of social cognitive development in this book, seeing for example, that older children think differently than younger children about what they are like as individuals and about how males and females differ. Here we focus on developmental changes in the ability to understand human psychology, describe other people, and adopt other people's perspectives (see Harris, 2006).

Developing a Theory of Mind

Imagine that you are a young child, are brought to the laboratory, and are led through the research scenario portrayed in ■ Figure 13.1. A girl named Sally, you are told, puts her marble in her basket and leaves the room. While she is gone, Anne moves the marble to her box. Sally returns to the room. Where will Sally look for her marble?

This task, called a **false belief task,** assesses the understanding that people can hold incorrect beliefs and that these beliefs, even though incorrect, can influence their behavior. The task was used in a pioneering study by Simon Baron-Cohen, Alan Leslie, and Uta Frith (1985) to determine whether young children, children with Down syndrome, and children with autism have a theory of mind. A **theory of mind** is the understanding that people have mental states such as desires, beliefs, and intentions and that these mental states guide (or cause, if you like) their behavior. We all rely on a theory of mind, also called mind-reading skills, to predict and explain human behavior. We refer

Sally places her marble in a basket.

Sally leaves the room.

The child being tested watches as Anne transfers Sally's marble to the box.

Sally returns.

The child being tested is asked the critical question: Where will Sally look for her marble?

■ **FIGURE 13.1** The false belief task involving Sally and Anne. The child who has developed a theory of mind should say that Sally will look in the basket based on her *false belief* that the marble is there. The child who fails this false belief task says that Sally will look in the box (where the child knows the marble has been moved).
SOURCE: Adapted from Baron-Cohen et al. (1985).

to mental states every day, saying, for example, that people did what they did because they wanted to, intended to, or believed that doing so would have a desired effect.

Children who pass the false belief task in Figure 13.1, and therefore show evidence of having a theory of mind to explain human behavior, say that Sally will look for her marble in the basket (where she falsely believes it to be) rather than in the box (where it was moved without her knowledge). Children who have a theory of mind believe that Sally's behavior will be guided by her false belief about the marble's location. They are able to set aside their own knowledge of where the marble ended up after Anne moved it. In a similar false belief task, children may be shown a candy box that, surprisingly, has pencils rather than candy in it, then asked what another child would think was in the candy box upon seeing it.

In the study by Baron-Cohen and his colleagues, about 85% of 4-year-olds of normal intelligence and older children with Down syndrome passed the false belief task about Sally and her marble. Yet despite mental ages greater than those of the children with Down syndrome, 80% of the children with autism failed. They incorrectly said Sally would look where they knew the marble to be (in the box) rather than where Sally had every reason to believe it was (in the basket).

This study served as the basis for hypothesizing that children with autism display severe social deficits because they lack a theory of mind and suffer from a kind of "mind blindness" (Baron-Cohen, 1995; and see Chapter 16). Imagine trying to understand and interact with people if you were unable to appreciate such fundamentals of human psychology as people look for things where they believe they are, choose things that they want and reject things that they dislike, and sometimes attempt to plant false beliefs in others (that is, lie). Temple Grandin, a woman with autism who is intelligent enough to be a professor of animal sciences, describes what it is like to lack a theory of mind: she must create a memory bank of how people behave and what emotions they express in various situations and then "compute" how people might be expected to behave in similar situations (Sacks, 1993). Just as we cannot understand falling objects without employing the concept of gravity, we cannot hope to understand humans without invoking the concept of mental states.

First Steps

The idea that humans develop and rely on a theory of mind in understanding the world of people has stimulated exciting research on the nature and causes of autism and on when and how normal children develop the components of a theory of mind. Although children normally do not pass false belief tasks until about age 4, researchers have detected forerunners of a theory of mind in the first year of life and believe that a theory of mind begins to form long before children pass false belief tasks (Flavell, 1999; Gopnik, Capps, & Meltzoff, 2000). Four abilities are considered important early signs of a theory of mind: joint attention, pretend play, imitation, and emotional understanding (Charman, 2000). All four, it turns out, are deficient in children with autism.

First, starting around 9 months, infants and their caregivers begin to engage in much *joint attention*, both looking at the same object at the same time. At this age, infants sometimes point to toys then look toward their companions, encouraging others to look at what they are looking at. By doing so, infants show awareness that other people have different perceptual experiences than they do—and that two people can share a perceptual experience. It turns out that an infant's ability to get involved in bouts of joint attention is a good predictor of later social competence (Van Hecke et al., 2007).

Second, when infants engage in their first simple *pretend play*, between 1 and 2 years, they show at least a primitive understanding of the difference between pretense (a kind of false belief) and reality (see Chapter 14). They show that they know the difference between a pretend tea party and a real one, for example, when they make exaggerated lip-smacking noises as they drink tea at a pretend tea party.

Third, *imitation* of other people in the first year of life reveals an ability to mentally represent their actions and possibly the goals or intentions behind them. Finally, *emotional understanding*, as evidenced by comforting a playmate who is crying (see a later section) or teasing a sibling in the second year of life, reflects an understanding that other people have emotions and that these emotions can be influenced for good or bad (Flavell, 1999).

We have even more solid evidence that children are developing theories of mind when they begin to refer to mental states in their speech starting around age 2 (Bretherton & Beeghly, 1982). For example, Ross (at 2 years, 7 months) was asked why he keeps asking why and replied, "I want to say 'why,'" explaining his behavior in terms of his desire; Adam (at 3 years, 3 months) commented about a bus, "I thought it was a taxi," showing awareness that he held a false belief about the bus (Wellman & Bartsch, 1994, p. 345).

In addition, some research suggests that very young children are capable of deception. Children as young as 2½ years old will attempt to deceive an adult about which of several containers holds a bag of gold coins and jewels (Chandler, Fritz, & Hala, 1989). They seem capable of trying to plant a false belief in another person if they are shown how to erase telltale footprints leading toward the hiding place and to lay new footprints heading in the wrong direction. So, joint attention, pretend play, imitation, and emotional understanding, as well as deception, show

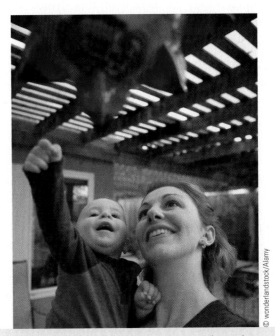

Even 1-year-olds show awareness that other people can have mental states (perceptions) different from their own when they point at objects so that their companions and they can jointly attend to the same object.

that children understand perceptions, desires, goals, and other aspects of human psychology before they pass false belief tasks. A theory of mind forms gradually, starting in infancy (Charman, 2000; Wellman, Phillips, & Rodriguez, 2000).

Desire and Belief–Desire Psychologies

Henry Wellman (1990) has theorized that children's theories of mind first take shape around age 2 as a **desire psychology.** Toddlers talk about what they want and explain their own behavior and that of others in terms of wants or desires. This early desire psychology could be seen even among 18-month-olds in a clever study by Betty Repacholi and Alison Gopnik (1997). An experimenter tried two foods—Goldfish crackers and broccoli florets—and expressed happiness in response to one but disgust in response to the other. Because the toddlers almost universally preferred the crackers to the broccoli, the acid test was a scenario in which toddlers saw the experimenter express her liking for broccoli but her disgust at the crackers ("Eww! Crackers! I tasted crackers! Eww!"). When confronted with the two bowls of food and asked to give the experimenter some, would these toddlers give her broccoli or crackers? The 14-month-olds in the study either did not comply with the request or gave the experimenter crackers, despite her distaste for them. However, the 18-month-olds gave her broccoli (undoubtedly against their better judgment), showing that they were able to infer her desire from her previous emotional reactions to the two foods.

By age 4, children normally progress to a **belief–desire psychology.** They appreciate that people do what they do because they *desire* certain things and because they *believe* that certain actions will help them fulfill their desires. They now pass false belief tasks like the one about Sally and her marble, demonstrating an understanding that beliefs, true or false, guide people's behavior just as desires do (Wellman, Cross, & Watson, 2001; Wellman & Liu, 2004).

Notice, then, that the 4-year-olds described by theory-of-mind researchers, and even younger children, are far more sophisticated students of psychology than the egocentric preschoolers described by Jean Piaget. However, it is better to think of a theory of mind as a set of understandings that children begin to develop well before age 4, and continue to refine and learn to use long afterward, than to view it as something children "have" at 4 years (Wellman & Liu, 2004). In late elementary school, children are still mastering the complexities of thinking about other people's beliefs (Harris, 2006; Keenan, 2003)—for example, making sense of statements such as, "Mary thinks that Jeff thinks that she hates him." Moreover, it is not until then that children grasp that different human minds construct different views of reality and that their interpretations of events are influenced by these views (Flavell, 1999).

Nature and Nurture

What roles do nature and nurture play in the development of theory of mind? On the nature side, evolutionary theorists argue that having a theory of mind proved adaptive to our ances-

tors and became part of our biological endowment as a species through natural selection (Bjorklund & Pellegrini, 2002). You can easily appreciate that theory-of-mind skills would help humans function as members of a social group, gain resources, and therefore survive. Social behaviors such as bargaining, conflict resolution, cooperation, and competition depend on understanding other people and predicting their behavior accurately.

Some support for an evolutionary perspective on theory of mind skills comes from studies of other primates. As it turns out, chimpanzees, gorillas, and other great apes share with humans basic, although not advanced, theory-of-mind skills, including a capacity to deceive others to get what they want (Tomasello, Call, & Hare, 2003). In one study, chimps deliberately chose to approach banana pieces that they knew might be snatched away by a human competitor by a route that would be hidden from the human's view rather than by a visible and more direct route (Hare, Call, & Tomasello, 2006). Yet human children have more advanced skills and are more successful than chimps at participating in games in which they must cooperate with others to achieve a goal (Warneken, Chen, & Tomasello, 2006).

Developing a theory of mind also requires a certain level of biological maturation, especially neurological and cognitive development. This may be why children everywhere develop a theory of mind and progress from a desire psychology to a belief–desire psychology in the same manner at about the same age (Tardif & Wellman, 2000). Abnormal brain development in children with autism is suspected to be behind their great difficulty passing theory-of-mind tasks. One view is that evolution may have equipped the normal human brain with a specialized module or modules devoted to understanding mental states (Leslie, 1994; Scholl & Leslie, 2001). Neuropsychologists are now exploring this possibility, as the Explorations box illustrates.

Finally, some twin research suggests that differences among children in behaviors, such as helping those in distress, that require understanding another person's perspective are partly genetic in origin (Ronald, Happé, Hughes, & Plomin, 2005). However, other research suggests that environmental influences may be more important than genes in shaping theory-of-mind skills (Hughes et al., 2005), so we cannot be sure yet how important genetic endowment is.

On the nurture side of the nature–nurture debate is evidence that acquiring a theory of mind, much like acquiring language, requires not only a normal human brain but also experience interacting with other humans and participating in a "community of minds" (Nelson et al., 2003). Children do not construct their theories of mind on their own; instead, they construct them jointly with others during conversations about mental states (Thompson, 2006).

Evidence? Children with siblings seem to grasp the elements of a theory of mind earlier than children without siblings (Jenkins & Astington, 1996; McAlister & Peterson, 2006). Engaging in pretend play with siblings may be especially valuable because the players must have shared beliefs (Taylor &

THEORY OF MIND AND THE BRAIN

Might there be an area of our brains dedicated to the important human task of understanding the perceptions, emotions, and thoughts of other human beings? We know that the human brain has areas that specialize in language. Might humans also have evolved to have areas that specialize in social cognition? Using neuroimaging techniques, researchers are beginning to identify areas in the prefrontal cortex and temporoparietal areas of the brain that are activated during theory-of-mind tasks and that seem to be uniquely involved in thinking about people's beliefs (Gallagher & Frith, 2003; Sabbagh, 2006; Saxe, Carey, & Kanwisher, 2004).

The researchers use functional magnetic resonance imaging (fMRI) to get a picture of the blood's oxygen content, which is high when an area of the brain is active and its neurons are firing. Using fMRI, Rebecca Saxe and Nancy Kanwisher (2003) found that the areas of adults' brains that respond strongly during tasks that require understanding a person's false beliefs (tasks like the one involving Sally and her marble described in Figure 13.1) do not respond when people are asked questions about "false photographs" (for example, when they are shown a photo of chocolate in a green cupboard after the chocolate had been moved to a blue cupboard). In another study (Saxe & Powell, 2006), the right temporoparietal area, along with a couple of other brain areas, was activated when adults read stories about people's thoughts (for example, "He guessed that the leash had come untied"), but not when they read stories about a person's appearance ("He was balding and combed his blond hair

over the top of his head") or bodily sensations ("By the time she got off the train, she was starving").

Recently neuroscientists have also been making fascinating and important discoveries about **mirror neurons,** neurons that are activated both when we perform an action and when we observe someone else perform the same action (Iacoboni & Dapretto, 2006; Oberman & Ramachandran, 2007). Thus, observing someone grasp a ball activates the same neurons that fire when we grasp a ball ourselves, and mirror neuron systems may therefore facilitate imitation of what we see and hear. Mirror neurons, which are evident in multiple areas of the brain, may also be critical in allowing us to quickly infer another person's internal state (she's thirsty, she wants a drink, she's happy to have that first sip) based on our own experiences of the same states. Very simply, we may understand other people primarily by drawing on what we know of ourselves. Mirror neuron systems make this possible through a mirroring process in which we simulate or reproduce within ourselves the actions, expressions of emotion, and other states we observe in other people and, through this simulation process, come to understand them (Oberman & Ramachandran, 2007).

Mirror neurons have now been implicated not only in imitation, but in language, empathy, and theory of mind—all, interestingly, areas in which individuals with autism have difficulty (Iacoboni & Dapretto, 2006; Oberman & Ramachandran, 2007). Consistent with the hypothesis that mirror neuron systems do not work properly in people with autism, research-

ers have discovered that the mirror neurons of individuals with autistic disorder are not as active as those of nonautistic people while observing or imitating others' actions (Oberman & Rachandran, 2007). The difference is especially noticeable in the right temporoparietal area—one of the areas that Saxe found is involved in processing information about other people's beliefs and thoughts (Williams et al., 2006). In addition, individuals with autism do not automatically and subtly mimic other people's facial expressions of emotion the way the rest of us do (McIntosh et al., 2006). Such mimicry, involving mirror neurons, appears to help us recognize other people's emotions and empathize with them.

So, exciting progress is being made in identifying areas of the brain and neuron systems that may be critical to theory-of-mind skills, empathy, and other very human abilities—and that do not function properly in people with autism. It is too simple to think that a particular "brain module" for theory of mind will be located; instead, whole systems of neurons spanning multiple areas of the brain are likely involved. A final warning: Most research to date on the neural basis of theory-of-mind skills has been done with adults rather than children (Sabbagh, 2006), despite some evidence that children and adults may rely on different brain areas to perform some theory-of-mind tasks (Kobayashi, Glover, & Temple, 2007). Progress in the neuroscience of social cognition is spectacular—but much more remains to be learned.

Carlson, 1997; Youngblade & Dunn, 1995). In multichild families, there may also be more talk about mental states ("She thought you were done with your ice cream," "He didn't mean to step on your head"). This kind of "mind talk" contributes to early mastery of a theory of mind (Dunn et al., 1991).

Parents are important, too. They can contribute positively to the development of theory-of-mind skills by forming secure attachments with their children and being sensitive to their needs and perspectives (Symons & Clark, 2000; Thompson, 2006). Even more important may be the parent's "mind-mindedness." Mothers who talk in elaborated and appropriate ways about their children's mental states ("You were probably sad because you thought Grandma would stay with us instead

of going home so soon") tend to have children with advanced theory-of-mind skills (Meins et al., 2002; Peterson & Slaughter, 2003). So do mothers who encourage their children to imagine what others may have thought or felt after the child misbehaved (Pears & Moses, 2003).

Experience with language is critical too. Deaf children of hearing parents, who usually do not have an opportunity to converse in sign language from an early age, sometimes struggle with false belief tasks even at ages 8 to 10 (Peterson & Siegal, 1999; Peterson, Wellman, & Liu, 2005). Deaf children of deaf parents, who can communicate with their companions using sign language, develop theory-of-mind skills on schedule. That deaf children with limited language experience show deficits in theory-of-mind performance rivaling those of children with autism casts doubt on the defective brain module view of autism (Wellman & Lagattuta, 2000). It could be instead that autistic children lack the social input they need to develop a theory of mind.

Finally, cultural influences are evident: Where there is not much talk about mental states, children are slow to develop theory-of-mind skills, though they generally develop skills in the same order. Among the Junin Quechua people of Peru, for example, adults rarely talk about beliefs and thoughts and have few words in their language for them. The result is that children as old as 8 years have trouble understanding that beliefs can be false (Vinden & Astington, 2000).

In sum, acquiring a theory of mind—the foundation for all later social cognitive development—begins in infancy and toddlerhood with first steps such as joint attention, pretend play, imitation, and emotional understanding and advances from a desire psychology to a belief–desire psychology universally. It is the product of both nature and nurture; that is, it is an evolved set of skills that requires normal neurological and cognitive growth, but also depends on social and language experiences that involve talking about mental states with parents, siblings, and other companions.

Formulating a theory of mind has many important consequences for development. Children who have mastered theory-of-mind tasks generally tend to have more advanced social skills and better social adjustment than those who have not (Keenan, 2003; Repacholi et al., 2003). They can understand that others' emotional responses might differ from their own (Harwood & Farrar, 2006), and, as you will see later, they think more maturely about moral issues. However, theory-of-mind

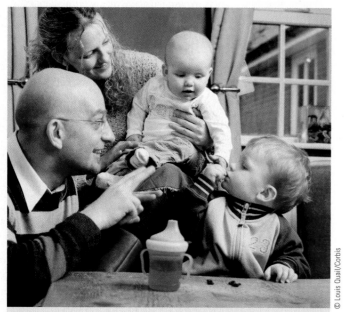

Deaf children who can communicate with their companions through sign language develop theory-of-mind skills on schedule.

skills can be used for evil and good ends; bullies and manipulative children often prove as adept as socially competent children at this sort of "mind reading" (Repacholi et al., 2003), so there is no guarantee that good "mind readers" will be socially well-adjusted.

Describing Other People

Although research on theory of mind shows that even preschool children are budding psychologists, they still have a way to go to understand other people in terms of their enduring personality traits and predict how others will react and behave. Consider first how children of different ages describe people they know—parents, friends, disliked classmates, and so on.

As you discovered in Chapter 11, children younger than 7 or 8 describe themselves primarily in physical rather than psychological terms. They describe other people that way, too (Livesley & Bromley, 1973; Yuill, 1993). Thus, 4-year-old Evan says of his father, "He has one nose, one Mom, two eyes, brown hair." And 5-year-old Keisha says, "My daddy is big. He has hairy legs and eats mustard. Yuck! My daddy likes dogs—do you?" Not much of a personality profile there.

Young children perceive others in terms of their physical appearance, possessions, and activities. When they use psychological terms, the terms are often global, evaluative ones such as "nice" or "mean," "good" or "bad," rather than specific personality-trait labels (Ruble & Dweck, 1995). Moreover, they do not yet understand traits as enduring qualities that predict how a person will behave in the future or explain why a person behaves as he does. The 5-year-old who describes a friend as "dumb" may be using this trait label only to describe that friend's recent "dumb" behavior; he may expect "smart" behavior tomorrow. Indeed, young children tend to be optimists, believing that negative traits today are likely to change into positive ones tomorrow (Lockhart, Chang, & Story, 2002).

Around age 7 or 8, children's descriptions of people suggest that they are more able to "get below the surface" and infer people's enduring psychological traits. Thus, 10-year-old Juanita describes her friend Tonya: "She's funny and friendly to everyone, and she's in the gifted program because she's smart, but sometimes she's too bossy." As children reach age 11 or 12, they make more use of psychological traits to explain why people behave as they do, saying, for instance, that Mike pulled the dog's tail *because* he is cruel (Gnepp & Chilamkurti, 1988). Clearly, then, children become more psychologically minded as their emerging social cognitive abilities permit them to make inferences about enduring inner qualities from the concrete behavior they observe in the people around them.

When asked to describe people they know, adolescents offer personality profiles that are even more psychological than those provided by children (Livesley & Bromley, 1973). They see people as unique individuals with distinctive personality traits, interests, values, and feelings. Moreover, they are able to create more integrated, or organized, person descriptions, analyzing how an individual's diverse and often inconsistent traits fit together and make sense as a whole personality. Dan, for example, may notice that Noriko brags about her abilities at times but seems unsure of herself at other times, and he may integrate these seemingly discrepant impressions by concluding that Noriko is basically insecure and boasts to hide her insecurity. Some adolescents spend hours psychoanalyzing people, trying to figure out what makes them tick.

As was the case for self-descriptions, then, you can detect a progression in perceptions of other people from (1) physical descriptions and global evaluations of other people as good or bad during the preschool years to (2) more differentiated descriptions that refer to specific personality traits starting at age 7 or 8 and, finally, to (3) more integrated personality profiles that show how even seemingly inconsistent traits fit together during adolescence.

Role-Taking Skills

Another important aspect of social cognitive development involves outgrowing the egocentrism that characterizes young children and developing **role-taking skills**—the ability to adopt another person's perspective and understand her thoughts and feelings in relation to your own. Role-taking skills are really an example of theory of mind in action (Blair, 2003). They are essential in thinking about moral issues from different points of view, predicting the consequences of a person's actions for others, and empathizing with others (Gibbs, 2003). Robert Selman (1976, 1980; Yeates & Selman, 1989) contributed greatly to our understanding of role-taking abilities by asking children questions about interpersonal dilemmas like this one (Selman, 1976, p. 302):

> Holly is an 8-year-old girl who likes to climb trees. She is the best tree climber in the neighborhood. One day while climbing down from a tall tree, she falls. . . . but does not hurt herself. Her father sees her fall. He is upset and asks her to promise not to climb trees anymore. Holly promises.
>
> Later that day, Holly and her friends meet Shawn. Shawn's kitten is caught in a tree and can't get down. Something has to be done right away or the kitten may fall. Holly is the only one who climbs trees well enough to reach the kitten and get it down but she remembers her promise to her father.

To assess how well a child understands the perspectives of Holly, her father, and Shawn, Selman asks: "Does Holly know how Shawn feels about the kitten? How will Holly's father feel if he finds out she climbed the tree? What does Holly think her father will do if he finds out she climbed the tree? What would you do in this situation?" Children's responses to these questions led Selman (1976) to conclude that role-taking abilities develop in a stagelike manner:

- Consistent with Piaget's theory, children 3 to 6 years old are largely egocentric, assuming that others share their point of view. If young children like kittens, for example,

they assume that Holly's father does, too, and therefore will be delighted if Holly saves the kitten.
- By age 8 to 10, as concrete-operational cognitive abilities solidify, children appreciate that two people can have different points of view even if they have access to the same information. Children are able to think about their own thoughts and about the thoughts of another person, and they realize that their companions can do the same. Thus, they can appreciate that Holly may think about her father's concern for her safety but conclude that he will understand her reasons for climbing the tree.
- Adolescents who have reached the formal-operational stage of cognitive development, at roughly age 12, become capable of mentally juggling multiple perspectives, including the perspective of the "generalized other," or the broader social group. The adolescent might consider how fathers in general react when children disobey them and consider whether Holly's father is similar to or different from the typical father. Adolescents thus become mental jugglers, keeping in the air their own perspective, that of another person, and that of an abstract "generalized other" representing a larger social group.

These advances in social cognition are made more likely if parents are good models of social perspective taking, consider their children's feelings and thoughts, and rely on explanation rather than punishment in disciplining their children. This may be why maltreated children and adolescents often prove to be more egocentric and less able to take others' perspectives than their peers when they are given a set of Selman's scenarios to think about (Burack et al., 2006).

Adolescents who have advanced role-taking, or social perspective-taking, skills are better able than those who do not to resolve conflicts with their parents (Selman et al., 1986). They are better able to adopt the perspectives of their parents (and parents in general) and to identify a mutually beneficial agreement.

Social perspective-taking skills have important implications for children's and adolescents' relationships. Experience interacting with peers seems to sharpen role-taking skills; sophisticated role-taking skills, in turn, help make children more sensitive and desirable companions. Children with advanced role-taking skills are more likely than age-mates with less advanced skills to be sociable and popular and to enjoy close relationships with peers (Kurdek & Krile, 1982; LeMare & Rubin, 1987). What is more, coaching in perspective taking can help improve the social behavior of disruptive children (Grizenko et al., 2000).

Social Cognition in Adulthood

As you saw in earlier chapters, nonsocial cognitive abilities, such as those used in remembering readings and testing scientific hypotheses, tend to improve during early and middle adulthood and decline in later life. Do important social cognitive skills, such as the ability to think through theory-of-mind problems or adopt other people's perspectives, also increase to a peak in middle age and decline later?

Social cognitive development during adulthood appears to involve more gains than losses (Blanchard-Fields, 1996; Hess, 1999). For example, Fredda Blanchard-Fields (1986) presented adolescents, young adults, and middle-aged adults with three dilemmas that required them to engage in role taking and to integrate discrepant perspectives: two conflicting historical accounts, a conflict between a teenage boy and his parents over whether he must visit his grandparents with the family, and a disagreement between a man and a woman about an unintended pregnancy. Adults, especially middle-aged ones, were better able than adolescents to see both sides of the issues and to integrate the perspectives of both parties into a workable solution. Here, then, is evidence that the social cognitive skills of adults may continue to improve after adolescence. Through a combination of social experience and cognitive growth, middle-aged adults have the potential to become very sophisticated students of human psychology. As you saw in Chapter 9, a few even gain a kind of wisdom that gives them exceptional insight into the complexities of human existence.

Do elderly people continue to display the sophisticated social cognitive skills that middle-aged adults display? The evidence is mixed but, overall, social cognitive skills hold up quite well late in life, better than other cognitive abilities. Thomas Hess and his colleagues found that both middle-aged and elderly adults were more adept than young adults at reading a person's behavior to infer whether he possessed traits such as honesty or intelligence (Hess, Osowski, & Leclerc, 2005). The older individuals studied seemed to have built up expertise in judging the diagnostic value of information about people. Elderly adults appear to perform as well as young and/or middle-aged adults on many social cognitive tasks (Hess, 1994; Keightley et al., 2006; Pratt & Norris, 1999).

Yet some researchers detect deficiencies in the performance of older adults (Blanchard-Fields, 1996; Pratt et al.,

1996). Consider studies in which adults are given theory-of-mind tasks suitable for adults. Susan Sullivan and Ted Ruffman (2004) used one in which a burglar leaving a crime scene is stopped by a policeman who saw the burglar drop his glove. The burglar turns himself in, and the research participant is asked what the burglar was thinking about the policeman's thoughts. Adults who averaged age 73 years of age performed less well than adults who averaged 30, and the poorer performance of older adults could be traced to age differences in fluid intelligence. In certain other studies, elderly adults perform as well as young adults on theory-of-mind tasks if the effects of older adults' memory limitations are taken into account (Happé, Winner, & Brownell, 1998; Keightley et al., 2006). Together these findings suggests that the declines in working memory and processing speed that limit the performance of older adults on nonsocial cognitive tasks sometimes take a toll on their ability to take in and manipulate social information (Hess, 1999).

For the most part, though, nonsocial and social cognition are distinct, and social cognitive abilities hold up better in later life (Keightley et al., 2006). A possible explanation is that the areas of the cortex that support social cognition and emotional understanding age more slowly than the areas that support nonsocial cognition (MacPherson, Phillips, & Della Sala, 2002). Yet possibly the most important finding is that older

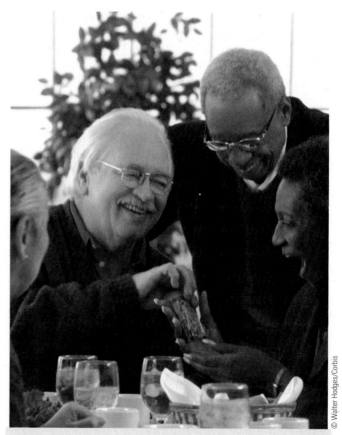

Social cognitive skills hold up well when older adults are socially active.

adults differ greatly in their social cognitive abilities. Those who have the sharpest social cognitive skills tend to be socially active and involved in meaningful social roles such as spouse, grandparent, church member, and worker (Dolen & Bearison, 1982; Hess et al., 2005). It is mainly when elderly people become socially isolated or inactive that their social cognitive skills become rusty.

Having examined some important and dramatic changes in social cognition over the life span, let us now focus on an important area of development in which social cognitive skills play a crucial role: moral development.

SUMMING UP

▌ Social cognition takes shape in infancy through joint attention, pretend play, imitation, and emotional understanding—precursors of a theory of mind.

▌ Children progress from a desire psychology to a belief–desire psychology in developing theory-of-mind skills, which depend on both nature (normal neurological functioning and cognitive maturation) and nurture (social and language experience).

▌ Children's descriptions of other people progress from a focus on physical features and activities to a focus on inner traits to the integration of trait descriptions; role-taking skills also improve with age.

▌ Social cognitive skills often improve in early and middle adulthood and hold up well in old age if adults remain socially active.

CRITICAL THINKING

1. Listen closely to a conversation in which your friends talk about people, and write down any statements in which they refer to people's beliefs, desires, intentions, and the like in attempting to explain someone's behavior. Find and analyze evidence that your friends have and use a theory of mind.

13.2 PERSPECTIVES ON MORAL DEVELOPMENT

Although we could debate endlessly what **morality** is (see Gibbs, 2003; Turiel, 2006), most of us might agree that it involves the ability to distinguish right from wrong, to act on this distinction, and to experience pride when we do the right things and guilt or shame when we do not. Accordingly, three basic components of morality have been of interest to developmental scientists:

1. The *affective*, or emotional, component consists of the feelings (guilt, concern for others' feelings, and so on) that surround right or wrong actions and that motivate moral thoughts and actions.

2. The *cognitive* component centers on how we conceptualize right and wrong and make decisions about how to behave, drawing on social cognitive skills such as role taking.

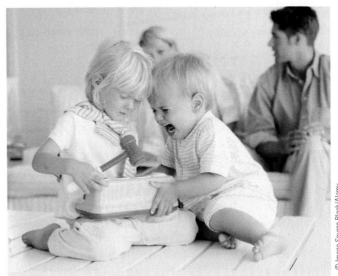

Learning to resist the temptation to break moral rules (here, one about taking turns) is an important part of moral development.

© Image Source Black/Alamy

3. The *behavioral* component reflects how we behave when, for example, we experience the temptation to cheat or are called upon to help a needy person.

Each of the three major theoretical perspectives on moral development focuses on a different component of morality. So, we will look at what psychoanalytic theory says about moral affect, what cognitive developmental theory says about moral cognition or reasoning, and what social learning (or social cognitive) theory reveals about moral behavior. Then we will look at morality from a broad, evolutionary perspective.

Moral Affect: Psychoanalytic Theory and Beyond

What kind of **moral affect,** or emotion related to matters of right and wrong, do you feel if you contemplate cheating or lying? Chances are you experience such negative feelings as shame, guilt, anxiety, and fear of being detected—feelings that keep you from doing what you know is wrong. You may also experience disgust or righteous anger when witnessing harmful acts and injustices (Tangney, Stuewig, & Mashek, 2007). Positive emotions, such as pride and self-satisfaction when you have done the right thing, and admiration or gratitude when you witness moral acts, are also an important part of morality (Turiel, 2006). Moral emotions, both positive and negative, require being able to evaluate whether you have exceeded or fallen short of standards of behavior (Tangney et al., 2007). We are generally motivated to avoid negative moral emotions and to experience positive ones by acting in moral ways.

Empathy is the vicarious experiencing of another person's feelings (for example, smiling at another person's good fortune or experiencing another person's distress). Although it is not a specific emotion, it is an emotional process believed to be especially important in moral development (Hoffman, 2000; Tangney et al., 2007). Empathizing with individuals who are suffering—not only taking their perspective but also feeling their pain—can motivate **prosocial behavior**—positive social acts, such as helping or sharing, that reflect a concern for the welfare of others. Empathy can also keep us from doing harm to others, as when a teenager can relate to the feelings of a disabled or overweight classmate and refrains from picking on this individual.

Young infants are unlikely to experience moral emotions, so when do they arise? Sigmund Freud's (1960) psychoanalytic theory offered an early answer (see Chapter 2). As you will recall, Freud believed that the mature personality has three components: the selfish and irrational id, the rational ego, and the moralistic superego. The *superego*, or conscience, has the important task of ensuring that any plans formed by the ego to gratify the id's urges are morally acceptable. Infants and toddlers, Freud said, lack a superego and are essentially "all id." They will therefore act on their selfish motives unless their parents control them.

The superego is formed during the phallic stage (ages 3–6), when children are presumed to experience an emotional conflict over their love for the other-sex parent. To resolve his Oedipus complex, Freud said, a boy identifies with and patterns himself after his father, particularly if the father is a threatening figure who arouses fear. Not only does he learn his masculine role in this manner, but through the process of identification, he also takes on his father's moral standards as his own. Similarly, a girl resolves her Electra complex by identifying with her mother and internalizing her mother's moral standards. However, Freud believed that, because girls do not experience the intense fear of castration that boys experience, females develop weaker superegos than males do.

Having a superego, then, is like having a parent inside your head—there, even when your parent is not, to tell you what is right or wrong and to arouse emotions such as shame and guilt if you so much as think about doing wrong. The only problem is that the specifics of Freud's theory are largely unsupported:

1. Cold, threatening, and punitive parents who make their children anxious about losing their parents' love do not raise morally mature youngsters; instead, as modern psychoanalytic thinkers appreciate, children form strong consciences when they are securely attached to warm and responsive parents (Hoffman, 2000).

2. Males do not appear to have stronger superegos than females; if anything, females are more able to resist temptation (Silverman, 2003).

3. Moral development begins well before the phallic stage and extends long after age 6 or 7.

Although the particulars of Freud's theory of moral development lack support, his main themes are taken very seriously today, as you will see shortly, because research has shown that: (1) moral emotions are an important part of morality, (2) early relationships with parents contribute to moral development,

and (3) children must somehow internalize moral standards if we want them to behave morally even when no authority figure is present to detect and punish their misbehavior (Kochanska & Aksan, 2006; Turiel, 2006).

Moral Reasoning: Cognitive Developmental Theory

Cognitive developmental theorists study morality by looking at the development of **moral reasoning**—the thinking process involved in deciding whether an act is right or wrong. These theorists assume that moral development depends on social cognitive development, particularly role-taking or perspective-taking skills that allow us to picture how our victims might react to our misdeeds or how people in distress must feel. These skills also allow us to get beyond our egocentric perspective to construct a concept of **reciprocity,** or mutual give and take by both parties in a human relationship (Gibbs, 2003).

Moral reasoning is said to progress through an invariant sequence—a fixed and universal order of stages, each of which represents a consistent way of thinking about moral issues that is different from the stage preceding or following it. To cognitive developmental theorists, what is of interest is how we decide what to do, not what we decide or what we actually do. A young child and an adult may both decide not to steal a pen, but the reasons they give for their decision may be entirely different. Jean Piaget paved the way for the influential theory of moral development put forth by Lawrence Kohlberg.

Piaget's View

Piaget (1965) studied children's concepts of rules by asking Swiss children about their games of marbles and explored children's concepts of justice by presenting them with moral dilemmas to ponder. For example, he told children about two boys: John, who accidentally knocked over a tray of 15 cups when coming to dinner as requested, and Henry, who broke only one cup when sneaking jam from the cupboard. The key question Piaget posed was which child was naughtier, and why.

Based on children's responses to such questions, Piaget formulated a theory of moral development that included a premoral period and two moral stages:

- **Premoral period.** During the preschool years, children show little awareness or understanding of rules and cannot be considered moral beings.
- **Heteronomous morality.** Children 6 to 10 years old take rules seriously, believing that they are handed down by parents and other authority figures and are sacred and unalterable (the term *heteronomous* means under the rule of another). They also judge rule violations as wrong based on the extent of damage done, not taking into account whether the violator had good or bad intentions.

- **Autonomous morality.** At age 10 or 11, Piaget said, most children enter a final stage of moral development in which they begin to appreciate that rules are agreements between individuals—agreements that can be changed through a consensus of those individuals. In judging actions, they pay more attention to whether the person's intentions were good or bad than to the consequences of his act; thus, they see Henry, the misbehaving boy who broke one cup, as naughtier than John, the well-intentioned boy who broke 15.

Kohlberg's View

Inspired by Piaget's pioneering work, Lawrence Kohlberg (1963, 1981, 1984; Colby & Kohlberg, 1987) formulated a highly influential cognitive developmental theory of moral development. Kohlberg began his work by asking 10-, 13-, and 16-year-old boys questions about various moral dilemmas to assess how they thought about these issues. Careful analysis of the responses led Kohlberg to conclude that moral growth progresses through a universal and invariant sequence of three broad moral levels,

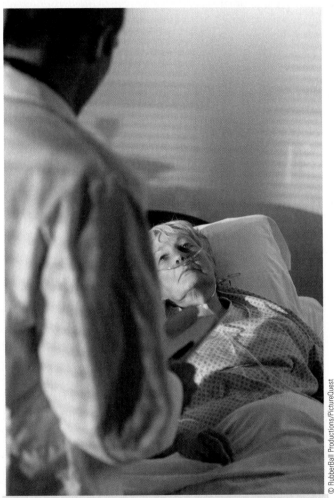

Moral dilemma: Should a doctor give a pain-ridden and terminal patient a drug that would hasten her death?

© RubberBall Productions/PictureQuest

each of which is composed of two distinct stages. Each stage grows out of the preceding stage and represents a more complex way of thinking about moral issues. According to Kohlberg, a person cannot skip stages, and a person who has reached a higher stage will not regress to earlier stages.

Think about how you would respond to the following moral dilemma posed by Kohlberg and his colleagues (Colby et al., 1983, p. 79):

> There was a woman who had very bad cancer, and there was no treatment known to medicine that would save her. Her doctor, Dr. Jefferson, knew that she had only about 6 months to live. She was in terrible pain, but she was so weak that a good dose of a pain killer like ether or morphine would make her die sooner. She was delirious and almost crazy with pain, and in her calm periods she would ask Dr. Jefferson to give her enough ether to kill her. She said she couldn't stand the pain and she was going to die in a few months anyway. Although he knows that mercy killing is against the law, the doctor thinks about granting her request.

Should Dr. Jefferson give her the drug that would make her die? Why or why not? Should the woman have the right to make the final decision? Why or why not? These are among the questions that people are asked after hearing the dilemma. You may want to answer them for yourself before reading further so that you can then analyze your own moral thinking. Remember, Kohlberg's goal is to understand how an individual thinks, not whether she is for or against providing the woman with the drug. Individuals at each stage of moral reasoning might endorse either of the alternative courses of action, but for different reasons. Following are Kohlberg's three levels of moral reasoning, and the two stages within each level.

Level 1: Preconventional Morality. At the level of **preconventional morality,** rules are external to the self rather than internalized. The child conforms to rules imposed by authority figures to avoid punishment or to obtain personal rewards. The perspective of the self dominates: What is right is what one can get away with or what is personally satisfying.

- *Stage 1: Punishment-and-Obedience Orientation.* The goodness or badness of an act depends on its consequences. The child will obey authorities to avoid punishment but may not consider an act wrong if it will not be punished. The greater the harm done or the more severe the punishment, the more "bad" the act is.
- *Stage 2: Instrumental Hedonism.* A person at the second stage of moral development conforms to rules to gain rewards or satisfy personal needs. There is some concern for the perspectives of others, but it is motivated by the hope of benefit in return. "You scratch my back and I'll scratch yours" and "an eye for an eye" are the guiding philosophies.

Level 2: Conventional Morality. At the level of **conventional morality,** the individual has internalized many moral values.

He strives to obey the rules set by others (parents, peers, the government), at first to win their approval, later to maintain social order. The perspectives of other people are clearly recognized and given serious consideration.

- *Stage 3: "Good Boy" or "Good Girl" Morality.* What is right is now what pleases, helps, or is approved by others. People are often judged by their intentions; "meaning well" is valued, and being "nice" is important. Other people's feelings should be considered.
- *Stage 4: Authority and Social Order–Maintaining Morality.* Now what is right is what conforms to the rules of legitimate authorities. The reason for conforming is not so much a fear of punishment as a belief that rules and laws maintain a social order worth preserving. Doing one's duty and respecting law and order are valued.

Level 3: Postconventional Morality. At the final level of moral reasoning, **postconventional morality**, the individual defines what is right in terms of broad principles of justice that have validity apart from the views of particular authority figures. The individual may distinguish between what is morally right and what is legal, recognizing that some laws—for example, the racial segregation laws that Dr. Martin Luther King Jr. challenged—violate basic moral principles. Thus, the person transcends the perspectives of particular social groups or authorities and begins to take the perspective of *all* individuals.

- *Stage 5: Morality of Contract, Individual Rights, and Democratically Accepted Law.* At this "social contract" stage, there is an understanding of the underlying purposes served by laws and a concern that rules should be arrived at through a democratic consensus so that they express the will of the majority and maximize social welfare. Whereas the person at stage 4 is unlikely to challenge an established law, the moral reasoner at stage 5 might call for democratic change in a law that compromises basic rights.
- *Stage 6: Morality of Individual Principles of Conscience.* At this "highest" stage of moral reasoning, the individual defines right and wrong on the basis of self-generated principles that are broad and universal in application. The stage 6 thinker does not just make up whatever principles she chooses. She discovers, through reflection, abstract principles of respect for all individuals and for their rights that all religions or moral authorities would view as moral. Kohlberg (1981) described stage 6 thinking as a kind of "moral musical chairs" in which the person facing a moral dilemma is able to take the "chair," or perspective, of each person and group and social system that could potentially be affected by a decision and to arrive at a solution that would be regarded as just from every chair. Stage 6 is Kohlberg's vision of ideal moral reasoning, but it is so rarely observed that Kohlberg stopped attempting to measure its existence.

In the Explorations box, we present examples of how people at the preconventional, conventional, and postconventional

levels might reason about the mercy-killing dilemma. Note that progress through Kohlberg's stages of moral reasoning depends partly on the development of perspective-taking abilities. Specifically, as individuals become more able to consider perspectives other than their own, moral reasoning progresses from an egocentric focus on personal welfare at the preconventional level, to a concern with the perspectives of other people (parents, friends, and other members of society) at the conventional level, and to an ability to coordinate multiple perspectives and determine what is right from the perspective of all people at the postconventional level (Carpendale, 2000).

Moral Behavior: Social Learning Theory

Social learning theorists such as Albert Bandura (1991, 2002; Bandura et al., 2001), whose social cognitive theory was introduced in Chapter 2, have been primarily interested in the behavioral component of morality—in what we actually do when faced with temptation or with an opportunity to behave prosocially. These theorists say that moral behavior is learned in the same way that other social behaviors are learned: through observational learning and reinforcement and punishment principles. They also consider moral behavior to be strongly influenced by situational factors—for example, by how closely a professor watches exam takers, by whether jewelry items are on the counter or behind glass in a department store.

Applying his social cognitive perspective, Bandura goes on to emphasize that moral cognition is linked to moral action through self-regulatory mechanisms that involve monitoring and evaluating our own actions (or anticipated actions), disapproving of ourselves when we contemplate doing wrong, and

How many students in your class would admit to having cheated in high school? Fifty years ago, only about one in five college students admitted to it, but in recent surveys at least three in five, and often more, admit to having cheated in high school (Kleiner & Lord, 1999). Cheating is also rampant in college and graduate school; 56% of MBA students admit to cheating or plagiarizing in the past year (McCabe, Butterfield, & Trevino, 2006). Use of preprogrammed calculators and handheld computers, cell phones to relay information about the test, hidden miniature cameras, and online term-paper mills suggest that cheating has gone "high-tech." Why do you think cheating is so rampant today?

SAMPLE RESPONSES TO THE MERCY-KILLING DILEMMA AT KOHLBERG'S THREE LEVELS OF MORAL REASONING

Preconventional Morality

Give the Drug

Stage 1: The doctor should give the terminally ill woman a drug that will kill her because there is little chance that he will be found out and punished.

Stage 2: He should give her the drug; he might benefit from the gratitude of her family if he does what she wants. He should think of it as the right thing to do if it serves his purposes to be for mercy killing.

Do Not Give the Drug

Stage 1: The doctor runs a big risk of losing his license and being thrown in prison if he gives her the drug.

Stage 2: He has little to gain by taking such a big chance. If the woman wants to kill herself, that is her business, but why should he help her if he stands to gain little in return?

Conventional Morality

Give the Drug

Stage 3: Most people would understand that the doctor was motivated by concern for the woman rather than by self-interest. They would be able to forgive him for what was essentially an act of kindness.

Stage 4: The doctor should give the woman the drug because of the Hippocratic oath, which spells out a doctor's duty to relieve suffering. This oath is binding and should be taken seriously by all doctors.

Do Not Give the Drug

Stage 3: Most people are likely to disapprove of mercy killing. The doctor would clearly lose the respect of his colleagues and friends if he administered the drug. A good person simply would not do this.

Stage 4: Mercy killing is against the laws that citizens are obligated to uphold. The Bible is another compelling authority, and it says, "Thou shalt not kill." The doctor simply cannot take the law into his own hands; rather, he has a duty to uphold the law.

Postconventional Morality

Give the Drug

Stage 5: Although most of our laws have a sound basis in moral principle, laws against mercy killing do not. The doctor's act is morally justified because it relieves the suffering of an agonized human without harming other people. Yet if he breaks the law in the service of a greater good, he should still be willing to be held legally accountable because society would be damaged if everyone simply ignored laws they do not agree with.

Stage 6: We must consider the effects of this act on everyone concerned—the doctor, the dying woman, other terminally ill people, and all people everywhere. Basic moral principle dictates that all people have a right to dignity and self-determination as long as others are not harmed by their decisions. Assuming that no one else will be hurt, then, the dying woman has a right to live and die as she chooses. The doctor may be doing right if he respects her integrity as a person and saves her, her family, and all of society from needless suffering.

Do Not Give the Drug

Stage 5: The laws against mercy killing protect citizens from harm at the hands of unscrupulous doctors and selfish relatives and should be upheld because they serve a positive function for society. If the laws were to be changed through the democratic process, that might be another thing. But right now the doctor can do the most good for society by adhering to them.

Stage 6: If we truly adhere to the principle that human life should be valued above all else and all lives should be valued equally, it is morally wrong to "play God" and decide that some lives are worth living and others are not. Before long, we would have a world in which no life has value.

approving of ourselves when we behave responsibly or humanely. By applying consequences to ourselves in this way, we become able to exert self-control, inhibit urges to misbehave, and keep our behavior in line with internalized standards of moral behavior. Sometimes this system of moral self-regulation can triumph over strong situational influences pushing us to do wrong. However, according to Bandura we have also devised mechanisms of **moral disengagement** that allow us, even though we know the difference between right and wrong, to avoid condemning ourselves when we engage in immoral behavior. For example, a store clerk who feels underpaid and mistreated by her employer may convince herself that she is justified in pilfering things from the store, and people may disengage morally from the use of military force by their country by dehumanizing their foes (McAlister, Bandura, & Owen, 2006). Many of us learn the right moral standards, but some people hold themselves strictly to those standards while others find ways to disengage morally.

The Functions of Morality: Evolutionary Theory

Moral development is also being looked at today from the broad perspective of evolutionary theory by researchers such as Dennis Krebs and others (Fry, 2006; Krebs, 2005). The focus is on what aspects of morality might be universal and how modes of moral thought, emotion, and behavior may have helped humans adapt to their environments over the course of evolution. Just as having a theory of mind helps humans get along with others and adapt to living in groups, prosocial behaviors such as sharing, cooperating, and helping may have evolved because they helped our ancestors obtain food and protect themselves from predators. Similarly, mechanisms for controlling and inhibiting harm-doing may have evolved in human societies because they enhanced survival (Hauser, 2006).

The phrase "survival of the fittest" implies raw selfishness, though. How can evolutionary theorists explain how humans might have evolved to be altruistic when altruists who sacrifice their lives for others die rather than pass on their genes? Evolutionary theorists have argued that it can be in our genetic self-interest to act altruistically toward kin because they will pass on the family's genes if we help them survive (Verbeek, 2006). Even helping nonrelatives may be adaptive, though, if we have reason to believe that the help we give will be reciprocated. Cooperating with other people to obtain resources that the individual could not obtain alone also makes good genetic sense, as does abiding by society's rules in order to avoid punishment. As Douglas Fry (2006) notes, reciprocity is key to explaining morality from an evolutionary perspective: Genes predisposing humans to act morally could become part of our evolutionary heritage as long as "humans repay good deeds and revenge bad ones" (p. 416).

Adopting an evolutionary perspective, Dennis Krebs (2005) notes that Kohlberg's stages of moral reasoning lead from selfishness to sensitivity to the welfare of other people. The fact that we do not always use the highest level of moral reasoning of which we are capable in everyday conflict situations, however, suggests that we retain immature forms of moral thinking rather than abandoning them as we progress in our moral development. We may use these different forms of moral reasoning like strategies, selecting whichever best fits the situation—for example, using stage 2, tit-for-tat reasoning in making business deals, but expressing stage 3 concern for others in family discussions, and stage 4 law-and-order reasoning in debating national policy issues.

Whereas Freud emphasized the dark, selfish side of human nature, evolutionary theorists argue that humans have an evolved genetic makeup that predisposes them to empathy and moral behavior. Indeed, humans may be a uniquely altruistic species. Research with chimpanzees suggests that they too show empathy for injured peers and engage in a variety of cooperative behaviors. However, they do not show the same motivation to benefit others even at a cost to themselves that humans display. Given the opportunity to get food for themselves *and* give food to another chimp at no cost to themselves, they

would just as soon get food only for themselves (Silk et al., 2005). In further support of an evolutionary perspective, empathy emerges very early in life (Hoffman, 2000; and see section 13.3 of this chapter). In addition, research with twins suggests that empathy and prosocial behavior are heritable traits (Knafo & Plomin, 2006; Verbeek, 2006).

To highlight differences among the four theoretical perspectives on moral development we have discussed, consider how different theorists might try to predict whether a teenager (we will call him Bart) will cheat on his upcoming math test. Freud would want to know whether Bart developed a strong superego; Kohlberg would be more interested in the stage at which he reasons about moral dilemmas. Notice that both the psychoanalytic perspective and the cognitive developmental perspective view morality as a traitlike quality that consistently influences an individual's judgments and actions.

By contrast, Bandura would see it this way: If Bart's parents have consistently reinforced moral behavior and punished misbehavior and have served as models of moral behavior, if he has well-developed self-regulatory mechanisms that cause him to take responsibility for his actions rather than to disengage morally, and if situational forces discourage cheating, Bart is likely to behave in morally acceptable ways.

Finally, evolutionary theorists like Krebs might look into the adaptive functions that cheating—or refraining from cheating—serve for an individual and his or her group. Like Bandura, Krebs might look at the classroom environment and conclude that so much cheating is going on that it is almost in Bart's self-interest to cheat too—or that the professor and students in the class have developed good control systems to discourage cheating. Moral emotion, thought, and behavior would all be considered (see ● **Table 13.1** for a comparison of theories).

We are now ready to trace the development of morality from infancy to old age. Our coverage charts the development of the self as a moral being, examining moral affect, cognition, and behavior over the life span.

● **TABLE 13.1   COMPARISON OF THEORETICAL PERSPECTIVES ON MORAL DEVELOPMENT**

PERSPECTIVE	THEORIST(S)	FOCUS	MESSAGE
Psychoanalytic theory	Freud	Moral emotion	Early parenting and emotional conflicts forge the superego and guilt.
Cognitive developmental theory	Piaget Kohlberg	Moral reasoning	Cognitive maturation and experience with peers bring stage like changes in thinking about moral issues.
Social learning theory	Bandura	Moral behavior	Observational learning, reinforcement, self-regulation processes, and situational influences affect what we do.
Evolutionary theory	Krebs	Moral emotion, reasoning, and behavior	Humans have evolved so that either immoral or moral behavior can be in their genetic self-interest depending on the context.

- Morality has affective, cognitive, and behavioral components.
- Moral emotion is the focus of Freudian psychoanalytic theory, with its emphasis on the formation of the superego during the preschool years.
- Moral reasoning is the focus of Piaget's premoral, heteronomous, and autonomous stages of moral development and of Kohlberg's preconventional, conventional, and postconventional levels of morality, each with two stages.
- Social cognitive theorist Bandura views morality as learned behavior influenced by basic learning processes, self-regulatory cognitive processes, and situational influences.
- Evolutionary theorists ask how morality may have evolved and what adaptive functions it serves.

CRITICAL THINKING

1. A preconventional thinker, a conventional thinker, and a postconventional thinker all face a moral dilemma the night before the final examination: A friend has offered them a key to the examination. Should they take it and use it or not? Provide examples of the reasoning you might expect at each of the three main levels of moral development—one argument in favor of cheating and one against it at each level. Are any of these arguments especially easy or difficult to make?

2. Jamal decides to become a kidney donor so that his brother Malcolm can live. How do you think Freud, Kohlberg, Bandura, and Krebs would explain his altruistic action?

13.3   THE INFANT

Do infants have a sense of right or wrong? If a baby takes a teddy bear that belongs to another child, would you label the act stealing? If an infant bashes another child on the head with a sippy cup, would you insist that the infant be put on trial for assault? Of course not. Adults in our society, including psychologists, view infants as **amoral**—that is, lacking any sense of morality. Because we do not believe that infants are capable of evaluating their behavior in relation to moral standards, we do not hold them responsible for wrongs they commit (although we certainly attempt to prevent them from harming others). Nor do we expect them to be "good" when we are not around to watch them. Yet it is now clear that these initially amoral creatures begin to learn fundamental moral lessons during their first 2 years of life.

Early Moral Training

Moral socialization begins early. Roger Burton (1984) relates how his daughter Ursula, age 1½, was so taken by the candy that she and her sisters had gathered on Halloween that she snatched some from her sisters' bags. The sisters immediately said, "No,

that's mine," and conveyed their outrage in the strongest terms. A week later, the sisters again found some of their candy in Ursula's bag and raised a fuss, and it was their mother's turn to explain the rules to Ursula. The problem continued until finally Burton came upon Ursula looking at some forbidden candy. Ursula looked up and said, "No, this is Maria's, not Ursula's" (p. 199).

It is through such social learning experiences, accumulated over years, that children come to understand and internalize moral rules and standards. Infants begin to learn that their actions have consequences, some good, some bad; they learn a lot by watching their companions' reactions to their missteps (Thompson, Meyer, & McGinley, 2006). They also begin to learn to associate negative emotions with violating rules and to exert self-control, or inhibit their impulses, when they are tempted to violate rules (Kochanska, 1993, 2002). Ursula and other young children learn from being reprimanded or punished to associate taking others' belongings with negative emotional responses. As they near age 2, children are already beginning to show visible signs of distress when they break things, spill their drinks, or otherwise violate standards of behavior (Cole, Barrett, & Zahn-Waxler, 1992; Kagan, 1981). Made to think that they have caused a doll's head to fall off, some toddlers even show signs of guilt, as opposed to mere distress, and try frantically to make amends (Kochanska, Casey, & Fukumoto, 1995). This means 18- to 24-month-old children are beginning to internalize rules and to anticipate disapproval when they fail to comply with them.

Grazyna Kochanska (1997, 2002; Kochanska & Aksan, 2006) has found that early moral socialization goes best when a **mutually responsive orientation** develops between caregiver and child—when there is a close, emotionally positive, and cooperative relationship in which child and caregiver are attached to each other and are sensitive to each other's needs. Such a relationship makes children want to comply with caregivers' rules and adopt their values and standards. These children then learn

Children learn early that some acts have distressing consequences.

moral emotions such as guilt and empathy, develop the capacity for advanced moral reasoning, and become able to resist temptation even when no one is around to catch them. It is also important for parents to discuss their toddlers' behavior in an open way, expressing their feelings and evaluating acts as good or bad (Laible & Thompson, 2000). By establishing a close, mutual relationship, setting out clear rules, discussing the emotional consequences of the child's behavior, and working during everyday conversations toward mutual understandings of what is acceptable and what is not, parents help their children develop a conscience (Emde et al., 1991; Thompson et al., 2006).

Empathy and Prosocial Behavior

Not only are infants capable of internalizing rules of behavior, but they are not so selfish, egocentric, and unconcerned about other people as Freud, Piaget, Kohlberg, and many other theorists have assumed. Perhaps the strongest evidence of this comes from studies of empathy and prosocial behavior. Even newborns display a primitive form of empathy: They become distressed by the cries of other newborns, supporting the view that empathy is part of our evolutionary heritage (Hoffman, 2000; Martin & Clark, 1982). It is unlikely that young infants distinguish between another infant's distress and their own, however.

From age 1 to age 2, according to Martin Hoffman (2000), infants become capable of a truer form of empathy that is likely a key motivator of moral behavior and that becomes more sophisticated with age as role-taking skills develop (Eisenberg et al., 2006). Toddlers begin to understand that someone else's distress is different from their own, and they try to comfort the person in distress. Consider some concrete examples described by Hoffman (2000). One 10-month-old, watching a peer cry, looked sad and buried her head in her mother's lap, as she often did when she was distressed. A 2-year-old brought his own teddy bear to comfort a distressed friend; when that failed, he offered the friend's teddy instead, beginning to show an ability to take the perspective of the friend.

Carolyn Zahn-Waxler and her colleagues (1992) report that more than half of the 13- to 15-month-old infants they observed engaged in at least one act of prosocial behavior—helping, sharing, expressing concern, comforting, and so on. These behaviors became increasingly common from age 1 to age 2, when all but one child in the study acted prosocially. In another study, about half of 1½- to 3-year-olds dealt with episodes of distress on the part of a peer who was visiting their home by trying to comfort, distract, or help the friend; however, 40% seemed more amused than concerned or even became aggressive, possibly because they found their playmate's crying irritating (Demetriou & Hay, 2004).

SUMMING UP

- Infants are amoral initially but moral socialization begins in infancy and by age 2, children have internalized rules of conduct.

- A mutually responsive orientation between parent and child and emotion-centered talk about the child's behavior contribute to the development of a conscience.
- Toddlers feel empathy for and try to help distressed peers.

CRITICAL THINKING

1. Suppose you want to study how toddlers in a day care center react when their peers are upset. How might you distinguish between true empathy for a classmate and personal distress in reaction to the classmate's crying?

13.4 | THE CHILD

Research on moral development during childhood has explored how children of different ages think about moral issues, how children behave when their moral values are tested, and how parents can raise moral children. This research shows that children's moral thinking is more sophisticated than Piaget and Kohlberg believed but that getting children to behave morally day in and day out is challenging.

Thinking through Kohlberg's Dilemmas

As we saw earlier, Piaget believed that children do not shift from heteronomous to autonomous morality, and thus to a more complete understanding of rules and of the importance of assessing a wrongdoer's intentions, until age 10 or 11. The hypothetical moral dilemmas that Lawrence Kohlberg devised to assess stages of moral reasoning (for example, the mercy-killing dilemma presented earlier) were intended primarily for adolescents and adults; the youngest individuals Kohlberg studied were age 10.

As a result, Kohlberg did not have much to say about children except that they are mostly preconventional moral reasoners who take an egocentric perspective on morality and define as right those acts that are rewarded and as wrong those acts that are punished (Colby et al., 1983). At best, older school-age children are beginning to make the transition to conventional moral reasoning by displaying a stage 3 concern with being a good boy or a good girl who takes others' perspectives and is concerned with others' approval. As we will now see, both Piaget and Kohlberg underestimated children. Other researchers have looked more closely at the moral reasoning of children and find that they engage in some sophisticated thinking about right and wrong from an early age.

Weighing Intentions

Consider Piaget's claim that young children (heteronomous moral thinkers) judge acts as right or wrong on the basis of their consequences, whereas older children (autonomous thinkers) judge on the basis of the intentions that guided the act. His moral-decision story about the two boys and the cups—asking whether a child who causes a small amount of damage in the service of bad intentions is naughtier than a child who causes a large amount of damage despite good intentions—was flawed in that it confounded the two issues, goodness of intentions and amount of damage done.

Sharon Nelson (1980) overcame this flaw in an interesting experiment. In the study, 3-year-olds listened to stories in which a boy threw a ball to a playmate. The boy's motive was described as *good* (his friend had nothing to play with) or *bad* (the boy was mad at his friend), and the consequences of his act were either *positive* (the friend caught the ball and was happy to play with it) or *negative* (the ball hit his friend in the head and made him cry). To make the task simpler, Nelson showed children drawings of what happened (see ■ **Figure 13.2** for an example).

Not surprisingly, the 3-year-olds in the study judged acts that had positive consequences more favorably than acts that caused harm. However, they also judged the well-intentioned child who had wanted to play more favorably than the child who intended to hurt his friend, regardless of the consequences of his actions. Apparently, then, even young children can base their moral judgments on both a person's intentions and the consequences of his act.

Overall, Piaget was correct to conclude that young children have less understanding of, and place less emphasis on, the intentions behind actions than older children do (Lapsley, 2006). However, he was wrong to conclude that young children are incapable of considering both intentions and consequences when they evaluate others' conduct.

Understanding Rules

Piaget also claimed that 6- to 10-year-old heteronomous children view rules as sacred prescriptions laid down by respected authority figures. These moral absolutes cannot be questioned or changed. However, Elliot Turiel (1978, 1983, 2006) has argued and observed that even young children distinguish sharply between different kinds of rules. Most importantly, they distinguish between **moral rules,** or standards that focus on the welfare and basic rights of individuals, and **social-conventional rules,** standards determined by social consensus that tell us what is appropriate in particular social settings. Moral rules include rules against hitting, stealing, lying, and otherwise harming others or violating their rights. Social-conventional rules are more like rules of social etiquette; they include the rules of games and school rules that forbid eating snacks in class or using the restroom without permission.

From their preschool years, children understand that moral rules are more compelling and unalterable than social-conventional rules (Turiel, 2006; Smetana, 2006). Judith Smetana (1981), for example, discovered that children as young as age 2 regard moral transgressions such as hitting, stealing, or refusing to share as more serious and deserving of punishment than social-conventional violations such as not staying in their seats in preschool or not saying grace before eating. Remarkably, these youngsters also indicated that it was always wrong to hit people or commit other moral transgressions, rule or no rule, whereas they felt that it would be okay for children to get out of their seats at preschool or violate other social conventions if there were no rules against it.

Piaget also claimed that 6- to 10-year-old children view any law laid down by adults as sacred. Instead, children appear to be quite capable of questioning adult authority (Tisak & Tisak, 1990). School-age children say it is fine for parents to enforce rules against stealing and other moral violations, but they believe that it can be inappropriate and unjustifiable for parents to arbitrarily restrict their children's friendship choices, which are viewed as a matter of personal choice. And they maintain that not even God can proclaim that stealing is morally right and make it so (Nucci & Turiel, 1993). In other words, school-age children will not blindly accept any dictate offered by an authority figure as legitimate.

Applying Theory of Mind

As you have probably guessed, children's moral thinking becomes quite a bit more sophisticated once they have the basics of a theory of mind down at about age 4. Showing that they understand that intentions matter, 4-year-old children who have a theory of mind and pass false belief tasks may cry, "I didn't mean it! I didn't mean it!" when they stand to be punished. Moreover, their understandings of a wrongdoer's beliefs at the time he committed a harmful act ("Spencer didn't know Lauren was in the box when he pushed it down the stairs!") influence their judgments about whether the act was intentional and therefore how bad it was (Chandler, Sokol, & Wainryb, 2000). Preschool children who pass theory-of-mind tasks are also more able than those who fail them to distinguish between lying (deliberately promoting false beliefs) and simply having one's facts wrong (Peterson & Siegal, 2002).

Theory-of-mind skills also help young children understand people's emotional reactions to others' actions, an important consideration in judging right and wrong. At only 3 years, for

■ **FIGURE 13.2** Examples of drawings used by Sharon Nelson to convey a character's intentions to preschool children. Here you see negative intent and a negative consequence.
SOURCE: From S. A. Nelson, Factors influencing young children's use of motives and outcomes as moral criteria, *Child Development*, 51, pp. 823–829. Copyright © 1980 Blackwell Publishing. Reprinted with permission.

example, children can use their emerging theory of mind to figure out that Lewis, who likes tarantulas but fears puppies, will be upset if his friend gives him a puppy—and that it is therefore "bad" to give Lewis a puppy, even though it may be "nice" to give almost any other child a puppy (Helwig, Zelazo, & Wilson, 2001). Children who have mastered theory-of-mind tasks are also more attuned than those who have not to other people's feelings and welfare when they think through the morality of snatching a friend's toy or calling a friend a bad name (Dunn, Cutting, & Demetriou, 2000).

Young children have things to learn, however—for example, about linkages between behavioral choices and emotions (Lagattuta, 2005; and see Arsenio, Gold, & Adams, 2006). Imagine that Ben wants to run into the street to get his ball but is not allowed to run out into the street, one of the scenarios used by Kristin Lagattuta (2005) in an interesting study of how children think story characters will feel after they either transgress or resist temptation. As shown in ■ Figure 13.3, 7-year-olds and adults responding to stories like this were more likely than 4- and 5-year-olds to recognize that rule breakers often experience mixed emotions, feeling good about getting what they wanted but bad about breaking the rule. Similarly, older children and adults appreciate that resisting temptation also generates mixed emotions: feeling good about abiding by the rule but also unhappy about not getting to do what you wanted to do. Young children were more focused on whether the individuals in the stories got what they wanted. So, research on theory of mind reinforces the theme that much moral growth

occurs during early childhood but that more occurs later in childhood.

Overall, then, both Piaget and Kohlberg failed to appreciate how much moral growth takes place during childhood. We now know that even preschool children are capable of judging acts as right or wrong according to whether the actor's intentions were good or bad; view only some rules as absolute, sacred, and unchangeable; challenge adult authority when they believe it is illegitimate; and use their theories of mind to analyze people's motives and the emotional consequences of their acts.

Behaving Morally

To many people, the goal of moral socialization is to produce an individual who not only has internalized moral rules but also will abide by them. Can children be trusted to do so? In a classic study of moral behavior, Hugh Hartshorne and Mark May (1928–1930) investigated the moral character of 10,000 children (ages 8–16) by tempting them to lie, cheat, or steal in a variety of situations. It readily became apparent that almost all children expressed "sound" moral values, saying that honesty was good, that cheating and stealing were wrong, and so on. Yet most children cheated or otherwise broke one of their moral rules in at least one of the situations the researchers created to test their moral behavior. In other words, Hartshorne and May had a tough time finding children who not only held the right values but consistently acted according to those values. Most children's moral behavior was inconsistent from situation to situation.

New analyses of these data and more recent studies suggest that children are somewhat more consistent in their behavior than Hartshorne and May concluded (Burton, 1963; Hoffman, 2000; Kochanska & Aksan, 2006). Moreover, across a set of situations, some children are more honest, more likely to resist temptation, and more helpful than other children. Still, moral thought, affect, and behavior are not as closely interrelated in childhood as they will be by adolescence or adulthood (Blasi, 1980).

Why are children more inconsistent in their moral behavior than older individuals? One explanation may be that they are reasoning at Kohlberg's preconventional level. When punishment and reward are the primary considerations in defining acts as right or wrong, perhaps it is not surprising that a child may see nothing much wrong with cheating when the chances of detection and punishment are slim. In addition, if children have not yet solidified their moral values, they may be especially swayed by situational factors.

Moral Socialization

How, then, can parents best raise a child who can be counted on to behave morally in most situations? You have already seen that a mutually responsive orientation between parent and child helps (Kochanska & Aksan, 2006). Social learning theo-

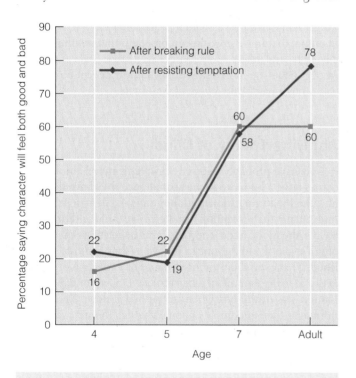

■ FIGURE 13.3 Age differences in appreciation that both giving into temptation and resisting temptation can make a person feel both good and bad about what he or she has done.
SOURCE: Based on data in Lagattuta (2005).

rists like Bandura would also advise parents to reinforce moral behavior, punish immoral behavior (but mildly and with caution, as discussed in Chapter 2), and serve as models of moral behavior.

The important work of Martin Hoffman (2000) has provided additional insights into how to foster not only moral behavior but also moral thought and affect. As you saw earlier, Hoffman (2000) believes that empathy is a key motivator of moral behavior and that the key task in moral socialization, therefore, is to foster empathy. Many years ago, Hoffman (1970) reviewed the child-rearing literature to determine which approaches to discipline were associated with high levels of moral development. Three major approaches were compared:

1. **Love withdrawal.** Withholding attention, affection, or approval after a child misbehaves—in other words, creating anxiety by threatening a loss of reinforcement from parents.
2. **Power assertion.** Using power to threaten, administer spankings, take away privileges, and so on—in other words, using punishment.
3. **Induction.** Explaining to a child why the behavior is wrong and should be changed by emphasizing how it affects other people.

Suppose that little Angel has just put the beloved family cat through a cycle in the clothes dryer. Using love withdrawal, a parent might say, "How could you do something like that? I can't even bear to look at you!" Using power assertion, a parent might say, "Get to your room this minute; you're going to get it." Using induction, a parent might say, "Angel, look how scared Fluffball is. You could have killed her, and you know how sad we'd be if she died." Induction, then, is a matter of providing rationales or explanations that focus special attention on the consequences of wrongdoing for other people (or cats).

Which approach best fosters moral development? Induction is more often positively associated with children's moral maturity than either love withdrawal or power assertion (Brody & Shaffer, 1982). In Hoffman's (2000) view, induction works well because it breeds empathy. Anticipating empathic distress if we contemplate harming someone keeps us from doing harm; empathizing with individuals in distress motivates us to help them.

Love withdrawal has been found to have positive effects in some studies but negative effects in others. The use of power assertion is more often associated with moral immaturity than with moral maturity. Children whose parents are physically abusive feel less guilt than other children and engage in more immoral behaviors such as stealing (Koenig, Cicchetti, & Rogosch, 2004). Even the use of power tactics such as restraining and commanding to keep young children from engaging in prohibited acts is associated with less rather than more moral behavior in other contexts (Kochanska, Aksan, & Nichols, 2003).

Despite evidence that power assertion interferes with the internalization of moral rules and the development of self-control, Hoffman (2000) concludes that power assertion can be useful occasionally, if it arouses some but not too much fear

Most youngsters can be tempted to steal if the situational factors are right. Children's moral conduct is fairly inconsistent from situation to situation.

and motivates a child to pay close attention to inductions. Like other techniques, it works best in the context of a loving and mutually responsive parent–child relationship.

Hoffman's work provides a fairly clear picture of how parents can best contribute to the moral growth of their children. As he puts it, the winning formula is "a blend of frequent inductions, occasional power assertions, and a lot of affection" (Hoffman, 2000, p. 23). Effective parents also use proactive strategies to prevent misbehavior and reduce the need for correction or discipline—techniques such as distracting young children from temptations and explicitly teaching older children values (Thompson et al., 2006). In the Explorations box on page 392, you can see in action a parent who knows how to foster moral growth.

Yet parents do not rely on just one approach all the time. Both the likelihood that a particular moral socialization technique will be used and its effectiveness depend on a host of factors such as the particular misdeed, child, parent, situation, and cultural context (Critchley & Sanson, 2006; Grusec, Goodnow, & Kuczynski, 2000). There is no one best discipline method for all occasions; instead, what may be most important is a parent's ability to maintain a high-quality relationship with his or her children and know which approach to use in which situation with which child (Grusec, 2006).

Consider just one example. A child's temperament turns out to be an important influence on how morally trainable she is and what motivates her to comply with parents' rules and requests (Thompson et al., 2006). Grazyna Kochanska has found that children are likely to be easiest to socialize if (1)

RAISING A MORAL CHILD

It takes only a few observations at the day care center to see that Doug, father of 3-year-old Trina, has mastered everything developmental psychologists have learned about how to foster moral development. He is sensitive to his daughter's emotional needs, often staying when he drops her off in the morning until he is sure she is ready for him to leave. He asks her to look after the new teacher because it's her first day and she might need help. As they hug and kiss, he tells Trina how happy it makes him to get hugs and kisses from her.

One day, Doug witnessed a little boy grab an 18-month-old girl, causing her to cry. He separated the two children, comforted the girl, and explained to the boy that grabbing hurts and that the girl was crying because she was hurt. He asked the boy to say he was sorry and to give the girl a hug because it might make her feel better. Another day, he was telling some of the girls a story and told them how good it makes him feel to share with Trina's friends.

As you might predict, Trina is following in her father's footsteps. She frequently comforts children who cry when their mothers drop them off in the morning, regularly offers toys to children who are upset, often hugs and pats and holds the hand of a smaller, more timid girl, and cheerfully cleans up all the toys when play time is over. Her father not only models and reinforces prosocial behavior but fosters empathy by talking about his feelings and those of other people and pointing out that antisocial behavior makes others feel bad whereas prosocial behavior makes them feel good. Using the discipline technique of induction, he explains why hurtful behaviors are wrong by emphasizing their consequences for other people. In short, he follows Martin Hoffman's advice regarding the importance of empathy in moral development and the effectiveness of induction in moral training. What might the world be like if it were full of parents like Doug?

---

they are by temperament fearful or inhibited (see Chapter 11), and therefore are more likely than fearless or uninhibited children to become appropriately anxious and distressed when they are disciplined and to want to avoid such distress in the future, and (2) they are capable of effortful control, and therefore are able to inhibit their urges to engage in wrongdoing or to stop themselves from doing something once they have begun (Kochanska, Murray, & Coy, 1997; Kochanska & Knaack, 2003). Children high in both fearfulness and effortful control can be socialized easily using positive disciplinary techniques such as induction. As a result, their parents are likely to use induction frequently and may rarely need to resort to power assertion (Keller & Bell, 1979). However, children who are not easily led to associate guilt and other negative emotions with their wrongdoings or who have difficulty controlling their impulses may drive their parents to use more power-assertive (and ineffective) discipline (Anderson, Lytton, & Romney, 1986; Lytton, 1990).

Moral socialization may go best when parents understand a child's biologically based temperament and act accordingly. Kochanska and her colleagues have found that fearful, inhibited children can be taught to refuse to touch certain toys and to comply cheerfully with requests through a gentle approach to discipline that capitalizes on their anxiety but does not terrorize them (Fowles & Kochanska, 2000). Toddlers who are fearless or uninhibited do not respond to the gentle reprimands that work with inhibited children, but they do not respond to being treated harshly, either. These fearless children are most likely to learn to comply with rules and requests when the parent–child relationship is characterized by a mutually responsive orientation and the child is therefore motivated to please the parent and maintain a good relationship (Fowles & Kochanska, 2000; and see Kochanska, Aksan, & Joy, 2007). Here, then, is another example of the importance of the goodness of fit between a child's temperament and her social environment. Socialized in a way that suits them, most children will internalize rules of conduct, experience appropriate moral emotions, and learn to regulate their behavior.

SUMMING UP

▮ Children experience a good deal of moral growth long before Piaget's autonomous stage and Kohlberg's stage 3 (conventional level) of moral reasoning are likely to be reached.

▮ Even preschool children consider whether an actor's intentions were good or bad, view only some rules (moral ones) as sacred and unchangeable, challenge adult authority, and use their theories of mind to analyze people's motives and the emotional consequences of their acts.

▮ Preconventional thinking and situational influences make for a good deal of inconsistency in moral behavior during childhood.

▮ Reinforcement, modeling, and the disciplinary approach of induction (as opposed to power assertion and love withdrawal) can foster moral growth; a child's socialization history and temperament also influence his response to moral training.

CRITICAL THINKING

1. How do you think power assertion and love withdrawal could contribute to moral development, and why do you think these socialization techniques are not as effective as induction in doing so?

13.5 THE ADOLESCENT

As adolescents gain the capacity to think about abstract and hypothetical ideas, and as they begin to chart their future identities, many of them reflect on their values and moral standards.

At the other extreme are the adolescents who end up engaging in serious antisocial behavior.

Changes in Moral Reasoning

Adolescence is a period of significant moral growth. Consider first the results of a 20-year longitudinal study by Kohlberg and his colleagues that involved repeatedly asking the 10-, 13-, and 16-year-old boys originally studied by Kohlberg to respond to moral dilemmas (Colby et al., 1983). ■ **Figure 13.4** shows the percentage of judgments offered at each age that reflected each of Kohlberg's six stages.

Several interesting developmental trends can be seen here. Notice that the preconventional reasoning (stage 1 and 2 thinking) that dominates among 10-year-olds decreases considerably during the teen years. During adolescence, conventional reasoning (stages 3 and 4) becomes the dominant mode of moral thinking. So, among 13- to 14-year-olds, most moral judgments reflect either a stage 2 (instrumental hedonism) approach—"You scratch my back and I'll scratch yours"—or a stage 3 (good boy or good girl) concern with being nice and earning approval. More than half of the judgments offered by 16- to 18-year-olds embody stage 3 reasoning, and about a fifth were scored as stage 4 (authority and social order–maintaining morality) arguments. These older adolescents were beginning to take a broad societal perspective on justice and were concerned about acting in ways that would help maintain the social system.

In short, the main developmental trend in moral reasoning during adolescence is a shift from preconventional to con-

Gangs in inner-city areas are only part of the larger problem of youth violence.

ventional reasoning. During this period, most individuals seem to rise above a concern with external rewards and punishments. They begin to express a genuine concern with living up to the moral standards that parents and other authorities have taught them and ensuring that laws designed to make human relations just and fair are taken seriously and maintained. Postconventional reasoning does not emerge until adulthood if at all.

Many teens also come to view being a moral person who is caring, fair, and honest as an important part of their identity. Their moral identity then motivates their behavior, and they end up being more capable of advanced moral reasoning and more likely to display moral behavior and to engage in community service than adolescents who do not incorporate morality into their sense of who they are (Aquino & Reed, 2002; Hart, 2005).

Antisocial Behavior

Although most adolescents internalize society's moral standards, a few youths are involved in serious antisocial conduct— muggings, rapes, armed robberies, knifings, or drive-by shootings. Indeed, crime rates peak during adolescence in most societies, especially for "hell-raising" crimes such as vandalism (Agnew, 2003).

Most severely antisocial adults started their antisocial careers in childhood and continued them in adolescence. The consequences of their early misbehavior cumulate, they become juvenile delinquents, and they find themselves leaving school early, participating in troubled relationships, having difficulty keeping jobs, and committing crimes as adults (Maughan & Rutter, 2001). Yet most children and adolescents who engage in aggressive behavior and other antisocial acts do not grow up to be antisocial adults. There seem to be at least two subgroups of antisocial youths, then: one group that is recognizable in childhood and persistently antisocial across the life span and a larger group that behaves antisocially mainly during adolescence, perhaps in response to peer pressures, and outgrows this behavior in adulthood (Moffitt & Caspi, 2001; Quinsey et al., 2004). Our focus here is mainly on the chroni-

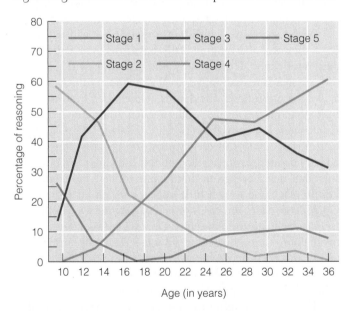

■ **FIGURE 13.4** Average percentage of moral reasoning at each of Lawrence Kohlberg's stages for males from age 10 to age 36.

SOURCE: From A. Colby, L. Kohlberg, J. Gibbs, & M. Lieberman, A longitudinal study of moral judgement, *Monographs of the Society for Research in Child Development, 48,* (1–2, Serial No. 200). Copyright © 1983 Blackwell Publishing. Reprinted with permission.

cally and seriously aggressive adolescents (see Dodge, Coie, & Lynam, 2006).

What causes some youths to become menaces to society? Might adolescents who engage repeatedly in aggressive, antisocial acts be cases of arrested moral development who have not internalized conventional values? Juvenile delinquents are indeed more likely than nondelinquents to rely on preconventional, egocentric moral reasoning (Gregg, Gibbs, & Basinger, 1994; Raaijmakers, Engels, & Van Hoof, 2005). Some juvenile offenders, then, lack a well-developed sense of right and wrong. Yet many delinquents are capable of conventional moral reasoning but commit illegal acts anyway. So, to understand the origins of antisocial conduct, we must consider a wider range of factors than immature moral reasoning (see Gibbs, 2003; Quinsey et al., 2004).

What about the moral emotions of antisocial youth? Adolescents who are aggressive or who are diagnosed with conduct disorders are less likely than other adolescents to show empathy and concern for others in distress (Blair, 2003; Lovett & Sheffield, 2007). They also report happiness and excitement, not guilt and fear, in response to vignettes about delinquent acts (Cimbora & McIntosh, 2003). Antisocial youth, then, feel little concern for others and little remorse about their criminal acts, suggesting that their moral emotions have not been socialized in ways that would promote moral behavior. As will now become clear, these adolescents also process social information differently than other adolescents do.

Dodge's Social Information-Processing Model

Kenneth Dodge and his colleagues have advanced our understanding by offering a social information-processing model of behavior that has been used to analyze contributors to aggressive behavior (Crick & Dodge, 1994; Dodge, 1986). Imagine that you are walking down the aisle in a classroom, trip over a classmate's leg, and end up in a heap on the floor. As you fall, you are not sure what happened. Dodge and other social information-processing theorists believe that the individual's reactions to frustration, anger, or provocation depend not so much on the social cues in the situation as on the ways in which she processes and interprets this information.

An individual who is provoked (as by being tripped) progresses through six steps in information processing, according to Dodge:

1. *Encoding of cues:* Taking in information
2. *Interpretation of cues:* Making sense of this information and deciding what caused the other person's behavior
3. *Clarification of goals:* Deciding what to achieve in the situation
4. *Response search:* Thinking of possible actions to achieve the goal
5. *Response decision:* Weighing the pros and cons of these alternative actions
6. *Behavioral enactment:* Doing something

People do not necessarily go through these steps in precise order; we can cycle among them or work on two or more simultaneously (Crick & Dodge, 1994). And at any step, we may draw not only on information available in the immediate situation but also on a stored database that includes memories of previous social experiences and information about the social world.

As you might imagine, the skills involved in carrying out these six steps in social information processing improve with age (Dodge & Price, 1994; Mayeux & Cillessen, 2003). Older children are more able than younger ones to encode and interpret all the relevant cues in a situation to determine why another person behaved as he did, generate a range of responses, and carry off intended behaviors skillfully. Why, then, are some children more aggressive than other children the same age?

Highly aggressive youths, including adolescents incarcerated for violent crimes, show deficient or biased information processing at every step (Dodge, 1993; Slaby & Guerra, 1988). For example, a highly aggressive adolescent who is tripped by a classmate is likely to (1) process relatively few of the available cues in the situation and show a bias toward information suggesting that the tripping was deliberate (for example, noticing a fleeting smirk on the classmate's face); (2) make an "attribution of hostile intent," inferring that the classmate meant to cause harm; (3) set a goal of getting even (rather than a goal of smoothing relations); (4) think of only a few possible ways to react, mostly aggressive ones; (5) conclude, after evaluating alternative actions, that an aggressive response will have favorable outcomes (or perhaps not think through the possible negative consequences of an aggressive response); and (6) carry out the particular aggressive response selected (see ● **Table 13.2**).

Many aggressive youths act impulsively, "without thinking"; they respond automatically based on their database of past experiences. These youths tend to see the world as a hostile place and are easily angered. If a situation is ambiguous (as a tripping or bumping incident is likely to be), they are more likely than nonaggressive youths to quickly attribute hostile intent to whoever harms them (Crick & Dodge, 1994; Orobio de Castro et al., 2002). Severely violent youths have often experienced abandonment, neglect, abuse, bullying, and other insults that may have given them cause to view the world as a hostile place and to feel little concern for others (Arsenio & Gold, 2006; Margolin & Gordis, 2000). Aggressive youths also tend to evaluate the consequences of aggression more positively than other adolescents do and feel morally justified in taking antisocial action because they believe they are only retaliating against individuals who are "out to get them" (Coie et al., 1991; Smithmyer, Hubbard, & Simons, 2000).

Dodge's social information-processing model is helpful in understanding why children and adolescents might behave aggressively in particular situations. However, it leaves somewhat unclear the extent to which the underlying problem is *how one thinks* (how skilled the person is at processing social information), *what one thinks* (for example, whether the individual believes that other people are hostile or that aggression pays), or *whether one thinks* (how impulsive the person is). The role of

STEP	BEHAVIOR	LIKELY RESPONSE OF AGGRESSIVE YOUTH
1. Encoding of cues	Search for, attend to, and register cues in the situation	Focus on cues suggesting hostile intent; ignore other relevant information
2. Interpretation of cues	Interpret situation; infer other's motive	Infer that provoker had hostile intent
3. Clarification of goals	Formulate goal in situation	Make goal to retaliate
4. Response search	Generate possible responses	Generate few options, most of them aggressive
5. Response decision	Assess likely consequences of responses generated; choose the best	See advantages in responding aggressively rather than nonaggressively (or fail to evaluate consequences)
6. Behavioral enactment	Carry out chosen response	Behave aggressively

Social information processors use a database of information about past social experiences, social rules, and social behavior at each step of the process and skip from step to step.
SOURCE: From N. R. Crick & K. A. Dodge, A review and reformulation of social information-processing mechanisms in children's social adjustment, *Psychological Bulletin, 115,* pp. 74–101. Copyright © 1994 American Psychological Association. Reprinted with permission from the American Psychological Association.

emotions also needs more attention. Children who are by temperament high in emotionality but low in emotional control are especially likely to show deficiencies in social information processing and to engage in problem behavior, possibly because their strong emotions cloud their thinking (Eisenberg et al., 1996; Lemerise & Arsenio, 2000). Finally, we need more research, like the work we will describe next, to tell us why only some children develop the social information-processing styles associated with aggressive behavior.

Patterson's Coercive Family Environments

Gerald Patterson and his colleagues have found that highly antisocial children and adolescents often experience **coercive family environments** in which family members are locked in power struggles, each trying to control the others through negative, coercive tactics (Kiesner, Dishion, & Poulin, 2001; Patterson, DeBaryshe & Ramsey, 1989). Parents learn (through negative reinforcement) that they can stop their children's misbehavior, temporarily at least, by threatening, yelling, and hitting. Meanwhile, children learn (also through negative reinforcement) that they can get their parents to lay off them by ignoring requests, whining, throwing full-blown temper tantrums, and otherwise being as difficult as possible. As both parents and children learn to rely on coercive tactics, parents increasingly lose control over their children's behavior until even the loudest lectures and hardest spankings have little effect and the child's conduct problems spiral out of control. It is easy to see how a child who has grown up in a coercive family environment might attribute hostile intent to other people and rely on aggressive tactics to resolve disputes.

Growing up in a coercive family environment sets in motion the next steps in the making of an antisocial adolescent, according to Patterson and his colleagues (see ■ **Figure 13.5**): The child, already aggressive and unpleasant to be around, ends up performing poorly in school and being rejected by other children. Having no better options, he becomes involved in a peer group made up of other low-achieving, antisocial, and

■ **FIGURE 13.5** Gerald Patterson's model of the development of antisocial behavior starts with poor discipline and coercive cycles of family influence.
SOURCE: Adapted from Patterson et al. (1989).

COMBATING YOUTH VIOLENCE

How can our society prevent youth violence and treat seriously aggressive children and adolescents? Many believe that violence prevention needs to start in infancy or toddlerhood with a strong emphasis on positive, noncoercive parenting (Dodge et al., 2006; Tremblay, 2000). School-based prevention programs aimed at teaching social information-processing and social skills can also be effective (Fraser et al., 2005; Wilson, Lipsey, & Derzon, 2003), as can approaches that focus on understanding the cultural context in which antisocial behavior develops and working to change children's communities (Guerra & Smith, 2006). Here, we focus on how three perspectives described in this chapter—Lawrence Kohlberg's theory of moral reasoning, Kenneth Dodge's social information-processing model, and Gerald Patterson's coercive family environment model—have been applied to the challenge of treating youths who have already become antisocial.

Improving Moral Reasoning (Kohlberg)

How can we foster stronger moral values and more advanced moral thinking among not-so-moral children and adolescents? If, as both Jean Piaget and Lawrence Kohlberg said, peers are especially important in stimulating moral growth, a sensible approach is to harness "peer power." This is what many psychologists and educators have tried to do in putting children or adolescents in small groups to discuss hypothetical moral dilemmas and in creating school-based programs that involve discussing rules and rule breaking (Nucci, 2001, 2006). The rationale is simple: Opportunities to take other people's perspectives and exposure to forms of moral reasoning more mature than their own will create cognitive disequilibrium in youth, which will motivate them to devise more mature modes of thinking.

Does participation in group discussions of moral issues produce more mature moral reasoning? It appears so (Rest et al., 1999). Average changes that are the equivalent of about 4 to 5 years of natural development have been achieved in programs lasting only 3 to 12 weeks. Researchers have learned that it is important that students be exposed to reasoning that is more mature than their own (Lapsley, 1996) and that moral growth is most likely when students actively transform, analyze, or otherwise act upon what their conversation partners have said—when they say things like "You're missing an important difference here" or "Here's something I think we can agree on" (Berkowitz & Gibbs, 1983; Nucci, 2001).

Participation in Kohlbergian moral discussion groups can even raise the level of moral

Discussion of moral dilemmas may increase complexity of moral reasoning but does not necessarily reduce delinquency.

unpopular youths, who positively reinforce one another's delinquency (Dodge, Dishion, & Lansford, 2006; Kiesner et al., 2001). Rejection by peers may further reinforce a tendency to attribute hostile intent to others and in the process strengthen aggressive tendencies (Dodge et al., 2003). Overall, there is much support for the view that ineffective parenting in childhood contributes to behavior problems, peer rejection, involvement with antisocial peers, and, in turn, antisocial behavior in adolescence.

Nature and Nurture

In the final analysis, severe antisocial behavior is the product of a complex interplay between genetic predisposition and social learning experiences (Dodge & Pettit, 2003; Quinsey et al., 2004). We can start by putting aggression in an evolutionary context. For example, males are more aggressive overall than females and engage in three or four times as much crime; the male edge in violence is evident in many cultures and in many species (Barash, 2002). It has been argued that aggression evolved in males because it serves adaptive functions in mate selection (Hilton, Harris, & Rice, 2000; Pellegrini & Long, 2003). Becoming dominant in the male peer group enables adolescent males to compete with other males for mates, bearing many offspring and therefore succeeding in passing their genes to future generations. Adolescent females can bear only so many children and therefore may not need to be as competitive (Barash, 2002). However, even females may boost their chances of finding mates by engaging in subtle and indirect forms of aggression such as spreading rumors about and "trashing" other females (Pellegrini & Long, 2003).

In addition, we now know that some individuals are more genetically predisposed than others to have difficult, irritable temperaments, impulsive tendencies, and other response tendencies and personality traits that contribute to aggressive, delinquent, and criminal behavior (Rhee & Waldman, 2002; Simonoff, 2001). Genetic differences among us account for about 40% of individual differences in antisocial behavior, en-thinking of institutionalized delinquents (Niles, 1986). However, unless it is combined with efforts to combat self-serving cognitions and teach social skills, fostering mature moral judgment is unlikely to cause delinquents to cease being delinquent (Gibbs, 2003; Niles, 1986). This may be in part because programs that put antisocial adolescents together in treatment groups or in detention facilities can backfire and increase problem behavior if they provide antisocial youths with opportunities to reinforce one another's deviance (Dodge et al., 2006). A better strategy may be to form groups with a mix of well-adjusted and aggressive youths—and hope that the well-adjusted ones prevail.

Building Social Information-Processing Skills (Dodge)

As you saw earlier, Dodge's social information-processing model identifies six steps at which highly aggressive youth display deficient or biased information processing. Nancy Guerra and Ronald Slaby (1990) coached small groups of incarcerated and violent juveniles of both sexes to (1) look for situational cues other than those suggesting hostile intentions, (2) control their impulses so that they do not lash out without considering the consequences, and (3) generate more nonaggressive solutions to conflicts. After a 12-week intervention, these adolescents showed dramatic improvements in social information-processing skills, believed

less strongly in the value of aggression, and behaved less aggressively in their interactions with authority figures and other inmates.

Trained offenders were only somewhat less likely than untrained offenders (34% versus 46%) to violate their paroles after release, however, suggesting that they may have reverted to their antisocial ways once back in the environment in which their aggressive tendencies originated. Indeed, for young African American and Hispanic males in gang-dominated inner-city neighborhoods, being quick to detect others' hostile intentions and take defensive action may be an important survival skill (Hudley & Graham, 1993).

Breaking Coercive Cycles (Patterson)

Patterson and his colleagues maintain that the secret to working with violent youths is to change the dynamics of interactions in their families so that aggressive tactics of controlling other family members are no longer reinforced and the cycle of coercive influence is broken. In one study, Patterson and his team (Bank et al., 1991) randomly assigned adolescent boys who were repeat offenders to either a special parent-training intervention guided by sound learning theory or the service usually provided by the juvenile court. In the parent-training program, therapy sessions held with each family taught parents how to observe both prosocial and antisocial behaviors in their son, to gather and use teachers' reports on his performance and

behavior at school, and to establish behavioral contracts that detail the reinforcement for prosocial behavior and the punishment (e.g., loss of privileges) for antisocial behavior he can expect.

The parent-training intervention was judged at least a partial success. It improved family processes, although it did not fully resolve the problems these dysfunctional families had. Rates of serious crime among this group dropped and remained lower even 3 years after the intervention ended. The usual juvenile services program also reduced crime rates but took longer to take effect. Overall, interventions designed to decrease children's aggressive behavior by equipping their parents with sound parenting skills have been quite successful (Dodge et al., 2006).

In sum, efforts to treat aggressive youths have included attempts to apply the work of Kohlberg (by discussing moral issues to raise levels of moral reasoning), Dodge (by teaching effective social information-processing skills), and Patterson (by replacing coercive cycles in the family with positive behavioral management techniques). The most promising approaches to preventing and treating aggression appear to recognize that modifying patterns of antisocial behavior requires adopting a biopsychosocial perspective and seeking to change not only the individual but also his family, peers, school, and community (Curtis, Ronan, & Bourduin, 2004; Dodge et al., 2006).

vironmental influences for the remaining 60% of the variation (Rhee & Waldman, 2002). The genes underlying antisocial behavior may make for an individual whose brain does not react normally to stress, who craves stimulation and gets it by engaging in risky behavior, and who has not learned to inhibit antisocial impulses in order to avoid negative emotional consequences (van Goozen et al., 2007).

Through the mechanism of *gene–environment interaction*, children with certain genetic predispositions may become antisocial only if they also grow up in a dysfunctional family and receive poor parenting (Button et al., 2005). Through the mechanism of *gene–environment correlation*, children who inherit a genetic predisposition to become aggressive may actually evoke the coercive parenting that Patterson and his colleagues find breeds aggression. This evocative gene–environment correlation effect is evident even when aggression-prone children grow up with adoptive parents rather than with their biological parents. Meanwhile, the coercive parenting they evoke further strengthens their aggressive tendencies (Lytton,

2000; O'Connor et al., 1998). In this way, child misbehavior and parenting influence one another reciprocally over time.

Once a coercive cycle is established, parents sometimes become so frustrated that they throw up their hands and monitor their child's behavior less to avoid the unpleasant battles of will that result when they try to impose discipline (Dodge & Pettit, 2003). And some parents, influenced at first by their child's conduct problems, not only use ineffective discipline techniques but make what Kenneth Dodge calls hostile attributions about their child's misbehavior, seeing it as the product of a "selfish," "hostile," or "evil" child (Snyder et al., 2005). Parents who are hostile and do not monitor their child's activities set the stage for involvement with a deviant peer group, the most important immediate predictor of antisocial behavior in adolescence (Chung & Steinberg, 2006).

Many other risk and protective factors in the environment can help determine whether a child genetically predisposed to be aggressive ends up on a healthy or unhealthy developmental trajectory (Guerra & Williams, 2006). The prenatal envi-

Some school environments breed aggressive behavior.

instead of writing it off as normal child behavior (Strauss, 2001).

Kenneth Dodge and Gregory Pettit (2003) have attempted to integrate all these influences into a biopsychosocial model of aggression, illustrated in ■ Figure 13.6. It is based primarily on their research tracing the development of aggression among 585 boys and girls who were studied from preschool age to early adulthood. In the model, biological factors such as genes associated with aggression and sociocultural factors such as living in a violent area put certain children at risk from birth. Then, experiences with harsh and coercive parents, antisocial peers, and dysfunctional social institutions such as violence-ridden schools translate risk into reality. Interactions between person and environment over time determine whether the developmental path leads toward more or less antisocial behavior over the years. As suggested by Dodge's social information-processing model, children build databanks of social knowledge about such things as norms for responding to aggression and aggressive tactics, and they establish information-processing habits such as attributing hostile intent to others. The more risk factors at work and interacting with each other, the greater the odds of an aggressive adult.

In sum, many interacting factors, both biological and environmental, can put an individual on a path to an antisocial adulthood. Then, unfortunately, he or she stands a good chance of contributing to the intergenerational transmission of aggression—of becoming the kind of negative and coercive parent who helps raise another generation of aggressive children, who apply the same coercive style to their own children (Conger et al., 2003; Dogan et al., 2007). Because many factors contribute to aggression, violence prevention and treatment programs can take many forms, as the Applications box on page 396 suggests.

ronment—for example, exposure to alcohol, opiate drugs, and lead poisoning—has been linked to conduct problems (Dodge & Pettit, 2003). Complications during delivery may also contribute, especially if the child later grows up in a deprived home (Arseneault et al., 2002).

Some cultural contexts are more likely to breed aggression than others. In Japan, a collectivist culture in which children are taught early to value social harmony, children are less angered by interpersonal conflicts and less likely to react to them aggressively than American children are (Zahn-Waxler et al., 1996). Hispanic American youths who have been brought up with traditional Hispanic cultural values such as the importance of family are less likely than those who are more acculturated into American society to engage in antisocial behavior (Cota-Robles, 2003; Soriano et al., 2004). This could be partly because children in the United States are so heavily exposed to violence on television, a known contributor to aggression (Anderson et al., 2003; Huesmann et al., 2003). More generally, the United States is a relatively violent country (Lim, Bond, & Bond, 2005). For example, the homicide rate is only 0.5 homicides per 1 million people in Iceland; it is closer to 10 per 1 million in Europe and more than 100 per 1 million in the United States (Barash, 2002).

Subcultural and neighborhood factors can also contribute to youth violence (Guerra & Williams, 2006). Rates of aggression and violent crime are two to three times higher in lower socioeconomic neighborhoods and communities, especially transient ones, than in middle-class ones (Elliott & Ageton, 1980; Maughan, 2001). Certain schools also have higher rates of delinquency and aggression than others, even when socioeconomic factors are controlled (Maughan, 2001). In school environments that breed aggression, peer influences can turn even an adolescent without a genetic predisposition toward aggression into an aggressive youth (Rowe, Almeida, & Jacobson, 1999). Because both bullies and victims of bullies are more likely than other youths to commit violent acts later in life, many schools today are taking active steps to combat bullying

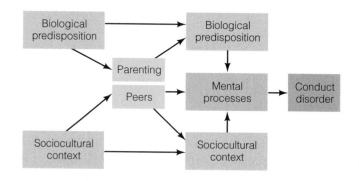

■ **FIGURE 13.6** A biopsychosocial model of aggression highlights biological and sociocultural factors that predispose a child to aggression and combine with parent and peer influences to affect mental processes that directly cause a conduct disorder.
SOURCE: Dodge & Pettit (2003, p. 351, Figure 1).

Summing Up

- Adolescents normally shift from preconventional to conventional moral reasoning and incorporate morality into their identities.

- Severe antisocial behavior is more than a matter of preconventional moral reasoning, however; it can be traced to deficiencies in social information-processing skills (Dodge), and to coercive family environments and subsequent peer group influences (Patterson).

- Genes and their interactions and correlations with prenatal, school, neighborhood, and cultural environments all contribute to antisocial behavior, as suggested by the biopsychosocial model.

Critical Thinking

1. To demonstrate to yourself that Dodge's social information-processing model can be applied not only to antisocial behavior but to prosocial behavior, picture a situation in which you see a student a couple of seats from you in class slump forward in his seat and drop his pen. Show how considerations at each of the six steps of Dodge's model (see Table 13.2) might contribute to your helping this student—and then how they might keep you from helping.

2. You pick up the newspaper and see that yet another teenage boy has gone on a shooting rampage at his school. Drawing on material in this chapter, why do you think he might have done what he did? Profile him in terms of (a) his likely temperament, (b) his stage of moral reasoning, (c) his social information-processing style, (d) the discipline approaches his parents used, and (e) other factors you think may have been significant contributors to his actions.

13.6 | The Adult

When adults assume responsibilities as parents, work supervisors, and community leaders, their moral decisions affect more people. How does moral thinking change during adulthood and what can we conclude overall about moral development across the life span?

Changes in Moral Reasoning

Most research on moral development in adulthood has been guided by Kohlberg's theory. As you have discovered (see Figure 13.4), Kohlberg's postconventional moral reasoning appears to emerge only during the adult years (if it emerges). In Kohlberg's 20-year longitudinal study (Colby et al., 1983), most adults in their 30s still reasoned at the conventional level, although many of them had shifted from stage 3 to stage 4. A minority of individuals—one-sixth to one-eighth of the sample—had begun to use stage 5 postconventional reasoning, showing a deeper understanding of the basis for laws and distinguishing between just and unjust laws. Clearly, there is opportunity for moral growth in early adulthood.

Do these growth trends continue into later adulthood? Most studies find no major age differences in complexity of moral reasoning, at least when relatively educated adults are studied and when the age groups compared have similar levels of education (Pratt & Norris, 1999). Older adults sometimes do less well than younger adults at gathering and coordinating information about the different perspectives that can be taken on a moral issue, perhaps because of declines in working memory or perhaps because they rely more on general rules in judging what is right and wrong and are not as interested in the details of different people's points of view (Pratt & Norris, 1999). However, even up to age 75, elderly adults seem to reason about moral issues as complexly as younger adults do, whether they are given Kohlberg's hypothetical dilemmas to ponder or asked to discuss real-life situations in which they were "unsure about the right thing to do" (Pratt et al., 1991, 1996). This, then, is further evidence that social-cognitive skills hold up well across the life span.

In addition, older adults are more likely than younger adults to feel that they have learned important lessons from moral dilemmas they have faced during their lives, suggesting that later life may be a time for making sense of one's experiences (Pratt & Norris, 1999). **Spirituality,** a search for ultimate meaning in life that may be carried out within or outside the context of religion, is a measurable quality, and it appears to increase from middle age to later adulthood (Wink & Dillon, 2002). Spirituality is especially evident among adults who are reflective seekers of knowledge and who have experienced adversity in their lives. Interestingly, both postconventional moral reasoning (Pasupathi & Staudinger, 2001) and spirituality (Wink & Dillon, 2003) are correlated with the attainment of wisdom (see Chapter 9). It seems, then, that moral reasoning is an aspect of social cognitive development that holds up well in later life and that advanced moral reasoning may go hand in hand with increased spirituality and wisdom in adulthood.

Influences on Moral Thinking

Following in Piaget's footsteps, Kohlberg argued that the two main influences on moral development are cognitive growth and social experiences, particularly interactions with peers. As Kohlberg predicted, reaching the conventional level of moral reasoning and becoming concerned about living up to the moral standards of parents and society requires the ability to take other people's perspectives. Gaining the capacity for postconventional or "principled" moral reasoning requires still more cognitive growth—namely, a solid command of formal-operational thinking (Tomlinson-Keasey & Keasey, 1974; Walker, 1980; and see Chapter 7). The person who bases moral judgments on abstract principles must be able to reason abstractly and to take all possible perspectives on a moral issue.

Kohlberg also stressed the need for social experiences that require taking the perspectives of others and involve growth-

Adults in rural societies may have no need for postconventional moral reasoning if they share the same moral perspective.

© Kal Muller/Woodfin Camp & Associates, Inc.

and may never have any need to question conventional moral standards.

In sum, advanced moral reasoning is most likely to develop if the individual has acquired the necessary cognitive skills (particularly perspective-taking skills and, later, formal operational thinking). Moreover, an individual's moral development is highly influenced by social learning experiences, such as interactions with parents, discussions with peers, exposure to higher education, and participation in democracy.

Kohlberg's Theory and Beyond

Because Kohlberg's theory has dominated the study of moral development, especially during adolescence and adulthood, it is time to evaluate its strengths and weaknesses. You have now seen that children think about hypothetical moral dilemmas primarily in a preconventional manner, that adolescents adopt a conventional mode of moral reasoning, and that a minority of adults progress to the postconventional level. Kohlberg claimed that his stages form an invariant and universal sequence of moral growth, and longitudinal studies of moral growth in several countries support him (Colby & Kohlberg, 1987; Rest et al., 1999).

However, support for some parts of the stage theory is stronger than support for other parts. As you saw earlier, young children are more sophisticated moral thinkers than either Piaget or Kohlberg appreciated. Moreover, the idea that everyone progresses from preconventional to conventional reasoning is better supported than the idea that people continue to progress from conventional to postconventional reasoning, as few make it that far (Boom, Brugman, & van der Heijden, 2001). Finally, contrary to expectations, some individuals "regress" from conventional reasoning to a stage 2 relativism in which they believe almost anything can be right depending on the circumstances (Lapsley, 2006). In addition, questions have been raised about whether the theory is biased against people from non-Western cultures, political conservatives, and women, as you will now see.

Biases in Kohlberg's Theory

Detecting *culture bias* in Kohlberg's theory, critics charge that his highest stages reflect a Western ideal of justice centered on individual rights, making the stage theory biased against people who live in non-Western societies (Shweder, Mahapatra, &

promoting cognitive disequilibrium when one's own ideas conflict with those of other people. First Piaget and then Kohlberg maintained that interactions with peers or equals, in which we experience and must work out differences between our own and others' perspectives, probably contribute more to moral growth than one-sided interactions with adult authority figures in which children are expected to bow to the adult's power. Research suggests that discussions of moral issues with peers *do* contribute to moral growth, especially when peers challenge our ideas, but that Piaget and Kohlberg failed to appreciate that discussions with parents also advance moral development (Walker, Hennig, & Krettenauer, 2000). As we saw earlier, parents' inductions, or explanations of why acts are wrong, are especially important.

Another social experience that contributes to moral growth is advanced schooling. Adults who go on to college think more complexly about moral issues than do those who obtain less education (Pratt et al., 1991). Advanced educational experiences not only contribute to cognitive growth but also provide exposure to the diverse ideas and perspectives that produce cognitive disequilibrium and soul-searching.

Finally, participating in a complex, diverse, and democratic society can stimulate moral development. Just as we learn from discussing issues with friends, we learn in a diverse democracy that the opinions of many groups must be weighed and that laws reflect a consensus of the citizens rather than the arbitrary rulings of a dictator. Indeed, cross-cultural studies suggest that postconventional moral reasoning emerges primarily in Western democracies (Snarey, 1985). Adults in homogeneous communities in traditional, non-Western societies may have less experience with political conflicts and compromises

CULTURAL DIFFERENCES IN MORAL THINKING

Is each of the following acts wrong? If so, how serious is the violation?

1. A young married woman is beaten by her husband after going to a movie without his permission despite having been warned not to do so.
2. A brother and sister decide to marry and have children.
3. The day after his father died, the oldest son in a family gets a haircut and eats chicken.

These are 3 of 39 acts presented by Richard Shweder, Manamohan Mahapatra, and Joan Miller (1990, pp. 165–166) to children ages 5 to 13 and adults in India and the United States. You may be surprised to learn that Hindu children and adults rated the son's getting a haircut and eating chicken after his father's death among the most morally offensive of the 39 acts they rated. The husband's beating of his "disobedient" wife was not considered wrong. American children and adults, of course, viewed wife beating as far more serious than breaking seemingly arbitrary rules about appropriate mourning behavior. Although Indians and Americans agreed that a few acts, such as brother–sister incest, were serious moral violations, they did not agree on much else.

Moreover, Indian children and adults viewed the Hindu ban against behavior disrespectful of a dead father as a universal moral rule; they thought it would be best if everyone in the world followed it, and they strongly disagreed that it would be acceptable to change the rule if most people in their society wanted to change it. For similar reasons, they believed it is a serious moral offense for a widow to eat fish or for

a woman to cook food for her family during her menstrual period. To orthodox Hindus, rules against such behaviors are required by natural law; they are not arbitrary social-conventional rules. Similarly, Hindus regard it as morally necessary for a man to beat his disobedient wife to uphold his obligations as head of the family.

Shweder also observed different developmental trends in moral thinking in India and the United States, as the figure shows. As age increased, Indians, whether they were from the Brahmin caste (priests, scholars, teachers) or were "Untouchables" (members of the Dalit group at the bottom of the social order), saw more issues as matters of universal moral principle, whereas American children saw fewer issues this way. Based on these and other cross-cultural findings, Shweder calls into question Lawrence Kohlberg's claims that all children everywhere construct similar moral codes at similar ages and that certain universal moral principles exist. In addition, Shweder questions Elliot Turiel's claim that children everywhere make similar distinctions from an early age between moral rules and more arbitrary social-conventional rules. Overall, then, these fascinating findings challenge the cognitive developmental position that important aspects of moral development

are universal. Instead, they support a social learning or contextual perspective on moral development and suggest that children's moral judgments are shaped by the social context in which they develop.

How do we make sense of such conflicting findings? It seems likely that children all over the world think in more complex ways about moral issues as they age, as Kohlberg said, but that they also adopt different notions about what is right and what is wrong depending on what they are taught, as Shweder says. Thus, people everywhere may develop an understanding that doing harm is morally wrong but have different notions of what precisely constitutes harm (Miller, 2006). In addition, people in different cultures may emphasize different moral considerations such as rights, caring, and duty (Miller, 2006). In the end, morality and moral development have both universal and culture-specific aspects.

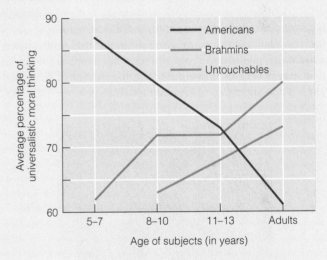

Miller, 1990; Turiel, 2006). People in *collectivist cultures*, which emphasize social harmony and place the good of the group ahead of the good of the individual, may look like stage 3 conventional moral thinkers in Kohlberg's system, yet have sophisticated concepts of justice that focus on the individual's responsibility for others' welfare (Snarey, 1985; Tietjen & Walker, 1985). Cultural influences on moral development are explored further in the Explorations box.

Regarding *liberal bias*, critics charge that Kohlberg's theory is biased not only against non-Westerners but also against political conservatives. A person must hold liberal values—for example, opposing capital punishment or supporting civil disobedience in the name of human rights—to be classified as a postconventional moral reasoner, they say. As Brian de Vries

and Lawrence Walker (1986) note, it could be that opposition to capital punishment is a more valid moral position than support of capital punishment in that it involves valuing life. However, it could also be that the theory is unfair to law-and-order conservatives (Lapsley et al., 1984).

Charges of culture bias and liberal bias may have some merit, but no criticism of Kohlberg's theory has caused more stir than the charge that it is plagued by *gender bias*. Psychologist and feminist Carol Gilligan (1977, 1982, 1993) was disturbed that Kohlberg's stages were developed based on interviews with males only and that, in some studies, women seemed to reason at stage 3 when men usually reasoned at stage 4. She hypothesized that females develop a distinctly feminine orientation to moral issues, one that is no less mature than the orientation adopted by most men and incorporated into Kohlberg's theory.

Gilligan argues that boys, who traditionally are raised to be independent, assertive, and achievement oriented, come to view moral dilemmas as conflicts between the rights of two or more parties and to view laws and other social conventions as necessary for resolving these inevitable conflicts (a perspective reflected in Kohlberg's stage 4 reasoning). Girls, Gilligan argues, are brought up to be nurturant, empathic, and concerned with the needs of others and to define their sense of "goodness" in terms of their concern for other people (a perspective that approximates stage 3 in Kohlberg's scheme). What this difference boils down to is the difference between a "masculine" **morality of justice** (focused on laws and rules, individual rights, and fairness) and a "feminine" **morality of care** (focused on an obligation to be selfless and look after the welfare of other people).

Despite the appeal of Gilligan's ideas, there is little support for her claim that Kohlberg's theory is systematically biased against females. In most studies, women reason just as complexly about moral issues as men do (Jaffee & Hyde, 2000; Walker, 2006). Moreover, although a few studies support Gilligan, most have found that males and females do not differ in their approaches to thinking about morality (Jaffee & Hyde, 2000). Instead, both men and women use both of Gilligan's types of reasoning—for example, care-based reasoning when they ponder dilemmas involving relationships, justice-based reasoning when issues of rights arise. The nature of the moral dilemma is far more important than the gender of the moral reasoner (Walker, 2006). Finally, there is surprisingly little sup-

port for Gilligan's view that boys and girls are socialized differently in the area of morality (Lollis, Ross, & Leroux, 1996).

Although her hypotheses about sex differences in moral reasoning and their origin have not received much support, Gilligan's work has increased our awareness that both men and women often think about moral issues in terms of their responsibilities for the welfare of other people. Kohlberg emphasized only one way—a legalistic and abstract way—of thinking about right and wrong. Gilligan called attention to the value of tracing the development of both a morality of justice and a morality of care in both males and females (Brabeck, 1983).

Overall, Kohlberg's theory may not be quite as biased as critics charge but it may well put too much emphasis on thinking about rules and rights, and too little on thinking about responsibility for others' welfare. Its biggest limitation, however, may be that it looks primarily at moral thinking and slights moral emotions and moral behavior.

Thought, Emotion, and Behavior

Kohlberg's theory of moral development, valuable as it has been, can rightly be criticized for saying too little about moral affect and behavior (Gibbs, 2003; Turiel, 2006). Developmentalists today are trying to remedy that by exploring the emotional and behavioral components of morality more fully, as well as interactions among thought, emotion, and behavior.

As Martin Hoffman (2000) emphasizes, empathy provides the motivation to take others' perspectives and needs seriously and to act to improve their welfare. Similarly, the anticipation of guilt motivates us to avoid doing wrong. Recognizing this, researchers today are looking more closely at what emotions children and adults experience when they engage in immoral and moral behavior and at how they learn to regulate these emotions (Eisenberg, 2000; Eisenberg, Spinrad, & Sadovsky, 2006; Gibbs, 2003). They are also looking at how morality becomes central to some people's identities and motivates them to live up to their values (Hart, 2005).

In addition, researchers are looking more closely at the relationship between moral reasoning and moral behavior. Although a person may decide to uphold or to break a law at any of Kohlberg's stages of moral reasoning, Kohlberg argued that more advanced moral reasoners are more likely to behave morally than less advanced moral reasoners are. He would predict, for example, that the preconventional thinker might readily decide to cheat if the chances of being detected were small and the potential rewards were high. The postconventional thinker would be more likely to appreciate that cheating is wrong in principle, regardless of the chances of detection, because it infringes on the rights of others and undermines social order.

Research supports Kohlberg's arguments and confirms that individuals at higher stages of moral reasoning are more likely than individuals at lower stages to behave prosocially (Gibbs, 2003), to do good through their involvement in social organizations (Matsuba & Walker, 2004), and to be helpful in everyday life (Midlarsky et al., 1999). Advanced moral reasoners are also less likely to cheat and to engage in delinquent and

© David Young-Wolff/PhotoEdit

Carol Gilligan maintains that girls are socialized into a morality of care rather than the morality of justice that interested Lawrence Kohlberg.

criminal activity (Judy & Nelson, 2000; Rest et al., 1999). Yet relationships between stage of moral reasoning and moral behavior are usually not very strong, and researchers have sought to explain inconsistencies between thought and action (Hart, Atkins, & Donnelly, 2006; Walker, 2004).

As Albert Bandura (2002) emphasizes, we not only develop self-regulatory mechanisms that help us adhere to our internalized moral standards but also devise tactics of moral disengagement that let us distort reality, slither out from under responsibility for our actions, and commit acts that violate our moral values. Moreover, our motives for prosocial behavior such as volunteering to feed the homeless or tutor inner city youth can include not only altruism but more selfish reasons such as an interest in padding our resumes or impressing our friends (Hart et al., 2006).

Emotions can also get in the way. We reason less maturely, for example, in real interpersonal conflicts with romantic partners, when our egos are threatened and our self-interests are at stake, than we do when pondering hypothetical moral dilemmas of the sort Kohlberg posed (Krebs et al., 2002). In the end, we do best recognizing that the moral reasoning of interest to Piaget and Kohlberg, the moral emotions of interest to Freud and Hoffman, and the self-regulatory and moral disengagement processes of interest to Bandura—together with many other personal and situational factors—all help predict whether a person will behave morally or immorally in daily life.

We have now completed our series of chapters on the development of the self, or the person as an individual, looking at the development of self-conceptions and distinctive personality traits (Chapter 11), identities as males or females (Chapter 12), and now social cognition and morality. But individual development does not occur in a vacuum. Repeatedly, you have seen that an individual's development may take different paths depending on the social and cultural context in which it occurs. Our task in upcoming chapters will be to put the individual even more squarely in social context. It should become clear that throughout our lives we are both independent and interdependent—separate from and connected to other developing persons.

SUMMING UP

▌ A minority of adults progress from the conventional to the postconventional level of moral reasoning during adulthood; moral reasoning skills are maintained in old age and may be tied to spirituality and wisdom for some.

▌ Kohlberg's stages and his view that both cognitive growth and perspective-taking experiences contribute to moral growth are largely supported, but his theory has been criticized for showing Western, liberal, and male biases, capturing a morality of justice better than what Gilligan calls a morality of care.

▌ Further, the focus in Kohlberg's theory on moral reasoning needs to be supplemented with attention to moral emotion and behavior.

CRITICAL THINKING

1. Play the part of Lawrence Kohlberg and defend yourself against charges that your theory is biased against non-Westerners, political conservatives, and women.

CHAPTER SUMMARY

13.1 SOCIAL COGNITION

- Social cognition (thinking about self and others) is involved in all social behavior, including moral behavior. Starting in infancy with milestones such as joint attention and pretend play, children develop a theory of mind—a desire psychology at age 2, and a belief-desire psychology by age 4 as evidenced by false belief tasks. Developing a theory of mind requires a normal brain (mirror neuron systems) and appropriate social and communication experience.

- In characterizing other people, preschool children focus on physical features and activities, children 8 years and older on inner psychological traits, and adolescents on integrating trait descriptions to create personality profiles. With age, children also become more adept at role taking. Social cognitive skills often improve during adulthood and hold up well but may decline late in life if a person is socially isolated.

13.2 PERSPECTIVES ON MORAL DEVELOPMENT

- Morality has cognitive, affective, and behavioral components. Sigmund Freud's psychoanalytic theory emphasized the superego and moral emotions. Cognitive developmental theorist Jean Piaget distinguished premoral, heteronomous, and autonomous stages of moral thinking, and Lawrence Kohlberg proposed three levels of moral reasoning—preconventional, conventional, and postconventional—each with two stages. Social cognitive theorist Albert Bandura focused on how moral behavior is influenced by past learning, situational forces, self-regulatory processes, and moral disengagement, and evolutionary theorists examine how morality and prosocial behavior may have proven adaptive for the human species.

13.3 THE INFANT

- Although infants are amoral in some respects, they begin learning about right and wrong through their early disciplinary encounters, internalize rules, and display empathy and prosocial behavior by age 2. Their moral growth is facilitated by what Grazyna Kochanska calls a mutually responsive orientation between parent and child.

13.4 THE CHILD

- Kohlberg and Piaget underestimated the moral sophistication of young children (for example, their ability to consider intentions, to distinguish between moral and social-conventional rules, and to question adult authority); most children display preconventional moral reasoning. Situational influences contribute to moral inconsistency in childhood. Reinforcement, modeling, and the disciplinary approach of induction can foster moral growth, and a child's temperament interacts with the approach to moral training parents adopt to influence outcomes.

13.5 THE ADOLESCENT

- During adolescence, a shift from preconventional to conventional moral reasoning is evident, and many adolescents incorporate moral values into their sense of identity.
- Antisocial behavior can be understood in terms of Kenneth Dodge's social information-processing model, Gerald Patterson's coercive family environments and the negative peer influences they set in motion, and, more generally, a biopsychosocial model involving the interaction of genetic predisposition with social–environmental influences. Attempts to prevent and reduce youth violence have applied the work of Kohlberg (through moral discussion groups), Dodge (by teaching effective social information-processing skills), and Patterson (by altering coercive family environments).

13.6 THE ADULT

- A minority of adults progress from the conventional to the postconventional level of moral reasoning; elderly adults typically do not regress in their moral thinking, and some display advanced moral reasoning, spirituality, and wisdom.
- Kohlberg's stages of moral reasoning form an invariant sequence, with progress through them influenced by cognitive growth and social experiences that involve taking others' perspectives. It has been charged that Kohlberg's theory is biased against people from non-Western cultures, conservatives, and women who rely on Gilligan's morality of care rather than a morality of justice. Today, researchers emphasize that a full understanding of moral development requires attention not only to moral reasoning but also to moral affect and behavior.

KEY TERMS

social cognition 374	conventional morality 383
false belief task 374	postconventional morality 384
theory of mind 374	moral disengagement 385
desire psychology 376	amoral 387
belief–desire psychology 376	mutually responsive
mirror neurons 377	orientation 387
role-taking skills 379	moral rules 389
morality 381	social-conventional rules 389
moral affect 381	love withdrawal 391
empathy 381	power assertion 391
prosocial behavior 382	induction 391
moral reasoning 382	coercive family
reciprocity 382	environment 395
premoral period 382	spirituality 399
heteronomous morality 382	morality of justice 402
autonomous morality 383	morality of care 402
preconventional morality 383	

MEDIA RESOURCES

BOOK COMPANION WEBSITE

academic.cengage.com/psychology/sigelman
Find online quizzes, flash cards, animations, video clips, experiments, interactive assessments, and other helpful study aids for this text at **academic.cengage.com/psychology/sigelman**. You can also connect directly to the following sites:

ARCHIVES OF GENERAL PSYCHIATRY: ANTISOCIAL BEHAVIOR AND MORAL DEVELOPMENT

The homepage of the Archives of General Psychiatry is a great place to search for research on most areas of psychology. Use the search engine to find articles on either "antisocial behavior" or "moral development." Using the "Advanced Search" feature allows you to refine your search in many ways (e.g., by year of publication).

ETHICS UPDATES ON GENDER DIFFERENCES

Housed in the Values Institute at the University of San Diego, Ethics Updates bills itself as a website "dedicated to promoting the thoughtful discussion of difficult moral issues." It contains a wealth of resources on ethics-related theories and applied ethics dilemmas such as poverty and welfare and bioethics. In its theory section, you can more thoroughly explore the ethical theory related to gender differences, including Gilligan's ideas.

MORAL DEVELOPMENT: AT ANSWERS.COM

This Answers.com site provides a solid review of the major theories of moral development (for example, Piaget and Kohlberg). One special feature of the site is a built in dictionary that allows the visitor to get a definition of a highlighted word with just a click.

PSI CAFÉ: MORAL DEVELOPMENT

This Psi Café-hosted site provides the visitor access to information on the major theory of moral development. Be sure to check out sections on moral development in education and parental influences on moral development.

UNDERSTANDING THE DATA: EXERCISES ON THE WEB

academic.cengage.com/psychology/sigelman
For additional insight on the data presented in this chapter, try out the exercise for this figure at **academic.cengage.com/psychology/sigelman**:

> **Figure 13.4** Average percentage of moral reasoning at each of Lawrence Kohlberg's stages for males from age 10 to age 36

CENGAGENOW

academic.cengage.com/login
Go to **academic.cengage.com/login** to link to CengageNOW, your online study tool. First take the Pre-Test for this chapter to get your Personalized Study Plan, which will identify topics you need to review and direct you to online resources. Then take the Post-Test to determine what concepts you have mastered and what you still need work on.

© Joel Gordon

CHAPTER

14

Attachment and Social Relationships

MIKE POHLE WAS ABOUT TO GRADUATE and wanted to find a job close to his fiancée, Marcy Crevonis (Jones, 2007). He slept every night in a Phillies jersey she gave him; filled her dorm room with chocolate kisses and rose petals on Valentine's Day, and had already named the five children they hoped to have together. They were soulmates. As Marcy put it, "We were the same person. We shared the same thoughts. We finished each other's sentences" (Jones, 2007, p. C1).

Mike Pohle was one of the 32 victims of the mass murders at Virginia Tech University April 16, 2007. Marcy had walked him part of the way to his German class that morning; later they exchanged text messages about the apparent shooting in her dorm. She raced to find him when his class

was to end but was blocked by the police. Told of Mike's death, she went back to his apartment, put on the Phillies jersey, and wept.

The shooter, Seung Hui Cho, had no soulmates. His relatives said he was an unusually quiet child who did not respond to greetings; his classmates and suitemates said he never talked to them; one high school classmate recalled jokes about him: "We would just say, 'Did you see Seung say nothing again today?'" (Cho & Gardner, 2007, p. A8). Cho spent his time writing stories of violence and death. Most certainly he suffered from intense social anxiety all his life; most likely he was seriously mentally ill (Cho & Gardner, 2007). Whatever the causes, he was almost completely isolated from the human community. He

seemingly knew nothing of bonds of love like those that bound Mike and Marcy, or bonds of community like those that tied members of Virginia Tech's "Hokie Nation" to one another after the killings—and tied many of us around the world to them.

One loner shattered many relationships at Virginia Tech.

■ ■ ■

How did their developmental experiences prepare Mike and Marcy to fall in love? What kept Seung from developing close human relationships and what made him so angry at his fellow humans? Think about Mike Pohle and Seung Hui Cho as you read this chapter. It concerns our closest emotional relationships across the life span and their implications for development. We should not have to work hard to convince you that close interpersonal relationships play a critical role in our lives and in development. The poet John Donne wrote, "No man is an island, entire of itself"; it seems equally true that no human can *become* entire without the help of other humans.

This chapter addresses questions such as the following: What social relationships are especially important during different phases of the life span, and what is the character of these relationships? When and how do we develop the social competence it takes to interact smoothly with other people and to enter into intimate relationships with them? What are the developmental implications of being deprived of close relationships? How are social relationships and emotional development interrelated? We begin with some broad perspectives on social relationships.

14.1 PERSPECTIVES ON RELATIONSHIPS

Relationships are important in human development for an endless range of reasons, but developmental theorists have disagreed about which relationships are most critical. Many noted theorists have argued that no social relationship is more impor-

tant than the first: the bond between parent and infant. Sigmund Freud (1930) left no doubt about his opinion: a stable mother–child relationship is essential for normal personality development. His follower Erik Erikson tended to agree, emphasizing the importance of responsive parenting to the development of trust in the parent–infant relationship. These theorists, in turn, influenced the architect of today's most influential theory of close human relationships, attachment theory, to emphasize the lasting significance of the parent–infant relationship. As you will see later, though, other theorists believe that peers are at least as significant as parents in the developmental process.

Attachment Theory

Attachment theory was formulated by British psychiatrist John Bowlby (1969, 1973, 1980, 1988), and it was elaborated on by his colleague Mary Ainsworth, an American developmental psychologist (1989; Ainsworth et al., 1978). The theory was based primarily on ethological theory and therefore asked how attachment might have evolved (see Chapter 2). It also drew on concepts from psychoanalytic theory (Bowlby was a therapist trained in psychoanalytic thinking about the contribution of mother–child relationships to psychopathology and studied war orphans separated from their mothers) and cognitive theory (Bowlby called attention to expectations about self and other, as you will see).

According to Bowlby (1969), an **attachment** is a strong affectional tie that binds a person to an intimate companion. It is also a behavioral system through which humans regulate their emotional distress when under threat and achieve security by seeking proximity to another person. For most of us, the first attachment we form, around 6 or 7 months of age, is to a parent. How do we know when baby Alberto becomes attached to his mother? He will try to maintain proximity to her—crying, clinging, approaching, following, doing whatever it takes to maintain closeness to her and expressing his displeasure when he cannot. He will prefer her to other individuals, reserving his biggest smiles for her and seeking her when he is upset, discomforted, or afraid; she is irreplaceable in his eyes. He will also be confident about exploring his environment as long as he knows that his mother is there to provide the security he needs.

Notice that an infant attached to a parent is rather like an adult "in love" (like Mike or Marcy at the start of the chapter). True, close emotional ties are expressed in different ways, and serve different functions, at different points in the life span. Adults, for example, do not usually feel compelled to follow their mates around the house, and they look to their loved ones for more than comforting hugs and smiles. Nonetheless, there are basic similarities among the infant attached to a caregiver, the child attached to a best friend, and the adolescent or adult attached to a mate or lover. Throughout the life span, the objects of our attachments are special, irreplaceable people to whom we want to be close and from whom we derive a sense of security (Ainsworth, 1989).

Nature, Nurture, and Attachment

Drawing on ethological theory and research, Bowlby argued that infants—and parents—are biologically predisposed to form attachments. As you saw in Chapter 2, ethologists and evolutionary theorists assume that all species, including humans, are born with behavioral tendencies that have been built into their species over the course of evolution because they have contributed to survival. It makes sense to think, for example, that young birds tended to survive if they stayed close to their mothers so that they could be fed and protected from predators—but that they starved or were gobbled up, and therefore failed to pass their genes to future generations, if they strayed. Thus, chicks, ducks, and goslings may have evolved so that they engage in **imprinting,** an innate form of learning in which the young will follow and become attached to a moving object (usually the mother) during a critical period early in life.

Groundbreaking ethologist Konrad Lorenz (1937) observed imprinting in young goslings and noted that it is automatic (young fowl do not have to be taught to follow), it occurs only within a critical period shortly after the bird has hatched, and it is irreversible—once the gosling begins to follow a particular object, whether its mother or Lorenz, it will remain attached to the object. The imprinting response is a prime example of a species-specific and largely innate behavior that has evolved because it has survival value.

What about human infants? Babies may not become imprinted to their mothers, but they certainly form attachments in infancy and follow their love objects around. Bowlby argued

that they come equipped with several other behaviors besides following, or proximity seeking, that help ensure adults will love them, stay with them, and meet their needs. Among these behaviors are sucking and clinging, smiling and vocalizing (crying, cooing, and babbling), and expressions of negative emotion (fretting and crying). Moreover, Bowlby argued, just as infants are programmed to respond to their caregivers, adults are biologically programmed to respond to an infant's signals. Indeed, it is difficult for an adult to ignore a baby's cry or fail to warm to a baby's grin. In short, both human infants and human caregivers have evolved in ways that predispose them to form close attachments, and this ensures that infants will receive the care, protection, and stimulation they need to survive and thrive.

Just as the imprinting of goslings occurs during a critical period, human attachments form during what Bowlby viewed as a sensitive period for attachment, the first 3 years of life. But attachments do not form automatically. According to Bowlby, a responsive social environment is critical: An infant's preprogrammed signals to other people may eventually wane if caregivers are unresponsive to them. Ultimately, the security of an attachment relationship depends on the ongoing interaction between infant and caregiver and on the sensitivity of each partner to the other's signals.

Attachment and Later Development

Bowlby maintained that the quality of the early parent–infant attachment has lasting impacts on development, including the kinds of relationships people have with their friends, romantic partners, and children. He proposed that, based on their interactions with caregivers, infants construct expectations about relationships in the form of **internal working models**—cognitive representations of themselves and other people that guide their processing of social information and behavior in relationships (Bowlby, 1973; see also Bretherton, 1996). Securely attached infants who have received responsive care will form internal working models suggesting that they are lovable

Ethologist Konrad Lorenz demonstrated that goslings would become imprinted to him rather than to their mother if he was the first moving object they encountered during their critical period for imprinting. Human attachment is more complex.

and that other people can be trusted to care for them. By contrast, insecurely attached infants subjected to insensitive, neglectful, or abusive care may conclude that they are difficult to love, that other people are unreliable, or both. These insecure infants would be expected to have difficulty participating in close relationships later in life. They may, for example, be wary of getting too close to anyone or become jealous and overly dependent partners if they do.

In sum, attachment theory, as developed by Bowlby and elaborated by Ainsworth, claims that (1) the capacity to form attachments is part of our evolutionary heritage; (2) attachments unfold through an interaction of biological and environmental forces during a sensitive period early in life; (3) the first attachment relationship, the one between infant and caregiver, shapes later development and the quality of later relationships; and (4) internal working models of self and other serve as the mechanism through which early experience affects later development.

Peers and the Two Worlds of Childhood

A **peer** is a social equal, someone who functions at a similar level of behavioral complexity—often someone of similar age (Lewis & Rosenblum, 1975). Although the parent–infant relationship is undoubtedly important in development, some theorists argue that relationships with peers are at least as significant. In effect, they argue, there are "two social worlds of childhood"—one involving adult–child relationships and the other involving peer relationships—and these two worlds contribute differently to development (Harris, 1998, 2006; Youniss, 1980). From an evolutionary perspective, it makes sense to think that humans evolved to live as members of groups, just as they evolved to form close one-on-one attachments to parents. Consider the perspectives of two strong believers in peer influence: Jean Piaget and Judith Rich Harris.

Jean Piaget (1965) observed that relationships with peers are different in quality from relationships with parents. Because parents have more power than children do, children are in a subordinate position and must defer to adult authority. By contrast, two children have equal power and influence and must learn to appreciate each other's perspectives, to negotiate and compromise, and to cooperate with each other if they hope to get along. For this reason, Piaget believed that peers can make a unique contribution to social development that adult authority figures cannot make. Indeed, as you saw in Chapter 13, peer relations help children understand that relationships are reciprocal, force them to hone their role-taking skills, and contribute to their social-cognitive and moral development.

More recently, Judith Rich Harris (1998, 2000b, 2006) has stirred up controversy by arguing that peers are far more important than parents in shaping development. In *The Nurture Assumption*, Harris (1998) made this strong claim: "Children would develop into the same sort of adults if we left their lives outside the home unchanged and left them in their schools and their neighborhoods—but switched all the parents around" (Harris, 1998, p. 359). She cites the example of immigrant chil-

dren, who readily learn the local culture and language from peers even though their parents come from a different culture and speak a different language.

Harris argues that parent influence is overrated; she observes that genes contribute to virtually all aspects of human development, that a child's genes influence the parenting she receives, and that parents do little to make different children growing up in the same home more alike. Moreover, even when parenting behaviors can be shown to affect children, she claims, they do so mainly in the home environment; learning rarely generalizes outside the home and beyond childhood.

Harris maintains that most important socialization for the world outside the home takes place in peer groups. Children figure out which social category they belong to based on age, sex, and other characteristics and then want to be like members of their social group. They adopt the norms of behavior that prevail in their peer group, learn by observing other children, and take on their attitudes, speech, dress styles, and behavior. When children later gravitate toward peers who are similar to themselves, their genetically based tendencies are magnified; the budding delinquent becomes more delinquent, and the studious child becomes more studious.

Many developmental scientists have reacted strongly to Harris's message, charging that she overstates her case and offers too little evidence that peers are more important than parents (Collins et al., 2000; Vandell, 2000). Moreover, they say, she overlooks solid evidence that, even when genetic influences are taken into account, parenting matters and that intervening to change how parents treat children can alter the course of development. Despite such criticisms, Harris deserves credit for stimulating greater attention to peer-group influences and for challenging developmentalists to demonstrate more convincingly, through research designs that take genes into account, how parents really influence their children's development.

SUMMING UP

▌ Following in Freud's footsteps, John Bowlby and Mary Ainsworth's attachment theory maintains that caregiver–infant attachment evolved to ensure survival, develops through an interaction of nature and nurture during a sensitive period, and results in internal working models that shape later relationships and development.

▌ Piaget (with his emphasis on peers as equals) and Harris (with her emphasis on genes and socialization by neighborhood peers) have argued that relationships with peers are at least as significant as attachments to parents.

CRITICAL THINKING

1. Ethological theory, psychoanalytic theory, and cognitive psychology all influenced John Bowlby as he formulated attachment theory. Which elements of attachment theory do you think most reflect each of these three theoretical perspectives, and why?

Human infants are social beings from the start, but their social relationships change dramatically once they form close attachments to caregivers and develop the social skills that allow them to coordinate their own activities with those of other infants. Because attachments involve strong emotions, both positive and negative, and because attachment figures are critical in shaping emotional development, we begin by setting the development of parent–infant attachment in the context of early emotional development.

Early Emotional Development

Emotions are complex phenomena that involve a subjective feeling (I'm furious), physiological changes (a pounding heart), and behavior (an enraged face). Carroll Izard (1982; Izard & Ackerman, 2000) and his colleagues maintain that basic emotions develop early and play critical roles in motivating and organizing behavior. By videotaping infants' responses to such events as having a toy taken away or seeing their mothers return after a separation, analyzing specific facial movements (such as the raising of the brows and the wrinkling of the nose), and asking raters to judge what emotion a baby's face reveals, Izard has established that very young infants express distinct emotions in response to different experiences and that adults can readily interpret which emotions they are expressing.

Developmentalists today appreciate that the face is not always a reliable indicator of the emotion being experienced (Saarni et al., 2006). Still, the work of Izard and others allows us to piece together an account of the early development of a number of "primary" emotions (Lewis, 2000; also see ■ **Figure 14.1**).

At birth, babies show contentment (by smiling), interest (by staring intently at objects), and distress (grimaces in response to pain or discomfort). Within the first 6 months, more specific

Can you find anger, disgust, fear, interest, joy, and sadness in these faces?

a. interest; b. fear; c. disgust; d. anger; e. sadness; f. joy.

emotions evolve from these three. By 3 months of age or so, contentment becomes joy, or excitement at the sight of something familiar such as Mom's face. Interest becomes surprise, such as when expectations are violated in games of peek-a-boo. Distress soon evolves into a range of negative emotions, starting with disgust (in response to foul-tasting foods) and sadness. Angry expressions appear as early as 4 months—about the time infants acquire enough control of their limbs to push unpleasant stimuli away. Fear makes its appearance as early as 5 months.

Next, as Figure 14.1 shows, come the so-called secondary or **self-conscious emotions.** These emotions, such as embarrassment, require an awareness of self and emerge around 18 months of age, when infants become able to recognize

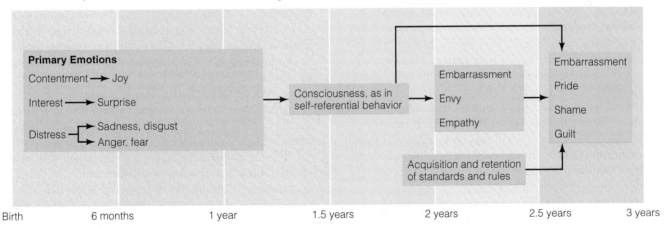

Primary Emotions

Contentment → Joy

Interest → Surprise

Distress → Sadness, disgust
Distress → Anger, fear

Consciousness, as in self-referential behavior

Embarrassment
Envy
Empathy

Acquisition and retention of standards and rules

Embarrassment
Pride
Shame
Guilt

Birth   6 months   1 year   1.5 years   2 years   2.5 years   3 years

■ **FIGURE 14.1** The emergence of different emotions. Primary emotions emerge in the first 6 months of life; secondary or self-conscious emotions emerge starting from about 18 months to 2 years.

SOURCE: From M. Lewis, The emergence of human emotions. In M. Lewis & J. M. Haviland-Jones (EDs.), *Handbook of emotions* (2nd ed.). Copyright © 2000 Guilford. Reprinted with permission.

themselves in a mirror (see Chapter 11). At this age, they begin to show embarrassment when they are asked to perform for guests (Lewis, 2000). Finally, when toddlers become able to judge their behavior against standards of performance, around age 2, they become capable of the self-conscious emotions of pride, shame, and guilt (Lewis, 2000). They can feel proud if they catch a ball because they know that's what you're supposed to do when a ball is tossed your way—or guilty if they spill their milk because they know you are not supposed to make messes.

Nature, Nurture, and Emotions

Primary or basic emotions such as interest and fear seem to be biologically programmed. They emerge in all normal infants at roughly the same ages and are displayed and interpreted similarly in all cultures (Izard, 1982; Malatesta et al., 1989). The timing of their emergence is tied to cognitive maturation; for example, babies cannot fear strangers until they are able to represent mentally what familiar companions look like (Lewis, 2000). As Charles Darwin recognized long ago, basic emotions probably evolved in humans because they helped our ancestors appraise and respond appropriately to novel stimuli and situations (Cole, Martin, & Dennis, 2004). As Bowlby emphasized, infants' emotional signals—whether expressions of joy or distress—also prompt their caregivers to respond to them (Kopp & Neufield, 2003).

Whether an infant tends to be predominantly happy and eager to approach new stimuli or irritable and easily distressed depends in part on his individual genetic makeup (Goldsmith, 2003). However, nurture is also important in emotional development; through the attachment relationship, caregivers help shape infants' predominant patterns of emotional expression. How do we know? Observational studies of face-to-face interactions between mothers and infants suggest that young infants display a range of positive and negative emotions, changing their expressions with lightning speed (once every 7 seconds) while their mothers do the same (Malatesta et al., 1986; Malatesta et al., 1989). Mothers mainly display interest, surprise, and joy, thus serving as models of positive emotions and eliciting positive emotions from their babies. Mothers also respond selectively to their babies' expressions; over the early months, they become increasingly responsive to their babies' expressions of happiness, interest, and surprise and less responsive to their negative emotions. Through basic learning processes, then, infants are trained to show happy faces more often than unhappy, grumpy ones—and they do just that over time. They are beginning to learn what emotional expressions mean in their sociocultural environment and which are socially acceptable (Saarni, 1999; Sroufe, 1996).

Toward the end of the first year, infants also begin to monitor their companions' emotional reactions in ambiguous situations and use this information to decide how they should feel and behave—a phenomenon called **social referencing** (Feinman, 1992). If their mothers are wary when a stranger approaches, so are they; if their mothers smile at the stranger, so may they. It is not just that 1-year-olds are imitating their par-

ents' emotions. They are able to understand what triggered these emotions and to regulate their behavior accordingly. Infants are especially attentive to stimuli that provoke negative emotional reactions such as fear or anger in their caregivers, as if they know already that these emotions are warning signals (Carver & Vaccaro, 2007). Parents also socialize their children's emotions by reacting (for example, sympathetically or critically) to their children's expressions of emotion and by talking about emotions in everyday conversations (Thompson & Meyer, 2007). Gradually, in the context of a secure parent–child relationship in which there is healthy emotional communication, infants and young children learn to understand emotions and express them appropriately.

Emotion Regulation

To conform to their culture's rules and their caregiver's rules about when and how different emotions should be expressed, and most importantly to keep themselves from being overwhelmed by their emotions, infants must develop strategies for **emotion regulation**—the processes involved in initiating, maintaining, and altering emotional responses (Bridges & Grolnick, 1995; and see Calkins & Hill, 2007; Gross, 2007). Infants are active from the start in regulating their emotions, but at first they have only a few, simple emotion regulation strategies.

Very young infants are able to reduce their negative arousal by turning from unpleasant stimuli or by sucking vigorously on a pacifier (Mangelsdorf, Shapiro, & Marzolf, 1995). By the end of the first year, infants can also regulate their emotions by rocking themselves or moving away from upsetting events. They also actively seek their attachment figures when they are upset because the presence of these individuals has a calming effect.

By 18 to 24 months, toddlers will try to control the actions of people and objects, such as mechanical toys, that upset them (Mangelsdorf et al., 1995). They are able to cope with the frustration of waiting for snacks and gifts by playing with toys and otherwise distracting themselves (Grolnick, Bridges, & Connell, 1996). They have been observed knitting their brows or compressing their lips in an attempt to suppress their anger or sadness (Malatesta et al., 1989). Finally, as children gain the capacity for symbolic thought and language, they become able to regulate their distress symbolically—for example, by repeating the words, "Mommy coming soon, Mommy coming soon," after Mom goes out the door (Thompson, 1994).

The development of emotion regulation skills is influenced by both the infant's temperament and his or her caregiver's behavior (Grolnick, McMenamy, & Korowski, 2006). Attachment figures play critical roles in helping infants regulate their emotions and in teaching them how to do so on their own. When infants are very young and have few emotion regulation strategies of their own, they rely heavily on caregivers to help them—for example, by stroking them gently or rocking them when they are distressed (Calkins & Hill, 2007; Cole, Michel, & Teti, 1994). As infants age, they gain control of emotion regulation strategies first learned in the context of the parent–child relationship and can regulate their emotions on their own (for example by rocking themselves rather than looking to be rocked). As you might guess, children who are not able to get a grip on their negative emotions tend to experience stormy relationships with both caregivers and peers and are at risk to develop behavior problems (Saarni et al., 2006).

Attachment figures also arouse powerful emotions, positive and negative, that need to be controlled; infants can become uncomfortably overstimulated during joyful bouts of play with parents, and they can become highly distressed when their parents leave them. Finally, as we shall soon discover, infants develop their own distinct styles of emotional expression designed to keep attachment figures close (Bridges & Grolnick, 1995). One infant may learn to suppress negative emotions such as fear and anger to avoid angering an irritable caregiver, whereas another may learn to scream loud and long to keep an unreliable caregiver close. By being sensitive, responsive caregivers, parents can help keep fear, anger, and other negative emotions to a minimum in infancy (Pauli-Pott, Mertesacker, & Beckmann, 2004). Clearly, then, emotions and emotion regulation develop in the context of attachment relationships and both affect and are affected by the quality of these relationships.

An Attachment Forms

Like any relationship, the parent–infant attachment is reciprocal. Parents become attached to their infants, infants become attached to their parents.

The Caregiver's Attachment to the Infant

Parents often begin to form emotional attachments to their babies before birth. Moreover, mothers who have an opportunity for skin-to-skin contact with their babies during the first few hours after birth often feel a special bond forming (Klaus & Kennell, 1976). Studies of other primates suggest that the first 2 or 3 weeks of life is a sensitive period for bonding in which mothers are especially ready to respond to an infant (Maestripieri, 2001). Moreover, premature human infants who have a daily session of skin-to-skin contact lying between their mothers' breasts develop more rapidly neurologically, tolerate stress better, and later receive more sensitive parenting from their parents than similar babies who do not receive this contact (Feldman & Eidelman, 2003; Feldman et al., 2003). Secure attachments can develop without such early contact, however, so it is neither crucial nor sufficient for the development of strong parent–infant attachments among humans.

What else helps a parent fall in love? Not only are babies cute, but their early reflexive behaviors such as sucking, rooting, and grasping help endear them to their parents (Bowlby, 1969). Smiling is an especially important social signal. Although it is initially a reflexive response to almost any stimulus, it is triggered by voices at 3 weeks of age and by faces at 5 or 6

weeks (Bowlby, 1969; Wolff, 1963). Babies are also endearing because they are responsive. Over the weeks and months, caregivers and infants develop **synchronized routines** much like dances, in which the partners take turns responding to each other's leads (Stern, 1977; Tronick, 1989). Note the synchrony as this mother plays peek-a-boo with her infant (Tronick, 1989, p. 112):

> The infant abruptly turns away from his mother as the game reaches its "peak" of intensity and begins to suck on his thumb and stare into space with a dull facial expression. The mother stops playing and sits back watching. . . . After a few seconds the infant turns back to her with an inviting expression. The mother moves closer, smiles, and says in a high-pitched, exaggerated voice, "Oh, now you're back!" He smiles in response and vocalizes. As they finish crowing together, the infant reinserts his thumb and looks away. The mother again waits. [Soon] the infant turns. . . . to her and they greet each other with big smiles.

Rhythmic, synchronized interactions like this depend in part on the infant's temperament and on whether she has developed organized biological rhythms such as sleep–wake cycles (Feldman, 2006). Caregiver–infant synchrony is also most likely to develop when caregivers are sensitive, providing social stimulation when a baby is alert and receptive but not pushing their luck when the infant's message is "Cool it—I need a break from all this stimulation." When synchrony between parent and infant can be achieved, a secure attachment relationship later in infancy is more likely (Jaffe et al., 2001).

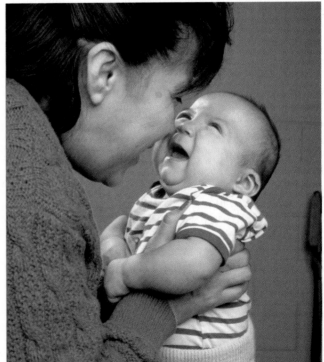

Smiling is one behavior that helps ensure adults will fall in love with babies.

The Infant's Attachment to the Caregiver

Infants progress through the following phases in forming attachments (Ainsworth, 1973; Bowlby, 1969):

1. *Undiscriminating social responsiveness (birth to 2 or 3 months).* Very young infants are responsive to voices, faces, and other social stimuli, but any human interests them. They do not yet show a clear preference for one person over another.

2. *Discriminating social responsiveness (2 or 3 months to 6 or 7 months).* Infants begin to express preferences for familiar companions. They direct their biggest grins and most enthusiastic babbles toward those companions, although they are still friendly toward strangers.

3. *Active proximity seeking or true attachment (6 or 7 months to about 3 years).* Around 6 or 7 months, infants form their first clear attachments, most often to their mothers. Now able to crawl, an infant will follow her mother to stay close, protest when her mother leaves, and greet her mother warmly when she returns. Soon most infants become attached to other people as well—fathers, siblings, grandparents, and regular baby-sitters (Schaffer & Emerson, 1964).

4. *Goal-corrected partnership (3 years and older).* By about age 3, partly because they have more advanced social cognitive abilities, children can participate in a **goal-corrected partnership,** taking a parent's goals and plans into consideration and adjusting their behavior to achieve the all-important goal of maintaining optimal proximity to the attachment figure. Thus, a 1-year-old cries and tries to follow when Dad leaves the house to talk to a neighbor, whereas a 4-year-old probably understands where Dad is going and can control the need for his attention until Dad returns. This final, goal-corrected partnership phase lasts a lifetime.

Attachment-Related Fears

Infants no sooner experience the pleasures of love than they discover the agonies of fear. One form of fear is **separation anxiety;** once attached to a parent, a baby often becomes wary or fretful when separated from that parent. Separation anxiety normally appears when infants are forming their first genuine attachments, peaks between 14 and 18 months, and gradually becomes less frequent and less intense (Weinraub & Lewis, 1977). Still, even children and adolescents may become homesick and distressed when separated from their parents for a long time (Thurber, 1995).

A second fearful response that often emerges shortly after an infant becomes attached to someone is **stranger anxiety**—a wary or fretful reaction to the approach of an unfamiliar person (Schaffer & Emerson, 1964). Anxious reactions to strangers—often mixed with signs of interest—become common between 8 and 10 months, continue through the first year, and gradually decline in intensity over the second year (Sroufe, 1996). The Explorations box describes the circumstances under which stranger anxiety is most and least likely to occur and suggests how baby-sitters and health-care professionals can head off outbreaks of fear and trembling.

Exploratory Behavior

The formation of a strong attachment to a caregiver has another important consequence: It facilitates exploratory behavior. Ainsworth and her colleagues (1978) emphasized that an attachment figure serves as a **secure base** for exploration—a point of safety from which an infant can feel free to venture and a safe haven to which she can return if frightened for some "emotional refueling" (Mercer, 2006). Thus Isabelle, a securely attached infant visiting a neighbor's home with Mom, may be comfortable cruising the living room as long as she can check occasionally to see that Mom is still on the couch but may freeze and fret and stop crawling about or playing if Mom disappears into the bathroom.

Quality of Attachment

Ainsworth's most important contribution to attachment theory was to devise a way to assess differences in the quality of parent–infant attachments, making Bowlby's hypotheses testable (Thompson & Raikes, 2003). She and her associates created the **Strange Situation,** a now-famous procedure for measuring the quality of an attachment (Ainsworth et al., 1978). It consists of eight episodes that gradually escalate the amount of stress infants experience as they react to the approach of an adult stranger and the departure and return of their caregiver (see ● **Table 14.1**). On the basis of an infant's pattern of behavior across the episodes, the quality of his attachment to a parent can be characterized as one of four types: secure, resistant, avoidant, or disorganized–disoriented.

1. **Secure attachment.** About 60 to 65% of 1-year-olds in our society are securely attached to their mothers or primary caregivers (Colin, 1996). The securely attached infant actively explores the room when alone with his mother because she serves as a secure base. The infant may be upset by separation but greets his mother warmly and is comforted by her presence when she returns. The securely attached child is outgoing with a stranger when his mother is present. As Cindy Hazan and her colleagues (Hazan, Campa, & Gur-Yaish, 2006) summarize the Bowlby–Ainsworth view, the securely attached infant ". . . stays close and continuously monitors [the caregiver's] whereabouts *(proximity maintenance),* retreats to her for comfort if needed *(safe haven),* resists and is distressed by separations from her *(separation distress),* and explores happily as long as she is present and attentive *(secure base)*" (p. 190).

2. **Resistant attachment.** About 10% of 1-year-olds show a resistant attachment, an insecure attachment characterized by anxious, ambivalent reactions (and also called anxious/ambivalent attachment). The resistant infant does not dare venture off to play even when his mother is present; she does not seem to serve as a secure base for exploration. Yet this infant becomes distressed when his mother departs, often showing stronger separation anxiety than the securely attached infant—perhaps because he is uncertain whether his mother will return. When his mother returns, the infant is ambivalent: He

PREVENTING STRANGER ANXIETY

It is not unusual for 1- or 2-year-olds meeting a new baby-sitter or being approached by a nurse or doctor at the doctor's office to break into tears and cling to their parents. Stranger-wary infants often stare at the stranger for a moment then turn away, whimper, and seek the comfort of their parents. Occasionally, infants become terrified and highly upset. Obviously, it is in the interests of baby-sitters, health care professionals, and other "strangers" to be able to prevent such negative reactions. What might we suggest?

- *Keep familiar companions available.* Stranger anxiety is less likely to occur if an attachment figure is nearby to serve as a secure base. In one study, less than one-third of 6- to 12-month-olds were wary of an approaching stranger when they were seated on their mothers' laps (Morgan & Ricciuti, 1969). Yet about two-thirds of these infants frowned, turned away, whimpered, or cried if they were seated only 4 feet from their mothers. A security blanket or beloved stuffed animal can have much the same calming effect as a parent's presence for some infants (Passman, 1977).

- *Arrange for the infant's companions to respond positively to the stranger.* As you have seen, infants about 9 months or older engage in social referencing, using other people's emotional reactions to guide their own responses to a situation. By implication, infants are likely to respond favorably to a stranger's approach if their mothers or fathers greet the stranger warmly.

- *Make the setting more "familiar."* Stranger anxiety is less likely to occur in familiar settings than in unfamiliar ones (Sroufe, Waters, & Matas, 1974). Stranger anxiety should be less severe if the baby-sitter comes to the child's home than if the child is taken to the baby-sitter's home or some other unfamiliar place. Yet an unfamiliar environment can become a familiar one if infants are given the time to get used to it. L. Alan Sroufe and his colleagues (1974) found that over 90% of 10-month-olds became upset if a stranger approached within 1 minute after they had been placed in an unfamiliar room, but only 50% did so when they were given 10 minutes to become accustomed to the room.

- *Be a sensitive, unobtrusive stranger.* Encounters with a stranger go best if the stranger initially keeps her distance and then approaches slowly while smiling, talking, and offering a familiar toy or suggesting a familiar activity (Bretherton, Stolberg, & Kreye, 1981; Sroufe, 1977). It also helps if the stranger, like any sensitive caregiver, takes her cues from the infant (Mangelsdorf, 1992). Babies prefer strangers they can control!

- *Try not to look any stranger than need be.* Finally, infants are most likely to be afraid of people who violate their mental schemas or expectations (Kagan, 1972). Baby-sitters who favor faddish dress or hairstyles, and health care professionals who don surgical masks, stethoscopes, and uniforms, might ask themselves whether they are violating babies' schemas!

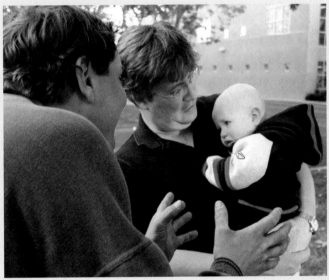

Christina Kennedy/PhotoEdit

---

may try to remain near his mother but seems to resent her for having left, may resist if she tries to make physical contact, and may even hit and kick her in anger (Ainsworth et al., 1978). Resistant infants are also wary of strangers, even when their mothers are present. It seems, then, that resistant or ambivalent infants are never sure that the affection and comfort they crave will be forthcoming.

3. **Avoidant attachment.** Infants with avoidant attachments (up to 15% of 1-year-olds) seem uninterested in exploring, show little distress when separated from their mothers, and avoid contact when their mothers return. These insecurely attached infants are not particularly wary of strangers but sometimes avoid or ignore them, much as these babies avoid or ig-

nore their mothers. Avoidant infants seem to have distanced themselves from their parents, almost as if they were denying their need for affection or had learned not to express their emotional needs.

4. **Disorganized–disoriented attachment.** Ainsworth's work initially focused on secure, resistant, and avoidant attachment styles, but some infants do not develop any of these consistent ways of coping with their need for proximity to their caregiver when they are stressed and seem confused. Up to 15% of infants—more in high-risk families—display what is now recognized as a fourth attachment classification, one that seems to be associated with later emotional problems (van IJzendoorn, Schuengel, & Bakermans-Kranenburg, 1999).

EPISODE	EVENTS	ATTACHMENT BEHAVIOR OBSERVED
1	Experimenter leaves parent and baby to play	
2	Parent sits while baby plays	Use of parent as secure base
3	Stranger enters, talks to parent	Stranger anxiety
4	Parent leaves; stranger lets baby play, offers comfort if needed	Separation anxiety
5	Parent returns, greets baby, offers comfort if needed; stranger leaves	Reactions to reunion
6	Parent leaves	Separation anxiety
7	Stranger enters, offers comfort	Stranger anxiety; ability to be soothed by stranger
8	Parent returns, greets baby, offers comfort, lets baby return to play	Reactions to reunion

SOURCE: Based on Ainsworth et al., 1978.

Reunited with their mothers after a separation, these infants may act dazed and freeze or lie on the floor immobilized—or they may seek contact but then abruptly move away as their mothers approach them, only to seek contact again (Main & Solomon, 1990). One infant may approach the parent with her head turned to the side; another may back his way slowly toward the parent. Unlike secure, resistant, or avoidant infants, infants with a disorganized–disoriented attachment have not been able to devise a consistent strategy for regulating negative emotions such as separation anxiety; they seem frightened of their parent and stuck between approaching and avoiding this frightening figure (Hesse & Main, 2006).

● **Table 14.2** summarizes the features of these four patterns of attachment, which have been the subject of considerable research. What determines which of these attachment patterns will characterize a parent–infant relationship? Early studies of the quality of attachments focused almost entirely on the qualities of caregivers that make infants form secure attachments to them, but we now know that infants also contribute to the attachment bond.

The Caregiver's Contributions

According to Freud, infants in the oral stage of psychosexual development become attached to the individual who provides them with oral pleasure, and the attachment bond will be most secure if a mother is relaxed and generous in her feeding practices. Early learning theorists put it differently but also believed that an infant learns positive emotional responses to her mother by associating her with food. In a classic study conducted by Harry Harlow and Robert Zimmerman (1959), the psychoanalytic and learning theory views dominant at the time were put to the test. Monkeys were reared with two surrogate mothers: a wire "mother" and a cloth "mother" wrapped in foam rubber and covered with terrycloth (see the photo on page 415). Half the infants were fed by the cloth mother, and the remaining

infants were fed by the wire mother. To which mother did these infants become attached? There was no contest: Infants strongly preferred the cuddly cloth mother, regardless of which mother had fed them. Even if their food came from the wire mother, they spent more time clinging to the cloth mother, ran to her when they were upset or afraid, and showed every sign of being attached to her.

Harlow's research demonstrated that **contact comfort,** the pleasurable tactile sensations provided by a soft and cuddly "parent," is a more powerful contributor to attachment in monkeys than feeding or the reduction of hunger. Contact comfort also promotes human attachments (Anisfeld et al., 1990); moreover, many infants become attached to someone other than the adult who feeds them, and variations in feeding schedules and the age at which infants are weaned have little effect on the quality of infants' attachments (Schaffer & Emerson, 1964).

Styles of parenting strongly influence the infant attachment styles described in Table 14.2. Infants who enjoy *secure* attachments to their parents have parents who are sensitive and responsive to their needs and emotional signals, as Bowlby proposed (Ainsworth et al., 1978; De Wolff & van IJzendoorn, 1997). Babies who show a *resistant* pattern of attachment often have parents who are inconsistent in their caregiving; they react enthusiastically or indifferently, depending on their moods, and are frequently unresponsive (Isabella, 1993; Isabella & Belsky, 1991). Mothers who are depressed, for example, often have difficulty responding sensitively to their babies and do not provide the comforting that helps babies regulate their negative emotions (Dawson & Ashman, 2000). The infant copes with unreliable caregiving by trying desperately—through clinging, crying, and other attachment behaviors—to obtain emotional support and comfort, and then becomes saddened and resentful when these efforts fail.

The parents of infants with an *avoidant* attachment tend to provide either too little or too much stimulation. Some are re-

	TYPE OF ATTACHMENT			
CHILD BEHAVIOR	SECURE	RESISTANT	AVOIDANT	DISORGANIZED– DISORIENTED
Explores when caregiver is present to provide a secure base for exploration?	Yes, actively	No, clings	Yes, but play is not as constructive as that of secure infant	No
Responds positively to stranger?	Yes, comfortable if caregiver is present	No, fearful even when caregiver is present	No, often indifferent, as with caregiver	No, confused responses
Protests when separated from caregiver?	Yes, at least mildly distressed	Yes, extremely upset	No, seemingly unfazed	Sometimes; unpredictable
Responds positively to caregiver at reunion?	Yes, happy to be reunited	Yes and no, seeks contact, but resents being left; ambivalent, sometimes angry	No, ignores or avoids caregiver	Confused; may approach or avoid caregiver or do both
Parenting style	Sensitive, responsive	Inconsistent, often unresponsive (e.g., depressed)	Rejecting–unresponsive or intrusive–overly stimulating	Frightened (e.g., overwhelmed) and frightening (e.g., abusive)

jecting; they are impatient, unresponsive, and resentful when the infant interferes with their plans (Ainsworth, 1979; Isabella, 1993). Some of these parents find an infant's crying extremely aversive and are unresponsive as a result (Mills-Koonce et al., 2007). Others have been called "intrusive"; they are overzealous and provide high levels of stimulation even when their babies become uncomfortably aroused and need a break so that they can regain control of their emotions (Isabella & Belsky, 1991). Infants with an avoidant attachment style may learn to avoid and make few emotional demands on adults who seem to dislike their company or who bombard them with stimulation they cannot handle.

Finally, a *disorganized–disoriented* style of attachment is evident in as many as 80% of infants who have been physically abused or maltreated (Carlson et al., 1989; and see Baer & Martinez, 2006). It is also common among infants whose mothers are severely depressed or abuse alcohol and drugs (Beckwith, Rozga, & Sigman, 2002). The parents of infants with a disorganized attachment pattern have been described as frightening and frightened—as fragile and fearful adults who are not up to the challenge of caring for an infant and create an unpredictable, scary environment for their babies (Hesse & Main, 2006). Infants with a disorganized attachment are understandably confused about whether to approach or avoid a parent who can be loving one minute but angry and abusive or indifferent the next. Each of the four types of attachment, then, reflects a reasonable way of coping with a particular brand of parenting.

The wire and cloth surrogate "mothers" used in Harlow's research. This infant monkey has formed an attachment to the cloth mother that provides "contact comfort," even though it must stretch to the wire mother in order to feed.

Harlow Primate Laboratory, University of Wisconsin

The Infant's Contributions

Clearly, the ways in which parents interact with their babies relate in predictable ways to the quality of the attachments that form. The infant's characteristics also have a bearing. Cognitive developmental theorists emphasize that the ability to form attachments depends partly on the infant's cognitive development. For example, the infant must recognize that close companions continue to exist even when they are absent to experience separation anxiety when a caregiver leaves the room (Kohlberg, 1969; Lester et al., 1974). That is, infants will not form attachments until they have acquired some concept of person permanence, a form of Jean Piaget's object permanence concept (see Chapter 7).

An infant's temperament also matters: Attachments tend to be insecure when infants are by temperament fearful, irritable, or unresponsive (Beckwith et al., 2002). Which has a stronger bearing on the quality of the attachment, then—the caregiver's style of parenting or the infant's temperament? Both are significant, and the two often interact. To illustrate, ■ **Figure 14.2** shows the percentages of 12-month-olds who tested as securely attached as a function of whether they were difficult-to-read infants born prematurely and whether their mothers were depressed (Poehlmann & Fiese, 2001). Only when a depressed mother was paired with a difficult-to-read, premature infant did the odds of a secure attachment become low. Similarly, the combination of a mother with a low sense of self-efficacy as a parent and an infant with colic who cries endlessly makes for an insecure attachment (Stifter, 2003).

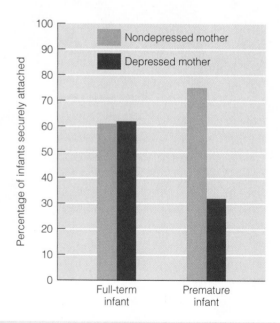

■ **FIGURE 14.2** The combination of a depressed mother and a premature infant means low odds that a secure attachment will form.

SOURCE: Data from J. Poehlmann & B. H. Fiese, The interaction of maternal and infant vulnerabilities on developing attachment relationships, *Development and Psychopathology*, 13, pp. 1–11. Copyright © 2001 Guilford. Reprinted by permission from Cambridge University Press.

Japanese infants become anxious in the Strange Situation because they are rarely separated from their mothers.

Overall, the caregiver has more to do than the infant with the quality of the attachment that forms (Goldberg et al., 1986; Vaughn et al., 1989). If the infant's temperament were the main influence on security of attachment, (1) we would not see so many infants securely attached to one parent but insecurely attached to the other (van IJzendoorn & De Wolff, 1997), (2) we would not have evidence that an infant's genes, which influence temperament, influence quality of attachment only minimally (Fearon et al., 2006), and (3) it would not be possible for caregivers who are patient and adjust to their baby's temperamental quirks to establish secure relationships with temperamentally difficult babies (Mangelsdorf et al., 1990). Consistent with the goodness of fit concept introduced in Chapter 11, secure bonds evolve when parents can respond sensitively to whatever temperamental characteristics their babies display.

Contextual Contributors

Finally, the broader social context surrounding caregiver and infant can affect how they react to each other. For example, the stresses associated with living in poverty or experiencing marital difficulties may make it difficult for parents to provide sensitive care and may contribute to insecure attachments (Howes & Markman, 1989; Murray et al., 1996). The cultural context in which caregiver and baby interact also colors their relationship. For instance, German parents strongly encourage independence and discourage clingy behavior, fearing that if they are responsive to cries they will spoil their infants. This may explain why many German infants make few emotional demands on their parents and are often classified as avoidantly attached in the Strange Situation (Grossmann, Grossmann, & Keppler, 2005). The Strange Situation may underestimate the number of securely attached infants in Germany—and also among U.S. babies who regularly receive nonmaternal care and who learn not to be bothered much by separations (Clarke-Stewart, Goossens, & Allhusen, 2001). By contrast, Japanese babies, who are rarely separated from their mothers early in life and are encouraged to be dependent on their mothers, become highly distressed by separations such as those they must endure

IS DAY CARE GOOD FOR INFANT DEVELOPMENT?

With more than 60% of mothers in the United States working outside the home at least part-time, questions have naturally arisen about the effects of care outside the home on infant and child development. Do infants who receive day care suffer compared with infants who stay at home with a parent? Not usually, but the effects of day care depend on many factors (Clarke-Stewart & Allhusen, 2005).

A major longitudinal study supported by the National Institute of Child Health and Human Development involving teams of researchers in 10 cities in the United States is our best source of evidence (NICHD Early Child Care Research Network [ECCRN], 1997, 2003b, 2005, 2006; NICHD, 2006). Of the 6-month-olds in this national sample at the outset of the study, 36% were cared for by their mothers, 9% attended day care centers (center attendance increased with age), 22% were in child-care or family-care homes (in which a caregiver takes children into her home), 10% received in-home care (provided in the child's home by a nanny, baby-sitter, or other nonrelative), 13% were tended by their fathers, and 10% were tended by grandparents (NICHD, 2006). Efforts were made in the study to control for child characteristics such as cognitive and language ability and social competence, as well as for family characteristics such as mother's education and quality of parenting, in assessing the effects of day care on development.

Overall, infants who experienced routine care by someone other than their mothers were not much different than infants cared for almost exclusively by their mothers. Quality of parenting was a stronger influence on these children's development than day care experience, but quality of day care, defined in terms of sensitive caregiving and cognitive and language stimulation, had impacts as well. Importantly, infants who received alternative forms of care were no less securely attached to their mothers overall than infants tended by their mothers (NICHD ECCRN, 1997). A mother's sensitivity to her infant had a lot more to do with attachment security than whether or not an infant was in alternative care.

Otherwise, findings from the NICHD study are somewhat mixed. On the one hand, children who spent a good deal of time in quality day care performed better than home-reared children on measures of cognitive and language skills and some measures of social skills. On the other hand, amount of time spent in day care also tended to be associated with higher levels of behavior problems (NICHD ECCRN, 2006). These effects were still evident to some extent in fifth or sixth grade (Belsky et al., 2007).

The most important finding of the NICHD study is that quality of care matters. Good developmental outcomes are likely in high-quality day care that has a reasonable child-to-caregiver ratio (up to three infants, four toddlers, or eight preschoolers per adult); caregivers who have been well trained and who are warm and responsive; little staff turnover so that children can become attached to their caregivers; and planned, age-appropriate stimulation activities (Burchinal et al., 2000; Clarke-Stewart & Allhusen, 2005). An infant's development clearly will suffer if he ends up with an alcoholic baby-sitter or must compete for adult attention as one of many infants in a large, understaffed center.

Some children also do better than others in day care. Infants from disadvantaged homes that offer little intellectual stimulation are especially likely to benefit from a stimulating day care program (Campbell & Ramey, 1994; Love et al., 2003). Girls tend to adapt better to day care than boys (Baydar & Brooks-Gunn, 1991; Belsky & Rovine, 1988), and infants and toddlers with easy temperaments adjust better than children who have difficult or slow-to-warm-up temperaments (Belsky & Rovine, 1988).

Finally, quality of the home environment interacts with quality of the day care environment to influence outcomes. In the NICHD (1997) study, for example, infants fared poorly if their mothers were insensitive and unresponsive *and* they were subjected to poor-quality day care on top of it. Under these circumstances, about half of the infants were insecurely attached to their mothers. By contrast, infants who received either good parenting or good day care were usually securely attached. Overall, infants and young children who receive day care do not turn out much different from infants and young children cared for at home— but are likely to thrive when they interact with both sensitive and stimulating parents and sensitive and stimulating substitute caregivers.

---

in the Strange Situation. They are more likely than American babies to be classified as resistant as a result (Takahashi, 1990; van IJzendoorn & Sagi, 1999).

Could findings like this mean that research on infant attachment is culturally biased? Fred Rothbaum and his colleagues (Rothbaum, Weisz et al., 2000; Rothbaum & Morelli, 2005) think so. They observe that in Western, *individualistic cultures*, such as Germany, optimal development means becoming an autonomous being, whereas in Eastern, *collectivist cultures*, such as Japan, the goal is to become integrated into the group, and this leads to differences in parenting and in the meaning of a secure attachment. Rothbaum appreciates that many of the predictions of attachment theory, such as the relationship between parental sensitivity and security of attachment, hold up in a variety of cultures (Rothbaum & Morelli, 2005). Still, characteristics of the caregiver, the baby, and the surrounding social environment all affect the quality of the emerging attachment, and what represents an adaptive attachment relationship in one culture may not be viewed as such in another.

Implications of Early Attachment

From Freud on, almost everyone has assumed that the parent–child relationship is critical in human development. Just how important is it? Two lines of research offer some answers: studies of socially deprived infants and studies of the later development of securely and insecurely attached infants.

Effects of Social Deprivation

What becomes of babies who are separated from their caregivers as a result of illness, death, or other unforeseen circumstances? Worse yet, what happens to infants who never have an opportunity to form an attachment bond? The daily separations from their parents that infants who attend day care centers experience are unlikely to keep them from forming or maintaining close relationships with their parents. As the Explorations box on page 417 illustrates, day care can have positive or negative effects on child development, depending on several factors, but normally does not damage attachments to parents or longer-term development.

Infants who experience long-term separations from caregivers because of hospitalizations, war, natural disasters, and the like go through a grieving process in which they may be sad and anxious but normally recover once reunited with their loved one. One man described by Jean Mercer (2006) recalls being traumatized, though, because when he was growing up adults did not appreciate the need to prepare children for long separations: "His mother brought him to the hospital, handed him to a nurse, and then left, returning for him as instructed ten days later. He did not speak again for a year after this event" (p. 21).

Infants who are permanently separated from a caregiver normally recover if they are able to maintain or form an attachment with someone else (Bowlby, 1960, 1980; and see Chapter 17). Studies of adopted children, though, suggest that the earlier permanent separation takes place the better (van IJzendoorn & Juffer, 2006). Children exposed to neglect or maltreatment in dysfunctional families or orphanages and then adopted before 1 year of age show remarkable catch-up growth physically, cognitively, behaviorally, and socially. Children adopted later than 1 year of age tend to form insecure attachments, possibly because they experienced a loss of trust when they were separated from their original caregivers, and show other developmental delays. Infants who experience a series of separations from caregivers may be permanently marred by their experiences of loving and losing (Colin, 1996; Ward, Munro, & Dearden, 2006).

It is better to have loved and lost, however, than never to have loved at all, say studies of infants who grow up in deprived institutional settings and are never able to form attachments (MacLean, 2003; Rutter & O'Connor, 2004). In the 1990s, children from deprived institutions in Romania were adopted into homes in the United States, the United Kingdom, and Canada after the fall of the Romanian government (Gunnar, Bruce, & Grotevant, 2000). These adoptees reportedly spent their infancies in orphanages with 20 to 30 children in a room and only one caregiver for every 10 to 20 children; they spent most of their time rocking in their cribs with little human contact, much less hugs, bouts of play, and synchronous routines (L. Fisher et al., 1997). How have they turned out?

Infants who spent 8 months or more in deprived orphanages displayed eating problems and medical problems; many were withdrawn and seemed overwhelmed in interactions with their new siblings and peers (L. Fisher et al., 1997). For a substantial number, physical, cognitive, and social–emotional development were compromised (Gunnar et al., 2000; MacLean, 2003). Rapid recovery was evident once the children were adopted and some children overcame their developmental problems entirely (Judge, 2003). Yet many children institutionalized for more than 6 months never achieved normal levels of cognitive development, possibly because they lacked the intellectual stimulation necessary for normal brain development during infancy (Rutter & O'Connor, 2004). Generally, the longer children had experienced deprivation, the more likely they were to experience long-term difficulties.

Continuing problems in interpersonal relationships were evident, too; these children have tended to be emotionally withdrawn, indiscriminately friendly, or both (Smyke, Dumitrescu, & Zeanah, 2002). For example, Thomas O'Connor and his colleagues (2003) compared attachment quality at age 4 among children who started their lives in deprived institutions in Romania and were adopted into British homes (either before 6 months or between 6 and 24 months of age) and British children who were adopted before 6 months of age. As ■ Figure 14.3 shows, the longer the Romanian children had experienced early deprivation, the less likely they were to be securely attached and the more likely they were to show an abnormal pattern of insecure behavior that O'Connor and his associates called *disinhibited attachment*.

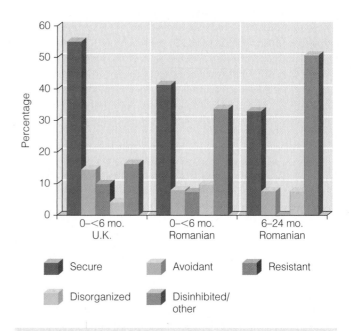

■ **FIGURE 14.3** Percentages of secure, avoidant, resistant, disorganized, and "disinhibited or other" attachments among nondeprived British children adopted before 6 months of age, deprived Romanian children adopted in the United Kingdom before 6 months, and deprived Romanian children adopted between 6 and 24 months.

SOURCE: From M. J. O'Connor & S. E. Whaley, Alcohol use in pregnant low-income women, *Journal of Studies in Alcohol*, 64, pp.773–783. Copyright © 2003. Reprinted with permission of Alcohol Research Documentation, Inc.

The children with a disinhibited attachment pattern were often indiscriminately friendly toward both a stranger and their parent in a Strange Situation test. They would eagerly approach the stranger in a coy or silly manner but then back off warily (rather than showing the normal pattern of wariness first and approach second). They were unable to regulate their emotions well enough to participate in real, reciprocal social interactions. Interviews with their adoptive parents revealed that these children sometimes went off with a stranger in a new situation without ever checking back with the parent. Although some of them had clearly formed secure attachments to their adoptive parents, the abnormal, disinhibited pattern of attachment was evident in half of the children deprived for more than 6 months.

What is it about institutional deprivation that damages development? Lack of proper nutrition, hygiene, and medical care; lack of stimulation; and lack of stable attachment relationships may all contribute (Gunnar et al., 2000). The deficits are probably not entirely caused by lack of sensory and intellectual stimulation; institutionalized children who are provided with such stimulation but lack a stable team of caregivers are still developmentally delayed and have emotional difficulties even as adolescents (Hodges & Tizard, 1989). Nor is the problem lack of a single "mother figure." In adequately staffed institutions and communes, infants cared for by a few responsive caregivers turn out quite normal (Groark et al., 2005; Smyke et al., 2002). Apparently, then, normal development requires sustained interactions with responsive caregivers—whether one or a few. Apparently too, children are resilient, provided that they are given reasonable opportunities to socialize and to find someone to love, but, as Bowlby claimed, early social experiences can sometimes leave lasting marks on development.

Later Development of Securely and Insecurely Attached Infants

How much difference does having secure rather than an insecure attachment to caregivers in infancy make later in life? According to Bowlby and Ainsworth's attachment theory, a secure attachment allows exploration from a secure base. This implies that securely attached children should be more cognitively competent (because they will be curious, explore the environment freely, and not shy from challenges) and more socially and emotionally competent (because they will explore the world of people freely, expect positive reactions from others because of the positive internal working models they form, and have learned in the parent–child relationship how to regulate their emotions). Does research support these predictions?

Indeed it does. In an early longitudinal study, Everett Waters and his associates (Waters, Wippman, & Sroufe, 1979) measured the quality of infants' attachments to their mothers at 15 months, then observed these children in preschool at 3 years. Securely attached infants turned into children whom teachers described as curious, self-directed, and eager to learn, whereas insecurely attached children were less independent.

Children who had been securely attached as infants were also more socially competent in the preschool setting than children who had been insecurely attached: They often initiated play activities, were sensitive to the needs and feelings of other children, and were popular (see also Schneider, Atkinson, & Tardif, 2001). Finally, research suggests that secure attachment in infancy is linked to positive emotional development and a greater capacity to cope with stress and regulate emotions later in childhood (Gunnar, 1998, 2000; Kochanska, 2001).

Do the effects of quality of attachment in infancy on intellectual curiosity, social competence, and emotional development last? In late childhood and adolescence, children who have enjoyed secure relationships with their parents continue to be well adjusted. They are self-confident and do well in school (Jacobsen & Hofmann, 1997); they are accepted by peers and have close friends (Elicker, Englund, & Sroufe, 1992). In a revealing longitudinal study, Jeffrey Simpson and his colleagues (2007) studied 78 individuals from infancy to their early 20s. These researchers were able to link secure attachment in the Strange Situation at 12 months of age to the quality of a child's peer relations in elementary school, which in turn predicted quality of friendships in adolescence, which in turn predicted the emotional quality of romantic relationships in early adulthood (as assessed by daily reports of emotions experienced in the relationship and emotions actually displayed while partners discussed problems in their relationship). Although quality of attachment during infancy and quality of romantic relationship in adulthood were not directly linked, they were indirectly associated through a chain of influence in which the quality of relationships in each developmental period affects the quality of relationships in the next period, as shown in ▪ **Figure 14.4.**

How can researchers be sure that relationships between attachment security and later adjustment are not the product of genes shared by parent and child that make some individuals well adjusted and others not? Geert-Jan Stams and his colleagues (2002) reasoned that a study of children and parents who were genetically unrelated might provide answers and followed a group of children placed in adoptive homes before 6 months of age until they were 7 years old. Children with a genetically influenced easy temperament were better adjusted than children with a difficult temperament. However, maternal sensitivity to the infant and the infant's attachment security also contributed to positive developmental outcomes, more than temperament did.

How do we know that later adjustment is the product of early parenting rather than later parenting? In another study of adopted infants (these infants were followed longitudinally from infancy to age 14), both early and current sensitivity on the part of parents affected the social development of adolescents (Jaffari-Bimmel et al., 2006). Early sensitivity on the part of a mother and a secure attachment in infancy had a positive impact on social development in adolescence through their contribution to social development in childhood. Evidence like this suggests that early parenting makes a difference in development—but that later experiences count too.

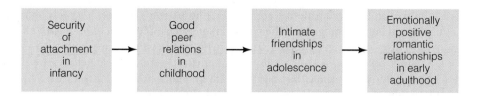

```
┌──────────────┐    ┌──────────────┐    ┌──────────────┐    ┌──────────────┐
│   Security   │    │     Good     │    │   Intimate   │    │  Emotionally │
│      of      │    │     peer     │    │  friendships │    │   positive   │
│  attachment  │───▶│  relations   │───▶│      in      │───▶│   romantic   │
│      in      │    │      in      │    │  adolescence │    │relationships │
│    infancy   │    │   childhood  │    │              │    │   in early   │
│              │    │              │    │              │    │  adulthood   │
└──────────────┘    └──────────────┘    └──────────────┘    └──────────────┘
```

■ **FIGURE 14.4** In the study by Simpson et al. (2007), relationship quality at each step in development affected relationship quality at the next step.
SOURCE: From J. A. Simpson, W. A. Collins, S. Tran, & K. C. Haydon, Attachment and the experience and expression of emotions in romantic relationships: A developmental perspective, *Journal of Personality and Social Psychology, 92*, pp. 355–367. Copyright © 2007 American Psychological Association. Reprinted with permission from the American Psychological Association.

In sum, children are unlikely to develop normally if their first relationships in life are repeatedly severed or if they never have the opportunity to form an attachment. By contrast, a secure attachment during infancy has many positive implications for social, emotional, and intellectual development. Yet you must avoid concluding that infants who are insecurely attached to their mothers are doomed—or that infants who are securely attached to their mothers are forever blessed.

First, affectionate ties to fathers (or siblings or grandparents) can compensate for insecure mother–infant relationships (Main & Weston, 1981). Second, early attachments may have no long-term consequences if they change in quality later. Stressful life events such as divorce and illness often convert secure attachments into insecure ones, and positive life changes can make insecure attachments more secure (Waters et al., 2000; Weinfield, Sroufe, & Egeland, 2000). Internal working models are just that—working models, subject to revision based on later social experiences (Sroufe et al., 2005).

All things considered, the Bowlby–Ainsworth attachment theory is well supported. Studies of the long-term consequences of early attachment support Bowlby's claim that internal working models formed early in life shape later relationships and development. Still, many of us learn new social skills and different attitudes toward relationships in our later interactions not only with parents but also with peers, close friends, lovers, and spouses. It is time, then, to supplement this description of parent–child relations with a look at the "second world of childhood"—the world of peer relations.

First Peer Relations

Evolution seems to have equipped human infants not only with a capacity for forming attachments to caregivers but also with a capacity for establishing social relationships with peers (Nash & Hay, 2003; Rubin, Bukowski, & Parker, 2006). Babies show an interest in other babies from an early age and begin to interact with them in earnest in about the middle of the first year. By then, infants will often smile or babble at their tiny companions, vocalize, offer toys, and gesture to one another, although many of their friendly gestures go unnoticed and unreciprocated (Hay, Nash, & Pedersen, 1983; Vandell, Wilson, & Buchanan, 1980). By around 6 months, infants even show

signs that they are biologically prepared for life in social groups: they can relate meaningfully to more than one peer at a time (Selby & Bradley, 2003).

By about 18 months, infants are able to engage in simple forms of reciprocal, complementary play with peers (Mueller & Lucas, 1975). They turn rounds of imitation into social games (Howes & Matheson, 1992). They can also adopt and reverse roles in their play. Thus, the toddler who receives a toy may immediately offer a toy in return, or the one who has been the chaser will become the chasee. Toward the end of the second year, infants have become proficient at this kind of turn-taking and reciprocal exchange, especially if they are securely attached to their parents (Fagot, 1997).

Surprising as it may seem, some infants also form special relationships with preferred playmates—friendships (Rubin et al., 2006). On Israeli kibbutzim, where children are cared for in groups, Martha Zaslow (1980) discovered that many pairs of infants as young as 1 year became truly attached to each other. Hadara and Rivka, for instance, consistently sought each other as playmates, mourned each other's absence, and disturbed everyone with their loud babbling "conversations" when they were confined to their cribs. Clearly the caregiver–infant relationship is not the only important social relationship that develops during infancy; peer relations are well under way, too.

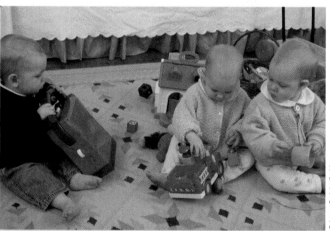

Even before 1 year of age, infants seem ready to engage in social interactions, not only in dyads but in groups.

▌ Primary emotions emerge in a universal sequence over the first months of life; secondary, or self-conscious emotions, follow, and emotions are increasingly socialized by caregivers.

▌ As infants age, they rely less on caregivers and more on their own emotion regulation strategies to manage the emotions aroused in their social relationships.

▌ Social from the start, as evidenced by synchronized routines, infants progress through phases of undiscriminating social responsiveness, discriminating social responsiveness, active proximity seeking, and goal-corrected partnership. The first attachment at 6 or 7 months brings with it both separation anxiety and stranger anxiety and use of the attachment figure as a secure base for exploration.

▌ Caregiver–infant interactions influence whether a secure, resistant, avoidant, or disorganized–disoriented attachment is evident in Ainsworth's Strange Situation. Secure attachments are associated with sensitive, responsive parenting.

▌ Although long-term consequences of early attachments on development are evident, early experience rarely makes or breaks later development, except perhaps for infants who experience repeated permanent separations or live in deprived institutions with no consistent caregivers.

CRITICAL THINKING

1. Some years ago, a 2-year-old named Baby Jessica was taken suddenly from the parents who thought they had adopted her and awarded by the court to her biological parents. What would attachment theory and research on attachment predict about Jessica's development? Was she able to form close attachments to her biological parents? What kind of child did she become? Then speculate about why Jessica apparently turned into a happy, well-adjusted child instead (Ingrassia & Springen, 1994).

2. Explain how infants with resistant attachments, avoidant attachments, and disorganized attachments are each trying to cope as best they can with the parenting they receive.

14.3 | THE CHILD

How do relationships with parents and peers change from infancy to childhood as children become more involved in play activities and try to gain acceptance by their peers? And how do changing social relationships in childhood contribute to development?

Parent–Child Attachments

The parent–child attachment changes qualitatively during childhood. According to John Bowlby (1969), it becomes a goal-corrected partnership in which parent and child accommodate to each other's needs; the child becomes a more sensi-

tive partner and grows more independent of the parent. Young preschool children want separations to be predictable and controllable and will negotiate with their parents to make sure that certain rituals such as the reading of a favorite book occur before bedtime or before parents go out for the evening (Mercer, 2006). Children continue to seek attention and approval from their parents, and they rush to their parents for comfort when they are frightened or hurt, but they also become increasingly dependent on peers for social and emotional support (Furman & Buhrmester, 1992). The result during the elementary school years is that children continue to perceive their parents as available to them, and turn to them when they really need comfort, but rely on their parents less and less frequently as they get older (Kerns, Tomich, & Kim, 2006).

Peer Networks

From age 2 to age 12, children spend more time with peers and less time with adults; about 10% of social interactions in toddlerhood but 30% of those in middle childhood are with peers (Rubin et al., 2006). Sharri Ellis and her colleagues (Ellis, Rogoff, & Cromer, 1981) observed 436 children playing in their homes and around the neighborhood. Youngsters of all ages spent less time with age-mates (defined as children whose ages were within 1 year of their own) than with children who were more than 1 year older or younger, suggesting that peer groups typically contain children of different levels of competence. In addition, even 1- to 2-year-olds played more often with same-sex companions than with other-sex companions. This gender segregation became increasingly strong with age (see Chapter 12). Moreover, the same trend toward increased gender segregation is evident in a variety of cultures, as shown in ■ Figure 14.5 (Munroe & Romney, 2006).

Once in their sex-segregated worlds, boys and girls experience different kinds of social relationships and interactions (Munroe & Romney, 2006). For example, there seems to be truth to the saying that boys travel in packs, girls in pairs: boys spend more time than girls in groups, and girls spend more time than boys in dyads (Fabes, Martin, & Hanish, 2003). Overall, then, children spend an increasing amount of time with peers as they get older, typically same-sex children only roughly similar in age who enjoy the same sex-typed activities.

Play

So important is play in the life of the child from age 2 to age 5 that these years are sometimes called *the play years*. This is when children hop about the room shrieking with delight, don capes and go off on dragon hunts, and whip up cakes and cookies made of clay, sand, or air. We can detect two major changes in play between infancy and age 5: it becomes more social, and it becomes more imaginative. After age 5 or so, the exuberant and fanciful play of the preschool years gives way to somewhat more serious play (Cohen, 2006; P. K. Smith, 2005).

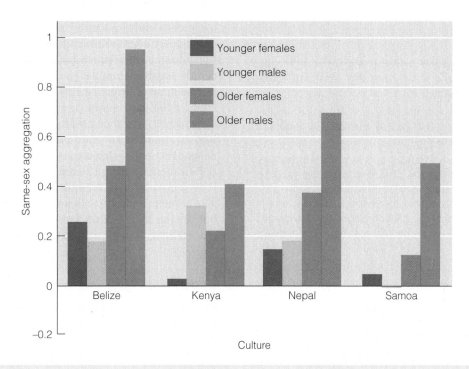

■ **FIGURE 14.5** Extent of same-sex group composition among younger (3- to 5-year-old) and older (7- to 9-year-old) boys and girls in four cultures. Scores represent mean number of same-sex group coparticipants minus mean number of different-sex coparticipants. Notice that the trend toward greater gender segregation with age is especially strong for boys.

SOURCE: From R. L. Munroe & A. K. Romney, Figure 1, p. 11 in Gender and age differences in same-sex aggregation and social behavior: A four-culture study, *Journal of Cross Cultural Psychology*, 31, pp. 3–16. Copyright © 2006 Sage. Reprinted with permission.

Play Becomes More Social

Years ago, Mildred Parten (1932) devised a method for classifying the types of play engaged in by preschool children of different ages. Her six categories of activity, arranged from least to most social, are as follows:

1. *Unoccupied play.* Children stand idly, look around, or engage in apparently aimless activities such as pacing.
2. *Solitary play.* Children play alone, typically with objects, and appear to be highly involved in what they are doing.
3. *Onlooker play.* Children watch others play, taking an active interest in and perhaps even talking to the players but not directly participating.
4. *Parallel play.* Children play next to one another, doing much the same thing, but they interact little (for example, two girls might sit near each other, both drawing pictures, without talking to each other to any extent).
5. *Associative play.* Children interact by swapping materials, conversing, or following each other's lead, but they are not united by the same goal (for example, the two girls may swap crayons and comment on each other's drawings as they draw).
6. *Cooperative play.* Children join forces to achieve a common goal; they act as a pair or group, dividing their labor and coordinating their activities in a meaningful way (for example, the two girls collaborate to draw a mural for their teacher).

The major message of Parten's study (and of others like it) is that play becomes increasingly social and socially skilled

from age 2 to age 5 (Barnes, 1971; P. K. Smith, 1978). Unoccupied and onlooker activities are evident at all ages, solitary and parallel play become less frequent with age, and associative and cooperative play, the most social and complex of the types of play, become more frequent with age (see ■ **Figure 14.6**).

The picture is more complex than Parten's work suggests. Older children continue to engage in solitary play, often to build skills. They also work their way into play groups by first being an onlooker and then playing in parallel with the other children before trying to join the ongoing activity (Rubin et al., 2006). Thus, all of Parten's forms of play can serve useful functions for children young and old depending on the occasion.

Play Becomes More Imaginative

The first **pretend play**—play in which one actor, object, or action symbolizes or stands for another—occurs around age 1, when an infant may raise an empty cup, or perhaps a forbidden treat, to her lips, smile, give a parent a knowing glance, and make loud lip-smacking sounds (Nicolich, 1977). The earliest pretend play is just like this: The infant performs actions that symbolize familiar activities such as eating, sleeping, and washing. By age 2, toddlers readily join in pretense; if you hand them a towel and suggest that they wipe up the imaginary tea you just spilled, they will (Harris & Kavanaugh, 1993). Because there is no tea in sight, this willingness to clean it up is remarkable. It means that toddlers are capable of using their new sym-

■ **FIGURE 14.6** Frequency of activities engaged in by preschool children of different ages. With age, solitary and parallel play occur less frequently, whereas associative and cooperative play occur more frequently.
SOURCE: Adapted from Barnes (1971).

bolic capacity to construct a mental representation of a pretend event and of acting according to this representation.

Pretend play fully blossoms from age 2 to age 5, increasing in both frequency and sophistication (Howes & Matheson, 1992; Rubin et al., 2006). As children age, they can depict heroes and heroines more different from themselves and can enact their dramas using fewer props. Most important, children combine their capacity for increasingly social play and their capacity for pretense to create **social pretend play,** play in which they cooperate with caregivers or playmates to enact dramas (Howes & Matheson, 1992). Social pretend play episodes can become quite sophisticated and require a good deal of social competence, including the theory-of-mind or people-reading skills discussed in Chapter 13. Consider the following example, in which a 5-year-old (M) wants her partner (E), playing the role of a mother, to leave her babies and come to M's house. The two girls negotiate what will happen next, managing to stay in role and keep in mind the other's role as they do so (Garvey, 1990, p. 137):

M: You come here. The babies are sleeping now and. . . . (interrupted).
E: No, they'll cry when I leave 'cause they'll hear the car.
M: Nooo. The car's broken. I have the car.
E: All right, but one baby will have to take care of these little babies.

Although social pretend play is universal, the quality of preschoolers' play is shaped by the culture in which they live (Haight et al., 1999). For example, U.S. children like to play superheroes and act out themes of danger and fantasy, whereas Korean children take on family roles and enact everyday activities (Farver & Lee-Shin, 1997). American children also talk a lot about their own actions, reject other children's ideas, and boss others around, whereas Korean children are more focused on their partners' activities and are more prone to make polite requests and agree with one another. Through their play, then, children in the United States (an individualistic culture) learn to assert their identities as individuals, whereas children in Korea (a collectivist culture) learn how to keep their egos and emotions under control to achieve group harmony.

Play Becomes More Rule-Governed

After they enter school, children engage less frequently in symbolic play. Now they spend more of their time playing organized games with rules—board and computer games, games of tag or hide-and-seek, organized sports, and so on (P. K. Smith, 2005). They also develop individual hobbies, such as building model cars, collecting coins, or making scrapbooks, that help them acquire skills and knowledge.

According to Jean Piaget (1965), it is not until children enter the stage of concrete operations, around age 6 or 7, that they become capable of cooperating with other children to follow the rules of games. Older children—11- and 12-year-olds who are entering the stage of formal operations—gain a more flexible concept of rules, recognizing that rules are arbitrary agreements that can be changed as long as the players agree. Partly because of cognitive gains, then, the play of the school-age child is more organized and rule-governed—and less fanciful—than that of the preschool child.

What Good Is Play?

In 19th-century America, child's play was discouraged because it was viewed as a frivolous waste of time (Athey, 1984). Today's parents who program their children's lives in hopes of molding little Einsteins may also have lost sight of the importance of play for children's development (Singer, Golinkoff, & Hirsh-

Pasek, 2006). Play contributes to virtually all areas of children's development. Indeed, that playful activity occurs among the young of so many species strongly suggests that play is an evolved behavior that helps the young adapt during childhood and prepare for adulthood (Cohen, 2006; P. K. Smith, 2005). It is easy to see how girls playing with dolls might be grooming themselves for traditional roles as mothers or how the rough-and-tumble play of boys, like the playful fights observed in young males of many species, might prepare them to compete with other males later in life.

In addition, play fosters cognitive, motor, and social skills and helps children cope with emotional problems (Singer et al., 2006; P. K. Smith, 2005). Physical play, from the leg kicking of infants to the rough and tumble play of childhood, contributes to neural maturation and the development of motor skills (P. K. Smith, 2005). Engaging in lots of pretend play has been linked to better performance on tests of cognitive development, language skills, and creativity (E. P. Fisher, 1992; Farver, Kim, & Lee-Shin, 2000). Engaging in social pretend play helps children construct their theories of mind, understand others' perspectives, and hone their social skills (Lillard, 2001). Perhaps as a result, preschoolers who engage in a lot of social pretend play tend to be more popular and socially skilled than children who do not (Connolly & Doyle, 1984; Farver et al., 2000).

Finally, play contributes to healthy emotional development by providing opportunities to express bothersome feelings, resolve emotional conflicts, and master challenges (Landreth & Homeyer, 1998). If Yoko, for example, has recently been scolded by her mother for drawing on the dining

Social pretend play during the preschool years contributes to intellectual, social, and emotional development.

room wall, she may gain control of the situation by scolding her "child" for doing the same thing. And Jackie, an abused 5-year-old, apparently coped with his abuse by having an alligator puppet swallow a small child doll and then smashing the alligator with a mallet and burying it in the sandbox (Landreth & Homeyer, 1998).

Let it never be said, then, that play is useless; it is truly the child's work. Although children play because it is fun, not because it sharpens their skills, they contribute to their own development by doing so. Parents can support their children's development by becoming involved in the social give and take that play episodes require (Lindsey & Mize, 2000).

Peer Acceptance and Popularity

Being accepted by peers means having the opportunity to play and interact with other children and in the process to develop normally. Researchers study peer-group acceptance through **sociometric techniques**—methods for determining who is liked and who is disliked in a group. In a sociometric survey, children in a classroom may be asked to nominate several classmates whom they like and several whom they dislike or to rate all of their classmates in terms of their desirability as companions (Cillessen & Mayeux, 2004; Hymel, McDougall, & Renshaw, 2002). It is important to find out both who is liked and who is disliked; this allows children to be classified into the following, distinct categories of social status (Coie, Dodge, & Coppotelli, 1982):

1. *Popular.* Well liked by most and rarely disliked.
2. *Rejected.* Rarely liked and often disliked.
3. *Neglected.* Neither liked nor disliked; these isolated children seem to be invisible to their classmates.
4. *Controversial.* Liked by many but also disliked by many; for example, the fun-loving child with leadership skills who also has a nasty habit of starting fights.
5. *Average.* In the middle on both the liked and disliked scales.

Why are some children more popular than others, and why are some children rejected by their peers? Popularity is affected by some personal characteristics that a child can do little to change. For instance, physically attractive children are usually more popular than physically unattractive children, and children who are relatively intelligent tend to be more socially accepted than those who are not (Bellanti, Bierman, & Conduct Problems Prevention Research Group, 2000). Social competence—the successful use of social cognitive skills in initiating social interactions, responding positively to peers, resolving interpersonal conflicts smoothly, and so on—strongly predicts popularity (Coie, Dodge, & Kupersmidt, 1990; Rubin et al., 2006). Well-liked children are also able to regulate their emotions well (Graziano, Keane, & Calkins, 2007).

"Rejected" children are often highly aggressive, although some are socially isolated, submissive children who are overly sensitive to teasing and are seen by others as "easy to push

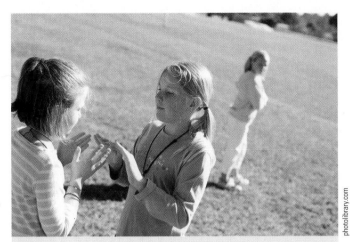
Children in the neglected category of sociometric status are shy and tend to hover on the fringes of a group without daring to enter it.

around" (Parkhurst & Asher, 1992; Rubin et al., 2006). Children who fall into the neglected category of sociometric status often have reasonably good social skills; they are usually nonaggressive and tend to be shy, withdrawn, and unassertive (Coie et al., 1990). As a result, no one really notices them. Controversial children are interesting: They often show leadership qualities, like popular children, but they are also viewed as aggressive bullies, like many rejected children (DeRosier & Thomas, 2003; Miller-Johnson et al., 2003). Their social skills may allow them to con some classmates into liking them even though others dislike their bullying.

To appreciate how social skills contribute to popularity, consider what happens when children try to enter and gain acceptance in play groups (Dodge et al., 1990; Putallaz & Wasserman, 1989). When children who ultimately become popular want to join a group's activity, they first hold back and assess what is going on, then smoothly blend into the group, commenting pleasantly about whatever the other children are discussing. By contrast, children who are eventually rejected by their peers tend to be pushy and disruptive. Jimmy, for example, may sit beside two boys who are playing a computer game and distract them by talking about a TV program he saw the night before. Even worse, he may criticize the way the boys are playing, start pecking computer keys at random, or threaten to turn off the computer if he is not allowed to play. By contrast, children who end up being neglected by their peers often hover around the edges of a group without taking positive steps to initiate contact, and they shy away from peers who attempt to make contact with them.

Influences on popularity vary from social context to social context. For example, children who are shy have been found to be unpopular in Canada but popular in China, where being quiet and reserved is more socially desirable (Chen, Rubin, & Sun, 1992; Chen et al., 2006). This pattern may be changing as China moves to a capitalistic economic system and expects children to be more assertive. The ingredients of popularity

also change with age: establishing close relationships with members of the other sex may enhance popularity during adolescence, but consorting with "the enemy," and thereby violating norms of gender segregation, can detract from popularity during childhood (Sroufe et al., 1993).

In sum, popularity or peer acceptance is affected by many factors. It helps to have an attractive face and cognitive skills, but it is probably more important to behave in socially competent ways and to be able to regulate one's emotions. As you have seen, children who enjoy secure relationships with their parents as infants tend to become popular children because they have learned social skills and styles of interacting in the parent–child relationship that shape the quality of their relationships with peers.

Do the outcomes of childhood popularity polls matter? Very much so, especially for the 10 to 15% of children who are rejected by their peers (Rubin et al., 2006). Children who are neglected by peers often gain greater acceptance later, but those who are rejected, especially because of aggressive behavior, are likely to maintain their rejected status from grade to grade (Bierman, 2004; Cillessen et al., 1992). More significantly, rejected children may end up even more poorly adjusted as a result of the experience of being rejected (Wentzel, 2003). Their self-esteem suffers, they lose opportunities to learn social skills, they develop negative attitudes toward others, they are negatively influenced by the other antisocial children they end up hanging out with, and their academic performance suffers (Coie, 2004; Flook, Repetti, & Ullman, 2005; Ladd & Troop-Gordon, 2003).

Friendships

Being accepted by the wider peer group and having close friends are distinct and serve different functions for children. Popular children are more likely than unpopular children to have friends, but many unpopular children have at least one reciprocated friendship and many popular children do not. In one study of 7- and 8-year-olds, for example, 39% of children rejected by peers had at least one mutual friendship, whereas 31% of popular children lacked a friendship (Gest, Graham-Bermann, & Hartup, 2001).

Having friends increases the odds that a child will be happy and socially competent, especially if the friendships are with peers who are well adjusted and supportive (Vaughn et al., 2000), and it reduces the odds that a child will be lonely and depressed (Nangle et al., 2003). As psychoanalytic theorist Harry Stack Sullivan (1953) theorized, having a close friend or chum is critical for children because it teaches them how to participate in emotionally intimate relationships and may pave the way for romantic relationships in adolescence. Friends also provide social support and comfort that can help children feel better about themselves, weather stressful events such as a divorce, and cope with challenges such as the first day of kindergarten (Ladd, 1999; Rubin et al., 2006). True friends become true attachment figures; maybe that is why having a secure attachment to a parent predicts having friends even better than it predicts being accepted by the wider peer group (Schneider et al., 2001).

SUMMING UP

▌ Children participate in goal-corrected partnerships with their parents and continue to rely on parents as needed but spend increasing amounts of time with peers, with boys running in packs, girls in pairs.

▌ Play becomes more social and imaginative during the preschool years and more often involves organized games and hobbies in elementary school.

▌ Physical attractiveness, cognitive ability, and especially social competence influence sociometric status. Peer acceptance may be critical for the learning of normal social behavior, whereas friends prepare children for intimate relationships and lend emotional support.

CRITICAL THINKING

1. Darren's sociometric status is neglected, whereas Alonzo's is rejected. What coaching would you give each boy to help him become more popular and why?

14.4 THE ADOLESCENT

Although children are already highly involved in peer activities, adolescents spend even more time with peers and less time with parents. The quality of the individual's attachment to parents continues to be highly important throughout adolescence, but peers, including romantic partners, begin to rival or surpass parents as sources of intimacy and support (Furman & Buhrmester, 1992). Moreover, the quality of peer relations changes. Not only do adolescents begin to form boy–girl friendships and go on dates, but they also become more capable of forming deep and intimate attachments.

Attachments to Parents

Just as infants must have a secure base if they are to explore, adolescents seem to need the security, as well as the encouragement to explore, provided by supportive parents to become independent and autonomous individuals (Scharf, Mayseless, & Kivenson-Baron, 2004). Adolescents who enjoy secure attachment relationships with their parents generally have a stronger sense of identity, higher self-esteem, greater social competence, better emotional adjustment, and fewer behavioral problems than their less securely attached peers (Arbona & Power, 2003; Kenny & Rice, 1995).

For many youths in our society, going off to college qualifies as a "naturally occurring Strange Situation"—a potentially

stressful separation that activates the attachment system (Kenny, 1987). Students who go home on weekends or talk to Mom or Dad on their cell phones every day during their first semester are engaging in attachment behavior just as surely as the infant who whimpers for his mommy. From an attachment theory perspective, experiencing separation anxiety in this situation is normal and adaptive. Preoccupation with parents typically decreases over the first semester and predicts adjustment problems only when it is extreme (Berman & Sperling, 1991).

College students who are securely attached to their parents display better psychological and social adjustment and academic performance during the potentially difficult transition to college than students who are insecurely attached (Lapsley, Rice, & FitzGerald, 1990; Larose, Bernier, & Tarabulsy, 2005). In one study (Mayseless, Danieli, & Sharabany, 1996), securely attached students proved able to maintain close, caring relationships with their parents while also forming new relationships with romantic partners. Lacking a secure base for exploration, resistantly attached students had more difficulty entering into romantic relationships and found even minor separations from their parents upsetting. And, true to form, avoidant youths claimed not to be bothered much by separation, as if denying that they could need their parents for anything. (Disorganized–disoriented attachments were not studied.) Knowing that attachments to parents provide a secure base for exploration, one can understand why parents who form secure relationships with their adolescents and grant them autonomy have adolescents who leave home when they should rather than leaving late or returning to the nest (Seiffe-Krenke, 2006) and adolescents who are capable of forming close relationships with both romantic partners and friends once they leave (Scharf et al., 2004).

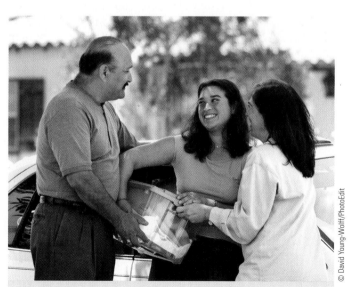

Going to college is a "Strange Situation" that activates attachment behaviors, such as hugging and e-mailing, designed to maintain contact with attachment figures.

© David Young-Wolff/PhotoEdit

Friendships

Friendships change qualitatively with age, being based on: (1) enjoyment of common activities in early childhood, (2) mutual loyalty and caring in late childhood, and (3) intimacy and self-disclosure in adolescence (Collins & Madsen, 2006; Rubin et al., 2006). Like children, teenagers form friendships with peers who are similar to themselves in observable ways. For example, most high school students choose friends of the same ethnic background (Hamm, 2000). However, adolescents increasingly choose friends whose psychological qualities—interests, attitudes, values, and personalities—match their own. In adolescence, friends are like-minded individuals who confide in each other.

Although same-sex friendships remain important throughout adolescence, teenagers increasingly form close cross-sex friendships too. Ruth Sharabany and her colleagues (Sharabany, Gershoni, & Hofman, 1981) asked 5th- to 11th-graders to assess their same-sex and cross-sex friendships in terms of such aspects of emotional intimacy as spontaneity, trust, loyalty, sensitivity to the other's feelings, and attachment. Same-sex friendships were highly intimate in most respects throughout this age range, whereas cross-sex friendships did not attain a high level of intimacy until 11th grade. These findings support neo-Freudian theorist Harry Stack Sullivan's view that children learn lessons about intimate attachments in their same-sex chumships that they later apply in their heterosexual relationships (Buhrmester & Furman, 1986). Finally, girls tended to report higher degrees of intimacy in their friendships than boys did, and they achieved emotional intimacy in their cross-sex relationships at earlier ages.

Changing Social Networks

Elementary-school children take interest in members of the other sex, talk at length about who likes whom, develop crushes, and in the process prepare themselves for heterosexual relationships (Thorne, 1993). Still, how do boys and girls who live in their own, gender-segregated worlds arrive at the point of dating each other?

Cliques and Crowds

Some time ago, Dexter Dunphy (1963) offered a plausible account of how peer-group structures change during adolescence to pave the way for dating relationships. His five stages are still helpful today in understanding how peer relations lay the foundation for romantic attachments (see also Collins & Madsen, 2006; Connolly, Furman, & Konarski, 2000):

1. In late childhood, boys and girls become members of same-sex **cliques,** or small friendship groups, and have little to do with the other sex.

2. Boy cliques and girl cliques then begin to interact. Just as parents provide a secure base for peer relationships, relationships with same-sex peers provide a secure base for romantic relationships. For an adolescent boy, talking to a girl at the mall with his friends and her friends there is far less threatening than doing so on his own.

3. The most popular boys and girls form a heterosexual clique.

4. As less popular peers also form mixed-sex cliques, a new peer-group structure, the **crowd,** completes its evolution. The crowd, a collection of several heterosexual cliques, is involved in arranging organized social activities—parties, outings to the lake or mall, and so on. Those adolescents who become members of a mixed-sex clique and a crowd (not all do) have many opportunities to get to know members of the other sex as both friends and romantic partners.

5. Couples form and the crowd disintegrates in late high school having served its purpose of bringing boys and girls together.

High school crowds not only bring boys and girls together but give adolescents a social identity and place in the social order. The names may vary, but every school has its crowds of, for example, "populars," "jocks," "druggies," and "losers," each consisting of adolescents who are similar to one another in some way (Brown, Mory, & Kinney, 1994). Everyone in high school seems to recognize these differences: "[The brains] all wear glasses and 'kiss up' to teachers and after school they all tromp uptown to the library" (Brown et al., 1994, p. 128), "The partiers goof off a lot more than the jocks do, but they don't come to school stoned like the burnouts do" (p. 133).

Which crowd or crowds an adolescent belongs to has important implications for her social identity and self-esteem; it is easier for her to feel good about herself if she is a "popular" or a "jock" than if she is a "dweeb," a "druggie," or a social isolate (like Seung Hui Cho of Virginia Tech) who does not belong to any crowd (Brown & Lohr, 1987). Indeed, self-perceived crowd membership in high school predicts later development; "brains" tend to graduate from college and have high self-esteem at age 24; "basket cases" are more likely than their peers to have seen a psychologist and attempted suicide; "jocks" achieve financial success but share with "criminals" a tendency to drink too much; and "criminals" are the least well adjusted (Barber, Eccles, & Stone, 2001). Crowd membership partly reflects personality traits, abilities, and values that existed before the adolescent ever got involved with a particular crowd but experiences in a crowd also help shape future development (Giordano, 2003).

A common misconception is that peers are typically a negative influence on adolescents. As it turns out, peers typically do more to foster positive behavior than to encourage antisocial behavior (Berndt & Murphy, 2002; Rubin et al., 2006). Yet much depends on the crowd to which an adolescent belongs: "Druggies" may encourage drug use, but "brains" discourage it. Adolescents are less likely to engage in delinquent behavior, become depressed, or feel lonely if they have friends and if those friends refrain from delinquent behavior than if they have delinquent friends or no friends (Brendgen, Vitaro, & Bukowski, 2000). There is a time, around the age of 14 or 15, when adolescents are quite dependent on their peers and may "go along with the crowd" and take risks when with friends that they would not take when alone (Berndt & Murphy, 2002; Gardner & Steinberg, 2005). Getting in trouble by conforming to peers is much less likely when adolescents have secure attachments to warm and authoritative parents who establish and enforce clear rules and are neither too lax nor too strict (Brown et al., 1993; Goldstein, Davis-Kean, & Eccles, 2005). Clearly, the influences of peers and friends can be healthy or destructive, depending on which cliques and crowds an adolescent belongs to and how much she needs the security of peer acceptance.

Dating

As Dunphy's model suggests, the transition to dating takes place in the context of the larger peer group (Collins & Laursen, 2004; Rubin et al., 2006). About 25% of 12-year-olds, 50% of 15-year-olds, and 70% of 18-year-olds say that they have been involved in a "special romantic relationship" in the past 18 months (Carver, Joyner, & Udry, 2003).

Dating relationships in early adolescence are more superficial and short lived than later dating relationships (Brown, Feiring, & Furman, 1999). Evolutionary psychologists suggest that humans have an evolved tendency to compete with peers for mates and to engage in sexual experimentation with several partners before they narrow in on a steady mate (Weisfeld & Woodward, 2004). This is evident in B. Bradford Brown's (1999) view that adolescent romantic relationships evolve through the following four phases:

Adolescents who end up in the wrong crowd often lack secure attachments to parents.

1. *Initiation phase.* In early adolescence, the focus is on the self—specifically, on coming to see oneself as a person capable of relating to members of the other sex in a romantic way.

2. *Status phase.* In midadolescence, peer approval is what counts; having a romantic relationship, and having it with the "right kind" of partner, is important for the status it brings in the larger peer group.

3. *Affection phase.* In late adolescence, the focus is on the relationship rather than on self-concept or peer acceptance. Romantic relationships become more personal, caring relationships; they are set in the context of a small, mixed-sex clique rather than in the context of the larger crowd, with friends providing advice and emotional support.

4. *Bonding phase.* In the transition to early adulthood, the emotional intimacy achieved in the affection phase is coupled with a long-term commitment to create a lasting attachment bond.

Brown's phases were evident in an 8-year longitudinal study of German adolescents who were age 13 at the start of the study. The 13-year-olds who had romantic relationships tended to have relatively low-quality and unstable, although emotionally intense, relationships that lasted an average of only about 3 months (Seiffge-Krenke, 2003). With age, relationships lasted longer (an average of 21 months by age 21) and became more emotionally intimate and supportive. Moreover, having a committed romantic relationship at age 21 was associated with having a positive self-concept at age 13, supportive peer relationships at age 15, and a supportive romantic relationship at age 17. Parents contributed too; supportive relationships with both mother and father proved to be at least as important as supportive relationships with peers in predicting involvement in a love relationship in early adulthood (see also Miller & Hoicowitz, 2004). This may go back to attachment: adolescents who have secure attachment styles based on their early experiences with their parents have more positive experiences dating than do adolescents with resistant attachment styles, who fall in love and have sex a lot but are ever fearful of abandonment, and adolescents with avoidant styles, who are reluctant to get emotionally involved (Tracy et al., 2003).

How does dating affect adolescent adjustment and development? Dating at an early age appears to have more negative than positive effects on social and emotional adjustment, either because troubled adolescents start dating early or because early daters get hurt or become involved in teenage problem behavior before their time (Collins, 2003; Compian, Gowen, & Hayward, 2004). However, both positive relationships with parents and positive relationships with same-gender peers can protect young adolescents from the negative effects of early dating (Brendgen et al., 2002; Doyle et al., 2003). And overall, dating typically has more positive than negative effects on development and can even compensate for a poor relationship with parents. Involvement in a steady relationship is good for self-esteem (although breakups hurt it), and adolescents who date tend to be better adjusted overall than those who do not (Collins, 2003; Furman & Shaffer, 2003).

THE DARK SIDE OF PEER RELATIONS

The 2004 film *Mean Girls* painted a vivid picture of the treacherous world of teenage peer relations. The film concerns the tribulations of Cady, a newcomer to North Shore High School who was homeschooled in Africa and has much to learn about this high school's social world. The center of this world is Regina George, the "queen bee" of a clique called the Plastics. Cady is told this about Regina by a classmate: "And evil takes a human form in Regina George. Don't be fooled, because she may seem like your typical selfish, back-stabbing slut-faced ho-bag, but in reality she's so much more than that." No one escapes the insults, vicious rumors, and betrayals in this society of mean girls.

After focusing for years on the positive contributions of peer acceptance and friendship to child and adolescent development, developmentalists have begun to appreciate that peer relationships have a dark side (Hartup, 2006; Rubin et al., 2006). One of your authors has only to conjure up memories of Sunday school bully Norma T. to appreciate the point! The kind of "relational aggression" at which Regina George excelled—subtle and indirect aggression such as gossiping about and ignoring and excluding others—has been studied by Amanda Rose and her colleagues (Rose,

Swenson, & Waller, 2004). These researchers found that relational aggression works for girls (though not boys) in early adolescence (though not in middle childhood) to enhance perceived popularity (Rose et al., 2004). Perceived popularity also predicted more use of relational aggression later for both males and females, suggesting that adolescents who become popular may discover that they can use their social power to exclude or hurt others—and do just that.

As you have seen already, rejection by the peer group in childhood can have long-lasting negative effects on a child's development (Bierman, 2004). Rejection by a dating partner can similarly derail adolescent development. In one study, adolescents who were or were not involved in romantic relationships were interviewed twice. Involvement in a romantic relationship, especially among girls, was associated with a rise in depression symptoms from the first to the second interview, probably because these relationships can be stressful and their breakups shattering (Joyner & Udry, 2000; Rubin et al., 2006).

Then there are the peer relationships that are inherently negative: bully–victim relationships and enemy relationships. Bullies are both verbally and physically aggressive, but

not toward everyone—just toward well-chosen victims. A bully's victims tend to be either weak and socially withdrawn or aggressive themselves (Olweus, 1993; Rubin et al., 2006). Partly as a result of their painful victimization experiences, victims of bullies are at significant risk for low self-esteem, depression, and poor performance in school (Smetana, Campione-Barr, & Metzger, 2006).

Most of us can also recall having enemies at some point in our lives. Enemies, by definition, express mutual dislike for one another on sociometric surveys (Hodges & Card, 2003). Figures vary greatly, but around 30% of children may be involved in enemyships (Hartup, 2006). Enemy relationships often start with conflict; sometimes they are friendships turned bad (Card, 2007). Children who are rejected by peers are especially likely to have enemies (Rodkin & Hodges, 2003).

Being excluded or rejected by peers, victimized by bullies, dumped by romantic partners, and detested by enemies are all, it seems, part of the normal landscape of peer relations in childhood and adolescence. Nonetheless, we must still conclude that peer relations are an essential—and in the end mostly positive—force in human development.

Adolescence is clearly an important time of change in attachment relationships. As adolescents get older, they look more to peers, both friends and romantic partners, to fulfill some of the attachment needs that parents fulfilled when they were younger. In a study of three age groups (12–15, 16–19, and 20–28), Dorothy Markiewicz and her colleagues (2006) asked adolescents who they most liked to spend time with (proximity seeking), most want to be with when they are feeling down (safe haven), and feel will always be there for them (secure base). Mothers were important to all age groups, especially as a secure base for exploration; fathers were less central in meeting attachment needs. With age, best friends became an important safe haven and source of reassurance when adolescents had problems, and romantic partners increasingly met needs for proximity or closeness. By early adulthood, romantic partners had become central to those who had them in meeting a variety of attachment needs. Parents are still there, however, in a backup role (Hazan et al., 2006).

Although human development could not proceed normally without peers, friends, and romantic partners, developmentalists now appreciate that there is also a dark side to peer relations, examined in the Explorations box.

SUMMING UP

▪ During adolescence, same-sex, and later cross-sex, relationships increasingly involve emotional intimacy and self-disclosure.

▪ According to Dunphy's model, the peer group is transformed from same-sex cliques to mixed-sex cliques and the crowd structure, and finally to dating relationships, with the type of crowd an adolescent belongs to having implications for self-esteem and development.

▪ According to Brown, dating relationships progress through initiation, status, affection, and bonding phases as romantic partners become increasingly important attachment figures.

CRITICAL THINKING

1. Analyze the clique and crowd structure in your high school, where you fit in it, and how you might have been affected by it.

2. Billy never had a best friend and is now in college and dating. What implications might the lack of a friend in childhood have for Billy's dating behavior?

Relationships with family and friends are no less important during adulthood than they are earlier in life, but they take on different qualities over the adult years. How do people's social networks change over the adult years and why, and what is the character of their romantic relationships and friendships?

Social Networks

Some years ago, Robert Kahn and Toni Antonucci (1980) proposed that each of us has a **social convoy,** a social network and support system that accompanies us during our life's journey, changing as we go. An infant's social convoy may consist only of parents. The social convoy enlarges over the years as others (relatives, friends, supportive teachers, romantic partners, colleagues, and so on) join it, then typically shrinks in later life (Carstensen, Mikels & Mather, 2006; Levitt, Weber, & Guacci, 1993). As new members are added, some members drift away. Others remain in the convoy, but our relationships with them change, as when the infant son thoroughly dependent on his mother becomes the adolescent son clamoring for his independence—and later the middle-aged son on whom his aging mother depends for help when she needs it.

Social Interaction Patterns

With whom do adults of different ages interact, and how socially active are they? Young adults are busily forming romantic relationships and friendships. The trend toward greater intimacy with the other sex that began in adolescence continues (Reis et al., 1993). Young women form closer friendship ties than men do. This sex difference may have evolved because women increase the odds that their children will survive if they can attract social support when they are bearing and raising children (S. E. Taylor, 2002).

Young adults, especially single ones, tend to have more friends than middle-aged and older adults do. As adults marry, have children, take on increasing job responsibilities, and age, their social networks shrink (J. L. Fischer et al., 1989). The trend toward smaller social networks with age can be seen in many ethnic groups, but ethnic group differences are also evident. For example, from early adulthood on, African American adults' networks tend to be smaller, to be more dominated by kin, and to involve more frequent contact than those of European Americans (Ajrouch, Antonucci, & Janevic, 2001).

Socioemotional Selectivity

You may be guessing that the shrinking of the social convoy in later adulthood is the result of increased disease, disability, and social isolation. However, Laura Carstensen's (1992) **socioemotional selectivity theory** explains it quite differently—as a choice older adults make to better meet their emotional needs (also see Charles & Carstensen, 2007; Lang & Carstensen,

2002). The perception that one has little time left to live is critical, according to Carstensen. It prompts older adults to put less emphasis on the goal of acquiring knowledge for future use and more emphasis on the goal of fulfilling current emotional needs. As a result, older adults actively choose to narrow their range of social partners to those who bring them emotional pleasure, usually family members and close friends, and they let other social relationships fall by the wayside. Whereas younger adults need the social stimulation and new information that contacts with strangers and acquaintances often provide—and are even willing to sacrifice some emotional well-being to have many social contacts—older adults put their emotional well-being first.

Does the evidence support socioemotional selectivity theory? In one study, cancer patients of various ages preferred familiar to unfamiliar social partners more than control adults who were not ill did (Pinquart & Silbereisen, 2006). Moreover, if their therapy was successful, they showed increased interest in interacting with people they did not know, suggesting that perceived time left to live was important, as Carstensen theorizes.

Pickiness about social partners also increases with age. Middle-aged adults interact less frequently with acquaintances and friends than young adults do, but they interact often with their spouses and siblings and feel closer emotionally to the most significant people in their lives than younger adults do (Carstensen, 1992). Elderly adults drop even more friends and acquaintances from their networks, but they usually maintain a core of "very close" relationships. If they do not have living spouses or children, they strengthen relationships with other relatives or friends to maintain an inner circle of intimates (Lang & Carstensen, 1994).

The quality of an older adult's emotional life appears to benefit from socioemotional selectivity, as Carstensen theorizes. She and her colleagues (2000) sampled the emotional experiences of African American and European American adults between age 18 and age 94 by paging them at random times over a 1-week period as they went about their lives. Contrary to ageist stereotypes, older adults did not have more dismal, depressing emotional lives than younger adults. Younger and older adults differed little in the frequency with which they experienced positive emotions; and negative emotions were actually less common among older adults. Older adults also experienced longer-lasting positive emotions and more fleeting negative moods, suggesting that they are more able than younger adults to regulate their emotions, savoring the happy experiences while cutting short the sad and angry ones (see also Kliegel, Jager, & Phillips, 2007). Finally, older adults appeared to have more complex emotional experiences, more often blending different emotions together. It is amply clear now that older adults lead rich and rewarding emotional lives and that they are able to experience and express emotions fully, and also regulate them effectively (Carstensen, Mikels, & Mather, 2006; Magai et al., 2006; Mroczek, 2004). Whether it is because of socioemotional selectivity or other factors, older adults end up at least as satisfied as young adults with their relationships (Lansford,

Contrary to stereotype, elderly adults lead rich and generally positive emotional lives.

Sherman, & Antonucci, 1998) and less likely to find them emotionally unpleasant (Akiyama et al., 2003).

Attachment Styles

Intrigued by parallels between an infant's attachment to a parent figure and a young adult's love for a romantic partner, researchers have been studying adult romantic relationships from the perspective of attachment theory (Mikulincer & Shaver, 2003; Shaver & Mikulincer, 2007). Following the lead of Bowlby, Phillip Shaver (2006) and others believe that romantic relationships involve at least three interrelated motivational–behavioral systems: the attachment system, the caregiving system, and the sex system. Basically, when we're in love, we want

to be close to our partner (attachment), care for this cherished person (caregiving), and express our love sexually (sex).

By any account, attachment is an important component of a love relationship. Like the infant who is attached to a parent, the adult who is in love experiences a strong emotional bond to her partner, wants to be close, takes comfort from the bond, and is upset by separations, as illustrated by the story of Mike and Marcy at the start of the chapter. Like the parent–child attachment, the attachment between romantic partners is also biologically adaptive; it increases the odds of having children and the odds that these children will have two parents to help them survive (H. Fisher, 2006). Perhaps it is not surprising, then, that the concept of romantic love is not just a Western phenomenon or a modern phenomenon, as some people incorrectly believe (Hatfield & Rapson, 2006). The phenomenon of romantic love has been documented in at least 88% of the world's cultures, including many in which marriages are arranged by family elders (Jankowiak & Fischer, 1992).

■ Figure 14.7 shows a way of thinking about how the internal working models that we construct from our experiences in the parent–child relationship may affect our romantic relationships (Bartholomew & Horowitz, 1991; Crowell, Fraley, & Shaver, 1999). Adults with a *secure* working model feel good about both themselves and others; they are not afraid of entering intimate relationships or of being abandoned once they do. People with a *preoccupied* internal working model have a positive view of other people but feel unlovable. Like resistantly attached infants, they crave closeness to others as a means of validating their self-worth, are highly fearful of abandonment, and tend to become overly dependent on their partners.

Adults with a *dismissing* style of attachment have a positive view of self but do not trust other people and dismiss the importance of close relationships (Beckwith, Cohen, & Hamilton,

MODEL OF SELF		
	POSITIVE	**NEGATIVE**
MODEL OF OTHER — POSITIVE	**SECURE** *Secure attachment history* Healthy balance of attachment and autonomy; freedom to explore	**PREOCCUPIED** *Resistant attachment history* Desperate for love to feel worthy as a person; worry about abandonment; express anxiety and danger openly
MODEL OF OTHER — NEGATIVE	**DISMISSING** *Avoidant attachment history* Shut out emotions; defend against hurt by avoiding intimacy, dismissing the importance of relationships, and being "compulsively self-reliant"	**FEARFUL** *Disorganized–disoriented attachment history* Need relationships but doubt own worth and fear intimacy; lack a coherent strategy for meeting attachment needs

■ **FIGURE 14.7** Internal working models of self and other people arising from early experiences in relationships.
SOURCE: Adapted from Bartholomew & Horowitz, 1991. It is also possible to look at these four types of attachment in terms of anxiety and avoidance dimensions (Gallo, Smith, & Ruiz, 2003; Mikulincer & Shaver, 2003). The secure type is low in both anxiety over relationships (fear of abandonment) and avoidance of relationships (discomfort over being intimate with and dependent on someone); the preoccupied type is high in anxiety but low in avoidance; the dismissing type is low in anxiety but high in avoidance; and the fearful type is high in both anxiety and avoidance.

INTERNAL WORKING MODELS OF ATTACHMENT

Which of the internal working models of attachment in Figure 14.7—secure, dismissing, preoccupied, or fearful—is expressed in each of the following statements (Bartholomew & Horowitz, 1991, p. 244, adapted from Hazan & Shaver, 1987)? And which internal working model best describes you?

1. "I want to be completely emotionally intimate with others, but I often find that others are reluctant to get as close as I would like. I am uncomfortable being without

close relationships, but I sometimes worry that others don't value me as much as I value them."

2. "I am somewhat uncomfortable getting close to others. I want emotionally close relationships, but I find it difficult to trust others completely or to depend on them. I sometimes worry that I will be hurt if I allow myself to become too close to others."

3. "It is relatively easy for me to become emotionally close to others. I am comfort-

able depending on others and having others depend on me. I don't worry about being alone or having others not accept me."

4. "I am comfortable without close emotional relationships. It is very important to me to feel independent and self-sufficient, and I prefer not to depend on others or have others depend on me."

1. Preoccupied, 2. Fearful, 3. Secure, 4. Dismissing

1999). Like avoidantly attached infants, they defend themselves against hurt by not expressing their need for love or their fear of abandonment. They downplay the importance of their relationships, find it hard to trust partners, feel that others want them to be more intimate than they wish to be, and keep partners at a distance. Bowlby (1973) described dismissing or avoidant individuals as "compulsively self-reliant." Finally, adults with a *fearful* internal working model resemble infants with a disorganized–disoriented attachment; they take a dim view of both themselves and other people and display a confusing, unpredictable mix of neediness and fear of closeness. You may wish to see if you can identify the internal working models expressed by the statements in the Explorations box.

Mary Main and her colleagues have stimulated much research on adult attachment styles with their Adult Attachment Interview (AAI). It asks adults about their childhood experiences with attachment figures and about their current relationships with their parents and romantic partners, including their experiences with separation and rejection. Respondents are then classified into categories similar to those in Figure 14.7 (Main, Kaplan, & Cassidy, 1985). Much is learned by seeing how freely and coherently adults talk about their early relationships. For example, dismissing adults prove unable to reflect on their early relationships with their parents; they may say all was great but provide no supporting evidence. Preoccupied adults have a lot to say, much of it emotionally charged, but they have difficulty integrating and gaining a perspective on their experiences. Secure adults are able to reflect on their family experience and make sense of it—even when they have had miserable childhoods.

Research using the AAI and other instruments suggests that adults do have predominant styles of attachment. In a pioneering study conceptualizing romantic love as attachment, Cindy Hazan and Phillip Shaver (1987) classified 56% of the adults they studied as having a secure attachment style, 19% as resistant, and 25% as avoidant. (They did not measure the fearful or disorganized–disoriented attachment style.) Adults' styles of attachment were related to the quality of their romantic relationships. For example, adults with a secure attachment style experience a good deal of trust and many positive emotions in their

current love relationships, and their relationships tend to last longer than those of adults with insecure attachment styles. Avoidant lovers fear intimacy, whereas resistant individuals tend to be obsessed with their partners. Both avoidant and resistant adults report a lot of jealousy and emotional extremes of love and pain in their romantic relationships. In a recent study in which engaged and married partners discussed problems in their relationships (Roisman, 2007), adults with a secure attachment style calmly shared their feelings and thoughts; avoidant-style adults showed physiological signs of shutting down or inhibiting their true feelings; and resistant-style adults became highly emotionally aroused, as indicated by high heart rates.

The quality of the parent–child relationship an adult experienced earlier in life predicts both adult attachment style and romantic relationship quality. In a longitudinal study spanning the years from infancy to adulthood, adults who had experi-

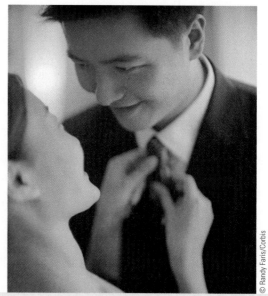

Romantic attachment shares qualities with parent–infant attachment.

enced sensitive maternal care in infancy had more positive mental representations of their romantic relationships than did other adults (Grossmann et al., 2002b). In addition, the quality of the parent–child attachment, especially after infancy, predicted the quality of an adult's romantic relationship. Similarly, and as we saw earlier, Jeffrey Simpson and his colleagues (2007) found that a secure attachment at 1 year of age was linked, in turn, to social competence in childhood, close friendships in adolescence, and an emotionally positive romantic relationship in early adulthood. So, as Bowlby theorized, internal working models of self and other formed on the basis of parent–child interactions affect the quality of later relationships (Fraley, 2002; Mayseless & Scharf, 2007).

Internal working models also predict the capacity for exploration—the extent to which adults have the confidence and curiosity to explore and master their environments (Mikulincer & Shaver, 2003). A secure attachment style in adulthood is associated with strong achievement motivation and a focus on mastering challenges as opposed to avoiding failure (Elliot & Reis, 2003). Securely attached adults also enjoy their work and are good at it, whereas preoccupied (resistantly attached) adults want approval and grumble about not being valued enough, and dismissing (avoidantly attached) adults bury themselves in their work and do little socializing with coworkers (Hazan & Shaver, 1990).

Internal working models also affect an adult's capacity for caregiving—most importantly, for being a sensitive and responsive parent (Mikulincer & Shaver, 2003). Mothers and fathers who had secure relations with their parents tend to interact more sensitively with their children and form more secure attachment relationships with them than parents whose early attachments were insecure (van IJzendoorn, 1995). Mothers with a dismissing attachment style seem to derive little pleasure from their infants, whereas preoccupied mothers are anxious and behave irritably and intrusively with theirs (Adam, Gunnar, & Tanaka, 2004). Attachment styles are even transmitted across multiple generations. In one study, grandmothers who completed the AAI, mothers-to-be who completed the AAI when pregnant, and infants tested in the Strange Situation with their mothers all fell in the same attachment category in 64% of the cases (Benoit & Parker, 1994).

Finally, attachment styles have a bearing on adjustment even in old age. Older adults who recall loving relationships with their parents during childhood tend to have better physical and mental health than those who recall unsupportive relationships (Shaw et al., 2004). Interestingly, whereas most young and middle-aged adults appear to have secure adult attachment styles, Carol Magai and her colleagues (2001) found that most European American and African American elderly adults fall in the dismissing–avoidant attachment category; they express some discomfort with closeness and tend to be compulsively self-reliant. Elderly people with either a secure or a dismissive (avoidant) attachment style tend to be happier than those whose styles are preoccupied or fearful, suggesting that the independent, dismissive style may be adaptive in old age, possibly helping adults who have lost spouses manage life on their own (Webster, 1998).

Overall, internal working models, past and present, have implications for romantic relationships, exploration and work, relationships with children, and overall adjustment in adulthood. Research on secure, preoccupied, dismissing, and fearful styles of attachment in adulthood has taught us a good deal about adult relationships.

Adult Friendships

Friendships are important across the life span, although they take on different characters at different ages (Blieszner & Roberto, 2004). Young adults typically have more friends than older adults do, but even very old adults usually have one or more close friend and are in frequent contact with their friends (Ueno & Adams, 2006). The friends of elderly adults are generally elderly; in one study, 68% of adults over age 75 had no one in their social network younger than 35, suggesting a good deal of age segregation (Uhlenberg & de Jong-Gierveld, 2004). Elderly adults seem fine with this, however: Almost three-fourths of the women Rebecca Adams (1985–1986) interviewed claimed that "old friends are the best friends," even though they continued to make new friends late in life.

Friendships can have a negative side too, however, especially as older adults begin to develop significant health problems and disabilities (Ueno & Adams, 2006). When one friend needs more aid than the other and is able to give less aid in return, this imbalance can strain the relationship. Social psychologists have long emphasized the importance of **equity,** or a balance of contributions and gains, to satisfaction in relationships (Walster, Walster, & Berscheid, 1978). A person who receives more from a relationship than he gives is likely to feel guilty; a person who gives a great deal and receives little in return may feel angry or resentful.

Consistent with equity theory, involvement in relationships in which the balance of emotional support given and received is unequal is associated with lower emotional well-being and more symptoms of depression than involvement in more balanced relationships (Keyes, 2002; Ramos & Wilmoth, 2003). Interestingly, overbenefited, or dependent, friends often experience more distress than underbenefited, or support-giving, friends (Roberto & Scott, 1986). Being able to help other people, or at least to reciprocate help, tends to boost the self-esteem and reduce the depressive symptoms of elderly adults (Krause & Shaw, 2000; Ramos & Wilmoth, 2003). Perhaps because of gender-role norms, men who have a strong desire to be independent react especially negatively to receiving help (Nagumey, Reich, & Newsom, 2004). Perhaps because inequity threatens friendships, older adults usually call on family before friends when they need substantial help (Felton & Berry, 1992; Kendig et al., 1988).

Adult Relationships and Adult Development

We have emphasized throughout this chapter that close attachments to other people are essential to normal cognitive, social, and emotional development. It should not surprise you to

BUILDING STRONGER SOCIAL RELATIONSHIPS

How might knowledge of social relationships be applied to help humans develop more satisfying relationships across the life span? As you have seen, parents who are likely to be insensitive to their infants, as well as infants who have difficult temperaments, are at risk for forming insecure attachments. Naturally there has been a good deal of interest in discovering how to help them form secure attachment bonds (Berlin, 2005). In one study (van den Boom, 1995), low-income mothers in Holland with irritable babies were given a series of three, 2-hour training sessions designed to make them more sensitive and responsive caregivers. Home visitors worked with the mothers during everyday interactions to help them recognize, interpret, and respond appropriately to their infants' signals.

Not only did the trained mothers become more sensitive caregivers, but their infants also were more likely than those of mothers who received no training to be able to soothe themselves when upset, to be securely attached at age 1, and to remain securely attached at age 3. What is more, these children had more positive relationships with peers. It is now clear that parents can be trained in only a few sessions to be more sensitive caregivers and, as a result, to build more secure attachments with even

difficult infants (Bakermans-Kranenburg, van IJzendoorn, & Juffer, 2003; Berlin, 2005; Velderman et al., 2006).

Also promising is toddler–parent psychotherapy based on attachment theory (Cicchetti, Toth, & Rogosch, 2004; Cicchetti, Rogosch, & Toth, 2006). In this approach, depressed or abusive parents are helped to understand how their internal working models (for example, lingering anger at a mother who was not there for them in childhood) affect their interactions with their infants and how they can improve those interactions. Such therapy can change disorganized attachments into secure ones.

Children who are neglected or, worse, rejected by their peers are another group at risk of having relationship difficulties. They can be helped through coaching programs designed to teach them the social and social cognitive skills they lack (Bierman, 2004; Ladd, 1999). In social-skills coaching programs, an adult therapist models or displays social skills, explains why they are useful, allows children to practice them, and offers feedback to help children improve their skills. In a pioneering study, Sherrie Oden and Steven Asher (1977) coached third- and fourth-grade social isolates in how to play, how to take turns and share, how to communicate effectively, and how to provide attention and help to peers. Children

who were coached developed more outgoing and positive social behavior and achieved gains in sociometric status within the classroom.

For some individuals, though, the real problem is a restricted social environment rather than a lack of social skills (Rook, 1984, 1991). Such was the case for the socially isolated elderly people described by Marc Pilisuk and Meredith Minkler (1980). Living in inner-city hotels in San Francisco, these individuals were often prisoners in their rooms because of disability, poverty, and fear of crime. To change this situation, public health nurses began to offer free blood pressure checkups in the lobby of one hotel. As the nurses got to know the residents, they were able to draw them into conversations and to link individuals who had common interests. After about a year, the residents formed their own activities club; organized discussions, film showings, and parties; and were well on their way out of their social isolation. Programs in which home visitors befriend lonely elderly adults can also help (Andrews et al., 2003), as can senior centers that allow isolated elders to meet and form friendships with other isolated elders (Aday, Kehoe, & Farney, 2006). The message may be this: To improve social relationships, change the individual, the social environment, or both as appropriate.

learn, then, that adults are better off in many ways when they enjoy meaningful social relationships. Research tells us this: The quality rather than the quantity of an individual's social relationships is most closely related to that person's sense of well-being or life satisfaction (O'Connor, 1995; Pinquart & Sorensen, 2000). Just as people can feel lonely despite being surrounded by other people, adults apparently can feel deprived of social support even though they receive a lot of it—or they can have restricted social networks yet be highly satisfied with their relationships.

The size of an adult's social network is not nearly as important as whether it includes at least one **confidant**—a spouse, relative, or friend to whom the individual feels especially attached and with whom thoughts and feelings can be shared (de Jong-Gierveld, 1986; Levitt, 1991). For most married adults in our society, spouses are the most important confidants, and the quality of an adult's marriage is one of the strongest influences on overall satisfaction with life (Fleeson, 2004). Men are particularly dependent on their spouses; women rely more on friends, siblings, and children for emotional support (Gurung, Taylor, & Seeman, 2003). Of concern is a recent finding that

the percentage of adults in the United States who say they have no one with whom to discuss important matters increased from 10% in 1985 to almost 25% in 2004 and the number of confidants the average person had dropped from about three to two over this same time span (McPherson, Smith-Lovin, & Brashears, 2006).

Also important to life satisfaction is whether interacting with close companions is rewarding or stressful (Krause, 1995). Perhaps because of their personality traits, people who have positive (or negative) interactions in one relationship tend to have similar experiences in other relationships, creating a constellation of supportive (or stressful) relationships (Krause & Rook, 2003). Relationships with spouses, children, or other significant companions can undermine rather than bolster emotional well-being if they involve mostly negative exchanges (Newsom et al., 2003).

So, a small number of close and harmonious relationships can improve the quality of an adult's life, whereas negative relationships (or none) can make life unpleasant. It is more than that, however: Social support, especially from family members, has positive effects on the cardiovascular, endocrine, and immune systems, keeps blood pressure in the normal range, improves the body's ability to cope with stress, and can contribute to better physical functioning and a longer life, especially in old age (Charles & Mavandadi, 2004; Uchino, Cacioppo, & Keicolt-Glaser, 1996). Close relationships with family and friends can also help people maintain high levels of cognitive functioning (Béland et al., 2005; Zunzunegui et al., 2003). By contrast, both being socially isolated and feeling lonely, whether one is isolated or not, have been linked to cognitive decline and even to signs of dementia (Wilson et al., 2007).

Susan Charles and Shahrzad Mavandadi (2004), noting that emotions and social relationships are closely linked throughout life starting in infancy, suggest that they may have evolved together. They go on to suggest that social relationships affect health and well-being through their effects, good or bad, on emotions and emotion regulation. Thus, separations from caregivers, abuse, and social deprivation raise stress hormone levels in infants and can disrupt neural development and make children more reactive to stress later in life (Gunnar & Quevedo, 2007). By contrast, warm, responsive parenting can help even infants who are highly emotionally reactive to stressors cope better, and close relationships later in life can help people keep their emotions in check and avoid stress-related illnesses (Charles & Mavandadi, 2004). Whatever the mechanisms, and whatever our ages, our well-being and development hinge considerably on the quality of our ties to our fellow humans—particularly on having a close emotional bond with at least one person. It is fitting, then, that we conclude this chapter by illustrating, in the Applications box, approaches to improving social relationships across the life span.

SUMMING UP

▌ Social networks shrink from early to later adulthood; according to Carstensen's socioemotional selectivity theory, this is because older adults, seeing less time ahead, focus on emotional fulfillment rather than acquisition of information for future use.

▌ As revealed by the AAI and other tools, adults have secure, preoccupied, dismissing, or fearful internal working models or attachment styles that are rooted in their early attachment experiences and that affect the quality of their romantic relationships, ability to work productively, relationships with their own children, and adjustment.

▌ Adults continue to value friends, but disability and disease can introduce inequity into relationships, so older adults often turn first to family for help.

▌ Life satisfaction, physical health, and cognitive functioning are maintained better in old age when people have at least one close confidant to help them regulate their emotions.

CRITICAL THINKING

1. Laura Carstensen's socioemotional selectivity theory suggests that adults narrow their social networks with age to better meet

their emotional needs. Develop some alternative hypotheses about why young adults have larger social networks than elderly adults.

2. Focusing on Pete the Preoccupied and Dwight the Dismissing, compare their behavior in past and current relationships and at work.

CHAPTER SUMMARY

14.1 PERSPECTIVES ON RELATIONSHIPS

- The developmental significance of early parent–child relationships is emphasized in the Bowlby–Ainsworth attachment theory, which argues that attachments are built into the human species, develop through an interaction of nature and nurture during a sensitive period, and affect later development by shaping internal working models of self and other.

- The second world of childhood, the peer world, is believed to be especially important by Jean Piaget, who emphasized the reciprocal nature of peer relations, and Judith Rich Harris, who argues that children are socialized more by peers than by parents.

14.2 THE INFANT

- Biologically based emotions such as anger and fear appear in the first year of life, self-conscious emotions in the second year. Attachment figures arouse strong emotions, socialize emotions, and help infants regulate their emotions until they can develop their own emotion regulation strategies.

- Parents typically become attached to infants before or shortly after birth and parent and child quickly establish synchronized routines. Infants progress through phases of undiscriminating social responsiveness, discriminating social responsiveness, active proximity seeking, and goal-corrected partnership. The formation of a first attachment around 6 or 7 months is accompanied by separation anxiety and stranger anxiety, as well as by exploration from a secure base.

- Research using Mary Ainsworth's Strange Situation classifies the quality of parent–infant attachment as secure, resistant, avoidant, or disorganized–disoriented. Harry Harlow demonstrated that contact comfort is more important than feeding in attachment; secure attachments are also associated with sensitive, responsive parenting. Infant characteristics (temperament and achievement of person permanence) also contribute.

- Repeated long-term separations and social deprivation can make it difficult for an infant to form normal attachments, though recovery is evident. Attending day care normally does not disrupt parent–child attachments, although quality of care matters. Secure attachments contribute to later cognitive and social competence, but attachment quality often changes over time, and insecurely attached infants are not doomed to a lifetime of poor relationships.

- Infants are interested in peers and become increasingly able to coordinate their own activity with that of their small companions; by 18 months, they participate in complementary interactive exchanges and form friendships.

14.3 THE CHILD

- From ages 2 to 12, children participate in goal-corrected partnerships with their parents and spend increasing amounts of time with peers, especially same-sex ones, engaging in increasingly social and imaginative play, including social pretend play, and later in organized games and hobbies.

- Physical attractiveness, cognitive ability, social competence, and emotion regulation skills contribute to popular—rather than rejected, neglected, or controversial—sociometric status. Children who are rejected by their peers or who have no friends are especially at risk for future problems.

14.4 THE ADOLESCENT

- During adolescence, same-sex and cross-sex friendships increasingly involve emotional intimacy and self-disclosure, and a transition is made from same-sex cliques, to mixed-sex cliques and larger crowds, and finally to dating relationships, which at first meet self-esteem and status needs and later become more truly affectionate. Although susceptibility to negative peer pressure peaks around age 14 or 15, peers are more often a positive than a negative force in development, unless poor relationships with parents lead to association with an antisocial crowd.

14.5 THE ADULT

- Adult social networks shrink with age, possibly because of increased socioemotional selectivity. Adults have secure, preoccupied, dismissing, or fearful internal working models that appear to be rooted in their early attachment experiences and that affect their romantic relationships, approaches to work, attachments with their own children, and adjustment.

- Although adults are highly involved with their spouses or romantic partners, they continue to value friendships, especially long-lasting and equitable ones. Having at least one confidant has beneficial effects on life satisfaction, as well as on physical health and cognitive functioning.

KEY TERMS

attachment theory 406
attachment 406
imprinting 407
internal working model 407
peer 408
self-conscious emotion 409
social referencing 410
emotion regulation 410
synchronized routines 411
goal-corrected partnership 412
separation anxiety 412
stranger anxiety 412
secure base 412
Strange Situation 412
secure attachment 412

resistant attachment 412
avoidant attachment 413
disorganized–disoriented
    attachment 413
contact comfort 414
pretend play 422
social pretend play 423
sociometric techniques 424
clique 427
crowd 427
social convoy 430
socioemotional selectivity
    theory 430
equity 433
confidant 434

MEDIA RESOURCES

BOOK COMPANION WEBSITE

academic.cengage.com/psychology/sigelman
Find online quizzes, flash cards, animations, video clips, experiments, interactive assessments, and other helpful study aids for this text at **academic.cengage.com/psychology/sigelman.** You can also connect directly to the following sites:

ABOUT.COM PSYCHOLOGY: ATTACHMENT STYLES

The About.com Psychology website on attachment styles offers the visitor an excellent overview of numerous types of attachments. Unique to this site are tables that describe how characteristics of each type of attachment are manifested in childhood and adulthood.

ADULT ATTACHMENT LAB

This University of California at Davis-housed site contains links to many respected attachment research labs and numerous research publications on attachment.

ONLINE DATING SERVICES

Even those not looking for a date or a mate might be interested in the newest fad in dating, the online service. Of particular interest are the types of characteristics that each of the services uses to sort for potential partners.

SOCIAL AND EMOTIONAL DEVELOPMENT

This PBS-sponsored site offers visitors access to links on a wide variety of topics related to early social development including milestones in social and emotional development, self-esteem and identity, and self-control.

UNDERSTANDING THE DATA: EXERCISES ON THE WEB

academic.cengage.com/psychology/sigelman
For additional insight on the data presented in this chapter, try out the exercise for this figure at **academic.cengage.com/psychology/sigelman:**

> **Figure 14.6** Frequency of activities engaged in by preschool children of different ages

CENGAGENOW

academic.cengage.com/login
Go to **academic.cengage.com/login** to link to CengageNOW, your online study tool. First take the Pre-Test for this chapter to get your Personalized Study Plan, which will identify topics you need to review and direct you to online resources. Then take the Post-Test to determine what concepts you have mastered and what you still need work on.

© Ronnie Kaufman/Corbis

15 CHAPTER

The Family

▪ ▪ ▪

For good or bad, we are all bound to our families. We are born into them, work our way toward adulthood in them, start our own as adults, and continue to be bound to them in old age. We are part of our families, and they are part of us. James Garbarino (1992) has gone so far as to call the family the "basic unit of human experience" (p. 7).

This chapter examines the family and its central roles in human development throughout the life span. How has the family changed in recent years? How do infants, children, and adolescents experience family life, and how are they affected by their relationships with parents and siblings? How is adult development affected by such family transitions as marrying, becoming a parent, watching children leave the nest, and becoming a grandparent? Finally, what are the implications of the diversity that characterizes today's family lifestyles—and of such decisions as remaining childless or divorcing?

15.1 | UNDERSTANDING THE FAMILY

The family is a system—and a system within other systems. It is also a changing system—and a changing system in a changing world.

The Family as a System within Systems

Debate rages in the United States today about whether the marriage that forms the basis of a family must be between husband and wife or can be between two men or two women. This illustrates that it may not be possible to define *family* in a way that applies across all cultures and eras; many forms of family life have worked and continue to work for humans (Coontz, 2000a; Leeder, 2004). However we define it, proponents of **family systems theory** conceptualize a family as a system. This means that the family, like the human body, is truly a whole consisting of interrelated parts, each of which affects and is affected by every other part, and each of which contributes to the functioning of the whole (Bornstein & Sawyer, 2006; Parke & Buriel, 2006). Moreover, the family is a dynamic system—a self-organizing system that adapts itself to changes in its members and to changes in its environment (Maccoby, 2007). In the past, developmentalists did not adopt this family systems perspective. They typically focused almost entirely on the mother–child relationship, assuming that the only process of interest within the family was the mother's influence on the child's development.

The **nuclear family** typically consists of father, mother, and at least one child. Even a simple man, woman, and infant "system" can be complex. An infant interacting with her mother is already involved in a process of reciprocal influence: The baby's smile is greeted by a smile from Mom, and Mom's smile is reciprocated by the infant's grin. However, the presence of both parents means that we must consider husband–wife, mother–infant, and father–infant relationships (Belsky, 1981). Every individual and every relationship within the family affects every other individual and relationship through reciprocal influence.

Now think about how complex the family system becomes if we add another child (or two or six) to it. We must then understand the husband–wife relationship, the relationships between each parent and each of their children, and the relationships between siblings. The family now becomes a system with subsystems—in this case the marital, parent–child, and sibling subsystems (Parke & Buriel, 2006). In addition, researchers have begun to focus on another subsystem, **coparenting,** the ways in which the two parents coordinate their parenting and function well (or poorly) as a team in relation to their children (J. McHale et al., 2002; Parke & Buriel, 2006). Do they talk to each other about the children, are they consistent in the rules they set, do they back one another up—or do they contradict one another, compete for their children's affection, and undermine each other's parenting? Mutually supportive coparenting can make a big difference in development, beyond the impact of a close marital relationship.

Now consider the complexity of an **extended family household,** in which parents and their children live with other kin—some combination of grandparents, siblings, aunts, uncles, nieces, and nephews. Extended family households are common in many cultures of the world (Ruggles, 1994), and humans may have evolved to involve the whole "village," or at least many members of the extended family, rather than just the mother and father in raising children (Hrdy, 2005). In the United States, African Americans, Hispanic Americans, and other ethnic minorities tend to place more emphasis on extended family bonds than European Americans do (Parke & Buriel, 2006). For example, economically disadvantaged single mothers can obtain needed help with child care and social support by living with their mothers (Burton, 1990; Oberlander, Black, & Starr, 2007). Even when members of the

Extended families have many paths of reciprocal influence.

extended family live in their own nuclear family households, they often interact frequently and share responsibility for raising children, often to the benefit of the children.

The family is also a *system within other systems*; whether it is of the nuclear or the extended type, it does not exist in a vacuum. Urie Bronfenbrenner's bioecological model (see Chapter 1) emphasizes that the family is a system embedded in larger social systems such as a neighborhood, a community, a subculture, and a broader culture (Bronfenbrenner & Morris, 2006). The family experience in our culture is different from that in cultures where new brides become underlings in the households of their mothers-in-law or where men can have several wives. There is an almost infinite variety of family forms and family contexts in the world and a correspondingly wide range of developmental experiences within the family.

The Family as a Changing System

It would be difficult enough to study the family as a system if it kept the same members and continued to perform the same activities for as long as it existed. However, family membership changes as new children are born and as grown children leave the nest. Moreover, each family member is a developing individual, and the relationships between husband and wife, parent and child, and sibling and sibling change in systematic ways over time. Because the family is truly a system, changes in family membership and changes in any individual or relationship within the family affect the dynamics of the whole.

The earliest theories of family development featured the concept of a **family life cycle**—a sequence of changes in family composition, roles, and relationships from the time people marry until they die (Hill & Rodgers, 1964). Family theorist Evelyn Duvall (1977), for example, outlined eight stages of the family life cycle, from the married couple without children through the family with children to the aging family. In each stage, family members were said to play distinctive roles—

husband, wife, daughter, and so on—and carry out distinctive developmental tasks—for example, establishing a satisfying relationship in the newlywed phase, adjusting to the demands of new parenthood in the childbearing phase, and adapting to the departure of children in the "launching" phase.

In this chapter, we look at the effect of these family transitions on adults, and we examine how the child's experience of the family changes as she develops. You will see, however, that an increasing number of people do not experience this traditional family life cycle. They remain single or childless, they marry multiple times, or they otherwise deviate from a scenario in which a man and woman form a nuclear family, raise children, and grow old together (Patterson & Hastings, 2007). As a result, many family researchers reject the overly simple concept of the family life cycle with its set stages. However, they have embraced the concept that we lead "linked lives" across the life course—that our development is intertwined with that of other family members (Elder & Shanahan, 2006). They have also embraced the concept that families function as systems and, like the individuals in them, develop and change over the life span.

A Changing System in a Changing World

Not only is the family a system embedded within systems, and not only is it a developing system, but the world in which it is embedded is ever changing. During the second half of the 20th century, several dramatic social changes altered the makeup of the typical family and the quality of family experience. Drawing on analyses of U.S. Census Bureau data and other surveys, we will highlight some of these trends (see Bryant et al., 2006; Teachman, 2000; U.S. Census Bureau, 2006; Whitehead & Popenoe, 2003; Wilmoth & Longino, 2006):

1. *More single adults.* More adults are living as singles today than in the past; often they are living with a partner or a partner and children but are unmarried. Do not conclude that marriage is out of style: more than 90% of adults can still be expected to marry at some time in their lives (Whitehead & Popenoe, 2003). The percentage of the population that is married at any given time has been dropping, though, especially among African Americans with little education (Schoen & Cheng, 2006).

2. *Postponed marriage.* Many adults are not rejecting marriage but are simply delaying it while they pursue educational and career goals. The average age of first marriage decreased during the first half of the 20th century, but it has since risen to about 25 for women and 27 for men (Whitehead & Popenoe, 2003). This has meant that more babies—about 35%—are being born outside marriage (U.S. Census Bureau, 2006).

3. *Fewer children.* Today's adults are also having fewer children and therefore spend fewer years of their lives raising children. Increasing numbers of young women are also remaining childless; in 1998, 19% of women ages 40 to 44 were childless, compared with 10% in 1980 (Whitehead & Popenoe, 2003).

4. *More women working.* In 1950, 12% of married women with children younger than 6 years worked outside the home; in 2005, the figure was about 60%, a truly dramatic social change (U.S. Census Bureau, 2006). Fewer children today have a mother whose full-time job is that of homemaker.

5. *More divorce.* The divorce rate has also increased over the past several decades, although it leveled off around 1980. At least 4 in 10 newly married couples can expect to divorce (Schoen & Canudas-Romo, 2006).

6. *More single-parent families.* Partly because of more out-of-wedlock births, but mostly because of the rise in divorce, more children live in single-parent families. In 1960, only 9% of children lived with one parent, usually a widowed one (Whitehead & Popenoe, 2003); in 2002, 23% of children younger than 18 years lived with their mothers only and 5% lived with their fathers only (U.S. Census Bureau, 2006).

7. *More children living in poverty.* The higher number of single-parent families has meant an increase in the proportion of children living in poverty. About 17% of children in the United States live in poverty today (U.S. Census Bureau, 2006). Fully 33% of African American children and almost 29% of Hispanic American children are poor.

8. *More remarriages.* As more married couples have divorced, more adults have been remarrying. Often they form new, **reconstituted families** that include at least a parent, a stepparent, and a child; sometimes they blend multiple children from two families into a new family.

9. *More years without children.* Because modern couples are compressing their childbearing into a shorter time span, because some divorced adults do not remarry, and mainly because people are living longer, adults today spend more of their later years as couples—or, especially if they are women, as single adults—without children in their homes (Johnson & Troll, 1996). Of adults age 65 and older, 30% live alone, 55% live with a spouse or partner, and 15% live with someone else, such as a sibling or adult child (U.S. Census Bureau, 2006).

10. *More multigenerational families.* As a result of these same trends, more children today than in the past know their grandparents and even their great-grandparents, parent–child and grandparent–child relationships are lasting longer, and multigenerational bonds are becoming more important (Bengtson, 2001). As three- and even four-generation families have become more common, the result has been dubbed the **beanpole family,** characterized by more generations, but smaller ones, than in the past (Bengtson, Rosenthal, & Burton, 1990).

11. *Fewer caregivers for aging adults.* Smaller families with fewer children, increases in the numbers of adults living alone, increased longevity, and the large Baby Boom generation poised to enter old age mean that more and more aging adults need care from relatives and have fewer relatives to provide it (E. Brody, 2004).

Clearly, many important changes have been occurring. Some observers view these changes as evidence of a "decline of marriage and the family," noting the negative effects on children of increased divorce, single-parent families, and poverty, and the problem of more elderly adults having fewer children to support them. Observers also worry because most Americans now view marriage as an institution whose purpose is more to meet the emotional needs of adults than to raise children (Whitehead & Popenoe, 2003).

Other scholars, though, find good news with the bad in these trends (Teachman, 2000; L. White & Rogers, 2000). For example, postponing marriage improves its chances of success, men's and women's roles in the family are more equal than they used to be, more children have relationships with their grandparents and great-grandparents, and families are better off financially with two wage earners than with only one. From this perspective, the family is not dying; it is just different. It can even be characterized as a highly "adaptable institution" in that it has survived despite many social changes that could have done it in (Amato et al., 2003).

Whether it is in decline or not, the American family is more diverse than ever before. Our stereotyped image of the family—the traditional, stereotypical nuclear family with a breadwinner–father, a full-time housewife–mother, and children—has become just that: a stereotype. By one estimate, about 45% of families in 1960, but only 12% of families by 1995, conformed to this pattern (Hernandez, 1997). Today only about one-fourth of all households are married couples with children, most of which are dual-earner families (U.S. Census Bureau, 2006). Clearly, we must broaden our image of the family to include the many dual-career, single-parent, reconstituted, childless, and other nontraditional families that exist today. We must also avoid assuming that families that do not fit the stereotypical family model are deficient.

SUMMING UP

▪ Family systems theorists view the family as a system with subsystems, embedded in other systems (as Bronfenbrenner emphasizes), changing over time (as family life cycle theorists note), and changing in a changing world.

▪ Changes in the last half century include trends toward more single adults, postponed marriage, fewer children, more women working, more divorce, more single-parent families, more children in poverty, more reconstituted families, more years without children, more multigenerational families, and fewer caregivers for aging adults.

▪ Given increased diversity of family forms, the stereotypical nuclear family is hard to find.

CRITICAL THINKING

1. If present trends continue, do you think the family will be stronger or weaker in 2050 than it is now? What statistics would you cite to make your case?

We begin this look at family development by adopting a child's perspective and tracing a child's development in the family from infancy to adolescence. Later, we will adopt the perspective of this child's parents and see how the events of the family life cycle look to them.

Mother–Infant and Father–Infant Relationships

Once developmentalists took seriously the idea that the family is a system, they discovered the existence of fathers and began to look more carefully at how both mothers and fathers interact with their children and at what each parent contributes to a child's development. They have also asked how mothers' and fathers' roles have changed as more mothers have gone to work and as divorce rates have climbed.

Gender stereotypes would suggest that fathers are not cut out to care for infants and young children; however, the evidence suggests that they are (Lamb & Tamis-Lemonda, 2004; Parke, 1996). Researchers repeatedly find that fathers and mothers are more similar than different in the ways they interact with infants and young children. For example, when mothers and fathers are observed feeding their babies, fathers prove to be no less able than mothers to perform this caregiving task effectively and to ensure that the milk is consumed (Parke & Sawin, 1976). And, fathers, like mothers, provide sensitive parenting, become objects of attachment, and serve as secure bases for their infants' explorations (Cox et al., 1992; Schoppe-Sullivan et al., 2006). We have no basis for thinking that moth-

Fathers are just as capable as mothers of sensitive, responsive parenting.

© Ariel Skelley/Corbis

ers are uniquely qualified to parent or that men are hopelessly inept around babies.

However, that fathers are capable of sensitive parenting does not mean that they play the same roles as mothers in their children's lives. Fathers and mothers differ in both the quantity and the style of the parenting they provide (Lamb & Tamis-Lemonda, 2004; Marsiglio et al., 2000), and we can ask how nature and nurture contribute to these differences. Consider first differences in quantity: Mothers spend more time with children than fathers do (Bianchi, 2000). This gender difference is common across cultures, causing some to argue that it has been built into our genes during the course of evolution; it may even be related to the biological fact that mothers are more certain their children are theirs than fathers are (Bjorklund & Pellegrini, 2002).

True, fathers today are more involved with their children than fathers of the past were (Marsiglio et al., 2000; Pleck & Masciadrelli, 2004). Some are even sharing responsibility for child care equally with their spouses rather than just "helping," especially if they hold egalitarian views about gender roles (Bulanda, 2004; Deutsch, 2001). Yet there is still a gap.

Now consider differences in style or type of parenting provided. Mothers and fathers differ in their typical styles of interacting with young children. When mothers interact with their babies, a large proportion of their time is devoted to caregiving: offering food, changing diapers, wiping noses, and so on. Fathers spend much of their time with children in playful interaction. They specialize in tickling, poking, bouncing, and surprising infants, whereas mothers hold, talk to, and play quietly with infants (Laflamme, Pomerleau, & Malcuit, 2002; Neville & Parke, 1997). Yet fathers are able to adopt a "motherlike" caregiver role if they have primary responsibility for their children, so their playful parenting may be more about being in the role of the "backup" parent than about being male rather than female (Phares, 1999). It seems, then, that both nature (evolution) and nurture (societal gender-role norms) contribute to mother–father differences in parental involvement and styles of interacting with young children.

In view of the roles that fathers play in their children's lives, what are their contributions to child development? Fathers contribute to healthy development by supporting their children financially, whether they live together or not (Marsiglio et al., 2000). They also contribute by being warm and effective parents, just as mothers do. Babies are likely to be more socially competent if they are securely attached to both parents than if they are securely attached to just one (Main & Weston, 1981). In addition, children whose fathers are warm and involved with them tend to become high achievers in school (Cabrera et al., 2000). A father's tendency to challenge his young children during play, egging them on to take risks, may be particularly important, breeding a secure attachment style later in life and encouraging exploration (Grossmann et al., 2002b). Finally, children generally have fewer psychological disorders and problems if their fathers are caring, involved, and effective parents than if they are not (Cabrera et al., 2000; Marsiglio et al., 2000).

Mothers, Fathers, and Infants: The System at Work

We now need to view the new family as a three-person system functioning in a social context (Bornstein & Sawyer, 2006). The mother–child relationship cannot be understood without considering the father; nor can the father–child relationship be understood without taking the mother into account. This is because parents have **indirect effects** on their children through their ability to influence the behavior of their spouses. More generally, indirect effects within the family are instances in which the relationship or interaction between two individuals is modified by the behavior or attitudes of a third family member.

Fathers indirectly influence the mother–infant relationship in many ways. For example, mothers who have close, supportive relationships with their husbands tend to interact more patiently and sensitively with their babies than do mothers who are experiencing marital tension and who feel that they are raising their children largely without help (Cox et al., 1992; Lamb & Tamis-Lemonda, 2004). Meanwhile, mothers indirectly affect the father–infant relationship. For example, fathers are more likely to become involved in their children's education when their wives are involved (Flouri & Buchanan, 2003), and fathers who have just had arguments with their wives are less supportive and engaged when they interact with their children than fathers who have just had pleasant conversations with their wives (Kitzmann, 2000). As you can imagine, infant development goes best when parents get along well and truly coparent, or work as a team (Parke & Buriel, 2006). When parents compete rather than cooperate—for example, when one parent tries to capture the child's attention while she is being engaged by the other parent—their infants may show signs of insecure attachment or may become securely attached to one parent but be blocked from enjoying close relationships with both parents (Caldera & Lindsey, 2006).

SUMMING UP

- Mothers and fathers are tremendously important forces in human development. Although they spend less time than mothers with their children, and often adopt a playful rather than a caregiving role, fathers are capable of sensitive and responsive parenting and contribute in many ways to their children's development.

- Both mothers and fathers affect their children not only directly but also through indirect effects on their spouses. Overall, children are best off when the marital relationship is solid and couples provide mutual support and encouragement that allow both to be more sensitive and responsive parents.

CRITICAL THINKING

1. Parents are not the only members of the family who can have indirect effects on other family members. Imagine how Little Raoul could have both (a) direct positive effects on his father and (b) indirect positive effects on his father through his effects on his mother.

15.3 | THE CHILD

As children reach age 2 or 3, parents continue to be caregivers and playmates, but they also become more concerned with teaching their offspring how (and how not) to behave, using some approach to child rearing and discipline to achieve this end. Siblings also serve as socialization agents and become an important part of the child's experience of the family.

Parenting Styles

How can I be a good parent? Certainly this question is uppermost in most parents' minds. You can go far in understanding which parenting styles are effective by considering just two dimensions of parenting: acceptance–responsiveness and demandingness–control (Darling & Steinberg, 1993; Maccoby & Martin, 1983; Schaefer, 1959; and see Maccoby, 2007).

Parental **acceptance–responsiveness** refers to the extent to which parents are supportive, sensitive to their children's needs, and willing to provide affection and praise when their children meet their expectations. Accepting, responsive parents are affectionate and often smile at, praise, and encourage their children, although they also let children know when they misbehave. Less accepting and responsive parents are often quick to criticize, belittle, punish, or ignore their children and rarely communicate to children that they are loved and valued.

Demandingness–control (sometimes called *permissiveness–restrictiveness*) refers to how much control over decisions lies with the parent as opposed to with the child. Controlling and demanding parents set rules, expect their children to follow them, and monitor their children closely to ensure that the rules are followed. Less controlling and demanding parents (often called *permissive parents*) make fewer demands and allow their children a great deal of autonomy in exploring the environment, expressing their opinions and emotions, and making decisions about their activities.

By crossing the acceptance and demandingness dimensions, we have four basic patterns of child rearing to consider, as shown in ■ Figure 15.1:

1. **Authoritarian parenting.** This is a restrictive parenting style combining high demandingness–control and low acceptance–responsiveness. Parents impose many rules, expect strict obedience, rarely explain why the child should comply with rules, and often rely on power tactics such as physical punishment to gain compliance.

2. **Authoritative parenting.** Authoritative parents are more flexible; they are demanding and exert control, but they are also accepting and responsive. They set clear rules and consistently enforce them, but they also explain the rationales for their rules and restrictions, are responsive to their children's needs and points of view, and involve their children in family decision making. They are reasonable and democratic in their approach; although it is clear that they are in charge, they communicate respect for their children.

Parental acceptance–responsiveness

	High	Low
High	**Authoritative** Reasonable demands, consistently enforced, with sensitivity to and acceptance of the child	**Authoritarian** Many rules and demands; few explanations and little sensitivity to the child's needs and perspectives
Low	**Permissive** Few rules and demands; children are allowed much freedom by indulgent parents	**Neglectful** Few rules and demands; parents are uninvolved and insensitive to their children's needs

Parental demandingness–control

■ **FIGURE 15.1** The acceptance–responsiveness and demandingness–control dimensions of parenting. Which combination best describes your parents' approach? SOURCE: From E. E. Maccoby & J. A. Martin, Socialization in the context of the family: Parent-child interaction. In E. M. Hetherington (Ed.), P. H. Mussen (Editor in Chief), *Handbook of child psychology: Vol.4, socialization, personality, and social development* (4th Ed.). Copyright © 1983 by Wiley. Reprinted with permission.

3. **Permissive parenting.** This style is high in acceptance–responsiveness but low in demandingness–control. Permissive parents are indulgent; they have relatively few rules and make relatively few demands, encourage children to express their feelings and impulses, and rarely exert control over their behavior.

4. **Neglectful parenting.** Finally, parents who combine low demandingness–control and low acceptance–responsiveness are relatively uninvolved in their children's upbringing. They seem not to care much about their children and may even reject them—or else they are so overwhelmed by their own problems that they cannot devote sufficient energy to setting and enforcing rules (Maccoby & Martin, 1983).

We assume that you have no difficulty deciding that parental acceptance and responsiveness are preferable to parental rejection and insensitivity. As you have seen in this book, warm, responsive parenting is associated with secure attachments to parents, academic competence, high self-esteem, good social skills, peer acceptance, a strong sense of morality, and many other virtues. By contrast, lack of parental acceptance and affection contributes to depression and other psychological problems (Ge et al., 1996).

The degree of demandingness and control is also important. The authoritarian, authoritative, and permissive parenting styles were originally identified and defined by Diana Baumrind (1967, 1977, 1991). In a pioneering longitudinal study, Baumrind found that children raised by authoritative parents were the best adjusted: They were cheerful, socially responsible, self-reliant, achievement oriented, and cooperative with adults and peers. Children of authoritarian parents tended to be moody and seemingly unhappy, easily annoyed,

relatively aimless, and unpleasant to be around. Finally, children of permissive parents were often impulsive, aggressive, self-centered, rebellious, without self-control, aimless, and low in independence and achievement, although a warm, permissive style can be effective with an older, more independent child.

Subsequent research has shown that the worst developmental outcomes are associated with a neglectful, uninvolved style of parenting. Children of neglectful parents display behavioral problems such as aggression and frequent temper tantrums as early as age 3 (Miller et al., 1993). They tend to become hostile and antisocial adolescents who abuse alcohol and drugs and get in trouble (Lamborn et al., 1991; Weiss & Schwarz, 1996). Parents who provide little guidance and communicate that they do not care breed children who are resentful and prone to strike back at their uncaring parents and other authority figures.

In short, children develop best when they have love and limits. If they are indulged or neglected and given little guidance, they will not learn self-control and may become selfish and lacking in direction. If they receive too much guidance, as the children of authoritarian parents do, they will have few opportunities to learn self-reliance and may lack confidence in their own decision-making abilities. The link between authoritative parenting and positive developmental outcomes is evident in most ethnic groups and socioeconomic groups studied to date in the United States (Glasgow et al., 1997; Steinberg, 2001) and in a variety of other cultures (Scott, Scott, & McCabe, 1991; Vazsonyi, Hibbert, & Snider, 2003). Yet the effectiveness of different parenting approaches still differs depending on the cultural or subcultural context in which they are used, as illustrated in the Explorations box on page 444.

Social Class, Economic Hardship, and Parenting

Middle-class and lower-class parents as groups have been found to pursue different goals, emphasize different values, and rely on different parenting styles in raising children—with some important implications. Compared with middle-class and upper-class parents, lower-class and working-class parents tend to stress obedience and respect for authority, be more restrictive and authoritarian, reason with their children less frequently, and show less warmth and affection (Conger & Dogan, 2007; McLoyd, 1990). Although you will find a range of parenting styles in any social group, these average social-class differences in parenting have been observed in many cultures and across racial and ethnic groups in the United States. Moreover, they help explain social class differences in developmental outcomes such as school achievement, adjustment, and life success (Conger & Dogan, 2007).

Why might these socioeconomic differences in parenting exist? One possibility is that personal traits that influence socioeconomic status (SES) and life outcomes are passed genetically from parents to children (Conger & Dogan, 2007). A genetically influenced trait such as aggression, for example, could help explain both a parent's difficulty holding jobs and a child's difficulty succeeding in school.

PARENTING IN CULTURAL AND SUBCULTURAL CONTEXT

Although much research tells us that an authoritative style of parenting is effective in a variety of cultural contexts, it remains important to understand parenting in its cultural and subcultural context. Parents of different cultures and ethnic backgrounds are socialized to hold different beliefs and values about child rearing that shape their parenting practices and, in turn, affect their children's development (MacPhee, Fritz, & Miller-Heyl, 1996; McLoyd et al., 2000; Parke & Buriel, 2006; Rothbaum & Trommsdorff, 2007). For example, some traditional Native American groups such as the Mayan and Navajo Indians believe that the freedom and autonomy of young children must be respected. As a result, although parents may try to persuade young children to do things, they feel it would be wrong to force them (Rogoff, 2003). Their children seem to do fine with this relatively permissive parenting style, learning at an early age to cooperate with their parents and with other people.

By contrast, Asian and African American parents sometimes rely on a more authoritarian approach to parenting than most European American parents would use, but get good results with it (Parke & Buriel, 2006). Ruth Chao (1994, 2000), for example, was puzzled by findings suggesting that Asian students do no better in school when their parents use an authoritative style of parenting than when they use an authoritarian style, even though the authoritative style is associated with higher achievement in other ethnic groups (Steinberg, Dornbusch, & Brown, 1992). Chao's analysis led her to conclude that what Chinese parents do is not well described by the Western concept of authoritarian parenting. These parents offer their children clear and specific guidelines for behavior, believing that this is the best way to express their love and train their children properly. Although the style seems controlling or authoritarian to European American eyes, Chinese parents and children view it as warm, caring parenting and children respond well to it as a result (see also Rothbaum & Trommsdorff, 2007). Similarly, the use of physical, coercive discipline (short of abuse) is not as strongly linked to aggression and antisocial behavior among African American youths as it is among European Americans—probably because it is

viewed by African American children as a sign that their parents care rather than as a sign of hostility and rejection (Deater-Deckard et al., 1996; Deater-Deckard, Dodge, & Sorbring, 2005).

Is the acceptability of a parenting approach in a particular cultural context the key to its success then? This hypothesis was put directly to the test by Jennifer Lansford and her colleagues (2005). Interviews with mothers and children and adolescents in six countries were conducted to study the relationship between physical discipline and child outcomes as a function of how common the use of physical punishment was in the country. Mothers were asked how often they used various discipline strategies, and both mothers and children were asked how often parents in general use these strategies. The study focused on three punitive methods: spanking or slapping, grabbing or shaking, and beating up.

Receiving lots of physical punishment rather than little was more closely associated with having behavior problems (aggression and anxiety) in countries where physical punishment was rare than in countries where it was widely used by mothers and perceived as normal by parents and children. The graph shows the effects of frequent or infrequent use of physical punishment in relation to children's average scores on an aggressive behavior checklist in each of the six countries studied. In Thailand, where physical punishment is rarely used, there was a strong relationship between being physically punished and being aggressive, whereas in Kenya, where physical punishment is commonly used, children who were physically punished frequently were not much more aggressive than chil-

dren who were hardly ever physically punished. Children's perceptions of how normal physical punishment is proved to be more important than their mothers' perceptions. When children view spanking as something that most parents do, it may not be as emotionally upsetting to them as being singled out for a practice that no other children in their social world experience.

In this study, frequent use of physical discipline was correlated to some extent with child aggression and anxiety in all of the countries. As a result, we would continue to recommend against heavy reliance on physical discipline, just as we would continue to recommend in favor of authoritative parenting, in most settings. Still, it is important to understand parenting in its cultural context and appreciate that parenting practices can be more or less effective depending on how they are interpreted by those who use and experience them.

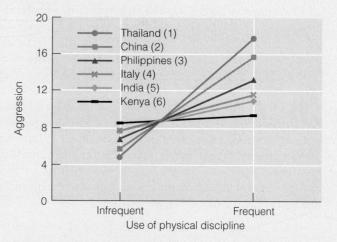

Frequent use of physical discipline is more strongly linked to high levels of aggression in children in cultures like Thailand where the use of physical discipline is infrequent, than in cultures like Kenya where physical discipline is widely used and accepted as normal. Numbers in parentheses after the countries show their ranking based on how frequently mothers report using physical discipline (with 1 being the country in which it is least normal and 6 being the country in which it is most normal).

SOURCE: From J. E. Lansford, L. Chang, K. A. Dodge, P. S. Malone, P. Oburu, K. Palmerus, D. Bacchini, C. Pastorelli, A. S. Bombi, A. Zelli, S. Tapanya, N. Chaudhary, K. Deater-Deckard, B. Manke, & N. Quinn, Physical discipline and children's adjustment: Cultural normativeness as a moderator, *Child Development*, 76, pp. 1234–1246 (Figure 6 top graph, p. 1242). Copyright © 2005 Blackwell Publishing. Reprinted with permission.

Another explanation centers on the negative effects of financial stresses (Conger & Dogan, 2007; McLoyd, 1990). Rand Conger and his associates (1992, 1995, 2002), for example, have shown that parents experiencing financial problems (economic pressure) tend to become depressed, which increases conflict between them. Marital conflict, in turn, disrupts each partner's ability to be a supportive, involved, and effective parent—another example of indirect effects within the family. This breakdown in parenting then contributes to negative child outcomes such as low self-esteem, poor school performance, poor peer relations, and adjustment problems such as depression and aggression, as summarized in ■ **Figure 15.2.**

Stresses are magnified for families living below the poverty line or moving in and out of poverty as a result of economic crises. Parents living in poverty tend to be restrictive, punitive, and inconsistent, sometimes to the point of being abusive and neglectful (Brooks-Gunn, Britto, & Brady, 1999; Seccombe, 2000). In high-crime poverty areas, parents may feel the need to be more authoritarian and controlling to protect their children from danger (Taylor et al., 2000). In addition, parents and children may be coping with a physical environment characterized by pollution, noise, and crowded, unsafe living conditions and a social environment characterized by family instability and violence (Evans, 2004). The effects of poverty on child development include health problems, emotional and behavioral problems, and school failure (Bradley & Corwyn, 2002; Evans, 2004).

In addition to personal traits and financial stress, a third explanation of social class differences in parenting and child outcomes is that low SES parents have fewer resources to invest in their children's development than high SES parents do (Conger & Dogan, 2007). Wealthier parents can invest more in getting their children a good education, providing books, computers, and other learning materials in the home, and taking their children to cultural events, and they may be able to devote more time to stimulating their children's minds as well (Conger & Dogan, 2007).

Finally, high and low SES parents may emphasize different qualities in preparing their children for the world of work based on their own work experiences. Sociologist Melvin Kohn (1969) observed that parents from lower socioeconomic groups tend to emphasize obedience to authority figures because that is what is required in jobs like their own. Middle-class and upper-class parents may reason with their children and foster initiative and creativity more because these are the attributes that count for business executives, professionals, and other white-collar workers.

In sum, low family socioeconomic status may be associated with poor developmental outcomes because of genes that contribute to both parents' low socioeconomic status and children's poor life outcomes, economic stresses that result in use of a harsher, more authoritarian parenting style, limited investment of resources, financial and otherwise, in children's development, and an orientation toward preparing children to obey a boss rather than be the boss.

Models of Influence in the Family

In thinking about influences within the family, we will bet that you, like most developmental scientists, think first about parents affecting children. But consider three different models of influence in the family: the parent effects, child effects, and transactional models.

Parent Effects Model

The study of human development has been guided through most of its history by a simple **parent effects model** of family influence (Maccoby, 2007). This model assumes that influences run one way, from parent (particularly mother) to child. You have just reviewed research demonstrating effects of parenting styles on child development. But what if you turn things around: Could it be that a child's behavior influences the style of parenting his parents adopt and that what appear to be parent effects are instead child effects?

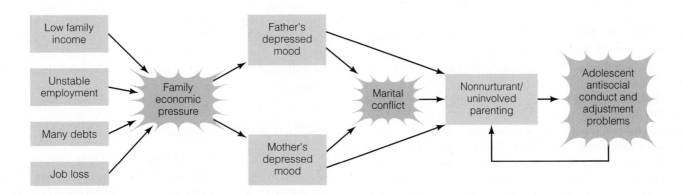

■ **FIGURE 15.2** A model of the relationship among family economic stress, patterns of parenting, and adolescent adjustment.
SOURCE: Adapted from Conger et al. (1992).

Child Effects Model

A **child effects model** of family influence highlights the influences of children on their parents (Crouter & Booth, 2003; Sanson, Hemphill, & Smart, 2004). One good example of a child effect is the influence of a child's age and competence on the style of parenting used with that child. For example, infants in their first year of life require and elicit sensitive care, whereas older infants who are asserting their wills and toddling here and there force parents to provide more instruction and set more limits (Fagot & Kavanaugh, 1993). Normally, parents then become less restrictive as their children mature and gradually, with parental guidance, become capable of making their own decisions (Steinberg, 2002).

Now consider the possibility that a child's personality influences the parenting she receives. Is it not possible that easygoing, manageable children cause their parents to be warm and authoritative? Could not difficult, stubborn, and aggressive children help mold parents who are rejecting rather than accepting—and who either rule with an authoritarian iron hand or throw up their hands in defeat and become neglectful?

Recall the description in Chapter 13 of the discipline techniques of induction, power assertion, and love withdrawal. In an early demonstration of child effects, Barbara Keller and Richard Bell (1979) set out to challenge the finding that a parent's use of induction (explanations emphasizing the consequences of a child's behavior for other people) fosters moral maturity. Is it not possible instead, they reasoned, that children who are already "good" are more likely than less responsive children to elicit inductive explanations from adults? Keller and Bell had female college students attempt to convince 9-year-old girls to behave altruistically (for example, to spend more time sewing a pillow for a handicapped child than sewing a pillow for themselves). The girls had been coached to respond either attentively or inattentively. As expected, students confronted with an attentive child used a great deal of induction, pointing out how other children might feel if the child behaved selfishly. By contrast, college students who interacted with an inattentive child relied on power-assertion techniques such as promising rewards for altruism and threatening penalties for selfishness.

A study of budding juvenile delinquents from age 14 to age 16 also revealed child effects on parents (Kerr & Stattin, 2003). In response to their delinquent child's difficult behavior at age 14, parents became less warm and emotionally supportive and less in control of their adolescents by the time the adolescents were 16. In contrast, these researchers could detect few links between the parenting these young delinquents received when they were 14 and their behavior at age 16. Not all child effects are this predictable; for example, a child's difficult temperament sometimes prompts parents to be warmer and more nurturing rather than more hostile (Bates & Pettit, 2007). Still, there do seem to be many instances in which children influence the parenting they receive.

Transactional Model

As the research reviewed in Chapter 13 indicated, antisocial behavior most likely results when a child genetically predisposed to be aggressive behaves in ways that elicit negative, coercive parenting and when that parenting causes the child to become even more aggressive (Ge et al., 1996; O'Connor et al., 1998). When such a destructive family process develops, it becomes impossible to say who is more influential, parent or child. This scenario is best described by a **transactional model** of family influence, in which parent and child are seen as influencing one another reciprocally (Kuczynski & Parkin, 2007; Sameroff, 1975). According to this model, child problems can develop if the relationship between parent and child goes bad as the two interact over time. Optimal child development is likely to result when parent–child transactions evolve in more positive directions.

Genes play a role in these transactional processes. For example, Jenae Neiderhiser and her colleagues (2004) found that a mother's genes influence her positivity toward all her children and children's genes influence how positively their mothers treat them in particular. As Chapter 3 showed, a child's genetic endowment influences many aspects of the parenting style and the home environment she experiences (Collins et al., 2000; Reiss et al., 2000). Through the process of gene–environment correlation (Scarr & McCartney, 1983; see Chapter 3), the genes children inherit (and share with their parents) influence how their parents and other people react to them and what experiences they seek and have. If a child's genes predispose him to antisocial behavior, the child's hostile behavior and the coercive parenting it is likely to elicit will feed on each other through a transactional process that ends up aggravating the child's behavioral problems (Ge et al., 1996).

Demonstrations of child effects and transactional effects within the family are tremendously important. They mean that parents do not singlehandedly control the developmental process. Yet parents' effects on their children's development remain significant; indeed, parents probably have more influence than children do on how the parent–child relationship unfolds over time (Kuczynski & Parkin, 2007). Still, we should not assume, as early child development researchers did, that parents are solely responsible for whether their children turn out "good" or "bad." We must remind ourselves repeatedly that the family is a system in which family members are influenced in reciprocal ways by both their genetic endowments and the environments they create for one another.

Sibling Relationships

A family system consisting of mother, father, and child is changed by the arrival of a new baby and becomes a new—and considerably more complex—family system. How do children adapt to a new baby in the house, how does the sibling relationship change as children age, and what do brothers and sisters contribute to development in the final analysis?

A New Baby Arrives

When Judy Dunn and Carol Kendrick (1982; see also Dunn, 1993, 2007) carefully studied young children's reactions to a new sibling, they found that mothers typically pay less attention to their firstborns after the new baby arrives than before. Partly for this reason, firstborns often find being "dethroned" a stressful experience. They become more difficult and demanding, or more dependent and clingy, and they often develop problems with their sleeping, eating, and toileting routines. Most of their battles are with their mothers, but a few firstborns are not above hitting, poking, and pinching their younger brothers or sisters. Secure attachments can become insecure, especially if firstborns are 2 years old or older and can fully appreciate how much they have lost (Teti et al., 1996). Although positive effects such as an increased insistence on doing things independently are also common, it is clear that many firstborns are not thrilled to have an attention-grabbing new baby in the house. They resent losing their parents' attention, and their own difficult behavior may alienate their parents further.

How can problems be minimized? Adjustment to a new sibling is easier if the marital relationship is good and if the firstborn had secure relationships with both parents before the younger sibling arrived—and continues to enjoy close relationships with them afterward (Dunn, 2007; Teti et al., 1996). Parents are advised to guard against ignoring their firstborn, to continue providing love and attention, and to maintain the child's routines as much as possible. Increased involvement in parenting by the father can be critical (Volling, 2005). Parents can also encourage older children to become aware of the new baby's needs and feelings and to assist in her care (Dunn & Kendrick, 1982; Howe & Ross, 1990).

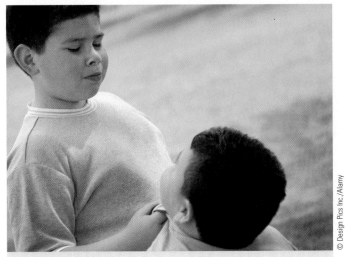

Sibling relationships are ambivalent—close but rivalrous.

Ambivalence in Sibling Relationships

Fortunately, most older siblings adjust fairly quickly to having a new brother or sister. Yet even in the best of sibling relationships, **sibling rivalry**—the spirit of competition, jealousy, and resentment between brothers and sisters—is normal. It may be rooted in an evolutionary fact: Although siblings share half their genes on average and are therefore more motivated to help one another than to help genetically unrelated individuals, siblings also compete with one another for their parents' time and resources to ensure their own survival and welfare (Bjorklund & Pellegrini, 2002). As a result, sibling relationships are typically ambivalent—they tend to involve both closeness and conflict.

The number of skirmishes between very young siblings can be as high as 56 per hour (Dunn, 1993). Jealousies, bouts of teasing, shouting matches, and occasional kicks and punches continue to be part of the sibling relationship throughout childhood; squabbles are most often about possessions (McGuire et al., 2000). Each combatant, of course, feels that he is blameless and has been terribly wronged (Wilson et al., 2004). Thankfully, levels of conflict decrease after early adolescence as teenagers spend more time away from the family (Furman & Buhrmester, 1992; Larson et al., 1996).

Some sibling relationships are consistently closer than others over the years (Dunn, 2007). Sibling relationships are friendlier and less conflictual if mothers and fathers get along well as a couple and if they respond warmly and sensitively to all their children rather than unfairly favoring one over another (Dunn, 2007). Children are able to accept that differences in treatment can be fair, and therefore not objectionable, if they are based on differences in the ages, competencies, and personalities of the siblings, but they do not like unfairness (Kowal et al., 2002).

Sibling Influences on Development

For most children, the sibling relationship is close, interactions with siblings are mostly positive, and siblings play mostly positive roles in one another's development. It is only when sibling relationships are extremely hateful and destructive, or when older siblings are poor role models, that parents should worry that siblings may contribute negatively to development (Ardelt & Day, 2002; Garcia et al., 2000).

One of the important positive functions of siblings is to provide *emotional support.* Brothers and sisters confide in one another, often more than they confide in their parents (Howe et al., 2000). They protect and comfort one another in rough times. Even preschoolers jump in to comfort their infant siblings when their mothers leave them or when strangers approach (Stewart & Marvin, 1984).

Second, older siblings often provide *caregiving* services for younger siblings; they babysit and tend young children. Indeed, in a study of 186 societies, older children were the principal caregivers for infants and toddlers in 57% of the cultures studied (Weisner & Gallimore, 1977). In many societies, chil-

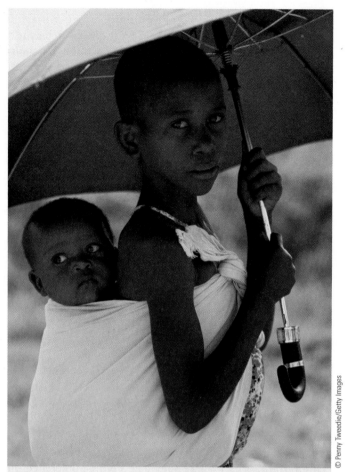

In many societies, older siblings are major caregivers for young children.

dren as young as 5 years are involved in meaningful ways in the care of infants and toddlers (Rogoff, 2003).

Older siblings also serve as *teachers*. One 5-year-old was aware of how much her 2-year-old sister acquired from her through observational learning: "See. I said, 'Bye, I'm going on the slide,' and she said, 'Bye.' She says whatever I say." Although older brothers and sisters are not always as skilled in teaching as parents are (Perez-Granados & Callanan, 1997), they clearly feel a special responsibility to teach, and younger siblings actively seek their guidance on any number of things.

Finally, siblings provide *social experience*. Although having a large number of siblings has negative implications for cognitive development, most likely because each child receives less intellectual stimulation from adults, having at least one sibling to interact with has positive effects on a child's social cognitive development and social skills (Dunn, 2007; S. McHale, Kim, & Whiteman, 2006; and see Chapter 13). In their interactions with siblings, especially all those skirmishes, children learn how to take others' perspectives, read others' minds, express their feelings, negotiate, and resolve conflicts.

Finally, note that an older sibling can affect a younger sibling not only directly but also through the indirect effects he has on parents. Gene Brody (2003, 2004) has discovered that,

if an older sibling is competent, this contributes positively to his mother's psychological functioning (possibly because she feels good about herself as a parent), which makes her more likely to provide supportive parenting to a younger sibling, which in turn increases the odds that the younger sibling will also be competent. By contrast, an incompetent older sibling can set in motion a negative chain of events involving less supportive parenting and less positive outcomes for the younger sibling.

SUMMING UP

- Parents who adopt an authoritative parenting style (as opposed to an authoritarian, permissive, or neglectful one) generally influence their children's development positively.

- Economic hardship undermines effective parenting because of the negative effects of family stress and limited resources.

- Children, through transactional effects, help influence where their parents fall on the acceptance and demandingness dimensions of parenting.

- Adjusting to a little sister or brother can be difficult. Involving both closeness and rivalry, sibling relationships provide emotional support, caretaking, teaching, and social experience and have both direct and indirect effects on development.

CRITICAL THINKING

1. Alison, a 16-year-old teenager who was drunk at the time, plowed the family car into a Dairy Queen and is being held at the police station for driving under the influence. Her father must pick her up. What would you expect an authoritarian, authoritative, permissive, and neglectful father to say and do in this situation? What implications might these contrasting approaches to parenting have for this young women's development?

2. How might a believer in the parent effects model, the child effects model, and the transactional model explain a relationship between a mother's warmth toward a child and the child's sociability?

15.4 | THE ADOLESCENT

When you picture the typical relationship between a teenager and her parents, do you envision a teenager who is out all the time with friends, resents every rule and restriction, and talks back at every opportunity? Do you imagine parents wringing their hands in despair and wondering if they will survive their children's adolescent years? Many people believe that the period of the family life cycle during which parents have adolescents in the house is a particularly stressful time, with close parent–child relationships deteriorating into bitter tugs-of-war. How much truth is there to these characterizations?

Ripples in the Parent–Child Relationship

Although many people believe that adolescents lose respect for their parents and feel less close to them than they did as children, these beliefs are largely unfounded. Parents of adolescents, especially mothers, often speak positively about their relationships with their adolescents (Collins & Laursen, 2006). They note positive changes such as increased independence and maturity in their children as they become teenagers and feel that the parent–child relationship becomes closer rather than chillier (Shearer, Crouter, & McHale, 2005). Most parent–adolescent relationships are close, and most retain whatever quality they had in childhood (Collins & Laursen, 2006).

Still, though, the parent–child relationship does change during adolescence. Time spent together decreases, and this can make adolescents feel less emotionally close to their parents (Collins & Laursen, 2006). A modest increase in parent–child conflict is also common at the onset of puberty (Steinberg, 2002). Young adolescents assert themselves, and they and their parents squabble more. However, the bickering is mainly about relatively minor matters such as disobedience, homework, household chores, and access to privileges, and the frequency of conflicts decreases from early to late adolescence, possibly having served a purpose in helping the adolescent become more independent (Collins & Laursen, 2006). By any account, adolescence is not the time of "storm and stress" that pioneering psychologist G. Stanley Hall believed it was.

A study by Matthew McGue and his colleagues (2005) offers interesting insights into why parent–adolescent relationships change as they do. The study focused on twins who were 11 years old and were then assessed again 3 years later when they were 14. As in other studies, parent–child conflict increased during this early adolescence period; in this study, warmth decreased as well on average, although there were wide differences among families in the tone of relationships. As in other studies, perceived parent–child closeness and conflict turned out to be heritable characteristics—more similar for identical twin pairs than for fraternal twins pairs.

Most interesting, genes became an even stronger influence on both perceived closeness and conflict between the ages of 11 and 14. McGue and his colleagues suggest that this reflects the workings of gene–environment correlations. As adolescents gain power in the parent–child relationship, they increasingly shape the quality of the relationship in ways that reflect their genetically influenced traits (for example, the temperamentally hot-headed child contributes to increased parent–child warfare). This interpretation fits with other evidence that 13- and 14-year-olds become more active than younger children in initiating and controlling interactions with their parents (Granic et al., 2003).

Renegotiating the Relationship

Conflicts now and then help bring about change in the parent–child relationship, not so much in its closeness as in the balance of power between parents and adolescents. Most theorists agree that a key developmental task of adolescence is to achieve **autonomy**—the capacity to make decisions independently and manage life tasks without being overly dependent on other people. If adolescents are to "make it" as adults, they cannot be rushing home for reassuring hugs after every little setback or depending on parents to get them to work on time or manage their checkbooks.

As children reach puberty and become more physically and cognitively mature and more capable of acting autonomously, they assert themselves more. As they do so, parents turn over more power to them, and the parent–child relationship changes from one in which parents are dominant to one in which parents and their sons and daughters are on a more equal footing (Steinberg, 2002). It is usually best for their development if adolescents maintain close attachments with their parents even as they are gaining autonomy and preparing to leave the nest (Kobak et al., 1993; Lamborn & Steinberg, 1993). Gaining some separation from parents is healthy; becoming detached from them is not (Beyers et al., 2003). Some combination of autonomy and attachment, or independence and interdependence, is most desirable.

How much autonomy parents grant differs from culture to culture. Andrew Fuligni (1998) found that adolescents from different ethnic groups in the United States differ considerably in their beliefs about how much authority parents should have and how much autonomy adolescents should have. For example, Filipino and Mexican American adolescents are more likely than European American adolescents to believe that they should not disagree with their parents, and Chinese Americans are less likely to expect the freedom to go to parties and to date at a young age. Adolescents in Japan are even more strongly socialized to expect limited autonomy. They remain closer to their mothers and fathers than American adolescents throughout the adolescent years, do not feel as much need to distance themselves from their parents, and spend less time with peers (Rothbaum, Pott, et al., 2000). In collectivist Asian cultures,

Parent–child conflict escalates in early adolescence.

then, parents continue to impose many rules and the balance of power does not change as much, or at least as early, during adolescence as it does in the United States.

Across cultures, adolescents are most likely to become autonomous, achievement oriented, and well adjusted if their parents consistently enforce a reasonable set of rules, involve their teenagers in decision making, recognize their need for greater autonomy, monitor their comings and goings, gradually loosen the reins, and continue to be warm, supportive, and involved throughout adolescence (Collins & Laursen, 2006; Lamborn et al., 1991). In other words, the winning approach is usually an authoritative style of parenting, although in some cultures and subcultures a more authoritarian style can also achieve good outcomes (Steinberg et al., 1992). Although you should remind yourself that children also affect their parents, an authoritative parenting style gives adolescents opportunities to strengthen their independent decision-making skills but retain the benefit of their parents' guidance and advice. It creates a climate in which teenagers confide in their parents—and parents, therefore, do not have to spy to monitor where their children are and who they are with (Kerr & Stattin, 2003). When parents are extremely strict and stifle autonomy, or when they are extremely lax and fail to monitor their adolescents, teenagers are likely to become psychologically distressed, socialize with the wrong crowds, and get into trouble (Goldstein, Davis-Kean, & Eccles, 2005; Knoester, Haynie, & Stephens, 2006; Lamborn et al., 1991).

SUMMING UP

▌ Most parents and their teenagers are able to work through minor conflicts at puberty and maintain positive feelings for each other while renegotiating their relationship to allow the adolescent more freedom.

▌ With the help of an authoritative parenting style, most adolescents shift toward a more mutual relationship with their parents and become more autonomous.

CRITICAL THINKING

1. At age 13, Miki moved from Japan to the United States with her family and now finds her relationship with her parents strained. Drawing on the material in this section, how would you analyze what is going on?

15.5 | THE ADULT

So far we have offered a child's-eye view of family life. How do adults experience the family life cycle? We will look at the establishment, new parenthood, child-rearing, empty nest, and grandparenthood phases of family life.

Establishing the Marriage

In U.S. society, more than 90% of adults choose to marry at some point in their lives (Whitehead & Popenoe, 2003). Most choose to marry partners they love. Marriages in many other cultures are not formed on the basis of love but are arranged by leaders of kin groups who are concerned with acquiring property, allies, and the rights to any children the marriage produces (Ingoldsby & Smith, 1995). As Corinne Nydegger (1986) put it, "These matters are too important to be left to youngsters" (p. 111). So, in reading what follows, remember that our way of establishing families is not the only way.

Marriage is a significant life transition for most adults: It involves taking on a new role (as husband or wife) and adjusting to life as a couple. We rejoice at weddings and view newlyweds as supremely happy beings. Indeed, they feel on top of the world, their self-esteem rises, and at least some of them adopt a more secure orientation toward attachment relationships as a result of marrying (Crowell, Treboux, & Waters, 2002; Giarrusso et al., 2000). Yet individuals who have just been struggling to achieve autonomy and assume adult roles soon find that they must compromise with their partners and adapt to each other's personalities and preferences.

Ted Huston and his colleagues have found that the honeymoon is short (Huston, McHale, & Crouter, 1986; Huston et al., 2001; also see Kurdek, 1999). In a longitudinal study of newlywed couples, these researchers discovered that perceptions of the marital relationship became less favorable during the first year after the wedding. For example, couples became less satisfied with their marriages and with their sex lives; they less frequently said "I love you," complimented each other, or disclosed their feelings to each other. Although they spent only somewhat less time together, more of that time was devoted to getting tasks done and less to having fun or just talking.

The honeymoon is great, but it often ends quickly.

Although most couples are far more satisfied than dissatisfied with their relationships after the "honeymoon" is over, adapting to marriage clearly involves strains. Blissfully happy relationships evolve into still happy but less idealized ones (Huston et al., 2001). Whether this happens because couples begin to see "warts" that they did not notice before marriage, stop trying to be on their best behavior, have run-ins as an inevitable part of living together, or start to take each other for granted, it is normal.

Does the quality of a couple's relationship early in their marriage have any implications for their later marital adjustment? Apparently it does. Huston and his colleagues (2001) assessed couples 2 months, 1 year, and 2 years into their marriages and again 13 to 14 years after the wedding. It is commonly believed that marriages crumble when negative feelings build up and conflicts escalate, but Huston's findings provide little support for this escalating conflict view. Compared with couples who were happily married after 13 years, couples who remained married but were unhappy had had relatively poor relationships all along. Even as newlyweds, and probably even before they married, these couples were less blissfully in love and more negative toward each other than were couples who stayed married and remained happy in their marriages. Apparently, it is not the case that all marriages start out blissfully happy and then some turn sour; some start out sour. Even couples who divorced did not usually experience escalating conflict over time; rather, they lost their positive feelings for each other.

So, the establishment phase of the family life cycle involves a loss of enthusiasm for most couples. Some couples are already on a path to long-term marital satisfaction, whereas others are headed for divorce or for staying in a marriage that will continue to be less than optimal. Couples seem best off when they can maintain a high level of positive and supportive interactions to help them weather the conflicts that inevitably arise in any relationship (Fincham, 2003). Participating in a premarital education program can help couples remain happy and keep conflict to a minimum (Stanley et al., 2006).

New Parenthood

How does the arrival of a new baby affect a wife, a husband, and their marital relationship? Some people believe that having children draws a couple closer together; others believe that children strain a relationship. Which is it?

On average, new parenthood is best described as a stressful life transition that involves both positive and negative changes (Cowan & Cowan, 2000; Nomaguchi & Milkie, 2003). On the positive side, parents claim that having a child brings them joy and fulfillment and contributes to their own growth as individuals (Emery & Tuer, 1993; Palkovitz, 2002). But couples have added new roles (as mothers and fathers) to their existing roles (as spouses, workers, and so on); new parents often find juggling work and family responsibilities challenging. They not only have a lot of new work to do as caregivers, but they also

lose sleep, worry about their baby, find that they have less time to themselves, and sometimes face financial difficulties. In addition, even egalitarian couples who previously shared household tasks begin to divide their labors along more traditional lines. She specializes in the "feminine" role by becoming the primary caregiver and housekeeper, often reducing her involvement in work outside the home, and he concentrates on his "masculine" role as provider (Cowan & Cowan, 2000; Noller, 2006).

What are the effects of increased stress and of sharper gender role differentiation? Marital satisfaction typically declines somewhat in the first year after a baby is born (Belsky, Lang, & Rovine, 1985; Gottman & Notarius, 2000). This decline is usually steeper for women than for men, primarily because child care responsibilities typically fall more heavily on mothers and they may resent what they regard as an unfair division of labor (Levy-Shiff, 1994; Noller, 2006). Overall, women often experience more of both the positive and negative impacts of new parenthood (Nomaguchi & Milkie, 2003).

However, individuals vary widely in their adjustment to new parenthood. Some new parents experience the transition as a bowl of cherries, others as the pits—as a full-blown crisis in their lives. What might make this life event easier or harder to manage? Characteristics of the baby, the parent, and the support the parent has available all count.

A *baby* who is difficult (for example, cries endlessly) creates more stresses and anxieties for parents than an infant who is quiet, sociable, responsive, and otherwise easy to love (Levy-Shiff, 1994; Meredith & Noller, 2003). *Parent characteristics* matter too. Parents who have good problem-solving and communication skills and find adaptive ways to restructure and organize their lives to accommodate a new baby adjust well (Cox et al., 1999; Levy-Shiff, 1994). Similarly, parents who have realistic expectations about how parenthood will change their lives and about children tend to adjust more easily than those who expect the experience to be more positive than it turns out to be (Kalmuss, Davidson, & Cushman, 1992; Mylod, Whitman, & Borkowski, 1997). Mentally healthy parents also fare better than parents who are experiencing mental health problems such as depression going into new parenthood (Cox et al., 1999).

Attachment styles are also important. New parents who remember their own parents as warm and accepting are likely to experience a smoother transition to new parenthood than couples who recall their parents as cold or rejecting (Florsheim et al., 2003; van IJzendoorn, 1992). Mothers who have a preoccupied (resistant) style of attachment—emotionally needy and dependent individuals who express a lot of anxiety and ambivalence about romantic relationships—are likely to become increasingly depressed from before the birth to 6 months after and to become less satisfied with their marriages if they perceive that their husbands give them little support and are angry (Rholes et al., 2001; Simpson et al., 2003). Women with other attachment styles are not as vulnerable to depression and drops in marital satisfaction, even when they go into parenthood feeling that their partners are not supportive.

Finally, *support* can make a great deal of difference to the new parent. Most important is partner support: As suggested already, things go considerably better for a new mother when she has a good relationship with the father, and when he shares the burden of child care and housework, than when she has no partner or an unsupportive one (Demo & Cox, 2000; Levy-Shiff, 1994). Social support from friends and relatives can also help new parents cope (Stemp, Turner, & Noh, 1986), as can interventions designed to help expecting mothers and fathers prepare realistically for the challenges ahead and support one another as they deal with these challenges (Doherty, Erickson, & LaRossa, 2006; Schulz, Cowan, & Cowan, 2006).

In sum, parents who have an easy baby to contend with; who possess positive personal qualities and coping skills, including a secure attachment style; and who receive reliable support from their partners and other people are in the best position to cope adaptively with new parenthood, a transition normally both satisfying and stressful that can undermine marital satisfaction, especially for women.

The Child-Rearing Family

The child-rearing family is the family with children in it. What can parents look forward to as they have additional children and as their children age? A heavier workload! The stresses and strains of caring for a toddler are greater than those of caring for an infant, and the arrival of a second child means additional stress (O'Brien, 1996). Parents must not only devote time to the new baby but also deal with their firstborn child's normal anxieties about this intruder. Mothers complain of the hassles of cleaning up food and toys, constantly keeping an eye on their children, and dealing with their perfectly normal but irritating demands for attention, failures to comply with requests, and bouts of whining (O'Brien, 1996). Because the workload increases, fathers often become more involved in child care after a second child is born (Dunn, 2007). However, the mother who is raising multiple children as a single parent or the mother whose partner is not very involved may find herself without a moment's rest as she tries to keep up with two or more active, curious, mobile, and dependent youngsters.

Additional challenges sometimes arise for parents when their children enter adolescence. As you saw earlier, parent–child conflicts become more frequent for a while as children enter adolescence. In addition, there is intriguing evidence that living with adolescents who are becoming physically and sexually mature and beginning to date may cause parents to engage in more than the usual amount of midlife questioning about what they have done with their lives and what they can expect next (Silverberg & Steinberg, 1990). Middle-aged parents are clearly affected by how well their children are doing and have difficulty maintaining a sense of well-being if their children are experiencing problems (Greenfield & Marks, 2006). Here, then, may be another example of child effects within the family system. But it works the other way, too: When parents are unhappy or are experiencing marital problems,

adolescents are at greater risk for problems such as delinquency, alcohol and drug use, and anxiety and depression, probably because the parenting they receive deteriorates (Cui, Conger, & Lorenz, 2005).

Children clearly complicate their parents' lives by demanding everything from fresh diapers and close monitoring to college tuition. By claiming time and energy that might otherwise go into nourishing the marital relationship and by adding stresses to their parents' lives, children seem to have a negative—although typically only slightly negative—effect on marital satisfaction (Kurdek, 1999; Rollins & Feldman, 1970). Yet when parents are interviewed about the costs and benefits of parenthood, they generally emphasize the positives and feel that parenthood has contributed a great deal to their personal development, making them more responsible and caring people (Palkovitz, 2002).

The Empty Nest

As children reach maturity, the family becomes a "launching pad" that fires adolescents and young adults into the world to work and start their own families. The term **empty nest** describes the family after the departure of the last child—a phase of the family life cycle that became common only starting in the 20th century (Fox, 2001a). Clearly, the emptying of the nest involves changes in roles and lifestyle for parents, particularly for mothers who have centered their lives on child rearing. There can be moments of deep sadness (Span, 2000, p. 15):

TELL ME ABOUT IT ®

DON'T GET DISCOURAGED. DEVELOPMENTALLY, ALL PARENTS PROGRESS AT A DIFFERENT PACE.

Pamela automatically started to toss Doritos and yucky dip into her cart—and then remembered. "I almost burst into tears," she recalls. "I wanted to stop some complete stranger and say, 'My son's gone away to college.' I had such a sense of loss."

Overall, however, parents react positively to the emptying of the nest. Whereas the entry of children into the family causes modest decreases in marital satisfaction, the departure of the last child seems to be associated with either modest increases in marital satisfaction or at least a slowing of the decline in marital satisfaction that began early in the marriage (White & Edwards, 1990; Van Laningham, Johnson, & Amato, 2001). After the nest empties, women often feel that their marriages are more equitable and that their spouses are more accommodating to their needs (Mackey & O'Brien, 1995; Suitor, 1991). Only a few parents find this transition disturbing.

Why are parents generally not upset by the empty nest? Possibly it is because they have fewer roles and responsibilities and, therefore, experience less stress and strain. Empty nest couples also have more time to focus on their marital relationship and to enjoy activities together and more money to spend on themselves. Moreover, parents are likely to view the emptying of the nest as evidence that they have done their job of raising children well and have earned what Erik Erikson called a sense of generativity. One 44-year-old mother put it well: "I have five terrific daughters who didn't just happen. It took lots of time to mold, correct, love, and challenge them. It's nice to see such rewarding results." Finally, most parents continue to enjoy a good deal of contact with their children after the nest empties, so it is not as if they are really losing the parent–child relationship (White & Edwards, 1990).

In recent years, an increasing number of adult children have been remaining in the nest or leaving then "refilling" it, often because of unemployment, limited finances, divorce, or other difficulties getting their adult lives on track (Ward & Spitze, 1992; White & Rogers, 1997). Compared to emerging adults who leave the nest on time, those who stay put or leave only to return are less likely to have experienced a secure parent–child attachment that allowed them room to develop autonomy (Seiffge-Krenke, 2006). Parents can find having these adult children in the house distressing (Aquilino, 1991; Umberson, 1992). However, most empty nesters adapt, especially if their children are responsible young adults who are attending school or working rather than freeloading and seem to be making progress toward greater independence (Aquilino, 2006; Ward & Spitze, 2004).

Grandparenthood

Although we tend to picture grandparents as white-haired, jovial elders who knit mittens and bake cookies, most adults become grandparents when they are middle-aged, not elderly, and when they are likely to be highly involved in work and community activities (Conner, 2000). Grandparenting styles are diverse, as illustrated by the results of a national survey of grandparents of teenagers conducted by Andrew Cherlin and Frank Furstenberg (1986). These researchers identified three major styles of grandparenting:

1. *Remote.* Remote grandparents (29% of the sample) were symbolic figures seen only occasionally by their grandchildren. Primarily because they were geographically distant, they were emotionally distant as well.

2. *Companionate.* This was the most common style of grandparenting (55% of the sample). Companionate grandparents saw their grandchildren frequently and enjoyed sharing activities with them. They only rarely played a parental role. Like most grandparents, they were reluctant to meddle in the way their adult children were raising their children and were happy not to have child care responsibilities. As one put it, "You can love them and then say, 'Here, take them now, go on home'" (Cherlin & Furstenberg, 1986, p. 55).

3. *Involved.* Finally, 16% of the grandparents took on a parentlike role. Like companionate grandparents, they saw their grandchildren frequently and were playful with them, but unlike companionate grandparents, they often helped with child care, gave advice, and played other practical roles in their grandchildren's lives. Indeed some involved grandparents lived with and served as substitute parents for their grandchildren because their daughters or sons were unmarried or recently divorced and could not tend the children themselves.

You can see, then, that grandparenting takes many forms but that most grandparents see at least some of their grandchildren frequently and prefer a companionate role that is high in enjoyment and affection but low in responsibility. Most grandparents find the role gratifying, especially if they see their grandchildren frequently (Reitzes & Mutran, 2004). Like grandparents, grandchildren report a good deal of closeness in

Most grandparents prefer and adopt a companionate style of grandparenting.

the grandparent–grandchild relationship and only wish they could see their grandparents more (Block, 2000).

Grandparents have been called "the family national guard" because they must be ever ready to come to the rescue when there is a crisis in the family and they never know when they will be called (Hagestad, 1985). Grandmothers often help their daughters adjust to new parenthood and help with child care when their grandchildren are young (Dunn, Fergusson, & Maughan, 2006). When a teenage daughter becomes pregnant, grandmother and grandfather may become the primary caregivers for the baby—sometimes in their 30s or even late 20s when they are not yet ready to become grandparents (Burton, 1996b). Similarly, grandparents may step in to help raise their grandchildren after a divorce (Dunn et al., 2006). If their child does not obtain custody, however, their access to their grandchildren may suddenly be reduced or even cut off, causing them much anguish (Ahrons, 2007; Cooney & Smith, 1996).

Grandparents who do get "called to duty" sometimes make a real contribution to their grandchildren's development. A grandmother who mentors an adolescent mother and coparents with her can help her gain competence as a parent (Oberlander et al., 2007). Teenagers raised by single mothers tend to have low educational attainment and high rates of problem behavior, but they resemble children raised by two parents if they are raised by a single mother and at least one grandparent (DeLeire & Kalil, 2002). A close grandparent–grandchild relationship can even protect the child of a depressed mother from becoming depressed (Silverstein & Ruiz, 2006).

Involved grandparenting can take a toll, however: Grandmothers sometimes show symptoms of depression when grandchildren move in with them and they must become substitute parents (Szinovacz, DeViney, & Atkinson, 1999). In one study of African American grandparents raising grandchildren, 94% reported significant levels of stress (Ross & Aday, 2006). Although grandparents may benefit from the intellectual challenges and emotional rewards that parenting brings (Ehrle, 2001), their development and well-being can suffer if they become overwhelmed by their responsibilities.

Changing Family Relationships

All family relationships develop and change with time. What becomes of relationships between spouses, siblings, and parents and children during the adult years?

Marital Relationships

As you have seen, marital satisfaction, although generally high for most couples throughout their lives together, dips somewhat after the honeymoon period is over, dips still lower in the new-parenthood phase, continues to drop as new children are added to the family, and recovers only when the children leave the nest. Women, because they have traditionally been more involved than men in rearing children, tend to be more strongly

affected by these family life transitions—for good or for bad—than men are. Women are typically less happy with their marriages than men (Amato et al., 2003), and their general happiness also depends more on how well their marriage is going (Kiecolt-Glaser & Newton, 2001).

The quality of marital relationships changes over the years. Although frequency of sexual intercourse decreases, psychological intimacy often increases. The love relationship often changes from one that is passionate to one that is companionate, more like a best-friends relationship (Bierhoff & Schmohr, 2003). Elderly couples are often even more affectionate than middle-aged couples, have fewer conflicts, and are able to resolve their conflicts without venting as many negative emotions (Carstensen, Levenson, & Gottman, 1995; Gagnon et al., 1999).

Overall, however, knowing what stage of the family life cycle an adult is in does not allow us to predict accurately how satisfied that person is with his marriage. Personality is more important. Happily married people have more pleasant personalities than unhappily married people; for example, they are more emotionally stable and vent negative feelings less often (Robins, Caspi, & Moffitt, 2000). Moreover, in happy marriages, the personalities of marriage partners are similar, and are likely to remain similar over the years, as each partner reinforces in the other the traits that brought them together (Caspi, Herbener, & Ozer, 1992). It is when "opposites attract" and find their personalities clashing day after day that marital problems tend to arise (Kurdek, 1991a; Russell & Wells, 1991).

The family life cycle ends with widowhood. Marriages face new challenges if one of the partners becomes seriously ill or impaired and needs care. Wives may suffer ill effects when they must care for a dying husband, but they generally cope reasonably well with their spouse's death, often feeling afterward that they have grown (Seltzer & Li, 2000; and see Chapter 17). By the time they reach age 65 or older, about 72% of men are still married and living with their wives; only 42% of women live with their husbands (U.S. Census Bureau, 2006).

Without question, the marital relationship is centrally important in the lives and development of most adults. Overall, married adults tend to be "happier, healthier, and better off financially" than other adults and are likely to remain so if they can weather bad times in their marriages (Waite & Gallagher, 2000).

Sibling Relationships

Relationships between brothers and sisters often change for the better once siblings no longer live together in the same home. Conflict and rivalry diminish as brothers and sisters forge their own lives. Sibling relationships tend to become warmer and more equal from adolescence to adulthood (Cicirelli, 1995; Scharf, Shulman, & Avigad-Spitz, 2005). Siblings often grow even closer in old age (Cicirelli, 1995). Most adult siblings are in frequent contact and have positive feelings toward one another (Spitze & Trent, 2006). They do not often discuss intimate problems or help one another, but they usually feel that they can count on each other in a crisis (Cicirelli, 1982, 1995).

Some of the ambivalence that characterizes sibling relationships during childhood carries over into adulthood. Emotional closeness persists despite decreased contact, but the potential for sibling rivalry persists, too (Cicirelli, 1995). Siblings who enjoyed a close relationship during childhood are likely to be drawn closer after significant life events such as a parent's illness or death, whereas siblings who had poor relationships during childhood may clash in response to the same life events (Lerner et al., 1991; Ross & Milgram, 1982). Even in middle age, siblings feel closer to each other, and to their parents, when they feel that their parents do not unfairly favor one of them over the other (Boll, Ferring, & Filipp, 2005).

The sibling relationship is typically the longest-lasting relationship we have, linking us to individuals who share many of our genes and experiences (Cicirelli, 1991). It is a relationship that can be close, conflictual, or, for most of us, some of both.

Parent–Child Relationships

Parent and child generations in most families are in close contact and enjoy affectionate give-and-take relationships throughout the adult years. When aging parents eventually need support, children are there to help.

Forming More Mutual Relationships. Parent–child relationships in adulthood take many forms—some are strained or conflictual, some are built more on obligation than love, and

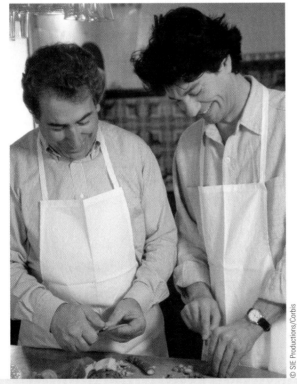

Young adults and their parents often negotiate a more mutual, friendlike relationship.

some are very close and friendlike (Van Gaalen & Dykstra, 2006). Usually the quality of the parent–child relationship stays much the same as adolescents become adults (Aquilino, 2006). However, as young adults leave the nest, they have an opportunity to negotiate a new phase of their relationship with their parents in which they move beyond playing out their roles as child and parent and become more like friends (Lefkowitz, 2005; Shulman & Ben-Artzi, 2003). Still under their parents' roof, emerging adults sometimes feel that they are being treated like children and cross horns with their parents; once they move out, it becomes easier for parents to give their emerging adults more freedom and for emerging adults to develop greater autonomy (Arnett, 2007). A more mutual and warm relationship is especially likely to develop when children are married (but are still childless) and are employed (Aquilino, 1997; Belsky et al., 2003). Relationships are also closer and less conflictual if parents were supportive, authoritative parents earlier in the child's life (Belsky et al., 2001).

When children are middle-aged and their parents elderly, the two generations typically continue to care about, socialize with, and help each other (Umberson & Slaten, 2000). Aging mothers enjoy closer relations and more contact with their children, especially their daughters, than aging fathers do (Umberson & Slaten, 2000). And Hispanic American, African American, and other minority group elders often enjoy more supportive relationships with their families than European Americans do, especially with regard to living together or near one another and providing mutual help (Bengtson, Rosenthal, & Burton, 1996; Sarkisian, Gerena, & Gerstel, 2007). Most elderly people in our society prefer to live close to but not with their children; they enjoy their independence and do not want to burden their children when their health fails (E. Brody, 2004).

Relationships between the generations are not only close and affectionate, but they also are generally equitable: each generation gives something, and each generation gets something in return (Conner, 2000; Markides, Boldt, & Ray, 1986). If anything, aging parents give more (E. Brody, 2004). Contrary to myth, then, most aging families do not experience what has been called **role reversal**—a switching of roles late in life such that the parent becomes the needy, dependent one and the child becomes the caregiver (E. Brody, 2004). Only when parents reach advanced ages and begin to develop serious physical or mental problems does the parent–child relationship sometimes become lopsided.

Caring for Aging Parents. Elaine Brody (1985, 2004) uses the term **middle generation squeeze** (others call it the *sandwich generation* phenomenon) to describe the situation of middle-aged adults pressured by demands from both the younger and the older generations simultaneously (see also Grundy & Henretta, 2006). Imagine a 50-year-old woman caring for her daughter's children (and maybe her granddaughter's children) as well as for her own ailing parents (and possibly her grandparents); it can happen in today's beanpole family.

Adults with children do increasingly find themselves caring for their aging parents (Gallagher & Gerstel, 2001); about one-third of women ages 55–69 report helping members of both the older and younger generations (Grundy & Henretta, 2006). Spouses are the first in line to care for frail elders, assuming they are alive and up to the challenge, but most caregivers of ailing elders are daughters or daughters-in-law in their 40s, 50s, and 60s. Daughters are more likely than sons to assist aging parents. This gender imbalance exists partly because, according to traditional gender-role norms, women are the "kinkeepers" of the family and therefore feel obligated to provide care (E. Brody, 2004) and partly because women are less likely than men to have jobs that prevent them from helping (Sarkisian & Gerstel, 2004).

In many Asian societies, daughters-in-law are the first choice. Aging parents are often taken in by a son, usually the oldest, and cared for by his wife (Youn et al., 1999). In our society, where most aging parents do not want to have to live with their children, much elder care is provided from a distance (Bengtson et al., 1996). Either way, families are the major providers of care for the frail elderly today. We see little support here for the view that today's families have abandoned their elders or that adult children have failed to meet their **filial responsibility,** a child's obligation to his parents (E. Brody, 2004; Conner, 2000).

Middle-aged adults who must foster their children's (and possibly their grandchildren's) development while tending to their own development and caring for aging parents sometimes find their situation overwhelming. They may experience **caregiver burden**—psychological distress associated with the demands of providing care for someone with physical or cognitive impairments. Although caring for an aging parent can be rewarding, many adult children providing such care experience emotional, physical, and financial strains (Hebert & Schulz, 2006; Pinquart & Sorensen, 2006). A woman who is almost wholly responsible for a dependent elder may feel angry and resentful because she has no time for herself. She may experience role conflict between her caregiver role and her roles as wife, mother, and employee that undermines her sense of well-being (Stephens et al., 2001). She is at risk for depression.

Caregiver burden is likely to be perceived as especially weighty if the elderly parent engages in the disruptive and socially inappropriate behaviors often shown by people with dementia (Gaugler et al., 2000; Pinquart & Sorensen, 2003). The caregiver's personality also makes a difference; caregivers who lack a sense of mastery or control may have difficulty coping (Li, Seltzer, & Greenberg, 1999). Cultural factors also enter in: for example, white caregivers devote fewer hours but feel more burdened than do African American caregivers, possibly because of differences in feelings of filial responsibility (Kosberg et al., 2007). Finally, the strain is likely to be worse if a caregiving daughter is unmarried and, therefore, does not have a husband to lean on for practical and emotional support (E. Brody et al., 1992); if her marriage is an unsupportive one; or if her family life is otherwise conflict ridden (Scharlach, Li, & Dalvi, 2006).

Do the caregiver's motivations matter? In an interesting attempt to find out, Cicirelli (1993) assessed whether daugh-

Caring for an ailing parent can result in middle generation squeeze and caregiving burden.

ters helped their aging mothers out of love ("I feel lonely when I don't see my mother often") or out of a sense of duty ("I feel that I should do my part in helping"). Both daughters who were highly motivated to help based on a strong attachment to their mothers and daughters who were motivated by a sense of obligation spent more time helping than women whose motivations to help were weaker. However, those who helped out of love experienced helping as less stressful and burdensome than those who helped mainly out of a sense of duty (see also Lyonette & Yardley, 2003).

So, the caregivers most likely to experience psychological distress are those who must care for parents or spouses with behavioral problems, who lack coping skills and social support, and whose assistance is not motivated by love. Interventions such as behavior management training, anger management training, and cognitive-behavioral therapy can help them sharpen their caregiving skills, learn to react less negatively to the difficult behavior often shown by elderly adults with dementia, and cope with the stress associated with their role (Gallagher-Thompson & Coon, 2007; Hebert & Schulz, 2006).

Summing Up

▌ Marital satisfaction declines soon after the honeymoon period and again in response to new parenthood—a rewarding but also stressful transition especially if the baby is difficult, the parent is ill equipped to cope, and social support is lacking.

▌ The empty nest transition is generally smooth, and middle-aged adults enjoy playing a companionate grandparental role. Women are especially affected by family life cycle transitions.

▌ Family relationships evolve. Marital satisfaction is more strongly influenced by personalities than by stage of family life but tends to drop until the nest empties. Adult siblings continue to be both close and rivalrous, and the parent–child relationship becomes more mutual in adulthood until some middle-aged adults, particularly daughters, are overburdened when they must care for an ailing parent.

CRITICAL THINKING

1. Martha has just married George and wonders how her experience of the family life cycle is likely to differ from his. Can you enlighten her?

2. Is the term "middle generation squeeze" too negative a characterization of middle age? Comment, referring to relevant research.

15.6 DIVERSITY IN FAMILY LIFE

Useful as it is, the concept of a family life cycle does not capture the diversity of adult lifestyles and family experiences. Many of today's adults do not progress in a neat and orderly way through the stages of the traditional family life cycle—marrying, having children, watching them leave the nest, and so on. A small number never marry; a larger number never have children. Some continue working when their children are young, others stop or cut back. And many adults move in and out of wedded life by marrying, divorcing, and remarrying. Let us examine some of these variations in family life (and see Patterson & Hastings, 2007).

Singles

It is nearly impossible to describe the "typical" single adult. This category includes not only young adults who have not yet married but also middle-aged and elderly people who experienced divorce or the death of a spouse or who never married. It is typical to start adulthood as a single person though; the large majority of adults in the 18 to 29 age range are unmarried and have never been (U.S. Census Bureau, 2006). Because adults have been postponing marriage, the number of young, single adults has been growing.

Cohabitation, living with a romantic partner without being married, is also on the rise (Amato et al., 2003). Some never-married people live together as a matter of convenience—because they are in a romantic relationship, need a place to live, and want to save money; they may later contemplate marriage if the relationship is working (Sassler, 2004). Other cohabiters see living together as a trial marriage; still others have seen their marriages end and are looking for an alternative to marriage (Seltzer, 2000). Many have children; by one estimate, 4 out of 10 children will live in a family headed by a cohabiting couple sometime during childhood (Whitehead & Popenoe, 2003).

It makes sense to think that couples who live together before marrying would have more opportunity than those who do not to determine whether they are truly compatible. Yet couples who live together and then marry seem to be more dissatisfied with their marriages and more likely to divorce overall than couples who do not live together before marrying, especially if they have had multiple cohabitation experiences before they marry (Teachman, 2003). It is unlikely that the experience of cohabitation itself is responsible (Booth & Johnson, 1988). Instead, it seems that people who choose to cohabit with multiple partners may be more susceptible to marital problems and less committed to the institution of marriage than people who do not. They tend, for example, to be less religious, less conventional in their family attitudes, less committed to the idea of marriage as a permanent arrangement, and more open to the idea of divorcing (Axinn & Barber, 1997; DeMaris & MacDonald, 1993).

What of the 5% of adults who never marry? Stereotypes suggest that they are miserably lonely and maladjusted, but they often make up for their lack of spouse and children by forming close bonds with siblings, friends, or younger adults who become like sons or daughters to them (Rubinstein et al., 1991). As "old-old" people in their 80s and 90s, never-married people sometimes lack relatives who can assist or care for them (Johnson & Troll, 1996). Yet it is divorced or widowed rather than never-married single adults who tend to be least happy with their singlehood in old age (Pudrovska, Schieman, & Carr, 2006).

Childless Married Couples

Like single adults who never marry, married couples who remain childless do not experience all the phases of the traditional family life cycle. Many childless couples want children but cannot have them. However, a growing number of adults, especially highly educated adults with high-status occupations, voluntarily decide to delay having children or decide not to have them at all (Heaton, Jacobson, & Holland, 1999).

How are childless couples faring when their peers are having, raising, and launching children? Generally, they do well. Their marital satisfaction tends to be higher than that of couples with children during the child-rearing years (Kurdek, 1999). And middle-aged and elderly childless couples seem to be no less satisfied with their lives than parents whose children have left the nest (Allen, Blieszner, & Roberto, 2000; Rempel, 1985). However, elderly women who are childless and widowed may find themselves without anyone to help them if they develop health problems (Johnson & Troll, 1996). It seems, then, that childless couples derive satisfaction from their marriages and are happier than single adults as a result but may suffer from a lack of social support late in life after their marriages end.

Dual-Career Families

As more mothers have gone to work outside the home, developmental scientists have asked what effect having two employed parents has on families and on child development.

Some have focused on the concept of **spillover effects**—ways in which events at work affect home life and events at home carry over into the workplace. Most of their research has focused on negative spillover effects from work to home (Barnett, 1994; Crouter, 2006). When adults are asked to keep daily diaries, it becomes clear that negative interactions and stressful workloads at work can precipitate angry confrontations with partners at home (Story & Repetti, 2006). Positive spillover effects can also occur: A good marriage and rewarding interactions with children can protect a woman from the negative psychological effects of stresses at work and increase her job satisfaction (Barnett, 1994; Rogers & May, 2003), and a rewarding, stimulating job can have positive effects on her interactions within the family (Greenberger, O'Neil, & Nagel, 1994).

Despite negative spillover effects, dual-career families are faring well overall (Gottfried & Gottfried, 2006). Women are giving up personal leisure time (not to mention sleep) and cutting back on housework to make time for their children; meanwhile, their husbands are slowly but steadily increasing their participation in household and child care activities (Cabrera et al., 2000; Coltrane, 2000). There is no indication that a mother's decision to work, in itself, has damaging effects on child development; it can have positive or negative effects depending on the age of the child and the family's circumstances (Gottfried & Gottfried, 2006). Living in a dual-career family is likely to be best for children when it means an increase in family income, when mothers are happy with the choice they have made, when fathers become more involved, and when children are adequately supervised after school (Hoffman, 2000; Lerner & Noh, 2000).

Having two working parents can be a negative experience, however, if working parents are unable to remain warm and involved parents who share "quality time" with their children

Dual-career families work best when partners share the workload.

(Beyer, 1995; Parke & Buriel, 2006). For example, Martha Moorehouse (1991) found that 6-year-olds whose mothers began working full-time were more cognitively and socially competent (according to their teachers) than children whose mothers were homemakers if these youngsters frequently shared activities such as reading, telling stories, and talking with their mothers. However, they fared worse than children with stay-at-home mothers if they lost out on such opportunities.

Fortunately, most working mothers, by reducing housework and leisure time, manage to spend almost as much time interacting with their children as nonworking mothers do, and their husbands are more involved than ever in child care (Bianchi, 2000). As a result, most dual-career couples are able to enjoy the personal and financial benefits of working without compromising their children's development. They might be able to do so even more successfully if the United States, like other industrialized nations, did more to support paid leave for parents, flexible work hours, day care and preschool programs, after-school programs, and other support systems for working parents and their children (Heymann, Penrose, & Earle, 2006).

Gay and Lesbian Families

The family experiences of gay men and lesbian women are most notable for their diversity (Patterson & Hastings, 2007; Peplau & Fingerhut, 2007). In the United States, several million gay men and lesbian women are parents, most through previous heterosexual marriages, others through adoption or artificial insemination. Some no longer live with their children, but others raise them as single parents and still others raise them in families that have two mothers or two fathers. Other gay men and lesbian women remain single and childless or live as couples without children throughout their lives. Gay and lesbian families face special challenges, as the national controversy over the legality of gay marriages suggests, because they are not fully recognized as families by society and are sometimes the target of discrimination (Peplau & Fingerhut, 2007).

Those gay and lesbian adults who live as couples debunk many stereotypes that associate homosexuality with unhappiness, loneliness, and difficulty sustaining romantic relationships (Peplau & Fingerhut, 2007). Gay and lesbian couples also do not follow traditional gender stereotypes in which one is the "husband" and one the "wife." Instead, relationships are egalitarian; partners share responsibilities equally and tend to work out a division of labor, through trial and error, based on who is especially talented at or who hates doing certain tasks (Huston & Schwartz, 1995). Even the transition to parenthood does not cause partners to divide housework less equally; most couples report that their child has two equally involved parents (Goldberg & Perry-Jenkins, 2007). Generally, gay and lesbian relationships evolve through the same stages of development, are satisfying or dissatisfying for the same reasons, and are typically as rewarding as those of married or cohabiting heterosexuals (Kurdek, 1995, 2006; Peplau & Fingerhut, 2007).

What are the implications for children of being raised by gay or lesbian parents? Comparing lesbian mothers with heterosexual mothers in two-parent and single-parent homes, Susan Golombok and her colleagues (2003) found that lesbian mothers tend to hit children less and to engage in imaginative and domestic play more but are otherwise similar to heterosexual mothers. Moreover, their lesbian partners are as involved in co-parenting as fathers typically are. Finally, children who lived with two parents of the same sex were better off in terms of developmental outcomes than children living with a single mother, and they were no different than children living with two heterosexual parents. This study and others suggest that gay and lesbian adults who raise children are as likely as heterosexual parents to produce competent and well-adjusted children (Patterson & Hastings, 2007). Moreover, contrary to what many people believe, their children display the usual gender-role behavior and are no more likely than the children of heterosexual parents to develop a homosexual or bisexual orientation.

Divorcing Families

Orderly progress through the family life cycle is disrupted when a couple divorces. Divorce is not just one life event; rather, it is a series of stressful experiences for the entire family that begins with marital conflict before the divorce and includes a complex of life changes as the marriage unravels and its members reorganize their lives (Amato, 2000; Hetherington & Kelly, 2002). Why do people divorce? What effects does divorce typically have on family members? And how can we explain, as illustrated by the two contrasting quotes at the start of this chapter, why some adults and children thrive after a divorce whereas others experience persisting problems?

Before the Divorce

Gay Kitson and her colleagues (Kitson, Babri, & Roach, 1985; Kitson, 1992) and Jay Teachman (2002) have pieced together a profile of the couples at highest risk for divorce. Generally, they are young adults, in their 20s and 30s, who have been married for an average of 7 years and often have young children. These days, only about 70% of marriages make it to the 10-year mark (Teachman, 2002). Couples are especially likely to divorce if they married as teenagers, had a short courtship, conceived a child before marrying, or are low in socioeconomic status—all factors that might suggest an unreadiness for marriage and unusually high financial and psychological stress accompanying new parenthood.

Contrary to the notion that today's couples do not give their marriages a chance to work, research suggests that most divorcing couples experience a few years of marital distress and conflict and often try separations before they make the final decision to divorce (Kitson, 1992). They typically divorce because they feel their marriages lack communication, emotional fulfillment, or compatibility. Wives tend to have longer lists of complaints than their husbands do and often have more to do

with initiating the breakup (Hewitt, Western, & Baxter, 2006; Thompson & Amato, 1999).

After the Divorce

Most families going through a divorce experience it as a genuine crisis—a period of considerable disruption that often lasts at least 1 to 2 years (Amato, 2000; Hetherington, 2006; Hetherington & Kelly, 2002). The wife, who usually obtains custody of any children, is likely to be angry, depressed, and otherwise distressed, although often she is relieved as well. The husband is also likely to be distressed, particularly if he did not want the divorce and feels shut off from his children. Both individuals must revise their identities and their relationship. Both may feel isolated from former friends and unsure of themselves as they try out new romantic relationships. Divorced women with children are likely to face the added problem of getting by with considerably less money (Amato, 2000).

Because of all these stressors, divorced adults are at higher risk than married adults for depression and other forms of psychological distress, physical health problems, and even death (Amato, 2000; Lillard & Panis, 1996). Their adjustment is especially likely to be poor if they have little income, do not find a new relationship, take a dim view of divorce, and did not initiate the divorce (Wang & Amato, 2000). The consequences of divorce for adult well-being are also worse if there are young children in the home than if there are not (Williams & Dunne-Bryant, 2006). Some adults actually feel better about themselves and more in control of their lives after extracting themselves from a miserable marriage. Thus, divorce is at least temporarily stressful for most adults, but it can have negative or positive effects in the long run depending on the individual and the circumstances (Amato, 2000).

As you might suspect, psychologically distressed adults do not make the best parents. Moreover, children going through a

INTERESTING. WHAT ABOUT THAT, PHIL? HOW DO YOU FEEL ABOUT BECOMING SOMEONE ELSE ENTIRELY?

divorce do not make the best children because they, too, are suffering. They are often angry, fearful, depressed, and guilty, especially if they fear that they were somehow responsible for what happened (Hetherington, 1981). They are also likely to be whiny, dependent, disobedient, and disrespectful. A vicious circle of the sort described by the transactional model of family influence can result: children's behavioral problems and parents' ineffective parenting styles feed on each other.

Mavis Hetherington and her associates (Hetherington, Cox, & Cox, 1982; Hetherington & Kelly, 2002) have found that stressed custodial mothers often become impatient and insensitive to their children's needs. In terms of the major dimensions of child rearing, they become less accepting and responsive, less authoritative, and less consistent in their discipline. They occasionally try to seize control of their children with a heavy-handed, authoritarian style of parenting, but more often they fail to carry through in enforcing rules and make few demands that their children behave maturely. Noncustodial fathers, meanwhile, are likely to be overly permissive, indulging their children during visitations (Amato & Sobolewski, 2004).

This is not the formula for producing well-adjusted, competent children. The behavioral problems that children display undoubtedly make effective parenting difficult, but deterioration in parenting style aggravates those behavioral problems. When this breakdown in family functioning occurs, children are likely to display not only behavioral problems at home but also strained relations with peers, low self-esteem, academic problems, and adjustment difficulties at school (Amato, 2001; Hetherington, 2006). Children are especially vulnerable to developing behavior problems, adolescents to drops in their performance at school (Lansford et al., 2006).

Families typically begin to pull themselves back together about 2 years after the divorce, and by the 6-year mark most differences between children of divorce and children of intact families have disappeared (Hetherington & Kelly, 2002). Yet even after the crisis phase has passed and most children and parents have adapted, divorce can leave a residue of negative effects on at least some individuals that lasts years (Amato, 2006; Hetherington & Kelly, 2002). For example, as adolescents, children of divorce are less likely than other youth to perceive their relationships with their parents, especially their fathers, as close and caring, and many are still negative about what divorce has done to their lives (Emery, 1999; Woodward, Fergusson, & Belsky, 2000). About 20 to 25% of Hetherington's children of divorce still had emotional scars and psychological problems as young adults (Hetherington & Kelly, 2002). And a study of middle-aged adults revealed that 24% of those whose parents had divorced when they were younger had never married, compared with 14% of adults from intact families (Maier & Lachman, 2000). Adults whose parents divorced are also more likely than adults from intact families to experience marital conflict and divorce themselves (Amato, 2006).

On a more positive note, not all families experience divorce as a major crisis; of those that do, most parents and children rebound from their crisis period and adapt well in the long run, sometimes even undergoing impressive growth as a result of their experience (Hetherington & Kelly, 2002; and see Harvey & Fine, 2004). A conflict-ridden two-parent family is usually more detrimental to a child's development than a cohesive single-parent family (Amato, 2006). Perhaps the most important message of research on divorce is that the outcomes of divorce vary widely. As Alan Booth and Paul Amato (2001) conclude, "divorce may be beneficial or harmful to children, depending on whether it reduces or increases the amount of stress to which children are exposed" (p. 210). As you can see in the Explorations box, several factors can help facilitate a positive adjustment to divorce and prevent lasting damage—among them adequate finances, effective parenting, minimal conflict between parents, social support, and minimal additional changes and stressors.

Remarriage and Reconstituted Families

Within 3 to 5 years of a divorce, about 75% of single-parent families experience yet another major transition when a parent remarries and the children acquire a stepparent—and sometimes new siblings (Hetherington, 1989; Hetherington & Stanley-Hagan, 2000). Because about 60% of remarried couples divorce, some adults and children today find themselves in a recurring cycle of marriage, marital conflict, divorce, single status, and remarriage.

Most children adjust to being part of a reconstituted family, but boys have an easier time than girls do.

"GOOD" AND "BAD" DIVORCES: FACTORS INFLUENCING ADJUSTMENT

Some adults and children thrive after a divorce, whereas others suffer long-lasting negative effects. Why is this? Here are some factors that can make a big difference.

1. *Adequate financial support.* Families fare better after a divorce if the father pays child support and the family therefore has adequate finances (Amato & Sobolewski, 2004; Marsiglio et al., 2000). Adjustment is likely to be more difficult for mother-headed families that fall into poverty and must struggle to survive.

2. *Good parenting by the custodial parent.* If the custodial parent can continue to be warm, authoritative, and consistent, children are far less likely to experience problems (Hetherington, 2006). It is difficult for parents to be effective when they are depressed and under stress, but parents who understand the stakes may be more able to give their children the love and guidance they need. Interventions can help them. Marion Forgatch and David DeGarmo (1999) randomly assigned divorced mothers of boys either to a parenting skills program designed to prevent them from becoming less positive and more coercive toward their children or to a control group. Training helped mothers rely less on coercive methods and remain positive toward their sons over a 12-month period. Better yet, these positive

changes in their parenting behaviors were linked to improvements in their children's adjustment at school and at home (see also Wolchik et al., 2000).

3. *Good parenting by the noncustodial parent.* Children may suffer when they lose contact with their noncustodial parent. A quarter or more of children living with their mothers lose contact with their fathers, and many others see their fathers only rarely (Demo & Cox, 2000). More important than amount of contact, however, is quality of contact. Fathers who are authoritative and remain emotionally close to their children can help them make a positive adjustment to life in a single-parent home (Amato & Sobolewski, 2004; King & Sobolewski, 2006).

4. *Minimal conflict between parents.* However their mothers and fathers parent, children should be protected from continuing marital conflict. If parents continue to squabble after the divorce and are hostile toward each other, both will likely be upset, their parenting will suffer, and children will feel torn in their loyalties and experience behavioral problems (Amato, 1993). When parents can agree on joint custody, children's adjustment tends to be better than when custody is granted to one parent or the other (Bauserman, 2002). When the mother has custody, positive coparenting in which parents co-

ordinate and cooperate helps keep fathers close to and involved with their children (Sobolewski & King, 2005).

5. *Additional social support.* Divorcing adults are less depressed if they have close confidants than if they do not (Menaghan & Lieberman, 1986). Children also benefit from having close friends (Lustig, Wolchik, & Braver, 1992) and from participating in peer-support programs in which they and other children of divorce can share their feelings and learn positive coping skills (Grych & Fincham, 1992). Friends, relatives, school personnel, and other sources of social support outside the family can all help families adjust to divorce.

6. *Minimal other changes.* Generally families do best if additional changes are kept to a minimum—for example, if parents do not have to move, get new jobs, cope with the loss of their children, and so on (Buehler et al., 1985–1986). It is easier to deal with a couple of stressors than a mountain of them.

Here, then, are some insights into why some divorces are less disruptive than others. As Paul Amato (1993) concludes, adjustment to divorce will depend on the "total configuration" of stressors the individual faces and on the resources he has available to aid in coping, including both personal strengths and social supports.

How do children fare when their custodial parent remarries? The first few years are a time of conflict and disruption as new family roles and relationships are ironed out (Hetherington & Stanley-Hagan, 2000). Interviewed 20 years after their parents divorced, about one-third of the adults interviewed in one study recalled the remarriage as more stressful than the divorce (Ahrons, 2007). The difficulties are likely to be worse if both parents bring children to the family (or the couple has children of their own) than if only one parent does (Hetherington, 2006). Girls are often so closely allied with their mothers that they may resent either a stepfather competing for their mother's attention or a stepmother attempting to play a substitute-mother role and can become sullen and hostile. Although most children adapt and fare better with time,

adolescents from complex reconstituted families blending children from more than one marriage, like children of divorce living in single-families, are less well adjusted and show more problems such as depression and antisocial behavior on average than adolescents from intact two-parent families (Hetherington, 2006). Children in reconstituted families in which all the children came from one parent fare much better. Outcomes are also better if children develop positive relationships with their fathers—both their noncustodial biological fathers and, even more importantly, their new stepfathers (King, 2006). As Mavis Hetherington concludes, though, "It is family process rather than family structure that is critical to the well-being of children" (p. 232); children and adolescents can thrive in any type of family if they receive good parenting.

SUMMING UP

▌ Single adults are diverse, and cohabitation tends to be associated with later marital problems.

▌ Childless married couples and gay and lesbian families generally fare well, and dual-career families can be good or bad for children depending on the quality of parenting they receive.

▌ Divorce creates a family crisis for 1 or 2 years and has long-term negative effects on some children; becoming part of a reconstituted family can also be a difficult transition, especially when children from multiple parents are involved.

CRITICAL THINKING

1. Three months after her divorce, Blanca has become depressed and increasingly withdrawn. Her son Carlos, age 7, has become a terror around the house and a discipline problem at school. From the perspective of (a) the parent effects model, (b) the child effects model, and (c) the transactional model of family influence, how would you explain what is going on in this single-parent family?

15.7 | THE PROBLEM OF FAMILY VIOLENCE

As this chapter makes clear, family relationships normally contribute positively to human development at every point in the life span. At the same time, families can be the cause of much anguish and of development gone astray. Nowhere is this more obvious than in cases of family violence (St. George, 2001, p. A20):

> From a young age, I have had to grow up fast. I see families that are loving and fathers who care for their children, and I find myself hating them. . . . I have nightmares pertaining to my father. I get angry and frustrated when family is around.

These sobering words were written by Sonyé Herrera, an abused adolescent who for years had been hit, threatened with guns, choked, and otherwise victimized—and had witnessed her mother abused—by an alcoholic father. The abuse continued even after the couple divorced. At age 15, unable to stand any more, Herrera had her father charged with assault, but he returned one afternoon, hit her, and shot and killed both her and her mother before turning his gun on himself (St. George, 2001, p. A21).

Child abuse is perhaps the most visible form of family violence. Every day, infants, children, and adolescents are burned, bruised, beaten, starved, suffocated, sexually abused, or otherwise mistreated by their caretakers (Miller & Knudsen, 2007). Accurate statistics are hard to come by, but in 2005 almost 900,000 children in the United States were determined to be victims of child maltreatment, a rate of about 12 of every 1000 children (U.S. Department of Health and Human Services, 2007). Of the 900,000 children, 63% were neglected, 17%

physically abused, 9% sexually abused, 7% emotionally or psychologically abused, and 16% experienced still other types of maltreatment (and many children experienced more than one of the preceding types). Surveys reveal even higher rates, because much child abuse goes unreported. According to a national survey of U.S. families, for example, 11% of children had reportedly been kicked, bitten, hit, hit with an object, beaten, burned, or threatened or attacked with a knife or gun by a parent in the past year (Wolfner & Gelles, 1993).

Child abuse commands a good deal of attention, but the potential for abuse exists in all possible relationships within the family (Tolan, Gorman-Smith, & Henry, 2006). Children and adolescents batter, and in rare cases kill, their parents (Agnew & Huguley, 1989). Siblings, especially brothers, abuse one another in countless ways, especially if there is violence elsewhere in the family (Hoffman, Kiecolt, & Edwards, 2005). And spousal or partner abuse, rampant in our society, appears to be the most common form of family violence worldwide. Globally, it is estimated that about one-third of women are beaten, coerced into sex, or emotionally abused by their partners (Murphy, 2003). An anthropological analysis of family violence in 90 nonindustrial societies by David Levinson (1989) revealed that wife beating occurred in 85% of them; in almost half of these societies, it occurred in most or all households, suggesting that it was an accepted part of family life.

Although spousal abuse is viewed as intolerable in most segments of U.S. society, Murray Straus and Richard Gelles (1986, 1990) nonetheless estimate 16% of married couples in the United States experience some form of marital violence in a year's time—often "only" a shove or a slap, but violence nonetheless—and that almost 6% experience at least one instance of severe vio-

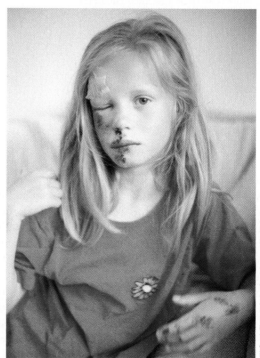

Child abuse occurs in all ethnic and racial groups.

lence (such as kicking or beating). Much "mild" spousal abuse is mutual. In rarer and more serious cases, the violence is one-sided: Men batter their female partners, usually in an attempt to control them (Johnson & Ferraro, 2000; Tolan et al., 2006). Millions of children witness this violence (McDonald et al., 2006).

Elderly adults are also targets of family violence. Frail or impaired older people are physically or psychologically mistreated, neglected, financially exploited, and stripped of their rights—most often by adult children or spouses serving as their caregivers (Flannery, 2003; Jayawardena & Liao, 2006; Wolf, 2000). Around 5% of elderly adults are probably neglected or abused in various ways, and all agree that many cases go unreported (Tolan et al., 2006). The most common scenario is neglect of an impaired elder near the end of life by a stressed caregiver, often motivated by financial considerations (Jayawardena & Liao, 2006).

This is not a pretty picture. Here is a social problem of major dimensions that causes untold suffering and harms the development of family members of all ages. What can be done to prevent it, or to stop it once it has started? To answer this question, we must understand why family violence occurs.

Why Does Family Violence Occur?

Various forms of family violence have many similarities, and the contributors are often similar (Tolan et al., 2006). Because child abuse has been studied the longest, we will look at what has been learned about how characteristics of the abuser, abused, and social context contribute to child abuse.

The Abuser

Hard as it may be to believe, only about 1 child abuser in 10 appears to have a severe psychological disorder (Kempe & Kempe, 1978). Rather, the abusive parent is most often a young mother who tends to have many children, to live in poverty, to be unemployed, and to have no partner to share her load (U.S. Department of Health and Human Services, 2007; Wolfner & Gelles, 1993). Yet child abusers come from all races, ethnic groups, and social classes. Many of them appear to be fairly typical, loving parents—except for their tendency to become extremely irritated with their children and to do things they will later regret.

A few reliable differences between parents who abuse their children and those who do not have been identified. First, child abusers tend to have been *abused as children*; abusive parenting, like effective parenting, tends to be passed from generation to generation (Conger et al., 2003; van IJzendoorn, 1992). Although most maltreated children do not abuse their own children when they become parents, roughly 30% do (Kaufman & Zigler, 1989). They are also likely to become spousal abusers; about 60% of men who abuse their partners report that they either were abused or witnessed abuse as children, compared with about 20% of nonviolent men (Delsol & Margolin, 2004). All forms of witnessing or being the target of violence in adults' families of origin predict all forms of perpe-

tration and victimization later in life, suggesting that what children from violent homes learn is that violence is an integral part of human relationships (Kwong et al., 2003). The cycle of abuse is not inevitable, however; it can be broken if abused individuals receive emotional support from parent substitutes, therapists, or spouses and are spared from severe stress as adults (Egeland, Jacobvitz, & Sroufe, 1988; Vondra & Belsky, 1993).

Second, abusive mothers are often *battered by their partners* (Coohey & Braun, 1997; McCloskey, Figueredo, & Koss, 1995). Adults are more likely to be in an abusive romantic relationship or marriage if they were abused or witnessed abuse as a child (Stith et al., 2000). Thus, abusive mothers may have learned through their experiences both as children and as wives that violence is the way to solve problems, or they may take out some of their frustrations about being abused on their children.

Third, abusers are often insecure individuals with *low self-esteem*. Their unhappy experiences in insecure attachment relationships with their parents, reinforced by their negative experiences in romantic relationships, may lead them to formulate negative internal working models of themselves and others (Pianta, Egeland, & Erickson, 1989; and see Chapter 14). These adults often see themselves as victims and feel powerless as parents (Bugental & Beaulieu, 2003). However, they have also learned to be victimizers (Pianta et al., 1989).

Fourth, abusive parents often have *unrealistic expectations* about what children can be expected to do at different ages and have difficulty tolerating the normal behavior of young children (Haskett, Johnson, & Miller, 1994). For example, when infants cry to communicate needs such as hunger, nonabusive mothers correctly interpret these cries as signs of discomfort, but abusive mothers often infer that the baby is somehow criticizing or rejecting them (Egeland, 1979; Egeland, Sroufe, & Erickson, 1983).

In short, abusive parents tend to have been exposed to harsh parenting and abusive relationships themselves, to have low self-esteem, and to find caregiving more stressful, and threatening to their egos, than other parents do. Still, it has been difficult to identify a particular kind of person who is highly likely to turn into a child abuser. Could some children bring out the worst in parents?

The Abused

An abusive parent sometimes singles out only one child in the family as a target; this offers a hint that child characteristics might matter (Gil, 1970). No one is suggesting that children are to blame for being abused, but some children appear to be more at risk than others. For example, children who have medical problems or who have difficult temperaments are more likely to be abused than quiet, healthy, and responsive infants who are easier to care for (Bugental & Beaulieu, 2003). Yet many difficult children are not mistreated, and many seemingly cheerful and easygoing children are.

Just as characteristics of the caregiver cannot fully explain why abuse occurs, then, neither can characteristics of children. There is now intriguing evidence that the *combination* of a high-risk parent and a high-risk child spells trouble. For example, a mother who feels powerless to deal with her child who confronts a child who has a disability or illness or is otherwise difficult is prone to overreact emotionally when the child cannot be controlled and to use harsh discipline such as spanking or, in the extreme, to become abusive (Bugental, 2001). Such powerless parents experience higher levels of stress than most parents, as indicated by high cortisol levels, when interacting with children who are unresponsive and that is what provokes the use of power tactics (Martorell & Bugental, 2006). However, even the match between child and caregiver may not be enough to explain abuse. We must, as always, consider the ecological context surrounding the family system (Cicchetti & Valentino, 2006).

The Context

Consistently, abuse is most likely to occur when a parent is under great stress and has little social support (Cano & Vivian, 2003; Egeland et al., 1983). Life changes such as the loss of a job or a move to a new residence can disrupt family functioning and contribute to abuse or neglect (Wolfner & Gelles, 1993). Abuse rates are highest in deteriorating neighborhoods where families are poor, transient, socially isolated, and lacking in community services and informal social support. These high-risk neighborhoods are areas in which adults do not feel a sense of community and do not look after each other's children, neighborhoods in which the motto "It takes a village to raise a child" has little meaning (Korbin, 2001).

Finally, the larger macroenvironment is important. Ours is a violent society in which the use of physical punishment is common and the line between physical punishment and child abuse can be difficult to draw (Whipple & Richey, 1997). Parents who believe strongly in the value of physical punishment are more at risk than those who do not to become abusive if they are under stress (Crouch & Behl, 2001). Child abuse is less common in societies that discourage physical punishment and advocate nonviolent ways of resolving interpersonal conflicts (Gilbert, 1997; Levinson, 1989). Child abuse is particularly rare in Scandinavian countries, where steps have been taken to outlaw corporal (physical) punishment of children not only in schools but also at home (Finkelhor & Dziuba-Leatherman, 1994).

As you can see, child abuse is a complex phenomenon with a multitude of causes and contributing factors. It is not easy to predict who will become a child abuser and who will not, but abuse seems most likely when a vulnerable individual faces overwhelming stress with insufficient social support. Much the same is true of spousal abuse, elder abuse, and other forms of family violence.

What Are the Effects of Family Violence?

As you might imagine, child abuse is not good for human development. Physically abused and otherwise maltreated children tend to have many problems, ranging from physical injuries and impaired brain development to cognitive and social deficits, behavioral problems, and psychological disorders (Cicchetti & Valentino, 2006; Margolin & Gordis, 2000).

Intellectual deficits and academic difficulties are common among mistreated children (Malinosky-Rummell & Hansen, 1993; Shonk & Cicchetti, 2001). A particularly revealing study focused on 5-year-old identical and fraternal twins to rule out possible genetic influences on the association between exposure to domestic violence and intellectual development (Koenen et al., 2003). Children exposed to high levels of domestic violence had IQ scores 8 points lower, on average, than those of children who were not exposed to domestic violence, even taking genetic influences on IQ into account.

Behavioral problems are also common among physically abused and other maltreated children (Flores, Cicchetti, & Rogosch, 2005). Many tend to be explosively aggressive youngsters, rejected by their peers for that reason (Bolger & Patterson, 2001). They learn from their experience with an abusive parent to be supersensitive to angry emotions; as a result, they may perceive anger in peers where there is none and lash out to protect themselves (Reynolds, 2003). Even as adults, individuals who were abused as children not only tend to be violent, both inside and outside the family, but also tend to have higher-than-average rates of depression, anxiety, and other psychological problems (Margolin & Gordis, 2000). Children who witness parental violence display as many behavior problems as those who are the targets of violence; the odds of problems are greatest when children both witness parental violence and experience it directly (K. J. Sternberg et al., 2006).

Finally, the social and emotional development of many abused children is disrupted (Darwish et al., 2001). One of the most disturbing consequences of physical abuse is a lack of normal empathy in response to the distress of others. When Mary Main and Carol George (1985) observed the responses of abused and nonabused toddlers to the fussing and crying of peers, they found that nonabused children typically attended carefully to the distressed child, showed concern, and attempted to provide comfort. As shown in ■ **Figure 15.3,** not one abused child showed appropriate

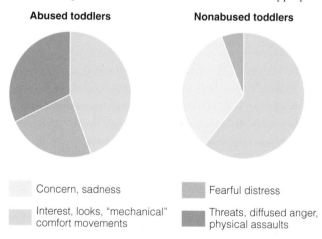

Abused toddlers   **Nonabused toddlers**

Concern, sadness

Fearful distress

Interest, looks, "mechanical" comfort movements

Threats, diffused anger, physical assaults

■ **FIGURE 15.3** Responses to distressed peers observed in abused and nonabused toddlers in day care. Abused children distinguish themselves by a lack of concern and a tendency to become upset, angry, and aggressive when other children cry.
SOURCE: Adapted from Main & George (1985).

BATTLING FAMILY VIOLENCE

That family violence has many causes is discouraging. Where do we begin to intervene, and just how many problems must we correct before we can prevent or stop the violence? Despite the complexity of the problem, progress is being made.

Consider first the task of preventing violence before it starts. This requires identifying high-risk families—a task greatly aided by the kinds of studies you have reviewed. For example, once we know that an infant is at risk for abuse because she is particularly irritable or unresponsive, it makes sense to help the child's parents appreciate the baby's positive qualities (Widmayer & Field, 1980).

Better yet, efforts to prevent abuse can be directed at the combination of a high-risk parent and a high-risk child. Daphne Bugental and her colleagues (Bugental & Beaulieu, 2003; Bugental et al., 2002) have focused on parents who feel powerless as parents and as a result often believe that their children are deliberately trying to annoy or get the best of them. Such parents are especially likely to become abusive if they face the challenge of raising a child who is unresponsive and difficult. In an intervention study, Bugental and her colleagues focused on high-risk mothers who had recently emigrated from Mexico to California and who scored high on a measure of family stress. Some had infants who were high risk (who were born prematurely or scored low on the Apgar examination at birth and were therefore at risk for future health problems), and others had infants who were low risk. The researchers designed a home visitation program aimed at empowering these mothers by teaching them to analyze the causes of caregiving problems without blaming either themselves or their children and to devise and try solutions to caregiving problems. Families were randomly assigned to the empowerment program, another home visitation program without the empowerment training, or a control condition

in which families were referred to regular community services.

After the intervention period, mothers in the empowerment training condition had more of a sense of power in the family than mothers in the other conditions did, and they reported fewer postpartum depression symptoms. The rate of physical abuse, including spanking and slapping, was only 4% in the empowerment group compared with 23% in the other home visitation group and 26% in the community referral group. Moreover, the children in the empowerment group were in better health and were better able to manage stress. Importantly, the benefits of the program were greatest for families with high-risk children. As the graph here shows, after empowerment training, harsh parenting was unlikely whether the child was at risk for health problems or not, whereas in the control conditions, children at risk were treated far more harshly than low-risk children, suggesting that they were headed for trouble developmentally.

What about parents who are already abusive? Here the challenge is more difficult. Occasional visits from a social worker are unlikely to solve the problem. A more promising approach is Parents Anonymous, a self-help program based on Alcoholics Anonymous that helps caregivers understand their problems and gives them the emotional support they often lack. However, Robert Emery and Lisa Laumann-Billings (1998) argue that the social service sys-

tem needs to distinguish more sharply between milder forms of abuse, for which supportive interventions such as Parents Anonymous are appropriate, and severe forms, where it may be necessary to prosecute the abuser and protect the children from injury and death by removing them from the home. Courts traditionally have been hesitant to break up families, but too often children who have been seriously abused are repeatedly abused.

A comprehensive approach is likely to be most effective. Abusive parents need emotional support and the opportunity to learn more effective parenting, problem-solving, and coping skills, and the victims of abuse need day care programs and developmental training to help them overcome cognitive, social, and emotional deficits caused by abuse (Malley-Morrison & Hines, 2004). The goal in combating child abuse and other forms of family violence must be to convert a pathological family system into a healthy one.

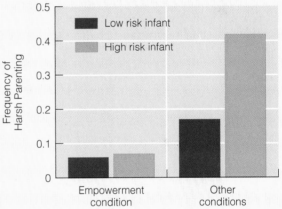

Empowerment training for low-income mothers under stress reduces harsh parenting practices, especially among mothers who are the most at risk of being abusive because their babies had medical problems or were born prematurely.

SOURCE: Reprinted from *Advances in child development and behavior*, Vol. 31, Kail, Empowerment training for low-income mothers, Page 252, Copyright 2003, with permission from Elsevier.

---

concern in this situation. Instead, abused toddlers were likely to become angry and attack the crying child, reacting to the distress of peers much as their abusive parents react to their distress (Main & George, 1985, p. 410; see also Klimes-Dougan & Kistner, 1990):

Martin (an abused boy of 32 months) tried to take the hand of the crying other child, and when she resisted, he slapped her on the arm with his open hand. He then turned away from her to

look at the ground and began vocalizing very strongly, "Cut it out! CUT IT OUT!," each time saying it a little faster and louder. He patted her, but when she became disturbed by his patting, he retreated, hissing at her and baring his teeth. He then began patting her on the back again, his patting became beating, and he continued beating her despite her screams.

Remarkable as it may seem, many other neglected and abused children turn out fine. What distinguishes these children from the ones who have long-term problems? Part of the reason may be that they have genes that protect them from the negative psychological effects of abuse and possibly other stressful life events. Avshalom Caspi and his colleagues (Caspi et al., 2003) found that maltreatment during childhood increases the likelihood of clinical depression among individuals with a genetic makeup that predisposes them to depression but not among individuals with a genetic makeup known to protect against depression. Indeed, among individuals whose genes protect against depression, the rate of depression is no higher among adults who were mistreated as children than among adults who were not. Similarly, maltreatment increases the risk of aggression, or conduct disorder, in children, but only among children who have a high genetic risk to behave antisocially (Jaffee et al., 2005). It seems, then, that genes and environment interact to determine the life outcomes of abused and maltreated children and that some children's genes protect them. Environmental factors can also make a big difference; for example, a close relationship with at least one nonabusive adult helps protect children against the destructive effects of abuse (Egeland et al., 1988).

Knowing what we know about the causes and effects of abuse, what can be done to prevent it, stop it, and undo the damage? What would you propose? The Applications box on page 465 offers some solutions. Meanwhile, we hope this examination of diverse family experiences has convinced you that the family is indeed centrally important in human development.

SUMMING UP

▌ Family violence occurs in all possible relationships within the family. A closer look at child abuse reveals that parent characteristics such as a history of abuse and low self-esteem, child characteristics such as medical problems or a difficult temperament, and contextual factors such as lack of social support and a culture that condones violence all contribute.

▌ Prevention efforts should therefore focus on empowering high-risk parents to deal with difficult and unresponsive children and treatment efforts on either strengthening social support for mild abusers or removing children from the reach of chronic, severe abusers.

CRITICAL THINKING

1. Given what you now know about the roles of the abuser, the abused, and the context in child abuse, how do you think these three sets of factors might enter into spouse violence?

CHAPTER SUMMARY

15.1 UNDERSTANDING THE FAMILY

- The family, whether nuclear or extended, is best viewed as a changing social system embedded in larger social systems that are also changing and in ways that have resulted in more single adults, fewer children, more working women, more divorce, and fewer caregivers for aging adults.

15.2 THE INFANT

- Infants affect and are affected by their parents. Fathers are less involved in caregiving than mothers and specialize in challenging play. Developmental outcomes are likely to be positive when parents have positive indirect effects on development because of their positive influence on each other.

15.3 THE CHILD

- Parenting styles can be described in terms of the dimensions of acceptance–responsiveness and demandingness–control; children are generally more competent when their parents adopt an authoritative style. Genes, socioeconomic status and economic hardship, and culture all affect parenting styles.
- Research on the parent effects, child effects, and transactional models of family influence reminds us that children's problem behaviors are not always solely caused by ineffective parenting.
- When a second child enters the family system, firstborns find the experience stressful; sibling relationships are characterized by both affection and rivalry and siblings play important roles as providers of emotional support, caregiving, teaching, and social experience.

15.4 THE ADOLESCENT

- Parent–child relationships typically remain close in adolescence but involve increased conflict initially before they are renegotiated to become more equal.

15.5 THE ADULT

- Marital satisfaction declines somewhat as newlyweds adjust to each other and become parents, whereas the empty nest transition and a companionate style of grandparenthood are generally positive experiences. Marital satisfaction is more affected by personality than phase of the family life cycle, though.
- In adulthood, siblings have less contact but normally continue to feel both emotionally close and rivalrous. Young adults often establish more mutual relationships with their parents, and most middle-aged adults continue to experience mutually supportive relationships with their elderly parents until some experience middle generation squeeze and caregiver burden.

15.6 DIVERSITY IN FAMILY LIFE

- Inadequately described by the traditional family life cycle concept are single adults (some of whom cohabitate), childless married couples, dual-career families, and gay and lesbian adults.
- Divorce creates a crisis in the family for 1 or 2 years; some children of divorce in single-parent and reconstituted families experience long-lasting adjustment problems.

15.7 THE PROBLEM OF FAMILY VIOLENCE

- Parent characteristics, child characteristics, and contextual factors all contribute to child abuse and must be considered in formulating prevention and treatment programs.

KEY TERMS

MEDIA RESOURCES

BOOK COMPANION WEBSITE

academic.cengage.com/psychology/sigelman
Find online quizzes, flash cards, animations, video clips, experiments, interactive assessments, and other helpful study aids for this text at **academic.cengage.com/psychology/sigelman.** You can also connect directly to the following sites:

CENTER FOR EFFECTIVE DISCIPLINE

This site is designed to help parents identify non-violent means of disciplining their children.

ELDERLY RIGHTS AND RESOURCES: ELDERLY ABUSE

This site, located within the United States Department of Health and Human Services: Administration on Aging web page, is a great resource for accessing information related to elder abuse.

SEPARATION AND DIVORCE

This site hosted by the Department of Family Relations and Human Development at The Ohio State University offers some excellent information on the impact of divorce on child development.

STEPFAMILY ASSOCIATION OF AMERICA

A nice site with information on stepfamilies that includes links to support groups and other available resources. It also contains information about other types of families.

UNDERSTANDING THE DATA: EXERCISES ON THE WEB

academic.cengage.com/psychology/sigelman
For additional insight on the data presented in this chapter, try out the exercises for these figures at **academic.cengage.com/psychology/sigelman:**

> **Figure 15.3** Responses to distressed peers observed in abused and nonabused toddlers in day care

> **Unnumbered Figure** in Applications box "Battling Family Violence." Empowerment training for low-income mothers under stress reduces harsh parenting practices.

CENGAGENOW

academic.cengage.com/login
Go to **academic.cengage.com/login** to link to CengageNOW, your online study tool. First take the Pre-Test for this chapter to get your Personalized Study Plan, which will identify topics you need to review and direct you to online resources. Then take the Post-Test to determine what concepts you have mastered and what you still need work on.

16 CHAPTER

Developmental Psychopathology

PEGGY, A 17-YEAR-OLD FEMALE, was referred by her pediatrician to a child psychiatry clinic for evaluation of an eating disorder. She had lost 10 pounds in 2 months and her mother was concerned. . . . At the clinic she stated that she was not trying to lose weight, had begun to sleep poorly about 2 months ago unless she had several beers, and that she and friends "got trashed" on weekends. Her relationship with her parents was poor; she had attempted suicide a year previously with aspirin and was briefly hospitalized. The day before this evaluation she had taken a razor to school to try to cut her wrists, but it was taken away by a friend. She admitted being depressed and wanting to commit suicide and finally told of discovering that she was pregnant 4 months earlier. Her boyfriend wanted her to abort, she was ambivalent, and then she miscarried spontaneously about 2 months after her discovery. After that, "It didn't really matter how I felt about anything" (Committee on Adolescence, 1996, pp. 71–72).

■ ■ ■

We do not all have as many problems as Peggy, but it is the rare person who makes it through the life span without having at least some difficulty adapting to the challenges of living. Each phase of life poses unique challenges, and some of us inevitably run into trouble mastering them. This chapter is about psychopathology or psychological disorder—about some of the ways in which human development can go awry. It is about how development influences psychopathology and how psychopathology influences development. By applying knowledge of life-span human development to the study of psychological disorders, we understand them better. And by learning more about abnormal patterns of development, we gain new perspectives on the forces that guide and channel—or block and distort—human development more generally.

16.1 | WHAT MAKES DEVELOPMENT ABNORMAL?

Clinical psychologists, psychiatrists, and other mental health professionals struggle to define the line between normal and abnormal behavior and diagnose psychological disorders, often using three broad criteria to do so:

1. *Statistical deviance.* Does the person's behavior fall outside the normal range of behavior? By this criterion, a mild case of the "blahs" or "blues" would not be diagnosed as clinical depression because it is so statistically common, but a more enduring, severe, and persistent case might be.
2. *Maladaptiveness.* Does the person's behavior interfere with adaptation or pose a danger to self or others? Psychological disorders disrupt functioning and create problems for the individual, other people, or both.
3. *Personal distress.* Does the behavior cause personal anguish or discomfort? Many psychological disorders involve personal suffering and are of concern for that reason alone.

Although these guidelines provide a start at defining abnormal behavior, they are vague. We must identify specific forms of statistical deviation, failures of adaptation, and personal distress.

DSM-IV Diagnostic Criteria

Professionals who diagnose and treat psychological disorders use the more specific diagnostic criteria in the *Diagnostic and Statistical Manual of Mental Disorders*, published in 1994 by the American Psychiatric Association (with an update, or text revision, DSM-IV-TR, in 2000). The fourth edition of this manual, known as **DSM-IV,** spells out defining features and symptoms for the range of psychological disorders. Because we will be looking closely at depression in this chapter, we will use it here as an example of how DSM-IV-TR defines disorders. Depression is a family of several affective or mood disorders, some relatively mild and some severe. One of the most important is **major depressive disorder,** defined in DSM-IV-TR as at least one episode of feeling profoundly depressed, sad, and hopeless, and/or losing interest in and the ability to derive pleasure from almost all activities, for at least 2 weeks (American Psychiatric Association, 2000). To qualify as having a major depressive episode, the individual must experience at least five of the following symptoms, including one of the first two, persistently during a 2-week period:

1. Depressed mood (or irritable mood in children and adolescents) nearly every day
2. Greatly decreased interest or pleasure in usual activities
3. Significant weight loss or weight gain (or in children, failure to make expected weight gains)
4. Insomnia or sleeping too much
5. Psychomotor agitation or sluggishness/slowing of behavior
6. Fatigue and loss of energy
7. Feelings of worthlessness or extreme guilt
8. Decreased ability to concentrate or indecisiveness
9. Recurring thoughts of death, suicidal ideas, or a suicide attempt

By these criteria, a man suffering from major depression might, for example, feel extremely discouraged, no longer seem to care about his job or even about sexual relations with his wife, lose weight or have difficulty sleeping, speak and move slowly as though lacking the energy to perform even the simplest actions, have trouble getting his work done, dwell on how guilty he feels about his many failings, and even begin to think he would be better off dead. Major depressive disorder would not be diagnosed if this man were merely a little "down," if his symptoms were directly caused by drug abuse or a medical condition, or if he were going through the normal grieving process after the death of a loved one. Many more people experience depressive symptoms than qualify as having a clinically defined depressive disorder.

Some think DSM-IV-TR does not say enough about cultural and developmental considerations (Christensen, Emde, & Fleming, 2004; Doucette, 2002), but it does note that both should be taken into account in making a diagnosis of major depressive disorder. For example, DSM-IV-TR indicates that Asians who are depressed tend to complain of bodily ailments such as tiredness rather than talking about psychological symptoms such as guilt (American Psychiatric Association, 2000). And although DSM-IV-TR takes the position that depression in a child is fundamentally similar to depression in an adult, it points out that some depressed children express their depression by being irritable rather than sad.

Developmental Psychopathology

Psychologists and psychiatrists have long brought major theories of human development to bear in attempting to understand and treat psychological disorders. Freudian psychoanalytic theory once guided most thinking about psychopathology and clinical practice; behavioral theorists have applied learning principles to the understanding and treatment of behavioral problems; and cognitive psychologists have called attention to how individuals interpret their experiences and perceive themselves.

More recently, evolutionary psychologists have begun asking interesting questions about the adaptive functions of psychological disorders—about how they may help people cope with abuse and other stressors or may otherwise carry advantages (Mealey, 2005; Nesse, 2000). For example, depression may be an adaptive response after loss, helping us to conserve energy and avoid further stress (Mealey, 2005). And genes that tend to make humans restless, energetic, and willing to take risks—like those implicated in attention deficit hyperactivity disorder—may have proved adaptive earlier in our evolutionary history (Selikowitz, 2004). Inheriting too many of these genes may not be as adaptive today; although some successful entrepreneurs credit their attention deficit hyperactivity disorder with helping them to think nonlinearly and creatively and take risks where others might hesitate (Underwood, 2005).

Psychologists have now forged a new field devoted to the study of abnormal behavior from a developmental perspective— **developmental psychopathology** (Cicchetti, 2006; Cummings, Davies, & Campbell, 2000; Rutter & Sroufe, 2000). As defined by pioneers L. Alan Sroufe and Michael Rutter (1984), developmental psychopathology is the study of the origins and course of maladaptive behavior. Developmental psychopathologists appreciate the need to evaluate abnormal development in relation to normal development and to study the two in tandem. They want to know how disorders arise and how their expression changes as the individual develops, and they search for causal

pathways and mechanisms involving genes, the nervous system, the person, and the social environment that lead to normal or abnormal adjustment (Rutter & Sroufe, 2000). In doing so, they bring both a life-span perspective and a systems perspective to the study of abnormal behavior.

Psychopathology as Development, Not Disease

Some developmental psychopathologists fault DSM-IV and similar diagnostic systems for being rooted in a medical or disease model of psychopathology that views psychological problems as diseaselike entities that people either have or do not have. Alan Sroufe (1997) argues that psychopathology is better seen as development rather than as disease; it is a pattern of adaptation that unfolds over time. From this perspective, a researcher cannot understand psychological disorder without understanding not only the person's characteristics, developmental status, and history of adaptation but also the interactions over time between person and environment that either support or undermine healthy development (Cummings et al., 2000; Sameroff, 2000).

■ **Figure 16.1** illustrates the concept of psychopathology as development. It portrays progressive branchings that lead development on either an optimal or a less-than-optimal course. Start with the assumption that normal human genes and normal human environments normally work to push development along a normal course and pull it back on course if it strays (Grossman et al., 2003). Some individuals—even some whose genes or experiences put them at risk to develop a disorder—manage to stay on a route to competence and good adjustment. Some start out poorly but get back on a more adaptive course later; others start off well but deviate later. Still others start on a maladaptive course and deviate further from developmental norms as they age because their early problems make it hard for them to master later developmental tasks and challenges. They may experience a developmental cascade in which genetic risk and early experiences such as living in a disturbed family environment lead to more negative experiences, lack of social support, and ultimately disorder (Kendler, Gardner, & Prescott, 2002).

Now picture Figure 16.1 with many more roadways. In the developmental pathways model, change is possible at many points, and the lines between normal and abnormal development are blurred. A model of this sort may seem complex, but it fits the facts of development. Diagnostic interviews with adults in the United States indicate that about half of us can expect to have some diagnosable disorder involving anxiety, mood, impulse control, or substance abuse by age 75, although more likely a mild than a severe one (Kessler, Berglund, et al., 2005). Half of these cases of disorder will surface by age 14, three-fourths by age 24.

Social Norms and Age Norms

Developmental psychopathologists appreciate that behaviors are abnormal or normal only within particular social and developmental contexts (Cummings et al., 2000; Lopez &

■ **FIGURE 16.1** Developmental pathways leading to normal and abnormal outcomes. Some individuals start on a maladaptive course and deviate further from developmental norms as they age (route A); some start poorly but return to a more adaptive course later (route B); others stay on a route to competence and good adjustment all along (route C); and still others start off well but deviate later in life (route D).

SOURCE: Adapted from Sroufe (1997).

Guarnaccia, 2000). **Social norms** are expectations about how to behave in a particular social context—whether a culture, a subculture, or an everyday setting. What is normal in one social context may be abnormal in another. For example, John Weisz and his colleagues (1997) have discovered that Thai children are more likely than American children to have (or to be reported to have) symptoms of inner distress such as anxiety and depression and are less likely to engage in aggression and other forms of "acting out." One reason for the difference may be that the Thai culture places high value on emotional control and socializes children to internalize rather than vent their negative emotions. The definitions and meanings, the rates, and the developmental courses and correlates of abnormal behavior vary from culture to culture, from subculture to subculture, and from historical period to historical period (Serafica & Vargas, 2006). Although there are universal aspects of psychopathology too, it is shaped by its social context.

In addition, developmental psychopathologists recognize that abnormal behavior must be defined in relation to age norms—societal expectations about what behavior is appropriate or normal at various ages. The 4-year-old boy who frequently cries, acts impulsively, wets his bed, is afraid of the dark, and talks to his imaginary friend may be perceived as—and may

be—normal. The 40-year-old who does the same things needs serious help. You simply cannot define abnormal behavior and development without having a solid grasp of normal behavior and development.

Developmental Issues

As they attempt to understand developmental pathways to adaptive or maladaptive functioning, developmental psychopathologists grapple with the same developmental issues that have concerned us throughout this book—most notably, the nature–nurture issue (Rutter, Moffitt, & Caspi, 2006) and the issue of continuity and discontinuity in development (Rutter, Kim-Cohen, & Maughan, 2006; and see Chapter 2). Addressing the nature–nurture issue involves asking important questions such as these:

- How do biological, psychological, and social factors interact over time to give rise to psychological disorders?
- What are the important risk factors for psychological disorders—and what are the protective factors that keep some individuals who are at risk from developing disorders?

As Japanese mothers have increased pressure on their children to succeed in school, cases of children refusing to attend school have become more prevalent (Kameguchi & Murphy-Shigematsu, 2001). This unhappy student may be reacting to his mother's overinvolvement in his schoolwork.

Addressing the continuity–discontinuity issue means asking these sorts of questions:

- Are most childhood problems passing phases that have no bearing on adjustment in adulthood, or does poor functioning in childhood predict poor functioning later in life?
- How do expressions of psychopathology change as the developmental status of the individual changes?

The Diathesis–Stress Model

In their efforts to understand how nature and nurture contribute to psychopathology, developmental psychopathologists have found a **diathesis–stress model** of psychopathology useful (Coyne & Whiffen, 1995; Ingram & Price, 2001). This model proposes that psychopathology results from the interaction over time of a predisposition or vulnerability to psychological disorder (called a *diathesis* that can involve a particular genetic makeup, physiology, cognitions, personality, or a combination of these) and the experience of stressful events. This model helps to explain why "'bad' things have 'bad' effects among some—but not all—people, some—but not all—of the time" (Steinberg & Avenevoli, 2000, p. 66).

Consider depression. We know that certain people are genetically predisposed to become depressed. Genetic factors account for about 40% of the variation in a group of people in symptoms of major depressive disorder; environmental factors unique to the individual account for the rest (Glowinski et al., 2003). A genetic vulnerability to depression manifests itself as imbalances in serotonin and other key neurotransmitters that affect mood and in such characteristics as high emotional reactivity to stress, including high production of the stress hormone cortisol, and self-defeating patterns of thinking in the face of negative events (Garber & Flynn, 2001; Gotlib et al., 2006).

According to the diathesis–stress model, however, individuals predisposed to become depressed are not likely to do so unless they experience significant losses or other stressful events, as illustrated in ■ Figure 16.2. One stressful life event (such as the death of a loved one or a divorce) is usually not enough to trigger major depression, but when negative events pile up or become chronic, a vulnerable person may succumb. Meanwhile, individuals who do not have a diathesis—a vulnerability to depression—may be able to withstand high levels of stress without becoming depressed.

Researchers can now pinpoint some of these diathesis–stress, or gene–environment, interactions. For example, inheriting a particular variant of a gene involved in controlling levels of the neurotransmitter serotonin and experiencing multiple stressful events in early adulthood results in an especially high probability of major depression (Caspi, Sugden et al., 2003; and see Chapter 3). Among people with one or two of the high-risk genes, about 10% became depressed if they experienced no negative life events between ages 21 and 26, but 33% became depressed if they experienced four or more such events. By comparison, even when exposed to many stressful events, only 17% of individuals with two low-risk versions of the gene became depressed (see Jokela et al., 2007, for a similar example).

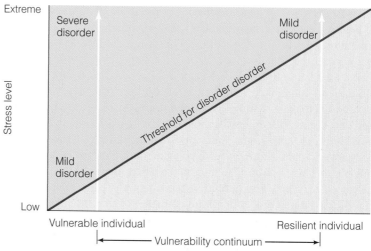

■ **FIGURE 16.2** The diathesis–stress model. For a vulnerable individual, even mild stress can result in disorder. For an individual who is resilient and does not have a vulnerability or diathesis to disorder, it would take extremely high levels of stress to cause disorder; even then, the disorder might be only mild and temporary.
SOURCE: Adapted from Ingram & Price (2001).

Depressive disorders (and many other psychological disorders) evolve from an interaction of diathesis and stress—or, to use familiar developmental terms, from the interplay of nature and nurture. It is messier than Figure 16.2 suggests, though. For example, it is clear that genes not only predispose some people to depression but also influence the extent to which they experience stressful life events (Rice, Harold, & Thapar, 2003). Moreover, the relationship between stress and disorder is reciprocal: Life stress aggravates disorder, but disorder also makes lives more stressful (Grant et al., 2004). Finally, in a person genetically predisposed to depression, a depressive episode early in life in response to intense stress may bring about changes in gene activity and in the neurobiology of the stress response system (the hypothalamic–pituitary–adrenal axis). These changes may lower the threshold for a future depressive episode (the diagonal line in Figure 16.2) so that later in life even mild stress can trigger depression (Grossman et al., 2003).

For some disorders we examine in this chapter, the diathesis for disorder is strong, probably more important than environmental influences in causing disorder. Environment may still play an important role, however, by shaping the course of the disorder and its effects on functioning and later development (Steinberg & Avenevoli, 2000). The depressed adolescent growing up in a hostile, disturbed family context, for example, is likely to fare worse than the depressed adolescent who receives parental support and appropriate professional treatment.

This chapter highlights a sampling of developmental problems associated with each phase of the life span (for example, autism to illustrate disorders arising in infancy; attention deficit hyperactivity disorder, or ADHD, to illustrate childhood disorders; anorexia nervosa to illustrate disorders linked to adolescence; and Alzheimer's disease to illustrate disorders of old age). In addition, we look at depression in every developmental period to see how its symptoms and significance change over the life span.

Summing Up

▪ Diagnosing a psychological disorder such as major depressive disorder involves the broad criteria of statistical deviance, maladaptiveness, and personal distress and the application of specific DSM-IV diagnostic criteria.

▪ Developmental psychopathology, the study of the origins and course of maladaptive behavior, offers a more developmental approach to psychological disorders, considering both social norms and age norms in diagnosis and charting developmental pathways leading to adaptive or maladaptive developmental outcomes.

▪ Questions about nature and nurture and about continuity and discontinuity must be answered, and diathesis–stress models must be developed, if researchers want to understand the development of psychological disorders.

CRITICAL THINKING

1. How are the criteria of statistical deviance, maladaptiveness, and personal distress reflected in the DSM-IV-TR definition of major depressive disorder?

16.2 THE INFANT

Adults worry about infants who do not eat properly, who cry endlessly, or who seem overly withdrawn and timid. Because infant development is strongly channeled by biological maturation, few infants develop severe psychological problems. Yet psychopathology exists in infancy, and its effects can be tragic.

Autism

Jeremy, 3½ years old, has big brown eyes and a sturdy body. His mother carries him down the corridor toward the examiner, who greets them. Jeremy glances at the examiner's face but does not smile or say hello. They walk together into a playroom. Jeremy's mother puts him down, and he sits on the carpet in front of some toys. He picks up two blocks, bangs them together, and begins to stack the blocks, one on top of the other, not stopping until he has used the entire set. Jeremy does not look at the examiner or his mother while he works, nor when he finishes. And he does not make a sound. The examiner asks him to give her a red block. He does not respond. On their way out, Jeremy and his mother stop to look at a poster of a waterfall surrounded by redwood trees. "Yosemite Valley," Jeremy reads out—the name beneath the picture. His voice sounds automated, almost robotic (Sigman & Capps, 1997, p. 1).

Autism, first identified and described by Leo Kanner in 1943, is a serious disorder that begins in infancy and is characterized by abnormal social development, impaired language and communication, and repetitive behavior. Picture the typical infant that we have described in this book: a social being who responds to others and forms close attachments starting at 6 or 7 months of age, a linguistic being who babbles and later uses one- and two-word sentences to converse, and a curious explorer who is fascinated by new objects and experiences. Now consider the three defining features of autism highlighted in DSM-IV-TR (American Psychiatric Association, 2000; also see Bowler, 2007; Frith, 2003):

1. *Abnormal social development.* Autistic children have difficulty forming normal social relationships, responding appropriately to social cues, and sharing social experiences with other people. Like Jeremy, they seem to live in a world of their own, as though they find social contact aversive rather than pleasurable. They are far less likely than other infants to make eye contact, jointly attend to something with a social partner, seek other people for comfort, snuggle when held, and make friends. They also have great difficulty reading other people's minds and emotions, responding with empathy when others are distressed, and demonstrating self-awareness and self-

conscious emotions such as embarrassment and guilt. It has been suggested that they lack self-awareness and have difficulty identifying, as one self to another, with someone else's attitudes and feelings (Hobson et al., 2006). Although many autistic children form secure attachments to their parents, many others display what Chapter 14 described as a disorganized–disoriented pattern of attachment (Sigman & Capps, 1997). Interestingly, Marinus van IJzendoorn and his colleagues (2007) have found that the parents of children with autism are no less sensitive than the parents of children without it, but that the usual relationship between sensitive parenting and secure attachment does not hold true for families with a child who has autism. Instead, the child's social deficits largely govern how secure the parent–child relationship can become.

2. *Impaired language and communicative skills.* Some autistic children are mute; others acquire language skills with some degree of success but still cannot communicate—that is, carry on a true conversation (Tager-Flusberg, 2000). As infants, autistic children often do not babble, gesture, or speak single words at the normal ages (Filipek et al., 2000). When they do speak, they may use a flat, robotlike tone; reverse pronouns (for example, use "you" to refer to the self); and engage in **echolalia** (a parroting of what someone else says).

3. *Repetitive, stereotyped behavior and restricted interests.* Autistic children seek sameness and repetition. They engage in stereotyped behaviors such as rocking, flapping their hands in front of their faces, or spinning toys; if they are more intellectually able, they may carry out elaborate rituals such as a particular sequence of getting-dressed activities. They also become obsessed with particular objects and interests and can become highly distressed when their physical environment is altered (as when a chair in the living room is moved a few feet).

Many individuals with autism continue to function poorly as adolescents and adults, but some improve with age. One "improver," Jerry, described his childhood as a reign of "confusion and terror" in which "nothing seemed constant; everything was unpredictable and strange" (Bemporad, 1979, p. 192).

It is important to recognize that individuals with autism vary greatly in the degree and nature of their deficits. There is a whole family of autistic conditions, called **autism spectrum disorders (ASDs),** within the DSM-IV category labeled "pervasive developmental disorders," which includes these and additional conditions that affect many aspects of functioning and have social and communication problems at their core (Bregman, 2005). Autism is an ASD; so is **Asperger syndrome,** in which the child has normal or above-average intelligence and good verbal skills, and clearly wants to establish social relationships, but has seriously deficient social-cognitive and social skills. Affected children are sometimes called "little professors" because they talk rather stiffly and formally, and at mind-numbing length, about the particular subjects that obsess them. They have been largely invisible until recently, although people around them tend to view them as odd and socially aloof. Other ASDs are Rett syndrome and childhood disintegrative disorder, both of which involve declines in multiple areas of functioning after birth.

Rates of autism appear to be rising. Autism in the narrow sense now affects about 20 of 10,000 children, and autism in the broader sense of a spectrum of disorders affects almost 60 children per 10,000, or 1 in 166 (Chakrabarti & Fombonne, 2005). Three or 4 boys are affected for every girl, with affected girls often having severe impairments and low IQ scores (Dawson & Toth, 2006). The Explorations box takes up the question of whether there is an autism epidemic.

Autistic children are autistic before age 3 and probably from birth. However, because at first they often seem to be normal and exceptionally good babies, or because physicians are slow to make the diagnosis even when parents express concerns about their child's development, many autistic children are not diagnosed until preschool (Klin et al., 2004). Researchers are working furiously to improve early screening and detection so that these children can receive early treatment. Autistic infants are given away by their lack of normal social responsiveness— for example, by failure to display normal infant behaviors such as orientation to human voices, babbling, preference for human over nonhuman stimuli, eye contact and visual focus on faces in a scene (autistic babies tend to focus on objects in the background), joint attention (a key precursor of theory-of-mind skills), and reciprocity or taking turns, as in mutual smiling and peek-a-boo games (Klin et al., 2004; Lord, 2007; Zwaigenbaum et al., 2005).

Many people believe that most autistic individuals are exceptionally intelligent. Some have average or above average IQs, but many are mentally retarded. With more higher-functioning children being diagnosed today, the percentage of children with autism who are also mentally retarded has dropped to under half but is still significant (Chakrabarti & Fombonne, 2001; Volkmar et al., 2004). Meanwhile, some autistic individuals, whether their IQs are high or low, show special talents such as the ability to quickly calculate days of the week corresponding to dates on the calendar or to memorize incredible amounts of information about train schedules (see Heaton & Wallace, 2004, and the description of savant syndrome in Chapter 9).

IS THERE AN AUTISM EPIDEMIC?

A debate has raged in recent years about why rates of autism seem to be increasing. There is no question that they are. For example, Christopher Gillberg and his colleagues (2006) have been studying the prevalence of autism in an area of Sweden for a number of years (see graph). Their data clearly show an increase in the prevalence of autism and other autistic spectrum disorders such as Asperger syndrome from the 1970s to the 1990s, as shown in the graph. In the United States, the rate has zoomed from around 5 out of 10,000 before 1990 to 60 out of 10,000, recently (Chakrabarti & Fombonne, 2005).

The question is why. You may have seen in the press charges that either the measles virus or a mercury-based preservative in the vaccinations children receive for measles, mumps, and rubella is the culprit. The evidence simply does not support this charge, which unfortunately has made some parents fear having their children immunized. To cite just one piece of evidence, rates of autism continued to climb after the mercury-based preservative was removed from vaccines in 1999 (Costello, Foley, & Angold, 2006; Vedantam, 2007). Still, because the vaccination is normally given to infants at about 15 months of age and children with autism often seem normal at birth and do not display their autistic symptoms until about that age, the vaccine myth has persisted.

Most researchers, including Gillberg and his colleagues, believe that increased rates of autistic spectrum disorders are mainly a result of increased awareness of autism, broader definitions of it, and better recognition and diagnosis of cases by parents and teachers as well as clinicians—especially cases at the mild end of the spectrum (Gillberg et al., 2006; Grinker, 2007). In Sweden, for example, legislation on autism was enacted in 1981 and services were made available but a diagnosis was necessary to receive them. Gillberg applied DSM-IV criteria in his study, but the addition of Asperger syndrome to DSM-IV in 1994 is also believed to have contributed to the increase in autism diagnoses since then. Moreover, in the United States, autism was not added to a government list of disabilities eligible for special education services until 1991 (Grinker, 2007).

In sum, it can be difficult to interpret changes in the prevalence of a psychological disorder. In the case of autism spectrum disorders, the recent rise in prevalence seems to be more about better detection of cases that were there all along than about new cases and causes.

The number of diagnosed cases of autism spectrum disorder has been increasing. These data are from Göteberg, Sweden. Of 546 cases identified over the 18-year period, 38% had autism, 17% Asperger syndrome, and 44% "pervasive developmental disorder not otherwise specified." These numbers of cases translate into a prevalence rate of 53 cases per 10,000 population for the entire period, but 80 per 10,000 in the last 6-year period. The male (light blue) to female (dark blue) ratio was almost 3 to 1.

SOURCE: From C. Gillberg, M. Cederlund, K. Lamberg, & L. Zeijlon, The autism epidemic: The registered prevalence of autism in a Swedish urban area, *Journal of Autism and Developmental Disorders*, 36, 429–435. Copyright 2006 Springer. Reprinted with permission.

Autism used to be seen as a clear example of development that is qualitatively different from normal development. No more. The social impairment that defines autism is increasingly viewed as the extreme end of a genetically influenced continuum of social responsiveness, quantitatively rather than qualitatively different from normal social behavior (Constantino & Todd, 2003). In other words, many of us have some of the traits associated with autism to some degree, and the dividing line between normality and abnormality is arbitrary. Instead of apples and oranges—normal functioning versus autistic functioning—there are only degrees of appleness, a principle that appears to hold for most other psychological disorders.

Suspected Causes

Interest in solving the mysteries of autism is intense, and some fascinating hypotheses have been put forward in recent years to explain why individuals with autistic spectrum disorders show the symptoms they do. Early theorists suggested that rigid and cold parenting by "refrigerator moms" caused autism, but this harmful myth has long been put to rest (Achenbach, 1982). It is now understood that interacting with an autistic child can easily cause parents to be tense and frustrated and that the parents of autistic children, the source of genes that contribute to autism, sometimes have mild forms of some autistic spectrum traits themselves. Bad parenting is not responsible for autism; rather, autism has a biological basis. Genes contribute strongly to autism (Veenstra-Vanderweele & Cook, 2003). One research team found that if one identical twin was autistic, the other was autistic in 60% of the twin pairs studied; the concordance rate for fraternal twin pairs was 0% (Bailey et al., 1995). Moreover, when the broader spectrum of autism-related deficits was considered, 92% of the identical twins but only 10% of the fraternal twins were alike.

Many genes on several chromosomes have been implicated; in some cases genes related to neural communication appear to have been copied too many times or left out during meiosis (Autism Genome Project Consortium, 2007). Most likely individuals with autism inherit several genes that put them at risk. It also appears that the three major impairments associated with autism—social impairments, communication disorders, and repetitive behaviors—are associated with distinct genetic causes (Ronald, Happé, Bolton et al., 2006). That one identical twin can be autistic although the other is not suggests that early environmental influences also contribute, although it is not clear how. An environmental trigger like a virus or chemicals in the environment could interact with a genetic predisposition to cause it.

Many autistic children display neurological abnormalities, and many of them have epilepsy (Volkmar et al., 2004). However, the neurological abnormalities are varied, and it is not yet clear which are most central to autism or how they arise. It has been observed, for example, that autistic children experience especially rapid and extensive brain growth during the first year of life, starting out with small heads and brains at birth but experiencing faster-than-normal growth during the first year of life and then a slowing of growth so that by adulthood they have normal-sized brains (Courchesne, Carper, & Akshoomoff, 2003; Redcay & Courchesne, 2005). It is hypothesized that neurons in the frontal cortex proliferate wildly during the early sensitive period for brain development but do not become properly interconnected (Volkmar et al., 2004).

Recognizing that knowledge is changing rapidly, we will outline one promising view that has emerged recently. As we have seen, individuals with autism regularly show limited understanding of mental states such as feelings, desires, beliefs, and intentions and of their role in human behavior—that is, they lack what was characterized in Chapter 13 as a theory of mind (Baron-Cohen, 2000). As infants, they also do not show some of the early precursors of theory of mind such as empathy, joint attention, pretend play, and imitation (Charman, 2000). Researchers have therefore been looking more closely at the brain mechanisms involved in social cognition (Oberman & Ramachandran, 2007), and they are now actively exploring a **mirror neuron simulation hypothesis** of autism. This view holds that malfunctioning of mirror neuron systems located in a number of brain areas account for the deficits individuals with autism show in imitation, theory-of-mind skills, empathy, and language (Oberman & Ramachandran, 2007; and see Chapter 13).

Mirror neuron systems allow us to make sense of other people's feelings and thoughts by relating them to feelings and thoughts we have experienced ourselves. By internally simulating what another person may be experiencing, we connect with that person (see Chapter 13). In one study (McIntosh et al., 2006), autistic and nonautistic adults watched pictures of happy and angry facial expressions so that the researchers could see if their faces automatically and subtly mimicked the expressions they saw—a good example of how mirror neurons allow us to simulate other people's emotions and relate them to our own. Although people with autistic disorders could mimic the faces they saw if asked to do so, they did not do so spontaneously—one example of accumulating evidence suggesting that their mirror neuron systems do not function properly (Oberman & Ramachandran, 2007).

It is not clear whether lack of properly functioning mirror neuron systems or some other neural impairment will prove to be at the heart of the problems autistic children display; the disorder clearly involves multiple cognitive impairments. Autistic individuals not only have social cognitive deficits but they have difficulty with certain **executive functions,** the higher-level control functions based in the prefrontal cortex of the brain that allow us to plan, change flexibly from one course of action to another, and inhibit actions (Bowler, 2007; Frith, 2003). This may explain their repetitive behavior (they often become fixated on doing an activity again and again and may not be able to switch to another activity easily), something the mirror neuron simulation theory does not explain well. Their tendency to focus on details and miss "the big picture" is another key cognitive impairment (Bowler, 2007; Frith, 2003). To make the mystery more intriguing, Simon Baron-Cohen (2003) has put forth an extreme male brain hypothesis regarding autistic spectrum disorders, described in the Explorations box. Perhaps it is not surprising that a number of cognitive and social deficits have been nominated as the "core" deficit in autism and a number of aspects of brain functioning are believed to be impaired; autism is, after all, a *pervasive* disorder.

Developmental Outcomes and Treatment

What becomes of children with autism as they get older? The long-term outcome in the past has usually been poor, especially if autism is accompanied by mental retardation. Most individuals with autism improve in functioning, but they are autistic for life, showing limited social skills even as adults, although about a third are employed in their 20s (Howlin et al., 2004). Positive outcomes are most likely among those who have IQ scores above 70 and reasonably good communication skills by age 5.

Can treatment help autistic children overcome their problems? Researchers continue to search for drugs that will correct the suspected brain dysfunctions of these children, but they are a long way from discovering a "magic pill." Some autistic children are given drugs to control behavioral problems such as hyperactivity or obsessive–compulsive behavior, drugs that

IS AUTISM AN EXTREME VERSION OF THE MALE BRAIN?

Many years ago, the discoverer of Asperger syndrome, Hans Asperger, suggested that the syndrome might reflect an extreme version of stereotypically masculine intelligence (Baron-Cohen, 2003). More recently, Simon Baron-Cohen (2003, 2005) has fleshed out Asperger's suggestion and proposed an **extreme male brain hypothesis** about autism. In his book *The Essential Difference,* Baron-Cohen lays out evidence that females tend to excel in empathizing (identifying people's thoughts and emotions and responding to them with appropriate emotions), males in systemizing (analyzing things to figure out how they work, extracting rules that determine what leads to what, and understanding systems). So, for example, little girls tend to be more interested than little boys in faces and in interacting with people, and women tend to be more able than men to read facial expressions of emotions and more likely to enter the helping professions. Meanwhile, little boys are more likely than little girls to enjoy playing with cars and trucks and building blocks and are more likely as adults to go into math, science, and engineering fields where they can work with predictable systems of objects rather than with ever-unpredictable people. Even when they are only a day old, girls prefer to look at a woman's face rather than a mechanical-looking mobile with some of the features of a face incorporated into it in a scrambled arrangement; by contrast, boys prefer the mechanical mobile (Connellan et al., 2000).

Baron-Cohen is quick to point out that not all women excel at empathizing and not all men excel at systemizing; there are simply average differences between the sexes, most likely caused by a combination of biological and environmental factors. Moreover, some people are strong at both or weak in both skills. Of interest to us here are the individuals who are extremely weak in empathizing and extremely strong in systemizing. They, Baron-Cohen argues, have the traits associated with autistic spectrum disorders. Much evidence suggests that individuals with autism and autism spectrum disorders are weak at empathizing and reading other people's mental states (Baron-Cohen, 2003; Golan et al., 2006). Moreover, their repetitive actions (spinning plates or dropping sand through their fingers for hours) could be interpreted as attempts to systemize, to figure out the rules, and their desire for sameness an attempt to keep the world orderly and rule governed.

To assess empathizing and systemizing in high-functioning individuals within the autism spectrum, John Lawson, Simon Baron-Cohen, and Sally Wheelwright (2004) gave males with Asperger syndrome, normal males, and normal females tasks to measure empathizing (understanding social outcomes when one person says something likely to upset another character in a story) and systemizing (predicting in mechanical diagrams how two levers or bobs will respond to the movement of another lever connected to them). On the empathizing tasks, females did better than males without Asperger syndrome, who in turn outperformed males with Asperger syndrome. On the systemizing tasks, by contrast, both male groups outperformed the women.

Baron-Cohen also cites concrete cases of the extreme male brain at work. Richard, an award-winning mathematician, has Asperger syndrome. Despite his understanding of the mechanics of phones, he did not know how to begin or end a phone conversation or what to say in between. He much preferred dealing with people one at a time rather than in groups, because people, unlike numbers, were too unpredictable for him. Noting that Isaac Newton and Albert Einstein had some similar traits, Baron-Cohen points out that Asperger syndrome is common in families with many "male-brained" scientists and engineers. Exposure to a high dose of the male hormone testosterone during the prenatal period has been linked to strong spatial and mechanical abilities, and Baron-Cohen and others are now pursuing the possibility that high exposure to testosterone prenatally may be implicated in autism spectrum disorders and may also explain why these conditions are so much more common among males than among females (see Ingudomnukul et al., 2007).

The extreme male brain hypothesis suggests that autism, once thought to be a prime example of truly deviant human development, may instead just represent the extreme end of a continuum of intellectual functioning. The extreme male brain hypothesis also calls attention to the strengths of individuals with autism and suggests that, if accommodations are made for their cognitive style, they can learn better and can be steered toward the kinds of mechanical and detail-oriented jobs that suit them. It is too soon to say, however, how valid the extreme male brain view of autism is; at this point, Baron-Cohen is still developing the concepts of empathizing and systemizing and has not yet reconciled his theory with evidence of the roles of genes in autism (Bowler, 2007; Ronald, Happé, & Plomin, 2006).

---

help them benefit from educational programs but do not cure autism (Volkmar, 2001).

The most effective approach to treating autism is intensive and highly structured behavioral and educational programming, beginning as early as possible, continuing throughout childhood, and involving the family (Koegel, Koegel, & McNerney, 2001; Simpson & Otten, 2005). The goal is to make the most of the plasticity of the young brain during its sensitive period, so early intervention is key. O. Ivar Lovaas and his colleagues pioneered the application of reinforcement principles to shape social and language skills in autistic chil-

dren (Lovaas & Smith, 2003). In an early study, Lovaas (1987) compared two groups of children with autism treated at the University of California at Los Angeles. One group received intensive treatment—more than 40 hours a week of one-on-one treatment for 2 or more years during their preschool years. Trained student therapists worked with these children using reinforcement principles to reduce their aggressive and self-stimulatory behavior and to teach them developmentally appropriate skills such as how to imitate others, play with toys and with peers, use language, and master academic concepts. The training procedures involve many repetitions of simple learning tasks and the delivery of reinforcers such as bits of cereal for successful performance. Parents were taught to use the same behavioral techniques at home. The children who received this intensive treatment were compared with a control group of similarly disturbed children who, because of staff shortages or transportation problems, received a similar treatment program but were exposed to it for only 10 or fewer hours a week.

Lovaas reported astounding results—for example, IQ scores about 30 points higher in the treatment group than in the control group. Other researchers have criticized this study's design, however, because it was not a true experiment with random assignment to treatment and control groups. As it turns out, early behavioral interventions usually do not convert autistic children into normally functioning ones (Volkmar et al., 2004). However, many children with autism, especially those who are young and are not severely retarded, can make good gains if they receive intensive cognitive and behavioral training and comprehensive family services starting early in life (Lovaas & Smith, 2003). In any case, training programs for the growing number of adults with autism and support services for their families are needed.

Depression

Does it seem possible to you that an infant could experience major depressive disorder as defined in DSM-IV-TR? Infants are surely not capable of the negative cognitions common among depressed adults—the low self-esteem, guilt, worthlessness, hopelessness, and so on (Garber, 1984). After all, they have not yet acquired the capacity for symbolic thought or self-awareness that would allow them to reflect on their experience. Yet infants can exhibit some of the behavioral symptoms (such as loss of interest in activities or psychomotor slowing) and **somatic symptoms** (bodily symptoms such as loss of appetite and disruption of normal sleep patterns) of depression. Researchers are still debating whether true depressive disorders can occur in infancy, but it is clear that babies can and do experience depression-like states and symptoms (Cytryn & McKnew, 1996; Wasserman, 2006).

Depressive symptoms are most likely to be observed in infants who lack a secure attachment relationship or who experience a disruption of an all-important emotional bond (Boris & Zeanah, 1999; Lyons-Ruth, Zeanah, & Benoit, 2003). It has long been observed that infants permanently separated from their mothers between 6 and 12 months of age tend to become sad, weepy, listless, unresponsive, and withdrawn and to show delays in virtually all aspects of their development (Spitz, 1946). Infants who display a disorganized pattern of attachment, in which they do not seem to know whether to approach or avoid the attachment figure (see Chapter 14)—an attachment style common among abused children—are especially likely to show symptoms of depression (Egeland & Carlson, 2004; Lyons-Ruth et al., 2003).

Infants whose mothers—or fathers—are depressed are also at risk (Gotlib et al., 2006; Ramchandani et al., 2005). They

adopt an interaction style that resembles that of their depressed caregivers; they vocalize little and look sad, even when interacting with women other than their mothers, and they begin to show developmental delays by age 1 (Field, 1995a). They are at increased risk of becoming clinically depressed themselves later in life and of developing other psychological disorders. This may be because of a combination of genes and stressful experiences with their unpredictable mothers (that is, because of diathesis–stress). Stress early in life can produce children with an overactive stress-response system who are easily distressed and unable to regulate their negative emotions effectively (Goodman, 2002; Gotlib et al., 2006). Interventions can help depressed parents understand and deal with their problems and interact more sensitively with their babies (Cicchetti, Toth, & Rogosch, 2004).

Some infants who are neglected, abused, separated from attachment figures, or otherwise raised in a stressful or unaffectionate manner by a mother who may be stressed or depressed herself not only display depression-like symptoms but also develop the life-threatening disorder called **failure to thrive** (Benoit & Coolbear, 2004; Chatoor & Ganiban, 2004). These youngsters fail to grow normally, lose weight, and become seriously underweight for their age—and are often developmentally delayed as a result. In some cases a physical cause such as a heart defect or swallowing problem can be identified, but in other cases, labeled nonorganic failure to thrive, the causes seem to be more emotional than physical (Chatoor & Ganiban, 2004; Lyons-Ruth, Zeanah, & Benoit, 2003). Babies with nonorganic failure to thrive may gain weight and overcome their depression-like emotional symptoms quickly when they are removed from their homes but can relapse if they are returned to the insensitive care they were receiving (Bauchner,

Failure to thrive can have either physical (organic) or emotional (nonorganic) causes.

1996). The long-term development of these infants is likely to be especially poor if they have a history of both failure to thrive and maltreatment (Kerr, Black, & Krishnakumar, 2000). Intervening to change the family system is therefore critical.

SUMMING UP

▌ Autism is characterized by abnormal social development, impaired language and communication skills, and repetitive behavior. There are other autistic spectrum disorders, including Asperger syndrome; the "autism epidemic" is mainly a result of better identification of mild cases within the autism spectrum.

▌ Genetics plays a strong role in autism; hypotheses about the brain dysfunctions and cognitive impairments at the root of this disorder include the mirror neuron simulation theory of social cognitive deficits and extreme male brain hypothesis. Early behavioral intervention is the preferred treatment.

▌ Even babies can display many of the symptoms of depression, especially the behavioral and somatic ones, or nonorganic failure to thrive if they experience long-term or permanent separation from an attachment figure or are brought up by depressed, unresponsive, or rejecting caregivers.

CRITICAL THINKING

1. How do you think the now discredited view that autism is caused by cold, "refrigerator" mothers arose, and how would you now characterize parents of children with autism?

2. You believe that 1-year-old Luis is depressed: Why do you think so?

16.3 | THE CHILD

Many children experience developmental problems—fears, recurring stomachaches, temper tantrums, and so on. A much smaller proportion are officially diagnosed as having one of the psychological disorders that typically begins in infancy, childhood, or adolescence—or as having one of the psychological disorders (such as major depressive disorder) that can occur at any age. ● Table 16.1 lists the major childhood disorders categorized in DSM-IV-TR. In a study assessing children longitudinally from age 9 to age 16 through detailed interviews with both parents and children, more than one-third of children were judged to have experienced at least one diagnosable psychological disorder by age 16 (Costello et al., 2003). In addition, 1 in 5 young children and 1 in 10 older children qualified as having a diagnosable disorder in any given 3-month window (problems were at their lowest at age 12 before a rise in rates during adolescence).

Many developmental problems of childhood can be placed in one of two broad categories that reflect whether the child's behavior is out of control or overly controlled (Achenbach & Edelbrock, 1978). When children have **externalizing problems,** or undercontrolled disorders, they act out in ways that disturb other people and violate social expectations. They may be aggressive, disobedient, difficult to control, or disruptive (see aggressive behavior discussion in Chapter 13). If their problems are severe, they may be diagnosed as having a conduct disorder or as hyperactive. **Internalizing problems,** or overcontrolled disorders, involve inner distress; they are more disruptive to the child than to other people and include anxiety disorders (such as persistent worrying about separation from loved ones), phobias, severe shyness and with-

● **TABLE 16.1** **SOME PSYCHOLOGICAL DISORDERS USUALLY FIRST DIAGNOSED IN INFANCY, CHILDHOOD, OR ADOLESCENCE**

DSM-IV-TR CATEGORY	MAJOR EXAMPLES
Mental retardation	Subaverage general intellectual functioning
Learning disorders	Reading, math, and writing difficulties
Motor skill disorder	Developmental coordination disorder (extreme clumsiness, lack of coordination)
Communication disorders	Expressive language disorder; stuttering
Pervasive developmental disorders	Autism; similarly severe conditions
Attention deficit and disruptive behavioral disorders	Attention deficit hyperactivity disorder; conduct disorders (persistent antisocial behavior); oppositional defiant disorder
Feeding and eating disorders	Pica (eating nonnutritive substances such as paint or sand)
Tic disorders	Tourette's disorder (involuntary grimaces, grunts, foul language)
Elimination disorders	Enuresis (inappropriate urination); encopresis (inappropriate defecation)

SOURCE: Based on *DSM-IV-TR*, American Psychiatric Association, 2000.

drawal, and depression. Externalizing behaviors decrease from age 4 to age 18, whereas internalizing difficulties increase (Bongers et al., 2003). Externalizing problems are more common among boys, whereas internalizing problems are more prevalent among girls—across cultures (Crijnen, Achenbach, & Verhulst, 1997). Here we will look at one problem of externalization, attention deficit hyperactivity disorder, and one problem of internalization, depression.

Attention Deficit Hyperactivity Disorder

The first year of proper school was a disaster for Greg. He spent most of the time being punished for getting out of his seat, for calling out, and for disrupting other children. The other children called him a "naughty Greg" and he became more and more discouraged and defiant. He did not seem to be learning anything at school at all. He was always in trouble. . . . At the end of the year the teacher told me that if she had to teach Greg for another year she would have resigned! (Selikowitz, 2004, p. 34)

When it was first identified, hyperactivity was defined principally as a problem of excess motor activity, and the term was used to describe children who could not seem to sit still and who were continually on the go. Now hyperactivity is viewed mainly as a problem of attentional control. According to DSM-IV-TR criteria, a child has **attention deficit hyperactivity disorder (ADHD)** if some combination of the following three symptoms is present (see also Selikowitz, 2004; Weyandt, 2007):

1. *Inattention.* The child does not seem to listen, is easily distracted, and does not stick to activities or finish tasks.
2. *Impulsivity.* The child acts before thinking and cannot inhibit urges to blurt something out in class or have a turn in a group activity.
3. *Hyperactivity.* The child is restless and is perpetually fidgeting, finger tapping, or chattering.

About 3 to 7% of school-age children, possibly more, are diagnosable as ADHD (American Psychiatric Association, 2000) and at least two boys for every girl have the disorder, although girls may in some cases be underdiagnosed because they often do not show as much of the hyperactivity and acting out associated with ADHD as boys do (Weyandt, 2007). Some critics believe that ADHD is overdiagnosed in the United States and even question whether ADHD is a valid diagnosis, but rates are actually quite similar around the world when similar diagnostic definitions are applied (Moffitt & Melchior, 2007). One recent study estimated that ADHD affects 5.3% of children worldwide (Polancyzk et al., 2007).

Some children with ADHD, about as many of them girls as boys, are mainly inattentive but not hyperactive and impulsive; but, because they are not disruptive, they often go unrecognized, even though they clearly have problems that affect their school performance (Weyandt, 2007). Those children with ADHD who are hyperactive and impulsive as well as inattentive often have conduct disorders or other externalizing problems. They are likely to irritate adults and become locked in coercive power struggles with their parents, interactions that then aggravate their problems (Barkley et al., 1991; Buhrmester et al., 1992). Because their behavior is so disruptive, they are also rejected by peers, which can have its own damaging effects on their adjustment and later development (Deater-Deckard, 2001; Whalen et al., 1989).

Not only do many children with ADHD have conduct disorders and behave aggressively, but many also have diagnosable learning disabilities, and some suffer from depression or anxiety disorders (Brassett-Harknett & Butler, 2007). This co-occurrence of two or more conditions in the same individual is called **comorbidity** and is extremely common, especially during childhood. That is, many troubled individuals (like Peggy at the start of the chapter) have multiple psychiatric diagnoses rather than just one (Clark, Watson, & Reynolds, 1995). Comorbidity complicates the task of understanding the causes and consequences of any particular psychological disorder.

Developmental Course

ADHD expresses itself differently at different ages (Pelham et al., 2004; Weyandt, 2007). The condition often reveals itself in infancy. As infants, children with ADHD are often very active, have difficult temperaments, and show irregular feeding and sleeping patterns (Teeter, 1998). As preschool children, they are in perpetual motion, quickly moving from one activity to another. Because most young children are energetic and have short attention spans, behavior must be evaluated in relation to developmental norms; otherwise, we might mistake most average 3- and 4-year-olds for hyperactive children. Finally, by the grade-school years, overactive behavior is less of a problem, but children with ADHD are fidgety, restless, and inattentive to schoolwork (American Psychiatric Association, 2000).

Hyperactive children test the patience of their parents.

What becomes of hyperactive children later in life? It used to be thought that they outgrew their problems, so parents sometimes delayed getting help, expecting their children's difficulties to go away by adolescence. Most children with ADHD do outgrow their overactive behavior (DuPaul & Stoner, 2003). However, adolescents with ADHD continue to be restless, to have difficulty concentrating on their academic work, and to behave impulsively; they often perform poorly in school or drop out, and they are prone to committing reckless delinquent acts without thinking about the consequences (Brassett-Harknett & Butler, 2007; Wallander & Hubert, 1985).

The picture is more positive by early adulthood; yet many individuals with ADHD get in trouble because they have lapses of concentration, make impulsive decisions, and procrastinate (Brassett-Harknett & Butler, 2007; Wender, 1995). In one study following hyperactive and control children from about age 7 to age 21, the hyperactive adults had lower educational attainment and achievement, had been fired more and received lower performance ratings from their employers, had fewer close friends and more problems in social relations, and had become involved in sexual activity and parenthood earlier (Barkley et al., 2006). Outcomes were especially poor for those who had conduct disorders along with their ADHD as children; this subgroup is also likely to have more than its share of car accidents and law breaking, to abuse alcohol and drugs, and to have emotional problems as adults (Selikowitz, 2004; Weiss & Hechtman, 1993). The more severe the ADHD symptoms and associated problems such as aggression in childhood, the more likely it is that later life outcomes will be poor (Pelham et al., 2004). Overall, an estimated 20% of ADHD children outgrow their problems, 20% continue to have severe problems as adults, and 60% continue to have at least mild problems throughout their lives (Selikowitz, 2004). More than 4% of adults in the United States appear to have diagnosable ADHD, and many could benefit from treatment (Kessler et al., 2006).

Suspected Causes

What causes this disorder? Researchers have long agreed that ADHD has a neurological basis, but they have had difficulty pinpointing it until recently. No consistent evidence of brain damage or of structural defects in the brain is found in most children with ADHD. Many cannot even be distinguished clearly from non-ADHD children on the basis of neuropsychological tests because they do not all show clear deficits in neuropsychological functions or show them in the same areas (Doyle & Biederman et al., 2000). Still, it is widely agreed that the brains of children with ADHD work differently than the brains of other children do and that the cause is most likely differences in brain chemistry rather than physical brain damage.

Russell Barkley (1997, 2000) put forth the view that the frontal lobes of individuals with ADHD do not function properly, resulting in deficiencies in executive functions, most importantly difficulty inhibiting and otherwise regulating one's behavior. This view has received a good deal of support, al-

though not all individuals with ADHD show executive function impairments and not all executive functions are impaired (Seidman, 2006). Low levels of dopamine and related neurotransmitters involved in communication among neurons in the frontal lobes may be at the root of executive function impairments (Selikowitz, 2004; Weyandt, 2007).

Genes predispose some individuals to develop ADHD and probably underlie the physiological problems that give rise to it. One identical twin is highly likely to have it if the other does, and first-degree relatives of someone with ADHD (including parents) have four to five times the usual risk (Thapar, 2003). Genes account for 60 to 90% of the variation in ADHD among individuals, nonshared environmental factors for the rest (Waldman & Gizer, 2006). There is not one ADHD gene, however. Instead, researchers have identified several gene variants common in individuals with ADHD that influence levels of dopamine, serotonin, and other relevant neurotransmitters in their brains (Waldman & Gizer, 2006).

Environmental influences are also important, not so much as the main cause of ADHD but as forces that help determine whether a genetic potential turns into a reality and whether the individual adapts well or poorly as she develops (Harknett-Brassett & Butler, 2007). Misconceptions that ADHD is due to consuming sugar or food additives such as red food coloring have long been put to rest, although allergies are an issue for a small number of children with ADHD (Weyandt, 2007). Carefully controlled studies comparing diets with and without the suspected culprit foods typically offer no support for diet theories. Low birth weight and maternal smoking, both associated with a shortage of oxygen prenatally, do appear to contribute to some cases of ADHD (Lehn et al., 2007; Linnet et al., 2003). Family risk factors such as marital conflict, an intrusive parenting style, and socioeconomic disadvantage may also worsen the outcomes of children with ADHD (Biederman et al., 1995; Jacobvitz & Sroufe, 1987). And genes and environment may interact: Individuals who inherit genes that adversely affect dopamine levels and who also experience family adversity show more ADHD symptoms than children who do not have both genes and environment working against them (Laucht et al., 2007).

Treatment

Many children with ADHD are given stimulant drugs such as methylphenidate (Ritalin), and most are helped by these drugs. Although it may seem odd to give overactive children stimulants, the brains of individuals with ADHD are actually underaroused and these drugs increase levels of dopamine and other neurotransmitters in the frontal lobes of the brain to normal levels and, by doing so, allow these children to concentrate (Selikowitz, 2004). Listen to Greg's mother (she described his behavioral problems at the beginning of this section) on the topic: "The change in his behavior and mood was miraculous. One hour after the tablet I had my first proper conversation with Greg. For the first time in his life he was able to sit still and look at a book" (Selikowitz, 2004, p. 34).

Why, then, does controversy surround the use of stimulants with ADHD children? Some critics feel that these drugs are prescribed to too many children, including some who do not have ADHD. Although it is probably true that Ritalin and other stimulants are overprescribed in some communities, it is also true that many children with ADHD who could benefit from drug treatment go untreated (Jensen, 2000). Others are concerned that stimulant drugs have undesirable side effects such as loss of appetite and headaches (see Weyandt, 2007). Moreover, they do not cure ADHD; they improve functioning only until their effects wear off. And so far, there is not much evidence that individuals with ADHD who took stimulants as children function better as adolescents or adults than those who did not, although some studies are beginning to show beneficial longer-term effects on attention and behavior (Weyandt, 2007). Many experts have concluded that stimulant drugs cannot resolve all the difficulties faced by individuals with ADHD and their families but that they are part of the answer, not only in childhood but continuing into adulthood.

Might behavioral treatment work better than drug treatment? The Multimodal Treatment of Attention Deficit Hyperactivity Disorder Study, a national study of 579 children with ADHD ranging in age from 7 to 9, is the best source of information about the pros and cons of medication and behavioral treatment for ADHD (Jensen et al., 2001). This study compared children who received optimally delivered medication, state-of-the-art behavioral treatment (a combination of parent training, child training through a summer program, and school intervention), a combination of the two approaches, or routine care in the community. The findings were clear: Medication alone was more effective than behavioral treatment alone or routine care in reducing ADHD symptoms. However, a combination of medication and behavioral treatment was superior to medication alone when the goal was defined as not only reducing ADHD symptoms but also improving academic performance, social adjustment, and parent–child relations. Behavioral programs designed to teach children with ADHD to stay focused on tasks, control their impulsiveness, and interact socially; parent training designed to help parents understand and manage the behavior of these often-difficult youngsters; and interventions at school to structure the learning environment can all help (Chronis, Jones, & Raggi, 2006; Weyandt, 2007).

Depression

Whereas ADHD illustrates an externalizing disorder, depression is an example of an internalizing disorder in childhood. As you saw earlier, the depression-like symptoms displayed by deprived or traumatized infants probably do not qualify as major depressive disorder. When, then, can children experience true clinical depression? For years many psychologists and psychiatrists, especially those influenced by psychoanalytic theory, argued that young children simply could not be depressed. Feelings of worthlessness, hopelessness, and self-blame were not believed to be possible until the child was older (Garber, 1984).

Besides, childhood is supposedly a happy, carefree time, right?

We now know that young children—as early as age 3—can meet the same criteria for major depressive disorder that are used in diagnosing adults (Garber & Flynn, 2001; Wasserman, 2006). Depression in children is rarer than depression in adolescents and adults, but an estimated 2% of children have diagnosable depressive disorders (Gotlib & Hammen, 1992). It used to be thought that depression in children was expressed in a masked manner as other problems. Many youngsters who show the key symptoms of depression do have comorbid problems such as conduct disorder, ADHD, and anxiety disorder. These disorders are distinct, comorbid problems, however, not just veiled symptoms of depression (Kaslow et al., 2000).

Developmentalists appreciate that depression expresses itself somewhat differently in a young child than in an adult, however (Weiss & Garber, 2003). Like depressed infants, depressed preschool children are more likely to display the behavioral and somatic symptoms of depression (losing interest in activities, eating poorly, and so on) than to display cognitive symptoms like hopelessness or to talk about being depressed (American Psychiatric Association, 2000; Kaslow et al., 2000). They are also prone to be anxious (Moffitt et al., 2007). Yet even young children who are depressed sometimes express excessive guilt, claiming that they are bad (Weiss & Garber, 2003), or act out themes of death and suicide in their play (Luby, 2004). Most important, depressed children are sad or irritable and show the same lack of interest in usually enjoyable activities that depressed adults do (Luby, 2004). Observers can reliably identify the depressed children in a group based on their lack of enthusiasm (Luby et al., 2006).

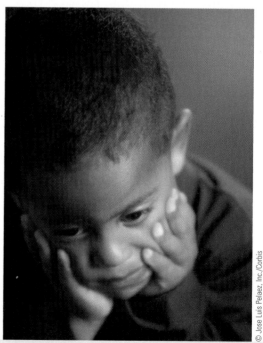

Even young children can experience a major depressive episode.

CHALLENGES IN TREATING CHILDREN AND ADOLESCENTS

According to the Surgeon General of the United States, fewer than one in five U.S. children with psychological disorders receives treatment (Shute, 2001). Sometimes the child does not think she has a problem and resists; sometimes parents cannot face reality. Other times, parents are dismissed by doctors or other professionals who say that that they are worrying too much or that their child is only going through "a phase" (Carter, Briggs-Gowan, & Davis, 2004). The fact that children are developing and their disorders are changing with them also makes diagnosis tricky (Carter et al., 2004).

When children and adolescents do enter treatment, their therapists must recognize that they are not adults and cannot be treated as such (Holmbeck, Greenley, & Franks, 2003; Kazdin, 2003). First, children rarely seek treatment on their own; they are usually referred for treatment by parents who are disturbed by their behavior. This means that therapists must view the child and her parents as the "client."

Second, children's therapeutic outcomes often depend greatly on the cooperation and involvement of their parents (Bailey, 2000; Heru, 2006). Sometimes all members of the family must be treated for any enduring change in the child's behavior to occur—a principle derived from family systems theory. However, not all parents cooperate.

Third—a point familiar to students of human development—children function at different levels of cognitive and emotional development than adults do, and this must be taken into consideration in both diagnosing and treating their problems (Kazdin, 2000). For example, young children cannot easily participate in therapies that require them to verbalize their problems and gain insight into the causes of their behavior. More developmentally appropriate techniques include play therapy, in which disturbed children are encouraged to act out concerns that they cannot easily express in words, and behavioral approaches that do not require insight and verbal skills.

Is psychotherapy for children and adolescents effective? John Weisz and Bahr Weiss (1993) pulled together research on two major categories of psychotherapy: behavioral therapies (those using reinforcement principles and modeling techniques) and nonbehavioral therapies (primarily psychoanalytic therapies based on Freudian theory and other "talking cures" in which therapists help clients to express, understand, and solve their problems). These studies examined a range of problems (both externalizing and internalizing) and measured a range of outcomes (anxiety, cognitive skills and school achievement, personality and self-concept, social adjustment). Judging from Weisz and Weiss's analysis, these forms of therapy for children and adolescents work for a range of problems—at least as well as they work with adults—and the benefits are lasting (Kazdin, 2003). Behavioral therapies proved to be more effective with children than "talk therapies," but more recent work suggests that children can benefit from cognitive behavioral therapy too, even though it requires more cognitive and linguistic ability that strictly behavioral therapy (Kazdin, 2003). In a recent meta-analysis of studies specifically focused on treating depression in children and adolescents, Weisz, McCarty, and Valeri (2006) found again that a variety of psychotherapies can be effective, although treatment effects were often modest and did not always last.

Although the safety of antidepressants for children is now in question, both psychological and pharmacological treatments for children and adolescents with psychological disorders clearly achieve positive results. Yet they do not always work; by one reckoning, 40% or more of clinically depressed children and adolescents do not respond to psychotherapy, and about the same percentage do not respond to antidepressant medications (Asarnow et al., 2001). Apparently, then, we have much left to learn about the special challenges of treating children and adolescents with psychological problems.

© Michael Newman/PhotoEdit

Play therapy can help young children who lack verbal skills express their feelings.

Children as young as age 2 or 3 are even capable of attempting suicide (Rosenthal & Rosenthal, 1984; Shaffer & Pfeffer, 2001). At age 3, Jeffrey repeatedly hurled himself down a flight of stairs and banged his head on the floor; upset by the arrival of a new brother, he was heard to say, "Jeff is bad, and bad boys have to die" (Cytryn & McKnew, 1996, p. 72). An 8-year-old, after writing her will, approached her father with a large rock and asked in all seriousness, "Daddy, would you crush my head, please?" (Cytryn & McKnew, 1996, pp. 69–70). Other children have jumped from high places, run into traffic, and stabbed themselves, often in response to abuse, rejection, or neglect. Moreover, children who attempt suicide once often try again (Shaffer & Pfeffer, 2001). The moral is clear: Parents, teachers, and human service professionals need to appreciate that childhood is not always a happy, carefree time and that children can develop serious depressive disorders and suicidal tendencies. Children's claims that they want to die should be taken dead seriously.

Do depressed children tend to have recurring bouts of depression, becoming depressed adolescents and adults? Most children make it through mild episodes of sadness, and carryover of depression problems from childhood to adulthood is not as strong as carryover from adolescence to adulthood (Rutter, Kim-Cohen, & Maughan, 2006). However, 5- and 6-year-olds who report many depression symptoms are more likely than their peers to be depressed, to think suicidal thoughts, to struggle academically, and to be perceived as in need of mental health services when they are adolescents (Ialongo, Edelsohn, & Kellam, 2001). Moreover, it is estimated that half of children and adolescents diagnosed as having major depressive disorder have recurrences in adulthood (Kessler, Avenevoli, & Merikangas, 2001). Even if depressed children do not have further episodes, their depression can disrupt their intellectual development, school achievement, and social adjustment for years (Kovacs & Goldston, 1991).

Fortunately, most depressed children respond well to psychotherapy. Cognitive behavioral therapies that focus on changing distorted thinking have proved especially effective (Asarnow, Jaycox, & Tompson, 2001). But because children are not adults, treating children with depression and other psychological disorders poses several challenges for psychotherapists, as the Applications box on page 483 reveals. Many depressed children have also been treated with antidepressant drugs such as Prozac (called *selective serotonin reuptake inhibitors*) that correct for low levels of the neurotransmitter serotonin in the brains of depressed individuals, but concerns about the use of antidepressants with children have been raised (Vitiello, Zuvekas, & Norquist, 2006). These drugs do not appear to be as effective with children as with adults, and some research indicates they increase the risk of suicide among child and adolescent users, causing a warning to that effect to be put out by the U.S. government in 2004 (Vedantam, 2006). Antidepressants are still prescribed because they do help seriously depressed youth who may be at greater risk of suicide if they are not put on drugs, but they are prescribed less often and with more careful monitoring of the patient's reactions (Nemeroff et al., 2007).

Nature and Nurture

Most of us have a strong belief in the power of the social environment, particularly the family, to shape child development. This belief often leads us to blame parents—especially mothers—if their children are sad and withdrawn, uncontrollable and "bratty," or otherwise different from most children (see Chapter 15). Parents whose children develop problems often draw the same conclusion, feeling guilty because they assume they are at fault.

It is essential to view developmental disorders from a family systems perspective and to appreciate how emerging problems affect and are affected by family interactions—to understand that problems are located not in an individual family member but in a whole family (Cowan & Cowan, 2006). From a family systems perspective, parents are important but they both influence and are influenced by their children.

On the one hand, youngsters with depression and many other psychological disorders tend to come from problem-ridden families and to have insecure attachments to their parents (Graham & Easterbrooks, 2000). They are also more likely than other children to have mothers, fathers, or both who have histories of psychological disorder (Connell & Goodman, 2002; Ramchandani et al., 2005). Surely this means that children develop problems because they live in disturbed family environments with adults whose own psychological problems and marital conflicts make it difficult for them to parent effectively.

Or are there other interpretations? A child may have a genetic predisposition to disorder that would be expressed even if the child were adopted into another home early in life. In addition, "poor parenting" can be partly the effect of a child's disorder rather than its cause; children's problem behaviors can negatively affect their parents' moods, marital relationships, and parenting behaviors (Cowan & Cowan, 2006).

Unquestionably, family disruption and conflict and ineffective parenting contribute to and aggravate many childhood problems. Indeed, there is evidence that the children of parents who have psychological disorders may or may not develop disorders themselves depending on whether their parents use an ineffective or effective parenting approach (Johnson et al., 2001). As the diathesis–stress model suggests, then, disorders often arise from the interaction of a genetic predisposition and a stressful environment. Abnormal development, like normal development, is the product of both nature and nurture and of a history of complex transactions between person and environment in which each influences the other (Rutter, Moffitt, & Caspi, 2006).

Continuity and Discontinuity

The parents of children who develop psychological problems want to know this: Will my child outgrow these problems, or will they persist? These parents are understandably concerned with the issue of continuity versus discontinuity in development, which concerns in part the extent to which traits carry over from one developmental period to another. You have already seen that autism, ADHD, and major depression tend to persist beyond childhood in many individuals. To answer the continuity–discontinuity question more fully, consider the spectrum of childhood problems.

Avshalom Caspi and his colleagues (1996) used data from a longitudinal study in New Zealand to determine whether children's behavioral styles, or temperamental characteristics, at age 3 predicted their susceptibility to psychological disorders at age 21—a span of 18 years. As Part A of ■ **Figure 16.3** shows, children who had externalizing problems (such as aggression)

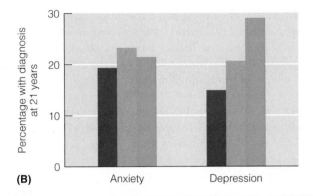

(A)

(B)

■ **FIGURE 16.3** Relationships between behavior at age 3 and psychosocial disorders at age 21. Part A shows that children with uncontrolled, externalizing behavioral styles are more likely than other children to show antisocial behavior and repeated criminal behavior at age 21. Part B shows that inhibited, internalizing children are at high risk of depression, but not anxiety disorders, at 21.
SOURCE: Adapted from Caspi et al. (1996).

as young children and were described as irritable, impulsive, and rough were more likely than either inhibited, overcontrolled children or well-adjusted children to be diagnosed as having antisocial personality disorder and to have records of criminal behavior as young adults.

Meanwhile, as Part B of Figure 16.3 shows, inhibited, internalizing children who were shy, anxious, and easily upset at age 3 were more likely than other children to be diagnosed as depressed later in life; contrary to prediction, they were not at significantly higher risk for anxiety disorders. This study and others point to _continuity_ in susceptibility to problems over the years and suggest that early problems tend to have significance for later development (Costello et al., 2003; Mesman, Bongers, & Koot, 2001).

Relationships between early behavioral problems and later psychopathology in this study and others tend to be weak, however, so there is also _discontinuity_ in development. Notice that most children with temperaments that put them at risk did not have diagnosable problems as adults. Similarly, in a 14-year follow-up of children and adolescents with behavioral and

emotional problems, about 40% still had significant problems in adulthood, but most did not (Hofstra, Van der Ende, & Verhulst, 2000). In other words, having serious psychological problems as a child does not doom most individuals to a life of maladjustment.

Why might we see continuity of problem behavior in some children but discontinuity in others? If children have mild rather than severe psychological problems and receive help, their difficulties are likely to disappear. Some children also show remarkable resilience, functioning well despite exposure to risk factors for disorder or overcoming even severe early problems to become well adjusted (Garmezy, 1994; Small & Memmo, 2004). Such children appear to benefit from protective factors that keep them from becoming maladjusted in the face of risk. These protective factors include their own competencies (especially intellectual ability and social skills) and strong social support (especially a stable family situation with at least one caring parent figure).

SUMMING UP

▌ ADHD, characterized by inattention, impulsivity, and hyperactivity, manifests itself from infancy into the adult years but is expressed differently at different ages.

▌ Genetically predisposed to ADHD, children with it have difficulty with executive functions and are helped most by a combination of stimulant drugs that increase dopamine levels in their brains and behavioral therapy.

▌ Even young children can meet DSM-IV criteria for depression and become suicidal (although rarely).

▌ Nature and nurture, diathesis and stress conspire to produce such childhood disorders; they are not just the products of bad parenting. There is also both continuity and discontinuity in development: Some children remain maladapted, whereas others, especially those with mild problems and many protective factors, outgrow their difficulties.

CRITICAL THINKING

1. Using ADHD and depression as examples, compare and contrast externalizing problems and internalizing problems in childhood.

2. If your child had ADHD or were depressed, would you allow her to be treated with medication? Why or why not?

16.4 | THE ADOLESCENT

If any age group has a reputation for having problems and causing trouble, it is adolescents. This is supposedly the time when angelic children are transformed into emotionally unstable, unruly, problem-ridden delinquents. The view that adolescence is a time of emotional storm and stress was set forth by the founder of developmental psychology, G. Stanley Hall (1904). It has been with us ever since.

Storm and Stress?

Are adolescents really more likely than either children or adults to experience psychological problems? In truth, adolescents have a worse reputation than they deserve. Most adolescents are not emotionally disturbed and do not develop serious problem behaviors such as drug abuse and chronic delinquency. Instead, significant mental health problems—real signs of storm and stress—characterize about 20% of adolescents (Ford, Goodman, & Meltzer, 2003; Kazdin, 2000). Moreover, many of these adolescents were maladjusted before they reached puberty and continue to be maladjusted during adulthood (Reinherz et al., 1999).

Yet adolescence is a period of heightened vulnerability to some forms of psychological disorder (Cicchetti & Rogosch, 2002). The 20% rate of diagnosable psychological disorder among adolescents is higher than an estimated rate of about 10% among children (Ford et al., 2003), although it is no higher than that for adults (Kazdin, 2000). Teenagers face greater stress than children; they must cope with physical maturation, changing brains and cognitive abilities, tribulations of dating, changes in family dynamics, moves to new and more complex school settings, societal demands to become more responsible and to assume adult roles, and more (Cicchetti & Rogosch, 2002; Hill, 1993). Most adolescents cope with these challenges remarkably well, maintain the level of adjustment they had when they entered adolescence, and undergo impressive psychological growth, although it is not unusual for them to feel depressed, anxious, and irritable occasionally. For a minority, a buildup of stressors during adolescence can precipitate serious psychopathology. Their problems should not be dismissed as adolescent moodiness and irritability.

Many adolescents of both sexes get themselves into trouble by overusing alcohol and drugs, engaging in delinquent behavior, and displaying other so-called adolescent problem behaviors. These problem behaviors, although common and often correlated with each other, usually do not reach the level of seriousness to qualify as psychological disorders (Boles, Biglan, & Smolkowski, 2006; Jessor, 1998). Here we focus on two serious disorders that clearly become more prevalent in adolescence. Diagnosable eating disorders such as anorexia nervosa can make the adolescent period treacherous, and rates of depression increase dramatically from childhood to adolescence. These problems interfere with normal adolescent development; yet they become far more understandable when you view them in the context of this developmental period.

Eating Disorders

Perhaps no psychological disorders are more associated with adolescence than the eating disorders that disproportionately strike adolescent girls, either during the transition from childhood to adolescence or during the transition from adolescence to adulthood (Keel & Fulkerson, 2001; and see Bryant-Waugh, 2007). Both anorexia nervosa and bulimia nervosa have be-

come more common in recent years in several industrialized countries (Gordon, 2000; Milos et al., 2004). And both are serious—indeed, potentially fatal—conditions that are difficult to cure.

Anorexia nervosa, which literally means "nervous loss of appetite," has been defined as a refusal to maintain a weight that is at least 85% of the expected weight for the person's height and age (American Psychiatric Association, 2000). Anorexic individuals are also characterized by a strong fear of becoming overweight, a distorted body image (a tendency to view themselves as fat even when they are emaciated), and, if they are females, an absence of regular menstrual cycles. The typical individual with anorexia may begin dieting soon after reaching puberty and simply continue, insisting, even when she weighs only 60 or 70 pounds and resembles a cadaver, that she is well nourished and could stand to lose a few more pounds (Hsu, 1990). Praised at first for losing weight, she becomes increasingly obsessed with dieting and exercising and gains a sense of control by resisting the urging of parents and friends to eat more (Levenkron, 2000). Fewer than 3 in every 1000 adolescent girls suffer from this condition, and there are about 11 female victims for every 1 male victim (van Hoeken, Seidell, & Hoek, 2003). The victims are getting younger; one third-grader was so severely affected that she considered five Cheerios a meal (Tyre, 2005).

Anorexia nervosa can be distinguished from **bulimia nervosa,** the so-called binge–purge syndrome, which involves recurrent episodes of consuming huge quantities of food followed by purging activities such as self-induced vomiting, use of laxatives, or rigid dieting and fasting (American Psychiatric Association, 2000; and see Pinhas et al., 2007). Bulimia is especially prevalent in late adolescence (college age), affecting about 1% of adolescents, most of them females (Pinhas et al., 2007). A bulimic girl or woman typically binges on the foods that are taboo to dieters, eating entire half gallons of ice cream, multiple bags of cookies and potato chips, or whole pies and cakes—

Anorexia can be life threatening.

as much as *55,000 calories* in a single binge session (Johnson et al., 1982). Whereas individuals with anorexia are by definition underweight, individuals with bulimia can be found in all weight ranges. It is a myth that these eating disorders are restricted to European American females from upper middle-class backgrounds. They are evident at all socioeconomic levels (Gard & Freeman, 1996) and in all racial and ethnic groups, although African American females are less concerned with being thin and dieting than European American and Asian American females and have much lower rates of eating disorders (Wildes, Emery, & Simons, 2001).

Suspected Causes

Both nature and nurture contribute to eating disorders. On the nurture side, cultural factors are significant. We live in a society obsessed with thinness as the standard of physical attractiveness that makes it hard for young women to feel good about themselves (Gordon, 2000; Keel & Klump, 2003). As the Western ideal of thinness has spread to other countries, rates of eating disorders in those countries have risen (Gordon, 2000). Interestingly, exposure to television on the island of Fiji converted girls raised to view plump bodies as a status symbol associated with the generous sharing of food into girls who feel too fat and try to control their weight (Becker et al., 2002).

Well before they reach puberty, starting as early as preschool, girls in our society begin to associate being thin with being attractive, fear becoming fat, and wish they were thinner (Hill, 2007; Ricciardelli & McCabe, 2001). Their desire to be thin and feelings about themselves and their bodies are influenced by how much emphasis they think their peers place on thinness and how much television focused on appearance they watch (Dohnt & Tiggemann, 2006). Ultrathin Barbie dolls with unattainable body proportions also contribute to young girls' dissatisfaction with their bodies (Dittmar, Halliwell, & Ive, 2006). Perhaps all these cultural messages explain why about a fourth of second-grade girls in one study dieted (Thelen et al., 1992; and see Hill, 2007). As girls experience normal pubertal changes, they naturally gain fat and become, in their minds, less attractive; they have more reason than ever to be obsessed with controlling their weight (Murnen & Smolak, 1997). This may be why adolescence is a prime time for the emergence of eating disorders.

But why do relatively few adolescent females in our society develop anorexia or bulimia, even though almost all of them experience social pressure to be thin? Genes serve as a diathesis, predisposing certain individuals to develop eating disorders, at least if they live in a sociocultural context that encourages weight concern and if other environmental influences come into play (Keel & Klump, 2003). Twin studies suggest that more than half of the variation in risk for eating disorders is attributable to genes (Bulik et al., 2006; Klump & Culbert, 2007). A number of biochemical abnormalities have been found in individuals with anorexia (Klump & Culbert, 2007; Wilson, Becker, & Heffernan, 2003). Genes may contribute to the low levels of the neurotransmitter serotonin, which is in-

volved in both appetite and mood and has been linked to both eating disorders and mood disorders (Keel & Fulkerson, 2001; Klump & Culbert, 2007). Other genes involved not only in food intake but in the regulation of emotion, especially anxiety level, have been implicated (Klump & Culbert, 2007). Perhaps owing in part to their genes, anorexic females also have a personality profile that puts them at risk; they tend to be highly anxious and obsessive perfectionists who desperately want to be thin (Lilenfeld et al., 2006).

Yet an eating disorder may still not emerge unless a genetically susceptible girl living in a weight-conscious culture experiences disturbed family relationships or other stressful events—that is, unless heredity and environment interact to produce a disorder (Keel & Fulkerson, 2001). Girls who are overly concerned about their weight tend to come from families preoccupied with weight (Gordon, 2000; Strober et al., 2000). They are often insecurely attached to their parents (Sharpe et al., 1998). Much emphasis has been placed on disturbed mother–daughter relationships, but poor father–daughter relationships may also contribute (Dominy, Johnson, & Koch, 2000). So, family dynamics may contribute to anorexia (and to bulimia as well), although it is not always clear whether disturbed family dynamics are contributors to, or effects of, the condition (Gowers & Bryant-Waugh, 2004). Ultimately, it may take a pileup of stressors to push a young woman over the edge. For example, vulnerable adolescents who are experiencing pubertal changes and weight gains, becoming involved in mixed-sex relationships, and changing schools may have more than they can handle and may then develop an eating disorder (Smolak & Levine, 1996). Emotional, sexual, or physical abuse can also precipitate the disorder (Kent & Waller, 2000). In anorexia nervosa, then, we have another clear example of the diathesis–stress model at work. A young woman who is at risk for it partly because of her genetic makeup may not develop anorexia unless she also grows up in a culture that overvalues thinness and in a family that makes it hard to forge a positive identity—and then faces an accumulation of stressful events. Similarly, bulimia is likely rooted in a combination of genetic risk and dysfunctional family dynamics (Pinhas et al., 2007).

Treatment

Individuals with bulimia respond better to treatment than those with anorexia, but both can be successfully treated (Wilson et al., 2003). Cognitive behavioral therapy and antidepressant drugs often work well with bulimic patients (Gowers & Bryant-Waugh, 2004). Effective therapies for individuals with anorexia start with behavior modification programs designed to bring their eating behavior under control, help them gain weight, and deal with any medical problems they may have, in a hospital or treatment facility if necessary (Patel, Pratt, & Greydarms, 2003). Then it is possible to move on to individual psychotherapy designed to help them understand and gain control of their problem, family therapy designed to help build healthier parent–child relationships, and medication for depression and related psychological problems (see Jaffa & McDermott, 2007). Women with anorexia are difficult to treat because they so strongly resist admitting that they have a problem and because the drugs that have been tried so far do not seem to have reliable benefits. However, many people in treatment overcome their eating disorders, or at least get somewhat better; although fewer than half fully recover, many others significantly improve (Gowers & Bryant-Waugh, 2004; Steinhausen, 2007).

Can eating disorders be prevented? C. Barr Taylor and his colleagues (2006) developed an 8-week, Internet-based prevention program based on cognitive behavioral principles called Student Bodies and tested it out with at-risk female college students who were highly concerned about their weight and body shape. The program provided information about healthy eating and body image, had students keep journals, and involved them in interactive discussions with a psychologist. A 2-year follow-up suggested that the program did not affect everyone but did reduce rates of eating disorder among women who, at the start of the program, were overweight or were already engaged in risky behaviors such as self-induced vomiting or obsessive exercising. A similar Internet-based prevention program proved effective with adolescent girls who identified themselves as having body image or eating problems (Heinicke et al., 2007).

Depression and Suicidal Behavior

Before puberty, boys and girls have similarly low rates of depression; after puberty, rates climb and the rate for girls becomes higher than that for boys (Wasserman, 2006). In one study of female adolescents, the rate of major depressive disorder at some time in the individual's life was 1% among girls younger than age 12 but 17% among young women age 19 and older (Glowinski et al., 2003). Up to 35% of adolescents experience depressed moods at some time, and as many as 7% have diagnosable depressive disorders at any given time (Petersen et al., 1993). Symptoms are mostly like those displayed by depressed adults, although depressed adolescents sometimes act out and look more like delinquents than like victims of depression.

Why is adolescence a depressing period for some? For one thing, research suggests that genetic influences on symptoms of depression become stronger in adolescence than they were in childhood (Rutter, Kim-Cohen, & Maughan, 2006; Scourfield et al., 2003). Pubertal changes may be responsible or may provide another part of the answer: Being an early maturer, especially for females, is associated with high levels of depression symptoms (Ge et al., 2003).

Social factors also put adolescent females at risk for depression. Individuals, especially females, who have experienced family disruption and loss in childhood may be especially vulnerable to interpersonal stress after they reach puberty (Rudolph & Flynn, 2007). Girls are also more likely than males to experience a cumulation of stressful events in early adolescence (Ge et al., 1994; Nolen-Hoeksema & Girgus, 1994), and

stressful events—especially interpersonal ones such as divorce in the family and relationship breakups—predict increases in depressive symptoms during adolescence (Ge, Natsuaki, & Conger, 2006). Girls are also more likely than boys to engage in **ruminative coping,** dwelling on their problems in an attempt to analyze them (Nolen-Hoeksema, 1990). Ruminative coping can be counterproductive for adolescent girls, perhaps because it makes one's problems seem worse. Indeed, ruminative coping predicts future depression and binge eating in adolescent girls; those conditions in turn make ruminating about one's problems more likely, creating a vicious circle (Nolen-Hoeksema et al., 2007; and see Papadakis et al., 2006). Adolescent girls may even push one another toward depression by co-ruminating about their problems; although frequent discussion of personal problems with friends serves the positive function of strengthening friendships, it also predicts more depression and anxiety symptoms over time and sets the stage for more co-rumination as well (Rose, Carlson, & Waller, 2007). For boys, co-ruminating improves friendships without aggravating depression and anxiety symptoms.

As depression becomes more common from childhood to adolescence, so do suicidal thoughts, suicide attempts, and actual suicides. Suicide is the third leading cause of death for this age group, far behind accidental injuries and just behind homicides; the yearly rate is 10 per 100,000 15- to 24-year-olds, quite a bit higher than it was in 1950 (Freid et al., 2003). For every adolescent suicide, there are many unsuccessful attempts, and suicidal thoughts are even more common (Shaffer & Pfeffer, 2001). National data indicate that almost 12% of males and 22% of females in grades 9 to 12 had seriously considered suicide in the past year; 6% of males and almost 11% of females had attempted it (National Center for Health Statistics, 2006b).

Before you conclude that adolescence is the peak time for suicidal behavior, however, consider the suicide rates for different age groups, as shown in ■ Figure 16.4. It is clear that adults are more likely to commit suicide than adolescents are. The suicide rate for females peaks in middle age, and the suicide rate for white males climbs throughout adulthood, making elderly white men the group most likely to commit suicide. As a result, increased attention is being focused on the problem of late-life suicide (Heisel & Duberstein, 2005; Pearson, 2000).

Overall, males are more likely to commit suicide than females, by a ratio of at least three to one—a difference that holds up across most cultures studied (Girard, 1993; Shaffer & Pfeffer, 2001). When we look at suicide attempts, this ratio is reversed, with females leading males by a ratio of about three to one. Apparently, then, females attempt suicide more often than males do, but males more often commit suicide when they try, probably because they use more lethal techniques (especially guns).

If suicide rates are higher in adulthood than in adolescence, why do we hear so much about teenage suicide? Probably because adolescents attempt suicide more frequently than adults do. The typical adolescent suicide attempt has been characterized as a "cry for help"—a desperate effort to get others to notice and help resolve problems that have become unbearable (Berman & Jobes, 1991). The adolescent who at-

■ FIGURE 16.4 Number of suicides per 100,000 people by age and sex among European Americans and African Americans in the United States. SOURCE: Data from Freid et al. (2003).

tempts suicide often wants a better life rather than death (Lester, 1994). This by no means suggests that adolescent suicide attempts should be taken lightly. Their message is clear: "I've got serious problems; wake up and help me!" Indeed, even suicidal thoughts during adolescence should be taken seriously; adolescents who have such thoughts are more likely than those who do not to have attempted suicide, to have psychological disorders, and to display difficulties in functioning at age 30 (Reinherz et al., 2006).

Suicidal behavior in adolescence is the product of diathesis–stress. Four key risk factors are youth psychological disorder, family pathology and psychopathology, stressful life events, and access to firearms (Gould et al., 2003; and see Beautrais, 2003). More than 90% of adolescent suicide victims, partly because of genetic predisposition, suffered from depression, substance use disorder, anxiety disorder, or another diagnosable psychological problem at the time of their death, so screening teenagers for depression and other psychological disorders makes great sense as an approach to prevention (Shaffer & Pfeffer, 2001). Indeed, the more problem behaviors, such as binge drinking, risky sexual behavior, eating disorders, aggression, and so on, an adolescent displays, the more likely she is to go from thinking suicidally to taking action (Miller & Taylor, 2005).

Many suicide attempters also have histories of troubled family relationships, and often psychopathology and even suicide run in the family. In the period leading up to a suicide attempt, the adolescent has often experienced a buildup of stressful life events—deteriorating relationships with parents and peers, academic and social failures, run-ins with the law—and begun to feel incapable of coping (Berman & Jobes, 1991). The availability of firearms makes it easy to act on suicidal im-

pulses. The adolescent who attempts suicide once may try again if he receives little help and continues to feel incapable of coping with problems; as a result, professional help is called for after an unsuccessful suicide attempt (Rotheram-Borus et al., 2000).

SUMMING UP

■ Although most adolescents do not experience storm and stress, rates of psychological disorder climb from about 10% in childhood to 20% in adolescence.

■ Females with anorexia nervosa are genetically predisposed to it but also tend to experience a culture obsessed with thinness, a disturbed family, and overwhelming stress.

■ Depression and suicide are also associated with diathesis–stress—with a genetically based vulnerability and a pileup of stressors. Still, most adolescents, even though they may diet or think a depressive or even suicidal thought now and then, emerge from this period as well-adjusted and competent young adults.

CRITICAL THINKING

1. Peggy, the young woman described at the beginning of the chapter, attempted suicide. Using the material on suicide in this section, explain why she might have done so, showing how both diathesis and stress may have contributed.

16.5 THE ADULT

Stressful experiences in childhood and adolescence increase a person's chances of psychological disorder later in life (Turner & Lloyd, 2004). Psychological problems then emerge when a vulnerable individual, perhaps one with a history of adversity, faces overwhelming stress. As it turns out, adults typically experience the greatest number of life strains in early adulthood (McLanahan & Sorensen, 1985; Pearlin, 1980). Life strains decrease from early to middle adulthood, perhaps as adults settle into more stable lifestyles. And, despite increased stress related to health problems, elderly adults report fewer hassles and strains overall than middle-aged adults do (Almeida & Horn, 2004; Martin, Grunendahl, & Martin, 2001). This may be because they have fewer roles and responsibilities to juggle or because they have learned to take more problems in stride.

Age differences in stressful experiences may help explain age differences in rates of psychological disorder. A major government-funded study suggests that about one-fourth of all Americans experienced a mental illness in the past year (Kessler, Chiu, et al., 2005). In another major study, adults age

18 or older were interviewed in their homes about the psychological symptoms they were experiencing, and the researchers then estimated the numbers of respondents who met the criteria for several psychological disorders (Myers et al., 1984; Robins & Regier, 1991). Rates of affective disorders (major depression and related mood disorders), alcohol abuse and dependence, schizophrenia, anxiety disorders, and antisocial personality all decreased from early adulthood to late adulthood. (As you appreciate, this could be either a true age effect or a cohort effect suggesting that recent generations are more vulnerable than previous generations to psychological disorder or report it more.) The only type of impairment that increased with age was cognitive impairment, undoubtedly because some older adults were developing Alzheimer's disease and other forms of dementia (to be described shortly).

Mainly, it appears that young adults, because they experience more stress than older adults, are a group at high risk for mental health problems. With that as background, we can look more closely at one of the disorders to which young adults are especially susceptible, depression, and then turn to an examination of Alzheimer's disease and related cognitive impairments in later life.

Depression

Major depression and other affective disorders are among the most common psychological problems experienced by adults. Who gets depressed, and what does this reveal?

Age and Sex Differences

About 28% of Americans can expect to experience a diagnosable mood disorder by age 75 (Kessler, Berglund et al., 2005). Contrary to stereotypes of elderly people, older adults tend to be less vulnerable to major depression and other severe affective disorders than young or middle-aged adults are (Blazer, 2003). Unless older adults develop physical health problems

Although few elderly adults have diagnosed depression, a sizable minority experiences at least some symptoms of depression.

that contribute to depression or experience increasing rather than decreasing levels of stress as they age, their mental health is likely to be good (Lynch & George, 2002; Wrosch, Schulz, & Heckhausen, 2004).

Still, there are good reasons to be concerned about depression in old age. First, we know that depressed elderly adults are more likely than depressed adolescents to take their own lives. Second, reports of depression symptoms, if not diagnosable disorders, increase when people reach their 70s (Nguyen & Zonderman, 2006; Teachman, 2006). Although only about 1 to 2% of elderly adults have major depressive disorder at a given time, about 15% experience symptoms of depression (Knight et al., 2006). Might some of the individuals who report symptoms of depression have a more serious but undiagnosed depressive disorder?

It's possible: Depression can be difficult to diagnose in later adulthood (Charney et al., 2003). Think about it: Symptoms of depression include fatigue and lack of energy, sleeping difficulties, cognitive deficits, and somatic (bodily) complaints. What if a clinician notes these symptoms in an elderly person but interprets them as nothing more than normal aging, as the result of the chronic illnesses so common in old age, or as signs of dementia? A case of depression can easily be missed. Diagnosis is even more complex because elderly adults who are depressed express their depression differently than younger adults do; they tend to deny that they are sad and mention only their somatic symptoms (Nguyen & Zonderman, 2006). Yet overdiagnosis of depression in older adults can also occur if bodily complaints that are actually caused by physical disease or disability are interpreted as symptoms of depression (Grayson et al., 2000).

Depression in elderly individuals is not so different from depression in young and middle-aged adults that different criteria must be developed to detect it. Still, clinicians working with elderly adults need to be sensitive to the differences between normal aging processes, disease, and psychopathology. Moreover, the fact that relatively few elderly people suffer from severe, diagnosable depression should not blind us to the fact that a much larger number feel depressed or demoralized and could benefit from treatment (Lynch & George, 2002). This is especially true of very old women who are physically ill, poor, socially isolated, or a combination of these (Blazer, 1993; Falcon & Tucker, 2000).

Gender differences in depression are also significant. Starting in adolescence, and in a variety of cultures, females are more likely than males to be diagnosed as depressed—by a margin of about two to one (Kuehner, 2003). This is not just because women are more likely than men to admit they are depressed or to seek help when they are depressed (Kessler, 2000). Instead, higher rates of depression in females than in males may be linked to gender differences in a variety of factors (Kuehner, 2003; Nolen-Hoeksema, 2002): hormones and biological reactions to stress, levels of stress (including more exposure to interpersonal stressors among women), ways of expressing distress (women being more likely to express classic depression symptoms, men being more likely to become angry or overindulge in alcohol and drugs), and styles of coping with distress (especially the tendency for women to engage in more ruminative coping, overanalyzing their despair, whereas men distract themselves from problems and may be better off for it). In short, there is no easy answer, but women are clearly more at risk than men for depression—at least until old age, when male and female rates become more similar (Wasserman, 2006).

Treatment

One of the biggest challenges in treating adults with major depression and other psychological disorders is getting them to seek treatment; many eventually do but they often go years without help (Wang et al., 2005). Elderly adults are especially likely to go undiagnosed and untreated, particularly if they are African Americans and other minority group members (Charney et al., 2003; Neighbors et al., 2007). Older adults and members of their families may believe, wrongly, that problems such as depression and anxiety are a normal part of getting older or becoming ill or that it is somehow shameful to have psychological problems. Mental health professionals may perceive elderly individuals as less treatable than younger adults and may underdiagnose or misdiagnose their problems (Graham et al., 2003). Medicare regulations also favor drug treatments over psychotherapy and counseling (Knight et al., 2006).

Despite these barriers, depressed elderly adults who seek psychotherapy benefit from it (Scogin et al., 2005). Moreover, those treated with antidepressant drugs, assuming they keep taking them, not only overcome their depression in most cases but also show improved cognitive functioning (Blazer, 2003; Butters et al., 2000). As with many psychological problems, the

most effective approach is often a combination of drug treatment and psychotherapy (Hollon, Thase, & Markowitz, 2002).

Aging and Dementia

Perhaps nothing scares us more about aging than the thought that we will become "senile." **Dementia,** the technical term for senility, is a progressive deterioration of neural functioning associated with memory impairment, declines in tested intellectual ability, poor judgment, difficulty thinking abstractly, and often personality changes. Becoming senile is not a normal part of the aging process. Yet rates of dementia increase steadily with age. Overall, dementia affects 6 to 8% of elderly adults age 65 and older (Knight et al., 2006). Rates climb steeply with age, though—from less than 1% in the 60-to-64 age group to around 30% for people 85 and older (Ferri et al., 2005). It is estimated that there are more than 24 million people with dementia in the world today and there will be more than 81 million by 2040 (Ferri et al., 2005).

Dementia is not a single disorder. Much damage can be done by labeling any older person with cognitive impairments as senile—or even as having Alzheimer's disease—and then assuming that she is a lost cause. Many different conditions can produce the symptoms we associate with senility, and some of them are curable or reversible (Thompson, 2006). It is also a mistake to assume that any elderly person who becomes forgetful or absentminded—who occasionally misplaces keys or cannot remember someone's name—is becoming senile. As you saw in Chapter 8, small declines in memory capacities in later life are common and usually have little effect on daily functioning. If this were all it took to warrant a diagnosis of dementia, many young and middle-aged adults, not to mention textbook writers, would qualify. Let us look at some of the specific forms of dementia.

Alzheimer's Disease

With Alzheimer's disease, you just know you're going to forget things, and it's impossible to put things where you can't forget them because people like me can always find a place to lose things and we have to flurry all over the house to figure where in the heck I left whatever it was. . . . It's usually my glasses. . . . You've got to have a sense of humor in this kind of business, and I think it's interesting how many places I can find to lose things. . . . [People with Alzheimer's] want things like they used to be. And we just hate the fact that we cannot be what we used to be. It hurts like hell. (Cary Henderson, age 64, former history professor diagnosed with Alzheimer's disease at age 55; Rovner, 1994, pp. 12–13)

Alzheimer's disease, or *dementia of the Alzheimer's type* as it is termed in DSM-IV-TR, is the most common cause of dementia, accounting for about 70% of all cases, including former President Ronald Reagan's (Tanzi & Parson, 2000). Dementia can strike in middle

Ronald Reagan, who died in 1994 of complications of Alzheimer's disease, brought attention to the tragedy of the disease.

© AP/Wide World Photos

Positron emission tomography (PET scanning) shows metabolic activity in the brain and reveals areas of high brain activity (in red and yellow) and low brain activity (in blue or black). Here we see more activity in a normally functioning brain (left) than in the brain of a person with Alzheimer's disease (right).

© Dr. Robert Friedland/Science Photo Library/ Photo Researchers, Inc.

age but becomes increasingly likely with advancing age. Because more people are living into advanced old age, more will end up with the disease unless ways of preventing it or slowing its progress are found.

Alzheimer's disease leaves two telltale signs in the brain (Selkoe, 1997; Williams, 1995): *senile plaques* (masses of dying neural material with a toxic protein called **beta-amyloid** at their core that injures neurons), and *neurofibrillary tangles* (twisted strands of neural fibers within the bodies of neural cells). Elderly adults without Alzheimer's disease have senile plaques and neurofibrillary tangles, too; it is not only the number but their type and location that mark the difference between Alzheimer's disease and normal aging (Snowdon, 1997). The results of Alzheimer's disease—deterioration of neurons,

increasingly impaired mental functioning, and personality changes—are progressive (and neither reversible nor curable).

The first sign of Alzheimer's disease, detectable 2 to 3 years before dementia can be diagnosed, is usually difficulty learning and remembering verbal material such as names and phone numbers (Howieson et al., 1997). As you saw in Chapter 8, mild cognitive impairment in some older adults is often an early warning that dementia will follow; this is especially true if the person with mild cognitive impairment has both memory problems and other cognitive deficits such as reduced processing speed and deficits in executive functions such as planning ahead (Tabert et al., 2006). In the early stages, free recall tasks are difficult but memory is good if cues to recall are provided; over time, individuals cannot recall even with the aid of cues and become increasingly frustrated (Grober & Kawas, 1997; Williams, 1995). As the disorder progresses, Alzheimer's patients have more trouble coming up with the words they want during conversations and may forget what to do next midway through making a sandwich or getting ready for bed. If tested, they may be unable to answer simple questions about where they are, what the date is, and who the president of the United States is. Eventually, they become incapable of caring for themselves, no longer recognize loved ones, lose all verbal abilities, and die, some earlier and some later, but on average about 8 to 10 years after onset (National Institute on Aging, 2000; and see ■ Figure 16.5). Not only do patients with Alzheimer's disease become increasingly unable to function, but they also often test the patience of caregivers by forgetting they have left something cooking on the stove, wandering away and getting lost, accusing people of stealing the items they have misplaced, or taking off their clothes in public. Many become highly agitated and uncontrollable; large numbers suffer from depression; and some experience psychotic symptoms such as hallucinations (Gillick, 1998).

■ **FIGURE 16.5** Alzheimer's disease emerges gradually over the adult years; brain cells are damaged long before noticeable cognitive impairment results in old age. Changes in brain functioning are significantly different from those associated with normal aging.
SOURCE: Adapted from Okie (2001).

What causes Alzheimer's disease? It has a genetic basis, but there is no single "Alzheimer's gene" (Gatz, 2007; Tanzi & Parson, 2000). Alzheimer's disease strikes repeatedly and early in some families. By analyzing blood samples from families with many Alzheimer's victims, genetic researchers made a big breakthrough when they located a gene for the disease on the 21st pair of chromosomes. Anyone who inherits just one of these apparently dominant genes will develop the disease. A couple of other genes of this sort associated with early-onset Alzheimer's disease have since been discovered, but these single-gene mutations account for only 2% of all cases of Alzheimer's disease (Gatz, 2007).

Genetic contributors to late-onset Alzheimer's disease, by far more common than the early-onset variety, are not as clear-cut or strong. Rather than making Alzheimer's disease inevitable, they only increase a person's risk (Gatz, 2007). One variant of a gene on Chromosome 19 may be especially important; it is responsible for the production of ApoE, a protein involved in processing cholesterol. Having two of the risk-inducing ApoE4 variants of the gene means having up to eight times the normal risk of Alzheimer's disease; having one of the genes means two to four times the normal risk (Hendrie, 2001). Having another variant of the ApoE gene means having a good chance of maintaining good cognitive functioning into very late adulthood (Riley et al., 2000).

Signs of brain atrophy can be detected in people with two ApoE4 genes before they show cognitive impairment (Chen et al., 2007). It is believed that the ApoE4 gene may increase the buildup of beta-amyloid—the damaging substance in senile plaques—and therefore speed the progression of Alzheimer's disease (National Institute on Aging, 2000). Yet not everyone with the ApoE4 gene, or even a pair of them, develops Alzheimer's disease, and many people with Alzheimer's disease lack the gene; other genes, environmental factors, or both apparently play a role.

Twin studies tell us that concordance rates for identical twins, though higher than those for fraternal twins, are in the vicinity of 50%, meaning that in half the cases one identical twin has Alzheimer's but the other does not (Gatz, 2007). Environmental factors must explain this, but which ones? It has not been easy to pinpoint gene–environment interactions (Gatz, 2007). Head injuries in earlier adulthood increase the risk of Alzheimer's disease (Plassman et al., 2000), and a diet that increases the odds of high cholesterol and cardiovascular disease is another contributor (Hendrie, 2001; Nourhashemi et al., 2000). Moreover, people with little education are more at risk than people with lots of education, probably because they have less "cognitive reserve" or brain power to fall back on as aging and disease begin to take a toll on brain functioning (Gatz et al., 2001).

What is being done to prevent and treat Alzheimer's disease? Because victims have a deficit in the neurotransmitter acetylcholine, which is essential for normal learning and memory, researchers have developed drugs to correct this problem and related problems in neural functioning. No pill to prevent or reverse Alzheimer's disease has yet been discovered, but some drugs are regularly prescribed (for example, Aricept, or donepezil, and Namenda, or memantine). They modestly improve cognitive functioning, reduce behavioral problems, and slow the progression of the disease in some patients (Grossberg & Desai, 2003). More such drugs are likely to follow.

Another promising approach attempts to combat the buildup of beta-amyloid in the brain. Antioxidants such as vitamins E and C may delay the onset and progression of Alzheimer's disease by inhibiting the damaging oxidating effects of beta-amyloid (National Institute on Aging, 2000). And lending support to the view that high cholesterol levels associated with the ApoE4 gene contribute to dementia, it has been found that statin drugs, widely prescribed to combat high cholesterol, improve cognitive functioning in people with dementia (Hajjar et al., 2002). It is beginning to look as though the same lifestyle factors that contribute to cardiovascular disease (eating too much and not getting enough exercise, which would limit oxygen to the brain) increase the risk of dementia and that we can reduce our odds of Alzheimer's disease by living a healthy lifestyle from an early age (Pope, Shue, & Beck, 2003; Underwood, 2004). Both physical and mental exercise have been shown to delay cognitive decline in later life and may delay the onset of dementia as well (Larson et al., 2006; Willis et al., 2006; and see Chapter 8).

Even if Alzheimer's disease cannot be prevented entirely, researchers are hopeful that its onset and progression can be slowed, especially if it is detected early. And, even though deterioration leading to death must be expected in today's Alzheimer's patients, a great deal can be done through the use of medications for behavioral problems, educational programs and psychological interventions for patients and their caregivers, and memory training to help people with the disease and their family members understand and cope with dementia and function better (Grossberg & Desai, 2003; Kasl-Godley & Gatz, 2000).

Other Causes of Cognitive Impairment

The second most common type of dementia, often occurring with Alzheimer's disease, is **vascular dementia** (Thompson, 2006). Also called multi-infarct dementia, it is caused by a series of minor strokes that cut off the blood supply to areas of the brain. Whereas Alzheimer's disease usually progresses slowly and steadily, vascular dementia often progresses in a steplike manner, with deterioration followed by improvement after each small stroke. Whereas Alzheimer's disease impairs memory most, vascular dementia may do its greatest damage to executive functions (Román, 2003). And whereas Alzheimer's disease is more strongly influenced by genes, vascular dementia is more closely associated with environmental risk factors for cerebrovascular diseases that affect blood flow in the brain—smoking, eating a fatty diet, and so on (Thompson, 2006). Huntington's disease (a genetic disorder described in Chapter 3), Parkinson's disease, and multiple sclerosis are among the other possible causes of irreversible dementia (Thompson, 2006).

Some cases of dementia—perhaps 10% or more—are not related to any of these causes and, more important, are reversible or curable (Gurland, 1991; Lipton & Weiner, 2003). Such problems as alcoholism, toxic reactions to medication, infections, metabolic disorders, and malnutrition can cause symptoms of dementia. If these problems are corrected—for example, if the individual is taken off a recently prescribed medicine or is placed on a proper diet—a once "senile" person can be restored to normal mental functioning. By contrast, if that same person is written off as senile or as a victim of Alzheimer's disease, a potentially curable condition may become a progressively worse and irreversible one.

Similarly, some elderly adults are mistakenly diagnosed as suffering from irreversible dementia when they are experiencing **delirium**. This reversible condition, which emerges more rapidly than dementia and comes and goes over the course of the day, is a disturbance of consciousness characterized by periods of disorientation, wandering attention, confusion, and hallucinations (American Psychiatric Association, 2000; Cole, 2004). Up to 50% of elderly hospital patients experience it in reaction to any number of stressors—illness, surgery, drug overdoses, interactions of different drugs, or malnutrition (Cole, 2004). It is essential to watch for signs of delirium, identify possible causes such as an incorrect drug prescription, and intervene to change them quickly (Flaherty & Morley, 2004). Unfortunately the condition is often undetected or misdiagnosed; elderly patients who experience delirium, are not identified, and are sent home from the hospital without treatment for it have high death rates (Kakuma et al., 2003; Moraga & Rodriguez-Pascual, 2007).

Finally, elderly adults who are depressed are sometimes misdiagnosed as suffering from dementia because depression is associated with cognitive impairments such as being forgetful and mentally slow (Butters et al., 2004). As you have seen, treatment with antidepressant drugs and psychotherapy can dramatically improve the functioning of such individuals. However, if their depression goes undetected and they are written off as senile, they may deteriorate further. A history of depression increases the risk of dementia and the two often co-occur (Ownby et al., 2006).

The moral is clear: It is critical to distinguish among irreversible dementias (notably, dementia of the Alzheimer's type and vascular dementia), reversible dementias, delirium, depression, and other conditions that may be mistaken for irreversible dementias—including old age itself. This requires a thorough assessment, including a medical history, physical and neurological examinations, and assessments of cognitive functioning (Thompson, 2006). Only after all other causes, especially potentially treatable ones, have been ruled out should a diagnosis of Alzheimer's disease be made.

So ends our tour of psychopathology across the life span. It can be discouraging to read about the countless ways in which genes and environment can conspire to make human development go awry and about the high odds that most of us will experience a psychological disorder sometime during our lives. Yet research provides an increasingly solid basis for attempting to prevent developmental psychopathology through a two-pronged strategy of eliminating risk factors (such as abusive parenting) and strengthening protective factors (such as social support). If prevention proves impossible, most psychological disorders and developmental problems can be treated successfully, enabling the individual to move back onto a healthier developmental pathway.

SUMMING UP

▌ Probably because young adults experience more life strains and stressors than older adults do, most psychological disorders besides those involving dementia or cognitive impairment are more common in early adulthood than in later adulthood.

▌ Rates of diagnosed depression decrease with age but adults over 70 may experience more depressive symptoms than younger adults and may be underdiagnosed; depression is also more common among women than men for a variety of reasons.

▌ The most common types of dementia are Alzheimer's disease, in which a buildup of beta-amyloid within senile plaques damages neurons, and vascular dementia. These irreversible dementias must be carefully distinguished from correctible conditions such as reversible dementias, delirium, and depression.

CRITICAL THINKING

1. Lula has struggled with major depressive disorder on and off for her entire life. Describe how she may have expressed her depression as an infant, preschool child, school-age child, adolescent, adult, and elderly adult.

2. Grandpa Fred is starting to display memory problems; sometimes he asks questions that he just asked, forgets where he left his car keys, and cannot come up with the names of visiting grandchildren. Fred's son Will is convinced that his father has Alzheimer's disease and is a lost cause. What possibilities would you like to rule out before accepting that conclusion—and why?

CHAPTER SUMMARY

16.1 WHAT MAKES DEVELOPMENT ABNORMAL?

• To diagnose psychological disorders, clinicians consider statistical deviance, maladaptiveness, and personal distress and use DSM-IV.

• Developmental psychopathology is concerned with the origins and course of maladaptive behavior; a diathesis–stress model has proved useful in understanding how nature and nurture contribute to psychological disorders.

16.2 THE INFANT

• Autism is characterized by deviant social responses, language and communication deficits, and repetitive behavior. It is genetically influenced, involves impairments in social cognition and mirror neuron functioning, and responds to early behavioral training.

- Infants who have been maltreated or separated from attachment figures, infants whose parents are depressed, and infants suffering from failure to thrive display depression-like symptoms.

16.3 THE CHILD

- Children with ADHD, an externalizing disorder, display inattention, impulsivity, and hyperactivity. Stimulant drugs and behavioral training help, but many with ADHD do not entirely outgrow their problems.
- Diagnosable depression, an internalizing disorder, can occur during early childhood; it manifests itself somewhat differently at different ages, tends to recur, and can be treated.
- It is too simple to view "bad" parenting as the cause of all childhood problems, because genes and gene–environment interactions also contribute and children affect parents. Many childhood problems, especially mild ones, are only temporary, whereas others persist.

16.4 THE ADOLESCENT

- Adolescents are more vulnerable than children but no more vulnerable than adults to psychological disorders; most do not experience storm and stress.
- Anorexia nervosa arises when a genetically predisposed female who lives in a society that strongly encourages dieting experiences stressful events.
- Risks of depression rise during adolescence, especially among females. Adolescents, in a cry for help, are more likely to attempt but less likely to commit suicide than adults.

16.5 THE ADULT

- Young adults experience both more life strains and more psychological disorders, including depression, than older adults.
- Dementia, a progressive deterioration in neural functioning associated with significant cognitive decline, increases with age. Alzheimer's disease, the most common cause of dementia, and vascular dementia, another irreversible dementia, must be carefully distinguished from correctible conditions such as reversible dementias, delirium, and depression.

KEY TERMS

DSM-IV 469
major depressive disorder 469
developmental
    psychopathology 470
social norm 471
diathesis–stress model 472
autism 473
echolalia 474
autism spectrum disorders
    (ASDs) 474
Asperger syndrome 474
mirror neuron simulation
    hypothesis 476
executive functions 476
extreme male brain
    hypothesis 477

somatic symptoms 478
failure to thrive 478
externalizing problem 479
internalizing problem 479
attention deficit hyperactivity
    disorder (ADHD) 480
comorbidity 480
anorexia nervosa 486
bulimia nervosa 486
ruminative coping 488
dementia 491
Alzheimer's disease 491
beta-amyloid 492
vascular dementia 493
delirium 494

MEDIA RESOURCES

BOOK COMPANION WEBSITE

academic.cengage.com/psychology/sigelman
Find online quizzes, flash cards, animations, video clips, experiments, interactive assessments, and other helpful study aids for this text at **academic.cengage.com/psychology/sigelman**. You can also connect directly to the following sites:

ALZHEIMER'S ASSOCIATION

This is a one-stop-shop for anyone interested in Alzheimer's disease. Be sure to check out the education section that contains sections on the basics of the disorder, behavioral changes associated with the disorder, and a "tour" of the brain changes associated with the disorder.

ATTENTION DEFICIT/HYPERACTIVITY DISORDER

The organization Children and Adults with Attention-Deficit/Hyperactivity Disorder provides support and information to individuals with AD/HD.

AUTISM

The Autism Society of America promotes research, education, advocacy, and awareness of issues related to this condition. Its website provides access to several informative articles.

DEPRESSION

The National Institute of Mental Health site contains some excellent information for anyone interested in clinical depression.

NATIONAL EATING DISORDERS ASSOCIATION

As its header states, the NEDA site is dedicated to the expanding public knowledge of eating disorders. The site contains both general information as well as ways to seek treatment.

UNDERSTANDING THE DATA: EXERCISES ON THE WEB

academic.cengage.com/psychology/sigelman
For additional insight on the data presented in this chapter, try out the exercises for these figures at **academic.cengage.com/psychology/sigelman**:

    Figure 16.3 Relationships between behavior at age 3 and psychosocial disorders at age 21

    Figure 16.4 Number of suicides per 100,000 people of age and sex among European Americans and African Americans in the United States

CENGAGENOW

academic.cengage.com/login
Go to **academic.cengage.com/login** to link to CengageNOW, your online study tool. First take the Pre-Test for this chapter to get your Personalized Study Plan, which will identify topics you need to review and direct you to online resources. Then take the Post-Test to determine what concepts you have mastered and what you still need work on.

© AP/Wide World Photos

17^{CHAPTER}

The Final Challenge: Death and Dying

KELLY COLASANTI'S HUSBAND CHRIS was one of the unlucky people working in the World Trade Center on September 11, 2001. The next morning, Kelly's 4-year-old daughter Cara stood outside her bedroom, and Kelly had to say something (Maraniss, Hull, & Schwartzman, 2001, p. A18):

> Cara had not wanted to accept her mother's word at first. "Maybe Daddy fainted," she said hours after she had been told. "If he did faint," Kelly answered, "he also stopped breathing and died." She could not believe her own words, but if nothing else, Cara had to know the truth.
>
> When the house emptied, Kelly gave Cara a bath, dressed her in pajamas and helped her into bed. She lay down in the adjoining trundle bed and started to tell a story that Chris loved to tell about his childhood—only she couldn't tell it so well. At the end of the story, the 4-year-old ordered her to leave and suggested that she go into the other room and read Harry Potter. Kelly was crushed; she wanted to sleep right there next to her daughter. She wandered across the hall and fell into bed, then got up and went to the closet for Chris's blue and green flannel bathrobe, the one he'd had forever. She took the robe to bed, burying her face in the cloth, again trying to smell him. Her chest went cold and her ribs ached and she opened her eyes, staring at the ceiling. My husband is dead, she said. I'm alone.

∎ ∎ ∎

Death hurts. Whether we are 4, 34, or 84 when death strikes a loved one, it still hurts. By adulthood, most of us have experienced a significant loss, even if it was "only" the death of a beloved pet. Even when death is not striking so closely, it is there, lurking somewhere in the background as we go about the tasks of living—in the newspaper, on television, fleeting through our minds. Some psychologists argue that much of human behavior is an effort to defend against the terror of death (Pyszczynski, Solomon, & Greenberg, 2003). Yet sooner or later we all face the ultimate developmental task: the task of dying.

This chapter explores death and its place in life-span human development, starting with what death is and why it happens. How have theorists characterized the experiences of dying and bereaved people? How is death experienced in infancy, childhood, adolescence, and adulthood? Why do some individuals cope more ably with death than others do? You will discover that death is part of the human experience throughout the life span, but that each person's experience of it depends on his level of development, personality, life circumstances, and sociocultural context. Finally, you will see what can be done to help dying and bereaved individuals.

17.1 | MATTERS OF LIFE AND DEATH

What is death? When are we most vulnerable to it, and what kills us? And why is it that all of us eventually die of "old age" if we do not die earlier?

What Is Death?

There is a good deal of confusion in our society today about when life begins and when it ends. Proponents and opponents of legalized abortion argue vehemently about when life really begins. And we hear similarly heated debates about whether a person in an irreversible coma is truly alive and whether a terminally ill patient who is in agonizing pain should be kept alive with the help of life support machines or allowed to die naturally. Definitions of death as a biological phenomenon change; so do the social meanings attached to death.

Biological Definitions of Death

Biological death is hard to define because it is not a single event but a process (Medina, 1996). Different systems of the body die at different rates, and some individuals who have stopped breathing or who lack a heartbeat or pulse, and who would have been declared dead in earlier times, can now be revived before their brains cease to function. Moreover, basic bodily processes such as respiration and blood circulation can be maintained by life support machines in patients who have fallen into a coma and whose brains have ceased to function.

In 1968 a special committee of the Harvard Medical School offered a definition of biological death that has influenced modern legal definitions of death (Berger, 1993). The Harvard group defined biological death in terms of brain functioning and insisted that there be **total brain death:** an irreversible loss of functioning in the entire brain, both the higher centers of the cerebral cortex that are involved in thought and the lower centers of the brain that control basic life processes such as breathing. Specifically, to be judged dead a person must meet the following criteria:

1. Be totally unresponsive to stimuli, including painful ones
2. Fail to move for 1 hour and fail to breathe for 3 minutes after being removed from a ventilator
3. Have no reflexes (for example, no eye blink and no constriction of the eye's pupil in response to light)
4. Register a flat electroencephalogram, indicating an absence of electrical activity in the cortex of the brain.

As an added precaution, the testing procedure is repeated 24 hours later. Moreover, because a coma is sometimes reversible if the cause is either a drug overdose or an abnormally low body temperature, these conditions must be ruled out before a coma victim is pronounced dead.

Ever since there has been much debate about which parts of the brain must cease to function for a person to be dead. In 1975, a now famous young woman named Karen Ann Quinlan lapsed into a coma at a party, probably as the result of alcohol and drug consumption (Cantor, 2001; Urofsky, 1993). Quinlan was unconscious, but her bodily functioning was maintained with the aid of a ventilator and other life support systems. When a court finally granted her parents permission to turn off the respirator, on the grounds that patients are entitled to choose their own course of treatment (or to have their surrogates do so on their behalf), Quinlan continued to breathe without it, much to everyone's surprise. She lived on in a "persistent vegetative state," lacking all consciousness and being fed through a tube, for 10 years.

More recently, the nation debated the question of whether the feeding and hydration of Terri Schiavo of Florida should be stopped (Cerminara, 2006; Preston & Kelly, 2006). In 1990, she had suffered a cardiac arrest, possibly as a result of an eating disorder, that caused irreversible and massive brain damage. Like Karen Quinlan, she was not dead by the Harvard criteria; part of her brain stem allowed her to breathe, swallow, and undergo sleep–wake cycles. Her husband wanted to remove her feeding tube as he believed she would have wanted, but her parents believed that she retained some awareness of her environment and fought a court decision to remove the tube. After the issue was debated at length in legislative bodies, courts, and the media, the tube was removed after appeals of the court's decision failed. Ms. Schiavo died at the age of 41 in 2005.

These famous right-to-die cases highlight the different positions people can take on the issue of when a person is dead. The position laid out in the Harvard definition of total brain death (and in the laws of most states and nations) is quite conservative. By the Harvard criteria, neither Quinlan nor Schiavo was dead, even though both were in irreversible comas, because their brain stems were still functioning enough to support breathing and other basic bodily functions. Shouldn't we keep such seemingly hopeless patients alive in case we discover ways to revive them? A more liberal position is that a person

Do you believe Terri Schiavo, who could breathe but suffered massive brain damage, should or should not have been taken off her feeding tube?

Associated Press

should be declared dead when the cerebral cortex is irreversibly dead, even if some bodily functions are still maintained by the more primitive portions of the brain. After all, is a person really a person if she lacks any awareness and if there is no hope that conscious mental activity will be restored?

Defining life and death became more complicated still when Adrian Owen and his colleagues (2006) demonstrated that at least some people in comas may have more awareness than suspected. These researchers asked a young woman who had been in a vegetative state for 5 months as a result of a car accident to imagine playing tennis or visiting the rooms of her house. Brain imaging showed that her brain responded exactly as healthy adults' brains respond, suggesting that she could understand and respond intentionally to instructions and implying that she had some degree of consciousness. Although comatose patients with more severe brain damage would probably not respond as well, this research opens up a new methodology for communicating with people who are in comas and determining what cognitive capacities they may still have.

Cases such as Quinlan's and Schiavo's raise issues concerning **euthanasia**—a term meaning "happy" or "good" death that usually refers to hastening the death of someone suffering from an incurable illness or injury. The Explorations box on page 500 explores some of these issues. Clearly, we as a society must continue to grapple with defining life and death and deciding whether euthanasia is morally and legally acceptable (Cantor, 2001; Emanuel, 2001).

Social Meanings of Death

Death is not only a biological process but also a psychological and social one. The social meanings attached to death vary widely from historical era to historical era and from culture to culture (Rosenblatt, 2001). Indeed, you have just discovered that society defines who is dead and who is alive. True, people everywhere die, and people everywhere grieve deaths. Moreover, all societies have evolved some manner of reacting to this universal experience—of interpreting its meaning, disposing of corpses, and expressing grief. Beyond these universals, however, the similarities end.

As Phillippe Ariès (1981) has shown, the social meanings of death have changed over the course of history. In Europe during the Middle Ages, people were expected to recognize that their deaths were approaching so that they could bid their farewells and die with dignity surrounded by loved ones. Since the late 19th century, Ariès argues, Western societies have engaged in a "denial of death." We have taken death out of the home and put it in the hospital and funeral parlor to be managed by physicians and funeral directors; as a result, we have less direct experience with it than our ancestors did (Röcke & Cherry, 2002; Taylor, 2003). Right-to-die and death-with-dignity advocates have been arguing forcefully that we should return to the old ways, bringing death into the open, allowing it to occur more naturally, and making it again a normal life experience to be shared with family rather than a medical failure.

SHOULD WE HASTEN DEATH?

Do you believe in euthanasia if a person is terminally ill and in constant pain? Before you answer, note that there are two very different forms of euthanasia. *Active euthanasia*, or "mercy killing," is deliberately and directly causing a person's death—for example, by administering a lethal dose of drugs to a pain-racked patient in the late stages of cancer or smothering a spouse who is in the late stages of Alzheimer's disease. *Passive euthanasia*, by contrast, means allowing a terminally ill person to die of natural causes—for example, by withholding extraordinary life-saving treatments (as happened when Terri Schiavo's feeding tube was removed). Between active euthanasia and passive euthanasia is **assisted suicide**—not killing someone, as in active euthanasia, but making available to a person who wishes to die the means by which she may do so. This includes physician-assisted suicide—for example, a doctor's writing a prescription for sleeping pills at the request of a terminally ill patient who has made known her desire to die, in full knowledge that she will probably take an overdose (Quill, 1993).

How do we as a society view these options? There is overwhelming support among medical personnel and members of the general public for passive euthanasia (Shannon, 2006; Stillion & McDowell, 1996). And more than 68% of a Texas sample expressed support for assisted suicide, especially when the assistance is provided by a doctor rather than by a relative or friend (Worthen & Yeatts, 2000–2001). In addition, a surprising majority of Americans support active euthanasia in which a doctor ends a patient's life by some painless means if the patient and his family request it (Caddell & Newton, 1995). African Americans and other minority group members seem less accepting of actions to hasten death than European Americans, possibly because they do not trust the medical establishment or possibly for religious or philosophical reasons (Kwak & Haley, 2005; Werth et al., 2002).

Although active euthanasia is still viewed as murder in the United States and most countries, it is now legal in most states to withhold extraordinary life-extending treatments from terminally ill patients and to "pull the plug" on life support equipment when that is the wish of the dying person or when the immediate family can show that the individual expressed, when she was able to do so, a desire to reject life support measures (Cantor, 2001). A **living will,** also called an advance directive, allows people to state that they do not want any extraordinary medical procedures applied if they become hopelessly ill.

In 1997, Oregon became the first state to legalize physician-assisted suicide and allow terminally ill adults with 6 or fewer months to live to request lethal medication, as patients in some European countries such as the Netherlands can do. People who request physician-assisted suicide usually suffer from terminal cancer and believe that they face only hopeless pain and suffering and a loss of dignity with no chance of recovery (Georges et al., 2007). Although few people in Oregon have used this option (Wineberg & Werth, 2003), several states have since passed laws *against* assisted suicide (Emanuel, 2001). This caution may be warranted. Terminally ill patients are sometimes in no shape to make life-or-death decisions, and others speaking for them may not always have their best interests at heart (Cantor, 2001; Mishara, 1999). It's also possible that some conditions that are terminal now will become curable tomorrow.

On many life-or-death issues, right-to-die advocates, who maintain that people should have a say in how they die, fight right-to-life advocates, who say that everything possible should be done to maintain life and that nothing should be done to cut it short. It makes sense to think through these issues now in case you must someday decide whether you or a loved one should live or die (see Shannon, 2006).

The experience of dying also differs from culture to culture, anthropologists tell us. If we look at how people in other cultures grieve and mourn a death, we quickly realize that there are many alternatives to our Western ways and no single, biologically mandated grieving process (Klass, 2001; Rosenblatt, 2001). Depending on the society, "funerals are the occasion for avoiding people or holding parties, for fighting or having sexual orgies, for weeping or laughing, in a thousand different combinations" (Metcalf & Huntington, 1991, p. 24). In most societies, there is some concept of spiritual immortality. Yet here, too, there is much variety, from concepts of heaven and hell to the idea of reincarnation to a belief in ancestral ghosts who meddle in the lives of the living (Rosenblatt, 1993).

We need not look beyond North America to find considerable variation in the social meanings of death. Different ethnic and racial groups clearly have different rules for expressing grief. For exam-

Mourning rituals differ considerably from culture to culture.

ple, it is customary among Puerto Ricans, especially women, to display intense, hysterical emotions after a death (Cook & Dworkin, 1992). Japanese Americans, by contrast, are likely to have been taught to restrain their grief—to smile so as not to burden others with their pain and to avoid the shame associated with losing self-control (Cook & Dworkin, 1992).

Different ethnic and racial groups also have different mourning practices. Irish Americans have traditionally believed that the dead deserve a good send-off, a wake with food, drink, and jokes—the kind of party the deceased might have enjoyed (McGoldrick et al., 1991). African Americans tend to regard the funeral not as a time for rowdy celebration but as a forum for expressing grief, in some congregations by wailing and singing spirituals (McGoldrick et al., 1991; Perry, 1993). Jewish families are even more restrained; they quietly withdraw from normal activities for a week of mourning, called *shivah*, then honor the dead again at the 1-month and 1-year marks (Cytron, 1993).

In short, the experiences of dying individuals and of their survivors are shaped by the historical and cultural contexts in which death occurs. Death may be universal, and the tendency to react negatively to loss may be too (Parkes, 2000). Otherwise, death is truly what we humans make of it; there is no one "right" way to die or to grieve a death.

What Kills Us and When?

How long are we likely to live, and what is likely to kill us? In the United States the **life expectancy** at birth—the average number of years a newborn can be expected to live—is almost 78 years (U.S. Census Bureau, 2006). This average life expectancy disguises important differences between males and females, among racial and ethnic groups, and among social classes. The life expectancy for white males has risen to 76 years, the life expectancy for white females to 81 years. Female hormones seem to protect women from high blood pressure and heart problems, and they are less vulnerable than men to violent deaths and accidents and to the effects of smoking, drinking, and similar health hazards (Kaplan & Erickson, 2000). No one is sure of all the reasons, but females live longer than men in most other countries as well (United Nations, 2007). Meanwhile, life expectancies for African Americans, many of whom experience the health hazards associated with poverty, are a good deal lower than those for European Americans: 70 years for males, 76.5 years for females. Life expectancies are also lower—and have been rising less rapidly—in poor areas than in affluent areas (Malmstrom et al., 1999).

Life expectancies have increased steadily over the centuries, from 30 years in ancient Rome to around 80 years in modern affluent societies (Harman, 2001). Despite improvements in all regions of the world, life expectancies in some parts of the world lag behind life expectancies in others, however, as illustrated in ■ **Figure 17.1**. In less developed countries plagued by malaria, famine, AIDS, and other such killers—in African countries such as Mozambique and Zambia, for example—the life expectancy barely exceeds 40 years (United Nations, 2007). The effect of AIDS in hard-hit countries in Africa has been to subtract about 30 years from the average life expectancy (Kinsella, 2005). By contrast, the life expectancy at birth is over 80 now in Asian countries such as Japan and China and in

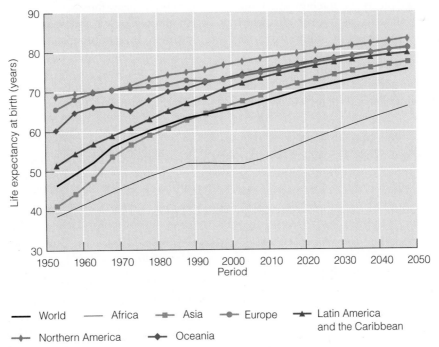

■ **FIGURE 17.1** Life expectancy at birth for the world and the major areas, 1950–2050.

SOURCE: United Nations, Department of Economic and Social Affairs, Population Division (2007). *World population prospects: The 2006 revision, highlights.* Working Paper No. ESA/P/WP.202.

European countries such as Sweden and Switzerland (United Nations, 2007).

Death rates change over the life span. Infants are relatively vulnerable; infant mortality in the United States has dropped considerably, however, and now stands at 7 out of 1000 live births—lower for whites, higher for African Americans (U.S. Census Bureau, 2006). Assuming that we survive infancy, we have a relatively small chance of dying during childhood or adolescence. Death rates then climb steadily throughout adulthood.

What kills us? The leading causes of death change dramatically over the life span, as shown in ● Table 17.1 (National Center for Health Statistics, 2006b). Infant deaths are mainly associated with complications in the period surrounding birth and congenital abnormalities that infants bring with them to life. The leading cause of death among preschool and school-age children is unintentional injuries or accidents (especially car accidents but also poisonings, falls, fires, drownings, and so on). Adolescence and early adulthood are generally periods of good health. Accidents (especially car accidents), homicides, and suicides are the leading killers of adolescents; accidents and cancers kill young adults, and heart diseases also begin to take a toll.

Starting in the 45-to-64 age group, cancers are the leading cause of death, followed by heart diseases, probably because certain individuals' genetic endowments, unhealthy lifestyles, or both put them at risk to develop these and other diseases prematurely (Horiuchi et al., 2003). The incidence of chronic diseases climbs steadily with age. Among adults 65 and older, heart diseases lead the list by far, accounting for more than a third of all deaths, followed by cancers and cerebrovascular diseases (strokes). By this age, general aging processes that affect all of us increase the odds that one disease or another will strike (Horiuchi et al., 2003).

In sum, life expectancies are higher than ever. After we make it through the vulnerable period of infancy, we are at low risk of death through early adulthood and are most likely to die suddenly because of an accident if we do die. As we age, we become more vulnerable to chronic diseases. But now a more fundamental question: Why is it that all of us die? Why does no one live to be 200 or 600?

Theories of Aging: Why Do We Age and Die?

There is no simple answer to the question of why we age and die. However, several theories have been proposed, and each of them says something important about the aging process. These theories can be divided into two main categories: **Programmed theories of aging** emphasize the systematic genetic control of aging processes; **damage theories of aging** call attention to more haphazard processes that cause errors in cells to accumulate and organ systems to deteriorate (Arking, 2006; Hayflick, 2004; Wickens, 1998). The question, really, is whether aging and death are the result of a biological master plan or of random insults to the body while we live.

Programmed Theories

Humans, like other species, have a characteristic **maximum life span**—a ceiling on the number of years that anyone lives. The longest documented and verified life so far is that of Jeanne Louise Calment, a French woman who died in 1997 at age 122 (Coles, 2004). Nearly blind and deaf and confined to a wheelchair, she maintained her sense of humor to the end, attributing her longevity to everything from having a stomach "like an ostrich's" to being forgotten by God (Trueheart, 1997). Calment and others who live almost as long are the basis for setting the maximum human life span around 120 years. The maximum life span has not increased much, despite the fact that the average life expectancy increased 30 some years during the 20th century and more and more people today are living to be centenarians (Kinsella, 2005).

● TABLE 17.1   LEADING CAUSES OF DEATH FOR DIFFERENT AGE GROUPS IN THE UNITED STATES

AGE GROUP	TOTAL DEATHS	NO. 1 CAUSE	NO. 2 CAUSE	NO. 3 CAUSE
Under 1 year	27,936	Congenital abnormalities	Short gestation, low birth weight	Sudden infant death syndrome
1 to 4 years	4,785	Unintentional injuries	Congenital abnormalities	Cancers
5 to 14 years	6,834	Unintentional injuries	Cancers	Congenital abnormalities
15 to 24 years	33,421	Unintentional injuries	Homicide	Suicide
25 to 44 years	126,230	Unintentional injuries	Cancers	Heart diseases
45 to 64 years	442,394	Cancers	Heart diseases	Unintentional injuries
65 years and older	1,755,669	Heart diseases	Cancers	Cerebrovascular diseases

SOURCE: Based on data from National Center for Health Statistics (2006b), Table 32, pp. 191–192.

Humans are long-lived compared with most species. The maximum life span for the mouse is 3½ years, for the dog 20, for the chimpanzee 50, and for the long-lived Galapagos tortoise 150 (Walford, 1983). The fact that each species has its own characteristic maximum life span should convince us that specieswide genes influence how long people generally live.

Beyond that, the individual's genetic makeup, combined with environmental factors, influences how rapidly he ages and how long he lives compared with other humans. For example, genetic differences among us account for more than 50% of differences in the ability to stay free of major chronic diseases at age 70 or older (Reed & Dick, 2003) and for up to about a third of the variation in longevity (Melzer, Hurst, & Frayling, 2007). A fairly good way to estimate how long you will live is to average the longevity of your parents and grandparents (Medvedev, 1991).

It is not clear yet exactly how genes influence aging and longevity, though. There are almost certainly many genes involved in aging and death but research findings to date are inconsistent about which specific genes might be most important (Arking, 2006; Melzer et al., 2007). The suspect genes are not just genes that increase or decrease susceptibility to the diseases that tend to kill people; they include genes that influence the human life span itself. Evolutionary theorists point to a puzzle, though: In the course of evolution, genes that act late in life to extend life will not be selected for, and genes that act late in life to shorten life will not be selected against, because they do not affect adaptation until after the person has reproduced (Arking, 2006). However, genes that proved adaptive to our ancestors early in life but have negative effects later in life *could* have become common in our species over time (Olshansky & Carnes, 2004). For example, recent research suggests that a gene that protects against cancer early in life may contribute to cell aging later in life by holding cell division in check (Dumble et al., 2004; Ferbeyre & Lowe, 2002). If other such intriguing findings emerge, aging and death may prove to be the by-products of genes that served humans well during their reproductive years.

Biological researchers have also been exploring for some time the possibility that we are programmed with an "aging clock" in every cell of our bodies. Their work has built on that of Leonard Hayflick (1976, 1994), who grew cells in cultures, allowed them to divide in two, and measured the number of cell divisions that occurred. He discovered that cells from human embryos could divide only a certain number of times—50 times, plus or minus 10—an estimate referred to as the **Hayflick limit.** Hayflick also demonstrated that cells taken from human adults divide even fewer times, presumably because they have already used up some of their capacity for reproducing themselves. Moreover, the maximum life span of a species is related to the Hayflick limit for that species: The short-lived mouse's cells can go through only 14 to 28 doublings; the long-lived Galapagos tortoise's cells can manage 90 to 125. It is believed that this limit on cell division evolved because it helps prevent precancerous cells from dividing enough times to become error-ridden and malignant (Wright & Shay, 2005).

The mechanism behind the cellular aging clock suggested by Hayflick's limit on cell division is **telomeres**—the stretches of DNA that form the tips of chromosomes and that shorten with every cell division (Klapper, Parwaresch, & Krupp, 2001; Wright & Shay, 2005). When a cell divides, each of its chromosomes replicates itself, but the chromosome's telomere does not. Instead, half of the telomere goes to one of the newly formed chromosomes and half goes to the other. The result is shorter telomeres as we age; eventually, the theory goes, this progressive shortening of telomeres makes cells unable to replicate and causes them to malfunction and die. Chronic stress, such as that involved in caring for an ill child, is not only associated with risk factors for cardiovascular disease but with shorter than normal telomeres (Epel et al., 2004, 2006). Many of us believe that stress ages people; now there is concrete evidence that stress increases the rate of cellular aging.

Using techniques of modern genetic analysis, researchers are now identifying specific genes that become either more or less active from middle age to old age and that therefore may be implicated in the basic aging process (Ly et al., 2000). As it turns out, many of these genes regulate cell division. And many

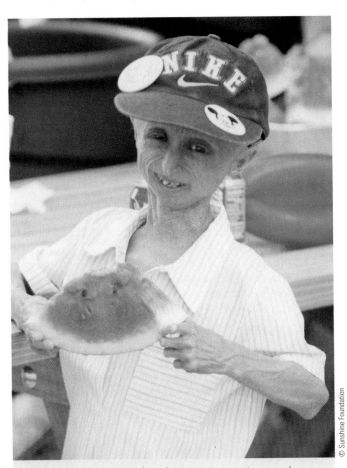

Children with the genetic disorder progeria experience early graying, wrinkling, and hair loss, cardiovascular problems, Alzheimer's disease, and death. They provide clues to the genetic basis of aging.

© Sunshine Foundation

of the genes that become less active with age in normal adults are also inactive in children who have **progeria,** a genetic disorder caused by a spontaneous (rather than inherited) gene mutation that makes babies who appear normal at first age prematurely and die in their teens, often of heart disease (Arking, 2006; DeBusk, 1972; Eriksson et al., 2003). Researchers are looking closely at the effects of the progeria gene, which makes cell nuclei abnormal in shape and functioning, and its possible role in cardiovascular diseases (Kuehn, 2006).

Other programmed theories of aging have centered on genetically guided changes in the neuroendocrine system and the immune system (Cristofalo, 1996; Knight, 2000). We know that the hypothalamus of the brain, guided by a genetic program, sets in motion the hormonal changes responsible for puberty and menopause (see Chapter 5). Possibly the hypothalamus also serves as an aging clock, systematically altering levels of hormones and brain chemicals in later life so that we die. Or perhaps aging is related to genetically governed changes in the immune system that decrease its ability to defend against potentially life-threatening foreign agents such as infections and cause it to mistake normal cells for invaders (Wickens, 1998). All of these programmed theories of aging hold that aging and dying are the inevitable products of our biological endowment as humans, and all have some support.

Damage Theories

In contrast to programmed theories of aging, damage theories generally propose that wear and tear—an accumulation of haphazard or random damage to cells and organs over the years—ultimately causes death. Like cars, we may have a limited warranty and simply give out after a certain number of years of use and abuse (Olshansky & Carnes, 2004). Early in life, DNA strands and cells replicate themselves faithfully; later in life, this fidelity is lost and cells become increasingly damaged. Damage theorists believe that biological aging is about random damage rather than genetically programmed change (Hayflick, 2004; Olshansky & Carnes, 2004).

According to the most promising damage theory, **free radical theory,** damage to cells that compromises their functioning is done by free radicals, which are toxic by-products of normal metabolism, or the everyday chemical reactions in cells such as those involved in the breakdown of food (Harman, 2001; Wickens, 1998). Free radicals are produced when oxygen reacts with certain molecules in the cells. They have an extra, or "free," electron, are chemically unstable, and react with still other molecules in the body to produce substances that damage normal cells, including their DNA. Over time, the genetic code contained in the DNA of more cells becomes scrambled, and the body's mechanisms for repairing such genetic damage simply cannot keep up with the chaos. More cells then function improperly or cease to function, and the organism eventually dies.

"Age spots" on the skin of older people are a visible sign of the damage free radicals can cause. Free radicals have also been implicated in some of the major diseases that become more common with age—most notably, cardiovascular diseases, cancer, and Alzheimer's disease (Harman, 2001). Moreover, they are implicated in the aging of the brain (Poon et al., 2004). However, the damage of most concern is damage to DNA because the result is more defective cells replicating themselves. Unfortunately, we cannot live and breathe without manufacturing free radicals. **Antioxidants** such as vitamins E and C (or foods high in them such as raisins, spinach, and blueberries) prevent oxygen from combining with other molecules to produce free radicals. At least when they are produced by the body or consumed in foods rather than taken in pill form, antioxidants may increase longevity, although not for long, by inhibiting free radical activity and in turn helping prevent age-related diseases (Meydani, 2001). Caution is advised, though: Taking exceptionally high doses of vitamin E may shorten rather than prolong life (Miller et al., 2005).

Nature and Nurture Conspiring

The theories just described are some of the most promising explanations of why we age and die. Programmed theories of aging generally say that aging and dying are as much a part of nature's plan as sprouting teeth or uttering first words and may be the by-products of genes that contributed to early growth, development, and reproduction. The maximum life span, the role of individual genetic makeup in longevity, the Hayflick limit on cell replication timed by telomeres, changes in the activity of certain genes as we age, and systematic changes in the neuroendocrine and immune systems all suggest that aging and dying are genetically controlled. By contrast, damage theories of aging hold that we eventually succumb to haphazard destructive processes, most notably those caused by free radicals, that result in increasingly faulty DNA and abnormal cell functioning and ultimately a breakdown in bodily functioning.

Neither of these broad theories of aging has proved to be *the* explanation; instead, many interacting mechanisms involving both aging processes and disease processes are at work (Arking, 2006; Knight, 2000). For example, genes influence the capacity of cells to repair environmentally caused damage, and the random damage caused by free radicals alters genetic material. John Medina (1996) put it this way: "Toxic waste products accumulate because genes shut off. Genes shut off because toxic waste products accumulate" (p. 291). In short, nature and nurture, biological and environmental factors, interact to bring about aging and dying—just as they interact to produce development.

The Applications box explores efforts to apply research on theories of aging to the task of extending life, or finding the elusive fountain of youth. However, none of our efforts to delay death will keep us from dying and having to cope with death and dying, our next topic.

CAN WE DELAY DEATH?

What does research on the basic causes of aging and death say about our prospects for finding the long-sought fountain of youth, or extending the human life span? Aging Baby Boomers want to know, and in response a bustling field of anti-aging medicine has sprung forth, bringing with it hucksters offering magic diets, cosmetic changes, and countless pills of no proven value (Binstock, 2004).

It is not unthinkable that researchers might discover genetic mechanisms behind aging and dying and then devise ways of manipulating genes to increase longevity or even the maximum life span (Arking, 2006). Life spans of 200 to 600 years are probably not possible, but some think researchers could raise the average age of death to around 112 years and allow 112-year-olds to function more like 78-year-olds (Miller, 2004). For example, stem cell researchers may discover ways to replace aging cells or modify aging processes (Snyder & Loring, 2005). Researchers are also looking at whether the enzyme telomerase can be used to keep telomeres from shortening and thus keep cells replicating and refreshing the body longer. They realize, however, that telomerase treatments could backfire and make cancerous cells multiply wildly (Wright & Shay, 2005). Other researchers are trying to genetically engineer antioxidant enzymes that would slow the damage caused by free radicals or to activate genes involved in the repair of such damage.

If aging is the result of random damage rather than a genetic program, or if many genetic and environmental factors contribute to it, the odds of long life through genetic engineering may be low because it will not be a simple matter of tinkering with a few "aging" genes. Moreover, what works for fruit flies or mice does not always work for humans; gene therapy experiments with humans have been disappointing so far, maybe because gene–environment interactions are complex and have unpredictable outcomes (Chapman, 2004).

At present, the most successful life-extension technique is **caloric restriction**—a highly nutritious but severely restricted diet representing a 30 to 40% or more cut in normal total caloric intake (Arking, 2006; Casadesus et al., 2004; Roth, 2005). Labora-

tory studies involving rats and even primates suggest that caloric restriction extends both the average longevity and the maximum life span of a species and that it delays or slows the progression of many age-related diseases (Bodkin et al., 2003; Lane et al., 2001). By one estimate, a 40% reduction in daily calories results in a 40% decrease in body weight, a 40% increase in average longevity, and a 49% increase in the maximum life span of diet-restricted rats (Harman, 2001).

How does caloric restriction achieve these results? It clearly reduces the number of free radicals and other toxic products of metabolism. A restricted diet appears to alter gene activity and trigger hormones that slow metabolism and put more emphasis on protecting cells against oxidative damage (Antebi, 2007; Arking, 2006). These changes help the half-starved organism hang on to life as long as possible.

However, we do not know whether caloric restriction works as well for humans as it apparently has for rats, what calorie counts and combinations of nutrients are optimal, or whether humans who have a choice would put up with being half-starved for most of their lives. We do know that centenarians are rarely obese (Arking, 2006). We also have some intriguing evidence from four men and four women who lived for 2 years in Biosphere II, a sealed ecological dome in Arizona. Crop shortages had them eating as little as about 1800 calories a day for the first 6 months and then about 2000 calories a day for the rest of their stay, mostly vegetables they grew themselves (Walford et al., 2002). They underwent a 15 to 20% weight loss.

Measurements such as the one for cholesterol shown in the graph in this box indicated that these adults experienced significant improvements in several of the physiological indicators that change

in positive ways in calorie-restricted mice and monkeys. However, their improvements in physiological functioning disappeared after they left Biosphere II and went back on normal diets (Coles, 2004). Because starvation without good nutrition is bad for humans (and no fun), experimenting with self-starvation before more evidence is in is unwise. Besides, researchers may develop drugs that would mimic the effects of caloric restriction without making us give up our beloved calories (Roth, 2005).

Some think the search for the fountain of youth is misguided and will prove futile. Others worry about the social and economic consequences if average longevity were to be pushed up to 100, 110, or 120 years—about high health care expenses, overpopulation, bankruptcy of the Social Security system, and the like (Louria, 2005). Leonard Hayflick (2004) is one of the skeptics: "If our society would learn to value old age to the same extent as we presently value youth," he concludes, "then the drive to slow, stop, or reverse the aging process would be as unthinkable as intervening in the developmental processes of our youth" (p. 578). For now, then, maybe it is best to concentrate on reducing our chances of dying young by not smoking, drinking only in moderation, eating nutritious food, and exercising regularly.

Cholesterol levels in 8 adults before, during, and after their 2-year residence in Biosphere II, when they were on a low-calorie but high-nutrition diet. Many other physiological measures show similarly dramatic change.

SOURCE: From *Journal of Gerontology*, 57A, pages B211–B224, 2002. Copyright © The Gerontological Society of America. Reproduced by permission of the publisher.

- In defining death as a biological process, the Harvard definition of total brain death has been influential; meanwhile, active euthanasia and assisted suicide are controversial.

- Our society tends to deny death, but the social meanings of death vary widely.

- The average life expectancy for a newborn in the United States is 78 years and is higher for women than men and for whites than blacks.

- Death rates decline after infancy and rise dramatically after early adulthood, when accidents give way to chronic diseases as primary causes of death.

- Programmed theories of aging claim that aging is governed largely by species heredity and individual genetic endowment and include evidence that the shortening of telomeres is behind the Hayflick limit on cell division.

- Damage theories of aging focus on random damage caused by destructive free radicals and other agents. In the end, genetic and environmental factors interact to bring about aging and death.

CRITICAL THINKING

1. What would you have decided about whether Terri Schiavo should have been taken off her feeding tube and why—and what does this imply about how you think death should be defined?

2. What arguments would you make for, and what arguments would you make against, having the federal government invest heavily in research aimed at extending the human life span?

17.2 | THE EXPERIENCE OF DEATH

People who die suddenly may be blessed, because those who develop life-threatening illnesses face the challenge of coping with the knowledge that they are seriously ill and are likely to die. What is it like to be dying, and how does the experience compare and contrast with the experience of losing a loved one to death?

Kübler-Ross's Stages of Dying

Perhaps no one has done more to focus attention on the emotional needs of dying patients than psychiatrist Elisabeth Kübler-Ross, whose "stages of dying" are widely known and whose 1969 book *On Death and Dying* revolutionized the care of dying people. In interviews with terminally ill patients, Kübler-Ross (1969, 1974) detected a common set of emotional responses to the knowledge that one has a serious, and probably fatal, illness. She believed that similar reactions might occur in response to any major loss, so bear in mind that the family and friends of the dying person may experience some of these emotional reactions during the loved one's illness and after the death.

The Stages

Kübler-Ross's five "stages of dying" are as follows:

1. *Denial and isolation.* A common first response to dreadful news is to say, "No! It can't be!" **Denial** is a defense mechanism in which anxiety-provoking thoughts are kept out of, or "isolated" from, conscious awareness. A woman who has just been diagnosed as having lung cancer may insist that the diagnosis is wrong—or accept that she is ill but be convinced that she will beat the odds and recover. Denial can be a marvelous coping device: It can get us through a time of acute crisis until we are ready to cope more constructively. Even after dying patients face the facts and become ready to talk about dying, care providers and family members often engage in their own denial.

2. *Anger.* As the bad news begins to register, the dying person asks, "Why me?" Feelings of rage or resentment may be directed at anyone who is handy—doctors, nurses, or family members. Kübler-Ross advises those close to the dying person to be sensitive to this reaction so that they will not try to avoid this irritable person or become angry in return.

3. *Bargaining.* When the dying person bargains, he says, "Okay, me, but please. . . ." The bargainer begs for some concession from God, the medical staff, or family members—if not for a cure, perhaps for a little more time, a little less pain, or provision for his children.

4. *Depression.* As the dying person becomes even more aware of the reality of the situation, depression, despair, and a sense of hopelessness become the predominant emotional responses. Grief focuses on the losses that have already occurred (for example, the loss of the ability to function as she once did) and the losses to come (separation from loved ones, the inability to achieve her dreams, and so on).

5. *Acceptance.* If the dying person is able to work through the emotional reactions of the preceding stages, he may accept the inevitability of death in a calm and peaceful manner. Kübler-Ross (1969) describes the acceptance stage this way: "It

Psychiatrist Elisabeth Kübler-Ross called on physicians to emphasize caring rather than curing.

is almost void of feelings. It is as if the pain had gone, the struggle is over, and there comes a time for 'the final rest before the long journey,' as one patient phrased it" (p. 100).

In addition to these five stages of dying, Kübler-Ross emphasized a sixth response that runs throughout the stages: *hope*. She believed that it is essential for terminally ill patients to retain some sense of hope, even if it is only the hope that they can die with dignity.

Problems with Kübler-Ross's Theory

Kübler-Ross, who died in 2004, deserves immense credit for sensitizing our society to the emotional needs of dying people. She convinced medical professionals to emphasize caring rather than curing in working with such people. At the same time, there are flaws in her account of the dying person's experience (Kastenbaum, 2000). Among the most important points made by critics are these: dying is not stagelike; the nature and course of an illness affects reactions to it; and individuals differ widely in their emotional responses to dying.

The major problem with Kübler-Ross's stages is that the dying process is simply not stagelike. Although dying patients often display symptoms of depression as death nears, the other emotional reactions Kübler-Ross describes seem to affect only minorities of dying people (Schulz & Aderman, 1974). Moreover, when these responses occur, they do not unfold in a standard order. It might have been better if Kübler-Ross had, from the start, described her stages simply as emotional reactions to dying. Unfortunately, some overzealous medical professionals have tried to push dying patients through the "stages" in order, believing incorrectly that their patients would never accept death unless they experienced the "right" emotions at the "right" times (Kastenbaum, 2000).

Edwin Shneidman (1973, 1980) offered an alternate view, arguing that dying patients experience a complex and ever-changing interplay of emotions, alternating between denial and acceptance of death. One day a patient may seem to understand that death is near; the next day she may talk of getting better and going home. Along the way many reactions—disbelief, hope, terror, bewilderment, rage, apathy, calm, anxiety, and others—come and go and are even experienced simultaneously. According to Shneidman, then, dying people experience many unpredictable emotional swings rather than distinct stages of dying. Research supports him and further suggests that anxiety and depression are common among dying patients and should be treated more often than they are to improve the quality of the person's last days (Chochinov & Schwartz, 2002). Many dying people also experience the confusion of delirium in their last weeks (Pessin, Rosenfeld, & Breitbart, 2002).

A second major problem in Kübler-Ross's theory is that it does not allow for differences in emotional responses to dying associated with the disease and its course or trajectory and the specific events that occur along the way (Glaser & Strauss, 1968). When a patient is slowly and gradually worsening over time, the patient, family members, and staff can all become accustomed to the death that lies ahead, whereas when the path toward death is more erratic, emotional ups or downs are likely each time the patient's condition takes a turn for better or worse. Kübler-Ross expects different patients to experience similar responses even when their diseases and pathways to death differ.

Finally, Kübler-Ross's approach overlooks the influences of each individual's personality on how she experiences dying. People cope with dying much as they have coped with life (Schulz & Schlarb, 1987–1988). For example, cancer patients who faced life's problems directly and effectively, were satisfied with their lives, and maintained good interpersonal relationships before they became ill displayed less anger and were less depressed and withdrawn during their illnesses than patients who were not so well adjusted before their illnesses (Hinton, 1975). Depending on their predominant personality traits, coping styles, and social competencies, some dying people may deny until the bitter end, some may "rage against the dying of the light," some may quickly be crushed by despair, and still others may display incredible strength. Most will display combinations of these responses, each in his own unique way. There is no right way to die.

The Experience of Bereavement

Most of us know more about the process of grieving a death than about the process of dying. To describe responses to the death of a loved one, we must distinguish among three terms: **Bereavement** is a state of loss, **grief** is an emotional response to loss, and **mourning** is a culturally prescribed way of displaying reactions to death. Thus, we can describe a bereaved person who grieves by experiencing such emotions as sadness, anger, and guilt and who mourns by attending the funeral and laying flowers on the grave each year.

Unless a death is sudden, relatives and friends, like the dying person, will experience many painful emotions before the death, from the initial diagnosis through the last breath (Grbich, Parker, & Maddocks, 2001). They, too, may alternate between acceptance and denial. They also may experience what has been termed **anticipatory grief**—grieving before death occurs for what is happening and for what lies ahead (Rando, 1986).

Yet no amount of preparation and anticipatory grief can eliminate the need to grieve after the death occurs. How, then, do we grieve?

The Parkes/Bowlby Attachment Model

Pioneering research on the grieving process was conducted by Colin Murray Parkes and his colleagues in Great Britain (Parkes, 1991, 1996, 2006; Parkes & Weiss, 1983). John Bowlby (1980), whose influential theory of attachment was outlined in Chapter 14, and Parkes have conceptualized grieving in the context of attachment theory as a reaction to separation from a loved one. As Parkes (2006) notes, "love and loss are two sides of the same coin. We cannot have one without risking the other" (p. 1). The grieving adult is very much like the infant who experiences separation anxiety when her mother disappears from view and tries to retrieve her. As humans, we have evolved not only to form attachments but also to protest their loss.

The **Parkes/Bowlby attachment model of bereavement** describes four predominant reactions. They overlap considerably and therefore should not be viewed as clear-cut stages even though the frequencies of different reactions change over time. These reactions are numbness, yearning, disorganization and despair, and reorganization (see also Jacobs et al., 1987–1988).

1. *Numbness.* In the first few hours or days after the death, the bereaved person is often in a daze—gripped by a sense of unreality and disbelief and almost empty of feelings. He may make plane reservations, call relatives, or order flowers—all as if in a dream. Underneath this state of numbness and shock is a sense of being on the verge of bursting, and occasionally painful emotions break through. The bereaved person is struggling to defend himself against the full weight of the loss; the bad news has not fully registered.

2. *Yearning.* As the numbing sense of shock and disbelief diminishes, the bereaved person experiences more agony. Grief comes in pangs or waves that typically are most severe from 5 to 14 days after the death. The grieving person has feelings of panic, bouts of uncontrollable weeping, and physical aches and pains. She is likely to be extremely restless, unable to concentrate or to sleep, and preoccupied with thoughts of the loved one and of the events leading to the death.

According to Parkes and Bowlby, the reaction that most clearly makes grieving different from other kinds of emotional distress is separation anxiety—the distress of being parted from the object of attachment. The bereaved person pines and yearns for the loved one and searches for the deceased. A widow may think she heard her husband's voice or saw him in a crowd; she may sense his presence in the house and draw comfort from it; she may be drawn to his favorite chair or wear his bathrobe. Ultimately, the quest to be reunited is doomed to fail.

Both anger and guilt are also common reactions during these early weeks and months of bereavement. Bereaved people often feel irritable and sometimes experience intense rage—at the loved one for dying, at the doctors for not doing a better job, at almost anyone. They seem to need to pin blame somewhere. Unfortunately, they often find reason to blame themselves—to feel guilty. A father may moan that he should have spent more time teaching his son gun safety; the friend of a young man who dies of AIDS may feel that he was not a good enough friend. One of the London widows studied by Parkes felt guilty because she never made her husband bread pudding.

3. *Disorganization and despair.* As time passes, pangs of intense grief and yearning become less frequent, although they still occur. As it sinks in that a reunion with the loved one is impossible, depression, despair, and apathy increasingly predominate. During most of the first year after the death, and longer in many cases, bereaved individuals often feel apathetic and may have difficulty managing and taking interest in their lives.

4. *Reorganization.* Eventually, bereaved people begin to pull themselves together again as their pangs of grief and periods of apathy become less frequent. They invest less emotional energy in their attachment to the deceased and more in their attachments to the living. If they have lost a spouse, they begin to make the transition from being a wife or husband to being a widow or widower, revising their identities. They begin to feel ready for new activities and possibly for new relationships or attachments.

Patterns of Bereavement

Coming sections of this chapter will examine grief responses across the life span. For now, note that some researchers disagree with the specifics of the Parkes/Bowlby view of bereavement. Like responses to dying, responses to bereavement tend to be messier and more individualized than the Parkes/Bowlby phases suggest (Röcke & Cherry, 2002). For example, Margaret Stroebe and Henk Schut (1999; and see Hansson & Stroebe, 2007) have put forth a **dual process model** of coping with bereavement in which the bereaved oscillate between coping with the emotional blow of the loss, coping with the practical challenges of living and reorganizing their lives, and taking breaks from coping in order to reenergize. Loss-oriented coping involves dealing with one's emotions and reconciling oneself to the loss, whereas restoration-oriented coping is focused on managing daily living and mastering new roles and challenges. The bereaved need to grieve but they also need to figure out their finances, take over household tasks that the loved one used to do, and manage other challenges. Over time, the evidence suggests, emphasis shifts from loss-oriented to restoration-oriented coping and less time and energy need to be devoted to coping (Hansson & Stroebe, 2007). The model is somewhat like Schneidman's view that dying patients oscillate between acceptance and denial and suggests that adjustment to bereavement, like adjustment to dying, is not very stagelike or even phaselike.

Most researchers would agree that bereavement is a complex and multidimensional process that varies greatly from person to person and often takes a long time. Many emotional reactions are involved, and their course and intensity differ from person to person. An analysis of research on adjustment to bereavement by George Bonanno and Stacey Kaltman (2000) suggests that modest disruptions in cognitive, emotional, physical, and interpersonal functioning are common, that they usually last for a year, and that less severe, recurring grief reactions may then continue for several years; see the "common grief" reaction in ■ Figure 17.2. Although not captured in the Parkes/Bowlby model, positive thoughts about the deceased, expressions of love, and feelings of gaining from the loss are also part of the typical picture.

As Figure 17.2 shows, a surprisingly high proportion of bereaved people, from 15 to 50% depending on the study, can be described as resilient. They experience minimal grief even in the early months after the death and minimal grief later on; they feel the loss but apparently cope effectively with it (Bonanno, 2004). About 15% can be characterized as chronic

First year of bereavement | Second year of bereavement

Loss

15–50%
Minimal grief

85%
Minimal grief

50–85%
Common grief
  Cognitive disorganization
  Dysphoria
  Health deficits
  Disrupted social and
    occupational functioning
  Positive experiences

15%
Chronic grief
  Major depression
  Generalized anxiety
  Posttraumatic stress disorder

■ **FIGURE 17.2** Patterns of grief differ greatly from person to person. Some people show little grief; many experience disrupted functioning for about a year and then minimal grief in the second year; and about 15% experience chronic and significant psychological problems.
SOURCE: From G. A. Bonanno, C. B. Wortman, & R. M. Nesse, Prospective patterns of resilience and maladjustment during widowhood, *Psychology and Aging, 19*, pp. 260–271. Copyright © 2004 American Psychological Association. Reprinted with permission from the American Psychological Association.

grievers: They continue to experience serious disruptions in functioning 1 to 2 or even more years after their loss, often have diagnosable major depression or anxiety disorder, and may therefore be candidates for treatment.

Meanwhile, we are sympathetic toward the bereaved immediately after a death—eager to help in any way we can—but we quickly grow weary of someone who is depressed, irritable, or preoccupied. We begin to think, sometimes after only a few days or weeks, that it is time for the bereaved person to cheer up and get on with life. We are wrong. To be of help to bereaved people, we must understand that their reactions of numbness and disbelief, yearning, and despair and their needs to engage in loss-oriented and restoration-oriented coping may linger a long time. Indeed, two-thirds of a sample of adults whose spouses died in car accidents indicated that they had been unable to find any meaning in the death and many continued to experience symptoms of depression, hostility, and anxiety even 4 to 7 years after the death (Lehman, Wortman, & Williams, 1987). Even 20 years after their loss, widowed men and women report thinking about their spouses once every week or two (Carnelley et al., 2006).

We have now presented some of the major theories of how people experience dying and bereavement. However, these theories have been based primarily on the responses of adults. How do infants, children, and adolescents respond to death? What does death even mean to infants and young children? A life-span perspective on death and dying is needed.

SUMMING UP

■ Kübler-Ross stimulated much concern for dying patients by describing five stages of dying (denial and isolation, anger, bargaining, depression, and acceptance).

■ However, dying is not stagelike; as Shneidman emphasized, swings between acceptance and denial and shifting emotions are common. Moreover, experiences differ depending on the nature and course of the individual's condition and the individual's personality and coping style.

■ Bereavement precipitates grief and mourning, which are expressed, according to the Parkes/Bowlby attachment model, in overlapping phases of numbness, yearning, disorganization and despair, and finally, after a year or more, reorganization.

■ Research suggests that emotional reactions to bereavement are diverse, that many people are resilient and never experience crippling grief, and that dual process oscillation between loss-oriented and restoration-oriented coping is common.

CRITICAL THINKING

1. Look carefully at the five stages of dying that Elisabeth Kübler-Ross believes terminally ill patients experience and at the four phases of adjustment bereaved people experience according to Colin Murray Parkes and John Bowlby. What common themes do you see? How do they differ?

2. If you worked in a hospital with terminally ill adults, how might you use Kübler-Ross's perspective—and how might you avoid misusing it?

17.3 THE INFANT

Looking at bereavement from an attachment theory perspective makes us wonder how infants understand and cope with the death of an attachment figure. Infants surely do not comprehend death as the cessation of life, but they do gain an understanding of concepts that pave the way for an understanding of death. Infants may, for example, grasp the concepts of being and nonbeing, here and "all gone," from such experiences as watching objects and people appear and disappear, playing peek-a-boo, and even going to sleep and "coming alive" again in the morning (Maurer, 1961). Possibly, infants first form a global category of things that are "all gone" and later divide it into subcategories, one of which is "dead" (Kastenbaum, 2000). Infants lack the concept of death as permanent separation or loss, however, and the cognitive capacity to interpret what has happened.

The experience most directly relevant to an emerging concept of death is the disappearance of a loved one, and it is here that Bowlby's theory of attachment is helpful. After infants form their first attachments around 6 or 7 months, they begin to display signs of separation anxiety when their beloved caregivers leave them. Consistent with Piaget's cognitive developmental theory, they have begun to grasp the concept that people, like objects, have permanent existence, and they expect a loved one who has disappeared to reappear. According to Bowlby, they are biologically programmed to protest separations by crying, searching for their loved one, and attempting to follow, thereby increasing the chances that they will be reunited with the caregiver and protected from harm.

Bowlby (1980) observed that infants separated from their attachment figures display many of the same reactions that bereaved adults do. Infants first engage in vigorous *protest*— yearning and searching for the loved one and expressing outrage when they fail. One 17-month-old girl said only, "Mum, Mum, Mum" for 3 days after her mother died. She was willing to sit on a nurse's lap but would turn her back, as if she did not want to see that the nurse was not "Mum" (Freud & Burlingham cited in Bowlby, 1980).

If, after some hours or days of protest, an infant has not succeeded in finding the loved one, he begins to *despair*, displaying depression-like symptoms. The baby loses hope, ends

Games of peek-a-boo help infants understand the concept of "all gone" and later the concept of death.

the search, and becomes apathetic and sad. Grief may be reflected in a poor appetite, a change in sleeping patterns, excessive clinginess, or regression to less mature behavior (Furman, 1984; and see the description of infant depression in Chapter 16). After some days—longer in some cases—the bereaved infant enters a *detachment* phase, in which he takes renewed interest in toys and companions and may begin to seek new relationships. Infants will recover from the loss of an attachment figure most completely if they can rely on an existing attachment figure (for example, the surviving parent) or have the opportunity to attach themselves to someone new.

SUMMING UP

▪ Infants who are at least 6 months of age and who have formed genuine attachment bonds are old enough to experience intense grief and depression-like symptoms when a parent or other loved one dies—protest and yearning, despair or depression, and detachment or reorganization similar to adult grief responses.

▪ However, infants lack the concept of death as permanent loss and cannot understand what has happened when a caregiver dies.

CRITICAL THINKING

1. Baby Seth was a year old when his mother died in a car accident. How would you expect him to react?

17.4 | THE CHILD

Much as parents would like to shelter their children from unpleasant life experiences, children encounter death in their early years, if only of bugs and birds. How do they come to understand and cope with their experiences of death?

Grasping the Concept of Death

Contrary to what many adults would like to believe, young children are highly curious about death, think about it with some frequency, and are willing to talk about it (Kastenbaum, 2000). Yet their beliefs about death often differ considerably from those of adults. In our society, a "mature" understanding of death has several components (Brent et al., 1996; Hoffman & Strauss, 1985; Kenyon, 2001; Slaughter, Jaakkola, & Carey, 1999). We see death as characterized by the following:

- *Finality.* It is the cessation of life and of all life processes, such as movement, sensation, and thought.
- *Irreversibility.* It cannot be undone.
- *Universality.* It is inevitable and happens to all living beings.
- *Biological causality.* It is the result of natural processes internal to the organism, even if external causes set off these internal changes.

Researchers have studied children's conceptions of death by asking them the sorts of questions contained in ● Table 17.2. Children between age 3 and age 5 have some understanding of death, especially of its universality (Brent et al., 1996). Rather than viewing death as a final cessation of life functions, however, many of them picture the dead as living under altered circumstances and retaining at least some of their capacities (Slaughter et al., 1999). According to these preschoolers, the dead may have hunger pangs, wishes, and beliefs and may continue to love their Moms (Bering & Bjorklund, 2004).

Some preschool-age children also view death as reversible rather than irreversible. They may liken it to sleep (from which a person can awaken) or to a trip (from which a person can return). With the right medical care, the right chicken soup, or a bit of magic, a dead person might be brought back to life (Speece & Brent, 1984). Finally, young children think death is caused by one external agent or another; one may say that people die because they eat aluminum foil; another may say the cause is eating a dirty bug or a Styrofoam cup (Koocher, 1974). They do not grasp the ultimate biological cause of death.

Children ages 5 to 7 make considerable progress in acquiring a mature concept of death. Most children this age understand that death is characterized by finality (cessation of life functions), irreversibility, and universality (Grollman, 1995; Speece & Brent, 1992). Even preschool children are capable of grasping these concepts if they understand that the function of the human body is to sustain life and that it needs food, air, and water to do so. They can then begin to infer that death is the opposite of life and that dead people no longer need to eat food or drink water (Bering & Bjorklund, 2004; Slaughter & Lyons, 2003).

Understanding the biological causality of death is the hardest concept of death for children to master but is typically mastered by about age 10 (Kenyon, 2001). Paula, age 12, had clearly mastered the concept that all deaths ultimately involve a failure of internal biological processes: "When the heart stops, blood stops circulating, you stop breathing and that's it. . . . there's lots of ways it can get started, but that's what really happens" (Koocher, 1974, pp. 407–408).

Children's level of understanding of death appears to be influenced by both their level of cognitive development and their cultural and life experiences. Major breakthroughs in the understanding of death occur in the 5-to-7 age range—when according to Piaget's theory children progress from the preoperational stage of cognitive development to the concrete operational stage. Mature understanding of death is also correlated with IQ (Kenyon, 2001).

In addition, children's concepts of death are influenced by the cultural context in which they live and the specific cultural and religious beliefs to which they are exposed (Sagara-Rosemeyer & Davies, 2007; Stambrook & Parker, 1987). For example, Jewish and Christian children in Israel, who are taught our Western concept of death, provide more "mature" answers to questions about death than Druze children, who are taught to believe in reincarnation (Florian & Kravetz, 1985). Understandably, a child who is taught that dead people are reincarnated may not view death as an irreversible cessation of life processes.

After the September 11 attack on the World Trade Center, the Sesame Workshop asked school-age children to draw pictures of their fears and worries. As one child wrote, "My worries is that terrist [sic] will harm my family, and I will be left with no family like the kids in New York" (Stepp, 2001, p. C4). Another child said: "I'm afraid we will be bombed again and it will be World War III. I hate technology" (Stepp, 2001, p. C1). Children's concepts of death are clearly affected by their sociocultural context and events like 9/11, the Southeast Asian tsunami, Hurricane Katrina, and the Virginia Tech massacre.

● **TABLE 17.2   WESTERN CHILDREN'S CONCEPTS OF DEATH AND QUESTIONS PERTAINING TO THEM**

CONCEPT	QUESTIONS
Finality	Can a dead person move? Get hungry? Speak? Think? Dream? Do dead people know that they are dead?
Irreversibility	Can a dead person become a live person again? Is there anything that could make a dead animal come back to life?
Universality	Does everyone die at some time? Will your parents die someday? Your friends? Will you die?
Biological causality	What makes a person die? Why do animals die?

SOURCES: Based on Hoffman & Strauss, 1985; Florian & Kravetz, 1985; and other sources.

Within any society, children's unique life experiences will also affect their understanding of death. Children who have life-threatening illnesses or who have encountered violence and death in their own lives sometimes grasp death sooner than other children (O'Halloran & Altmaier, 1996). How parents and others communicate with children about death can also make a difference. How is a young child to overcome the belief that death is temporary, for example, if parents and other adults claim that relatives who have died are "asleep"? And if a child is told that "Grandma has gone away," is it not logical to ask why she cannot hop a bus and return?

Experts on death insist that adults only make death more confusing and frightening to young children when they use such euphemisms. They point out that children often understand more than we think, as illustrated by the 3-year-old who, after her father explained that her long-ill and just deceased grandfather had "gone to live on a star in the sky," looked at him quizzically and said, "You mean he is dead?" (Silverman, 2000, pp. 2–3). Experts recommend that parents give children simple but honest answers to the many questions they naturally ask about death and capitalize on events such as the death of a pet to teach children about death and help them understand and express their emotions (Silverman, 2000). Appropriate educational programs can also help familiarize children with the concepts of life and death and accelerate the development of a mature understanding of death (Schonfeld & Kappelman, 1990; Slaughter & Lyons, 2003).

The Dying Child

Parents and doctors often assume that terminally ill children are unaware that they will die and are better off remaining so. Yet research shows that dying children are far more aware of what is happening to them than adults realize (Essa & Murray, 1994). Consider what Myra Bluebond-Langner (1977) found when she observed children ranging in age from 2 to 14 who had leukemia. Even many preschool children arrived, over time, at an understanding that they were going to die and that death is irreversible. Despite the secretiveness of adults, these children noticed changes in their treatments and subtle changes in the way adults interacted with them, and they paid close attention to what happened to other children who had the same disease and were receiving the same treatments. Over time, many of these ill children stopped talking about the long-term future and wanted to celebrate holidays such as Christmas early. A doctor trying to get one boy to cooperate with a procedure said, "I thought you would understand, Sandy. You told me once you wanted to be a doctor." Sandy threw an empty syringe at the doctor and screamed, "I'm not going to be anything!" (p. 59).

How do terminally ill children cope with the knowledge that they are dying? They are not all the models of bravery that some people suppose them to be. Instead, they experience many of the emotions that dying adults

experience (Waechter, 1984). Preschool children may not talk about dying, but they may reveal their fears by having temper tantrums or portraying violent acts in their pretend play. School-age children understand more about their situation and can talk about their feelings if given an opportunity to do so. They want to participate in normal school and sports activities so that they will not feel inadequate compared with their peers, and they want to maintain a sense of control or mastery, even if the best they can do is take charge of deciding which finger should be pricked for a blood sample.

Children with terminal illnesses need the love and support of parents, siblings, and other significant individuals in their lives. In particular, they benefit from a strong sense that their parents are there to care for them (Worchel, Copeland, & Barker, 1987). It is not as clear whether parents should talk to their children about dying. In one study of Swedish families (Kreicbergs et al., 2004), about a third of parents of terminally ill children talked to their children. None regretted it; by comparison, 27% of the parents who did not talk with their children regretted not having done so, especially if they sensed their child was aware of dying (as over half the parents did). Perhaps the best advice to parents is to follow the child's lead, enabling children to talk about their feelings if they wish (Faulkner, 1997).

The Bereaved Child

Children's coping capacities are also tested when a parent, sibling, pet, or other loved one dies. Four major messages have emerged from studies of bereaved children: children grieve, they express their grief differently than adults do, they lack some of the coping resources that adults command, and they are vulnerable to long-term negative effects of bereavement (Osterweis, Solomon, & Green, 1984; Lieberman et al., 2003; Silverman, 2000).

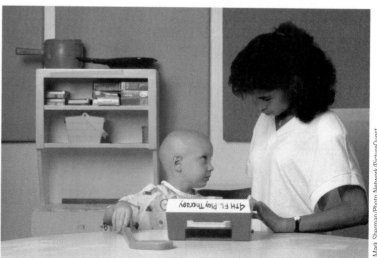

Children who are dying need to know that they are loved and to have opportunities to express their concerns and fears.

Consider some of the reactions that have been observed in young children whose parents have died (Lewis & Lippman, 2004; Lieberman et al., 2003; Silverman, 2000). These children often misbehave or strike out in rage at their surviving parent; they can become unglued when routines such as playing airplane when eating their oatmeal are not honored (Lieberman et al., 2003). They ask endless questions: Where is Daddy? When is he coming back? Will I get a new Daddy? Anxiety about attachment and separation are common; more than half of the bereaved children in one study reported being scared that other family members might die (Sanchez et al., 1994). Yet at other times bereaved children go about their activities as if nothing had happened, denying the loss or distracting themselves from it by immersing themselves in play. Alicia Lieberman and her colleagues (2003) characterize young children's responses as "cycles of intense distress, emotional withdrawal, anger, and emotional detachment" (p. 11). You can readily see how caregivers might be disturbed by some of these behaviors.

Because they lack the cognitive abilities and coping skills that older individuals command, it is natural that young children might have trouble grasping what has happened and attempt to deny and avoid emotions too overwhelming to face. Young children also have mainly behavioral or action coping strategies at their disposal (Skinner & Zimmer-Gembeck, 2007). For example, 2-year-old Reed found comfort by taking out a picture of his mother and putting it on his pillow at night, then returning it carefully to the photo album in the morning (Lieberman et al., 2003). Older children are able to use cognitive coping strategies such as conjuring up mental representations of their lost parents (Compas et al., 2001; Skinner & Zimmer-Gembeck, 2007).

Grief reactions differ greatly from child to child, but the preschooler's grief is likely to manifest itself in problems with sleeping, eating, toileting, and other daily routines (Osterweis et al., 1984; Oltjenbruns, 2001). Negative moods, dependency, and temper tantrums are also common. Older children express their sadness, anger, and fear more directly, although somatic symptoms such as headaches and other physical ailments are also common (Worden & Silverman, 1996).

Well beyond the first year after the death, some bereaved children continue to display problems such as unhappiness, low self-esteem, social withdrawal, difficulty in school, and problem behavior (Worden & Silverman, 1996; Osterweis et al., 1984). In a longitudinal study of school-age children, one in five children who had lost a parent had serious adjustment problems 2 years after the death (Worden & Silverman, 1996; see also Dowdney, 2000). Some children even develop psychological problems that carry into adulthood—for example, depression or insecurity in later attachment relationships (Harris & Bifulco, 1991; Miralt, Bearor, & Thomas, 2001–2002).

However, most bereaved children—especially those who have effective coping skills and solid so-cial support—adjust quite well. They are especially likely to fare well if their surviving parent or someone else is able to provide them with positive parenting (Haine et al., 2006), if caregivers communicate that the child will be loved and cared for (Lieberman et al., 2003), and if children have opportunities to talk about and share their grief (Lewis & Lippman, 2004, p. xii).

SUMMING UP

▌ Young children are naturally curious about death and form ideas about it from an early age.

▌ By age 5 to 7, they have mastered the concepts that death is final, irreversible, and universal; they will later appreciate that death is ultimately caused by a failure of internal biological processes.

▌ Each child's grasp of death depends on her level of cognitive development, culture, and personal experiences of death.

▌ Terminally ill children often become aware that they are dying and find this upsetting.

▌ Bereaved young children sometimes act out their grief and sometimes deny the death because their coping skills are limited; some experience unhappiness, academic difficulties, and behavioral problems well beyond the first year mark, but most adjust with time.

CRITICAL THINKING

1. How might parents impede children from developing a mature concept of death, and how might they facilitate such understanding?

2. If your child had untreatable cancer, would you talk to him about dying? Why or why not?

The death of a friend can be a transformational experience for adolescents.

© Najlah Feamry/CORBIS SABA

Adolescents typically understand death as the irreversible cessation of biological processes and are able to think in more abstract ways about it as they progress from Piaget's concrete-operational stage to his formal-operational stage (Corr, 1995; Koocher, 1973). They use their new cognitive capacities to ponder and discuss the meaning of death and such hypotheticals as an afterlife (Noppe & Noppe, 1997; Wass, 1991). However, studies by Jesse Bering and David Bjorklund (2004) suggest that many adolescents and adults, although they clearly know that biological processes cease at death, share with young children a belief that psychological functions such as knowing, believing, and feeling continue even after bodily functions have ceased. This is because they have acquired a belief in an afterlife—a belief that is so common, these researchers suggest, that it could be a product of evolution.

Just as children's reactions to death and dying reflect their developmental capacities and needs, adolescents' reactions to becoming terminally ill are likely to reflect the themes of adolescence (Adams & Deveau, 1986; Stevens & Dunsmore, 1996). Concerned about their body images as they experience physical and sexual maturation, adolescents may be acutely disturbed if their illness brings hair loss, weight gain, amputation, or other such physical changes. Wanting to be accepted by peers, they may feel like "freaks" or become upset when friends who do not know what to say or do abandon them. Eager to become more autonomous, they may be distressed by having to depend on parents and medical personnel and may struggle to assert their will and maintain a sense of control. Wanting to establish their own identities and chart future goals, adolescents may be angry and bitter at having their dreams snatched from them.

Similarly, the reactions of adolescents to the deaths of family members and friends are likely to reflect the themes of the adolescent period (Balk & Corr, 2001; Tyson-Rawson, 1996). For example, still being dependent on their parents for emotional support and guidance, adolescents who lose a parent to death may carry on an internal dialogue with the dead parent for years (Silverman & Worden, 1993). And, given the importance of peers in this developmental period, it is not surprising that adolescents are often devastated when a close friend dies in a car accident, commits suicide, or succumbs to a deadly disease (Servaty-Seib & Pistole, 2006). In one study, 32% of teenagers who lost a friend to suicide experienced clinical depression during the month after the suicide (Bridge et al., 2003). Yet grief over the loss of a friend is often not taken as seriously as grief over the loss of a family member (Ringler & Hayden, 2000).

Adolescents mostly grieve much as adults do. However, they are sometimes reluctant to express their grief for fear of seeming abnormal or losing control and may express their anguish instead through delinquent behavior and somatic ailments (Clark, Pynoos, & Goebel, 1994; Osterweis et al., 1984). The adolescent who yearns for a dead parent may feel that he is being sucked back into the dependency of childhood and may therefore bottle up these painful feelings (Raphael, 1983, p. 176):

> "When my mother died I thought my heart would break," recalled Geoffrey, age 14. "Yet I couldn't cry. It was locked inside. It was private and tender and sensitive like the way I loved her. They said to me, 'You're cool man, real cool, the way you've taken it,' but I wasn't cool at all. I was hot—hot and raging. All my anger, all my sadness was building up inside me. But I just didn't know any way to let it out."

SUMMING UP

▪ By adolescence, youth have acquired a mature and more abstract concept of death, understanding it as a final cessation of life that is irreversible, universal, and biologically caused—yet often believing in an afterlife as well.

▪ Whereas young children often express their grief indirectly through their behavior, older children and adolescents more directly express painful thoughts and emotions.

▪ In each period, children's reactions to dying or bereavement reflect their developmental needs and the developmental tasks that they are facing; thus, when a life-threatening illness strikes, the young child may most want reassurance of parental love and protection, the school-age child may most wish to keep up with peers, and the adolescent may most want a sense of identity and autonomy.

CRITICAL THINKING

1. Miki (age 3), Rosario (age 9), and Jasmine (age 16) have all been diagnosed with cancer. They have been given chemotherapy and radiation treatments for several months but seem to be getting worse rather than better. Write a short monologue for each child conveying how she understands death.

2. Think about Miki (3), Rosario (9), and Jasmine (16) again but this time focus on each girl's major concerns and wishes based on what you know of normal development at each age.

17.6 THE ADULT

For adults, dealing with the loss of a spouse or partner and accepting their own mortality can be considered normal developmental tasks (Röcke & Cherry, 2002). We have already introduced models describing adults' experiences of dying and bereavement. Here we will elaborate by examining bereavement from a family systems perspective, then trying to define differences between normal and abnormal grief reactions.

Death in the Family Context

To fully understand bereavement, it is useful to adopt a family systems perspective and examine how a death alters relationships, roles, and patterns of interaction within the family, as well as interactions between the family and its environment (Shapiro, 2001; Silverman, 2000; Traylor et al., 2003). Consider some of the special challenges associated with three kinds of death in the family: the loss of a spouse or partner, the loss of a child, and the loss of a parent.

The Loss of a Spouse or Partner

Most of what we know about bereavement is based on studies of widows and widowers. Experiencing the death of a spouse or partner becomes increasingly likely as we age; in heterosexual relationships, it is something most women can expect to endure because women tend both to live longer than men and to marry men who are older than they are. The marital relationship is a central one for most adults, and the loss of a marriage partner or other romantic attachment figure can mean the loss of a great deal. Moreover, the death of a partner often precipitates other changes—the need to move, enter the labor force or change jobs, assume responsibilities that the partner formerly performed, parent single-handedly, and so on. Thus, bereaved partners must redefine their roles and even their identities in fundamental ways (Lopata, 1996; Parkes, 1996). If they are women, their income is also likely to decline substantially (Zick & Holden, 2000).

As noted earlier in this chapter, Colin Murray Parkes, in extensive research on widows and widowers younger than age 45, concluded that bereaved adults progress through overlapping phases of numbness, yearning, disorganization and despair, and reorganization. What tolls does this grieving process take on physical, emotional, and cognitive functioning? ● Table 17.3 shows some of the symptoms that widows and widowers commonly report (Parkes, 1996; also see Bonanno & Kaltman, 2000). They are at risk for illness and physical symptoms such as loss of appetite and sleep disruption, and they tend to overindulge in alcohol, tranquilizers, and cigarettes. Cognitive functions such as memory and decision making are often impaired, and emotional problems such as loneliness and anxiety are common. Most bereaved partners do not become clinically depressed, but many display increased symptoms of depression in the year after the death (Wilcox et al., 2003). Widows and widowers as a group have higher-than-average rates of illness and death as well (Stroebe, 2001b).

Yet research on bereaved elderly adults by George Bonanno and his colleagues reveals much diversity in patterns of response to loss. Adults who lost a partner were studied longitudinally from an average of 3 years before the death to 6 and 18 months afterward (Bonanno et al., 2002; Bonanno, Wortman, & Nesse, 2004). The sample was assessed again 4 years after their loss to examine the longer-term implications of different patterns of grieving (Boerner, Wortman, & Bonanno, 2005; and see Ott et al., 2007). Gathering data both before and after the death of a partner revealed patterns of adjustment over time that had not been evident in studies focused only on adjustment after a loss. ■ Figure 17.3 graphs the average depression symptom scores displayed by five subgroups of widows and widowers identified in the study:

● **TABLE 17.3   PERCENTAGES OF BEREAVED AND NONBEREAVED ADULTS REPORTING VARIOUS SYMPTOMS WITHIN 14 MONTHS OF LOSS**

SYMPTOMS	BEREAVED	NONBEREAVED
Admitted to hospital	12%	4%
Awakened during the night	27	8
Experienced changes in appetite	34	40
Increased alcohol consumption	19	2
Sought help for emotional problems	23	5
Wondered if anything is worthwhile	34	18
Worried by loneliness	44	17
Depressed or very unhappy (in past few weeks)	33	20
Felt restless	33	15
Believed memory was not all right	20	6
Found it hard to make up mind	36	22
Felt somewhat apart or remote even among friends	23	10

Responses were gathered in the Harvard Bereavement Study from men and women younger than age 45 who had lost their spouses 14 months before the interviews. Nonbereaved respondents were married adults matched to members of the bereaved sample so that they were similar in age, sex, family size, geographic area, nationality, and socioeconomic status.

SOURCE: Based on Parkes, 1996, Appendix Table 3.

- A resilient pattern in which distress is at low levels all along
- Common grief, with heightened then diminishing distress after the loss
- Chronic grief in which loss brings distress and the distress lingers
- Chronic depression in which individuals who were depressed before the loss remain so after it
- A depressed–improved pattern in which individuals who were depressed before the loss become less depressed after the death.

The biggest surprise in this study was that the resilient pattern of adjustment involving low levels of distress turned out to be the most common pattern of response, characterizing almost half the sample. The resilient grievers were not just cold, unfeeling people who did not really love their partners. Rather,

■ FIGURE 17.3 Depression symptom scores of five subgroups of elderly widows and widowers an average of 3 years before, 6 months after, and 18 months after the death of their spouse. In parentheses are the percentages of the sample showing each pattern. Notice that resilience—a low level of depression all along—is the most common response, contrary to our belief that all bereaved people must go through a period of significant distress.

as indicated by the data collected before their partners died, they seemed to be well adjusted and happily married people with good coping resources (Bonanno et al., 2002). Nor was there any sign that they were defensively denying or avoiding painful feelings initially and would pay for it by having delayed grief reactions later (Boerner et al., 2005). Rather, although they experienced emotional pangs in the first months after the death, they were more comforted than most by positive thoughts of their partners and simply coped effectively with their loss.

This study also helps us understand that some bereaved people who display symptoms of depression after a loss were depressed even before the death, whereas others become depressed in response to their loss. Those who are depressed before the loss tend to remain depressed even 4 years later and are in the most need of help. Those who become depressed in response to the loss tend to recover from their depression by the 4-year mark (Boerner et al., 2005).

Finally the "depressed–improved" individuals in Bonanno's study who were depressed before the death but recovered afterward are intriguing. Most likely they were experiencing caregiver burden (see Chapter 15) before the death and were relieved of stress after it. Richard Schulz and his colleagues (2003) found that it is common among those who carry the burden of caring for family members with dementia to experience more depression before their partner's death than after;

indeed, more than 70% admit that the death came as a relief to both themselves and their loved one.

Do the partners of gay men who die of AIDs experience patterns of bereavement similar to those experienced by widows and widowers? Bonanno and his colleagues (2005) wondered whether resilience would be as common in this group, as many of these men were not only experiencing the burden of caring for their dying partners but were HIV infected themselves and therefore stressed by thoughts of their own imminent deaths. In a sample of adults who lost marriage partners or children to death, about half proved to be resilient, showing levels of depression and other bereavement reactions within range of those of nonbereaved people. Among partners of gay men who died of AIDS, about half also showed resilience; whether they were HIV positive themselves did not seem to matter. Otherwise, most of these men experienced significant depression symptoms both before and after the partner's death, almost half remained depressed 8 months after the death, and about one-fourth were judged candidates for psychotherapy. It seems, then, that gay adults who lose a life partner grieve at least as strongly as other bereaved partners but that they too show a good deal of resilience in the face of loss.

Many bereaved individuals who experience significant grief begin to show signs of recovery in the second year after the death. Yet for a minority, grieving and psychological distress may continue for many years (Parkes, 2006; Hansson & Stroebe, 2007). In such cases psychologists speak of **complicated grief**, grief that is unusually prolonged or intense and that impairs functioning (Parkes, 2006). People who have difficulty coping with loss are often diagnosed as having a depressive disorder or, if the death was traumatic, posttraumatic stress disorder. However, some experts have concluded that complicated grief, with its unique symptoms such as intense yearning for the deceased, is distinct from these other conditions, has distinct effects on functioning, and should be added as a distinct disorder to the DSM-IV psychiatric manual (Bonanno et al., 2007; Prigerson & Jacobs, 2001).

In sum, the loss of a spouse or partner can be a painful and damaging experience. During the first weeks and months after the death, the psychological pain is typically most acute, and the risks of developing physical or mental health problems or even dying are at a peak. Some widows and widowers experience emotional aftereffects for years, yet up to half of elderly widows and widowers show resilience and manage to cope without becoming highly distressed.

The Loss of a Child

> My child has died! My heart is torn to shreds. My body is screaming. My mind is crazed. The question is always present on my mind. Why? How could this possibly have happened? The anger is ever so deep, so strong, so frightening. (Bertman, 1991, p. 323, citing a mother's reflections on how she reacted to her 16-year-old daughter's death in a car accident after the initial numbness wore off)

No loss is more difficult for an adult than the death of a child (Parkes, 2006). Even when there is forewarning, the loss of a child seems unexpected, untimely, and unfair. Understandably, parents experience a raging anger and often feel that they failed as parent and protector (Rando, 1991). In one study, only 12% of parents whose adolescent or young adult child died of an accident, suicide, or homicide had found meaning in the death 1 year later, and only 57% had found it 5 years later (Murphy, Johnson, & Lohan, 2003b). The age of the child who dies has little effect on the severity of the grief: parents, especially mothers, can experience severe grief reactions even after a miscarriage or the loss of a premature baby (Broen et al., 2004; Buchi et al., 2007). Grief is likely to be especially intense if the parents have no other children (Wijngaards-de-Meij et al., 2005).

The death of a child alters the family system, affecting the marital relationship, parenting, and the well-being of surviving siblings and grandparents. The marital relationship is likely to be strained because each partner grieves in a unique way and is not always able to provide emotional support for the other (Bohannon, 1990–1991). Strains are likely to be especially severe if the marriage was shaky before the death. The odds of marital problems and divorce tend to increase after the death of a child, although most couples stay together and some feel closer than ever (Dijkstra & Stroebe, 1998; Najman et al., 1993).

Grieving parents may have difficulty giving their surviving children the love and support they need to cope with their loss. Children are deeply affected when a brother or sister dies, but their grief is often not fully appreciated (Lohan & Murphy, 2001–2002; Silverman, 2000). Siblings of children battling cancer, for example, may resent it if they are neglected by their parents, may be anxious about their own health, may feel guilty about some of the unsavory feelings of rivalry they have, and may feel pressure to replace the lost child in their parents' eyes (Adams & Deveau, 1987). One 12-year-old boy whose brother

died described his experience this way: "My dad can't talk about it, and my mom cries a lot. It's really hard on them. I pretend I'm O.K. I usually just stay in my room" (Wass, 1991, p. 29). If siblings are isolated from their understandably upset parents or if their grief is not taken seriously, they may have an especially hard time recovering, whereas if their parents can remain warm and supportive, they are likely to fare better (Applebaum & Burns, 1991; Graham-Pole et al., 1989). Many bereaved children and adolescents continue their relationship with their sibling after the death by, for example, "discussing" problems with the sibling and find it a comfort (Packman et al., 2006).

Finally, grandparents also grieve following the death of a child, both for their grandchild and for their child, the bereaved parent. As one grandparent said, "It's like a double whammy!" (DeFrain, Jakub, & Mendoza, 1991–1992, p. 178). Grandparents are likely to feel guilty about surviving their grandchildren and helpless to protect their adult children from pain (Fry, 1997). Clearly, then, those who are attempting to help bereaved families need to include the whole family in their efforts.

The Loss of a Parent

Even if we escape the death of a child or spouse, the death of a parent is a normative life transition that most of us will experience. As noted already, some children experience long-lasting problems after the death of a parent. Fortunately, most of us do not have to face this event until we are in middle age. We are typically less emotionally dependent on our parents by then, and most of us are heavily invested in our own families. Moreover, we expect that our parents will die someday and have prepared ourselves, at least to some degree.

Perhaps for all of these reasons, adjusting to the death of a parent is usually not as difficult as adjusting to the death of a romantic partner or child (Parkes, 2006). Yet it can be a turning point in an adult's life with effects on his identity and relationships with his partner, children (who are grieving the loss of their grandparent), surviving parent, and siblings (Umberson, 2003). Adult children may feel vulnerable and alone in the world when their parents no longer stand between them and death. Guilt about not doing enough for the parent who died is also common (Moss et al., 1993). Compared with adults who are not bereaved, adults who have lost a parent in the past 3 years have higher rates of psychological distress, alcohol use, and health problems (Umberson, 2003).

Challenges to the Grief Work Perspective

It's time to step back and reflect. The view that has guided much of the research on bereavement we have described has come to be called the **grief work**

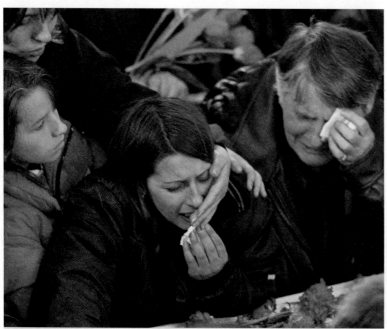

The death of a child can be devastating for parents.

© Oleg Popov/Reuters/Corbis

perspective—the view that to cope adaptively with death, bereaved people must confront their loss, experience painful emotions, work through those emotions, and move toward a detachment from the deceased (Stroebe, 2001a). This view, which grew out of Freudian psychoanalytic theory, is widely held in our society, not only among therapists but among people in general, and it influences what we view as an abnormal reaction to death (Wortman & Silver, 2001). From the grief work perspective, either a chronic grief that lasts longer, is more intense than usual, or both, or an absence, inhibition, or delay of grief, in which the bereaved denies the loss and never seems to confront and express painful feelings, is viewed as pathological or complicated grief (see, for example, Raphael, 1983). This grief work perspective has now come under serious attack. Questions have been raised about its assumptions that there is a right way to grieve, that bereaved people must experience intense grief to recover, and that they must sever their bonds with the deceased to move on with their lives (Bonanno, 2004; Wortman & Boerner, 2007).

First, cross-cultural studies reveal that there are many ways to grieve and suggest that the grief work model of bereavement may be culturally biased. An Egyptian mother may be conforming to her culture's norms of mourning if she sits alone, withdrawn and mute, for months or even years after a child's death. Likewise, a Balinese mother is following the rules of her culture if she is calm, composed, and even seemingly cheerful soon after a child's death (Wikan, 1988, 1991). We would be wrong to conclude, based on our own society's norms, that the Egyptian mother is suffering from chronic grief or the Balinese mother from absent or inhibited grief.

Second, there is surprisingly little support for the grief work perspective's assumption that bereaved individuals must confront their loss and experience painful emotions to cope successfully (Bonanno, 2004; Wortman & Silver, 2001). As you saw earlier, bereaved individuals who fail to show much emotional distress during the early months after the loss do not seem to pay for their lack of grief with a delayed grief reaction later, as the grief work model says they should. Delayed grief is extremely rare, and the individuals who adjust best to death are the resilient ones who display relatively little distress at any point in their bereavement, experience many positive emotions and thoughts, and manage to carry on with life despite their loss (Bonanno, 2004; Bonanno & Field, 2001). In fact, there is growing evidence that too much "grief work" may, like ruminative coping that involves overanalyzing one's problems, backfire and *prolong* psychological distress rather than relieve it (Bonanno et al., 2005).

Finally, the grief work view that we must break our bonds to the deceased to overcome our grief is being challenged. Freud believed that bereaved people had to let go in order to invest their psychic energy elsewhere. However, John Bowlby (1980) noticed that many bereaved individuals revise their internal working models of self and others and continue their relationships with their deceased loved ones on new terms (Bonanno & Kaltman,

1999). Recent research supports Bowlby, suggesting that many bereaved individuals maintain their attachments to the deceased indefinitely through **continuing bonds.** They reminisce and share memories of the deceased, derive comfort from the deceased's possessions, consult with the deceased and feel his or her presence, and so on. Bereavement rituals in some cultures (in Japan and China, for instance) are actually designed to ensure a continued bond between the living and the dead (Klass, 2001).

Individuals who continue their bonds rather than severing them do not necessarily show poorer adjustment than those who do not. In fact, many enjoyed a secure attachment with the deceased before the death and benefit from the continuing relationship (Field et al., 1999; Waskowic & Chartier, 2003). Evidence on the value of continuing bonds is mixed, however. In one study, maintaining continuing bonds was related to better adjustment in China but poorer adjustment in the United States, possibly because continuing a relationship with the deceased is perceived as more appropriate in China (Lalande & Bonanno, 2006). Moreover, Nigel Field and his colleagues (1999) discovered that some forms of continuing attachment are healthier than others. They investigated whether continuing attachment to a deceased spouse was positively or negatively related to levels of grief symptoms among widows and widowers at 6 months, 14 months, and 25 months after their loss. Those who expressed their continuing attachment by having and sharing fond memories of the deceased and by sensing

Is it pathological to maintain a relationship with a deceased parent for many years? Probably not. It is common practice in Japan to remember each morning during worship ancestors who have died, to leave them food and otherwise care for them, and to tell them about one's triumphs and disasters (Klass, 2001). A continuing bond with rather than detachment from the deceased is normal in some cultural contexts.

that their loved one was watching over and guiding them experienced relatively low levels of distress, but those who used their spouse's possessions to comfort themselves showed high levels of distress at the 6-month mark and little decrease in grief over the coming months. Apparently maintaining continuing bonds is adaptive for some people but a sign of complicated grief for others (Field, 2006).

Overall, the traditional grief work perspective is flawed. Norms for expressing grief vary widely across cultures; it is not clear that bereaved people must do "grief work" or that those who do not do it will pay later with a delayed grief reaction; and people do not need to sever their attachment to the deceased to adjust to a loss and sometimes benefit from continuing bonds. More fundamentally, researchers are now questioning the idea, embedded in the grief work model, that grief is a pathological process—like a disease that we catch, suffer from, and eventually get over (Bonanno, 2001). As you saw earlier, only about 15% of bereaved individuals experience complications of grief so severe that they can be described as pathological (Bonanno & Kaltman, 2000). What is more, it is common to experience positive emotions along with the negative ones and to feel in the end that one has benefited from one's loss in some way—for example, by becoming a stronger or better person (Davis & Nolen-Hoeksema, 2001; Folkman & Moskowitz, 2004). Overall, we must conclude that grief is more complex and less pathological than the grief work model implies.

Who Copes and Who Succumbs?

Even if it is difficult to find the line between normal grief and pathological or complicated grief, we can still ask what risk and protective factors distinguish people who cope well with loss from people who cope poorly. Coping with bereavement is influenced by the individual's personal resources, the nature of the loss, and the surrounding context of support and stressors.

Just as some individuals are better able to cope with their own dying than others are, some are better equipped to handle the stresses of bereavement. Bowlby's attachment theory emphasizes that *early experiences in attachment relationships* influence the internal working models we form of self and other, how we later relate to others, and how we handle losses of relationships. Colin Parkes (2006) has studied the internal working models of adults who seek help as they cope with bereavement. His research and other studies paint a picture consistent with attachment theory.

If infants and young children receive loving and responsive care, they form internal working models of self and other that tell them that they are lovable and that other people can be trusted (see Chapter 14). Having a secure attachment style is associated with coping relatively well with the death of a loved one (Parkes, 2006; Waskowic & Chartier, 2003). In a study of people affected by the 9/11 attacks on the World Trade Center, those with secure attachment styles suffered fewer symptoms of depression and posttraumatic stress disorder than those with insecure attachment styles, for example (Fraley et

al., 2006). Individuals who develop a resistant (or preoccupied) style of attachment tend to be overly dependent on others and display extreme and chronic grief and anxiety after a loss (Parkes, 2006). Those who develop an avoidant (or dismissing) attachment style tend to have difficulty expressing their emotions or seeking comfort from other people (Fraley & Bonanno, 2004; Parkes, 2006). Finally, those who have a disorganized attachment style rooted in unpredictable and sometimes abusive parenting appear to be especially unequipped to cope with loss; they may turn inward, harm themselves, or abuse alcohol or drugs (Parkes, 2006).

Personality and coping style also influence how successfully people cope with death. For example, individuals who have difficulty coping tend to have low self-esteem (Lund et al., 1985–1986) and lack a sense that they are in control of their lives (Haas-Hawkings et al., 1985). They often score high on measures of neuroticism (Wijngaards-de-Meij et al., 2007; Robinson & Marwit, 2006), and many were experiencing chronic psychological problems such as depression before they were bereaved (Bonanno, Wortman, & Nesse, 2004). Many also rely on ineffective coping strategies such as denial and escape through alcohol and drugs (Murphy, Johnson, & Lohan, 2003a). By contrast, people who are optimistic, find positive ways of interpreting their loss, and use active coping strategies experience less intense grief reactions and are more likely to report personal growth after their losses than other bereaved adults (Riley et al., 2007).

Bereavement outcomes are influenced not only by the individual's personal resources but also by the nature of the loss. The closeness of the person's *relationship to the deceased* is a key factor. For example, spouses grieve especially hard if they were highly dependent on their partners (Johnson et al., 2007). The *cause of death* can also influence bereavement outcomes. One reason the death of a child is so painful is that children's deaths are often the result of "senseless" and violent events such as car accidents, homicides, and suicides.

Finally, grief reactions are influenced positively by the presence of a strong social support system and negatively by additional life stressors (Parkes, 2006; Hansson & Stroebe, 2007). Social support is crucial at all ages. It is especially important for the young child whose parent dies to have good parenting (Haine et al., 2006). Brothers and sisters can help each other cope (Hurd, 2002). Indeed, family members of all ages recover best when the family is cohesive and family members can share their emotions (Traylor et al., 2003). As the Applications box on page 520 suggests, there are also simple things that friends and colleagues can do to be supportive.

Just as social support helps the bereaved, additional stressors hurt. For example, outcomes tend to be poor for widows who must cope with financial problems after bereavement and for widowers who must manage household tasks without their wives (Lopata, 1996). Widows and widowers may have more than the usual difficulty adjusting if they must also care single-handedly for young children, find a new job, or move (Parkes, 1996; Worden & Silverman, 1993). These kinds of stressors all demand what the dual process model of bereavement calls restoration-

WHAT SHOULD I SAY?

Many of us are clueless about how to support bereaved friends and colleagues—about how to find the right words, whether in person or in sympathy cards, about how to provide comfort. Meanwhile, bereaved people have plenty of ideas about what's helpful and what's not. Jess Decourcy Hinds (2007) was so irritated by some of the responses she received after her father's death that she wrote a column in *Newsweek* on the subject. She especially did not appreciate the people who tried to talk her out of her grief ("You should be happy you have your memories," "It's good he's not suffering anymore") or sought to distract her from it ("How's your teaching going?"). Among her recommendations are these:

- Say simply and directly that you're sorry to hear of the death.
- Ask, "How are you?" or "How are you feeling?" rather than telling the person how she should feel.

- Don't give advice about how the person should cope; people differ greatly in their ways of grieving, and their needs change from day to day.

Research is on her side. Bereaved individuals report that they are helped most by family and friends who say they are sorry to hear of the loss, make themselves available to serve as confidants, and let the bereaved express painful feelings freely when they wish to (Herkert, 2000; Lehman, Ellard, & Wortman, 1986). Because so many of us have no idea

Sensitive social support can make all the difference to the bereaved.

what to do or say, it often falls to the bereaved person to teach us (Dyregrov, 2003–2004).

---

oriented coping; they take energy and resources that elderly widows in poor health, especially those living in poverty with little social support, may not have (Hansson & Stroebe, 2007).

By taking into account the person who has experienced a death, the nature of the death, and the context surrounding it, we can put together a profile of the individuals who are most likely to have long-term problems after bereavement. These individuals have had an unfortunate history of interpersonal relationships, perhaps suffering the death of a parent when they were young or experiencing insecurity in their early attachments. They have had previous psychological problems and generally have difficulty coping effectively with adversity. The person who died is someone on whom they depended greatly, and the death was untimely and seemingly senseless. Finally, these high-risk individuals lack the kinds of social support that can aid them in overcoming their loss, and they are burdened by multiple stressors.

Bereavement and Human Development

The grief work perspective on bereavement has tended to put the focus on the negative side of bereavement—on the damaging effects of loss and the need to "recover" from "symptoms"

of grief. As you have seen, however, psychologists are coming to appreciate that bereavement and other life crises also have positive consequences and sometimes foster personal growth (Davis & Nolen-Hoeksema, 2001; Tedeschi & Calhoun, 2004). Granted, it can be a painful way to grow, and we could hardly recommend it as a plan for optimizing human development. Still, the literature on death and dying is filled with testimonials about the lessons that can be learned.

Many bereaved individuals believe that they have become stronger, wiser, more loving, and more religious people with a greater appreciation of life (Tedeschi & Calhoun, 2004). Many widows master new skills, become more independent, and emerge with new identities and higher self-esteem, especially those who depended heavily on their spouses and then discover that they can manage life on their own (Carr, 2004; Lopata, 1996). An example is Lisa Beamer, a young widow with three young children who wrote a book about her husband, a heroic 9/11 victim, established a foundation to help children in her husband's name, and became a motivational speaker (Scannell-Desch, 2005). A mother whose infant died said it all: "Now I can survive anything" (DeFrain, Taylor, & Ernst, 1982, p. 57). So perhaps it is by encountering tragedy that we learn to cope with tragedy, and perhaps it is by struggling to find meaning in death that we come to find meaning in life.

SUMMING UP

▮ All deaths in the family, including the death of a partner, have the potential to cause emotional damage and to alter the family system, although many widows and widowers are resilient. The death of a child often takes a greater toll than the death of a parent.

▮ Recent research challenges the grief work perspective, which holds that grieving involves experiencing and working through painful emotions and breaking the bond to the deceased.

▮ Prolonged grief is especially likely among individuals who have insecure attachment styles or ineffective coping skills; who had close relationships with loved ones who died senselessly; and who lack social support, face additional stressors, or both. Yet positive emotions and personal growth are common among the bereaved.

CRITICAL THINKING

1. Many people have misconceptions about what is normal and what is abnormal when it comes to grieving, as this chapter has illustrated. Identify two such misconceptions and, using relevant research, show why they are just that—misconceptions.

2. Anna is doing well after her husband's death. What about her and her situation might account for her resilience in the face of death?

17.7 TAKING THE STING OUT OF DEATH

Several efforts are under way to help children and adults who are dying or who are bereaved grapple with death and their feelings about it. Here is a sampling.

For the Dying

Dramatic changes in the care of dying people have occurred with the past few decades, thanks partly to the efforts of Elisabeth Kübler-Ross and others. Still, many signs suggest that hospital personnel continue to place emphasis on curing terminally ill patients and keeping them alive rather than on controlling their pain and allowing them to "die with dignity." Families feel that doctors are "missing in action" and that staff are more task focused than person focused (Wetle et al., 2005). Out of such concerns arose the hospice movement.

A **hospice** is a program that supports dying people and their families through a philosophy of "caring" rather than "curing" (Connor, 2000; Saunders, 2002). One of the founders of the hospice movement and of St. Christopher's Hospice in London, Dr. Cicely Saunders (2002), put it this way: "I remain committed to helping people find meaning in the end of life and not to helping them to a hastened death" (p. 289).

The hospice concept spread quickly to North America, where hospices have been established in most communities to serve individuals with cancer, AIDS, and other life-threatening diseases. In many hospice programs today, however, there is no care facility like St. Christopher's; instead, dying patients stay at home and are visited by hospice workers. Hospices are part of a larger movement to provide **palliative care,** care aimed not at curing but at meeting the physical, psychological, and spiritual needs of patients with incurable illnesses (Shannon, 2006).

What makes hospice care different from hospital care? Whether hospice care is provided in a facility or at home, it entails these key features (Connor, 2000; Corr & Corr, 1992; Siebold, 1992):

- The dying person and his family—not the "experts"—decide what support they need and want.
- Attempts to cure the patient or prolong his life are deemphasized (but death is not hastened either).
- Pain control is emphasized.
- The setting for care is as normal as possible (preferably the patient's own home or a homelike facility that does not have the sterile atmosphere of many hospital wards).
- Bereavement counseling is provided to the family before and after the death.

Do dying patients and their families fare better when they spend their last days together receiving hospice care? Hospice leaders point to suggestive evidence that patients have less interest in physician-assisted suicide when they have access to hospice care and their pain is better controlled (Foley & Hendin, 2002). In one study, a third of individuals cared for by

Hospice care helps people live even while they are dying.

a home health care agency, nursing home, or hospital felt they received too little emotional support, whereas only about 20% of those receiving home hospice services felt this way (Teno et al., 2004). And an evaluation of hospice facility care, at-home hospice care, and conventional hospital care in Great Britain found that hospice patients spent more of their last days without pain, underwent fewer medical interventions and operations, and received nursing care that was more oriented to their emotional needs (Seale, 1991). Moreover, spouses and partners, parents, and other relatives of dying people who received hospice care appear to display fewer symptoms of grief and have a greater sense of well-being 1 to 2 years after the death than similar relatives who coped with a death without benefit of hospice care (Ragow-O'Brien, Hayslip, & Guarnaccia, 2000).

The hospice approach may not work for all, but for some it means an opportunity to die with dignity, free of pain and surrounded by loved ones. The next challenge may be to extend the hospice philosophy of caring rather than curing to more children (Davies et al., 2007). Many children who die of cancer die in a hospital where their pain is not adequately controlled, possibly because their doctors and parents cannot accept that the child is dying and so continue to treat the cancer aggressively (Stillion & Papadatou, 2002; Wolfe et al., 2000).

For the Bereaved

Most bereaved individuals do not need psychological interventions to help them cope with death; they deal with this normal life transition on their own and with support from significant others. At the same time, there are many options for bereaved individuals, ranging from counseling intended to prevent problems before they arise to interventions designed to treat serious psychological disorders precipitated by a loss (Kazak & Noll, 2004; Raphael, Minkov, & Dobson, 2001). Bereaved individuals at risk for depression—because of a history of losses, a history of depression or other psychological disorders, or other factors—can clearly benefit from therapy or counseling aimed at preventing or treating their depression (Murray et al., 2000; Schulz et al., 2006; Zisook & Shuchter, 2001).

Because death takes place in a family context, family therapy often makes a good deal of sense (Kazak & Noll, 2004; Moore & Carr, 2000). Family therapy and other interventions designed for families can help bereaved parents and children communicate more openly and support one another. It can also help parents deal with their own emotional issues so that they can provide the warm and supportive parenting that can be so critical in facilitating their children's recovery. In one well-planned preventive program, the Family Bereavement Program (Sandler et al., 2003; Schmiege et al., 2006), children and adolescents who had lost a parent and the surviving parent met for 2 hours a week for 12 weeks, sometimes separately in their own age groups, sometimes in joint parent–child sessions. The aims of the program included helping the children cope and helping the surviving parent manage stressful life events

and maintain close parent–child relationships and effective discipline at home. A behavioral approach involving modeling and role-playing of target skills and homework assignments to apply skills was used. Like some other interventions, this one helped girls more than boys, allowing them to overcome their mental health and behavior problems faster than girls whose families were randomly assigned to an innocuous control treatment. Boys improved over the year with or without treatment.

Another approach to helping the bereaved is the mutual support or self-help group (Goodkin et al., 2001; Silverman, 2000; Zisook & Shuchter, 2001). One such program is Compassionate Friends, serving parents whose children have died. Parents without Partners, THEOS (They Help Each Other Spiritually), the Widowed Persons Service, and similar groups bring widows and widowers and other bereaved partners together to offer everything from practical advice on such matters as settling finances to emotional support and friendship.

Participation in mutual support groups can be beneficial for bereaved parents, helping them find meaning in the death of their child (Murphy et al., 2003a). And, compared with widows who do not participate in support groups, participants tend to be less depressed and anxious, use less medication, and have a greater sense of well-being and self-esteem (Lieberman & Videka-Sherman, 1986). Perhaps this is because other bereaved people are in the best position to understand what a bereaved person is going through and to offer effective social support. One widow summed it up this way: "What's helpful? Why, people who are in the 'same boat'" (Bankoff, 1983, p. 230).

Taking Our Leave

We have reached the end not only of the life span but of this book and want to leave you with a few parting words. Notice that the book's inside back cover provides a chart summarizing key developments in different periods of the life span; it will help you put the "whole person" back together again and see at a glance relationships among the domains of physical, cognitive, personal, and social development. Also notice the appendix on Careers in Human Development—a resource for those of you who think you may want to make a life of studying development or intervening to change it.

Finally, we leave you with a reminder of some of the themes echoed throughout this book, many of them part of the life-span perspective on development (Baltes, 1987; and see Chapter 1). We hope you can now think of many illustrations of each:

1. **Nature and Nurture Truly Interact in Development:** It's clear that both biology and environment, reciprocally influencing each other all the way, steer development.

2. **We Are Whole People throughout the Life Span:** Advances in one area of development (motor development, for example) have implications for other areas of development (cognitive development through exploration, for example); we must understand interrelationships among domains of development to understand whole human beings.

3. **Development Proceeds in Multiple Directions:** We experience gains and losses, along with changes that simply make us different than we were, at every age.

4. **There Is Both Continuity and Discontinuity in Development:** Each of us is at once "the same old person" and a new person, qualitatively different from the person who came before; development is also both gradual and stagelike.

5. **There Is Much Plasticity in Development:** We can change in response to experience at any age, getting off one developmental pathway and onto another.

6. **We Are Individuals, Becoming Even More Diverse with Age:** Developing humans are diverse from the start—and become even more diverse by old age.

7. **We Develop in a Cultural and Historical Context:** Human development takes different forms in different times and cultures, in different socioeconomic and racial/ethnic groups, and in different social niches.

8. **We Are Active in Our Own Development:** We help create our environments, influence those around us, and, by doing so, contribute to our own development.

9. **Development Is a Lifelong Process:** We never stop developing, and behavior during any one phase of life is best understood in relation to what came before and what is to come.

10. **Development Is Best Viewed from Multiple Perspectives:** Many disciplines have something to contribute to a comprehensive understanding of human development—and we need them all.

We hope that you are intrigued enough by the mysteries of life-span human development to observe more closely your own development and that of those around you—or even to seek further course work and practical experience in the field. And we sincerely hope that you will use what you learn to steer your own and others' development in positive directions.

SUMMING UP

▌ Successful efforts to take the sting out of death have included hospice programs for dying patients and their families, part of the larger palliative care movement that emphasizes caring over curing.

▌ Individual therapy, family therapy, and mutual support groups can help the bereaved.

▌ This book has illustrated a number of themes, many associated with the life-span perspective on development introduced in Chapter 1.

CRITICAL THINKING

1. On what can proponents of assisted suicide (see the first Explorations box) and proponents of hospice care agree—and how do they differ?

2. Which of the life-span development themes illustrated throughout this book can you detect in this chapter on death and dying?

CHAPTER SUMMARY

17.1 MATTERS OF LIFE AND DEATH

- In defining death as a biological process, the Harvard definition of total brain death has been influential. Many controversies surround issues of active and passive euthanasia and assisted suicide; meanwhile, the social meanings of death vary widely.

- The average life expectancy for a newborn in the United States has risen to 78 years, higher than that in less developed countries. Death rates decline after infancy but rise after early adulthood as accidents give way to chronic diseases as the primary causes of death.

- Programmed theories of aging hold that aging is governed by species heredity, a telomere-controlled cellular aging clock, and individual heredity, whereas damage theories of aging focus on an accumulation of random damage caused by destructive free radicals and other agents.

17.2 THE EXPERIENCE OF DEATH

- Elisabeth Kübler-Ross stimulated much concern for dying patients by describing five stages of dying, but, as Edwin Shneidman emphasized, the dying experience ever-changing emotions, depending on the course of their disease and on their personality.

- Bereavement precipitates grief and mourning, which are expressed, according to the Parkes/Bowlby attachment model, in overlapping phases of numbness, yearning, disorganization and despair, and reorganization. The dual process model describes oscillation between loss-oriented coping, restoration-oriented coping, and respites from coping.

17.3 THE INFANT

- Infants may not comprehend death but clearly grieve, protesting, despairing, and then detaching after separations.

17.4 THE CHILD

- Children are curious about death and usually understand by age 5 to 7 that it is a final cessation of life functions that is irreversible and universal, later realizing that it is ultimately caused by internal biological changes.

- Terminally ill children often become very aware of their plight, and bereaved children often experience bodily symptoms, academic difficulties, and behavioral problems.

17.5 THE ADOLESCENT

- Adolescents understand death more abstractly, believe in an afterlife, and cope with dying and bereavement in ways that reflect the developmental themes of adolescence.

17.6 THE ADULT

- Widows and widowers experience many physical, emotional, and cognitive symptoms and are at increased risk of dying; the death of a child is often even more difficult for an adult to bear, whereas the death of a parent is often easier.

- The grief work perspective has been challenged; what is normal depends on the cultural context, and many people display resilience, never doing "grief work" and continuing rather than severing their attachment bonds.

- Complicated grief is especially likely among individuals who have insecure attachment styles, who have neurotic personalities and limited coping skills, who had dependent relationships with individuals who died violently and senselessly, and who lack social support or face additional stressors.

17.7 TAKING THE STING OUT OF DEATH

- Successful efforts to take the sting out of death have included hospices and other forms of palliative care for dying patients and their families and individual therapy, family therapy, and mutual support groups for the bereaved.

KEY TERMS

total brain death 498	caloric restriction 505
euthanasia 499	denial 506
assisted suicide 500	bereavement 507
living will 500	grief 507
life expectancy 501	mourning 507
programmed theories of aging 502	anticipatory grief 507
damage theories of aging 502	Parkes/Bowlby attachment model of bereavement 508
maximum life span 502	dual process model 508
Hayflick limit 503	complicated grief 516
telomere 503	grief work perspective 517
progeria 504	continuing bonds 518
free radical theory 504	hospice 521
antioxidants 504	palliative care 521

MEDIA RESOURCES

BOOK COMPANION WEBSITE

academic.cengage.com/psychology/sigelman
Find online quizzes, flash cards, animations, video clips, experiments, interactive assessments, and other helpful study aids for this text at **academic.cengage.com/psychology/sigelman**. You can also connect directly to the following sites:

AGING UNDER THE MICROSCOPE

This National Institute on Aging-hosted site presents a superb discussion of the biological aging process at both the global and individual systems levels. This colorful and informative site is a "must-see" for those interested in the process of biological aging.

DEATH-RELATED SITES

This St. Olaf College-hosted site contains links to dozens of interesting websites and articles related to issues of death and dying. These links cover a wide range of topics including "American Way of Dying," "Children and Death Attitudes," and "Euthanasia and Biomedical Issues."

ELISABETH KÜBLER-ROSS

The Elisabeth Kübler-Ross site contains a wealth of information on the woman who made the concept of stages of dying part of both medical practice and popular culture. One special aspect of this site is several video clip interviews focusing on issues like unconditional love and spirituality.

HOSPICE FOUNDATION OF AMERICA

This is a great site for those interested in the hospice alternative to dying. Be sure to check out the sections on "Grief & Loss" and "End of Life Info."

UNDERSTANDING THE DATA: EXERCISES ON THE WEB

academic.cengage.com/psychology/sigelman
For additional insight on the data presented in this chapter, try out the exercises for these figures at **academic.cengage.com/psychology/sigelman**:

Table 17.1 Leading Causes of Death for Different Age Groups in the United States

Figure 17.3 Depression symptom scores of five subgroups of elderly widows and widowers an average of 3 years before, 6 months after, and 18 months after the death of their spouse

CENGAGENOW

academic.cengage.com/login
Go to **academic.cengage.com/login** to link to CengageNOW, your online study tool. First take the Pre-Test for this chapter to get your Personalized Study Plan, which will identify topics you need to review and direct you to online resources. Then take the Post-Test to determine what concepts you have mastered and what you still need work on.

Appendix

Careers in Human Development

What career possibilities exist for students interested in understanding or optimizing human development? Being developmentalists ourselves, we would argue that *anyone* who works with people can benefit from an understanding of life-span human development. We are not alone in our belief: Preparation for many "people" professions—teaching, counseling, nursing and other allied health professions—includes course work in human development. Indeed, some of you are taking this course because it is required for your chosen career.

If you think you are interested in a career in human development, you might first ask yourself some basic questions:

What *level of education* do you seek—bachelor's, master's, or doctoral?

Are you interested in a particular *age group*—infants, children, adolescents, adults, elderly people?

Are you interested in a particular *aspect of development*—physical, cognitive, or social development, normal or abnormal development?

Are you most interested in *research, teaching, or practice* (work as a helping professional of some kind)?

We will sketch out some career possibilities within the broad areas of research, teaching, and professional practice, illustrating as we go how the level of education you seek and the age groups and aspects of development of interest to you come into play. Much information is drawn from the Bureau of Labor Statistics (2006) guide, *Occupational Outlook Handbook, 2006-07 edition*, available online or as a book; you may want to consult it to learn more about the employment outlook and average salaries in some of the professions discussed (see Resources at the end of this Appendix).

RESEARCH

Depending on what level of authority and responsibility you seek, you can conduct research on human development with a bachelor's degree, master's degree (typically 2 years of course work and either a comprehensive examination or completion of a thesis), or doctoral degree (typically 5 to 7 years of work, including courses, a qualifying or comprehensive exam, and completion of a doctoral dissertation research project). Research on normal life-span development and aging, abnormal development, and genetic and environmental influences on development is conducted in a variety of settings: colleges and universities; medical schools, hospitals, and other health care facilities; government institutes and agencies (for example, the National Institutes of Health, including the National Institute of Child Health and Human Development and the National Institute on Aging, and state and local health and human services agencies), social research organizations (some of the larger ones that conduct research on children, families, aging, and social policy are Abt Associates, SRI International, Mathematica, MDRC, RAND, and Westat), and various for-profit and nonprofit organizations.

With a bachelor's degree, you could be hired as a research assistant or another member of a research team to conduct interviews or telephone surveys, test children, observe and code behavior, analyze physiological data, compile tables and graphs, or complete the many other tasks involved in research. With additional work experience—or with a master's degree in a relevant field such as developmental psychology, including course work in research methods and statistics—you would become eligible for positions of greater responsibility. For example, you might be hired as the project coordinator for an investigator's study, responsible for implementing the data collection plan and supervising the work of research assistants, or you might become a specialist in testing infants, administering tasks to elderly adults, or analyzing data.

Finally, with a doctor of philosophy (PhD) degree in developmental psychology or a related field, you would qualify to be a principal investigator and head a research team—to be the one who designs research projects, submits research proposals to the federal government or foundations to obtain funding, guides implementation of the study, supervises the research staff, analyzes data, writes up findings, and submits papers for publication in a professional journal (publications that are then cited in textbooks like this one). Because research is conducted in so many settings, your options as a PhD include many besides becoming a college or university professor who combines teaching and research. And the topics you can study are as wide ranging as those in this book.

How can you get a start on a career in human development research now? You might ask professors at your college or university about graduate programs and job opportunities in areas of development that interest you. Seek as much research experience as you can get, too:

- Ask your professors whether they need help with their research and be on the lookout for notices about research projects that need student assistants on either a voluntary or paid basis.
- Sign up for an independent study course that would allow you to conduct a literature review or do a research project with guidance from a professor.
- Seek undergraduate research fellowships that might allow you to do a research project with financial support, possibly a summer living stipend; some colleges and universities offer such research fellowships to their own students or even to students from other universities (for example, through the National Science Foundation's Research Experiences for Undergraduates program).
- Do a senior thesis or capstone project if it is an option in your major.
- If you are seeking work, look for jobs that involve research, program evaluation, or policy analysis; even if the research is not directly related to human development, you may learn useful research skills.
- Attend professional conferences to gain exposure to researchers in your area of interest and hear about the latest research they are conducting.

These sorts of activities will help you find out whether you like research and what aspects of it you like (or don't). They will also help you acquire research skills, get to know professors who can write reference letters for you and otherwise help you pursue your career plans, and demonstrate to graduate programs or employers that you are interested in research and have some familiarity with it. Increasingly, admission to doc-

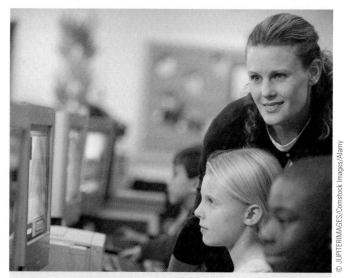

Getting research experience as an undergraduate student is good preparation for graduate school.

toral programs requires experience assisting with research, presenting papers at professional conferences, or even publishing articles with professors.

Some students seek paid research staff positions after completing their bachelor's degree, do well, and work their way up to more responsible positions. Others work for a while and go on for an advanced degree after they have gained some experience. Others enter master's programs, and still others who are certain they want a research career apply directly to doctoral programs as college seniors. In most graduate programs, students gain hands-on experience by serving as research assistants for professors while they are taking courses; they then draw on this apprenticeship experience in designing and conducting a master's thesis or doctoral dissertation project of their own.

TEACHING

Teachers clearly need to understand the developmental characteristics and learning capacities of their students to teach effectively and make a difference in their students' lives. As a result, course work in human development is a required part of teacher training at the bachelor's and master's levels. Colleges of education offer teacher preparation programs in preschool or early childhood, kindergarten, elementary school, middle school, secondary school, and adult education; in the teaching of specific subjects such as English or science; and in special education (the teaching of students with developmental disabilities, behavior disorders, and other special learning needs). Teachers normally need to complete a teacher education program leading to a bachelor's or master's degree and then obtain certification from the state in which they will teach by demonstrating that they have taken the required course work and passing a standardized teacher exam.

To teach at the college or university level, a doctoral degree, usually a doctor of philosophy (PhD) degree, is normally required. Much of what we said above about doctoral education for researchers applies to doctoral education for professors. Most PhD programs are highly research-oriented and involve both learning about the field through course work and learning how to contribute to the field through research. Some community colleges hire professors with master's degrees in certain areas but more and more hire only PhDs. In schools of education, either a PhD or an EdD (doctor of education) can qualify an individual for a faculty position; the PsyD degree, discussed later, prepares people to be practicing psychologists and is not the right choice for those interested primarily in research and teaching positions.

Students may get the impression that their professors do nothing but teach, but the job description of a faculty member often includes not only teaching and advising students but also conducting research and providing service to the college or university (for example, through committee work or involvement in university governance) as well as to the local community and profession (for example, by consulting with local non-profit organizations or schools, or by serving as a reviewer for a journal that publishes research in one's field or as an officer in a professional organization). Specific responsibilities vary considerably depending on the type of institution; generally teaching responsibilities are heavy and research responsibilities are light at a community college, whereas research may be the first and foremost responsibility of a professor at a large research university, who may teach only a course or two a semester. Large universities also appoint some PhDs as "research professors," who typically spend virtually all of their time doing research supported by grants from the federal government and other sources.

If you are considering applying to doctoral programs, we would strongly recommend that you do serious research to identify programs that are a good fit to your interests and qualifications. Doctoral-level training in human development can be found in a bewildering array of departments, schools, centers, and institutes within universities. The American Psychological Association's (2007) publication *Graduate Study in Psychology* is an excellent resource for students seeking a graduate program in developmental psychology (typically located in a psychology department), human development (typically an interdisciplinary program located in its own department or even school), family studies or family and consumer sciences (also interdisciplinary, sometimes attached to a school of agriculture because the field originated in connection with agricultural extension services), educational psychology (in either schools of education or psychology departments), or gerontology (also often interdisciplinary and sometimes based in a center or institute).

Most professors who teach human development or aging did their doctoral work in either psychology or education, but some departments of sociology and anthropology around the country also have strength in the study of families or aging. Moreover, graduate programs in biology often have faculty who specialize in developmental biology, and neuroscience and cognitive neuroscience programs often have specialists in developmental neurobiology, dementia, and other topics relevant to development and aging. The more you know about your specific research and teaching interests, the better; you will then be able to seek programs in the right field that have scholars whose interests match yours and can even apply to particular programs because you want to work with specific professors. Doctoral programs are competitive but many doctoral students have their education paid for by fellowships and teaching and research assistantships.

PROFESSIONAL PRACTICE

By "professional practice," we mean the application of knowledge of human development in order to optimize development. Opportunities for professional practice are even more varied than those for research and teaching.

Bachelor's Level Positions

If you decide you want to enter one of the many helping professions, it makes sense to seek applied experience while you are completing your bachelor's degree or afterwards—for example, through unpaid or paid internships or jobs in counseling centers, hospitals, human services agencies, treatment facilities for children or adolescents, or senior centers or nursing homes, depending on your interests. This is a great way to gauge your interests and abilities and develop skills. Some relevant jobs available to individuals with a bachelor's degree or less include:

- **Child care worker:** The pay is not good, but individuals who love working with children can, with a bachelor's degree or less, work in day care and preschool facilities, before- and after-school programs, camps and recreation programs, and residential programs for disturbed children (Bureau of Labor Statistics, 2006).
- **Human services worker:** Countless entry-level positions in human services, mental health, and health care are available, carrying diverse titles such as case management aide, community outreach worker, life skills counselor, and gerontology aide. These workers may assist psychologists, nurses, and social workers in hospitals, mental health centers and facilities, and government agencies, performing such tasks as assessing client needs, conducting intake interviews, keeping case records, processing paperwork, teaching life skills, supervising clients in residential facilities, and leading group or family sessions.

Most of the following career options require graduate course work in areas such as assessment and treatment approaches; practicum and internship experiences in which learning is put to practice; and the passing of an examination after completion of studies in order to be licensed or certified by a state to practice.

Some human service workers organize and lead activities at senior day care centers and residential facilities for elderly adults.

Applied Developmental Psychologist

If you want to be squarely in the field of human development and have a positive impact on development but do not want to become a therapist or counselor, you might look into master's or doctoral programs in applied developmental psychology, a fairly new subfield of psychology. Although many graduate programs in developmental psychology, human development, and family studies engage in real-world, policy-relevant research, applied developmental psychology programs make a point of it. Applied developmental psychologists may be trained to conduct research on practical problems such as improving early childhood education, supporting at-risk families, or reducing childhood injuries; assess the developmental status of infants and children; design, implement, and evaluate interventions aimed at preventing or treating problems such as alcohol and drug abuse, aggression, or abusive parenting; and consult or serve as expert witnesses in juvenile court proceedings, custody hearings, and the like (Kuther & Morgan, 2007).

Counselor, Psychologist, or Therapist

Now consider some options if you want to provide counseling or psychotherapy to individuals or families as a state-licensed or certified psychologist. Wearing the title "psychologist" generally requires doctoral-level training in the United States. Individuals with master's degrees in fields such as clinical or counseling psychology are needed in mental health centers and facilities, but they are hired as "psychological assistants" or "psychological associates" and must be supervised by doctoral-level psychologists or psychiatrists (see Bureau of Labor Statistics, 2006). Here are three types of practicing psychologists:

Clinical Psychologist

Clinical psychologists are trained to diagnose and treat individuals with psychological disorders. Some of them, such as child clinical psychologists and pediatric psychologists (who usually work in hospitals and other health care facilities), focus on infants, children, and adolescents; others (geropsychologists) specialize in problems of the elderly. Becoming a clinical psychologist normally requires earning a PhD or PsyD (the doctor of psychology degree, a more practice-oriented and less research-oriented degree than the PhD that often involves a culminating project rather than a research dissertation). You should look closely at the extent to which a program of interest is practice-oriented versus research-oriented and decide whether you want to be primarily a scientist, primarily a practitioner, or a scientist–practitioner who integrates the two roles. You should also understand that clinical psychology programs are extremely selective, requiring high grades, high scores on the Graduate Record Examinations (GREs), relevant experience, and excellent recommendations.

Counseling Psychologist

Counseling psychologists may earn a PhD, EdD, or PsyD. Like clinical psychologists, they qualify to be licensed as psychologists. Compared to clinical psychologists, though, they tend to emphasize optimizing mental health and more often work with everyday problems of adjustment (for example, as a counselor in a college or university, company, or community mental health center).

School Psychologist

After completing either an education specialist (EdS) degree (which requires about 3 years of study and a yearlong internship) or a PhD, EdD, or PsyD in school psychology, a school psychologist is prepared to administer IQ tests and other assessment instruments to students believed to have learning disabilities or other special educational needs or to be gifted, consult with teachers and parents on how best to educate them, and provide other supportive psychological services in schools.

Now consider some additional possibilities for careers in counseling and therapy, some of which do not require doctoral-level education:

Psychiatrist

Becoming a psychiatrist involves earning a doctor of medicine (MD) degree; job descriptions and employment opportunities are much like those of clinical psychologists, but psychiatrists can prescribe medications for psychological disorders.

Counselor

A wide range of counseling programs exist in psychology departments, schools of education, and family studies programs, and many provide opportunities for independent practice after earning a master's degree and passing a state licensing examination. Subareas of counseling include school counseling (which may involve helping students who have academic or personal problems or, at the secondary school level, helping high school students plan their futures), vocational or career counseling, rehabilitation counseling (work in the vocational rehabilitation field helping adults with disabilities deal with their disabilities and find appropriate jobs), substance abuse or addiction counselors, mental health or community counselors, marriage and family therapists, genetic counselors, gerontological (aging) counselors, and more (see Bureau of Labor Statistics, 2006, on Counselors).

Social Worker

Careers in social work normally require at least a master's degree in social work (MSW). Specialties include child, family, and school social work; medical social work; and mental health or clinical social work (Bureau of Labor Statistics, 2006). Some social workers are employed by human services agencies as caseworkers who work with families on welfare, neglected or abused children and their families, or aging adults and their families; medical social workers are based in health care facilities and support patients and their families. Clinical social workers are trained in diagnosing personal and family problems and in providing counseling and therapy. Clinical social workers with an MSW can practice independently, whereas psychologists must have a doctoral degree to do so.

Mindful of the steady growth of the aging population, the Bureau of Labor Statistics (2006) notes that career opportunities for psychologists, counselors, and social workers with training in gerontology are expanding. A number of universities offer certificates or minors in gerontology that students can combine with their academic major to position themselves to work with elderly people; other universities offer bachelor's, master's, and even doctoral programs in gerontology. Services for older adults are varied and are expanding, providing plenty of opportunities for individuals with bachelor's and master's degrees. Our society clearly needs more individuals in a variety of disciplines and professions who care about and have expertise in aging.

Health Professionals

Our limited space here allows only a brief look at the topic, but a wide range of careers in medicine and allied health professions provide opportunities to apply knowledge of human development and aging to practice. Physicians can focus their careers on newborns, children, adolescents, or elderly adults, as they choose, selecting specialties such as pediatrics or geriatrics in medical school and seeking positions that allow them to work with the age groups and health problems of greatest interest to them. Similarly, nurses can become hospice or palliative care nurses who work with terminally ill patients, developmental disabilities nurses, or psychiatric nurses—or can specialize in the care of a particular age group. Other allied health professions such as speech therapy, physical therapy, and occupational therapy also allow for specialization in particular age groups and type of problems.

Other Options

Finally, we need an "Other" category to say that individuals with training in developmental psychology, counseling, and other human development fields land in surprising places. Many people who enter the occupations we have discussed here advance by becoming administrators; for example, a teacher may become a principal, a psychologist, counselor, or social worker may become the director of a treatment facility or human service agency. Some of these helping professionals seek further education relevant to their administrative roles (for example, a master's degree in business administration, public administration, or heath care management); others simply take on higher administrative roles and learn on the job.

People with training in human development also find their way into business and industry. One may become a book editor in a company that publishes books on psychology, another may test toys or other products for children, another may advise a company's employees on retirement issues, another may advise on architectural design for the elderly. Many also work as self-employed consultants, offering help to agencies, organizations, and businesses in areas in which they have expertise. ● **Table A.1** summarizes some of the career options we have discussed.

We hope this is enough to get you thinking and dreaming—and, better yet, taking concrete steps now to gain the knowledge, skills, and experience that will help you formulate and realize your dream. We are confident that the need for individuals who understand the complexities and marvels of life-span human development and can steer it in healthy directions will remain strong as long as humans develop and age.

● TABLE A.1   SOME CAREER OPTIONS IN HUMAN DEVELOPMENT

DEGREE REQUIRED	RESEARCH	TEACHING	PROFESSIONAL PRACTICE
Bachelor's or master's degree	Research assistant Research staff member Project coordinator	Teacher's aide Teacher in preschool, elementary, secondary, or adult education	Child care worker Human services worker Psychological assistant or associate Social worker* School psychologist*
Doctoral degree	Research professor Principal investigator in. . . . university, hospital, health or mental health facility, research organization	Professor of. . . . developmental psychology, human development, family studies Professor of. . . . clinical psychology, counseling psychology, social work, etc.	Applied developmental psychologist Clinical psychologist Counseling psychologist Psychiatrist Counselor Health professional (medicine, allied health)

*Master's degree required.

Family therapy may be provided by clinical or counseling psychologists or by clinical social workers.

RESOURCES

American Psychological Association Careers in Psychology in the 21st Century: A short overview of careers in psychology, including profiles of psychologists in different types of jobs. Available at: www.apa.org/topics/psychologycareer.html.

American Psychological Association. (2007). *Graduate Study in Psychology: 2008 Edition.* Washington, DC: American Psychological Association. This invaluable guide for students looking for appropriate graduate programs profiles over 600 graduate programs in the United States and Canada, noting program emphases, admission standards, information about the employment of graduates, and the like. The website of the American Psychological Association, www.apa.org, also has information relevant to careers in psychology (see especially the Student section).

Bureau of Labor Statistics. (2006). *Occupational Outlook Handbook, 2006-07.* A wonderful resource describing, for each of many occupational fields, the nature of the work involved, working conditions, training and other qualifications, employment data, job prospects, and average earnings. Available free at www.bls.gov/oco or as a book published by JIST Works.

Careers in Aging. The website of the Association for Gerontology in Higher Education describes educational programs from the associate degree level to the doctoral level in gerontology (the study of aging) and geriatrics (health care for the aging) and includes information about career possibilities. The website is www.careersinaging.com.

GradSchools.com. This website allows you to search for graduate programs at the master's and doctoral levels in various fields and link to the web pages of those programs efficiently. The web address is http://GradSchools.com.

JobWeb.com. This site of the National Association of Colleges and Employers is aimed at new college graduates and provides useful guidance on resume preparation and job search strategies, as well as job listings. The web address is www.JobWeb.com.

Kuther, T. L. (2006). *The Psychology Major's Handbook* (2nd ed.). Belmont, CA: Thomson Wadsworth. A good general guide to succeeding as a psychology major and preparing for graduate school and careers.

Kuther, T. L., & Morgan, R. D. (2007). *Careers in Psychology: Opportunities in a Changing World* (2nd ed.). Belmont, CA: Thomson Wadsworth. A survey of opportunities in the various subfields of psychology, including developmental psychology.

Glossary

A-not-B error The tendency of 8- to 12-month-old infants to search for a hidden object in the place they last found it (A) rather than in its new hiding place (B).

ability grouping The practice in education of grouping students according to ability and educating them in classes with students of comparable academic or intellectual standing; also called ability tracking or simply tracking.

acceptance–responsiveness A dimension of parenting capturing the extent to which parents are supportive, sensitive to their children's needs, and willing to provide affection and praise when their children meet their expectations.

accommodation In Piaget's cognitive developmental theory, the process of modifying existing schemes to incorporate or adapt to new experiences. Contrast with *assimilation*. In vision, a change in the shape of the eye's lens to bring objects at differing distances into focus.

acquired immunodeficiency syndrome (AIDS) The life-threatening disease in which the human immunodeficiency virus (HIV) destroys the immune system and makes victims susceptible to rare, so-called opportunistic, infections that eventually kill them. AIDS is transmitted through sexual activity, drug needle sharing, and from mother to child before or during birth.

activity–passivity issue The issue in developmental theory centering on whether humans are active contributors to their own development or are passively shaped by forces beyond their control.

activity theory A perspective holding that aging adults will find satisfaction to the extent that they maintain an active lifestyle. Contrast with *disengagement theory*.

adaptation In Piaget's cognitive developmental theory, a person's inborn tendency to adjust to the demands of the environment, consisting of the complementary processes of *assimilation* and *accommodation*.

adolescence The transitional period between childhood and adulthood that begins with puberty and ends when the individual has acquired adult competencies and responsibilities.

adolescent egocentrism A characteristic of adolescent thought that involves difficulty differentiating between the person's own thoughts and feelings and those of other people; evident in the *personal fable* and *imaginary audience* phenomena.

adolescent growth spurt The rapid increase in physical growth that occurs during adolescence.

age effects In developmental research, the effects of getting older or of developing. Contrast with *cohort effects* and *time of measurement effects*.

age grades Socially defined age groups or strata, each with different statuses, roles, privileges, and responsibilities in society.

age norms Expectations about what people should be doing or how they should behave at different points in the life span.

age of viability A point (around the 24th prenatal week) when a fetus may survive outside the uterus if the brain and respiratory system are well enough developed and if excellent medical care is available.

ageism Prejudice against elderly people.

agency An orientation toward individual action and achievement that emphasizes traits of dominance, independence, assertiveness, and competitiveness; considered masculine.

age-related macular degeneration Damage to cells in the retina responsible for central vision.

aging To most developmentalists, positive, negative, and neutral changes in the mature organism; different from *biological aging*.

alphabetic principle The idea that the letters in printed words represent the sounds in spoken words.

Alzheimer's disease A pathological condition of the nervous system that results in an irreversible loss of cognitive capacities; the leading cause of dementia in later life.

amniocentesis A method of extracting amniotic fluid from a pregnant woman so that fetal body cells within the fluid can be tested for chromosomal abnormalities and other genetic defects.

amnion A watertight membrane that surrounds the developing embryo, regulating its temperature and cushioning it against injuries.

amoral Lacking any sense of morality; without standards of right and wrong.

androgenized female A genetic female who was exposed to male sex hormones during the prenatal period and therefore developed malelike external genitals and some masculine behaviors.

androgens Male hormones that help trigger the adolescent growth spurt and the development of the male sex organs, secondary sex characteristics, and sexual motivation.

androgyny A gender-role orientation in which the person blends both positive masculine-stereotyped and positive feminine-stereotyped personality traits.

androgyny shift A psychological change that begins in midlife, when parenting responsibilities are over, in which both men and women retain their gender-typed qualities but add to them qualities traditionally associated with the other sex, thus becoming more androgynous.

andropause The slower and less-dramatic male counterpart of *menopause*, characterized by decreasing levels of testosterone and symptoms that include low libido, fatigue and lack of energy, erection problems, memory problems, and loss of pubic hair.

anencephaly Condition in which the top of the neural tube fails to close and the main portion of the brain above the brain stem fails to develop properly.

anorexia nervosa A life-threatening eating disorder characterized by failure to maintain a normal weight, a strong fear of weight gain, and a distorted body image; literally, "nervous lack of appetite."

anoxia A lack of sufficient oxygen to the brain that may result in neurological damage or death.

anticipatory grief Grieving before death for what is happening and for what lies ahead.

antioxidant Vitamins C, E, and similar substances that may increase longevity, although not for long, by inhibiting the free radical activity associated with oxidation and in turn preventing age-related diseases.

Apgar test A test routinely used to assess a newborn's heart rate, respiration, color, muscle tone, and reflexes immediately after birth and 5 minutes later; used to identify high-risk babies.

artificial insemination A method of conception that involves injecting sperm from a woman's partner or from a donor into the uterus.

Asperger syndrome An autistic spectrum disorder in which the child has normal or above-average intelligence, has good verbal skills, and wants to establish social relationships but has seriously deficient mind-reading and social skills.

assimilation Piaget's term for the process by which children interpret new experiences in terms of their existing schemata. Contrast with *accommodation*.

assisted reproductive technologies (ARTs) A range of methods used to help a couple conceive a child, from fertility drugs to in vitro fertilization.

assisted suicide Making available to individuals who wish to commit suicide the means by which they may do so, such as when a physician provides a terminally ill patient who wants to die with enough medication to overdose.

at risk Children who have a higher than normal chance of either short-term or long-term problems because of genetic defects, prenatal hazards, or perinatal damage.

attachment A strong affectional tie that binds a person to an intimate companion and is characterized by affection and a desire to maintain proximity.

attachment theory The theory of close relationships developed by Bowlby and Ainsworth and grounded in ethological theory (with psychoanalytic theory and cognitive theory); it says that close emotional bonds such as parent–child attachments are biologically based and contribute to species survival.

attention Focusing perception and cognition on something in particular.

attention deficit hyperactivity disorder (ADHD) A disorder characterized by attentional difficulties, impulsive behavior, and overactive or fidgety behavior.

authoritarian parenting A restrictive style of parenting combining high demandingness–control and low acceptance–responsiveness in which adults impose many rules, expect strict obedience, and often rely on power tactics rather than explanations to elicit compliance.

authoritative parenting A flexible style of parenting combining high demandingness–control and high acceptance–responsiveness in which adults lay down clear rules but also grant a fair amount of autonomy to their children and explain the rationale for their restrictions.

autism A pervasive and severe developmental disorder that begins in infancy and is characterized by such problems as an aversion to social contact, deviant communication or mutism, and repetitive, stereotyped behavior.

autism spectrum disorders (ASDs) Also called pervasive developmental disorders because they affect many aspects of functioning, these disorders, which include autism, Asperger syndrome, Rett syndrome, and others, all involve social and communication problems.

autobiographical memory Memory of everyday events that the individual has experienced.

automatization The process by which information processing becomes effortless and highly efficient as a result of continued practice or increased expertise.

autonomous morality The most mature Piagetian stage of morality in which rules are viewed as agreements between individuals that can be changed through a consensus of those individuals and in which the older child or adolescent pays more attention to intentions than to consequences in judging actions. Contrast with *heteronomous morality*.

autonomy The capacity to make decisions independently, serve as one's own source of emotional strength, and otherwise manage life tasks without being overdependent on other people; an important developmental task of adolescence.

autonomy versus shame and doubt The psychosocial conflict in which toddlers attempt to demonstrate their independence from and control over other people; second of Erikson's stages.

avoidant attachment An insecure infant-caregiver bond or other intimate relationship characterized by little separation anxiety and a tendency to avoid or ignore the attachment object upon reunion.

babbling An early form of vocalization that appears between 4 and 6 months of age and involves repeating consonant–vowel combinations such as "baba" or "dadada."

baby biographies Carefully recorded observations of the growth and development of children by their parents over a period; the first scientific investigations of development.

baby boom generation The huge generation of people born between 1946 (the close of World War II) and 1964.

beanpole family A multigenerational family structure characterized by many small generations.

behavioral genetics The scientific study of the extent to which genetic and environmental differences among individuals are responsible for differences among them in traits such as intelligence and personality.

behavioral inhibition A temperamental characteristic reflecting a person's tendency to withdraw from unfamiliar people and situations.

behaviorism A school of thinking in psychology that holds that conclusions about human development should be based on controlled observations of overt behavior rather than on speculation about unconscious motives or other unobservable phenomena; the philosophical underpinning of early theories of learning.

belief–desire psychology The theory of mind reflecting an understanding that people's desires and beliefs guide their behavior and that their beliefs are not always an accurate reflection of reality; evident by age 4. Contrast with *desire psychology*.

bereavement A state of loss that provides the occasion for grief and mourning.

beta-amyloid A toxic protein that injures neurons and is located in the senile plaques associated with Alzheimer's disease.

big-fish–little-pond effect The phenomenon in which a student's academic self-concept and performance are likely to be more positive in an academically unselective school than in a highly selective one with many high-achieving students.

Big Five The five major dimensions used to characterize people's personalities: neuroticism, extraversion, openness to experience, agreeableness, and conscientiousness.

bioecological model Bronfenbrenner's model of development that emphasizes the roles of both nature and nurture as the developing person interacts with a series of environmental systems (microsystem, mesosystem, exosystem, and macrosystem).

biological aging The deterioration of organisms that leads inevitably to their death.

blastocyst A hollow sphere of about 100 to 150 cells that the zygote forms by rapid cell division as it moves through the fallopian tube.

breech presentation A delivery in which the fetus emerges feet first or buttocks first rather than head first.

bulimia nervosa A life-threatening eating disorder characterized by recurrent eating binges followed by purging activities such as vomiting.

caloric restriction A technique demonstrated to extend the life span of laboratory animals involving a highly nutritious but severely calorie-restricted diet.

caregiver burden The psychological distress associated with providing care for someone with physical, cognitive, or both types of impairment.

carrier In genetics, individuals who possesses a recessive gene associated with a disease and who, although they do not have the disease, can transmit the gene for it to offspring.

case study method An in-depth examination of an individual that often involves compiling and analyzing information from a variety of sources such as observing, testing, and interviewing the person or people who know the individual.

cataracts A pathologic condition of the eye involving opacification (clouding) of the lens that can impair vision or cause blindness.

catch-up growth A phenomenon in which children who have experienced growth deficits will grow rapidly and catch up to the growth trajectory they are genetically programmed to follow.

categorical self A person's classification of the self along socially significant dimensions such as age and sex.

centenarian An individual who lives to be 100 years of age.

centration In Piaget's theory, the tendency to focus on only one aspect of a problem when two or more aspects are relevant.

cephalocaudal principle The principle that growth proceeds from the head (cephalic region) to the tail (caudal region).

cerebral palsy A neurological disability caused by anoxia that is associated with difficulty controlling muscle movements.

cesarean section A surgical procedure in which an incision is made in the mother's abdomen and uterus so that the baby can be removed through the abdomen.

characteristic adaptations Compared to traits, more situation-specific and changeable aspects of personality; ways in which people adapt to their roles and environments, including motives, goals, plans, schemas, self-conceptions, stage-specific concerns, and coping mechanisms.

child-directed speech Speech used by adults speaking with young children, it involves short, simple sentences spoken slowly and in a high-pitched voice, often with much repetition and with exaggerated emphasis on key words.

childhood amnesia A lack of memory for the early years of a person's life.

child effects model A model of family influence in which children are believed to influence their parents rather than vice versa.

chorion A membrane that surrounds the amnion and becomes attached to the uterine lining to gather nourishment for the embryo.

chorionic villus sampling (CVS) An alternative to amniocentesis in which a catheter is inserted through the cervix to withdraw fetal cells from the chorion for prenatal testing to detect genetic defects.

chromosome A threadlike structure made up of genes; in humans, there are 46 chromosomes in the nucleus of each cell.

chromosome abnormalities Conditions in which a child has too few, too many, or incomplete chromosomes because of errors in the formation of sperm or ova.

chronosystem In Bronfenbrenner's bioecological approach, the system that captures the way changes in environmental systems, such as social trends and life events, are patterned over a person's lifetime.

class inclusion The logical understanding that parts or subclasses are included in the whole class and that the whole is therefore greater than any of its parts.

classical conditioning A type of learning in which a stimulus that initially had no effect on the individual comes to elicit a response because of its association with a stimulus that already elicits the response.

clinical method An unstandardized interviewing procedure used by Piaget in which a child's response to each successive question (or problem) determines what the investigator will ask next.

clique A small friendship group that interacts frequently. See *crowd*.

cochlear implant A surgically implanted amplification device that stimulates the auditory nerve to provide the sensation of hearing to a deaf individual.

codominance In genetics, an instance in which two different but equally powerful genes produce a phenotype in which both genes are expressed.

coercive family environment A home in which family members are locked in power struggles, each trying to control the other through aggressive tactics such as threatening, yelling, and hitting.

cognition The activity of knowing and the processes through which knowledge is acquired (for example, attending, perceiving, remembering, and thinking).

cohabitation When two single adults live together as an unmarried couple.

cohort A group of people born at the same time; a particular generation of people.

cohort effects In cross-sectional research, the effects on findings that the different age groups (cohorts) being compared were born at different times and had different formative experiences. Contrast with *age effects* and *time of measurement effects*.

collectivist culture A culture in which people define themselves in terms of group memberships, give group goals higher priority than personal goals, and socialize children to seek group harmony. Contrast with *individualistic culture*.

communality An orientation that emphasizes the well-being of others and includes traits of emotionality and sensitivity to others; considered feminine.

comorbidity The co-occurrence of two or more psychiatric conditions in the same individual.

complicated grief An emotional response to a death that is unusually prolonged or intense and that impairs functioning; pathological grief.

componential subtheory An aspect of Sternberg's triarchic theory of intelligence that focuses on the information-processing skills used to arrive at answers and their efficiency.

conception The moment of fertilization, when a sperm penetrates an ovum, forming a zygote.

concordance rate The percentage of cases in which a particular attribute is present for both members of a pair of people (for example, twins) if it is present for one member.

concrete operations stage Piaget's third stage of cognitive development, lasting from about age 7 to age 11, when children are acquiring logical operations and can reason effectively about real objects and experiences.

conditioned response (CR) A learned response to a stimulus that was not originally capable of producing the response.

conditioned stimulus (CS) An initially neutral stimulus that elicits a particular response after it is paired with an unconditioned stimulus that always elicits the response.

confidant A spouse, relative, or friend to whom a person feels emotionally close and with whom that person can share thoughts and feelings.

congenital malformations Defects that are present at birth and are caused by genetic factors, prenatal events, or both.

conservation The recognition that certain properties of an object or substance do not change when its appearance is altered in some superficial way.

consolidation In information processing, the processing and organizing of information into a form suitable for long-term storage.

constraint-seeking questions In the Twenty Questions task and similar hypothesis-testing tasks, questions that rule out more than one answer to narrow the field of possible choices rather than asking about only one hypothesis at a time.

constructivism The position taken by Piaget and others that humans actively create their own understandings of the world from their experiences, as opposed to being born with innate ideas or being programmed by the environment.

contact comfort The pleasurable tactile sensations provided by a parent or a soft, terry cloth mother substitute; believed to foster attachments in infant monkeys and possibly humans.

contextual subtheory An aspect of Sternberg's triarchic theory of intelligence that defines whether behavior is intelligent or unintelligent in terms of the sociocultural context in which it is displayed.

continuing bond Maintenance of attachment to a loved one after the person's death through reminiscence, use of the person's possessions, consultation with the deceased, and the like.

continuity–discontinuity issue The debate among theorists about whether human development is best characterized as gradual and continuous or abrupt and stagelike.

contour The amount of light-dark transition or boundary area in a visual stimulus.

conventional morality Kohlberg's term for the third and fourth stages of moral reasoning in which societal values are internalized and judgments are based on a desire to gain approval or uphold law and social order.

convergent thinking Thinking that involves "converging" on the one best answer to a problem; what IQ tests measure. Contrast with *divergent thinking*.

cooing An early form of vocalization that involves repeating vowel-like sounds.

cooperative learning Procedures that involve assigning students, usually of different races or ability levels, to work teams that are reinforced for performing well as teams and that encourage cooperation among teammates.

coordination of secondary schemes During Piaget's sensorimotor period, the infant's combining of actions to solve problems, using one scheme as a means to an end, as in batting aside a barrier in order to grasp a toy.

coparenting The extent and manner in which the two parents coordinate their parenting and function as a team in relation to their children.

correlation coefficient A measure, ranging from $+1.00$ to -1.00, of the extent to which two variables or attributes are systematically related to each other in either a positive or a negative way.

correlational method A research technique that involves determining whether two or more variables are related. It cannot indicate that one thing caused another, but it can suggest that a causal relationship exists or allow us to predict one characteristic from our knowledge of another.

couvade Sympathetic pregnancy, or the experiencing by fathers of some of the same physiological symptoms their pregnant partners experience (for example, bloating, weight gain, fatigue, insomnia, and nausea).

creativity The ability to produce novel responses or works.

critical period A defined period in the development of an organism when it is particularly sensitive to certain environmental influences; outside this period, the same influences will have far less effect.

crossing over A process in which genetic material is exchanged between pairs of chromosomes during meiosis.

cross-modal perception The ability to use one sensory modality to identify a stimulus or a pattern of stimuli already familiar through another modality.

cross-sectional design A developmental research design in which different age groups are studied at the same point and compared.

crowd A network of heterosexual cliques that forms during adolescence and facilitates mixed-sex social activities. See *clique*.

crystallized intelligence Those aspects of intellectual functioning that involve using knowledge acquired through experience. Contrast with *fluid intelligence*.

cued recall memory Recollecting objects, events, or experiences in response to a hint or cue. Contrast with pure *recall memory* and *recognition memory*.

cultural–familial retardation Mental retardation that appears to be caused by some combination of low genetic potential and a poor family environment rather than by a specific biological cause. Contrast with *organic retardation*.

culture A system of meanings shared by a population of people and transmitted from one generation to the next.

culture bias The situation that arises in testing when one cultural or subcultural group is more familiar with test items than another group and therefore has an unfair advantage.

cumulative-deficit hypothesis The notion that impoverished environments inhibit intellectual growth and that these inhibiting effects accumulate over time.

damage theories of aging Theories that emphasize several haphazard processes that cause cells and organ systems to deteriorate. Contrast with *programmed theories of aging.*

dark adaptation The process by which the eyes become more sensitive to light over time as they remain in the dark.

decentration The ability to focus on two or more dimensions of a problem at one time.

decontextualize To separate the demands of a task at hand from prior beliefs and knowledge.

decontextualized language Language that is not bound to the immediate conversational context and that is about past or remote events.

defense mechanisms Mechanisms used by the ego to defend itself against anxiety caused by conflict between the id's impulses and social demands.

deferred imitation The ability to imitate a novel act after a delay.

delirium A clouding of consciousness characterized by alternating periods of disorientation and coherence.

demandingness–control A dimension of parenting reflecting the extent to which parents as opposed to children exert control over decisions and set and enforce rules; also called permissiveness-restrictiveness.

dementia A progressive loss of cognitive capacities such as memory and judgment that affects some aging individuals and that has a variety of causes.

denial A defense mechanism in which anxiety-provoking thoughts are kept out of, or isolated from, conscious awareness.

dependent variable The aspect of behavior measured in an experiment and assumed to be under the control of, or dependent on, the independent variable.

depression See *major depressive disorder.*

desire psychology The earliest theory of mind: an understanding that desires guide behavior (for example, that people seek things they like and avoid things they hate). Contrast with *belief–desire psychology.*

development Systematic changes in the individual occurring between conception and death; such changes can be positive, negative, or neutral.

developmental norm The age at which half of a large group of infants or children master a skill or display a behavior; the average age for achieving a milestone in development.

developmental psychopathology A field of study concerned with the origins and course of maladaptive or psychopathological behavior.

developmental quotient (DQ) A numerical measure of an infant's performance on a developmental test relative to the performance of other infants the same age.

developmental stage A distinct phase within a larger sequence of development; a period characterized by a particular set of abilities, motives, behaviors, or emotions that occur together and form a coherent pattern.

diathesis–stress model The view that psychopathology results from the interaction of a person's predisposition to psychological problems and the experience of stressful events.

differentiation In brain development, the progressive diversification of cells that results in their taking on different characteristics and functions.

difficult temperament Characteristic mode of response in which the individual is irregular in habits and adapts slowly, often with vigorous protest, to changes in routine or new experiences. Contrast with *easy temperament* and *slow-to-warm-up temperament.*

diffusion status Identity status characterizing individuals who have not questioned who they are and have not committed themselves to an identity.

disengagement theory A perspective that holds that successful aging involves a mutually satisfying withdrawal of the aging individual and society from each other. Contrast with *activity theory.*

disorganized–disoriented attachment An insecure infant–caregiver bond, common among abused children, that combines features of the resistant and avoidant attachment styles and is characterized by the infant's dazed response to reunion and confusion about whether to approach or avoid the caregiver.

dispositional traits Relatively enduring dimensions or qualities of personality along which people differ (for example, extraversion, aloofness).

divergent thinking Thinking that requires coming up with a variety of ideas or solutions to a problem when there is no one right answer. Contrast with *convergent thinking.*

dominant gene A relatively powerful gene that is expressed phenotypically and masks the effect of a less-powerful recessive gene.

double standard The view that sexual behavior appropriate for members of one gender is inappropriate for members of the other.

Down syndrome A chromosomal abnormality in which the child has inherited an extra 21st chromosome and is, as a result, mentally retarded; also called trisomy 21.

DSM-IV The fourth edition of the *Diagnostic and Statistical Manual of Mental Disorders*, which spells out defining features and symptoms for the range of psychological disorders.

dual process model A theory of coping with bereavement in which the bereaved oscillate between loss-oriented coping in which they deal with their emotions, restoration-oriented coping in which they try to manage practical tasks and reorganize their lives, and periods of respite from coping.

dynamic assessment An approach to assessing intelligence that evaluates how well individuals learn new material when an examiner provides them with competent instruction.

dynamic systems theory A perspective on development applied to motor development which proposes that more sophisticated patterns of motor behavior emerge over time through a "self-organizing" process in which children modify their motor behavior in adaptive ways on the basis of the sensory feedback they receive when they try different movements.

dyslexia Serious difficulties learning to read in children who have normal intellectual ability and no sensory impairments or emotional difficulties that could account for their learning problems.

easy temperament Characteristic mode of response in which the individual is even-tempered, content, and open and adaptable to new experiences. Contrast with *difficult temperament* and *slow-to-warm-up temperament.*

echolalia The repetition of sounds, such as when an autistic child parrots what someone else says.

eclectic In the context of science, an individual who recognizes that no single theory can explain everything but that each has something to contribute to our understanding.

effortful control Dimension of temperament pertaining to being able to sustain attention, control one's behavior, and regulate one's emotions (as opposed to unable to regulate one's arousal and stay calm and focused). See *negative affectivity* and *surgency/extraversion*.

ego Psychoanalytic term for the rational component of the personality.

egocentrism The tendency to view the world from the person's own perspective and fail to recognize that others may have different points of view.

elaboration A strategy for remembering that involves adding something to or creating meaningful links between the bits of information the person is trying to retain.

Electra complex Female version of the *Oedipus complex*, in which a 4- to 6-year-old girl is said to envy her father for possessing a penis and would choose him as a sex object in the hope of sharing this valuable organ that she lacks.

embryo See *embryonic period*.

embryonic period Second phase of prenatal development, lasting from the third through the eighth prenatal week, during which the major organs and anatomical structures begin to develop.

emergent literacy The developmental precursors of reading skills in young children, including knowledge, skills, and attributes that will facilitate the acquisition of reading competence.

emerging adulthood Newly identified period of the life span extending from about age 18 to age 25, when young people are neither adolescents nor adults and are exploring their identities, careers, and relationships.

emotion regulation The processes involved in initiating, maintaining, and altering emotional responses.

empathy The vicarious experiencing of another person's feelings.

empty nest The term used to describe the family after the last child departs the household.

encoding The first step in learning and remembering something, it is the process of getting information into the information-processing system, or learning it, and organizing it in a form suitable for storing.

endocrine gland A type of gland that secretes chemicals called hormones directly into the bloodstream. Endocrine glands play

critical roles in stimulating growth and regulating bodily functions.

environment Events or conditions outside the person that are presumed to influence and be influenced by the individual.

epigenesis The process through which nature and nurture, genes and environment, jointly bring forth development in ways that are difficult to predict at the outset, according to Gottlieb's epigenetic psychobiological systems perspective.

epigenetic psychobiological systems perspective Gilbert Gottlieb's view that development is the product of interacting biological and environmental forces that form a larger, dynamic system, both over the course of evolution and during the individual's life.

equilibration In Piaget's theory, the process of seeking a state of mental stability in which our thoughts (schemes) are consistent with the information we receive from the external world.

equity A balance of contributions and gains in a social relationship that results in neither partner feeling over- or underbenefited.

estrogen The female hormone responsible for the development of the breasts, the female sex organs, and secondary sex characteristics and for the beginning of menstrual cycles.

ethnic identity A sense of personal identification with the individual's ethnic group and its values and cultural traditions.

ethnocentrism The belief that one's own cultural or ethnic group is superior to others.

ethology A discipline and theoretical perspective that focuses on the evolved behavior of different species in their natural environments.

euthanasia Literally, "good death"; specifically, hastening, either actively or passively, the death of someone suffering from an incurable illness or injury.

executive control processes Processes that direct and monitor the selection, organization, manipulation, and interpretation of information in the information-processing system, including executive functions.

executive functions The planning and organizational functions that reside in the prefrontal cortex of the brain.

exosystem In Bronfenbrenner's bioecological approach, settings not experienced directly by individuals still influence their development (for example, effects of events at a parent's workplace on children's development).

expansion A conversational tactic used by adults in speaking to young children in which they respond to a child's utterance with a more grammatically complete expression of the same thought.

experiential subtheory An aspect of Sternberg's triarchic theory of intelligence that highlights the role of experience in intelligence and distinguishes between what is smart in response to novelty and what is smart in response to familiar tasks.

experiment A research strategy in which the investigator manipulates or alters some aspect of a person's environment to measure its effect on the individual's behavior or development.

experimental control The holding of all other factors besides the independent variable in an experiment constant so that any changes in the dependent variable can be said to be caused by the manipulation of the independent variable.

explicit memory Memory that involves consciously recollecting the past. Contrast with *implicit memory*.

extended family household A family unit composed of parents and children living with other kin such as grandparents, aunts and uncles, cousins, or a combination of these. Compare with *nuclear family*.

externalizing problem Childhood behavioral problem that involves "undercontrolled" behavior such as aggression or acting out difficulties that disturb other people. Contrast with *internalizing problem*.

extinction The gradual weakening and disappearance of a learned response when it is no longer reinforced.

extreme male brain hypothesis Baron-Cohen's theory that individuals with autism have brains that are more masculine, or skilled at systemizing, than feminine, or skilled at empathizing.

eyewitness memory Remembering and reporting events the person has witnessed or experienced.

failure to thrive A condition observed in infants who, because of either physical causes or emotional deprivation, are characterized by stunted growth, weight loss, and delays in cognitive and socioemotional development.

false belief task A research paradigm used to assess an important aspect of a theory of mind, mainly the understanding that people can hold incorrect beliefs and be influenced by them.

family life cycle The sequence of changes in family composition, roles, and relationships that occurs from the time people marry until they die.

family systems theory The conceptualization of the family as a whole consisting of interrelated parts, each of which affects and is affected by every other part, and each of which contributes to the functioning of the whole.

fetal alcohol syndrome (FAS) A group of symptoms commonly observed in the offspring of mothers who use alcohol heavily during pregnancy, including a small head, widely spaced eyes, and mental retardation.

fetal period The third phase of prenatal development, lasting from the ninth prenatal week until birth; during this period, the major organ systems begin to function effectively and the fetus grows rapidly.

fetus See *fetal period*.

filial responsibility Children's obligation to their parents.

fine motor skills Skills that involve precise movements of the hands and fingers or feet and toes. Contrast with *gross motor skills*.

fixation In psychoanalytic theory, a defense mechanism in which development is arrested and part of the libido remains tied to an early stage of development.

fluid intelligence Aspects of intelligence that involve actively thinking and reasoning to solve novel problems. Contrast with *crystallized intelligence*.

Flynn effect The rise in average IQ scores over the 20th century.

foreclosure status An identity status characterizing individuals who appear to have committed themselves to a life direction but who have adopted an identity prematurely, without much thought.

formal operations stage Piaget's fourth and final stage of cognitive development (from age 11 or 12), when the individual begins to think more rationally and systematically about abstract concepts and hypothetical ideas.

fragile X syndrome A chromosome abnormality in which one arm of the X chromosome is only barely connected to the rest of the chromosome; the most common hereditary cause of mental retardation.

fraternal twins Twins who are not identical and who result when a mother releases two ova at roughly the same time and each is fertilized by a different sperm.

free radical theory The theory of aging that views it as damage caused by free radicals, chemically unstable byproducts of metabolism that have an extra electron and react with other molecules to produce toxic substances that damage cells.

functional grammar An analysis of the semantic relations (meanings such as naming and locating) that children express in their earliest sentences.

fuzzy-trace theory The view that verbatim and general or gistlike accounts of an event are stored separately in memory.

gender consistency The stage of gender typing in which children realize that their sex is stable across situations or despite changes in activities or appearance.

gender identity Individuals' basic awareness that they are either a male or a female.

gender intensification A magnification of differences between males and females during adolescence associated with increased pressure to conform to traditional gender roles.

gender role A pattern of behaviors and traits that defines how to act the part of a female or a male in a particular society.

gender-role norms Society's expectations or standards concerning what males and females should be like and how they should behave.

gender-role stereotypes Overgeneralized and largely inaccurate beliefs about what males and females are like.

gender schema (plural: schemata) Organized sets of beliefs and expectations about males and females that guide information processing.

gender segregation The formation of separate boys' and girls' peer groups during childhood.

gender stability The stage of gender typing in which children realize that their sex remains the same over time.

gender typing The process by which children become aware of their gender and acquire the motives, values, and behaviors considered appropriate for members of their biological sex.

gene A functional unit of heredity made up of DNA and transmitted from generation to generation.

gene–environment correlation A systematic interrelationship between an individual's genes and that individual's environment; ways in which genes influence the kind of home environment provided by parents (passive gene–environment correlation), the social reactions to the individual (evocative gene–environment correlation), and the types of experiences the individual seeks (active gene–environment correlation).

gene–environment interaction The phenomenon in which the effects of people's genes depend on the kind of environment they experience and in which the effects of the environment depend on their genetic endowment.

gene expression The activation of particular genes in particular cells of the body at particular times in life.

gene therapy Interventions that involve substituting normal genes for the genes associated with a disease or disorder; otherwise altering a person's genetic makeup.

generativity versus stagnation The psychosocial conflict in which middle-aged adults must gain the sense that they have produced something that will outlive them and genuinely care for younger generations to avoid self-preoccupation; seventh of Erikson's stages.

genetic counseling A service designed to inform people about genetic conditions they or their unborn children are at risk of inheriting.

genetic epistemology The study of how humans come to know reality and basic dimensions of it such as space, time, and causality; Piaget's field of interest.

genotype The genetic endowment that an individual inherits. Contrast with *phenotype*.

germinal period First phase of prenatal development, lasting about 2 weeks from conception until the developing organism becomes attached to the wall of the uterus.

gerontology The study of aging and old age.

giftedness The possession of unusually high general intellectual potential or of special abilities in such areas as creativity, mathematics, or the arts.

glaucoma A condition in which increased fluid pressure in the eye damages the optic nerve and causes progressive loss of peripheral vision and ultimately blindness.

goal-corrected partnership In Bowlby's attachment theory, the most mature phase of attachment in which parent and child accommodate to each other's needs and the child becomes more independent.

goodness of fit The extent to which the child's temperament and the demands of the child's social environment are compatible or mesh, according to Thomas and Chess; more generally, a good match between person and environment.

grief The emotional response to loss. Contrast with *mourning*.

grief work perspective The view commonly held, but now challenged, that to cope adaptively with death bereaved people must confront their loss, experience painful emotions, work through these emotions, and move toward a detachment from the deceased.

gross motor skills Skills that involve large muscles and whole body or limb movements (for example, kicking the legs or drawing large circles). Contrast with *fine motor skills*.

growth The physical changes that occur from conception to maturity.

growth hormone Hormone produced by the pituitary gland that stimulates childhood physical growth and the adolescent growth spurt.

guided participation A process in which children learn by actively participating in culturally relevant activities with the aid and support of their parents and other knowledgeable individuals.

habituation A simple form of learning that involves learning not to respond to a repeated stimulus; learning to be bored by the familiar.

Hayflick limit The estimate that human cells can double only 50 times, plus or minus 10, and then will die.

hemophilia A deficiency in the blood's ability to clot. It is more common among males than females because it is associated with a sex-linked gene on the X chromosome.

heritability The amount of variability in a population on some trait dimension that is attributable to genetic differences among those individuals.

heteronomous morality A term meaning subject to authority and referring to the childhood beliefs that rules are handed down by authority figures and are sacred and unalterable and that wrongness should be judged on the basis of consequences rather than intentions; typical of children ages 6 to 10, according to Piaget. Contrast with *autonomous morality*.

holophrase A single-word utterance used by an infant that represents an entire sentence's worth of meaning.

Home Observation for Measurement of the Environment (HOME) inventory A widely used instrument that allows an observer to determine how intellectually stimulating or impoverished a home environment is.

horizontal décalage A term used by Piaget to characterize that different cognitive skills related to the same stage of cognitive development emerge at different times.

hormone replacement therapy (HRT) Taking estrogen and progestin to compensate for hormone loss because of menopause in women.

hospice A program that supports dying persons and their families through a philosophy of caring rather than curing, either in a facility or at home.

hot flash A sudden experience of warmth and sweating, often followed by a cold shiver, that occurs in a menopausal woman.

human agency Ways in which humans deliberately exercise cognitive control over their environments and lives, according to Bandura.

Human Genome Project A massive, government-sponsored effort to decipher the human genetic code.

Huntington's disease A genetic disease caused by a single, dominant gene that strikes in middle age to produce a deterioration of physical and mental abilities and premature death.

hyperactivity See *attention deficit hyperactivity disorder (ADHD)*.

hypothesis A theoretical prediction about what will hold true if we observe a phenomenon.

hypothetical-deductive reasoning A form of problem solving in which a person starts with general or abstract ideas and deduces or traces their specific implications; "if–then" thinking.

id A psychoanalytic term for the inborn component of the personality that is driven by the instincts or selfish urges.

ideal self Idealized expectations of what one's attributes and personality should be like.

identical twins Monozygotic twins who develop from a single zygote that later divides to form two genetically identical individuals.

identification Freud's term for the individual's tendency to emulate, or adopt the attitudes and behaviors of, another person, particularly the same-sex parent.

identity A self-definition or sense of who one is, where one is going, and how one fits into society.

identity achievement status An identity status characterizing individuals who have carefully thought through identity issues and made commitments or resolved their identity issues.

identity versus role confusion The psychosocial conflict in which adolescents must form a coherent self-definition or remain confused about their life directions; fifth of Erikson's stages.

imaginary audience A form of adolescent egocentrism that involves confusing one's own thoughts with the thoughts of a hypothesized audience for behavior and concluding that others share these preoccupations.

imaginary companion A play companion invented by a child in the preoperational stage who has developed the capacity for symbolic thought.

implicit memory Memory that occurs unintentionally and without consciousness or awareness. Contrast with *explicit memory*.

imprinting An innate form of learning in which the young of certain species will follow and become attached to moving objects (usually their mothers) during a critical period early in life.

inclusion The educational practice of integrating handicapped students into regular classrooms rather than placing them in segregated special education classes; also called mainstreaming.

incomplete dominance A condition in which a stronger gene fails to mask all the effects of a weaker partner gene; a phenotype results that is similar but not identical to the effect of the stronger gene.

independent variable The aspect of the environment that a researcher deliberately changes or manipulates in an experiment to see its effect on behavior; a causal variable. Contrast with *dependent variable*.

indirect effect The instance in which the relationship between two individuals in a family is modified by the behavior or attitudes of a third family member.

individualistic culture A culture in which individuals define themselves as individuals and put their own goals ahead of their group's goals, and one in which children are socialized to be independent and self-reliant. Contrast with *collectivist culture*.

induction A form of discipline that involves explaining why a child's behavior is wrong and should be changed by emphasizing its effects on other people.

industry versus inferiority The psychosocial conflict in which school-aged children must master important cognitive and social skills or feel incompetent; fourth of Erikson's stages.

infant states Coherent patterns of waking and sleeping evident in the fetus and young infant (for example, quiet sleep, active sleep, and active waking).

information-processing approach An approach to cognition that emphasizes the fundamental mental processes involved in attention, perception, memory, and decision making.

initiative versus guilt The psychosocial conflict in which preschool children must learn to initiate new activities and pursue bold plans or become self-critical; third of Erikson's stages.

instinct An inborn biological force assumed to motivate a particular response or class of responses.

integrity versus despair The psychosocial conflict in which elderly adults attempt to find a sense of meaning in their lives and to accept the inevitability of death; eighth of Erikson's stages.

intelligence quotient (IQ) A numerical measure of a person's performance on an intelligence test relative to the performance of other examinees of the same age, typically with a score of 100 defined as average.

internal working model In attachment theory, cognitive representation of self and other that children construct from their interactions with caregivers and that shape their expectations about relationships.

internalizing problem Childhood behavioral problem that represents an "overcontrolled" pattern of coping with difficulties and is expressed in anxiety, depression, and other forms of inner distress. Contrast with *externalizing problem*.

intimacy versus isolation The psychosocial conflict in which young adults must commit themselves to a shared identity with another person or remain aloof and unconnected to others; sixth of Erikson's stages.

intonation Variations in pitch, loudness, and timing when saying words or sentences.

intuitive theories Organized systems of knowledge, believed to be innate, that allow children to make sense of the world in areas such as physics and psychology.

in vitro fertilization (IVF) Procedure in which several eggs are removed from a woman's ovary, fertilized by sperm in a petri dish in the laboratory, then transferred to the woman's uterus in hopes that one will implant on the wall of the uterus.

joint attention The act of looking at the same object at the same time with someone else; a way in which infants share perceptual experiences with their caregivers.

karyotype A chromosomal portrait created by staining chromosomes, photographing them under a high-power microscope, and arranging them into a predetermined pattern.

Klinefelter syndrome A sex chromosome abnormality in which males inherit two or more X chromosomes (XXY or XXXY); these males fail to develop secondary sex characteristics and often show deficiencies on tests of verbal abilities.

knowledge base A person's existing information about a content area, significant for its influence on how well that individual can learn and remember.

Lamaze method Prepared childbirth in which parents attend classes and learn mental exercises and relaxation techniques to ease delivery.

language A symbolic system in which a limited number of signals can be combined according to rules to produce an infinite number of messages.

language acquisition device (LAD) A set of linguistic processing skills that nativists believe to be innate; presumably the LAD enables a child to infer the rules governing others' speech and then use these rules to produce language.

lateralization The specialization of the two hemispheres of the cerebral cortex of the brain.

learned helplessness orientation A tendency to avoid challenges and to cease trying in the face of failure primarily because of a tendency to attribute failure to lack of ability and therefore to believe that little can be done to improve the results. Contrast with *mastery orientation*.

learning A relatively permanent change in behavior (or behavioral potential) that results from a person's experiences or practice.

learning goal A goal adopted by learners in which they seek to learn new things so that they can improve their abilities. Contrast with *performance goal*.

libido Freud's term for the biological energy of the sex instinct.

life expectancy The average number of years a newborn baby can be expected to live; now almost 78 years in the United States.

life review Process in which elderly adults reflect on unresolved conflicts of the past and evaluate their lives; it may contribute to a sense of integrity and readiness for death.

life-span perspective A perspective that views development as a lifelong, multidirectional process that involves gain and loss, is characterized by considerable plasticity, is shaped by its historical-cultural context, has many causes, and is best viewed from a multidisciplinary perspective.

literacy The ability to use printed information to function in society, achieve goals, and develop potential.

living will A document in which people state in advance that they do not wish to have extraordinary medical procedures applied if they are hopelessly ill.

longitudinal design A developmental research design in which one group of subjects is studied repeatedly over months or years.

long-term memory Memory store in which information that has been examined and interpreted is stored relatively permanently.

looking-glass self The idea that a person's self-concept is largely a reflection of the ways in which other people respond to that person.

love withdrawal A form of discipline that involves withholding attention, affection, or approval after a child misbehaves.

low birth weight (LBW) A weight at birth of less than 2500 grams, or 5½ pounds, associated with increased risk of developmental problems.

macrosystem In Bronfenbrenner's bioecological approach, the larger cultural or subcultural context of development.

macular degeneration See *age-related macular degeneration*.

major depressive disorder An affective or mood disorder characterized by at least one episode of feeling profoundly sad and hopeless, losing interest in almost all activities, or both.

mastery motivation An intrinsic motive to master and control the environment evident early in infancy.

mastery orientation A tendency to thrive on challenges and persist in the face of failure because of healthy attributions that lead to the belief that increased effort will pay off. Contrast with *learned helplessness orientation*.

maternal blood sampling A noninvasive method of prenatal diagnosis involving testing for substances in maternal blood; more recently, analysis of fetal cells that have slipped through the placenta into the mother's blood.

maturation Developmental changes that are biologically programmed by genes rather than caused primarily by learning, injury, illness, or some other life experience.

maximum life span A ceiling on the number of years that any member of a species lives; 120 years for humans.

mediation deficiency The initial stage of mastery of memory strategies in which children cannot spontaneously use or benefit from strategies even if they are taught to use them.

meiosis The process in which a germ cell divides, producing sperm or ova, each containing half of the parent cell's original complement of chromosomes; in humans, the products of meiosis normally contain 23 chromosomes.

menarche A female's first menstrual period.

menopause The ending of a woman's menstrual periods and reproductive capacity around age 51.

mental age A measure of intellectual development that reflects the level of age-graded problems that a child is able to solve; the age at which a child functions intellectually.

mental retardation Significant subaverage general intellectual functioning associated with impairments in adaptive behavior and manifested during the developmental period.

mesosystem In Bronfenbrenner's bioecological approach, interrelationships between microsystems or immediate environments (for example, ways in which events in the family affect a child's interactions at a day care center).

meta-analysis A research method in which the results of multiple studies addressing the same question are synthesized to produce overall conclusions.

metacognition Knowledge of the human mind and of the range of cognitive processes, including thinking about personal thought processes.

metalinguistic awareness Knowledge of language as a system.

metamemory A person's knowledge about memory and about monitoring and regulating memory processes.

microsystem In Bronfenbrenner's bioecological approach, the immediate settings in which the person functions (for example, the family).

middle generation squeeze The phenomenon in which middle-aged adults sometimes experience heavy responsibilities for both the younger and the older generations in the family.

midlife crisis A period of major questioning, inner struggle, and re-evaluation hypothesized to occur in an adult's early 40s.

mild cognitive impairment A level of memory loss between normal loss with age and pathological loss from disease.

mirror neuron simulation hypothesis Theory of autism that holds that the malfunctioning of behavior-simulating mirror neuron systems accounts for the deficits individuals with autism show in imitation, theory of mind skills, empathy, and language.

mirror neurons Neural cells in several brain areas that are activated when we perform an action or observe someone else performing it.

mitosis The process in which a cell duplicates its chromosomes and then divides into two genetically identical daughter cells.

molecular genetics The analysis of particular genes and their effects, including the identification of specific genes that influence particular traits and the comparison of animals or humans who have these specific genes and those who do not.

moral affect The emotional component of morality, including feelings of guilt, shame, and pride regarding one's conduct.

moral disengagement According to Bandura, the ability to avoid self condemnation when engaged in immoral behavior by justifying, minimizing, or blaming others for one's actions.

moral reasoning The cognitive component of morality; the thinking that occurs when people decide whether acts are right or wrong.

moral rules Standards of conduct that focus on the basic rights and privileges of individuals. Contrast with *social-conventional rules*.

morality The ability to distinguish right from wrong, to act on this distinction, and to experience pride when doing something right and to experience guilt or shame when doing something wrong. Morality has affective, cognitive, and behavioral components.

morality of care Gilligan's term for what she says is the dominant moral orientation of females, in which the individual emphasizes concern and responsibility for the welfare of other people rather than abstract rights. Contrast with *morality of justice*.

morality of justice Gilligan's term for what she says is the dominant moral orientation of males, in which moral dilemmas are viewed as inevitable conflicts between the rights of two or more parties that must be settled by law. Contrast with *morality of care*.

moratorium period A period of time in high school or college when young adults are relatively free of responsibilities and can experiment with different roles to find their identities.

moratorium status Identity status characterizing individuals who are experiencing an identity crisis or actively exploring identity issues but who have not yet achieved an identity.

morphology Rules governing the formation of words from sounds (for example, rules for forming plurals and past tenses).

mourning Culturally prescribed ways of displaying reactions to a loss. Contrast with *grief*.

mutation A change in the structure or arrangement of one or more genes that produces a new phenotype.

mutually responsive orientation A close, affectively positive, and cooperative relationship in which child and parent are attached to each other and are sensitive to each other's needs; a contributor to moral development.

myelin A fatty sheath that insulates neural axons and thereby speeds the transmission of neural impulses.

myelination The depositing of a fatty sheath around neural axons that insulates them and thereby speeds the transmission of neural impulses.

narrative identities Unique and integrative "life stories" that we construct about our pasts and futures to give ourselves an identity and our lives meaning; an aspect of personality.

nativist An individual whose approach to human development emphasizes the contribution of genetic factors; specifically, a person who believes that infants enter the world equipped with knowledge that allows them to perceive a meaningful world from the start. Contrast with *empiricist*.

natural selection The evolutionary principle that individuals who have characteristics advantageous for survival in a particular environment are most likely to survive and reproduce. Over many generations, this process of "survival of the fittest" will lead to changes in a species and the development of new species.

naturalistic observation A research method in which the scientist observes people as they engage in common everyday activities in their natural habitats. Contrast with *structured observation*.

nature–nurture issue The debate over the relative importance of biological predispositions (nature) and environmental influences (nurture) as determinants of human development.

negative affectivity Dimension of temperament that concerns the tendency to be sad, fearful, easily frustrated, and irritable (as opposed to laid back and adaptable). See *effortful control* and *surgency/extraversion*.

negative punishment The process in operant conditioning in which a response is weakened or made less probable when its consequence is the removal of a pleasant stimulus from the situation.

negative reinforcement The process in operant conditioning in which a response is strengthened or made more probable when its consequence is the removal of an unpleasant stimulus from the situation.

neglectful parenting A parenting style low in demandingness–control and low in acceptance–responsiveness; uninvolved parenting.

neonatal Pertaining to events or developments in the first month after birth.

neuron The basic unit of the nervous system; a nerve cell.

nonshared environmental influences Experiences unique to the individual that are not shared by other members of the family and that tend to make members of the same family different. Contrast with *shared environmental influences*.

normal distribution A symmetrical (bell-shaped) curve that describes the variability of characteristics within a population. Most people fall at or near the average score; there are relatively few high or low scores.

nuclear family A family unit consisting of husband–father, wife–mother, and at least one child. Compare with *extended family household*.

obesity Condition of being overweight; specifically, being 20% or more above the "ideal" weight for one's height, age, and sex.

object permanence The understanding that objects continue to exist when they are no longer visible or otherwise detectable to the senses; fully mastered by the end of infancy.

observational learning Learning that results from observing the behavior of other people; emphasized in Bandura's social cognitive theory.

Oedipus complex Freud's term for the conflict that 4- to 6-year-old boys experience when they develop an incestuous desire for their mothers and a jealous and hostile rivalry with their fathers.

olfaction The sense of smell, made possible by sensory receptors in the nasal passage that react to chemical molecules in the air.

operant conditioning Also called instrumental conditioning, a form of learning in which freely emitted acts (or operants) become more or less probable depending on the consequences they produce.

oral sex Sexual activity involving contact between the mouth and genitals.

organic retardation Mental retardation because of some identifiable biological cause associated with hereditary factors, diseases, or injuries. Contrast with *cultural–familial retardation*.

organization In Piaget's cognitive developmental theory, a person's inborn tendency to combine and integrate available schemes into more coherent and complex systems or bodies of knowledge; as a memory strategy, a technique that involves grouping or classifying stimuli into meaningful clusters.

organogenesis The process, occurring during the period of the embryo, in which every major organ takes shape in a primitive form.

orthogenetic principle Werner's principle that development proceeds from global and undifferentiated states toward more differentiated and integrated patterns of response.

osteoarthritis A joint problem among older adults resulting from a gradual deterioration of the cartilage that cushions the bones and keeps them from rubbing together.

osteoporosis A disease affecting older adults in which bone tissue is lost, leaving bones fragile and easily fractured.

overextension The young child's tendency to use a word to refer to a wider set of objects, actions, or events than adults do (for example, using the word *car* to refer to all motor vehicles). Contrast with *underextension*.

overlapping waves theory Siegler's view that the development of problem-solving skills is not a matter of moving from one problem-solving approach to a better one with age but of knowing and using a variety of strategies at each age, becoming increasingly selective with experience about which strategies to use in particular situations, and adding new strategies to one's collection.

overregularization The overgeneralization of observed grammatical rules to irregular cases to which the rules do not apply (for example, saying *mouses* rather than *mice*).

palliative care Care aimed not at curing but at meeting the physical, psychological, and spiritual needs of dying patients.

parent effects model A model of family influence in which parents (particularly mothers) are believed to influence their children rather than vice versa.

parental imperative The notion that the demands of parenthood cause men and women to adopt distinct roles and psychological traits.

Parkes/Bowlby attachment model of bereavement Model of grieving describing four predominant reactions to loss of an attachment figure: numbness, yearning, disorganization and despair, and reorganization.

peer A social equal; a person who functions at a level of behavioral complexity similar to that of the self, often someone of similar age.

perception The interpretation of sensory input.

perceptual salience Phenomenon in which the most obvious features of an object or situation have disproportionate influence on the perceptions and thought of young children.

performance goal A goal adopted by learners in which they attempt to prove their ability rather than to improve it. Contrast with *learning goal*.

perinatal environment The environment surrounding birth.

permissive parenting A lax style of parenting combining low demandingness–control and high acceptance–responsiveness in which adults love their children but make few demands on them and rarely attempt to control their behavior.

perseveration error Mistake made when an information processor continues to use the same strategy that was successful in the past over and over despite the strategy's lack of success in the current situation.

personal fable A form of adolescent egocentrism that involves thinking that oneself and one's thoughts and feelings are unique or special.

personality The organized combination of attributes, motives, values, and behaviors that is unique to each individual.

phenotype The way in which a person's genotype is expressed in observable or measurable characteristics.

phenylketonuria (PKU) A genetic disease in which the child is unable to metabolize phenylalanine; if left untreated, it soon causes hyperactivity and mental retardation.

phoneme One of the basic units of sound used in a particular spoken language.

phonological awareness The understanding that spoken words can be decomposed into some number of basic sound units, or phonemes; an important skill in learning to read.

pincer grasp A grasp in which the thumb is used in opposition to the fingers, enabling an infant to become more dexterous at lifting and manipulating objects.

pituitary gland The "master gland" located at the base of the brain that regulates the other endocrine glands and produces growth hormone.

placenta An organ, formed from the chorion and the lining of the uterus, that provides for the nourishment of the unborn child and the elimination of its metabolic wastes.

plasticity An openness of the brain cells (or of the organism as a whole) to positive and negative environmental influence; a capacity to change in response to experience.

polygenic trait A characteristic influenced by the action of many gene pairs rather than a single pair.

population A well-defined group that a researcher who studies a sample of individuals is interested in drawing conclusions about.

positive punishment The process in operant conditioning whereby a response is weakened when its consequence is an unpleasant event.

positive reinforcement The process in operant conditioning whereby a response is strengthened when its consequence is a pleasant event.

postconventional morality Kohlberg's term for the fifth and sixth stages of moral reasoning, in which moral judgments are based on a more abstract understanding of democratic social contracts or on universal principles of justice that have validity apart from the views of particular authority figures.

postformal thought Proposed stages of cognitive development that lie beyond formal operations.

postpartum depression An episode of severe, clinical depression lasting for months in a woman who has just given birth; to be contrasted with milder cases of the "baby blues," in which a new mother is tearful and moody in the first days after birth.

posttraumatic stress disorder A psychological disorder involving flashbacks to traumatizing events, nightmares, and feelings of helplessness and anxiety in the face of danger experienced by victims of extreme trauma such as soldiers in combat and sexually abused children.

power assertion A form of discipline that involves the use of superior power to administer spankings, withhold privileges, and so on.

pragmatics Rules specifying how language is to be used appropriately in different social contexts to achieve goals.

preconventional morality Kohlberg's term for the first two stages of moral reasoning, in which society's rules are not yet internalized and judgments are based on the punishing or rewarding consequences of an act.

preimplantation genetic diagnosis Prenatal diagnostic procedure in which a mother's eggs are fertilized in the laboratory using in vitro fertilization techniques, DNA tests are conducted on the first cells that result from mitosis of each fertilized egg, and only eggs that do not have chromosome abnormalities or genes associated with disorders are implanted in the uterus.

premenstrual syndrome (PMS) Several symptoms experienced shortly before each menstrual period that include having tender breasts, feeling bloated, and being irritable and moody.

premoral period According to Piaget, a period during the preschool years when children show little awareness or understanding of rules and cannot be considered to be moral beings.

prenatal environment The physical environment of the womb.

preoperational stage Piaget's second stage of cognitive development, lasting from about age 2 to age 7, when children think at a symbolic level but have not yet mastered logical operations.

presbycusis Problems of the aging ear, which commonly involve loss of sensitivity to high-frequency or high-pitched sounds.

presbyopia Problems of the aging eye, especially loss of near vision related to a decreased ability of the lens to accommodate to objects close to the eye.

pretend play Symbolic play in which one actor, object, or action symbolizes or stands for another.

primary circular reaction During Piaget's sensorimotor period, the infant's repetition of interacting acts centered on his or her own body (e.g., repeatedly kicking).

private speech Nonsocial speech, or speech for the self, commonly used by preschoolers to guide their activities and believed by Vygotsky to be the forerunner of inner speech, or silent thinking in words.

problem solving The use of the information-processing system to achieve a goal or arrive at a decision.

production deficiency A phase in the mastery of memory strategies in which children can use strategies they are taught but cannot produce them on their own.

progeria A genetic disorder caused by a single dominant gene that makes victims age prematurely and die early.

programmed theories of aging Theories that emphasize the systematic genetic control of aging processes. Contrast with *damage theories of aging*.

prosocial behavior Positive actions toward other people such as helping and cooperating.

protective factors Factors such as personal resources and a supportive postnatal environment that work to prevent at-risk individuals from developing problems.

proximodistal principle In development, the principle that growth proceeds from the center of the body (or the proximal region) to the extremities (or the distal regions).

psychoanalytic theory The theoretical perspective associated with Freud and his followers that emphasizes unconscious motivations for behavior, conflicts within the personality, and stages of psychosexual development.

psychometric approach The research tradition that spawned standardized tests of intelligence and that views intelligence as a trait or a set of traits that can be measured and that varies from person to person.

psychosexual stages Freud's five stages of development, associated with biological maturation and shifts in the libido: oral, anal, phallic, latency, and genital.

psychosocial stages Erikson's eight stages of development (trust, autonomy, initiative, industry, identity, intimacy, generativity, and integrity), emphasizing social influences more and biological urges less than Freud's psychosexual stages.

puberty The point at which a person reaches sexual maturity and is physically capable of conceiving a child.

quasi experiment An experiment-like study that evaluates the effects of different treatments but does not randomly assign individuals to treatment groups.

random assignment A technique in which research participants are placed in experimental conditions in an unbiased or random way so that the resulting groups are not systematically different.

random sample A sample formed by identifying all members of the larger population of interest and then selecting a portion of them in an unbiased or random way to participate in the study; a technique to ensure that the sample studied is representative or typical of the larger population of interest.

reaction time The interval between the presentation of a stimulus and a response to it.

recall memory Recollecting or actively retrieving objects, events, and experiences when examples or cues are not provided. Contrast with *cued recall memory* and *recognition memory*.

recessive gene A less powerful gene that is not expressed phenotypically when paired with a *dominant gene*.

reciprocal determinism The notion in social cognitive theory that the flow of influence between people and their environments is a two-way street; the environment may affect the person, but the person's characteristics and behavior will also influence the environment.

reciprocity The mutual give and take by both parties in a human relationship that forms an important basis for morality.

recognition memory Identifying an object or event as one that has been experienced before, such as when a person must select the correct answer from several options. Contrast with *cued recall memory* and *recall memory*.

reconstituted family A new family that forms after the remarriage of a single parent, sometimes involving the blending of two families into a new one.

reflex An unlearned and automatic response to a stimulus.

regression A defense mechanism that involves retreating to an earlier, less traumatic stage of development.

rehearsal A strategy for remembering that involves repeating the items the person is trying to retain.

relativistic thinking A form of postformal-operational thought in which it is understood that there are multiple ways of viewing a problem and that the solutions people arrive at will depend on their starting assumptions and perspective.

REM sleep A state of active, irregular sleep associated with dreaming; named for the rapid eye movements associated with it.

research ethics Standards of conduct that investigators are ethically bound to honor to protect their research participants from physical or psychological harm.

reserve capacity The ability of many organ systems to respond to demands for extraordinary output, such as when the heart and lungs work at maximal capacity.

resistant attachment An insecure infant-caregiver bond or other intimate relationship characterized by strong separation anxiety and a tendency to show ambivalent reactions to the attachment object upon reunion, seeking and yet resisting contact.

retinitis pigmentosa (RP) A group of hereditary disorders that involve gradual deterioration of the light-sensitive cells of the retina.

retrieval The process of retrieving information from long-term memory when it is needed.

reversibility In Piaget's theory, the ability to reverse or negate an action by mentally performing the opposite action.

rhythmic stereotypies Repetitive movements observed in infants shortly before a new motor skill emerges.

role reversal A switching of child and parent roles late in life such that the parent becomes dependent and the child becomes the caregiver.

role-taking skills The ability to assume other people's perspectives and understand their thoughts, feelings, and behaviors.

rubella A disease that has little effect on a pregnant woman but may cause several serious birth defects, such as blindness, deafness, and mental retardation, in unborn children exposed in the first 3 to 4 months of gestation; German measles.

rule assessment approach Siegler's approach to studying the development of problem solving that determines what information about a problem children take in and what rules they then formulate to account for this information.

ruminative coping Way of managing stress that involves dwelling on problems and attempting to analyze them; may help explain higher rates of depression in females than in males.

sample The group of individuals chosen to be the subjects of a study.

savant syndrome The phenomenon in which extraordinary talent in a particular area is displayed by a person who is otherwise mentally retarded.

scheme (or schema; plural: schemes or schemata) A cognitive structure or organized pattern of action or thought used to deal with experiences.

schizophrenia A serious form of mental illness characterized by disturbances in logical thinking, emotional expression, and interpersonal behavior.

scientific method An attitude or value about the pursuit of knowledge that dictates that investigators must be objective and must allow their data to decide the merits of their theorizing.

script A mental representation of a typical sequence of actions related to an event that is created in memory and that then guides future behaviors in similar settings.

secondary circular reaction During Piaget's sensorimotor period, the infant's repetition of interesting actions on objects (e.g., repeatedly shaking a rattle to make a noise).

secular trend A trend in industrialized society toward earlier maturation and greater body size.

secure attachment An infant–caregiver bond or intimate relationship in which the individual welcomes close contact, uses the attachment object as a source of comfort, and dislikes but can manage separations.

secure base A point of safety, represented by an infant's attachment figure, that permits exploration of the environment.

selective attention Deliberately concentrating on one thing and ignoring something else.

selective breeding A method of studying genetic influence that involves deliberately determining whether a trait can be bred in animals through selective mating.

selective optimization with compensation (SOC) The concept that older people cope with aging through a strategy that involves focusing on the skills most needed, practicing those skills, and developing ways to avoid the need for other skills.

self-concept People's perceptions of their unique attributes or traits.

self-conscious emotion A "secondary emotion" such as embarrassment or pride that requires an awareness of self; unlikely to emerge until about 18 months of age.

self-efficacy The belief that one can effectively produce desired outcomes in a particular area of life.

self-esteem People's overall evaluation of their worth as based on an assessment of the qualities that make up the self-concept.

self-recognition The ability to recognize oneself in a mirror or photograph, which occurs in most infants by 18 to 24 months of age.

semantics The aspect of language centering on meanings.

semenarche A boy's first ejaculation.

sensation The process by which information is detected by the sensory receptors and transmitted to the brain; the starting point in perception.

sensitive period As compared to a critical period, a period of life during which the developing individual is especially susceptible to the effects of experience or has an especially high level of plasticity.

sensorimotor stage Piaget's first stage of cognitive development, spanning the first 2 years of life, in which infants rely on their senses and motor behaviors in adapting to the world around them.

sensory register The first memory store in information processing in which stimuli are noticed and are briefly available for further processing.

sensory threshold The point at which low levels of stimulation can be detected.

separation anxiety A wary or fretful reaction that infants display when separated from their attachment objects.

sequential design A developmental research design that combines the cross-sectional approach and the longitudinal approach in a single study to compensate for the weaknesses of each.

seriation A logical operation that allows a person to mentally order a set of stimuli along a quantifiable dimension such as height or weight.

sex-linked characteristic An attribute determined by a gene that appears on one of the two types of sex chromosomes, usually the X chromosome.

sexual orientation A person's preference for sexual partners of the same or other sex, often characterized as primarily heterosexual, homosexual, or bisexual.

shared environmental influences Experiences that individuals living in the same home environment share and that work to make them similar. Contrast with *nonshared environmental influences*.

short-term memory The memory store in which limited amounts of information are temporarily held; called *working memory* when its active quality is being emphasized.

sibling rivalry A spirit of competition, jealousy, or resentment that may arise between two or more brothers or sisters.

sickle-cell disease A genetic blood disease in which red blood cells assume an unusual sickle shape and become inefficient at distributing oxygen throughout the body.

single gene-pair inheritance The genetic mechanism through which a characteristic is influenced by only one pair of genes, one gene from the mother and its partner from the father.

size constancy The tendency to perceive an object as the same size despite changes in its distance from the eyes.

slow-to-warm-up temperament A characteristic mode of response in which the individual is relatively inactive and moody and displays mild resistance to new routines and experiences but gradually adapts. Contrast with *easy temperament* and *difficult temperament*.

social clock A personal sense of when things should be done in life and when the individual is ahead of or behind the schedule dictated by age norms.

social cognition Thinking about the thoughts, feelings, motives, and behavior of the self and other people.

social cognitive theory Bandura's social learning theory, which holds that children and adults can learn novel responses merely by observing the behavior of a model, making mental notes on what they have seen, and then using these mental representations to reproduce the model's behavior; more broadly, a theory emphasizing the importance of cognitive processing of social experiences.

social comparison The process of defining and evaluating the self through comparisons with other people.

social convoy The changing cadre of significant people who serve as sources of social support to the individual during the life span.

social learning theory See *social cognitive theory*.

social norm A socially defined expectation about how people should behave in particular social contexts.

social pretend play A form of play that involves both cooperation with playmates and pretend or symbolic activity.

social referencing Infants' monitoring of companions' emotional reactions in ambiguous situations and use of this information to decide how they should feel and behave.

social-conventional rules Standards of conduct determined by social consensus that indicate what is appropriate within a particular social setting. Contrast with *moral rules*.

social-role hypothesis Eagly's view that gender-role stereotypes are created and maintained by differences in the roles that men and women play in society rather than being inherent in males and females.

sociocultural perspective Vygotsky's contextual theory of development, which maintains that cognitive development is shaped by the sociocultural context in which it occurs and grows out of children's social interactions with members of their culture.

socioeconomic status (SES) The position people hold in society based on such factors as income, education, occupational status, and the prestige of their neighborhoods.

socioemotional selectivity theory Carstensen's notion that our needs change as we grow older and that we actively choose to narrow our range of social partners to those who can best meet our emotional needs.

sociometric techniques Methods for determining who is well liked and popular and who is disliked or neglected in a group.

somatic symptoms Physical or bodily signs of emotional distress such as loss of appetite or disruption of normal sleep patterns.

species heredity The genetic endowment that members of a particular species have in common; a contributor to universal species traits and patterns of maturation.

spillover effects Events at work affect home life, and events at home carry over into the work place.

spina bifida Condition in which the bottom of the neural tube fails to fully close during prenatal development and part of the spinal cord is not fully encased in the protective covering of the spinal column.

spirituality A search for ultimate meaning in life that may or may not be carried out in the context of religion.

standard deviation A measure of the dispersion or spread around the mean of a distribution of scores; in the case of IQ tests with a mean score of 100, the standard deviation is 15, meaning that about two-thirds of people taking the test have scores between 85 and 115.

static thought In Piaget's theory, the thought characteristic of the preoperational period that is fixed on end states rather than on the changes that transform one state into another. Contrast with *transformational thought*.

stem cell Undifferentiated, primitive cells that have the ability both to multiply and to differentiate into a variety of specific cells.

stereotype threat An individual's fear of being judged to have the qualities associated with negative stereotypes of his or her social group.

storage In information processing, the holding of information in the long-term memory store.

storm and stress Hall's term for the emotional ups and downs and rapid changes that he believed characterize adolescence.

stranger anxiety A wary or fretful reaction that infants often display when approached by an unfamiliar person.

Strange Situation A series of mildly stressful experiences involving the departure of the parent and exposure to a stranger to which infants are exposed to determine the quality of their attachments; developed by Ainsworth.

structured observation A research method in which scientists create special conditions designed to elicit the behavior of interest to achieve greater control over the conditions under which they gather behavioral data. Contrast with *naturalistic observation*.

successful intelligence Sternberg's concept that people are intelligent to the extent that they are able to succeed in life in their sociocultural context.

sudden infant death syndrome (SIDS) The death of a sleeping baby because of a failure of the respiratory system; linked to maternal smoking.

superego The psychoanalytic term for the component of the personality that consists of the individual's internalized moral standards.

surfactant A substance that aids breathing by preventing the air sacs of the lungs from sticking together.

surgency/extraversion Dimension of temperament that involves the tendency to actively and energetically approach new experiences in an emotionally positive way (rather than to be inhibited and withdrawn). See *negative affectivity* and *effortful control*.

symbolic capacity The capacity to use symbols such as words, images, or actions to represent or stand for objects and experiences; representational thought.

synapse The point at which the axon or dendrite of one neuron makes a connection with another neuron.

synchronized routine Harmonious, dance-like interaction between infant and caregiver in which each adjusts behavior in response to that of the other.

syntax Rules specifying how words can be combined to form meaningful sentences in a language.

syphilis A common sexually transmitted disease that may cross the placental barrier in the middle and later stages of pregnancy, causing miscarriage or serious birth defects.

systemize The brain's ability to analyze and explore how things work.

systems theories Theories of development holding that changes over the life span arise from the ongoing interrelationships between a changing organism and a changing environment, both of which are part of a larger, dynamic system.

tabula rasa The idea that the mind of an infant is a "blank slate" and that all knowledge, abilities, behaviors, and motives are acquired through experience.

telegraphic speech Early sentences that consist primarily of content words and omit the less meaningful parts of speech such as articles, prepositions, pronouns, and auxiliary verbs.

telomere A stretch of DNA that forms the tip of a chromosome and that shortens after each cell division, possibly timing the death of cells.

temperament A genetically based pattern of tendencies to respond in predictable ways; building blocks of personality such as activity level, sociability, and emotionality.

teratogen Any disease, drug, or other environmental agent that can harm a developing fetus.

terminal drop A rapid decline in intellectual abilities that people within a few years of dying often experience.

tertiary circular reaction During Piaget's sensorimotor period, the infant's experimenting with actions to find new ways to solve problems or produce interesting effects.

test norms Standards of normal performance on psychometric instruments based on the average scores and range of scores obtained by a large, representative sample of test takers.

testosterone The most important of the male hormones, or androgens; essential for normal sexual development during the prenatal period and at puberty.

thalidomide A mild tranquilizer that, taken early in pregnancy, can produce a variety of malformations of the limbs, eyes, ears, and heart.

theory A set of concepts and propositions designed to organize, describe, and explain a set of observations.

theory of mind The understanding that people have mental states (feelings, desires, beliefs, intentions) and that these states underlie and help explain their behavior.

time of measurement effects In developmental research, the effects on findings of historical events occurring when the data for a study are being collected (for example, psychological changes brought about by an economic depression rather than as a function of aging). Contrast with *age effects* and *cohort effects*.

tinnitus Condition caused by exposure to high noise levels that involves ringing sounds in one or both ears and that can last for days, weeks, or indefinitely.

total brain death An irreversible loss of functioning in the entire brain, both the higher centers of the cerebral cortex that are involved in thought and the lower centers of the brain that control basic life processes such as breathing.

transactional model A model of family influence in which parent and child are believed to influence each other reciprocally.

transformational grammar Rules of syntax that allow a person to transform declarative statements into questions, negatives, imperatives, and other kinds of sentences.

transformational thought In Piaget's theory, the ability to conceptualize transformations, or processes of change from one state to another, which appears in the stage of concrete operations. Contrast with *static thought*.

transitivity The ability to recognize the necessary or logical relations among elements in a serial order (for example, that if A is taller than B, and B is taller than C, then A must be taller than C).

triarchic theory of intelligence An information-processing theory of intelligence that emphasizes three aspects of intelligent behavior: the *context* in which people display intelligence, the previous *experience* they have with cognitive tasks, and the *information-processing components* they use to solve problems.

trust versus mistrust The psychosocial conflict of infancy in which infants must learn to trust others to meet their needs in order

to trust themselves; first stage in Erikson's theory.

Turner syndrome A sex chromosome abnormality in which females inherit only one X chromosome (XO); they remain small in stature, fail to develop secondary sex characteristics, and may show some mental deficiencies.

ultrasound Method of examining physical organs by scanning them with sound waves—for example, scanning the womb and thereby producing a visual outline of the fetus to detect gross abnormalities.

umbilical cord A soft tube containing blood vessels that connects the embryo to the placenta and serves as a source of oxygen and nutrients and as a vehicle for the elimination of wastes.

unconditioned response (UR) The unlearned response elicited by an unconditioned stimulus.

unconditioned stimulus (UCS) A stimulus that elicits a particular response without prior learning.

unconscious motivation Freud's term for feelings, experiences, and conflicts that influence a person's thinking and behavior even though they cannot be recalled.

underextension The young child's tendency to use general words to refer to a smaller set of objects, actions, or events than adults do (for example, using *candy* to refer only to mints). Contrast with *overextension*.

universality–context-specificity issue The debate over the extent to which developmental changes are common to everyone (universal, as in most stage theories) or different from person to person (particularistic).

utilization deficiency The third phase in mastery of memory strategies in which children fail to benefit from a memory strategy they are able to produce.

vascular dementia The deterioration of functioning and cognitive capacities caused by a series of minor strokes that cut off the blood supply to areas of the brain; also called multi-infarct dementia.

vicarious reinforcement In observational learning, the consequences experienced by models, because of their behavior, that affect the learner's likelihood of engaging in the behavior.

visual accommodation The ability of the lens of the eye to change shape to bring objects at different distances into focus.

visual acuity The ability to perceive detail in a visual stimulus.

visual cliff An elevated glass platform that creates an illusion of depth and is used to test the depth perception of infants.

vocabulary spurt A phenomenon occurring around 18 months of age when the pace of word learning quickens dramatically.

word segmentation In language development, the ability to break the stream of speech sounds into distinct words.

working memory A memory store, often referred to as a mental "scratch pad," that temporarily holds information when it is being actively operated upon; the active use of the short-term memory store.

X chromosome The longer of the two sex chromosomes; normal females have two X chromosomes, whereas normal males have only one.

Y chromosome The shorter of the two sex chromosomes; normal males have one Y chromosome, whereas females have none.

zone of proximal development Vygotsky's term for the difference between what a learner can accomplish independently and what a learner can accomplish with the guidance and encouragement of a more skilled partner.

zygote A single cell formed at conception from the union of a sperm and an ovum.

References

A

Aarons, S. J., & Jenkins, R. R. (2002). Sex, pregnancy, and contraception-related motivators and barriers among Latino and African-American youth in Washington, D.C. *Sex Education, 2,* 5–30.

Abe, J. A. A. (2005). The predictive validity of the Five-Factor Model of personality with preschool age children: A nine year follow-up study. *Journal of Research in Personality, 39,* 423–442.

Ablard, K. E., & Mills, C. J. (1996). Implicit theories of intelligence and self-perceptions of academically talented adolescents and children. *Journal of Youth and Adolescence, 25,* 137–148.

Abraham, J. D., & Hansson, R. O. (1995). Successful aging at work: An applied study of selection, optimization, and compensation through impression management. *Journals of Gerontology: Psychological Sciences, 50,* P94–P103.

Achenbach, T. M. (1982). *Developmental psychopathology* (2nd ed.). New York: Wiley.

Achenbach, T. M., & Edelbrock, C. S. (1978). The classification of child psychopathology: A review and analysis of empirical efforts. *Psychological Bulletin, 85,* 1275–1301.

Achenbaum, W. A., & Bengtson, V. L. (1994). Re-engaging the disengagement theory of aging: On the history and assessment of theory development in gerontology. *Gerontologist, 34,* 756–763.

Achter, J. A., Benbow, C. P., & Lubinski, D. (1997). Rethinking multipotentiality among the intellectually gifted: A critical review and recommendations. *Gifted Child Quarterly, 41,* 5–15.

Acredolo, L., & Goodwyn, S. (1988). Symbolic gesturing in normal infants. *Child Development, 59,* 450–466.

Adam, E. K., Gunnar, M. R., & Tanaka, A. (2004). Adult attachment, parent emotion, and observed parenting behavior: Mediator and moderator models. *Child Development, 75,* 110–122.

Adams, C. (1991). Qualitative age differences in memory for text: A life-span developmental perspective. *Psychology and Aging, 6,* 323–336.

Adams, D. W., & Deveau, E. J. (1986). Helping dying adolescents: Needs and responses. In C. A. Corr & J. N. McNeil (Eds.), *Adolescence and death.* New York: Springer.

Adams, D. W., & Deveau, E. J. (1987). When a brother or sister is dying of cancer: The vulnerability of the adolescent sibling. *Death Studies, 11,* 279–295.

Adams, M. J. (1990). *Beginning to read: Learning and thinking about print.* Cambridge, MA: MIT Press.

Adams, M. J., Treiman, R., & Pressley, M. (1998). Reading, writing, and literacy. In I. E. Sigel & K. A. Renninger (Vol. Eds.), W. Damon (Editor-in-Chief), *Handbook of child psychology: Vol. 4. Child psychology in practice* (5th ed., pp. 275–355). New York: Wiley.

Adams, R. (2003, December 9). Baby's first pictures. *The Washington Post,* pp. F1, F5.

Adams, R. E., & Bukowski, W. M. (2007). Relationships with mothers and peers moderate the association between childhood sexual abuse and anxiety disorders. *Child Abuse and Neglect, 31,* 645–656.

Aday, R. H., Kehoe, G. C., & Farney, L. A. (2006). Impact of senior center friendships on aging women who live alone. *Journal of Women & Aging, 18,* 57–73.

Adey, P. S., & Shayer, M. (1992). Accelerating the development of formal thinking in middle and high school students: II. Postproject effects on science achievement. *Journal of Research in Science Teaching, 29,* 81–92.

Adler, J. (2005, November 14). The Boomer Files: Hitting 60. *Newsweek,* 50–58.

Adler, S. R., Fosket, J. R., Kagawa-Singer, M., McGraw, S. A., Wong-Kim, E., Gold, E., et al. (2000). Conceptualizing menopause and midlife: Chinese American and Chinese women in the U.S. *Maturitas, 35,* 11–23.

Adolph, K. E., & Avolio, A. M. (2000). Walking infants adapt locomotion to changing body dimensions. *Journal of Experimental Psychology: Human Perception and Performance, 26,* 1148–1166.

Adolph, K. E., & Berger, S. E. (2006). Motor Development. In D. Kuhn & R. Siegler (Vol. Eds.), *Handbook of child psychology: Cognition, perception, and language* (6th ed.). Hoboken, NJ: Wiley and Sons.

Agnew, R. (2003). An integrated theory of the adolescent peak in offending. *Youth & Society, 34,* 263–299.

Agnew, R., & Huguley, S. (1989). Adolescent violence toward parents. *Journal of Marriage and the Family, 51,* 699–711.

Aguiar, A., & Baillargeon, R. (1999). 2.5-month-old infants' reasoning about when objects should and should not be occluded. *Cognitive Psychology, 39,* 116–157.

Aguiar, A., & Baillargeon, R. (2002). Developments in young infants' reasoning about occluded objects. *Cognitive Psychology, 45,* 267–336.

Ahbe-Rappe, K. (2006). "I no longer believe": Did Freud abandon seduction theory? *Journal of the American Psychoanalytic Association, 54,* 171–199.

Ahluwalia, I. B., Morrow, B., & Hsia, J. (2006). Why do women stop breastfeeding? Findings from the pregnancy risk assessment and monitoring system. *Journal of the American Academy of Child and Adolescent Psychiatry, 45,* 699–700.

Ahrons, C. R. (2007). Family ties after divorce: Long-term implications for children. *Family Process, 46,* 53–65.

Ainscough, C. E. (1990). Premenstrual emotional changes: A prospective study of symptomatology in normal women. *Journal of Psychosomatic Research, 34,* 35–45.

Ainsworth, M. D. S. (1973). The development of infant–mother attachment. In B. M. Caldwell & H. N. Ricciuti (Eds.), *Review of child development research* (Vol. 3). Chicago: University of Chicago Press.

Ainsworth, M. D. S. (1979). Attachment as related to mother–infant interaction. In J. G. Rosenblatt, R. A. Hinde, C. Beer, & M. Busnel (Eds.), *Advances in the study of behavior* (Vol. 9). New York: Academic Press.

Ainsworth, M. D. S. (1989). Attachments beyond infancy. *American Psychologist, 44,* 709–716.

Ainsworth, M. D. S., Blehar, M., Waters, E., & Wall, S. (1978). *Patterns of attachment.* Hillsdale, NJ: Erlbaum.

Ajrouch, K. J., Antonucci, T. C., & Janevic, M. R. (2001). Social networks among blacks and whites: The interaction between race and age. *Journals of Gerontology: Psychological Sciences and Social Sciences, 56,* S112–S118.

Akiyama, H., Antonucci, T., Takahashi, K., & Langfahl, E. S. (2003). Negative interactions in close relationships across the life span. *Journals of Gerontology: Psychological Sciences and Social Sciences, 58,* P70–P79.

Albers, L. L. (1999). The duration of labor in healthy women. *Journal of Perinatology, 19,* 114–119.

Albert, R. S. (1996). Some reasons why childhood creativity often fails to make it past puberty into the real world. In M. A. Runco (Ed.), *Creativity from childhood through adulthood: The developmental issues.* San Francisco: Jossey-Bass.

Aldwin, C. M., Spiro, A., & Park, C. L. (2006). Health, behavior, and optimal aging. In J. E. Birren & K. W. Schaie (Eds.), *Handbook of the psychology of aging.* Boston: Elsevier Academic Press.

Alexander, G. M. (2003). An evolutionary perspective of sex–typed toy preferences: Pink, blue, and the brain. *Archives of Sexual Behavior, 32,* 7–14.

Alfieri, T., Ruble, D. N., & Higgins, E. T. (1996). Gender stereotypes during adolescence: Developmental changes and the transition to junior high school. *Developmental Psychology, 32,* 1129–1137.

Alford, J. R., Funk, C. L., & Hibbing, J. R. (2005). Are political orientations genetically transmitted? *American Political Science Review, 99,* 153–167.

Allen, J. P., Seitz, V., & Apfel, N. H. (2007). The sexually mature teen as a whole person: New directions in prevention and intervention for teen pregnancy and parenthood. In J. L. Aber, S. J. Bishop-Josef, S. M. Jones, K. T. McLearn, & D. A. Phillips, D. A. (Eds.), *Child development and social policy: Knowledge for action.* Washington, DC: American Psychological Association.

Allen, K. R., Blieszner, R., & Roberto, K. A. (2000). Families in the middle and later years: A review and critique of research in the 1990s. *Journal of Marriage and the Family, 62,* 911–926.

Allen, M. C., & Capute, A. J. (1986). Assessment of early auditory and visual abilities of extremely premature infants. *Developmental Medicine and Child Neurology, 28,* 458–466.

Alloway, T. P., Gathercole, S. E., & Pickering, S. J. (2006). Verbal and visuospatial short-term and working memory in children: Are they separable? *Child Development, 77,* 1698–716.

Allum, J. H., Greisiger, R., Straubhaar, S., & Carpenter, M. G. (2000). Auditory perception and speech identification in children with cochlear implants tested with the EARS protocol. *British Journal of Audiology, 34,* 293–303.

Almeida, D. M., & Horn, M. C. (2004). Is daily life more stressful during middle adulthood? In O. G. Brim, C. D. Ryff, & R. C. Kessler (Eds.), *How healthy are we? A national study of well-being at midlife.* Chicago: University of Chicago Press.

Almli, C. R., Ball, R. H., & Wheeler, M. E. (2001). Human fetal and neonatal movement patterns: Gender differences and fetal-to-neonatal continuity. *Developmental Psychobiology, 38,* 252–273.

Amara, C. E., Rice, C. L., Coval, J. J., Paterson, D. H., Winter, E. M., & Cunningham, D. A. (2003). Allometric scaling of strength in an independently living population age 55–86 years. *American Journal of Human Biology, 15,* 48–60.

Amato, P. R. (1993). Children's adjustment to divorce: Theories, hypotheses, and empirical support. *Journal of Marriage and the Family, 55,* 23–38.

Amato, P. R. (2000). The consequences of divorce for adults and children. *Journal of Marriage and the Family, 62,* 1269–1287.

Amato, P. R. (2001). Children of divorce in the 1990s: An update of the Amato and Keith (1991) meta-analysis. *Journal of Family Psychology, 15,* 355–370.

Amato, P. R. (2006). Marital discord, divorce, and children's well-being: Results from a 20-year longitudinal study of two generations. In A. Clarke-Stewart & J. Dunn (Eds.), *Families count: Effects on child and adolescent development.* New York: Cambridge University Press.

Amato, P. R., Johnson, D. R., Booth, A., & Rogers, S. J. (2003). Continuity and change in marital quality between 1980 and 2000. *Journal of Marriage and the Family, 65,* 1–22.

Amato, P. R., & Sobolewski, J. M. (2004). The effects of divorce on fathers and children: Nonresidential fathers and stepfathers. In M. E. Lamb (Ed.), *The role of the father in child development* (4th ed.). Hoboken, NJ: John Wiley & Sons.

American Academy of Pediatrics. (2000). Prevention and management of pain and stress in the neonate (RE9945). *Pediatrics, 105,* 454–461.

American Academy of Pediatrics Committee on Injury and Poison Prevention. (2001). Injuries associated with infant walkers. *Pediatrics, 108,* 790–92.

American Association on Intellectual and Developmental Disabilities (2007). *Welcome to AAIDD.* Available at: www.aamr.org. Accessed September 10, 2007.

American Psychiatric Association. (2000). *Diagnostic and statistical manual of mental disorders DSM–IV–TR* (4th ed., text revision). Arlington, VA: American Psychiatric Association.

Amstutz, D. D., & Sheared, V. (2000). The crisis in adult basic education. *Education and Urban Society, 32,* 155–166.

Anand, K. J., & Hickey, P. R. (1992). Halothane-morphine compared with high-dose sufentanil for anesthesia and postoperative analgesia in neonatal cardiac surgery. *New England Journal of Medicine, 326,* 1–9.

Anastasi, A. (1958). Heredity, environment, and the question, "how?" *Psychological Review, 65,* 197–208.

Anderman, E. M., & Midgley, C. (1997). Changes in achievement goal orientations, perceived academic competence, and grades across the transition to middle-level schools. *Contemporary Educational Psychology, 22,* 269–298.

Anderson, C. A., Berkowitz, L., Donnerstein, E., Huesmann, L. R., Johnson, J. D., Linz, D., et al. (2003). The influence of media violence on youth. *Psychological Science in the Public Interest, 4,* 81–110.

Anderson, C. A., & Bushman, B. J. (2002, March 29). The effects of media violence on society. *Science, 295,* 2377–2379.

Anderson, D. A., & Hamilton, M. (2007). Gender role stereotyping of parents in children's picture books: The invisible father. *Sex Roles, 52,* 145–151.

Anderson, K. E., Lytton, H., & Romney, D. M. (1986). Mothers' interactions with normal and conduct-disordered boys: Who affects whom? *Developmental Psychology, 22,* 604–609.

Anderson, S. E., Dallal, G. E., & Must, A. (2003). Relative weight and race influence average age at menarche: Results from two nationally representative surveys of US girls studied 25 years apart. *Pediatrics, 111,* 844–854.

Andersson, A. M., Carlsen, E., Petersen, J. H., & Skakkebaek, N. E. (2003). Variation in levels of serum inhibin B, testosterone, estradiol, luteinizing hormone, follicle-stimulating hormone, and sex hormone-ginding globulin in monthly samples from healthy men during a 17-month period: Possible effects of seasons. *Journal of Clinical Endocrinology and Metabolism, 88,* 932–937.

Andrade, J. Q., Bunduki, V., Curti, S. P., Figueiredo, C. A., de Oliveria, M. I., & Zugaib, M. (2006). Rubella in pregnancy: Intrauterine transmission and perinatal outcome during a Brazilian epidemic. *Journal of Clinical Virology: The Official Publication of the Pan American Society for Clinical Virology, 35,* 285–291.

Andrews, G., Clark, M., & Luszcz, M. (2002). Successful aging in the Australian Longitudinal Study of Aging: Applying the MacArthur model cross-nationally. *Journal of Social Issues, 58,* 749–765.

Andrews, G. J., Gavin, N., Begley, S., & Brodie, D. (2003). Assisting friendships, combating loneliness: Users' views on a "befriending" scheme. *Ageing & Society, 23,* 349–362.

Anglin, J. M. (1993). Vocabulary development: A morphological analysis. *Monographs of the Society for Research in Child Development, 58* (Serial No. 10).

Anisfeld, E., Casper, V., Nozyce, M., & Cunningham, N. (1990). Does infant carrying promote attachment? An experimental study of the effects of increased physical contact on the development of attachment. *Child Development, 61,* 1617–1627.

Anstey, K. J., Hofer, S. M., & Luszcz, M. A. (2003). A latent growth curve analysis of late-life sensory and cognitive function over 8 years: Evidence for specific and common factors underlying change. *Psychology and Aging, 18,* 714–726.

Antebi, A. (2007). Ageing: When loss is more. *Nature, 447,* 536–537.

Anthis, K., & LaVoie, J. C. (2006). Readiness to change: A longitudinal study of changes in adult identity. *Journal of Research in Personality, 40,* 209–219.

Aoki, K. (1986). A stochastic model of gene-culture coevolution suggested by the "culture historical hypothesis" for the evolution of adult lactose absorption in humans. *Proceedings of the National Academy of Sciences, 83,* 2929–2933.

Apgar, V., & Beck, J. (1974). *Is my baby all right?* New York: Pocket Books.

Applebaum, D. R., & Burns, G. L. (1991). Unexpected childhood death: Posttraumatic stress disorder in surviving siblings and parents. *Journal of Clinical Child Psychology, 20,* 114–120.

Appollonio, I., Carabellese, C., Frattola, L., & Trabucchi, M. (1996). Effects of sensory aids on the quality of life and mortality of elderly people: A multivariate analysis. *Age and Ageing, 25,* 89–96.

Aquilino, W. S. (1991). Predicting parents' experiences with coresident adult children. *Journal of Family Issues, 12,* 323–342.

Aquilino, W. S. (1997). From adolescent to young adult: A prospective study of parent–child relations during the transition to adulthood. *Journal of Marriage and the Family, 59,* 670–686.

Aquilino, W. S. (2006). Family relationships and support systems in emerging adulthood. In J. J. Arnett & J. L. Tanner (Eds.), *Coming of age in the 21st century.* Washington, DC: American Psychological Association.

Aquino, K., & Reed, A. (2002). The self-importance of moral identity. *Journal of Personality & Social Psychology, 83,* 1423–1440.

Arana-Ward, M. (1997, May 11). As technology advances, a bitter debate divides the deaf. *The Washington Post,* p. A1.

Arber, S., & Ginn, J. (1991). *Gender and later life: A sociological analysis of resources and constraints.* London: Sage.

Arbona, C., & Power, T. G. (2003). Parental attachment, self-esteem, and antisocial behaviors among African American, European American, and Mexican American adolescents. *Journal of Counseling Psychology, 50,* 40–51.

Archer, J. (1991). The influence of testosterone on human aggression. *British Journal of Psychology, 82,* 1–28.

Archer, J. (1992). *Ethology and human development.* Hertfordshire, England: Harvester Wheatsheaf.

Archer, J. (1996). Sex differences in social behavior: Are the social role and evolutionary explanations compatible? *American Psychologist, 51,* 909–917.

Archer, S. L. (1982). The lower age boundaries of identity development. *Child Development, 53,* 1551–1556.

Archer, S. L. (1992). A feminist's approach to identity research. In G. R. Adams, T. P. Gullotta, & R. Montemayor (Eds.), *Adolescent identity formation: Vol. 4. Advances in adolescent development.* Newbury Park, CA: Sage.

Ardelt, M. (2000). Antecedents and effects of wisdom in old age. *Research on Aging, 22,* 360–394.

Ardelt, M., & Day, L. (2002). Parents, siblings, and peers: Close social relationships and adolescent deviance. *Journal of Early Adolescence, 22,* 310–349.

Arden, R., & Plomin, R. (2006). Sex differences in variance of intelligence across childhood. *Personality and Individual Differences, 41,* 39–48.

Arendt, R., Singer, L., Angelopoulos, J., Bass-Busdiecker, O., & Mascia, J. (1998). Sensorimotor development in cocaine-exposed infants. *Infant Behavior and Development, 21,* 627–640.

Ariès, P. (1962). *Centuries of childhood.* New York: Knopf.

Ariès, P. (1981). *The hour of our death* (H. Weaver, Trans.). New York: Knopf. (Original work published 1977).

Arking, R. (2006). *The biology of aging: Observations and principles* (3rd ed.). New York: Oxford University Press.

Arlt, W., Callies, F., van Vlijmen, J. C., Koehler, I., Reincke, M., Bidlingmaier, M., Huebler, D., Oettel, M., Ernst, M., Schulte, H. M., & Allolio, B. (1999). Dehydroepiandrosterone replacement in women with adrenal insufficiency. *New England Journal of Medicine, 341,* 1013–1020.

Armstrong, E. M. (2003). *Conceiving risk, bearing responsibility: Fetal alcohol syndrome and the diagnosis of moral disorder.* Baltimore, MD: The Johns Hopkins University Press.

Armstrong, P. I., & Crombie, G. (2000). Compromises in adolescents' occupational aspirations and expectations from grades 8 to 10. *Journal of Vocational Behavior, 56,* 82–98.

Armstrong, V. L., Brunet, P. M., He, C., Nishimura, M., Poole, H. L. & Spector, F. (2006). What is so critical?: A commentary on the reexamination of critical periods. *Developmental Psychobiology, 48,* 326–331.

Arnett, J. J. (1999). Adolescent storm and stress, reconsidered. *American Psychologist, 54,* 317–326.

Arnett, J. J. (2000). Emerging adulthood: A theory of development from the late teens through the twenties. *American Psychologist, 55,* 469–480.

Arnett, J. J. (2006). Emerging adulthood: Understanding the new way of coming of age. In J. J. Arnett & J. L. Tanner (Eds.), *Emerging adults in America: Coming of age in the 21st century.* Washington, DC: American Psychological Association.

Arnett, J. J. (2007). Socialization in emerging adulthood: From the family to the wider world, from socialization to self-socialization. In J. E. Grusec & P. D. Hastings (Eds.), *Handbook of socialization theory and research.* New York: Guilford.

Arnett, J. J., & Tanner, J. L. (Eds.) (2006). *Emerging adults in America: Coming of age in the 21st century.* Washington, DC: American Psychological Association.

Aronson, J., Lustina, M. J., Good, C., Keough, K., Steele, C. M., & Brown, J. (1999). When white men can't do math: Necessary and sufficient factors in stereotype threat. *Journal of Experimental Social Psychology, 35,* 29–46.

Aros, S., Mills, J. L., Torres, C., Henriquez, C., Fuentes, A., Capurro, T., Mena, M., Conley, M., Cox, C., Signore, C., Klebanoff, M., & Cassoria, F. (2006). Prospective identification of pregnant women drinking four or more standard drinks (> or = 48g) of alcohol per day. *Substance Use & Misuse, 41,* 193–197.

Arroyo, C. G., & Zigler, E. (1995). Racial identity, academic achievement, and the psychological well-being of economically disadvantaged adolescents. *Journal of Personality and Social Psychology, 69,* 903–914.

Arseneault, L., Tremblay, R. E., Boulerice, B., & Saucier, J. (2002). Obstetrical complications and violent delinquency: Testing two developmental pathways. *Child Development, 73,* 496–508.

Arsenio, W. F., & Gold, J. (2006). The effects of social injustice and inequality on children's moral judgments and behavior: Towards a theoretical model. *Cognitive Development, 21,* 388–400.

Arsenio, W. F., Gold, J., & Adams, E. (2006). Children's conceptions and displays of moral emotions. In M. Killen & J. G. Smetana (Eds.), *Handbook of moral development.* Mahwah, NJ: Erlbaum.

Asarnow, J. R., Jaycox, L. H., & Tompson, M. C. (2001). Depression in youth: Psychosocial interventions. *Journal of Clinical Child Psychology, 30,* 33–47.

Asbury, K., Dunn, J. F., Pike, A., & Plomin, R. (2003). Nonshared environmental influences on individual differences in early behavioral development: A monozygotic twin differences study. *Child Development, 74,* 933–943.

Asbury, K., Dunn, J. F., & Plomin, R. (2006). Birthweight-discordance and differences in early parenting relate to monozygotic twin differences in behaviour problems and academic achievement at age 7. *Developmental Science, 9,* F22–F31.

Asendorpf, J. B., Warkentin, V., & Baudonnière, P. M. (1996). Self-awareness and other-awareness: 2. Mirror self-recognition, social contingency awareness, and synchronic imitation. *Developmental Psychology, 32,* 313–321.

Aspelmeier, J. E., Elliott, A. N., & Smith, C. H. (2007). Childhood sexual abuse, attachment, and trauma symptoms in college females: The moderating role of attachment. *Child Abuse and Neglect, 31,* 549–566.

Associated Press. (2003, November 21). Women earn 20% less than men, GAO finds. *The Washington Post,* p. E4.

Associated Press. (2004, January 18). Woman delivers daughter after dispute over C-section. *Sunday Patriot News* (Harrisburg, PA), p. B11.

Atchley, R. C. (1976). *The sociology of retirement.* Cambridge, MA: Schenkman.

Athey, I. (1984). Contributions of play to development. In T. D. Yawkey & A. D. Pellegrini (Eds.), *Child's play: Developmental and applied.* Hillsdale, NJ: Erlbaum.

Atkinson, R. C. & Shiffrin, R. M. (1968). Human memory: A proposed system and its control processes. In K. W. Spence & J. T. Spence (Eds.), *The psychology of learning and motivation: Advances in research and theory* (Vol. 2). New York: Academic Press.

Austrian, S. G. (Ed). (2002). *Developmental theories through the life cycle.* New York: Columbia University.

Autism Genome Project Consortium (2007). Mapping autism risk loci using genetic linage and chromosomal rearrangements. *Nature Genetics, 39,* 319–328.

Autti-Rämö, I. (2000). Twelve-year follow-up of children exposed to alcohol in utero. *Developmental Medicine & Child Neurology, 42,* 406–411.

Avellar, S., & Smock, P. J. (2003). Has the price of motherhood declined over time? A cross-cohort comparison of the motherhood wage penalty. *Journal of Marriage and Family, 65,* 597–607.

Avert. (2006). *Preventing mother-to-child transmission of HIV.* Available at: www.avert.org/motherchild.htm. Accessed: October 2, 2006.

Avolio, B. J., & Sosik, J. J. (1999). A life-span framework for assessing the impact of work on white-collar workers. In S. L. Willis & J. D. Reid (Eds.), *Life in the middle: Psychological and social development in middle age.* San Diego: Academic Press.

Axinn, W. G., & Barber, J. S. (1997). Living arrangements and family formation attitudes in early adulthood. *Journal of Marriage and the Family, 59,* 595–561.

Azmitia, M. (1992). Expertise, private speech, and the development of self-regulation. In R. M. Diaz & L. E. Berk (Eds.), *Private speech: From social interaction to self-regulation.* Hillsdale, NJ: Erlbaum.

B

Bacharach, V. R., & Baumeister, A. A. (1998). Direct and indirect effects of maternal intelligence, maternal age, income, and home environment on intelligence of preterm, low-birth-weight children. *Journal of Applied Developmental Psychology, 19,* 361–375.

Bachman, J. G., Safron, D. J., Sy, S. R., & Schulenberg, J. E. (2003). Wishing to work: New perspectives on how adolescents' part-time work intensity is linked to educational disengagement, substance use, and other problem behaviors. *International Journal of Behavioral Development, 27,* 301–315.

Backhaus, J., Junghanns, K., Born, J., Hohaus, K., Faasch, F. & Hohagen, F. (2006). Impaired declarative memory consolidation during sleep in patients with primary insomnia: Influence of sleep architecture and nocturnal cortisol release. *Biological Psychiatry, 60,* 1324–1330.

Bada, H. S., Das, A., Bauer, C. R., Shankaran, S., Lester, B. M., Gard, C. C., Wright, L. L., Lagasse, L. L., & Higgins, R. (2005). Low birth weight and preterm births: Etiologic fraction attributable to prenatal drug exposure. *Journal of Perinatology: Official Journal of the California Perinatal Association, 25,* 631–637.

Baddeley, A. (1986). *Working memory.* Oxford: Oxford University Press.

Baddeley, A. (1992). Working memory. *Science, 255,* 556–559.

Baer, J. C., & Martinez, C. D. (2006). Child maltreatment and insecure attachment: A meta-analysis. *Journal of Reproductive and Infant Psychology, 24,* 187–197.

Bahrick, H. P., Bahrick, P. O., & Wittlinger, R. P. (1975). Fifty years of memory for names and faces: A cross-sectional approach. *Journal of Experimental Psychology: General, 104,* 54–75.

Bahrick, L. E., & Pickens, J. N. (1995). Infant memory for object motion across a period of three months: Implications for a four-phase attention function. *Journal of Experimental Child Psychology, 59,* 343–371.

Bailey, A., Lecouteur, A., Gottesman, I., Bolton, P., Simonoff, E., Yuzda, E., et al. (1995). Autism as a strongly genetic disorder: Evidence from a British twin study. *Psychological Medicine, 25,* 63–77.

Bailey, C. E. (Ed.) (2000). *Children in therapy: Using the family as a resource.* New York: W. W. Norton.

Bailey, J. M., Bechtold, K. T., & Berenbaum, S. A. (2002). Who are tomboys and why should we study them? *Archives of Sexual Behavior, 31,* 333–341.

Bailey, J. M., Dunne, M. P., & Martin, N. G. (2000). Genetic and environmental influences on sexual orientation and its correlates in an Australian twin sample. *Journal of Personality and Social Psychology, 78,* 524–536.

Bailey, J. M., & Pillard, R. C. (1991). A genetic study of male sexual orientation. *Archives of General Psychiatry, 48,* 1089–1096.

Bailey, J. M., Pillard, R. C., Neale, M. C., & Agyei, Y. (1993). Heritable factors influence sexual orientation in women. *Archives of General Psychiatry, 50,* 217–223.

Bailey, R. N., Indian, R. W., Zhang, X., Geiss, L. S., Duenas, M. R., & Saaddine, J. B. (2006). Visual impairment and eye care among older adults—five states, 2006. *Morbidity and Mortality Weekly Report, 55,* 1321–1325.

Baillargeon, R. (2002). The acquisition of physical knowledge in infancy: A summary in eight lessons. In U. Goswami (Ed.), *Blackwell handbook of child cognitive development* (pp. 47–83). Oxford: Blackwell.

Baillargeon, R. H., Zoccolillo, M., Keenan, K., Côté, S., Pérusse, D., Wu, H., Boivin, M., & Tremblay, R. E. (2007). Gender differences in physical aggression: A prospective population-based survey of children before and after 2 years of age. *Developmental Psychology, 43,* 13–26.

Bajpai, A., Kabra, M., Gupta, A. K., & Menon, P. S. (2006). Growth pattern and skeletal maturation following growth hormone therapy in growth hormone deficiency: Factors influencing outcome. *Indian Pediatrics, 43,* 593–599.

Baker, D. P., & Jones, D. P. (1992). Opportunity and performance: A sociological explanation for gender differences in academic mathematics. In J. Wrigley (Ed.), *Education and gender equality.* London: Falmer Press.

Baker, L., & Brown, A. L. (1984). Metacognitive skills and reading. In P. D. Pearson (Ed.), *A handbook of reading research.* New York: Longman.

Bakermans-Kranenburg, M. J., van IJzendoorn, M. H., & Juffer, F. (2003). Less is more: Meta-analyses of sensitivity and attachment interventions in early childhood. *Psychological Bulletin, 129,* 195–215.

Baker-Ward, L., Gordon, B. N., Ornstein, P. A., Larus, D. M., & Clubb, P. A. (1993). Young children's long-term retention of a pediatric examination. *Child Development, 64,* 1519–1533.

Baker-Ward, L., Ornstein, P. A., & Holden, D. J. (1984). The expression of memorization in

early childhood. *Journal of Experimental Child Psychology, 37,* 555–575.

Balk, D. E., & Corr, C. A. (2001). Bereavement during adolescence: A review of research. In M. S. Stroebe, R. O. Hansson, W. Stroebe, & H. Schut (Eds.), *Handbook of bereavement research: Consequences, coping, and care.* Washington, DC: American Psychological Association.

Baltes, P. B. (1987). Theoretical propositions of life-span developmental psychology: On the dynamics between growth and decline. *Developmental Psychology, 23,* 611–626.

Baltes, P. B., & Baltes, M. M. (1990). Psychological perspectives on successful aging: The model of selective optimization with compensation. In P. B. Baltes & M. M. Baltes (Eds.), *Successful aging: Perspectives from the behavioral sciences.* New York: Cambridge University Press.

Baltes, P. B., & Carstensen, L. L. (2003). The process of successful aging: Selection, optimization and compensation. In U. M. Staudinger & U. Lindenberger (Eds.), *Understanding human development: Dialogues with life-span psychology.* Dordecht, Netherlands: Kluwer Academic Press.

Baltes, P. B., & Freund, A. M. (2003). Human strengths as the orchestration of wisdom and selective optimization with compensation. In L. G. Aspinwall & U. M. Staudinger (Eds.), *A psychology of human strengths: Fundamental questions and future directions for a positive psychology.* Washington, DC: American Psychological Association.

Baltes, P. B., & Lindenberger, U. (1997). Emergence of a powerful connection between sensory and cognitive functions across the adult life span: A new window to the study of cognitive aging? *Psychology and Aging, 12,* 12–21.

Baltes, P. B., Lindenberger, U., & Staudinger, U. M. (1998). Life-span theory in developmental psychology. In R. M. Lerner (Vol. Ed.), W. Damon (Editor-in-Chief), *Handbook of child psychology: Vol. 1. Theoretical models of human development* (5th ed.). New York: Wiley.

Baltes, P. B., Lindenberger, U., & Staudinger, U. M. (2006). Life span theory in developmental psychology. In W. Damon & R. M. Lerner (Eds. in Chief) & R. M. Lerner (Vol. Ed.), *Handbook of child psychology: Vol. 1. Theoretical models of human development* (6th ed.). Hoboken, NJ: Wiley.

Baltes, P. B., Reese, H. W., & Lipsitt, L. P. (1980). Life-span developmental psychology. *Annual Review of Psychology, 31,* 65–110.

Baltes, P. B., Smith, J., & Staudinger, U. M. (1992). Wisdom and successful aging. In T. B. Sonderegger (Ed.), *Nebraska Symposium on Motivation: Vol. 39. Psychology and aging.* Lincoln: University of Nebraska Press.

Baltes, P. B., & Staudinger, U. M. (2000). Wisdom: A metaheuristic (pragmatic) to orchestrate mind and virtue toward excellence. *American Psychologist, 55,* 122–136.

Baltes, P. B., Staudinger, U. M., Maercker, A., & Smith, J. (1995). People nominated as wise: A comparative study of wisdom-related knowledge. *Psychology and Aging, 10,* 155–166.

Bandura, A. (1965). Influence of models' reinforcement contingencies on the acquisition of imitative responses. *Journal of Personality and Social Psychology, 1,* 589–595.

Bandura, A. (1971). An analysis of modeling processes. In A. Bandura (Ed.), *Psychological modeling.* New York: Lieber-Atherton.

Bandura, A. (1977). *Social learning theory.* Englewood Cliffs, NJ: Prentice-Hall.

Bandura, A. (1986). *Social foundations of thought and action: A social cognitive theory.* Englewood Cliffs, NJ: Prentice-Hall.

Bandura, A. (1989). Social cognitive theory. In R. Vasta (Ed.), *Annals of child development: Vol. 6. Theories of child development: Revised formulations and current issues.* Greenwich, CT: JAI Press.

Bandura, A. (1991). Social cognitive theory of moral thought and action. In W. M. Kurtines & J. L. Gewirtz (Eds.), *Handbook of moral behavior and development: Vol. 1. Theory.* Hillsdale, NJ: Erlbaum.

Bandura, A. (2000). Social cognitive theory: An agentic perspective. *Annual Review of Psychology, 52,* 1–26.

Bandura, A. (2002). Selective moral disengagement in the exercise of moral agency. *Journal of Moral Education, 31,* 101–119.

Bandura, A. (2006). Toward a psychology of human agency. *Perspectives on Psychological Science, 1,* 164–180.

Bandura, A., Caprara, G. V., Barbaranelli, C., Pastorelli, C., & Regalia, C. (2001). Sociocognitive self-regulatory mechanisms governing transgressive behavior. *Journal of Personality & Social Psychology, 80,* 125–135.

Banerjee, R., & Lintern, V. (2000). Boys will be boys: The effect of social evaluation concerns on gender-typing. *Social Development, 9,* 397–408.

Bank, L., Marlowe, J., Reid, J., Patterson, G., & Weinrott, M. (1991). A comparative evaluation of parent-training interventions for families of chronic delinquents. *Journal of Abnormal Child Psychology, 19,* 15–33.

Bankoff, E. A. (1983). Aged parents and their widowed daughters: A support relationship. *Journal of Gerontology, 38,* 226–230.

Banks, M. S., & Ginsburg, A. P. (1985). Infant visual preferences: A review and new theoretical treatment. In H. W. Reese (Ed.), *Advances in child development and behavior* (Vol. 19). Orlando, FL: Academic Press.

Banks, M. S. & Salapatek, P. (1983). Infant visual perception. In M. M. Haith & J. J. Campos (Eds.) & P. H. Mussen (Gen Ed.), *Handbook of child psychology: Vol 2. Infancy and developmental psychobiology* (4th ed.), New York: Wiley.

Banks, M. S., & Shannon, E. (1993). Spatial and chromatic visual efficiency in human neonates. In C. E. Granrud (Ed.), *Visual perception and cognition in infancy.* Hillsdale, NJ: Erlbaum.

Barack, J. A., Hodapp, R. M., & Zigler, E. (Eds.) (1998). *Handbook of mental retardation and development.* New York: Cambridge University Press.

Barash, D. P. (2002, May 24). Evolution, males, and violence. *The Chronicle of Higher Education,* pp. B7–B9.

Barash, D. P. (2006, April 7). The case for evolution, in real life. *The Chronicle of Higher Education, 52*(31), B10.

Barber, B. L., Eccles, J. S., & Stone, M. R. (2001). Whatever happened to the jock, the brain, and the princess? Young adult pathways linked to adolescent activity involvement and social identity. *Journal of Adolescent Research, 16,* 429–455.

Barclay, L., & Lupton, D. (1999). The experiences of new fatherhood: A socio-cultural analysis. *Journal of Advanced Nursing, 29,* 1013–1020.

Bar-Haim, Y., Ziv, T., Lamy, D., & Hodes, R. M. (2006). Nature and nurture in own-race face processing. *Psychological Science, 17,* 159–163.

Barker, D. J. P. (1998). *Mothers, babies, and disease in later life* (2nd ed.). New York: Churchill Livingstone.

Barkley, R. A. (1997). Behavioral inhibition, sustained attention, and executive functions: Constructing a unifying theory of ADHD. *Psychological Bulletin, 121,* 65–94.

Barkley, R. A. (2000). Genetics of childhood disorders: XVII. ADHD, Part 1: The executive functions and ADHD. *Journal of the American Academy of Child and Adolescent Psychiatry, 39,* 1064–1068.

Barkley, R. A., Fischer, M., Edelbrock, C., & Smallish, L. (1991). The adolescent outcome of hyperactive children diagnosed by research criteria. Mother–child interactions, family conflicts and maternal psychopathology. *Journal of Child Psychology and Psychiatry and Allied Disciplines, 32,* 233–255.

Barkley, R. A., Fischer, M., Smallish, L., & Fletcher, K. (2006). Young adult outcome of hyperactive children: Adaptive functioning in major life activities. *Journal of the American Academy of Child and Adolescent Psychiatry, 45,* 192–202.

Barnes, D. E., Yaffe, K., Satariano, W. A., & Tager, I. B. (2003). A longitudinal study of cardiorespiratory fitness and cognitive function in healthy older adults. *Journal of the American Geriatrics Society, 51,* 459–465.

Barnes, K. E. (1971). Preschool play norms: A replication. *Developmental Psychology, 5,* 99–103.

Barnett, R. C. (1994). Home-to-work spillover revisited: A study of full-time employed women in dual-earner couples. *Journal of Marriage and the Family, 56,* 647–656.

Barnett, W. S. (2002). Early childhood education. In A. Molnar (Ed.), *School reform proposals: The research evidence* (pp. 1–26). Greenwich, CT: Information Age Publishing.

Barnett, W. S., Brown, K. C., Finn-Stevenson, M., & Henrich, C. (2007). From visions to systems of universal prekindergarten. In J. L. Aber, S. J. Bishop-Josef, S. M. Jones, K. T. McLearn, & D. A. Phillips (Eds.), *Child development and social policy: Knowledge for action.* Washington, DC: American Psychology Association.

Baron, N. S. (1992). Growing up with language: How children learn to talk. Reading, MA: Addison-Wesley.

Baron-Cohen, S. (1995). *Mindblindness: An essay on autism and theory of mind.* Cambridge, MA: MIT Press.

Baron-Cohen, S. (2000). Theory of mind and autism: A 15 year review. In S. Baron-Cohen, H. Tager-Flusberg, & D. J. Cohen (Eds.), *Understanding other minds: Perspectives from developmental cognitive neuroscience* (2nd ed.). Oxford: Oxford University Press.

Baron-Cohen, S. (2003). *The essential difference: The truth about the male and female brain.* New York: Basic Books.

Baron-Cohen, S. (2005). The empathizing system: A revision of the 1994 model of the mind-reading system. In B. J. Ellis & D. F. Bjorklund (Eds.), *Origins of the social mind.* New York: Guilford Press.

Baron-Cohen, S., Leslie, A. M., & Frith, U. (1985). Does the autistic child have a "theory of mind"? *Cognition, 21,* 37–46.

Barr, H. M., & Streissguth, A. P. (1991). Caffeine use during pregnancy and child outcome: A 7-year prospective study. *Neurotoxicology and Teratology, 13,* 441–448.

Barr, R. G., Pantel, M. S., Young, S. N., Wright, J. H., Hendricks, L. A., & Gravel, R. (1999). The response of crying newborns to sucrose: Is it a "sweetness" effect? *Physiological Behavior, 66,* 409–417.

Barr, R., Dowden, A., & Hayne, H. (1996). Developmental changes in deferred imitation by 6- to 24-month-old infants. *Infant Behavior & Development, 19,* 159–170.

Barrett, T. R., & Wright, M. (1981). Age-related facilitation in recall following semantic processing. *Journal of Gerontology, 36,* 194–199.

Bartels, M., Rietveld, M. J. H., van Baal, G. C. M., & Boomsma, D. I. (2002). Genetic and environmental influences on the development of intelligence. *Behavior Genetics, 32,* 237–249.

Bartholomew, K., & Horowitz, L. M. (1991). Attachment styles among young adults: A test of a four-category model. *Journal of Personality and Social Psychology, 61,* 226–244.

Bartlett, D. (1997). Primitive reflexes and early motor development. *Journal of Developmental and Behavioral Pediatrics, 18,* 151–157.

Basow, S. A., Cahill, K. F., Phelan, J. E., Longshore, K., & McGillicuddy-DeLisi, A. (2007). Perceptions of relational and physical aggression among college students: Effects of gender of perpetrator, target, and perceiver. *Psychology of Women Quarterly, 31,* 85–95.

Basseches, M. (1984). Dialectical thinking and adult development. Norwood, NJ: Ablex.

Bates, E., O'Connell, B., & Shore, C. (1987). Language and communication in infancy. In J. D. Osofsky (Ed.), *Handbook of infant development* (2nd ed.). New York: Wiley.

Bates, J. E., & Pettit, G. S. (2007). Temperament, parenting, and socialization. In J. E. Grusec & P. D. Hastings (Eds.), *Handbook of socialization: Theory and research.* New York: Guilford.

Batshaw, M. L. (2002). *Children with disabilities* (5th ed.). Baltimore: Paul H. Brookes.

Bauchner, H. (1996). Failure to thrive. In R. E. Behrman, R. M. Kliegman, & A. M. Arvin (Eds.), *Nelson textbook of pediatrics* (15th ed.). Philadelphia: W. B. Saunders.

Bauer, P. J. (1996). What do infants recall of their lives? Memory for specific events by one- to two-year-olds. *American Psychologist, 51,* 29–41.

Bauer, P. J. (2007). *Remembering the times of our lives: Memory in infancy and beyond.* Mahwah, NJ: Lawrence Erlbaum.

Bauer, P. J., Hertsgaard, L. A., & Wewerka, S. S. (1995). Effects of experience and reminding on long-term recall in infancy: Remembering not to forget. *Journal of Experimental Child Psychology, 59,* 260–298.

Bauer, P. J., Wenner, J. A., Dropik, P. L., & Wewerka, S. S. (2000). Parameters of remembering and forgetting in the transition from infancy to early childhood. *Monographs of the Society for Research in Child Development, 65* (Serial No. 263).

Baumrind, D. (1967). Child care practices anteceding three patterns of preschool behavior. *Genetic Psychology Monographs, 75,* 43–88.

Baumrind, D. (1977, March). *Socialization determinants of personal agency.* Paper presented at the biennial meeting of the Society for Research in Child Development, New Orleans.

Baumrind, D. (1991). Effective parenting during the early adolescent transition. In P. A. Cowan & M. Hetherington (Eds.), *Family transitions.* Hillsdale, NJ: Erlbaum.

Bauserman, R. (2002). Child adjustment in joint-custody versus sole-custody arrangements: A meta-analytic review. *Journal of Family Psychology, 16,* 91–102.

Baxter, J. (2006). Women's experience of infant feeding following birth by caesarean section. *British of Journal of Midwifery, 14,* 290–295.

Baydar, N., & Brooks-Gunn, J. (1991). Effects of maternal employment and child-care arrangements on preschoolers' cognitive and behavioral outcomes: Evidence from the children of the National Longitudinal Survey of Youth. *Developmental Psychology, 27,* 932–945.

Bayley, N. (1993). *Bayley scales of infant development* (2nd ed.). San Antonio: Psychological Corporation.

Beal, C. R. (1990). The development of text evaluation and revision skills. *Child Development, 61,* 247–258.

Beal, C. R. (1994). *Boys and girls: The development of gender roles.* New York: McGraw-Hill.

Bear, M. F., Connors, B. W., & Paradiso, M. A. (2001). *Neuroscience: Exploring the brain* (2nd ed.). Philadelphia, PA: Lippincott, Williams & Wilkins.

Beautrais, A. L. (2003). Life course factors associated with suicidal behaviors in young people. *American Behavioral Scientist, 46,* 1137–1156.

Becker, A. E., Burwell, R. A., Herzog, D. B., Hamburg, P., & Gilman, S. E. (2002). Eating behaviours and attitudes following prolonged exposure to television among ethnic Fijian adolescent girls. *British Journal of Psychiatry, 180,* 509–514.

Beckwith, L., Cohen, S. E., & Hamilton, C. E. (1999). Maternal sensitivity during infancy and subsequent life events relate to attachment representation at early adulthood. *Developmental Psychology, 35,* 693–700.

Beckwith, L., Rozga, A., & Sigman, M. (2002). Maternal sensitivity and attachment in atypical groups. In R. V. Kail (Ed.), *Advances in child development and behavior* (Vol. 30). San Diego: Academic Press.

Beehr, T. A., Glazer, S., Nielson, N. L., & Farmer, S. J. (2000). Work and nonwork predictors of employee's retirement age. *Journal of Vocational Behavior, 57,* 206–225.

Beemsterboer, S. N., Homburg, R., Gorter, N. A., Schats, R., Hompes, P. G., & Lambalk, C. B. (2006). The paradox of declining fertility but increasing twinning rates with advancing maternal age. *Human Reproduction, 21,* 1531–1532.

Behrend, D. A., Rosengren, K., & Perlmutter, M. (1989). A new look at children's private speech: The effects of age, task difficulty, and parent presence. *International Journal of Behavioral Development, 12,* 305–320.

Beilin, H. (1992). Piaget's enduring contribution to developmental psychology. *Developmental Psychology, 28,* 191–204.

Beitchman, J. H., Zucker, K. J., Hood, J. E., daCosta, G. A., & Akman, D. (1991). A review of the short-term effects of child sexual abuse. *Child Abuse & Neglect, 15,* 537–556.

Béland, F., Zunzunegui, M., Alvarado, B., Otero, A., & del Ser, T. (2005). Trajectories of cognitive decline and social relations. *Journal of*

Gerontology: Psychological Sciences, 60B, P320–P330.

Bell, J. H., & Bromnick, R. D. (2003). The social reality of the imaginary audience: A grounded theory approach. *Adolescence, 38,* 205–219.

Bell, M. A., & Wolfe, C. D. (2007). Changes in brain functioning from infancy to early childhood: Evidence from EEG power and coherence working memory tasks. *Developmental Neuropsychology, 31,* 21–38.

Bellanti, C. J., Bierman, K. L., & Conduct Problems Prevention Research Group. (2000). Disentangling the impact of low cognitive ability and inattention on social behavior and peer relationships. *Journal of Clinical Child Psychology, 29,* 66–75.

Bellinger, D., Leviton, A., Waternaux, C., Needleman, H., & Rabinowitz, M. (1987). Longitudinal analyses of prenatal and postnatal lead exposure and early cognitive development. *New England Journal of Medicine, 316,* 1037–1043.

Bellugi, U. (1988). The acquisition of a spatial language. In F. S. Kessel (Ed.), *The development of language and language researchers: Essays in honor of Roger Brown.* Hillsdale, NJ: Erlbaum.

Belsky, J. (1981). Early human experience: A family perspective. *Developmental Psychology, 17,* 3–23.

Belsky, J., Jaffee, S. R., Caspi, A., Moffitt, T., & Silva, P. A. (2003). Intergenerational relationships in young adulthood and their life course, mental health, and personality correlates. *Journal of Family Psychology, 17,* 460–471.

Belsky, J., Jaffee, S., Hsieh, K., & Silva, P. A. (2001). Child-rearing antecedents of intergenerational relations in young adulthood: A prospective study. *Developmental Psychology, 37,* 801–813.

Belsky, J., Lang, M. E., & Rovine, M. (1985). Stability and change in marriage across the transition to parenthood: A second study. *Journal of Marriage and the Family, 47,* 855–865.

Belsky, J., & Rovine, M. J. (1988). Nonmaternal care in the first year of life and the security of infant–parent attachment. *Child Development, 59,* 157–167.

Belsky, J., Vandell, D. L., Burchinal, M., Clark-Stewart, K. A., McCartney, K., & Owen, M. T. (2007). Are there long-term effects of early child care? *Child Development, 78,* 681–701.

Bem, S. L. (1974). The measurement of psychological androgyny. *Journal of Consulting and Clinical Psychology, 42,* 155–162.

Bem, S. L. (1975). Sex-role adaptability: One consequence of psychological androgyny. *Journal of Personality and Social Psychology, 31,* 634–643.

Bem, S. L. (1978). Beyond androgyny: Some presumptuous prescriptions for a liberated sexual identity. In J. A. Sherman & F. L. Denmark (Eds.), *The psychology of women: Future directions in research.* New York: Psychological Dimensions.

Bem, S. L. (1989). Genital knowledge and gender constancy in preschool children. *Child Development, 60,* 649–662.

Bemporad, J. R. (1979). Adult recollections of a formerly autistic child. *Journal of Autism and Developmental Disorders, 9,* 179–197.

Benbow, C. P., & Arjmand, O. (1990). Predictors of high academic achievement in mathematics and science by mathematically talented students: A longitudinal study. *Journal of Educational Psychology, 82,* 430–441.

Benenson, J. F., Philippoussis, M., & Leeb, R. (1999). Sex differences in neonates' cuddliness. *Journal of Genetic Psychology, 160,* 332–342.

Benes, F. M. (1998). Human brain growth spans decades. *American Journal of Psychiatry, 155,* 1489.

Bengtson, V. L. (2001). Beyond the nuclear family: The increasing importance of multigenerational bonds. *Journal of Marriage and Family, 63,* 1–16.

Bengtson, V., Rosenthal, C., & Burton, L. (1990). Families and aging: Diversity and heterogeneity. In R. H. Binstock & L. K. George (Eds.), *Handbook of aging and the social sciences* (3rd ed.). San Diego: Academic Press.

Bengtson, V., Rosenthal, C., & Burton, L. (1996). Paradoxes of families and aging. In R. H. Binstock, L. K. George, V. W. Marshall, G. C. Myers, & J. H. Schulz (Eds.), *Handbook of aging and the social sciences* (4th ed.). San Diego: Academic Press.

Benjet, C., & Hernández-Guzmán, L. (2002). A short-term longitudinal study of pubertal change, gender, and psychological well-being of Mexican early adolescents. *Journal of Youth and Adolescence, 31,* 429–442.

Benjet, C., & Kazdin, A. E. (2003). Spanking children: The controversies, findings, and new directions. *Clinical Psychology Review, 23,* 197–224.

Bennett, I., Switzer, J., Aguirre, A., Evans, K., & Barg, F. (2006). 'Breaking it down': Patient-clinician communication and prenatal care among African American women of low and higher literacy. *Annals of Family Medicine, 4,* 334–340.

Benoit, D., & Coolbear, J. (2004). Disorders of attachment and failure to thrive. In L. Atkinson & S. Goldberg (Eds.), *Attachment issues in psychopathology and intervention.* Mahwah, NJ: Erlbaum.

Benoit, D., & Parker, K. C. (1994). Stability and transmission of attachment across three generations. *Child Development, 65,* 1444–1456.

Benson, M. J., McWey, L. M., & Ross, J. J. (2006). Parental attachment and peer relations in adolescence: A meta-analysis. *Research in Human Development, 3,* 33–43.

Berg, C. A. (2000). Intellectual development in adulthood. In R. J. Sternberg (Ed.), *The handbook of intelligence* (pp. 117–137). New York: Cambridge University Press.

Berg, C. A., & Klaczynski, P. A. (1996). Practical intelligence and problem solving: Searching for perspectives. In F. Blanchard-Fields & T. M. Hess (Eds.), *Perspectives on cognitive change in adulthood and aging.* New York: McGraw-Hill.

Berger, A. S. (1993). *Dying and death in law and medicine: A forensic primer for health and legal professionals.* Westport, CT: Praeger.

Berger, S. E., & Adolph, K. E. (2003). Infants use handrails as tools in locomotor task. *Developmental Psychology, 39,* 594–605.

Berger, S. E., Adolph, K. E., & Lobo, S. A. (2005). Out of the toolbox: Toddlers differentiate wobbly and wooden handrails. *Child Development, 76,* 1294–1307.

Bering, J. M., & Bjorklund, D. F. (2004). The natural emergence of reasoning about the afterlife as a developmental regularity. *Developmental Psychology, 40,* 217–233.

Berk, L. E. (1992). Children's private speech: An overview of theory and the status of research. In R. M. Diaz & L. E. Berk (Eds.), *Private speech: From social interaction to self-regulation.* Hillsdale, NJ: Erlbaum.

Berk, L. E., & Landau, S. (1993). Private speech of learning disabled and normally achieving children in classroom academic and laboratory contexts. *Child Development, 64,* 556–571.

Berk, L. E., & Winsler, A. (1995). *Scaffolding children's learning: Vygotsky and early childhood education.* Washington, DC: National Association for the Education of Young Children.

Berkowitz, G., Wolff, M., Janevic, T., Holzman, I., Yehunda, R., & Landrigan, P. (2003). The World Trade Center disaster and intrauterine growth restriction. *Journal of the American Medical Association, 290,* 595–596.

Berkowitz, M. W., & Gibbs, J. C. (1983). Measuring the developmental features of moral discussion. *Merrill-Palmer Quarterly, 29,* 399–410.

Berlin, L. J. (2005). Interventions to enhance early attachments. The state of the field today. In L. J. Berlin, Y. Ziv, L. Amaya-Jackson, & M. T. Greenberg (Eds.), *Enhancing early attachments: Theory, research, intervention, and policy.* New York: Guilford.

Berman, A. L., & Jobes, D. A. (1991). *Adolescent suicide: Assessment and intervention.* Washington, DC: American Psychological Association.

Berman, W. H., & Sperling, M. B. (1991). Parental attachment and emotional distress in the transition to college. *Journal of Youth and Adolescence, 20,* 427–440.

Bernal, M. E., & Knight, G. P. (1997). Ethnic identity of Latino children. In J. G. Garcia & M. C. Zea (Eds.), *Psychological interventions and research with Latino populations.* Boston: Allyn & Bacon.

Berndt, T. J., & Murphy, L. M. (2002). Influences of friends and friendships: Myths, truths, and research recommendations. In R. V. Kail (Ed.), *Advances in child development and behavior* (Vol. 30). San Diego: Academic Press.

Bernstein, A. C., & Cowan, P. A. (1975). Children's concepts of how people get babies. *Child Development, 46,* 77–91.

Berry, J. W., Poortinga, Y. H., Segall, M., & Dasen, P. R. (1992). *Cross-cultural psychology: research and applications.* Cambridge, England: Cambridge University Press.

Berson, E. L. (2000). Nutrition and retinal degenerations. *International Ophthalmology Clinic, 40,* 93–111.

Bertenthal, B. I., & Fischer, K. W. (1978). Development of self-recognition in the infant. *Developmental Psychology, 14,* 44–50.

Berthier, N. E., & Keen, R. (2006). Development of reaching in infancy. *Experimental Brain Research, 169,* 507–518.

Bertman, S. L. (1991). Children and death: Insights, hindsights, and illuminations. In D. Papadatou & C. Papadatos (Eds.), *Children and Death.* New York: Hemisphere.

Berzonsky, M. D., & Kuk, L. S. (2000). Identity status, identity processing style, and the transition to university. *Journal of Adolescent Research, 15,* 81–98.

Bess, F. H., & McConnell, F. E. (1981). *Audiology, education, and the hearing impaired child.* St. Louis: Mosby.

Best, D. L. (1993). Inducing children to generate mnemonic organizational strategies: An examination of long-term retention and materials. *Developmental Psychology, 29,* 324–336.

Best, D. L., & Williams, J. E. (1993). A cross-cultural viewpoint. In A. E. Beall & R. J. Sternberg (Eds.), *The psychology of gender* (pp. 215–248). New York: Guilford Press.

Beyer, S. (1995). Maternal employment and children's academic achievement: Parenting styles as mediating variable. *Developmental Review, 15,* 212–253.

Beyers, J. M., Bates, J. E., Pettit, G. S., & Dodge, K. A. (2003). Neighborhood structure, parenting processes, and the development of youths' externalizing behaviors: A multilevel analysis. *American Journal of Community Psychology, 31,* 35–53.

Bhatara, V., Loudenberg, R., & Ellis, R. (2006). Association of attention deficit hyperactivity disorder and gestational alcohol exposure: An exploratory study. *Journal of Attention Disorders, 9,* 515–522.

Bianchi, S. M. (2000). Maternal employment and time with children: Dramatic change or surprising continuity? *Demography, 37,* 401–414.

Bianchi, S. M., Milkie, M. A., Sayer, L. C., & Robinson, J. P. (2000). Is anyone doing the housework? Trends in the gender division of household labor. *Social Forces, 79,* 191–228.

Bick, D. P., & Lau, E. C. (2006). Preimplantation genetic diagnosis. *Pediatric Clinics of North America, 53,* 559–577.

Biederman, I., Cooper, E. E., Fox, P. W., & Mahadevan, R. S. (1992). Unexceptional spatial memory in an exceptional memorist. *Journal of Experimental Psychology: Learning, Memory, and Cognition, 18,* 654–657.

Biederman, J., Milberger, S., Faraone, S. V., Kiely, K., Guite, J., Mick, E., et al. (1995). Family-environment risk factors for attention-deficit hyperactivity disorder: A test of Rutter's indicators of adversity. *Archives of General Psychiatry, 52,* 464–470.

Bierhoff, H., & Schmohr, M. (2003). Romantic and marital relationships. In F. R. Lang & K. L. Fingerman (Eds.), *Growing together. Personal relationships across the life span.* Cambridge, UK: Cambridge University Press.

Bierman, K. L. (2004). *Peer rejection: Developmental processes and intervention strategies.* New York: Guilford.

Bigler, R. S., & Liben, L. S. (1990). The role of attitudes and interventions in gender-schematic processing. *Child Development, 61,* 1440–1452.

Billing, L., Eriksson, M., Jonsson, B., Steneroth, G., & Zetterstrom, R. (1994). The influence of environmental factors on behavioral problems in 8-year-old children exposed to amphetamine during fetal life. *Child Abuse and Neglect, 18,* 3–9.

Binstock, R. H. (2004). The search for prolongevity: A contentious pursuit. In S. G. Post & R. H. Binstock (Eds.), *The fountain of youth: Cultural, scientific, and ethical perspectives on a biomedical goal.* New York: Oxford University Press.

Bird, A., & Reese, E. (2006). Emotional reminiscing and the development of an autobiographical self. *Developmental Psychology, 42,* 613–626.

Birdsong, D. (1999). Introduction: Whys and why nots of the critical period hypothesis for second language acquisition. In D. Birdsong (Ed.), *Second language acquisition and the critical period hypothesis.* Mahwah, NJ: Erlbaum.

Birdsong, D. (2005). Interpreting age effects in second language acquisition. In J. Kroll & A.

de Groot (Eds.), *Handbook of bilingualism: Psycholinguistic approaches.* New York: Oxford University Press.

Birnbacher, R., Messerschmidt, & Pollak, A. P. (2002). Diagnosis and prevention of neural tube defects. *Current Opinion in Urology, 12,* 461–464.

Biro, S. & Leslie, A. M. (2007). Infants' perception of goal-directed actions: Development through cue-based bootstrapping. *Developmental Science, 10,* 379–398.

Birren, J. E., Butler, R. N., Greenhouse, S. W., Sokoloff, L., & Yarrow, M. R. (Eds.). (1963). *Human aging: A biological and behavioral study.* Washington, DC: U.S. Government Printing Office.

Birren, J. E., & Fisher, L. M. (1995). Aging and speed of behavior: Possible consequences for psychological functioning. *Annual Review of Psychology, 46,* 329–353.

Birren, J. E., & Schroots, J. J. F. (2006). Autobiographical memory and the narrative self over the life span. In J. E. Birren & K. W. Schaie (Eds.), *Handbook of the psychology of aging* (6th ed.). Burlington, MA: Elsevier Academic Press.

Bishop, J. A., & Cooke, L. M. (1975). Moths, melanism and clean air. *Scientific American, 232,* 90–99.

Bishop, J. E., & Waldholz, M. (1990). *Genome. The story of the most astonishing scientific adventure of our time: The attempt to map all the genes in the human body.* New York: Simon & Schuster.

Bivens, J. A., & Berk, L. E. (1990). A longitudinal study of the development of elementary school children's private speech. *Merrill-Palmer Quarterly, 36,* 443–463.

Bjork, J. M., Knutson, B., Fong, G. W., Caggiano, D. M., Bennett, S. M., & Hommer, D. W. (2004). Incentive-elicited brain activation in adolescents: Similarities and differences from young adults. *The Journal of Neuroscience, 24,* 1793–1802.

Bjork, R. A., & Bjork, E. L. (Eds.) (1998). *Memory.* New York: Academic Press.

Bjorklund, D. F. (1985). The role of conceptual knowledge in the development of organization in children's memory. In C. J. Brainerd & M. Pressley (Eds.), *Basic processes in memory development: Progress in cognitive development research.* New York: Springer-Verlag.

Bjorklund, D. F. (1995). *Children's thinking: Developmental function and individual differences.* Pacific Grove, CA: Brooks/Cole.

Bjorklund, D. F. (1997). In search of a metatheory for cognitive development (or, Piaget is dead and I don't feel so good myself). *Child Development, 68,* 144–148.

Bjorklund, D. F., Brown, R. D., & Bjorklund, B. R. (2002). Children's eyewitness memory: Changing reports and changing representations. In P. Graf & N. Ohta (Eds.), *Life-span development of human memory* (pp. 101–126). Cambridge, MA: Massachusetts Institute of Technology.

Bjorklund, D. F., Miller, P. H., Coyle, T. R., & Slawinski, J. L. (1997). Instructing children to use memory strategies: Evidence of utilization deficiencies in memory training studies. *Developmental Review, 17,* 411–441.

Bjorklund, D. F., & Pellegrini, A. D. (2002). *The origins of human nature.* Washington, DC: American Psychological Association.

Black, J. E., Isaacs, K. R., & Greenough, W. T. (1991). Usual vs. successful aging: Some notes on experiential factors. *Neurobiology of Aging, 12,* 325–328.

Blackburn, J. A. (1984). The influence of personality, curriculum, and memory correlates on formal reasoning in young adults and elderly persons. *Journal of Gerontology, 39,* 207–209.

Blackburn, J. A., & Papalia, D. E. (1992). The study of adult cognition from a Piagetian perspective. In R. J. Sternberg & C. A. Berg (Eds.), *Intellectual development.* New York: Cambridge University Press.

Blair, R. J. R. (2003). Did Cain fail to represent the thoughts of Abel before he killed him? The relationship between theory of mind and aggression. In B. Repacholi & V. Slaughter (Eds.), *Individual differences in theory of mind: Implications for typical and atypical development.* New York: Psychology Press.

Blake, S. M., Simkin, L., Ledsky, R., Perkins, C., & Calabrese, J. M. (2001). Effects of a parent–child communications intervention on young adolescents' risk for early onset of sexual intercourse. *Family Planning Perspectives, 33,* 52–62.

Blakemore, J. E. O. (2003). Children's beliefs about violating gender norms: Boys shouldn't look like girls, and girls shouldn't act like boys. *Sex Roles, 49,* 411–420.

Blanchard, R., Cantor, J. M., Bogaert, A. F., Breedlove, S. M., & Ellis, L. (2006). Interaction of fraternal birth order and handedness in the development of male homosexuality. *Hormonal Behavior, 49,* 405–414.

Blanchard, R., & Lippa, R. A. (2007). Birth order, sibling sex ratio, handedness, and sexual orientation of male and female participants in a BBC internet research project. *Archives of Sexual Behavior, 36,* 163–176.

Blanchard-Fields, F. (1986). Reasoning on social dilemmas varying in emotional saliency: An adult developmental perspective. *Psychology and Aging, 1,* 325–333.

Blanchard-Fields, F. (1996). Social cognitive development in adulthood and aging. In F. Blanchard-Fields & T. M. Hess (Eds.), *Perspectives on cognitive change in adulthood and aging.* New York: McGraw-Hill.

Blanchard-Fields, F., Chen, Y., & Norris, L. (1997). Everyday problem solving across the adult life span: Influence of domain specificity and cognitive appraisal. *Psychology and Aging, 12,* 684–693.

Blasi, A. (1980). Bridging moral cognition and moral action: A critical review of the literature. *Psychological Bulletin, 88,* 1–45.

Blatchford, P., Moriarty, V., Edmonds, S., & Martin, C. (2002). Relationships between class size and teaching: A multimethod analysis of English infant schools. *American Educational Research Journal, 39,* 101–132.

Blazer, D. G. (1993). *Depression in late life.* St. Louis: Mosby.

Blazer, D. G. (2003). Depression in late life: Review and commentary. *Journal of Gerontology: Medical Sciences, 58A,* 249–265.

Blieszner, R., & Roberto, K. A. (2004). Friendship across the life span: Reciprocity in individual and relationship development. In F. R. Lang & K. L. Fingerman (Eds.), *Growing together: Personal relationships across the life span.* Cambridge, UK: Cambridge University Press.

Block, C. E. (2000). Dyadic and gender differences in perceptions of the grandparent–grandchild relationship. *International Journal of Aging and Human Development, 51,* 85–104.

Bloom, L. (1998). Language acquisition in its developmental context. In D. Kuhn & R. S. Siegler (Vol. Eds.), W. Damon (Editor-in-Chief), *Handbook of child psychology: Vol. 2. Cognition, perception, and language* (5th ed., pp. 309–370). New York: Wiley.

Bloom, L., & Tinker, E. (2001). The intentionality model and language acquisition: Engagement, effort, and the essential tension. *Monographs of the Society for Research in Child Development, 66* (Serial No. 267).

Bluebond-Langner, M. (1977). Meanings of death to children. In H. Feifel (Ed.), *New meanings of death.* New York: McGraw-Hill.

Blumberg, E. S. (2003). The lives and voices of highly sexual women. *The Journal of Sex Research, 40,* 146–157.

Blumberg, F., & Torenberg, M. (2005). The effects of spatial configuration on preschoolers' attention strategies, selective attention, and incidental learning. *Infant and Child Development, 14,* 243–258.

Boatella-Costa, E., Costas-Moragas, C., Botet-Mussons, F., Fornieles-Deu, A., & De Cáceres-Zurita, M. L. (2007). Behavioral gender differences in the neonatal period according to the Brazelton scale. *Early Human Development, 83,* 91–97.

Bock, J. (2005). Farming, foraging, and children's play in the Okavango Delta, Botswana. In A. D. Pellegrini & P. K. Smith (Eds.), *The nature of play: Great apes and humans.* New York: Guilford Press.

Bodkin, N. L., Alexander, T. M., Ortmeyer, H. K., Johnson, E., & Hansen, B. C. (2003). Morbidity and mortality in laboratory-maintained rhesus monkeys and effects of long-term dietary restriction. *Journal of Gerontology: Biological Sciences, 58A,* 212–219.

Bodrova, E., & Leong, D. J. (1996). *Tools of the mind: The Vygotskian approach to early childhood education.* Englewood Cliffs, NJ: Prentice Hall.

Boerner, K., Wortman, C. B., & Bonanno, G. A. (2005). Resilient or at risk? A 4-year study of older adults who initially showed high or low distress following conjugal loss. *Journal of Gerontology: Psychological Sciences, 60B,* P67–P73.

Bogenschneider, K. (1997). Parental involvement in adolescent schooling: A proximal process with transcontextual validity. *Journal of Marriage and the Family, 59,* 718–733.

Boggiano, A. K., & Katz, P. (1991). Maladaptive achievement patterns in students: The role of teachers' controlling strategies. *Journal of Social Issues, 47(4),* 35–51.

Bogoch, I. I., House, R. A., & Kudla, I. (2005). Perceptions about hearing protection and noise-induced hearing loss of attendees of rock concerts. *Canadian Journal of Public Health, 96,* 69–72.

Bohannon, J. N., & Bonvillian, J. D. (2005). Theoretical approaches to language development. In J. Berko-Gleason (Ed.), *The development of language* (6th ed.). Needham Heights, MA: Allyn & Bacon.

Bohannon, J. N., & Stanowicz, L. (1988). The issue of negative evidence: Adult responses to children's language errors. *Developmental Psychology, 24,* 684–689.

Bohannon, J. R. (1990–1991). Grief responses of spouses following the death of a child: A longi-

tudinal study. *Omega: Journal of Death and Dying, 22,* 109–121.

Boldizar, J. P. (1991). Assessing sex-typing and androgyny in children: The children's sex-role inventory. *Developmental Psychology, 27,* 505–515.

Boles, S., Biglan, A., & Smolkowski, K. (2006). Relationships among negative and positive behaviours in adolescence. *Journal of Adolescence, 29,* 33–52.

Bolger, K. E., & Patterson, C. J. (2001). Developmental pathways from child maltreatment to peer rejection. *Child Development, 72,* 549–568.

Boll, T., Ferring, D., & Filipp, S. (2005). Effects of parental differential treatment on relationship quality with siblings and parents: Justice evaluations as mediators. *Social Justice Research, 18,* 155–182.

Bollag, B. (2006). The debate over deaf education. *The Chronicle of Higher Education, 52,* A18–A21.

Boloh, Y., & Champaud, C. (1993). The past conditional verb form in French children: The role of semantics in late grammatical development. *Journal of Child Language, 20,* 169–189.

Bonanno, G. A. (2001). Introduction. New direction in bereavement research and theory. *American Behavioral Scientist, 44,* 718–725.

Bonanno, G. A. (2004). Loss, trauma, and human resilience: Have we underestimated the human capacity to thrive after extremely aversive events? *American Psychologist, 59,* 20–28.

Bonanno, G. A., & Field, N. P. (2001). Examining the delayed grief hypothesis across 5 years of bereavement. *American Behavioral Scientist, 44,* 798–816.

Bonanno, G. A., & Kaltman, S. (1999). Toward an integrative perspective on bereavement. *Psychological Bulletin, 125,* 760–776.

Bonanno, G. A., & Kaltman, S. (2000). The varieties of grief experience. *Clinical Psychology Review, 21,* 705–734.

Bonanno, G. A., Neria, Y., Mancini, A., Coifman, K.G., Litz, B., & Insel, B. (2007). Is there more to complicated grief than depression and posttraumatic stress disorder? A test of incremental validity. *Journal of Abnormal Psychology, 116,* 342–351.

Bonanno, G. A., Papa, A., Lalande, K., Zhang, N., & Noll, J. G. (2005). Grief processing and deliberate grief avoidance: A prospective comparison of bereaved spouses and parents in the United States and the People's Republic of China. *Journal of Consulting and Clinical Psychology, 73,* 86–98.

Bonanno, G. A., Wortman, C. B., Lehman, D. R., Tweed, R. G., Haring, M., Sonnega, J., et al. (2002). Resilience to loss and chronic grief: A prospective study from preloss to 18 months postloss. *Journal of Personality and Social Psychology, 83,* 1150–1164.

Bonanno, G. A., Wortman, C. B., & Nesse, R. M. (2004). Prospective patterns of resilience and maladjustment during widowhood. *Psychology and Aging, 19,* 260–271.

Bongers, I. L., Koot, H. M., van der Ende, J., & Verhulst, F. C. (2003). The normative development of child and adolescent problem behavior. *Journal of Abnormal Psychology, 112,* 179–192.

Boodman, S. G. (2006, June 13). Too much information. Results of home DNA tests can shock, misinform some users. *The Washington Post,* pp. F1, F4.

Books, S. (Ed.) (2007). *Invisible children in the society and its schools* (3rd ed.). Mahwah, New Jersey: Lawrence Erlbaum Associates.

Boom, J., Brugman, D., & van der Heijden, P. G. M. (2001). Hierarchical structure of moral stages assessed by a sorting task. *Child Development, 72,* 535–548.

Booth, A., & Amato, P. R. (2001). Parental predivorce relations and offspring postdivorce well-being. *Journal of Marriage and the Family, 63,* 197–212.

Booth, A., & Johnson, D. (1988). Premarital cohabitation and marital success. *Journal of Family Issues, 9,* 255–272.

Boothe, D., Sethna, B. W., & Stanley, J. C. (2000). Special educational opportunities for able high school students: A description of residential early-college-entrance programs. *Journal of Secondary Gifted Education, 26.*

Borders, A. E., Grobman, W. A., Amsden, L. B., Holl, J. L. (2007). Chronic stress and low birth weight neonates in a low-income population of women. *Obstetrics and Gynecology, 109,* 331–338.

Boris, N. W., & Zeanah, C. H. (1999). Disturbances and disorders of attachment in infancy: An overview. *Infant Mental Health Journal, 20,* 1–9.

Borkenau, P., Riemann, R., Angleitner, A., & Spinath, F. M. (2001). Genetic and environmental influences on observed personality: Evidence from the German Observational Study of Adult Twins. *Journal of Personality and Social Psychology, 80,* 655–668.

Born, J., Rasch, B., & Gais, S. (2006). Sleep to remember. *Neuroscientist, 12,* 410–424.

Bornstein, M. H., & Bradley, R. H. (2003). *Socioeconomic status, parenting, and child development.* Mahwah, NJ: Erlbaum.

Bornstein, M. H., & Sawyer, J. (2006). Family systems. In K. McCartney & D. Phillips (Eds.), *Blackwell handbook of early childhood development.* Malden, MA: Blackwell.

Bornstein, M. H., Putnick, D. L., Suwalsky, J. T. D., & Gini, M. (2006). Maternal chronological age, prenatal and prenatal history, social support, and parenting of infants, *Child Development, 77,* 875–892

Boston Retinal Implant Project. (2004). Available online http://www.bostonretinalimplant.org/ (retrieved September 8, 2004).

Botkin, D. R., Weeks, M. O., & Morris, J. E. (2000). Changing marriage role expectations: 1961–1996. *Sex Roles, 42,* 933–942.

Bouchard, T. J., Jr. (1984). Twins reared together and apart: What they tell us about human diversity. In S. W. Fox (Ed.), *Individuality and determinism: Chemical and biological bases.* New York: Plenum.

Bouchard, T. J., Jr. (2004). Genetic influence on human psychological traits: A survey. *Current Directions in Psychological Science, 13,* 148–151.

Bouchard, T. J., Jr., Lykken, D. T., McGue, M., Segal, N. L., & Tellegen, A. (1990). Sources of human psychological differences: The Minnesota Study of Twins Reared Apart. *Science, 250,* 223–228.

Bouchard, T. J., Jr., & McGue, M. (1981). Family studies of intelligence: A review. *Science, 212,* 1055–1059.

Bouchard, T. J., Jr., & Pedersen, N. (1999). Twins reared apart: Nature's double experiment. In M. C. LaBuda & E. L. Grigorenko (Eds.), *On* the way to individuality: *Methodological issues in behavioral genetics.* Commack, NY: Nova Science Publishers.

Bouldin, P. (2006). An investigation of fantasy predisposition and fantasy style of children with imaginary companions. *The Journal of Genetic Psychology, 167,* 17–29.

Boulet, S. L., Alexander, G. R., Salihu, H. M., Kirby, R. S., & Carlo, W. A. (2006). Fetal growth risk curves: Defining levels of fetal growth restriction by neonatal death risk. *American Journal of Obstetrics and Gynecology, 195,* 572–1577.

Bowen, B. A. (1999). Four puzzles in adult literacy: Reflections on the national adult literacy survey. *Journal of Adolescent & Adult Literacy, 42,* 314–323.

Bower, T. G. R., Broughton, J. M., & Moore, M. K. (1970). The coordination of vision and tactile input in infancy. *Perception and Psychophysics, 8,* 51–53.

Bowlby, J. (1960). Separation anxiety. *International Journal of Psychoanalysis, 41,* 89–113.

Bowlby, J. (1969). *Attachment and loss: Vol. 1. Attachment.* New York: Basic Books.

Bowlby, J. (1973). *Attachment and loss: Vol. 2. Separation.* New York: Basic Books.

Bowlby, J. (1980). *Attachment and loss: Vol. 3. Loss, sadness and depression.* New York: Basic Books.

Bowlby, J. (1988). *A secure base: Parent–child attachment and healthy human development.* New York: Basic Books.

Bowler, D. (2007). *Autism spectrum disorders: Psychological theory and research.* West Sussex, UK: Wiley.

Boyce, P. M. (2003). Risk factors for postnatal depression: A review and risk factors in Australian populations. *Archives of Women's Mental Health, Supplement 2,* S43–S50.

Bracey, J. R., Bamaca, M. Y., & Umana-Taylor, A.J. (2004). Examining ethnic identity and self-esteem among biracial and monoracial adolescents. *Journal of Youth and Adolescence, 33,* 123–132.

Brabeck, M. (1983). Moral judgment: Theory and research on differences between males and females. *Developmental Review, 3,* 274–291.

Brabyn, J. (2000). Visual function in the oldest old. Papers from the 15th Biennial Eye Research Seminar. New York: *Research to Prevent Blindness.* [Available online: http://www.rpbusa.org/new/pdf/jbrabyn1.pdf].

Bradbard, M. R., Martin, C. L., Endsley, R. C., & Halverson, C. F. (1986). Influence of sex stereotypes on children's exploration and memory: A competence versus performance distinction. *Developmental Psychology, 22,* 481–486.

Braddock, J. H., II, & McPartland, J. M. (1993). Education of early adolescents. *Review of Educational Research, 19,* 135–170.

Bradley, R. H., Caldwell, B. M., Rock, S. L., Ramey, C. T., Barnard, K. E., Gray, C., et al. (1989). Home environment and cognitive development in the first 3 years of life: A collaborative study involving six sites and three ethnic groups in North America. *Developmental Psychology, 25,* 217–235.

Bradley, R. H., Convyn, R. F., Burchinal, M., McAdoo, H. P., & Coll, C. G. (2001). The home environments of children in the United States, Part II: Relations with behavioral development through age thirteen. *Child Development, 72,* 1868–1886.

Bradley, R. H., & Corwyn, R. F. (2002). Socioeconomic status and child development. *Annual Review of Psychology, 53,* 371–399.

Bradmetz, J., & Mathy, F. (2006). An estimate of the Flynn Effect: Changes in IQ and subtest gains of 10-year-old French children between 1965 and 1988. *Psychological Reports, 99,* 743–746.

Brady, S. S., & Halpern-Fisher, B. L. (2007). Adolescents' reported consequences of having oral sex versus vaginal sex. *Pediatrics, 119,* 229–236.

Brainerd, C. J., & Gordon, L. L. (1994). Development of verbatim and gist memory for numbers. *Developmental Psychology, 30,* 163–177.

Brainerd, C. J. & Reyna, V. F. (1993). Domains of fuzzy trace theory. In M. L. Howe & R. Pasnak (Ed.), *Emerging themes in cognitive development: Vol. 1. Foundations.* New York: Springer-Verlag.

Braithwaite, V. (2002). Reducing ageism. In T. D. Nelson (Ed.), *Ageism: Stereotyping and prejudice against older persons.* Cambridge, MA: The MIT Press.

Brandtstädter, J., & Greve, W. (1994). The aging self: Stabilizing and protective processes. *Developmental Review, 14,* 52–80.

Brassett-Harknett, A., & Butler, N. (2007). Attention-deficit/hyperactivity disorder: An overview of the etiology and a review of the literature relating to the correlates and lifecourse outcomes for men and women. *Clinical Psychology Review, 27,* 188–210.

Bratberg, G. H., Nilsen, T. I., Holmen, T. L., & Vatten, L. J. (2005). Sexual maturation in early adolescence and alcohol drinking and cigarette smoking in late adolescence: A prospective study of 2,129 Norwegian girls and boys. *European Journal of Pediatrics, 164,* 621–625.

Braude, P. (2006, August 10). Preimplantation diagnosis for genetic susceptibility. *New England Journal of Medicine, 355,* 541–543.

Braver, E. R., & Trempel, R. E. (2004). Are older drivers actually at higher risk of involvement in collisions resulting in deaths or non-fatal injuries among their passengers and other road users? *Injury Prevention, 10,* 27–32.

Bray, N. W., Hersh, R. E., & Turner, L. A. (1985). Selective remembering during adolescence. *Developmental Psychology, 21,* 290–294.

Brazelton, T. B. (1979). Behavioral competence of the newborn infant. *Seminars in Perinatology, 3,* 35–44.

Breedlove, S. M. (1994). Sexual differentiation of the human nervous system. *Annual Review of Psychology, 45,* 389–418.

Bregman, J. D. (2005). Definitions and characteristics of the spectrum. In D. Zager (Ed.), *Autism spectrum disorders: Identification, education, and treatment* (3rd ed.). Mahwah, NJ: Erlbaum.

Brehmer, Y., Li, S., Müller, V., von Oertzen, T., Lindenberger, U. (2007). Memory plasticity across the life-span: Uncovering children's latent potential. *Developmental Psychology, 43,* 465–478.

Bremner, J. D., & Narayan, M. (1998). The effects of stress on memory and the hippocampus throughout the life cycle: Implications for childhood development and aging. *Development and Psychopathology, 10,* 871–886.

Bremner, J. G., Johnson, S. P., Slater, A., Mason, U., Foster, K., Cheshire, A., & Spring, J. (2005). Conditions for young infants' perception of object trajectories. *Child Development, 76,* 1029–1043.

Brendgen, M., Vitaro, F., & Bukowski, W. M. (2000). Deviant trends and early adolescents' emotional and behavioral adjustment. *Journal of Research on Adolescence, 10,* 173–189.

Brendgen, M., Vitaro, F., Doyle, A. B., Markiewicz, D., & Bukowski, W. M. (2002). Same-sex peer relations and romantic relationships during early adolescence: Interactive links to emotional, behavioral, and academic adjustment. *Merrill-Palmer Quarterly, 48,* 77–103.

Brenick, A., Henning, A., Killen, M., O'Connor, A., & Collins, M. (2007). Social evaluations of stereotypic images in video games: Unfair, legitimate, or 'just entertainment'? *Youth & Society, 38,* 395–419.

Brent, S. B., Speece, M. W., Lin, C. G., Dong, Q., & Yang, C. M. (1996). The development of the concept of death among Chinese and U.S. children 3–17 years of age: From binary to "fuzzy" concepts? *Omega: Journal of Death and Dying, 33,* 67–83.

Bretherton, I. (1996). Internal working models of attachment relationships as related to resilient coping. In G. G. Noam, & K. W. Fischer (Eds.), *Development and vulnerability in close relationships.* Mahwah, NJ: Erlbaum.

Bretherton, I., & Beeghly, M. (1982). Talking about internal states: The acquisition of an explicit theory of mind. *Developmental Psychology, 18,* 906–921.

Bretherton, I., Stolberg, U., & Kreye, M. (1981). Engaging strangers in proximal interaction: Infants' social initiative. *Developmental Psychology, 17,* 746–755.

Brewster, K. L., & Padavic, I. (2000). Changes in gender-ideology, 1977–1996: The contributions of intracohort change and population turnover. *Journal of Marriage and the Family, 62,* 477–487.

Bridge, J. A., Day, N. L., Day, R., Richardson, G. A., Birmaher, B., & Brent, D. A. (2003). Major depressive disorder in adolescents exposed to a friend's suicide. *Journal of the American Academy of Child and Adolescent Psychiatry, 42,* 1294–1300.

Bridges, L. J., & Grolnick, W. S. (1995). The development of emotional self-regulation in infancy and early childhood. In N. Eisenberg (Ed.), *Social development: Vol. 15. Review of personality and social psychology.* Thousand Oaks, CA: Sage.

Bright, J. E. H., Pryor, R. G. L., & Harpham, L. (2005). The role of chance events in career decision making. *Journal of Vocational Behavior, 66,* 561–576.

Brilleslijper-Kater, S. N., & Baartman, H. E. M. (2000). What do young children know about sex? Research on the sexual knowledge of children between the ages of 2 and 6 years. *Child Abuse Review, 9,* 166–182.

Broberg, A. G., Wessels, H., Lamb, M. E., & Hwang, C. P. (1997). Effects of day care on the development of cognitive abilities in 8-year-olds: A longitudinal study. *Developmental Psychology, 33,* 62–69.

Brody, E. B., & Brody, N. (1976). *Intelligence: Nature, determinants, and consequences.* New York: Academic Press.

Brody, E. M. (1985). Parent care as a normative family stress. *Gerontologist, 25,* 19–29.

Brody, E. M. (2004). *Women in the middle: Their parent care years* (2nd ed.). New York: Springer.

Brody, E. M., Litvin, S. J., Hoffman, C., & Kleban, M. H. (1992). Differential effects of daughters' marital status on their parent care experiences. *Gerontologist, 32*, 58–67.

Brody, G. H. (2003). Parental monitoring: Action and reaction. In A. C. Crouter, & A. Booth (Eds.), *Children's influence on family dynamics: The neglected side of family relationships.* Mahwah, NJ: Erlbaum.

Brody, G. H. (2004). Siblings' direct and indirect contributions to child development. *Current Directions in Psychological Science, 13*, 124–126.

Brody, G. H., & Shaffer, D. R. (1982). Contributions of parents and peers to children's moral socialization. *Developmental Review, 2*, 31–75.

Brody, J. A., Grant, M. D., Frateschi, L. J., Miller, S. C., & Zhang, H. (2000). Reproductive longevity and increased life expectancy. *Age and Ageing, 29*, 75–78.

Broen, A. N., Moum, T., Bodtker, A. S., & Ekeberg, O. (2004). Psychological impact on women of miscarriage versus induced abortion: A 2-year follow-up study. *Psychosomatic Medicine, 66*, 265–271.

Bronfenbrenner, U. (1979). *The ecology of human development: Experiments by nature and design.* Cambridge, MA: Harvard University Press.

Bronfenbrenner, U. (1989). Ecological systems theory. In R. Vasta (Ed.), *Annals of child development: Vol. 6. Theories of child development: Revised formulations and current issues.* Greenwich, CT: JAI Press.

Bronfenbrenner, U., & Morris, P. A. (2006). The bioecological model of human development. In W. Damon & R. M. Lerner (Eds. in Chief) & R. M. Lerner (Vol. Ed.), *Handbook of child psychology: Vol. 1. Theoretical models of human development* (6th ed.). Hoboken, NJ: Wiley.

Brooks-Gunn, J., Britto, P. R., & Brady, C. (1999). Struggling to make ends meet: Poverty and child development. In M. E. Lamb (Ed.), *Parenting and child development in "nontraditional" families.* Mahwah, NJ: Erlbaum.

Brooks-Gunn, J., Klebanov, P. K., & Duncan, G. J. (1996). Ethnic differences in children's intelligence test scores: Role of economic deprivation, home environment, and maternal characteristics. *Child Development, 67*, 396–408.

Brooks-Gunn, J., & Lewis, M. (1981). Infant social perception: Responses to pictures of parents and strangers. *Developmental Psychology, 17*, 647–649.

Brown, A. L., & Smiley, S. S. (1978). The development of strategies for studying text. *Child Development, 49*, 1076–1088.

Brown, B. B. (1999). "You're going out with who?" Peer group influences on adolescent romantic relationships. In W. Furman, B. B. Brown, & C. Feiring (Eds.), *The development of romantic relationships in adolescence.* Cambridge, England: Cambridge University Press.

Brown, B. B., Feiring, C., & Furman, W. (1999). Missing the love boat. Why researchers have shied away from adolescent romance. In W. Furman, B. B. Brown, & C. Feiring (Eds.), *The development of romantic relationships in adolescence.* Cambridge, England: Cambridge University Press.

Brown, B. B., & Lohr, M. J. (1987). Peer-group affiliation and adolescent self-esteem: An integration of ego–identity and symbolic-interaction theories. *Journal of Personality and Social Psychology, 52*, 47–55.

Brown, B. B., Mory, M. S., & Kinney, D. (1994). Casting adolescent crowds in a relational perspective: Caricature, channel, and context. In R. Montemayor, G. R. Adams, & T. P. Gulotta (Eds.), *Personal relationships during adolescence.* Thousand Oaks, CA: Sage.

Brown, B. B., Mounts, N., Lamborn, S. D., & Steinberg, L. (1993). Parenting practices and peer group affiliation in adolescence. *Child Development, 64*, 467–482.

Brown, D. (2005, September 5). Study suggests 'Y' the male chromosome will endure. *The Washington Post*, p. A13.

Brown, J. D., L'Engle, K. D., Pardun, C. J., Guang, G., Kenneavy, K., & Jackson, C. (2006). Sexy media matter: Exposure to sexual content in music, movies, television, and magazines predicts black and white adolescents' sexual behavior. *Pediatrics, 117*, 1018–1027.

Brown, J. L. (1964). States in newborn infants. *Merrill-Palmer Quarterly, 10*, 313–327.

Brown, R., Cazden, C., & Bellugi, U. (1969). The child's grammar from I to III. In J. P. Hill (Ed.), *Minnesota Symposia on child psychology* (Vol. 2). Minneapolis: University of Minnesota Press.

Brown, R., & Hanlon, C. (1970). Derivational complexity and order of acquisition. In J. R. Hayes (Ed.), *Cognition and the development of language.* New York: Wiley.

Brown, S. M. (with contributions by J. G. Hay & H. Ostrer) (2003). *Essentials of medical genomics.* Hoboken, NJ: Wiley-Liss.

Brownell, C. A., & Carriger, M. S. (1990). Changes in cooperation and self/other differentiation during the second year. *Child Development, 61*, 1164–1174.

Bruck, M. (1990). Word recognition skills of adults with childhood diagnoses of dyslexia. *Developmental Psychology, 26*, 439–454.

Bruck, M. (1992). Persistence of dyslexics' phonological awareness deficits. *Developmental Psychology, 28*, 874–886.

Bruck, M., & Ceci, S. J. (1999). The suggestibility of children's memory. *Annual Review of Psychology, 50*, 419–439.

Bruer, J. T. (1999). The myth of the first three years: A new understanding of early brain development and lifelong learning. New York: Free Press.

Brugman, G. M. (2006). Wisdom and aging. In J. E. Birren & K. W. Schaie (Eds.), *Handbook of the psychology of aging* (6th ed.). Boston: Elsevier.

Bruner, J. S. (1983). *Child's talk: Learning to use language.* New York: Norton.

Bruner, J. S. (1997). Celebrating divergence: Piaget and Vygotsky. *Human Development, 40*, 63–73.

Bryant, C. M., Bolland, J. M., Burton, L. M., Hurt, T., & Bryant, B. M. (2006). The changing social context of relationships. In P. Noller & J. A. Feeney (Eds.), *Close relationships: Functions, forms, and processes.* New York: Psychology Press.

Bryant, P. (1998). Sensitivity to onset and rhyme does predict young children's reading: A comment on Muter, Hulme, Snowling, and Taylor (1997). *Journal of Experimental Child Psychology, 71*, 39–44.

Bryant-Waugh, R. (2007). Anorexia nervosa in children and adolescents. In T. Jaffa & B. McDermott (Eds.), *Eating disorders in children and adolescents.* Cambridge, UK: Cambridge University Press.

Buchanan, C. M., Eccles, J. S., & Becker, J. B. (1992). Are adolescents the victims of raging hormones? Evidence for activational effects of hormones on moods and behavior at adolescence. *Psychological Bulletin, 111*, 62–107.

Buchi, S., Morgeli, H., Schnyder, U., Jenewein, J., Hepp, U., Jina, E., Neuhaus, R., Fauchere, J., Bucher, H. U., & Sensky, T. (2007). Grief and post-traumatic growth in parents 2–6 years after the death of their extremely premature baby. *Psychotherapy and Psychosomatics, 76*, 106–114.

Buehler, C. A., Hogan, M. J., Robinson, B. E., & Levy, R. J. (1985–1986). The parental divorce transition: Divorce-related stressors and well-being. *Journal of Divorce, 9*, 61–81.

Bugental, D. B. (2001). *Parental cognitions as predictors of dyadic interaction with very young children.* Paper presented at the biennial meeting of the Society for Research in Child Development, Minneapolis, MN.

Bugental, D. B., & Beaulieu, D. A. (2003). A bio-social-cognitive approach to understanding and promoting the outcomes of children with medical and physical disorders. In R. V. Kail (Ed.), *Advances in child development and behavior* (Vol. 31). San Diego: Academic Press.

Bugental, D. B., Ellerson, P. C., Lin, E. K., Rainey, B., Kokotovic, A., & O'Hara, N. (2002). A cognitive approach to child abuse prevention. *Journal of Family Psychology, 16*, 243–258.

Buhrmester, D., Camparo, L., Christensen, A., Gonzales, L. S., & Hinshaw, S. P. (1992). Mothers and fathers interacting in dyads and triads with normal and hyperactive sons. *Developmental Psychology, 28*, 500–509.

Buhrmester, D., & Furman, W. (1986). The changing functions of friends in childhood: A neo-Sullivanian perspective. In V. J. Derlega & B. A. Winstead (Eds.), *Friendship and social interaction.* New York: Springer-Verlag.

Buitelaar, J., Huizink, A. C., Mulder, E., de Medina, P., & Visser, G. (2003). Prenatal stress and cognitive development and temperament in infants. *Neurobiological Aging, 24* (Suppl. 1), S53–S60.

Bulanda, R. E. (2004). Paternal involvement with children: The influence of gender ideologies. *Journal of Marriage and Family, 66*, 40–45.

Bulcroft, R. A. (1991). The value of physical change in adolescence: Consequences for the parent–adolescent exchange relationship. *Journal of Youth and Adolescence, 20*, 89–105.

Bulik, C. M., Sullivan, P. F., Tozzi, F., Furberg, H., Lichtenstein, P., & Pedersen, N. L. (2006). Prevalence, heritability, and prospective risk factors for anorexia nervosa. *Archives of General Psychiatry, 63*, 305–312.

Burack, J. A., Enns, J. T., Iarocci, G., & Randolph, B. (2000). Age differences in visual search for compound patterns: Long- versus short-range grouping. *Developmental Psychology, 36*, 731–740.

Burack, J. A., Flanagan, T., Peled, T., Sutton, H. M., Zygmuntowicz, C., & Manly, J. T. (2006). Social perspective-taking skills in maltreated children and adolescents. *Developmental Psychology, 42*, 207–217.

Burchinal, M. R., Roberts, J. E., Riggins, R., Zeisel, S. A., Neebe, E., & Bryant, D. (2000). Relating quality of center-based child care to early cognitive and language development longitudinally. *Child Development, 71*, 339–357.

Burgess, R. L., & MacDonald, K. (Eds.). (2005). *Evolutionary perspectives on human development*. Thousand Oaks, CA: Sage.

Burhans, K. K., & Dweck, C. S. (1995). Helplessness in early childhood: The role of contingent worth. *Child Development, 66,* 1719–1738.

Burke, T. M., Abramovitch, R., & Zlotkin, S. (2005). Children's understanding of the risks and benefits associated with research. *Journal of Medical Ethics, 31,* 715–720.

Burleson, M. H., Trevathan, W. R., & Todd, M. (2007). In the mood for love or vice versa? Exploring the relations among sexual activity, physical affection, affect, and stress in the daily lives of mid-aged women. *Archives of Sexual Behavior, 36,* 357–368.

Burn, S., O'Neil, A. K., & Nederend, S. (1996). Childhood tomboyishness and adult androgyny. *Sex Roles, 34,* 419–428.

Burns, G. W., & Bottino, P. J. (1989). *The science of genetics* (6th ed.). New York: Macmillan.

Burt, C. D. B., Kemp, S., & Conway, M. A. (2003). Themes, events, and episodes in autobiographical memory. *Memory & Cognition, 31,* 317–325.

Burt, S. A., McGue, M., DeMarte, J. A., Krueger, R. F., & Iacono, W. G. (2006). Timing of menarche and the origins of conduct disorder. *Archives of General Psychiatry, 63,* 890–896.

Burton, L. A., Hafetz, J., & Henninger, D. (2007). Gender differences in relational and physical aggression. *Social Behavior and Personality, 35,* 41–50.

Burton, L. M. (1990). Teenage childrearing as an alternative life-course strategy in multigenerational black families. *Human Nature, 1,* 123–143.

Burton, L. M. (1996a). Age norms, the timing of family role transitions, and intergenerational caregiving among aging African American women. *Gerontologist, 36,* 199–208.

Burton, L. M. (1996b). The timing of childbearing, family structure, and the role responsibilities of aging black women. In E. M. Hetherington & E. A. Blechman (Eds.), *Stress, coping, and resiliency in children and families.* Mahwah, NJ: Erlbaum.

Burton, R. V. (1963). The generality of honesty reconsidered. *Psychological Review, 70,* 481–499.

Burton, R. V. (1984). A paradox in theories and research in moral development. In W. M. Kurtines & J. L. Gewirtz (Eds.), *Morality, moral behavior, and moral development.* New York: Wiley.

Bus, A. G., & van Ijzendoorn, M. H. (1999). Phonological awareness and early reading: A meta-analysis of experimental training studies. *Journal of Educational Psychology, 91,* 403–414.

Busch-Rossnagel, N. A. (1997). Mastery motivation in toddlers. *Infants and Young Children, 9,* 1–11.

Bushman, B. J., & Anderson, C. A. (2001). Media violence and the American public. Scientific facts versus media misinformation. *American Psychologist, 56,* 477–489.

Bushnell, E. W., & Baxt, C. (1999). Children's haptic and cross-modal recognition with familiar and unfamiliar objects. *Journal of Experimental Psychology: Human Perception and Performance, 25,* 1867–1881.

Buss, A. H., & Perry, M. (1992). The aggression question. *Journal of Personality and Social Psychology, 63,* 452–459.

Buss, A. H., & Plomin, R. (1984). *Temperament: Early developing personality traits.* Hillsdale, NJ: Erlbaum.

Buss, D. M. (1995). Psychological sex differences: Origins through sexual selection. *American Psychologist, 50,* 164–168.

Butcher, P. R., Kalverboer, A. F., & Geuze, R. H. (2000). Infants' shifts of gaze from a central to a peripheral stimulus: A longitudinal study of development between 6 and 26 weeks. *Infant Behavior & Development, 23,* 3–21.

Butler, R. (1990). The effects of mastery and competitive conditions on self-assessment at different ages. *Child Development, 61,* 201–210.

Butler, R. (1999). Information seeking and achievement motivation in middle childhood and adolescence: The role of conceptions of ability. *Developmental Psychology, 35,* 146–163.

Butler, R. N. (1963). The life review: An interpretation of reminiscence in the aged. *Psychiatry, 26,* 65–76.

Butters, M. A., Becker, J. L., Nebes, R. D., Zmuda, M. D., Mulsant, B. H., Pollock, B. G., et al. (2000). Changes in cognitive functioning following treatment of late-life depression. *American Journal of Psychiatry, 157,* 1949–1954.

Butters, M. A., Whyte, E. M., Nebes, R. D., Begley, A. E., Dew, M. A., Mulsant, B. H., et al. (2004). The nature and determinants of neuropsychological functioning in late-life depression. *Archives of General Psychiatry, 61,* 587–595.

Button, T. M. M., Scourfield, J., Martin, N., Purcell, S., & McGuffin, P. (2005). Family dysfunction interacts with genes in the causation of antisocial symptoms. *Behavior Genetics, 35,* 115–120.

Buysse, V., & Bailey, D. B. (1993). Behavioral and developmental outcomes in young children with disabilities in integrated and segregated settings: A review of comparative studies. *Journal of Special Education, 26,* 434–461.

Bybee, R. W. (1995). Science curriculum reform in the United States. In R. W. Bybee & J. D. McInerney (Eds.), *Redesigning the science curriculum.* Colorado Springs, Colorado: Biological Sciences Curriculum Study.

Byne, W. (1994). The biological evidence challenged. *Scientific American, 270,* 50–55.

Byrnes, J. P. (1996). *Cognitive development and learning in instructional contexts.* Boston: Allyn & Bacon.

Byrne, B. (1998). *The foundation of literacy: The child's acquisition of the alphabetic principle.* East Sussex, UK: Psychology Press.

C

Cabrera, N. J., Tamis-LeMonda, C. S., Bradley, R. H., Hofferth, S., & Lamb, M. E. (2000). Fatherhood in the twenty-first century. *Child Development, 71,* 127–136.

Caddell, D. P., & Newton, R. R. (1995). Euthanasia: American attitudes toward the physician's role. *Social Science and Medicine, 40,* 1671–1681.

Cairns, R. B., & Cairns, B. (2006). The making of developmental psychology. In W. Damon & R. M. Lerner (Eds. in Chief) & R. M. Lerner (Vol. Ed.), *Handbook of child psychology: Vol. 1. Theoretical models of human development* (6th ed.). Hoboken, NJ: Wiley.

Caldera, Y. M., Huston, A. C., & O'Brien, M. (1989). Social interactions and play patterns of parents and toddlers with feminine, masculine, and neutral toys. *Child Development, 60,* 70–76.

Caldera, Y. M., & Lindsey, E. W. (2006). Coparenting, mother–infant interaction, and infant–parent attachment relationships in two-parent families. *Journal of Family Psychology, 20,* 275–283.

Caldwell, B. M., & Bradley, R. H. (1984). *Manual for the home observation for measurement of the environment.* Little Rock: University of Arkansas.

Caldwell, P. (1996). Child survival: Physical vulnerability and resilience in adversity in the European past and the contemporary third world. *Social Science and Medicine, 43,* 609–619.

Calkins, S. D., & Hill, A. (2007). Caregiver influences on emerging emotion regulation: Biological and environmental transactions in early development. In J. J. Gross (Ed.), *Handbook of emotion regulation.* New York: Guilford.

Call, K. T., Mortimer, J. T., & Shanahan, M. (1995). Helpfulness and the development of competence in adolescence. *Child Development, 66,* 129–138.

Callaghan, W. M., MacDorman, M. F., Rasmussen, S. A., Qin, C., Lackritz, E. M. (2006). The contribution of preterm birth to infant mortality rates in the United States. *Pediatrics, 118,* 1566–1573.

Camaioni, L. (2004). Early language. In G. Bremner & A. Fogel (Eds.), *Blackwell handbook of infant development* (pp. 404–426). Malden, MA: Blackwell Publishing.

Cameron, N. (2002). Human growth curve, canalization, and catch-up growth. In N. Cameron (Ed.), *Human growth and development* (pp. 19). New York: Academic Press.

Camp, C. J., Foss, J. W., O'Hanlon, A. M., & Stevens, A. B. (1996). Memory interventions for persons with dementia. *Applied Cognitive Psychology, 10,* 193–210.

Camp, C. J., & McKitrick, L. A. (1992). Memory interventions in Alzheimer's-type dementia populations: Methodological and theoretical issues. In R. L. West & J. D. Sinnott (Eds.), *Everyday memory and aging: Current research and methodology* (pp. 155–172). New York: Springer-Verlag.

Campbell, A., Shirley, L., & Caygill, L. (2002). Sex-typed preferences in three domains: Do two-year-olds need cognitive variables? *British Journal of Psychology, 93,* 203–217.

Campbell, F. A., Pungello, E. P., Miller-Johnson, S., Burchinal, M., & Ramey, C. T. (2001). The development of cognitive and academic abilities: Growth curves from an early childhood educational experiment. *Developmental Psychology, 37,* 231–242.

Campbell, F. A., & Ramey, C. T. (1994). Effects of early intervention on intellectual and academic achievement: A follow-up study of children from low-income families. *Child Development, 65,* 684–698.

Campbell, F. A., & Ramey, C. T. (1995). Cognitive and school outcomes for high-risk African-American students at middle adolescence: Positive effects of early intervention. *American Educational Research Journal, 32,* 743–772.

Campbell, V. A., Crews, J. E., Moriarty, D. G., Zack, M. M., & Blackman, D. K. (1999). Surveillance for sensory impairment, activity limitation, and health-related quality of life among older adults: United States, 1993–1997. *CDC MMWR Surveillance Summaries, 48* (SS08), 131–156.

Campos, J. J., Bertenthal, B. I., & Kermoian, R. (1992). Early experience and emotional development: The emergence of wariness of heights. *Psychological Science, 3,* 61–64.

Campos, J. J., Langer, A., & Krowitz, A. (1970). Cardiac responses on the visual cliff in prelocomotor human infants. *Science, 170,* 196–197.

Canfield, R. L., Henderson, C. R., Cory-Slechta, D. A., Cox, C., Jusko, T. A., & Lanphaer, B. P. (2003). Intellectual impairment in children with blood lead concentrations below 10 microg per deciliter. *New England Journal of Medicine, 348,* 1517–1526.

Canfield, R. L., & Smith, E. G. (1996). Number-based expectations and sequential enumeration by 5-month-old infants. *Developmental Psychology, 32,* 269–279.

Cannon, M., Kendell, R., Susser, E., & Jones, P. (2003). Prenatal and perinatal risk factors for schizophrenia. In R. M. Murray, P. B. Jones, E. Susser, J. van Os, & M. Cannon (Eds.), *The epidemiology of schizophrenia.* Cambridge, UK: Cambridge University Press.

Cano, A., & Vivian, D. (2003). Are life stressors associated with marital violence? *Journal of Family Psychology, 17,* 302–314.

Cantor. N. L. (2001). Twenty-five years after Quinlan: A review of the jurisprudence of death and dying. *Journal of Law, Medicine, and Ethics, 29,* 182–196.

Caplan, L. J., & Schooler, C. (2001). Age effects on analogy-based memory for text. *Experimental Aging Research, 27,* 151–165.

Card, N. A. (2007). "I hated her guts!": Emerging adults' recollections of the formation, maintenance, and termination of antipathetic relationships during high school. *Journal of Adolescent Research, 22,* 32–57.

Card, N. A., & Hodges, E. V. E. (2003). Parent-child relationships and enmity with peers: The role of avoidant and preoccupied attachment. In E. V. E. Hodges, & N. A. Card (Eds.), *Enemies and the darker side of peer relations.* San Francisco: Jossey-Bass.

Cardno, A., & Murray, R. M. (2003). The "classical" genetic epidemiology of schizophrenia. In R. M. Murray, P. B. Jones, E. Susser, J. van Os, & M. Cannon (Eds.), *The epidemiology of schizophrenia.* Cambridge, UK: Cambridge University Press.

Carlesimo, G. A., Mauri, M., Graceffa, A. M. S., Fadda, L., Loasses, A., Lorusso, S., et al. (1998). Memory performances in young, elderly, and very old healthy individuals versus patients with Alzheimer's disease: Evidence for discontinuity between normal and pathological aging. *Journal of Clinical and Experimental Neuropsychology, 20,* 14–29.

Carlson, V., Cicchetti, D., Barnett, D., & Braunwald, K. (1989). Disorganized/disoriented attachment relationships in maltreated infants. *Developmental Psychology, 25,* 525–531.

Carmichael, M. (2004, May 10). Have it your way: Redesigning birth. *Newsweek,* pp. 70–72.

Carmichael, S. L., Shaw, G. M., Schaffer, D. M, Laurent, C., & Selvin, S. (2003). Dieting behaviors and risk of neural tube defects. *American Journal of Epidemiology, 158,* 1127–1131.

Carnelley, K. B., Wortman, C. B., Bolger, N., & Burke, C. T. (2006). The time course of grief reactions to spousal loss: Evidence from a national probability sample. *Journal of Personality and Social Psychology, 91,* 476–492.

Carnethon, M., Gulati, M., & Greenland, P. (2005). Prevalence and cardiovascular disease correlates of low cardiorespiratory fitness in adolescents and adults. *Journal of the American Medical Association, 294,* 2981–2988.

Caron, S. L., & Moskey, E. G. (2002). Changes over time in teenage sexual relationships: Comparing the high school class of 1950, 1975, and 2000. *Adolescence, 37,* 515–526.

Carpendale, J. I. M. (2000). Kohlberg and Piaget on stages and moral reasoning. *Developmental Review, 20,* 181–205.

Carpenter, M., Nagell, K., & Tomasello, M. (1998). Social cognition, joint attention, and communicative competence from 9 to 15 months of age. *Monographs of the Society for Research in Child Development, 63* (Serial No. 255).

Carr, C. L. (2007). Where have all the tomboys gone? Women's accounts of gender in adolescence. *Sex Roles, 56,* 439–448.

Carr, D. (2004). Gender, preloss marital dependence, and older adults' adjustment to widowhood. *Journal of Marriage and Family, 66,* 220–235.

Carr, P. L., Ash, A. S., Friedman, R. H., Scaramucci, A., Barnett, R. C., Szalacha, L., et al. (1998). Relation of family responsibilities and gender to the productivity and career satisfaction of medical faculty. *Annals of Internal Medicine, 129,* 532–538.

Carrera, M., Kaye, J. W., Philliber, S., & West, E. (2000). Knowledge about reproduction, contraception, and sexually transmitted infections among young adolescents in American cities. *Social Policy, 30,* 41–50.

Carroll, D. W. (2008). *Psychology of language* (5th ed.). Belmont, CA: Wadsworth.

Carroll, J. B. (1993). *Human cognitive abilities: A survey of factor–analytic studies.* Cambridge, England: Cambridge University Press.

Carroll, J. M., Snowling, M. J., Hulme, C., & Stevenson, J. (2003). The development of phonological awareness in preschool children. *Developmental Psychology, 39,* 913–925.

Carstensen, L. L. (1992). Social and emotional patterns in adulthood: Support for socio-emotional selectivity theory. *Psychology and Aging, 7,* 331–338.

Carstensen, L. L., & Freund, A. M. (1994). Commentary: The resilience of the aging self. *Developmental Review, 14,* 81–92.

Carstensen, L. L., Levenson, R. W., & Gottman, J. M. (1995). Emotional behavior in long-term marriages. *Psychology and Aging, 10,* 140–149.

Carstensen, L. L., Mikels, J. A., & Mather, M. (2006). Aging and the intersection of cognition, motivation, and emotion. In J. E. Birren & K. W. Schaie (Eds.), *Handbook of the psychology of aging* (6th ed). Burlington, MA: Elsevier Academic Press.

Carstensen, L. L., Pasupathi, M., Mayr, U., & Nesselroade, J. R. (2000). Emotional experience in everyday life across the adult life span. *Journal of Personality and Social Psychology, 79,* 644–655.

Carter, A. S., Briggs-Gowan, M. J., & Davis, N. O. (2004). Assessment of young children's social-emotional development and psychopathology: Recent advances and recommendations for practice. *Journal of Child Psychology and Psychiatry and Allied Disciplines, 45,* 109–134.

Carver, K., Joyner, K., & Udry, J. R. (2003). National estimates of adolescent romantic relationships. In P. Florsheim (Ed.), *Adolescent romantic relations and sexual behavior: Theory,* *research, and practical implications.* Mahwah, NJ: Erlbaum.

Carver, L. J., & Vaccaro, B. G. (2007). 12-month-old infants allocate increased neural resources to stimuli associated with negative adult emotion. *Developmental Psychology, 43,* 54–69.

Casadesus, G., Perry, G., Joseph, J. A., & Smith, M. A. (2004). Eat less, eat better, and live longer: Does it work and is it worth it? The role of diet in aging and disease. In S. G. Post & R. H. Binstock (Eds.), *The fountain of youth: Cultural, scientific, and ethical perspectives on a biomedical goal.* New York: Oxford University Press.

Case, R. (1985). *Intellectual development: Birth to adulthood.* Orlando, FL: Academic Press.

Case, R. (1998). The development of conceptual structures. In D. Kuhn & R. S. Siegler (Vol. Eds.), W. Damon (Editor-in-Chief), *Handbook of child psychology: Vol. 2. Cognition, perception, and language* (5th ed., pp. 745–800). New York: Wiley.

Case, T. I., Repacholi, B. M., & Stevenson, R. J. (2006). My baby doesn't smell as bad as yours: The plasticity of disgust. *Evolution and Human Behavior, 27,* 357–365.

Casey, B. M., McIntire D. D., & Leveno, K. J. (2001). The continuing value of the Apgar score for the assessment of newborn infants. *New England Journal of Medicine, 344,* 467–471.

Caspi, A. (1998). Personality development across the life course. In R. M. Lerner (Vol. Ed.), W. Damon (Editor-in-Chief), *Handbook of child psychology: Vol. 1. Theoretical models of human development* (5th ed.). New York: Wiley.

Caspi, A. (2000). The child is father of man: Personality continues from childhood to adulthood. *Journal of Personality and Social Psychology, 78,* 158–172.

Caspi, A., Harrington, H., Milne, B., Amell, J. W., Theodore, R. F., & Moffitt, T. E. (2003). Children's behavioral styles at age 3 are linked to their adult personality traits at age 26. *Journal of Personality, 71,* 495–513.

Caspi, A., Herbener, E. S., & Ozer, D. J. (1992). Shared experiences and the similarity of personalities: A longitudinal study of married couples. *Journal of Personality and Social Psychology, 62,* 281–291.

Caspi, A., Moffitt, T. E., Newman, D. L., & Silva, P. A. (1996). Behavioral observations at age 3 years predict adult psychiatric disorders: Longitudinal evidence from a birth cohort. *Archives of General Psychiatry, 53,* 1033–1039.

Caspi, A., & Roberts, B. W. (2001). Personality development across the life course: The argument for change and continuity. *Psychological Inquiry, 12,* 49–66.

Caspi, A., Sugden, K., Moffitt, T. E., Taylor, A., Craig, I. W., Harrington, H., et al. (2003, July 18). Influence of life stress on depression: Moderation by a polymorphism in the 5-HTT gene. *Science, 301,* 386–389.

Cassia, V. M., Kuefner, D., Westerlund, A., & Nelson, C. A. (2006). A behavioural and ERP investigation of 3-month-olds' face preferences. *Neuropsychologia, 44,* 2113–2125.

Cassia, V. M., Turati, C., & Simion, F. (2004). Can a nonspecific bias toward top-heavy patterns explain newborns' face preference? *Psychological Science, 15,* 379–383.

Cassidy, T. (2006). *Birth: The surprising history of how we are born.* New York: Atlantic Monthly Press.

Cattell, R. B. (1963). Theory of fluid and crystallized intelligence: A critical experiment. *Journal of Educational Psychology, 54,* 1–22.

Cavanaugh, J. C. (1996). Memory self-efficacy as a moderation of memory change. In F. Blanchard-Fields & T. M. Hess (Eds.), *Perspectives on cognitive change in adulthood and aging.* New York: McGraw-Hill.

Cavanaugh, J. C., Grady, J. G., & Perlmutter, M. (1983). Forgetting and use of memory aids in 20 to 70 year olds' everyday life. *International Journal of Aging and Human Development, 17,* 113–122.

Ceci, S. J., & Bruck, M. (1998). Children's testimony: Applied and basic issues. In I. E. Sigel & K. A. Renninger (Vol. Eds.), W. Damon (Editor-in-Chief), *Handbook of child psychology: Vol. 4. Child psychology in practice* (5th ed., pp. 713–774). New York: Wiley.

Ceci, S. J., & Williams, W. M. (1997). Schooling, intelligence, and income. *American Psychologist, 52,* 1051–1058.

Centers for Disease Control and Prevention. (2005). *Assisted reproductive technology success rates: National summary and fertility clinic reports.* Atlanta, GA: U.S. Department of Health and Human Services.

Centers for Disease Control and Prevention. (2006a). Improved national prevalence estimates for 18 selected major birth defects—United States, 1999–2001. *MMWR Weekly, 54*(51 & 52), 1301–1305.

Centers for Disease Control and Prevention. (2006b). *Percentage of births attended by midwives in the United States.* Available at: www.cdc.gov/nchs/births.htm. Accessed: September 6, 2006.

Centers for Disease Control and Prevention. (2006c). *Reported cases of HIV/AIDS in infants born to HIV-infected mothers, by year of report and selected characteristics, 1994–2004.* Available at: www.cdc.gov/hiv/topics/surveillance/resources/reports/2004report/table23.htm. Accessed: October 2, 2006.

Centers for Disease Control and Prevention. (2006d). Table 23. *Reported cases of HIV/AIDS in infants born to HIV-infected mothers, by year of report and selected characteristics, 1994–2004: 25 states with confidential name-based HIV infection reporting.* Available at: http://www.cdc.gov/hiv/topics/surveillance/resources/reports/2004report/pdf/table23.pdf. Accessed: July 1, 2007.

Centers for Disease Control and Prevention. (2006e). *Healthy youth!* Available at: www.cdc.gov/Healthy Youth/healthtopics/index.htm. Accessed: December 14, 2006.

Centers for Disease Control and Prevention. (2007a). *Possible health effects of radiation exposure on unborn babies.* Available at: www.bt.cdc.gov/radiation/prenatal.asp. Accessed: February 14, 2007.

Centers for Disease Control and Prevention. (2007b). Smoking during pregnancy—United States, 1990–2002. *Morbidity and Mortality Weekly Report, 53,* 911–915.

Centers for Disease Control and Prevention. (2007c). *Healthy youth!* Available at: www.cdc.gov/healthyyouth/healthtopics/index.htm. Accessed: April 17, 2007.

Centers for Disease Control and Prevention. (2007d). *National youth risk behavior survey: 1991–2005.* Available at: www.cdc.gov/healthyyouth/yrbs/pdf/trends/2005_YRBS_Risk_Behaviors.pdf. Accessed: March 7, 2007.

Cerminara, K. L. (2006). Theresa Marie Schiavo's long road to peace. *Death Studies, 30,* 101–112.

Cernoch, J. M., & Porter, R. H. (1985). Recognition of maternal axillary odors by infants. *Child Development, 56,* 1593–1598.

Chakrabarti, S., & Fombonne, E. (2001). Pervasive developmental disorders in preschool children. *Journal of the American Medical Association, 285,* 3093–3099.

Chakrabarti, S., & Fombonne, E. (2005). Pervasive developmental disorders in preschool children: Confirmation of high prevalence. *American Journal of Psychiatry, 162,* 1133–1141.

Chall, J. S. (1967). *Learning to read: The great debate.* New York: McGraw-Hill.

Chambers, W. C. (2007). Oral sex: Varied behaviors and perceptions in a college population. *Journal of Sex Research, 44,* 28–42.

Chandler, M., Fritz, A. S., & Hala, S. (1989). Small-scale deceit: Deception as a marker of two-, three-, and four-year-olds' early theories of mind. *Child Development, 60,* 1263–1277.

Chandler, M. J., Sokol, B. W., & Wainryb, C. (2000). Beliefs about truth and beliefs about rightness. *Child Development, 71,* 91–97.

Chandler, S., & Field, P. A. (1997). Becoming a father: First-time fathers' experience of labor and delivery. *Journal of Nurse-Midwifery, 42,* 17–24.

Chao, R. K. (1994). Beyond parental control and authoritarian parenting style: Understanding Chinese parenting through the cultural notion of training. *Child Development, 65,* 1111–1119.

Chao, R. K. (2000). Cultural explanations for the role of parenting in the school success of Asian American children. In R. D. Taylor & M. C. Wang (Eds.), *Resilience across contexts: Family, work, culture, and community.* Mahwah, NJ: Erlbaum.

Chapman, A. R. (2004). The social and justice implications of extending the human life span. In S. G. Post & R. H. Binstock (Eds.), *The fountain of youth: Cultural, scientific, and ethical perspectives on a biomedical goal.* New York: Oxford University Press.

Chapman, L. L. (2000). Expectant fathers and labor epidurals. *American Journal of Maternity and Child Nursing, 25,* 133–138.

Chapman, M., & Lindenberger, U. (1988). Functions, operations, and décalage in the development of transitivity. *Developmental Psychology, 24,* 542–551.

Charach, A., Figueroa, M., Chen, S., Ickowicz, A., & Schachar, R. (2006). Stimulant treatment over 5 years: Effects on growth. *Journal of the American Academy of Child and Adolescent Psychiatry, 45,* 415–421.

Charles, S. T., & Carstensen, L. L. (2007). Emotion regulation and aging. In J. J. Gross, J. J. (Ed.), *Handbook of emotion regulation.* New York: Guilford.

Charles, S. T., Mather, M., & Carstensen, L. L. (2003). Aging and emotional memory: The forgettable nature of negative images for older adults. *Journal of Experimental Psychology: General, 132,* 310–324.

Charles, S. T., & Mavandadi, S. (2004). Social support and physical health across the life span: Socioemotional influences. In F. R. Lang & K. L. Fingerman (Eds.), *Growing together: Personal relationships across the life span.* Cambridge, UK: Cambridge University Press.

Charlesworth, W. R. (1992). Darwin and developmental psychology: Past and present. *Developmental Psychology, 28,* 5–16.

Charman, T. (2000). Theory of mind and the early diagnosis of autism. In S. Baron-Cohen, H. Tager-Flusberg, & D. J. Cohen (Eds.), *Understanding other minds. Perspectives from developmental cognitive neuroscience* (2nd ed.). Oxford: Oxford University Press.

Charney, D. S., Reynolds, C. F., Lewis, L., Lebowitz, B. D., Sunderland, T., Alexopoulos, G. S., et al. (2003). Depression and Bipolar Support Alliance consensus statement on the unmet needs in diagnosis and treatment of mood disorders in late life. *Archives of General Psychiatry, 60,* 664–672.

Chatoor, I., & Ganiban, J., (2004). The diagnostic assessment and classification of feeding disorders. In R. DelCarmen-Wiggins & A. Carter (Eds.), *Handbook of infant, toddler, and preschool mental health assessment.* New York: Oxford University Press.

Chavous, T. M., Bernat, D. H., Schmeelk-Cone, K., Caldwell, C. H., Kohn-Wood, L., & Zimmerman, M. A. (2003). Racial identity and academic attainment among African American adolescents. *Child Development, 74,* 1076–1090.

Chen, A. (2007). Learning to map: Strategy discovery and strategy change in young children. *Developmental Psychology, 43,* 386–403.

Chen, C., & Stevenson, H. W. (1995). Motivation and mathematics achievement: A comparative study of Asian-American, Caucasian-American, and East Asian high school students. *Child Development, 66,* 1214–1234.

Chen, D. (1996). Parent–infant communication: Early intervention for very young children with visual impairment or hearing loss. *Infants and Young Children, 9,* 1–12.

Chen, E., Martin, A. D., & Matthews, K. A. (2006). Understanding health disparities: The role of face and socioeconomic status in children's health. *American Journal of Public Health, 96,* 702–708.

Chen, J. Q., & Gardner, H. (1997). Alternative assessment from a multiple intelligences theoretical perspective. In D. P. Flanagan, J. Genshaft, & P. L. Harrison (Eds.), *Contemporary intellectual assessment: Theories, tests, and issues.* New York: Guilford.

Chen, K., Reiman, E. M., Alexander, G. E., Caselli, R. J., Gerkin, R., Bandy, D., Domb, A., Osborne, D., Fox, N., Crum, W. R., Saunders, A. M., & Hardy, J. (2007). Correlations between apolipoprotein E 4 gene dose and whole brain atrophy rates. *American Journal of Psychiatry, 164,* 916–921.

Chen, L. C., Metcalfe, J. S., Jeka, J. J., & Clark, J. E. (2007). Two steps forward and one back: Learning to walk affects infants' sitting posture. *Infant Behavioral Development, 30,* 16–25.

Chen, X., Cen, G., Li, D., & He, Y. (2005). Social functioning and adjustment in Chinese children: The imprint of historical time. *Child Development, 76,* 182–195.

Chen, X., DeSouza, A. T., Chen, H., & Wang, L. (2006). Reticent behavior and experiences in peer interactions in Chinese and Canadian children. *Developmental Psychology, 42,* 656–665.

Chen, X., Rubin, K. H., & Sun, Y. (1992). Social reputation in Chinese and Canadian children: A cross-cultural study. *Child Development, 63,* 1336–1343.

Cheng, A. K., Rubin, H. R., Powe, N. R., Mellon, M. K., Francis, H. W., & Niparko, J. K. (2000). Cost–utility analysis of the cochlear implant in children. *Journal of the American Medical Association, 284,* 850–856.

Cherlin, A. J., & Furstenberg, F. F., Jr. (1986). *The new American grandparent: A place in the family, a life apart.* New York: Basic Books.

Cherney, I. D. (2005). Children's and adults' recall of sex-stereotyped toy pictures: Effects of presentation and memory task. *Infant and Child Development, 14,* 11–27.

Cherney, I. D., Harper, H. J., & Winter, J. A. (2006). Nouveaux jouets: Ce que les enfants identifient comme 'jouets de garçons' et 'jouets de filles.' *Enfance, 58,* 266–282.

Cherney, I. S., & London, K. (2006). Gender-linked differences in the toys, television shows, computer games, and outdoor activities of 5- to 13-year-old children. *Sex Roles, 54,* 717–726.

Cherry, K. E., & LeCompte, D. C. (1999). Age and individual differences influence prospective memory. *Psychology and Aging, 14,* 60–76.

Cherry, K. E., & Morton, M. R. (1989). Drug sensitivity in older adults: The role of physiologic and pharmacokinetic factors. *International Journal of Aging and Human Development, 28,* 159–174.

Cherry, K. E., & Smith, A. D. (1998). Normal memory aging. In M. Hersen & V. B. Van Hasselt (Eds.), *Handbook of clinical geropsychology* (pp. 87–110). New York: Plenum.

Chess, S., & Thomas, A. (1984). *Origins and evolution of behavior disorders: From infancy to early adult life.* New York: Brunner/Mazel.

Chess, S., & Thomas, A. (1999). *Goodness of fit: Clinical applications from infancy through adult life.* Ann Arbor, MI: Edwards Brothers.

Chi, M. T. H. (1978). Knowledge structures and memory development. In R. Siegler (Ed.), *Children's thinking: What develops?* Hillsdale, NJ: Erlbaum.

Chia, E. M., Wang, J. J., Rochtchina, E., Smith, W., Cumming, R. R., & Mitchell, P. (2004). Impact of bilateral visual impairment on health-related quality of life: The Blue Mountains Eye Study. *Investigations in Ophthalmology & Visual Science, 45,* 71–76.

Child Prodigies (2006, December 27). *60 Minutes.*

Child Trends Databank (undated). *Attitudes toward spanking.* Available at www.childtrendsdatabank.org/indicators/51AttitudesTowardsSpanking.cfm. Accessed: May 31, 2007.

Childbirth Connection (2007). *Vaginal birth and cesarean birth: How do the risks compare?* Available at: www.childbirthconnection.org. Accessed: February 14, 2007.

Chimpanzee Sequencing and Analysis Consortium (2005). Initial sequence of the chimpanzee genome and comparison with the human genome. *Nature, 437,* 69–87.

Chiu, R. W. K., & Lo, Y. M. (2006). Noninvasive prenatal diagnosis by analysis of fetal DNA in maternal plasma. *Methods in Molecular Biology, 336,* 101–109.

Chiu, S., & Alexander, P. A. (2000). The motivational function of preschoolers' private speech. *Discourse Processes, 30,* 133–152.

Cho, D., & Gardner, A. (2007, April 21). Virginia Tech killer: An isolated boy in a world of strangers. *The Washington Post,* pp. A1, A8.

Chochinov, H. M., & Schwartz., L. (2002). Depression and the will to live in the psychological landscape of terminally ill patients. In K. Foley, & H. Hendin (Eds.), *The case against assisted suicide: For the right to end-of-life care.* Baltimore: The Johns Hopkins Press.

Choi, J., & Silverman, I. (2003). Processes underlying sex differences in route-learning strategies in children and adolescents. *Personality and Individual Differences, 34,* 1153–1166.

Chomsky, N. (1968). *Language and mind.* New York: Harcourt Brace & World.

Chomsky, N. (1975). *Reflections on language.* New York: Pantheon Books.

Chomsky, N. (1995). *The minimalist program.* Cambridge: MIT Press.

Christensen, M., Emde, R., & Fleming, C. (2004). Cultural perspectives for assessing infants and young children. In R. DelCarmen-Wiggins & A. Carter (Eds.), *Handbook of infant, toddler, and preschool mental health assessment.* New York: Oxford University Press.

Christiansen, S. L., & Palkovitz, R. (1998). Exploring Erikson's psychosocial theory of development: Generativity and its relationship to parental identity, intimacy, and involvement with others. *Journal of Men's Studies, 7,* 133–156.

Christianson, A., Howson, C. P., & Modell, B. (2006). *March of Dimes Global report on birth defects: The hidden toll of dying and disabled children.* White Plains, NY: March of Dimes Birth Defects Foundation.

Christie, F. (2002). The development of abstraction in adolescence in subject English. In M. J. Schleppegrell & Colombi, M. C. (Eds.), *Developing advanced literacy in first and second languages: Meaning with power* (pp. 45–66). Mahwah, NJ: Lawrence Erlbaum Associates.

Chronis, A. M., Jones, H. A., & Raggi, V. L. (2006). Evidence-based psychosocial treatments for children and adolescents with attention-deficit/hyperactivity disorder. *Clinical Psychology Review, 26,* 486–502.

Chumlea, W. C., Schubert, C. M., Roche, A. F., Kulin, H. E., Lee, P. A., Himes, J. H., et al. (2003). Age at menarche and racial comparisons in US girls. *Pediatrics, 111,* 110–113.

Chung, H. L., & Steinberg, L. (2006). Relations between neighborhood factors, parenting behaviors, peer deviance, and delinquency among serious juvenile offenders. *Developmental Psychology, 42,* 319–331.

Chung, J. H., Des Roches, C. M., Meunier, J., & Eavey, R. D. (2005). Evaluation of noise-induced hearing loss in young people using a web-based survey technique. *Pediatrics, 115,* 861–867.

Cicchetti, D. (2006). Development and psychopathology. In D. Cicchetti & D. J. Cohen (Eds.). *Developmental psychopathology: Vol. 1. Theory and method* (2nd ed.). Hoboken, NJ: Wiley.

Cicchetti, D., & Rogosch, F. A. (2002). A developmental psychopathology perspective on adolescence. *Journal of Consulting and Clinical Psychology, 70,* 6–20.

Cicchetti, D., Rogosch, F. A., & Toth, S. L. (2006). Fostering secure attachment in infants in maltreating families through preventive interventions. *Development and Psychopathology, 18,* 623–649.

Cicchetti, D., Toth, S. L., & Rogosch, F. A. (2004). Toddler–parent psychotherapy for depressed mothers and their offspring: Implications for attachment theory. In L. Atkinson & S. Goldberg (Eds.), *Attachment issues in psychopathology and intervention.* Mahwah, NJ: Erlbaum.

Cicchetti, D., & Valentino, K. (2006). An ecological–transactional perspective on child maltreatment: Failure of the average expectable environment and its influence on child development. In D. Cicchetti & D. J. Cohen (Eds.), *Developmental psychopathology: Vol. 3. Risk, disorder, and adaptation* (2nd ed.). Hoboken, NJ: Wiley.

Cicirelli, V. G. (1982). Sibling influence throughout the life span. In M. E. Lamb & B. Sutton-Smith (Eds.), *Sibling relationships: Their nature and significance across the lifespan.* Hillsdale, NJ: Erlbaum.

Cicirelli, V. G. (1991). Sibling relationships in adulthood. *Marriage and Family Review, 16,* 291–310.

Cicirelli, V. G. (1993). Attachment and obligation as daughters' motives for caregiving behavior and subsequent effect on subjective burden. *Psychology and Aging, 8,* 144–155.

Cicirelli, V. G. (1995). *Sibling relationships across the life span.* New York: Plenum.

Cillessen, A. H., Van IJzendoorn, H. W., Van Lieshout, C. F., & Hartup, W. W. (1992). Heterogeneity among peer-rejected boys: Subtypes and stabilities. *Child Development, 63,* 893–905.

Cillessen, A. H. N., & Mayeux, L. (2004). Sociometric status and peer group behavior: Previous findings and current directions. In J. B. Kupersmidt & K. A. Dodge (Eds.), *Children's peer relations: From development to intervention.* Washington, DC: American Psychological Association.

Cimbora, D. M., & McIntosh, D. N. (2003). Emotional responses to antisocial acts in adolescent males with conduct disorder: A link to affective morality. *Journal of Clinical Child and Adolescent Psychology, 32,* 296–301.

Cipriani, N. (2002, Nov. 1). What kids should know when. *Parenting, 16,* 150.

Clark, D. C., Pynoos, R. S., & Goebel, A. E. (1994). Mechanisms and processes of adolescent bereavement. In R. J. Haggerty, L. R. Sherrod, N. Garmezy, & M. Rutter (Eds.), *Stress, risk, and resilience in children and adolescents: Processes, mechanisms, and interventions.* Cambridge, England: Cambridge University Press.

Clark, D. O., & Maddox, G. L. (1992). Racial and social correlates of age-related changes in functioning. *Journal of Gerontology: Social Sciences, 47,* S222–S232.

Clark, H. H., & Clark, E. V. (1977). *Psychology and language: An introduction to psycholinguistics.* New York: Harcourt Brace Jovanovich.

Clark, L. A., Watson, D., & Reynolds, S. (1995). Diagnosis and classification of psychopathology: Challenges to the current system and future directions. *Annual Review of Psychology, 46,* 121–153.

Clarke-Stewart, A., & Allhusen, V. D. (2005). *What we know about child care.* Cambridge, MA: Harvard University Press.

Clarke-Stewart, A., & Dunn, J. (2006). *Families count: Effects on child and adolescent development.* New York: Cambridge University Press.

Clarke-Stewart, K. A. (1998). Reading with children. *Journal of Applied Developmental Psychology, 19,* 1–14.

Clarke-Stewart, K. A., Goossens, F. A., & Allhusen, V. D. (2001). Measuring infant-mother attachment: Is the strange situation enough? *Social Development, 10,* 143–169.

Clarkson, M. G., & Berg, W. K. (1983). Cardiac orienting and vowel discrimination in newborns: Crucial stimulation parameters. *Child Development, 54,* 162–171.

Claxton, A. F., Pannells, T. C., & Rhoads, P. A. (2005). Developmental trends in the creativity of school-age children. *Creativity Research Journal, 17,* 327–335.

Cleary-Goldman, J., Malone, F. D., Vidaver, J., Ball, R. H., Nyberg, D. A., Comstock, C. H., Saade, G. R., Eddleman, K. A., Klugman, S., Dugoff, L., Timor-Tritsch, E. I., Craigo, S. D., Carr. S. R., Wolfe, H. M., Bianchi, D. W., & D'Alton, M., for the First and Second Trimester Evaluation of Risk (FASTER) Trial Research Consortium. (2005). Impact of maternal age on obstetric outcome. *Obstetrics & Gynecology, 105,* 983–990.

Cleckner-Smith, C. S., Doughty, A. S., & Grossman, J. A. (1998). Premenstrual symptoms: Prevalence and severity in an adolescent sample. *Journal of Adolescent Health, 22,* 403–408.

Cleveland, H. H., Jacobson, K. C., Lipinski, J. J., & Rowe, D. C. (2000). Genetic and shared environmental contributions to the relationship between the home environment and child and adolescent achievement. *Intelligence, 28,* 69–86.

Coats, P. B., & Overman, S. J. (1992). Childhood play experiences of women in traditional and nontraditional professions. *Sex Roles, 26,* 261–271.

Cobb, R. W., & Coughlin, J. F. (1998). Are elderly drivers a road hazard? Problem definition and political impact. *Journal of Aging Studies, 12,* 411–420.

Cohen, B. B., Friedman, D. J., Zhang, A., Trudeau, E. B., Walker, D. K., Anderka, M., et al. (1999). Impact of multiple births on low birth weight: Massachusetts, 1989–1996. *Morbidity & Mortality Weekly Report, 48,* 289–293.

Cohen, D. (2006). *The development of play* (3rd ed.). London: Routledge.

Cohen, G. D. (2005). *The mature mind: The positive power of the aging brain.* New York: Basic Books.

Cohen, L. B., & Cashon, C. H. (2006). Infant cognition. In D. Kuhn & R. Siegler (Vol. Eds.), *Handbook of child psychology: Cognition, perception, and language.* Hoboken, NJ: Wiley.

Cohen, M. (1996). Preschoolers' practical thinking and problem solving: The acquisition of an optimal solution strategy. *Cognitive Development, 11,* 357–373.

Coie, J. D. (2004). The impact of negative social experiences on the development of antisocial behavior. In J. B. Kupersmidt & K. A. Dodge (Eds.), *Children's peer relations: From development to intervention.* Washington, DC: American Psychological Association.

Coie, J. D., Dodge, K. A., & Coppotelli, H. (1982). Dimensions and types of social status: A cross-age perspective. *Developmental Psychology, 18,* 557–570.

Coie, J. D., Dodge, K. A., & Kupersmidt, J. B. (1990). Peer group behavior and social status. In S. R. Asher & J. D. Coie (Eds.), *Peer rejection in childhood.* Cambridge, England: Cambridge University Press.

Coie, J. D., Dodge, K. A., Terry, R., & Wright, V. (1991). The role of aggression in peer rela-

tions: An analysis of aggression episodes in boys' play groups. *Child Development, 62,* 812–826.

Colapinto, J. (1997, December 11). The true story of John Joan. *Rolling Stone,* 54–97.

Colapinto, J. (2000). *As nature made him: The boy who was raised as a girl.* New York: Harper Collins.

Colapinto, J. (2004, June 3). What were the real reasons behind David Reimer's suicide? Available at: www.slate.com/id/2101678. Accessed: August 25, 2007.

Colburn, D. (2000, October 3). Wired for sound. *The Washington Post—Health,* 13–18.

Colby, A., & Kohlberg, L. (1987). *The measurement of moral judgment. Vol. 1: Theoretical foundations and research validation.* Cambridge, England: Cambridge University Press.

Colby, A., Kohlberg, L., Gibbs, J., & Lieberman, M. (1983). A longitudinal study of moral judgment. *Monographs of the Society for Research in Child Development, 48* (1–2, Serial No. 200).

Colcombe, S. J., Kramer, A. F., Erickson, K. I., Scalf, P., McAuley, E., Cohen, N. J., Webb, A., Jerome, G. J., Marquez, D. X., & Elavsky, S. (2004). Cardiovascular fitness, cortical plasticity, and aging. *Proceedings of the National Academy of Sciences, 101,* 3316–3321.

Cole, D. A., Maxwell, S. E., Martin, J. M., Peeke, L. G., Seroczynski, A. D., Tram, J. M., et al. (2001). The development of multiple domains of child and adolescent self-concept: A cohort sequential longitudinal design. *Child Development, 72,* 1723–1746.

Cole, M. G. (2004). Delirium in elderly patients. *American Journal of Geriatric Psychiatry, 12,* 7–21.

Cole, P. M., Barrett, K. C., & Zahn-Waxler, C. (1992). Emotion displays in two-year-olds during mishaps. *Child Development, 63,* 314–324.

Cole, P. M., Martin, S. E., & Dennis, T. A. (2004). Emotion regulation as a scientific construct: Methodological challenges and directions for child development research. *Child Development, 75,* 317–333.

Cole, P. M., Michel, M. K., & Teti, L. O. (1994). The development of emotion regulation and dysregulation: A clinical perspective. In N. Fox (Ed.), *The development of emotion regulation: Biological and behavioral considerations. Monographs of the Society for Research in Child Development, 59* (Nos. 2–3, Serial No. 240).

Cole, P. M., & Putnam, F. W. (1992). Effect of incest on self and social functioning: A developmental psychopathology perspective. *Journal of Consulting and Clinical Psychology, 60,* 174–184.

Cole, T. R. (1992). *The journey of life. A cultural history of aging in America.* Cambridge, England: Cambridge University Press.

Coleman, J. (1961). *The adolescent society.* New York: Free Press.

Coles, L. S. (2004). Demography of human supercentenarians. *Journal of Gerontology: Biological Sciences, 59A,* 579–586.

Colin, V. (1996). *Human attachment.* New York: McGraw-Hill.

Colley, A., Griffiths, D., Hugh, M., Landers, K., & Jaggli, N. (1996). Childhood play and adolescent leisure preferences: Associations with gender typing and the presence of siblings. *Sex Roles, 35,* 233–245.

Collins, W. A. (2003). More than myth: The developmental significance of romantic relationships during adolescence. *Journal of Research on Adolescence, 13,* 1–24.

Collins, W. A., & Laursen, B. (2004). Changing relationships, changing youth: Interpersonal contexts of adolescent development. *Journal of Early Adolescence, 24,* 55–62.

Collins, W. A., & Laursen, B. (2006). Parent–adolescent relationships. In P. Noller & J. A. Feeney (Eds.), *Close relationships: Functions, forms, and processes.* New York: Psychology Press.

Collins, W. A., Maccoby, E. E., Steinberg, L., Hetherington, E. M., & Bornstein, M. H. (2000). Contemporary research on parenting. The case for nature and nurture. *American Psychologist, 55,* 218–232.

Collins, W. A., & Madsen, S. D. (2006). Personal relationships in adolescence and early adulthood. In A. L. Vangelisti & D. Perlman (Eds.), *The Cambridge handbook of personal relationships.* New York: Cambridge University Press.

Coltrane, S. (2000). Research on household labor: Modeling and measuring the social embeddedness of routine family work. *Journal of Marriage and the Family, 62,* 1208–1233.

Columbo, J. (1993). *Infant cognition: Predicting later intellectual functioning.* Newbury Park, CA: Sage.

Colombo, J. (2001). The development of visual attention in infancy. *Annual Review of Psychology, 52,* 337–367.

Colwell, M. J., & Lindsey, E. W. (2005). Preschool children's pretend and physical play and sex of play partner: Connections to peer competence. *Sex Roles, 52,* 497–509.

Comer, J. P. (1997). *Waiting for a miracle: Why schools can't solve our problems—and how we can.* New York: Plume.

Commons, M. L., Richards, F. A., & Armon, C. (Eds.). (1984). *Beyond formal operations. Late adolescent and adult cognitive development.* New York: Praeger.

Compas, B. E., Connor-Smith, J. K., Saltzman, H., Thomsen, A. H., & Wadsworth, M. E. (2001). Coping with stress during childhood and adolescence: Problems, progress, and potential in theory and research. *Psychological Bulletin, 127,* 87–127.

Compian, L., Gowen, L. K., & Hayward, C. (2004). Peripubertal girls' romantic and platonic involvement with boys: Associations with body image and depression symptoms. *Journal of Research on Adolescence, 14,* 23–47.

Condon, J. T. (1993). The premenstrual syndrome: A twin study. *British Journal of Psychiatry, 162,* 481–486.

Condon, J. T., Boyce, P., & Corkindale, C. J. (2004). The first-time fathers study: A prospective study of the mental health and wellbeing of men during the transition to parenthood. *Australia Psychiatry, 38,* 56–64.

Condry, J., & Condry, S. (1976). Sex differences: A study in the eye of the beholder. *Child Development, 47,* 812–819.

Congdon, N., O'Colmain, B., Klaver, C. C., Klein, R., Munoz, B., Friedman, D. S., et al. (2004). Causes and prevalence of visual impairment among adults in the United States. *Archives of Ophthalmology, 122,* 477–485.

Conger, R. D., Conger, K. J., Elder, G. H., Jr., Lorenz, F. O., Simons, R. L., & Whitbeck, L. B. (1992). A family process model of economic hardship and adjustment of early adolescent boys. *Child Development, 63,* 526–541.

Conger, R. D., & Dogan, S. J. (2007). Social class and socialization in families. In J. E. Grusec & P. D. Hastings (Eds.), *Handbook of socialization theory and research.* New York: Guilford.

Conger, R. D., & Donnellan, M. B. (2007). An interactionist perspective on the socioeconomic context of human development. *Annual Review of Psychology, 58,* 175–199.

Conger, R. D., Neppl, T., Kim, K. J., & Scaramella, L. (2003). Angry and aggressive behavior across three generations: A prospective, longitudinal study of parents and children. *Journal of Abnormal Child Psychology, 31,* 143–160.

Conger, R. D., Patterson, G. R., & Ge, X. (1995). It takes two to replicate: A mediational model for the impact of parents' stress on adolescent adjustment. *Child Development, 66,* 80–97.

Conger, R. D., Wallace, L. E., Sun, Y., Simons, R. L., McLoyd, V. C., & Brody, G. H. (2002). Economic pressure in African American families: A replication and extension of the family stress model. *Developmental Psychology, 38,* 179–193.

Conklin, H. M., Luciana, M., Hooper, C. J., & Yarger, R. S. (2007). Working memory performance in typically developing children and adolescents: Behavioral evidence of protracted frontal lobe development. *Developmental Neuropsychology, 31,* 103–128.

Connell, A. M., & Goodman, S. H. (2002). The association between psychopathology in fathers versus mothers and children's internalizing and externalizing behavior problems: A meta-analysis. *Psychological Bulletin, 128,* 746–773.

Connellan, J., Baron-Cohen, S., Wheelwright, S., Batki, A., & Ahluwalia, J. (2000). Sex differences in human neonatal social perception. *Infant Behavior and Development, 23,* 113–118.

Conner, K. A. (2000). *Continuing to care. Older Americans and their families.* New York: Falmer Press.

Connolly, C. (2005, April 14). As teen pregnancy dropped, so did child poverty. *Washington Post,* p. A10.

Connolly, J. A., & Doyle, A. B. (1984). Relation of social fantasy play to social competence in preschoolers. *Developmental Psychology, 20,* 797–806.

Connolly, J., Furman, W., & Konarski, R. (2000). The role of peers in the emergence of heterosexual romantic relationships in adolescence. *Child Development, 71,* 1395–1408.

Connor, S. R. (2000). Hospice care and the older person. In A. Tomer (Ed.), *Death attitudes and the older adult: Theories, concepts, and applications.* Philadelphia, PA: Brunner-Routledge.

Conrade, G., & Ho, R. (2001). Differential parenting styles for fathers and mothers: Differential treatment for sons and daughters. *Australian Journal of Psychology, 53,* 29–35.

Constantino, J. N., & Todd, R. D. (2003). Autistic traits in the general population: A twin study. *Archives of General Psychiatry, 60,* 524–530.

Conway, M., & Vartanian, L. R. (2000). A status account of gender stereotypes: Beyond communality and agency. *Sex Roles, 43,* 181–199.

Coohey, C., & Braun, N. (1997). Toward an integrated framework for understanding child physical abuse. *Child Abuse and Neglect, 21,* 1081–1094.

Cook, A. S., & Dworkin, D. S. (1992). *Helping the bereaved. Therapeutic interventions for children,* adolescents, *and adults.* New York: Basic Books.

Cook, B. G., & Semmel, M. I. (1999). Peer acceptance of included students with disabilities as a function of severity of disability and classroom composition. *Journal of Special Education, 33,* 50–61.

Cooley, C. H. (1902). *Human nature and the social order.* New York: Scribner's.

Cooney, T. M., & Smith, L. A. (1996). Young adults' relations with grandparents following recent parental divorce. *Journal of Gerontology: Social Sciences, 51B,* S91–S95.

Coontz, S. (2000a). Historical perspectives on family diversity. In D. H. Demo, K. R. Allen, & M. A. Fine (Eds.), *Handbook of family diversity.* New York: Oxford University Press.

Coontz, S. (2000b). Historical perspectives on family studies. *Journal of Marriage and the Family, 62,* 283–297.

Cooper, P. J., & Murray, L. (1998). Postnatal depression. *British Medical Journal, 316,* 1884–1886.

Cooper, R. P., Abraham, J., Berman, S., & Staska, M. (1997). The development of infants' preference for motherese. *Infant Behavior and Development, 20,* 477–488.

Coopersmith, S. (1967). *The antecedents of self-esteem.* San Francisco: W. H. Freeman.

Cornelius, S. W., & Caspi, A. (1987). Everyday problem solving in adulthood and old age. *Psychology and Aging, 2,* 144–153.

Cornell, D., Delcourt, M., Goldberg, M., & Bland, L. (1992). Characteristics of elementary students entering gifted programs: The Learning Outcomes Project at the University of Virginia. *Journal for the Education of the Gifted, 15,* 309–331.

Corr, C. A. (1995). Entering into adolescent understanding of death. In E. A. Grollman (Ed.), *Bereaved children and teens.* Boston: Beacon Press.

Corr, C. A., & Corr, D. M. (1992). Children's hospice care. *Death Studies, 16,* 431–449.

Corwin, J., Loury, M., & Gilbert, A. N. (1995). Workplace, age, and sex as mediators of olfactory function: Data from the National Geographic Smell Survey. *Journals of Gerontology Series B: Psychological Sciences and Social Sciences, 50,* 179–186.

Costa, P. T., Jr., & McCrae, R. R. (1992). Trait psychology comes of age. In T. B. Sonderegger (Ed.), *Nebraska symposium on motivation: Vol 39. Psychology and aging.* Lincoln, NE: University of Nebraska Press.

Costello, E. J., Foley, D. L., & Angold, A. (2006). 10-year research update review: The epidemiology of child and adolescent psychiatric disorders: II. Developmental epidemiology. *Journal of the American Academy of Child and Adolescent Psychiatry, 45,* 8–25.

Costello, E. J., Mustillo, S., Erkanli, A., Keeler, G., & Angold, A. (2003). Prevalence and development of psychiatric disorders in childhood and adolescence. *Archives of General Psychiatry, 60,* 837–844.

Cota-Robles, S. (2003, April). *Traditional Mexican cultural values and the reduced risk for delinquency: Acculturation, familism and parent–adolescent process.* Poster presented at the biennial meeting of the Society for Research in Child Development, Tampa, FL.

Coté, J. E. (2006). Emerging adulthood as an institutionalized moratorium: Risks and benefits to identity formation. In J. J. Arnett, & J. L. Tanner (Eds.), *Emerging adults in America:* Coming of age in the 21st century. Washington, D.C.: American Psychological Association.

Cote, J. E., & Levine, C. (1988). A critical examination of the ego identity status paradigm. *Developmental Review, 8,* 147–184.

Courage, M. L., Reynolds, G. D., & Richards, J. E. (2006). Infants' attention to patterned stimuli: Developmental change from 3 to 12 months of age. *Child Development, 77,* 680–695.

Courchesne, E., Carper, R., & Akshoomoff, N. (2003). Evidence of brain overgrowth in the first year of life in autism. *Journal of the American Medical Association, 290,* 337–344.

Courchesne E., Chisum, H. J., Townsend, J., Cowles, A., Covington, J., Egaas, B., et al. (2000). Normal brain development and aging: Quantitative analysis at in vivo MR imaging in healthy volunteers. *Radiology, 216,* 672–682.

Covington, M. V. (1998). *The will to learn.* New York: Cambridge University Press.

Covington, M. V. (2000). Goal theory, motivation, and school achievement: An integrative review. *Annual Review of Psychology, 51,* 171–200.

Cowan, C. P., & Cowan, P. A. (2000). *When partners become parents: The big life change for couples.* Mahwah, NJ: Erlbaum.

Cowan, P. A., & Cowan, C. P. (2006). Developmental psychopathology from family systems and family risk factors perspectives: Implications for family research, practice, and policy. In D. Cicchetti & D. J. Cohen (Eds.), *Developmental psychopathology: Vol. 1. Theory and method* (2nd ed.). Hoboken, NJ: Wiley.

Cox, M. J., Owen, M. T., Henderson, V. K., & Margand, N. A. (1992). Prediction of infant-father and infant-mother attachment. *Developmental Psychology, 28,* 474–483.

Cox, M. J., Paley, B., Burchinal, M., & Payne, C. C. (1999). Marital perceptions and interactions across the transition to parenthood. *Journal of Marriage and the Family, 61,* 611–625.

Cox, T. H., & Harquail, C. V. (1991). Career paths and career success in the early career stages of male and female MBAs. *Journal of Vocational Behavior, 39,* 54–75.

Coyle, T. R., & Bjorklund, D. F. (1996). The development of strategic memory: A modified microgenetic assessment of utilization deficiencies. *Cognitive Development, 11,* 295–314.

Coyne, J. C., & Whiffen, V. E. (1995). Issues in personality as diathesis for depression: The case of sociotropy dependency and autonomy self-criticism. *Psychological Bulletin, 118,* 358–378.

Crago, M. B., Allen, S. E., & Hough-Eyamir, W. P. (1997). Exploring innateness through cultural and linguistic variation. In M. Gopnik (Ed.), *The inheritance and innateness of grammars* (pp. 70–90). New York: Oxford University Press.

Crawford, M., & Popp, D. (2003). Sexual double standards: A review and methodological critique of two decades of research, *The Journal of Sex Research, 40,* 13–26.

Creasey, G. L. (2006). *Research methods in life span development.* Boston, MA: Pearson Education.

Creusere, M. A. (1999). Theories of adults' understanding and use of irony and sarcasm: Applications to and evidence from research with children. *Developmental Review, 19,* 213–262.

Crews, F. (1996). The verdict on Freud [Review of *Freud evaluated: The completed arc*]. *Psychological Science, 7,* 63–68.

Crick, N. R., & Bigbee, M. (1998). Relational and overt forms of peer victimization: A multiinformant approach. *Journal of Consulting and Clinical Psychology, 66*, 337–347.

Crick, N. R., & Dodge, K. A. (1994). A review and reformulation of social information-processing mechanisms in children's social adjustment. *Psychological Bulletin, 115*, 74–101.

Crijnen, A. A. M., Achenbach, T. M., & Verhulst, F. C. (1997). Comparisons of problems reported by parents of children in 12 cultures: Total problems, externalizing, and internalizing. *Journal of the American Academy of Child and Adolescent Psychiatry, 36*, 1269–1277.

Cristofalo, V. J. (1996). Ten years later: What have we learned about human aging from studies of cell cultures? *Gerontologist, 36*, 737–741.

Critchley, C. R., & Sanson, A. V. (2006). Is parent disciplinary behavior enduring or situational? A multilevel modeling investigation of individual and contextual influences on power assertive and inductive reasoning behaviors. *Journal of Applied Developmental Psychology, 27*, 370–388.

Crockenberg, S., & Leerkes, E. (2003). Infant negative emotionality, caregiving, and family relationships. In A. C. Crouter & A. Booth (Eds.), *Children's influence on family dynamics. The neglected side of family relationships.* Mahwah, NJ: Erlbaum.

Crooks, R. L., & Baur, K. (2008). *Our sexuality* (10th ed.). Pacific Grove, CA: Wadsworth.

Cross, S. E. (2000). What does it mean to "know thyself" in the United States and Japan? The cultural construction of the self. In T. J. Owens (Ed.), *Self and identity through the life course in cross-cultural perspective.* Stamford, CT: JAI Press.

Crouch, J. L., & Behl, L. E. (2001). Relationships among parental beliefs in corporal punishment, reported stress, and physical child abuse potential. *Child Abuse and Neglect, 25*, 413–419.

Crouter, A. C. (2006). Mothers and fathers at work: Implications for families and children. In A. Clarke-Stewart & J. Dunn (Eds.), *Families count: Effects on child and adolescent development.* New York: Cambridge University Press.

Crouter, A. C., & Booth, A. (Eds.) (2003). *Children's influence on family dynamics. The neglected side of family relationships.* Mahwah, NJ: Erlbaum.

Crouter, A. C., Manke, B. A., & McHale, S. M. (1995). The family context of gender intensification in early adolescence. *Child Development, 66*, 317–329.

Crowell, J. A., Fraley, R. C., & Shaver, P. R. (1999). Measurement of individual differences in adolescent and adult attachment. In J. Cassidy & P. R. Shaver (Eds.), *Handbook of attachment: Theory, research, and clinical applications.* New York: Guilford.

Crowell, J. A., Treboux, D., & Waters, E. (2002). Stability of attachment representations: The transition to marriage. *Developmental Psychology, 38*, 467–479.

Csikszentmihalyi, M., & Nakamura, J. (2006). Creativity through the life span from an evolutionary systems perspective. In C. Hoare (Ed.), *Handbook of adult development and learning.* New York: Oxford University Press.

Cui, M., Conger, R. D., & Lorenz, F. O. (2005). Predicting change in adolescent adjustment from change in marital problems. *Developmental Psychology, 41*, 812–823.

Cumming, E., & Henry, W. E. (1961). *Growing old, the process of disengagement.* New York: Basic Books.

Cummings, E. M., Davies, P. T., & Campbell, S. B. (2000). *Developmental psychopathology and family process. Theory, research, and clinical implications.* New York: Guilford.

Cummings, S. M., Williams, M. M., & Ellis, R. A. (2003). Impact of an intergenerational program on 4th graders' attitudes toward elders and school behaviors. *Journal of Human Behavior in the Social Environment, 6*, 91–107.

Cunningham, H. (1996). The history of childhood. In C. P. Hwang, M. E. Lamb, & I. E. Sigel (Eds.), *Images of childhood.* Mahwah, NJ: Erlbaum.

Curtis, N. M., Ronan, K. R., & Bourduin, C. M. (2004). Multisystemic treatment: A meta-analysis of outcome studies. *Journal of Family Psychology, 18*, 411–419.

Cytron, B. D. (1993). To honor the dead and comfort the mourners: Traditions in Judaism. In D. P. Irish, K. F. Lundquist, & V. J. Nelson (Eds.), *Ethnic variations in dying, death, and grief: Diversity in universality.* Washington, D.C.: Taylor & Francis.

Cytryn, L., & McKnew, D. H., Jr. (1996). *Growing up sad: Childhood depression and its treatment.* New York: W. W. Norton.

D

D'Antonio, M. (2006). *Hershey.* New York: Simon Schuster.

D'Onofrio, B. M., Turkheimer, E., Emery, R. E., Slutske, W. S., Heath, A. C., Madden, P. A., & Martin, N. G. (2006). A genetically informed study of the processes underlying the association between parental marital instability and offspring adjustment. *Developmental Psychology, 42*, 486–499.

Dabbs, J. M., & Morris, R. (1990). Testosterone, social class, and antisocial behavior in a sample of 4462 men. *Psychological Science, 1*, 209–211.

Dahl, R. E. (1999). The consequences of insufficient sleep for adolescents: Links between sleep and emotional regulation. *Phi Delta Kappan, 80*, 354–359.

Dalton, D. S., Cruickshanks, K. J., Klein, B. E. K., Klein, R., Wiley, R. L., & Nondahl, D. M. (2004). The impact of hearing loss on quality of life in older adults. *Gerontologist, 43*, 661–668.

Damon, W. (1977). *The social world of the child.* San Francisco: Jossey-Bass.

Damon, W. (1994). *Greater expectations: Overcoming the culture of indulgence in America's homes and schools.* New York: Free Press.

Damon, W., & Hart, D. (1988). *Self-understanding in childhood and adolescence.* New York: Cambridge University Press.

Damon, W., & Hart, D. (1992). Self-understanding and its role in social and moral development. In M. H. Bornstein & M. E. Lamb (Eds.), *Developmental psychology: An advanced textbook.* Hillsdale, NJ: Erlbaum.

Dang-Vu, T. T., Desseilles, M., Peigneux, P., & Maquet, P. (2006). A role for sleep in brain plasticity. *Pediatric Rehabilitation, 9*, 98–118.

Daniluk, J. C. (2001). Reconstructing their lives: A longitudinal, qualitative analysis of the transition to biological childlessness for infertile people. *Journal of Counseling Development, 79*, 439–449.

Darling, C. A., Davidson, J. K., & Passarello, L. C. (1992). The mystique of first intercourse among college youth: The role of partners, contraceptive practices, and psychological reactions. *Journal of Youth and Adolescence, 21*, 97–117.

Darling, N., & Steinberg, L. (1993). Parenting style as context: An integrative model. *Psychological Bulletin, 113*, 487–496.

Darwin, C. (1859). *The origin of species.* New York: Modern Library.

Darwin, C. A. (1877). A biographical sketch of an infant. *Mind, 2*, 285–294.

Darwish, D., Esquivel, G. B., Houtz, J. C., & Alfonso, V. C. (2001). Play and social skills in maltreated and non-maltreated preschoolers during peer interactions. *Child Abuse and Neglect, 25*, 13–31.

Davidson, R. G. (2002). *PDQ medical genetics.* Hamilton, ONT: B. C. Decker.

Davies, B., Collins, J., Steele, R., Cook, K., Distler, V., & Brenner, A. (2007). Parents' and children's perspectives of a children's hospice bereavement program. *Journal of Palliative Care, 23*, 14–23.

Davies, S. L., DiClemente, R. J., Wingood, G. M., Harrington, K. F., Crosby, R. A., & Sionean, C. (2003). Pregnancy desire among disadvantaged African American adolescent females. *American Journal of Health Behavior, 27*, 55–62.

Davis, C. G., & Nolen-Hoeksema, S. (2001). Loss and meaning: How do people make sense of loss? *American Behavioral Scientist, 44*, 726–741.

Dawson, G., & Ashman, S. B. (2000). On the origins of a vulnerability to depression: The influence of the early social environment on the development of psychobiological systems related to risk for affective disorder. In C. A. Nelson (Ed.), *Minnesota Symposium on Child Psychology: Vol. 31. The effects of early adversity on neurobehavioral development.* Mahwah, NJ: Erlbaum.

Dawson, G., & Toth, K. (2006). Autism spectrum disorders. In D. Cicchetti & D. J. Cohen (Eds.), *Developmental psychopathology: Vol. 3. Risk, disorder, and adaptation.* Hoboken, NJ: Wiley.

Day, R. D., & Peterson, G. W. (1998). Predicting spanking of younger and older children by mothers and fathers. *Journal of Marriage & the Family, 60*, 79–92.

de Bode, S., & Curtiss, S. (2000). Language after hemispherectomy. *Brain Cognition, 43*, 135–138.

de Gaston, J. F., Jensen, L., & Weed, S. (1995). A closer look at adolescent sexual activity. *Journal of Youth and Adolescence, 24*, 465–479.

de Gaston, J. F., Weed, S., & Jensen, L. (1996). Understanding gender differences in adolescent sexuality. *Adolescence, 31*, 217–232.

de Jong-Gierveld, J. (1986). Loneliness and the degree of intimacy in interpersonal relationships. In R. Gilmour & S. Duck (Eds.), *The emerging field of personal relationships.* Hillsdale, NJ: Erlbaum.

De Lisi, R., & Staudt, J. (1980). Individual differences in college students' performance on formal operations tasks. *Journal of Applied Developmental Psychology, 1*, 163–174.

de Mol, A. C., Vrancken, S., Eggink, A. J., Verduyn Lunel, F. M., & Warris, A. (2006). The first newborn with congenital rubella syndrome during the rubella epidemic in the Netherlands in 2004/'05. *Nederlands Tijdschrift Voor Geneeskundel, 150*, 741–746.

de St. Aubin, E., McAdams, D. P., & Kim, T. (2004). The generative society: An introduction. In E. de St. Aubin, D. P. McAdams, & T. Kim (Eds.), *The generative society: Caring for future generations*. Washington, D.C.: American Psychological Association.

de Vries, B., & Walker, L. J. (1986). Moral reasoning and attitudes toward capital punishment. *Developmental Psychology, 22*, 509–513.

de Weerth, C., van Hees, Y., & Buitelaar, J. K. (2003). Prenatal maternal cortisol levels and infant behavior during the first 5 months. *Early Human Development, 74*, 139–151.

De Wolff, M. S., & van IJzendoorn, M. H. (1997). Sensitivity and attachment: A meta-analysis on parental antecedents of infant attachment. *Child Development, 68*, 571–591.

Deardorff, J., Gonzales, N. A., Christopher, F. S., Roosa, M. W., & Millsap, R. E. (2005). Early puberty and adolescent pregnancy: The influence of alcohol use. *Pediatrics, 116*, 1451–1456.

Deary, I. J., Strand, S., Smith, P., & Fernandes, C. (2007). Intelligence and educational achievement. *Intelligence, 35*, 13–21.

Deary, I. J., Whalley, L. J., & Starr, J. M. (2003). IQ at age 11 and longevity: Results from a follow up of the Scottish Mental Survey of 1932. In C. E. Finch, J. M. Robine, & Y. Christen (Eds.), *Brain and longevity: Perspectives in longevity* (pp. 153–164). Berlin, Germany: Springer.

Deary, I. J., Whiteman, M. C., Starr, J. M., Whalley, L. J., & Fox, H. C. (2004). The impact of childhood intelligence on later life: Following up the Scottish Mental Surveys of 1932 and 1947. *Journal of Personality and Social Psychology, 86*, 130–147.

Deater-Deckard, K. (2001). Recent research examining the role of peer relationships in the development of psychopathology. *Journal of Child Psychiatry and Allied Disciplines, 42*, 565–579.

Deater-Deckard, K., Dodge, K. A., Bates, J. E., & Pettit, G. S. (1996). Physical discipline among African-American and European American mothers: Links to children's externalizing behaviors. *Developmental Psychology, 32*, 1065–1072.

Deater-Deckard, K., Dodge, K. A., & Sobring, E. (2005). Cultural differences in the effects of physical punishment. In M. Rutter & M. Tienda (Eds.), *Ethnicity and causal mechanisms*. New York: Cambridge University Press.

Deaux, K., & Major, B. (1990). A social-psychological model of gender. In D. L. Rhode (Ed.), *Theoretical perspectives on sexual difference*. New Haven, CT: Yale University Press.

DeBusk, F. L. (1972). The Hutchinson-Gilford progeria syndrome: Report of 4 cases and review of the literature. *Journal of Pediatrics, 80*, 697–724.

DeCasper, A. J., & Fifer, W. P. (1980). Of human bonding: Newborns prefer their mothers' voices. *Science, 208*, 1174–1176.

DeCasper, A. J., & Spence, M. J. (1986). Prenatal maternal speech influences newborns' perception of speech sounds. *Infant Behavior and Development, 9*, 133–150.

Deci, E. L., Koestner, R., & Ryan, R. M. (1999). A meta-analytic review of experiments examining the effects of extrinsic rewards on intrinsic motivation. *Psychological Bulletin, 125*, 627–668.

Deci, E. L., & Ryan, R. M. (1992). The initiation and regulation of intrinsically motivated learning and achievement. In A. K. Boggiano & T. S. Pittman (Eds.), *Achievement and motivation: A social developmental perspective* (pp. 9–36). New York: Cambridge University Press.

DeFrain, J., Taylor, J., & Ernst, L. (1982). *Coping with sudden infant death*. Lexington, MA: Lexington Books.

DeFrain, J. D., Jakub, D. K., & Mendoza, B. L. (1991–1992). The psychological effects of sudden infant death on grandmothers and grandfathers. *Omega: Journal of Death and Dying, 24*, 165–182.

DeLamater, J. D., & Sill, M. (2005). Sexual desire in later life. *The Journal of Sex Research, 42*, 138–149.

Delaunay-El Allam, M., Marlier, L., & Schaal, B. (2006). Learning at the breast: Preference formation for an artificial scent and its attraction against the odor of material milk. *Infant Behavioral Development, 29*, 308–321.

DeLeire, T. C., & Kalil A. (2002). Good things come in threes: Single-parent multigenerational family structure and adolescent adjustment. *Demography, 39*, 393–413.

DeLoache, J. S., Cassidy, D. J., & Brown, A. L. (1985). Precursors of mnemonic strategies in very young children's memory. *Child Development, 56*, 125–137.

DeLoache, J. S., Miller, K. F., & Pierroutsakos, S. L. (1998). Reasoning and problem solving. In D. Kuhn & R. Siegler (Vol. Eds.), W. Damon (Editor-in-Chief), *Handbook of child psychology: Vol. 2. Cognition, perception, and language* (5th ed., pp. 801–850). New York: Wiley.

Delsol, C., & Margolin, G. (2004). The role of family-of-origin violence in men's marital violence perpetration. *Clinical Psychology Review, 24*, 99–122.

DeMarie, D., & Ferron, J. (2003). Capacity, strategies, and metamemory: Tests of a three-factor model of memory development. *Journal of Experimental Child Psychology, 84*, 167–193.

DeMarie, D., Norman, A., & Abshier, D. W. (2000). Age and experience influence different verbal and nonverbal measures of children's scripts for the zoo. *Cognitive Development, 15*, 241–262.

DeMaris, A., & MacDonald, W. (1993). Premarital cohabitation and marital instability: A test of the unconventionality hypothesis. *Journal of Marriage and the Family, 55*, 399–407.

Demetriou, H., & Hay, D. F. (2004). Toddlers' reactions to the distress of familiar peers: The importance of context. *Infancy, 6*, 299–318.

Demo, D. H., & Cox, M. J. (2000). Families with young children: A review of research in the 1990s. *Journal of Marriage and the Family, 62*, 876–895.

Denney, N. W. (1982). Aging and cognitive changes. In B. B. Wolman (Ed.), *Handbook of developmental psychology*. Englewood Cliffs, NJ: Prentice-Hall.

Denney, N. W. (1989). Everyday problem solving: Methodological issues, research findings, and a model. In L. W. Poon, D. C. Rubin, & B. A. Wilson (Eds.), *Everyday cognition in adulthood and late life*. Cambridge, England: Cambridge University Press.

Denney, N. W., & Pearce, K. A. (1989). A developmental study of practical problem solving in adults. *Psychology and Aging, 4*, 438–442.

Dennis, W. (1966). Creative productivity between the ages of 20 and 80 years. *Journal of Gerontology, 21*, 1–8.

Denworth, L. (2006, April 10). The sun has finally come out for Alex. *Newsweek*, p. 26.

DeRosier, M. E., & Thomas, J. M. (2003). Strengthening sociometric prediction: Scientific advances in the assessment of children's peer relations. *Child Development, 74*, 1379–1392.

DESAction (2007). *DES Daughters*. Available at: www.desaction.org/desdaughers.htm. Accessed: June 9, 2007.

DesRosiers, F., Vrsalovic, W. T., Knauf, D. E., Vargas, M., & Busch-Rossnagel, N. A. (1999). Assessing the multiple dimensions of the self-concept of young children: A focus on Latinos. *Merrill-Palmer Quarterly, 45*, 543–566.

Deutsch, F. M. (1999). *Having it all: How equally shared parenting works*. Cambridge, MA: Harvard University Press.

Deutsch, F. M. (2001). Equally shared parenting. *Current Directions in Psychological Science, 10*, 25–28.

Devenny, D. A., Silverman, W. P., Hill, A. L., Jenkins, E., Sersen, E. A., & Wisniewski, K. E. (1996). Normal ageing in adults with Down's syndrome: A longitudinal study. *Journal of Intellectual Disability Research, 40*, 208–221.

Deveny, K. (2003, June 30). We're not in the mood. *Newsweek*, 40–46.

Devlin, B., Daniels, M., & Roeder, K. (1997). The heritability of IQ. *Nature, 388(6641)*, 468–471.

DeVries, M. W. (1984). Temperament and infant mortality among the Masai of East Africa. *American Journal of Psychiatry, 141*, 1189–1194.

DeVries, R. (2000). Vygotsky, Piaget, and education: A reciprocal assimilation of theories and educational practices. *New Ideas in Psychology, 18*, 187–213.

Dewar, R. E., Kline, D. W., & Swanson, H. A. (1995). Age differences in the comprehension of traffic sign symbols. *Transportation Research Record, 1456*, 1–10.

Dews, S., Winner, E., Kaplan, J., Rosenblatt, E., Hunt, M., Lim, K., Mcgovern, A., Qualter, A., & Smarsh, B. (1996). Children's understanding of the meaning and functions of verbal irony. *Child Development, 67*, 3071–3085.

Diamond, M., & Sigmundson, H. K. (1997). Sex reassignment at birth: Long-term review and clinical implications. *Archives of Pediatric and Adolescent Medicine, 151*, 298–304.

Diaz, J. (1997). *How drugs influence behavior: A neuro-behavioral approach*. Upper Saddle River, NJ: Prentice-Hall.

Dickens, W. T., & Flynn, J. R. (2006). Black Americans reduce the racial IQ gap: Evidence from standardization samples. *Psychological Science, 17*, 913–920.

Dickinson, J. E., Paech, M. J., McDonald, S. J., & Evans, S. F. (2002). The impact of intrapartum analgesia on labour and delivery outcomes in nulliparous women. *Department of Obstetrics and Gynaecology, 42*, 59–66.

Diego, M. A., Field, T., & Hernandez-Reif, M. (2005). Vagal activity, gastric motility, and weight gain in massaged preterm neonates. *The Journal of Pediatrics, 147*, 50–55.

Diekman, A. B., & Murnen, S. K. (2004). Learning to be little women and little men: The inequitable gender equality of nonsexist children's literature. *Sex Roles, 50*, 373–385.

Digman, J. M. (1990). Personality structure: Emergence of the 5-factor model. *Annual Review of Psychology, 41*, 417–440.

Dijkstra, I. C., & Stroebe, M. S. (1998). The impact of a child's death on parents: A myth (not yet) disproved? *Journal of Family Studies, 4*, 159–185.

DiLalla, L. F., Kagan, J., & Reznick, S. J. (1994). Genetic etiology of behavioral inhibition among 2-year-old children. *Infant Behavior and Development, 17*, 405–412.

DiMatteo, M. R., Morton, S. C., Lepper, H. S., & Damush, T. M. (1996). Cesarean childbirth and psychosocial outcomes: A meta-analysis. *Health Psychology, 15*, 303–314.

Dimmock, P. W., Wyatt, K. M., Jones, P. W., & O'Brien, P. M. S. (2000). Efficacy of selective serotonin-reuptake inhibitors in premenstrual syndrome: A systematic review. *Lancet, 356*, 1131–1136.

Dinmore, I. (1997). Interdisciplinarity and integrative learning: An imperative for adult education. *Education, 117*, 452–468.

DiPietro, J. A., Costigan, K. A., & Gurewitsch, E. D. (2003). Fetal response to induced maternal stress. *Early Human Development, 74*, 125–138.

DiPietro, J. A., Hilton, S. C., Hawkins, M., Costigan, K. A., & Pressman, E. K. (2002). Maternal stress and affect influence fetal neurobehavioral development. *Developmental Psychology, 38*, 659–668.

DiPietro, J. A., Hodgson, D. M., Costigan, K. A., Hilton, S. C., & Johnson, T. R. B. (1996a). Fetal antecedents of infant temperament. *Child Development, 67*, 2568–2583.

DiPietro, J. A., Hodgson, D. M., Costigan, K. A., Hilton, S. C., & Johnson, T. R. B. (1996b). Fetal neurobehavioral development. *Child Development, 67*, 2553–2567.

DiPietro, J. A., Novak, M., F. S. X., Costigan, K. A., Atella, L. D., & Reusing, S. P. (2006). Maternal psychological distress during pregnancy in relation to child development at age two. *Child Development, 77*, 573–587.

Dittman, R. W., Kappes, M. E., & Kappes, M. H. (1992). Sexual behavior in adolescent and adult females with congenital adrenal hyperplasia. *Psychoneuroendocrinology, 17*, 153–170.

Dittmar, H., Halliwell, E., & Ive, S. (2006). Does Barbie make girls want to be thin? The effect of experimental exposure to images of dolls on the body image of 5- to 8-year-old girls. *Developmental Psychology, 42*, 283–292.

Division of Vital Statistics. (2004). *Infant mortality rates.* Hyattsville, MD: National Center for Health Statistics, Centers for Disease Control and Prevention, U.S. Department of Health and Human Services. Available online: http://www.cdc.gov/nchs/data/hus/tables/2001/01hus023.pdf (retrieved September 2, 2004).

Dixon, R. A. (1992). Contextual approaches to adult intellectual development. In R. J. Sternberg & C. A. Berg (Eds.), *Intellectual development.* New York: Cambridge University Press.

Dixon, R. A. (2003). Themes in the aging of intelligence: Robust decline with intriguing possibilities. In R. J. Sternberg, J. Lautrey, & T. I. Lubart (Eds.), *Models of intelligence: International perspectives* (pp. 151–167). Washington, D.C.: American Psychological Association.

Dodge, K. A. (1986). A social information processing model of social competence in children. In M. Perlmutter (Ed.), *Minnesota Symposia on Child Psychology* (Vol. 18). Hillsdale, NJ: Erlbaum.

Dodge, K. A. (1993). Social-cognitive mechanisms in the development of conduct disorder and depression. *Annual Review of Psychology, 44*, 559–584.

Dodge, K. A., Coie, J. D., & Lynam, D. (2006). Aggression and antisocial behavior in youth. In N. Eisenberg (Vol. Ed.), & W. Damon & R. M. Lerner (Eds. in Chief), *Handbook of child psychology: Vol. 3. Social, emotional, and personality development* (6th ed). Hoboken, NJ: Wiley.

Dodge, K. A., Coie, J. D., Pettit, G. S., & Price, J. M. (1990). Peer status and aggression in boys' groups: Developmental and contextual analysis. *Child Development, 61*, 1289–1309.

Dodge, K. A., Dishion, T. J., & Lansford, J. E. (Eds.) (2006). *Deviant peer influences in programs for youth: Problems and solutions.* New York: Guilford.

Dodge, K. A., Lansford, J. E., Burks, V. S., Bates, J. W., Pettit, G. S., Fontaine, R., & Price, J. M. (2003). Peer rejection and social information-processing factors in the development of aggressive behavior problems in children. *Child Development, 74*, 374–393.

Dodge, K. A., & Pettit, G. S. (2003). A biopsychosocial model of the development of chronic conduct problems in adolescence. *Developmental Psychology, 39*, 349–371.

Dodge, K. A., & Price, J. M. (1994). On the relation between social information processing and socially competent behavior in early school-aged children. *Child Development, 65*, 1385–1397.

Dodson, C. S., Bawa, S., & Krueger, L. E. (2007). Aging, metamemory, and high-confidence errors: A misrecollection account. *Psychological Aging, 22*, 122–133.

Dogan, S. J., Conger, R. D., Kim, K. J., & Masyn, K. E. (2007). Cognitive and parenting pathways in the transmission of antisocial behavior from parents to adolescents. *Child Development, 78*, 335–349.

Doherty, W. J., Erickson, M. F., & LaRossa, R. (2006). An intervention to increase father involvement and skills with infants during the transition to parenthood. *Journal of Family Psychology, 20*, 438–447.

Dohnt, H., & Tiggemann, M. (2006). The contribution of peer and media influences to the development of body satisfaction and self-esteem in young girls: A prospective study. *Developmental Psychology, 42*, 929–936.

Dolen, L. S., & Bearison, D. J. (1982). Social interaction and social cognition in aging. *Human Development, 25*, 430–442.

Dominy, N. L., Johnson, W. B., & Koch, C. (2000). Perception of parental acceptance in women with binge-eating disorder. *Journal of Psychology, 134*, 23–36.

Domjan, M. J. (1993). *Principles of learning and behavior* (3rd ed.). Pacific Grove, CA: Brooks/Cole.

Donnellan, M. B., Trzesniewski, K. H., & Robins, R. W. (2006). Personality and self-esteem development in adolescence. In D. K. Mroczek & T. D. Little (Eds.), *Handbook of personality development.* Mahwah, NJ: Erlbaum.

Donnelly, N., Cave, K., Greenway, R., Hadwin, J. A., Stevenson, J., & Sonuga-Barke, E. (2007). Visual search in children and adults: top-down and bottom-up mechanisms. *Quarterly Journal of Experimental Psychology, 60*, 120–136.

Dorn, L. D., Susman, E. J., & Ponirakis, A. (2003). Pubertal timing and adolescent adjustment and behavior: Conclusions vary by rater. *Journal of Youth and Adolescence, 32*, 157–167.

Dosoky, M., & Amoudi, F. (1997). Menarcheal age of school girls in the city of Jeddah, Saudia Arabia. *Journal of Obstetrics and Gynaecology, 17*, 195–198.

Doucette, A. (2002). Child and adolescent diagnosis: The need for a model-based approach. In L. E. Beutler & M. L. Malik (Eds.), *Rethinking the DSM: A psychological perspective.* Washington, D.C.: American Psychological Association.

Dougherty, T. M., & Haith, M. M. (1997). Infant expectations and reaction time as predictors of childhood speed of processing and IQ. *Developmental Psychology, 33*, 146–155.

Dowdney, L. (2000). Annotation: Childhood bereavement following parental death. *Journal of Child Psychology and Psychiatry and Allied Disciplines, 41*, 819–830.

Downey, D. B. (2002). Parental and family involvement in education. In A. Molnar (Ed.), *School reform proposals: The research evidence* (pp. 113–134). Greenwich, CT: Information Age Publishing.

Downey, J., Elkin, E. J., Ehrhardt, A. A., Meyer-Bahlburg, H. F., Bell, J. J., & Morishima, A. (1991). Cognitive ability and everyday functioning in women with Turner syndrome. *Journal of Learning Disabilities, 24*, 32–39.

Doyle, A. B., Brendgen, M., Markiewicz, D., & Kamkar, K. (2003). Family relationships as moderators of the association between romantic relationships and adjustment in early adolescence. *Journal of Early Adolescence, 23*, 316–340.

Doyle, A. B., Markiewicz, D., Brendgen, M., Lieberman, M., & Voss, K. (2000). Child attachment security and self-concept: Associations with mother and father attachment style and marital quality. *Merrill-Palmer Quarterly, 46*, 514–539.

Doyle, A. E., Biederman, J., Seidman, L. J., Weber, W., & Faraone, S. V. (2000). Diagnostic efficiency of neuropsychological test scores for discriminating boys with and without Attention Deficit-Hyperactivity Disorder. *Journal of Counseling and Clinical Psychology, 68*, 477–488.

Doyle, L. W., & Anderson, P. J. (2005). Improved neurosensory outcome at 8 years of age of extremely low birthweight children born in Victoria over three distinct years. *Archives of Disease in Childhood–Fetal and Neonantal Edition, 90*, 484–488.

Draper, J. (2002). It's the first scientific evidence: A man's experience of pregnancy confirmation. *Journal of Advanced Nursing, 39*, 563–570.

Dubas, J. S., Graber, J. A., & Petersen, A. C. (1991). The effects of pubertal development on achievement during adolescence. *American Journal of Education, 99*, 444–460.

Dublin, L. I., & Lotka, A. J. (1936). *Length of life. A study of the life table.* New York: Ronald Press.

Dumble, M., Gatza, C., Tyner, S., Venkatachalam, S., & Donehower, L. A. (2004). Insights into aging obtained from p53 mutant mouse models. *Annals of the New York Academy of Sciences, 1019*, 171–177.

Duncan, H., & Dick, T. (2000). Collaborative workshops and student academic performance in introductory college mathematics courses: A study of a Treisman model math excel program. *School Science and Mathematics, 100,* 365–373.

Duncan, R. M., & Pratt, M. W. (1997). Microgenetic change in the quantity and quality of preschoolers' private speech. *International Journal of Behavioral Development, 20,* 367.

Dunn, J. (1993). *Young children's close relationships. Beyond attachment.* Newbury Park, CA: Sage.

Dunn, J. (2007). Siblings and socialization. In J. E. Grusec & P. D. Hastings (Eds.), *Handbook of socialization: Theory and research.* New York: Guilford.

Dunn, J., Brown, J., Slomkowski, C., Tesla, C., & Youngblade, L. (1991). Young children's understanding of other people's feelings and beliefs: Individual differences and their antecedents. *Child Development, 62,* 1352–1366.

Dunn, J., Cutting, A. L., & Demetriou, H. (2000). Moral sensibility, understanding others, and children's friendship interactions in the preschool period. *British Journal of Developmental Psychology, 18,* 159–177.

Dunn, J., Fergusson, E., & Maughan, B. (2006). Grandparents, grandchildren, and family change in contemporary Britain. In A. Clarke-Stewart & J. Dunn (Eds.), *Families count: Effects on child and adolescent development.* New York: Cambridge University Press.

Dunn, J., & Kendrick, C. (1982). *Siblings: Love, envy, and understanding.* Cambridge, MA: Harvard University Press.

Dunn, J., & Plomin, R. (1990). *Separate lives. Why siblings are so different.* New York: Basic Books.

Dunphy, D. C. (1963). The social structure of urban adolescent peer groups. *Sociometry, 26,* 230–246.

DuPaul, G. J., & Stoner, G. (2003). *ADHD in the schools. Assessment and intervention strategies* (2nd ed.). New York: Guilford.

Durik, A. M., Hyde, J. S., & Clark, R. (2000). Sequelae of cesarean and vaginal deliveries: Psychosocial outcomes for mothers and infants. *Developmental Psychology, 36,* 251–260.

Durston, L., Davidson, M. C., Tottenham, N., Galvan, A., Spicer, J., Fossella, J. A., & Casey, B. J. (2006). A shift from diffuse to focal cortical activity with development. *Developmental Science, 9,* 1–8.

Dustman, R. E., Emmerson, R. Y., Steinhaus, L. A., Shearer, D. E., & Dustman, T. J. (1992). The effects of videogame playing on neuropsychological performance of elderly individuals. *Journal of Gerontology, 47,* 168–171.

Dustman, R. E., Ruhling, R. O., Russell, E. M., Shearer, D. E., Bonekat, H. W., Shigeoka, J. W., Wood, J. S., & Bradford, D. C. (1989). Neurobiology of aging. In A. C. Ostrow (Ed.), *Aging and motor behavior.* Indianapolis: Benchmark Press.

Duvall, E. M. (1977). *Marriage and family development* (5th ed.). Philadelphia: J. B. Lippincott.

Duyme, M., Dumaret, A., & Tomkiewicz, S. (1999). How can we boost IQs of "dull children"? A late adoption study. *Proceedings of the National Academy of Sciences of the United States of America, 96,* 8790–8794.

Dweck, C. S. (2002). The development of ability conceptions. In A. Wigfield & J. S. Eccles (Eds.), *Development of achievement motivation* (pp. 57–91). San Diego: Academic Press.

Dweck, C. S., & Leggett, E. L. (1988). A social-cognitive approach to motivation and personality. *Psychological Review, 95,* 256–273.

Dyk, P. H., & Adams, G. R. (1990). Identity and intimacy: An initial investigation of three theoretical models using cross-lag panel correlations. *Journal of Youth and Adolescence, 19,* 91–110.

Dyregrov, K. (2003–2004). Micro-sociological analysis of social support following traumatic bereavement: Unhelpful and avoidant responses from the community. *Omega: Journal of Death and Dying, 48,* 23–44.

E

Eagly, A. H. (1987). *Sex differences in social behavior: A social-role interpretation.* Hillsdale, NJ: Erlbaum.

Eagly, A. H., & Steffen, V. J. (2000). Gender differences stem from the distribution of women and men into social roles. In C. Stangor (Ed.), *Stereotypes and prejudice: Essential readings* (pp. 142–160). Philadelphia: Taylor & Francis.

Earles, J. L., & Salthouse, T. A. (1995). Interrelations of age, health, and speed. *Journal of Gerontology: Psychological Sciences and Social Sciences, 50,* 33–41.

Early, D. M., Maxwell, K. L., Burchinal, M., Alva, S., Bender, R. H., Bryant, D., Cai, K., Clifford, R. M., Ebanks, C., Griffin, J. A., Henry, G. T., Howes, C., Irondo-Perez, J., Jeon, H-J., Mashburn, A. J., Peisner-Feinberg, E., Pianta, R. C., Vandergrift, N., & Zill, N. (2007). Teachers' education, classroom quality, and young children's academic skills: Results from seven studies of preschool programs. *Child Development, 78,* 558–580.

Easterbrook, M. A., Kisilevsky, B. S., Muir, D. W., & Laplante, D. P. (1999). Newborns discriminate schematic faces from scrambled faces. *Canadian Journal of Experimental Psychology, 53,* 231–241.

Eaton, D. K., Kann, L., Kinchen, S., Ross, J., Hawkins, J., Harris, W. A., Lowry, R., McManus, T., Chyen, D., Shanklin, S., Lim, C., Grunbaum, J. A., & Wechsler, H. (2006, June 9). Youth risk behavior surveillance—United States, 2005. *Morbidity and Mortality Weekly Report, 55,* 1–108.

Eaton, W. O., & Ritchot, K. F. M. (1995). Physical maturation and information-processing speed in middle childhood. *Developmental Psychology, 31,* 967–972.

Eaves, L., Martin, N., Heath, A., Schieken, R., Meyer, J., Silberg, J., Neale, M., & Corey, L. (1997). Age changes in the causes of individual differences in conservatism. *Behavior Genetics, 27,* 121–124.

Ebbeck, M. (1996). Parents' expectations and child rearing practices in Hong Kong. *Early Child Development and Care, 119,* 15–25.

Eberstadt, N. (2006). Growing old the hard way: China, Russia, India. *Policy Review, 136.* Available at: www.policyreview.org/136/eberstadt.html. Accessed: July 22, 2006.

Ebstein, R. P., Benjamin, J., & Belmaker, R. H. (2003). Behavioral genetics, genomics, and personality. In R. Plomin, J. C. DeFries, I. W. Craig, & P. McGuffin (Eds.), *Behavioral genetics in the postgenomic era.* Washington, D.C.: American Psychological Association.

Eccles, J. S., Jacobs, J. E., & Harold, R. D. (1990). Gender role stereotypes, expectancy effects, and parents' socialization of gender differences. *Journal of Social Issues, 46,* 183–201.

Eccles, J. S., Lord, S., & Midgley, C. (1991). What are we doing to early adolescents? The impact of educational contexts on early adolescents. *American Journal of Education, 99,* 521–542.

Eccles, J. S., Midgley, C., Wigfield, A., Buchanan, C. M., Reuman, D., Flanagan, C., & Mac Iver, D. (1993). Development during adolescence: The impact of stage–environment fit on young adolescents' experiences in schools and in families. *American Psychologist, 48,* 90–101.

Ecklund-Flores, L., & Turkewitz, G. (1996). Asymmetric headturning to speech and nonspeech in human newborns. *Developmental Psychobiology, 29,* 205–217.

Eddleman, K. A., Malone, F. D., Sullivan, L., Dukes, K., Berkowitz, R. L., Kharbutli, Y., Porter, F., Luthy, D. A., Comstock, C. H., Saade, G. R., Klugman, S., Dugoff, L., Craigo, S. D., Timor-Tritsch, I. E., Carr, S. R., Wolfe, H. M., D'Alton, M. E., for the First and Second Trimester Evaluation of Risk (FASTER) Trial Research Consortium. (2006). Pregnancy loss rates after midtrimester amniocentesis. *Obstetrics & Gynecology, 108,* 1067–1072.

Eder, R. A. (1989). The emergent personologist: The structure and content of $3\frac{1}{2}$-, $5\frac{1}{2}$-, and $7\frac{1}{2}$-year-olds' concepts of themselves and other persons. *Child Development, 60,* 1218–1228.

Egeland, B. (1979). Preliminary results of a prospective study of the antecedents of child abuse. *International Journal of Child Abuse and Neglect, 3,* 269–278.

Egeland, B., & Carlson, E. A. (2004). Attachment and psychopathology. In L. Atkinson & S. Goldberg (Eds.), *Attachment issues in psychopathology and intervention.* Mahwah, NJ, Erlbaum.

Egeland, B., Jacobvitz, D., & Sroufe, L. A. (1988). Breaking the cycle of abuse. *Child Development, 59,* 1080–1088.

Egeland, B., Sroufe, L. A., & Erickson, M. (1983). The developmental consequences of different patterns of maltreatment. *International Journal of Child Abuse and Neglect, 7,* 459–469.

Ehrenberg, R. G., Brewer, D. J., Gamoran, A., & Willms, J. D. (2001). Class size and student achievement. *Psychological Science in the Public Interest, 2,* 1–30.

Ehrhardt, A. A. (1985). The psychobiology of gender. In A. S. Rossi (Ed.), *Gender and the life course.* New York: Aldine.

Ehrhardt, A. A., & Baker, S. W. (1974). Fetal androgens, human central nervous system differentiation, and behavioral sex differences. In R. C. Friedman, R. M. Rickard, & R. L. Van de Wiele (Eds.), *Sex differences in behavior.* New York: Wiley.

Ehri, L. C. (1999). Phases of development in learning to read words. In J. Oakhill & R. Beard (Eds.), *Reading development and the teaching of reading* (pp. 79–108). Oxford: Blackwell.

Ehrle, G. M. (2001). Grandchildren as moderator variables in the family, social, physiological, and intellectual development of grandparents who are raising them. In E. L. Grigorenko & R. J. Sternberg (Eds.), *Family environment and intellectual functioning: A life-span perspective.* Mahwah, NJ: Erlbaum.

Eiger, M. S. & Olds, S. W. (1999). *The complete book of breastfeeding* (3rd ed.). New York: Workman Publishing & Bantam Books.

Eimas, P. D. (1975a). Auditory and phonetic cues for speech: Discrimination of the (r-l) distinction by young infants. *Perception and Psychophysics, 18,* 341–347.

Eimas, P. D. (1975b). Speech perception in early infancy. In L. B. Cohen & P. Salapatek (Eds.), *Infant perception: From sensation to cognition.* New York: Academic Press.

Eimas, P. D. (1985). The perception of speech in early infancy. *Scientific American, 252,* 46–52.

Eisenberg, N. (2000). Emotion, regulation, and moral development. *Annual Review of Psychology, 51,* 665–697.

Eisenberg, N., Fabes, R. A., Guthrie, I. K., Murphy, B. C., Maszk, P., Holmgren, R., & Suh, K. (1996). The relations of regulation and emotionality to problem behavior in elementary school children. *Development and Psychopathology, 8,* 141–162.

Eisenberg, N., Spinrad, T. L., & Sadovsky, A. (2006). Empathy-related responding in children. In M. Killen & J. G. Smetana (Eds.), *Handbook of moral development.* Mahwah, NJ: Erlbaum.

Ekerdt, D. J., Bossé, R., & Levkoff, S. (1985). Empirical test for phases of retirement: Findings from the Normative Aging Study. *Journal of Gerontology, 40,* 95–101.

Ekerdt, D. J., Kosloski, K., & DeViney, S. (2000). The normative anticipation of retirement by older adults. *Research on Aging, 22,* 3–22.

Elbourne, D., & Wiseman, R. A. (2000). Types of intra-muscular opioids for maternal pain relief in labor. *Cochrane Database Systems Review 2000* (CD001237).

Elder, G. H., Jr. (1998). The life course as developmental theory. *Child Development, 69,* 1–12.

Elder, G. H., Jr., Liker, J. K., & Cross, C. E. (1984). Parent–child behavior in the Great Depression: Life course and intergenerational influences. In P. B. Baltes & O. G. Brim Jr. (Eds.), *Life-span development and behavior* (Vol. 6). Orlando, FL: Academic Press.

Elder, G. H., Jr., & Shanahan, M. J. (2006). The life course and human development. In W. Damon & R. M. Lerner (Eds. in Chief) & R. M. Lerner (Vol. Ed.), *Handbook of child psychology: Vol. 1. Theoretical models of human development* (6th ed.). Hoboken, NJ: Wiley.

Elicker, J., Englund, M., & Sroufe, L. A. (1992). Predicting peer competence and peer relationships in childhood from early parent–child relationships. In R. D. Parke & G. W. Ladd (Eds.), *Family-peer relationships: Modes of linkage.* Hillsdale, NJ: Erlbaum.

Eliot, L. (1999). What's going on in there? How the brain and mind develop in the first five years of life. New York, NY: Bantam Books.

Elkind, D. (1967). Egocentrism in adolescence. *Child Development, 38,* 1025–1034.

Elkind, D. (1987). *Miseducation: Preschoolers at risk.* New York: Knopf.

Elkind, D. (1992, May/June). The future of childhood. Waaah!! Why kids have a lot to cry about. *Psychology Today,* 38–41, 80–81.

Elkind, D., & Bowen, R. (1979). Imaginary audience behavior in children and adolescents. *Developmental Psychology, 15,* 38–44.

Ella Galbraith Miller. Va. woman lived to 119. (2000, November 23). *The Washington Post,* B6.

Elliot, A. J., & Church, M. A. (1997). A hierarchical model of approach and avoidance achievement motivation. *Journal of Personality and Social Psychology, 72,* 218–232.

Elliot, A. J., & Reis, H. T. (2003). Attachment and exploration in adulthood. *Journal of Personality & Social Psychology, 85,* 317–331.

Elliott, D. S., & Ageton, S. S. (1980). Reconciling race and class differences in self-reported and official estimates of delinquency. *American Sociological Review, 45,* 95–110.

Elliott, E. S., & Dweck, C. S. (1988). Goals: An approach to motivation and achievement. *Journal of Personality and Social Psychology, 54,* 5–12.

Elliott, J. G. (1999). School refusal: Issues of conceptualization, assessment, and treatment. *Journal of Child Psychology and Psychiatry, 40,* 1001–1012.

Ellis, B. J., & Bjorklund, D. F. (Eds.). (2005). *Origins of the social mind.* New York: Guilford.

Ellis, L., Ames, M. A., Peckham, W., & Burke, D. M. (1988). Sexual orientation in human offspring may be altered by severe emotional distress during pregnancy. *Journal of Sex Research, 25,* 152–157.

Ellis, B. J., & Garber, J. (2000). Psychosocial antecedents of variation in girls' pubertal timing: Maternal depression, stepfather presence, and marital and family stress. *Child Development, 71,* 485–501.

Ellis, S., Rogoff, B., & Cromer, C. C. (1981). Age segregation in children's social interactions. *Developmental Psychology, 17,* 399–407.

Ellison, P. T. (2002). Puberty. In N. Cameron (Ed.), *Human growth and development* (pp. 65–84). New York: Academic Press.

Else-Quest, N. M., Hyde, J. S., & DeLamater, J. D. (2005). Context counts: Long-term sequelae of premarital intercourse or abstinence. *The Journal of Sex Research, 42,* 102–112.

Ely, R. (1997). Language and literacy in the school years. In J. K. Gleason (Ed.), *The development of language* (4th ed.). Boston: Allyn & Bacon.

Ely, R. (2001). Language and literacy in the school years. In J. B. Gleason (Ed.), *The development of language* (5th ed.). Boston: Allyn & Bacon.

Ely, R. (2005). Language development in the school years. In J. B. Gleason (Ed.), *The development of language* (6th ed.). Boston: Allyn & Bacon.

Emanuel, E. J. (2001). Euthanasia: Where the Netherlands leads will the world follow? *British Medical Journal, 322,* 1376–1377.

Emde, R. N., Biringen, Z., Clyman, R. B., & Oppenheim, D. (1991). The moral self of infancy: Affective core and procedural knowledge. *Developmental Review, 11,* 251–270.

Emery, R. E. (1999). Post divorce family life for children. An overview of research and some implications for policy. In R. A. Thompson & P. R. Amato (Eds.), *The post divorce family. Children, parenting, & society.* Thousand Oaks, CA: Sage.

Emery, R. E., & Laumann-Billings, L. (1998). An overview of the nature, causes, and consequences of abusive family relationships: Toward differentiating maltreatment and violence. *American Psychologist, 53,* 121–135.

Emery, R. E., & Tuer, M. (1993). Parenting and the marital relationship. In T. Luster & L. Okagaki (Eds.), *Parenting. An ecological perspective.* Hillsdale, NJ: Erlbaum.

England, P., Reid, L. L., & Kilbourne, B. S. (1996). The effect of the sex composition of jobs on starting wages in an organization: Findings from the NLSY. *Demography, 33,* 511–521.

Englander-Golden, P., Sonleitner, F. J., Whitmore, M. R., & Corbley, G. J. M. (1986). Social and menstrual cycles: Methodological and substantive findings. In V. L. Olesen & N. F. Woods (Eds.), *Culture, society, and menstruation.* Washington, D.C.: Hemisphere.

Enright, R., Lapsley, D., & Shukla, D. (1979). Adolescent egocentrism in early and late adolescence. *Adolescence, 14,* 687–695.

Ensminger, M. E., & Slusarcick, A. L. (1992). Paths to high school graduation or dropout: A longitudinal study of a first-grade cohort. *Sociology of Education, 65,* 95–113.

Epel, E. S., Blackburn, E. H., Lin, J., Dhabhar, F. S., Adler, N. E., Morrow, J. D., & Cawthon, R. M. (2004). Accelerated telomere shortening in response to life stress. *Proceedings of the National Academy of Sciences, 101,* 17312–17315.

Epel, E. S., Lin, J., Wilhelm, F. H., Wolkowitz, O. M., Cawthon, R., Adler, N. E., Dolbier, C., Mendes, W. B., & Blackburn, E. H. (2006). Cell aging in relation to stress arousal and cardiovascular disease risk factors. *Psychoneuroendrocrinology, 31,* 277–287.

Eppler, M. A. (1995). Development of manipulatory skills and the deployment of attention. *Infant Behavior & Development, 18,* 391–405.

Epstein, H. T. (2001). An outline of the role of brain in human cognitive development. *Brain and Cognition, 45,* 44–51.

Epstein, R. (1995). *Creativity games for trainers: A handbook of group activities for jumpstarting workplace creativity.* New York: McGraw Hill.

Erber, J. T. (2005). *Aging and older adulthood.* Belmont, CA: Wadsworth.

Erdley, C. A., Loomis, C. C., Cain, K. M., & Dumas-Hines, F. (1997). Relations among children's social goals, implicit personality theories, and responses to social failure. *Developmental Psychology, 33,* 263–272.

Ericsson, K. A. (1996). The acquisition of expert performance: An introduction to some of the issues. In K. A. Ericsson (Ed.), *The road to excellence: The acquisition of expert performance in the arts and sciences, sports, and games.* Mahwah, NJ: Erlbaum.

Ericsson, K. A., Chase, W. G., & Faloon, S. (1980). Acquisition of a memory skill. *Science, 208,* 1181–1182.

Ericsson, K. A., & Kintsch, W. (1995). Long-term working memory. *Psychological Review, 102,* 211–245.

Erikson, E. H. (1963). *Childhood and society* (2nd ed.). New York: Norton.

Erikson, E. H. (1968). *Identity: Youth and crisis.* New York: Norton.

Erikson, E. H. (1982). *The life cycle completed: A review.* New York: Norton.

Erikson, E. H., Erikson, J. M., & Kivnick, H. Q. (1986). *Vital involvement in old age.* New York: Norton.

Eriksson, M., Brown, W. T., Gordon, L. B., Glynn, M. W., Singer, J., Scott, L., Erdos, M. R., Robbins, C. M., Moses, T. Y., Berglund, P., Dutra, A., Pak, E., Durkin, S., Csoka, A. B., Boehnke, M., Glover, T. W., & Collins, F. S. (2003). Recurrent *de novo* point mutations in lamin A cause Hutchinson-Gilford progeria syndrome. *Nature, 423,* 239–298.

Eriksson, M., Rasmussen, F., & Tynelius, P. (2006). Genetic factors in physical activity and the equal environment assumption: The Swedish young male twins study. *Behavior Genetics, 36,* 238–247.

Escalona, S. (1968). *The roots of individuality: Normal patterns of individuality.* Chicago: Aldine.

Eskritt, M., & Lee, K. (2002). "Remember where you last saw that card": Children's production of external symbols as a memory aid. *Developmental Psychology, 38,* 254–266.

Espy, K. A., Molfese, V. J., & DiLalla, L. F. (2001). Effects of environmental measures on intelligence in young children: Growth curve modeling of longitudinal data. *Merrill-Palmer Quarterly, 47,* 42–73.

Essa, E. L., & Murray, C. I. (1994). Young children's understanding and experience with death. *Young Children, 49,* 74–81.

Etaugh, C., & Liss, M. B. (1992). Home, school, and playroom: Training grounds for adult gender roles. *Sex Roles, 26,* 129–147.

Estourgie-van Burk, G. F., Bartels, M., van Beijsterveldt, T. C., Delemarre-van de Waal, H. A., & Boomsma, D. I. (2006). Body size in five-year-old twins: Heritability and comparison to singleton standards. *Twin Research and Human Genetics, 9,* 646–655.

Evans, G. W. (2004). The environment of childhood poverty. *American Psychologist, 59,* 77–92.

Evans, G. W. (2006). Child development and the physical environment. *Annual Review of Psychology, 57,* 423–451.

Evans, G. W., Gonnella, C., Marcynyszyn, L. A., Gentile, L., & Salpekar, N. (2005). The role of chaos in poverty and children's socioemotional adjustment. *Psychological Science, 16,* 560–565.

Evans, J. R. (2001). Risk factors for age-related macular degeneration. *Progress in Retinal and Eye Research, 20,* 227.

Evans, J. R., Fletcher, A. E., Wormald, R. P., Ng, E. S., Stirling, S., Smeeth, L., Breeze, E., Bulpitt, C. J., Nunes, M., Jones, D., & Tulloch, A. (2002). Prevalence of visual impairment in people aged 75 years and older in Britain: Results from the MRC trial of assessment and management of older people in the community. *Ophthalmology,* 795–800.

F

Faber, C. E., & Grontved, A. M. (2000). Cochlear implantation and change in quality of life. *Acta Otolaryngology Supplement, 543,* 151–153.

Fabes, R. A., Martin, C. L., & Hanish, L. D. (2003). Young children's play qualities in same-, other-, and mixed-sex peer groups. *Child Development, 74,* 921–932.

Fagot, B. I. (1978). The influence of sex of child on parental reactions to toddler children. *Child Development, 49,* 459–465.

Fagot, B. I. (1985). Beyond the reinforcement principle: Another step toward understanding sex-role development. *Developmental Psychology, 21,* 1097–1104.

Fagot, B. I. (1997). Attachment, parenting, and peer interactions of toddler children. *Developmental Psychology, 33,* 489–499.

Fagot, B. I., & Kavanaugh, K. (1993). Parenting during the second year: Effects of children's age, sex, and attachment classification. *Child Development, 64,* 258–271.

Fagot, B. I., & Leinbach, M. D. (1989). The young child's gender schema: Environmental input, internal organization. *Child Development, 60,* 663–672.

Fagot, B. I., & Leinbach, M. D. (1993). Gender-role development in young children: From discrimination to labeling. *Developmental Review, 13,* 205–224.

Fagot, B. I., Leinbach, M. D., & Hagan, R. (1986). Gender labeling and the adoption of sex-typed behaviors. *Developmental Psychology, 22,* 440–443.

Fagot, B. I., Leinbach, M. D., & O'Boyle, C. (1992). Gender labeling, gender stereotyping, and parenting behaviors. *Developmental Psychology, 28,* 225–230.

Falcon, L. M., & Tucker, K. L. (2000). Prevalence and correlates of depressive symptoms among Hispanic elders in Massachusetts. *Journal of Gerontology: Social Sciences, 55,* S108–S116.

Fantz, R. L., & Fagan, J. F. (1975). Visual attention to size and number of pattern details by term and preterm infants during the first six months. *Child Development, 46,* 3–18.

Farber, N. (2003). *Adolescent pregnancy. Policy and prevention services.* New York: Springer.

Farroni, T., Johnson, M. H., Menon, E., Zulian, L., Faraguna, D., & Csibra, G. (2005). Newborns' preference for face-relevant stimuli: Effects of contrast polarity. *Proceedings of the National Academy of Sciences, 102,* 17245–17250.

Farver, J. A. M., & Lee-Shin, Y. (1997). Social pretend play in Korean and Anglo American preschoolers. *Child Development, 68,* 544–556.

Farver, J. A. M., Kim, Y. K., & Lee-Shin, Y. (2000). Within cultural differences: Examining individual differences in Korean American and European American preschoolers' social pretend play. *Journal of Cross-Cultural Psychology, 31,* 583–602.

Faulkner, D., Joiner, R., Littleton, K., Miell, D., & Thompson, L. (2000). The mediating effect of task presentation on collaboration and children's acquisition of scientific reasoning. *European Journal of Psychology of Education, 15,* 417–430.

Faulkner, K. W. (1997). Talking about death with a dying child. *American Journal of Nursing, 97,* 64, 66, 68–69.

Faust, M. A., & Glenzer, N. (2000). "I could read those parts over and over": Eighth graders rereading to enhance enjoyment and learning with literature. *Journal of Adolescent and Adult Literacy, 44,* 234–239.

Favilla, M. (2006). Reaching movements in children: Accuracy and reaction time development. *Journal of Experimental Brain Research, 169,* 122–125.

Fearon, R. M., P., van IJzendoorn, M. H., Fonagy, P., Bakermans-Kranenburg, M. J., Schuengel, C., & Bokhorst, C. L. (2006). In search of shared and nonshared environmental factors in security of attachment: A behavior-genetic study of the association between sensitivity and attachment security. *Developmental Psychology, 42,* 1026–1040.

Federal Interagency Forum on Aging (2006). *Older Americans update 2006: Key indicators of well-being.* Available at: http://www.agingstats.gov/agingstatsdotnet/main_site/default.aspx. Accessed: March 23, 2007.

Fehlings, D., Hunt, C., & Rosenbaum, P. (2007). Cerebral palsy (pp. 279–286). In I. Brown & M. Percy (Eds.), *A comprehensive guide to intellectual & developmental disabilities.* Baltimore, MD: Paul H. Brookes.

Feingold, A. (1992). Sex differences in variability in intellectual abilities: A new look at an old controversy. *Review of Educational Research, 62,* 61–84.

Feingold, A. (1994a). Gender differences in intellectual abilities: A cross-cultural perspective. *Sex Roles, 30,* 81–92.

Feingold, A. (1994b). Gender differences in personality: A meta-analysis. *Psychological Bulletin, 116,* 429–456.

Feinman, S. (1992). *Social referencing and the social construction of reality in infancy.* New York: Plenum.

Feldman, D. H. (1986). *Nature's gambit: Child prodigies and the development of human potential.* New York: Basic Books.

Feldman, D. H., & Fowler, R. C. (1997). The nature(s) of developmental change: Piaget, Vygotsky, and the transition process. *New Ideas in Psychology, 3,* 195–210.

Feldman, R. (2006). From biological rhythms to social rhythms: Physiological precursors of mother–infant synchrony. *Developmental Psychology, 42,* 175–188.

Feldman, R. D. (1982). *Whatever happened to the Quiz Kids? Perils and profits of growing up gifted.* Chicago: Chicago Review Press.

Feldman, R., & Eidelman, A. I. (2003). Skin-to-skin contact (kangaroo care) accelerates autonomic and neurobehavioral maturation in preterm infants. *Developmental Medicine and Child Neurology, 45,* 274–281.

Feldman, R., & Eidelman, A. I. (2005). Does a triplet pose a special risk for infant development? Assessing cognitive development in relation to intrauterine growth and mother–infant interaction across the first two years. *Pediatrics, 115,* 443–452.

Feldman, R., & Eidelman, A. I. (2006). Neonatal state organization, neuromaturation, mother–infant interaction, and cognitive development in small-for-gestational-age premature infants. *Pediatrics, 118,* 869–879.

Feldman, R., Weller, A., Sirota, L., & Eidelman, A. (2003). Testing a family intervention hypothesis: The contribution of mother–infant skin-to-skin contact (kangaroo care) to family interaction, proximity, and touch. *Journal of Family Psychology, 17,* 94–107.

Feldman, S. S., Biringen, Z. C., & Nash, S. C. (1981). Fluctuations of sex-related self-attributions as a function of stage of family life cycle. *Developmental Psychology, 17,* 24–35.

Felton, B. J., & Berry, C. A. (1992). Do the sources of the urban elderly's social support determine its psychological consequences? *Psychology and Aging, 7,* 89–97.

Fenson, L., Dale, P. S., Reznick, J. S., Bates, E., Thal, D. J., & Pethick, S. J. (1994). Variability in early communicative development. *Monographs of the Society for Research in Child Development, 59* (Serial No. 242).

Ferbeyre, G., & Lowe, S. W. (2002). Ageing: The price of tumour suppression? *Nature, 415,* 26–27.

Ferguson., R. F. (2002). *What doesn't meet the eye: Understanding and addressing racial disparities in high-achieving suburban schools.* Oakbrook, IL: North Central Regional Educational Laboratory. Available at http://www.tripodproject.org/uploads/file/What_doesnt_meet_the_eye.pdf. Accessed: November 2, 2007.

Fernald, A. (2004). Auditory development in infancy. In G. Bremner, & A. Fogel (Eds.),

Blackwell handbook of infant development (pp. 35–70). Malden, MA: Blackwell Publishing.

Ferri, B., & Connor, D. J. (2005). Tools of exclusion: Race, disability, and (re)segregated education. *Teachers College Record, 107,* 453–474.

Ferri, C. P., Prince, M., Brayne, C., Brodaty, H., Fratiglioni, L., Ganguli, M., Hall, K., Hasegawa, K., Hendrie, H., Huang, Y., Jorm, A., Mathers, C., Menezes, P. R., Rimmer, E., & Scazufca, M. (2005). Global prevalence of dementia: A Delphi consensus study. *Lancet, 366,* 2112–2117.

Feuerstein, R., Feuerstein, R., & Gross, S. (1997). The learning potential assessment device. In D. P. Flanagan, J. Genshaft, & P. L. Harrison (Eds.), *Contemporary intellectual assessment: Theories, tests, and issues.* New York: Guilford.

Field, D. (1981). Can preschool children really learn to conserve? *Child Development, 52,* 326–334.

Field, D., & Gueldner, S. H. (2001). The oldest-old: How do they differ from the old-old? *Journal of Gerontological Nursing, 27,* 20–27.

Field, J., Muir, D., Pilon, R., Sinclair, M., & Dodwell, P. (1980). Infants' orientation to lateral sounds from birth to three months. *Child Development, 51,* 295–298.

Field, N. P. (2006). Unresolved grief and continuing bonds: An attachment perspective. *Death Studies, 30,* 739–756.

Field, N. P., Nichols, C., Holen, A., & Horowitz, M. J. (1999). The relation of continuing attachment to adjustment in conjugal bereavement. *Journal of Consulting & Clinical Psychology, 67,* 212–218.

Field, T., Diego, M. A., Hernandez-Reif, M., Deeds, O., & Figuereido, B. (2006). Moderate versus light pressure massage therapy leads to greater weight gain in preterm infants. *Infant Behavior and Development, 2006,* 574–578.

Field, T. M. (1990). *Infancy.* Cambridge, MA: Harvard University Press.

Field, T. M. (1995). Infants of depressed mothers. *Infant Behavior and Development, 18,* 1–13.

Fifer, W. P., Monk, C. E.,. & Grose-Fifer, J. (2004). Prenatal development and risk. In G. Bremner, & A. Fogel (Eds.), *Blackwell handbook of infant development* (pp. 505–542). Malden, MA: Blackwell Publishing.

Filipek, P. A., Accardo, P. J., Ashwal, S., & Baranek, G. T. (2000). Practice parameter: Screening and diagnosis of autism: Report of the Quality Standards Subcommittee of the American Academy of Neurology and the Child Neurology Society. *Neurology, 55,* 468–479.

Filipp, S. H. (1996). Motivation and emotion. In J. E. Birren, K. W. Schaie, R. P. Abeles, M. Gatz, & T. A. Salthouse (Eds.), *Handbook of the psychology of aging* (4th ed.). San Diego: Academic Press.

Fincham, F. D. (2003). Marital conflict: Correlates, structure, and context. *Current Directions in Psychological Science, 12,* 23–27.

Finitzo, T., Gunnarson, A. D., & Clark, J. L. (1990). Auditory deprivation and early conductive hearing loss from otitis media. *Topics in Language Disorders, 11,* 29–42.

Finkel, D., Pedersen, N. L., Reynolds, C. A., Berg, S., de Faire, U., & Svartengren, M. (2003). Genetic and environmental influences on decline in biobehavioral markers of aging. *Behavior Genetics, 33,* 107–123.

Finkelhor, D., & Berliner, L. (1995). Research on the treatment of sexually abused children: A review and recommendations. *Journal of the American Academy of Child and Adolescent Psychiatry, 34,* 1408–1423.

Finkelhor, D., & Dziuba-Leatherman, J. (1994). Victimization of children. *American Psychologist, 49,* 173–183.

Finkelstein, J. A., & Schiffman, S. S. (1999). Workshop on taste and smell in the elderly: An overview. *Physiological Behavior, 66,* 173–176.

Finn, J. D. (2002). Class-size reduction in grades K–3. In A. Molnar (Ed.), *School reform proposals: The research evidence* (pp. 27–48). Greenwich, CT: Information Age Publishing.

Fisch, H., Hyun, G., Golder, R., Hensle, T. W., Olsson, C. A., & Liberson, G. L. (2003). The influence of paternal age on Down syndrome. *Journal of Urology, 169,* 2275–2278.

Fischer, J. L., Sollie, D. L., Sorell, G. T., & Green, S. K. (1989). Marital status and career stage influences on social networks of young adults. *Journal of Marriage and the Family, 51,* 521–534.

Fischer, J. S. (2000, February 14). Best hope or broken promise? After a decade, gene therapy goes on trial. *U.S. News and World Report,* 46.

Fischer, K. W. (1980). A theory of cognitive development: The control and construction of hierarchies of skills. *Psychological Review, 87,* 477–531.

Fischer, K. W., & Bidell, T. (1991). Constraining nativist inferences about cognitive capacities. In S. Carey & Gelman (Eds.), *The epigenesis of mind: Essays on biology and cognition.* Hillsdale, NJ: Erlbaum.

Fischer, K. W., Kenny, S. L., & Pipp, S. L. (1990). How cognitive processes and environmental conditions organize discontinuities in the development of abstractions. In C. N. Alexander & E. J. Langer (Eds.), *Higher stages of human development: Perspectives on adult growth.* New York: Oxford Univeristy Press.

Fischer, P., Jungwirth, S., Zehetmayer, S., Weissgram, S., Hoenigschnabl, S., Gelpi, E., Krampla, W., & Tragl, K. H. (2007). Conversion from subtypes of mild cognitive impairment to Alzheimer dementia. *Neurology, 68,* 288–291.

Fischer, R. B., Blazey, M. L., & Lipman, H. T. (1992). *Students of the third age.* New York: Macmillan.

Fisher, C., & Tokura, H. (1996). Acoustic cues to grammatical structure in infant-directed speech: Cross-linguistic evidence. *Child Development, 67,* 3192–3218.

Fisher, E. P. (1992). The impact of play on development: A meta-analysis. *Play and Culture, 5,* 159–181.

Fisher, H. (2006). The drive to love: The neural mechanism for mate selection. In R. J. Sternberg & K. Weis (Eds.), *The new psychology of love.* New Haven, CT: Yale University Press.

Fisher, L., Ames, E. W., Chisholm, K., & Savoie, L. (1997). Problems reported by parents of Romanian orphans adopted to British Columbia. *International Journal of Behavioral Development, 20,* 67–82.

Fisher, S., & Greenberg, R. P. (1977). *The scientific credibility of Freud's theories and therapy.* New York: Basic Books.

Fitzgerald, J. M. (1999). Autobiographical memory and social cognition: Development of the remembered self in adulthood. In T. M. Hess & F. Blanchard-Fields (Eds.), *Social cognition and aging* (pp. 143–171). San Diego: Academic Press.

Fivush, R. (2002). Children's long-term memory of childhood events. In P. Graf & N. Ohta (Eds.), *Lifespan development of human memory* (pp. 83–100). Cambridge, MA: MIT Press.

Fivush, R., & Hammond, N. R. (1989). Time and again: Effects of repetition and retention interval on 2-year-olds' event recall. *Journal of Experimental Child Psychology, 47,* 259–273.

Fivush, R., Gray, J. T., & Fromhoff, F. A. (1987). Two-year-olds talk about the past. *Cognitive Development, 2,* 393–409.

Flaherty, J. H., & Morley, J. E. (2004). Delirium: A call to improve current standards of care. *Journal of Gerontology: Medical Sciences, 59A,* M341–M343.

Flannery, R. B., Jr. (2003). Domestic violence and elderly dementia sufferers. *American Journal of Alzheimer's Disease and Other Dementias, 18,* 21–23.

Flavell, J. H. (1963). *The developmental psychology of Jean Piaget.* New York: Van Nostrand Reinhold.

Flavell, J. H. (1985). *Cognitive development* (2nd ed.). Englewood Cliffs, NJ: Prentice Hall.

Flavell, J. H. (1996). Piaget's legacy. *Psychological Science, 7,* 200–203.

Flavell, J. H. (1999). Cognitive development: Children's knowledge about the mind. *Annual Review of Psychology, 50,* 21–45.

Flavell, J. H., Beach, D. R., & Chinsky, J. M. (1966). Spontaneous verbal rehearsal in a memory task as a function of age. *Child Development, 37,* 283–299.

Flavell, J. H., Everett, B. H., Croft, K., & Flavell, E. R. (1981). Young children's knowledge about visual perception: Further evidence for the level 1–level 2 distinction. *Developmental Psychology, 17,* 99–103.

Flavell, J. H., Miller, P. H., & Miller, S. A. (1993). *Cognitive development.* Englewood Cliffs, NJ: Prentice Hall.

Flavell, J. H., & Wellman, H. M. (1977). Metamemory. In R. V. Kail & J. W. Hagen (Eds.), *Perspectives on the development of memory and cognition.* Hillsdale, NJ: Erlbaum.

Fleeson, W. (2004). The quality of American life at the end of the century. In O. G. Brim, C. D. Ryff, & R. C. Kessler (Eds.), *How healthy are we? A national study of well-being at midlife.* Chicago: University of Chicago Press.

Fletcher, K. L., & Bray, N. W. (1996). External memory strategy use in preschool children. *Merrill-Palmer Quarterly, 42,* 379–396.

Flieller, A. (1999). Comparison of the development of formal thought in adolescent cohorts aged 10 to 15 years (1967–1996 and 1972–1993). *Developmental Psychology, 35,* 1048–1058.

Flint, M. (1982). Male and female menopause: A cultural put-on. In A. M. Voda, M. Dinnerstein, & S. R. O'Donnell (Eds.), *Changing perspectives on menopause.* Austin: University of Texas Press.

Flook, L., Repetti, R. L., & Ullman, J. B. (2005). Classroom social experiences as predictors of academic performance. *Developmental Psychology, 41,* 319–327.

Floor, P., & Akhtar, N. (2006). Can 18-month-old infants learn words by listening in on conversations? *Infancy, 9,* 327–339.

Flores, E., Cicchetti, D., & Rogosch, F. A. (2005). Predictors of resilience in maltreated and nonmaltreated Latino children. *Developmental Psychology, 41,* 338–351.

Florian, V., & Kravetz, S. (1985). Children's concepts of death. A cross-cultural comparison among Muslims, Druze, Christians, and Jews in Israel. *Journal of Cross-Cultural Psychology, 16*, 174–189.

Florida, R. (2002). *The rise of the creative class.* New York: Basic Books.

Florsheim, P., Sumida, E., McCann, C., Winstanley, M., Fukui, R., Seefeldt, T., & Moore, D. (2003). The transition to parenthood among young African American and Latino couples: Relational predictors of risk for parental dysfunction. *Journal of Family Psychology, 17*, 65–79.

Flouri, E., & Buchanan, A. (2003). What predicts fathers' involvement with their children? A prospective study of intact families. *British Journal of Developmental Psychology, 21*, 81–97.

Flum, H., & Blustein, D. L. (2000). Reinvigorating the study of vocational research. *Journal of Vocational Behavior, 56*, 380–404.

Flynn, J. R. (1987). Massive IQ gains in 14 nations: What IQ tests really measure. *Psychological Bulletin, 101*, 171–191.

Flynn, J. R. (1998). IQ gains over time: Toward finding the causes. In U. Neisser (Ed.), *The rising curve: Long-term gains in IQ and related measures.* Washington, D.C.: American Psychological Association.

Flynn, J. R. (1999). Search for justice: The discovery of IQ gains over time. *American Psychologist, 54*, 5–20.

Foley, K., & Hendin, H. (2002). Conclusion: Changing the culture. In K. Foley, & H. Hendin (Eds.), *The case against assisted suicide: For the right to end-of-life care.* Baltimore: The Johns Hopkins Press.

Folkman, S., & Moskowitz, J. T. (2004). Coping: Pitfalls and promise. *Annual Review of Psychology, 55*, 745–774.

Fonagy, P., & Target, M. (2000). The place of psychodynamic theory in developmental psychopathology. *Development and Psychopathology, 12*, 407–425.

Foorman, B. R. (1995). Research on "The Great Debate": Code-oriented versus whole language approaches to reading instruction. *School Psychology Review, 24*, 376–392.

Foorman, B. R., Francis, D. J., Fletcher, J. M., Schatschneider, C., & Mehta, P. (1998). The role of instruction in learning to read: Preventing reading failure in at-risk children. *Journal of Educational Psychology, 90*, 37–55.

Foos, P. W., & Sarno, S. J. (1998). Adult age differences in semantic and episodic memory. *Journal of Genetic Psychology, 159*, 297–312.

Ford, T., Goodman, R., & Meltzer, H. (2003). The British child and adolescent mental health survey 1999: The prevalence of DSM-IV disorders. *Journal of the American Academy of Child and Adolescent Psychiatry, 42*, 1203–1211.

Fordham, S., & Ogbu, J. U. (1986). Black students' school success: Coping with the "burden of 'acting white.'" *Urban Review, 18*, 176–206.

Forgatch, M. S., & DeGarmo, D. S. (1999). Parenting through change: An effective prevention program for single mothers. *Journal of Consulting and Clinical Psychology, 67*, 711–724.

Forys, K., & Rider, E. (2000, April). *Factors influencing self-esteem during the transition from elementary to middle school.* Paper presented at the Annual Meeting of the Eastern Psychological Association, Baltimore.

Fouquereau, E., Fernandez, A., Fonseca, A. M., Paul, M. C., & Uotinen, V. (2005). Perceptions of and satisfaction with retirement: A comparison of six European Union countries. *Psychology and Aging, 20*, 524–528.

Fowles, D. C., & Kochanska, G. (2000). Temperament as a moderator of pathways to conscience in children: The contribution of electrodermal activity. *Psychophysiology, 37*, 788–795.

Fox, B. (2001). As times change: A review of trends in personal and family life. In B. J. Fox (Ed.), *Family patterns, gender relations* (2nd ed.). Don Mills, Ont.: Oxford University Press.

Fox, N. A., Henderson, H. A., Marshall, P. J., Nichols, K. E., & Ghera, M. M. (2005). Behavioral inhibition: Linking biology and behavior within a developmental framework. *Annual Review of Psychology, 56*, 235–262.

Fox, N. A., Henderson, H. A., Rubin, K. H., Calkins, S. D., & Schmidt, L. A. (2001). Continuity and discontinuity of behavioral inhibition and exuberance: Psychophysiological and behavioral influences across the first four years of life. *Child Development, 72*, 1–21.

Fozard, J. L., & Gordon-Salant, T. (2001). Changes in vision and hearing with aging. In J. E. Birren & K. W. Schaie (Eds.), *Handbook of the psychology of aging, 5th ed* (pp. 241-266). San Diego: Academic Press.

Fraga, M. F., Ballestar, E., Paz, M. F., Ropero, S., Setien, F., Ballestar, M. L., Heine-Suner, D., Cigudosa, J. C., Urioste, M., Benitez, J., Boix-Chormet, M., Sanchez-Aguilera, A., Ling, C., Carlsson, E., Poulsen, P., Vaag, A., Stephan, Z., Spector, T. D., Wu, Y-Z., Plass, C., & Esteller, M. (2005). Epigenetic differences arise during the lifetime of monozygotic twins. *Proceedings of the National Academy of Sciences, 102*, 10604–10609.

Fraley, R. C. (2002). Attachment stability from infancy to adulthood: Meta-analysis and dynamic modeling of developmental mechanisms. *Personality and Social Psychology Review, 6*, 123–151.

Fraley, R. C., & Bonanno, G. A. (2004). Attachment and loss: A test of three competing models on the association between attachment-related avoidance and adaptation to bereavement. *Personality and Social Psychology Bulletin, 30*, 878–890.

Fraley, R. C., Fazzari, D. A., Bonanno, G. A., & Dekel, S. (2006). Attachment and psychological adaptation in high exposure survivors of the September 11th attack on the World Trade Center. *Personality and Social Psychology Bulletin, 32*, 538–551.

Francis, K. L., & Spirduso, W. W. (2000). Age differences in the expression of manual asymmetry. *Experimental Aging Research, 26*, 169–180.

Frank, S. M., Raja, S. N., Bulcao, C., & Goldstein, D. S. (2000). Age-related thermoregulatory differences during core cooling in humans. *American Journal of Physiological Regulation, Integration, and Comparative Physiology, 279*, R349-354.

Frankel, E. B., & Gold, S. (2007). Principles and practices of early intervention. In I. Brown & M. Percy (Eds.), *A comprehensive guide to intellectual & developmental disabilities.* Baltimore: Paul H. Brookes.

Frankenburg, W. K., Dodds, J. B., Archer, P., Shapiro, H., & Bresnick, B. (1992). The Denver II: A major revision and restandardization of the Denver Development Screening Test. *Pediatrics, 89*, 91–97.

Franklin, C., & Corcoran, J. (2000). Preventing adolescent pregnancy: A review of programs and practices. *Social Work, 45*, 40–52.

Franklin, Z., Pilling, M., & Davies, I. (2005). The nature of infant color categorization: Evidence from eye movements on a target detection task. *Journal of Experimental Child Psychology, 91*, 227–248.

Fraser, M. W. (2004). The ecology of childhood: A multisystems perspective. In M. W. Fraser (Ed.), *Risk and resilience in childhood: An ecological perspective, 2nd ed.* (1-9). Washington, D. C. NASW Press.

Fraser, M. W., Galinsky, M. J., Smokowski, P. R., Day, S. H., Terzian, M. A., Rose, R. A., & Guo, S. (2005). Social information-processing skills training to promote social competence and prevent aggressive behavior in the third grade. *Journal of Consulting and Clinical Psychology, 73*, 1045–1055.

Frawley, W. (1997). *Vygotsky and cognitive science: Language and the unification of the social and computational mind.* Cambridge, MA: Harvard University Press.

Fredriksen, K., Rhodes, J., Reddy, R., & Niobe, W. (2004). Sleepless in Chicago: Tracking the effects of adolescent sleep loss during the middle school years. *Child Development, 75*, 84–95.

Freedman, D. S., Khan, L. K., Serdula, M. K., Ogden, C. L., & Dietz, W. H. (2006). Racial and ethnic differences in secular trends for childhood BMI, weight, and height. *Obesity, 14*, 301–308.

Freedman-Doan, C., Wigfield, A., Eccles, J. S., Blumenfeld, P., Arbreton, A., & Harold, R. D. (2000). What am I best at? Grade and gender differences in children's beliefs about ability improvement. *Journal of Applied Developmental Psychology, 21*, 379–402.

Freeman, S. F. N. (2000). Academic and social attainments of children with mental retardation in general education and special education settings. *Remedial and Special Education, 21*, 3–19.

Freid, V. M., Prager, K., MacKay, A. P., & Xia, H. (2003). *Health, United States, 2003, with Chartbook on trends in the health of Americans.* Hyattsville, MD: National Center for Health Statistics. Available at: http://www.cdc.gov/nchs/hus.htm.

Fremont, W. P. (2003). School refusal in children and adolescents. *American Family Physician, 68*, 1555–1560.

Freud, S. (1930). *Three contributions to the theory of sex.* New York: Nervous and Mental Disease Publishing Company. (Original work published 1905).

Freud, S. (1933). *New introductory lectures in psychoanalysis.* New York: Norton.

Freud, S. (1960). *A general introduction to psychoanalysis.* New York: Washington Square Press. (Original work published 1935).

Freud, S. (1964). An outline of psychoanalysis. In J. Strachey (Ed.), *The standard edition of the complete psychological works of Sigmund Freud* (Vol. 23). London: Hogarth Press. (Original work published 1940).

Freund, A., & Riediger, M. (2006). Goals as building blocks of personality and development in adulthood. In D. K. Mroczek & T. D. Little

(Eds.), *Handbook of personality development*. Mahwah, NJ: Erlbaum.

Freund, L. S. (1990). Maternal regulation of children's problem solving behavior and its impact on children's performance. *Child Development, 61*, 113-126.

Frey, K. S., & Ruble, D. N. (1985). What children say when the teacher is not around: Conflicting goals in social comparison and performance assessment in the classroom. *Journal of Personality and Social Psychology, 48*, 550–562.

Frey, K. S., & Ruble, D. N. (1992). Gender constancy and the cost of sex-typed behavior: A test of the conflict hypothesis. *Developmental Psychology, 28*, 714–721.

Friedman, J. M., & Polifka, J. E. (1996). *The effects of drugs on the fetus and nursing infant: A handbook for health care professionals*. Baltimore: Johns Hopkins University Press.

Friedman, L. J. (1999). *Identity's architect: A biography of Erik H. Erikson*. New York: Scribner.

Friedrich, L. K., & Stein, A. H. (1973). Aggressive and prosocial television programs and the natural behavior of preschool children. *Monographs of the Society for Research in Child Development, 38* (4, Serial No. 51).

Frieswijk, N., Buunk, B. P., Steverink, N., & Slaets, J. P. J. (2004). The effect of social comparison information on the life satisfaction of frail older persons. *Psychology and Aging, 19*, 183–190.

Frith, Uta. (2003). *Autism: Explaining the enigma* (2nd ed.). Malden, MA: Blackwell.

Frost, M. (2000). Ella Miller dies at age 119, *Rogersville Review*. Available at: http://www.grg.org/emiller.htm.

Fry, C. L. (1985). Culture, behavior, and aging in the comparative perspective. In J. E. Birren & K. W. Schaie (Eds.), *Handbook of the psychology of aging* (2nd ed.). New York: Van Nostrand Reinhold.

Fry, C. L. (1999). Anthropological theories of age and aging. In V. L. Bengtson & K. W. Schaie (Eds.), *Handbook of theories of aging*. New York: Springer.

Fry, D. P. (2006). Reciprocity: The foundation stone of morality. In M. Killen & J. G. Smetana (Eds.), *Handbook of moral development*. Mahwah, NJ: Erlbaum.

Fry, P. S. (1992). Major social theories of aging and their implications for counseling concepts and practice: A critical review. *Counseling Psychologist, 20*, 246–329.

Fry, P. S. (1997). Grandparents' reactions to the death of a grandchild: An exploratory factor analytic study. *Omega: Journal of Death and Dying, 35*, 119–140.

Fryauf-Bertschy, H., Tyler, R. S., Kelsay, D. M. R., Gantz, B. J., & Woodworth, G. G. (1997). Cochlear implant use by prelingually deafened children: The influence of age at implant and length of device use. *Journal of Speech, Language, and Hearing Research, 40*, 183–199.

Fryer, S. L., McGee, C. L., Matt, G. E., Riley, E. P., and Mattson, S. N. (2007). Evolution of psychopathological conditions in children with heavy prenatal alcohol exposure. *Pediatrics, 119*, E733–E741.

Fuligni, A. J. (1998). Authority, autonomy, and parent–adolescent conflict and cohesion: A study of adolescents from Mexican, Chinese, Filipino, and European backgrounds. *Developmental Psychology, 34*, 782–792.

Fuligni, A. J., & Stevenson, H. W. (1995). Time use and mathematics achievement among American, Chinese, and Japanese high school students. *Child Development, 66*, 830–842.

Fullilove, R. E., & Treisman, E. M. (1990). Mathematics achievement among African American undergraduates at the University of California, Berkeley: An evaluation of the mathematics workshop. *Journal of Negro Education, 59*, 463–478.

Furman, E. (1984). Children's patterns in mourning the death of a loved one. In H. Wass & C. A. Corr (Eds.), *Childhood and death*. Washington, D.C.: Hemisphere.

Furman, W., & Buhrmester, D. (1992). Age and sex differences in perceptions of networks of personal relationships. *Child Development, 63*, 103–115.

Furman, W., & Shaffer, L. (2003) The role of romantic relationships in adolescent development. In P. Florsheim (Ed.), *Adolescent romantic relations and sexual behavior: Theory, research, and practical implications*. Mahwah, NJ: Erlbaum.

Furstenberg, F. F. (2005). Non-normative life course transitions: Reflections on the significance of demographic events on lives. In R. Levy, P. Ghisletta, J. Le Goff, D. Spini, & E. Widmer (Eds.), *Advances in life course research: Vol. 10. Towards an interdisciplinary perspective on the life course*. Amsterdam: Elsevier.

Furstenberg, F. F., Jr. (2000). The sociology of adolescence and youth in the 1990s: A critical commentary. *Journal of Marriage and the Family, 62*, 896–910.

Furstenberg, F. F., Jr., Brooks-Gunn, J., & Chase-Lansdale, L. (1989). Teenage pregnancy and childbearing. *American Psychologist, 44*, 313–320.

Furstenberg, F. F., Jr., Brooks-Gunn, J., & Morgan, S. P. (1987). *Adolescent mothers in later life*. New York: Cambridge University Press.

Furstenberg, F. F., Jr., Kennedy, S., McLoyd, V. C., Rumbaut, R. G., & Settersten, R. A., Jr. (2004). Growing up is harder to do. *Contexts, 3*(3), 33–41.

G

Gable, S., & Lutz, S. (2000). Household, parent, and child contributions to childhood obesity. *Family Relations, 49*, 293–300.

Gabriel, K., Hofmann, C., Glavas, M., & Weinberg, J. (1998). The hormonal effects of alcohol use on the mother and fetus. *Alcohol Health & Research World, 22*, 170–177.

Gagnon, M. D., Hersen, M., Kabacoff, R. I., & Vanhasselt, V. B. (1999). Interpersonal and psychological correlates of marital dissatisfaction in late life: A review. *Clinical Psychology Review, 19*, 359–378.

Gais, S., & Born, J. (2004). Declarative memory consolidation: Mechanisms acting during human sleep. *Learning and Memory, 11*, 679–685.

Galambos, N. L., Almeida, D. M., & Petersen, A. C. (1990). Masculinity, femininity, and sex role attitudes in early adolescence: Exploring gender intensification. *Child Development, 61*, 1905–1914.

Gall, T. L., Evans, D. R., & Howard, J. (1997). The retirement adjustment process: Changes in the well-being of male retirees across time.

Journals of Gerontology: Psychological Sciences, 52, 110–117.

Gallagher, H. L., & Frith, C. D. (2003). Functional imaging of "theory of mind." *Trends in Cognitive Sciences, 7*, 77–83.

Gallagher, J. M., & Easley, J. A., Jr. (Eds.). (1978). *Knowledge and development: Vol. 2. Piaget and education*. New York: Plenum.

Gallagher, S. K., & Gerstel, N. (2001). Connections and constraints: The effects of children on caregiving. *Journal of Marriage and the Family, 63*, 265–275.

Gallagher-Thompson, D., & Coon, D. W. (2007). Evidence-based psychological treatments for distress in family caregivers of older adults. *Psychology and Aging, 22*, 37–51.

Gallo, L. C., Smith, T. W., & Ruiz, J. M. (2003). An interpersonal analysis of adult attachment style: Circumplex descriptions, recalled developmental experiences, self-representations, and interpersonal functioning in adulthood. *Journal of Personality, 71*, 141–181.

Gallup, G. G., Jr. (1979). Self-recognition in chimpanzees and man: A developmental and comparative perspective. In M. Lewis & L. A. Rosenblum (Eds.), *Genesis of behavior: Vol. 2. The child and its family*. New York: Plenum.

Galsworthy, M. J., Dionne, G., Dale, P. S., & Plomin, R. (2000). Sex differences in early verbal and non-verbal cognitive development. *Developmental Science, 3*, 206–215.

Galvan, A., Hare, T., Voss, H., Gover, G., & Casey, B. J. (2007). Risk-taking and the adolescent brain: Who is at risk? *Developmental Science, 10*, F8–F14.

Gamé, F., Carchon, I., & Vital-Durand, F. (2003). The effect of stimulus attractiveness on visual tracking in 2- to 6-month-old infants. *Infant Behavior & Development, 26*, 135–150.

Gamoran, A., Porter, A. C., Smithson, J., & White, P. A. (1997). Upgrading high school mathematics instruction: Improving learning opportunities for low-achieving, low-income youth. *Educational Evaluation and Policy Analysis, 19*, 325–338.

Ganahl, D. J., Prinsen, T. J., & Netzley, S. B. (2003). A content analysis of prime time commercials: A contextual framework of gender representation. *Sex Roles, 49*, 545–551.

Ganchrow, J. R., Steiner, J. E., & Daher, M. (1983). Neonatal facial expressions to different qualities and intensities of gustatory stimuli. *Infant Behavior and Development, 6*, 189–200.

Gannon, L., & Ekstrom, B. (1993). Attitudes toward menopause: The influence of sociocultural paradigms. *Psychology of Women Quarterly, 17*, 275–288.

Garbarino, J. (1992). *Children and families in the social environment* (2nd ed.). New York: Aldine de Gruyter.

Garber, J. (1984). The developmental progression of depression in female children. In D. Cicchetti & K. Schneider-Rosen (Eds.), *Childhood depression* (New Directions for Child Development, No. 26). San Francisco: Jossey-Bass.

Garber, J., & Flynn, C. (2001). Vulnerability to depression in childhood and adolescence. In R. E. Ingram & J. M. Price (Eds.), *Vulnerability to psychopathology. Risk across the lifespan*. New York: Guilford.

Garcia, M. M., Shaw, D. S., Winslow, E. B., & Yaggi, K. E. (2000). Destructive sibling conflict and the development of conduct problems in young boys. *Developmental Psychology, 36,* 44–53.

Garciaguirre, J. S., Adolph, K. E., & Shrout, P. E. (2007). Baby carriage: Infants walking with loads. *Child Development, 78,* 664–680.

Gard, M. C. E., & Freeman, C. P. (1996). The dismantling of a myth: A review of eating disorders and socioeconomic status. *International Journal of Eating Disorders, 20,* 1–12.

Gardner, H. (1982). *Art, mind, and brain: A cognitive approach to creativity.* New York: Basic Books.

Gardner, H. (1985). *The mind's new science: A history of the cognitive revolution.* New York: Basic Books.

Gardner, H. (1993). *Frames of mind: The theory of multiple intelligences* [Tenth anniversary edition]. New York: Basic Books.

Gardner, H. (1999/2000). *Intelligence reframed: Multiple intelligences for the 21st century.* New York: Basic Books.

Gardner, M., & Steinberg, L. (2005). Peer influence on risk taking, risk preference, and risky decision making in adolescence and adulthood: An experimental study. *Developmental Psychology, 41,* 625–635.

Garmezy, N. (1994). Reflections and commentary on risk, resilience, and development. In R. J. Haggerty, L. R. Sherrod, N. Garmezy, & M. Rutter (Eds.), *Stress, risk and resilience in children and adolescents: Processes, mechanisms, and interventions.* Cambridge, England: Cambridge University Press.

Garner, R. (1999, November 15). Failing at four. *New York Times Magazine,* 26.

Garvey, C. (1990). *Play* (enlarged ed.). Cambridge, MA: Harvard University Press.

Gatz, M. (2007). Genetics, dementia, and the elderly. *Current Directions in Psychological Science, 16,* 123–127.

Gatz, M., Reynolds, C. A., Fratiglioni, L., Johansson, B., Mortimer, J. A., Berg, S., Fiske, A., & Pedersen, N. L. (2006). Role of genes and environments for explaining Alzheimer disease. *Archives of General Psychiatry, 63,* 168–174.

Gatz, M., Svedberg, P., Pedersen, N. L., Mortimer, J. A., Berg, S., & Johansson, B. (2001). Education and the risk of Alzheimer's disease: Findings from the study of dementia in Swedish twins. *Journal of Gerontology: Psychological Sciences, 56B,* 292–300.

Gaugler, J. E., Davey, A., Pearlin, L. I., & Zarit, S. H. (2000). Modeling caregiver adaptation over time: The longitudinal impact of behavior problems. *Psychology and Aging, 15,* 437–450.

Gauvain, M., & Rogoff, B. (1989). Collaborative problem-solving and children's planning skills. *Developmental Psychology, 25,* 139–151.

Gazzaniga, M. S. (1998). The split brain revisited. *Scientific American, 279,* 50–55.

Ge, X., Best, K. M., Conger, R. D., & Simons, R. L. (1996). Parenting behaviors and the occurrence and co-occurrence of adolescent depressive symptoms and conduct problems. *Developmental Psychology, 32,* 717–731.

Ge, X., Kim, I. J., Brody, G. H., Conger, R. D., Simons, R. L., Gibbons, F. X., & Cutrona, C. E. (2003). It's about timing and change: Pubertal transition effects on symptoms of major depression among African American youths. *Developmental Psychology, 39,* 430–439.

Ge, X., Lorenz, F. O., Conger, R. D., Elder, G. H., Jr., & Simons, R. L. (1994). Trajectories of stressful life events and depressive symptoms during adolescence. *Developmental Psychology, 30,* 467–483.

Ge, X., Natsuaki, M. N., & Conger, R. D. (2006). Trajectories of depressive symptoms and stressful life events among male and female adolescents in divorced and nondivorced families. *Development and Psychopathology, 18,* 253–273.

Geithner, C. A., Satake, T., Woynarowska, B., & Malina, R. M. (1999). Adolescent spurts in body dimensions: Average and modal sequences. *American Journal of Human Biology, 11,* 287–295.

Gelman, R. (1972). The nature and development of early number concepts. In H. W. Reese (Ed.), *Advances in Child Development and Behavior* (Vol. 7). New York: Academic Press.

Gelman, R. (1978). Cognitive development. *Annual Review of Psychology, 29,* 297–332.

Gelman, S. A. (1996). Concepts and theories. In R. Gelman & T. K. Au (Eds.), *Perceptual and cognitive development.* San Diego: Academic Press.

Genc, M., & Ledger, W. J. (2000). Syphilis in pregnancy. *Sexual Transmission Information, 76,* 73–79.

George, L., Granath, F., Johansson, A. L., Annerén, G., & Cnattinguis, S. (2006). Environmental tobacco smoke and risk of spontaneous abortion. *Epidemiology, 17,* 500–505.

Georges, J., Onwuteaka-Philipsen, B. D., Muller, M. T., van der Wal, G., van der Heide, A., & van der Maas, P. J. (2007). Relatives' perspective on the terminally ill patients who died after euthanasia or physician-assisted suicide: A retrospective cross-sectional interview study in the Netherlands. *Death Studies, 31,* 1–15.

Gershoff, E. T. (2002). Corporal punishment by parents and associated child behaviors and experiences: A meta-analytic and theoretical review. *Psychological Bulletin, 128,* 539–579.

Gest, S. D., Graham-Bermann, S. A., & Hartup, W. W. (2001). Peer experience: Common and unique features of number of friendships, social network centrality, and sociometric status. *Social Development, 10,* 23–40.

Getzels, J. W., & Jackson, P. W. (1962). Creativity and intelligence: Explorations with gifted children. New York: Wiley.

Ghetti, S., & Alexander, K. W. (2004). "If it happened, I would remember it": Strategic use of event memorability in the rejection of false autobiographical events. *Child Development, 75,* 542–560.

Giampaoli S. (2000). Epidemiology of major age-related diseases in women compared to men. *Aging, 12,* 93–105.

Giarrusso, R., Feng, D., Silverstein, M., & Bengtson, V. L. (2000). Self in the context of the family. In K. W. Schaie & J. Hendrick (Eds.), *The evolution of the aging self. The societal impact on the aging process.* New York: Springer.

Gibbs, J. C. (2003). *Moral development and reality: Beyond the theories of Kohlberg and Hoffman.* London, England: Sage Publications Ltd.

Gibson, E. J. (1988). Exploratory behavior in the development of perceiving, acting, and the acquiring of knowledge. *Annual Review of Psychology, 39,* 1–41.

Gibson, E. J., & Pick, A. D. (2000). *An ecological approach to perceptual learning and development.* New York: Oxford University Press.

Gibson, E. J., & Walk, R. D. (1960). The "visual cliff." *Scientific American, 202,* 64–71.

Gibson-Davis, C. M., & Brooks-Gunn, J. (2006). Couples' immigration status and ethnicity as determinants of breastfeeding. *American Journal of Public Health, 96,* 4684–4689.

Giedd, J. N. (2004). Structural magnetic resonance imaging of the adolescent brain. *Annals of the New York Academic of Sciences, 1021,* 77–85.

Gil, D. G. (1970). *Violence against children.* Cambridge, MA: Harvard University Press.

Gilbert, N. (1997). *Combating child abuse: International perspectives and trends.* New York: Oxford University Press.

Gillberg, C., Cederlund, M., Lamberg, K., & Zeijlon, L. (2006). "The autism epidemic." The registered prevalence of autism in a Swedish urban area. *Journal of Autism and Developmental Disorders, 36,* 429–435.

Gillick, M. R. (1998). *Tangled minds. Understanding Alzheimer's disease and other dementias.* New York: Penguin.

Gilligan, C. (1977). In a different voice: Women's conceptions of self and morality. *Harvard Educational Review, 47,* 481–517.

Gilligan, C. (1982). *In a different voice: Psychological theory and women's development.* Cambridge, MA: Harvard University Press.

Gilligan, C. (1993). Adolescent development reconsidered. In A. Garrod (Ed.), *Approaches to moral development: New research and emerging themes.* New York: Teachers College Press.

Gillis, J. R. (2003). The birth of the virtual child. A Victorian progeny. In W. Koops & M. Zuckerman. (Eds.), *Beyond the century of the child. Cultural history and developmental psychology.* Philadelphia: University of Pennsylvania Press.

Ginsburg, G. S., & Bronstein, P. (1993). Family factors related to children's intrinsic/extrinsic motivational orientation and academic performance. *Child Development, 64,* 1461–1474.

Ginsburg, H. P. & Opper, S. (1988). *Piaget's theory of intellectual development* (3rd ed.). Upper Saddle River, NJ: Prentice-Hall.

Ginzberg, E. (1972). Toward a theory of occupational choice: A restatement. *Vocational Guidance Quarterly, 20,* 169–176.

Ginzberg, E. (1984). Career development. In D. Brown, L. Brooks, & Associates (Eds.), *Career choice and development.* San Francisco: Jossey-Bass.

Giordano, P. C. (2003). Relationships in adolescence. *Annual Review of Sociology, 29,* 257–281.

Girard, C. (1993). Age, gender, and suicide: A cross-national analysis. *American Sociological Review, 58,* 553–574.

Glascock, J. (2001). Gender roles on prime-time network television: Demographics and behaviors. *Journal of Broadcasting & Electronic Media, 45,* 656–669.

Glaser, B. G., & Strauss, A. L. (1968). *Time for dying.* Chicago: Aldine.

Glaser, R., & Chi, M. T. H. (1988). Overview. In M. T. H. Chi, R. Glaser, & M. Farr (Eds.), *The nature of expertise.* Hillsdale, NJ: Erlbaum.

Glasgow, K. L., Dornbusch, S. M., Troyer, L., Steinberg, L., & Ritter, P. L. (1997). Parenting styles, adolescents' attributions, and educational outcomes in nine heterogeneous high schools. *Child Development, 68,* 507–529.

Glass, G. V. (2002a). Grouping students for instruction. In A. Molnar (Ed.), *School reform proposals: The research evidence* (pp. 95–112). Greenwich, CT: Information Age Publishing.

Glass, G. V. (2002b). Teacher characteristics. In A. Molnar (Ed.), *School reform proposals: The research evidence* (pp. 155–174). Greenwich, CT: Information Age Publishing.

Glass, G. V. (2002c). Time for school: Its duration and allocation. In A. Molnar (Ed.), *School reform proposals: The research evidence* (pp. 79–93). Greenwich, CT: Information Age Publishing.

Glass, G. V., McGaw, B., & Smith, M. L. (1981). *Meta-analysis in social research.* Beverly Hills, CA: Sage.

Glick, J. C. (1975). Cognitive development in cross-cultural perspective. In F. Horowitz (Ed.), *Review of child development research* (Vol. 1). Chicago: University of Chicago Press.

Glick, M., & Zigler, E. (1985). Self-image: A cognitive developmental approach. In R. L. Leahy (Ed.), *The Development of the self.* Orlando, FL: Academic Press.

Gloth, F. M. (2000). Geriatric pain: Factors that limit pain relief and increase complications. *Geriatrics, 55,* 51–54.

Glowinski, A. L., Madden, P. A. F., Bucholz, K. K., Lynskey, M. T., & Heath, A. C. (2003). Genetic epidemiology of self-reported lifetime DSM-IV major depressive disorder in a population-based twin sample of female adolescents. *Journal of Child Psychology and Psychiatry and Allied Disciplines, 44,* 988–996.

Gluckman, P. D., & Hanson, M. A. (2006). Evolution, development and timing of puberty. *Trends in Endocrinology and Metabolism, 17,* 7–12.

Gnepp, J., & Chilamkurti, C. (1988). Children's use of personality attributions to predict other people's emotional and behavioral reactions. *Child Development, 59,* 743–754.

Goertzel, V., & Goertzel, M. G. (1962). *Cradles of eminence.* Boston: Little, Brown.

Golan, O., Baron-Cohen, S., Hill, J. J., Golan, Y. (2006). The "Reading the Mind in Films" task: Complex emotion recognition in adults with and without autism spectrum conditions. *Social Neuroscience, 1,* 111–123.

Gold, E. B., Sternfeld, B., Kelsey, J. L., Brown, C., Mouton, C., Reame, N., Salamone, L., & Stellato, R. (2000). Relation of demographic and lifestyle factors to symptoms in a multi-racial/ethnic population of women 40–55 years of age. *American Journal of Epidemiology, 152,* 463–473.

Goldberg, A. E., Perry-Jenkins, M. (2007). The division of labor and perceptions of parental roles: Lesbian couples across the transition to parenthood. *Journal of Social and Personal Relationships, 24,* 297–318.

Goldberg, A. P., & Hagberg, J. M. (1990). Physical exercise in the elderly. In E. L. Schneider & J. W. Rowe (Eds.), *Handbook of the biology of aging* (3rd ed.). San Diego: Academic Press.

Goldberg, G. R., & Prentice, A. M. (1994). Maternal and fetal determinants of adult diseases. *Nutrition Reviews, 52,* 191–200.

Goldberg, S., Perrotta, M., Minde, K., & Corter, C. (1986). Maternal behavior and attachment in low–birth-weight twins and singletons. *Child Development, 57,* 34–46.

Golden, J. (2005). *Message in a bottle: The making of fetal alcohol syndrome.* Cambridge, MA: Harvard University Press.

Goldenberg, R. L., & Culhane, J. F. (2007). Low birth weight in the United States. *The American Journal of Clinical Nutrition, 85,* 584–590.

Goldhaber, D. E. (2000). *Theories of human development. Integrative perspectives.* Mountain View, CA: Mayfield.

Goldin-Meadow, S. (2003). *The resilience of language: What gesture creation in deaf children can tell us about how all children learn language.* New York: Psychology Press.

Goldin-Meadow, S. (2005). What language creation in the manual modality tells us about the foundations of language. *Linguistic Review, 22,* 199–225.

Goldsmith, H. H. (2003). Genetics of emotional development. In R. J. Davidson, K. R. Scherer, & H. H. Goldsmith (Eds.), *Handbook of affective sciences.* New York: Oxford University Press.

Goldstein, D. B., & Cavalleri, G. L. (2005, October 27). Understanding human diversity. *Nature, 437,* 1241–1242.

Goldstein, E. B. (2007). *Sensation and perception* (7th ed.). Belmont, CA: Wadsworth.

Goldstein, S. E., Davis-Kean, P. E., & Eccles, J. S. (2005). Parents, peers, and problem behavior: A longitudinal investigation of the impact of relationship perceptions and characteristics on the development of adolescent problem behavior. *Developmental Psychology, 41,* 401–413.

Goldwater, O. D., & Nutt, R. L. (1999). Teachers' and students' work-culture variables associated with positive school outcome. *Adolescence, 34,* 653–664.

Golinkoff, R. M., & Hirsh-Pasek, K. (2006). Baby wordsmith: From associationist to social sophisticate. *Current Directions in Psychological Science, 15,* 30–33.

Golombok, S., MacCallum, F., Murray, C., Lycett, E., & Jadva, V. (2005). Surrogacy families: Parental functioning, parent–child relationships and children's psychological developmental at age 2. *Journal of Child Psychology and Psychiatry, 47,* 213–222.

Golombok, S., Murray, C., Jadva, V., Lycett, E., MacCallum, F., & Rust, J. (2006). Non-genetic and non-gestational parenthood: Consequences for parent–child relationships and the psychological well-being of mothers, fathers, and children at age 3. *Human Reproduction, 21,* 1918–1924.

Golombok, S., Perry, B., Burston, A., Murray, C., Mooney-Somers, J., Stevens, M., & Golding, J. (2003). Children with lesbian parents: A community study. *Developmental Psychology, 39,* 20–33.

Good, C., Aronson, J., & Inzlicht, M. (2003). Improving adolescents' standardized test performance: An intervention to reduce the effects of stereotype threat. *Journal of Applied Developmental Psychology, 24,* 645–662.

Goodkin, K., Baldewicz, T. T., Blaney, N. T., Asthana, D., Kumar, M., Shapshak, P., Leeds, B., Burkhalter, J. E., Rigg, D., Tyll, M. D., Cohen, J., & Zheng, W. L. (2001). Physiological effects of bereavement and bereavement support group interventions. In M. S. Stroebe, & R. O. Hansson (Eds.), *Handbook of bereavement research: Consequences, coping, and care.* Washington, D.C.: American Psychological Association.

Goodman, S. H. (2002). Depression and early adverse experiences. In I. H. Gotlib & C. L. Hammen (Eds.), *Handbook of depression.* New York: Guilford.

Gooren, L. (2006). The biology of human psychosexual differentiation. *Hormonal Behavior, 50,* 589–601.

Gopnik, A. (1996). The post-Piaget era. *Psychological Science, 7,* 221–225.

Gopnik, A., Capps, L., & Meltzoff, A. N. (2000). Early theories of mind: What the theory can tell us about autism. In S. Baron-Cohen, H. Tager-Flusberg, & D. J. Cohen (Eds.), *Understanding other minds. Perspectives from developmental cognitive neuroscience* (2nd ed.). Oxford: Oxford University Press.

Gopnik, A., & Choi, S. (1995). Names, relational words, and cognitive development in English and Korean speakers: Nouns are not always learned before verbs. In M. Tomasello & W. E. Merriman (Eds.), *Beyond names for things: Young children's acquisition of verbs* (pp. 83–90). Hillsdale, NJ: Erlbaum.

Gordon, B. N., Schroeder, C. S., & Abrams, J. M. (1990). Children's knowledge of sexuality: A comparison of sexually abused and non-abused children. *American Journal of Orthopsychiatry, 60,* 250–257.

Gordon, R. A. (2000). *Eating disorders. Anatomy of a social epidemic* (2nd ed.). Oxford, England: Blackwell.

Gorey, K. M., & Leslie, D. (1997). The prevalence of child sexual abuse: Integrative review adjustment for potential response and measurement bias. *Child Abuse and Neglect, 21,* 391–398.

Gortmaker, S. L., Must, A., Sobol, A. M., Peterson, K., Colditz, G. A., & Dietz, W. H. (1996). Television viewing as a cause of increasing obesity among children in the United States. *Archives of Pediatric and Adolescent Medicine, 150,* 356–362.

Gostin, L. O. (2001). National health information privacy: Regulations under the Health Insurance Portability and Accountability Act. *Journal of the American Medical Association, 23,* 3015–3021.

Goswami, U. (1999). Causal connections in beginning reading: The importance of rhyme. *Journal of Research in Reading, 22,* 217–241.

Gotlib, I. H., & Hammen, C. L. (1992). *Psychological aspects of depression. Toward a cognitive-interpersonal integration.* Chichester, England: John Wiley & Sons.

Gotlib, I. H., & Hammen, C. L. (2002). Introduction. In I. H. Gotlib & C. L. Hammen (Eds.), *Handbook of depression.* New York: Guilford.

Gotlib, I. H., Joormann, J., Minor, K. L., & Cooney, R. E. (2006). Cognitive and biological functioning in children at risk for depression. In T. Canli (Ed.), *Biology of personality and individual differences.* New York: Guilford.

Gott, M., & Hinchliff, S. (2003). How important is sex in later life? The views of older people. *Social Science & Medicine, 56,* 1617–1628.

Gottesman, I. I. (1991). *Schizophrenia genesis: The origins of madness.* New York: W. H. Freeman.

Gottesman, I. I., & Hanson, D. R. (2005). Human development: Biological and genetic processes. *Annual Review of Psychology, 56,* 263–286.

Gottfredson, L. S. (1996). Gottfredson's theory of circumscription and compromise. In D. Brown, L. Brooks, & Associates (Eds.), *Career choice and development* (3rd ed.). San Francisco: Jossey-Bass.

Gottfredson, L. S. (1997). Why g matters: The complexity of everyday life. *Intelligence, 24,* 79–132.

Gottfredson, L. S. (2002). G: Highly general and highly practical. In R. J. Sternberg & E. L.

Grigorenko (Eds.), *The general factor in intelligence: How general is it?* Mahwah, NJ: Erlbaum.

Gottfredson, L. S. (2004). Intelligence: Is it the epidemiologists' elusive "fundamental cause" of social class inequalities in health? *Journal of Personality and Social Psychology, 86,* 174–199.

Gottfredson, L. S., & Deary, I. (2004). Intelligence predicts health and longevity, but why? *Current Directions in Psychological Science, 13,* 1–4.

Gottfried, A. E., Fleming, J. S., & Gottfried, A. W. (1998). Role of cognitively stimulating home environment in children's academic intrinsic motivation: A longitudinal study. *Child Development, 69,* 1448–1460.

Gottfried, A. E., & Gottfried, A. W. (2006). A long-term investigation of the role of maternal and dual-earner employment in children's development: The Fullerton Longitudinal Study. *American Behavioral Scientist, 49,* 1310–1327.

Gottfried, A. W. (1984). Home environment and early cognitive development: Integration, meta-analyses, and conclusions. In A. W. Gottfried (Ed.), *Home environment and early cognitive development: Longitudinal research.* Orlando, FL: Academic Press.

Gottfried, A. W., & Gottfried, A. E. (1984). Home environment and cognitive development in young children of middle-socioeconomic-status families. In A. W. Gottfried (Ed.), *Home environment and early cognitive development: Longitudinal research.* Orlando, FL: Academic Press.

Gottfried, A. W., Gottfried, A. E., Bathurst, K., & Guerin, D. W. (1994). *Gifted IQ: Early developmental aspects: The Fullerton Longitudinal Study.* New York: Plenum.

Gottlieb, G. (1991). Experiential canalization of behavioral development: Theory. *Developmental Psychology, 27,* 4–13.

Gottlieb, G. (1992). *Individual development and evolution: The genesis of novel behavior.* New York: Oxford University Press.

Gottlieb, G. (2000). Environmental and behavioral influences on gene activity. *Current Directions in Psychological Science, 9,* 93–97.

Gottlieb, G. (2002). Developmental-behavioral initiation of evolutionary change. *Psychological Review, 109,* 211–218.

Gottlieb, G. (2003). On making behavioral genetics truly developmental. *Human Development, 46,* 337–355.

Gottlieb, G., & Blair, C. (2004). How early experience matters in intellectual development in the case of poverty. *Prevention Science, 5,* 245–252.

Gottlieb, G., Wahlsten, D., & Lickliter, R. (1998). The significance of biology for human development: A developmental psychobiological systems view. In R. M. Lerner (Vol. Ed.), William Damon (Editor-in-Chief), *Handbook of Child Psychology: Vol. 1. Theoretical Models of Human Development* (5th ed.). New York: Wiley.

Gottlieb, G., Wahlsten, D., & Lickliter, R. (2006). The significance of biology for human development: A developmental psychobiological systems view. In W. Damon & R. M. Lerner (Eds. in Chief) & R. M. Lerner (Vol. Ed.), *Handbook of child psychology: Vol. 1. Theoretical models of human development* (6th ed.). Hoboken, NJ: Wiley.

Gottlieb, L. (2000). *Luring a child into this life: A Beng path for infant care* (Session on cultural differences in infant care). Presented at the International Society on Infant Studies Conference.

Gottman, J. M., & Notarius, C. I. (2000). Decade review: Observing marital interaction. *Journal of Marriage and the Family, 62,* 927–947.

Goubet, N., Rochat, P., Maire-Leblond, C., & Poss, S. (2006). Learning from others in 9–18-month-old infants. *Infant and Child Development, 15,* 161–177.

Gould, D. C., Petty, R., & Jacobs, H. S. (2000). The male menopause—does it exist? *British Medical Journal, 320,* 858–861.

Gould, M. S., Greenberg, T., Velting, D. M., & Shaffer, D. (2003). Youth suicide risk and preventive interventions: A review of the past 10 years. *Journal of the American Academy of Child and Adolescent Psychiatry, 42,* 386–405.

Gowers, S., & Bryant-Waugh, R. (2004). Management of child and adolescent eating disorders: The current evidence base and future directions. *Journal of Child Psychology and Psychiatry and Allied Disciplines, 45,* 63–83.

Graber, J. A., Lewinsohn, P. M., Seeley, J. R., & Brooks-Gunn, J. (1997). Is psychopathology associated with the timing of pubertal development? *Journal of the American Academy of Child and Adolescent Psychiatry, 36,* 1768–1776.

Graber, J. A. & Sontag, L. M. (2006). Puberty and girls' sexuality: Why hormones are not the complete answer. *New Directions for Child and Adolescent Development, 112,* 23–38.

Grady, D. (2006, May 3). Study finds few therapies work well on hot flashes. *The New York Times,* p. A22.

Graf, P., Squire, L. R., & Mandler, G. (1984). The information that amnesic patients do not forget. *Journal of Experimental Psychology: Learning, Memory, and Cognition, 10,* 164–178.

Graham, C. A., & Easterbrooks, M. A. (2000). School-aged children's vulnerability to depressive symptomatology: The role of attachment security, maternal depressive symptomatology, and economic risk. *Development and Psychopathology, 12,* 201–213.

Graham, N., Lindesay, J., Katona, C., Bertolote, J. M., Camus, V., Copeland, J. R. M., de Mendonca Lima, C. A., Gaillard, M., Nargeot, M. C. G., Gray, J., Jacobsson, L., Kingma, M., Kuhne, N., O'Loughlin, A., Rutz, W., Saraceno, B., Taintor, Z., & Wancata, J. (2003). Reducing stigma and discrimination against older people with mental disorders: A technical consensus statement. *International Journal of Geriatric Psychiatry, 18,* 670–678.

Graham-Pole, J., Wass, H., Eyberg, S., Chu, L., & Olejnik, S. (1989). Communicating with dying children and their siblings: A retrospective analysis. *Death Studies, 13,* 463–483.

Granic, I., Hollenstein, T., Dishion, T. J., & Patterson, G. R. (2003). Longitudinal analysis of flexibility and reorganization in early adolescence: A dynamic systems study of family interactions. *Developmental Psychology, 39,* 606–617.

Granrud, C. E. (2006). Size constancy in infants: 4-month-olds' responses to physical versus retinal image size. *Journal of Experimental Psychology: Human Perception and Performance, 32,* 1398–1404.

Grant, K. E., Compas, B. E., Thurm, A. E., McMahon, S. D., & Gipson, P. Y. (2004). Stressors and child and adolescent psychopathology: Measurement issues and prospective effects. *Journal of Clinical Child and Adolescent Psychology, 33,* 412–425.

Gray, S. W., Ramsey, B. K., & Klaus, R. A. (1982). *From 3 to 20: The Early Training Project.* Baltimore: University Park Press.

Gray, W. M., & Hudson, L. M. (1984). Formal operations and the imaginary audience. *Developmental Psychology, 20,* 619–627.

Gray-Little, B., & Carels, R. A. (1997). The effect of racial dissonance on academic self-esteem and achievement in elementary, junior high, and high school students. *Journal of Research on Adolescence, 7,* 109–131.

Gray-Little, B., & Hafdahl, A. R. (2000). Factors influencing racial comparisons of self-esteem: A quantitative review. *Psychological Bulletin, 126,* 26–54.

Grayson, D. A., Mackinnon, A., Jorm, A. F., Creasey, H., & Broe, G. A. (2000). Item bias in the Center for Epidemiologic Studies Depression Scale: Effects of physical disorders and disability in an elderly community sample. *Journal of Gerontology: Psychological Sciences, 55,* 273–282.

Graziano, P. A., Keane, S. P., & Calkins, S. D. (2007). Cardiac vagal regulation and early peer status. *Child Development, 78,* 264–278.

Grbich, C., Parker, D., & Maddocks, I. (2001). The emotions and coping strategies of caregivers of family members with a terminal cancer. *Journal of Palliative Care, 17,* 30–36.

Green, C. R. (2001). *Total memory workout: 8 easy steps to maximum memory fitness.* New York: Bantam Doubleday.

Green, R. (1987). *The "sissy boy syndrome" and the development of homosexuality.* New Haven, CT: Yale University Press.

Green, R. E., Krause, J., Ptak, S. E., Briggs, A. W., Ronan, M. T., Egholm, J., Rothberg, J. M., Paunovic, M., & Pääbo, S. (2006). Analysis of one million base pairs of Neanderthal DNA. *Nature, 444,* 330–336.

Greenberger, E., & Steinberg, L. (1986). *When teenagers work: The psychological and social costs of adolescent employment.* New York: Basic Books.

Greenberger, E., O'Neil, R., & Nagel, S. K. (1994). Linking workplace and homeplace: Relations between the nature of adults' work and their parenting behaviors. *Developmental Psychology, 30,* 990–1002.

Greene, J. G. (1984). *The social and psychological origins of the climacteric syndrome.* Hants, England & Brookfield, VT: Gower.

Greene, K., Rubin, D. L., Hale, J. L., & Walters, L. H. (1996). The utility of understanding adolescent egocentrism in designing health promotion messages. *Health Communication, 8,* 131–152.

Greenfield, E. A., & Marks, N. F. (2006). Linked lives: Adult children's problems and their parents' psychological and relational well-being. *Journal of Marriage and Family, 68,* 442–454.

Greenfield, P. M., & Savage-Rumbaugh, E. S. (1993). Comparing communicative competence in child and chimp: The pragmatics of repetition. *Journal of Child Language, 20,* 1–26.

Greenhalgh, R., Slade, P., & Spiby, H. (2000). Fathers' coping style, antenatal preparation, and experiences of labor and the postpartum. *Birth, 27,* 177–184.

Greenough, W. T., Black, J. E., & Wallace, C. S. (1987). Experience and brain development. *Child Development, 58,* 539–559.

Greenspan, S. I. (1997). *The growth of the mind.* Reading, MA: Addison-Wesley.

Gregg, V., Gibbs, J. C., & Basinger, K. S. (1994). Patterns of developmental delay in moral judgment by male and female delinquents. *Merrill-Palmer Quarterly, 40,* 538–553.

Gregory, A. M., Rijsdijk, F. V., & Eley, T. C. (2006). A twin-study of sleep difficulties in school-aged children. *Child Development, 77,* 1668–1679.

Greve, F. (2006, Feb 3). Rise in average IQ scores makes kids today exceptional by earlier standards. *Knight Ridder Washington Bureau.*

Griesenbach, U., Geddes, D. M., & Alton, E. W. (2006). Gene therapy progress and prospects: Cystic fibrosis. *Gene Therapy, 13,* 1061–1067.

Grilo, C. M., & Pogue-Geile, M. F. (1991). The nature of environmental influences on weight and obesity: A behavior genetic analysis. *Psychological Bulletin, 110,* 520–537.

Grinker, R. R. (2007). *Unstrange minds: Remapping the world of autism.* New York: Basic Books.

Grizenko, N., Zappitelli, M., Langevin, J. P., Hrychko, S., El-Messidi, A., Kaminester, D., Pawliuk, N., & Stepanian, M. T. (2000). Effectiveness of a social skills training program using self/other perspective-taking: A nine-month follow-up. *American Journal of Orthopsychiatry, 70,* 501–509.

Groark, C. J., Muhamedrahimov, R. J., Palmov, O. I., Nikiforova, N. V., & McCall, R. B. (2005). Improvements in early care in Russian orphanages and their relationship to observed behaviors. *Infant Mental Health Journal, 26,* 96–109.

Grober, E., & Kawas, C. (1997). Learning and retention in preclinical and early Alzheimer's disease. *Psychology and Aging, 12,* 183–188.

Grollman, E. A. (1995). Explaining death to young children: Some questions and answers. In E. A. Grollman (Ed.), *Bereaved children and teens.* Boston: Beacon Press.

Grolnick, W. S., Bridges, L. J., & Connell, J. P. (1996). Emotion regulation in two-year-olds: Strategies and emotional expression in four contexts. *Child Development, 67,* 928–941.

Grolnick, W. S., McMenamy, J. M., & Kurowski, C. O. (2006). Emotional self-regulation in infancy and toddlerhood. In L. Balter & C. S. Tamis-LeMonda (Eds.), *Child psychology: A handbook of contemporary issues* (2nd ed.). New York: Psychology Press.

Gros-Louis, J., West, M. J., Goldstein, M. H., & King, A. P. (2006). Mothers provide differential feedback to infants' prelinguistic sounds. *International Journal of Behavioral Development, 30,* 509–516.

Gross, J. J. (Ed.) (2007). *Handbook of emotion regulation.* New York: Guilford.

Grossberg, G. T., & Desai, A. K. (2003). Management of Alzheimer's disease. *Journal of Gerontology: Medical Sciences, 58A,* 331–353.

Gross-Loh, C. (2006). Caring for your premature baby: Find out why breastfeeding and skin-to-skin contact are key components in making sure your premature infant thrives. *Mothering, 135,* 38–47.

Grossman, A. W., Churchill, J. D., McKinney, B. C., Kodish, I. M., Otte, S. L., & Greenough, W. T. (2003). Experience effects on brain development: Possible contributions to psychopathology. *Journal of Child Psychology and Psychiatry and Allied Disciplines, 44,* 33–63.

Grossmann, K., Grossmann, K. E., Fremmer-Bombik, E., Kindler, H., Scheuerer-Englisch, H., & Zimmermann, P. (2002). The uniqueness of the child-father attachment relationship: Fathers' sensitive and challenging play as a pivotal variable in a 16-year longitudinal study. *Social Development, 11,* 307–331.

Grossmann, K. E., Grossmann, K., & Keppler, A. (2005). Universal and culture-specific aspects of human behavior: The case of attachment. In W. Friedlmeier, P. Chakkarath, & B. Schwarz (Eds.), *Culture and human development. The importance of cross-cultural research for the social sciences.* New York: Psychology Press.

Grotevant, H. D., & Cooper, C. R. (1986). Individuation in family relations. A perspective on individual differences in the development of identity and role-taking skills in adolescence. *Human Development, 29,* 82–100.

Gruber-Baldini, A. L., Schaie, K. W., & Willis, S. L. (1995). Similarity in married couples: A longitudinal study of mental abilities and rigidity–flexibility. *Journal of Personality and Social Psychology, 69,* 191–203.

Grundy, E., & Henretta, J. C. (2006). Between elderly parents and adult children: A new look at the intergenerational care provided by the 'sandwich generation.' *Ageing and Society, 26,* 707–722.

Grusec, J. E. (2006). The development of moral behavior and conscience from a socialization perspective. In M. Killen & J. G. Smetana (Eds.), *Handbook of moral development.* Mahwah, NJ: Erlbaum.

Grusec, J. E., Goodnow, J. J., & Kuczynski, L. (2000). New directions in analyses of parenting contributions to children's acquisition of values. *Child Development, 71,* 205–211.

Grych, J. H., & Fincham, F. D. (1992). Interventions for children of divorce: Toward greater integration of research and action. *Psychological Bulletin, 111,* 434–454.

Guay, F., Marsh, H. W., & Boivin, M. (2003). Academic self-concept and academic achievement: Developmental perspectives on their causal ordering. *Journal of Educational Psychology, 95,* 124–136.

Guerin, D. W., Gottfried, A. W., Oliver, P. H., & Thomas, C. W. (2003). *Temperament: Infancy through adolescence: The Fullerton Longitudinal Study.* New York: Kluwer Academic/Plenum Publishers.

Guerra, N. G., & Slaby, R. G. (1990). Cognitive mediators of aggression in adolescent offenders: 2. Intervention. *Developmental Psychology, 26,* 269–277.

Guerra, N. G., & Smith, E. P. (Eds.). (2006). *Preventing youth violence in a multicultural society.* Washington, D.C.: American Psychological Association.

Guerra, N. G., & Williams, K. R. (2006). Ethnicity, youth violence, and the ecology of development. In N. G. Guerra, & E. P. Smith (Eds.), *Preventing youth violence in a multicultural society.* Washington, D.C.: American Psychological Association.

Guilford, J. P. (1950). Creativity. *American Psychologist, 5,* 444–445.

Gunnar, M., & Quevedo, K. (2007). The neurobiology of stress and development. *Annual Review of Psychology, 58,* 145–173.

Gunnar, M. R. (1998). Quality of early care and buffering of neuroendocrine stress reactions: Potential effects on the developing human brain. *Preventive Medicine, 27,* 208–211.

Gunnar, M. R. (2000). Early adversity and the development of stress reactivity and regulation. In C. A. Nelson (Ed.), *Minnesota Symposium on Child Psychology: Vol. 31. The effects of early adversity on neurobehavioral development.* Mahwah, NJ: Erlbaum.

Gunnar, M. R., Bruce, J., & Grotevant, H. D. (2000). International adoption of institutionally reared children: Research and policy. *Development and Psychopathology, 12,* 677–693.

Guralnick, M. J. (Ed.). (1997). *The effectiveness of early intervention.* Baltimore: Brookes.

Gurland, B. (1991). Epidemiology of psychiatric disorders. In J. Sadavoy, L. W. Lazarus, & L. F. Jarvik (Eds.), *Comprehensive review of geriatric psychiatry.* Washington, D.C.: American Psychiatric Press.

Gurung, R. A. R., Taylor, S. E., & Seeman, T. E. (2003). Accounting for changes in social support among married older adults: Insights from the MacArthur Studies of Successful Aging. *Psychology and Aging, 18,* 487–496.

Guterl, F. (2002, November 11). What Freud got right. *Newsweek,* 50–51.

Gutman, L. (2006). How student and parent goal orientations and classroom goal structures influence the math achievement of African Americans during the high school transition. *Contemporary Educational Psychology, 31,* 44–63.

Gutman, L. M., Sameroff, A. J., & Cole, R. (2003). Academic growth curve trajectories from 1st grade to 12th grade: Effects of multiple social risk factors and preschool child factors. *Developmental Psychology, 39,* 777–790.

Gutman, L. M., Sameroff, A. J., & Eccles, J. S. (2002). The academic achievement of African American students during early adolescence: An examination of multiple risk, promotive, and protective factors. *American Journal of Community Psychology, 39,* 367–399.

Gutmann, D. (1987). *Reclaimed powers: Toward a new psychology of men and women in later life.* New York: Basic Books.

Gutmann, D. (1997). *The human elder in nature, culture, and society.* Boulder, CO: Westview.

Guyer, B., Freedman, M. A., Strobino, D. M., & Sondik, E. J. (2000). Annual summary of vital statistics: Trends in the health of Americans during the 20th century. *Pediatrics, 106,* 1307–1317.

H

Haas-Hawkings, G., Sangster, S., Ziegler, M., & Reid, D. (1985). A study of relatively immediate adjustment to widowhood in later life. *International Journal of Women's Studies, 8,* 158–166.

Habek, D., Habek, J. C., Ivanisevic, M., & Djelmis, J. (2002). Fetal tobacco syndrome and perinatal outcome. *Fetal Diagnosis and Therapy, 17,* 367–371.

Haber, D. (1994). *Health promotion and aging.* New York: Springer.

Haber, D. (2006). Life review: Implementation, theory, research, and therapy. *International Journal of Aging & Human Development, 63,* 153–171.

Hack, M., & Fanaroff, A. A. (1999). Outcomes of children of extremely low birth weight and gestational age in the 1990's. *Early Human Development, 53,* 193–218.

Haegerstrom-Portnoy, G., Schneck, M. E., & Brabyn, J. A. (2000). Seeing into old age: Vision function beyond acuity. *Optometry and Vision Science, 76,* 141–158.

Hagan, L. K., & Kuebli, J. (2007). Mothers' and fathers' socialization of preschoolers' physical risk taking. *Journal of Applied Developmental Psychology, 28,* 2–14.

Hagekull, B., & Bohlin, G. (1998). Preschool temperament and environmental factors related to the five-factor model of personality in middle childhood. *Merrill-Palmer Quarterly, 44,* 194–215.

Hagen, E. W., Palta, M., Albanese, A., & Sadek-Badawi, M. (2006). School achievement in a regional cohort of children born very low birthweight. *Developmental & Behavioral Pediatrics, 27,* 112–119.

Hagestad, G. O. (1985). Continuity and connectedness. In V. L. Bengtson & J. F. Robertson (Eds.), *Grandparenthood.* Beverly Hills, CA: Sage.

Hahn, C., & DiPietro, J. A. (2001). In vitro fertilization and the family: Quality of parenting, family functioning, and child psychosocial adjustment. *Developmental Psychology, 37,* 37–48.

Haight, W. L., Wong, X., Fung, H. H., Williams, K., & Mintz, J. (1999). Universal, developmental, and variable aspects of young children's play: A cross-cultural comparison of pretending at home. *Child Development, 70,* 1477–1488.

Haine, R. A., Wolchik, S. A., Sandler, I. N., & Milsap, R. E. (2006). Positive parenting as a protective resource for parentally bereaved children. *Death Studies, 30,* 1–28.

Hainline, L. (1998). The development of basic visual abilities. In A. Slater (Ed.), *Perceptual development: Visual, auditory and speech perception in infancy* (pp. 37–44). Hove, East Sussex, U.K.: Psychology Press.

Hainline, L., & Abramov, I. (1992). Assessing visual development: Is infant vision good enough? *Advances in Infancy Research, 7,* 39–102.

Haith, M. M., & Benson, J. B. (1998). Infant cognition. In D. Kuhn & R. S. Siegler (Vol. Eds.), W. Damon (Editor-in-Chief), *Handbook of child psychology: Vol. 2. Cognition, perception, and language* (5th ed., pp. 199–254). New York: Wiley.

Hajjar, I., Schumpert, J., Hirth, V., Wieland, D., & Eleazer, G. P. (2002). The impact of the use of statins on the prevalence of dementia and the progression of cognitive impairment. *Journal of Gerontology: Medical Sciences, 57A,* M414–M418.

Halford, G. S. (2004). Information-processing models of cognitive development. In U. Goswami (Ed.), *Blackwell handbook of childhood cognitive development* (pp. 555-574). Malden, MA: Blackwell Publishing.

Hall, C. S. (1954). *A primer of Freudian psychology.* New York: New American Library.

Hall, E. (2001). Babies, books and "impact": Problems and possibilities in the evaluation of a Bookstart project. *Educational Review, 53,* 57–64.

Hall, G. S. (1891). The contents of children's minds on entering school. *Pedagogical Seminary, 1,* 139–173.

Hall, G. S. (1904). *Adolescence* (2 vols.). New York: Appleton.

Hall, G. S. (1922). *Senescence: The last half of life.* New York: Appleton.

Hall, J. A., & Halberstadt, A. G. (1980). Masculinity and femininity in children: Development of the Children's Personal Attributes Questionnaire. *Developmental Psychology, 16,* 270–280.

Hall, W. G., Arnold, H. M., & Myers, K. P. (2000). The acquisition of an appetite. *Psychological Science, 11,* 101–105.

Hallgren, A., Kihlgren, M., Forslin, L., & Norberg, A. (1999). Swedish fathers' involvement in and experiences of childbirth preparation and childbirth. *Midwifery, 15,* 6–15.

Halligan, S. L., Herbert, J., Goodyer, I. M., & Murray, L. (2004). Exposure to postnatal depression predicts elevated cortisol in adolescent offspring. *Biological Psychiatry, 55,* 376–381.

Halpern, C. J. T., Udry, J. R., Suchindran, C., & Campbell, B. (2000). Adolescent males' willingness to report masturbation. *Journal of Sex Research* [Special Issue], 37, 327–332.

Halpern, C. T. (2006). Integrating hormones and other biological factors into a developmental systems model of adolescent female sexuality. *New Directions for Child and Adolescent Development, 112,* 9–22.

Halpern, S. H., Leighton, B. L., Ohlsson A., Barrett, J. F., & Rice, A. (1998). Effect of epidural vs. parenteral opioid analgesia on the progress of labor: A meta-analysis. *Journal of the American Medical Association, 280,* 2105–2110.

Halverson, C. F., Havill, V. L., Deal, J., Baker, S. R., Victor, J. B., Pavlopoulous, V., Besevegis, E., & Wen, L. (2003). Personality structure as derived from parental ratings of free descriptions of children: The Inventory of Child Individual Differences. *Journal of Personality, 71,* 995–1026.

Hamilton, B. E., Miniño, A. M., Martin, J. A., Kochanek, K. D., Strobino, D. M., & Guyer, B. (2007). Annual summary of vital statistics: 2005. *Pediatrics, 119,* 345–360.

Hamm, J. V. (2000). Do birds of a feather flock together? The variable bases for African American, Asian American, and European American adolescents' selection of similar friends. *Developmental Psychology, 36,* 209–219.

Hanawalt, B. A. (2003). The child in the Middle Ages and Renaissance. In W. Koops & M. Zuckerman. (Eds.), *Beyond the century of the child. Cultural history and developmental psychology.* Philadelphia: University of Pennsylvania Press.

Hansen, D., Lou, H. C., & Olsen, J. (2001). Serious life events and congenital malformations: A national study with complete follow-up. *Obstetrical and Gynecological Survey, 56,* 68–69.

Hansson, R. O., DeKoekkoek, P. D., Neece, W. M., & Patterson, D. W. (1997). Successful aging at work: Annual review, 1992–1996: The older worker and transitions to retirement. *Journal of Vocational Behavior, 51,* 202–233.

Hansson, R. O., & Stroebe, M. S. (2007). *Bereavement in late life: Coping, adaptation, and developmental influences.* Washington, D.C.: American Psychological Association.

Hanushek, E. A. (1997). Assessing the effects of school resources on student performance: An update. *Educational Evaluation and Policy Analysis, 19,* 141–164.

Hanushek, E. A. (1998). The evidence on class size: Occasional paper. ERIC: 443158.

Happé, F. G. E., Winner, E., & Brownell, H. (1998). The getting of wisdom: Theory of mind in old age. *Developmental Psychology, 34,* 358–362.

Hare, B., Call, J., & Tomasello, M. (2006). Chimpanzees deceive a human competitor by hiding. *Cognition, 101,* 495–514.

Harley, K., & Eskenazi, B. (2006). Time in the United States, social support and health behaviors during pregnancy among women of Mexican descent. *Social Science & Medicine, 62,* 3048–3061.

Harley, K., & Reese, E. (1999). Origins of autobiographical memory. *Developmental Psychology, 35,* 1338–1348.

Harlow, H. F., & Zimmerman, R. R. (1959). Affectional responses in the infant monkey. *Science, 130,* 421–432.

Harman, D. (2001). Aging: An overview. In S. C. Park, E. S. Hwang, H. Kim, & W. Park (Eds.), *Annals of the New York Academy of Sciences: Vol. 928. Molecular and cellular interactions in senescence.* New York: The New York Academy of Sciences.

Harman, S. M., & Talbert, G. B. (1985). Reproductive aging. In C. E. Finch & E. L. Schneider (Eds.), *Handbook of the biology of aging* (2nd ed.). New York: Van Nostrand Reinhold.

Harper, G., & Kember, D. (1986). Approaches to study of distance education students. *British Journal of Educational Technology, 17,* 211–212.

Harper, L. V. (2005). Epigenetic inheritance and the intergenerational transfer of experience. *Psychological Bulletin, 131,* 340–360.

Harrington, D. M., Block, J. H., & Block, J. (1987). Testing aspects of Carl Rogers's theory of creative environments: Child-rearing antecedents of creative potential in young adolescents. *Journal of Personality and Social Psychology, 52,* 851–856.

Harris, J. R. (1998). *The nurture assumption. Why children turn out the way they do.* New York: Free Press.

Harris, J. R. (2000) Socialization, personality development, and the child's environments: Comment on Vandell (2000). *Developmental Psychology, 36,* 711–723.

Harris, J. R. (2006). *No two alike: Human nature and human individuality.* New York: W. W. Norton.

Harris, J. R., Pedersen, N. L., McClearn, G. E., Plomin, R., & Nesselroade, J. R. (1992). Age differences in genetic and environmental influences for health from the Swedish Adoption/Twin Study of Aging. *Journal of Gerontology: Psychological Sciences, 47,* 213–220.

Harris, M. (1992). Language experience and early language development: From input to uptake. Hove, UK: Erlbaum.

Harris, P. L. (2006). Social cognition. In D. Kuhn & R. S. Siegler (Eds.), & W. Damon & R. M. Lerner (Eds. in Chief), *Handbook of child psychology: Vol. 2. Cognition, perception, and language* (6th ed). Hoboken, NY: Wiley.

Harris, P. L., & Kavanaugh, R. D. (1993). Young children's understanding of pretense. *Monographs of the Society for Research in Child Development, 58* (1, Serial No. 181).

Harris, P. L., Pasquini, E. S., Duke, S., Asscher, J. J., & Pons, F. (2006). Germs and angels: The role of testimony in young children's ontology. *Developmental Science, 9,* 76–96.

Harris, T., & Bifulco, A. (1991). Loss of parent in childhood, attachment style, and depression in adulthood. In C. M. Parkes, J. Stevenson-

Hinde, & P. Marris (Eds.), *Attachment across the life cycle*. London: Tavistock/Routledge.

Harrison, R. V., Gordon, K. A., & Mount, R. J. (2005). Is there a critical period for cochlear implantation in congenitally deaf children? Analyses of hearing and speech perception performance after implantation. *Developmental Psychobiology, 46,* 252–261.

Hart, D. (2005). The development of moral identity. *Nebraska Symposium on Motivation, 51,* 165–196.

Hart, D., Atkins, R., & Donnelly, T. M. (2006). Community service and moral development. In M. Killen & J. G. Smetana (Eds.), *Handbook of moral development*. Mahwah, NJ: Erlbaum.

Hart, M. A., & Foster, S. N. (1997). Couples' attitudes toward childbirth participation: Relationship to evaluation of labor and delivery. *Journal of Perinatal & Neonatal Nursing, 11,* 10–20.

Harter, S. (1996). Historical roots of contemporary issues involving self-concept. In B. A. Bracken (Ed.), *Handbook of self-concept: Developmental, social, and clinical considerations*. New York: Wiley.

Harter, S. (1999). *The construction of the self. A developmental perspective*. New York: Guilford.

Harter, S. (2003). The development of self-representations during childhood and adolescence. In M. R. Leary & J. P. Tangney (Eds.), *Handbook of self and identity*. New York: Guilford.

Harter, S. (2006). The self. In N. Eisenberg (Ed.) & W. Damon & R. M. Lerner (Series Ed.), *Handbook of child psychology: Vol. 3. Social, emotional, and personality development* (6th ed.). Hoboken, NJ: Wiley.

Harter, S., & Monsour, A. (1992). Development analysis of conflict caused by opposing attributes in the adolescent self-portrait. *Developmental Psychology, 28,* 251–260.

Hartley, A. (2006). Changing role of the speed of processing construct in the cognitive psychology of human aging. In J. E. Birren & K. W. Schaie (Eds.), *Handbook of the psychology of aging*. Boston: Elsevier Academic Press.

Hartshorne, H., & May, M. S. (1928–1930). *Studies in the nature of character: Vol. 1. Studies in deceit. Vol. 2. Studies in self-control. Vol. 3. Studies in the organization of character*. New York: Macmillan.

Hartshorne, J. K., & Ullman, M. T. (2006). Why girls say 'holded' more than boys. *Developmental Science, 9,* 21–32.

Hartung, P. J., Porfeli, E. J., & Vondracek, F. W. (2005). Child vocational development: A review and reconsideration. *Journal of Vocational Behavior, 66,* 385–419.

Hartup, W. W. (2006). Relationships in early and middle childhood. In A. L. Vangelisti & D. Perlman (Eds.), *The Cambridge handbook of personal relationships*. New York: Cambridge University Press.

Harvey, J. H., & Fine, M. A. (2004). *Children of divorce. Stories of loss and growth*. Mahwah, NJ: Erlbaum.

Harwood, M. D., & Farrar, M. J. (2006). Conflicting emotions: The connection between affective perspective taking and theory of mind. *British Journal of Developmental Psychology, 24,* 401–418.

Haskett, M. E., Johnson, C. A., & Miller, J. W. (1994). Individual differences in risk of child abuse by adolescent mothers: Assessment in the perinatal period. *Journal of Child Psychology and Psychiatry and Allied Disciplines, 35,* 461–476.

Hatfield, E., & Rapson, R. L. (2006). Passionate love, sexual desire, and mate selection: Cross-cultural and historical perspectives. In P. Noller & J. A. Feeney (Eds.), *Close relationships: Functions, forms, and processes*. New York: Psychology Press.

Hattie, J., Biggs, J., & Purdie, N. (1996). Effects of learning skills interventions on student learning: A meta-analysis. *Review of Educational Research, 66,* 99–136.

Haught, P. A., Hill, L. A., Nardi, A. H., & Walls, R. T. (2000). Perceived ability and level of education as predictors of traditional and practical adult problem solving. *Experimental Aging Research, 26,* 89–101.

Hausdorff, J. M., Levy, B. R., & Wei, J. Y. (1999). The power of ageism on physical function of older persons: Reversibility of age-related gait changes. *Journal of the American Geriatrics Society, 47,* 1346–1349.

Hauser, M. D. (2006). Moral ingredients: How we evolved the capacity to do the right thing. In S. C. Levinson & J. Pierre (Eds.), *Evolution and culture: A Fyssen Foundation symposium*. Cambridge, MA: MIT Press.

Havighurst, R. J., Neugarten, B. L., & Tobin, S. S. (1968). Disengagement and patterns of aging. In B. L. Neugarten (Ed.), *Middle age and aging*. Chicago: University of Chicago Press.

Hawley, R. S., & Mori, C. A. (1999). *The human genome. A user's guide*. San Diego: Academic Press.

Hay, D. F., Nash, A., & Pedersen, J. (1983). Interaction between six-month-old peers. *Child Development, 54,* 557–562.

Hay, D. F., Pawlby, S., Angold, A., Harold, G. T., & Sharp, D. (2003). Pathways to violence in the children of mothers who were depressed postpartum. *Developmental Psychology, 39,* 1083–1094.

Hayflick, L. (1976). The cell biology of human aging. *New England Journal of Medicine, 295,* 1302–1308.

Hayflick, L. (1994). *How and why we age*. New York: Ballantine.

Hayflick, L. (2004). "Anti-aging" is an oxymoron. *Journal of Gerontology: Biological Sciences, 59A,* 573–578.

Hayne, H. (2004). Infant memory development: Implications for childhood amnesia. *Developmental Review, 24,* 33–73.

Hayward, C., Killen, J. D., Wilson, D. M., Hammer, L. D., Litt, I. F., Kraemer, H. C., Haydel, F., Varady, A., & Taylor, C. B. (1997). Psychiatric risk associated with early puberty in adolescent girls. *Journal of the American Academy of Child and Adolescent Psychiatry, 36,* 255–262.

Haywood, H. C., & Tzuriel, D. (2002). Applications and challenges in dynamic assessment. *Peabody Journal of Education, 77,* 40–63.

Hazan, C., Campa, M., & Gur-Yaish, N. (2006). Attachment across the lifespan. In P. Noller & J. A. Feeney (Eds.), *Close relationships: Functions, forms, and processes*. New York: Psychology Press.

Hazan, C., & Shaver, P. (1987). Romantic love conceptualized as an attachment process. *Journal of Personality and Social Psychology, 52,* 511–524.

Hazan, C., & Shaver, P. (1990). Love and work: An attachment-theoretical perspective. *Journal of Personality and Social Psychology, 59,* 270–280.

Heaton, P., & Wallace, G. L. (2004). Annotation: The savant syndrome. *Journal of Child Psychology and Psychiatry, 45,* 899–911.

Heaton, T. B., Jacobson, C. K., & Holland, K. (1999). Persistence and change in decisions to remain childless. *Journal of Marriage and the Family, 61,* 531–539.

Hebert, R. S., & Schulz, R. (2006). Caregiving at the end of life. *Journal of Palliative Medicine, 9,* 1174–1187.

Hedge, J. W., Borman, W. C., & Lammlein, S. E. (Eds.) (2006). *The aging workforce: Realities, myths, and implications for organizations*. Washington, DC: American Psychological Association.

Hedlund, B., & Ebersole, P. (1983). A test of Levinson's midlife reevaluation. *Journal of Genetic Psychology, 143,* 189–192.

Heh, S. S. (2003). Relationship between social support and postnatal depression. *Kaohsiung Journal of Medical Science, 19,* 491–496.

Heinicke, B. E., Paxton, S. J., McLean, S. A., & Wertheim, E. H. (2007). Internet-delivered targeted group intervention for body dissatisfaction and disordered eating in adolescent girls: A randomized controlled trial. *Journal of Abnormal Child Psychology, 35,* 379–391.

Heisel, M. J., & Duberstein, P. R. (2005). Suicide prevention in older adults. *Clinical Psychology: Science and Practice, 12,* 242–259.

Helderman, R. S. (2003, June 13). Inseparable sisters say a first goodbye. *The Washington Post,* B5.

Helgeson, V. S., & Mickelson, K. (2000). Coping with chronic illness among the elderly: Maintaining self-esteem. In S. B. Manuck, R. Jennings, B. S. Rabin, & A. Baum (Eds.), *Behavior, health, and aging*. Mahwah, NJ: Erlbaum.

Helmreich, R. L., Sawin, L. L., & Carsrud, A. L. (1986). The honeymoon effect in job performance: Temporal increases in the predictive power of achievement motivation. *Journal of Applied Psychology, 71,* 185–188.

Helms, J. E. (1992). Why is there no study of cultural equivalence in standardized cognitive-ability testing? *American Psychologist, 47,* 1083–1101.

Helms, J. E. (1997). The triple quandary of race, culture, and social class in standardized cognitive ability testing. In D. P. Flanagan, J. Genshaft, & P. L. Harrison (Eds.), *Contemporary intellectual assessment: Theories, tests, and issues*. New York: Guilford.

Helms, J. E., Jernigan, M., & Mascher, J. (2005). The meaning of race in psychology and how to change it. *American Psychologist, 60,* 27–36.

Helson, R., Jones, C., & Kwan, V. S. Y. (2002). Personality change over 40 years of adulthood: Hierarchical linear modeling analyses of two longitudinal samples. *Journal of Personality and Social Psychology, 83,* 752–766.

Helwig, C. C., Zelazo, P. D., & Wilson, M. (2001). Children's judgments of psychological harm in normal and noncanonical situations. *Child Development, 72,* 66–81.

Henderson, J., Hockley, C., Petrou, S., Goldacre, M., & Davidson, L. (2004). Economic implications of multiple births: Inpatient hospital cost in the first 5 years of life. *Archives of Dis-*

ease in Childhood Fetal and Neonatal Edition, 89, 542–545.

Hendrie, H. C. (2001). Exploration of environmental and genetic risk factors for Alzheimer's disease: The value of cross-cultural studies. *Current Directions in Psychological Science, 10,* 98–101.

Henker, B., & Whalen, C. K. (1989). Hyperactivity and attention deficits. *American Psychologist, 44,* 216–223.

Henrich, C. C., Brookmeyer, K. A., Shrier, L. A., & Shahar, G. (2006). Supportive relationships and sexual risk behavior in adolescence: An ecological–transactional approach. *Journal of Pediatric Psychology, 31,* 286–297.

Henry, D. B., Schoeny, M. E., Deptula, D. P., & Slavick, J. T. (2007). Peer selection and socialization effects on adolescent intercourse without a condom and attitudes about the costs of sex. *Child Development, 78,* 825–838.

Henry, D. B., Schoeny, M. E., Deptula, D. P., & Slavick, J. T. (2007). Peer selection and socialization effects on adolescent intercourse without a condom and attitudes about the costs of sex. *Child Development, 78,* 825–838.

Henry, J. D., MacLeod, M. S., Phillips, L. H., & Crawford, J. R. (2004). A meta-analytic review of prospective memory and aging. *Psychology and Aging, 19,* 27–39.

Herbert, J., & Hayne, H. (2000). Memory retrieval by 18–30-month-olds: Age-related changes in representational flexibility. *Developmental Psychology, 36,* 473–484.

Herdt, G., & Davidson, J. (1988). The Sambia "turnim-man": Sociocultural and clinical aspects of gender formation in male pseudohermaphrodites with 5-alpha-reductase deficiency in Papua New Guinea. *Archives of Sexual Behavior, 17,* 33–56.

Herdt, G., & McClintock, M. (2000). The magical age of 10. *Archives of Sexual Behavior, 29,* 587–606.

Herkert, B. M. (2000). Communicating grief. *Omega: Journal of Death and Dying, 41,* 93–115.

Herman-Giddens, M. E., Slora, E. J., Wasserman, R. C., Bourdony, C. J., Bhapkar, M. V., Koch, G. G., & Hasemeier, C. M. (1997). Secondary sexual characteristics and menses in young girls seen in office practice: A study from the Pediatric Research in Office Settings network. *Pediatrics, 99,* 505–512.

Hermans, H. J., & Oles, P. K. (1999). Midlife crisis in men: Affective organization of personal meanings. *Human Relations, 52,* 1403–1426.

Hermelin, B. (with foreword by M. Rutter). (2001). *Bright splinters of the mind: A personal story of research with autistic savants.* London: Jessica Kingsley Publishers, Ltd.

Hernandez, D. J. (1997). Child development and the social demography of childhood. *Child Development, 68,* 149–169.

Herrnstein, R. J., & Murray, C. (1994). *The bell curve: Intelligence and class structure in American life.* New York: Free Press.

Heru, A. M. (2006). Family psychiatry: From research to practice. *American Journal of Psychiatry, 163,* 962–968.

Hess, T. M. (1994). Social cognition in adulthood: Age-related changes in knowledge and processing mechanisms. *Developmental Review, 14,* 373–412.

Hess, T. M. (1999). Cognitive and knowledge-based influences on social representations. In T. M. Hess & F. Blanchard-Fields (Eds.), *Social cognition and aging.* San Diego: Academic Press.

Hess, T. M. (2006). Attitudes toward aging and their effects on behavior. In J. E. Birren & K. W. Schaie (Eds.), *Handbook of the psychology of aging* (6th ed.). Burlington, MA: Elsevier Academic Press.

Hess, T. M., Osowski, N. L., & Leclerc, C. M. (2005). Age and experience influences on the complexity of social inferences. *Psychology and Aging, 20,* 447–459.

Hesse, E., & Main, M. (2006). Frightened, threatening, and dissociative parental behavior in low-risk samples: Description, discussion, and interpretations. *Development and Psychopathology, 18,* 309–343

Heston, L. L. (1970). The genetics of schizophrenia and schizoid disease. *Science, 167,* 249–256.

Hetherington, E. M. (1981). Children and divorce. In R. W. Henderson (Ed.), *Parent–Child Interaction: Theory, Research and Prospects.* New York: Academic Press.

Hetherington, E. M. (1989). Coping with family transitions: Winners, losers, and survivors. *Child Development, 60,* 1–14.

Hetherington, E. M. (2006). The influence of conflict, marital problem solving and parenting on children's adjustment in nondivorced, divorced and remarried families. In A. Clarke-Stewart & J. Dunn (Eds.), *Families count: Effects on child and adolescent development.* New York: Cambridge University Press.

Hetherington, E. M., Cox, M., & Cox, R. (1982). Effects of divorce on parents and children. In M. E. Lamb (Ed.), *Nontraditional families.* Hillsdale, NJ: Erlbaum.

Hetherington, E. M., & Frankie, G. (1967). Effect of parental dominance, warmth, and conflict on imitation in children. *Journal of Personality and Social Psychology, 6,* 119–125.

Hetherington, E. M., & Kelly, J. (2002). *For better or for worse: Divorce reconsidered.* New York: Norton.

Hetherington, E. M., & Stanley-Hagen, M. (2000). Diversity among stepfamilies. In D. H. Demo, K. R. Allen, & M. A. Fine (Eds.), *Handbook of family diversity.* New York: Oxford University Press.

Hewitt, B., Western, M., & Baxter, J. (2006). Who decides? The social characteristics of who initiates marital separation. *Journal of Marriage and Family, 68,* 1165–1177.

Hewlett, B. S. (1996). Diverse contexts of human infancy. In C. Ember & M. Ember (Eds.), *Cross-cultural research for social science.* Englewood Cliffs, NJ: Prentice Hall.

Heyman, G. D., Dweck, C. S., & Cain, K. M. (1992). Young children's vulnerability to self-blame and helplessness: Relationship to beliefs about goodness. *Child Development 63,* 401–415.

Heymann, S. J., Penrose, K., & Earle, A. (2006). Meeting children's needs: How does the United States measure up? *Merrill-Palmer Quarterly, 52,* 189–215.

Heyne, D., King, N. J., & Tonge, B. (2004). School refusal. In T. H. Ollendick & J. S. March (Eds.), *Phobic and anxiety disorders in children and adolescents: A clinician's guide to effective psychosocial and pharmacological interventions.* New York: Oxford University Press.

Hicks, B. M., Blonigen, D. M., Kramer, M. D., Krueger, R. F., Patrick, C. J., Iacono, W. G., & McGue, M. (2007). Gender differences and developmental change in externalizing disorders from late adolescence to early adulthood: A longitudinal twin study. *Journal of Abnormal Psychology, 116,* 433–447.

Hilgard, E. R., & Loftus, E. F. (1979). Effective interrogation of the eyewitness. *International Journal of Clinical and Experimental Psychology, 27,* 342–357.

Hill, A. J. (2007). The development of children's shape and weight concerns. In T. Jaffa & B. McDermott (Eds.), *Eating disorders in children and adolescents.* Cambridge, UK: Cambridge University Press.

Hill, J. B. & Haffner, W. H. J. (2002). Growth before birth. In M. L. Batshaw (Ed.), *Children with disabilities* (5th ed.). Baltimore: Paul H. Brookes.

Hill, J. P., & Lynch, M. E. (1983). The intensification of gender-related role expectations during early adolescence. In J. Brooks-Gunn & A. C. Petersen (Eds.), *Girls at puberty: Biological and psychosocial perspectives.* New York: Plenum.

Hill, N. E., & Craft, S. A. (2003). Parent–school involvement and school performance: Mediated pathways among socioeconomically comparable African American and Euro-American families. *Journal of Educational Psychology, 95,* 74–83.

Hill, N. E., & Taylor, L. C. (2004). Parent–school involvement and children's academic achievement: Pragmatics and issues. *Current Directions in Psychological Science, 13,* 161–164.

Hill, P. (1993). Recent advances in selected aspects of adolescent development. *Journal of Child Psychology and Psychiatry and Allied Disciplines, 34,* 69–99.

Hill, R., & Rodgers, R. H. (1964). The developmental approach. In H. Christensen (Ed.), *Handbook of marriage and the family.* Chicago: Rand-McNally.

Hill, S. D., & Tomlin, C. (1981). Self-recognition in retarded children. *Child Development, 52,* 145–150.

Hill, S. E. & Flom, R. (2007). 18- and 24-month-olds' discrimination of gender-consistent and inconsistent activities. *Infant Behavior & Development, 30,* 168–173.

Hilton, N. Z., Harris, G. T., & Rice, M. E. (2000). The functions of aggression by male teenagers. *Journal of Personality and Social Psychology, 79,* 988–994.

Himes, C. (2001). Elderly Americans. *Population Bulletin, 56(4),* 3–40.

Hinde, R. A. (1983). Ethology and child development. In M. M. Haith & J. J. Campos (Vol. Eds.), P. H. Mussen (Editor-in-Chief), *Handbook of child psychology: Vol. 2. Infancy and developmental psychobiology* (4th ed.). New York: Wiley.

Hinds, J. D. (2007, May 28). 'I'm sorry' shouldn't be the hardest words. *Newsweek,* p. 20.

Hine, T. (1999). *The rise and fall of the American teenager.* New York: Bard.

Hinton, J. (1975). The influence of previous personality on reactions to having terminal cancer. *Omega: Journal of Death and Dying, 6,* 95–111.

Hirsh-Pasek, K., Golinkoff, R. M., & Hollich, G. (1999). Trends and transitions in language development: Looking for the missing piece. *Developmental Neuropsychology, 16,* 139–162.

Hoare, C. H. (2005). Erikson's general and adult developmental revisions of Freudian thought: "Outward, forward, upward." *Journal of Adult Development, 12,* 19–31.

Hobbs, F. B. (with B. L. Damon). (1996). *65 in the United States.* Washington, D.C.: U.S. Bureau of the Census.

Hobson, R. P., Chidambi, G., Lee, A., & Meyer, J. (2006). Foundations for self-awareness: An exploration through autism. *Monographs of the Society for Research in Child Development, 71*(2, Serial No. 284).

Hodges, E. V. E., & Card, N. A. (Eds.). (2003). *Enemies and the darker side of peer relations.* San Francisco: Jossey-Bass.

Hodges, J., & Tizard, B. (1989). IQ and behavioral adjustment of exinstitutional adolescents. *Journal of Child Psychology and Psychiatry, 30,* 53–75.

Hodgson, J. W., & Fischer, J. L. (1979). Sex differences in identity and intimacy development in college youth. *Journal of Youth and Adolescence, 8,* 37–50.

Hodnett, E. D., Gates, S., Hofmeyr, G. J., & Sakala, C. (2003). Continuous support for women during childbirth. *Cochrane Database System Review: CD003766.*

Hodnett, E. D., & Osborn, R. W. (1989). A randomized trial of the effects of monitrice support during labor: Mothers' views two to four weeks postpartum. *Birth, 16,* 177–183.

Hof, P., & Mobbs, C. (2001). *Functional neurobiology of aging.* Academic Press.

Hofer, S. M., Christensen, H., MacKinnon, A. J., Korten, A. E., Jorm, A. F., Henderson, A. S., & Easteal, S. (2002). Change in cognitive functioning associated with ApoE genotype in a community sample of older adults. *Psychology and Aging, 17,* 194–208.

Hoff, E. (2005). *Language development* (3rd ed.). Belmont, CA: Wadsworth.

Hoff, E. V. (2005a). A friend living inside me— The forms and functions of imaginary companions. *Imagination, Cognition, and Personality, 24,* 151–189.

Hoff, E. V. (2005b). Imaginary companions, creativity, and self-image in middle childhood. *Creativity Research Journal, 17,* 167–180.

Hoffman, B. J., & Woehr, D. J. (2006). A quantitative review of the relationship between person-organization fit and behavioral outcomes. *Journal of Vocational Behavior, 68,* 389–399.

Hoffman, K. L., Kiecolt, K. J., & Edwards, J. N. (2005). Physical violence between siblings: A theoretical and empirical analysis. *Journal of Family Issues, 26,* 1103–1130.

Hoffman, L. W. (2000). Maternal employment: Effects of social context. In R. D. Taylor & M. C. Wang (Eds.), *Resilience across contexts: Family, work, culture, and community.* Mahwah, NJ: Erlbaum.

Hoffman, M. L. (1970). Moral development. In P. H. Mussen (Ed.), *Carmichael's manual of child psychology* (Vol. 2). New York: Wiley.

Hoffman, M. L. (2000). *Empathy and moral development: Implications for caring and justice.* Cambridge, UK: Cambridge University Press.

Hoffman, M., Levy-Shiff, R., & Malinski, D. (1996). Stress and adjustment in the transition to adolescence: Moderating effects of neuroticism and extroversion. *Journal of Youth and Adolescence, 25,* 161–175.

Hoffman, S. I., & Strauss, S. (1985). The development of children's concepts of death. *Death Studies, 9,* 469–482.

Hofstra, M. B., Van der Ende, J., & Verhulst, F. C. (2000). Continuity and change of psychopathology from childhood into adulthood. *Journal of the American Academy of Child & Adolescent Psychiatry, 39,* 850–858.

Hogan, D. P., & Park, J. M. (2000). Family factors and social support in the developmental outcomes of very low-birth weight children. *Clinical Perinatology, 27,* 433–459.

Hohm, E., Jennen-Steinmetz, C., Schmidt, M. H., Laucht, M. (2007). Language development at ten months: Predictive of language outcome and school achievement ten years later? *European Child & Adolescent Psychiatry, 16,* 149–156.

Holahan, A., & Costenbader, V. (2000). A comparison of developmental gains for preschool children with disabilities in inclusive and self-contained classrooms. *Topics in Early Childhood Special Education, 20,* 224-235.

Holahan, C., & Sears, R. (1995). *The gifted group in later maturity.* Stanford, CA: Stanford University Press.

Holland, J. L. (1985). *Making vocational choices: A theory of vocational personalities and work environments* (2nd ed.). Englewood Cliffs, NJ: Prentice-Hall.

Hollich, G. J., Hirsh-Pasek, K., & Golinkoff, R. M. (2000). Breaking the language barrier: An emergentist coalition model for the origins of word learning. *Monographs of the Society for Research in Child Development, 65* (No. 262).

Hollon, S. D., Thase, M. E., & Markowitz, J. C. (2002). Treatment and prevention of depression. *Psychological Science in the Public Interest, 3,* 39–77.

Holmbeck, G. N., Crossman, R. E., Wandrei, M. L., & Gasiewski, E. (1994). Cognitive development, egocentrism, self-esteem, and adolescent contraceptive knowledge, attitudes, and behavior. *Journal of Youth and Adolescence, 23,* 169–193.

Holmbeck, G. N., Greenley, R. N., & Franks, E. A. (2003). Developmental issues and considerations in research and practice. In A. E. Kazdin (Ed.), *Evidence-based psychotherapies for children and adolescents.* New York: Guilford Press.

Holowka, S., & Petitto, L. A. (2002). Left hemisphere cerebral specialization for babies while babbling. *Science, 297,* 1515.

Holzrichter, A. S., & Meier, R. P. (2000). Child-directed signing in American Sign Language. In C. Chamberlain, J. P. Morford, & R. Mayberry (Eds.), *Language acquisition by eye.* Mahwah, NJ: Lawrence Erlbaum.

Honey, K. L., Bennett, P., & Morgan, M. (2003). Predicting postnatal depression. *Journal of Affective Disorders, 76,* 201–210.

Honzik, M. P. (1983). Measuring mental abilities in infancy: The value and limitations. In M. Lewis (Ed.), *Origins of intelligence: Infancy and early childhood* (2nd ed.). New York: Plenum.

Hooker, K., & Siegler, I. C. (1993). Life goals, satisfaction, and self-rated health: Preliminary findings. *Experimental Aging Research, 19,* 97–110.

Hooper, F. H., Hooper, J. O., & Colbert, K. K. (1985). Personality and memory correlates of intellectual functioning in adulthood: Piaget-ian and psychometric assessments. *Human Development, 28,* 101–107.

Hopfer, C. J., Crowley, T. J., & Hewitt, J. K. (2003). Review of twin and adoption studies of adolescent substance use. *Journal of the American Academy of Child and Adolescent Psychiatry, 42,* 710–719.

Horiuchi, S., Finch, C. E., Mesle, F., & Vallin, J. (2003). Differential patterns of age-related mortality increase in middle age and old age. *Journal of Gerontology: Biological Sciences, 58A,* 495–507.

Horn, J. L., & Cattell, R. B. (1967). Age differences in fluid and crystallized intelligence. *Acta Psychologica, 26,* 107–129.

Horn, J. L., & Noll, J. (1997). Human cognitive capabilities: Gf-Gc theory. In D. P. Flanagan, J. Genshaft, & P. L. Harrison (Eds.), *Contemporary intellectual assessment: Theories, tests, and issues.* New York: Guilford.

House, J. D. (2006). Mathematics beliefs, instructional strategies, and algebra achievement of adolescent students in Japan: Results from the TIMSS 1999 Assessment. *International Journal of Instructional Media, 33,* 443–462.

Houston, D. M., Pisoni, D. B., Kirk, K. I., Ying, E. A., & Miyamoto, R. T. (2005). Speech perception skills of deaf infants following cochlear implantation: A first report. *International Journal of Pediatric Otorhinolaryngology, 67,* 1479–495.

Houx, P. J., Vreeling, F. W., & Jolles, J. (1991). Rigorous health screening reduces age effect on memory scanning task. *Brain and Cognition, 15,* 246–260.

Howe, M. (2006). Developmental invariance in distinctiveness effects in memory. *Developmental Psychology, 42,* 1193–1205.

Howe, M. L. (2000). *The fate of early memories: Developmental science and the retention of childhood experiences.* Washington, D.C.: American Psychological Association.

Howe, M. L., & Courage, M. L. (1993). On resolving the enigma of infantile amnesia. *Psychological Bulletin, 113,* 305–326.

Howe, M. L., & Courage, M. L. (1997). The emergence and early development of autobiographical memory. *Psychological Review, 104,* 499–523.

Howe, M. L., Courage, M. L., & Peterson, C. (1994). How can I remember when "I" wasn't there: Long-term retention of traumatic experiences and emergence of the cognitive self. *Consciousness and Cognition, 3,* 327–355.

Howe, M. L., & Lewis, M. D. (2005). The importance of dynamic systems approaches for understanding development. *Developmental Review, 25,* 247–251.

Howe, N., Aquan-Assee, J., Bukowski, W. M., Rinaldi, C. M., & Lehoux, P. M. (2000). Sibling self-disclosure in early adolescence. *Merrill-Palmer Quarterly, 46,* 653–671.

Howe, N., & Ross, H. S. (1990). Socialization, perspective-taking, and the sibling relationship. *Developmental Psychology, 26,* 160–165.

Howell, K. K., Lynch, M. E., Platzman, K. A., Smith, G. H., & Coles, C. D. (2006). Prenatal alcohol exposure and ability, academic achievement, and school functioning in adolescence: A longitudinal follow-up. *Journal of Pediatric Psychology, 31,* 116–126.

Howes, C. (1988). Same- and cross-sex friends: Implications for interaction and social skills. *Early Childhood Research Quarterly, 3,* 21–37.

Howes, C., & Matheson, C. C. (1992). Sequences in the development of competent play with peers: Social and social pretend play. *Developmental Psychology, 28*, 961–974.

Howes, P., & Markman, H. J. (1989). Marital quality and child functioning: A longitudinal investigation. *Child Development, 60*, 1044–1051.

Howieson, D. B., Dame, A., Camicioli, R., Sexton, G., Payami, H., & Kaye, J. A. (1997). Cognitive markers preceding Alzheimer's dementia in the healthy oldest old. *Journal of the American Geriatrics Society, 45*, 584–589.

Howieson, N. (1981). A longitudinal study of creativity: 1965–1975. *Journal of Creative Behavior, 15*, 117–134.

Howlin, P., Goode, S., Hutton, J., & Rutter, M. (2004). Adult outcome for children with autism. *Journal of Child Psychology and Psychiatry, 45*, 212–229.

Hoyer, W. J., & Verhaeghen, P. (2006). Memory aging. In J. E. Birren & K. W. Schaie (Eds.), *Handbook of the psychology of aging*. Boston: Elsevier Academic Press.

Hrdy, S. B. (2005). On why it takes a village. Cooperative breeders, infant needs, and the future. In R. L. Burgess & K. MacDonald (Eds.), *Evolutionary perspectives on human development*. Thousand Oaks, CA: Sage.

Hsu, L. K. G. (1990). *Eating disorders*. New York: Guilford Press.

Hubbard, J. A., Smithmyer, C. M., Ramsden, S. R., Parker, E. H., Flanagan, K. D., Dearing, K. F., Relyea, N., & Simons, R. F. (2002). Observational, physiological, and self-report measures of children's anger: Relations to reactive versus proactive aggression. *Child Development, 73*, 1101–1118.

Hubel, D. H., & Wiesel, T. N. (1970). The period of susceptibility to the physiological effects of unilateral eye-closure in kittens. *Journal of Physiology, 206*, 419–436.

Hudley, C., & Graham, S. (1993). An attributional intervention to reduce peer-directed aggression among African American boys. *Child Development, 64*, 124–138.

Huesmann, L. R., Moise-Titus, J., Podolski, C., & Eron, L. D. (2003). Longitudinal relations between children's exposure to TV violence and their aggressive and violent behavior in young adulthood: 1977–1992. *Developmental Psychology, 39*, 201–221.

Huesmann, L. R., & Taylor, L. D. (2006). The role of media violence in violent behavior. *Annual Review of Public Health, 27*, 393–415.

Hughes, C., Jaffee, S. R., Happe, F., Taylor, A., Caspi, A., & Moffitt, T. E. (2005). Origins of individual differences in theory of mind: From nature to nurture? *Child Development, 76*, 356–370.

Hughes, D., Rodriguez, J., Smith, E. P., Johnson, D. J., Stevenson, H. C., & Spicer, P. (2006). Parents' ethnic socialization practices: A review of research and directions for future study. *Developmental Psychology, 42*, 747–770.

Hughes, D., & Simpson, L. (1995). The role of social change in preventing low birth weight. *The Future of Children, 5*, 87–102.

Hughes, F. M., & Seta, C. E. (2003). Gender stereotypes: Children's perceptions of future compensatory behavior following violations of gender roles. *Sex Roles, 49*, 685–691.

Huijbregts, S. C. J., Seguin, J. R., Zelazo, P. D., Parent, S., Japel, C., & Tremblay, R. E. (2006).

Interrelations between maternal smoking during pregnancy, birth weight, and sociodemographic factors in the prediction of early cognitive abilities. *Infant and Child Development, 15*, 593–607.

Hultsch, D. F., Hammer, M., & Small, B. J. (1993). Age differences in cognitive performance in later life: Relationships to self-reported health and activity life style. *Journal of Gerontology: Psychological Sciences, 48*, 1–11.

Hunt, P., & Goetz, L. (1997). Research on inclusive educational programs, practices, and outcomes for students with severe disabilities. *Journal of Special Education, 31*, 3–29.

Hurd, L. C. (1999). "We're not old!" Older women's negotiation of aging and oldness. *Journal of Aging Studies, 13*, 419–439.

Hurd, R. C. (2002). Sibling support systems in childhood after a parent dies. *Omega: Journal of Death and Dying, 45*, 299–320.

Huston, M., & Schwartz, P. (1995). The relationships of lesbians and gay men. In J. T. Wood & S. Duck (Eds.), *Under-studied relationships: Off the beaten track*. Thousand Oaks, CA: Sage.

Huston, T. L., Caughlin, J. P., Houts, R. M., Smith, S. E., & George, L. J. (2001). The connubial crucible: Newlywed years as predictors of marital delight, distress, and divorce. *Journal of Personality and Social Psychology, 80*, 237–252.

Huston, T. L., McHale, S. M., & Crouter, A. C. (1986). When the honeymoon's over: Changes in the marriage relationship over the first year. In R. Gilmour & S. Duck (Eds.), *The emerging field of personal relationships*. Hillsdale, NJ: Erlbaum.

Hutchinson, K. E., Stallings, M., McGeary, J., & Bryan, A. (2004). Population stratification in the candidate gene study: Fatal threat or red herring? *Psychological Bulletin, 130*, 66–79.

Hyde, J. S. (1984). How large are gender differences in aggression? A developmental meta-analysis. *Developmental Psychology, 20*, 722–736.

Hyde, J. S., & DeLamater, J. D. (2006). *Understanding human sexuality* (9th ed.). New York: McGraw-Hill.

Hyde, J. S., Fennema, E., & Lamon, S. J. (1990). Gender differences in mathematics performance: A meta-analysis. *Psychological Bulletin, 107*, 139–155.

Hymel, S., McDougall, P., & Renshaw, P. (2002). Peer acceptance–rejection. In P. K. Smith & C. H. Hart (Eds.), *Blackwell handbook of childhood social development*. Malden, MA: Blackwell.

Hyson, M. C., Hirsh-Pasek, K., & Rescorla, L. (1989). *Academic environments in early childhood: Challenge or pressure?* Summary report to the Spencer Foundation.

I

Iacoboni, M., & Dapretto, M. (2006). The mirror neuron system and the consequences of its dysfunction. *Nature Reviews Neuroscience, 7*, 942–951.

Ialongo, N. S., Edelsohn, G., & Kellam, S. G. (2001). A further look at the prognostic power of young children's reports of depressed mood. *Child Development, 72*, 736–747.

Iervolino, A. C., Hines, M., Golombok, S. E., Rust, J., & Plomin, R. (2005). Genetic and environmental influences on sex-typed behavior

during the preschool years. *Child Development, 76*, 826–840.

Imel, S. (1996). Adult literacy education: Emerging directions in program development. ERIC Digest No. 179.

Imperato-McGinley, J., Peterson, R. E., Gautier, T., & Sturla, E. (1979). Androgens and the evolution of male gender identity among male pseudohermaphrodites with 5a-reductase deficiency. *New England Journal of Medicine, 300*, 1233–1237.

Ingoldsby, B. B., & Smith, S. (1995). *Families in multicultural perspective*. New York: Guilford.

Ingram, R. E., & Price, J. M. (2001). The role of vulnerability in understanding psychopathology. In R. E. Ingram & J. M. Price (Eds.), *Vulnerability to psychopathology. Risk across the lifespan*. New York: Guilford.

Ingrassia, M., & Springen, K. (1994, March 21). She's not baby Jessica anymore. *Newsweek, 123*, 60–66.

Ingudomnukul, E., Baron-Cohen, S., Wheelwright, S., & Knickmeyer, R. (2007). Elevated rates of testosterone-related disorders in women with autism spectrum conditions. *Hormones and Behavior, 51*, 597–604.

Inhelder, B. (1966). Cognitive development and its contribution to the diagnosis of some phenomena of mental deficiency. *Merrill-Palmer Quarterly, 12*, 299–319.

Inhelder, B., & Piaget, J. (1958). *The growth of logical thinking from childhood to adolescence: An essay on the construction of formal operational structures* (A. Parsons & S. Milgram, Trans.). New York: Basic Books.

Inhelder, B., & Piaget, J. (1964). *Early growth of logic in the child: Classification and seriation*. New York: Harper & Row.

Insurance Institute for Highway Safety, Highway Loss Data Institute (2007). *Fatality facts*. Available at: www.iihs.org/research/fatality_facts/gender.html. Accessed: April 15, 2007.

International Human Genome Sequencing Consortium (2004, October 21). Finishing the euchromatic sequence of the human genome. *Nature, 431*, 931–945.

Irwin, R. R. (1991). Reconceptualizing the nature of dialectical postformal operational thinking: The effects of affectively mediated social experiences. In J. D. Sinnott & J. C. Cavanaugh (Eds.), *Bridging paradigms: Positive development in adulthood and cognitive aging*. New York: Praeger.

Isabella, R. A. (1993). Origins of attachment: Maternal interactive behavior across the first year. *Child Development, 64*, 605–621.

Isabella, R. A., & Belsky, J. (1991). Interactional synchrony and the origins of infant-mother attachment: A replication study. *Child Development, 62*, 373–384.

Izard, C. E. (1982). *Measuring emotions in infants and children*. New York: Cambridge University Press.

Izard, C. E., & Ackerman, B. P. (2000). Motivational, organizational, and regulatory functions of discrete emotions. In M. Lewis & J. M. Haviland-Jones (Eds.), *Handbook of emotions* (2nd ed.). New York: Guilford.

J

Jacklin, C. N. (1989). Male and female: Issues of gender. *American Psychologist, 44*, 127–133.

Jacobs, J. E., & Klaczynski, P. A. (2002). The development of judgment and decision making during childhood and adolescence. *Current Directions in Psychological Science, 11,* 145–149.

Jacobs, J. E., Lanza, S., Osgood, D. W., Eccles, J. S., & Wigfield, A. (2002). Changes in children's self-competence and values: Gender and domain differences across grades one through twelve. *Child Development, 73,* 509–527.

Jacobs, S. C., Kosten, T. R., Kasl, S. V., Ostfeld, A. M., Berkman, L., & Charpentier, P. (1987–1988). Attachment theory and multiple dimensions of grief. *Omega: Journal of Death and Dying, 18,* 41–52.

Jacobsen, T., & Hofmann, V. (1997). Children's attachment representations: Longitudinal relations to school behavior and academic competency in middle childhood and adolescence. *Developmental Psychology, 33,* 703–710.

Jacobson, J. L., & Jacobson, S. W. (1999). Drinking moderately and pregnancy: Effects on child development. *Alcohol Research and Health, 25,* 25–30.

Jacobson, J. L., Jacobson, S. W., Sokol, R. J., Martier, S. S., Ager, J. W., & Kaplan-Estrin, M. G. (1993). Teratogenic effects of alcohol on infant development. *Alcoholism: Clinical and Experimental Research, 17,* 174–183.

Jacobvitz, D., & Sroufe, L. A. (1987). The early caregiver–child relationship and attention-deficit disorder with hyperactivity in kindergarten: A prospective study. *Child Development, 58,* 1496–1504.

Jaffa, T., & McDermott, B. (2007). (Eds.). *Eating disorders in children and adolescents.* Cambridge, UK: Cambridge University Press.

Jaffari-Bimmel, N., Juffer, F., van IJzendoorn, M. H., Bakermans-Kranenberg, M. J., & Mooijaart, A. (2006). Social development from infancy to adolescence: Lognitudinal and concurrent factors in an adoption sample. *Developmental Psychology, 42,* 1143–1153.

Jaffe, J., Beebe, B., Feldstein, S., Crown, C. L., & Jasnow, M. D. (2001). Rhythms of dialogue in infancy: Coordinated timing in development. *Monographs of the Society for Research in Child Development, 66* (2, Serial No. 265).

Jaffee, S., & Hyde, J. S. (2000). Gender differences in moral orientation: A meta-analysis. *Psychological Bulletin, 126,* 703–726.

Jaffee, S. R., Caspi, A., Moffitt, T. E., Dodge, K. A., Rutter, M., Taylor, A., & Tully, L. A. (2005). Nature X nurture: Genetic vulnerabilities interact with physical maltreatment to promote conduct problems. *Development and Psychopathology, 17,* 67–84.

James, J. B., & Zarrett, N. (2005). Ego integrity in the lives of older women: A follow-up of mothers from the Sears, Maccoby, and Levin (1951) Patterns of Child Rearing Study. *Journal of Adult Development, 12,* 155–167.

James, W. (1890). *Principles of psychology* (2 vols.). New York: Holt.

Jankowiak, W. R., & Fischer, E. F. (1992). A cross-cultural perspective on romantic love. *Ethnology, 31,* 149–155.

Janus, J. S., & Janus, C. L. (1993). *The Janus report on sexual behavior.* New York: Wiley.

Jaquish, G. A., & Ripple, R. E. (1981). Cognitive creative abilities and self-esteem across the adult life-span. *Human Development, 24,* 110–119.

Jastrzembski, T. S., Charness, N., & Vasyukova, C. (2006). Expertise and age effects on knowledge activation in chess. *Psychology and Aging, 21,* 401–405.

Jayawardena, K. M., & Liao, S. (2006). Elder abuse at the end of life. *Journal of Palliative Medicine, 9,* 127–136.

Jedrychowski, W., Jankowski, J., Flak, E., Skarupa, A., Mroz, E., Sochacka-Tatara, E., Lisowska-Miszczyk, I., Szpanowska-Wohn, A., Rauh, V., Skolicki, Z., Kaim, I., & Perera, F. (2006). Effects of prenatal exposure to mercury in cognitive and psychomotor function in one-year-old infants: Epidemiologic cohort study in Poland. *Annals of Epidemiology, 16,* 439–447.

Jeffery, R., & Jeffery, P. M. (1993). Traditional birth attendants in rural north India: The social organization of childbearing. In S. Lindenbaum & M. Lock (Eds.), *Knowledge, power and practice: The anthropology of medicine and everyday life.* Berkeley: University of California Press.

Jelliffe-Pawlowski, L. L., Miles, S. Q., Courtney, J. G., Materna, B., & Charlton, V. (2006). Effect of magnitude and timing of maternal pregnancy blood lead (Pb) levels on birth outcomes. *Journal of Perinatology, 26,* 154–162.

Jenkins, J. M., & Astington, J. W. (1996). Cognitive factors and family structure associated with theory of mind development in young children. *Developmental Psychology, 32,* 70–78.

Jenkins, S. R. (1989). Longitudinal prediction of women's careers: Psychological, behavioral, and social–structural influences. *Journal of Vocational Behavior, 34,* 204–235.

Jennings, K. D., & Dietz, L. J. (2003). Mastery motivation and goal persistence in young children. In M. H. Bornstein & Davidson, L. (Eds.), *Well-being: positive development across the life course* (pp. 295–309). Mahwah, NJ: Lawrence Erlbaum.

Jensen, A. R. (1969). How much can we boost IQ and scholastic achievement? *Harvard Educational Review, 39,* 1–123.

Jensen, A. R. (1977). Cumulative deficit in the IQ of blacks in the rural South. *Developmental Psychology, 13,* 184–191.

Jensen, A. R. (1980). *Bias in mental testing.* New York: Free Press.

Jensen, A. R. (1990). Speed of information processing in a calculating prodigy. *Intelligence, 14,* 259–274.

Jensen, A. R. (1993). Why is reaction time correlated with psychometric g? *Current Directions in Psychological Science, 2,* 53–56.

Jensen, P. S. (2000). Current concepts and controversies in the diagnosis and treatment of attention-deficit/hyperactivity disorder. *Current Psychiatry Reports, 2,* 102–109.

Jensen, P. S., Hinshaw, S. P., Swanson, J. M., Greenhill, L. L., Conners, C. K., Arnold, L. E., Abikoff, H. B., Elliott, G., Hechtman, L., Hoza, B., March, J. S., Newcorn, J. H., Severe, J. B., Vitiello, B., Wells, K., & Wigal, T. (2001). Findings from the NIMH Multimodal Treatment Study of ADHD (MTA): Implications and applications for primary care providers. *Journal of Developmental and Behavioral Pediatrics, 22,* 60–73.

Jessor, R. (Ed.) (1998). *New perspectives on adolescent risk behavior.* Cambridge, England: Cambridge University Press.

Jia, G., & Aaronson, D. (1999). Age differences in second language acquisition: The dominant language switch and maintenance hypothesis. In A. Greenhill, H. Littlefield, & C. Tano (Eds.), *Proceedings of the 23rd Annual Boston University Conference on Language Development* (pp. 301–312). Somerville, MA: Cascadilla Press.

Joh, A. S., & Adolph, K. E. (2006). Learning from falling. *Child Development, 77,* 89–102.

Johanson, R. B., & Menon, B. K. (2000). Vacuum extraction versus forceps for assisted vaginal delivery. *Cochrane Database System Review, 2:* CD000224.

Johansson, B., Zarit, S. H., & Berg, S. (1992). Changes in cognitive functioning of the oldest old. *Journal of Gerontology: Psychological Sciences, 47,* P75–P80.

Johnson, C. L., Stuckey, M. K., Lewis, L. D., & Schwartz, D. M. (1982). Bulimia: A descriptive survey of 316 cases. *International Journal of Eating Disorders, 2,* 3–16.

Johnson, C. L., & Troll, L. (1994). Constraints and facilitators to friendships in late life. *Gerontologist, 34,* 79–87.

Johnson, C. L., & Troll, L. (1996). Family structure and the timing of transitions from 70 to 103 years of age. *Journal of Marriage and the Family, 58,* 178–187.

Johnson, D. W., Johnson, R. T., & Maruyama, G. (1983). Interdependence and interpersonal attraction among heterogeneous and homogeneous individuals: A theoretical formulation and a meta-analysis of the research. *Review of Educational Research, 53,* 5–54.

Johnson, H. M. (2005). *Developmental cognitive neuroscience.* Malden, MA: Blackwell Publishing.

Johnson, J., & Newport, E. (1989). Critical period effects in second language learning: The influence of maturational state on the acquisition of English as a second language. *Cognitive Psychology, 21,* 60–99.

Johnson, J. G., Cohen, P., Kasen, S., Smailes, E., & Brook, J. (2001). Association of maladaptive parental behavior with psychiatric disorder among parents and their offspring. *Archives of General Psychology, 58,* 453–460.

Johnson, J. G., Zhang, B., Greer, J. A., & Prigerson, H. G. (2007). Parental control, partner dependency, and complicated grief among widowed adults in the community. *Journal of Nervous and Mental Disease, 195,* 26–30.

Johnson, M., & de Haan, M. (2001). Developing cortical specialization for visual-cognitive function: The case of face recognition. In J. L. McClelland & R. S. Siegler (Eds.), *Mechanisms of cognitive development: Behavioral and neural perspectives* (pp. 253–270). Mahwah, NJ: U Sum Associates Publishers.

Johnson, M. H. (1997). *Developmental cognitive neuroscience.* Cambridge, MA: Blackwell.

Johnson, M. P., & Ferraro, K. J. (2000). Research on domestic violence in the 1990s: Making distinctions. *Journal of Marriage and the Family, 62,* 948–963.

Johnson, S., Ring, W., Anderson, P., Marlow, N. (2005). Randomised trial of parental support for families with very preterm children: Outcome at 5 years. *Archives of Disease in Childhood, 90,* 909–915.

Johnson, S. P., & Aslin, R. N. (1995). Perception of object unity in 2-month-old infants. *Developmental Psychology, 31,* 739–745.

Johnson, S. P., Bremner, J. G., Slater, A. M., & Mason, U. (2000). The role of good form in young infants' perception of partly occluded objects. *Journal of Experimental Child Psychology, 76,* 1–25.

Johnson, W., & Bouchard, T. J. (2007). Sex differences in mental abilities: *g* masks the dimensions on which they lie. *Intelligence, 35,* 23–39.

John-Steiner, V. (1992). Private speech among adults. In R. M. Diaz & L. E. Berk (Eds.), *Private speech: From social interaction to self-regulation.* Hillsdale, NJ: Erlbaum.

Johnston, T. D., & Edwards, L. (2002). Genes, interactions, and the development of behavior. *Psychological Review, 109,* 26–34.

Joint Committee on Infant Hearing. (2000). Year 2000 position statement: Principles and guidelines for early hearing detection and intervention programs. *Pediatrics, 106,* 798–817.

Jokela, M., Keltikangas-Jarvinen, L., Kivimaki, M., Puttonen, S., Elovainio, M., Rontu, R., & Lehtimaki, T. (2007). Serotonin receptor 2A gene and the influence of childhood maternal nurturance on adulthood depressive symptoms. *Archives of General Psychiatry, 64,* 356–360.

Jones, E. J. H., & Herbert, J. S. (2006). Exploring memory in infancy: Deferred imitation and the development of declarative memory. *Infant and Child Development, 15,* 195–205.

Jones, M. C. (1924). A laboratory study of fear: The case of Peter. *Pedagogical Seminary, 31,* 308–315.

Jones, M., & Larson, E. (2003). Length of normal labor in women of Hispanic origin. *Journal of Midwifery, 48,* 2–9.

Jones, S. S. (1996). Imitation or exploration? Young infants' matching of adults' oral gestures. *Child Development, 67,* 1952–1969.

Joyner, K., & Udry, J. R. (2000). You don't bring me anything but down: Adolescent romance and depression. *Journal of Health and Social Behavior, 41,* 369–391.

Judge, S. (2003). Developmental recovery and deficit in children adopted from Eastern European orphanages. *Child Psychiatry and Human Development, 34,* 49–62.

Jones, T. (2007, April 18). A tragedy beyond the imagination. *The Washington Post,* pp. C1, C4.

Judge, T. A., & Bono, J. E. (2001). Relationship of core self-evaluation traits—self-esteem, generalized self-efficacy, locus of control, and emotional stability—with job satisfaction and job performance: A meta-analysis. *Journal of Applied Psychology, 86,* 80–92.

Judy, B., & Nelson, E. S. (2000). Relationship between parents, peers, morality, and theft in an adolescent sample. *High School Journal, 83,* 31–42.

Junaid, K. A., & Fellowes, S. (2006). Gender differences in the attainment of motor skills on the Movement Assessment Battery for Children. *Physical and Occupational Therapy in Pediatrics, 26,* 5–11.

Jung, C. G. (1933). *Modern man in search of a soul* (W. S. Dell & C. F. Baynes, Trans.). New York: Harcourt, Brace.

Jungblut, P. R., Ostorne, J. A., Quigg, R. J., McNeal, M. A., Clauser, J., Muster, A. J., & McPherson, D. D. (2000). Echocardiographic Doppler evaluation of left ventricular diastolic filling in older, highly trained male endurance athletes. *Echocardiography, 17,* 7–16.

Juola, J. F., Koshino, H., Warner, C. B., McMickell, M., & Peterson, M. (2000). Automatic and voluntary control of attention in young and older adults. *American Journal of Psychology, 113,* 159–178.

Jusczyk, P. W. & Aslin, R. N. (1995). Infants' detection of sound patterns of words in fluent speech. *Cognitive Psychology, 29,* 1–23.

Justice, E. M., Bakerward, L., Gupta, S., & Jannings, L. R. (1997). Means to the goal of remembering: Developmental changes in awareness of strategy use–performance relations. *Journal of Experimental Child Psychology, 65,* 293–314.

K

Kabir, A. A., Pridjian, G., Steinmann, W. C., Herrera, E. A., & Khan, M. M. (2005). Racial differences in cesareans: An analysis of U.S. 2001 national inpatient sample data. *Obstetrics & Gynecology, 105,* 710–718.

Kacew, S. (1999). Effect of over-the-counter drugs on the unborn child: What is known and how should this influence prescribing? *Pediatric Drugs, 1,* 75–80.

Kagan, J. (1972). Do infants think? *Scientific American, 226,* 74–82.

Kagan, J. (1981). *The second year: The emergence of self-awareness.* Cambridge, MA: Harvard University Press.

Kagan, J. (1989). Temperamental contributions to social behavior. *American Psychologist, 44,* 668–674.

Kagan, J. (1994). *Galen's prophecy: Temperament in human nature.* New York: Basic Books.

Kagan, J. (1998). *Three seductive ideas.* Cambridge, MA: Harvard University Press.

Kagan, J., & Snidman, N. (2004). *The long shadow of temperament.* Cambridge, MA: The Belknap Press of Harvard University Press.

Kahn, R. L., & Antonucci, T. C. (1980). Convoys over the life course: Attachment, roles, and social support. In P. B. Baltes & O. G. Brim Jr. (Eds.), *Life-span development and behavior* (Vol. 3). New York: Academic Press.

Kail, R. (1991). Developmental change in speed of processing during childhood and adolescence. *Psychological Bulletin, 109,* 490–501.

Kail, R., & Bisanz, J. (1992). The information-processing perspective on cognitive development in childhood and adolescence. In R. J. Sternberg & C. A. Berg (Eds.), *Intellectual development.* New York: Cambridge University Press.

Kail, R., & Salthouse, T. A. (1994). Processing speed as a mental capacity. *Acta Psychologica, 86,* 199–225.

Kaiser Family Foundation (2004, February). *The role of media in childhood obesity.* Publication #7030. Available at: www.kff.org/entmedia/upload/The-Role-Of-Media-in-Childhood-Obesity.pdf.

Kaiser Family Foundation (2007, March). *Food for thought: Television food advertising to children in the United States.* Publication #7618. Available at: www.kff.org/entmedia/upload/7618.pdf.

Kakuma, R., duFort, G. G., Arsenault, L., Perrault, A., Platt, R. W., Monette, J., Moride, Y., & Wolfson, C. (2003). Delirium in older emergency department patients discharged home: Effect on survival. *Journal of the American Geriatrics Society, 51,* 443–450.

Kalmuss, D., Davidson, A., & Cushman, L. (1992). Parenting expectancies, experiences, and adjustment to parenthood: A test of the violated expectations framework. *Journal of Marriage and the Family, 54,* 516–526.

Kaltiala-Heino, R., Marttunen, M., Rantanen, P., & Rimpela, M. (2003). Early puberty is associated with mental health problems in middle adolescence. *Social Science Medicine, 57,* 1055–1064.

Kamakura, T., Ando, J., & Ono, Y. (2007). Genetic and environmental effects on stability and change in self-esteem during adolescence. *Personality and Individual Differences, 42,* 181–190.

Kameguchi, K., & Murphy-Shigematsu, S. (2001). Family psychology and family therapy in Japan. *American Psychologist, 56,* 65–70.

Kandel, E. R., & Jessell, T. (1991). Early experience and the fine tuning of synaptic connections. In E. R. Kandel, J. H. Schwartz, & T. Jessell (Eds.), *Principles of neural science* (3rd ed., pp. 945–958). Norwalk, CT: Appleton & Lange.

Kane, H. D., & Brand, C. R. (2006). The variable importance of general intelligence (*g*) in the cognitive abilities of children and adolescents. *Educational Psychology, 26,* 751–767.

Kanellopoulos, T. A., Varvarigon, A. A., Karatza, A. A., & Beratis, N. G. (2007). Course of growth during the first 6 years in children exposed in utero to tobacco smoke. *European Journal of Pediatrics, 166,* 685–692.

Kannass, K. N., & Colombo, J. (2007). The effects of continuous and intermittent distractors on cognitive performance and attention in preschoolers. *Journal of Cognition and Development, 8,* 63–77.

Kaplan, A. S., & Murphy, G. L. (2000). Category learning with minimal prior knowledge. *Journal of Experimental Psychology: Learning, Memory, and Cognition, 26,* 829–845.

Kaplan, D. S., Damphousse, K. R., & Kaplan, H. B. (1994). Mental health implications of not graduating from high school. *Journal of Experimental Education, 62,* 105–123.

Kaplan, R. M., & Erickson, J. (2000). Quality adjusted life expectancy for men and women in the United States. In S. B. Manuck, R. Jennings, B. S. Rabin, & A. Baum (Eds.), *Behavior, health, and aging.* Mahwah, NJ: Erlbaum.

Karpov, Y. V. (2005). *The Neo-Vygotskian approach to child development.* New York: Cambridge University Press.

Karraker, K. H., Vogel, D. A., & Lake, M. A. (1995). Parents' gender-stereotyped perceptions of newborns: The eye of the beholder revisited. *Sex Roles, 33,* 687–701.

Kart, C. S., Metress, E. K., & Metress, S. P. (1992). *Human aging and chronic disease.* Boston: Jones and Bartlett.

Kasl-Godley, J., & Gatz, M. (2000). Psychosocial interventions for individuals with dementia: An integration of theory, therapy, and a clinical understanding of dementia. *Clinical Psychology Review, 20,* 755–782.

Kaslow, N., Mintzer, M. B., Meadows, L. A., & Grabill, C. M. (2000). A family perspective on assessing and treating childhood depression. In C. E. Bailey (Ed.), *Children in therapy. Using the family as a resource.* New York: W. W. Norton.

Kastenbaum, R. (2000). *The psychology of death.* New York: Springer.

Kasworm, C. E., & Medina, R. A. (1990). Adult competence in everyday tasks: A cross-sectional secondary analysis. *Educational Gerontology, 16,* 27–48.

Katz, P. A. (1986). Modification of children's gender-stereotyped behavior: General issues and research considerations. *Sex Roles, 14,* 591–602.

Katz, P. A., & Walsh, P. V. (1991). Modification of children's gender-stereotyped behavior. *Child Development, 62,* 338–351.

Kaufman, A. S. (2001). WAIS-III IQs, Horn's theory, and generational changes from young adulthood to old age. *Intelligence, 29,* 131–167.

Kaufman, A. S., Kamphaus, R. W., & Kaufman, N. L. (1985). New directions in intelligence testing: The Kaufman Assessment Battery for Children (K-ABC). In B. B. Wolman (Ed.), *Handbook of intelligence.* New York: Wiley.

Kaufman, A. S., & Kaufman, N. L. (1997). The Kaufman Adolescent and Adult Intelligence Test. In D. P. Flanagan, J. L. Genshaft, & P. L. Harrison (Eds.), *Contemporary intellectual assessment: Theories, tests, and issues.* New York: Guilford.

Kaufman, J., & Zigler, E. (1989). The intergenerational transmission of child abuse. In D. Cicchetti & V. Carlson (Eds.), *Child maltreatment. Theory and research on the causes and consequences of child abuse and neglect.* New York: Cambridge University Press.

Kaufman, R. H., Adam, E., Hatch, E. E., Noller, K., Herbst, A. L., Palmer, J. R., & Hoover, R. N. (2000). Continued follow-up of pregnancy outcomes in diethylstilbestrol-exposed offspring. *Obstetric Gynecology, 96,* 483–489.

Kaufman, S. B. (2007). Sex differences in mental rotation and spatial visualization ability: Can they be accounted for by differences in working memory capacity? *Intelligence, 35,* 211–223.

Kavsek, M., & Yonas, A. (2006). The perception of moving subjective contours by 4-month-old infants. *Perception, 35,* 215–227.

Kaye, R. A. (1993). Sexuality in the later years. *Aging and Society, 13,* 415–426.

Kayed, N. S., & van der Meer, A. L. (2007). Infants' timing strategies to optical collisions: A longitudinal study. *Infant Behavior and Development, 30,* 50–59.

Kazak, A. E., & Noll, R. B. (2004). Child death from pediatric illness: Conceptualizing intervention from a family/systems and public health perspective. *Professional Psychology: Research and Practice, 35,* 219–226.

Kazdin, A. E. (2000). *Psychotherapy for children and adolescents : Directions for research and practice.* New York: Oxford University Press.

Kazdin, A. E. (2003). Psychotherapy for children and adolescents. *Annual Review of Psychology, 54,* 253–276.

Kean, A. W. G. (1937). The history of the criminal liability of children. *Law Quarterly Review, 3,* 364–370.

Keel, P. K., & Fulkerson, J. A. (2001). Vulnerability to eating disorders in childhood and adolescence. In R. E. Ingram & J. M. Price (Eds.), *Vulnerability to psychopathology. Risk across the lifespan.* New York: Guilford.

Keel, P. K., & Klump, K. L. (2003). Are eating disorders culture-bound syndromes? Implications for conceptualizing their etiology. *Psychological Bulletin, 129,* 747–769.

Keenan, T. (2003). Individual differences in theory of mind. The preschool years and beyond. In B. Repacholi & V. Slaughter (Eds.). *Individual differences in theory of mind: Implications for typical and atypical development.* New York: Psychology Press.

Keightley, M. L., Winocur, G., Burianova, H., Hongwanishkul, D., & Grady, C. L. (2006). Age effects on social cognition: Faces tell a different story. *Psychology and Aging, 21,* 558–572.

Kelemen, W. L. (2000). Metamemory cues and monitoring accuracy: Judging what you know and what you will know. *Journal of Educational Psychology, 92,* 800–810.

Keller, B. B., & Bell, R. Q. (1979). Child effects on adult's method of eliciting altruistic behavior. *Child Development, 50,* 1004–1009.

Keller, H. (1954). *The story of my life.* New York: Doubleday.

Kelley-Buchanan, C. (1988). *Peace of mind during pregnancy: An A–Z guide to the substances that could affect your unborn baby.* New York: Facts on File.

Kellman, P. J., & Arterberry, M. E. (2006). Infant visual perception. In D. Kuhn & R. Siegler (Vol. Eds.), *Handbook of child psychology: Cognition, perception, and language.* Hoboken, NJ: Wiley.

Kellman, P. J., & Spelke, E. S. (1983). Perception of partly occluded objects in infancy. *Cognitive Psychology, 15,* 483–524.

Kelly, D. J., Quinn, P. C., Slater, A. M., Lee, K., Gibson, A., Smith, M., Ge, L. Z., & Pascalis, O. (2005). Three-month-olds, but not newborns, prefer own-race faces. *Developmental Science, 8,* F31–F36.

Kelsall, D. C., Shallop, J. K., & Burnelli, T. (1995). Cochlear implantation in the elderly. *American Journal of Otology, 16,* 609–615.

Kemler Nelson, D. G., Hirsh-Pasek, K., Jusczyk, P. W., & Cassidy, K. W. (1989). How the prosodic cues in motherese might assist in language learning. *Journal of Child Language, 16,* 55–68.

Kempe, R. S., & Kempe, C. H. (1978). *Child abuse.* Cambridge, MA: Harvard University Press.

Kemper, S. & Mitzner, T. L. (2001). Production and comprehension. In J. E. Birren & K. W. Schaie (Eds.), *Handbook of the psychology of aging* (5th ed.). San Diego, CA: Academic Press.

Kemtes, K. A., & Kemper, S. (1997). Younger and older adults' on-line processing of syntactically ambiguous sentences. *Psychology and Aging, 12,* 362–371.

Kendall-Tackett, K. A., Williams, L. M., & Finkelhor, D. (1993). Impact of sexual abuse on children: A review and synthesis of recent empirical studies. *Psychological Bulletin, 113,* 164–180.

Kendig, H. L., Coles, R., Pittelkow, Y., & Wilson, S. (1988). Confidants and family structure in old age. *Journal of Gerontology: Social Sciences, 43,* S31–S40.

Kendler, K. S. (2003). Of genes and twins. *Psychological Medicine, 33,* 763–768.

Kendler, K. S., Gardner, C. O., & Prescott, C. A. (2002). Toward a comprehensive developmental model for major depression in women. *American Journal of Psychiatry, 159,* 1133–1145.

Kendler, K. S., Neale, M., Kessler, R., Heath, A., & Eaves, L. (1993). A twin study of recent life events and difficulties. *Archives of General Psychiatry, 50,* 789–796.

Kendler, K. S., Silberg, J. L., Neale, M. C., Kessler, R. C., Heath, A. C., & Eaves, L. J. (1992). Genetic and environmental factors in the aetiology of menstrual, premenstrual and neurotic symptoms: A population-based twin study. *Psychological Medicine, 22,* 85–100.

Keniston, K. (1970). Youth: A "new" stage of life. *American Scholar, 39,* 631–654.

Kennell, J., Klaus, M., McGrath, S., Robertson, S., & Hinkley, C. (1991). Continuous emotional support during labor in a US hospital: A randomized controlled trial. *Journal of the American Medical Association, 265,* 2197–2201.

Kenney-Benson, G. A., Pomerantz, E. M., Ryan, A. M., & Patrick, H. (2006). Sex differences in math performance: The role of children's approach to schoolwork. *Developmental Psychology, 42,* 11–26.

Kenny, M. E. (1987). The extent and function of parental attachment among first-year college students. *Journal of Youth and Adolescence, 16,* 17–29.

Kenny, M. E., & Rice, K. G. (1995). Attachment to parents and adjustment in late adolescent college students: Current status, applications, and future considerations. *The Counseling Psychologist, 23,* 433–456.

Kent, A., & Waller, G. (2000). Childhood emotional abuse and eating psychopathology. *Clinical Psychology Review, 20,* 887–903.

Kenyon, B. L. (2001). Current research in children's conceptions of death: A critical review. *Omega: Journal of Death and Dying, 43,* 63–91.

Keough, J., & Sugden, D. (1985). *Movement skill development.* New York: Macmillan.

Kerka, S. (1995). Adult learner retention revisited. ERIC Clearinghouse on Adult, Career, and Vocational Education, Digest No. 166.

Kerns, K. A., Tomich, P. L., & Kim, P. (2006). Normative trends in children's perceptions of availability and utilization of attachment figures in middle childhood. *Social Development, 15,* 1–22.

Kerr, M. A., Black, M. M., & Krishnakumar, A. (2000). Failure to thrive, maltreatment, and the behavior and development of 6-year-old children from low-income, urban families: A cumulative risk model. *Child Abuse and Neglect, 24,* 587–598.

Kerr, M., & Stattin, H. (2003). Parenting of adolescents: Action or reaction? In A. C. Crouter, & A. Booth (Eds.), *Children's influence on family dynamics: The neglected side of family relationships.* Mahwah, NJ: Erlbaum.

Kessler, R. C. (2000). Gender differences in major depression. Epidemiological finding through the world. In E. Frank (Ed.), *Gender and its effects on psychopathology.* Washington, D.C.: American Psychiatric Press.

Kessler, R. C., Adler, L., Barkley, R., Biederman, J., Conners, C. K., Demler, O., Faraone, S. V., Greenhill, L. L., Howes, M. J., Secnik, K., Spencer, T., Ustun, T. B., Walters, E. E., & Zaslavsky, A. M. (2006). The prevalence and correlates of adult ADHD in the United States: Results from the National Comorbidity Survey Replication. *American Journal of Psychiatry, 163,* 716–723.

Kessler, R. C., Avenevoli, S., & Merikangas, K. R. (2001). Mood disorders in children and adolescents: An epidemiologic perspective. *Biological Psychiatry, 49,* 1002–1014.

Kessler, R. C., Berglund, P., Demler, O., Jin, R., & Walters, E. E. (2005). Lifetime prevalence and age-of-onset distributions of DSM-IV disorders in the National Comorbidity Survey Replication. *Archives of General Psychiatry, 62,* 593–602.

Kessler, R. C., Chiu, W. T., Demler, O., & Walters, E. E. (2005). Prevalence, severity, and comorbidity of 12-month DSM–IV disorders in the National Comorbidity Survey Replication. *Archives of General Psychiatry, 62,* 617–627.

Kett, J. F. (1977). *Rites of passage. Adolescence in America 1790 to the present.* New York: Basic Books.

Kettlewell, H. B. D. (1959). Darwin's missing evidence. *Scientific American, 200 (3),* 48–53.

Keyes, C. L. M. (2002). The exchange of emotional support with age and its relationship with emotional well-being by age. *Journals of Gerontology: Psychological Sciences and Social Sciences, 57,* 518–525.

Kiecolt-Glaser, J. K., & Newton, T. L. (2001). Marriage and health: His and hers. *Psychological Bulletin, 127,* 472–503.

Kiesner, J., Dishion, T. J., & Poulin, F. (2001). A reinforcement model of conduct problems in children and adolescents: Advances in theory and intervention. In J. Hill & B. Maughan (Eds.), *Conduct disorders in childhood and adolescence.* New York: Cambridge University Press.

Kim, K., & Spelke, E. J. (1992). Infants' sensitivity to effects of gravity on visible object motion. *Journal of Experimental Psychology: Human Perception and Performance, 18,* 385–393.

Kim, S. Y. H., Appelbaum, P. S., Jeste, D. V., & Olin, J. T. (2004). Proxy and surrogate consent in geriatric neuropsychiatric research: Update and recommendations. *American Journal of Psychiatry, 161,* 797–806.

Kimura, D. (1992). Sex differences in the brain. *Scientific American, 267,* 119–125.

King, A. C., Castro, C., Wilcox, S., Eyler, A. A., Sallis, J. F., & Brownson, R. C. (2000). Personal and environmental factors associated with physical inactivity among different racial-ethnic groups of U.S. middle-aged and older-aged women. *Health Psychology, 19,* 354–364.

King, S. M., Forbes, J., Singer, J., Lapointe, N., Samson, L., Embree, J., & Vaudry, W. (2002, July). *Survival of perinatally HIV-infected children in Canada.* Presented at: XIV International AIDS Conference, Barcelona.

King, V. (2006). The antecedents and consequences of adolescents' relationships with stepfathers and nonresident fathers. *Journal of Marriage and Family, 68,* 910–928.

King, V., & Sobolewski, J. M. (2006). Nonresident fathers' contributions to adolescent well-being. *Journal of Marriage and Family, 68,* 537–557.

Kinsella, K. G. (2005). Future longevity—Demographic concerns and consequences. *Journal of the American Geriatrics Society, 53,* S299–S303.

Kirby, D. (2002). Effective approaches to reducing adolescent unprotected sex, pregnancy, and childbearing. *Journal of Sex Research, 39,* 51–57.

Kirchmeyer, C. (2006). The different effects of family on objective career success across gender: A test of alternative explanations. *Journal of Vocational Behavior, 68,* 323–346.

Kirsh, S. J. (2006). *Children, adolescents, and media violence.* Thousand Oaks, CA: Sage.

Kisilevsky, B. S., & Muir, D. W. (1984). Neonatal habituation and dishabituation to tactile stimulation during sleep. *Developmental Psychology, 20,* 367–373.

Kisilevsky, B. S., Hains, S. M., Lee, K., Xie, X., Huang, H., Ye, H. H., Zhang, K., & Wang, Z. (2003). Effects of experience on fetal voice recognition. *Psychological Science, 14,* 220–224.

Kitamura, C., & Burnham, D. (2003). Pitch and communicative intent in mother's speech: Adjustments for age and sex in the first year. *Infancy, 4,* 85–110.

Kitchener, K. S., King, P. M., Wood, P. K., & Davison, M. L. (1989). Sequentiality and consistency in the development of reflective judgment: A six-year longitudinal study. *Journal of Applied Developmental Psychology, 10,* 73–95.

Kitson, G. C. (1992). *Portrait of divorce: Adjustment to marital breakdown.* New York: Guilford.

Kitson, G. C., Babri, K. B., & Roach, M. J. (1985). Who divorces and why. A review. *Journal of Family Issues, 6,* 255–293.

Kitzmann, K. M. (2000). Effects of marital conflict on subsequent triadic family interactions and parenting. *Developmental Psychology, 36,* 3–13.

Klaczynski, P. A. (2000). Motivated scientific reasoning biases, epistemological beliefs, and theory polarization: A two-process approach to adolescent cognition. *Child Development, 71,* 1347–1366.

Klaczynski, P. A. (2001). Analytic and heuristic processing influences on adolescent reasoning and decision-making. *Child Development, 72,* 844–861.

Klaczynski, P. A., & Gordon, D. H. (1996a). Everyday statistical reasoning during adolescence and young adulthood: Motivational, general ability, and developmental influences. *Child Development, 67,* 2873–2892.

Klaczynski, P. A., & Gordon, D. H. (1996b). Self-serving influences on adolescents' evaluations of belief-relevant evidence. *Journal of Experimental Child Psychology, 62,* 317–339.

Klaczynski, P. A., & Narasimham, G. (1998). Development of scientific reasoning biases: Cognitive versus ego-protective explanations. *Developmental Psychology, 34,* 175–187.

Klapper, W., Parwaresch, R., & Krupp, G. (2001). Telomere biology in human aging and aging syndromes. *Mechanisms of Ageing and Development, 122,* 695–712.

Klass, D. (2001). Continuing bonds in the resolution of grief in Japan and North America. *American Behavioral Scientist, 44,* 742–763.

Klaus, H. M., & Kennell, J. H. (1976). *Maternal-infant bonding.* St. Louis: C. V. Mosby.

Klein, P. J., & Meltzoff, A. N. (1999). Long-term memory, forgetting, and deferred imitation in 12-month-old infants. *Developmental Science, 2,* 102–113.

Klein, R., Klein, B. E., Lee, K. E., Cruickshanks, K. J., & Chappell, R. J. (2001). Changes in visual acuity in a population over a 10-year period: The Beaver Dam Eye Study. *Ophthalmology, 108,* 1757–1766.

Klein, W. (1996). Language acquisition at different ages. In D. Magnusson (Ed.), *The lifespan development of individuals: Behavioral, neurobiological, and psychosocial perspectives: A synthesis.* Cambridge, England: Cambridge University Press.

Kleiner, C., & Lord, M. (1999, November 22). The cheating game. 'Everyone's doing it,' from grade school to graduate school. *U.S. News & World Report,* 54–66.

Kleinhaus, K., Perrin, M., Friedlander, Y., Paltiel, O., Malaspina, D., & Harlap, S. (2006). Paternal age and spontaneous abortion. *Obstetrics and Gynecology, 108,* 369–377.

Kliegel, M., Jager, T., & Phillips, L. H. (2007). Emotional development across adulthood: Differential age-related emotional reactivity and emotion regulation in a negative mood induction procedure. *International Journal of Aging and Human Development, 64,* 217–244.

Klimes-Dougan, B., & Kistner, J. (1990). Physically abused preschoolers' responses to peers' distress. *Developmental Psychology, 26,* 599–602.

Klin, A., Chawarska, K., Rubin, E., & Volkmar F. (2004). Clinical assessment of young children at risk for autism. In R. DelCarmen-Wiggins & A. Carter (Eds.), *Handbook of infant, toddler, and preschool mental health assessment.* New York: Oxford University Press.

Kline, D. W., & Scialfa, C. T. (1996). Visual and auditory aging. In J. E. Birren & K. W. Schaie (Eds.), *Handbook of the psychology of aging* (4th ed.). San Diego: Academic Press.

Klineberg, O. (1963). Negro–white differences in intelligence test performance: A new look at an old problem. *American Psychologist, 18,* 198–203.

Kling, K. C., Ryff, C. D., Love, G., & Essex, M. (2003). Exploring the influence of personality on depressive symptoms and self-esteem across a significant life transition. *Journal of Personality and Social Psychology, 85,* 922–932.

Klinger, L. J., Hamilton, J. A., & Cantrell, P. J. (2001). Children's perceptions of aggressive and gender-specific content in toy commercials. *Social Behavior and Personality, 29,* 11–20.

Klump, K. L., & Culbert, K. M. (2007). Molecular genetic studies of eating disorders. Current status and future directions. *Current Directions in Psychological Science, 16,* 37–41.

Klump, K. L., McGue, M., & Iacono, W. G. (2003). Differential heritability of eating attitudes and behaviors in prepubertal versus pubertal twins. *International Journal of Eating Disorders, 33,* 287–292.

Knafo, A., & Plomin, R. (2006). Prosocial behavior from early to middle childhood: Genetic and environmental influences on stability and change. *Developmental Psychology, 42,* 771–786.

Knecht, S., Deppe, M., Drager, B., Bobe, L., Lohmann, H., Ringelstein, E., & Henningsen, H. (2000). Language lateralization in healthy right-handers. *Brain, 123,* 74–81.

Knight, B. G., Kaskie, B., Shurgot, G. R., & Dave, J. (2006). Improving the mental health of older adults. In J. E. Birren & K. W. Schaie (Eds.), *Handbook of the psychology of aging* (6th ed). Burlington, MA: Elsevier Academic Press.

Knight, J. A. (2000). The biochemistry of aging. *Advances in Clinical Chemistry, 35,* 1–62.

Knight, M., & Mather, M. (2006). The affective neuroscience of aging and its implications for cognition. In T. Canli (Ed.), *Biology of personality and individual differences.* New York; Guilford.

Knightley, P., Evans, H., Potter, E., & Wallace, M. (1979). *Suffer the children: The story of thalidomide.* NY: Viking Press.

Knoester, C., Haynie, D. L., & Stephens, C. M. (2006). Parenting practices and adolescents' friendship networks. *Journal of Marriage and Family, 68,* 1247–1260.

Kobak, R. R., & Esposito, A. (2004). Levels of processing in parent–child relationships: Implications for clinical assessment and treatment. In L. Atkinson & S. Goldberg (Eds.), *Attachment issues in psychopathology and intervention*. Mahwah, NJ, Erlbaum.

Kobayashi, C., Glover, G. H., & Temple, E. (2007). Children's and adults' neural bases of verbal and nonverbal 'theory of mind.' *Neuropsychologia, 45*, 1522–1532.

Kochanska, G. (1993). Toward a synthesis of parental socialization and child temperament in early development of conscience. *Child Development, 64*, 325–347.

Kochanska, G. (2001). Emotional development in children with different attachment histories: The first three years. *Child Development, 72*, 474–490.

Kochanska, G. (2002). Mutually responsive orientation between mothers and their young children: A context for the early development of conscience. *Current Directions in Psychological Science, 11(6)*, 191–195.

Kochanska, G., & Aksan, N. (2006). Children's conscience and self-regulation. *Journal of Personality, 74*, 1587–1617.

Kochanska, G., Aksan, N., & Joy, M. E. (2007). Children's fearfulness as a moderator of parenting in early socialization: Two longitudinal studies. *Developmental Psychology, 43*, 222–237.

Kochanska, G., Aksan, N., & Nichols, K. E. (2003). Maternal power assertion in discipline and moral discourse contexts: Commonalities, differences, and implications for children's moral conduct and cognition. *Developmental Psychology, 39*, 949–963.

Kochanska, G., Casey, R. J., & Fukumoto, A. (1995). Toddlers' sensitivity to standard violations. *Child Development, 66*, 643–656.

Kochanska, G., & Knaack, A. (2003). Effortful control as a personality characteristic of young children: Antecedents, correlates, and consequences. *Journal of Personality, 71*, 1087–1112.

Kochanska, G., Murray, K., Coy, K. C. (1997). Inhibitory control as a contributor to conscience in childhood: From toddler to early school age. *Child Development, 68*, 263–277.

Kochi, C., Longui, C. A., Lemos-Marini, S. H., Guerra-Junior, G., Melo, M. B., Calliari, L. E., & Monte, O. (2007). The influence of parental origin of X chromosome genes on the stature of patients with 45 X Turner syndrome. *Genetics and Molecular Research, 18*, 1–7.

Kodama, K., Mabuchi, K., & Shigematsu, I. (1996). A long-term cohort study of the atomic-bomb survivors. *Journal of Epidemiology, 6*, S95–S105.

Kodish, E. (2005). Ethics and research with children: An introduction. In E. Kodish (Ed.), *Ethics and research with children: A case-based approach*. Cary, NC: Oxford University Press.

Koegel, R. L., Koegel, L. K., & McNerney, E. K. (2001). Pivotal areas in intervention for autism. *Journal of Clinical Child Psychology, 30*, 19–32.

Koenen, K. C., Moffitt, T. E., Caspi, A., Taylor, A., & Purcell, S. (2003). Domestic violence is associated with environmental suppression of IQ in young children. *Development and Psychopathology, 15*, 297–311.

Koenig, A. L., Cicchetti, D., & Rogosch, F. A. (2000). Child compliance/noncompliance and maternal contributors to internalization in

maltreating and nonmaltreating dyads. *Child Development, 71*, 1018–1032.

Koff, E., & Rierdan, J. (1995). Early adolescent girls' understanding of menstruation. *Women and Health, 22*, 1–19.

Kogan, N. (1983). Stylistic variation in childhood and adolescence: Creativity, metaphor, and cognitive styles. In J. H. Flavell & E. H. Markman (Eds.), *Handbook of child psychology: Vol. 3. Cognitive development* (4th ed.). New York: Wiley.

Kogan, S. M. (2004). Disclosing unwanted sexual experiences: Results from a national sample of adolescent women. *Child Abuse & Neglect, 28*, 147–165.

Kohl, G. O., Lengua, L. J., McMahon, R. J., & the Conduct Problems Prevention Research Group. (2000). Parent involvement in school: Conceptualizing multiple dimensions and their relations with family and demographic risk factors. *Journal of School Psychology, 38*, 501–523.

Kohlberg, L. (1963). The development of children's orientations toward a moral order: I. Sequence in the development of moral thought. *Vita Humana, 6*, 11–33.

Kohlberg, L. (1966a). A cognitive-developmental analysis of children's sex-role concepts and attitudes. In E. E. Maccoby (Ed.), *The development of sex differences*. Stanford, CA: Stanford University Press.

Kohlberg, L. (1966b). Cognitive stages and preschool education. *Human Development, 9*, 5–17.

Kohlberg, L. (1969). Stage and sequence: The cognitive developmental approach to socialization. In D. A. Goslin (Ed.), *Handbook of socialization theory and research*. Chicago: Rand McNally.

Kohlberg, L. (1981). *Essays on moral development: Vol. 1. The philosophy of moral development*. San Francisco: Harper & Row.

Kohlberg, L. (1984). *Essays on moral development: Vol. 2. The psychology of moral development*. San Francisco: Harper & Row.

Kohn, M. L. (1969). *Class and conformity: A study of values*. Homewood, IL: Dorsey Press.

Kohn, M. L., & Schooler, C. (1982). Job conditions and personality: A longitudinal assessment of their reciprocal effects. *American Journal of Sociology, 87*, 1257–1286.

Kojima, H. (2003). The history of children and youth in Japan. In W. Koops & M. Zuckerman. (Eds.), *Beyond the century of the child. Cultural history and developmental psychology*. Philadelphia: University of Pennsylvania Press.

Kolb, B., & Whishaw, I. Q. (2006). *An introduction to brain and behavior* (2nd ed.). New York: Worth.

Kolev, V., Falkenstein, M., & Yordanova, J. (2006). Motor-response generation as a source of aging-related behavioural slowing in choice-reaction tasks. *Neurobiological Aging, 27*, 1719–1730.

Kolstad, V., & Aguiar, A. (1995, March). *Means–end sequences in young infants*. Paper presented at the biennial meeting of the Society for Research in Child Development, Indianapolis.

Konstantinidis, I., Hummel, T., & Larsson, M. (2006). Identification of unpleasant odors is independent of age. *Archives of Clinical Neuropsychology, 21*, 615–621.

Koocher, G. P. (1973). Childhood, death, and cognitive development. *Developmental Psychology, 9*, 369–375.

Koocher, G. P. (1974). Talking with children about death. *American Journal of Orthopsychiatry, 44*, 404–411.

Koopmans-van Beinum, F. J., Clement, C. J., & van den Dikkenberg-Pot, I. (2001). Babbling and the lack of auditory speech perception: A matter of coordination? *Developmental Science, 4*, 61–70.

Koops, W. (2003). Imaging childhood. In W. Koops & M. Zuckerman. (Eds.), *Beyond the century of the child. Cultural history and developmental psychology*. Philadelphia: University of Pennsylvania Press.

Kopka, T. L. C., & Peng, S. S. (1993). *Adult education: Main reasons for participating*. Statistics in Brief NCES-93–451. Washington, D.C.: National Center for Education Statistics.

Kopp, C. B., & Krakow, J. B. (1982). *The child: Development in a social context*. Reading, MA: Addison-Wesley.

Kopp, C. B., & Neufield, S. J. (2003). Emotional development during infancy. In R. J. Davidson, K. R. Scherer, & H. H. Goldsmith (Eds.), *Handbook of affective sciences*. New York: Oxford University Press.

Korbin, J. E. (2001). Context and meaning in neighborhood studies of children and families. In A. Booth, & A. C. Crouter (Eds.), *Does it take a village? Community effects on children, adolescents, and families*. Mahwah, NJ: Erlbaum.

Koriat, A., Goldsmith, M., & Pansky, A. (2000). Toward a psychology of memory accuracy. *Annual Review of Psychology, 51*, 481–538.

Kortenhaus, C. M., & Demarest, J. (1993). Gender role stereotyping in children's literature: An update. *Sex Roles, 28*, 219–232.

Kosberg, J. I., Kaufman, A. V., Burgio, L. D., Leeper, J. D., & Sun, F. (2007). Family caregiving to those with dementia in rural Alabama: Racial similarities and differences. *Journal of Aging and Health, 19*, 3–21.

Kothare S. V. & Kaleyias, J. (2007). The adverse effects of antiepileptic drugs in children *Expert Opinion On Drug Safety, 6*, 251–65.

Kotimaa, A. J., Moilanen, I., Taanila, A., Ebeling, H., Smalley, S. L., McGough, J. J., Hartikainen, A. L., & Jarvelin, M. R. (2003). Maternal smoking and hyperactivity in 8-year-old children. *Journal of the American Academy of Child and Adolescent Psychiatry, 42*, 826–833.

Koutstaal, W., Schacter, D. L., Johnson, M. K., Angell, K. E., & Gross, M. S. (1998). Post-event review in older and younger adults: Improving memory accessibility of complex everyday events. *Psychology and Aging, 13*, 277–296.

Kovacs, D. M., Parker, J. G., & Hoffman, L. W. (1996). Behavioral, affective, and social correlates of involvement in cross-sex friendships in elementary school. *Child Development, 67*, 2269–2286.

Kovacs, M., & Goldston, D. (1991). Cognitive and social cognitive development of depressed children and adolescents. *Journal of the American Academy of Child and Adolescent Psychiatry, 30*, 388–392.

Kowal, A., Kramer, L., Krull, J. L., & Crick N. R. (2002). Children's perceptions of the fairness of parental preferential treatment and their socioemotional well-being. *Journal of Family Psychology, 16*, 297–306.

Krafft, K. C., & Berk, L. E. (1998). Private speech in two preschools: Significance of open-ended activities and make-believe play for verbal self-regulation. *Early Childhood Research Quarterly, 13*, 637–658.

Krause, N. (1995). Negative interaction and satisfaction with social support among older adults. *Journal of Gerontology: Psychological Sciences, 50B*, 59–73.

Krause, N., & Rook, K. S. (2003). Negative interaction in late life: Issues in the stability and generalizability of conflict across relationships. *Journals of Gerontology: Psychological Sciences and Social Sciences, 58*, 88–99.

Krause, N., & Shaw, B. A. (2000). Role-specific feelings of control and mortality. *Psychology and Aging, 15*, 617–626.

Krebs, D. (2005). An evolutionary reconceptualization of Kohlberg's model of moral development. In R. L. Burgess & K. MacDonald (Eds.), *Evolutionary perspectives on human development.* Thousand Oaks, CA: Sage.

Krebs, D. L., Denton, K., Wark, G., Couch, R., Racine, T., & Krebs, D. L. (2002). Interpersonal moral conflicts between couples: Effects of type of dilemma, role, and partner's judgments on level of moral reasoning and probability of resolution. *Journal of Adult Development, 9*, 307–316.

Kreicbergs, U., Valdimarsdottir, U., Onelov, E., Henter, J., & Steineck, G. (2004). Talking about death with children who have severe malignant disease. *New England Journal of Medicine, 351*, 1175–1186.

Kroger, J. (1996). Identity, regression and development. *Journal of Adolescence, 19*, 203–222.

Kroger, J. (1997). Gender and identity: The intersection of structure, content, and context. *Sex Roles, 36*, 747–770.

Krogh, K. M. (1985). Women's motives to achieve and to nurture in different life stages. *Sex Roles, 12*, 75–90.

Krucoff, C. (May 16, 2000). Good to the bone. *The Washington Post—Health*, 8.

Krueger, R. F., Johnson, W., & Kling, K. C. (2006). Behavior genetics and personality development. In D. K. Mroczek & T. D. Little (Eds.), *Handbook of personality development.* Mahwah, NJ: Erlbaum.

Krueger, R. F., Markon, K. E., & Bouchard, T. J., Jr. (2003). The extended genotype: The heritability of personality accounts for the heritability of recalled family environments in twins reared apart. *Journal of Personality, 71*, 809–833.

Kruse, L., Denk, C. E., Feldman-Winter, L., & Mojita Rotondo, F. (2006). Longitudinal patterns of breastfeeding initiation. *Maternal & Child Health Journal, 10*, 13–18.

Kübler-Ross, E. (1969). *On death and dying.* New York: Macmillan.

Kübler-Ross, E. (1974). *Questions and answers on death and dying.* New York: Macmillan.

Kuczynski, L., & Parkin, C. M. (2007). Agency and bidirectionality in socialization. Interactions, transactions, and relational dialectics. In J. E. Grusec & P. D. Hastings (Eds.), *Handbook of socialization: Theory and research.* New York: Guilford.

Kuebli, J., & Fivush, R. (1994). Children's representation and recall of event alternatives. *Journal of Experimental Child Psychology, 58*, 25–45.

Kuehn, B. M. (2006). Gene discovery speeds progeria research. *JAMA, 295*, 876–878.

Kuehner, C. (2003). Gender differences in unipolar depression: An update of epidemiological findings and possible explanations. *Acta Psychiatrica Scandinavia, 108*, 163–174.

Kuhl, P. K., Stevens, E., Hayashi, A., Deguchi, T., Kiritani, S., & Iverson, P. (2006). Infants show a facilitation effect for native language phonetic perception between 6 and 12 months. *Developmental Science, 9*, F13–F21.

Kuhn, D. (1993). Connecting scientific and informal reasoning. *Merrill-Palmer Quarterly, 39*, 74–103.

Kuhn, D. (2000). Metacognitive development. *Current Directions in Psychological Science, 9*, 178–181.

Kulik, J. A., & Kulik, C. C. (1992). Meta-analytic findings on grouping programs. *Gifted Child Quarterly, 36*, 73–77.

Kuncel, N. R., Hezlett, S. A., & Ones, D. S. (2004). Academic performance, career potential, creativity, and job performance: Can one construct predict them all? *Journal of Personality and Social Psychology, 86*, 148–161.

Kurdek, L. A. (1991). Correlates of relationship satisfaction in cohabiting gay and lesbian couples: Integration of contextual investment, and problem-solving models. *Journal of Personality and Social Psychology, 61*, 910–922.

Kurdek, L. A. (1995). Lesbian and gay couples. In A. R. Augelli & C. J. Patterson (Eds.), *Lesbian and gay identities over the life span: Psychological perspectives on personal, relational, and community processes.* New York: Oxford University Press.

Kurdek, L. A. (1999). The nature and predictors of the trajectory of change in marital quality for husbands and wives over the first 10 years of marriage. *Developmental Psychology, 35*, 1283–1296.

Kurdek, L. A. (2006). Differences between partners from heterosexual, gay, and lesbian cohabiting couples. *Journal of Marriage and Family, 68*, 509–528.

Kurdek, L. A., & Krile, D. (1982). A developmental analysis of the relation between peer acceptance and both interpersonal understanding and perceived social self-competence. *Child Development, 53*, 1485–1491.

Kwak, J., & Haley, W. E. (2005). Current research findings on end-of-life decision making among racially and ethnically diverse groups. *Gerontologist, 45*, 634–641.

Kwon, Y., & Lawson, A. (2000). Linking brain growth with the development of scientific reasoning ability and conceptual change during adolescence. *Journal of Research in Science Teaching, 37*, 44–62.

Kwong, M. J., Bartholomew, K., Henderson, A. J. Z., & Trinke, S. J. (2003). The intergenerational transmission of relationship violence. *Journal of Family Psychology, 17*, 288–301.

L

La Sala, G. B., Gallinelli, A., Nicoli, A., Villani, M. T., & Nucera, G. (2006). Pregnancy loss and assisted reproduction: Preliminary results after the law 40/2004 in Italy. *Reproductive Biomedicine Online, 13*, 65–70.

Labbok, M., H. (2006). Trends in exclusive breastfeeding: Findings from the 1990s. *Journal of Human Lactation, 22*, 272–276.

Labinowicz, E. (1980). *The Piaget primer.* Menlo Park, CA: Addison-Wesley.

Labouvie-Vief, G. (1985). Intelligence and cognition. In J. E. Birren & K. W. Schaie (Eds.), *Handbook of the psychology of aging* (2nd ed.). New York: Van Nostrand Reinhold.

Labouvie-Vief, G. (1992). A neo-Piagetian perspective on adult cognitive development. In R. J. Sternberg & C. A. Berg (Eds.), *Intellectual development.* New York: Cambridge University Press.

Labouvie-Vief, G., Adams, C., Hakim-Larson, J., & Hayden, M. (1983, April). *Contexts of logic: The growth of interpretation from pre-adolescence to mature adulthood.* Paper presented at the biennial meeting of the Society for Research in Child Development, Detroit.

Lachance, J. A., & Mazzocco, M. M. (2006). A longitudinal analysis of sex differences in math and spatial skills in primary school age children. *Learning and Individual Differences, 16*, 195–216.

Ladd, G. W. (1999). Peer relationships and social competence during early and middle childhood. *Annual Review of Psychology, 50*, 333–359.

Ladd, G. W., Buhs, E. S., & Seid, M. (2000). Children's initial sentiments about kindergarten: Is school liking an antecedent of early classroom participation and achievement? *Merrill-Palmer Quarterly, 46*, 255–279.

Ladd, G. W., & Troop-Gordon, W. (2003). The role of chronic peer difficulties in the development of children's psychological adjustment problems. *Child Development, 74*, 1344–1367.

Laflamme, D., Pomerleau, A., & Malcuit, G. (2002). A comparison of fathers' and mothers' involvement in childcare and stimulation behaviors during free-play with their infants at 9 and 15 months. *Sex Roles, 47*, 507–518.

LaFranchi, S. H., Haddow, J. E., & Hollowell, J. G. (2005). Is thyroid inadequacy during gestation a risk factor for adverse pregnancy and developmental outcomes? *Thyroid, 15*, 60–71.

Lagattuta, K. H. (2005). When you shouldn't do what you want to do: Young children's understanding of desires, rules, and emotions. *Child Development, 76*, 713–733.

Laible, D. J., & Thompson, R. A. (2000). Mother–child discourse, attachment security, shared positive affect, and early conscience development. *Child Development, 71*, 1424–1440.

Lakatta, E. G. (1990). Heart and circulation. In E. L. Schneider & J. W. Rowe (Eds.), *Handbook of the biology of aging* (3rd ed.). San Diego: Academic Press.

Lalande, K. L., & Bonanno, G. A. (2006). Culture and continuing bonds: A prospective comparison of bereavement in the United States and the People's Republic of China. *Death Studies, 30*, 303–324.

Lamaze, F. (1958). *Painless childbirth: Psychoprophylactic method.* London: Burke.

Lamb, M. E., & Tamis-Lemonda, C. S. (2004). The role of the father: An introduction. In M. E. Lamb (Ed.), *The role of the father in child development* (4th ed.). Hoboken, NJ: John Wiley & Sons.

Lambert, S. R., & Drack, A. V. (1996). Infantile cataracts. *Survey of Ophthalmology, 40*, 427–458.

Lambert, S. R., Lynn, M. J., Reeves, R., Plager, D. A., Buckley, E. G., & Wilson, M. E. (2006). Is there a latent period for the surgical treatment of children with dense bilateral congenital cataracts? *Journal of the American Association for Pediatric Ophthalmology and Strabismus, 10*, 30–36.

Lamborn, S. D., Mounts, N. S., Steinberg, L., & Dornbusch, S. M. (1991). Patterns of competence and adjustment among adolescents from authoritative, authoritarian, indulgent, and neglectful families. *Child Development, 62,* 1049–1065.

Lamborn, S. D., & Steinberg, L. (1993). Emotional autonomy redux: Revisiting Ryan and Lynch. *Child Development, 64,* 483–499.

Lampinen, P., Heikkinen, R., & Ruoppila, I. (2000). Changes in intensity of physical exercise as predictors of depressive symptoms among older adults: An eight-year follow-up. *Preventive Medicine, 30,* 371–380.

Lampl, M. (2002). Saltation and stasis. In N. Cameron (Ed.), *Human growth and development* (pp. 253–270). New York: Academic Press.

Lamy, P. P. (1986). The elderly and drug interactions. *Journal of the American Geriatrics Society, 34,* 586–592.

Landon, M. B., Hauth, J. C., Leveno, K. J., Spong, C. Y., Leindecker, S., Varner, M. W., Moawad, A. H., Caritis, S. N., Harper, M., Wapner, R. J., Sorokin, Y., Miodovnik, M., Carpenter, M., Peaceman, A. M., O'Sullivan M. J., Sibai, B., Langer, O., Thorp, J. M., Ramin, S. M., Mercer, B. M., Gabbe, S. G., & the National Institute of Child Health and Human Development Maternal–Fetal Medicine Units Network. (2004). Maternal and perinatal outcomes associated with a trial of labor after prior cesarean delivery. *New England Journal of Medicine, 351,* 2581–2589.

Landreth, G., & Homeyer, L. (1998). Play as the language of children's feelings. In D. P. Fromberg & D. Bergen (Eds.), *Play from birth to twelve and beyond.* New York: Garland.

Lane, M. A., Black, A., Handy, A., Tilmont, E. M., Ingram, D. K., & Roth, G. S. (2001). Caloric restriction in primates. In S. C. Park, E. S. Hwang, H. Kim, & W. Park (Eds.), *Annals of the New York Academy of Sciences: Vol. 928. Molecular and cellular interactions in senescence.* New York: The New York Academy of Sciences.

Lang, F. R., & Carstensen, L. L. (1994). Close emotional relationships in late life: Further support for proactive aging in the social domain. *Psychology and Aging, 9,* 315–324.

Lang, F. R., & Carstensen, L. L. (2002). Time counts: Future time perspective, goals, and social relationships. *Psychology and Aging, 17,* 125–139.

Lange, G., & Pierce, S. H. (1992). Memory-strategy learning and maintenance in preschool children. *Developmental Psychology, 28,* 453–462.

Langley-Evans, A. J., & Langley-Evans, S. C. (2003). Relationship between maternal nutrient intakes in early and late pregnancy and infants' weight and proportions at birth: Prospective cohort study. *Journal of Research in Social Health, 123,* 210–216.

Langlois, J. A., Keyl, P. M., Guralnik, J. M., Foley, D. J., Marottoli, R. A., & Wallace, R. B. (1997). Characteristics of older pedestrians who have difficulty crossing the street. *American Journal of Public Health, 87,* 393–397.

Lansford, J. E., Chang, L., Dodge, K. A., Malone, P. S., Oburu, P., Palmerus, K., Bacchini, D., Pastorelli, C., Bombi, A. S., Zelli, A., Tapanya, S., Chaudhary, N., Deater-Deckard, K., Manke, B., & Quinn, N. (2005). Physical discipline and children's adjustment: Cultural normativeness as a moderator. *Child Development, 76,* 1234–1246.

Lansford, J. E., Malone, P. S., Castellino, D. R., Dodge, K. A., Pettit, G. S., & Bates, J. E. (2006). Trajectories of internalizing, externalizing, and grades for children who have and have not experienced their parents' divorce or separation. *Journal of Family Psychology, 20,* 292–301.

Lansford, J. E., Sherman, A. M., & Antonucci, T. C. (1998). Satisfaction with social networks: An examination of socioemotional selectivity theory across cohorts. *Psychology and Aging, 13,* 544–552.

Laplante, D. P., Barr, R. G., Brunet, A., Fort, G., Meaney, M. L., Saucier, J., Zelazo, P. R., King, S. (2004). Stress during pregnancy affects general intellectual and language functioning in human toddlers. *Pediatric Research, 56,* 400–410.

Lapsley, D. K. (1996). *Moral psychology.* Boulder, CO: Westview.

Lapsley, D. K. (2006). Moral stage theory. In M. Killen & J. G. Smetana (Eds.), *Handbook of moral development.* Mahwah, NJ: Erlbaum.

Lapsley, D. K., Harwell, M. R., Olson, L. M., Flannery, D., & Quintana, S. M. (1984). Moral judgment, personality, and attitude toward authority in early and late adolescence. *Journal of Youth and Adolescence, 13,* 527–542.

Lapsley, D. K., Milstead, M., Quintana, S. M., Flannery, D., & Buss, R. R. (1986). Adolescent egocentrism and formal operations: Tests of a theoretical assumption. *Developmental Psychology, 22,* 800–807.

Lapsley, D. K., Rice, K. G., & FitzGerald, D. P. (1990). Adolescent attachment, identity, and adjustment to college: Implications for the continuity of adaptation hypothesis. *Journal of Counseling and Development, 68,* 561–565.

Larose, S., Bernier, A., & Tarabulsy, G. M. (2005). Attachment state of mind, learning dispositions, and academic performance during the college transition. *Developmental Psychology, 41,* 281–289.

Larson, E. B., Wang, L., Bowen, J. D., McCormick, W. C., Teri, L., Crane, P., & Kukull, W. (2006). Exercise is associated with reduced risk for incident dementia among persons 65 years of age and older. *Annals of Internal Medicine, 144,* 73–81.

Larson, R. W., Richards, M. H., Moneta, G., Holmbeck, G., & Duckett, E. (1996). Changes in adolescents' daily interactions with their families from ages 10 to 18: Disengagement and transformation. *Developmental Psychology, 32,* 744–753.

Larsson, I. & Svedin, C. (2002). Sexual experiences in childhood: Young adults' recollections. *Archives of Sexual Behavior, 31,* 263-273.

Laucht, M., Skowronek, M. H., Becker, K., Schmidt M. H., Esser, G., Schulze, T. G., & Rietschel, M. (2007). Interacting effects of the dopamine transporter gene and psychosocial adversity on attention-deficit/hyperactivity disorder symptoms among 15-year-olds from a high-risk community sample. *Archives of General Psychiatry, 64,* 585–590.

Laumann, E. O., Gagnon, J. H., Michael, R. T., & Michaels, S. (1994). *The social organization of sexuality: Sexual practices in the United States.* Chicago: University of Chicago Press.

Laumann, E. O., Paik, A., & Rosen, R. C. (1999). Sexual dysfunction in the United States: Prevalence and predictors. *Journal of the American Medical Association, 281,* 537–544.

Laursen, B., & Williams, V. (2002). The role of ethnic identity in personality development. In L. Pulkkinen & A. Caspi (Eds.), *Paths to successful development. Personality in the life course.* Cambridge, UK: Cambridge University Press.

Lavigne, J. V., Arend, R., Rosenbaum, D., Smith, A., Weissbluth, M., Binns, H. J., & Christoffel, K. K. (1999). Sleep and behavior problems among preschoolers. *Journal of Developmental and Behavioral Pediatrics, 20,* 164–169.

Law, K. L., Stroud, L. R., LaGasse, L. L., Niaura, R., Liu, J., & Lester, B. M. (2003). Smoking during pregnancy and newborn neurobehavior. *Pediatrics, 111,* 1318–1323.

Lawson, J., Baron-Cohen, S., & Wheelwright, S. (2004). Empathizing and systemizing in adults with and without Asperger syndrome. *Journal of Autism and Developmental Disorders, 34,* 301–310.

Lawton, M. P., Moss, M. S., Winter, L., & Hoffman, C. (2002). Motivation in later life: Personal projects and well-being. *Psychology and Aging, 17,* 539–547.

Lazar, I., & Darlington, R. (1982). Lasting effects of early education: A report from the Consortium for Longitudinal Studies. *Monographs of the Society for Research in Child Development, 47* (2–3, Serial No. 195).

Leaper, C. (1994). *Childhood gender segregation: Causes and consequences* (New Directions for Child Development, Vol. 65). San Francisco: Jossey-Bass.

Lécuyer, R., Berthereau, S., Taïeb, A. B., & Tardif, N. (2004). Location of a missing object and detection of its absence by infants: Contribution of an eye-tracking system to the understanding of infants' strategies. *Infant and Child Development, 13,* 287–300.

Lederman, S.A., Rauh, V., Weiss, L., Stein, J.L., Hoepner, L.A., Becker, M., Perera, F.P. (2004). The effects of the World Trade Center event on birth outcomes among term deliveries at three lower Manhattan hospitals. *Environmental Health Perspectives, 112,* 1772–1778.

Lee, J. M., Appugliese, D., Kaciroti, N., Corwyn, R. F., Bradley, R. H., & Lumeng, J. C. (2007). Weight status in young girls and the onset of puberty. *Pediatrics, 119,* E624–E630.

Leeder, E. J. (2004). *The family in global perspective. A gendered journey.* Thousand Oaks, CA: Sage.

Lefkowitz, E. S. (2005). "Things have gotten better": Developmental changes among emerging adults after the transition to university. *Journal of Adolescent Research, 20,* 40–63.

Lefkowitz, E. S., & Zeldow, P. B. (2006). Masculinity and femininity predict optimal mental health: A belated test of the androgyny hypothesis. *Journal of Personality Assessment, 87,* 95–101.

Lehman, D. R., Ellard, J. H., & Wortman, C. B. (1986). Social support for the bereaved: Recipients' and providers' perspectives on what is helpful. *Journal of Consulting and Clinical Psychology, 54,* 438–446.

Lehman, D. R., Wortman, C. B., & Williams, A. F. (1987). Long-term effects of losing a spouse or child in a motor vehicle crash. *Journal of Personality and Social Psychology, 52,* 218–231.

Lehman, H. C. (1953). *Age and achievement.* Princeton, NJ: Princeton University Press.

Lehn, H., Derks, E. M., Hudziak, J. J., Heutink, P., van Beijsterveldt, T. C. E. M., & Boomsma, D. I. (2007). Attention problems and attention-deficit/hyperactivity disorder in discordant and concordant monozygotic twins: Evidence of environmental mediators. *Journal of the American Academy of Child and Adolescent Psychiatry, 46,* 83–91.

Leichtman, M. D., & Ceci, S. J. (1993). The problem of infantile amnesia: Lessons from fuzzy-trace theory. In M. L. Howe & R. Pasnak (Eds.), *Emerging themes in cognitive development: Vol. 1. Foundations.* New York: Springer-Verlag.

Lejarraga, H. (2002). Growth in infancy and childhood: A pediatric approach. In N. Cameron (Ed.), *Human growth and development* (pp. 21–44). New York: Academic Press.

Lemann, N. (1997, November). The reading wars. *Atlantic Monthly,* 128–134.

LeMare, L. J., & Rubin, K. H. (1987). Perspective taking and peer interaction: Structural and developmental analyses. *Child Development, 58,* 306–315.

Lemerise, E. A., & Arsenio, W. F. (2000). An integrated model of emotion processes and cognition in social information processing. *Child Development, 71,* 107–118.

Lenneberg, E. H. (1967). *Biological foundations of language.* New York: Wiley.

Leonard, K. E., & Das Eiden, R. (2002). Cognitive functioning among infants of alcoholic fathers. *Drug and Alcohol Dependence, 67,* 139–147.

Lerner, J. V., & Noh, E. R. (2000). Maternal employment influences on early adolescent development: A contextual view. In R. D. Taylor & M. C. Wang (Eds.), *Resilience across contexts: Family, work, culture, and community.* Mahwah, NJ: Erlbaum.

Lerner, M. J., Somers, D. G., Reid, D., Chiriboga, D., & Tierney, M. (1991). Adult children as caregivers: Egocentric biases in judgments of sibling contributions. *Gerontologist, 31,* 746–755.

Lerner, R. M. (2003). What are SES effects effects of?: A developmental systems perspective. In M. H. Bornstein & R. H. Bradley (Eds.), *Socioeconomic status, parenting, and child development.* Mahwah, NJ: Erlbaum.

Lerner, R. M. (2006). Developmental science, developmental systems, and contemporary theories of human development. In W. Damon & R. M. Lerner (Eds. in Chief) & R. M. Lerner (Vol. Ed.), *Handbook of child psychology: Vol. 1. Theoretical models of human development* (6th ed.). Hoboken, NJ: Wiley.

Lerner, R. M., Dowling, E., & Chaudhuri, J. (2005). Methods of contextual assessment and assessing contextual methods: A developmental systems perspective. In D. M. Teti (Ed.), *Handbook of research methods in developmental science.* Malden, MA: Blackwell Publishing.

Lerner, R. M., & Kauffman, M. B. (1985). The concept of development in contextualism. *Developmental Review, 5,* 309–333.

Leslie, A. M. (1994). ToMM, ToBy, and agency: Core architecture and domain specificity in cognition and culture. In L. Hirschfeld & S. Gelman (Eds.), *Mapping the mind: Domain specificity in cognition and culture.* New York: Cambridge University Press.

Lester, B. M., Kotelchuck, M., Spelke, E., Sellers, M. J., & Klein, R. E. (1974). Separation protest in Guatemalan infants: Cross-cultural and cognitive findings. *Developmental Psychology, 10,* 79–85.

Lester, D. (1994). Are there unique features of suicide in adults of different ages and developmental stages. *Omega: Journal of Death and Dying, 29,* 337–348.

Leung, A. K. C., & Robson, W. L. M. (1993). Childhood masturbation. *Clinical Pediatrics, 32,* 238–241.

LeVay, S. (1996). *Queer science: The use and abuse of research into homosexuality.* Cambridge, MA: MIT Press.

Leve, L. D., & Fagot, B. I. (1997). Gender-role socialization and discipline processes in one- and two-parent families. *Sex Roles, 36,* 1–21.

Levenkron, S. (2000). *Anatomy of anorexia.* New York: W. W. Norton.

Levinson, D. (1989). *Family violence in cross-cultural perspective.* Newbury Park, CA: Sage.

Levinson, D. J. (1986). A conception of adult development. *American Psychologist, 41,* 3–13.

Levinson, D. J. (in collaboration with J. D. Levinson) (1996). *The seasons of a woman's life.* New York: Alfred A. Knopf.

Levinson, D. J., Darrow, C. N., Klein, E. B., Levinson, M. H., & McKee, B. (1978). *The seasons of a man's life.* New York: Ballantine Books.

Levitt, M. J. (1991). Attachment and close relationships: A life-span perspective. In J. L. Gewirtz & W. M. Kurtines (Eds.), *Intersections with attachment.* Hillsdale, NJ: Erlbaum.

Levitt, M. J., Weber, R. A., & Guacci, N. (1993). Convoys of social support: An intergenerational analysis. *Psychology and Aging, 8,* 323–326.

Levy, B. (1996). Improving memory in old age through implicit self-stereotyping. *Journal of Personality and Social Psychology, 71,* 1092–1107.

Levy, B., & Langer, E. (1994). Aging free from negative stereotypes: Successful memory in China and among the American deaf. *Journal of Personality and Social Psychology, 66,* 989–997.

Levy, B. R. (2003). Mind matters: Cognitive and physical effects of aging self-stereotypes. *Journals of Gerontology: Psychological Sciences & Social Sciences, 58,* 203–211.

Levy, B. R., Slade, M. D., & Kasl, S. V. (2002). Longitudinal benefit of positive self-perceptions of aging on functional health. *Journals of Gerontology: Psychological Sciences and Social Sciences, 57,* 409–417.

Levy, G. D. (1999). Gender-typed and non-gender-typed category awareness in toddlers. *Sex Roles, 41,* 851–873.

Levy, G. D., Sadovsky, A. L., & Troseth, G. L. (2000). Aspects of young children's perceptions of gender-typed occupations. *Sex Roles, 42,* 993–1006.

Levy-Shiff, R. (1994). Individual and contextual correlates of marital change across the transition to parenthood. *Developmental Psychology, 30,* 591–601.

Lew, A. R., Hopkins, B., Owen, L. H., & Green, M. (2007, March 1). Postural change effects on infants' AB task performance: Visual, postural, or spatial? *Journal of Experimental Psychology, 97,* 1–13.

Lewandowsky, S., & Kirsner, K. (2000). Knowledge partitioning: Context-dependent use of expertise. *Memory & Cognition, 28,* 295–305.

Lewis, B. A., & Thompson, L. A. (1992). A study of developmental speech and language disorders in twins. *Journal of Speech and Hearing Research, 35,* 1086–1094.

Lewis, D. A., Sesack, S. R., Levey, A. I., & Rosenberg, D. R. (1998). Dopamine axons in primate prefrontal cortex: Specificity of distribution, synaptic targets, and development. *Advances in Pharmacology, 42,* 703–706.

Lewis, M. (2000). The emergence of human emotions. In M. Lewis & J. M. Haviland-Jones (Eds.), *Handbook of emotions* (2nd ed.). New York: Guilford.

Lewis, M., Alessandri, S. M., & Sullivan, M. W. (1990). Violation of expectancy, loss of control, and anger expressions in young infants. *Developmental Psychology, 26,* 745–751.

Lewis, M., & Brooks-Gunn, J. (1979). *Social cognition and the acquisition of self.* New York: Plenum.

Lewis, M., & Rosenblum, M. A. (1975). *Friendship and peer relations.* New York: Wiley.

Lewis, M., Sullivan, M. W., Stanger, C., & Weiss, M. (1989). Self-development and self-conscious emotions. *Child Development, 60,* 146–156.

Lewis, M., & Weinraub, M. (1979). Origins of early sex-role development. *Sex Roles, 5,* 135–153.

Lewis, P. G., & Lippman, J. G. (2004). *Helping children cope with the death of a parent. A guide for the first year.* Westport, CT: Praeger.

Lewis, T. L., & Maurer, D. (2005). Multiple sensitive periods in human visual development: Evidence from visually deprived children. *Developmental Psychobiology, 46,* 163–183.

Lewontin, R. C. (1976). Race and intelligence. In N. J. Block & G. Dworkin (Eds.), *The IQ controversy.* New York: Pantheon.

Lewontin, R. C., Rose, S., & Kamin, L. J. (1984). *Not in our genes.* New York: Pantheon.

Li, D., Liu, L., & Odouli, R. (2003). Exposure to non-steroidal anti-inflammatory drugs during pregnancy and risk of miscarriage: Population based cohort study. *British Medical Journal, 327,* 368.

Li, K. Z. H., Lindenberger, U., Freund, A. M., & Baltes, P. B. (2001). Walking while memorizing: Age-related differences in compensatory behavior. *Psychological Science, 12,* 230–237.

Li, L. W., Seltzer, M. M., & Greenberg, J. S. (1999). Change in depressive symptoms among daughter caregivers: An 18-month longitudinal study. *Psychology and Aging, 14,* 206–219.

Li, N. & Kirkup, G. (2007). Gender and cultural differences in Internet use: A study of China and the UK. *Computers & Education, 48,* 301–317.

Li, S. (2003). Biocultural orchestration of developmental plasticity across levels: The interplay of biology and culture in shaping the mind and behavior across the life span. *Psychological Bulletin, 129,* 171–194.

Liben, L. S., & Signorella, M. L. (1993). Gender-schematic processing in children: The role of initial interpretations of stimuli. *Developmental Psychology, 29,* 141–149.

Lidz, C. S. (1997). Dynamic assessment approaches. In D. P. Flanagan, J. Genshaft, & P. L. Harrison (Eds.), *Contemporary intellectual assessment: Theories, tests, and issues.* New York: Guilford.

Lidz, C. S., & Elliott, J. G. (Eds.). (2001). *Dynamic assessment: Prevailing models and applications.* Amsterdam: JAI/Elsevier Science.

Lidz, J., Waxman, S., & Freedman, J. (2003). What infants know about syntax but couldn't have learned: Experimental evidence for syntactic structure at 18 months. *Cognition, 89,* B65–B73.

Lie, E., & Newcombe, N. S. (1999). Elementary school children's explicit and implicit memory for faces of preschool classmates. *Developmental Psychology, 35,* 102–112.

Lieberman, A. F., Compton, N. C., Van Horn, P., & Ippen, C. G. (2003). *Losing a parent to death in the early years. Guidelines for the treatment of traumatic bereavement in infancy and early childhood.* Washington, D.C.: Zero to Three Press.

Lieberman, M. A., & Videka-Sherman, L. (1986). The impact of self-help groups on the mental health of widows and widowers. *American Journal of Orthopsychiatry, 56,* 435–449.

Lieven, E. V. M. (1994). Crosslinguistic and cross-cultural aspects of language addressed to children. In C. Gallaway & B. J. Richards (Eds.), *Input and interaction in language acquisition.* Cambridge, England: Cambridge University Press.

Light, L. L. (1991). Memory and aging: Four hypotheses in search of data. *Annual Review of Psychology, 42,* 333–376.

Lilenfeld, L. R. R., Wonderlich, S., Riso, L. P., Crosby, R., & Mitchell, J. (2006). Eating disorders and personality: A methodological and empirical review. *Clinical Psychology Review, 26,* 299–320.

Lillard, A. (2001). Pretend play as twin earth: A social-cognitive analysis. *Developmental Review, 21,* 495–531.

Lillard, A. S. (2005). *Montessori: The science behind the genius.* Oxford, UK: Oxford University Press.

Lillard, L. A., & Panis, C. W. A. (1996). Marital status and mortality: The role of health. *Demography, 33,* 313–327.

Lim, F., Bond, M. H., & Bond, M. K. (2005). Linking societal and psychological factors to homicide rates across nations. *Journal of Cross-Cultural Psychology, 36,* 515–536.

Lima, S. D., Hale, S., & Myerson, J. (1991). How general is general slowing? Evidence from the lexical domain. *Psychology and Aging, 6,* 416–425.

Lindau, S. T., Schumm, L. P., Laumann, E. O., Levinson, W., O'Muircheartaigh, C. A., & Waite, L. J. (2007). A study of sexuality and health among older adults in the United States. *New England Journal of Medicine, 357,* 762–774.

Lindenberger, U., Marsiske, M., & Baltes, P. B. (2000). Memorizing while walking: Increase in dual-task costs from young adulthood to old age. *Psychology and Aging, 15,* 417–436.

Lindsey, E. W., & Mize, J. (2000). Parent–child physical and pretense play: Links to children's social competence. *Merrill-Palmer Quarterly, 46,* 565–591.

Linnet, K. M., Dalsgaard, S., Obel, C., Wisborg, K., Henriksen, T. B., Rodriguez, A., Kotimaa, A., Moilanen, I., Thomsen, P. H., Olsen, J., & Jarvelin, M. R. (2003). Maternal lifestyle factors in pregnancy risk of attention deficit hyperactivity disorder and associated behaviors: Review of the current evidence. *American Journal of Psychiatry, 160,* 1028–1040.

Lipsey, M. W., & Wilson, D. B. (2001). *Practical meta-analysis.* Thousand Oaks, CA: Sage.

Lipsitt, L. P. (1990). Learning processes in the human newborn: Sensitization, habituation and classical conditioning. *Annals of the New York Academy of Sciences, 608,* 113–127.

Lipton, A. M., & Weiner, M. F. (2003). Differential diagnosis. In M. F. Weiner & A. M. Lipton (Eds.), *The dementias. Diagnosis, treatment, and research.* Washington, D.C.: American Psychiatric Publishing.

Lipton, J. S., & Spelke, E. S. (2003). Origins of number sense. Large-number discrimination in human infants. *Psychological Science, 14,* 396–401.

Little, J., Cardy, A., & Munger, R. G. (2004). Tobacco smoking and oral clefts: A meta-analysis. *Bulletin of the World Health Organization, 82,* 213–218.

Liu, C. (2003). Does quality of marital sex decline with duration? *Archives of Sexual Behavior, 32,* 55–60.

Livesley, W. J., & Bromley, D. B. (1973). *Person perception in childhood and adolescence.* London: Wiley.

Livson, F. B. (1976). Patterns of personality in middle-aged women: A longitudinal study. *International Journal of Aging and Human Development, 7,* 107–115.

Livson, F. B. (1981). Paths to psychological health in the middle years: Sex differences. In D. H. Eichorn, J. A. Clausen, N. Haan, M. P. Honzik, & P. H. Mussen (Eds.), *Present and past in middle life.* New York: Academic Press.

Lobel, T., Slone, M., & Winch, G. (1997). Masculinity, popularity, and self-esteem among Israeli preadolescent girls. *Sex Roles, 36,* 395–408.

Lock, A. (2004). Preverbal communication. In G. Bremner & A. Fogel (Eds.), *Blackwell handbook of infant development* (pp. 379–403). Malden, MA: Blackwell Publishing.

Lock, M. (1993). Encounters with aging: Mythologies of menopause in Japan and North America. Berkeley: University of California Press.

Locke, J. L. (1997). A theory of neurolinguistic development. *Brain and Language, 58,* 265–326.

Lockhart, K. L., Chang, B., & Story, T. (2002). Young children's beliefs about the stability of traits: Protective optimism? *Child Development, 73,* 1408–1430.

Lockheed, M. E. (1986). Reshaping the social order: The case of gender segregation. *Sex Roles, 14,* 617–628.

Lockl, K., & Schneider, W. (2007). Knowledge about the mind: Links between theory of mind and later metamemory. *Child Development, 78,* 148–167.

Loehlin, J. C. (1985). Fitting heredity–environment models jointly to twin and adoption data from the California Psychological Inventory. *Behavior Genetics, 15,* 199–221.

Loehlin, J. C. (1992). *Genes and environment in personality development (Individual differences and development series, Vol. 2).* Newbury Park, CA: Sage.

Loehlin, J. C., Horn, J. M., & Willerman, L. (1997). Heredity, environment, and IQ in the Texas Adoption Project. In R. J. Sternberg & E. L. Grigorenko (Eds.), *Intelligence, heredity, and environment.* New York: Cambridge University Press.

Loehlin, J. C., McCrae, R. R., Costa, P. T., Jr., & John, O. P. (1998). Heritabilities of common and measure-specific components of the Big Five personality factors. *Journal of Research in Personality, 32,* 431–453.

Loewenstein, G., & Furstenberg, F. (1991). Is teenage sexual behavior rational? *Journal of Applied Social Psychology, 21,* 957–986.

Lohan, J. A., & Murphy, S. A. (2001–2002). Parents' perceptions of adolescent sibling grief responses after an adolescent or young adult child's sudden, violent death. *Omega: Journal of Death and Dying, 44,* 77–95.

Lollis, S., Ross, H., & Leroux, L. (1996). An observational study of parents' socialization of moral orientation during sibling conflicts. *Merrill-Palmer Quarterly, 42,* 475–494.

Lonigan, C. J., Burgess, S. R., & Anthony, J. L. (2000). Development of emergent literacy and early reading skills in preschool children: Evidence from a latent-variable longitudinal study. *Developmental Psychology, 36(5),* 596–613.

Lonner, W. J. (2005). The psychological study of culture: Issues and questions of enduring importance. In W. Friedlmeier, P. Chakkarath, & B. Schwarz (Eds.), *Culture and human development: The importance of cross-cultural research for the social sciences.* New York: Psychology Press.

Loovis, E. M., & Butterfield, S. A. (2000). Influence of age, sex, and balance on mature skipping by children in grades K–8. *Perceptual and Motor Skills, 90,* 974–978.

Lopata, H. Z. (1996). *Current widowhood: Myths and realities.* Thousand Oaks, CA: Sage.

Lopez, E. C. (1997). The cognitive assessment of limited English proficient and bilingual children. In D. P. Flanagan, J. Genshaft, & P. L. Harrison (Eds.), *Contemporary intellectual assessment: Theories, tests, and issues.* New York: Guilford.

Lopez, S. R., & Guarnaccia, P. J. J. (2000). Cultural psychopathology: Uncovering the social world of mental illness. *Annual Review of Psychology, 51,* 571–598.

Lord, C. (2007). Early assessment of autistic spectrum disorders. In J. M. Perez, P. M. Gonzalez, M. Llorente Comi, & C. Nieto (Eds.), *New developments in autism: The future is today.* London: Jessica Kingsley.

Lorenz, K. Z. (1937). The companion in the bird's world. *Auk, 54,* 245–273.

Lorsbach, T. C., & Reimer, J. F. (1997). Developmental changes in the inhibition of previously relevant information. *Journal of Experimental Child Psychology, 64,* 317–342.

Lourenco, O., & Machado, A. (1996). In defense of Piaget's theory: A reply to 10 common criticisms. *Psychological Review, 103,* 143–164.

Louria, D. B. (2005). Extraordinary longevity: Individual and societal issues. *Journal of the American Geriatrics Society, 53,* S317–S319.

Lovaas, O. I. (1987). Behavioral treatment and normal educational and intellectual functioning in young autistic children. *Journal of Consulting and Clinical Psychology, 55,* 3–9.

Lovaas, O. I., & Smith, T. (2003). Early and intensive behavioral intervention in autism. In A. E. Kazdin & J. R. Weisz (Eds.), *Evidence-based psychotherapies for children and adolescents.* New York: Guilford.

Love, J. M., Harrison, L., Sagi-Schwartz, A., van IJzendoorn, M. H., Ross, C., Ungerer, J. A., Raikes, H., Brady-Smith, C., Boller, K., Brooks-Gunn, J., Constantine, J., Kisker, E. E., Paulsell, D., & Chazan-Cohen, R. (2003). Child care quality matters: How conclusions may vary with context. *Child Development, 74,* 1021–1033.

Lovering, J. S., & Percy, M. (2007). Down syndrome. In I. Brown & M. Percy (Eds.), *A comprehensive guide to intellectual & developmental disabilities*. Baltimore: Paul H. Brookes.

Lovett, B. J., & Sheffield, R. A. (2007). Affective empathy in aggressive children and adolescents: A critical review. *Clinical Psychology Review, 27,* 1–13.

Low, K. S. D., Yoon, M. J., Roberts, B. W., & Rounds, J. (2005). The stability of vocational interests from early adolescence to middle adulthood: A quantitative review of longitudinal studies. *Psychological Bulletin, 131,* 713–737.

Luby, J. L. (2004). Affective disorders. In R. DelCarmen-Wiggins & A. Carter (Eds.), *Handbook of infant, toddler, and preschool mental health assessment.* New York: Oxford University Press.

Luby, J. L., Sullivan, J., Belden, A., Stalets, M., Blankenship, S., & Spitznagel, E. (2006). An observational analysis of behavior in depressed preschoolers: Further validation of early-onset depression. *Journal of the American Academy of Child and Adolescent Psychiatry, 45,* 203–212.

Luciana, M., Conklin, H. M., Hooper, C. J., & Yarger, R. S. (2005). The development of nonverbal working memory and executive control processes in adolescents. *Child Development, 76,* 697–712.

Lueptow, L. B., Garovich-Szabo, L., & Lueptow, M. B. (2001). Social change and the persistence of sex typing: 1974–1997. *Social Forces, 80,* 1–36.

Lund, D. A., Dimond, M. F., Caserta, M. S., Johnson, R. J., Poulton, J. L., & Connelly, J. R. (1985–1986). Identifying elderly with coping difficulties after two years of bereavement. *Omega: Journal of Death and Dying, 16,* 213–224.

Lundy, B. L., Jones, N. A., Field, T., Nearing, G., Davalos, M., Pietro, P. A., Schanberg, S., & Kuhn, C. (1999). Prenatal depression effects on neonates. *Infant Behavior and Development, 22,* 119–129.

Luo, Y., Waite, L. J. (2005). The impact of childhood and adult SES on physical, mental, and cognitive well-being in later life. *Journals of Gerontology: Social Sciences, 60B,* S93–S101.

Lupsakko, T. A., Kautiainen, H. J., & Sulkava, R. (2005). The non-use of hearing aids in people aged 75 years and over in the city of Kuopio in Finland. *European Archives of Oto-Rhino-Laryngology, 262,* 165–169.

Luria, A. (1987). *The mind of a mnemonist.* MA: Harvard University Press.

Luria, A. R. (1974/1976). *Cognitive development: Its cultural and social foundations.* Cambridge, MA: Harvard University Press.

Lustig, J. L., Wolchik, S. A., & Braver, S. L. (1992). Social support in chumships and adjustment in children of divorce. *American Journal of Community Psychology, 20,* 393–399.

Ly, D. H., Lockhart, D. J., Lerner, R. A., & Schultz, P. G. (2000). Mitotic misregulation and human aging. *Science, 287,* 2486–2492.

Lykken, D. T., Tellegen, A., & Iacono, W. G. (1982). EEG spectra in twins: Evidence for a neglected mechanism of genetic determination. *Physiological Psychology, 10,* 60–65.

Lyman, S., Ferguson, S. A., Braver, E. R. , & Williams, A. F. (2002). Older driver involvements in police reported crashes and fatal crashes: Trends and projections. *Injury Prevention, 8,* 116–120.

Lynch, M. P., Eilers, R. E., Oller, D. K., & Urbano, R. C. (1990). Innateness, experience, and music perception. *Psychological Science, 1,* 272–276.

Lynch, S. K., Turkheimer, E., D'Onofrio, B. M., Mendle, J. Emery, R. E., Slutske, W. S., & Martin, N. G. (2006). A genetically informed study of the association between harsh punishment and offspring behavioral problems. *Journal of Family Psychology, 20,* 190–198.

Lynch, S. M., & George, L. K. (2002). Interlocking trajectories of loss-related events and depressive symptoms among elders. *Journal of Gerontology: Social Sciences, 57B,* S117–S125.

Lyonette, C., & Yardley, L. (2003). The influence on carer wellbeing of motivations to care for older people and the relationship with the care recipient. *Ageing & Society, 23,* 487–506.

Lyons-Ruth, K., Zeanah, C. H., & Benoit, D. (2003). Disorder and risk for disorder during infancy and toddlerhood. In E. J. Mash & R. A. Barkley (Eds.), *Child psychopathology* (2nd ed.). New York: Guilford Press.

Lytton, H. (1990). Child and parent effects in boys' conduct disorder: A reinterpretation. *Developmental Psychology, 26,* 683–697.

Lytton, H. (2000). Toward a model of family–environmental and child–biological influences on development. *Developmental Review, 20,* 150–179.

Lytton, H., & Romney, D. M. (1991). Parents' differential socialization of boys and girls: A meta-analysis. *Psychological Bulletin, 109,* 267–296.

M

Ma, H. H. (2006). A synthetic analysis of the effectiveness of single components and packages in creativity training programs. *Creativity Research Journal, 18,* 435–446.

Ma, L., & Lillard, A. S. (2006). Where is the real cheese? Young children's ability to discriminate between real and pretend acts. *Child Development, 77,* 1762–1777.

Macario, A., Scibetta, W. C., Navarro, J., & Riley, E. (2000). Analgesia for labor pain: A cost model. *Anesthesiology, 92,* 643–645.

Maccoby, E. E. (1980). *Social development.* New York: Harcourt Brace Jovanovich.

Maccoby, E. E. (1998). *The two sexes: Growing up apart, coming together.* Cambridge, MA: Harvard University Press.

Maccoby, E. E. (2000). Parenting and its effects on children: On reading and misreading behavior genetics. *Annual Review of Psychology, 51,* 1–28.

Maccoby, E. E. (2007). Historical overview of socialization research and theory. In J. E. Grusec & P. D. Hastings (Eds.), *Handbook of socialization theory and research.* New York: Guilford.

Maccoby, E. E., & Jacklin, C. N. (1974). *The psychology of sex differences.* Stanford, CA: Stanford University Press.

Maccoby, E. E., & Jacklin, C. N. (1987). Gender segregation in childhood. In H. W. Reese (Ed.), *Advances in child development and behavior* (Vol. 20). Orlando, FL: Academic Press.

Maccoby, E. E., & Martin, J. A. (1983). Socialization in the context of the family: Parent–child interaction. In E. M. Hetherington (Vol. Ed.), P. H. Mussen (Editor-in-Chief), *Handbook of child psychology: Vol. 4. Socialization, personality, and social development* (4th ed.). New York: Wiley.

MacDonald, K., & Hershberger, S. L. (2005). Theoretical issues in the study of evolution and development. In R. L. Burgess & K. MacDonald (Eds.), *Evolutionary perspectives on human development.* Thousand Oaks, CA: Sage.

MacDorman, M. F., Martin, J. A., Mathews, T. J., Hoyert, D. L., Ventura, S. J. (2005). Explaining the 2001–2002 infant mortality increase: Data from the linked birth/infant death data set. *National Vital Statistics Report, 53,* 1–22.

Machado, C. J. (2006). Impact of maternal age on birth outcomes: A population-based study of primiparous Brazilian women in the city of São Paulo. *Journal of Biosocial Science, 38,* 523–535.

Mac Iver, D. J. & Reuman, D. A. (1988, April). *Decision-making in the classroom and early adolescents' valuing of mathematics.* Paper presented at the annual meeting of the American Educational Research Association, New Orleans.

Mac Iver, D. J., Reuman, D. A., & Main, S. R. (1995). Social structuring of the school: Studying what is, illuminating what could be. *Annual Review of Psychology, 46,* 375–400.

Mackey, R. A., & O'Brien, B. A. (1995). *Lasting marriages: Men and women growing together.* Westport, CT: Praeger.

MacLean, K. (2003). The impact of institutionalization on child development. *Development and Psychopathology, 15,* 853–884.

Macmillan, M. (1991). *Freud evaluated: The completed arc.* New York: Elsevier.

MacPhee, D., Fritz, J., & Miller-Heyl, J. (1996). Ethnic variations in personal social networks and parenting. *Child Development, 67,* 3278–3295.

MacPherson, S. E., Phillips, L. H., & Della Sala, S. (2002). Age, executive function and social decision making: A dorsolateral prefrontal theory of cognitive aging. *Psychology and Aging, 17,* 598–609.

Madden, D. J. (2007). Aging and visual attention. *Current Directions in Psychological Science, 16,* 70–74.

Madden, D. J., Gottlob, L. R., & Allen, P. A. (1999). Adult age differences in visual search accuracy: Attentional guidance and target detectability. *Psychology and Aging, 14,* 683–694.

Madden, D. J., & Langley, L. K. (2003). Age-related changes in selective attention and perceptual load during visual search. *Psychology and Aging, 18,* 54–67.

Maddux, J. E. (2002). Self-efficacy: The power of believing you can. In C. R. Snyder & S. J. Lopez (Eds.), *Handbook of positive psychology* (pp. 277–287). New York: Oxford University Press.

Madigan, S., Bakermans-Kranenburg, M. J., van IJzendoorn, M. H., Moran, G., Pederson, D. R., & Benoit, D. (2006). Unresolved states of mind, anomalous parental behavior, and disorganized attachment: A review and meta-analysis of a transmission gap. *Attachment and Human Development, 8,* 89–111.

Maehr, M., & Meyer, H. (1997). Understanding motivation and schooling: Where we've been, where we are, and where we need to go. *Educational Psychology Review, 9,* 371–409.

Maestripieri, D. (2001). Is there mother–infant bonding in primates? *Developmental Review, 21*, 93–120.

Magai, C., Cohen, C., Milburn, N., Thorpe, B., McPherson, R., & Peralta, D. (2001). Attachment styles in older European American and African American adults. *Journals of Gerontology: Psychological Sciences and Social Sciences, 56*, S28–S35.

Magai, C., Consedine, N. S., Krivoshekova, Y. S., Kudadjie-Gyamfi, E., & McPherson, R. (2006). Emotion experience and expression across the adult life span: Insights from a multimodal assessment study. *Psychology and Aging, 21*, 303–317.

Magnus, K., Diener, E., Fujita, F., & Payot, W. (1993). Extraversion and neuroticism as predictors of objective life events: A longitudinal analysis. *Journal of Personality and Social Psychology, 65*, 1046–1053.

Magnusson, D. (1995). Individual development: A holistic, integrated model. In P. Moen, & G. H. Elder Jr. (Eds.), *Examining lives in context: Perspectives on the ecology of human development*. Washington, D.C.: American Psychological Association.

Magoni, M., Bassani, L., Okong, P., Kituuka, P., Germinario, E. P., Giuliano, M., & Vella, S. (2005). Mode of infant feeding and HIV infection in children in a program for prevention of mother-to-child transmission in Uganda. *AIDS, 19*, 433–437.

Mahaffy, K. A., & Ward, S. K. (2002). The gendering of adolescents' childbearing and educational plans: Reciprocal effects and the influence of social context. *Sex Roles, 46*, 403–417.

Maiden, R. J., Peterson, S. A., Caya, M., & Hayslip, B. (2003). Personality changes in the old-old: A longitudinal study. *Journal of Adult Development, 10*, 31–39.

Maier, E. H., & Lachman, M. E. (2000). Consequences of early parental loss and separation for health and well-being in midlife. *International Journal of Behavioral Development, 24*, 183–189.

Main, M., & George, C. (1985). Responses of abused and disadvantaged toddlers to distress in agemates: A study in the day-care setting. *Developmental Psychology, 21*, 407–412.

Main, M., Kaplan, N., & Cassidy, J. (1985). Security in infancy, childhood, and adulthood: A move to the level of representation. In I. Bretherton & E. Waters (Eds.), *Growing points in attachment theory and research. Monographs of the Society for Research in Child Development, 50* (1–2, Serial No. 209), 66–106.

Main, M., & Solomon, J. (1990). Procedures for identifying infants as disorganized/disoriented during the Ainsworth Strange Situation. In M. T. Greenberg, D. Cicchetti, & E. M. Cummings (Eds.), *Attachment in the preschool years: Theory, research, and intervention.* Chicago: University of Chicago Press.

Main, M., & Weston, D. R. (1981). The quality of the toddler's relationship to mother and to father: Related to conflict and the readiness to establish new relationships. *Child Development, 52*, 932–940.

Maioli, F., Coveri, M., Pagni, P., Chiandetti, C., Marchetti, C., Ciarrocchi, R., Ruggero, C., Nativio, V., Onesti, A., D'Anastasio, C., & Pedone, V. (2007). Conversion of mild cognitive impairment to dementia in elderly subjects: A preliminary study in a memory and cognitive disorder unit. *Archives of Gerontology and Geriatrics, 44*, 233–241.

Malatesta, C. Z., Culver, C., Tesman, J. R., & Shepard, B. (1989). The development of emotion expression during the first two years of life. *Monographs of the Society for Research in Child Development, 54* (1–2, Serial No. 219).

Malatesta, C. Z., Grigoryev, P., Lamb, C., Albin, M., & Culver, C. (1986). Emotional socialization and expressive development in preterm and full-term infants. *Child Development, 57*, 316–330.

Malinosky-Rummell, R., & Hansen, D. J. (1993). Long-term consequences of childhood physical abuse. *Psychological Bulletin, 114*, 68–79.

Malley-Morrison, K., & Hines, D. A. (2004). *Family violence in a cultural perspective. Defining, understanding, and combating abuse.* Thousand Oaks, CA: Sage.

Malmstrom, M., Sundquist, J., Bajekal, M., & Johansson, S. E. (1999). Ten-year trends in all-cause mortality and coronary heart disease mortality in socioeconomically diverse neighbourhoods. *Public Health, 113*, 279–284.

Malouf, M. A., Migeon, C. J., Carson, K. A., Petrucci, L., & Wisniewski, A. B. (2006). Cognitive outcome in adult women affected by congenital adrenal hyperplasia due to 21-hydroxylase deficiency. *Hormone Research, 65*, 142–150.

Mandoki, M. W., Sumner, G. S., Hoffman, R. P., & Riconda, D. L. (1991). A review of Klinefelter's syndrome in children and adolescents. *Journal of the American Academy of Child and Adolescent Psychiatry, 30*, 167–172.

Mangelsdorf, S. C. (1992). Developmental changes in infant-stranger interaction. *Infant Behavior and Development, 15*, 191–208.

Mangelsdorf, S. C., Gunnar, M., Kestenbaum, R., Lang, S., & Andreas, D. (1990). Infant proneness-to-distress temperament, maternal personality, and mother–infant attachment: Associations and goodness of fit. *Child Development, 61*, 820–831.

Mangelsdorf, S. C., Shapiro, J. R., & Marzolf, D. (1995). Developmental and temperamental differences in emotion regulation in infancy. *Child Development, 66*, 1817–1828.

Manning, M. A., Bear, G. G., & Minke, K. M. (2006). Self-concept and self-esteem. In G. G. Bear & K. M. Minke (Eds.), *Children's needs. Vol. 3: Development, prevention, and intervention.* Washington, DC: National Association of School Psychologists.

Manset, G., & Semmel, M. I. (1997). Are inclusive programs for students with mild disabilities effective? A comparative review of model programs. *Journal of Special Education, 31*, 155–180.

Mansi, G. Raimondi, F., Pichini, S., Campasso, L., Sarno, M., Zuccaro, P., Pacifici, R., Garcia-Algar, O., Romano, A., & Paludetto, R. (2007). Neonatal urinary cotinine correlates with behavioral alterations in newborns prenatally exposed to tobacco smoke. *Pediatric Research, 61*, 257–261.

Maraniss, D., Hull, A., & Schwartzman, P. (2001, September 30). The days after. *The Washington Post*, A1, A18.

Marchant, G., Robinson, J., Anderson, U., & Schadewald, M. (1991). Analogical transfer and expertise in legal reasoning. *Organizational Behavior & Human Decision Making, 48*, 272–290.

Marcia, J. E. (1966). Development and validation of ego identity status. *Journal of Personality and Social Psychology, 3*, 551–558.

Marcon, R. A. (1999). Positive relationships between parent school involvement and public school inner-city preschoolers' development and academic performance. *School Psychology Review, 28*, 395–412.

Marcovitch, S., & Zelazo, D. (1999). The A-not-B error: Results from a logistic meta-analysis. *Child Development, 70*, 1297–1313.

Marean, G. C., Werner, L. A., & Kuhl, P. K. (1992). Vowel categorization by very young infants. *Developmental Psychology, 28*, 396–405.

Margolin, G., & Gordis, E. B. (2000). The effects of family and community violence on children. *Annual Review of Psychology, 51*, 445–479.

Marian, V., & Neisser, U. (2000). Language-dependent recall of autobiographical memories. *Journal of Experimental Psychology: General, 129*, 361–367.

Marini, Z., & Case, R. (1994). The development of abstract reasoning about the physical and social world. *Child Development, 65*, 147–159.

Markides, K. S., Boldt, J. S., & Ray, L. A. (1986). Sources of helping and intergenerational solidarity: A three-generations study of Mexican Americans. *Journal of Gerontology, 41*, 506–511.

Markiewicz, D., Lawford, H., Doyle, A. B., & Haggart, N. (2006). Developmental differences in adolescents' and young adults' use of mothers, fathers, best friends, and romantic partners to fulfill attachment needs. *Journal of Youth and Adolescence, 35*, 127–140.

Marks, M. J., & Fraley, R. C. (2006). Confirmation bias and the sexual double standard. *Sex Roles, 54*, 19–26.

Markstrom-Adams, C. (1992). A consideration of intervening factors in adolescent identity formation. In G. R. Adams, T. P. Gullotta, & R. Montemayor (Eds.), *Adolescent identity formation* (Advances in Adolescent Development, Vol. 4). Newbury Park, CA: Sage.

Markstrom-Adams, C., & Adams, G. R. (1995). Gender, ethnic group, and grade differences in psychosocial functioning during middle adolescence. *Journal of Youth and Adolescence, 24*, 397–417.

Markus, H. R. (2004). Culture and personality: Brief for an arranged marriage. *Journal of Research in Personality, 38*, 75–83.

Markus, H. R., Mullally, P. R., & Kitayama, S. (1997). Self-ways: Diversity in modes of cultural participation. In U. Neisser & D. A. Jopling (Eds.), *The conceptual self in context. Culture, experience, self-understanding.* Cambridge, UK: Cambridge University Press.

Marlier, L., & Schaal, B. (2005). Human newborns prefer human milk: Conspecific milk odor is attractive without postnatal exposure. *Child Development, 76*, 155–168.

Marschark, M. (1993). *Psychological development of deaf children.* New York: Oxford University Press.

Marsh, H. W., & Ayotte, V. (2003). Do multiple dimensions of self-control become more differentiated with age? The differential distinctiveness hypothesis. *Journal of Educational Psychology, 95*, 687–706.

Marsh, H. W., Chessor, D., Craven, R., & Roche, L. (1995). The effect of gifted and talented programs on academic self-concept: The big fish strikes again. *American Educational Research Journal, 32*, 285–319.

Marsh, H. W., & Craven, R. G. (2006). Reciprocal effects of self-concept and performance from a multidimensional perspective: Beyond seductive pleasure and unidimensional perspectives. *Perspectives on Psychological Science, 1*, 133–163.

Marsh, H. W., Craven, R., & Debus, R. (1999). Separation of competency and affect components of multiple dimensions of academic self-concept: A developmental perspective. *Merrill-Palmer Quarterly, 45*, 567–701.

Marsh, H. W., & Hau, K. (2003). Big fish-little pond effect on academic self-concept: A cross-cultural (26-country) test of the negative effects of academically selective schools. *American Psychologist, 58*, 364–376.

Marsh, H. W., & Kleitman, S. (2005). Consequences of employment during high school: Character building, subversion of academic goals, or a threshold? *American Educational Research Journal, 42*, 331–470.

Marsiglio, W., Amato, P., Day, R. D., & Lamb, M. E. (2000). Scholarship on fatherhood in the 1990s and beyond. *Journal of Marriage and the Family, 62*, 1173–1191.

Marsiske, M., & Margrett, J. A. (2006). Everyday problem solving and decision making. In J. E. Birren & K. W. Schaie (Eds.), *Handbook of the psychology of aging*. Boston: Elsevier Academic Press.

Marsiske, M., & Willis, S. L. (1995). Dimensionality of everyday problem solving in older adults. *Psychology and Aging, 10*, 269–283.

Martin, C. L., & Fabes, R. A. (2001). The stability and consequences of young children's same-sex peer interactions. *Developmental Psychology, 37*, 431–446.

Martin, C. L., & Halverson, C. F., Jr. (1981). A schematic processing model of sex typing and stereotyping in children. *Child Development, 52*, 1119–1134.

Martin, C. L., & Halverson, C. F., Jr. (1983). The effects of sex-typing schemas on young children's memory. *Child Development, 54*, 563–574.

Martin, C. L., & Halverson, C. F., Jr. (1987). The roles of cognition in sex-roles and sex-typing. In D. B. Carter (Ed.), *Current conceptions of sex roles and sex-typing: Theory and research*. New York: Preager.

Martin, C. L., & Ruble, D. N., & Szkrybalo, J. (2002). Cognitive theories of early gender development, *Psychological Bulletin, 128*, 903–933.

Martin, F. N., & Clark, J. G. (2002). *Introduction to audiology* (8th ed.). New York: Allyn & Bacon.

Martin, G. B., & Clark, R. D., III. (1982). Distress crying in neonates: Species and peer specificity. *Developmental Psychology, 18*, 3–9.

Martin, J. A., Hamilton, B. E., Sutton, P. D., Ventura, S. J., Menacker, F., & Munson, M. L. (2005). *Births: Final data for 2003*. National Vital Statistics Reports, 54. Hyattsville, MD: National Center for Health Statistics. Available at: www.cdc.gov/nchs/data/nvsr/nvsr54/nvsr54_02.pdf. Accessed: February 14, 2007.

Martin, K. A. (1996). *Puberty, sexuality, and the self: Girls and boys at adolescence*. New York: Routledge.

Martin, M., Grunendahl, M., & Martin, P. (2001). Age differences in stress, social resources, and well-being in middle and old age. *Journal of Gerontology: Psychological Sciences, 56*, 214–222.

Martin, M., & Lantos, J. (2005). Bioethics meets the barrio: Community-based research involving children. In E. Kodish (Ed.), *Ethics and research with children: A case-based approach*. Cary, NC: Oxford University Press.

Martin, M. O., Mullis, I. V. S., Gonzalez, E. J., & Chrostowski, S. J. (2004). *TIMSS 2003 international science report: Findings from IEA's trends in international mathematics and science study at the fourth and eighth grades*. Chestnut Hill, MA: TIMSS & PIRLS International Study Center, Boston College.

Martin, R. A. (2007). *The psychology of humor: An integrative approach*. Burlington, MA: Elsevier Academic Press.

Martin, R. P., Dombrowski, S. C., Mullis, C., Wisenbaker, J., & Huttunen, M. O. (2006). Smoking during pregnancy: Association with childhood temperament, behavior, and academic performance. *Journal of Pediatric Psychology, 31*, 490–500.

Martinez, G. M., Chandra, A., Abma, J. C., Jones, J., & Mosher, W. D. (2006). Fertility, contraception, and fatherhood: Data on men and women from cycle 6 (2002) of the National Survey of Family Growth. *Vital Health Statistics, 23*. Available at: www.cdc.gov/nchs/nsfg.htm.

Martlew, M., & Connolly, K. J. (1996). Human figure drawings by schooled and unschooled children in Papua New Guinea. *Child Development, 67*, 2743–2762.

Martorano, S. C. (1977). A developmental analysis of performance on Piaget's formal operations tasks. *Developmental Psychology, 13*, 666–672.

Martorell, G. A., & Bugental, D. B. (2006). Maternal variations in stress reactivity: Implications for harsh parenting practices with very young children. *Journal of Family Psychology, 20*, 641–647.

Masataka, N. (2000). The role of modality and input in the earliest stage of language acquisition: Studies of Japanese sign language. In C. Chamberlain, J. Morford, & R. Mayberry, R. I. (Eds.), *Language acquisition by eye* (pp. 3–24). Mahwah, NJ: Lawrence Erlbaum.

Massie, R. K., & Massie, S. (1975). *Journey*. New York: Knopf.

Masson, J. M. (1984). *The assault on truth: Freud's suppression of the seduction theory*. New York: Farrar, Straus, and Giroux.

Masten, A. S., & Reed, M. J. (2002). Resilience in development. In C. R. Snyder & S. J. Lopez (Eds.), *Handbook of positive psychology* (pp. 74–88). New York: Oxford University Press.

Masters, W. H., & Johnson, V. E. (1966). *Human sexual response*. Boston: Little, Brown.

Masters, W. H., & Johnson, V. E. (1970). *Human sexual inadequacy*. Boston: Little, Brown.

Mathews, F., Youngman, L, & Neil, A. (2004). Maternal circulating nutrient concentrations in pregnancy: Implications for birth and placental weights of term infants. *American Journal of Clinical Nutrition, 79*, 103–110.

Mathews, J. (2003, Oct. 1). Not quite piling on the homework. *The Washington Post*, A1, A4.

Mathews, T. J., & MacDorman, M. F. (2006). Infant mortality statistics from the 2003 period linked birth/infant death data set. *National Vital Statistics Reports: From the Centers for Disease Control and Prevention National Center for Health Statistics, 54*, 1–29.

Matsuba, M. K., & Walker, L. J. (2004). Extraordinary moral commitment: Young adults involved in social organizations. *Journal of Personality, 72*, 413–436.

Mattes, R. D. (2002). The chemical senses and nutrition in aging: Challenging old assumptions. *Journal of the American Dietetic Association, 102*, 192–196.

Matthews, K. A. (1992). Myths and realities of the menopause. *Psychosomatic Medicine, 54*, 1–9.

Matthews, K. A., Wing, R. R., Kuller, L. H., Meilahn, E. N., Kelsey, S. F., Costello, E. J., & Caggiula, A. W. (1990). Influences of natural menopause on psychological characteristics and symptoms of middle-aged healthy women. *Journal of Consulting and Clinical Psychology, 58*, 345–351.

Matusov, E., & Hayes, R. (2000). Sociocultural critique of Piaget and Vygotsky. *New Ideas in Psychology, 18*, 215–239.

Maughan, B. (2001). Conduct disorder in context. In J. Hill & B. Maughan (Eds.), *Conduct disorders in childhood and adolescence*. New York: Cambridge University Press.

Maughan, B., & Rutter, M. (2001). Antisocial children grown up. In J. Hill & B. Maughan (Eds.), *Conduct disorders in childhood and adolescence*. New York: Cambridge University Press.

Maurer, A. (1961). The child's knowledge of non-existence. *Journal of Existential Psychiatry, 2*, 193–212.

Maurer, D., Lewis, T. L., Brent, H. P., & Levin, A. V. (1999). Rapid improvement in the acuity of infants after visual input. *Science, 286*, 108–110.

Maurer, D., & Maurer, C. (1988). *The world of the newborn*. New York: Basic Books.

Maurer, D., Mondloch, C. J., & Lewis, T. L. (2007). Sleeper effects. *Developmental Science, 10*, 40–47.

Maurer, D., Stager, C. L., & Mondloch, C. J. (1999). Cross-modal transfer of shape is difficult to demonstrate in one-month-olds. *Child Development, 70*, 1047–1057.

Maxon, A. B., & Brackett, D. (1992). *The hearing-impaired child: Infancy through high school years*. Boston: Andover Medical Publishers.

May, P. A., Fiorentiono, D., Gossage, P. J., Kalberg, W. O., Hoyme, E. H., Robinson, L. K., Coriale, G., Jones, K. L., del Campo, M., Tarani, L., Romeo, M., Kodituwakku, P. W., Deiana, L., Buckley, D., & Ceccanti, M. (2005). Epidemiology of FASD in a province in Italy: Prevalence and characteristics of children in a random sample of schools. *Alcoholism, Clinical and Experimental Research, 30*, 1562–1575.

Mayberry, R. I. (1994). The importance of childhood to language acquisition: Evidence from American Sign Language. In J. C. Goodman & H. C. Nusbaum (Eds.), *The development of speech perception: The transition from speech sounds to spoken words*. Cambridge, MA: MIT Press.

Mayberry, R. I., & Eichen, E. B. (1991). The long-lasting advantage of learning sign language in childhood: Another look at the critical period for language acquisition. *Journal of Memory and Language, 30*, 486–512.

Mayberry, R. I., Lock, E., & Kazmi, H. (2002). Linguistic ability and early language exposure. *Nature, 417*, 38.

Mayeux, L., & Cillessen, A. H. N. (2003). Development of social problem solving in early childhood: Stability, change, and associations with social competence. *Journal of Genetic Psychology, 164,* 153–173.

Mayseless, O., Danieli, R., & Sharabany, R. (1996). Adults' attachment patterns: Coping with separations. *Journal of Youth and Adolescence, 25,* 667–690.

Mayseless, O., & Scharf, M. (2007). Adolescents' attachment representations and their capacity for intimacy in close relationships. *Journal of Research on Adolescence, 17,* 23–50.

McAdams, D. P. (2005). Studying lives in time: A narrative approach. In R. Levy, P. Ghisletta, J. Le Goff, D. Spini, & E. Widmer (Eds.), *Advances in life course research. Vol. 10: Towards an interdisciplinary perspective on the life course.* Amsterdam: Elsevier.

McAdams, D. P., & Adler, J. M. (2006). How does personality develop? In D. K. Mroczek & T. D. Little (Eds.), *Handbook of personality development.* Mahwah, NJ: Erlbaum.

McAdams, D. P., Hart, H. M., & Maruna, S. (1998). The anatomy of generativity. In D. P. McAdams & E. de St. Aubin (Eds.), *Generativity and adult development: How and why we care for the next generation.* Washington, D.C.: American Psychological Association.

McAdams, D. P., & Logan, R. L. (2004). What is generativity? In E. de St. Aubin, D. P. McAdams, & T. Kim (Eds.), *The generative society: Caring for future generations.* Washington, D.C.: American Psychological Association.

McAdams, D. P., & Pals, J. L. (2006). A new Big Five: Fundamental principles for an integrative science of personality. *American Psychologist, 61,* 204–217.

McAdams, P. P., de St. Aubin, E., & Logan, R. L. (1993). Generativity among young, middle, and older adults. *Psychology and Aging, 8,* 221–230.

McAlister, A. L., Bandura, A., & Owen, S. V. (2006). Mechanisms of moral disengagement in support of military force: The impact of Sept. 11. *Journal of Social and Clinical Psychology, 25,* 141–165.

McAlister, A., & Peterson, C. C. (2006). Mental playmates: Siblings, executive functioning and theory of mind. *British Journal of Developmental Psychology, 24,* 733–751.

McCabe, D. L., Butterfield, K. D., & Trevino, L. K. (2006). Academic dishonesty in graduate business programs: Prevalence, causes, and proposed action. *Academy of Management Learning & Education, 5,* 294–305.

McCall, R. B. (1977). Challenges to a science of developmental psychology. *Child Development, 48,* 333–344.

McCall, R. B. (1981). Nature–nurture and the two realms of development: A proposed integration with respect to mental development. *Child Development, 52,* 1–12.

McCall, R. B. (1983). A conceptual approach to early mental development. In M. Lewis (Ed.), *Origins of intelligence: Infancy and early childhood* (2nd ed.). New York: Plenum.

McCall, R. B., Applebaum, M. I., & Hogarty, P. S. (1973). Developmental changes in mental test performance. *Monographs of the Society for Research in Child Development, 38* (3, Serial No. 150).

McCall, R. B., & Carriger, M. S. (1993). A meta-analysis of infant habituation and recognition memory performance as predictors of later IQ. *Child Development, 64,* 57–79.

McCartney, K. (2003). On the meaning of models: A signal amidst the noise. In A. C. Crouter & A. Booth (Eds.), *Children's influence on family dynamics. The neglected side of family relationships.* Mahwah, NJ: Erlbaum.

McCartney, K., Harris, M. J., & Bernieri, F. (1990). Growing up and growing apart: A developmental meta-analysis of twin studies. *Psychological Bulletin, 107,* 226–237.

McCarton, C. M., Brooks-Gunn, J., Wallace, I. F., Bauer, C. R., Bennett, F. C., Bernbaum, J. C., Broyles, S., Casey, P. H., McCormick, M. C., Scott, D. T., Tyson, J., Tonascia, J., & Meinert, C. L. (1997). Results at age 8 years of early intervention for low-birth-weight premature infants. *Journal of the American Medical Association, 277,* 126–132.

McCaul, E. J., Donaldson, G. A., Coladarci, T., & Davis, W. E. (1992). Consequences of dropping out of school: Findings from high school and beyond. *Journal of Educational Research, 85,* 198–207.

McClintock, M. K., & Herdt, G. (1996). Rethinking puberty: The development of sexual attraction. *Current Directions in Psychological Science, 5,* 178–183.

McCloskey, L. A., Figueredo, A. J., & Koss, M. P. (1995). The effects of systematic family violence on children's mental health. *Child Development, 66,* 1239–1261.

McConkie-Rosell, A., Finucane, B., Cronister, A., Abrams, L., Bennett, R. L., & Pettersen, B. J. (2005). Genetic counseling for Fragile X syndrome: Updated recommendations of the National Society of Genetic Counselors. *Journal of Genetic Counseling, 14,* 249–270.

McCormick, M. (1998). Mom's "BABY" vids sharpen new minds. *Billboard, 110,* 72–73.

McCormick, M. C., Brooks-Gunn, J., Buka, S. L., Goldman, J., Yu, J., Salganik, M., Scott, D. T., Bennett, F. C., Kay, L. L., Bernbaum, J. C., Bauer, C. R., Martin, C., Woods, E. R., Martin, A., & Casey, P. H. (2006). Early intervention in low birth weight infants: Results at 18 years of age for the Infant Health and Developmental Program. *Pediatrics, 117,* 771–780.

McCrae, R. R. (2004). Human nature and culture: A trait perspective. *Journal of Research in Personality 38,* 3–14.

McCrae, R. R., Arenberg, D., & Costa, P. T., Jr. (1987). Declines in divergent thinking with age: Cross-sectional, longitudinal, and cross-sequential analyses. *Psychology and Aging, 2,* 130–137.

McCrae, R. R., & Costa, P. T., Jr. (2003). *Personality in adulthood: A five-factor theory perspective* (2nd ed.). New York: Guilford Press.

McCrae, R. R., Costa, P. T., Jr., Ostendorf, F., Angleitner, A., Hrebickova, M., Avia, M. D., Sanz, J., Sanchez-Bernardos, M. L., Kusdil, M. E., Woodfield, R., Saunders, P. R., & Smith, P. B. (2000). Nature over nurture: Temperament, personality, and life span development. *Journal of Personality and Social Psychology, 78,* 173–186.

McCune, L., Vihman, M. M., Roug-Hellichius, L. Delery, D. B., & Gogate, L. L. (1996). Grunt communication in human infants (*Homo sapiens*). *Journal of Comparative Psychology, 110,* 27–27.

McDonald, R., Jouriles, E. N., Ramisetty-Mikler, S., Caetano, R., & Green, C. E. (2006). Estimating the number of American children living in partner-violent families. *Journal of Family Psychology, 20,* 137–142.

McFarlane, J. A., & Williams, T. M. (1990). The enigma of premenstrual syndrome. *Canadian Psychology, 31,* 95–108.

McGhee, P. E. (1979). *Humor: Its origin and development.* San Francisco: Freeman.

McGhee-Bidlack, B. (1991). The development of noun definitions: A metalinguistic analysis. *Journal of Child Language, 18,* 417–434.

McGoldrick, M., Almeida, R., Hines, P. M., Garcia-Preto, N., Rosen, E., & Lee, E. (1991). Mourning in different cultures. In F. Walsh & M. McGoldrick (Eds.), *Living beyond loss: Death in the family.* New York: W. W. Norton.

McGrath, E. P., & Repetti, R. L. (2000). Mothers' and fathers' attitudes toward their children's academic performance and children's perceptions of their academic competence. *Journal of Youth and Adolescence, 29,* 713–723.

McGue, M., Bouchard, T. J., Jr., Iacono, W. G., & Lykken, D. T. (1993). Behavioral genetics of cognitive ability: A life-span perspective. In R. Plomin & G. E. McClearn (Eds.), *Nature, nurture, and psychology.* Washington, D.C.: American Psychological Association.

McGue, M., Elkins, I., Walden, B., & Iacono, W. G. (2005). Perceptions of the parent–adolescent relationship: A longitudinal investigation. *Developmental Psychology, 41,* 971–984.

McGuire, S., Manke, B., Eftekhari, A., & Dunn, J. (2000). Children's perceptions of sibling conflict during middle childhood: Issues and sibling (dis)similarity. *Social Development, 9,* 173–190.

McHale, J., Khazan, I., Erera, P., Rotman, T., DeCourcey, W., & McConnell, M. (2002). Coparenting in diverse family systems. In M. H. Bornstein (Ed.), *Handbook of parenting: Vol. 3. Being and becoming a parent* (2nd ed.). Mahwah, NJ: Erlbaum.

McHale, S. M., Kim, J., & Whiteman, S. D. (2006). Sibling relationships in childhood and adolescence. In P. Noller & J. A. Feeney (Eds.), *Close relationships: Functions, forms, and processes.* New York: Psychology Press.

McIntosh, D. N., Reichmann-Decker, A., Winkielman, P., & Wilbarger, J. L. (2006). When the social mirror breaks: Deficits in automatic, but not voluntary, mimicry of emotional facial expressions in autism. *Developmental Science, 9,* 295–302.

McIntosh, G. C., Olshan, A. F., & Baird, P. A. (1995). Paternal age and the risk of birth defects in offspring. *Epidemiology, 6,* 282–288.

McKay, K. E., Halperin, J. M., Schwartz, S. T., & Sharma, V. (1994). Developmental analysis of three aspects of information processing: Sustained attention, selective attention, and response organization. *Developmental Neuropsychology, 10,* 121–132.

McKusick, V. A. (1990). *Mendelian inheritance in man* (9th ed.) Baltimore: Johns Hopkins Press.

McLanahan, S. S., & Sorensen, A. B. (1985). Life events and psychological well-being over the life course. In G. H. Elder Jr. (Ed.), *Life course dynamics: Trajectories and transitions, 1968–1980.* Ithaca, NY: Cornell University Press.

McLean, K. C., & Pratt, M. W. (2006). Life's little (and big) lessons: Identity statuses and meaning-making in the turning point narratives of emerging adults. *Developmental Psychology, 42,* 714–722.

McLoyd, V. C. (1990). The impact of economic hardship on black families and children: Psychological distress, parenting, and socioemotional development. *Child Development, 61,* 311–346.

McLoyd, V. C., Cauce, A. M., Takeuchi, D., & Wilson, L. (2000). Marital processes and parental socialization in families of color: A decade review of research. *Journal of Marriage and the Family, 62,* 1070–1093.

McMaster, J., Pitts, M., & Poyah, G. (1997). The menopausal experiences of women in a developing country—There is a time for everything—To be a teenager, a mother and a granny. *Women and Health, 26,* 1–14.

McNeill, D. (1970). *The acquisition of language.* New York: Harper & Row.

McNulty, J. K. & Fisher, T. D. (2007, July 20). Gender differences in response to sexual expectancies and changes in sexual frequency: A short-term longitudinal study of sexual satisfaction in newly married couples. *Archives of Sexual Behavior* (in press).

McPherson, M., Smith-Lovin, L., & Brashears, M. E. (2006). Social isolation in America: Changes in core discussion networks over two decades. *American Sociological Review, 71,* 353–375.

Mead, G. H. (1934). *Mind, self, and society.* Chicago: University of Chicago Press.

Meadows, S. (2006). *The child as thinker: The development and acquisition of cognition in childhood* (2nd ed). New York: Routledge.

Meadows-Orlans, K. P., & Orlans, H. (1990). Responses to loss of hearing in later life. In D. F. Moores & K. P. Meadows-Orlans, (Eds.), *Educational and developmental aspects of deafness.* Washington, D.C.: Gallaudet University Press.

Mealey, L. (2005). Evolutionary psychopathology and abnormal development. In R. L. Burgess & K. MacDonald (Eds.), *Evolutionary perspectives on human development.* Thousand Oaks, CA: Sage.

Measelle, J. R., John, O. P., Ablow, J. C., Cowan, P. A., & Cowan, C. P. (2005). Can children provide coherent, stable, and valid self-reports on the Big Five dimensions? A longitudinal study from ages 5 to 7. *Journal of Personality and Social Psychology, 89,* 90–106.

Medina, J. J. (1996). *The clock of ages: Why we age—how we age—winding back the clock.* Cambridge, England: Cambridge University Press.

Medvedev, Z. A. (1991). The structural basis of aging. In F. C. Ludwig (Ed.), *Life span extension: Consequences and open questions.* New York: Springer.

Meeus, W., Iedema, J., Helsen, M., & Vollebergh, W. (1999). Patterns of adolescent identity development: Review of literature and longitudinal analysis. *Developmental Review, 19,* 419–461.

Mehan, H., Villanueva, I., Hubbard, L., & Lintz, A. (1996). *Constructing school success: The consequences of untracking low-achieving students.* New York: Cambridge University Press.

Meier, R. P. (1991). Language acquisition by deaf children. *American Scientist, 79,* 69–70.

Meijer, J., & Elshout, J. J. (2001). The predictive and discriminant validity of the zone of proximal development. *British Journal of Educational Psychology, 71,* 93–113.

Meikle, S., Steiner, C. A., Zhang, J., Lawrence, W. L. (2005). A national estimate of the elective primary cesarean delivery rate. *Obstetrics & Gynecology, 105,* 751–756.

Meilman, P. W. (1979). Cross-sectional age changes in ego identity status during adolescence. *Developmental Psychology, 15,* 230–231.

Meins, E., Fernyhough, C., Wainwright, R., Gupta, M., Fradley, E., & Tuckey, M. (2002). Maternal mind-mindedness and attachment security as predictors of theory of mind understanding. *Child Development, 73,* 1715–1726.

Mellinger, J. C., & Erdwins, C. J. (1985). Personality correlates of age and life roles in adult women. *Psychology of Women Quarterly, 9,* 503–514.

Meltzoff, A. N. (1988). Infant imitation and memory: Nine-month-olds in immediate and deferred tests. *Child Development, 59,* 216-225.

Meltzoff, A. N. (1995). What infant memory tells us about infantile amnesia: Long-term recall and deferred imitation. *Journal of Experimental Child Psychology, 59,* 497–515.

Meltzoff, A. N. (2004). Imitation as a mechanism of social cognition: Origins of empathy, theory of mind, and the representation of action. In U. Goswami (Ed.), *Blackwell handbook of childhood cognitive development* (pp. 6–25). Malden, MA: Blackwell Publishing.

Meltzoff, A. N., & Moore, M. K. (1997). Explaining facial imitation: Theoretical model. *Early Development and Parenting, 6,* 179–192.

Melzer, D., Hurst, A. J., & Frayling, T. (2007). Genetic variation and human aging: Progress and prospects. *Journal of Gerontology: Medical Sciences, 62A,* 301–307.

Memon, A., & Vartoukian, R. (1996). The effects of repeated questioning on young children's eyewitness testimony. *British Journal of Psychology, 87,* 403–415.

Menaghan, E. G., & Lieberman, M. A. (1986). Changes in depression following divorce: A panel study. *Journal of Marriage and the Family, 48,* 319–328.

Mennella, J. A., & Beauchamp, G. K. (2002). Flavor experiences during formula feeding are related to preferences during childhood. *Early Human Development, 68,* 71–82.

Mennella, J. A., Giffin, C. E., & Beauchamp, G. K. (2004). Flavor programming during infancy. *Pediatrics, 113,* 840–845.

Mennella, J. A., Jagnow, C. P., & Beauchamp, G. K. (2001). Prenatal and postnatal flavor learning by human infants. *Pediatrics, 107,* E88.

Mennella, J. A., Kennedy, J. M., & Beauchamp, G. K. (2006). Vegetable acceptance by infants: Effects of formula flavors. *Early Human Development, 82,* 463–368.

Mennella, J. A., Pepino, M. Y., & Reed, D. R. (2005). Genetic and environmental determinants of bitter perception and sweet preferences. *Pediatrics, 115,* E216–222.

Ment, L. R., Vohr, B., Allan, W., Katz, K. H., Schneider, K. C., Westerveld, M., Duncan, C. C., & Makuch, R. W. (2003). Change in cognitive function over time in very low-birth-weight infants. *Journal of the American Medical Association, 289,* 705–711.

Mercer, J. (2006). *Understanding attachment: Parenting, child care, and emotional development.* Westport, CT: Praeger.

Meredith, P., & Noller, P. (2003). Attachment and infant difficultness in postnatal depression. *Journal of Family Issues, 24,* 668–686.

Merrick, J., Merrick, E., Morad, M., & Kandel, I. (2006). Fetal alcohol syndrome and its long-term effects. *Minerva Pediatrica, 58,* 211–218.

Merzenich, M. M., Jenkins, W. M., Johnston, P., Schreiner, C., Miller, S. L., & Tallal, P. (1996). Temporal processing deficits of language-learning impaired children ameliorated by training. *Science, 271,* 77–81.

Meschke, L. L., Zweig, J. M., Barber, B. L., & Eccles, J. S. (2000). Demographic, biological, psychological, and social predictors of the timing of first intercourse. *Journal of Research on Adolescence, 10,* 315–338.

Mesman, J., Bongers, I. L., & Koot, H. M. (2001). Preschool developmental pathways to preadolescent internalizing and externalizing problems. *Journal of Child Psychology and Psychiatry and Allied Disciplines, 42,* 679–689.

Messer, D. J., McCarthy, M. E., McQuiston, S., MacTurk, R. H., Yarrow, L. J., & Vietze, P. M. (1986). Relation between mastery behavior in infancy and competence in early childhood. *Developmental Psychology, 22,* 366–372.

Messinger-Rapport, B. J. (2003). Assessment and counseling of older drivers: A guide for primary care physicians. *Geriatrics, 58,* 16.

Metcalf, P., & Huntington, R. (1991). *Celebrations of death. The anthropology of mortuary ritual* (2nd ed.). Cambridge, England: Cambridge University Press.

Meydani, M. (2001). Nutrition interventions in aging and age-associated disease. In S. C. Park, E. S. Hwang, H. Kim, & W. Park (Eds.), *Annals of the New York Academy of Sciences: Vol. 928. Molecular and cellular interactions in senescence.* New York: The New York Academy of Sciences.

Meyer-Bahlburg, H. F., Dolezal, C., Baker, S. W., Ehrhardt, A. A., & New, M. I. (2006). Gender development in women with congenital adrenal hyperplasia as a function of disorder severity. *Archives of Sexual Behavior, 35,* 667–684.

Meyer-Bahlburg, H. F. L., Ehrhardt, A. A., Rosen, L. R., & Gruen, R. S. (1995). Prenatal estrogens and the development of homosexual orientation. *Developmental Psychology, 31,* 12–21.

Midgley, C., Feldlaufer, H., & Eccles, J. S. (1989). Student/teacher relations and attitudes toward mathematics before and after the transition to junior high school. *Child Development, 60,* 981–992.

Midlarsky, E., Kahana, E., Corley, R., Nemeroff, R., & Schonbar, R. A. (1999). Altruistic moral judgment among older adults. *International Journal of Aging and Human Development, 49,* 27–41.

Mikulincer, M., & Shaver, P. R. (2003). The attachment behavioral system in adulthood: Activation, psychodynamics, and interpersonal processes. In M. P. Zanna (Eds.), *Advances in experimental social psychology* (Vol. 35). San Diego: Academic Press.

Miller, A. (1985). A developmental study of the cognitive basis of performance impairment after failure. *Journal of Personality and Social Psychology, 49,* 529–538.

Miller, E. R., III, Pastor-Barriuso, R., Dalal, D., Riemersma, R. A. Appel, L. J., & Guallar, E. (2005). Meta-analysis: High-dosage vitamin E supplementation may increase all-cause mortality. *Annals of Internal Medicine, 142,* 37–46.

Miller, J., & Knudsen, D. D. (2007). *Family abuse and violence: A social problems perspective.* Lanham, MD: AltaMira Press.

Miller, J. A. (1995). Strictest diet avoids subtle detriments of PKU. *Bioscience, 45,* 244–245.

Miller, J. B., & Hoicowitz, T. (2004). Attachment contexts of adolescent friendship and romance. *Journal of Adolescence, 27,* 191–206.

Miller, J. G. (2006). Insight into moral development from cultural psychology. In M. Killen & J. G. Smetana (Eds.), *Handbook of moral development*. Mahwah, NJ: Erlbaum.

Miller, M. (2005). Refusal to undergo a cesarean section: A woman's right or a criminal act? *Health Matrix. Journal of Law-Medicine, 15,* 383–400.

Miller, N. B., Cowan, P. A., Cowan, C. P., Hetherington, E. M., & Clingempeel, W. G. (1993). Externalizing in preschoolers and early adolescents: A cross-study replication of a family model. *Developmental Psychology, 29,* 3–18.

Miller, P. H. (1990). The development of strategies of selective attention. In D. F. Bjorklund (Ed.), *Children's strategies: Contemporary views of cognitive development*. Hillsdale, NJ: Erlbaum.

Miller, P. H. (1994). Individual differences in children's strategic behavior: Utilization deficiencies. *Learning and Individual Differences, 6,* 285–307.

Miller, P. H. (2002). *Theories of developmental psychology* (4th ed.). New York: Worth.

Miller, P. H., & Seier, W. S. (1994). Strategy utilization deficiencies in children: When, where and why. In H. W. Reese (Ed.), *Advances in Child Development and Behavior* (Vol. 25, pp. 107–156). New York: Academic Press.

Miller, P. H., & Weiss, M. G. (1981). Children's attention allocation, understanding of attention, and performance on the incidental learning task. *Child Development, 52,* 1183–1190.

Miller, R. A. (2004). Extending life: Scientific prospects and political obstacles. In S. G. Post & R. H. Binstock (Eds.), *The Fountain of Youth: Cultural, scientific, and ethical perspectives on a biomedical goal*. New York: Oxford University Press.

Miller, R. A. (2005). Genetic approaches to the study of aging. *Journal of the American Geriatrics Society, 53,* S284–S286.

Miller, S. A. (1986). Parents' beliefs about their children's cognitive abilities. *Developmental Psychology, 22,* 276–284.

Miller, T. R., & Taylor, D. M. (2005). Adolescent suicidality: Who will ideate, who will act? *Suicide and Life-Threatening Behavior, 35,* 425–435.

Miller-Johnson, S., Costanzo, P. R., Coie, J. D., Rose, M. R., Browne, D. C., & Johnson, C. (2003). Peer social structure and risk-taking behaviors among African American early adolescents. *Journal of Youth and Adolescence, 32,* 375–384.

Miller-Loncar, C., Lester, B. M., Seifer, R., Lagasse, L. L., Bauer, C. R., Shankaran, S., Bada, H. S., Wright, L. L., Smeriglio, V. L., Bigsby, R. & Liu, J. (2005). Predictors of motor development in children prenatally exposed to cocaine. *Neurotoxicology and Teratology, 27,* 213–220.

Mills-Koonce, W. R., Gariepy, J., Propper, C., Sutton, K., Calkins, S., Moore, G., & Cox, M. (2007). Infant and parent factors associated with early maternal sensitivity: A caregiver-attachment systems approach. *Infant Behavior and Development, 30,* 114–126.

Milos, G., Spindler, A., Schnyder, U., Martz, J., Hoek, H. W., & Willi, J. (2004). Incidence of severe anorexia nervosa in Switzerland: 40 years of development. *International Journal of Eating Disorders, 35,* 250–258.

Minard, K. L., Freudigman, K., & Thoman, E. B. (1999). Sleep rhythmicity in infants: Index of stress or maturation. *Behavioral Processes, 47,* 189–206.

Mineka, S., & Zinbarg, R. (2006). A contemporary learning theory perspective on the etiology of anxiety disorders. *American Psychology, 61,* 10–26.

Mingroni, M. A. (2004). The secular rise in IQ: Giving heterosis a closer look. *Intelligence, 32,* 65–83.

Minnes, S., Singer, L. T., Arendt, R., & Satayathum, S. (2005). Effects of prenatal cocaine/polydrug use on maternal–infant feeding interactions during the first year of life. *Journal of Developmental and Behavioral Pediatrics, 26,* 194–200.

Miralt, G., Bearor, K., & Thomas, T. (2001–2002). Adult romantic attachment among women who experienced childhood maternal loss. *Omega: Journal of Death and Dying, 44,* 97–104.

Mischel, W. (1973). Toward a cognitive social learning reconceptualization of personality. *Psychological Review, 80,* 252–283.

Mishara, B. L. (1999). Synthesis of research and evidence on factors affecting the desire of terminally ill or seriously chronically ill persons to hasten death. *Omega: Journal of Death and Dying, 39,* 1–70.

Mishori, R. (2006, January 10). Increasingly, wired for sound. *The Washington Post,* pp. F1, F5.

Mitchell, P. (1997). *Introduction to theory of mind: Children, autism, and apes*. London: Arnold.

Miyamoto, R. T., Houston, D. M., & Bergeson, T. (2005). Cochlear implantation in deaf infants. *Laryngoscope, 115,* 1376–1380.

Miyawaki, K., Strange, W., Verbrugge, R., Liberman, A. M., Jenkins, J. J., & Fujimura, D. (1975). An effect of linguistic experience: The discrimination of [r] and [l] by native speakers of Japanese and English. *Perception and Psychophysics, 18,* 331–340.

MMWR. (2006a). Racial and socioeconomic disparities in breastfeeding—United States, 2004. *Morbidity and Mortality Weekly Report, 55,* 335–339.

MMWR. (2006b). Visual impairment and eye care among older adults—five states, 2005. *Mortality and Morbidity Weekly Report,* December 2006. Available at: www.cdc.gov/mmwr/preview/mmwrhtml/mm5549a1.htm. Accessed: June 19, 2007.

Modell, J., & Elder, G. H., Jr. (2002). Children develop in history: So what's new? In W. W. Hartup & R. A. Weinberg (Eds.), *Child psychology in retrospect and prospect. The Minnesota Symposium* (Vol. 32). Mahwah, NJ: Erlbaum.

Moen, P. (1992). *Women's two roles: A contemporary dilemma*. New York: Auburn House.

Moen, P., & Wethington, E. (1999). Midlife development in a life course context. In S. L. Willis & J. D. Reid (Eds.), *Life in the middle. Psychological and social development in middle age*. San Diego: Academic Press.

Moerk, E. L. (1989). The LAD was a lady and the tasks were ill-defined. *Developmental Psychology, 9,* 21–57.

Moffitt, T. E., & Caspi, A. (2001). Childhood predictors differentiate life-course persistent and adolescence-limited antisocial pathways among males and females. *Development and Psychopathology, 13,* 355–375.

Moffitt, T. E., Harrington, H., Caspi, A., Kim-Cohen, J., Goldberg, D., Gregory, A. M., & Poulton, R. (2007). Depression and generalized anxiety disorder: Cumulative and sequential comorbidity in a birth cohort followed prospectively to age 32 years. *Archives of General Psychiatry, 64,* 651–660.

Moffitt, T. E., & Melchior, M. (2007). Why does the worldwide prevalence of childhood attention deficit hyperactivity disorder matter? *American Journal of Psychiatry, 164,* 856–858.

Mohr, P. E., Feldman, J. J., Dunbar, J. L., McConkey-Robbins, A., Niparko, J. K., Rittenhouse, R. K., & Skinner, M. W. (2000). The societal costs of severe to profound hearing loss in the United States. *International Journal of Technology and Assessment of Health Care, 16,* 1120–1135.

Molfese, D. L. (2000). Predicting dyslexia at 8 years of age using neonatal brain responses. *Brain and Language, 72,* 238–245.

Molina, B. S. G., & Chassin, L. (1996). The parent–adolescent relationship at puberty: Hispanic ethnicity and parent alcoholism as moderators. *Developmental Psychology, 32,* 675–686.

Molinari, V. (1999). Using reminiscence and life review as natural therapeutic strategies in group therapy. In M. Duffy (Ed.), *Handbook of counseling and psychotherapy with older adults*. New York: Wiley.

Molyneux, C. S., Wassenaar, D. R., Peshu, N., & Marsh, K. (2005). 'Even if they ask you to stand by a tree all day, you will have to do it (laughter)...!': Community voices on the notion and practice of informed consent for biomedical research in developing countries. *Social Science and Medicine, 61,* 443–454.

Money, J. (1985). Pediatric sexology and hermaphroditism. *Journal of Sex and Marital Therapy, 11,* 139–156.

Money, J. (1988). *Gay, straight, and in-between: The sexology of erotic orientation*. New York: Oxford University Press.

Money, J., & Ehrhardt, A. (1972). *Man and woman, boy and girl*. Baltimore: Johns Hopkins University Press.

Money, J., & Tucker, P. (1975). *Sexual signatures: On being a man or a woman*. Boston: Little, Brown.

Montemayor, R., & Eisen, M. (1977). The development of self-conceptions from childhood to adolescence. *Developmental Psychology, 13,* 314–319.

Montgomery, M. J. (2005). Psychosocial intimacy and identity: From early adolescence to emerging adulthood. *Journal of Adolescent Research, 20,* 346–374.

Moore, D. S., & Cocas, L. A. (2006). Perception precedes computation: Can familiarity preferences explain apparent calculation by human babies? *Developmental Psychology, 42,* 666–678.

Moore, E. G. J. (1986). Family socialization and the IQ test performance of traditionally and transracially adopted black children. *Developmental Psychology, 22,* 317–326.

Moore, K. L. (1988). *The developing human*. Philadelphia: W. B. Saunders.

Moore, M., & Carr, A. (2000). Depression and grief. In A. Carr (Ed.), *What works with children and adolescents?: A critical review of psychological interventions with children, adolescents, and their families*. Florence, KY: Taylor & Francis/Routledge.

Moore, M. K., & Meltzoff, A. N. (1999). New findings on object permanence: A developmental difference between two types of occlusion. *British Journal of Developmental Psychology, 17,* 563–584.

Moore, S. M. (1995). Girls' understanding and social constructions of menarche. *Journal of Adolescence, 18,* 87–104.

Moorehouse, M. J. (1991). Linking maternal employment patterns to mother–child activities and children's school competence. *Developmental Psychology, 27,* 295–303.

Moraga, A. V., Rodriguez-Pascual, C. (2007). Accurate diagnosis of delirium in elderly patients. *Current Opinion in Psychiatry, 20,* 262–267.

Morgan, G. A., MacTurk, R. H., & Hrncir, E. J. (1995). Mastery motivation: Overview, definitions, and conceptual issues. In R. H. MacTurk & G. A. Morgan (Eds.), *Mastery motivation: Origins, conceptualizations, and applications.* Norwood, NJ: Ablex.

Morgan, G. A., & Ricciuti, H. N. (1969). Infants' responses to strangers during the first year. In B. M. Foss (Ed.), *Determinants of infant behavior* (Vol. 4). London: Methuen.

Morin, R. (2003, January 9). Words matter. *The Washington Post,* B5.

Morizot, J., & Le Blanc, M. (2003). Continuity and change in personality traits from adolescence to midlife: A 25-year longitudinal study comparing representative and adjudicated men. *Journal of Personality, 71,* 705–755.

Morrell, R. W., Park, D. C., & Poon, L. W. (1989). Quality of instructions on prescription drug labels: Effects on memory and comprehension in young and old adults. *Gerontologist, 29,* 345–354.

Morris, J. (1999, October 18). Assessing children's toxic risks. *U.S. News & World Report,* 80.

Morrongiello, B. A., Fenwick, K. D., Hillier, L., & Chance, G. (1994). Sound localization in newborn human infants. *Developmental Psychobiology, 27,* 519–538.

Morrongiello, B. A., & Hogg, K. (2004). Mothers' reactions to children misbehaving in ways that can lead to injury: Implications for gender differences in children's risk taking and injuries. *Sex Roles, 50,* 1003–1118.

Morrow, D., Leirer, V., Altieri, P., & Fitzsimmons, C. (1994). When expertise reduces age differences in performance. *Psychology and Aging, 9,* 134–148.

Morse, C. A., Dudley, E., Guthrie, J., & Dennerstein, L. (1998). Relationships between premenstrual complaints and perimenopausal experiences. *Journal of Psychosomatic Obstetrics and Gynecology, 19,* 182–191.

Mortimer, J. T., Finch, M. D., & Kumka, D. (1982). Persistence and change in development: The multidimensional self-concept. In P. B. Baltes & O. G. Brim Jr. (Eds.), *Life-span development and behavior* (Vol. 4). New York: Academic Press.

Mortimer, J. T., Finch, M. D., Ryu, S., Shanahan, M. J., & Call, K. T. (1996). The effects of work intensity on adolescent mental health, achievement, and behavioral adjustment: New evidence from a prospective study. *Child Development, 67,* 1243–1261.

Moss, M. S., Moss, S. Z., Rubinstein, R., & Resch, N. (1993). Impact of elderly mother's death on middle age daughters. *International Journal of Aging and Human Development, 37,* 1–22.

Mroczek, D. K. (2004). Positive and negative affect at midlife. In O. G. Brim, C. D. Ryff, & R. C. Kessler (Eds.), *How healthy are we? A national study of well-being at midlife.* Chicago: University of Chicago Press.

Mroczek, D. K., & Spiro, A., III (2003). Modeling intraindividual change in personality traits: Findings from the Normative Aging Study. *Journal of Gerontology: Psychological Sciences, 58B,* P153–P165.

Mroczek, D. K., & Spiro, A., III (2006). Personality and aging. In J. E. Birren & K. W. Schaie (Eds.), *Handbook of the psychology of aging* (6th ed.). Burlington, MA: Elsevier Academic Press.

Mueller, E., & Lucas, T. (1975). A developmental analysis of peer interactions among toddlers. In M. Lewis & L. Rosenblum (Eds.), *Friendship and peer relations.* New York: Wiley.

Mundy, P. C., & Acra, C. F. (2006). Joint attention, social engagement, and the development of social competence. In P. J. Marshall & N. A. Fox (Eds.), *The development of social engagement: Neurobiological perspectives.* Oxford, NY: Oxford University Press.

Munro, G., & Adams, G. R. (1977). Ego–identity formation in college students and working youth. *Developmental Psychology, 13,* 523–524.

Munroe, R. L., Hulefeld, R., Rodgers, J. M., Tomeo, D. L., & Yamazaki, S. K. (2000). Aggression among children in four cultures. *Cross-Cultural Research, 34,* 3–25.

Munroe, R. L., & Romney, A. K. (2006). Gender and age differences in same-sex aggregation and social behavior: A four-culture study. *Journal of Cross-Cultural Psychology, 37,* 3–19.

Murnen, S. K., & Smolak, L. (1997). Femininity, masculinity and disordered eating: A meta-analytic review. *International Journal of Eating Disorders, 22,* 231–242.

Murphy, C. (1985). Cognitive and chemosensory influences on age-related changes in the ability to identify blended foods. *Journal of Gerontology, 40,* 47–52.

Murphy, C., Nordin, S., & Acosta, L. (1997). Odor learning, recall, and recognition memory in young and elderly adults. *Neuropsychology, 11,* 126–137.

Murphy, D. R., Craik, F. I. M., Li, K. Z. H., & Schneider, B. A. (2000). Comparing the effects of aging and background noise on short-term memory performance. *Psychology and Aging, 15,* 323–334.

Murphy, D. R., Daneman, M., & Schneider, B. A. (2006). Why do older adults have difficulty following conversations? *Psychology and Aging, 21,* 49–61.

Murphy, E. M. (2003). Being born female is dangerous for your health. *American Psychologist, 58,* 205–210.

Murphy, S. A., Johnson, C., & Lohan, J. (2003a). The effectiveness of coping resources and strategies used by bereaved parents 1 and 5 years after the violent deaths of their children. *Omega: Journal of Death and Dying, 47,* 25–44.

Murphy, S. A., Johnson, C., & Lohan, J. (2003b). Finding meaning in a child's violent death: A five-year prospective analysis of parents' personal narratives and empirical data. *Death Studies, 27,* 381–404.

Murray, C. (2006). Changes over time in the black–white difference on mental tests: Evidence from the children of the 1979 cohort of the National Longitudinal Survey of Youth. *Intelligence, 34,* 527–540.

Murray, C. J. L., Kulkarni, S. C., Michaud, C., Tomijima, N., Bulzacchelli, M. T., Iandiorio, T. J., & Ezzati, M. (2006). Eight Americas: Investigating mortality disparities across races, counties, and race-counties in the United States. *PLoS Medicine, 3,* 1513–1524. Available at: http://www.plosmedicine.org.

Murray, J. A., Terry, D. J., Vance, J. C., Battistutta, D., & Connolly, Y. (2000). Effects of a program of intervention on parental distress following infant death. *Death Studies, 24,* 275–305.

Murray, L., Fiori-Cowley, A., Hooper, R., & Cooper, P. (1996). The impact of postnatal depression and associated adversity on early mother–infant interactions and later infant outcome. *Child Development, 67,* 2512–2526.

Murray, L., Sinclair, D., Cooper, P., Ducournau, P., Turner, P., & Stein, A. (1999). The socio-emotional development of 5-year-old children of postnatally depressed mothers. *Journal of Child Psychology and Psychiatry, 40,* 1259–1271.

Murray-Close, D., Ostrov, J. M., & Crick, N. R. (2007). A short-term longitudinal study of growth of relational aggression during middle childhood: Associations with gender, friendship intimacy, and internalizing problems. *Development and Psychopathology, 19,* 187–203.

Mussen, P. H., & Rutherford, E. (1963). Parent–child relations and parental personality in relation to young children's sex-role preferences. *Child Development, 34,* 589–607.

Must, A., Jacques, P. F., Dallal, G. E., Bajema, C. J., & Dietz, W. H. (1992). Long-term morbidity and mortality of overweight adolescents: A follow-up of the Harvard Growth Study of 1922 to 1935. *New England Journal of Medicine, 327,* 1350–1355.

Mwamwenda, T. S. (1999). Undergraduate and graduate students' combinatorial reasoning and formal operations. *Journal of Genetic Psychology, 160,* 503–506.

Mwamwenda, T. S., & Mwamwenda, B. A. (1989). Formal operational thought among African and Canadian college students. *Psychological Reports, 64,* 43–46.

Myers, J., Jusczyk, P. W., Nelson, D. G. K., Charles-Luce, J., Woodward, A. L., & Hirsh-Pasek, K. (1996). Infants' sensitivity to word boundaries in fluent speech. *Journal of Child Language, 23,* 1–30.

Myers, J. K., Weissman, M. M., Tischler, G. L., Holzer, C. E., III, Leaf, P. J., & Orvaschel, H. (1984). Six-month prevalence of psychiatric disorders in three communities. *Archives of General Psychiatry, 41,* 959–967.

Myers, K. P., & Sclafani, A. (2006). Development of learned flavor preferences. *Developmental Psychobiology, 48,* 380–388.

Mylod, D. E., Whitman, T. L., & Borkowski, J. G. (1997). Predicting adolescent mothers' transition to adulthood. *Journal of Research on Adolescence, 7,* 457–478.

N

Nagumey, A. J., Reich, J. W., & Newsom, J. (2004). Gender moderates the effects of independence and dependence desires during the social support process. *Psychology and Aging, 19,* 215–218.

Naigles, L. G., & Gelman, S. A. (1995). Overextensions in comprehension and production revisited: Preferential-looking in a study of dog, cat, and cow. *Journal of Child Language, 22,* 19–46.

Najman, J. M., Vance, J. C., Boyle, F., Embleton, G., Foster, B., & Thearle, J. (1993). The impact of a child death on marital adjustment. *Social Science and Medicine, 37,* 1005–1010.

Najman, J. M., Williams, G. M., Nikles, J., Spence, S., Bor, W., O'Callaghan, M., Le Brocque, R., & Andersen, M. J. (2000). Mothers' mental illness and child behavior problems: Cause–effect association or observation bias? *Journal of the American Academy of Child and Adolescent Psychiatry, 39,* 592–602.

Nakajima, S., Saijo, Y., Kato, S., Sasaki, S., Uno, A., Kanagami, N., Hirakawa, H., Hori, T., Tobiishi, K., Todaka, T., Nakamura, Y., Yanagiya, S., Sengoku, Y., Iida, T., Sata, F., & Kishi, R. (2006). Effects of prenatal exposure to polychlorinated biphenyls and dioxins on mental and motor development in Japanese children at 6 months of age. *Environmental Health Perspectives, 114,* 773–778.

NAMS (2006). *Menopause Guidebook* (6th ed.). Cleveland, OH: The North American Menopause Society.

Nanez, J. E., & Yonas, A. (1994). Effects of luminance and texture motion on infant defensive reactions to optical collision. *Infant Behavior and Development, 17,* 165–174.

Nash, A., & Hay, D. F. (2003). Social relations in infancy: Origins and evidence. *Human Development, 46,* 222–232.

National Academy of Sciences. (2000). *Sleep needs, patterns and difficulties of adolescents: Summary of a workshop.* Available online: http://www.nap.edu/openbook/030907177/html/3.html.

National Campaign to Prevent Teen Pregnancy. (2003). *The case for the cautious generation (#2).* Available at: www.teenpregnancy.org.

National Campaign to Prevent Teen Pregnancy. (2005a). *Science says: Teens' attitudes toward sexual activity, 2002 (#14).* Available at: www.teenpregnancy.org.

National Campaign to Prevent Teen Pregnancy. (2005b). *Teens and oral sex (#17).* Available at: www.teenpregnancy.org.

National Campaign to Prevent Teen Pregnancy. (2006). *Teens' sexual experience, 1995–2002 (#22).* Available at: www.teenpregnancy.org.

National Center for Education Statistics. (1998). National Household Education Survey (NHES), "Adult Education Interview," 1991, 1995, 1999; Projections of Education Statistics to 2008 (NCES 98-016).

National Center for Education Statistics. (2007). *Dropout rates in the United States: 2005.* Available at: http://nces.ed.gov/pubs2007/dropout05/tables/table_11.asp. Accessed: July 19, 2007.

National Center for Health Statistics. (2005). *Health, United States, 2005 with Chartbook on trends in the health of Americans with special feature on adults 55–64.* Available at: http://www.cdc.gov/nchs/hus.htm.

National Center for Health Statistics. (2006a). *Infant health.* Available at: www.cdc.gov/nchs/fastats/infant_health.htm. Accessed: December 14, 2006.

National Center for Health Statistics. (2006b). *Health, United States, 2006, with chartbook on trends in the health of Americans.* Hyattsville, MD: U.S. Government Printing Office.

National Center for Health Statistics. (2007a). *Clinical growth charts.* Available at: www.cdc.gov/nchs/about/major/nhanes/growthcharts/clinical_charts.htm. Accessed: March 1, 2007.

National Center for Health Statistics. (2007b). *Deaths: Preliminary data for 2004.* Available at: www.cdc.gov/nchs/products/pubs/pubd/hestats/prelimdeaths04/preliminarydeaths04.htm. Accessed: April 17, 2007.

National Center for Injury Prevention and Control. (2007). *10 leading causes of death by age group, United States–2003.* Available at: www.cdc.gov/ncipc/osp/charts.htm. Accessed: February 23, 2007.

National Institute on Aging. (2000). *Progress report on Alzheimer's disease 2000. Taking the next steps* (NIH Publication No. 00-4859). Available at:www.alzheimers.org/pubs/prog00.htm.

National Institutes of Health. (2000). Phenylketonuria (PKU): Screening and management. *NIH Consensus Statement 2000 October 16–18, 17*(3), 1–33.

National Institutes of Health. (2006). *Newborn hearing screening.* Available at: www.nih.gov/about/researchresultsforthepublic/Newborn.pdf. Accessed: April 15, 2007.

National Reading Panel. (1999). *Teaching children to read: An evidence-based assessment of the scientific literature on reading and its implications for reading instruction.* Washington, D.C.: National Institute of Child Health & Human Development.

National Research Council. (2001). *Preparing for an aging world: The case for cross-national research.* Panel on a Research Agenda and New Data for an Aging World, Community on Population and Committee on National Statistics, Division of Behavioral, Social Sciences and Education. Washington, D.C.: National Academy Press.

National Sleep Foundation. (2004). Adolescent sleep needs and patterns: Research report and resource guide. Washington, D.C.: Author.

National Sleep Foundation. (2007). *Sleep for all ages.* Available at: www.sleepfoundation.org/site/c.huIXKjM0IxF/b.2417429/k.BD15/Sleep_for_All_Ages.htm. Accessed: March 7, 2007.

Neale, M. C., & Martin, N. G. (1989). The effects of age, sex, and genotype on self-report drunkenness following a challenge dose of alcohol. *Behavior Genetics, 19,* 63–78.

Needham, A. (1999). The role of shape in 4-month-old infants' object segregation. *Infant Behavior and Development, 22,* 161–178.

Neiderhiser, J. M., Reiss, D., Pedersen, N. L., Lichtenstein, P., Spotts, E. L., Hansson, K., Cederblad, M., & Ellhammer, O. (2004). Genetic and environmental influences on mothering of adolescents: A comparison of two samples. *Developmental Psychology, 40,* 335–351.

Neighbors, H. W., Caldwell, C., Williams, D. R., Nesse, R., Taylor, R. J., Bullard, K. M., Torres, M., & Jackson, J. S. (2007). Race, ethnicity, and the use of services for mental disorders: Results from the National Survey of American Life. *Archives of General Psychiatry, 64,* 485–494.

Neimark, E. D. (1975). Longitudinal development of formal operations thought. *Genetic Psychology Monographs, 91,* 171–225.

Neimark, E. D. (1979). Current status of formal operations research. *Human Development, 22,* 60–67.

Neisser, U., Boodoo, G., Bouchard, T. J., Jr., Boykin, A. W., Brody, N., Ceci, S. J., Halpern, D. F., Loehlin, J. C., Perloff, R., Sternberg, R. J., & Urbina, S. (1996). Intelligence: Knowns and unknowns. *American Psychologist, 51,* 77–101.

Nelson, C. A. & Luciana, M. (Eds.) (2001). *Handbook of developmental cognitive neuroscience.* MA: The MIT Press.

Nelson, C. A., Thomas, K. M., & de Haan, M. (2006). Neural bases of cognitive development. In D. Kuhn & R. Siegler (Vol. Eds.), *Handbook of child psychology: Vol. 2. Theoretical models of human development* (6th ed.). Hoboken, NJ: Wiley.

Nelson, G., Westhues, A., & MacLeod, J. (2003). A meta-analysis of longitudinal research on preschool prevention programs for children. *Prevention & Treatment, 6.* Available at: http://journals.apa.org/prevention/volume6/toc-dec18-03.html.

Nelson, K. (1973). Structure and strategy in learning to talk. *Monographs of the Society for Research in Child Development, 38* (Serial No. 149).

Nelson, K. (1986). *Event knowledge: Structure and function in development.* Hillsdale, NJ: Erlbaum.

Nelson, K. (1997). Event representations then, now, and next. In P. W. van den Broek & P. J. Bauer (Eds.), *Developmental spans in event comprehension and representation: Bridging fictional and actual events* (pp. 1–26). Mahwah, NJ: Erlbaum.

Nelson, K. (2007). *Young minds in social worlds: Experience, meaning, and memory.* Cambridge, MA: Harvard University Press.

Nelson, K., Hampson, J., & Shaw, L. K. (1993). Nouns in early lexicons: Evidence, explanations and implications. *Journal of Child Language, 20,* 61–84.

Nelson, K., & Hudson, J. (1988). Scripts and memory: Functional relationship in development. In F. E. Weinert & M. Perlmutter (Eds.), *Memory development: Universal changes and individual differences.* Hillsdale, NJ: Erlbaum.

Nelson, K., Skwerer, D. P., Goldman, S., Henseler, S., Presler, N., & Walkenfeld, F. F. (2003). Entering a community of minds: An experiential approach to "theory of mind." *Human Development, 46,* 24–46.

Nelson, S. A. (1980). Factors influencing young children's use of motives and outcomes as moral criteria. *Child Development, 51,* 823–829.

Nemeroff, C. B., Kalai, A., Keller, M. B., Charney, D. S. Lenderts, S. E., Cascade, E. F., Stephenson, H., & Schatzberg, A. F. (2007). Impact of publicity concerning pediatric suicidality data on physician practice patterns in the United States. *Archives of General Psychiatry, 64,* 466–472.

Nes, S. L. (2003). Using paired reading to enhance the fluency skills of less-skilled readers. *Reading Improvement, 40,* 179–193.

Nesse, R. M. (2000). Is depression an adaptation? *Archives of General Psychiatry, 57,* 14–20.

Nettelbeck, T., & Young, R. (1996). Intelligence and savant syndrome: Is the whole greater than the sum of the fragments? *Intelligence, 22,* 49–68.

Neugarten, B. L. (1968). Adult personality: Toward a psychology of the life cycle. In B. L. Neugarten (Ed.), *Middle age and aging: A* reader in social psychology. Chicago: University of Chicago Press.

Neugarten, B. L., Moore, J. W., & Lowe, J. C. (1965). Age norms, age constraints, and adult socialization. American Journal of Sociology, 70, 710–717.

Neville, B., & Parke, R. D. (1997). Waiting for paternity: Interpersonal and contextual implications of the timing of fatherhood. Sex Roles, 37, 45–59.

Neville, H. J., Coffey, S. A., Lawson, D. S., Fischer, A., Emmorey, K., & Bellugi, U. (1997). Neural systems mediating American Sign Language: Effects of sensory experience and age of acquisition. Brain and Language, 57, 285–308.

Newell, A., & Simon, H. A. (1961). Computer simulation of human thinking. Science, 134, 2011–2017.

Newell, K. M., Vaillancourt, D. E., & Sosnoff, J. J. (2006). Aging, complexity, and motor performance. In J. E. Birren & K. W. Schaie (Eds.), Handbook of the psychology of aging. Boston: Elsevier Academic Press.

Newell, M. L. (2003). Antenatal and perinatal strategies to prevent mother-to-child transmission of HIV infection. Transactions of the Royal Society of Tropical Medicine and Hygiene, 97, 22–24.

Newman, C., Atkinson, J., & Braddick, O. (2001). The development of reaching and looking preferences in infants to objects of different sizes. Developmental Psychology, 37, 561–572.

Newman, R., Ratner, N. B., Jusczyk, A. M., Jusczyk, P. W., & Dow, K. A. (2006). Infants' early ability to segment the conversational speech signal predicts later language development: A retrospective analysis. Developmental Psychology, 42, 643–655.

Newport, E. L. (1991). Contrasting conceptions of the critical period for language. In S. Carey & R. Gelman (Eds.), The epigenesis of mind: Essays on biology and cognition. Hillsdale, NJ: Erlbaum.

Nguyen, H. T., & Zonderman, A. B. (2006). Relationship between age and aspects of depression: Consistency and reliability across two longitudinal studies. Psychology and Aging, 21, 119–126.

NICHD. (2006). The NICHD study of early child care and youth development: Findings for children up to age 4½ years. Available at: www.nichd.nih.gov/publications/pubs.cfm.

NICHD Early Child Care Research Network. (1997). The effects of infant child care on infant-mother attachment security: Results of the NICHD Study of Early Child Care. Child Development, 68, 860–879.

NICHD Early Child Care Research Network. (2003). Does quality of child care affect child outcomes at age 4½? Developmental Psychology, 39, 451–469.

NICHD Early Child Care Research Network. (2005). Child care and child development: Results from the NICHD study of early child care and youth development. New York: Guilford.

NICHD Early Child Care Research Network. (2006). Child-care effect sizes for the NICHD Study of Early Child Care and Youth Development. American Psychologist, 61, 99–116.

Nicholls, J. G., & Miller, A. T. (1984). Reasoning about the ability of self and others: A developmental study. Child Development, 55, 1990–1999.

Nichols, M. (1999). Clinging to life. Maclean's, 112, 66.

Nicolich, L. M. (1977). Beyond sensorimotor intelligence: Assessment of symbolic maturity through analysis of pretend play. Merrill-Palmer Quarterly, 23, 89–99.

Nielsen, M., Dissanayake, C., & Kashima, Y. (2003). A longitudinal investigation of self–other discrimination and the emergence of minor self-recognition. Infant Behavior and Development, 26, 213–226.

Niles, W. (1986). Effects of a moral development discussion group on delinquent and predelinquent boys. Journal of Counseling Psychology, 33, 45–51.

Nilsson, L., Adolfsson, R., Bäckman, L., Cruts, M., Edvardsson, H., Nyberg, L., & Van Broeckhoven, C. (2002). Memory development in adulthood and old age: The Betula prospective-cohort study. In P. Graf & N. Ohta (Eds.), Lifespan development of human memory (pp. 185–204). Cambridge, MA: Massachusetts Institute of Technology.

Nilsson, M., Perfilieva, E., Johansson, U., Orwar, O., & Eriksson, P. S. (1999). Enriched environment increases neurogenesis in the adult rat dentate gyrus and improves spatial memory. Journal of Neurobiology, 39, 569–578.

Nippold, M. A., Hegel, S. L., Sohlberg, M. M., & Schwarz, I. E. (1999). Defining abstract entities: Development in pre-adolescents, adolescents, and young adults. Journal of Speech, Language, and Hearing Research, 42, 473–481.

No Child Left Behind Act of 2002 (U.S. Public Law 107-110).

Nolen-Hoeksema, S. (1990). Sex differences in depression. Stanford, CA: Stanford University Press.

Nolen-Hoeksema, S. (2002). Gender differences in depression. In I. H. Gotlib & C. L. Hammen (Eds.), Handbook of depression. New York: Guilford.

Nolen-Hoeksema, S., & Girgus, J. S. (1994). The emergence of gender differences in depression during adolescence. Psychological Bulletin, 115, 424–443.

Nolen-Hoeksema, S., Stice, E., Wade, E., & Bohon, C. (2007). Reciprocal relations between rumination and bulimic, substance abuse, and depressive symptoms in female adolescents. Journal of Abnormal Psychology, 116, 198–207.

Noller, P. (2006). Marital relationships. In P. Noller & J. A. Feeney (Eds.), Close relationships: Functions, forms, and processes. New York: Psychology Press.

Nomaguchi, K. M., & Milkie, M. A. (2003). Costs and rewards of children: The effects of becoming a parent on adults' lives. Journal of Marriage and the Family, 65, 356–374.

Noppe, I. C., & Noppe, L. D. (1997). Evolving meanings of death during early, middle, and later adolescence. Death Studies, 21, 253–275.

Nordin, S., Razani, L. J., Markison, S., & Murphy, C. (2003). Age-associated increases in intensity discrimination for taste. Experimental Aging Research, 29, 371–381.

Nordstrom, B. B., Sood, B. G., Sokol, R. J., Ager, J., Janisse, J., Hannigan, J. H., Covington, C., & Delaney-Black, V. (2005). Gender and alcohol moderate prenatal cocaine effects on teacher-report of child behavior. Neurotoxicology and Teratology, 27, 181–190.

Nordvik, H., & Amponsah, B. (1998). Gender differences in spatial abilities and spatial activity among university students in an egalitarian educational system. Sex Roles, 38, 1009–1023.

Norenzayan, A., & Heine, S. J. (2005). Psychological universals: What are they and how can we know? Psychological Bulletin, 131, 763–784.

Nourhashemi, F., Gillette-Guyonnet, S., Andrieu, S., Ghisolfi, A., Ousset, P. J., Grandjean, H., Grand, A., Pous, J., Vellas, B., & Albarede, J. L. (2000). Alzheimer disease: Protective factors. American Journal of Clinical Nutrition, 71, 643s–649s.

Nowell, A., & Hedges, L. V. (1998). Trends in gender differences in academic achievement from 1960 to 1994: An analysis of differences in mean, variance, and extreme scores. Sex Roles, 39, 21–43.

Nsamenang, A. B. (1992). Human development in cultural context: A third world perspective. Newbury Park, CA: Sage.

Nucci, L., & Turiel, E. (1993). God's word, religious rules, and their relation to Christian and Jewish children's concepts of morality. Child Development, 64, 1475–1491.

Nucci, L. P. (2001). Education in the moral domain. Cambridge, UK: Cambridge University Press.

Nucci, L. (2006). Education for moral development. In M. Killen & J. G. Smetana (Eds.), Handbook of moral development. Mahwah, NJ: Erlbaum.

Nulman, I., Ickowicz, A., Koren, G., & Knittel-Keren, D. (2007). Fetal alcohol spectrum disorder. In I. Brown & M. Percy (Eds.), A comprehensive guide to intellectual & developmental disabilities. Baltimore, MD: Paul H. Brookes.

Nyborg, H., & Jensen, A. R. (2001). Occupation and income related to psychometric g. Intelligence, 29, 45–55.

Nyborg, V. M, & Curry, J. F. (2003). The impact of perceived racism: Psychological symptoms among African American boys. Journal of Clinical Child and Adolescent Psychology, 32, 258–266.

Nydegger, C. N. (1986). Asymmetrical kin and the problematic son-in-law. In N. Datan, A. L. Greene, & H. W. Reese (Eds.), Life-span developmental psychology. Intergenerational relations. Hillsdale, NJ: Erlbaum.

O

Oakhill, J., Garnham, A., & Reynolds, D. (2005). Immediate activation of stereotypical gender information. Memory and Cognition, 33, 972–983.

Oberlander, S. E., Black, M. M., & Starr, R. H., Jr. (2007). African American adolescent mothers and grandmothers: A multigenerational approach to parenting. American Journal of Community Psychology, 39, 37–46.

Oberman, L. M., & Ramachandran, V. S. (2007). The simulated social mind: The role of the mirror neuron system and simulation in the social and communicative deficits of autism spectrum disorders. Psychological Bulletin, 133, 310–327.

Obler, L. K. (2005). Language in adulthood. In J. B. Gleason (Ed.), The development of language (6th ed.). Boston: Allyn & Bacon.

O'Brien, L. T., & Hummert, M. L. (2006). Memory performance of late middle-aged adults: Contrasting self-stereotyping and stereotype threat accounts of assimilation to age stereotypes. Social Cognition, 24, 338–358.

O'Brien, M. (1996). Child-rearing difficulties reported by parents of infants and toddlers. *Journal of Pediatric Psychology, 21*, 433–446.

O'Brien, M., Peyton, V., Mistry, R., Hruda, L., Jacobs, A., Caldera, Y., Huston, A., & Roy, C. (2000). Gender-role cognition in three-year-old boys and girls. *Sex Roles, 42*, 1007–1025.

Ochs, E. (1982). Talking to children in western Samoa. *Language in Society, 11*, 77–104.

Ochse, R. (1990). *Before the gates of excellence: The determinants of creative genius.* Cambridge, England: Cambridge University Press.

O'Connor, B. P. (1995). Family and friend relationships among older and younger adults: Interaction motivation, mood, and quality. *International Journal of Aging and Human Development, 40*, 9–29.

O'Connor, B. P., & Nikolic, J. (1990). Identity development and formal operations as sources of adolescent egocentrism. *Journal of Youth and Adolescence, 19*, 149–158.

O'Connor, M. J., & Whaley, S. E. (2003). Alcohol use in pregnant low-income women. *Journal of Studies in Alcohol, 64*, 773–783.

O'Connor, T. G., Deater-Deckard, K., Fulker, D., Rutter, M., & Plomin, R. (1998). Genotype-environment correlations in late childhood and early adolescence: Antisocial behavioral problems and coercive parenting. *Developmental Psychology, 34*, 970–981.

O'Connor, T. G., Marvin, R. S., Rutter, M., Olrick, J. T., & Britner, P. A. (2003). Child–parent attachment following early institutional deprivation. *Development and Psychopathology, 15*, 19–38.

O'Dempsey, T. J. D. (1988). Traditional belief and practice among the Pokot people of Kenya with particular reference to mother and child health: 2. Mother and child health. *Annals of Tropical Pediatrics, 8*, 125.

Oden, M. H. (1968). The fulfillment of promise: 40-year follow-up of the Terman gifted group. *Genetic Psychology Monographs, 77*, 3–93.

Oden, S., & Asher, S. R. (1977). Coaching children in social skills for friendship making. *Child Development, 48*, 495–506.

O'Donnell, A. M., & O'Kelly, J. (1994). Learning from peers: Beyond the rhetoric of positive results. *Educational Psychology Review, 6*, 321–349.

Ogbu, J. U. (1981). Origins of human competence: A cultural–ethological perspective. *Child Development, 52*, 413–429.

Ogbu, J. U. (1994). From cultural differences to differences in cultural frames of reference. In P. M. Greenfield & R. R. Cocking (Eds.), *Cross-cultural roots of minority child development.* Hillsdale, NJ: Erlbaum.

Ogbu, J. U. (2003). *Black American students in an affluent suburb: A study of academic disengagement.* Lawrence Erlbaum.

Ogletree, S. M., & Drake, R. (2007). College students' video game participation and perceptions: Gender differences and implications. *Sex Roles, 56*, 537–542.

Ogletree, S. M., Martinez, C. N., Turner, T. R., & Mason, B. (2004). Pokemon: Exploring the role of gender. *Sex Roles, 50*, 851–859.

O'Grady, J. P., Pope, C. S., & Patel, S. S. (2000). Vacuum extraction in modern obstetric practice: A review and critique. *Current Opinion in Obstetric Gynecology, 12*, 475–480.

O'Halloran, C. M., & Altmaier, E. M. (1996). Awareness of death among children: Does a life-threatening illness alter the process of discovery? *Journal of Counseling and Development, 74*, 259–262.

Ohman, A., & Mineka, S. (2003). The malicious serpent: Snakes as a prototypical stimulus for an evolved module of fear. *Current Directions in Psychological Science, 12*, 5–9.

Okami, P., Olmstead, R., & Abramson, P. R. (1997). Sexual experiences in early childhood: 18-year longitudinal data from the UCLA family lifestyles project. *Journal of Sex Research, 34*, 339–347.

Okie, S. (2001, May 8). Confronting Alzheimer's. Promising vaccine targets ravager of minds. *The Washington Post*, A1, A4.

Oliveness, F., Golombok, S., Ramogida, C., & Rust, J. (2005). Behavioral and cognitive development as well as family functioning of twins conceived by assisted reproduction: Findings from a large population study. *Fertility and Sterility, 84*, 725–733.

Olshan, A. F., Schnitzer, P. G., & Baird, P. A. (1994). Paternal age and the risk of congenital heart defects. *Teratology, 50*, 80–84.

Olshansky, S. J., & Carnes, B. A. (2004). In search of the holy grail of senescence. In S. G. Post & R. H. Binstock (Eds.), *The fountain of youth: Cultural, scientific, and ethical perspectives on a biomedical goal.* New York: Oxford University Press.

Olson, C. M. (2002). *Weight gain in pregnancy: A major factor in the development of obesity in childbearing women?* Cornell University. Available online: http://www.cce.cornell.edu/food/expfiles/topics/olson2/olson2overview.html.

Olson, J. M., Vernon, P. A., Harris, J. A., & Jang, K. L. (2001). The heritability of attitudes: A study of twins. *Journal of Personality and Social Psychology, 80*, 845–860.

Oltjenbruns, K. A. (2001). Developmental context of childhood: Grief and regrief phenomena. In M. S. Stroebe, R. O. Hansson, W. Stroebe, & H. Schut (Eds.), *Handbook of bereavement research. Consequences, coping, and care.* Washington, D.C.: American Psychological Association.

Olweus, D. (1993). *Bullying at school.* Oxford, UK: Blackwell.

O'Mara, A. J., Marsh, H. W., Craven, R. G., & Debus, R. L. (2006). Do self-concept interventions make a difference? A synergistic blend of construct validation and meta-analysis. *Educational Psychologist, 41*, 181–206.

O'Mathúna, D. P. (2006). Human growth hormone for improved strength and increased muscle mass in athletes. *Alternative Medicine Alert, 8*, 97–101.

Oosterwegel, A., & Oppenheimer, L. (1993). *The self-system: Developmental changes between and within self-concepts.* Hillsdale, NJ: Erlbaum.

Oppliger, P. A. (2007). Effects of gender stereotyping on socialization. In R. W. Preiss, B. Mae, N. Burrell, M. Allen, J. Bryant (Eds.), *Mass media effects research: Advances through meta-analysis* (pp. 199–214). Mahwah, NJ: Lawrence Erlbaum.

Orobio de Castro, B., Veerman, J. W., Koops, W., Bosch, J. D., & Monshouwer, H. J. (2002). Hostile attribution of intent and aggressive behavior: A meta-analysis. *Child Development, 73*, 916–934.

Orth, L. C., & Martin, R. P. (1994). Interactive effects of student temperament and instruction method on classroom behavior and achievement. *Journal of School Psychology, 32*, 149–166.

Osterweis, M., Solomon, F., & Green, M. (Eds.). (1984). *Bereavement: Reactions, consequences, and care.* Washington, D.C.: National Academy Press.

Oswald, D. L., & Lindstedt, K. (2006). The content and function of gender self-stereotypes: An exploratory investigation. *Sex Roles, 54*, 447–458.

Ott, C. H., Lueger, R. J., Kelber, S. T., & Prigerson, H. G. (2007). Spousal bereavement in older adults: Common, resilient, and chronic grief with defining characteristics. *Journal of Nervous and Mental Disease, 195*, 332–341.

Otte, E., & van Mier, H. I. (2006). Bimanual interference in children performing a dual motor task. *Human Movement Science, 25*, 678–693.

Owen, A. M., Coleman, M. R., Boly, M., Davis, M. H., Laureys, S., & Pickard, J. D. (2006). Detecting awareness in the vegetative state. *Science, 313*(5792), 1402.

Owen, L., McNeill, A., & Callum, C. (1998). Trends in smoking during pregnancy in England, 1992-7: Quota sampling surveys. *British Medical Journal, 317*, 728–730.

Owen, M. J., & O'Donovan, M. C. (2003). Schizophrenia and genetics. In R. Plomin, J. C. DeFries, I. W. Craig, & P. McGuffin (Eds.), *Behavioral genetics in the postgenomic era.* Washington, D.C.: American Psychological Association.

Owens, J., Spirito, A., McGuinn, M., & Nobile, C. (2000). Sleep habits and sleep disturbance in elementary school-aged children. *Journal of Developmental and Behavioral Pediatrics, 21*, 27–36.

Ownby, R. L., Crocco, E., Acevedo, A., John, V., & Loewenstein, D. (2006). Depression and risk for Alzheimer disease: Systematic review, meta-analysis, and metaregression analysis. *Archives of General Psychiatry, 63*, 530–538.

Owsley, C., Ball, K., McGwin, G., Sloane, M. E., Roenker, D. L., White, M. F., & Overley, E. T. (1998). Visual processing impairment and risk of motor vehicle crash among older adults. *Journal of the American Medical Association, 279*, 1083–1088.

Ozer, D. J., & Benet-Martinez, V. (2006). Personality and the prediction of consequential outcomes. *Annual Review of Psychology, 57*, 401–421.

P

Packman, W., Horsley, H., Davies, B., & Kramer, R. (2006). Sibling bereavement and continuing bonds. *Death Studies, 30*, 817–841.

Page, T. (1996, December 22). "Shine," brief candle. *The Washington Post*, G1, G10–G11.

Paikoff, R. L., & Brooks-Gunn, J. (1991). Do parent–child relationships change during puberty? *Psychological Bulletin, 110*, 47–66.

Palkovitz, R. (2002). *Involved fathering and men's adult development: Provisional balances.* Mahwah, NJ: Erlbaum.

Palmore, E. B., Burchett, B. M., Fillenbaum, G. G., George, L. K., & Wallman, L. M. (1985). *Retirement. Causes and consequences.* New York: Springer.

Pan, B. A. (2005). Semantic development. In J. B. Gleason (Ed.), *The development of language* (6th ed.). Boston: Allyn & Bacon.

Papadakis, A. A., Prince, R. P., Jones, N. P., & Strauman, T. J. (2006). Self-regulation, rumination, and vulnerability to depression in adolescent girls. *Development and Psychopathology, 18,* 815–829.

Park, D. C., Lautenschlager, G., Hedden, T., Davidson, N. S., Smith, A. D., & Smith, P. K. (2002). Models of visuospatial and verbal memory across the adult life span. *Psychological Aging, 17,* 299–320.

Park, D. C., Morrell, R. W., Frieske, D., & Kincaid, D. (1992). Medication adherence behaviors in older adults: Effects of external cognitive supports. *Psychology and Aging, 7,* 252–256.

Park, F., & Gow, K. W. (2006). Gene therapy: Future or flop. *Pediatric Clinics of North America, 53,* 621–638.

Parke, R. D. (1996). *Fatherhood.* Cambridge, MA: Harvard University Press.

Parke, R. D., & Buriel, R. (2006). Socialization in the family: Ethnic and ecological perspectives. In N. Eisenberg (Ed.), W. Damon & R. M. Learner (Eds. in Chief), *Handbook of child psychology: Vol. 3. Social, emotional, and personality development.* Hoboken, NJ: Wiley.

Parke, R. D., Ornstein, P. A., Rieser, J. J., & Zahn-Waxler, C. (1994). The past as prologue: An overview of a century of developmental psychology. In R. D. Parke, P. A. Ornstein, J. J. Rieser, & C. Zahn-Waxler (Eds.), *A century of developmental psychology.* Washington, D.C.: American Psychological Association.

Parke, R. D., & Sawin, D. B. (1976). The father's role in infancy: A reevaluation. *Family Coordinator, 25,* 365–371.

Parker, F. L., Boak, A. Y., Griffin, K. W., Ripple, C., & Peay, L. (1999). Parent–child relationship, home learning environment, and school readiness. *School Psychology Review, 28,* 413–425.

Parkes, C. M. (1991). Attachment, bonding, and psychiatric problems after bereavement in adult life. In C. M. Parkes, J. Stevenson-Hinde, & P. Marris (Eds.), *Attachment across the life cycle.* London: Tavistock/Routledge.

Parkes, C. M. (1996). *Bereavement: Studies of grief in adult life* (3rd ed.). London: Routledge.

Parkes, C. M. (2000). Comments on Dennis Klass' article "Developing a cross-cultural model of grief." *Omega: Journal of Death and Dying, 41,* 323–326.

Parkes, C. M. (2006). *Love and loss. The roots of grief and its complications.* London: Routledge.

Parkes, C. M., & Weiss, R. S. (1983). *Recovery from bereavement.* New York: Basic Books.

Parkhurst, J. T., & Asher, S. R. (1992). Peer rejection in middle school: Subgroup differences in behavior, loneliness, and interpersonal concerns. *Developmental Psychology, 28,* 231–241.

Parnham, J. (2001). Lifelong learning: A model for increasing the participation of non-traditional adult learners. *Journal of Further and Higher Education, 25,* 57–65.

Parten, M. B. (1932). Social participation among preschool children. *Journal of Abnormal and Social Psychology, 27,* 243–269.

Passman, R. H. (1977). Providing attachment objects to facilitate learning and reduce distress: Effects of mothers and security blankets. *Developmental Psychology, 13,* 25–28.

Pasupathi, M., & Carstensen, L. L. (2003). Age and emotional experience during mutual reminiscing. *Psychology and Aging, 18,* 430–442.

Pasupathi, M., & Staudinger, U. M. (2001). Do advanced moral reasoners also show wisdom?

Linking moral reasoning and wisdom-related knowledge and judgment. *International Journal of Behavioral Development, 25,* 401–415.

Pasupathi, M., Staudinger, U. M., & Baltes, P. B. (2001). Seeds of wisdom: Adolescents' knowledge and judgment about difficult life problems. *Developmental Psychology, 37,* 351–361.

Patel, D. R., Pratt, H. D., & Greydanus, D. E. (2003). Treatment of adolescents with anorexia nervosa. *Journal of Adolescent Research, 18,* 244–260.

Patterson C. J. (2004). Gay fathers. In M. E. Lamb (Ed.), *The role of the father in child development* (4th ed.). Hoboken, NJ: John Wiley & Sons.

Patterson, C. J., & Hastings, P. D. (2007). Socialization in the context of family diversity. In J. E. Grusec & P. D. Hastings (Eds.), *Handbook of socialization: Theory and research.* New York: Guilford.

Patterson, C. J., Kupersmidt, J. B., & Vaden, N. A. (1990). Income level, gender, ethnicity, and household composition as predictors of children's school-based competence. *Child Development, 61,* 485–494.

Patterson, G. R., DeBaryshe, B. D., & Ramsey, E. (1989). A developmental perspective on antisocial behavior. *American Psychologist, 44,* 329–335.

Patton, J. R. (2000). Educating students with mild mental retardation. *Focus on Autism and Other Developmental Disabilities, 15,* 80–89.

Paul, D. A., Leef, K. H., Locke, R. G., Bartoshesky, L., Walrath, J., & Stefano, J. L. (2006). Increasing illness severity in very low birth weight infants over a 9-year period. *BMC Pediatrics, 6,* 1471–2431.

Paul, J. P. (1993). Childhood cross-gender behavior and adult homosexuality: The resurgence of biological models of sexuality. *Journal of Homosexuality, 24,* 41–54.

Pauli-Pott, U., Mertesacker, B., & Beckmann, D. (2004). Predicting the development of infant emotionality from maternal characteristics. *Development and Psychopathology, 16,* 19–42.

Paulson, J. F., Dauber, S., & Leiferman, J. A. (2006). Individual and combined effects of postpartum depression in mothers and fathers on parenting behavior. *Pediatrics, 118,* 659–668.

Paus, T. (2005). Mapping brain maturation and cognitive development during adolescence. *Trends in Cognitive Science, 9,* 60–68.

Paxton, S. J., Neumark-Sztainer, D., Hannan, P. J., Eisenberg, M. E. (2006). Body dissatisfaction prospectively predicts depressive mood and low self-esteem in adolescent girls and boys. *Journal of Clinical Child and Adolescent Psychology, 35,* 539–549.

Pearce, K. A., & Denney, N. W. (1984). A lifespan study of classification preference. *Journal of Gerontology, 39,* 458–464.

Pearlin, L. I. (1980). Life strains and psychological distress among adults. In N. J. Smelser & E. H. Erikson (Eds.), *Themes of work and love in adulthood.* Cambridge, MA: Harvard University Press.

Pears, K. C., & Moses, L. J. (2003). Demographics, parenting, and theory of mind in preschool children. *Social Development, 12,* 1–19.

Pearson, J. D., Morell, C. H., Gordon-Salant, S., Brant, L. J., Metter, E. J., Klein, L., & Fozard, J. L. (1995). Gender differences in a longitudinal study of age-associated hearing loss. *Journal*

of the Acoustical Society of America, 97, 1196–1205.

Pearson, J. L. (2000). Preventing late life suicide: National Institutes of Health initiatives. *Omega: Journal of Death and Dying, 42,* 9–20.

Pedersen, N. L., McClearn, G. E., Plomin, R., & Friberg, L. (1985). Separated fraternal twins: Resemblance for cognitive abilities. *Behavior Genetics, 15,* 407–419.

Pedula, K. L., Coleman, A. L., Hillier, T. A., Ensrud, K. E., Nevitt, M. C., Hochberg, M. C., Mangione, C. M., & Study of Osteoporotic Fractures Research Group. (2006). Visual acuity, contract sensitivity, and mortality in older women: Study of osteoporotic fractures. *Journal of American Geriatric Society, 54,* 1871–1877,

Pegg, J. E., Werker, J. F., & McLeod, P. J. (1992). Preference for infant-directed over adult-directed speech: Evidence from 7-week-old infants. *Infant Behavior and Development, 15,* 325–345.

Pelham, W., Chacko, A., & Wymbs, B. (2004). Diagnostic and assessment issues in ADHD in the young child. In R. DelCarmen-Wiggins & A. Carter (Eds.), *Handbook of infant, toddler, and preschool mental health assessment.* New York: Oxford University Press.

Pellegrini, A. D. (1996). *Observing children in their natural worlds: A methodological primer.* Mahwah, NJ: Erlbaum.

Pellegrini, A. D., & Long, J. D. (2003). A sexual selection theory longitudinal analysis of sexual segregation and integration in early adolescence. *Journal of Experimental Child Psychology, 85,* 257–278.

Pellegrini, A. D., Long, J. D., Roseth, C. J., Bohn, C. M., & Van Ryzin, M. (2007). A short-term longitudinal study of preschoolers' (*Homo sapiens*) sex segregation: The role of physical activity, sex, and time. *Journal of Comparative Psychology, 121,* 282–289.

Penner, S. G. (1987). Parental responses to grammatical and ungrammatical child utterances. *Child Development, 58,* 376–384.

Peplau, L. A., & Fingerhut, A. W. (2007). The close relationships of lesbians and gay men. *Annual Review of Psychology, 58,* 405–424.

Pepper, S. C. (1942). *World hypotheses: A study in evidence.* Berkeley, CA: University of California Press.

Percy, M. (2007). Factors that cause or contribute to intellectual and developmental disabilities. In I. Brown & M. Percy (Eds.), *A comprehensive guide to intellectual & developmental disabilities.* Baltimore, MD: Paul H. Brookes.

Percy, M., Lewkis, S. Z., & Brown, I. (2007). Introduction to genetics and development. In I. Brown & M. Percy (Eds.), *A comprehensive guide to intellectual & developmental disabilities.* Baltimore, MD: Paul H. Brookes.

Perez-Granados, D. R., & Callanan, M. A. (1997). Conversations with mothers and siblings: Young children's semantic and conceptual development. *Developmental Psychology, 33,* 120–134.

Perfetti, C. A. (1999). Cognitive research and the misconceptions of reading education. In J. Oakhill & R. Beard (Eds.), *Reading development and the teaching of reading* (pp. 42–58). Malden, MA: Blackwell.

Perkins, D. (1996). *Outsmarting IQ: The emerging science of learnable intelligence.* New York: Free Press.

Perkins, H. W., & DeMeis, D. K. (1996). Gender and family effects on the "second-shift" domestic activity of college educated young adults. *Gender & Society, 10*, 78–93.

Perlmutter, M. (1986). A life-span view of memory. In P. B. Baltes, D. L. Featherman, & R. M. Lerner (Eds.), *Life-span development and behavior* (Vol. 7). Hillsdale, NJ: Erlbaum.

Perry, D. G., & Parke, R. D. (1975). Punishment and alternative response training as determinants of response inhibition in children. *Genetic Psychology Monographs, 91*, 257–279.

Perry, H. L. (1993). Mourning and funeral customs of African Americans. In D. P. Irish, K. F. Lundquist, & V. J. Nelson (Eds.), *Ethnic variations in dying, death, and grief: Diversity in universality*. Washington, D.C.: Taylor and Francis.

Perry, W. G., Jr. (1970). *Forms of intellectual and ethical development in the college years: A scheme*. New York: Holt, Rinehart & Winston.

Persson, G., & Svanborg, A. (1992). Marital coital activity in men at the age of 75: Relation to somatic, psychiatric, and social factors at the age of 70. *Journal of the American Geriatrics Society, 40*, 439–444.

Pesonen, A., Raeikkoenen, K., Keskivaara, P., & Keltikangas-Jaervinen, L. (2003). Difficult temperament in childhood and adulthood: Continuity from maternal perceptions to self-ratings over 17 years. *Personality and Individual Differences, 34*, 19–31.

Pessin, H., Rosenfeld, B., & Breitbart, W. (2002). Assessing psychological distress near the end of life. *American Behavioral Scientist, 46*, 357–372.

Peters, A. (2002). The effects of normal aging on myelin and nerve fibers: A review. *Journal of Neurocytology, 31*, 581–593.

Petersen, A. C., Compas, B. E., Brooks-Gunn, J., Stemmler, M., Ey, S., & Grant, K. E. (1993). Depression in adolescence. *American Psychologist, 48*, 155–168.

Petersen, R. C., Smith, G. E., Waring, S. C., & Ivnik, R. J. (1997). Aging, memory, and mild cognitive impairment. *International Psychogeriatrics, 65* (Supplement).

Petersen, R. C., Stevens, J. C., Ganguli, M., Tangalos, E. G., Cummings, J. L., & DeKosky, S. T. (2001). Early detection of dementia: Mild cognitive impairment. *Neurology, 56*, 1133-1142.

Peterson, C. C., & Rideout, R. (1998). Memory for medical emergencies experienced by 1 and 2-year-olds. *Developmental Psychology, 34*, 1059–1072.

Peterson, C. C., & Siegal, M. (1999). Representing inner worlds: Theory of mind in autistic, deaf, and normal hearing children. *Psychological Science, 10*, 126–129.

Peterson, C. C., & Siegal, M. (2002). Mind reading and moral awareness in popular and rejected preschoolers. *British Journal of Developmental Psychology, 20*, 205–224.

Peterson, C. C., & Slaughter, V. (2003). Opening windows into the mind: Mothers' preferences for mental state explanations and children's theory of mind. *Cognitive Development, 18*, 399–429.

Peterson, C. & Steen, T. A. (2002). Optimistic explanatory style. In C. R. Snyder & S. J. Lopez (Eds.) *Handbook of positive psychology* (pp. 244–256). New York: Oxford University Press.

Peterson, C. C., Wellman, H. M., & Liu, D. (2005). Steps in theory-of-mind development for children with deafness or autism. *Child Development, 76*, 502–517.

Peterson, P. L. (1977). Interactive effects of student anxiety, achievement orientation, and teacher behavior on student achievement and attitude. *Journal of Educational Psychology, 69*, 779–792.

Petitto, L. A., & Marentette, P. F. (1991). Babbling in the manual mode: Evidence for the ontogeny of language. *Science, 251*, 1493–1496.

Pettitt, L. M. (2004). Gender intensification of peer socialization during puberty. *New Directions for Child and Adolescent Development, 106*, 23–34.

Pexman, P. M., & Glenwright, M. (2007). How do typically-developing children grasp the meaning of verbal irony? *Journal of Neurolinguistics, 20*, 178–196.

Phares, V. (1999). *"Poppa" psychology. The role of fathers in children's mental well-being*. Westport, CT: Praeger.

Phillips, M. (1997). What makes schools effective? A comparison of the relationships of communitarian climate and academic climate to mathematics achievement and attendance during middle school. *American Educational Research Journal, 34*, 633–662.

Phillips, S. D. (1982). Career exploration in adulthood. *Journal of Vocational Behavior, 20*, 129–140.

Phillips, T. M., & Pittman, J. F. (2003). Identity processes in poor adolescents: Exploring the linkages between economic disadvantage and the primary task of adolescence. *Identity, 3*, 115–129.

Phinney, J. S. (1993). A three-stage model of ethnic identity development in adolescence. In M. E. Bernal, & G. P. Knight (Eds.), *Ethnic identity: Formation and transmission among Hispanics and other minorities*. Albany, NY: State University of New York Press.

Phinney, J. S. (1996). When we talk about American ethnic groups, what do we mean? *American Psychologist, 51*, 918–927.

Phinney, J. S. (2006). Ethnic identity exploration in emerging adulthood. In J. J. Arnett, & J. L. Tanner (Eds.), *Emerging adults in America: Coming of age in the 21st century*. Washington, D.C.: American Psychological Association.

Phipps, M. G., Blume, J. D., & DeMonner, S. M. (2002). Young maternal age associated with increased risk of postneonatal death. *Obstetrics and Gynecology, 100*, 481–486.

Piaget, J. (1926). *The child's conception of the world*. New York: Harcourt, Brace & World.

Piaget, J. (1950). *The psychology of intelligence*. New York: Harcourt, Brace & World.

Piaget, J. (1952). *The origins of intelligence in children*. New York: International Universities Press.

Piaget, J. (1965). *The moral judgment of the child*. New York: Free Press. (Original work published 1932).

Piaget, J. (1970). Piaget's theory. In P. H. Mussen (Ed.), *Carmichael's manual of child psychology* (Vol. 1). New York: Wiley.

Piaget, J. (1971). *Biology and knowledge*. Edinburgh, UK: Edinburgh University Press.

Piaget, J. (1972). Intellectual evolution from adolescence to adulthood. *Human Development, 15*, 1–12.

Piaget, J. (1977). The role of action in the development of thinking. In W. F. Overton & J. M. Gallagher (Eds.), *Knowledge and development* (Vol. 1). New York: Plenum.

Piaget, J. (1978). *The development of thought: Equilibration of cognitive structures*. Oxford, UK: Blackwell.

Piaget, J. (1985). *The equilibration of cognitive structures: The central problem of intellectual development* (T. Brown & K. J. Thampy, Trans.). Chicago: University of Chicago Press.

Piaget, J., & Inhelder, B. (1956). *The child's conception of space*. New York: Norton.

Piaget, J., & Inhelder, B. (1969). *The psychology of the child* (H. Weaver, Trans.). New York: Basic Books. (Original work published 1966).

Pianta, R., Egeland, B., & Erickson, M. F. (1989). The antecedents of maltreatment: Results of the Mother–child Interaction Research Project. In D. Cicchetti & V. Carlson (Eds.), *Child maltreatment: Theory and research on the causes and consequences of child abuse and neglect*. Cambridge, England: Cambridge University Press.

Pickens, J. (1994). Perception of auditory-visual distance relations by 5-month-old infants. *Developmental Psychology, 30*, 537–544.

Pigott, T. A. (2002). Anxiety disorders. In S. G. Kornstein & A. H. Clayton (Eds.), *Women's mental health: A comprehensive textbook* (pp. 195–221). New York: The Guilford Press.

Pilisuk, M., & Minkler, M. (1980). Supportive networks: Life ties for the elderly. *Journal of Social Issues, 36(2)*, 95–116.

Pinhas, L., Katzman, D. K., Dimitropoulos, G., & Woodside, D. B. (2007). Bingeing and bulimia nervosa in children and adolescents. In T. Jaffa & B. McDermott (Eds.), *Eating disorders in children and adolescents*. Cambridge, UK: Cambridge University Press.

Pinheiro, R. T., Magalhaes, P. V., Horta, B. L., Pinheiro, K. A., da Silva, R. A., & Pinto, R. H. (2006). Is paternal postpartum depression associated with maternal postpartum depression? Population-based study in Brazil. *Acta Psychiatrica Scandinavica, 113*, 230–232.

Pinker, S. (1994). *The language instinct*. New York: HarperCollins.

Pinker, S. (1999). *Words and rules: The ingredients of language*. New York: HarperCollins.

Pinker, S. (2002). *The blank slate. The modern denial of human nature*. New York: Viking.

Pinquart, M., & Silbereisen, R. K. (2006). Socioemotional selectivity in cancer patients. *Psychology and Aging, 21*, 419–423.

Pinquart, M., & Sorenson, S. (2000). Influences of socioeconomic status, social network, competence, or subjective competence in later life: A meta-analysis. *Psychology and Aging, 15*, 187–224.

Pinquart, M., & Sorensen, S. (2003). Associations of stressors and uplifts of caregiving with caregiver burden and depressive mood: A meta-analysis. *Journal of Gerontology: Psychological Sciences, 58B*, 112–128.

Pinquart, M., & Sorensen, S. (2006). Gender differences in caregiver stressors, social resources, and health: An updated meta-analysis. *Journals of Gerontology: Psychological Sciences, 61B*, P33–P45.

Pipp, S., Easterbrooks, M. A., & Harmon, R. J. (1992). The relation between attachment and knowledge of self and mother in one-year-old infants to three-year-old infants. *Child Development, 63*, 738–750.

Pitts, M., & Rahman, Q. (2001). Which behaviors constitute "having sex" among university students in the UK? *Archives of Sexual Behavior, 30*, 169–176.

Pitts, S. C., Prost, J. H., & Winters, J. J. (2005). Quasi-experimental designs in developmental research: Design and analysis considerations. In D. M. Teti (Ed.), *Handbook of research methods in developmental science.* Malden, MA: Blackwell Publishing.

Plassman, B. L., Havlik, R. J., Steffens, D. C., Helms, M. J., Newman, T. N., Drosdick, D., Phillips, C., Gau, B. A., Welsh-Bohmer, K. A., Burke, J. R., Guralnik, J. M., & Breitner, J. C. (2000). Documented head injury in early childhood and risk of Alzheimer's disease and other dementias. *Neurology, 55*, 1158–1166.

Platt, M. J., Cans, C., Johnson, A., Surman, G., Topp, M., Torrioli, M. G., & Krageloh-Mann, I. (2007). Trends in cerebral palsy among infants of very low birthweight (<1500g) or born prematurely (<32weeks) in 16 European centres: A database study. *Lancet, 369*, 43–50.

Pleck, J. H., & Masciadrelli, B. P. (2004). Paternal involvement by U.S. residential fathers: Levels, sources, and consequences. In M. E. Lamb (Ed.), *The role of the father in child development* (4th ed.). Hoboken, NJ: John Wiley & Sons.

Plomin, R. (1990). *Nature and nurture. An introduction to human behavioral genetics.* Pacific Grove, CA: Brooks/Cole.

Plomin, R., & Bergeman, C. S. (1991). The nature of nurture: Genetic influence on environmental measures. *Behavioral and Brain Sciences, 14*, 373–385.

Plomin, R., Corley, R., DeFries, J. C., & Fulker, D. W. (1990). Individual differences in television viewing in early childhood: Nature as well as nurture. *Psychological Science, 1*, 371–377.

Plomin, R., DeFries, J. C., & Loehlin, J. C. (1977). Genotype–environment interaction and correlation in the analysis of human behavior. *Psychological Bulletin, 84*, 309–322.

Plomin, R., DeFries, J. C., Craig, I. W., & McGuffin, P. (2003). Behavioral genetics. In R. Plomin, J. C. DeFries, I. W. Craig, & P. McGuffin (Eds.), *Behavioral genetics in the postgenomic era.* Washington, D.C.: American Psychological Association.

Plomin, R., DeFries, J. C., McClearn, G. E., & McGuffin, P. (2001). *Behavioral genetics* (4th ed.). New York: Worth.

Plomin, R., Kennedy, J. K., & Craig, I. W. (2006). The quest for quantitative trait loci associated with intelligence. *Intelligence, 34*, 513–526.

Plomin, R., & McGuffin, P. (2003). Psychopathology in the postgenomic era. *Annual Review of Psychology, 54*, 205–228.

Plomin, R., Pedersen, N. L., McClearn, G. E., Nesselroade, J. R., & Bergeman, C. S. (1988). EAS temperaments during the last half of the life span: Twins reared apart and twins reared together. *Psychology and Aging, 3*, 43–50.

Plomin, R., & Spinath, F. M. (2004). Intelligence, genetics, genes, and genomics. *Journal of Personality and Social Psychology, 86*, 112–129.

Plotnik, J. M., de Waal, F. B. M., & Reiss, D. (2006). Self-recognition in an Asian elephant. *Proceedings of the National Academy of Sciences, 103*, 17053–17057.

Poehlmann, J., & Fiese, B. H. (2001). The interaction of maternal and infant vulnerabilities on developing attachment relationships. *Development and Psychopathology, 13*, 1–11.

Polanczyk, G., deLima, M. S., Horta, B. L., Biederman, J., & Rohde, L. A. (2007). The world wide prevalence of ADHD: A systematic review and metaregression analysis. *American Journal of Psychiatry, 164*, 942–948.

Pomerantz, E. M., Altermatt, E. R., & Saxon, J. L. (2002). Making the grade but feeling distressed: Gender differences in academic performance and internal distress. *Journal of Educational Psychology, 94*, 396–404.

Pomerantz, E. M., & Ruble, D. N. (1997). Distinguishing multiple dimensions of conceptions of ability: Implications for self-evaluation. *Child Development, 68*, 1165–1180.

Pomerantz, E. M., Ruble, D. N., Frey, K. S., & Grenlich, F. (1995). Meeting goals and confronting conflict: Children's changing perceptions of social comparison. *Child Development, 66*, 723–738.

Pomerleau, A., Bolduc, D., Malcuit, G., & Cossette, L. (1990). Pink or blue: Environmental gender stereotypes in the first two years of life. *Sex Roles, 22*, 359–367.

Ponton, L. (2001). *The sex lives of teenagers: Revealing the secret world of adolescent boys and girls.* New York: Plume.

Poon, H. F., Calabrese, V., Scapagnini, G., & Butterfield, D. A. (2004). Free radicals: Key to brain aging and heme oxygenase as a cellular response to oxidative stress. *Journal of Gerontology: Medical Science, 59A*, 478–493.

Pope, S. K., Shue, V. M., & Beck, C. (2003). Will a healthy lifestyle help prevent Alzheimer's disease? *Annual Review of Public Health, 24*, 111–132.

Porter, R. H. (1999). Olfaction and human kin recognition. *Genetica, 104*, 259–263.

Porter, R. H., Makin, J. W., Davis, L. B., & Christensen, K. M. (1992). Breast-fed infants respond to olfactory clues from their own mother and unfamiliar lactating females. *Infant Behavior and Development, 15*, 85–93.

Portes, A., & MacLeod, D. (1996). Educational progress of children of immigrants: The roles of class, ethnicity, and school context. *Sociology of Education, 69*, 255–275.

Posthuma, D., & de Geus, E. J. C. (2006). Progress in the molecular-genetic study of intelligence. *Current Directions in Psychological Science, 15*, 151–155.

Poulin-Dubois, D., & Goodz, N. (2001). Language differentiation in bilingual infants: Evidence from babbling. In J. Cenoz & F. Genesee (Eds.) *Trends in bilingual acquisition* (pp. 95–106). Amsterdam: Netherlandsing Company.

Poulin-Dubois, D., & Serbin, L. A. (2006). Infants' knowledge about gender stereotypes and categories. *Enfance, 58*, 283–310.

Poulin-Dubois, D., Serbin, L. A., Eichstedt, J. A., Sen, M. G., & Beissel, C. F. (2002). Men don't put on make-up: Toddlers' knowledge of the gender stereotyping of household activities. *Social Development, 11*, 166–181.

Pratt, M. W., Diessner, R., Hunsberger, B., Pancer, S. M., & Savoy, K. (1991). Four pathways in the analysis of adult development and aging: Comparing analyses of reasoning about personal-life dilemmas. *Psychology and Aging, 4*, 666–675.

Pratt, M. W., Diessner, R., Pratt, A., Hunsberger, B., & Pancer, S. M. (1996). Moral and social reasoning and perspective taking in later life: A longitudinal study. *Psychology and Aging, 11*, 66–73.

Pratt, M. W., & Norris, J. E. (1999). Moral development in maturity. Life-span perspectives on the processes of successful aging. In T. M. Hess & F. Blanchard-Fields (Eds.), *Social cognition and aging.* San Diego: Academic Press.

Pressley, M. (1983). Making meaningful materials easier to learn: Lessons from cognitive strategy research. In M. Pressley & J. R. Levin (Eds.), *Cognitive strategy research: Educational applications.* New York: Springer-Verlag.

Pressley, M., & Hilden, K. (2006). Cognitive strategies. In D. Kuhn & R. Siegler (Vol. Eds.), *Handbook of child psychology: Cognition, perception, and language: Vol. 2.* Hoboken, NJ: Wiley and Sons.

Pressley, M., & Levin, J. R. (1980). The development of mental imagery retrieval. *Child Development, 51*, 558–560.

Pressley, M., Levin, J. R., & Ghatala, E. S. (1984). Memory strategy monitoring in adults and children. *Journal of Verbal Learning and Verbal Behavior, 23*, 270–288.

Preston, T., & Kelly, M. (2006). A medical ethics assessment of the case of Terri Schiavo. *Death Studies, 30*, 121–133.

Price, D. W. W., & Goodman, G. S. (1990). Visiting the wizard: Children's memory for a recurring event. *Child Development, 61*, 664–680.

Prigerson, H., & Jacobs, S. (2001). Traumatic grief as a distinct disorder: A rationale, consensus criteria, and a preliminary empirical test. In M. S. Stroebe, R. O. Hansson, W. Stroebe, & H. Schut (Eds.), *Handbook of bereavement research: Consequences, coping, and care.* Washington, D.C.: American Psychological Association.

Prinstein, M. J., Meade, C. S., & Cohen, G. L. (2003). Adolescent oral sex, peer popularity, and perceptions of best friends' sexual behavior. *Journal of Pediatric Psychology, 28*, 243–249.

Proctor, M., Moore, L., Gao, D., Cupples, L., Bradlee, M., Hood, M., & Ellison, R. (2003). Television viewing and change in body fat from preschool to early adolescence: The Framingham Children's Study. *International Journal of Obesity, 27*, 827–833.

Proctor, R. M. J., & Burnett, P. C. (2004). Measuring cognitive and dispositional characteristics of creativity in elementary students. *Creativity Research Journal, 16*, 421–429.

Proffitt, J. B., Coley, J. D., & Medin, D. L. (2000). Expertise and category-based induction. *Journal of Experimental Psychology: Learning, Memory, and Cognition, 26*, 811–828.

Pruden, S. M., Hirsh-Pasek, K., Golinkoff, R. M., & Hennon, E. A. (2006). The birth of words: Ten-month-olds learn words through perceptual salience. *Child Development, 77*, 266–280.

Pudrovska, T., Schieman, S., & Carr, D. (2006). Strains of singlehood in later life: Do race and gender matter? *Journals of Gerontology: Social Sciences, 61B*, S315–S322.

Pujol, J. Soriano-Mas, C., Ortiz, H., Sebastián-Gallés, N., Losilla, J. M., Deus, J. (2006). Myelination of language-related areas in the developing brain. *Neurology, 66*, 339–343.

Purifoy, F. E., Grodsky, A., & Giambra, L. M. (1992). The relationship of sexual daydreaming to sexual activity, sexual drive, and sexual attitudes for women across the life-span. *Archives of Sexual Behavior, 21,* 369–385.

Putallaz, M., & Wasserman, A. (1989). Children's naturalistic entry behavior and sociometric status: A developmental perspective. *Developmental Psychology, 25,* 297–305.

Putnam, F. W. (2003). Ten-year research update review: Child sexual abuse. *Journal of the American Academy of Child and Adolescent Psychiatry, 42,* 269–278.

Putnam, S. P., Gartstein, M. A., & Rothbart, M. K. (2006). Measurement of fine-grained aspects of toddler temperament: The Early Childhood Behavior Questionnaire. *Infant Behavior and Development, 29,* 386–401.

Pyszczynski, T., Solomon, S., & Greenberg, J. (2003). *In the wake of 9/11: The psychology of terror.* Washington, D.C.: American Psychological Association.

Q

Quigley, B. A. (1997). Rethinking literacy education: The critical need for practice-based change. San Francisco: Jossey-Bass.

Quigley, B. A., & Uhland, R. L. (2000). Retaining adult learners in the first three critical weeks: A quasi-experimental model for use in ABE programs. *Adult Basic Education, 10,* 55–68.

Quill, T. E. (1993). *Death and dignity: Making choices and taking charge.* New York: W. W. Norton.

Quinsey, V. L. Skilling, T. A., Lalumiere, M. L., & Craig, W. M. (2004). *Juvenile delinquency. Understanding the origins of individual differences.* Washington, D.C.: American Psychological Association.

R

Raaijmakers, Q. A. W., Engels, R. C. M. E., & Van Hoof, A. (2005). Delinquency and moral reasoning in adolescence and young adulthood. *International Journal of Behavioral Development, 29,* 247–258.

Rabbitt, P., Chetwynd, A., & McInnes, L. (2003). Do clever brains age more slowly? Further exploration of a nun result. *British Journal of Psychology, 94,* 63–71.

Rader. D. (2006, April 9). After a painful childhood, Tom Cruise now believes... "I can create who I am." *Parade,* pp. 6–8.

Ragland, D. R., Satariano, W. A., & MacLeod, K. E. (2004). Reasons given by older people for limitation or avoidance of driving. *Gerontologist, 44,* 237–244.

Ragow-O'Brien, D., Hayslip, B., & Guarnaccia, C. A. (2000). The impact of hospice on attitudes toward funerals and subsequent bereavement adjustment. *Omega: Journal of Death and Dying, 41,* 291–305.

Ramchandani, P., Stein, A., Evans, J., O'Connor, T. G., & the ALSPAC Study Team (2005). Paternal depression in the postnatal period and child development: A prospective population study. *The Lancet, 365*(9478), 2201–2205.

Ramey, C. T., & Ramey, S. L. (1992). Effective early intervention. *Mental Retardation, 30,* 337–345.

Ramos, M., & Wilmoth, J. (2003). Social relationships and depressive symptoms among older adults in southern Brazil. *Journals of Gerontology: Psychological Sciences and Social Sciences, 58,* S253–S261.

Rando, T. A. (1986). A comprehensive analysis of anticipatory grief: Perspectives, processes, promises, and problems. In T. A. Rando (Ed.), *Loss and anticipatory grief.* Lexington, MA: Lexington Books.

Rando, T. A. (1991). Parental adjustment to the loss of a child. In D. Papadatou & C. Papadatos (Eds.), *Children and death.* New York: Hemisphere.

Raphael, B. (1983). *The anatomy of bereavement.* New York: Basic Books.

Raphael, B., Minkov, C., & Dobson, M. (2001). Psychotherapeutic and pharmacological intervention for bereaved persons. In M. S. Stroebe, & R. O. Hansson (Eds.), *Handbook of bereavement research: Consequences, coping, and care.* Washington, D.C.: American Psychological Association.

Rapkin, B. D., & Fischer, K. (1992). Personal goals of older adults: Issues in assessment and prediction. *Psychology and Aging, 7,* 127–137.

Rasmussen, F. (2006). Paternal age, size at birth, and size in young adulthood—risk factors for schizophrenia. *European Journal of Endocrinology, 155,* S65–S69.

Ratcliffe, S. D., Byrd, J. E., & Sakornbut, E. L. (1996). *Handbook of pregnancy and perinatal care in family practice: Science and practice.* Philadelphia: Hanley & Belfus.

Rattaz, C., Goubet, N., & Bullinger, A. (2005). The calming effect of a familiar odor on full-term newborns. *Journal of Developmental and Behavioral Pediatrics, 26,* 86–92.

Raz, S., Goldstein, R., Hopkins, T. L., Lauterbach, M. D., Shah, F., Porter, C. L., Riggs, W. W., Magill, L. H., & Sander C. J. (1994). Sex differences in early vulnerability to cerebral injury and their neurodevelopmental implications. *Psychobiology, 22,* 244–253.

Redcay, E., & Courchesne, E. (2005). When is the brain enlarged in autism? A meta-analysis of all brain size reports. *Biological Psychiatry, 58,* 1–9.

Redding, R. E., Harmon, R. J., & Morgan, G. A. (1990). Maternal depression and infants' mastery behaviors. *Infant Behavior and Development, 13,* 391–395.

Reddy, U. M., Ko, C., & Willinger, M. (2006). Maternal age and the risk of stillbirth throughout pregnancy in the United States. *American Journal of Obstetrics & Gynecology, 195,* 764–770.

Reder, L. M., Wible, C., & Martin, J. (1986). Differential memory changes with age: Exact retrieval versus plausible inference. *Journal of Experimental Psychology: Learning, Memory, and Cognition, 12,* 72–81.

Redon, R., et al. (2006). Global variation in copy number in the human genome. *Nature, 444,* 444–454.

Reed, R. (1996, Spring). Birthing fathers. *Mothering,* 50–55.

Reed, T., & Dick, D. M. (2003). Heritability and validity of healthy physical aging (wellness) in elderly male twins. *Twin Research, 6,* 227–234.

Rees, M. (1993). Menarche when and why? *Lancet, 342,* 1375–1376.

Reese, H. W., & Overton, W. F. (1970). Models of development and theories of development. In L. R. Goulet & P. B. Baltes (Eds.), *Life-span developmental psychology: Research and theory.* New York: Academic Press.

Reid, P. T., & Trotter, K. H. (1993). Children's self-presentations with infants: Gender and ethnic comparisons. *Sex Roles, 29,* 171–181.

Reid, T. R. (1993, January 16). 2 million accept duty of being 20. *The Washington Post,* A14, A24.

Reinherz, H. Z., Giaconia, R. M., Hauf, A. M. C., Wasserman, M. S., & Silverman, A. B. (1999). Major depression in the transition to adulthood: Risks and impairments. *Journal of Abnormal Psychology, 108,* 500–510.

Reinherz, H. Z., Tanner, J. L., Berger, S. R., Beardslee, W. R., & Fitzmaurice, G. M. (2006). Adolescent suicidal ideation as predictive of psychopathology, suicidal behavior, and compromised functioning at age 30. *American Journal of Psychiatry, 163,* 1226–1232.

Reis, H. T., Lin, Y., Bennett, M. E., & Nezlek, J. B. (1993). Change and consistency in social participation during early adulthood. *Developmental Psychology, 29,* 633–645.

Reis, O., & Youniss, J. (2004). Patterns of identity change and development in relationships with mothers and friends. *Journal of Adolescent Research, 19,* 31–44.

Reiss, D. (2005). The interplay between genotypes and family relationships. Reframing concepts of development and prevention. *Current Directions in Psychological Science, 14,* 139–143.

Reiss, D. (with J. M. Neiderhiser, E. M. Hetherington, & R. Plomin). (2000). *The relationship code. Deciphering genetic and social influences on adolescent development.* Cambridge, MA: Harvard University Press.

Reiss, D., & Neiderhiser, J. M. (2000). The interplay of genetic influences and social processes in developmental theory: Specific mechanisms are coming into view. *Development and Psychopathology, 12,* 357–374.

Reiss, S. (1994). Issues in defining mental retardation. *American Journal of Mental Retardation, 99,* 1–7.

Reiter, E. O., Price, D. A., Wilton, P., Albertsson-Wikland, K., & Ranke, M. B. (2006). Effect of growth hormone (GH) treatment on the near-final height of 1258 patients with idiopathic GH deficiency: Analysis of a large international database. *The Journal of Clinical Endocrinology and Metabolism, 91,* 2147–2054.

Reitzes, D. C., & Mutran, E. J. (2004). Grandparenthood: Factors influencing frequency of grandparent–grandchildren contact and grandparent role satisfaction. *Journal of Gerontology: Social Sciences, 59B,* S9–S16.

Reker, G. T., Peacock, E. J., & Wong, P. T. P. (1987). Meaning and purpose in life and well-being: A life-span perspective. *Journal of Gerontology, 42,* 44–49.

Rempel, J. (1985). Childless elderly: What are they missing? *Journal of Marriage and the Family, 47,* 343–348.

Rende, R., & Waldman, I. (2006). Behavioral and molecular genetics and developmental psychopathology. In D. Cicchetti & D. J. Cohen (Eds.), *Developmental psychopathology: Vol 2. Developmental neuroscience.* Hoboken, N. J.: Wiley.

Renzulli, J. S. (1998). The three-ring conception of giftedness. In S. M. Baum, S. M. Reis, & L. R. Maxfield (Eds.), *Nurturing the gifts and talents of primary grade students.* Mansfield Center, CT: Creative Learning Press.

Repacholi, B. M., & Gopnik, A. (1997). Early reasoning about desires: Evidence from 14- and

18-month-olds. *Developmental Psychology, 33,* 12–21.

Repacholi, B., Slaughter, V., Pritchard, M., & Gibbs, V. (2003). Theory of mind, Machiavellianism, and social functioning in childhood. In B. Repacholi & V. Slaughter (Eds.). *Individual differences in theory of mind: Implications for typical and atypical development.* New York: Psychology Press.

Rescorla, L. A., Achenbach, T. M., Ginzburg, S., Ivanova, M., Dumenci, L., Almqvist, F., Bathiche, M., Bilenberg, N., Bird, H., Domuta, A., Erol, N., Fombonne, E., Fonseca, A., Frigerio, A., Kanbayashi, Y., Lambert, M. C., Liu, X., Leung, P., Minaei, A., Roussos, A., Simsek, Z., Weintraub, S., Weisz, J., Wolanczyk, T., Zubrick, S. R., Zukauskiene, R., & Verhulst, F. (2007). Consistency of teacher-reported problems for students in 21 countries. *School Psychology Review, 36,* 91–110.

Resnick, S. M. (2000). One-year age changes in MRI brain volumes in older adults. *Cerebral Cortex, 10,* 464–472.

Resnick, S. M., Berenbaum, S. A., Gottesman, I. I., & Bouchard, T. J., Jr. (1986). Early hormonal influences on cognitive functioning in congenital adrenal hyperplasia. *Developmental Psychology, 22,* 191–198.

Rest, J., Narvaez, D., Bebeau, M. J., & Thoma, S. J. (1999). *Postconventional moral thinking. A neo-Kohlbergian approach.* Mahwah, NJ: Erlbaum.

Resta, R., Biesecker, B. B., Bennett, R. L., Blum, S., Hahn, S. E., Strecker, M. N., & Williams, J. L. (2006). A new definition of genetic counseling: National Society of Genetic Counselors' Task Force Report. *Journal of Genetic Counseling, 15,* 77–83.

Reuben, D. B., Walsh, K., Moore, A. A., Damesyn, M., & Greendale, G. A. (1998). Hearing loss in community-dwelling older persons: National prevalence data and identification using simple questions. *Journal of the American Geriatric Society, 46,* 1008–1011.

Reuter, M., Roth, S., Holve, K., & Hennig, J. (2006). Identification of first candidate genes for creativity: A pilot study. *Brain Research, 1069,* 190–197.

Reynolds, T. (2003, October). Understanding emotion in abused children. *APS Observer, 16,* 1, 31–33.

Reznick, J. S., Kagan, J., Snidman, N., Gersten, M., Baak, K., & Rosenberg, A. (1986). Inhibited and uninhibited children: A follow-up study. *Child Development, 57,* 660–680.

Reznikoff, M., Domino, G., Bridges, C., & Honeyman, M. (1973). Creative abilities in identical and fraternal twins. *Behavior Genetics, 3,* 365–377.

Rhee, S. H., & Waldman, I. D. (2002). Genetic and environmental influences on antisocial behavior: A meta-analysis of twin and adoption studies. *Psychological Bulletin, 128,* 490–529.

Rhodes, S. R. (1983). Age-related differences in work attitudes and behavior: A review and conceptual analysis. *Psychological Bulletin, 93,* 328–367.

Rholes, W. S., Simpson, Jeffry A., Campbell, L., & Grich, J. (2001). Adult attachment and the transition to parenthood. *Journal of Personality and Social Psychology, 81,* 421–435.

Ribeiro, F., de Mendonca, A., & Guerreiro, M. (2006). Mild cognitive impairment: Deficits in cognitive domains other than memory. *Dementia and Geriatric Cognitive Disorders, 21,* 284–290.

Ricciardelli, L. A., & McCabe, M. P. (2001). Children's body image concerns and eating disturbance: A review of the literature. *Clinical Psychology Review, 21,* 325–344.

Rice, F., Harold, G. T., & Thapar, A. (2003). Negative life events as an account of age-related differences in the genetic aetiology of depression in childhood and adolescence. *Journal of Child Psychology and Psychiatry and Allied Disciplines, 44,* 977–987.

Richard, J. F., Normandeau, J., Brun, V., & Maillet, M. (2004). Attracting and maintaining infant attention during habituation: Further evidence of the importance of stimulus complexity. *Infant and Child Development, 13,* 277–286.

Richards, F. A., & Commons, M. L. (1990). Postformal cognitive-developmental theory and research: A review of its current status. In C. N. Alexander & E. J. Langer (Eds.), *Higher stages of human development: Perspectives on adult growth.* New York: Oxford University Press.

Richards, R. (1996). Beyond Piaget: Accepting divergent, chaotic, and creative thought. In M. A. Runco (Ed.), *Creativity from childhood through adulthood: The developmental issues.* San Francisco: Jossey-Bass.

Riediger, M., Li, S., & Lindenberger, U. (2006). Selection, optimization, and compensation as developmental mechanisms of adaptive resource allocation: Review and preview. In J. E. Birren & K. W. Schaie (Eds.), *Handbook of the psychology of aging.* Boston: Elsevier Academic Press.

Riegel, K. F. (1973). Dialectic operations: The final period of cognitive development. *Human Development, 16,* 346–370.

Rieser, J., Yonas, A., & Wilkner, K. (1976). Radial localization of odors by human newborns. *Child Development, 47,* 856–859.

Rieser, P. & Underwood, L. E. (2004). *A guide to normal growth in children.* Available: http://www.andorrapediatrics.com/handouts/growth.html (retrieved 11/18/2004).

Riley, K. P., Snowdon, D. A., Saunders, A. M., Roses, A. D., Mortimer, J. A., & Nanayakkara, N. (2000). Cognitive function and apolipoprotein E in very old adults: Findings from the Nun Study. *Journal of Gerontology: Psychological Sciences & Social Sciences, 55B,* S69–S75.

Riley, L. P., LaMontagne, L. L., Hepworth, J. T., & Murphy, B. A. (2007). Parental grief responses and personal growth following the death of a child. *Death Studies, 31,* 277–299.

Rilling, M. (2000). John Watson's paradoxical struggle to explain Freud. *American Psychologist, 55,* 301–312.

Rimm-Kaufman, S., & Pianta, R. C. (1999). Patterns of family–school contact in preschool and kindergarten. *School Psychology Review, 28,* 426–438.

Ringler, L. L., & Hayden, D. C. (2000). Adolescent bereavement and social support: Peer loss compared to other losses. *Journal of Adolescent Research, 15,* 209–230.

Rivera-Gaxiola, M., Silva-Pereyra, J., & Kuhl, P. K. (2005). Brain potentials to native and non-native speech contrasts in 7- and 11-month-old American infants. *Developmental Science, 8,* 162–172.

Riviere, J., & Lecuyer, R. (2003). The C-not-B error: A comparative study. *Cognitive Development, 18,* 285–297.

Roberto, K. A., & Scott, J. P. (1986). Equity considerations in the friendships of older adults. *Journal of Gerontology, 41,* 241–247.

Roberts, B. W., & Caspi, A. (2003). The cumulative continuity model of personality development: Striking a balance between continuity and change in personality traits across the life course. In U. M. Staudinger & U. Lindenberger (Eds.), *Understanding human development: Dialogues with life-span psychology.* Dordrecht, Netherlands: Kluwer Academic.

Roberts, B. W., & DelVecchio, W. F. (2000). The rank-order consistency of personality traits from childhood to old age: A quantitative review of longitudinal studies. *Psychological Bulletin, 126,* 3–25.

Roberts, B. W., & Robins, R. W. (2004). Person-environment fit and its implications for personality development: A longitudinal study. *Journal of Personality, 72,* 89–110.

Roberts, B. W., Walton, K. E., & Viechtbauer, W. (2006). Patterns of mean-level change in personality traits across the life course: A meta-analysis of longitudinal studies. *Psychological Bulletin, 132,* 1–25.

Roberts, D., & Foehr, U. (2004). *Kids & media in America.* Cambridge, MA: University Press.

Roberts, L. R., Sarigiani, P. A., Petersen, A. C., & Newman, J. L. (1990). Gender differences in the relationship between achievement and self image during early adolescence. *Journal of Early Adolescence, 10,* 159–175.

Robertson, N. R. C. (1993). *A manual of neonatal intensive care* (3rd ed.). London: Edward Arnold.

Robins, L. N., & Regier, D. A. (Eds.). (1991). *Psychiatric disorders in America. The Epidemiologic Catchment Area Study.* New York: The Free Press.

Robins, R. W., Caspi, A., & Moffitt, T. E. (2000). Two personalities, one relationship: Both partners' personality traits shape the quality of their relationship. *Journal of Personality and Social Psychology, 79,* 251–259.

Robins, R. W., Trzesniewski, K. H., Tracy, J. L., Gosling, S. D., & Potter, J. (2002). Global self-esteem across the life span. *Psychology and Aging, 17,* 423–434.

Robinson, C. C., & Morris, J. T. (1986). The gender-stereotyped nature of Christmas toys received by 36-, 48-, and 60-month-old children: A comparison between nonrequested vs. requested toys. *Sex Roles, 15,* 21–32.

Robinson, N. M., Abbott, R. D., Berninger, V. W., & Busse, J. (1996). The structure of abilities in mathematically precocious young children: Gender similarities and differences. *Journal of Educational Psychology, 88,* 341–352.

Robinson, N. M., & Janos, P. M. (1986). Psychological adjustment in a college-level program of marked academic acceleration. *Journal of Youth and Adolescence, 15,* 51–60.

Robinson, P. K. (1983). The sociological perspective. In R. B. Weg (Ed.), *Sexuality in the later years: Roles and behavior.* New York: Academic Press.

Robinson, T. (1999). Reducing children's television to prevent obesity: A randomized control trial. *Journal of the American Medical Association, 282,* 1561–1567.

Robinson, T., & Marwit, S. J. (2006). An investigation of the relationship of personality, coping, and grief intensity among bereaved mothers. *Death Studies, 30,* 677–696.

Roccella, M., & Testa, D. (2003). Fetal alcohol syndrome in developmental age: Neuropsychiatric aspects. *Minerva Pediatrics, 55,* 63–69.

Rochat, P., & Striano, T. (2000). Perceived self in infancy. *Infant Behavior and Development, 23,* 513–530.

Röcke, C., & Cherry, K. E. (2002). Death at the end of the 20th century: Individual processes and developmental tasks in old age. *International Journal of Aging and Human Development, 54,* 315–333.

Rodin, J., & Langer, E. (1980). Aging labels: The decline of control and the fall of self-esteem. *Journal of Social Issues, 36,* 12–29.

Rodkin, P. C., & Hodges, E. V. E. (2003). Bullies and victims in the peer ecology: Four questions for psychological and school professionals. *School Psychology Review, 32,* 384–401.

Rogan, W. J., & Ware, J. H. (2003). Exposure to lead in children: How low is low enough? *New England Journal of Medicine, 384,* 1515–1516.

Rogers, M. T. (1986). *A comparative study of developmental traits of gifted and average children.* Unpublished doctoral dissertation, University of Denver.

Rogers, S. J., & May, D. C. (2003). Spillover between marital quality and job satisfaction: Long-term patterns and gender differences. *Journal of Marriage and the Family, 65,* 482–495.

Rogler, L. H. (2002). The case of the Great Depression and World War II. *American Psychologist, 57,* 1013–1023.

Rogoff, B. (1998). Cognition as a collaborative process. In D. Kuhn & R. S. Siegler (Vol. Eds.), W. Damon (Editor-in-Chief), *Handbook of child psychology: Cognition, perception, and language* (5th ed.). New York: Wiley.

Rogoff, B. (2003). *The cultural nature of human development.* New York: Oxford University Press.

Rogoff, B., Paradise, R., Arauz, R. M., Correa-Chavez, M., & Angelillo, C. (2003). Firsthand learning through intent participation. *Annual Review of Psychology, 54,* 175–203.

Roid, G. (2003). *Stanford-Binet Intelligence Scales* (5th ed.). Itasca, IL: Riverside Publishing.

Roisman, G. I. (2007). The psychopathology of adult attachment relationships: Autonomic reactivity in marital and premarital interactions. *Developmental Psychology, 43,* 39–53.

Roizen, N. J., & Patterson, D. (2003). Down's syndrome. *Lancet, 361,* 1281–1289.

Rollins, B. C., & Feldman, H. (1970). Marital satisfaction over the family life cycle. *Journal of Marriage and the Family, 32,* 20–28.

Rolls, B. J. (1999). Do chemosensory changes influence food intake in the elderly? *Physiological Behavior, 66,* 193–197.

Román, G. C. (2003). Neurological aspects of vascular dementia: Basic concepts, diagnosis, and management. In P. A. Lichtenberg, D. L. Murman, & A. M. Mellow (Eds.), *Handbook of dementia. Psychological, neurological, and psychiatric perspectives.* Hoboken, NJ: John Wiley & Sons.

Ronald, A., Happé, F., Bolton, P., Butcher, L. M., Price, T. S., Wheelright, S., Baron-Cohen, S., & Plomin, R. (2006). Genetic heterogeneity between the three components of the autism spectrum: A twin study. *Journal of the American Academy of Child and Adolescent Psychiatry, 45,* 691–699.

Ronald, A., Happé, F., Hughes, C., & Plomin, R. (2005). Nice and nasty theory of mind in pre-school children: Nature and nurture. *Social Development, 14,* 664–684.

Ronald, A., Happé, F., & Plomin, R. (2006). Genetic research into autism. *Science, 311,* 952.

Rönnlund, M., Nyberg, L., Bäckman, L., & Nillson, L-G. (2005). Stability, growth, and decline in adult life span development of declarative memory: Cross-sectional and longitudinal data from a population-based study. *Psychology and Aging, 20,* 3–18.

Rook, K. S. (1984). Promoting social bonding. Strategies for helping the lonely and socially isolated. *American Psychologist, 39,* 1389–1407.

Rook, K. S. (1991). Facilitating friendship formation in late life: Puzzles and challenges. *American Journal of Community Psychology, 19,* 103–110.

Rose, A. J., Carlson, W., & Waller, E. M. (2007). Prospective associations of co-rumination with friendship and emotional adjustment: Considering the socioemotional trade-offs of co-rumination. *Developmental Psychology, 43,* 1019–1031.

Rose, A. J., Swenson, L. P., & Waller, E. M. (2004). Overt and relational aggression and perceived popularity: Developmental differences in concurrent and prospective relations. *Developmental Psychology, 40,* 378–387.

Rose, S. A., & Feldman, J. F. (1997). Memory and speed: Their role in the relation of infant information processing to later IQ. *Child Development, 68,* 630–641.

Rose, S. A., Feldman, J. F., Futterweit, L. R., & Jankowski, J. J. (1997). Continuity in visual cognition memory: Infancy to 11 years. *Intelligence, 24,* 381–392.

Rose, S. A., Feldman, J. F., & Jankowski, J. J. (2003). Infant visual recognition memory: Independent contributions of speed and attention. *Developmental Psychology, 39,* 563–571.

Rose, S. A., Feldman, J. F., Jankowski, J. J., & Rossem, R. (2005). Pathways from prematurity and infant abilities to later cognition. *Child Development, 76,* 1172–1184.

Rose, S. A., Feldman, J. F., Wallace, I. F., & McCarton, C. (1989). Infant visual attention: Relation to birth status and developmental outcome during the first 5 years. *Developmental Psychology, 25,* 560–576.

Rosenberg, J. (2001). Exposure to multiple risk factors linked to delivery of underweight infants. *Family Planning Perspectives, 33,* 238.

Rosenberg, S. D., Rosenberg, H. J., & Farrell, M. P. (1999). The midlife crisis revisited. In S. L. Willis & J. D. Reid (Eds.), *Life in the middle. Psychological and social development in middle age.* San Diego: Academic Press.

Rosenblatt, P. C. (1993). Cross-cultural variation in the experience, expression, and understanding of grief. In D. P. Irish, K. F. Lundquist, & V. J. Nelson (Eds.), *Ethnic variations in dying, death, and grief: Diversity in universality.* Washington, D.C.: Taylor and Francis.

Rosenblatt, P. C. (2001). A social constructionist perspective on cultural differences in grief. In M. S. Stroebe, R. O. Hansson, W. Stroebe, & H. Schut (Eds.), *Handbook of bereavement research. Consequences, coping, and care.* Washington, D.C.: American Psychological Association.

Rosenbloom, C., & Bahns, M. (2006). What can we learn about diet and physical activity from master athletes? *Holistic Nursing Practice, 20,* 161–167.

Rosenfeld, R. G. (1997). Is growth hormone just a tall story? *Journal of Pediatrics, 130,* 172–174.

Rosenthal, P. A., & Rosenthal, S. (1984). Suicidal behavior by preschool children. *American Journal of Psychiatry, 141,* 520–525.

Roskos, K. A., Christie, J. F., & Richgels, D. J. (2003, March). The essentials of early literacy instruction. *Young Children,* 52–60.

Ross, C. A., Miler, S. D., Bjornson, L., Reagor, P., Fraser, G. A., & Anderson, G. (1991). Abuse histories in 102 cases of multiple personality disorder. *Canadian Journal of Psychiatry, 36,* 97–101.

Ross, E. E. T., & Aday, L. A. (2006). Stress and coping in African American grandparents who are raising their grandchildren. *Journal of Family Issues, 27,* 912–932.

Ross, H. G., & Milgram, J. I. (1982). Important variables in adult sibling relationships: A qualitative study. In M. E. Lamb & B. Sutton-Smith (Eds.), *Sibling relationships: Their nature and significance across the lifespan.* Hillsdale, NJ: Erlbaum.

Ross, M. T., et al. (2005). The DNA sequence of the human X chromosome. *Nature, 434,* 325–337.

Ross, R. T., Begab, M. J., Dondis, E. H., Giampicolo, J. S., Jr., & Meyers, C. E. (1985). *Lives of the mentally retarded: A forty-year follow-up study.* Stanford, CA: Stanford University Press.

Rossell, C. H., Armor, D. J., & Walberg, H. J. (Eds.) (2002). *School desegregation in the 21st century.* Westport, CT: Praeger.

Roth, F. P., Speece, D. L., & Cooper, D. H. (2002). A longitudinal analysis of the connection between oral language and early reading. *Journal of Educational Research, 95,* 259–272.

Roth, G. S. (2005). Caloric restriction and caloric restriction mimetics: Current status and promise for the future. *Journal of the American Geriatrics Society, 53,* S280–S283.

Roth, P. L., Bevier, C. A., Switzer, F. S., & Schippmann, J. S. (1996). Meta-analyzing the relationship between grades and job performance. *Journal of Applied Psychology, 81,* 548–556.

Rothbart, M. K., Ahadi, S. A., & Evans, D. E. (2000). Temperament and personality: Origins and outcomes. *Journal of Personality and Social Psychology, 78,* 122–135.

Rothbart, M. K., & Bates, J. E. (2006). Temperament. In N. Eisenberg (Vol. Ed.) & W. Damon & R. M. Lerner (Eds. in Chief), *Handbook of child psychology: Vol. 3. Social, emotional, and personality development* (6th ed.). Hoboken, NJ: Wiley.

Rothbart, M. K., & Derryberry, D. (2002). Temperament in children. In C. von Hofsten & L. Backman (Eds.), *Psychology at the turn of the millennium: Vol. 2. Social, developmental, and clinical perspectives.* New York: Taylor & Francis.

Rothbaum, F., & Morelli, G. (2005). Attachment and culture: Bridging relativism and universalism. In W. Friedlmeier, P. Chakkarath, & B. Schwarz (Eds.), *Culture and human development: The importance of cross-cultural research for the social sciences.* New York: Psychology Press.

Rothbaum, F., & Trommsdorff, G. (2007). Do roots and wings complement or oppose one another? The socialization of relatedness and autonomy in cultural context. In J. E. Grusec & P. D. Hastings (Eds.), *Handbook of socialization: Theory and research*. New York: Guilford.

Rothbaum, F., Weisz, J., Pott, M., Miyake, K., & Morelli, G. (2000). Attachment and culture: Security in the United States and Japan. *American Psychologist, 55*, 1093–1104.

Rothbaum, R., Pott, M., Azuma, H., Miyake, K., & Weisz, J. (2000). The development of close relationships in Japan and the United States: Paths of symbiotic harmony and generative tension. *Child Development, 71*, 1121–1142.

Rotheram-Borus, M. J., Piacentini, J., Cantwell, C., Belin, T. R., & Song, J. W. (2000). The 18-month impact of an emergency room intervention for adolescent female suicide attempters. *Journal of Consulting and Clinical Psychology, 68*, 1081–1093.

Rothermund, K. (2005). Effects of age stereotypes on self-views and adaptation. In W. Greve, K. Rothermund, & D. Wentura (Eds.), *The adaptive self: Personal continuity and intentional self-development*. Cambridge, MA: Hofgrefe & Huber.

Rothermund, K., & Brandtstädter, J. (2003a). Age stereotypes and self-views in later life: Evaluating rival assumptions. *International Journal of Behavioral Development, 27*, 549–554.

Rothermund, K., & Brandtstädter, J. (2003b). Coping with deficits and losses in later life: From compensatory action to accommodation. *Psychology and Aging, 18*, 896–905.

Rovee-Collier, C. (1997). Dissociations in infant memory: Rethinking the development of implicit and explicit memory. *Psychological Review, 104*, 467–498.

Rovee-Collier, C. (1999). The development of infant memory. *Current Directions in Psychological Science, 8*, 80–85.

Rovee-Collier, C. (2001). Information pick-up by infants: What is it, and how can we tell? *Journal of Experimental Child Psychology, 78*, 35–49.

Rovee-Collier, C., & Barr, R. (2004). Infant learning and memory. In G. Bremner & A. Fogel (Eds.), *Blackwell handbook of infant development* (pp. 139–168). Malden, MA: Blackwell Publishing.

Rovee-Collier, C., & Boller, K. (1995). Current theory and research on infant learning and memory: Application to early intervention. *Infants and Young Children, 7*, 1–12.

Rovner, S. (1994, March 29). An Alzheimer's journal. *The Washington Post—Health*, 12–15.

Rowe, D. C. (1994). *The limits of family influence: Genes, experience, and behavior*. New York: Guilford.

Rowe, D. C. (2003). Assessing genotype-environment interactions and correlations in the postgenomic era. In R. Plomin, J. C. DeFries, I. W. Craig, & P. McGuffin (Eds.), *Behavioral genetics in the postgenomic era*. Washington, D.C.: American Psychological Association.

Rowe, D. C., Almeida, D. M., & Jacobson, K. C. (1999). School context and genetic influences on aggression in adolescence. *Psychological Science, 10*, 277–280.

Rowe, D. C., & Jacobson, K. C. (1999). In the mainstream. Research in behavioral genetics. In R. A. Carson & M. A. Rothstein (Eds.), *Behavioral genetics. The clash of culture and biology*. Baltimore: Johns Hopkins University Press.

Rowe, D. C., Vesterdal, W. J., & Rodgers, J. L. (1999). Herrnstein's syllogism: Genetic and shared environmental influences on IQ, education, and income. *Intelligence, 26*, 405–423.

Rowe, J. W., & Kahn, R. L. (1998). *Successful aging*. New York: Pantheon.

Rowley, S. J., Jurtz-Costes, B., Mistry, R., & Feagans, L. (2007). Social status as a predictor of race and gender stereotypes in late childhood and early adolescence. *Social Development, 16*, 150–156.

Rubin, D. C. (2002). Autobiographical memory across the lifespan. In P. Graf & N. Ohta (Eds.), *Lifespan development of human memory* (pp. 159–184). Cambridge, MA: Massachusetts Institute of Technology.

Rubin, D. C., Rahhal, T. A., & Poon, L. W. (1998). Things learned in early adulthood are remembered best. *Memory and Cognition, 26*, 3–19.

Rubin, J. Z., Provenzano, F. J., & Luria, Z. (1974). The eye of the beholder: Parents' views on sex of newborns. *American Journal of Orthopsychiatry, 44*, 512–519.

Rubin, K. H., Bukowski, W. M., & Parker, J. G. (2006). Peer interactions, relationships, and groups. In N. Eisenberg (Vol. Ed.), & W. Damon & R. M. Lerner (Eds. in Chief), *Handbook of child psychology: Vol. 3. Social, emotional, and personality development* (6th ed.). Hoboken, NJ: Wiley.

Rubinow, D. R., & Schmidt, P. J. (1996). Androgens, brain, and behavior. *American Journal of Psychiatry, 153*, 974–984.

Rubinstein, R. L., Alexander, R. B., Goodman, M., & Luborsky, M. (1991). Key relationships of never married, childless older women: A cultural analysis. *Journal of Gerontology: Social Sciences, 46*, S270–S277.

Ruble, D. N., & Dweck, C. S. (1995). Self-conceptions, person conceptions, and their development. In N. Eisenberg (Ed.), *Social development*. Thousand Oaks, CA: Sage.

Ruble, D. N., Eisenberg, R., & Higgins, E. T. (1994). Developmental changes in achievement evaluation: Motivational implications of self–other differences. *Child Development, 65*, 1095–1110.

Ruble, D. N., Taylor, L. J., Cypers, L., Greulich, F. K., Lurye, L. E., & Shrout, P. E. (2007). The role of gender constancy in early gender development. *Child Development, 78*, 1121–1136.

Ruchlin, H. S., & Lachs, M. S. (1999). Prevalence and correlates of exercise among older adults. *Journal of Applied Gerontology, 18*, 341–356.

Rudolph, K. D., & Flynn, M. (2007). Childhood adversity and youth depression: Influence of gender and pubertal status. *Development and Psychopathology, 19*, 497–521.

Ruff, H. A., & Capozzoli, M. C. (2003). Development of attention and distractibility in the first 4 years of life. *Developmental Psychology, 39*, 877–890.

Ruff, H. A., & Lawson, K. R. (1990). Development of sustained, focused attention in young children during free play. *Developmental Psychology, 26*, 85–93.

Ruff, H. A., & Rothbart, M. K. (1996). *Attention in early development: Themes and variations*. New York: Oxford University Press.

Ruff, H. A., Saltarelli, L. M., Coppozzoli, M., & Dubiner, K. (1992). The differentiation of activity in infants' exploration of objects. *Developmental Psychology, 27*, 851–861.

Ruffman, T. K., & Olson, D. R. (1989). Children's ascriptions of knowledge to others. *Developmental Psychology, 25*, 601–606.

Ruffman, T., Slade, L., & Redman, J. (2005). Young infants' expectations about hidden objects. *Cognition, 97*, 835–843.

Ruffman, T., Slade, L., Sandino, J. C., & Fletcher, A. (2005). Are A-Not-B errors caused by a belief about object location? *Child Development, 76*, 122–136.

Ruggles, S. (1994). The origins of African-American family structure. *American Sociological Review, 59*, 136–151.

Rumberger, R. W., & Palardy, G. J. (2005). Does segregation still matter? The impact of student composition on academic achievement in high school. *Teachers College Record, 107*, 1999–2045.

Runco, M. A. (1992). Children's divergent thinking and creative ideation. *Developmental Review, 12*, 233–264.

Runco, M. A. (2006). Information, experience, and divergent thinking: An empirical test. *Creativity Research Journal, 18*, 269–277.

Runco, M. A. (2007). *Creativity—Theories and themes: Research, development, and practice*. Burlington, MA: Elsevier Academic Press.

Russ, S. W. (1996). Development of creative processes in children. In M. A. Runco (Ed.), *Creativity from childhood through adulthood: The developmental issues*. San Francisco: Jossey-Bass.

Russell, A., Aloa, V., Feder, T., Glover, A., Miller, H., & Palmer, G. (1998). Sex-based differences in parenting styles in a sample with preschool children. *Australian Journal of Psychology, 50*, 89–99.

Russell, R. J., & Wells, P. A. (1991). Personality similarity and quality of marriage. *Personality and Individual Differences, 12*, 407–412.

Rust, J., Golombok, S., Hines, M., Johnston, K., & Golding, J. (2000). The role of brothers and sisters in the gender development of preschool children. *Journal of Experimental Child Psychology, 77*, 292–303.

Ruth, J. E., & Coleman, P. (1996). Personality and aging: Coping and management of the self in later life. In J. E. Birren, K. W. Schaie, R. P. Abeles, M. Gatz, & T. A. Salthouse (Eds.), *Handbook of the psychology of aging* (4th ed.). San Diego: Academic Press.

Rutter, M. (1983). School effects on pupil progress: Research findings and policy implications. *Child Development, 54*, 1–29.

Rutter, M., Kim-Cohen, J., & Maughan, B. (2006). Continuities and discontinuities in psychopathology between childhood and adult life. *Journal of Child Psychology and Psychiatry, 47*, 276–295.

Rutter, M., & Maughan, B. (2002). School effectiveness findings 1979–2002. *Journal of School Psychology, 50*, 451–475.

Rutter, M., Maughan, B., Mortimore, P., Ouston, J., & Smith, A. (1979). *Fifteen thousand hours: Secondary schools and their effects on children*. Cambridge, MA: Harvard University Press.

Rutter, M., Moffitt, T. E., & Caspi, A. (2006). Gene–environment interplay and psychopathology: Multiple varieties but real effects. *Journal of Child Psychology and Psychiatry, 47*, 226–261.

Rutter, M., & O'Connor, T. G. (2004). Are there biological programming effects for psychological development? Findings from a study of Romanian adoptees. *Developmental Psychology, 40*, 81–94.

Rutter, M., & Sroufe, L. A. (2000). Developmental psychopathology: Concepts and challenges. *Development and Psychopathology, 12*, 265–296.

Ruusuvirta, T., Huotilainen, M., Fellman, V., & Naatanen, R. (2003). The newborn human brain binds sound features together. *Neuroreport, 14*, 2117–2119.

Ryabov, I., & Van Hook, J. (2007). School segregation and academic achievement among Hispanic children. *Social Science Research, 36*, 767–788.

Ryan, A. S. & Zhou, W. (2006). Lower breastfeeding rates persist among the special supplemental nutrition program for women, infants, and children participants, 1978–2003. *Pediatrics, 117*, 1136–1146.

Ryan, R. M., & Kuczkowski, R. (1994). The imaginary audience, self-consciousness, and public individuation in adolescence. *Journal of Personality, 62*, 219–238.

Rybash, J. M. (1999). Aging and autobiographical memory: The long and bumpy road. *Journal of Adult Development, 6*, 1–10.

Ryff, C. D. (1991). Possible selves in adulthood and old age: A tale of shifting horizons. *Psychology and Aging, 6*, 286–295.

S

Saarni, C. (1999). *The development of emotional competence*. New York: Guilford Press.

Saarni, C., Campos, J. J., Camras, L. A., & Withington, D. (2006). Emotional development: Action, communication, and understanding. In N. Eisenberg (Vol. Ed.), & W. Damon & R. M. Lerner (Eds. in Chief), *Handbook of child psychology: Vol. 3. Social, emotional, and personality development* (6th ed). Hoboken, NJ: Wiley.

Sabattini, L., & Leaper, C. (2004). The relation between mothers' and fathers' parenting styles and their division of labor in the home: Young adults' retrospective reports. *Sex Roles, 50*, 217–225.

Sabbagh, M. A. (2006). Neurocognitive bases of preschoolers' theory-of-mind development: Integrating cognitive neuroscience and cognitive development. In P. J. Marshall & N. A. Fox (Eds.), *The development of social engagement: Neurobiological perspectives*. New York: Oxford University Press.

Sackett, P. R., Hardison, C. M., & Cullen, M. J. (2004). On interpreting stereotype threat as accounting for African American-White differences on cognitive tests. *American Psychologist, 59*, 7–13.

Sacks, O. (1993, December 27). A neurologist's notebook: An anthropologist on Mars. *The New Yorker*, 106–125.

Sadeh, A., Gruber, R., & Raviv, A. (2003). The effects of sleep restriction and extension on school-age children: What a difference an hour makes. *Child Development, 74*, 444–455.

Sadler, T. W. (2004). *Langman's medical embryology* (9th ed.). Philadelphia: Lippincott, Williams, & Wilkins.

Saffran, J. R., Werker, J. F., & Werner, L. A. (2006). The infant's auditory world: Hearing, speech, and the beginnings of language. In D. Kuhn & R. Siegler (Vol. Eds.), *Handbook of child psychology: Cognition, perception, and language: Vol. 2* (6th ed.). Hoboken, NJ: Wiley.

Sagara-Rosemeyer, M., & Davies, B. (2007). The integration of religious traditions in Japanese children's view of death and afterlife. *Death Studies, 31*, 223–247.

Sai, F. Z. (2005). The role of the mother's voice in developing mother's face preference: Evidence for intermodal perception at birth. *Infant and Child Development, 14*, 9–50.

Saigal, S., Stoskopf, B., Boyle, M., Paneth, N., Pinelli, J., Streiner, D., & Godderis, J. (2007). Comparison of current health, functional limitations, and health care use of young adults who were born with extremely low birth weight and normal birth weight. *Pediatrics, 119*, e562–e573.

Salapatek, P. (1975). Pattern perception in early infancy. In L. B. Cohen & P. Salapatek (Eds.), *Infant perception: From sensation to cognition, Vol 1*. New York: Academic Press.

Salend, S. J. (1999). Facilitating friendships among diverse students. *Intervention in School and Clinic, 35*, 9–15.

Sales, B. D., & Folkman, S. (2000). *Ethics in research with human participants*. Washington, D.C.: American Psychological Association.

Salihu, H. M., Sharma, P. P., Ekundayo, O. J., Kristensen, S., Badewa, A. P., Kirby, R. S., & Alexander, G. R. (2006) Childhood pregnancy (10–14 years old) and risk of stillbirth in singletons and twins. *The Journal of Pediatrics, 148*, 522–566.

Salihu, H. M., Shumpert, M. N., Slay, M., Kirby, R. S., & Alexander, G. R. (2003). Childbearing beyond maternal age 50 and fetal outcomes in the United States. *Obstetrics and Gynecology, 102*, 1006–1014.

Salthouse, T. A. (1990). Cognitive competence and expertise in aging. In J. E. Birren & K. W. Schaie (Eds.), *The handbook of the psychology of aging* (3rd ed.). San Diego: Academic Press.

Salthouse, T. A. (1993). Speed and knowledge as determinants of adult age differences in verbal tasks. *Journal of Gerontology: Psychological Sciences, 48*, 29–36.

Salthouse, T. A. (1996). General and specific speed mediation of adult age differences in memory. *Journals of Gerontology: Psychological Sciences and Social Sciences, 51B*, 30–42.

Salthouse, T. A. (2000). Aging and measures of processing speed. *Biological Psychology, 54*, 35–54.

Salthouse, T. A., Hancock, H. E., Meinz, E. J., & Hambrick, D. Z. (1996). Interrelations of age, visual acuity, and cognitive functioning. *Journals of Gerontology: Psychological Sciences and Social Sciences, 51*, 317–330.

Sameroff, A. (1975). Early influences on development: Fact or fancy? *Merrill-Palmer Quarterly, 21*, 263–294.

Sameroff, A. J. (2000). Developmental systems and psychopathology. *Development and Psychopathology, 12*, 297–312.

Sameroff, A. J., Seifer, R., Baldwin, A., & Baldwin, C. (1993). Stability of intelligence from preschool to adolescence: The influence of social and family risk factors. *Child Development, 64*, 80–97.

Samson, M. M., Meeuwsen, I. B. A. E., Crowe, A., Dessens, J. A. G., Duursma, S. A., & Verhaar, H. J. J. (2000). Relationships between physical performance measures, age, height and body weight in healthy adults. *Age and Ageing, 29*, 235–242.

Samuelson, R. J. (2002, December 16). The "mature worker" glut. *Newsweek*, 55.

Samuolis, J., Layburn, K., & Schiaffino, K. M. (2001). Identity development and attachment to parents in college students. *Journal of Youth and Adolescence, 30*, 373–384.

Sanchez, L., Fristad, M., Weller, R. A., Weller, E. B., & Moye, J. (1994). Anxiety in acutely bereaved prepubertal children. *Annals of Clinical Psychiatry, 6*, 39–43.

Sandler, I. N., Ayers, T. S., Wolchik, S. A., Tein, J., Kwok, O., Haine, R. A., Twohey-Jacobs, J., Suter, J., Lin, K., Padgett-Jones, S., Weyer, J. L., Cole, E., Kriege, G., & Griffin, W. A. (2003). The Family Bereavement Program: Efficacy evaluation of a theory-based prevention program for parentally-bereaved children and adolescents. *Journal of Consulting and Clinical Psychology, 71*, 587–600.

Sanson, A., Hemphill, S. A., & Smart, D. (2004). Connections between temperament and social development: A review. *Social Development, 13*, 142–170.

Santos, L. L., Magalhaes, M. C., Januario, J. N., Aguiar, M. J., & Carvalho, M. R. (2006). The time has come: A new scene for PKU treatment. *Genetics & Molecular Research, 5*, 33–44.

Sargant, N., Field, J., Francis, H., Schuller, T., & Tuckett, A. (1997). *The learning divide*. Brighton, UK: National Organisation for Adult Learning.

Sarkisian, N., Gerena, M., & Gerstel, N. (2007). Extended family integration among Euro and Mexican Americans: Ethnicity, gender, and class. *Journal of Marriage and Family, 69*, 40–54.

Sarkisian, N., & Gerstel, N. (2004). Explaining the gender gap in help to parents: The importance of employment. *Journal of Marriage and Family, 66*, 431–451.

Sartor, C. E., & Youniss, J. (2002). The relationship between positive parental involvement and identity achievement during adolescence. *Adolescence, 37*, 221–234.

Sassler, S. (2004). The process of entering into cohabiting unions. *Journal of Marriage and Family, 66*, 491–505.

Satariano, W. A. (2006). *Epidemiology of aging: An ecological approach*. Sudbury, MA: Jones & Bartlett.

Saucier, G., & Simonds, J. (2006). The structure of personality and temperament. In D. K. Mroczek & T. D. Little (Eds.), *Handbook of personality development*. Mahwah, NJ: Erlbaum.

Saunders, C. (2002). A hospice perspective. In K. Foley, & H. Hendin (Eds.), *The case against assisted suicide: For the right to end-of-life care*. Baltimore: The Johns Hopkins Press.

Savage, J. S. (2001). Birth stories: A way of knowing in childbirth education. *Journal of Perinatal Education, 10*, 3–7.

Savin-Williams, R. C. (1995). An exploratory study of pubertal maturation timing and self-esteem among gay and bisexual male youths., *Developmental Psychology, 31*, 56-64.

Savin-Williams, R. C., & Ream, G. L. (2003). Sex variations in the disclosure to parents of same-sex attractions. *Journal of Family Psychology, 17*, 429–438.

Savin-Williams, R. C., & Ream, G. L. (2007). Prevalence and stability of sexual orientation components during adolescence and young adulthood. *Archives of Sexual Behavior, 36,* 385–394.

Saxe, R., Carey, S., & Kanwisher, N. (2004). Understanding other minds: Linking developmental psychology and functional neuroimaging. *Annual Review of Psychology, 55,* 87–124.

Saxe, R., & Kanwisher, N. (2003). People thinking about thinking people: The role of the temporo-parietal junction in "theory of mind." *NeuroImage, 19,* 1835–1842.

Saxe, R., & Powell, L. J. (2006). It's the thought that counts: Specific brain regions for one component of theory of mind. *Psychological Science, 17,* 692–699.

Saxton, M. (1997). The contrast theory of negative input. *Journal of Child Language, 24,* 139–161.

Sayal, K., Heron, J., Golding, J., & Emond, A. (2007). Prenatal alcohol exposure and gender differences in childhood mental health problems: A longitudinal population-based study. *Pediatrics, 119,* e426–e434.

Sayer, L. C. (2005). Gender, time and inequality: Trends in women's and men's paid work, unpaid work and free time. *Social Forces, 84,* 285–303.

Sayre, N. E., & Gallagher, J. D. (2001). *The young child and the environment.* Boston: Allyn & Bacon.

Scafidi, F. A., Field, T., & Schanberg, S. M. (1993). Factors that predict which preterm infants benefit most from massage therapy. *Journal of Developmental and Behavioral Pediatrics, 14,* 176–180.

Scannell-Desch, E. A. (2005). Prebereavement and postbereavement struggles and triumphs of midlife widows. *Journal of Hospice and Palliative Nursing, 7,* 15–22.

Scarr, S., & McCartney, K. (1983). How people make their own environments: A theory of genotype → environment effects. *Child Development, 54,* 424–435.

Scarr, S., & Weinberg, R. A. (1978). The influence of family background on intellectual attainment. *American Sociological Review, 43,* 674–692.

Scarr, S., & Weinberg, R. A. (1983). The Minnesota adoption studies: Genetic differences and malleability. *Child Development, 54,* 260–267.

Schaal, B., Barlier, L., & Soussignan, R. (1998). Olfactory function in the human fetus: Evidence from selective neonatal responsiveness to the odor of amniotic fluid. *Behavioral Neuroscience, 112,* 1438–1449.

Schacter, D. L. (1996). *Searching for memory: The brain, the mind, and the past.* New York: Basic Books.

Schaefer, E. S. (1959). A circumplex model for maternal behavior. *Journal of Abnormal and Social Psychology, 59,* 226–235.

Schaffer, H. R., & Emerson, P. E. (1964). The development of social attachments in infancy. *Monographs of the Society for Research in Child Development, 29* (3, Serial No. 94).

Schaie, K. W. (1994). Developmental designs revisited. In S. H. Cohen & H. W. Reese (Eds.), *Life-span developmental psychology: Methodological contributions.* Hillsdale, NJ: Erlbaum.

Schaie, K. W. (1996). *Intellectual development in adulthood: The Seattle Longitudinal Study.*

Cambridge, England: Cambridge University Press.

Schaie, K. W. (2000). The impact of longitudinal studies on understanding development from young adulthood to old age. *International Journal of Behavioral Development, 24,* 257–266.

Schaie, K. W. (2005). *Developmental influences on adult intelligence: The Seattle Longitudinal Study.* New York: Oxford University Press.

Schaie, K. W., & Caskie, G. I. L. (2005). Methodological issues in aging research. In D. M. Teti (Ed.), *Handbook of research methods in developmental science.* Malden, MA: Blackwell Publishing.

Schaie, K. W., & Parham, I. A. (1976). Stability of adult personality traits: Fact or fable? *Journal of Personality and Social Psychology, 34,* 146–158.

Schaie, K. W., & Willis, S. L. (1986). Can decline in adult intellectual functioning be reversed? *Developmental Psychology, 22,* 223–232.

Schaie, K. W., & Zanjani, F. A. K. (2006). Intellectual development across adulthood. In C. Hoare (Ed.), *Handbook of adult development and learning.* New York: Oxford University Press.

Schalock, R. L., Holl, C., Elliott, B., & Ross, I. (1992). A longitudinal follow-up of graduates from a rural special education program. *Learning Disability Quarterly, 15,* 29–38.

Schank, R. C., & Abelson, R. P. (1977). *Scripts, plans, goals, and understanding.* Hillsdale, NJ: Erlbaum.

Scharf, M., Mayseless, O., & Kivenson-Baron, I. (2004). Adolescents' attachment representations and developmental tasks in emerging adulthood. *Developmental Psychology, 40,* 430–444.

Scharf, M., Shulman, S., & Avigad-Spitz, L. (2005). Sibling relationships in emerging adulthood and in adolescence. *Journal of Adolescent Research, 20,* 64–90.

Scharlach, A., Li, W., & Dalvi, T. B. (2006). Family conflict as a mediator of caregiver strain. *Family Relations, 55,* 625–635.

Scheiber, F. (2006). Vision and aging. In J. E. Birren & K. W. Schaie (Eds.), *Handbook of the psychology of aging.* Boston: Elsevier Academic Press.

Schell, L. M., Gallo, M. V., Denham, M., & Ravenscroft, J. (2006). Effects of pollution on human growth and development: An introduction. *Journal of Physiological Anthropology, 25,* 103–112.

Schery, T. K., & Peters, M. L. (2003). Developing auditory learning in children with cochlear implants. *Topics in Language Disorders, 23,* 4–15.

Schiavi, R. C., Schreiner-Engel, P., White, D., & Mandeli, J. (1991). The relationship between pituitary-gonadal function and sexual behavior in healthy aging men. *Psychosomatic Medicine, 53,* 363–374.

Schick, B., de Villiers, P., de Villiers, J., & Hoffmeister, R. (2007). Language and theory of mind: A study of deaf children. *Child Development, 78,* 376–396.

Schieffelin, B. B. (1986). *How Kaluli children learn what to say, what to do, and how to feel.* New York: Cambridge University Press.

Schiff, A. R., & Knopf, I. J. (1985). The effect of task demands on attention allocation in children of different ages. *Child Development, 56,* 621–630.

Schiffman, H. R. (2000). *Sensation and perception* (5th ed.) New York: Wiley.

Schiffman, S. S. (1977). Food recognition by the elderly. *Journal of Gerontology, 32,* 586–592.

Schiffman, S. S., & Warwick, Z. S. (1993). Effect of flavor enhancement of foods for the elderly on nutritional status: Food intake, biochemical indices, and anthropometric measures. *Physiological Behavior, 53,* 395–402.

Schindl, M., Birner, P., Reingrabner, M., Joura, E., Husslein, P., & Langer, M. (2003). Elective cesarean section vs. spontaneous delivery: A comparative study of birth experience. *Acta Obstetrics and Gynecology of Scandinavia, 82,* 834–840.

Schleppenbach, M., Perry, M., Miller, K. F., Sims, L., & Fang, G. (2007). The answer is only the beginning: Extended discourse in Chinese and U.S. mathematics classrooms. *Journal of Educational Psychology, 99,* 380–396.

Schmidt, F. L., & Hunter, J. E. (1998). The validity and utility of selection methods in personnel psychology: Practical and theoretical implications of 85 years of research findings. *Psychological Bulletin, 124,* 262–274.

Schmidt, F. L., & Hunter, J. E. (2004). General mental ability in the world of work: Occupational attainment and job performance. *Journal of Personality and Social Psychology, 86,* 162–173.

Schmidt, L. (2006). Psychosocial burden of infertility and assisted reproduction. *The Lancet, 367,* 379–380.

Schmidt, P. J., Nieman, L. K., Danaceau, M. A., Adams, L. F., & Rubinow, D. R. (1998). Differential behavioral effects of gonadal steroids in women with and in those without premenstrual syndrome. *New England Journal of Medicine, 338,* 209–216.

Schmiege, S. J., Khoo, S. T., Sandler, I. N., Ayers, T. S., & Wolchik, S. A. (2006). Symptoms of internalizing and externalizing problems: Modeling recovery curves after the death of a parent. *American Journal of Preventive Medicine, 31*(6, Suppl. 1), 152–160.

Schmitt, S. K., Sneed, L., & Phibbs, C. S. (2006). Costs of newborn care in California: A population-based study. *Pediatrics, 117,* 154–160.

Schneider, B. H., Atkinson, L., & Tardif, C. (2001). Child–parent attachment and children's peer relations: A quantitative review. *Developmental Psychology, 37,* 86–100.

Schneider, W. (2004). Memory development in childhood. In U. Goswami (Ed.), *Blackwell handbook of childhood cognitive development* (pp. 236–256). Malden, MA: Blackwell Publishing.

Schneider, W., & Bjorklund, D. F. (1998). Memory. In D. Kuhn & R. S. Siegler (Vol. Eds.), W. Damon (Editor-in-Chief), *Handbook of child psychology: Vol. 2. Cognition, perception, and language* (5th ed., pp. 467–522). New York: Wiley.

Schneider, W., Bjorklund, D. F., & Maier-Bruckner, W. (1996). The effects of expertise and IQ on children's memory: When knowledge is, and when it is not enough. *International Journal of Behavioral Development, 19,* 773–796.

Schneider, W., Gruber, H., Gold, A., & Opwis, K. (1993). Chess expertise and memory for chess positions in children and adults. *Journal of Experimental Child Psychology, 56,* 328–349.

Schneider, W., & Pressley, M. (1997). *Memory development between two and 20* (2nd ed.). Mahwah, NJ: Erlbaum.

Schneider, W., & Sodian, B. (1988). Metamemory-memory behavior relationships in young children: Evidence from a memory-for-location task. *Journal of Experimental Child Psychology, 45,* 209–233.

Schneider, W., Roth, E., & Ennemoser, M. (2000). Training phonological skills and letter knowledge in children at risk for dyslexia: A comparison of three kindergarten intervention programs. *Journal of Educational Psychology, 92,* 284–295.

Schoen, R., & Canudas-Romo, V. (2006). Timing effects on divorce: 20th century experience in the United States. *Journal of Marriage and Family, 68,* 749–758.

Schoen, R., & Cheng, Y. A. (2006). Partner choice and the differential retreat from marriage. *Journal of Marriage and Family, 68,* 1–10.

Scholl, B. J., & Leslie, A. M. (2001). Minds, modules, and meta-analysis. *Child Development, 72,* 696–701.

Schonfeld, D. J., & Kappelman, M. (1990). The impact of school-based education on the young child's understanding of death. *Developmental and Behavioral Pediatrics, 11,* 247–252.

Schooler, C., Mulatu, M. S., & Oates, G. (1999). The continuing effects of substantively complex work on the intellectual functioning of older workers. *Psychology and Aging, 14,* 483–506.

Schoppe-Sullivan, S. J., Diener, M. L., Mangelsdorf, S. C., Brown, G. L., & McHale, J. L. (2006). Attachment and sensitivity in family context: The roles of parent and infant gender. *Infant and Child Development, 15,* 367–385.

Schott, J. M., & Rossor, M. N. (2003). The grasp and other primitive reflexes. *Journal of Neurology and Neurosurgical Psychiatry, 74,* 558–560.

Schulz, M. S., Cowan, C. P., & Cowan, P. A. (2006). Promoting healthy beginnings: A randomized controlled trial of a preventive intervention to preserve marital quality during the transition to parenthood. *Journal of Consulting and Clinical Psychology, 74,* 20–31.

Schulz, R., & Aderman, D. (1974). Clinical research and the stages of dying. *Omega: Journal of Death and Dying, 5,* 137–143.

Schulz, R., Belle, S. H., Czaja, S. J., Gitlin, L. N., Wisniewski, S. R., & Ory, M. G. (2003). Introduction to the special section on Resources for Enhancing Alzheimer's Caregiver Health (REACH). *Psychology and Aging, 18,* 357–360.

Schulz, R., Boerner, K., Shear, K., Zhang, S., & Gitlin, L. N. (2006). Predictors of complicated grief among dementia caregivers: A prospective study of bereavement. *American Journal of Geriatric Psychiatry, 14,* 650–658.

Schulz, R., & Schlarb, J. (1987–1988). Two decades of research on dying: What do we know about the patient? *Omega: Journal of Death and Dying, 18,* 299–317.

Schunn, C. D., & Anderson, J. R. (1999). The generality/specificity of expertise in scientific reasoning. *Cognitive Science, 23,* 337–370.

Schwartz, C. E., Wright, C. I., Shin, L. M., Kagan, J., & Rauch, S. L. (2003). Inhibited and uninhibited infants "grown up": Adult amygdalar response to novelty. *Science, 300,* 1952–1953.

Schwitzgebel, E. (1999). Gradual belief change in children. *Human Development, 42,* 283–296.

Scialfa, C. T., Esau, S. P., & Joffe, K. M. (1998). Age, target–distracter similarity, and visual search. *Experimental Aging Research, 24,* 337–358.

Scogin, F., Walsh, D., Hanson, A., Stump, J., & Coates, A. (2005). Evidence-based psychotherapies for depression in older adults. *Clinical Psychology: Science and Practice, 12,* 222–237.

Scott, G., Leritz, L. E., & Mumford, M. D. (2004). The effectiveness of creativity training: A quantitative review. *Creativity Research Journal, 16,* 361–388.

Scott, K. D., Klaus, P. H., & Klaus, M. H. (1999). The obstetrical and postpartum benefits of continuous support during childbirth. *Journal of Women's Health and Gender Based Medicine, 8,* 1257–1264.

Scott, W. A., Scott, R., & McCabe, M. (1991). Family relationships and children's personality: A cross-cultural, cross-source comparison. *British Journal of Social Psychology, 30,* 1–20.

Scourfield, J., Rice, F., Thapar, A., Harold, G. T., Martin, N., & McGuffin, P. (2003). Depressive symptoms in children and adolescents: Changing etiological influences with development. *Journal of Child Psychology and Psychiatry and Allied Disciplines, 44,* 968–976.

Seale, C. (1991). A comparison of hospice and conventional care. *Social Science and Medicine, 32,* 147–152.

Seaton, E. K., Scottham, K. M., & Sellers, R. M. The status model of racial identity development in African American adolescents: Evidence of structure, trajectories, and well-being. *Child Development, 77,* 1416–1426.

Seccombe, K. (2000). Families in poverty in the 1990s: Trends, causes, consequences, and lessons learned. *Journal of Marriage and the Family, 62,* 1094–1113.

Segal, N. L. (2000). Virtual twins: New findings on within-family environmental influences on intelligence. *Journal of Educational Psychology, 92,* 442–448.

Segal, N. L. (2005). Evolutionary studies of cooperation, competition, and altruism. A twin-based approach. In R. L. Burgess & K. MacDonald (Eds.), *Evolutionary perspectives on human development.* Thousand Oaks, CA: Sage.

Seger, J. Y., & Thorstensson, A. (2000). Muscle strength and electromyogram in boys and girls followed through puberty. *European Journal of Applied Physiology, 81,* 54–61.

Seiffge-Krenke, I. (1998). *Adolescents' health: A developmental perspective.* Mahwah, NJ: Erlbaum.

Seiffge-Krenke, I. (2003). Testing theories of romantic development from adolescence to young adulthood: Evidence of a developmental sequence. *International Journal of Behavioral Development, 27,* 519–531.

Seidl, A., & Johnson, E. K. (2006). Infant word segmentation revisited: Edge alignment facilitates target extraction. *Developmental Science, 9,* 565–573.

Seidman, L. J. (2006). Neuropsychological functioning in people with ADHD across the lifespan. *Clinical Psychology Review, 26,* 466–485.

Seiffe-Krenke, I. (2006). Leaving home or still in the nest? Parent–child relationships and psychological health as predictors of different leaving home patterns. *Developmental Psychology, 42,* 864–876.

Selby, J. M., & Bradley, B. S. (2003). Infants in groups: A paradigm for the study of early social experience. *Human Development, 46,* 197–221.

Seleen, D. R. (1982). The congruence between actual and desired use of time by older adults: A predictor of life satisfaction. *Gerontologist, 22,* 95–99.

Selikowitz, M. (2004). *ADHD: The facts.* Oxford: Oxford University Press.

Selkoe, D. J. (1997). Alzheimer's disease: From genes to pathogenesis. *American Journal of Psychiatry, 154,* 1198.

Selman, R. L. (1976). Social cognitive understanding: A guide to educational and clinical experience. In T. Lickona (Ed.), *Moral development and behavior: Theory, research and social issues.* New York: Holt, Rinehart & Winston.

Selman, R. L. (1980). *The growth of interpersonal understanding.* New York: Academic Press.

Seltzer, J. A. (2000). Families formed outside of marriage. *Journal of Marriage and the Family, 62,* 1247–1268.

Seltzer, M. M., & Li, L. W. (2000). The dynamics of caregiving: Transitions during a three-year prospective study, *Gerontologist, 40,* 165–178.

Senter, M. S., & Senter, R. (1997). Student outcomes and the adult learner. *Continuing Higher Education Review, 61,* 75–87.

Serafica, F. C., & Vargas, L. A. (2006). Cultural diversity in the development of child psychopathology. In D. Cicchetti & D. J. Cohen (Eds.), *Developmental psychopathology: Vol. 1. Theory and method* (2nd ed.). Hoboken, NJ: Wiley.

Serbin, L. A., & Karp, J. (2004). The intergenerational transfer of psychosocial risk: Mediators of vulnerability and resilience. *Annual Review of Psychology, 55,* 333–363.

Serbin, L. A., Poulin-Dubois, D., Colburne, K. A., Sen, M. G., & Eichstedt, J. A. (2001). Gender stereotyping in infancy: Visual preferences for and knowledge of gender-stereotyped toys in the second year. *International Journal of Behavioral Development, 25,* 7–15.

Serbin, L. A., Poulin-Dubois, D., & Eichstedt, J. A. (2002). Infants' response to gender-inconsistent events. *Infancy, 3,* 531–542.

Serbin, L. A., Powlishta, K. K., & Gulko, J. (1993). The development of sex typing in middle childhood. *Monographs of the Society for Research in Child Development, 58* (2, Serial No. 232).

Serbin, L. A., Tonick, I. J., & Sternglanz, S. H. (1977). Shaping cooperative cross-sex play. *Child Development, 48,* 924–929.

Servaty-Seib, H. L., & Pistole, M. C. (2006). Adolescent grief: Relationship category and emotional closeness. *Omega: Journal of Death and Dying, 54,* 147–167.

Servin, A., Bohlin, G., & Berlin, L. (1999). Sex differences in 1-, 3-, and 5-year-olds' toy-choice in a structured play-session. *Scandinavian Journal of Psychology, 40,* 43–48.

Settersten, R. A., Jr. (1998). A time to leave home and a time never to return? Age constraints on the living arrangements of young adults. *Social Forces, 76,* 1373–1400.

Settersten, R. A., Jr. (2005). Linking the two ends of life: What gerontology can learn from childhood studies. *Journals of Gerontology: Social Sciences, 60B,* S173–S180.

Shaffer, D., & Pfeffer, C. R. (2001). Practice parameters for the assessment and treatment of children and adolescents with suicidal behavior. *Journal of the American Academy of Child and Adolescent Psychiatry, 40,* 24S–51S.

Shaffer, D. R., Pegalis, L. J., & Cornell, D. P. (1992). Gender and self-disclosure revisited: Personal and contextual variations in self-disclosure to same-sex acquaintances. *Journal of Social Psychology, 132*, 307–315.

Shanahan, M. J. (2000). Pathways to adulthood in changing societies: Variability and mechanisms in life course perspective. *Annual Review of Sociology, 26*, 667–692.

Shanahan, M. J., Erickson, L. D., & Bauer, D. J. (2005). One hundred years of knowing: The changing science of adolescence, 1904 and 2004. *Journal of Research on Adolescence, 15*, 383–394.

Shanahan, M. J., Finch, M. D., Mortimer, J. T., & Ryu, S. (1991). Adolescent work experience and depressive affect. *Social Psychology Quarterly, 54*, 299–317.

Shannon, J. B. (2006). *Death and dying sourcebook* (2nd ed.). Detroit, MI: Omnigraphics.

Shapiro, E. R. (2001). Grief in interpersonal perspective: Theories and their implications. In M. S. Stroebe, R. O. Hansson, W. Stroebe, & H. Schut (Eds.), *Handbook of bereavement research. Consequences, coping, and care.* Washington, D.C.: American Psychological Association.

Sharabany, R., Gershoni, R., & Hofman, J. E. (1981). Girlfriend, boyfriend: Age and sex differences in intimate friendship. *Developmental Psychology, 17*, 800–808.

Sharpe, P. A., Jackson, K. L., White, C., Vaca, V. L., Hickey, T., Gu, J., & Otterness, C. (1997). Effects of a one-year physical activity intervention for older adults at congregate nutrition sites. *Gerontologist, 37*, 208–215.

Sharpe, T. M., Killen, J. D., Bryson, S. W., Shisslak, C. M., Estes, L. S., Gray, N., Crago, M., & Taylor, C. G. (1998). Attachment style and weight concerns in preadolescent and adolescent girls. *International Journal of Eating Disorders, 23*, 39–44.

Shaver, P. R. (2006). Dynamics of romantic love: Comments, questions, and future directions. In M. Mikulincer & G. S. Goodman (Eds.), *Dynamics of romantic love: Attachment, caregiving, and sex.* New York: Guilford.

Shaver, P. R., & Mikulincer, M. (2007). Adult attachment strategies and the regulation of emotion. In J. J. Gross (Ed.), *Handbook of emotion regulation.* New York: Guilford.

Shaw, B. A., Krause, N., Chatters, L. M., Connell, C. M., & Ingersoll-Dayton, B. (2004). Emotional support from parents early in life, aging, and health. *Psychology and Aging, 19*, 4–12.

Shaw, C. (1997). The perimenopausal hot flash: Epidemiology, physiology, and treatment. *Nurse Practitioner, 22*, 55–66.

Shaywitz, S. E., Fletcher, J. M., Holahan, J. M., Shneider, A. E., Marchione, K. E., Stuebing, K. K., Francis, D. J., Pugh, K. R., & Shaywitz, B. A. (1999). Persistence of dyslexia: The Connecticut Longitudinal Study at Adolescence. *Pediatrics, 104*, 1351–1359.

Shea, C. H., Park, J. H., & Braden, H. W. (2006). Age-related effects in sequential motor learning. *Physical Therapy, 86*, 478–488.

Shearer, C. L., Crouter, A. C., & McHale, S. M. (2005). Parents' perceptions of changes in mother–child and father–child relationships during adolescence. *Journal of Adolescent Research, 20*, 662–684.

Sheehy, G. (2005, December 11). Life begins at 60. *Parade*, 4–6.

Sheiner, E., Shoham-Vardi, I., Sheiner, E. K., Press, F., Hackmon-Ram, R., Mazor, M., & Katz, M. (2000). A comparison between the effectiveness of epidural analgesia and parenteral pethidine during labor. *Archives of Gynecology and Obstetrics, 263*, 95–98.

Shepard, R. J. (1997). Curricular physical activity and academic performance. *Pediatric Exercise Science, 9*, 113–126.

Shepard, R. N., & Metzler, J. (1971). Mental rotation of three-dimensional objects. *Science, 171*, 701–703.

Shepard, T. H. & Lemire, R. J. (2004). *Catalog of teratogenic agents* (11th ed.). Baltimore, MD: Johns Hopkins University Press.

Shih, M., Pittinsky, T. L., & Ambady, N. (1999). Stereotype susceptibility: Identity salience and shifts in quantitative performance. *Psychological Science, 10*, 80–83.

Shih, M., & Sanchez, D. T. (2005). Perspectives and research on the positive and negative implications of having multiple racial identities. *Psychological Bulletin, 131*, 569–591.

Shihadeh, A., & Al-Najdawi, W. (2001). Forceps or vacuum extraction: A comparison of maternal and neonatal morbidity. *Eastern Mediterranean Health, 7*, 106–114.

Shimamura, A. P., Berry, J. M., Mangels, J. A., Rusting, C. L., & Jurica, P. J. (1995). Memory and cognitive abilities in university professors: Evidence for successful aging. *Psychological Science, 6*, 271–277.

Shiner, R. (2006). Temperament and personality in childhood. In D. K. Mroczek & T. D. Little (Eds.), *Handbook of personality development.* Mahwah, NJ: Erlbaum.

Ship, J. A., Pearson, J. D., Cruise, L. J., Brant, L. J., & Metter, E. J. (1996). Longitudinal changes in smell identification. *Journals of Gerontology: Biological Sciences and Medical Sciences, 51*, M86–M91.

Ship, J. A., & Weiffenbach, J. M. (1993). Age, gender, medical treatment, and medication effects on smell identification. *Journal of Gerontology, 48*, M26–M32.

Shneidman, E. S. (1973). *Deaths of man.* New York: Quadrangle.

Shneidman, E. S. (1980). *Voices of death.* New York: Harper & Row.

Shoda, Y., & Mischel, W. (2000). Reconciling contextualism with the core assumptions of personality psychology. *European Journal of Personality, 14*, 407–428.

Shonk, S. M., & Cicchetti, D. (2001). Maltreatment, competency deficits, and risk for academic and behavioral maladjustment. *Developmental Psychology, 37*, 3–17.

Shulman, S., & Ben-Artzi, E. (2003). Age-related differences in the transition from adolescence to adulthood and links with family relationships. *Journal of Adult Development, 10*, 217–226.

Shurkin, J. N. (1992). *Terman's kids: The groundbreaking study of how the gifted grow up.* Boston: Little, Brown.

Shute, N. (2001, January 15). Children in anguish. A call for better treatment of kids' mental ills. *U.S. News & World Report*, 42.

Shweder, R. A., Goodnow, J., Hatano, G., LeVine, R., Markus, H., & Miller, P. (1998). The cultural psychology of development: One mind, many mentalities. In R. M. Lerner (Vol. Ed.), W. Damon (Editor-in-Chief), *Handbook of child psychology: Vol. 1. Theoretical models of human development* (5th ed.). New York: Wiley.

Shweder, R. A., Goodnow, J. J., Hatano, G., LeVine, R. A., Markus, H. R., & Miller, P. J. (2006). The cultural psychology of development: One mind, many mentalities. In W. Damon & R. M. Lerner (Eds. in Chief) & R. M. Lerner (Vol. Ed.), *Handbook of child psychology: Vol. 1. Theoretical models of human development* (6th ed.). Hoboken, NJ: Wiley.

Shweder, R. A., Mahapatra, M., & Miller, J. G. (1990). Culture and moral development. In J. W. Stigler, R. A. Shweder, & G. Herdt (Eds.), *Cultural psychology. Essays on comparative human development.* Cambridge, England: Cambridge University Press.

Sibulesky, L., Hayes, K. C., Pronczuk, A., Weigel-DiFranco, C., Rosner, B., & Berson, E. L. (1999). Safety of 7500 RE (25,000 IU) vitamin A daily in adults with retinitis pigmentosa. *American Journal of Clinical Nutrition, 69*, 656–663.

Siebenbruner, J., Zimmer-Gembeck, M. J., & Egeland, B. (2007). Sexual partners and contraceptive use: A 16-year prospective study predicting abstinence and risk behavior. *Journal of Research on Adolescence, 17*, 179–206.

Siebold, C. (1992). *The hospice movement. Easing death's pains.* New York: Twayne Publishers.

Siegel, A. C., & Burton, R. V. (1999). Effects of baby walkers on motor and mental development in human infants. *Journal of Developmental and Behavioral Pediatrics, 20*, 355–361.

Siegler, I. C., & Brummett, B. H. (2000). Associations among NEO personality assessments and well-being at mid-life: Facet-level analyses. *Psychology and Aging, 15*, 710–714.

Siegler, R. (2006). Microgenetic analysis of learning. In D. Kuhn & R. Siegler (Vol. Eds.), *Handbook of child psychology: Cognition, perception, and language: Vol. 2.* Hoboken, NJ: Wiley and Sons.

Siegler, R. S. (1981). Developmental sequences within and between concepts. *Monographs of the Society for Research in Child Development, 46* (2, Serial No. 189).

Siegler, R. S. (1989). Hazards of mental chronometry: An example from children's subtraction. *Journal of Educational Psychology, 81*, 497–506.

Siegler, R. S. (1996). *Emerging minds: The process of change in children's thinking.* New York: Oxford University Press.

Siegler, R. S. (2000). The rebirth of children's learning. *Child Development, 71*, 26–35.

Siegler, R. S., & Ellis, S. (1996). Piaget on childhood. *Psychological Science, 7*, 211–215.

Siegler, R. S., & Svetina, M. (2006). What leads children to adopt new strategies? A microgenetic/cross sectional study of class inclusion. *Child Development, 77*, 997–1015.

Sieving, R. E., McNeely, C. S., & Blum, R. W. (2000). Maternal expectations, mother–child connectedness, and adolescent sexual debut. *Archives of Pediatrics and Adolescent Medicine, 154*, 809–816.

Sigelman, C. K., Carr, M. B., & Begley, N. L. (1986). Developmental changes in the influence of sex-role stereotypes on person perception. *Child Study Journal, 16*, 191–205.

Sigman, M., & Capps, L. (1997). *Children with autism. A developmental perspective.* Cambridge, MA: Harvard University Press.

Signorielli, N., & Kahlenberg, S. (2001). Television's world of work in the nineties. *Journal of Broadcasting and Electronic Media, 45,* 4–22.

Signorielli, N., & Lears, M. (1992). Children, television, and conceptions about chores: Attitudes and behaviors. *Sex Roles, 27,* 157–170.

Silk, J. B., Brosnan, S. F., Vonk, J., Henrich, J., Povinelli, D. J., Richardson, A. S., Lambeth, S. P., Mascaro, J., & Schapiro, S. J. (2005). Chimpanzees are indifferent to the welfare of unrelated group members. *Nature, 437*(7063), 1357–1359.

Silverberg, S. B., & Steinberg, L. (1990). Psychological well-being of parents with early adolescent children. *Developmental Psychology, 26,* 658–666.

Silverman, I. W. (2003). Gender differences in resistance to temptation: Theories and evidence. *Developmental Review, 23,* 219–259.

Silverman, L. K., Chitwood, D. G., & Waters, J. L. (1986). Young gifted children: Can parents identify giftedness? *Topics in Early Childhood Special Education, 6,* 23–38.

Silverman, P. R. (2000). *Never too young to know. Death in children's lives.* New York: Oxford University Press.

Silverman, P. R., & Worden, J. W. (1993). Children's reactions to the death of a parent. In M. S. Stroebe, W. Stroebe, & R. O. Hansson (Eds.), *Handbook of bereavement. Theory, research, and intervention.* Cambridge, England: Cambridge University Press.

Silverstein, M., & Ruiz, S. (2006). Breaking the chain: How grandparents moderate the transmission of maternal depression to their grandchildren. *Family Relations, 55,* 601–612.

Simcock, G., & Hayne, H. (2002). Breaking the barrier? Children fail to translate their preverbal memories into language. *Psychological Science, 13,* 225–231.

Simcock, G., & Hayne, H. (2003). Age-related changes in verbal and nonverbal memory during early childhood. *Developmental Psychology, 39,* 805–814.

Simmons, R. G., & Blyth, D. A. (1987). *Moving into adolescence: The impact of pubertal change and school context.* New York: Hawthorne, Aldine de Gruyter.

Simmons, R. G., Burgeson, R., Carlton-Ford, S., & Blyth, D. A. (1987). The impact of cumulative change in early adolescence. *Child Development, 58,* 1220–1234.

Simon, H. A. (1995). The information-processing theory of mind. *American Psychologist, 50,* 507–508.

Simon, H. A. (2001). Creativity in the arts and sciences. *The Canyon Review and Stand, 23,* 203–220.

Simon, T. J. (1997). Reconceptualizing the origins of number knowledge: A "non-numerical" account. *Cognitive Development, 12,* 349–372.

Simon, T. J. (1999). The foundations of numerical thinking in a brain without numbers. *Trends in Cognitive Science, 3,* 363–365.

Simon, T. J., Hespos, S. J., & Rochat, P. (1995). Do infants understand simple arithmetic? A replication of Wynn (1992). *Cognitive Development, 10,* 253–269.

Simon, W., & Gagnon, J. (1998). Psychosexual development. *Society, 35,* 60–67.

Simonoff, E. (2001). Genetic influences on conduct disorder. In J. Hill & B. Maughan (Eds.), *Conduct disorders in childhood and adolescence.* New York: Cambridge University Press.

Simonoff, E., Bolton, P., & Rutter, M. (1996). Mental retardation: Genetic findings, clinical implications and research agenda. *Journal of Child Psychology and Psychiatry and Allied Disciplines, 37,* 259–280.

Simonton, D. K. (1984). *Genius, creativity, and leadership: Historiometric inquiries.* Cambridge, MA: Harvard University Press.

Simonton, D. K. (1990). Creativity in the later years: Optimistic prospects for achievement. *Gerontologist, 30,* 626–631.

Simonton, D. K. (1999). Creativity from a historiometric perspective. In R. J. Sternberg (Ed.), *Handbook of creativity.* New York: Cambridge University Press.

Simonton, D. K. (1999). *Origins of genius: Darwinian perspectives on creativity.* New York: Oxford University Press.

Simpson, J. A., Collins, W. A., Tran, S., & Haydon, K. C. (2007). Attachment and the experience and expression of emotions in romantic relationships: A developmental perspective. *Journal of Personality and Social Psychology, 92,* 355–367.

Simpson, J. A., Rholes, W. S., Campbell, L., Tran, S., & Wilson, C. L. (2003). Adult attachment, the transition to parenthood, and depressive symptoms. *Journal of Personality and Social Psychology, 84,* 1172–1187.

Simpson, J. L., & Elias, S. (2003). *Genetics in obstetrics and gynecology.* Philadelphia: Saunders.

Simpson, K. R., & Creehan, P. A. (1996). *Perinatal nursing.* Philadelphia: Lippincott-Raven.

Simpson, R., & Otten, K. (2005). Structuring behavior management strategies and building social competence. In D. Zager (Ed.), *Autism spectrum disorders. Identification, education, and treatment* (3rd ed.). Mahwah, NJ: Erlbaum.

Singer, D. G., Golinkoff, R. M., & Hirsh-Pasek, K. (Eds.) (2006). *Play = learning: How play motivates and enhances children's cognitive and social-emotional growth.* New York: Oxford University Press.

Singer, L. T., Arendt, R., Fagan, J., Minnes, S., Salvator, A., Bolek, T., & Becker, M. (1999). Neonatal visual information processing in cocaine-exposed and non-exposed infants. *Infant Behavior and Development, 22,* 1–15.

Singer, T., Verhaeghen, P., Ghisletta, P., Lindenberger, U., & Baltes, P. B. (2003). The fate of cognition in very old age: Six-year longitudinal findings in the Berlin Aging Study (BASE). *Psychology and Aging, 18,* 318–331.

Singh, B., Berman, B. M., Simpson, R. L., & Annechild, A. (1998). Incidence of premenstrual syndrome and remedy usage: A national probability sample study. *Alternative Therapeutic Health Medicines, 4,* 75–79.

Singh, K., & Ozturk, M. (2000). Effect of part-time work on high school mathematics and science course taking. *Journal of Educational Research, 94,* 67–74.

Sinnott, J. (1996). The developmental approach: Postformal thought as adaptive intelligence. In F. Blanchard-Fields & T. M. Hess (Eds.), *Perspectives on cognitive change in adulthood and aging.* New York: McGraw-Hill.

Skinner, B. F. (1953). *Science and human behavior.* New York: Macmillan.

Skinner, B. F. (1957). *Verbal behavior.* New York: Appleton-Century-Crofts.

Skinner, B. F. (1983). Intellectual self-management in old age. *American Psychologist, 38,* 239–244.

Skinner, E. A., & Zimmer-Gembeck, M. J. (2007). The development of coping. *Annual Review of Psychology, 58,* 119–144.

Slaby, R. G., & Guerra, N. G. (1988). Cognitive mediators of aggression in adolescent offenders: 1. Assessment. *Developmental Psychology, 24,* 580–588.

Slater, A. (2004). Visual perception. In G. Bremner & A. Fogel (Eds.), *Blackwell handbook of infant development* (pp. 5–34). Malden, MA: Blackwell Publishing.

Slater, C. L. (2003). Generativity versus stagnation: An elaboration of Erikson's adult stage of human development. *Journal of Adult Development, 10,* 53–65.

Slater, R., Cantarella, A., Gallella, S., Worley, A. Boyd, S., Meek, J., & Fitzgerald, M. (2006). Cortical pain responses in human infants. *The Journal of Neuroscience, 26,* 3662–3666.

Slaughter, V., Jaakkola, R., & Carey, S. (1999). Constructing a coherent theory: Children's biological understanding of life and death. In M. Siegal & C. C. Peterson (Eds.), *Children's understanding of biology and health.* Cambridge, U.K.: Cambridge University Press.

Slaughter, V., & Lyons, M. (2003). Learning about life and death in early childhood. *Cognitive Psychology, 46,* 1–30.

Slavin, R. E. (1986). Cooperative learning: Engineering social psychology in the classroom. In R. S. Feldman (Ed.), *The social psychology of education: Current research and theory.* Cambridge: Cambridge University Press.

Slavkin, M., & Stright, A. D. (2000). Gender role differences in college students from one- and two-parent families. *Sex Roles, 42,* 23–37.

Sliwinski, M., & Buschke, H. (1999). Cross-sectional and longitudinal relationships among age, cognition, and processing speed. *Psychology and Aging, 14,* 18–33.

Sliwinski, M., Buschke, H., Kuslansky, G., Senior, G., & Scarisbrick, D. (1994). Proportional slowing and addition speed in old and young adults. *Psychology and Aging, 9,* 72–80.

Slobin, D. I. (1979). *Psycholinguistics* (2nd ed.). Glenview, IL: Scott, Foresman.

Sloboda, D. M., Hart, R., Doherty, D. A., Pennell, C. E., & Hickey, M. (2007). Age at menarche: Influences of prenatal and postnatal growth. *Journal of Clinical Endocrinology and Metabolism, 92,* 46–50.

Slotkin, T. A. (1998). Fetal nicotine or cocaine exposure: Which one is worse? *Journal of Pharmacology and Experimental Therapy, 285,* 931–945.

Smagorinsky, P. (1995). The social construction of data: Methodological problems of investigating learning in the zone of proximal development. *Review of Educational Research, 65,* 191–212.

Smaldone, A., Honig, J. C., & Byrne, M. W. (2007). Sleepless in America: Inadequate sleep and relationships to health and well-being of our nation's children. *Pediatrics, 119,* S29–S37.

Small, M. (1999). *Our babies, ourselves: How biology and culture shape the way we parent.* New York: Anchor Publishing.

Small, S., & Memmo, M. (2004). Contemporary models of youth development and problem prevention: Toward an integration of terms, concepts, and models. *Family Relations, 53,* 3–11.

Smetana, J. G. (1981). Preschool children's conceptions of moral and social rules. *Child Development, 52,* 1333–1336.

Smetana, J. G. (2006). Social-cognitive domain theory: Consistencies and variations in children's moral and social judgments. In M. Killen & J. G. Smetana (Eds.), *Handbook of moral development.* Mahwah, NJ: Erlbaum.

Smetana, J. G., Campione-Barr, N., & Metzger, A. (2006). Adolescent development in interpersonal and societal contexts. *Annual Review of Psychology, 57,* 255–284.

Smith, A. D., & Earles, J. L. K. (1996). Memory changes in normal aging. In F. Blanchard-Fields & T. M. Hess (Eds.), *Perspectives on cognitive change in adulthood and aging.* New York: McGraw-Hill.

Smith, B., & Blass, E. M. (1996). Taste-mediated calming in premature, preterm, and full-term human infants. *Developmental Psychology, 32,* 1084–1089.

Smith, G. E., Petersen, R. C., Ivnik, R. J., Malec, J. F., & Tangalos, E. G. (1996). Subjective memory complaints, psychological distress, and longitudinal change in objective memory performance. *Psychology and Aging, 11,* 272–279.

Smith, G. J. W. (2005). How should creativity be defined? *Creativity Research Journal, 17,* 293–295.

Smith, G. J., & Carlsson, I. M. (1990). *The creative process: A functional model based on empirical studies from early childhood to middle age.* Madison, CT: International Universities Press.

Smith, J., & Baltes, P. B. (1990). Wisdom-related knowledge: Age/cohort differences in response to life-planning problems. *Developmental Psychology, 26,* 494–505.

Smith, J. B. (1997). Effects of eighth-grade transition programs on high school retention and experiences. *Journal of Educational Research, 90,* 144–152.

Smith, K. E., Landry, S. H., & Swank, P. R. (2000). Does the content of mothers' verbal stimulation explain differences in children's development of verbal and nonverbal cognitive skills? *Journal of School Psychology, 38,* 27–49.

Smith, K. E., Landry, S. H., & Swank, P. R. (2006). The role of early maternal responsiveness in supporting school-aged cognitive development for children who vary in birth status. *Pediatrics, 117,* 1608–1617.

Smith, L. B., & Thelen, E. (1993). *A dynamic systems approach to development: Applications.* Cambridge, MA: MIT Press.

Smith, P. K. (1978). A longitudinal study of social participation in preschool children: Solitary and parallel play reexamined. *Developmental Psychology, 14,* 517–523.

Smith, P. K. (2005). Types and functions of play in human development. In B. J. Ellis & D. F. Bjorklund (Eds.), *Origins of the social mind.* New York: Guilford Press.

Smith, P. K., & Daglish, L. (1977). Sex differences in parent and infant behavior in the home. *Child Development, 48,* 1250–1254.

Smith, T. W. (1991). Adult sexual behavior in 1989: Number of partners, frequency of intercourse and risk of AIDS. *Family Planning Perspectives, 23,* 102–107.

Smithmyer, C. M., Hubbard, J. A., & Simons, R. F. (2000). Proactive and reactive aggression in delinquent adolescents: Relations to aggression outcome expectancies. *Journal of Clinical Child Psychology, 29,* 86–93.

Smolak, L., & Levine, M. P. (1996). Adolescent transitions and the development of eating problems. In L. Smolak, M. P. Levine, & R. Striegel-Moore (Eds.), *The developmental psychopathology of eating disorders: Implications for research, prevention, and treatment.* Mahwah, NJ: Erlbaum.

Smoll, F. L., & Schutz, R. W. (1990). Quantifying gender differences in physical performance: A developmental perspective. *Developmental Psychology, 26,* 360–369.

Smotherman, W. P., & Robinson, S. R. (1996). The development of behavior before birth. *Developmental Psychology, 32,* 425–434.

Smyke, A. T., Dumitrescu, A., & Zeanah, C. H. (2002). Attachment disturbances in young children. I: The continuum of caretaking casualty. *Journal of the American Academy of Child and Adolescent Psychiatry, 41,* 972–982.

Snarey, J. R. (1985). Cross-cultural universality of social–moral development: A critical review of Kohlbergian research. *Psychological Bulletin, 97,* 202–232.

Snow, C. E., Arlman-Rupp, A., Hassing, Y., Jobse, J., Joosken, J., & Vorster, J. (1976). Mother's speech in three social classes. *Journal of Psycholinguistic Research, 5,* 1–20.

Snow, D. (2006). Regression and reorganization of intonation between 6 and 23 months. *Child Development, 77,* 281–296.

Snowdon, D. (2002). *Aging with grace: What the Nun Study teaches us about leading longer, healthier, and more meaningful lives.* New York: Bantam Books.

Snowdon, D. A. (1997). Aging and Alzheimer's disease: Lessons from the Nun Study. *Gerontologist, 37,* 150–156.

Snyder, E. Y., & Loring, J. F. (2005). A role for stem cell biology in the physiological and pathological aspects of aging. *Journal of the American Geriatrics Society, 53,* S287–S291.

Snyder, J., Cramer, A., Afrank, J., & Patterson, G. R. (2005). The contributions of ineffective discipline and parental hostile attributions of child misbehavior to the development of conduct problems at home and school. *Developmental Psychology, 41,* 30–41.

Sobolewski, J. M., & King, V. (2005). The importance of the coparental relationship for nonresident fathers' ties to children. *Journal of Marriage and Family, 67,* 1196–1212.

Somerville, S. C., Wellman, H. M., & Cultice, J. C. (1983). Young children's deliberate reminding. *Journal of Genetic Psychology, 143,* 87–96.

Son, L. K. (2004). Spacing one's study: Evidence for a metacognitive control strategy. *Journal of Experimental Psychology: Learning, Memory, and Cognition, 30,* 601–604.

Son, L. K., & Metcalfe, J. (2000). Metacognitive and control strategies in study-time allocation. *Journal of Experimental Psychology: Learning, Memory, and Cognition, 26,* 204–221.

Soriano, F. I., Rivera, L. M., Williams, K. J., Daley, S. P., & Reznik, V. M. (2004). Navigating between cultures: The role of culture in youth violence. *Journal of Adolescent Health, 34,* 169–176.

Sostek, A. M., Vietze, P., Zaslow, M., Kreiss, L., van der Waals, F., & Rubinstein, D. (1981). Social context in caregiver-infant interaction: A film study of Fais and the United States. In T. M. Field, A. M. Sostek, P. Vietze, & P. H. Liederman (Eds.), *Culture and early interactions.* Hillsdale, NJ: Erlbaum.

Sotomi, O., Ryan, C. A., O'Connor, G., & Murphy, B. P. (2007). Have we stopped looking for a red reflex in newborn screening? *Irish Medical Journal, 100,* 398–400.

Span, P. (2000, August 27). Home alone. *The Washington Post Magazine,* 12–15, 24–25.

Sparling, P. B., O'Donnell, E. M., & Snow, T. K. (1998). The gender difference in distance running performance has plateaued: An analysis of world rankings from 1980 to 1996. *Medicine and Science in Sports and Exercise, 30,* 1725–1729.

Sparrow, S. S., & Davis, S. M. (2000). Recent advances in the assessment of intelligence and cognition. *Journal of Child Psychology and Psychiatry, 41,* 117–131.

Spear, L. P. (2000a). The adolescent brain and age-related behavioral manifestations. *Neuroscience and Biobehavioral Reviews, 24,* 417–463.

Spear, L. P. (2000b). Neurobehavioral changes in adolescence. *Current Directions in Psychological Science, 9,* 111–114.

Spearman, C. (1927). *The abilities of man.* New York: Macmillan.

Speece, M. W., & Brent, S. B. (1984). Children's understanding of death: A review of three components of a death concept. *Child Development, 55,* 1671–1686.

Speece, M. W., & Brent, S. B. (1992). The acquisition of a mature understanding of three components of the concept of death. *Death Studies, 16,* 211–229.

Spelke, E. S. (1990). Principles of object perception. *Cognitive Science, 14,* 29-56.

Spelke, E. S. (1994). Initial knowledge: Six suggestions. *Cognition, 50,* 431–445.

Spelke, E. S., Breinlinger, K., Macomber, J., & Jacobson, K. (1992). Origins of knowledge. *Psychological Review, 99,* 605–632.

Spelke, E. S., & Hermer, L. (1996). Early cognitive development: Objects and space. In R. Gelman & T. Fong (Eds.), *Handbook of perception and cognition* (2nd ed.). New York: Academic Press.

Spence, J. T. (1985). Achievement American style: The rewards and costs of individualism. *American Psychologist, 40,* 1285–1295.

Spence, J. T., & Hall, S. K. (1996). Children's gender-related self-perceptions, activity preferences, and occupational stereotypes: A test of three models of gender constructs. *Sex Roles, 35,* 659–691.

Spence, J. T., & Helmreich, R. L. (1978). *Masculinity and femininity: Their psychological dimensions, correlates, and antecedents.* Austin: University of Texas Press.

Spencer, J. P., Corbetta, D., Buchanan, P., Clearfield, M., Ulrich, B., & Schoner, G. (2006). Moving toward a grand theory of development: In memory of Esther Thelen. *Child Development, 77,* 1521–1538.

Spencer, M. B. (2006). Phenomenology and ecological systems theory: Development of diverse groups. In W. Damon & R. M. Lerner (Eds. in Chief) & R. M. Lerner (Vol. Ed.), *Handbook of child psychology: Vol. 1. Theoretical models of human development* (6th ed.). Hoboken, NJ: Wiley.

Spencer, M. B., & Markstrom-Adams, C. (1990). Identity processes among racial and ethnic minority children in America. *Child Development, 61,* 290–310.

Spencer, P. E. (1996). The association between language and symbolic play at two years: Evidence from deaf toddlers. *Child Development, 67*, 867–876.

Spera, C. (2006). Adolescents' perceptions of parental goals, practices, and styles in relation to the motivation and achievement. *Journal of Early Adolescence, 26*, 456–490.

Spiby, H., Henderson, B., Slade, P., Escott, D., & Fraser, R. B. (1999). Strategies for coping with labour: Does antenatal education translate into practice? *Journal of Advanced Nursing, 29*, 388–394.

Spieler, D. H., & Griffin, Z. M. (2006). The influence of age on the time course of word preparation in multiword utterances. *Language and Cognitive Processes, 21*, 291–321.

Spilich, G. J., Vesonder, G. T., Chiesi, H. L., & Voss, J. F. (1979). Text processing of domain-related information for individuals with high and low domain knowledge. *Journal of Verbal Learning and Verbal Behavior, 18*, 275–290.

Spinath, B., Spinath, F. M., Harlaar, N., & Plomin, R. (2006). Predicting school achievement from general cognitive ability, self-perceived ability, and intrinsic value. *Intelligence, 34*, 363–374.

Spirduso, W. W., & MacRae, P. G. (1990). Motor performance and aging. In J. E. Birren & K. W. Schaie (Eds.), *Handbook of the psychology of aging* (3rd ed.). San Diego: Academic Press.

Spitz, R. A. (1946). Anaclitic depression: An inquiry into the genesis of psychiatric conditions in early childhood, II. *Psychoanalytic Study of the Child, 2*, 313–342.

Spitze, G., & Trent, K. (2006). Gender differences in adult sibling relations in two-child families. *Journal of Marriage and Family, 68*, 977–992.

Spokane, A. R., Meir, E. I., & Catalano, M. (2000). Person-environment congruence and Holland's theory: A review and reconsideration. *Journal of Vocational Behavior, 57*, 137–187.

Springen, K. (2004, January 26). The ancient art of making babies. *Newsweek*, 51.

Springer, S., & Deutsch, G. (1997). *Left brain, right brain: Perspectives from cognitive neuroscience* (5th ed.). New York: W. H. Freeman.

Squire, L. R. (2004). Memory systems of the brain: A brief history and current perspective. *Neurobiology of Learning and Memory, 82*, 171–177.

Sroufe, L. A. (1977). Wariness of strangers and the study of infant development. *Child Development, 48*, 1184–1199.

Sroufe, L. A. (1996). *Emotional development: The organization of emotional life in the early years.* Cambridge, England: University of Cambridge Press.

Sroufe, L. A. (1997). Psychopathology as an outcome of development. *Development and Psychopathology, 9*, 251–268.

Sroufe, L. A., Bennett, C., Englund, M., Urban, J., & Shulman, S. (1993). The significance of gender boundaries in preadolescence: Contemporary correlates and antecedents of boundary violation and maintenance. *Child Development, 64*, 455–466.

Sroufe, L. A., Egeland, B., Carlson, E., & Collins, W. A. (2005). Placing early attachment experiences in developmental context: The Minnesota Longitudinal Study. In K. E. Grossmann, K. Grossmann, & E. Waters (Eds.), *Attachment from infancy to adulthood: The major longitudinal studies.* New York: Guilford Press.

Sroufe, L. A., & Rutter, M. (1984). The domain of developmental psychopathology. *Child Development, 55*, 17–29.

Sroufe, L. A., Waters, E., & Matas, L. (1974). Contextual determinants of infant affectional response. In M. Lewis & L. A. Rosenblum (Eds.), *The origins of fear.* New York: Wiley.

Staddon, J. E. R., & Cerutti, D. T. (2003). Operant conditioning. *Annual Review of Psychology, 54*, 115–144.

Stake, J. E. (2006). The critical mediating role of social encouragement for science motivation and confidence among high school girls and boys. *Journal of Applied Social Psychology, 6*, 1017–1045.

Stambrook, M., & Parker, K. C. H. (1987). The development of the concept of death in childhood: A review of the literature. *Merrill-Palmer Quarterly, 33*, 133–157.

Stams, G. J. J. M., Juffer, F., & van IJzendoorn, M. (2002). Maternal sensitivity, infant attachment, and temperament in early childhood predict adjustment in middle childhood: The case of adopted children and their biologically unrelated parents. *Developmental Psychology, 38*, 806–821.

Stanley, S. M., Amato, P. R., Johnson, C. A., & Markman, H. J. (2006). Premarital education, marital quality, and marital stability: Findings from a large, random household survey. *Journal of Family Psychology, 20*, 117–126.

Stanovich, K. E. (1986). Matthew effects in reading: Some consequences of individual differences in the acquisition of literacy. *Reading Research Quarterly, 21*, 360–407.

Stanovich, K. E., & Stanovich, P. J. (1999). How research might inform the debate about early reading acquisition. In J. Oakhill & R. Beard (Eds.), *Reading development and the teaching of reading* (pp. 12–41). Oxford: Blackwell.

Stanovich, K. E., & West, R. F. (1997). Reasoning independently of prior belief and individual differences in actively open-minded thinking. *Journal of Educational Psychology, 89*, 342–357.

Staudinger, U. M., & Baltes, P. B. (1996). Interactive minds: A facilitative setting for wisdom-related performance? *Journal of Personality and Social Psychology, 71*, 746–762.

Staudinger, U. M., Smith, J., & Baltes, P. B. (1992). Wisdom-related knowledge in a life review task: Age differences and the role of professional specialization. *Psychology and Aging, 7*, 271–281.

Steele, C. M. (1997). A threat in the air: How stereotypes shape intellectual identity and performance. *American Psychologist, 52*, 613–629.

Steele, C. M. (1999). Thin ice: "Stereotype threat" and black college students. *Atlantic, 284*, 44–54.

Steele, C. M., & Aronson, J. (1995). Stereotype threat and the intellectual test performance of African Americans. *Journal of Personality and Social Psychology, 69*, 797–811.

Steenari, M., Vuontela, V., Paavonen, E. J., Carlson, S., Fjallberg, M., & Aronen, E. T. (2003). Working memory and sleep in 6- to 13-year-old schoolchildren. *Journal of the American Academy of Child and Adolescent Psychiatry, 42*, 85–92.

Steenland, K., Henley, J., & Thun, M. (2002). All-cause and cause-specific death rates by educational status for two million people in two American Cancer Society cohorts, 1959–1999. *American Journal of Epidemiology, 156*, 11–21.

Stein, J. H., & Reiser, L. W. (1994). A study of white middle-class adolescent boys' responses to "semenarche" (the first ejaculation). *Journal of Youth and Adolescence, 23*, 373–384.

Stein, Z. A., Susser, M. W., Saenger, G., & Marolla, F. (1975). *Famine and human development: The Dutch hunger winter of 1944–1945.* New York: Oxford University Press.

Steinberg, E. P., Holtz, P. M., Sullivan, E. M., & Villar, C. P. (1998). Profiling assisted reproductive technology: Outcomes and quality of infertility management. *Fertility and Sterility, 69*, 617–623.

Steinberg, L. (1989). Pubertal maturation and parent–adolescent distance: An evolutionary perspective. In G. R. Adams, R. Montemayor, & T. P. Gullotta (Eds.), *Advances in adolescent behavior and development* (pp. 71–97). Newbury Park, CA: Sage.

Steinberg, L. (2001). We know some things: Parent–adolescent relationships in retrospect and prospect. *Journal of Research on Adolescence, 11*, 1–19.

Steinberg, L. (2002). *Adolescence* (6th ed.). Boston: McGraw-Hill.

Steinberg, L. (2007). Risk taking in adolescence: New perspectives from brain and behavioural science. *Current Directions in Psychological Sciences, 16*, 55–59.

Steinberg, L., & Avenevoli, S. (2000). The role of context in the development of psychopathology: A conceptual framework and some speculative propositions. *Child Development, 71*, 66–74.

Steinberg, L., & Dornbusch, S. M. (1991). Negative correlates of part-time employment during adolescence: Replication and elaboration. *Developmental Psychology, 27*, 304–313.

Steinberg, L., Dornbusch, S. M., & Brown, B. B. (1992). Ethnic differences in adolescent achievement: An ecological perspective. *American Psychologist, 47*, 723–729.

Steinberg, L., Fegley, S., & Dornbusch, S. M. (1993). Negative impact of part-time work on adolescent adjustment: Evidence from a longitudinal study. *Developmental Psychology, 29*, 171–180.

Steiner, J. E. (1979). Human facial expressions in response to taste and smell stimulation. In H. W. Reese & L. P. Lipsitt (Eds.), *Advances in child development and behavior* (Vol. 13). New York: Academic Press.

Steinhausen, H.-C. (2007). Longitudinal perspectives, outcome and prognosis. In T. Jaffa & B. McDermott (Eds.), *Eating disorders in children and adolescents.* Cambridge, UK: Cambridge University Press.

Stemp, P. S., Turner, J., & Noh, S. (1986). Psychological distress in the postpartum period: The significance of social support. *Journal of Marriage and the Family, 48*, 271–277.

Stephens, M. A., Townsend, A. L., Martire, L. M., & Druley, J. A. (2001). Balancing parent care with other roles: Interrole conflict of adult daughter caregivers. *Journal of Gerontology: Psychological Sciences, 56B*, P24–34.

Stephenson, J. (2006). Early diet and heart health. *Journal of the American Medical Association, 295*, 265.

Stepp, L. S. (2001, November 2). Children's worries take new shape. *The Washington Post*, C1, C4.

Stern, D. (1977). *The first relationship: Infant and mother.* Cambridge, MA: Harvard University Press.

Stern, M., & Karraker, K. H. (1989). Sex stereotyping of infants: A review of gender labeling studies. *Sex Roles, 20,* 501–522.

Sternberg, K. J., Baradaran, L. P., Abbott, C. B., Lamb, M. E., & Guterman, E. (2006). Type of violence, age, and gender differences in the effects of family violence on children's behavior problems: A mega-analysis. *Developmental Review, 26,* 89–112.

Sternberg, R. J. (1985). *Beyond IQ: A triarchic theory of human intelligence.* Cambridge, MA: Cambridge University Press.

Sternberg, R. J. (1988). *The triarchic mind: A new theory of human intelligence.* New York: Viking.

Sternberg, R. J. (1997). Educating intelligence: Infusing the triarchic theory into school instruction. In R. J. Sternberg & E.L. Grigorenko (Eds.), *Intelligence, heredity, and environment.* New York: Cambridge University Press.

Sternberg, R. J. (1999). *Handbook of creativity.* New York: Cambridge University Press.

Sternberg, R. J. (Ed.). (1999). *Handbook of creativity.* New York: Cambridge University Press.

Sternberg, R. J. (2000). The concept of intelligence. In R. J. Sternberg (Ed.), *The handbook of intelligence* (pp. 3–15). New York: Cambridge University Press.

Sternberg, R. J. (2003). *Wisdom, intelligence, and creativity synthesized.* Cambridge, England: Cambridge University Press.

Sternberg, R. J. (2004). Culture and intelligence. *American Psychologist, 59,* 325–338.

Sternberg, R. J. (2006). The nature of creativity. *Creativity Research Journal, 18,* 87–98.

Sternberg, R. J., Grigorenko, E. L., & Bundy, D. A. (2001). The predictive value of IQ. *Merrill-Palmer Quarterly, 47,* 1–41.

Stevens, D. P., & Truss, C. V. (1985). Stability and change in adult personality over 12 and 20 years. *Developmental Psychology, 21,* 568–584.

Stevens, G. (1999). Age at immigration and second language proficiency among foreign-born adults. *Language in Society, 28,* 555–578.

Stevens, M. M., & Dunsmore, J. C. (1996). Adolescents who are living with a life-threatening illness. In C. A. Corr & D. E. Balk (Eds.), *Handbook of adolescent death and bereavement.* New York: Springer.

Stevens, R. J., & Slavin, R. E. (1995). The cooperative elementary school: Effects on students' achievement, attitudes, and social relations. *American Educational Research Journal, 32,* 321–351.

Stevenson, H. W., Chen, C., & Lee, S. (1993). Mathematics achievement of Chinese, Japanese, and American children: Ten years later. *Science, 259,* 53–58.

Stevenson, H. W., & Lee, S. Y. (1990). Contexts of achievement: A study of American, Chinese, and Japanese children. *Monographs of the Society for Research in Child Development, 55* (1–2, Serial No. 221).

Stevenson, H. W., Lee, S. Y., & Stigler, J. W. (1986). Mathematics achievement of Chinese, Japanese, and American children. *Science, 231,* 693–699.

Stevenson, H. W., & Stigler, J. W. (1994). *The learning gap: Why our schools are failing and what we can learn from Japanese and Chinese education.* New York: Simon & Schuster.

Stevenson, M. R., & Black, K. N. (1988). Paternal absence and sex-role development: A meta-analysis. *Child Development, 59,* 793–814.

Stevenson, R. J., Mahmut, M., & Sundqvist, N. (2007). Age related changes in odor discrimination. *Developmental Psychology, 43,* 253–260.

Stewart, R. B., & Marvin, R. S. (1984). Sibling relations: The role of conceptual perspective-taking in the ontogeny of sibling caregiving. *Child Development, 55,* 1322–1332.

St. George, D. (2001, June 8). A child's unheeded cry for help. *The Washington Post,* A1, A20–A21.

Stifter, C. (2003). Child effects on the family: An example of the extreme case and a question of methodology. In A. C. Crouter & A. Booth (Eds.), *Children's influence on family dynamics. The neglected side of family relationships.* Mahwah, NJ: Erlbaum.

Stigler, J. W., Lee, S. Y., & Stevenson, H. W. (1987). Mathematics classrooms in Japan, Taiwan, and the United States. *Child Development, 58,* 1272–1285.

Stillion, J. M., & McDowell, E. E. (1996). *Suicide across the life span: Premature exits* (2nd ed.). Washington, D.C.: Taylor & Francis.

Stillion, J. M., & Papadatou, D. (2002). Suffer the children: An examination of psychosocial issues in children and adolescents with terminal illness. *American Behavioral Scientist, 46,* 299–315.

Stine, E. A. L., Soederberg, L. M., & Morrow, D. G. (1996). Language and discourse processing through adulthood. In F. Blanchard-Fields & T. M. Hess (Eds.), *Perspectives on cognitive change in adulthood and aging.* New York: McGraw-Hill.

Stine-Morrow, E. A. L., Loveless, M. K., & Soederberg, L. M. (1996). Resource allocation in on-line reading by younger and older adults. *Psychology and Aging, 11,* 475–486.

Stipek, D., Gralinski, H., & Kopp, C. (1990). Self-concept development in the toddler years. *Developmental Psychology, 26,* 972–977.

Stipek, D., & Hakuta, K. (2007). Strategies to ensure that no child starts from behind. In J. L. Aber, S. J. Bishop-Josef, S. M. Jones, K. T. McLearn, & D. A. Phillips (Eds.), *Child development and social policy: Knowledge for action.* Washington, DC: American Psychology Association.

Stipek, D. J. (1984). The development of achievement motivation. In R. Ames & C. Ames (Eds.), *Research on motivation in education* (Vol. 1). Orlando, FL: Academic Press.

Stipek, D. J., & Gralinski, J. H. (1996). Children's beliefs about intelligence and school performance. *Journal of Educational Psychology, 88,* 397–407.

Stipek, D. J., & Mac Iver, D. J. (1989). Developmental change in children's assessment of intellectual competence. *Child Development, 60,* 521–538.

Stipek, D. J., Feiler, R., Daniels, D., & Milburn, S. (1995). Effects of different instructional approaches on young children's achievement and motivation. *Child Development, 66,* 209–223.

Stipek, D. J., Recchia, A., & McClintic, S. (1992). Self-evaluation in young children. *Monographs of the Society for Research in Child Development, 57* (1, Serial No. 226).

Stith, S. M., Rosen, K. H., Middleton, K. A., Busch, A. L., Lundeberg, K., & Carlton, R. P. (2000). The intergenerational transmission of spouse abuse: A meta-analysis. *Journal of Marriage and the Family, 62,* 640–654.

St. James-Roberts, I., & Plewis, I. (1996). Individual differences, daily fluctuations, and developmental changes in amounts of waking, fussing, crying, feeding, and sleeping. *Child Development, 67,* 2527–2540.

St. John, W., Cameron, C., & McVeigh, C. (2005). Meeting the challenge of new fatherhood during the early weeks. *Obstetrics and Gynaecology, 34,* 180–189.

Stoddart, T., & Turiel, E. (1985). Children's concepts of cross-gender activities. *Child Development, 56,* 1241–1252.

Stone, R. (1992). Can a father's exposure lead to illness in his children? *Science, 258,* 31.

Stones, M. J., & Kozma, A. (1985). Physical performance. In N. Charness (Ed.), *Aging and human performance.* Chichester, England & New York: Wiley.

Stoolmiller, M. (1999). Implications of the restricted range of family environments for estimates of heritability and nonshared environment in behavior-genetic adoption studies. *Psychological Bulletin, 125,* 392–409.

Storgaard, L., Bonde, J. P., Ernst, E., Spano, M., Andersen, C. Y., Frydenberg, M., & Olsen, J. (2003). Does smoking during pregnancy affect sons' sperm count? *Epidemiology, 14,* 278–286.

Story, L. B., & Repetti, R. (2006). Daily occupational stressors and marital behavior. *Journal of Family Psychology, 20,* 690–700.

Straus, M. A., & Gelles, R. J. (1986). Societal change and change in family violence from 1975 to 1985 as revealed by two national surveys. *Journal of Marriage and the Family, 48,* 465–479.

Straus, M. A., & Gelles, R. J. (Edited with C. Smith). (1990). *Physical violence in American families. Risk factors and adaptations to violence in 8145 families.* New Brunswick, NJ: Transaction Publishers.

Strauss, V. (2001, May 8). No beating the problem of bullies. Stubborn, pervasive schoolyard behavior leaves long-term scars on perpetrators and victims. *The Washington Post,* A11.

Streissguth, A. P., Barr, H. M., Bookstein, F. L., Sampson, P. D., & Olson, H. C. (1999). The long-term neurocognitive consequences of prenatal alcohol exposure: A 14-year study. *Psychological Science, 10,* 186–190.

Streissguth, A. P., & Dehaene, P. (1993). Fetal alcohol syndrome in twins of alcoholic mothers: Concordance of diagnosis and IQ. *American Journal of Medical Genetics, 47,* 857–861.

Streri, A. (2003). Cross-modal recognition of shape from hand to eyes in human newborns. *Somatosensory Motor Research, 20,* 13–18.

Streri, A., & Gentaz, E. (2004). Cross-modal recognition of shape from hand to eyes and handedness in human newborns. *Neuropsychologia, 42,* 1365–1369.

Streri, A., & Pecheux, M. (1986). Vision-to-touch and touch-to-vision transfer of form in 5-month-old infants. *British Journal of Developmental Psychology, 4,* 161–167.

Strigini, P., Sansone, R., Carobbi, S., & Pierluigi, M. (1990). Radiation and Down's syndrome. *Nature, 347,* 717.

Stringer, J. S., Sinkala, M., Goldenberg, R. L., Kumwenda, R., Acosta, E. P., Aldrovandi, G. M., Stout, J. P., & Vermund, S. H. (2004). Universal nevirapine upon presentation in labor to prevent mother-to-child HIV transmission in high prevalence settings. *AIDS, 18*, 939-943.

Strober, M., Freeman, R., Lampert, C., Diamond, J., & Kaye, W. (2000). Controlled family study of anorexia nervosa and bulimia nervosa: Evidence of shared liability and transmission of partial syndromes. *American Journal of Psychiatry, 157*, 393-401.

Stroebe, M. (2001a). Bereavement research and theory: Retrospective and prospective. *American Behavioral Scientist, 44*, 854-865.

Stroebe, M. (2001b). Gender differences in adjustment to bereavement: An empirical and theoretical review. *Review of General Psychology, 5*, 62-83.

Stroebe, M. S., & Schut, H. A. W. (1999). The dual process model of coping with bereavement: Rationale and description. *Death Studies, 23*, 197-224.

Stroebe, W., & Schut, H. (2001). Risk factors in bereavement outcome: A methodological and empirical review. In M. S. Stroebe, R. O. Hansson, W. Stroebe, & H. Schut (Eds.), *Handbook of bereavement research. Consequences, coping, and care.* Washington, D.C.: American Psychological Association.

Stumpf, H., & Stanley, J. C. (1996). Gender-related differences on the College Board's Advanced Placement and Achievement Tests, 1982-1992. *Journal of Educational Psychology, 88*, 353-364.

Sudhalter, V., & Braine, M. D. S. (1985). How does comprehension of passives develop? A comparison of actional and experiential verbs. *Journal of Child Language, 12*, 455-470.

Suitor, J. J. (1991). Marital quality and satisfaction with the division of household labor across the family life cycle. *Journal of Marriage and the Family, 53*, 221-230.

Sullivan, H. S. (1953). *The interpersonal theory of psychiatry.* New York: Norton.

Sullivan, S., & Ruffman, T. (2004). Social understanding: How does it fare with advancing years? *British Journal of Psychology, 95*, 1-18.

Sulloway, F. J. (2007). Birth order and intelligence. *Science, 316*, 1711-1717.

Super, D. E., Savickas, M. L., & Super, C. M. (1996). The life-span, life-space approach to careers. In D. Brown, L. Brooks, & Associates (Eds.), *Career choice and development* (3rd ed.). San Francisco: Jossey-Bass.

Susser, M., & Stein, Z. (1994). Timing in prenatal nutrition: A reprise of the Dutch Famine Study. *Nutrition Reviews, 52*, 84-94.

Sutton-Brown, M., & Suchowersky, O. (2003). Clinical and research advances in Huntington's disease. *Canadian Journal of Neurological Sciences, 30* (Suppl. 1), S45.

Swanson, H. L. (1999). What develops in working memory? A life span perspective. *Developmental Psychology, 35*, 986-1000.

Swarr, A. E., & Richards, M. H. (1996). Longitudinal effects of adolescent girls' pubertal development, perceptions of pubertal timing, and parental relations on eating problems. *Developmental Psychology, 32*, 636-646.

Symons, D. K., & Clark, S. E. (2000). A longitudinal study of mother-child relationships and theory of mind in the preschool period. *Social Development, 9*, 3-23.

Szinovacz, M. E., & Davey, A. (2005). Retirement and marital decision making: Effects on retirement satisfaction. *Journal of Marriage and the Family, 67*, 387-398.

Szinovacz, M. E., DeViney, S., & Atkinson, M. P. (1999). Effects of surrogate parenting on grandparents' well-being. *Journal of Gerontology: Social Sciences, 54B*, S376-S388.

T

Tabert, M. H., Manly, J. J., Liu, X., Pelton, G. H., Rosenblum, S., Jacobs, M., Zamora, D., Goodkind, M., Bell, K., Stern, Y., Devanand, D. P. (2006). Neuropsychological prediction of conversion to Alzheimer disease in patients with mild cognitive impairment. *Archives of General Psychiatry, 63*, 916-924.

Taddio, A. (2002). Conditioning and hyperalgesia in newborns exposed to repeated heel lances, *Journal of the American Medical Association, 288*, 857-861.

Tafarodi, R. W., Lo, C., Yamaguchi, S., Lee, W. W., & Katsura, H. (2004). The inner self in three countries. *Journal of Cross-Cultural Psychology, 35*, 97-117.

Taft, L. B., & Nehrke, M. F. (1990). Reminiscence, life review, and ego integrity in nursing home residents. *International Journal of Aging and Human Development, 30*, 189-196.

Tager-Flusberg, H. (2000). Language and understanding minds: Connections in autism. In S. Baron-Cohen, H. Tager-Flusberg, & D. J. Cohen (Eds.), *Understanding other minds. Perspectives from developmental cognitive neuroscience* (2nd ed.). Oxford: Oxford University Press.

Tager-Flusberg, H. (2005). Morphology and syntax in the preschool years. In J. B. Gleason (Ed.), *The development of language* (6th ed.). Boston: Allyn & Bacon.

Takahashi, K. (1990). Are the key assumptions of the "Strange Situation" procedure universal? A view from Japanese research. *Human Development, 33*, 23-30.

Tallal, P., Miller, S. L., Bedi, G., Byma, G., Wang, X., Nagarajan, S. S., Schreiner, C., Jenkins, W. M., & Merzenich, M. M. (1996). Language comprehension in language-learning impaired children improved with acoustically modified speech. *Science, 271*, 81-84.

Tam, C. S., de Zegher, R., Garnett, S. P., Baur, L. A., & Cowell, C. T. (2006). Opposing influences of prenatal and postnatal growth on the timing of menarche. *Journal of Clinical Endocrinology and Metabolism, 91*, 4369-4373.

Tan, R. S., & Pu, S. J. (2004). Is it andropause? Recognizing androgen deficiency in aging men. *Postgraduate Medicine, 115*, 62-66.

Tan, U., & Tan, M. (1999). Incidences of asymmetries for the palmar grasp reflex in neonates and hand preference in adults. *Neuroreport: For Rapid Communication of Neuroscience Research, 10*, 3254-3256.

Tangney, J. P., Stuewig, J., & Mashek, D. J. (2007). Moral emotions and moral behavior. *Annual Review of Psychology, 58*, 345-372.

Tanner, J. M. (1990). *Foetus into man: Physical growth from conception to maturity* (2nd ed.). Cambridge, MA: Harvard University Press.

Tanzi, R. E., & Parson, A. B. (2000). *Decoding darkness. The search for the genetic causes of Alzheimer's disease.* Cambridge, MA: Perseus Publishing.

Tardif, T., & Wellman, H. M. (2000). Acquisition of mental state language in Mandarin- and Cantonese-speaking children. *Developmental Psychology, 36*, 25-43.

Taylor, C. B., Bryson, S., Luce, K. H., Cunning, D., Doyle, A. C., Abascal, L. B., Rockwell, R., Dev, P., Winzelberg, A. J., & Wilfley, D. E. (2006). Prevention of eating disorders in at-risk college-age women. *Archives of General Psychiatry, 63*, 881-888.

Taylor, J. S., Risica, P. M., Geller, L., Kirtania, U., & Cabral, H. J. (2006). Duration of breastfeeding among first-time mothers in the United States: Results of a national survey. *Acta Paediatrica, 95*, 980-984.

Taylor, M., & Carlson, S. M. (1997). The relation between individual differences in fantasy and theory of mind. *Child Development, 68*, 436-455.

Taylor, M., Carlson, S. M., Maring, B. L., Gerow, L., & Charley, C. M. (2004). The characteristics and correlates of fantasy in school-age children: Imaginary companions, impersonation, and social understanding. *Developmental Psychology, 40*, 1173-1187.

Taylor, M. D., Frier, B. M., Gold, A. E., & Deary, I. J. (2003). Psychosocial factors and diabetes-related outcomes following diagnosis of Type 1 diabetes. *Diabetic Medicine, 20*, 135-146.

Taylor, M. G. (1996). The development of children's beliefs about social and biological aspects of gender differences. *Child Development, 67*, 1555-1571.

Taylor, M. R. (2003). Dealing with death: Western philosophical strategies. In C. D. Bryant (Ed.), *Handbook of death and dying.* Thousand Oaks, CA: Sage.

Taylor, R. D., Jacobson, L., Rodriquez, A. U., Dominguez, A., Cantic, R., Doney, J., Boccuti, A., Alejandro, J., & Tobon, C. (2000). Stressful experiences and the psychological functioning of African-American and Puerto Rican families and adolescents. In R. D. Taylor & M. C. Wang (Eds.), *Resilience across contexts: Family, work, culture, and community.* Mahwah, NJ: Erlbaum.

Taylor, R. E., & Richards, S. B. (1991). Patterns of intellectual differences of black, Hispanic, and white children. *Psychology in the Schools, 28*, 5-9.

Taylor, S. E. (2002). *The tending instinct: How nurturing is essential for who were are and how we live.* New York: Times Books.

Teachman, B. A. (2006). Aging and negative affect: The rise and fall and rise of anxiety and depression symptoms. *Psychology and Aging, 21*, 201-207.

Teachman, J. D. (2000). Diversity of family structure: Economic and social influences. In D. H. Demo, K. R. Allen, & M. A. Fine (Eds.), *Handbook of family diversity.* New York: Oxford University Press.

Teachman, J. D. (2002). Stability across cohorts in divorce risk factors. *Demography, 39*, 331-351.

Teachman, J. D. (2003). Premarital sex, premarital cohabitation and the risk of subsequent marital dissolution among women. *Journal of Marriage and the Family, 65*, 444-455.

Tedeschi, R. G., & Calhoun, L. G. (2004). Posttraumatic growth: Conceptual foundations and empirical evidence. *Psychological Inquiry, 15*, 1-18.

Teeter, P. A. (1998). *Interventions for ADHD. Treatment in developmental context.* New York: Guilford.

Temple, E., Poldrack, R. A., Protopapas, A., Nagarajan, S., Salz, T., Tallal, P., Merzenich,

M. M., & Gabrieli, J. D. (2000). Disruption of the neural response to rapid acoustic stimuli in dyslexia: Evidence from functional MRI. *Proceedings of the National Academy of Science, 97*, 13907–13912.

Tenenbaum, H. R., & Leaper, C. (2003). Parent–child conversations about science: The socialization of gender inequities. *Developmental Psychology, 39*, 34–47.

Tenenbaum, H. R., Poe, M. V., Snow, C. E., Tabors, P., & Ross, S. (2007). Maternal and child predictors of low-income children's educational attainment. *Journal of Applied Development Psychology, 28*, 227–238.

Teno, J. M., Clarridge, B. R., Casey, V., Welch, L. C., Wetle, T., Shield, R., & Mor, V. (2004). Family perspectives on end-of-life care at the last place of care. *Journal of the American Medical Association, 291*, 88–93.

Terman, L. M. (1954). The discovery and encouragement of exceptional talent. *American Psychologist, 9*, 221–238.

Teti, D. M. (Ed.) (2005). *Handbook of research methods in developmental science.* Malden, MA: Blackwell Publishing.

Teti, D. M., Sakin, J. W., Kucera, E., & Corns, K. M. (1996). And baby makes four: Predictors of attachment security among preschool-age firstborns during the transition to siblinghood. *Child Development, 67*, 579–596.

Thapar, A. (2003). Attention deficit hyperactivity disorder: New genetic findings, new directions. In R. Plomin, J. C. DeFries, I. W. Craig, & P. McGuffin (Eds.), *Behavioral genetics in the postgenomic era.* Washington, D.C.: American Psychological Association.

Tharinger, D. (1990). Impact of child sexual abuse on developing sexuality. *Professional Psychology: Research & Practice, 21*, 331–337.

Thelen, E. (1984). Learning to walk: Ecological demands and phylogenetic constraints. In L. P. Lipsitt & C. Rovee-Collier (Eds.), *Advances in infancy research* (Vol. 3). Norwood, NJ: Ablex.

Thelen, E. (1995). Motor development: A new synthesis. *American Psychologist, 50*, 79–95.

Thelen, E. (1996). The improvising infant: Learning about learning to move. In M. R. Merrens & G. G. Brannigan (Eds.). *The developmental psychologists: Research adventures across the life span* (pp. 21–35). McGraw-Hill.

Thelen, E., & Smith, L. B. (1994). *A dynamic systems approach to the development of cognition and action.* Cambridge, MA: MIT Press.

Thelen, M. H., Powell, A. L., Lawrence, C., & Kuhnert, M. E. (1992). Eating and body image concerns among children. *Journal of Clinical Child Psychology, 21*, 41–46.

Thiede, K. W., & Dunlosky, J. (1999). Toward a general model of self-regulated study: An analysis of selection of items for study and self-paced study time. *Journal of Experimental Psychology: Learning, Memory, and Cognition, 25*, 1024–1037.

Thiessen, E. D., & Saffran, J. R. (2007). Learning to learn: Infants' acquisition of stress-based strategies for word segmentation. *Language Learning and Development, 3*, 73–100.

Thomas, A., & Chess, S. (1986). The New York Longitudinal Study: From infancy to early adult life. In R. Plomin & J. Dunn (Eds.), *The study of temperament: Changes, continuities, and challenges.* Hillsdale, NJ: Erlbaum.

Thomas, A. K., & Bulevich, J. B. (2006). Effective cue utilization reduces memory errors in older adults. *Psychological Aging, 21*, 379–389.

Thomas, F., Renaud, F., Benefice, E., de Meeus, T., & Guegan, J. (2001). International variability of ages at menarche and menopause: Patterns and main determinants. *Human Biology, 73*, 271.

Thomas, J. (1998, May 13). Concerns heighten as U.S. teens work increasing numbers of hours. *The New York Times.* Retrieved online (January 15, 2005): http://mbhs.bergtraum.k12.ny.us/cybereng/opinion3/working-teens.html

Thomas, J. R., Yan, J. H., & Stelmach, G. E. (2000). Movement substructures change as a function of practice in children and adults. *Journal of Experimental Child Psychology, 75*, 228–244.

Thompson A. M., & Smart, J. L. (1993). A prospective study of the development of laterality: Neonatal laterality in relation to perinatal factors and maternal behavior. *Cortex, 29*, 649–659.

Thompson, J. R., & Chapman, R. S. (1977). Who is "Daddy" revisited? The status of two-year-olds' overextended words in use and comprehension. *Journal of Child Language, 4*, 359–375.

Thompson, R. A. (1994). Emotion regulation: A theme in search of definition. In N. A. Fox (Ed.), *The development of emotion regulation: Biological and behavioral considerations. Monographs of the Society for Research in Child Development, 59* (Nos. 2–3, Serial No. 240).

Thompson, R. A. (1998). Early sociopersonality development. In N. Eisenberg (Vol. Ed.), W. Damon (Editor-in-Chief), *Handbook of child psychology: Vol. 3. Social, emotional, and personality development.* New York: Wiley.

Thompson, R. A. (2006). Conversation and developing understanding: Introduction to the special issue. *Merrill-Palmer Quarterly, 52*, 1–16.

Thompson, R. A., & Amato, P. R. (1999). The post divorce family. An introduction to the issues. In R. A. Thompson & P. R. Amato (Eds.), *The post divorce family. Children, parenting, & society.* Thousand Oaks, CA: Sage.

Thompson, R. A., & Meyer, S. (2007). Socialization of emotion regulation in the family. In J. J. Gross (Ed.), *Handbook of emotion regulation.* New York: Guilford.

Thompson, R. A., Meyer, S., & McGinley, M. (2006). Understanding values in relationships: The development of conscience. In M. Killen & J. G. Smetana (Eds.), *Handbook of moral development.* Mahwah, NJ: Erlbaum.

Thompson, R. A., & Raikes, H. A. (2003). Toward the next quarter-century: Conceptual and methodological challenges for attachment theory. *Development and Psychopathology, 15*, 691–718.

Thompson, R.F. (1975). *Introduction to physiological psychology.* New York: Harper & Row.

Thompson, R. F. (2000). *The brain: An introduction to neuroscience* (3rd ed.). New York: Worth.

Thompson, S. B. N. (2006). *Dementia and memory: A handbook for students and professionals.* Hampshire, UK: Ashgate Publishing.

Thorndike, R. L. (1997). The early history of intelligence testing. In D. P. Flanagan, J. L. Genshaft, & P. L. Harrison (Eds.), *Contemporary intellectual assessment: Theories, tests, and issues.* New York: Guilford.

Thorne, B. (1993). *Gender play: Girls and boys in school.* New Brunswick, NJ: Rutgers University Press.

Thornton, R., & Light, L. L. (2006). Language comprehension and production in normal aging. In J. E. Birren & K. W. Schaie (Eds.), *Handbook of the psychology of aging.* Boston: Elsevier Academic Press.

Thurber, C. A. (1995). The experience and expression of homesickness in preadolescent and adolescent boys. *Child Development, 66*, 1162–1178.

Thurstone, L. L. (1938). *Primary mental abilities.* Chicago: University of Chicago Press.

Thurstone, L. L., & Thurstone, T. G. (1941). Factorial studies of intelligence. *Psychometric Monographs*, No. 2.

Thys-Jacobs, S. (2000). Micronutrients and the premenstrual syndrome: The case for calcium. *Journal of the American College of Nutrition, 19*, 220–227.

Tienari, P., Wynne, L. C., Sorri, A., Lahti, I., Laksy, K., Moring, J., Naarala, M., Nieminen, P., & Wahlberg, K. E. (2004). Genotype–environment interaction in schizophrenia-spectrum disorder. Long-term follow-up study of Finnish adoptees. *British Journal of Psychiatry, 184*, 216–222.

Tietjen, A. M., & Walker, L. J. (1985). Moral reasoning and leadership among men in a Papua New Guinea society. *Developmental Psychology, 21*, 982–992.

Timmer, E., Bode, C., & Dittmann-Kohli, F. (2003). Expectations of gains in the second half of life: A study of personal conceptions of enrichment in a lifespan perspective. *Ageing & Society, 23*, 3–24.

Tisak, M. S., & Tisak, J. (1990). Children's conceptions of parental authority, friendship, and sibling relations. *Merrill-Palmer Quarterly, 36*, 347–368.

Tolan, P., Gorman-Smith, D., & Henry, D. (2006). Family violence. *Annual Review of Psychology, 57*, 557–583.

Tomasello, M. (2006). Acquiring linguistic constructions. In D. Kuhn & R. Siegler (Vol. Eds.), *Handbook of child psychology: Cognition, perception, and language: Vol. 2* (6th ed.). Hoboken, NJ: Wiley and Sons.

Tomasello, M., Call, J., & Hare, B. (2003). Chimpanzees understand psychological states: The question is which ones and to what extent. *Trends in Cognitive Sciences, 7*, 153–156.

Tomlinson-Keasey, C., & Keasey, C. B. (1974). The mediating role of cognitive development in moral judgment. *Child Development, 45*, 291–298.

Tomlinson-Keasey, C., & Little, T. D. (1990). Predicting educational attainment, occupational achievement, intellectual skill, and personal adjustment among gifted men and women. *Journal of Educational Psychology, 82*, 442–455.

Tommiska, V., Heinonen, K., Lehtonen, L., Renlund, M., Saarela, T., Tammela, O., Virtanen, M., & Fellman, V. (2007). No improvement in outcome of nationwide extremely low birth weight infant populations between 1996–1997 and 1999–2000. *Pediatrics, 119*, 29–36.

Torner, N., Valerio, L., Costa, J., Parron, I., Dominguez, A. (2006). Rubella outbreak in young adults of Brazilian origin in a Barcelona suburb, October-December 2005. *Euro Surveill, 11*, (2):E060223.3. Available: http://www.

eurosurveillance.org/ew/2006/060223.asp#3. Accessed: February 10, 2007.Torrance, E. P. (1968). A longitudinal examination of the fourth grade slump in creativity. *Gifted Child Quarterly, 12,* 195–199.

Torrance, E. P. (1975). Creativity research in education: Still alive. In I. A. Taylor & J. W. Getzels (Eds.), *Perspectives in creativity.* Chicago: Aldine-Atherton.

Torrance, E. P. (1988). The nature of creativity as manifest in its testing. In R. J. Sternberg (Ed.), *The nature of creativity: Contemporary psychological perspectives.* Cambridge, England: Cambridge University Press.

Torvaldsen, S., Roberts, C. L., Bell, J. C., & Raynes-Greenow, C. H. (2004). Discontinuation of epidural analgesia late in labour for reducing the adverse delivery outcomes associated with epidural analgesia. *Cochrane Database of Systematic Reviews,* Art. No.: CD004457. DOI: 10.1002/14651858. CD004457.pub2.

Tousignant, M. (1995, November 17). The lesson of a lifetime: 2nd-graders thrill to 114-year-old Ella Miller's tales of growing up. *The Washington Post,* B1.

Tousignant, M. (1996, November 9). A seasoned voter speaks her mind: At 115 years old, Vienna woman says age of candidate is not an issue. *The Washington Post,* B5.

Trabasso, T. (1975). Representation, memory, and reasoning: How do we make transitive inferences? In A. D. Pick (Ed.), *Minnesota Symposia on Child Psychology* (Vol. 9). Minneapolis: University of Minnesota.

Tracy, J. L., Shaver, P. R., Albino, A. W., & Cooper, M. L. (2003). Attachment styles and adolescent sexuality. In P. Florsheim (Ed.), *Adolescent romantic relations and sexual behavior: Theory, research, and practical implications.* Mahwah, NJ: Erlbaum.

Trautner, H. M., Gervai, J., & Nemeth, R. (2003). Appearance-reality distinction and development of gender constancy understanding in children. *International Journal of Behavioral Development, 27,* 275–281.

Trautner, H. M., Ruble, D. N., Cyphers, L., Kirsten, B., Behrendt, R., & Hartmann, P. (2005). Rigidity and flexibility of gender stereotypes in childhood: Developmental or differential? *Infant and Child Development, 14,* 365–381.

Traylor, E. S., Hayslip, B. Jr., Kaminski, P. L., & York, C. (2003). Relationships between grief and family system characteristics: A cross lagged longitudinal analysis. *Death Studies, 27,* 575–601.

Treffert, D. A. (2000). *Extraordinary people: Understanding savant syndrome.* Available online: iUniverse.com.

Treiman, R. (2000). The foundations of literacy. *Current Directions in Psychological Science, 9,* 89–92.

Treiman, R., & Broderick, V. (1998). What's in a name? Children's knowledge about the letters in their own names. *Journal of Experimental Child Psychology, 70,* 97–116.

Tremblay, M. S., Inman, J. W., & Willms, J. D. (2000). The relationship between physical activity, self-esteem, and academic achievement in 12-year-old children. *Pediatric Exercise Science, 12,* 312–323.

Tremblay, R. E. (2000). The development of aggressive behaviour during childhood: What

have we learned in the past century? *International Journal of Behavioral Development. 24,* 129–141.

Triandis, H. C. (1989). Self and social behavior in differing cultural contexts. *Psychological Review, 96,* 269–289.

Triandis, H. C. (1995). *Individualism and collectivism.* Boulder, CO: Westview Press.

Trickett, P. K., & Putnam, F. W. (1993). Impact of child sexual abuse on females: Toward a developmental, psychobiological integration. *Psychological Science, 4,* 81–87.

Tronick, E. Z. (1989). Emotions and emotional communication in infants. *American Psychologist, 44,* 112–119.

Troseth, G. L., Saylor, M. M., & Archer, A. H. (2006). Toddlers have difficulty learning from video. *Child Development, 77,* 786–799.

Trueheart, C. (1997, August 5). Champion of longevity ends her reign at 122. *The Washington Post,* A1, A12.

Tryon, R. C. (1940). Genetic differences in maze learning in rats. *Yearbook of the National Society for Studies in Education, 39,* 111–119.

Trzesniewski, K. H., Donnellan, M. B., Moffitt, T. E., Robins, R. W., Poulton, R., & Caspi, A. (2006). Low self-esteem during adolescence predicts poor health, criminal behavior, and limited economic prospects during adulthood. *Developmental Psychology, 42,* 381–390.

Trzesniewski, K. H., Donnellan, M. B., & Robins, R. W. (2003). Stability of self-esteem across the lifespan. *Journal of Personality and Social Psychology, 84,* 205–220.

Tsuchiya, K. J., Takagai, S., Kawai, M., Matsumoto, H., Nakamura, K., Minabe, Y., Mori, N., & Takei, N. (2005). Advanced paternal age associated with an elevated risk for schizophrenia in offspring in a Japanese population. *Schizophrenia Research, 65,* 337–342.

Tucker, B. P. (1998). Deaf culture, cochlear implants, and elective disability. *Hastings Center Report, 28,* 6–14.

Tuckman, B. W. (1999). The effects of exercise on children and adolescents. In A. J. Goreczny & M. Hersen (Eds.), *Handbook of pediatric and adolescent health psychology* (pp. 275–286). Boston: Allyn & Bacon.

Turati, C. (2004). Why faces are not special to newborns: An alternative account of the face preference. *Current Directions in Psychological Science, 13,* 5–8.

Turiel, E. (1978). The development of concepts of social structure: Social convention. In J. Glick & A. Clarke-Stewart (Eds.), *The development of social understanding.* New York: Gardner Press.

Turiel, E. (1983). *The development of social knowledge. Morality and convention.* Cambridge, England: Cambridge University Press.

Turiel, E. (2006). The development of morality. In N. Eisenberg (Vol. Ed.), & W. Damon & R. M. Lerner (Eds. in Chief), *Handbook of child psychology: Vol. 3. Social, emotional, and personality development* (6th ed). Hoboken, NJ: Wiley.

Turk-Charles, S., & Carstensen, L. L. (1999). The role of time in the setting of social goals across the life span. In T. M. Hess & F. Blanchard-Fields (Eds.), *Social cognition and aging.* San Diego: Academic Press.

Turkheimer, E. (1991). Individual and group differences in adoption studies of IQ. *Psychological Bulletin, 110,* 392–405.

Turkheimer, E. (2000). Three laws of behavior genetics and what they mean. *Current Directions in Psychological Science, 9,* 160–164.

Turkheimer, E., Haley, A., Waldron, M., D'Onofrio, B., & Gottesman, I. I. (2003). Socioeconomic status modifies heritability of IQ in young children. *Psychological Science, 14,* 623–628.

Turner, P. J., & Gervai, J. (1995). A multidimensional study of gender typing in preschool children and their parents: Personality, attitudes, preferences, behavior, and cultural differences. *Developmental Psychology, 31,* 759–772.

Turner, R. J., & Lloyd, D. A. (2004). Stress burden and the lifetime incidence of psychiatric disorder in young adults racial and ethnic contrasts. *Archives of General Psychiatry, 61,* 481–488.

Turnpenny, P. D., & Ellard, S. (2005). *Emery's elements of medical genetics.* Edinburgh: Elsevier.

Twenge, J. M. (1997). Changes in masculine and feminine traits over time: A meta-analysis. *Sex Roles, 36,* 305–325.

Twenge, J. M. (2000). The age of anxiety? Birth cohort change in anxiety and neuroticism, 1952–1993. *Journal of Personality and Social Psychology, 79,* 1007–1021.

Tyre, P. (2005, December 5). No one to blame. *Newsweek,* pp. 50–59.

Tyson-Rawson, K. J. (1996). Adolescent responses to the death of a parent. In C. A. Corr & D. E. Balk (Eds.), *Handbook of adolescent death and bereavement.* New York: Springer.

U

Uchida, N., Fujita, K., & Katayama, T. (1999). Detection of vehicles on the other crossing path at an intersection: Visual search performance of elderly drivers. *Japanese Society of Automotive Engineers Review, 20,* 381.

Uchino, B. N., Cacioppo, J. T., & Keicolt-Glaser, J. K. (1996). The relationship between social support and physiological processes: A review with emphasis on underlying mechanisms and implications for health. *Psychological Bulletin, 119,* 488–531.

Ueno, K., & Adams, R. G. (2006). Adult friendship: A decade review. In P. Noller & J. A. Feeney (Eds.), *Close relationships: Functions, forms, and processes.* New York: Psychology Press.

Uhlenberg, P., & de Jong-Gierveld, J. (2004). Age-segregation in later life: An examination of personal networks. *Ageing & Society, 24,* 5–28.

Umana-Taylor, A. J., & Alfaro, E. C. (2006). Ethnic identity among U. S. Latino adolescents: Theory, measurement, and implications for well-being. In F. A. Villarruel & T. Luster (Eds.), *The crisis in youth mental health: Critical issues and effective programs: Vol 2. Disorders in adolescence.* Westport, CT: Praeger.

Umana-Taylor, A. J., Bhanot, R., & Shin, N. (2006). Ethnic identity formation during adolescence: The critical role of families. *Journal of Family Issues, 27,* 390–414.

Umberson, D. (1992). Relationships between adult children and their parents: Psychological consequences for both generations. *Journal of Marriage and the Family, 54,* 664–674.

Umberson, D. (2003). *Death of a parent: Transition to a new adult identity.* Cambridge, U.K.: Cambridge University Press.

Umberson, D., & Slaten, E. (2000). Gender and intergenerational relationships. In D. H. Demo, K. R. Allen, & M. A. Fine (Eds.),

Handbook of family diversity. New York: Oxford University Press.

Umberson, D., Wortman, C. B., & Kessler, R. C. (1992). Widowhood and depression: Explaining long-term gender differences in vulnerability. *Journal of Health and Social Behavior, 33,* 10–24.

Underwood, A. (2004, January 19). Now, reduce your risk of Alzheimer's. *Newsweek,* 72–73.

Underwood, A. (2005, March 14). The gift of ADHD? *Newsweek,* p. 48.

Unger, J. B., Molina, G. B., & Teran, L. (2000). Perceived consequences of teenage childbearing among adolescent girls in an urban sample. *Journal of Adolescent Health, 26,* 205–212.

United Nations, Department of Economic and Social Affairs, Population Division (2007). *World population prospects: The 2006 revision, highlights.* Working Paper No. ESA/P/WP.202. Available at: www.un.org/esa/population/publications/wpp2006/WPP2006_Highlights_rev.pdf.

Updegraff, K., & McHale, S. M., & Crouter, A. C. (1996). Gender roles in marriage: What do they mean for girls' and boys' school achievement? *Journal of Youth and Adolescence, 25,* 73–88.

Urdan, T., & Mestas, M. (2006). The goals behind performance goals. *Journal of Educational Psychology, 98,* 354–365.

Urofsky, M. I. (1993). *Letting go. Death, dying, and the law.* New York: Charles Scribner's Sons.

U.S. Census Bureau. (2005). *College degree nearly doubles annual earnings.* Washington, D.C.: U.S. Department of Commerce.

U.S. Census Bureau. (2006). *Statistical abstract of the United States 2007* (126th ed.). Washington, DC: U.S. Government Printing Office, 2006. Available at: www.census.gov/compendia/statab.

U.S. Census Bureau. (2007). *Educational attainment in the United States: 2004. Detailed Tables: Table 8.* Washington, DC: Government Printing Office. Available at www.census.gov/population/socdemo/education/cps2004/tab08-1.pdf. Accessed: September 25, 2007.

U.S. Department of Education. (1997). Digest of Education Statistics, 1997. Washington, D.C.: National Center for Education Statistics.

U.S. Department of Education. (2005). National Assessment of Educational Progress (NAEP). *The Nation's Report Card, Mathematics 2005.* Washington, DC: Office of Educational Research and Improvement, National Center for Education Statistics.

U.S. Department of Health and Human Services, Administration on Children, Youth, and Families. (2007). *Child maltreatment 2005.* Washington, DC: U.S. Government Printing Office. Available at: www.acf.hhs.gov/programs/cb/pubs/cm05/index.htm.

U.S. Department of Labor, Bureau of Labor Statistics. (2001). *Highlights of women's earnings in 2000* (Report 952). Washington, D.C.: Author.

Usher, J. A., & Neisser, U. (1993). Childhood amnesia and the beginnings of memory for four early life events. *Journal of Experimental Psychology: General, 122,* 155–165.

V

Vaillant, G. E. (1977). *Adaptation to life.* Boston: Little, Brown.

Vaillant, G. E. (1983). Childhood environment and maturity of defense mechanisms. In D.

Magnusson & V. L. Allen (Eds.), *Human development. An interactional perspective.* New York: Academic Press.

Vaillant, G. E., & Milofsky, E. (1980). Natural history of male psychological health. IX: Empirical evidence for Erikson's model of the life cycle. *American Journal of Psychiatry, 137,* 1348–1359.

Valenza, E., Leo, I., Gava, L., & Simion, F. (2006). Perceptual completion in newborn human infants. *Child Development, 77,* 1810–1821.

Van Beurden, E., Zask, A., Barnett, L. M., & Dietrich, U. C. (2002). Fundamental movement skills—How do primary school children perform? The "Move it, Groove it" program in rural Australia. *Journal of Science and Medicine on Sport, 5,* 244–252.

Van Beveren, T. T., Little, B. B., & Spence, M. (2000). Effects of prenatal cocaine exposure and postnatal environment on child development. *American Journal of Human Biology, 12,* 417–428.

Vandell, D. L. (2000). Parents, peer groups, and other socializing influences. *Developmental Psychology, 36,* 699–710.

Vandell, D. L., Wilson, K. S., & Buchanan, N. R. (1980). Peer interaction in the first year of life: An examination of its structure, content, and sensitivity to toys. *Child Development, 51,* 481–488.

van den Boom, D. C. (1995). Do first-year intervention effects endure? Follow-up during toddlerhood of a sample of Dutch irritable infants. *Child Development, 66,* 1798–1816.

van der Maas, H., & Jansen, B. R. J. (2003). What response times tell of children's behavior on the balance scale task. *Journal of Experimental Child Psychology, 85,* 141–177.

Van Gaalen, R. I., & Dykstra, P. A. (2006). Solidarity and conflict between adult children and parents: A latent class analysis. *Journal of Marriage and Family, 68,* 947–960.

van Galen, G. P. (1993). Handwriting: A developmental perspective. In A. F. Kalverboer, B. Hopkins, & R. H. Geuze (Eds.), *Motor development in early and later childhood: Longitudinal approaches.* Cambridge, England: Cambridge University Press.

Van Giffen, K., & Haith, M. M. (1984). Infant visual response to Gestalt geometric forms. *Infant Behavior and Development, 7,* 335–346.

Van Goozen, S. H. M., Fairchild, G., Snoek, H., & Harold, G. T. (2007). The evidence for a neurobiological model of childhood antisocial behavior. *Psychological Bulletin, 133,* 149–182.

Van Hecke, A. V., Mundy, P. C., Acra, C. F., Block, J. J., Delgado, C. E. F., Parlade, M. V., Meyer, J. A., Neal, A. R., & Pomares, Y. B. (2007). Infant joint attention, temperament, and social competence in preschool children. *Child Development, 78,* 53–69.

van Hoeken, D., Seidell, J., & Hoek, H. (2003). Epidemiology. In J. Treasure, U. Schmidt, & E. Van Furth (Eds.), *Handbook of eating disorders* (2nd ed.). Chicester, UK: Wiley.

van Hoof, A. (1999). The identity status field reviewed: An update of unresolved and neglected issues with a view on some alternative approaches. *Developmental Review, 19,* 497–556.

van IJzendoorn, M. H. (1992). Intergenerational transmission of parenting: A review of studies in nonclinical populations. *Developmental Review, 12,* 76–99.

van IJzendoorn, M. H. (1995). Adult attachment representations, parental responsiveness, and infant attachment: A meta-analysis on the predictive validity of the Adult Attachment Interview. *Psychological Bulletin, 117,* 387–403.

van IJzendoorn, M. H., & DeWolff, M. S. (1997). In search of the absent father: Meta-analyses of infant-father attachment: A rejoinder to our discussants. *Child Development, 68,* 604–609.

van IJzendoorn, M. H., & Juffer, F. (2005). Adoption is a successful natural intervention enhancing adopted children's IQ and school performance. *Current Directions in Psychological Science, 14,* 326–330.

van IJzendoorn, M. H., & Juffer, F. (2006). The Emanuel Miller Memorial Lecture 2006: Adoption as intervention: Meta-analytic evidence for massive catch-up and plasticity in physical, socio-emotional, and cognitive development. *Journal of Child Psychology and Psychiatry, 47,* 1228–1245.

van IJzendoorn, M. H., Rutgers, A. H., Bakermans-Kranenburg, M. J., Swinkels, S. H. N., van Daalen, E., Dietz, C., Naber, F. B. A., Buitelaar, J. K., & van Engeland, H. (2007). Parental sensitivity and attachment in children with autism spectrum disorder: Comparison with children with mental retardation, with language delays, and with typical development. *Child Development, 78,* 597–608.

van IJzendoorn, M. H., & Sagi, A. (1999). Cross-cultural patterns of attachment: Universal and contextual dimensions. In J. Cassidy & P. R. Shaver (Eds.), *Handbook of attachment.* New York: Guilford.

van IJzendoorn, M. H., Schuengel, C., & Bakermans-Kranenburg, M. J. (1999). Disorganized attachment in early childhood: Meta-analysis of precursors, concomitants, and sequelae. *Development and Psychopathology, 11,* 225–249.

van Kleeck, A., Gillam, R. B., Hamilton, L., & McGrath, C. (1997). The relationship between middle-class parents' book-sharing discussion and their preschooler's abstract language development. *Journal of Speech, Language, and Hearing Research, 40,* 1261–1271.

Van Laningham, J., Johnson, D., & Amato, P. (2001). Marital happiness, marital duration, and the U-shaped curve: Evidence from a five-wave panel study. *Social Forces, 79,* 1313–1341.

van Os, J., & Sham, P. (2003). Gene-environment correlation and interaction in schizophrenia. In R. M. Murray, P. B. Jones, E. Susser, J. van Os, & M. Cannon (Eds.), *The epidemiology of schizophrenia.* Cambridge, U.K.: Cambridge University Press.

van Solinge, H., & Henkens, K. (2005). Couples' adjustment to retirement: A multi-actor study. *Journal of Gerontology: Psychological and Social Sciences, 60B,* S11–S20.

Van Voorhis, B. J. (2006). Outcomes from assisted reproductive technology. *Obstetrics and Gynecology, 107,* 183–200.

Varea, C., Bernis, C., Montero, P., Arias, S., Barroso, A., & Gonzalez, B. (2000). Secular trend and intrapopulational variation in age of menopause in Spanish women. *Journal of Biosocial Science, 32,* 383–393.

Varendi, H., Christensson, K., Porter, R. H., & Winberg, J. (1998). Soothing effect of amniotic fluid smell in newborn infants. *Early Human Development, 51,* 47–55.

Vargha-Khadem, F., Gadian, D. G., Watkins, K. E., Connelly, A., Van Paesschen, W., & Mishkin, M. (1997). Differential effects of early hippocampal pathology on episodic and semantic memory. *Science, 277,* 376–380.

Vartanian, L. R., & Powlishta, K. K. (1996). A longitudinal examination of the social-cognitive foundations of adolescent egocentrism. *Journal of Early Adolescence, 16,* 157–178.

Vaughn, B. E., Azria, M. R., Krzysik, L., Caya, L. R., Bost, K. K., Newell, W., & Kazura, K. L. (2000). Friendship and social competence in a sample of preschool children attending head start. *Developmental Psychology, 36,* 326–338.

Vaughn, B. E., Lefever, G. B., Seifer, R., & Barglow, P. (1989). Attachment behavior, attachment security, and temperament during infancy. *Child Development, 60,* 728–737.

Vedantam, S. (2006, December 14). Antidepressants a suicide risk for young adults. *The Washington Post,* p. A16.

Vedantam, S. (2007, June 10). Fight over vaccine–autism link hits court. *The Washington Post,* A6.

Veenstra-Vanderweele, J., & Cook, E. H. (2003). Genetics of childhood disorders: XLVI. Autism, part 5: Genetics of autism. *Journal of the American Academy of Child and Adolescent Psychiatry, 42,* 116–118.

Velderman, M.K., Bakermans-Kranenburg, M. J., Juffer, F., & van IJzendoorn, M. H. (2006). Effects of attachment-based interventions on maternal sensitivity and infant attachment: Differential susceptibility of highly reactive infants. *Journal of Family Psychology, 20,* 266–274.

Vellutino, F. R. (1991). Introduction to three studies on reading acquisition: Convergent findings on theoretical foundations of code-oriented versus whole language approaches to reading instruction. *Journal of Educational Psychology, 83,* 437–443.

Vellutino, F. R., Scanlon, D. M., Sipay, E. R., & Small, S. G. (1996). Cognitive profiles of difficult-to-remediate and readily remediated poor readers: Early intervention as a vehicle for distinguishing between cognitive and experiential deficits as basic causes of specific reading disability. *Journal of Educational Psychology, 88,* 601–638.

Verbeek, P. (2006). Everyone's monkey: Primate moral roots. In M. Killen & J. G. Smetana (Eds.), *Handbook of moral development.* Mahwah, NJ: Erlbaum.

Verghese, J., Lipton, R. B., Katz, M. J., Hall, C. B., Derby, C. A., Kuslansky, G., Ambrose, A. F., Sliwinski, M., & Buschke, H. (2003). Leisure activities and the risk of dementia in the elderly. *New England Journal of Medicine, 348,* 2508–2516.

Verhaak, C. M., Smeenk, J. M., van Minnen, A., Kremer, J. A., & Kraaimaat, F. W. (2005). A longitudinal, prospective study on emotional adjustment before, during, and after consecutive fertility treatment cycles. *Human Reproduction, 20,* 2253–2260.

Verhaeghen, P. (2003). Aging and vocabulary scores: A meta-analysis. *Psychology and Aging, 18,* 332–339.

Verhaeghen, P. (2003). Aging and vocabulary scores: A meta-analysis. *Psychology and Aging, 18,* 332–339.

Verma, S., & Larson, R. (Eds.), (2003). *Examining adolescent leisure time across cultures: New directions for child and adolescent development, No. 99.* San Francisco: Jossey-Bass.

Vermeulen, A. (2000). Andropause. *Maturitas, 15,* 5–15.

Veroff, J., Reuman, D., & Feld, S. (1984). Motives in American men and women across the adult life span. *Developmental Psychology, 20,* 1142–1158.

Verquer, M. L., Beehr, T. A., & Wagner, S. H. (2003). A meta-analysis of relations between person-organization fit and work attitudes. *Journal of Vocational Behavior, 63,* 473–489.

Verrillo, R. T., & Verrillo, V. (1985). Sensory and perceptual performance. In N. Charness (Ed.), *Aging and human performance.* Chichester, England: Wiley.

Verschueren, K., Buyck, P., & Marcoen, A. (2001). Self-representations and socioemotional competence in young children: A 3-year longitudinal study. *Developmental Psychology, 37,* 126–134.

Vieweg, V. R., Johnston, C. H., Lanier, J. O., Fernandez, A., & Pandurangi, A. K. (2007). Correlation between high risk obesity groups and low socioeconomic status in school children. *Southern Medical Journal, 100,* 8–13.

Vinden, P. G., & Astington, J. W. (2000). Culture and understanding other minds. In S. Baron-Cohen, H. Tager-Flusberg, & D. J. Cohen (Eds.), *Understanding other minds. Perspectives from developmental cognitive neuroscience* (2nd ed.). Oxford: Oxford University Press.

Viner, R. (2002). Splitting hairs: Is puberty getting earlier in girls? *Archives of Disease in Childhood, 86,* 6–8.

Vining, E. P. G., Freeman, J. M., Pillas, D. J., Uematsu, S., Carson, B. S., Brandt, J., Boatman, D., Pulsifer, M. B., & Zuckerberg, A., (1997). Why would you remove half a brain? The outcome of 58 children after hemispherectomy—the Johns Hopkins experience: 1968 to 1996. *Pediatrics, 100,* 163–171.

Vita, A. J., Terry, R. B., Hubert, H. B., & Fries, J. F. (1998). Aging, health risks, and cumulative disability. *New England Journal of Medicine, 338,* 1035–1041.

Vitiello, B., Zuvekas, S. H., & Norquist, G. S. (2006). National estimates of antidepressant medication use among U.S. children. *Journal of the American Academy of Child and Adolescent Psychiatry, 45,* 271–279.

Vobejda, B., & Havemann, J. (1997, May 2). Teenagers less sexually active in U.S. *The Washington Post,* A1, A12.

Vogler, G. P. (2006). Behavior genetics and aging. In J. E. Birren & K. W. Schaie (Eds.), *Handbook of the psychology of aging* (6th ed). Burlington, MA: Elsevier Academic Press.

Vohr, B.R., Poindexter, B. B., Dusick, A. M., McKinely, L. T., Wright, L. L., Langer, J.C., & Poole, W. K. (2006). Beneficial effects of breast milk in the neonatal intensive care unit on the developmental outcome of extremely low birth weight infants at 18 months of age. *Pediatrics, 118,* 115–123.

Voight, B. F., Kudaravalli, S., Wen, X., & Pritchard, J. K. (2006). A map of recent positive selection in the human genome. *PLoS Biology, 4,* 0446–0458.

Volkmar, F. R. (2001). Pharmacological interventions in autism: Theoretical and practical issues. *Journal of Clinical Child Psychology, 30,* 80–87.

Volkmar, F. R., Lord, C., Bailey, A., Schultz, R. T., & Klin, A. (2004). Autism and pervasive developmental disorders. *Journal of Child Psychology and Psychiatry and Allied Disciplines, 45,* 135–170.

Volling, B. L. (2005). The transition to siblinghood: A developmental ecological systems perspective and directions for future research. *Journal of Family Psychology, 19,* 542–549.

Vondra, J., & Belsky, J. (1993). Developmental origins of parenting: Personality and relationship factors. In T. Luster & L. Okagaki (Eds.), *Parenting. An ecological perspective.* Hillsdale, NJ: Erlbaum.

von Hofsten, C. (1993). Studying the development of goal-directed behavior. In A. F. Kalverboer, B. Hopkins, & R. H. Geuze (Eds.), *Motor development in early and later childhood: Longitudinal approaches.* Cambridge, England: Cambridge University Press.

Von Hofsten, C. (2007). Action in development. *Developmental Science, 10,* 54–60.

Vouloumanos, A., & Werker, J. F. (2007). Listening to language at birth: Evidence for a bias for speech in neonates. *Developmental Science, 10,* 159–171.

Voyer, D., Postma, A., Brake, B., & Imperato-McGinley, J. (2007). Gender differences in object location memory: A meta-analysis. *Psychonomic Bulletin and Review, 14,* 23–38.

Vuorialho, A., Karinen, P., & Sorri, M. (2006). Effect of hearing aids on hearing disability and quality of life in the elderly. *International Journal of Audiology, 45,* 400–405.

Vurpillot, E. (1968). The development of scanning strategies and their relation to visual differentiation. *Journal of Experimental Child Psychology, 6,* 632–650.

Vygotsky, L. S. (1962). *Thought and language* (E. Hanfmann & G. Vakar, Eds. & Trans.). Cambridge, MA: MIT Press. (Original work published 1934).

Vygotsky, L. S. (1978). *Mind in society: The development of higher mental processes* (M. Cole, V. John-Steiner, S. Scribner, & E. Souberman, Eds.). Cambridge, MA: Harvard University Press. (Original work published 1930, 1933, 1935).

W

Wachs, T. D. (2000). *Necessary but not sufficient. The respective roles of single and multiple influences on individual development.* Washington, D.C.: American Psychological Association.

Wade, B., & Moore, M. (1998). An early start with books: Literacy and mathematical evidence from a longitudinal study. *Educational Review, 50,* 135–145.

Waechter, E. H. (1984). Dying children. Patterns of coping. In H. Wass & C. A. Corr (Eds.), *Childhood and death.* Washington, D.C.: Hemisphere.

Waite, L. J., & Gallagher, M. (2000). *The case for marriage. Why married people are happier, healthier, and better off financially.* New York: Doubleday.

Wakschlag, L. S., Leventhal, B. L., Pine, D., S., Pickett, K. E., & Carter, A. S. (2006a). Elucidating early mechanisms of developmental psychopathology: The case of prenatal smoking and disruptive behavior. *Child Development, 77,* 893–906.

Wakschlag, L. S., Pickett, K. E., Kasza, K. E., & Loeber, R. (2006b). Is prenatal smoking associated with a developmental pattern of conduct problems in young boys? *American Academy of Child and Adolescent Psychiatry, 45,* 461–467.

Waldenström, U., Borg, I., Olsson, B., Sköld, M., & Wall, S. (1996). The childbirth experience: A study of 295 new mothers. *Birth, 23,* 144–153.

Waldman, I. D., & Gizer, I. R. (2006). The genetics of attention deficit hyperactivity disorder. *Clinical Psychology Review, 26,* 396–432.

Walford, R. L. (1983). *Maximum life span.* New York: Norton.

Walford, R. L., Mock, D., Verdery, R., & MacCallum, T. (2002). Calorie restriction in Biosphere 2: Alterations in the physiologic, hematologic, hormonal, and biochemical parameters in humans restricted for a 2-year period. *Journal of Gerontology, 57A,* B211–B224.

Walker, L. J. (1980). Cognitive and perspective-taking prerequisites of moral development. *Child Development, 51,* 131–139.

Walker, L. J. (2004). Gus in the gap: Bridging the judgment-action gap in moral reasoning. In D. K. Lapsley & D. Narvaez (Eds.), *Moral development, self, and identity.* Mahwah, NJ: Erlbaum.

Walker, L. J. (2006). Gender and morality. In M. Killen & J. G. Smetana (Eds.), *Handbook of moral development.* Mahwah, NJ: Erlbaum.

Walker, L. J., Hennig, K. H., & Krettenauer, T. (2000). Parent and peer contexts for children's moral reasoning development. *Child Development, 71,* 1033–1048.

Walker, W. R., Skowronski, J. J., & Thompson, C. P. (2003). Life is good—and memory helps to keep it that way. *Review of General Psychology, 7,* 203–210.

Walker-Andrews, A. S. (1997). Infants' perception of expressive behaviors: Differentiation of multimodal information. *Psychological Bulletin, 121,* 437–456.

Wallace, P. S., & Whishaw, I. Q. (2003). Independent digit movements and precision grip patterns in 1–5-month-old human infants: Hand-babbling, including vacuous then self-directed hand and digit movements, precedes targeted reaching. *Neuropsychologia, 41,* 1912–1918.

Wallach, M. A. & Kogan, N. (1965). *Thinking in young children.* New York: Holt, Rinehart & Winston.

Wallach, M. A., & Wing, C. W. (1969). *The talented student: A validation of the creativity-intelligence distinction.* New York: Holt, Rinehart & Winston.

Wallander, J. L., & Hubert, N. C. (1985). Long-term prognosis for children with attention deficit disorder with hyperactivity (ADD/H). In B. B. Lahey & A. E. Kazdin (Eds.), *Advances in clinical child psychology* (Vol. 8). New York: Plenum.

Wallen, K. (1996). Nature needs nurture: The interaction of hormonal and social influences on the development of behavioral sex differences in rhesus monkeys. *Hormones and Behavior, 30,* 364–378.

Walls, R. T. (2000). Vocational cognition: Accuracy of 3rd-, 6th-, 9th-, and 12th-grade students. *Journal of Vocational Behavior, 56,* 137–144.

Walsh, C. E. (2003). Gene therapy progress and prospects: Gene therapy for the hemophilias. *Gene Therapy, 10,* 999–1003.

Walster, E., Walster, G. W., & Berscheid, E. (1978). *Equity: Theory and research.* Boston: Allyn & Bacon.

Wang, H. Y., & Amato, P. R. (2000). Predictors of divorce adjustment: Stressors, resources, and definitions. *Journal of Marriage and the Family, 62,* 655–668.

Wang, P. S., Berglund, P., Olfson, M., Pincus, H. A., Wells, K. B., & Kessler, R. C. (2005). Failure and delay in initial treatment contact after first onset of mental disorders in the National Comorbidity Survey Replication. *Archives of General Psychiatry, 62,* 603–613.

Wang, Q. (2004). Cultural self-constructions: Autobiographical memory and self-description in European American and Chinese children. *Developmental Psychology, 40,* 3–15.

Wang, Q. (2006). Culture and the development of self-knowledge. *Current Directions in Psychological Science, 15,* 182–187.

Wang, S. H., Baillargeon, R., & Brueckner, L. (2004). Young infants' reasoning about hidden objects: Evidence from violation-of-expectation tasks with test trials only. *Cognition, 93,* 167–198.

Wang, S. Y., & Chen, C. H. (2006). Psychosocial health of Taiwanese postnatal husbands and wives. *Journal of Psychosomatic Research, 60,* 303–307.

Ward, C. D., & Cooper, R. P. (1999). A lack of evidence in 4-month-old human infants for paternal voice preference. *Developmental Psychobiology, 35,* 49–59.

Ward, H., Munro, E. R., & Dearden, C. (2006). *Babies and young children in care: Life pathways, decision-making and practice.* London: Jessica Kingsley.

Ward, R., & Spitze, G. (1992). Consequences of parent–adult child coresidence. *Journal of Family Issues, 13,* 533–572.

Ward, R., & Spitze, G. (2004). Marital implications of parent–adult child coresidence: A longitudinal view. *Journal of Gerontology: Social Sciences, 59B,* S2–S8.

Warin, J. (2000). The attainment of self-consistency through gender in young children. *Sex Roles, 42,* 209–231.

Warneken, F., Chen, F., & Tomasello, M. (2006). Cooperative activities in young children and chimpanzees. *Child Development, 77,* 640–663.

Warren, J. R., LePore, P. C., & Mare, R. D. (2000). Employment during high school: Consequences for students' grades in academic courses. *American Educational Research Journal, 37,* 943–970.

Washburn, A. M., Sands, L. P., & Walton, P. J. (2003). Assessment of social cognition in frail older adults and its association with social functioning in the nursing home. *Gerontologist, 43,* 203–212.

Waskowic, T. D., & Chartier, B. M. (2003). Attachment and the experience of grief following the loss of a spouse. *Omega: Journal of Death and Dying, 47,* 77–91.

Wass, H. (1991). Helping children cope with death. In D. Papadatou & C. Papadatos (Eds.), *Children and death.* New York: Hemisphere.

Wasserman, D. (2006). *Depression: The facts.* Oxford, UK: Oxford University Press.

Waterman, A. S. (1982). Identity development from adolescence to adulthood: An extension of theory and a review of research. *Developmental Psychology, 18,* 341–358.

Waterman, A. S. (1992). Identity as an aspect of optimal psychological functioning. In G. R. Adams, T. P. Gullotta, & R. Montemayor

(Eds.), *Adolescent identity formation* (Advances in Adolescent Development, Vol. 4). Newbury Park, CA: Sage.

Waters, E., Merrick, S., Treboux, D., Crowell, J., & Albersheim, L. (2000). Attachment security in infancy and early adulthood: A twenty-year longitudinal study. *Child Development, 71,* 684–689.

Waters, E., Wippman, J., & Sroufe, L. A. (1979). Attachment, positive affect, and competence in the peer group: Two studies in construct validation. *Child Development, 50,* 821–829.

Watson, J. B. (1913). Psychology as the behaviorist views it. *Psychological Review, 20,* 158–177.

Watson, J. B. (1925). *Behaviorism.* New York: Norton.

Watson, J. B., & Raynor, R. (1920). Conditioned emotional reactions. *Journal of Experimental Psychology, 3,* 1–14.

Waxman, S. R., & Hatch, T. (1992). Beyond the basics: Preschool children label objects flexibly at multiple hierarchical levels. *Journal of Child Language, 19,* 153–166.

Waxman, S. R., & Lidz, J. L. (2006). Early word learning. In D. Kuhn & R. Siegler (Vol. Eds.), *Handbook of child psychology: Cognition, perception, and language: Vol. 2* (6th ed.). Hoboken, NJ: Wiley and Sons.

Wayne, A. J., & Youngs, P. (2003). Teacher characteristics and student achievement gains: A review. *Review of Educational Research, 73,* 89–122.

Webster, J. D. (1998). Attachment styles, reminiscence functions, and happiness in young and elderly adults. *Journal of Aging Studies, 12,* 315–330.

Webster, J. D., & Haight, B. K. (Eds.) (2002). *Critical advances in reminiscence work: From theory to application.* New York: Springer.

Wechsler, D. (1997). *Wechsler Adult Intelligence Scale* (3rd ed.). San Antonio: Harcourt.

Wechsler, D. (2002). *Wechsler Preschool and Primary Scale of Intelligence* (3rd ed.). The Psychological Corporation.

Wechsler, D. (2003). *Wechsler Intelligence Scale for Children, fourth edition* (WISC–IV). San Antonio, TX: The Psychological Corporation.

Weiffenbach, J. M., Cowart, B. J., & Baum, B. J. (1986). Taste intensity perception in aging. *Journal of Gerontology, 41,* 460–468.

Weinberg, K. M., Olson, K. L., Beeghly, M., & Tronick, E. Z. (2006). Making up is hard to do, especially for mothers with high levels of depressive symptoms and their infant sons. *Journal of Child Psychology and Psychiatry and Allied Disciplines, 47,* 670–683.

Weinberg, R. A., Scarr, S., & Waldman, I. D. (1992). The Minnesota transracial adoption study: A follow-up of IQ test performance at adolescence. *Intelligence, 16,* 117–135.

Weinert, F. E., & Hany, E. A. (2003). The stability of individual differences in intellectual development: Empirical evidence, theoretical problems, and new research questions. In R. J. Sternberg, J. Lautrey, & T. I. Lubart (Eds.), *Models of intelligence: International perspectives* (pp. 169–181). Washington, D.C.: American Psychological Association.

Weinert, F. E., & Schneider, W. (1999). *Individual development from 3 to 12: Findings from the Munich Longitudinal Study.* Cambridge, England: Cambridge University Press.

Weinfield, N. S., Sroufe, L. A., & Egeland, B. (2000). Attachment from infancy to early adulthood in a high-risk sample: Continuity, discontinuity, and their correlates. *Child Development, 71,* 695–702.

Weinraub, M., & Lewis, M. (1977). The determinants of children's responses to separation. *Monographs of the Society for Research in Child Development,* (4, Serial No. 172).

Weisberg, P. (1963). Social and nonsocial conditioning of infant vocalization. *Child Development, 34,* 377–388.

Weisfeld, G. E., & Woodward, L. (2004). Current evolutionary perspectives on adolescent romantic relations and sexuality. *Journal of the American Academy of Child and Adolescent Psychiatry, 43,* 11–19.

Weisner, T. S., & Gallimore, R. (1977). My brother's keeper: Child and sibling caretaking. *Current Anthropology, 18,* 169–190.

Weiss, B., & Garber, J. (2003). Developmental differences in the phenomenology of depression. *Development and Psychopathology, 15,* 403–430.

Weiss, G., & Hechtman, L. T. (1993). *Hyperactive children grown up* (2nd ed.). New York: Guilford.

Weiss, L. H., & Schwarz, J. C. (1996). The relationship between parenting types and older adolescents' personality, academic achievement, adjustment, and substance use. *Child Development, 67,* 2101–2114.

Weiss, R. (2000, May 23). For DNA, a defining moment. With code revealed, challenge will be to find its meaning and uses. *The Washington Post,* A1, A16–A17.

Weiss, R. (2003a, February 28). Dream unmet 50 years after DNA milestone. *The Washington Post,* A1, A10.

Weiss, R. (2003b, April 15). Genome Project completed. *The Washington Post,* A6.

Weiss, R., & Gillis, J. (2000, June 27). DNA-mapping milestone heralded. *The Washington Post,* A1, A12–A13.

Weisz, J. R., McCarty, C. A., Eastman, K. L., Chaiyasit, W., & Suwanlert, S. (1997). Developmental psychopathology and culture: Ten lessons from Thailand. In S. S. Luthar, J. A. Burack, D. Cicchetti, & J. R. Weisz (Eds.). *Developmental psychopathology: Perspectives on adjustment, risk and disorder.* Cambridge, England: Cambridge University Press.

Weisz, J. R., McCarty, C. A., & Valeri, S. M. (2006). Effects of psychotherapy for depression in children and adolescents: A meta-analysis. *Psychological Bulletin, 132,* 132–149.

Weisz, J. R., & Weiss, B. (1993). *Effects of psychotherapy with children and adolescents* (Vol. 27, Developmental Clinical Psychology and Psychiatry Series). Newbury Park, CA: Sage.

Weizman, A. O., & Snow, C. E. (2001). Lexical input as related to children's vocabulary acquisition: Effects of sophisticated exposure and support for meaning. *Developmental Psychology, 37,* 265–279.

Wellbery, C. (2006). Intervention to increase breastfeeding rates. *American Family Physician, 73,* 2047.

Wellman, H. M. (1990). *The child's theory of mind.* Cambridge, MA: MIT Press.

Wellman, H. M., & Bartsch, K. (1994). Before belief: Children's early psychological theory. In C. Lewis & P. Mitchell (Eds.), *Children's early understanding of mind: Origins and development.* Hove, England: Erlbaum.

Wellman, H. M., & Gelman, S. A. (1992). Cognitive development: Foundational theories of core domains. *Annual Review of Psychology, 43,* 337–375.

Wellman, H. M., & Lagattuta, K. H. (2000). Developing understandings of mind. In S. Baron-Cohen, H. Tager-Flusberg, & D. J. Cohen (Eds.), *Understanding other minds. Perspectives from developmental cognitive neuroscience* (2nd ed.). Oxford: Oxford University Press.

Wellman, H. M., & Liu, D. (2004). Scaling of theory-of-mind-tasks. *Child Development, 75,* 523–541.

Wellman, H. M., Cross, D., & Watson, J. (2001). Meta-analysis of theory-of-mind development: The truth about false-belief. *Child Development, 72,* 655–684.

Wellman, H. M., Phillips, A. T., & Rodriguez, T. (2000). Young children's understanding of perception, desire, and emotion. *Child Development, 71,* 895–912.

Wender, P. H. (1995). *Attention-deficit hyperactivity disorder in adults.* New York: Oxford University Press.

Wenglinsky, H. (1998). Finance equalization and within-school equity: The relationship between education spending and the social distribution of achievement. *Educational Evaluation and Policy Analysis, 20,* 269–283.

Wentzel, K. R. (2003). Sociometric status and adjustment in middle school: A longitudinal study. *Journal of Early Adolescence, 23,* 5–28.

Werker, J. F., & Desjardins, R. N. (1995). Listening to speech in the first year of life: Experiential influences on phoneme perception. *Current Directions in Psychological Science, 4,* 76–81.

Werker, J. F., Gilbert, J. H. V., Humphrey, K., & Tees, R. C. (1981). Developmental aspects of cross-language speech perception. *Child Development, 52,* 349–355.

Werker, J. F., & Tees, R. C. (2005). Speech perception as a window for understanding plasticity and commitment in language systems of the brain. *Developmental Psychobiology, 46,* 233–234.

Werner, E. E. (1989a). Children of the Garden Island. *Scientific American, 260,* 106–111.

Werner, E. E. (1989b). High-risk children in young adulthood: A longitudinal study from birth to 32 years. *American Journal of Orthopsychiatry, 59,* 72–81.

Werner, E. E., & Smith, R. S. (1982). *Vulnerable but invincible: A longitudinal study of resilient children and youth.* New York: McGraw-Hill.

Werner, E. E., & Smith, R. S. (1992). *Overcoming the odds: High risk children from birth to adulthood.* Ithaca, NY: Cornell University Press.

Werner, E. E., & Smith, R. S. (2001). *Journeys from childhood to midlife: Risk, resilience, and recovery.* Ithaca, NY: Cornell University Press.

Werner, H. (1957). The concept of development from a comparative and organismic point of view. In D. B. Harris (Ed.), *The concept of development: An issue in the study of human behavior.* Minneapolis: University of Minnesota Press.

Werth, J. L., Jr., Blevins, D., Toussaint, K. L., & Durham, M. R. (2002). The influence of cultural diversity on end-of-life care and decisions. *American Behavioral Scientist, 46,* 204–219.

Wetle, T., Shield, R., Teno, J., Miller, S. C., & Welch, L. (2005). Family perspectives on end-of-life care experiences in nursing homes. *Gerontologist, 45,* 642–650.

Wetzel, N., Widmann, A., Berti, S., & Schroger, E. (2006). The development of involuntary and voluntary attention from childhood to adulthood: A combined behavioral and event-related potential study. *Clinical Neurophysiology, 117,* 2191–2203.

Weyandt, L. L. (2007). *An ADHD primer* (2nd ed.). Mahwah, NJ: Erlbaum.

Whalen, C. K., Henker, B., Buhrmester, D., Hinshaw, S. P., Huber, A., & Laski, K. (1989). Does stimulant medication improve the peer status of hyperactive children? *Journal of Consulting and Clinical Psychology, 57,* 545–549.

Whalen, G., Griffin, M. R., Shintani, A., Mitchel, E., Cruz-Gervis, R., Forbes, B. L., & Hartet, T. V. (2006). Smoking rates among pregnant women in Tennessee, 1990–2001. *Preventive Medicine, 43,* 196–199.

Whipp, B. J., & Ward, S. A. (1992). Will women soon outrun men? *Nature, 355,* 25.

Whipple, E. E., & Richey, C. A. (1997). Crossing the line from physical discipline to child abuse: How much is too much? *Child Abuse and Neglect, 21,* 431–444.

Whitbourne, S. K. (2005). *Adult development and aging: Biopsychological perspectives* (2nd ed.). Hoboken, NJ: Wiley.

Whitbourne, S. K., & Tesch, S. A. (1985). A comparison of identity and intimacy statuses in college students and alumni. *Developmental Psychology, 21,* 1039–1044.

Whitbourne, S. K., & Willis, S. L. (Eds.). (2006). *The baby boomers grow up: Contemporary perspectives on midlife.* Mahwah, NJ: Erlbaum.

White, L., & Edwards, J. N. (1990). Emptying the nest and parental well-being: An analysis of national panel data. *American Sociological Review, 55,* 235–242.

White, L., & Rogers, S. J. (1997). Strong support but uneasy relationships: Coresidence and adult children's relationships with their parents. *Journal of Marriage and the Family, 59,* 62–76.

White, L., & Rogers, S. J. (2000). Economic circumstances and family outcomes: A review of the 1990s. *Journal of Marriage and the Family, 62,* 1035–1051.

White, S. H., & Pillemer, D. B. (1979). Childhood amnesia and the development of a socially accessible memory system. In J. F. Kihlstrom & F. J. Evans (Eds.), *Functional disorders of memory.* Hillsdale, NJ: Erlbaum.

Whitebread, D. (1999). Interactions between children's metacognitive abilities, working memory capacity, strategies and performance during problem-solving. *European Journal of Psychology of Education, 14,* 489–507.

Whitehead, B. D., & Popenoe, D. (2003). *The state of the unions. The social health of marriage in America 2003. Essay: Marriage and children: Coming together again?* The National Marriage Project, Rutgers University. Available from: http://marriage.rutgers.edu/Publications/Print/PrintSOOU2003.htm.

Whitehurst, G. J., & Lonigan, C. J. (1998). Child development and emergent literacy. *Child Development, 69,* 848–872.

Whitehurst, G. J., & Valdez-Menchaca, M. C. (1988). What is the role of reinforcement in early language acquisition? *Child Development, 59,* 430–440.

Whitelaw, E., & Garrick, D. (2006). Epigenetic mechanisms. In P. Gluckman & M. Hanson

(Eds.), *Developmental origins of health and disease*. New York: Cambridge University Press.

Whiting, B. B., & Edwards, C. P. (1988). *Children of different worlds: The formation of social behavior*. Cambridge, MA: Harvard University Press.

WHO Multicentre Growth Reference Study Group. (2006). WHO Motor Development Study: Windows of achievement for six gross motor development milestones. *Acta Paediatric Supplement, 450*, 86–95.

Wickens, A. P. (1998). *The causes of aging*. Amsterdam: Harwood Academic Publishers.

Widén, S. E., & Erlandsson, S. I. (2004). The influence of socio-economic status on adolescent attitude to social noise and hearing protection. *Noise Health, 7*, 59–70.

Widmayer, S., & Field, T. (1980). Effects of Brazelton demonstrations on early interactions of preterm infants and their teen-age mothers. *Infant Behavior and Development, 3*, 79–89.

Widmer, E. D., Treas, J., & Newcomb, R. (1998). Attitudes toward nonmarital sex in 24 countries. *Journal of Sex Research, 35*, 349–358.

Wigfield, A., Eccles, J. S., Yoon, K. S., & Harold, R. D. (1997). Change in children's competence beliefs and subjective task values across the elementary school years: A 3-year study. *Journal of Educational Psychology, 89*, 451–469.

Wiggins, S., Whyte, P., Huggins, M., Adam, S., Theilmann, J., Bloch, M., Sheps, S. B., Schechter, M. T., Hayden, M. R. (1992). The psychological consequences of predictive testing for Huntington's disease. *New England Journal of Medicine, 327*, 1401–1405.

Wijngaards-de-Meij, L., Stroebe, M., Schut, H., Stroebe, W., van den Bout, J., van der Heijden, P., & Dijkstra, I. (2005). Couples at risk following the death of their child: Predictors of grief versus depression. *Journal of Consulting and Clinical Psychology, 73*, 617–623.

Wijngaards-de-Meij, L., Stroebe, M., Schut, H., Stroebe, W., van den Bout, J., van der Heijden, P., & Dijkstra, I. (2007). Neuroticism and attachment insecurity as predictors of bereavement outcome. *Journal of Research in Personality, 41*, 498–505.

Wikan, U. (1988). Bereavement and loss in two Muslim communities: Egypt and Bali compared. *Social Science and Medicine, 27*, 451–460.

Wikan, U. (1991). *Managing turbulent hearts*. Chicago: University of Chicago Press.

Wilbur, J., Miller, A., & Montgomery, A. (1995). The influence of demographic characteristics, menopausal status, and symptoms on women's attitudes toward menopause. *Women and Health, 23*, 19–39.

Wilcock, A., Kobayashi, L., & Murray, I. (1997). Twenty-five years of obstetric patient satisfaction in North America: A review of the literature. *Journal of Perinatal and Neonatal Nursing, 10*, 36–47.

Wilcox, S., Evenson, K. R., Aragaki, A., Wassertheil-Smoller, S., Mouton, C. P., & Loevinger, B. L. (2003). The effects of widowhood on physical and mental health, health behaviors, and health outcomes: The Women's Health Initiative. *Health Psychology, 22*, 513–522.

Wildes, J. E., Emery, R. E., & Simons, A. D. (2001). The roles of ethnicity and culture in the development of eating disturbance and body dissatisfaction: A meta-analytic review. *Clinical Psychology Review, 21*, 521–551.

Willats, P. (1990). Development of problem solving strategies in infancy. In D. F. Bjorklund (Ed.), *Children's strategies*. Hillsdale, NJ: Erlbaum.

Williams, I. J., Rasmussen, S. A., Flores, A., Kirby, R. S., & Edmonds, L. D. (2005). Decline in the prevalence of spina bifida and anencephaly by race/ethnicity: 1995–2002. *Pediatrics, 116*, 580–586.

Williams, J. (2003). Dementia and genetics. In R. Plomin, J. C. DeFries, I. W. Craig, & P. McGuffin (Eds.), *Behavioral genetics in the postgenomic era*. Washington, D.C.: American Psychological Association.

Williams, J. E., & Best, D. L. (1990). *Measuring sex stereotypes: A multination study* (rev. ed.). Newbury Park, CA: Sage.

Williams, J. H., Waiter, G. D., Gilchrist, A., Perrett, D. I., Murray, A. D., & Whiten, A. (2006). Neural mechanisms of imitation and 'mirror neuron' functioning in autistic spectrum disorder. *Neuropsychologia, 44*, 610–621.

Williams, J. M., & Currie, C. (2000). Self-esteem and physical development in early adolescence: Pubertal timing and body image. *Journal of Early Adolescence, 20*, 129–149.

Williams, K. C. (1996). Piagetian principles: Simple and effective application. *Journal of Intellectual Disability Research, 40*, 110–119.

Williams, K., & Dunne-Bryant, A. (2006). Divorce and adult psychological well-being: Clarifying the role of gender and child age. *Journal of Marriage and Family, 68*, 1178–1196.

Williams, M. E. (1995). *The American Geriatrics Society's complete guide to aging and health*. New York: Harmony Books.

Williams, M. V., Baker, D. W., Parker, R. M., & Nurss, J. R. (1998). Relationship of functional health literacy to patients' knowledge of their chronic disease. *Archives of Internal Medicine, 158*, 166–172.

Williams, P. T. (1997). Evidence for the incompatibility of age-neutral overweight and age-neutral physical activity standards from runners. *American Journal of Clinical Nutrition, 65*, 1391–1396.

Willis, S. L., & Schaie, K. W. (1999). Intellectual functioning in midlife. In S. L. Willis & J. D. Reid (Eds.), *Life in the middle. Psychological and social development in middle age*. San Diego: Academic Press.

Willis, S. L., Tennstedt, S. L., Marsiske, M., Ball, K., Elias, J., Koepke, K. M., Morris, J. N., Rebok, G. W., Unverzagt, F. W., & Stoddard, A. M. for the ACTIVE Study Group (2006). Long-term effects of cognitive training on everyday functional outcomes in older adults. *Journal of the American Medical Association, 296*, 2805–2814.

Wilmoth, J. M., & Longino, C. F., Jr. (2006). Demographic trends that will shape U.S. policy in the twenty-first century. *Research on Aging, 28*, 269–288.

Wilson, A. E., Smith, M. D., Ross, H. S., & Ross, M. (2004). Young children's personal accounts of their sibling disputes. *Merrill-Palmer Quarterly, 50*, 39–60.

Wilson, G. T., Becker, C. B., & Heffernan, K. (2003). Eating disorders. In E. J. Mash & R. A. Barkley (Eds.), *Child psychopathology* (2nd ed.). New York: Guilford Press.

Wilson, R. (2003, December 5). How babies alter careers for academics. *The Chronicle of Higher Education*, A1, A6–A8.

Wilson, R. S. (1978). Synchronies in mental development: An epigenetic perspective. *Science, 202*, 939–948.

Wilson, R. S. (1983). The Louisville twin study: Developmental synchronies in behavior. *Child Development, 54*, 298–316.

Wilson, R. S., Arnold, S. E., Tang, Y. & Bennett, D. A. (2006). Odor identification and decline in different cognitive domains in old age, *Neuroepidemiology, 26*, 61–67.

Wilson, R. S., Krueger, K. R., Arnold, S. E., Schneider, J. A., Kelly, J. F., Barnes, L. L., Tang, Y., & Bennett, D. A. (2007). Loneliness and risk of Alzheimer disease. *Archives of General Psychiatry, 64*, 234–240.

Wilson, S. J., Lipsey, M. W., & Derzon, J. H. (2003). The effects of school-based intervention programs on aggressive behavior: A meta-analysis. *Journal of Consulting and Clinical Psychology, 71*, 136–149.

Wilson-Costello, D., Friedman, H., Minich, N., Siner, B., Taylor, G., Schluchter, M., & Hack, M. (2007). Improved neurodevelopmental outcomes for extremely low birth weight infants in 2000–2002. *Pediatrics, 119*, 37–45.

Wineberg, H., & Werth, J. L. Jr. (2003). Physician-assisted suicide in Oregon: What are the key factors? *Death Studies, 27*, 501–518.

Wingfield, A., Poon, L. W., Lombardi, L., & Lowe, D. (1985). Speed of processing in normal aging: Effects of speech rate, linguistic structure, and processing time. *Journal of Gerontology, 40*, 579–595.

Wink, P., & Dillon, M. (2002). Spiritual development across the adult life course: Findings from a longitudinal study. *Journal of Adult Development, 9*, 79–94.

Wink, P., & Dillon, M. (2003). Religiousness, spirituality, and psychosocial functioning in late adulthood: findings from a longitudinal study. *Psychology and Aging, 18*, 916–924.

Wink, P., & Helson, R. (1993). Personality change in women and their partners. *Journal of Personality and Social Psychology, 65*, 597–605.

Winkler, I., Kushnerenko, E., Horvath, J., Ceponiene, R., Fellman, V., Huotilainen, M., Naatanen, R., & Sussman, E. (2003). Newborn infants can organize the auditory world. *Proceedings of the National Academy of Sciences, 100*, 11812–11815.

Winn, H. N., & Hobbins, J. C. (Eds.). (2000). *Clinical maternal-fetal medicine*. London: Parthenon.

Winner, E. (1996). *Gifted children: Myths and realities*. New York: Basic Books.

Winsler, A., Carlton, M. P., & Barry, M. J. (2000). Age-related changes in preschool children's systematic use of private speech in a natural setting. *Journal of Child Language, 27*, 665–687.

Winsler, A., Naglieri, J., & Manfra, L. (2006). Children's search strategies and accompanying verbal and motor strategic behavior: Developmental trends and relations with task performance among children age 5 to 17. *Cognitive Development, 21*, 232–248.

Winterich, J. A., & Umberson, D. (1999). How women experience menopause: The importance of context. *Journal of Women and Aging, 11*, 57.

Witt, S. (1997). Parental influence on children's socialization to gender roles. *Adolescence, 32*, 253–259.

Witte, K. (2006, April 2). Untitled. *Washington Post*, p. D1.

Wlodkowski, R. J. (1999). *Enhancing adult motivation to learn : A comprehensive guide for teaching all adults*. San Francisco: Jossey-Bass Higher and Adult Education Series.

Wodrich, D. L. (2006). Sex chromosome anomalies. In L. Phelps (Ed.), *Chronic health–related disorders in children: Collaborative medical and psychoeducational interventions*. Washington, DC: American Psychological Association.

Wolchik, S. A., West, S. G., Sandler, I. N., Tein, J. Y., Coatsworth, D., Lengua, L., Weiss, L., Anderson, E. R., Greene, S. M., & Griffin, W. A. (2000). An experimental evaluation of theory-based mother and mother–child programs for children of divorce. *Journal of Consulting and Clinical Psychology, 68*, 843–856.

Wolf, R. S. (2000). Elder abuse. In V. B. Van Hasselt & M. Hersen (Eds.), *Aggression and violence: An introductory text*. Needham Heights, MA: Allyn & Bacon.

Wolfe, J., Grier, H. E., Klar, N., Levin, S. B., Ellenbogen, J. M., Salem-Schatz, S., Emanuel, E. J., & Weeks, J. C. (2000). Symptoms and suffering at the end of life in children with cancer. *New England Journal of Medicine, 342*, 326–333.

Wolff, P. H. (1963). Observations on the early development of smiling. In B. M. Foss (Ed.), *Determinants of infant behavior* (Vol. 2). London: Methuen.

Wolfner, G. D., & Gelles, R. J. (1993). A profile of violence toward children: A national study. *Child Abuse and Neglect, 17*, 197–212.

Wolfson, A. R., & Carskadon, M. A. (1998). Sleep schedules and daytime functioning in adolescents. *Child Development, 69*, 875–998.

Women's Health Initiative. (2004). *The estrogen-plus-progestin study*. Available online: http://www.nhlbi.nih.gov/whi/estro_pro.htm (retrieved September 9, 2004).

Wong, C. A., Eccles, J. S., & Sameroff, A. (2003). The influence of ethnic discrimination and ethnic identification on African American adolescents' school and socioemotional adjustment. *Journal of Personality, 71*, 1197–1232.

Wong, P. T. P., & Watt, L. M. (1991). What types of reminiscence are associated with successful aging? *Psychology and Aging, 6*, 272–279.

Wong, S. T., Yoo, G. J., & Stewart, A. L. (2006). The changing meaning of family support among older Chinese and Korean immigrants. *Journals of Gerontology: Social Sciences, 61B*, S4–S9.

Wood, E., Desmarais, S., & Gugula, S. (2002). The impact of parenting experience on gender stereotyped toy play of children. *Sex Roles, 47*, 39–49.

Woodhill, B. M., & Samuels, C. A. (2003). Positive and negative androgyny and their relationship with psychological health and well-being. *Sex Roles, 49*, 555–565.

Woodhill, B. M., & Samuels, C. A. (2004). Desirable and undesirable androgyny: A prescription for the twenty-first century. *Journal of Gender Studies, 13*, 15–28.

Woodward, A. L., & Markman, E. M. (1998). Early word learning. In D. Kuhn & R. S. Siegler (Vol. Eds.), W. Damon (Editor-in-Chief), *Handbook of child psychology: Vol. 2. Cognition, perception, and language* (5th ed., pp. 371–420). New York: Wiley.

Woodward, L., Fergusson, D. M., & Belsky, J. (2000). Timing of parental separation and attachment to parents in adolescence: Results of a prospective study from birth to age 16. *Journal of Marriage and the Family, 62*, 162–174.

Woolley, J. D., Boerger, E. A., & Markman, A. B. (2004). A visit from the Candy Witch: Factors influencing young children's belief in a novel fantastical being. *Developmental Science, 7*, 456–468.

Worchel, F. F., Copeland, D. R., & Barker, D. G. (1987). Control-related coping strategies in pediatric oncology patients. *Journal of Pediatric Psychology, 12*, 25–38.

Worden, J. W., & Silverman, P. R. (1996). Parental death and the adjustment of school-age children. *Omega: Journal of Death and Dying, 33*, 91–102.

Worden, J. W., & Silverman, P. S. (1993). Grief and depression in newly widowed parents with school-age children. *Omega: Journal of Death and Dying, 27*, 251–261.

Worfolk, J. B. (2000). Heat waves: Their impact on the health of elders. *Geriatric Nursing, 21*, 70–77.

Worthen, L. T., & Yeatts, D. E. (2000–2001). Assisted suicide: Factors affecting public attitudes. *Omega: Journal of Death and Dying, 42*, 115–135.

Wortman, C. B., & Boerner, K. (2007). Beyond the myths of coping with loss: Prevailing assumptions versus scientific evidence. In H. S. Friedman & R. C. Silver (Eds.), *Foundations of health psychology*. New York: Oxford University Press.

Wortman, C. B., & Silver, R. C. (2001). The myths of coping with loss revisited. In M. S. Stroebe, R. O. Hansson, W. Stroebe, & H. Schut (Eds.), *Handbook of bereavement research. Consequences, coping, and care*. Washington, D.C.: American Psychological Association.

Wright, K. (2000). Thalidomide is back. *Discover, 21*, 31–33.

Wright, W. E., & Shay, J. W. (2005). Telomere biology in aging and cancer. *Journal of the American Geriatrics Society, 53*, S292–S294.

Wrosch, C., Bauer, I., & Scheier, M. F. (2005). Regret and quality of life across the adult life span: The influence of disengagement and available future goals. *Psychology and Aging, 20*, 657–670.

Wrosch, C., Schulz, R., & Heckhausen, J. (2004). Health stresses and depressive symptomatology in the elderly: A control-process approach. *Current Directions in Psychological Science, 13*, 17–20.

Wu, C. H., Cheng, Y., Ip, H. M., & McBride-Change, C. (2005). Age differences in creativity: Task structure and knowledge base. *Creativity Research Journal, 17*, 321–326.

Wu, C. Y., Yu, T. J., & Chen, M. J. (2000). Age related testosterone level changes and male andropause syndrome. *Changgeng Yi Xue Za Zhi [Chinese Medical Journal], 23*, 348–353.

Wu, T., Mendola, P., & Buck, G. M. (2002). Ethnic differences in the presence of secondary sex characteristics and menarche among US girls: The Third National Health and Nutrition Examination Survey, 1988–1994. *Pediatrics, 110*, 752–757.

Wurmser, H., Rieger, M., Domogalla, C., Kahnt, A., Buchwald, J., Kowatsch, M., Kuehnert, N., Buske-Kirschbaum, A., Papousek, M., Pirke, K. M., & von Voss, H. (2006). Association between life stress during pregnancy and infant crying in the first six months of postpartum: A prospective longitudinal study. *Early Human Development, 82*, 341–349.

Wyly, M. V. (1997). *Infant assessment*. Boulder, CO: Westview.

Wynn, K. (1992). Addition and subtraction by human infants. *Nature, 358*, 749–750.

Wynn, K. (1995). Infants possess a system of numerical knowledge. *Current Directions in Psychological Science, 4*, 172–177.

X

Xiong, X., Wightkin, J., Magnus, J. H., Pridjian, G., Acuna, J. M., & Buekens, P. (2007). Birth weight and infant growth: Optimal infant weight gain versus optimal infant weight. *Maternal and Child Health, 11*, 57–63.

Xu, F., & Spelke, E. S. (2000). Large number discrimination in 6-month-old infants. *Cognition, 74*, B1–B11.

Xu, F., Spelke, E. S., & Goddard, S. (2005). Number sense in human infants. *Developmental Science, 8*, 88–101.

Y

Yaffe, K., Barnes, D., Nevitt, M., Lui, L., & Covinsky, K. (2001). A prospective study of physical activity and cognitive decline in elderly women. *Archives of Internal Medicine, 161*, 1703–1708.

Yamagata, S., Suzuki, A., Ando, J., Ono, Y., Kijima, N., Yoshimura, K., Ostendorf, F., Angleitner, A., Riemann, R., Spinath, F. M., Livesley, W. J., & Jang, K. L. (2006). Is the genetic structure of human personality universal? A cross-cultural twin study from North America, Europe, and Asia. *Journal of Personality and Social Psychology, 90*, 987–998.

Yan, B., & Arlin, P. K. (1995). Nonabsolute/relativistic thinking: A common factor underlying models of postformal reasoning? *Journal of Adult Development, 2*, 223–240.

Yan, J. H., Thomas, J. R., & Stelmach, G. E. (1998). Aging and rapid aiming arm movement control. *Experimental Aging Research, 24*, 155–168.

Yan, J. H., Thomas, J. R., Stelmach, G. E., & Thomas, K. T. (2000). Developmental features of rapid aiming arm movements across the lifespan. *Journal of Motor Behavior, 32*, 121–140.

Yang, Y. H., Kim, S. H., & Jung, J. E. (2002). Prenatal diagnosis of fetal cells in maternal blood by comparative genomic hybridization. In F. A. Chervenak, A. Kurjak, & Z. Papp (Eds.), *The fetus as a patient*. New York: Parthenon.

Yeates, K. O., MacPhee, D., Campbell, F. A., & Ramey, C. T. (1983). Maternal IQ and home environment as determinants of early childhood intellectual competence: A developmental analysis. *Developmental Psychology, 19*, 731–739.

Yeates, K. O., & Selman, R. L. (1989). Social competence in the schools: Toward an integrative developmental model for intervention. *Developmental Review, 9*, 64–100.

Yeh, Y., & Wu, J. (2006). The cognitive processes of pupils' technological creativity. *Creativity Research Journal, 18*, 213–227.

Yendovitskaya, T. V. (1971). Development of attention. In A. V. Zaporozhets & D. B. Elkonin (Eds.), *The psychology of preschool children*. Cambridge, MA: MIT Press.

Youn, G. Y., Knight, B. G., Jeong, H. S., & Benton, D. (1999). Differences in familism values and caregiving outcomes among Korean, Korean American, and White American dementia caregivers. *Psychology and Aging, 14,* 355–364.

Young, W. C., Goy, R. W., & Phoenix, C. H. (1964). Hormones and sexual behavior. *Science, 143,* 212–218.

Youngblade, L. M., & Dunn, J. (1995). Individual differences in young children's pretend play with mother and sibling: Links to relationships and understanding of other people's feelings and beliefs. *Child Development, 66,* 1472–1492.

Youniss, J. (1980). *Parents and peers in social development. A Sullivan–Piaget perspective.* Chicago: University of Chicago Press.

Yuill, N. (1993). Understanding of personality and dispositions. In M. Bennett (Ed.), *The development of social cognition: The child as psychologist.* New York: Guilford.

Yussen, S. R., & Levy, V. M. (1975). Developmental changes in predicting one's own memory span of short-term memory. *Journal of Experimental Child Psychology, 19,* 502–508.

Z

Zahn-Waxler, C., Friedman, R. J., Cole, P. M., Mizuta, I., & Himura, N. (1996). Japanese and United States preschool children's responses to conflict and distress. *Child Development, 67,* 2462–2477.

Zahn-Waxler, C., Radke-Yarrow, M., Wagner, E., & Chapman, M. (1992). Development of concern for others. *Developmental Psychology, 28,* 126–136.

Zajac, R., & Hayne, H. (2003). I don't think that's what really happened: The effect of cross-examination on the accuracy of children's reports. *Journal of Experimental Psychology: Applied, 9,* 187–195.

Zajonc, R. B. (2001a). Birth order debate resolved? *American Psychologist, 56,* 522–523.

Zajonc, R. B. (2001b). The family dynamics of intellectual development. *American Psychologist, 56,* 490–496.

Zander, L., & Chamberlain, G. (1999). Place of birth. *British Medical Journal, 318,* 721.

Zaporozhets, A. V. (1965). The development of perception in the preschool child. *Monographs of the Society for Research in Child Development, 30* (2, Serial No. 100), 82–101.

Zaslow, M. (1980). Relationships among peers in kibbutz toddler groups. *Child Psychiatry and Human Development, 10,* 178–189.

Zemach, I., Chang, S., & Teller, D. Y. (2006). Infant color vision: Prediction of infants' spontaneous color preferences. *Vision Research, 47,* 1368–1381.

Zemel, B. (2002). Body composition during growth and development. In N. Cameron (Ed.), *Human growth and development* (pp. 271–293). New York: Academic Press.

Zeskind, P. S., & Gingras, J. L. (2006). Maternal cigarette-smoking during pregnancy disrupts rhythms in fetal heart rate. *Journal of Pediatric Psychology, 31,* 5–14.

Zhang, L. (2002). Thinking styles and cognitive development. *Journal of Genetic Psychology, 163,* 179–195.

Zick, C. D., & Holden, K. (2000). An assessment of the wealth holdings of recent widows. *Journal of Gerontology: Social Sciences, 55,* S90–S97.

Zigler, E. (1995). Can we "cure" mild mental retardation among individuals in the lower socioeconomic stratum? *American Journal of Public Health, 85,* 302–304.

Zigler, E., Abelson, W. D., Trickett, P. K., & Seitz, V. (1982). Is an intervention program necessary to improve economically disadvantaged children's IQ scores? *Child Development, 53,* 340–348.

Zigler, E., & Hodapp, R. M. (1991). Behavioral functioning in individuals with mental retardation. *Annual Review of Psychology, 42,* 29–50.

Zimprich, D., & Martin, M. (2002). Can longitudinal changes in processing speed explain longitudinal age changes in fluid intelligence? *Psychology and Aging, 17,* 690–695.

Zisook, S., & Shuchter, S. R. (2001). Treatment of the depressions of bereavement. *American Behavioral Scientist, 44,* 782–797.

Zucker, A. N., Ostrove, J. M., & Stewart, A. J. (2002). College-educated women's personality development in adulthood: Perceptions and age differences. *Psychology and Aging, 17,* 236–244.

Zunzunegui, M. V., Alvarado, B. E., DelSer, T., & Otero, A. (2003). Social networks, social integration, and social engagement determine cognitive decline in community-dwelling Spanish older adults. *Journals of Gerontology: Psychological Sciences and Social Sciences, 58,* S93–S100.

Zvoch, K., & Stevens, J. J. (2006). Longitudinal effects of school context and practice on middle school mathematics achievement. *The Journal of Educational Research, 99,* 347–356.

Zwaigenbaum, L., Bryson, S., Rogers, T., Roberts, W., Brian, J., & Szatmari, P. (2005). Behavioral manifestations of autism in the first year of life. *International Journal of Developmental Neuroscience, 23,* 143–152.

Name Index

Smithmyer, C. M., 394
Smock, P. J., 336
Smolak, L., 487
Smolkowski, K., 486
Smoll, F. L., 147
Smotherman, W. P., 95
Smyke, A. T., 418–419
Snarey, J. R., 400, 401
Sneed, L., 116
Snider, J. B., 443
Snidman, N., 314
Snow, C. E., 280, 285
Snow, D., 278
Snow, T. K., 147
Snowdon, D. A., 154, 492
Snyder, J., 397
Sobolewski, J. M., 460–461
Sobring, E., 444
Sodian, B., 226
Soederberg, L. M., 235, 282
Sokol, B. W., 389
Solomon, F., 512
Solomon, J., 414
Solomon, S., 498
Somerville, S. C., 224
Son, L. K., 221, 232
Sorensen, A. B., 4, 489
Sorensen, S., 339, 434, 456
Soriano, F. I., 398
Sorri, M., 182
Sosik, J. J., 336
Sosnoff, J. J., 152
Sostek, A. M., 25
Sotomi, O., 171
Soussignan, R., 169
Span, P., 452
Sparling, P. B., 147
Sparrow, S. S., 249
Spear, L. P., 143
Speece, D. L., 292
Speece, M. W., 511
Spelke, E. J., 164
Spelke, E. S., 163–165
Spence, J. T., 303, 361, 363
Spence, M., 103
Spencer, J. P., 137, 138
Spencer, M. B., 25, 323
Spencer, P. E., 286
Spera, C., 299
Sperling, M. B., 426
Spiby, H., 105, 113
Spieler, D. H., 282
Spinath, B., 290
Spinath, F. M., 78, 265
Spinrad, T. L., 314, 402
Spirduso, W. W., 152
Spiro, A., 130
Spiro, A., III, 331
Spitz, R. A., 478
Spitze, G., 453–454
Spokane, A. R., 325
Springen, K., 98, 421
Springer, S., 127
Squire, L. R., 219
Sroufe, L. A., 350, 410, 412–413, 419–420, 425, 463, 470, 481
St. George, D., 462
St. John, W., 114
Staddon, J. E. R., 42
Stambrook, M., 511
Stanley, J. C., 273, 345
Stanley, S. M., 451
Stanley-Hagen, M., 460–461
Stanovich, K. E., 203, 291
Stanovich, P. J., 291
Stanowicz, L., 285
Starr, J. M., 260
Starr, R. H., Jr., 438
Stattin, H., 446, 450
Staudinger, U. M., 3, 11, 12, 23, 237, 241, 263, 337, 399
Steele, C. M., 269
Steen, T. A., 290
Steenari, M., 134
Steenland, K., 260
Steffen, V. J., 346

Stein, J. H., 145
Stein, Z., 107
Stein, Z. A., 107
Steinberg, E. P., 91
Steinberg, L., 145, 299, 302–303, 318, 397, 428, 442–444, 446, 449–450, 452, 472–473
Steiner, J. E., 168
Steinhausen, H. C., 488
Stelmach, G. E., 140, 152
Stemp, P. S., 452
Stephens, C. M., 450
Stephens, M. A., 456
Stephenson, J., 141
Stepp, L. S., 511
Stern, D., 411
Stern, M., 353
Sternberg, K. J., 464
Sternberg, R. J., 246, 250–251, 253, 257, 262–263, 265
Stevens, D. P., 304
Stevens, G., 286
Stevens, J. J., 295
Stevens, M. M., 514
Stevens, R. J., 297
Stevenson, H. W., 290, 300
Stevenson, M. R., 353
Stevenson, R. J., 169, 173
Stewart, A. J., 322
Stewart, R. B., 447
Stifter, C., 416
Stigler, J. W., 290, 300
Stillion, J. M., 500, 522
Stine, E. A. L., 282
Stine-Morrow, E. A. L., 235
Stipek, D., 255, 316
Stipek, D. J., 289–290, 298
Stith, S. M., 463
Stolberg, U., 413
Stone, M. R., 427
Stone, R., 108
Stoner, G., 481
Stoolmiller, M., 74
Storgaard, L., 102
Story, L. B., 458
Story, T., 378
Strauss, A. L., 507
Strauss, S., 510
Strauss, V., 398
Streissguth, A. P., 100–102
Streri, A., 170
Striano, T., 312
Stright, A. D., 362
Strigini, P., 69, 108
Stringer, J. S., 104
Strober, M., 487
Stroebe, M., 515, 518
Stroebe, M. S., 508, 516, 517, 519, 520
Stuewig, J., 381
Stumpf, H., 345
Suchowersky, O., 73
Sudhalter, V., 281
Sugden, D., 147
Sugden, K., 83, 472
Suitor, J. J., 453
Sulkava, R., 182
Sullivan, M. W., 312
Sulloway, F. J., 266
Sun, Y., 425
Sundqvist, N., 173
Super, C. M., 324, 335
Super, D. E., 324, 335
Susman, E. J., 146
Susser, M., 107
Sutton-Brown, M., 73
Svanborg, A., 370
Svedin, C., 364
Svetina, M., 197
Swank, P. R., 118, 119, 266
Swanson, H. A., 179
Swanson, H. L., 238
Swarr, A. E., 146
Swenson, L. P., 429
Symons, D. K., 377
Szinovacz, M. E., 338, 454
Szkrybalo, J., 349

Tabert, M. H., 492
Taddio, A., 169
Tafarodi, R. W., 328
Taft, L. B., 334
Tager-Flusberg, H., 281, 474
Takahashi, K., 417
Talbert, G. B. 149
Tallal, P., 294
Tam, C. S., 144
Tamis-Lemonda, C. S., 441
Tan, M., 127
Tan, R. S., 151
Tan, U., 127
Tanaka, A., 433
Tangney, J. P., 381, 382
Tanner, J. L., 8
Tanner, J. M., 127, 144, 145, 174
Tanzi, R. E., 491
Tarabulsy, G. M., 426
Tardif, C., 419
Tardif, T., 376
Target, M., 36, 37
Taylor, D. M., 489
Taylor, J., 520
Taylor, L. C., 295
Taylor, L. D., 20
Taylor, M. D., 260
Taylor, M. G., 351
Taylor, M. R., 499
Taylor, M., 194, 376
Taylor, R. D., 445
Taylor, R. E., 268
Taylor, S. E., 430, 434
Teachman, B. A., 490
Teachman, J. D., 439, 440, 457
Teeter, P. A., 480
Tellegen, A., 80
Teller, D. Y., 160
Temple, E., 293, 377
Tenenbaum, H. R., 299, 355–356
Teno, J. M., 522
Teran, L., 53
Terman, L. M., 272, 273
Testa, D., 100
Teti, D. M., 14, 447
Teti, L. O., 410
Thapar, A., 473, 481
Tharinger, D., 365
Thase, M. E., 491
Thelen, E., 137–138
Thelen, M. H., 487
Thiede, K. W., 232
Thiessen, E. D., 278
Thoman, E. B., 133
Thomas, A., 314
Thomas, A. K., 238
Thomas, F., 145
Thomas, J., 301
Thomas, J. M., 425
Thomas, J. R., 140, 152
Thomas, K. M., 94, 125–127
Thomas, T., 513
Thompson A. M., 127
Thompson, C. P., 234
Thompson, J. R., 279
Thompson, L. A., 284
Thompson, R. A., 312–313, 376–377, 387–388, 391, 410, 412, 491, 493
Thompson, R. F., 70, 126
Thorndike, R. L., 256
Thorne, B., 427
Thornton, R., 282
Thorstensson, A., 147
Thun, M., 260
Thurber, C. A., 412
Thurstone, L. L., 246
Thurstone, T. G., 246
Thys-Jacobs, S., 150
Tienari, P., 80
Tietjen, A. M., 401
Tiggemann, M., 487
Timmer, E., 334
Tinker, E., 279
Tisak, J., 389
Tisak, M. S., 389

Tobin, S. S., 338
Todd, M., 369
Todd, R. D., 475
Tokura, H., 277
Tolan, P., 462–463
Tomasello, M., 278–279, 283, 285–286
Tomasello, M., 376
Tomich, P. L., 421
Tomkiewicz, S., 268
Tomlin, C., 313
Tomlinson-Keasey, C., 273, 399
Tompson, M. C., 484
Tonge, B., 30
Torner, N., 104
Torrance, E. P., 254, 256, 258
Toth, K., 474
Toth, S. L., 434, 478
Tousignant, M., 2
Trabasso, T., 199
Tracy, J. L., 428
Trautner, H. M., 357
Traylor, E. S., 515, 519
Treas, J., 364
Treboux, D., 450
Treffert, D. A., 247
Treiman, R., 291–293
Treisman, E. M., 297
Tremblay, M. S., 142
Tremblay, R. E., 396
Trempel, R. E., 179
Trent, K., 454
Trevathan, W. R., 369
Trevino, L. K., 384
Triandis, H. C., 327
Trickett, P. K., 365
Troll, L., 440, 457
Trommsdorff, G., 443, 444
Tronick, E. Z., 411
Troop-Gordon, W., 425
Troseth, G. L., 16
Trotter, K. H., 345
Trueheart, C., 502
Truss, C. V., 304
Trzesniewski, K. H., 320–321, 326
Tucker, B. P., 167
Tucker, K. L., 490
Tucker, P. 354
Tuer, M., 451
Turati, C., 161
Turiel, E., 381, 389, 401–402
Turk-Charles, S., 339
Turkewitz, G., 168
Turkheimer, E., 74, 82, 267
Turner, J., 452
Turner, L. A., 231
Turner, P. J., 356
Turner, R. J., 489
Turnpenny, P. D., 62, 65, 68, 70, 72, 85
Tynelius, P., 80
Tyre, P., 486
Tyson-Rawson, K. J., 514
Tzuriel, D., 249

U.S. Census Bureau, 303, 439–440, 454, 457, 501, 502
U.S. Department of Education, 304, 345
U.S. Department of Labor, 346
Uchida, N., 179
Uchino, B. N., 435
Udry, J. R., 428–429
Ueno, K., 433
Uhland, R. L., 304
Uhlenberg, P., 433
Ullman, J. B., 425
Umana-Taylor, A. J., 322–324
Umberson, D., 151, 453, 455, 517
Underwood, A., 470, 493
Unger, J. B., 53
United Nations, 501, 502
Updegraff, K., 356
Urofsky, M. I., 498

Vaccaro, B. G., 410
Vaden, N. A., 270
Vaillancourt, D. E., 152
Vaillant, G. E., 333, 335

Subject Index

friendship, 425–426, 433
infant, 409–420
peer relations, 408, 420, 421, 424–425, 429
play, 421
quality of attachment, 412–417
social network, 427–428, 430–431
Attachment-related fears, 412
Attachment theory, 406–408
Attention
adolescent, 174
adult, 180
child, 173
Attention deficit hyperactivity disorder (ADHD), 480–482
Authoritarian parenting, 442
Authoritative parenting, 442
Autism, 473–478
Autism spectrum disorder (ASD), 474
Autobiographical memory, 227–229, 234–235
Automatization, 249
Autonomous morality, 383
Autonomy, 449
Autonomy *vs.* shame and doubt, 36, 332
Avoidant attachment, 413, 431

Babbling, 278
Babinski reflex, 132
Baby biographies, 11
Baby boom generation, 9
Bayley Scales of Infant Development, 252
Beanpole family, 440
Behavioral genetics, 73
Behavioral inhibition, 314–315
Behavioral observations, 15–16
Behaviorism, 39
Belief-desire psychology, 376
Beng, 114
Bereavement, 507, 508–509, 512–513, 520
Beta-amyloid, 492
Bidirectional influences, 50
Big-fish-little-pond effect, 320
Big Five, 310, 311
Binge-purge syndrome, 486
Bioecological model, 7
Biological aging, 3
Birthing process, 109–114
Blastocyst, 92
Bodily-kinesthetic intelligence, 247
Brain development, 125–129
Breast *vs.* bottle, 115
Breathing reflex, 132
Breech presentation, 109
Brown v. Board of Education of Topeka, 296
Bulimia nervosa, 486

C-section, 109, 111
Caloric restriction, 505
Careers, 525–530
applied developmental psychologist, 528
bachelor's level positions, 527
counselor, psychologist, therapist, 528–529
health professionals, 529
professional practice, 527–529
research, 525–526
teaching, 526–527
Caregiver burden, 456
Case study method, 11
Cat in the Hat, The, 292
Cataract, 171
Catch-up growth, 123
Categorical self, 313
Centenarian, 2
Centration, 195, 199
Cephalocaudal principle, 129
Cerebral palsy, 109
Cesarean section, 109, 111
Characteristic adaptation, 310
Chemotherapy drugs, 102
Chicken pox, 103
Child
achievement motivation, 289–291
attachment, 421–426
autobiographical memory, 227–229

cognition, 194–199
concrete operations period, 198–199
conservation, 198
creativity, 254–255
death and dying, 510–513
depression, 482–484
developmental psychopathology, 479–485
education, 289–297
eyewitness memory, 229
family, 442–448
friendships, 425–426
gender roles, 348–350
intelligence, 253–255
language, 289–297
memory, 223–231
moral development, 388–392
peer relations, 421, 424–425
perception, 173
personality, 316–319
physical development, 139–143
play, 421
preoperational period, 194–198, 199
reading, 291–294
rules, 389
scripts, 228–229
self, 316–319
seriation, 198
sexuality, 363–365
sibling relationships, 446–448
social cognition, 379
transitivity, 198
Child abuse, 462–466
Child care worker, 527
Child-directed speech, 285
Child effects model, 446
Childbirth, 109–114
Childhood, 8
Childhood amnesia, 227
Childhood sexual abuse, 364–365
Chlamydia, 103
Chorion, 92
Chorionic villus sampling (CVS), 72
Chromosome, 61
Chromosome abnormalities, 69–70
Chronosystem, 8
Cigarette smoking, 99–100
Class inclusion, 197
Classical conditioning, 40
Clinical method, 187
Clique, 427
Cocaine, 102–103
Cochlear implant, 167
Codominance, 67
Coercive family environment, 395–396, 397
Cognition, 186–215
adolescent, 200–205
adult, 205–208
aging, 207–208
child, 194–199
concrete operations period, 198–199
conservation, 194, 196, 198
defined, 187
formal operations period, 200–202
humor, 204
improving cognitive functioning, 212
infant, 190–193
intelligence, 187–189
object permanence, 191–193
Piaget's constructivist approach, 187–189, 208–209, 213
preoperational period, 194–198, 199
problem solving, 200–201
sensorimotor period, 190–193
seriation, 198
symbols, 193
transitivity, 198
Vygotsky's sociocultural perspective, 210–214
Cognitive developmental theory, 45–48
Cohabitation, 457
Cohort, 20
Cohort effects, 20
Collectivist culture, 327, 330
Communality, 344

Comorbidity, 480
Complicated grief, 516
Componential subtheory, 249
Conception, 61, 90–92
Concordance rates, 75
Concrete operations period, 46, 47, 198–199
Conditioned response (CR), 40
Conditioned stimulus (CS), 40
Conditioning phase, 40
Confidant, 434
Confidentiality, 26
Congenital malformations, 139
Conscientiousness, 311
Conservation, 194, 196, 198
Conservation-of-area task, 194, 196
Conservation-of-liquid task, 196, 198
Consolidation, 218
Constraint-seeking questions, 241
Constructivism, 46
Constructivist, 158
Contact comfort, 414
Contextual subtheory, 247
Continuing bonds, 518
Continuing education, 304–306
Continuity-discontinuity issue, 32
Contour, 161
Convergent thinking, 251
Cooing, 278
Cooperative learning, 297
Cooperative play, 422
Coordination of secondary schemes, 191
Coparenting, 438
Corpus callosum, 126
Correlation coefficient, 18
Correlational method, 18–20
Counseling psychologist, 528
Counselor, 528
Counting, 165
Couvade, 113
CR. *See* Conditioned response
Crawling, 136
Creativity
adolescent, 256–258
adult, 263–264
child, 254–255
defined, 250
fostering, 257
intelligence, 250–251
Critical period, 98
Critical period hypothesis of language acquisition, 285–287
Cross-modal perception, 170
Cross-sectional design, 21–22
Crossing over, 63
Crowd, 427
Crystallized intelligence, 246
CS. *See* Conditioned stimulus
Cued recall memory, 218
Cultural evolution, 60
Cultural-familial retardation, 271
Culture
childbirth, 112
defined, 7
IQ, 268–269
menopause, 151
moral thinking, 401
neonates, 114
parenting, 444
perception, 172
self-conceptions, 327–329
social cognition, 378
Culture bias, 268
Cumulative-deficit hypothesis, 253
CVS. *See* Chorionic villus sampling
Cystic fibrosis, 71
Cytomegalovirus, 103

Damage theories of aging, 502, 504
Dark adaptation, 177
Data collection, 14–15
Dating, 428–429
Day care, 417
Deaf children, 286, 377

Learned helplessness orientation, 289
Learning, 5
Learning goals, 290
Learning theories, 39–45
  classical conditioning, 39–40
  operant conditioning, 41–42
  school refusal, 44
  social cognitive theory, 42–44
  strengths/weaknesses, 44–45
  teenage pregnancy, 44
Lesbian family, 458–459
Levinson's stages of adult development, 335
Life expectancy, 501
Life review, 334
Life span. *See* Adolescent; Adult; Child; Infant;
  Neonatal environment
Life-span developmental model of health, 129–130
Life-span perspective, 11–13
Life stories, 323
Linguistic intelligence, 247
Living will, 500
Logical-mathematical intelligence, 247
Logical reasoning, 199
Long-term memory, 218
Longitudinal design, 21, 22–23
Looking-glass self, 313
Love withdrawal, 391
Low birth weight (LBW), 116–119

Macrosystem, 7
Macular degeneration, 178
Major depressive disorder, 469
Marijuana, 102
Marriage, 450–451
Mastery motivation, 287–288
Maternal blood sampling, 72
Maturation, 5
*Mature Mind: The Positive Power of the Aging
  Brain, The* (Cohen), 129
Maximum life span, 502
Mean Girls, 429
Mediation deficiency, 225
Meiosis, 61
Memory and information processing, 216–243
  adolescent, 231–232
  adult, 232–241
  autobiographical memory, 227–229, 234–235
  child, 223–231
  eyewitness memory, 229
  forgetting, 236
  habituation, 221
  imitation, 220–221
  implicit/explicit memory, 218–219
  improving memory/study skills, 240
  infant, 220–223
  information-processing approach, 217–220
  memory systems, 217–218
  metamemory, 232, 237–238
  operant conditioning, 221–222
  problem solving, 219–220, 222–223, 229–231,
    241–242
  recall, 222
  scripts, 228–229
  stereotyping, 238
Memory systems, 217–218
Menarche, 143
Mendelian heredity, 65
Menopause, 150–151
Menstruation, 143
Mental age, 248
Mental retardation, 270–272
Mercy killing, 385
Mesosystem, 7
*Message in a Bottle: The Making of Fetal Alcohol
  Syndrome* (Golden), 98
Meta-analysis, 20
Metacognition, 225
Metalinguistic awareness, 282
Metamemory, 225, 232, 237–238
Microsystem, 7
Middle generation squeeze, 455
Midlife crisis, 334–335
Mild cognitive impairment, 237

Mind of a Mnemonist, The (Luria), 217
Minnesota Twin Study, 80
Mirror neuron, 377
Mirror neuron simulation hypothesis, 476
Miseducation: Preschoolers at Risk (Elkind), 288
Mitosis, 61
Models, 42
Molecular genetics, 76–77
Monozygotic twins, 63
Moral affect, 381
Moral development, 381–403
  adolescent, 392–399
  adult, 399–403
  antisocial behavior, 393–399
  child, 388–392
  cognitive developmental theory, 382–384
  culture, 401
  Dodge's social information-processing model,
    394–395, 397
  evolutionary theory, 385–386
  infant, 387–388
  Kohlberg, 383–384, 396–397, 400
  moral socialization, 390–392
  Patterson's coercive family environment,
    305–396, 397
  Piaget, 382–383
  psychoanalytic theory, 381–382
  rules, 389
  social learning theory, 384–385
Moral disengagement, 385
Moral reasoning, 382
Moral rules, 389
Moral socialization, 390–392
Morality, 381
Morality of care, 402
Morality of justice, 402
Moratorium period, 321
Moratorium status, 322, 323
Moro reflex, 132
Morphology, 280
Mourning, 507
Multi-infarct dementia, 493
Multiple classification, 199
Musical intelligence, 247
Mutations, 68–69
Mutually responsive orientation, 387
Myelin, 96, 125
Myelination, 125

Narcotics, 102
Narrative identity, 310
Native Americans
  ethnic identity, 324
  IQ, 268
  parenting, 444
Nativist, 158
Natural selection, 60
Naturalist intelligence, 247
Naturalistic observation, 15
Nature-nurture issue, 5
  attachment, 407
  death and dying, 504
  emotions, 410
  perception, 158–159
  psychopathology, 484
  social cognition, 376–378
NCLB. *See* No Child Left Behind
Negative affectivity, 315
Negative punishment, 41
Negative reinforcement, 41
Neglectful parenting, 443
Neo-Freudian psychoanalytic theory, 37–39
Neonatal, 114
Neonatal environment
  at-risk newborns, 115–119
  behavioral states, 131–133
  breast *vs.* bottle, 115
  hearing, 166
  milestones, 136
  reflexes, 131, 132
  risk/residence, 119
  sensing/learning, 133
  speech perception, 168

Nervous system, 125
Neuron, 125
Neuroticism, 311
New parenthood, 451–452
Newborn. *See* Neonatal environment
No Child Left Behind (NCLB), 295
Nonshared environmental influences, 76
Nonsteroidal and anti-inflammatory drugs
  (NSAIDS), 102
Normal distribution, 248
NSAIDS. *See* Nonsteroidal and anti-inflammatory
  drugs
Nuclear family, 438
Nurture Assumption, The (Harris), 408

Obesity, 147
Object concept, 191
Object permanence, 191–193
Observational learning, 42, 356–357
Occupation, 258–259, 324–325, 335–338
Occupational success, 258–259
Oedipus complex, 353
Olfaction, 169
On Death and Dying (Kübler-Ross), 506
Onlooker play, 422
Openness to experience, 311
Operant conditioning, 41
  memory, 221–222
  perception, 160
Oral sex, 367
Oral stage, 36
Organic retardation, 271
Organization, 188, 224
Organogenesis, 92
Orthogenetic principle, 129
Osteoarthritis, 154
Osteoporosis, 153–154
Overextension, 279
Overlapping waves theory, 230
Overregularization, 281

Pain, 169, 183
Palliative care, 521
Papillary reflex, 132
Parallel play, 422
Parallel processing, 220
Parent effects model, 445
Parental imperative, 361
Parenting styles, 442–443
Parkes/Bowlby attachment model of bereavement,
  508
Passive gene-environment correlation, 83
Patterson's coercive family environment, 305–396,
  397
Peer, 408
Peer relations, 408
  adolescent, 429
  child, 424–425
  infant, 420
Pendulum problem, 201
Perception, 157–185
  adolescent, 174–175
  adult, 176–184
  attention, 173, 174
  child, 173
  cross-modal, 170
  defined, 158
  evoked potentials, 159
  habituation, 159
  hearing, 166–168
  infant, 159–172
  intuitive theories, 164
  nature *vs.* nurture, 158–159
  operant conditioning, 160
  preferential looking, 159
  taste/smell, 168–169
  vision, 160–164
Perceptual salience, 194, 199
Performance goals, 290
Perinatal environment, 108–114
Periods of the life span, 4
Permissive parenting, 443
Permissiveness-restrictiveness, 442